LO
69

PETERSON'S 440 GREAT COLLEGES FOR TOP STUDENTS

29th Edition

PETERSON'S

A **nelnet** COMPANY

About Peterson's

To succeed on your lifelong educational journey, you will need accurate, dependable, and practical tools and resources. That is why Peterson's is everywhere education happens. Because whenever and however you need education content delivered, you can rely on Peterson's to provide the information, know-how, and guidance to help you reach your goals. Tools to match the right students with the right school. It's here. Personalized resources and expert guidance. It's here. Comprehensive and dependable education content—delivered whenever and however you need it. It's all here.

For more information, contact Peterson's, 2000 Lenox Drive, Lawrenceville, NJ 08648; 800-338-3282; or find us on the World Wide Web at www.petersons.com/about.

© 2009 Peterson's, a Nelnet company

Previously published as *Competitive Colleges* © 1981, 1982, 1983, 1984, 1985, 1986, 1987, 1988, 1989, 1990, 1991, 1992, 1993, 1994, 1995, 1996, 1997, 1998, 1999, 2000, 2001, 2002, 2003, 2004, 2005; previously published as *440 Colleges for Top Students* © 2006, 2007, 2008

Stephen Clemente, President; Bernadette Webster, Director of Publishing; Mark D. Snider, Editor; Bret Bollmann, Copy Editor; Ward Brigham, Research Project Manager; Cathleen Fee, Research Associate; Phyllis Johnson, Programmer; Ray Golaszewski, Manufacturing Manager; Linda M. Williams, Composition Manager; Janet Garwo, Mimi Kaufman, Karen Mount, Danielle Vreeland

Peterson's makes every reasonable effort to obtain accurate, complete, and timely data from reliable sources. Nevertheless, Peterson's and the third-party data suppliers make no representation or warranty, either expressed or implied, as to the accuracy, timeliness, or completeness of the data or the results to be obtained from using the data, including, but not limited to, its quality, performance, merchantability, or fitness for a particular purpose, non-infringement or otherwise.

Neither Peterson's nor the third-party data suppliers warrant, guarantee, or make any representations that the results from using the data will be successful or will satisfy users' requirements. The entire risk to the results and performance is assumed by the user.

ISSN 0887-0152
ISBN-13: 978-0-7689-2686-6
ISBN-10: 0-7689-2686-6

Printed in the United States

10 9 8 7 6 5 4 3 2 1   11 10 09

Twenty-ninth Edition

By producing this book on recycled paper (40% post consumer waste) 96 trees were saved.

CONTENTS

A NOTE FROM THE PETERSON'S EDITORS

WHY SHOULD YOU CONSIDER A COMPETITIVE COLLEGE?

Excellent colleges typically take great care in admitting students. For them, selecting the entering class is, as Bill Fitzsimmons, Dean of Admissions and Financial Aid at Harvard University, describes it: a process of "sculpting" the best possible class from the pool of qualified applicants. The goal of an admission committee is to bring together a community of students who can learn from one another, each one bringing their own particular talents, skills, and experiences that will contribute to the development of all the others.

Students who have excelled in high school want to go on excelling. They need an educational environment that will push them, test them, help them go beyond their past accomplishments. They require a college that "fits," one that will help them develop into what they can uniquely become.

At the start, you'll likely find that everyone's list of "best" colleges is very much alike. Except for adding the most popular regional schools or schools serving an unusual interest or a family's traditional alma mater, your initial list probably will include the Ivy League schools and one or more of up to a dozen other similarly prestigious colleges and universities. The one quality shared by these schools is prestige. It certainly can be argued that it helps to graduate from a prestigious college. But prestige is a limited and very expensive factor upon which to base one's college choice. There are truly excellent college choices beyond the eight Ivy League schools and a newsstand magazine's designated top schools. One of these "other" college choices could very well be the best fit for your particular requirements and goals.

We make only one assumption in this guide. This is that the most influential factor in determining your experience on campus is the other students you will find there. In selecting colleges for inclusion in this book, we measure the competitiveness of the admission environment at colleges. This is measured over a meaningful period of time by entering-class statistics, such as GPA, class rank, and test scores. The 440 colleges selected for inclusion in this book routinely attract and admit an above-average share of the nation's high-achieving students.

Peterson's publishes a full line of resources to help guide you and your family through the college admission process. Peterson's publications can be found at your local bookstore or library and at your high school guidance office; you can access us online at **www.petersons.com**. Our Web-based resources for high school students can be found at **www.studentedge.com,** a personalized online resource center that helps you prepare for life after high school. It combines test preparation, college search, financial aid planning, and career exploration in one convenient location.

We welcome any comments or suggestions you may have about this publication and invite you to complete our online survey at **www.petersons.com/booksurvey.** Or you can fill out the survey at the back of this book, tear it out, and mail it to us at:

Publishing Department
Peterson's, a Nelnet company
2000 Lenox Drive
Lawrenceville, NJ 08648

Your feedback will help us to make your educational dreams possible.

Selecting a college is a great adventure, and colleges will be pleased to know that Peterson's helped you in your selection. Admissions staff members are more than happy to answer questions, address specific problems, and help in any way they can. The editors at Peterson's wish you great success in your college search!

GETTING INTO A COMPETITIVE COLLEGE

UNDERSTANDING THE COLLEGE ADMISSION PROCESS

TED SPENCER
Associate Vice Provost and Executive Director of Undergraduate Admissions at the University of Michigan

The process you are about to begin, that of choosing a college, can be very challenging, sometimes frustrating, but most often rewarding. As Executive Director of Undergraduate Admissions at a large, selective university, I would like to provide some basic information about the admission process that should help you get into the college of your choice. Although each competitive college or university has its own distinctive qualities and goals, the process of applying to them is strikingly similar. The following will give you the basic information you need to help you plan and apply to college.

GATHERING INFORMATION

How do you get the information you need to choose a college? Although colleges publish volumes of information about themselves that they are willing to mail or give out in person, another way to find out about them is through a guide such as this one.

The major difference between the college-published materials and this guide is that the colleges present only the most appealing picture of themselves and are perhaps, then, somewhat less objective. As a student seeking information about college, you should review both the information provided in guides like this one and the information sent by the colleges. Your goal should be to use all of the available literature to assist you in developing your list of the top five or ten colleges in which you are interested.

Chances are that if you are a top student and you have taken the PSAT, SAT, SAT Subject Tests, ACT, or AP (Advanced Placement) tests, you will receive a great deal of material directly from many colleges and universities. Colleges purchase lists of names of students taking these exams and then screen the list for students they think will be most successful at their institutions. Some colleges will also automatically mail course catalogs, posters, departmental brochures, and pamphlets, as well as DVDs. If you do not receive this information but would like a sample, write or call that particular college.

My advice is to take a look at the materials you receive and then use them to help you decide (if you don't already know) about the type of college you would like to attend. Allow the materials to help you narrow your list of top schools by comparing key facts and characteristics.

OTHER HELPFUL SOURCES

Published information about colleges, printed by the colleges, is certainly an important way to narrow your choices. But there are other means of learning more about colleges and universities:

- *High School Counselors.* Most high school counselors have established positive relationships with the college representatives in your state as well as with out-of-state universities where large numbers of their students apply. As you attempt to gain more information while narrowing your choice of colleges, the high school counselor can give you a fairly accurate assessment of colleges to which you will have the best chance of gaining admission.

- *Parents.* Because most prospective students and their parents are at that stage in life in which they view issues in different ways, students tend to be reluctant to ask parents' opinions about college choices. However, you may find that parents are very helpful because they often are actively gathering information about the colleges that they feel are best suited for you. And not only do they gather information—you can be sure that they have thoroughly read the piles of literature that colleges have mailed to you. Ask your parents questions about what they have read and also about the colleges from which they graduated. As alumni of schools on your list, parents can be a very valuable resource.

- *College Day/Night/Fairs Visitation.* One of the best ways to help narrow your college choices is to meet with a person representing a college while they are visiting your area or high school. In fact, most admission staff members spend a good portion of the late spring and fall visiting high schools and attending college fairs. In some cases, college fairs feature students, faculty members, and alumni. Before attending one of these sessions, you should prepare a list of questions you would like to ask the representatives. Most students want to know about five major areas:

1 Academic preparation

2 The admission process

3 Financial aid

4 Social life

5 Job preparation

Most college representatives can be extremely helpful in addressing these questions as well as the many others that you may have. It is then up to you to decide if their answers fit your criteria of the college you are seeking.

- *Alumni.* For many schools, alumni are a very important part of the admission process. In some cases, alumni conduct interviews and even serve as surrogate admission officers, particularly when admission office staff cannot travel. As recent graduates, alumni can talk about their own experience and can give balance to the materials you have received from the college or university.

- *Campus Visits.* Finally, try to schedule a campus visit as part of your information-gathering process in an effort to make sure that the reality lives up to whatever material you've read. Most colleges and universities provide daily campus tours to both prospective and admitted students. The tours for prospective students are generally set up to help you answer questions about the following: class size and student-to-teacher ratio; size of the library, residence halls, and computer centers; registration and faculty advising; and retention, graduation rates, and career placement planning. Since the tours may not cover

everything you came prepared to ask about, be sure to ask questions of as many staff, students, and faculty members as possible before leaving the campus.

THE ADMISSION PROCESS

ADMISSION CRITERIA

After you go through the process of selecting a college or narrowing your choices to a few schools, the admission process now focuses on you—your academic record and skills—and judgment will be passed on these pieces of information for admission to a particular school. The first four things you should find out about each college on your priority list are the admission criteria—what it takes to get in:

1 Does the college or university require standardized tests—the ACT or SAT? Do they prefer one or the other, or will they accept either?

2 Do they require SAT Subject Tests and, if so, which ones?

3 Are Advanced Placement scores accepted and, if so, what are the minimums needed?

4 In terms of grades and class rank, what is the profile of a typical entering student?

It is also important to find out which type of admission notification system the college uses—rolling or deferred admission. On a rolling system, you find out your status within several weeks of applying; with the deferred system, notification is generally made in the spring. For the most part, public universities and colleges use rolling admission and private colleges generally use deferred admission.

THE APPLICATION

The application is the primary vehicle used to introduce yourself to the admission office. As with any introduction, you want to make a good first impression. The first thing you should do in presenting your application is to find out what the college or university wants from you. This means you should read the application carefully to learn the following:

- Is there an application fee and, if so, how much is it?
- Is there a deadline and, if so, when is it?

- What standardized tests are required?
- Is an essay required?
- Is an interview required?
- Should you send letters of recommendation?
- How long will it take to find out the admission decision?
- What other things can you do to improve your chances for admission?

My advice is to submit your application early. It does not guarantee admission, but it is much better than submitting it late or near the deadline. Also, don't assume that colleges using rolling admission will always have openings close to their deadlines. Regardless of when you submit it, make sure that the application has all the information that is requested.

TRANSCRIPTS

While all of the components of the application are extremely important in the admission process, perhaps the single most important item is your transcript because it tells what courses you took, which courses were college-preparatory and challenging, class rank, and grades and test scores.

- *Required Course Work.* Generally speaking, most colleges look at the high school transcript to see if the applicant followed a college-preparatory track while in high school. So, if you have taken four years of English, math, natural science, social sciences, and foreign language, you are on the right track. Many selective colleges require four years of English; three years each of math, natural science, and social science; and two years of a foreign language. It is also true that some selective colleges believe students who are interested in majoring in math and science need more than the minimum requirements in those areas.
- *Challenging Courses.* As college admission staff members continue to evaluate your transcript, they also look to see how demanding your course load has been during high school. If the high school offered Advanced Placement or Honors courses, the expectation of most selective colleges is that students will have taken seven or more honors classes or four or more AP courses during their four years in high school. However, if you

do elect to take challenging courses, it is also important that you make good grades in those courses. Quite often, students ask, "If I take Honors and AP courses and get a 'C,' does that count more than getting a 'B' or higher in a strictly college-prep course?" It's a difficult question to answer, because too many C's and B's can outweigh mostly A's. On the other hand, students who take the more challenging courses will be better prepared to take the more rigorous courses in college. Consequently, many colleges will give extra consideration when making their selections to the students who take the more demanding courses.

- *Transcript Trends.* Because the courses you take in high school are such a critical part of the college decision-making process, your performance in those courses indicates to colleges whether you are following an upward or downward trend. Beginning with the ninth grade, admission staff look at your transcript to see if you have started to develop good academic habits. In general, when colleges review your performance in the ninth grade, they are looking to see if you are in the college-preparatory track.

By sophomore year, students should begin choosing more demanding courses and become more involved in extracurricular activities. This will show that you are beginning to learn how to balance your academic and extracurricular commitments. Many admission officers consider the sophomore year to be the most critical and telling year for a student's future success.

The junior year is perhaps the second-most-important year in high school. The grades you earn and the courses you take will help to reinforce the trend you began in your sophomore year. At the end of your junior year, many colleges will know enough about the type of student you are to make their admission decision.

The upward and positive trend must continue, however, during your senior year. Many selective schools do not use senior grades in making their admission decisions. However, almost all review the final transcript, so your last year needs to show a strong performance to the end. The research shows that students who finish their senior year with strong grades will start their freshman year in college with strong grades.

THE APPLICATION REVIEW PROCESS

WHAT'S NEXT?

At this point, you have done all you can do. So you might as well sit back and relax, if that's possible, and wait for the letters to come in the mail. Hopefully, if you've evaluated all the college materials you were sent earlier and you prepared your application carefully and sent it to several colleges, you will be admitted to either your first, second, or third choice. It may help your peace of mind, however, to know what happens to your application after the materials have been submitted.

Once your application is received by the admission office, it is reviewed, in most cases by noncounseling staff, to determine if you have completed the application properly. If items are missing, you will receive a letter of notification identifying additional information that must be provided. Be sure to send any additional or missing information the college requests back to them as soon as possible. Once your application is complete, it is then ready for the decision process.

READER REVIEW

The process by which the decision is finalized varies from school to school. Most private colleges and universities use a system in which each application is read by two or more admission staff members. In some cases, faculty members are also readers. If all of the readers agree on the decision, a letter is sent. Under this system, if the readers do not agree, the application will be reviewed by a committee or may be forwarded to an associate dean, dean, or director of admission for the final decision. One advantage to this process is that each applicant is reviewed by several people, thereby eliminating bias.

COMMITTEE REVIEW

At some universities, a committee reviews every application. Under that system, a committee member is assigned a number of applications to present. It is that member's responsibility to prepare background information on each applicant and then present the file to the committee for discussion and a vote. In this process, every applicant is voted on.

COUNSELOR REVIEW

The review process that many selective public institutions use is one in which the counselor responsible for a particular school or geographical territory makes the final decision. In this case, the counselor who makes the admission decision is also the one who identified and recruited the student, thereby lending a more personal tone to the process.

COMPUTER-GENERATED REVIEW

Many large state universities that process nearly 20,000 applications a year have developed computer-generated guidelines to admit their applicants. If applicants meet the required GPA and test scores, they are immediately notified of the decision.

A WORD OF ADVICE

When you start the admission process, do so with the idea of exploring as many college opportunities as you can. From the very beginning, avoid focusing on just one college or, for that matter, one type of college. Look at private, public, large, small, highly selective, selective—in short, a variety of colleges and universities. Take advantage of every available resource, including students, parents, counselors, and college materials, in order to help identify the colleges that will be a great fit for you.

Finally, the most important thing you can do is to build a checklist of what you want out of the college experience and then match your list with one of the many wonderful colleges and universities just waiting for you to enroll.

CRAFTING A COMPETITIVE COLLEGE APPLICATION OR WHAT CAN I DO TO GET IN?

Not to discourage you about applying to competitive colleges, but the number of students who are over-the-top qualified to get into these schools versus the number of available slots is mind-boggling! Recently, the University of Southern California had 34,000 applications for 2,700 freshman seats, while the eight Ivy League schools' admission rate is just below 10 percent. (Thirty percent is considered competitive—get the picture?)

Mickey Gilbert, Guidance Counselor at Passaic High School in New Jersey, throws out a few figures to his students to help them understand the competition: There are about 32,000 high schools in the United States and roughly 4,000 high schools outside the country with students who apply to U.S. colleges. Take the top ten students from each class—those who are the academically gifted and who have done everything, been everything, and won everything. Multiply those ten students from each class by the 36,000 worldwide high schools and you get 360,000 students who are in the pool of well-qualified applicants. Granted, all high schools are not alike, but this gives you an idea of what you face if you are applying to a competitive school.

WHY SO MUCH COMPETITION?

THE SHEER NUMBER OF WELL-QUALIFIED APPLICANTS
"Twenty years ago it was a student's market," notes Kathy Cleaver, Co-Director of College Counseling at Durham Academy, a private high school in North Carolina. Back then, students could pretty much pick and choose. Not anymore. Today, more exceptional students are applying to more competitive colleges.

However, colleges haven't fully increased the size of their freshman classes to meet the demand, nor do they want to. Like other competitive schools, the University of Denver is committed to keeping classes small so that teachers can be involved with their students, instead of lecturing to thousands. The University of Southern California also faces the same dilemma—whether or not to increase the number of classes and faculty members.

"If we're already going 8 a.m. to 6 p.m., Monday through Friday, and are busy on weekends, there are finite limitations to how many people a professor can teach, how many sections we can offer," comments Dr. Katharine Harrington, Dean of Admissions and Financial Aid at USC.

THE PRESTIGE FACTOR
"Competition has increased for spaces because more students think that certain schools are their only road to success," observes Doris Davis, Cornell University's Associate Provost for Admissions and Enrollment. Many top students have a short list of possibilities and won't consider schools they think aren't up to their expectations. Their list is based only on the name of the university.

JUST HOW BRILLIANT ARE YOU?
Once the "most" brilliant applicants are chosen, admitting committees are faced with choosing from the "less" brilliant applicants. You could have done exceptionally well in your high school, but you're up against many others who are more brilliant than you.

"The worst part of this job is that we have to say 'no' to three out of four applicants because we can't accept all the students who can do the work," says Harrington. "The hard choices come at the margin."

GETTING ADMITTED ISN'T ALL ABOUT GRADES OR ACTIVITIES
Don't assume that if you have achieved great grades and test scores, done all the activities that admissions

officers like to see, and written a dazzling essay, but you still weren't admitted, there's something wrong with you. There are other factors besides GPAs that count. Some admission officers say they "sculpt" or "shape" each freshman class. Schools don't just plug in grade averages and take the top students to fill their quota.

"Schools want to build racial, socioeconomic, religious, and geographic diversity into each class," says Cleaver. For instance, a prestigious school on the east coast might choose a student from Montana over someone with a higher GPA who lives in Massachusetts.

Those deciding whether you should or shouldn't be admitted are looking at the big picture of college life—not just what you'll learn in the classroom but also what you'll learn outside the classroom.

"A healthy community is one that is integrated along a number of points. We want to shape a class by identifying students who, together, will build a strong community," says Davis. "Students learn from each other. That's why it's so important to us."

Being exposed to people who look different, think differently, and act differently creates a "fabric or a stew," observes Cleaver, who uses the illustration to show that a greater variety of students becomes a flavorful and rich class. Admissions are looking for the mix of students from all kinds of backgrounds to give each incoming class the experience of studying, living, and playing with people who aren't all the same.

SO, HOW DO YOU GIVE YOURSELF THE EDGE?

Granted, the talk so far has been somewhat negative and it might sound like your chances are out of your control. That is not so. You do have control over a great deal of the process of getting into a competitive college.

HAVE YOU TAKEN CHALLENGING CLASSES?

Not all GPA's are equal to the people deciding to admit you. Admitting committees look at overall trends in your grades. Maybe you had a 3.5 GPA your first two years of high school, but in your junior and senior years, you have a 3.9 GPA.

"That's an upward trend that can help you if you're competing for those last spots in a freshman class at a competitive college," observes Todd Rinehart, Assistant Vice Chancellor/Director of Admission at the University of Denver.

ARE YOU LETTING OTHERS DECIDE WHICH COLLEGE IS BEST FOR YOU?

This includes your parents, your best friend who is applying to "The Best University," and your uncle who went to an Ivy League school, not to mention your own expectations that demand only one institution or else. When Harrington visits high schools to talk about the college application process, she makes sure parents know they can help facilitate their children getting into college, but the college choice is not about parents' bragging rights to their co-workers.

ARE YOU ONLY CONSIDERING THE NAME?

The schools heading the latest magazine list comprise a small percentage of colleges in the United States. Many outstanding students don't take full advantage of the tremendous range of schools but instead set their sights on only a few names. Do you assume smart, talented students only attend certain schools? Broaden your horizons and you'll find dozens of schools that match your needs.

"Look at your passion and what a school can offer you," advises Gilbert. He recalls one student who loved Civil War history and wanted to apply only to a competitive school that offered little to do with his fascination. Gilbert directed him to a small college that wasn't a brand name but was located in Gettysburg, right in the middle of his favorite period of history! He'll point another student who is leaning toward architecture to a school that isn't super competitive but has a terrific architecture program. "It's what you want to do, not its name," he says.

When counseling her high school students, Cleaver tells them that each college has a personality. Some get their identity from sports; others are more academically competitive, with a constant focus on grades. Some revolve around Greek life or religion or are known for their politically charged environment and student activism. Target a school because it matches your personality.

"If you bring a wonderful set of skills or a mindset that would strengthen a program, it will more easily help the admission office see why you would be a strong student at their institution," says Cleaver. Admitting committees want to find the best fit between your goals and their institution.

"We want students to find the best place for them," says Davis. "My goal is to make sure students are a good match with us."

DOES YOUR APPLICATION TELL WHO YOU ARE?

If your application speaks clearly about you, the admission people around the table (who have read hundreds of applications) will see you as a whole person, including your academic capabilities, what interests you, and what makes you unique. An application is the culmination of all the pieces that make up who you are.

"We're looking at your essay, your letters of recommendation, your responses to the questions on the application, your academics. If it all comes together, we know you're on to something," says Davis.

DOES YOUR ESSAY REVEAL WHAT MAKES YOU TICK?

Cleaver compares the essay to a hologram that stands on the table in front of the admitting committee to show you as a real person. Your essay can make you stand out from the student whose application they read half an hour ago. She offers an example of two essays. The first starts out, "I've done rock climbing 20 hours a week for the last three years." The second begins with, "I'm standing on a ledge, looking down hundreds of feet and wondering how I got there."

"Think about what you want someone to know about you," she advises. "Rather than repeat your grades or activities, show how you are a hard worker, overcame adversity, learned from failure, or faced your fears."

DO YOUR ACTIVITIES JUMP OFF THE PAGE?

Authenticity is what admitting committees look for when reading about your extracurricular activities. Just listing them doesn't tell who you are. Sure, you might have joined ten different clubs, volunteered at a soup kitchen for one semester and a hospital the next, and collected cans to save the environment, but that doesn't show your commitment. This is the time to brag about yourself, to bring out times when

you were responsible, whether it was as chairman of the clean-up committee or when you took care of a 4-year-old cousin for a summer.

DID YOU CHOOSE THE RIGHT TEACHER TO WRITE YOUR LETTER OF RECOMMENDATION?

The "right" teacher isn't necessarily the teacher who gave you the highest grades. Choose someone who understands what motivates you. Maybe you got a B in math because you were overcoming a tremendous challenge at the time and that teacher saw you persevere. Maybe it was someone who helped you develop leadership qualities and can write about how you will be an asset to a college.

"Ask a teacher who can write about both your academic interests and your skills," advises Cleaver.

AND HOW DO YOU LOSE THAT EDGE?

NOT HITTING THE SEND BUTTON

It can happen to the best students. You're rushing to get out those six applications to meet the deadline. You've made sure your information is correct, filled in the checklist, done the spell-check, and when everything was done, you sat back and relaxed. Sorry to say, you forgot to actually submit it! With more than 80 percent of applications submitted online, it's an easy mistake to make. So, call a week after you (think you) submitted your application to verify its receipt with the admission office.

HIRING SOMEONE TO WRITE YOUR APPLICATION ESSAY

Too bad the same person didn't write your SAT essay! Admission departments compare the essay you wrote for them and your SAT essay and can easily tell if the two match. It's okay to have your essay proofed by someone, but you should be the only author.

ALL MY LIFE I'VE WANTED TO GO TO (FILL IN THE BLANK)

Except the school you're applying to doesn't have that name! You can start with a standard application because much of the information is applicable to multiple schools, but make sure to customize each application—and then double-check everything to make sure all the school name references are correct. This is a more common mistake than you think.

FANCY FOLDERS AND COLORED PAPER DON'T IMPRESS

In fact, by the time your application gets to the people who will read it, they have probably already put it in a standard folder. The presentation of your application should concentrate on content, spelling, and grammar, not the packaging.

FORGET CLEVER AND CUTE

The applicant who had a chair delivered to the admissions office with the attached note, "Hope this reserves a chair for me," was creative, but no one was impressed. Same with the shoe another student sent saying, "Now that I have one foot in the door." Then there was the essay someone wrote on a football. Every admission office has stories of the crazy things applicants do to try to stand out. It isn't effective. Show your creativity and resourcefulness in presenting a detailed application and well-written essay.

Applying to Professional Colleges for Art and Music

Theresa Bedoya
Vice President of Admissions and Financial Aid, Maryland Institute College of Art

The term "competitive" will have a different meaning if you are applying to a professional college specializing in art or music. The goal of selective art and music colleges is to admit students of extraordinary talent. Since you are using this resource as part of your college search, you most likely have distinguished yourself academically. But to gain admission to the music and art colleges listed in this guide, you will also need to be competitive in your achievements in the arts.

ADMISSION CRITERIA

In order to choose the most talented students from those who apply, most professional art and music colleges require evidence of talent, skill, ability, experience, and desire as demonstrated in an audition or by a portfolio of artwork. Each art and music college has expectations and academic requirements particular to the program of study you choose.

Admission will be based upon the review of traditional criteria such as your grade point average, level of course work, test scores, essays, and interviews. However, for most professional colleges, the evaluation of your portfolio or your audition will supersede the review of all other criteria for admission. (Many visual arts colleges even prescreen potential applicants through review of the portfolio prior to application in order to determine eligibility for admission. This process, which occurs early in the senior year, allows students the opportunity to gain valuable guidance early in the admission process. It also creates a more "acceptable" pool of applicants and is the reason that acceptance rates at many visual arts colleges appear to be higher than other selective institutions.) In some cases, the evaluation of your talent and academic achievement will be given equal weight.

In contrast, most comprehensive colleges and universities offering majors in art and music will rely on academic criteria to make an admission decision. The portfolio or audition, if required, will play a secondary role. You should take these factors into account when deciding whether to apply to art and music schools or to colleges and universities that offer art and music programs.

PREPARING FOR YOUR PORTFOLIO REVIEW OR AUDITION

If you are interested in the visual arts, you should gain as much studio experience as possible in order to develop a strong portfolio. Take full advantage of your high school art program and enroll in Saturday or summer classes or seek private tutoring. Exhibit your artwork when the opportunity is provided. Become better informed as an artist by studying art history and the works of contemporary artists.

If you plan to study music, remember that experience and confidence need to be clearly evident in your audition. Therefore, become involved as much as possible in your own high school music activities as well as local, district, and state youth orchestras, choirs, and performance ensembles. The more you perform and study, the more confident you will be on stage.

Contact the schools to which you are applying early in the process to learn how and when they will receive your portfolio or conduct your audition.

PAYING FOR COLLEGE

DON BETTERTON
Former Director of Financial Aid at Princeton University

Regardless of which college a student chooses, higher education requires a major investment of time, energy, and money. By taking advantage of a variety of available resources, most students can bring the education that is right for them within reach.

A NOTE OF ENCOURAGEMENT

While there is no denying that the cost of an education at some competitive colleges can be high, it is important to recognize that, although the rate of increase in costs in recent years has outpaced gains in family income, there are more options available to pay for college than ever before.

Many families find it is economically wise to spread costs out over a number of years by borrowing money for college. A significant amount of government money, both federal and state, is available to students. Moreover, colleges themselves have expanded their own student aid efforts considerably. In spite of rapidly increasing costs, most competitive colleges are still able to provide financial aid to all admitted students with demonstrated need.

In addition, many colleges have developed ways to assist families who are not eligible for need-based assistance. These include an increasing number of merit scholarships as well as various forms of parental loans. There also are a number of organizations that give merit awards based on a student's academic record, talent, or special characteristics. Thus, regardless of your family's income, if you are academically qualified and knowledgeable about the many different sources of aid, you should be able to attend the college of your choice.

ESTIMATING COSTS

If you have not yet settled on specific colleges and you would like to begin early financial planning, estimate a budget. As reported in *Trends in College Pricing 2008* (College Board) the average New England region private college costs for 2008–09

include tuition and fees of $31,680 and room and board costs of $10,701 for total expenses of $42,381. Yet in the southwest, private school total costs are $28,511. Nationally, 2008–09 total costs at private school averaged about $34,132. Given this rather wide variation, it is best to check with each school you are considering. You can assume a 5 percent cost increase each year.

IDENTIFYING RESOURCES

There are essentially four sources of funds you can use to pay for college:

1. Money from your parents
2. Need-based scholarships or grants from federal and/or state programs, a college, or outside organization
3. Your own contribution from savings, loans, and jobs
4. Other forms of assistance unrelated to demonstrated financial need

All of these are considered by the financial aid office, and the aid "package" given to a student after the parental contribution has been determined usually consists of a combination of scholarships, loans, and campus work.

THE PARENTAL CONTRIBUTION

The financial aid policies of most colleges are based on the assumption that parents should contribute as much as they reasonably can to the education expenses of their children. The amount of this contribution varies greatly, according to a family's current financial situation.

Because there is no limit on aid eligibility based solely on income, the best rule of thumb is *apply for financial aid if there is any reasonable doubt about your ability to meet college costs*. Since it is generally true that applying for financial aid does not affect a student's chances of being admitted (known as "need-blind" admission), any candidate for admission should apply for aid if his or her family feels they will be unable to pay the entire cost of attendance. (In spite of considerable publicity on the subject, there are still only a handful of competitive colleges that practice need-sensitive admissions.)

Application for aid is made by completing the Free Application for Federal Student Aid (FAFSA). In addition, many competitive colleges will require you to also file a separate application called PROFILE®, since they need more detailed information to award their own funds. The financial aid section of a college's admission information booklet will tell you which financial aid application is required, when it should be filed, and whether a separate aid form of the college's own design is also necessary.

All colleges use the same government formula (the Federal Methodology) to determine eligibility for federal and state student aid. This process of coming up with an expected contribution from you (the student) and your parents is called "need analysis." The information on the FAFSA—parental and student income and assets, the number of family members, and the number attending college as well as other variables—is analyzed to derive the Expected Family Contribution (EFC). You can estimate how much your family will be expected to contribute by referring to the EFC calculator at http://www.finaid.org/calculators/quickefc.phtml. Keep in mind that the parental contribution is determined on campus by a financial aid officer, using the government formula as a guideline.

Competitive colleges that also require the PROFILE will have at their disposal information they will analyze in addition to what is reported on the FAFSA. The net result of this further examination (for example, adding the value of the family home to the equation) will usually increase the expected parental contribution compared to the Federal Methodology.

Parental Borrowing

Some families who are judged to have sufficient resources to be able to finance their children's college costs find that lack of cash at any moment prevents them from paying college bills without difficulty.

Other families prefer to use less current income by extending their payments over more than four years. In both instances, these families rely on borrowing to assist with college payments. Each year parental loans become a more important form of college financing.

The Federal PLUS program (PLUS), part of the Federal Family Education Loan Program (FFELP) and the Direct Loan (DL) program, is designed to help both aid and non-aid families. It allows parents to pay their share of education costs by borrowing at a reasonable interest rate, with the backing of the federal government. These loans are available through both the DL program, administered at the college or university, and FFELP, administered through banks and financial institutions. For 2008–09, the interest rate for Federal PLUS Loans is fixed at 8.5 percent and for Direct PLUS Loans it is fixed at 7.9 percent. Interest is charged on the loan from the date of the first disbursement until the loan is paid. Many competitive colleges, state governments, and commercial lenders also have their own parental loan programs patterned along the lines of PLUS. For more information about parent loans for students, contact a college financial aid office or your state higher education department.

NEED-BASED SCHOLARSHIP OR GRANT ASSISTANCE

Need-based aid is primarily available from federal and state governments and from colleges themselves. It is not necessary for a student to apply directly for a particular scholarship at a college; the financial aid office will match an eligible applicant with the appropriate fund.

The Federal Pell Grant is by far the largest single form of federal student assistance; an estimated 5.3 million students receive awards annually. Families with incomes of up to $50,000 (often higher when other family members are in college or family assets are relatively low) may be eligible for grants up to $5350 for the 2009–10 award year. By filing the FAFSA, you automatically apply for the Federal Pell Grant and the Federal Supplemental Educational Opportunity Grant. Students eligible for a Federal Pell Grant who complete a rigorous high school program (as defined by their state) may be eligible for an Academic Competitiveness Grant ($750 first-year students; $1300 second-year students). Federal Pell Grant students who major in science, math, and certain foreign languages and maintain a 3.0 GPA may be eligible for a SMART Grant ($4000 a year for up to 2 years). Further information is available from the financial aid office.

Most state-administered financial aid programs use the FAFSA as their application form. In general, state aid programs are usually not portable, meaning that they cannot be used out-of-state. Check with your state higher education department for additional information on application procedures and restrictions.

The Student's Own Contribution

All undergraduates, not only those who apply for financial aid, can assume responsibility for meeting a portion of their college expenses by borrowing, working during the academic year and the summer, and contributing a portion of their savings. Many private colleges require aid recipients to provide a "self-help" contribution before awarding grant and scholarship money because they believe students should pay a reasonable share of their own education costs.

Student Loans

Virtually every student will be able to borrow to help pay for college. Colleges administer three types of loans (all backed by the federal government):

1 Direct Stafford Loans

2 Federal Family Education Loan Program (FFELP) Stafford Loans

3 Federal Perkins Loans

Students must demonstrate financial need to be eligible for the Federal Perkins Loan. While every student is eligible for the Stafford Loan programs, financial need must be demonstrated to have the interest on the loan subsidized by the federal government.

Rather than providing FFELP Stafford Loans, some colleges have made arrangements to participate in the Direct Stafford Loan program. Under the Direct Loan program, the U.S. Department of Education serves as the lender, while under the FFELP, students and parents deal with a private lender, usually a bank or credit union. As far as the

student is concerned, the loan terms are essentially the same. Once you have selected your college, the financial aid office will guide you through the process.

Summer Employment

All students, whether or not they are receiving financial aid, should plan to work during the summer months. Students may be expected to save from $800 to $1850 before their freshman year and $1500 to $2550 each summer while enrolled in college. It is worthwhile for a student to begin working while in high school to increase the chance of finding summer employment during college vacations.

Term-Time Employment

Colleges have student employment offices that find jobs for students during the school year. Aid recipients on the Federal Work-Study Program receive priority in placement, but once they have been assisted, non-aid students are helped as well. Some jobs relate closely to academic interests; others should be viewed as a source of income rather than intellectual stimulation. A standard 8- to 15-hour-per-week job does not normally interfere with academic work or extracurricular activities and results in approximately $1500 to $2500 in earnings during the academic year.

Student Savings

Student assets accumulated prior to starting college are available to help pay college bills. The need-analysis system expects 20 percent of each year's student savings to go toward college expenses. This source can often be quite substantial, particularly when families have accumulated large sums in the student's name (or in a trust fund with the student as the beneficiary). If you have a choice whether to keep college savings in the parents' name or the student's name, you should realize that the contribution rate on parental assets can never be more than 5.6 percent, compared to 20 percent for the student's savings.

Aid Not Requiring Need as an Eligibility Criterion

There are scholarships available to students whether or not they are eligible for need-based financial aid. Awards based on merit are given by certain state scholarship programs, and National Merit Scholarship winners usually receive a $2500 stipend regardless of family financial circumstances. Scholarships and prizes are also awarded by community organizations and other local groups. In addition, some parents receive tuition payments for their children as employment benefits. Most colleges offer merit scholarships to a limited group of highly qualified applicants. The selection of recipients for such awards depends on unusual talent in a specific area or on overall academic excellence.

The Reserve Officers' Training Corps sponsors an extensive scholarship program that pays for tuition and books and provides an expense allowance of $300 a month for the first school year and increasing each subsequent year. The Army, Air Force, and Navy/Marine Corps have ROTC units at many colleges.

High school guidance offices have brochures describing ROTC application procedures. Since each branch of the service has a number of incentive programs, check with your ROTC recruiter for more information.

Students are encouraged to aggressively seek out private sources of financial aid. Many books are available, including *Peterson's Scholarships, Grants & Prizes*. Peterson's Web site, www.petersons.com, has scholarship search features and links to other financial aid-related topics.

Aid recipients are required to notify the college financial aid office about outside awards, as colleges take into consideration grants from all sources in developing the financial aid package for their students.

SPONSOR LIST

These sponsors arranged for copies of this guide to reach outstanding students—students eager to learn more about top schools. This icon appears in each sponsor's profile:

SPONSOR

Agnes Scott College
Albany College of Pharmacy and
    Health Sciences
Alfred University
Alma College
American University
Amherst College
Augustana College (IL)
Barnard College
Belmont University
Beloit College
Bethel University
Birmingham-Southern College
Boston College
Brown University
Bucknell University
Butler University
Calvin College
Canisius College
Carnegie Mellon University
Chapman University
Clarkson University
Clemson University
The College of New Jersey
College of the Atlantic
College of the Holy Cross
The College of Wooster
Colorado State University
Cornell College
Cornell University
Denison University
Dominican University
Drake University
Elizabethtown College
Emerson College
Eugene Lang College The New
    School for Liberal Arts
Florida Institute of Technology
Fordham University

Georgia State University
Gettysburg College
Grove City College
Hamilton College (NY)
Harding University
Haverford College
Hendrix College
Hillsdale College
Hobart and William Smith Colleges
Ithaca College
Juniata College
Kettering University
Lafayette College
Lawrence Technological University
Lebanon Valley College
Linfield College
List College, The Jewish
    Theological Seminary
Loyola College in Maryland
Loyola University New Orleans
Marietta College
Messiah College
Michigan State University
Mills College
Muhlenberg College
New College of Florida
New Jersey Institute of Technology
New York School of Interior Design
North Central College
Oberlin College
Oglethorpe University
Ohio Northern University
Ohio Wesleyan University
Pitzer College
Princeton University
Providence College
Quinnipiac University
Randolph College
Reed College

Rice University
Ripon College
Rochester Institute of Technology
Saint Francis University
St. John's College (MD)
St. John's College (NM)
Saint Joseph's University
St. Lawrence University
Saint Louis University
Saint Mary's College
St. Mary's College of Maryland
St. Norbert College
Samford University
Sarah Lawrence College
Seattle University
Siena College
Simpson College
Skidmore College
Smith College
Southern Methodist University
Southwestern University
State University of New York
    College of Environmental
    Science and Forestry
Stevens Institute of Technology
Susquehanna University
Sweet Briar College
Syracuse University
Texas Christian University
Transylvania University
Union College (NY)
Union University
United States Air Force Academy
United States Merchant Marine
    Academy
United States Military Academy
University at Buffalo, the State
    University of New York
University of Arkansas

University of Central Florida
University of Denver
University of Redlands
University of Rochester
University of St. Thomas (MN)
University of San Diego
University of South Carolina

University of the Sciences in
   Philadelphia
Valparaiso University
Villanova University
Virginia Military Institute
Wabash College
Washington College

Wellesley College
Wells College
Wesleyan College
Western Washington University
Westminster College (UT)
Williams College
Worcester Polytechnic Institute

How to Use This Guide

PROFILES OF COMPETITIVE COLLEGES

This section presents pertinent factual and statistical data for each college in a standard format for easy comparison. All college information presented was supplied to Peterson's by the colleges themselves. Any item that does not apply to a particular college or for which no information was supplied is omitted from that college's profile.

GENERAL INFORMATION

The first paragraph gives a brief introduction to the college, covering the following elements.

Campus setting: This indicates the size of the campus in acres or hectares and its location.

Institutional control: A *public* college receives its funding wholly or primarily from the federal, state, and/or local government. The term *private* indicates an independent, nonprofit institution, that is, one whose funding comes primarily from private sources and tuition. This category includes independent, religious colleges, which may also specify a particular religious denomination or church affiliation. Profit-making institutions are designated as *proprietary*.

Type of student body: The categories are *men's* (100 percent of the student body), *primarily men's*, *women's* (100 percent of the student body), *primarily women's*, and *coed*. A few schools are designated as *undergraduate: women only, graduate: coed* or *undergraduate: men only, graduate: coed*. A college may also be designated as coordinate with another institution, indicating that there are separate colleges or campuses for men and women, but facilities, courses, and institutional governance are shared.

Contact information: Along with the school's location and Web address, the name, title, mailing address, telephone, fax, and e-mail address of the person to contact for more information on application and admission procedures are given here.

ACADEMICS

This paragraph contains information on the following items.

Degree levels: An *associate* degree program may consist of either a college-transfer program, equivalent to the first two years of a bachelor's degree, or a one- to three-year terminal program that provides training for a specific occupation. A *bachelor's* degree program represents a three- to five-year liberal arts, science, professional, or preprofessional program. A *master's* degree is the first graduate degree in the liberal arts and sciences and certain professional fields and usually requires one to two years of full-time study. A *doctoral* degree is the highest degree awarded in research-oriented academic disciplines and usually requires from three to six years of full-time graduate study; the *first professional* degrees in such fields as law and medicine are also at the doctoral level. For colleges that award degrees in one field only, such as art or music, the field of specialization is indicated.

Challenging opportunities: *Advanced placement* gives credit for acceptable scores on College Board Advanced Placement tests. *Accelerated degree programs* allow students to earn a bachelor's degree in three academic years. *Self-designed major* is a program of study based on individual interests, designed by the student with the assistance of an adviser. *Freshmen honors college* is a separate academic program for talented freshmen. *Honors programs* are any special programs for very able students, offering the opportunity for educational enrichment, independent study, acceleration, or some combination of these. *Double major* consists of a program of study in which a student concurrently completes the requirements of two majors. *Independent study* consists of academic work, usually undertaken outside the regular classroom structure, chosen or designed by the student with departmental approval and instructor supervision. *Senior project* indicates a special advanced program is required for students.

Most frequently chosen baccalaureate fields: The most popular field or fields of study at the college, in terms of the number of undergraduate degrees conferred in 2008, are listed.

Faculty: The number of full-time and part-time faculty members as of fall 2008 is given, followed by the percentage of the full-time faculty members who hold doctoral, first professional, or terminal degrees and the student-faculty ratio. (Not all colleges calculate the student-faculty ratio in the same way; Peterson's prints the ratio as provided by the college.)

STUDENTS OF THE COLLEGE

The total number of students and undergraduates enrolled in degree programs as of fall 2008 are given. With reference to the undergraduate enrollment for fall 2008, the percentages of women and men and the number of states and countries from which students hail are listed. The following percentages are also provided: in-state, international, American Indian, African American, Hispanic American, and Asian American or Pacific Islander students, and the percentage of students who returned for their sophomore year.

FACILITIES AND RESOURCES

Computers/terminals: This paragraph includes information on the numbers of computers/terminals and ports available on campus for general student use and what computer technology is accessible to students. Information is also given on the availability of a campuswide network, the percentage of college-owned or -operated housing units wired for high-speed Internet access, and the availability of a wireless campus network.

Libraries: The numbers of books, serials, and audiovisual materials in the college's collections are listed.

CAMPUS LIFE

How many active organizations are represented on campus including information on drama-theater groups, student-run campus newspapers, student-run radio stations, student-run television stations, choral groups, and marching bands. National sorority and national fraternity representation is also provided.

Membership in one or more of the following athletic associations is indicated:

NCAA: National Collegiate Athletic Association

NAIA: National Association of Intercollegiate Athletics

NCCAA: National Christian College Athletic Association

NSCAA: National Small College Athletic Association

NJCAA: National Junior College Athletic Association

CIS: Canadian Interuniversity Sports

The overall NCAA division in which all or most intercollegiate teams compete may be designated by a roman numeral I, II, or III. All teams that do not compete in this division are listed as exceptions.

Intercollegiate sports offered by the college are designated as (m) or (w) following the name of each sport indicating that it is offered for men or women.

CAMPUS SAFETY

Campus safety measures including 24-hour emergency response devices (telephones and alarms) and patrols by trained security personnel, student patrols, late-night transport-escort service, and controlled dormitory access (key, security card, etc.).

APPLYING

The supporting data that a student must submit when applying for freshman admission are grouped into these categories: required for all, recommended, and required for some. They may include an essay, a high school transcript, high school course requirements (e.g., three years of math), letters of recommendation, an interview on campus or with local alumni, standardized test scores, and, for certain types of schools or programs, special requirements such as a musical audition or an art portfolio.

The most commonly required standardized tests are the ACT and the College Board's SAT and SAT Subject Tests. TOEFL (Test of English as a Foreign Language) is for international students whose native language is not English.

The application deadline for admission is given as either a specific date or *rolling*. Rolling means that applications are processed as they are received, and qualified students are accepted as long as there are openings. The application deadline for out-of-state students is indicated if it differs from the date for state residents. *Early decision* and *early action* deadlines are also given when applicable. Early decision is a program whereby students may apply early, are notified of acceptance or rejection well in advance of the usual notification date, and agree to accept an offer of admission, the assumption being that only one early application has been made. Early action is the same as early decision except that applicants are not obligated to accept an offer of admission. *Deferred admission* refers to the perogative of a student to defer admission to a future semester.

Financial aid application deadline: This deadline may be given as a specific date, as continuous processing up to a specific date or until all available aid has been awarded, or as a priority date rather than a strict deadline, meaning that students are encouraged to apply by that date in order to have the best chance of obtaining aid.

GETTING ACCEPTED

Figures are given for the number of students who applied for fall admission, the percentage of those who were accepted, and the number who enrolled. Freshman statistics include the percentage of students graduating in the top tenth of their high school class; average high school GPA; mean SAT critical reading score; mean SAT math score; mean SAT writing score; mean ACT score; the percentage of freshmen who took the SAT and received critical reading, math, and writing scores above 600, and above 700; the percentage who took the ACT and received scores above 24, and above 30; and the numbers of class presidents, valedictorians, and National Merit Scholars.

Graduation and after: Percentages are given for those graduating in four, five, or six years; pursuing further study (and most popular fields, if provided); and with job offers within six months. The number of organizations recruiting on campus is also detailed.

Financial matters: Annual expenses are expressed as a comprehensive fee (includes full-time tuition and mandatory fees) and as a separate figure for room and board. For public institutions where tuition differs

according to residence, separate figures are given for area and/or state residents and for nonresidents.

The tuition structure at some institutions is complex in that freshmen and sophomores may be charged a different rate from that for juniors and seniors or a professional or vocational division may have a different fee structure from the liberal arts division of the same institution. For colleges that report that room and board costs vary according to the type of accommodation and meal plan, the average costs are given. The phrase *no college housing* indicates that the college does not own or operate any housing facilities for its undergraduate students.

Also provided is the dollar amount of the average financial aid package, including scholarships, grants, loans, and part-time jobs, received by such undergraduates.

SPONSOR MESSAGE TO STUDENTS

These messages have been written by those sponsoring colleges that wished to supplement their profile data with additional information.

INDEXES

Specialized Indexes: Indexes are provided covering the following criteria: Twenty-Five Largest Colleges (by total enrollment), Twenty-Five Smallest Colleges (by total enrollment), Single-Sex Colleges: Men Only, Single-Sex Colleges: Women Only, Colleges with Religious Affiliation, Public Colleges, and Hispanic-Serving Institutions.

Majors by College: Listed here are the majors offered at the 440 profiled schools. The schools are listed alphabetically. Although the term "major" is used in this guide, some colleges may use other terms, such as "concentration," "program of study," or "field."

Geographical Listing of Colleges: This index gives the page locations of the colleges and universities included in this book.

DATA COLLECTION PROCEDURES

The data contained in the Profiles and Indexes were researched during the fall and winter of 2008–09 through *Peterson's Annual Survey of Undergraduate*

Institutions. All data included in this edition have been submitted by officials (usually admissions and financial aid officers, registrars, or institutional research personnel) at the colleges. In addition, many of the institutions that submitted data were contacted directly by the Peterson's research staff to verify unusual figures, resolve discrepancies, or obtain additional data. All usable information received in time for publication has been included. The omission of any particular item from an index or profile listing

signifies that the information is either not applicable to that institution or not available. Because of Peterson's comprehensive editorial review and because all material comes directly from college officials, we believe that the information presented in this guide is accurate. You should check with a specific college or university at the time of application to verify such figures as tuition and fees, which may have changed since the publication of this volume.

PROFILES OF COMPETITIVE COLLEGES AND UNIVERSITIES

SPONSOR

AGNES SCOTT COLLEGE
URBAN SETTING ■ PRIVATE ■ INDEPENDENT RELIGIOUS
■ UNDERGRADUATE: WOMEN ONLY; GRADUATE: COED
DECATUR, GEORGIA

Web site: www.agnesscott.edu
Contact: 141 East College Avenue, Decatur, GA 30030-3797
Telephone: 404-471-6285 or toll-free 800-868-8602
Fax: 404-471-6414
E-mail: admission@agnesscott.edu

Agnes Scott College educates women to think deeply, live honorably, and engage the intellectual and social challenges of their times through a twenty-first-century curriculum that emphasizes academic excellence in the liberal arts and sciences. Programs such as the First-Year Seminars, Global Awareness, and Global Connections enrich the Agnes Scott experience. In the last ten years, students have been awarded Gilman, Goldwater, and Fulbright Scholarships and the College has had an NCAA finalist. It ranks in the top 6 percent of 1,325 baccalaureate degree–granting institutions in the percentage of graduates who earn Ph.D.'s. Atlanta provides opportunities for internships, community service, and cultural events. Agnes Scott is an excellent value in terms of academic quality, personalized attention, and a residential community with a student-governed honor system.

Academics
Agnes Scott awards bachelor's and master's **degrees** and post-bachelor's certificates. **Challenging opportunities** include advanced placement credit, accelerated degree programs, student-designed majors, double majors, independent study, and a senior project. Special programs include internships, summer session for credit, off-campus study, study-abroad, and Army and Air Force ROTC.

The most frequently chosen **baccalaureate** fields are social sciences, psychology, and English. A complete listing of majors at Agnes Scott appears in the Majors by College index beginning on page 469.

The **faculty** at Agnes Scott has 83 full-time members, 96% with terminal degrees. The student-faculty ratio is 8:1.

Students of Agnes Scott
The student body totals 832, of whom 813 are undergraduates. 99.4% are women and 0.6% are men. Students come from 43 states and territories and 25 other countries. 53% are from Georgia. 6% are international students. 20.9% are African American, 0.1% American Indian, 4.4% Asian American, and 2.7% Hispanic American. 82% returned for their sophomore year.

Facilities and Resources
458 **computers/terminals** and 3,819 ports are available on campus for general student use. Students can access the following: campus intranet, computer help desk, free student e-mail accounts, online (class) grades, online (class) registration, online (class) schedules. Campuswide network is available. 100% of college-owned or -operated housing units are wired for high-speed Internet access. Wireless service is available via entire campus. The **library** has 228,320 books and 24,017 subscriptions.

Campus Life
There are 50 active organizations on campus, including a drama/theater group, newspaper, television station, choral group, and marching band. No national or local **sororities**.

Agnes Scott is a member of the NCAA (Division III). **Intercollegiate sports** include basketball, lacrosse, soccer, softball, tennis, volleyball.

Campus Safety
Student safety services include security systems in apartments, public safety facility, surveillance equipment, key required for residence hall entry, late-night transport/escort service, 24-hour emergency telephone alarm devices, 24-hour patrols by trained security personnel, and electronically operated dormitory entrances.

Applying
Agnes Scott requires an essay, SAT or ACT, a high school transcript, and 2 recommendations, and in some cases SAT and SAT Subject Tests or ACT. It recommends an interview and a minimum high school GPA of 3.0. Application deadline: 3/1; 5/1 for financial aid, with a 2/15 priority date. Early and deferred admission are possible.

Getting Accepted
1,593 applied
48% were accepted
179 enrolled (23% of accepted)
34% from top tenth of their h.s. class
3.61 average high school GPA
Mean SAT critical reading score: 605
Mean SAT math score: 556
Mean SAT writing score: 591
Mean ACT score: 25
57% had SAT critical reading scores over 600
30% had SAT math scores over 600
46% had SAT writing scores over 600
63% had ACT scores over 24
21% had SAT critical reading scores over 700
3% had SAT math scores over 700
12% had SAT writing scores over 700
21% had ACT scores over 30
1 National Merit Scholar
2 class presidents

Graduation and After
64% graduated in 4 years
6% graduated in 5 years
1% graduated in 6 years
57% had job offers within 6 months
27 organizations recruited on campus

Financial Matters
$30,105 tuition and fees (2009–10)
$9850 room and board
97% average percent of need met
$28,138 average financial aid amount received per undergraduate (2007–08 estimated)

ALBANY COLLEGE OF PHARMACY AND HEALTH SCIENCES

URBAN SETTING ■ PRIVATE ■ INDEPENDENT ■ COED
ALBANY, NEW YORK

Web site: www.acphs.edu
Contact: 106 New Scotland Avenue, Albany, NY 12208-3425
Telephone: 518-694-7221 or toll-free 888-203-8010
Fax: 518-445-7202
E-mail: admissions@acp.edu

SPONSOR

Academics

Albany College of Pharmacy awards bachelor's and first-professional **degrees**. Advanced placement credit is a **challenging opportunity.** Special programs include internships, summer session for credit, off-campus study, and Army, Navy, and Air Force ROTC.

The most frequently chosen **baccalaureate** field is health professions and related sciences. A complete listing of majors at Albany College of Pharmacy appears in the Majors by College index beginning on page 469.

The **faculty** at Albany College of Pharmacy has 76 full-time members.

Students of Albany College of Pharmacy

The student body totals 1,525, of whom 1,099 are undergraduates. 58.6% are women and 41.4% are men. Students come from 28 states and territories and 13 other countries. 85% are from New York. 9% are international students. 2.5% are African American, 0.3% American Indian, 12.8% Asian American, and 1.2% Hispanic American. 80% returned for their sophomore year.

Facilities and Resources

30 **computers/terminals** are available on campus for general student use. Students can access the following: campus intranet, computer help desk, free student e-mail accounts, online (class) grades, online (class) registration, online (class) schedules. Campuswide network is available. 100% of college-owned or -operated housing units are wired for high-speed Internet access. Wireless service is available via entire campus. The **library** has 16,124 books and 3,576 subscriptions.

Campus Life

There are 26 active organizations on campus, including a newspaper and choral group. 6% of eligible men and 5% of eligible women are members of national **fraternities** and national **sororities**.

Intercollegiate sports include basketball, soccer.

Campus Safety

Student safety services include 24-hour emergency telephone alarm devices, 24-hour patrols by trained security personnel, and electronically operated dormitory entrances.

Applying

Albany College of Pharmacy requires an essay, SAT or ACT, a high school transcript, and 2 recommendations, and in some cases an interview. It recommends a minimum high school GPA of 3.0. Application deadline: 2/1; 2/1 priority date for financial aid. Deferred admission is possible.

Albany College of Pharmacy and Health Sciences, one of the nation's premier health science institutions, has a single focus: preparing students for a rewarding career. In an array of medical, scientific, and research professions, the College ensures its students are equipped for a career that makes a difference. Through degree programs in pharmacy, pharmaceutical sciences, health and human sciences, and biomedical technology, students learn how to manage disease states, dispense knowledge, and seek cures. Students also become valuable medical team members who bring hope, knowledge, and well-being to society.

Getting Accepted

1,186 applied
62% were accepted
288 enrolled (39% of accepted)
41% from top tenth of their h.s. class
3.7 average high school GPA
Mean SAT critical reading score: 570
Mean SAT math score: 610
Mean ACT score: 26
34% had SAT critical reading scores over 600
61% had SAT math scores over 600
90% had ACT scores over 24
3% had SAT critical reading scores over 700
9% had SAT math scores over 700
18% had ACT scores over 30

Graduation and After

54% graduated in 4 years
45 organizations recruited on campus

Financial Matters

$22,640 tuition and fees (2008–09)
$7600 room and board
78% average percent of need met
$12,320 average financial aid amount received per undergraduate

ALBION COLLEGE

SMALL-TOWN SETTING ■ PRIVATE ■ INDEPENDENT RELIGIOUS ■ COED
ALBION, MICHIGAN

Web site: www.albion.edu
Contact: Mr. Doug Kellar, Associate Vice President for Enrollment, 611 East Porter Street, Albion, MI 49224
Telephone: 517-629-0600 or toll-free 800-858-6770
Fax: 517-629-0569
E-mail: admissions@albion.edu

Getting Accepted

1,958 applied
83% were accepted
485 enrolled (30% of accepted)
27% from top tenth of their h.s. class
3.55 average high school GPA
Mean SAT critical reading score: 586
Mean SAT math score: 570
Mean SAT writing score: 560
Mean ACT score: 25
49% had SAT critical reading scores over 600
45% had SAT math scores over 600
69% had ACT scores over 24
14% had SAT critical reading scores over 700
8% had SAT math scores over 700
10% had ACT scores over 30
2 National Merit Scholars
17 valedictorians

Graduation and After

63% graduated in 4 years
9% graduated in 5 years
1% graduated in 6 years
73% had job offers within 6 months

Financial Matters

$28,880 tuition and fees (2008–09)
$8190 room and board
91% average percent of need met
$22,108 average financial aid amount received per undergraduate (2007–08 estimated)

Academics

Albion awards bachelor's **degrees**. **Challenging opportunities** include advanced placement credit, student-designed majors, an honors program, double majors, independent study, and a senior project. Special programs include internships, summer session for credit, off-campus study, and study-abroad.

The most frequently chosen **baccalaureate** fields are social sciences, biological/life sciences, and psychology. A complete listing of majors at Albion appears in the Majors by College index beginning on page 469.

The **faculty** at Albion has 138 full-time members. The student-faculty ratio is 12:1.

Students of Albion

The student body is made up of 1,860 undergraduates. 53.5% are women and 46.5% are men. Students come from 28 states and territories and 18 other countries. 91% are from Michigan. 0.9% are international students. 2.6% are African American, 0.4% American Indian, 2.5% Asian American, and 0.8% Hispanic American. 86% returned for their sophomore year.

Facilities and Resources

435 **computers/terminals** and 25 ports are available on campus for general student use. Students can access the following: campus intranet, computer help desk, free student e-mail accounts, online (class) grades, online (class) registration, online (class) schedules, online student account and financial aid. Campuswide network is available. 100% of college-owned or -operated housing units are wired for high-speed Internet access. Wireless service is available via classrooms, computer centers, computer labs, dorm rooms, learning centers, libraries, student centers. The **library** has 363,870 books and 16,293 subscriptions.

Campus Life

There are 122 active organizations on campus, including a drama/theater group, newspaper, radio station, choral group, and marching band. 41% of eligible men and 39% of eligible women are members of national **fraternities** and national **sororities**.

Albion is a member of the NCAA (Division III). **Intercollegiate sports** include baseball (m), basketball, cheerleading, cross-country running, equestrian sports, football (m), golf, soccer, softball (w), swimming and diving, tennis, track and field, volleyball (w).

Campus Safety

Student safety services include late-night transport/escort service, 24-hour emergency telephone alarm devices, 24-hour patrols by trained security personnel, student patrols, and electronically operated dormitory entrances.

Applying

Albion requires an essay, SAT or ACT, a high school transcript, and 1 recommendation, and in some cases TOEFL and an interview. It recommends a minimum high school GPA of 3.2. Application deadline: 5/1; 3/1 priority date for financial aid. Deferred admission is possible.

ALBRIGHT COLLEGE

SUBURBAN SETTING ■ PRIVATE ■ INDEPENDENT RELIGIOUS ■ COED
READING, PENNSYLVANIA

Web site: www.albright.edu
Contact: Mr. Gregory Eichhorn, Vice President for Enrollment Management,
  PO Box 15234, 13th and Bern Streets, Reading, PA 19612-5234
Telephone: 610-921-7260 or toll-free 800-252-1856
Fax: 610-921-7294
E-mail: admission@albright.edu

Academics
Albright awards bachelor's and master's **degrees**. **Challenging opportunities** include advanced placement credit, accelerated degree programs, student-designed majors, an honors program, double majors, independent study, and a senior project. Special programs include internships, summer session for credit, off-campus study, and study-abroad.

The most frequently chosen **baccalaureate** fields are business/marketing, social sciences, and psychology. A complete listing of majors at Albright appears in the Majors by College index beginning on page 469.

The **faculty** at Albright has 118 full-time members, 81% with terminal degrees. The student-faculty ratio is 12:1.

Students of Albright
The student body totals 2,305, of whom 2,245 are undergraduates. 57.6% are women and 42.4% are men. Students come from 26 states and territories and 16 other countries. 65% are from Pennsylvania. 6% are international students. 9.7% are African American, 0.3% American Indian, 1.7% Asian American, and 4.8% Hispanic American. 73% returned for their sophomore year.

Facilities and Resources
800 **computers/terminals** and 1,600 ports are available on campus for general student use. Students can access the following: campus intranet, computer help desk, free student e-mail accounts, online (class) grades, online (class) registration, online (class) schedules. Campuswide network is available. 100% of college-owned or -operated housing units are wired for high-speed Internet access. Wireless service is available via classrooms, computer centers, computer labs, learning centers, libraries, student centers. The 2 **libraries** have 247,969 books and 6,068 subscriptions.

Campus Life
There are 72 active organizations on campus, including a drama/theater group, newspaper, radio station, television station, and choral group. 13% of eligible men and 24% of eligible women are members of national **fraternities** and national **sororities**.

Albright is a member of the NCAA (Division III). **Intercollegiate sports** include badminton (w), baseball (m), basketball, cheerleading, cross-country running, field hockey (w), football (m), golf (m), soccer, softball (w), swimming and diving, tennis, track and field, volleyball (w).

Campus Safety
Student safety services include late-night transport/escort service, 24-hour emergency telephone alarm devices, 24-hour patrols by trained security personnel, student patrols, and electronically operated dormitory entrances.

Applying
Albright requires an essay, standardized tests are optional, a high school transcript, 1 recommendation, and secondary school report (guidance department). It recommends an interview. Application deadline: rolling admissions. Early and deferred admission are possible.

Getting Accepted
4,561 applied
62% were accepted
509 enrolled (18% of accepted)
16% from top tenth of their h.s. class
3.29 average high school GPA
Mean SAT critical reading score: 502
Mean SAT math score: 505
14% had SAT critical reading scores over 600
14% had SAT math scores over 600
1% had SAT critical reading scores over 700
1 class president
2 valedictorians

Graduation and After
53% graduated in 4 years
6% graduated in 5 years
98% had job offers within 6 months
47 organizations recruited on campus

Financial Matters
$30,570 tuition and fees (2008–09)
$8670 room and board
76% average percent of need met
$19,785 average financial aid amount received
  per undergraduate (2007–08 estimated)

Alfred University is a selective, nondenominational, residential university nestled at the foothills of the Allegheny Mountains in Alfred, New York. With more than sixty majors and concentrations to choose from, students can combine majors or minors, complete a second degree, or even design their own major through the College of Business, the College of Liberal Arts and Sciences, the School of Art and Design, and the Inamori School of Engineering. Students enjoy an interactive education with professors who know their names, challenge them to excel, and care deeply about their success.

Getting Accepted
2,355 applied
74% were accepted
518 enrolled (30% of accepted)
18% from top tenth of their h.s. class
3.13 average high school GPA
Mean SAT critical reading score: 552
Mean SAT math score: 561
Mean SAT writing score: 529
Mean ACT score: 24
30% had SAT critical reading scores over 600
33% had SAT math scores over 600
21% had SAT writing scores over 600
57% had ACT scores over 24
4% had SAT critical reading scores over 700
2% had SAT math scores over 700
3% had SAT writing scores over 700
9% had ACT scores over 30
3 valedictorians

Graduation and After
47% graduated in 4 years
15% graduated in 5 years
2% graduated in 6 years
54 organizations recruited on campus

Financial Matters
$24,278 tuition and fees (2008–09)
$10,796 room and board
86% average percent of need met
$19,697 average financial aid amount received per undergraduate (2006–07)

ALFRED UNIVERSITY

RURAL SETTING ■ PRIVATE ■ INDEPENDENT ■ COED
ALFRED, NEW YORK

Web site: www.alfred.edu
Contact: Mr. Jeremy Spencer, Director of Admissions, Alumni Hall, Alfred, NY 14802-1205
Telephone: 607-871-2115 or toll-free 800-541-9229
Fax: 607-871-2198
E-mail: admissions@alfred.edu

Academics
Alfred awards bachelor's, master's, and doctoral **degrees** and post-master's certificates. **Challenging opportunities** include advanced placement credit, accelerated degree programs, student-designed majors, an honors program, double majors, independent study, and a senior project. Special programs include cooperative education, internships, summer session for credit, off-campus study, study-abroad, and Army ROTC.

The most frequently chosen **baccalaureate** fields are visual and performing arts, engineering, and business/marketing. A complete listing of majors at Alfred appears in the Majors by College index beginning on page 469.

The **faculty** at Alfred has 172 full-time members. The student-faculty ratio is 12:1.

Students of Alfred
The student body totals 2,436, of whom 2,030 are undergraduates. 50.7% are women and 49.3% are men. Students come from 45 states and territories. 69% are from New York. 1.3% are international students. 3.7% are African American, 0.4% American Indian, 2.2% Asian American, and 2.5% Hispanic American. 79% returned for their sophomore year.

Facilities and Resources
450 **computers/terminals** are available on campus for general student use. Students can access the following: computer help desk, free student e-mail accounts, online (class) grades, online (class) registration, online (class) schedules. Campuswide network is available. 100% of college-owned or -operated housing units are wired for high-speed Internet access. Wireless service is available via classrooms, computer labs, libraries, student centers. The 2 **libraries** have 288,667 books and 1,478 subscriptions.

Campus Life
There are 90 active organizations on campus, including a drama/theater group, newspaper, radio station, television station, and choral group. No national or local **fraternities** or **sororities**.

Alfred is a member of the NCAA (Division III). **Intercollegiate sports** include basketball, cross-country running, equestrian sports, football (m), lacrosse, skiing (downhill), soccer, softball (w), swimming and diving, tennis, track and field, volleyball (w).

Campus Safety
Student safety services include late-night transport/escort service, 24-hour emergency telephone alarm devices, and student patrols.

Applying
Alfred requires an essay, SAT or ACT, a high school transcript, and 1 recommendation, and in some cases an interview and portfolio. It recommends an interview. Application deadline: 2/1; 3/15 for financial aid. Early and deferred admission are possible.

ALLEGHENY COLLEGE
SMALL-TOWN SETTING ■ PRIVATE ■ INDEPENDENT ■ COED
MEADVILLE, PENNSYLVANIA

Web site: www.allegheny.edu
Contact: Ms. Jennifer Winge, Director of Admissions, 520 North Main
 Street, Box 5, Meadville, PA 16335
Telephone: 814-332-4351 or toll-free 800-521-5293
Fax: 814-337-0431
E-mail: admissions@allegheny.edu

Academics
Allegheny awards bachelor's **degrees. Challenging opportunities** include advanced placement credit, student-designed majors, double majors, independent study, and a senior project. Special programs include internships, off-campus study, and study-abroad.

The most frequently chosen **baccalaureate** fields are social sciences, biological/life sciences, and psychology. A complete listing of majors at Allegheny appears in the Majors by College index beginning on page 469.

The **faculty** at Allegheny has 150 full-time members, 94% with terminal degrees. The student-faculty ratio is 13:1.

Students of Allegheny
The student body is made up of 2,125 undergraduates. 55.9% are women and 44.1% are men. Students come from 42 states and territories and 33 other countries. 60% are from Pennsylvania. 1.2% are international students. 3.2% are African American, 0.2% American Indian, 2.7% Asian American, and 2.2% Hispanic American. 88% returned for their sophomore year.

Facilities and Resources
390 **computers/terminals** and 200 ports are available on campus for general student use. Students can access the following: campus intranet, computer help desk, free student e-mail accounts, online (class) grades, online (class) registration, online (class) schedules, online room selection, placement testing, course catalog, class lists, book buy, repair service, transcript review and ordering, billing, payroll time cards. Campuswide network is available. 100% of college-owned or -operated housing units are wired for high-speed Internet access. Wireless service is available via computer centers, computer labs, learning centers, libraries, student centers. The **library** has 306,660 books and 21,741 subscriptions.

Campus Life
There are 78 active organizations on campus, including a drama/theater group, newspaper, radio station, television station, and choral group. 21% of eligible men and 34% of eligible women are members of national **fraternities** and national **sororities**.

Allegheny is a member of the NCAA (Division III). **Intercollegiate sports** include baseball (m), basketball, cross-country running, football (m), golf, lacrosse (w), soccer, softball (w), swimming and diving, tennis, track and field, volleyball (w).

Campus Safety
Student safety services include local police patrol, late-night transport/escort service, 24-hour emergency telephone alarm devices, 24-hour patrols by trained security personnel, student patrols, and electronically operated dormitory entrances.

Applying
Allegheny requires an essay, SAT or ACT, a high school transcript, and 2 recommendations. It recommends an interview. Application deadline: 2/15; 2/15 priority date for financial aid. Early and deferred admission are possible.

Getting Accepted
4,243 applied
61% were accepted
565 enrolled (22% of accepted)
46% from top tenth of their h.s. class
3.74 average high school GPA
Mean SAT critical reading score: 601
Mean SAT math score: 603
Mean ACT score: 25
54% had SAT critical reading scores over 600
56% had SAT math scores over 600
72% had ACT scores over 24
11% had SAT critical reading scores over 700
6% had SAT math scores over 700
13% had ACT scores over 30
7 National Merit Scholars
16 valedictorians

Graduation and After
70% graduated in 4 years
4% graduated in 5 years
54% had job offers within 6 months
18 organizations recruited on campus

Financial Matters
$32,000 tuition and fees (2008–09)
$8000 room and board
92% average percent of need met
$24,183 average financial aid amount received
 per undergraduate (2007–08 estimated)

ALLEN COLLEGE

SUBURBAN SETTING ■ PRIVATE ■ INDEPENDENT ■ COED, PRIMARILY WOMEN
WATERLOO, IOWA

Web site: www.allencollege.edu
Contact: Dina Dowden, Education Secretary, Student Services, Barrett
   Forum, 1825 Logan Avenue, Waterloo, IA 50703
Telephone: 319-226-2000
Fax: 319-226-2051
E-mail: allencollegeadmissions@ihs.org

Academics

Allen awards associate, bachelor's, and master's **degrees** (liberal arts and general education courses offered at either University of North Iowa or Wartburg College). **Challenging opportunities** include advanced placement credit, accelerated degree programs, independent study, and a senior project. Special programs include cooperative education, internships, off-campus study, and Army ROTC.

The most frequently chosen **baccalaureate** field is health professions and related sciences. A complete listing of majors at Allen appears in the Majors by College index beginning on page 469.

The **faculty** at Allen has 27 full-time members, 22% with terminal degrees. The student-faculty ratio is 12:1.

Students of Allen

The student body totals 416, of whom 308 are undergraduates. 95.5% are women and 4.5% are men. Students come from 5 states and territories. 95% are from Iowa. 1% are African American, 0.6% American Indian, 0.3% Asian American, and 0.6% Hispanic American. 72% returned for their sophomore year.

Facilities and Resources

26 **computers/terminals** are available on campus for general student use. Students can access the following: campus intranet, computer help desk, free student e-mail accounts, online (class) grades, online (class) schedules. Campuswide network is available. Wireless service is available via entire campus. The **library** has 3,200 books and 199 subscriptions.

Campus Life

There are 4 active organizations on campus, including a newspaper and choral group. No national or local **fraternities** or **sororities**.

This institution has no intercollegiate sports.

Campus Safety

Student safety services include 24-hour patrols by trained security personnel and electronically operated dormitory entrances.

Applying

Allen requires an essay, ACT, a high school transcript, and 1 recommendation, and in some cases an interview. It recommends rank in upper 50% of high school class, minimum ACT score of 20 and a minimum high school GPA of 2.7. Application deadline: 7/1.

Getting Accepted
4 enrolled
3.62 average high school GPA
Mean ACT score: 23
25% had ACT scores over 24

Graduation and After
48% graduated in 4 years
7% graduated in 5 years
100% had job offers within 6 months
40 organizations recruited on campus

Financial Matters
$14,579 tuition and fees (2008–09)
$6816 room and board
51% average percent of need met
$7827 average financial aid amount received
   per undergraduate (2007–08 estimated)

ALMA COLLEGE

SMALL-TOWN SETTING ■ PRIVATE ■ INDEPENDENT RELIGIOUS ■ COED
ALMA, MICHIGAN

Web site: www.alma.edu
Contact: Mr. Evan Montague, Director of Admissions, Admissions Office,
  Alma, MI 48801-1599
Telephone: 800-321-ALMA or toll-free 800-321-ALMA
Fax: 989-463-7057
E-mail: admissions@alma.edu

SPONSOR

> Alma's undergraduates thrive on challenging academic programs in a supportive small-college atmosphere. The College is committed to a liberal arts and sciences curriculum, with opportunities for one-on-one research and publication with faculty members whose first priority is teaching. Students enjoy small classes in modern facilities, including the Alan J. Stone Center for Recreation. Alma College offers excellent preparation for professional careers in the arts, business, education, law, medicine, and a wide range of other fields.

Academics

Alma awards bachelor's **degrees**. **Challenging opportunities** include advanced placement credit, student-designed majors, an honors program, double majors, independent study, and a senior project. Special programs include internships, summer session for credit, off-campus study, study-abroad, and Army ROTC.

The most frequently chosen **baccalaureate** fields are business/marketing, biological/life sciences, and health professions and related sciences. A complete listing of majors at Alma appears in the Majors by College index beginning on page 469.

The **faculty** at Alma has 86 full-time members, 87% with terminal degrees. The student-faculty ratio is 13:1.

Students of Alma

The student body is made up of 1,384 undergraduates. 55.6% are women and 44.4% are men. Students come from 24 states and territories and 15 other countries. 96% are from Michigan. 0.8% are international students. 2.4% are African American, 0.7% American Indian, 1.4% Asian American, and 2.4% Hispanic American. 76% returned for their sophomore year.

Facilities and Resources

291 **computers/terminals** are available on campus for general student use. Students can access the following: campus intranet, computer help desk, free student e-mail accounts, online (class) grades, online (class) registration, online (class) schedules. Campuswide network is available. 100% of college-owned or -operated housing units are wired for high-speed Internet access. Wireless service is available via classrooms, dorm rooms, libraries, student centers. The **library** has 275,723 books and 1,500 subscriptions.

Campus Life

There are 75 active organizations on campus, including a drama/theater group, newspaper, radio station, choral group, and marching band. 19% of eligible men and 28% of eligible women are members of national **fraternities**, national **sororities**, local fraternities, and local sororities.

Alma is a member of the NCAA (Division III). **Intercollegiate sports** include baseball (m), basketball, cross-country running, football (m), golf, soccer, softball (w), swimming and diving, tennis, track and field, volleyball (w).

Campus Safety

Student safety services include 24-hour emergency telephone alarm devices and 24-hour patrols by trained security personnel.

Applying

Alma requires SAT or ACT, a high school transcript, minimum SAT score of 1030 or ACT score of 22, and a minimum high school GPA of 3.0, and in some cases an essay and 3 recommendations. It recommends an interview. Application deadline: rolling admissions; 3/1 priority date for financial aid. Deferred admission is possible.

Getting Accepted
1,854 applied
73% were accepted
429 enrolled (32% of accepted)
27% from top tenth of their h.s. class
3.49 average high school GPA
Mean ACT score: 23
46% had SAT critical reading scores over 600
46% had SAT math scores over 600
46% had SAT writing scores over 600
50% had ACT scores over 24
25% had SAT critical reading scores over 700
13% had SAT math scores over 700
25% had SAT writing scores over 700
8% had ACT scores over 30
7 National Merit Scholars
17 valedictorians

Graduation and After
61% graduated in 4 years
8% graduated in 5 years
1% graduated in 6 years

Financial Matters
$24,850 tuition and fees (2008–09)
$8120 room and board
85% average percent of need met
$20,805 average financial aid amount received per undergraduate (2007–08 estimated)

American University's (AU) academic excellence has been recognized by the *Fiske Guide to Colleges,* the Princeton Review, and *U.S. News & World Report,* among others. American University is located in the residential "Embassy Row" neighborhood of Washington, D.C. Nestled among embassies and ambassadorial residences, AU's campus offers a safe, suburban environment with easy access to Washington's countless cultural destinations via the Metrorail subway system. AU's faculty includes scholars, journalists, artists, diplomats, authors, and scientists in seventy programs across five undergraduate schools. Combining a liberal arts core curriculum with in-depth professional programs, academics at AU provide the necessary balance between theoretical study and hands-on experience. AU's Career Center works with students to enhance this experience with access to unique internship opportunities available only in Washington. With its diverse national and international student body and its world-class study-abroad program, AU can open a world of possibilities.

Getting Accepted
15,413 applied
53% were accepted
1,577 enrolled (19% of accepted)
46% from top tenth of their h.s. class
3.79 average high school GPA
Mean SAT critical reading score: 639
Mean SAT math score: 621
Mean SAT writing score: 632
Mean ACT score: 28
71% had SAT critical reading scores over 600
65% had SAT math scores over 600
71% had SAT writing scores over 600
90% had ACT scores over 24
25% had SAT critical reading scores over 700
17% had SAT math scores over 700
21% had SAT writing scores over 700
33% had ACT scores over 30

Graduation and After
70% graduated in 4 years
5% graduated in 5 years

Financial Matters
$33,283 tuition and fees (2008–09)
$12,418 room and board
57% average percent of need met
$24,294 average financial aid amount received per undergraduate (2007–08 estimated)

AMERICAN UNIVERSITY
SUBURBAN SETTING ■ PRIVATE ■ INDEPENDENT RELIGIOUS ■ COED
WASHINGTON, DISTRICT OF COLUMBIA

Web site: www.american.edu
Contact: Greg Grauman, Acting Director of Admissions, 4400 Massachusetts Avenue, NW, Washington, DC 20016-8001
Telephone: 202-885-6000
Fax: 202-885-6014
E-mail: admissions@american.edu

Academics
American awards bachelor's, master's, doctoral, and first-professional **degrees** and post-bachelor's certificates. **Challenging opportunities** include advanced placement credit, accelerated degree programs, student-designed majors, an honors program, double majors, independent study, and a senior project. Special programs include cooperative education, internships, summer session for credit, off-campus study, study-abroad, and Army and Air Force ROTC.

The most frequently chosen **baccalaureate** fields are social sciences, business/marketing, and communications/journalism. A complete listing of majors at American appears in the Majors by College index beginning on page 469.

The **faculty** at American has 578 full-time members, 94% with terminal degrees.

Students of American
The student body totals 11,684, of whom 6,311 are undergraduates. 61.5% are women and 38.5% are men. Students come from 54 states and territories and 137 other countries. 16% are from District of Columbia. 6.4% are international students. 4.3% are African American, 0.4% American Indian, 5.2% Asian American, and 4.4% Hispanic American. 88% returned for their sophomore year.

Facilities and Resources
700 **computers/terminals** are available on campus for general student use. Students can access the following: campus intranet, computer help desk, free student e-mail accounts, online (class) grades, online (class) registration, online (class) schedules, printers, scanners, online course support. Campuswide network is available. 100% of college-owned or -operated housing units are wired for high-speed Internet access. Wireless service is available via entire campus. The 2 **libraries** have 1,058,221 books and 34,838 subscriptions.

Campus Life
There are 220 active organizations on campus, including a drama/theater group, newspaper, radio station, television station, and choral group. 14% of eligible men and 16% of eligible women are members of national **fraternities** and national **sororities**.

American is a member of the NCAA (Division I). **Intercollegiate sports** (some offering scholarships) include basketball, cross-country running, field hockey (w), lacrosse (w), soccer, swimming and diving, tennis, track and field, volleyball (w), wrestling (m).

Campus Safety
Student safety services include late-night transport/escort service, 24-hour emergency telephone alarm devices, 24-hour patrols by trained security personnel, and electronically operated dormitory entrances.

Applying
American requires an essay, SAT or ACT, a high school transcript, and 2 recommendations. It recommends SAT Subject Tests and a minimum high school GPA of 3.0. Application deadline: 1/15; 2/15 for financial aid. Deferred admission is possible.

Amherst College

SMALL-TOWN SETTING ■ PRIVATE ■ INDEPENDENT ■ COED
AMHERST, MASSACHUSETTS

Web site: www.amherst.edu
Contact: Mr. Thomas H. Parker, Dean of Admission and Financial Aid, PO
  Box 5000, Amherst, MA 01002
Telephone: 413-542-2328
Fax: 413-542-2040
E-mail: admission@amherst.edu

SPONSOR

Academics

Amherst awards bachelor's **degrees**. **Challenging opportunities** include student-designed majors, an honors program, double majors, independent study, and a senior project. Special programs include off-campus study and study-abroad.

The most frequently chosen **baccalaureate** fields are social sciences, English, and foreign languages and literature. A complete listing of majors at Amherst appears in the Majors by College index beginning on page 469.

The **faculty** at Amherst has 202 full-time members. The student-faculty ratio is 8:1.

Students of Amherst

The student body is made up of 1,697 undergraduates. 51.1% are women and 48.9% are men. Students come from 48 states and territories and 41 other countries. 12% are from Massachusetts. 7.2% are international students. 10.2% are African American, 0.2% American Indian, 10.1% Asian American, and 9.4% Hispanic American. 96% returned for their sophomore year.

Facilities and Resources

182 **computers/terminals** are available on campus for general student use. Students can access the following: campus intranet, computer help desk, free student e-mail accounts, online (class) grades, online (class) schedules. Campuswide network is available. 100% of college-owned or -operated housing units are wired for high-speed Internet access. Wireless service is available via entire campus. The 6 **libraries** have 1,023,085 books and 12,190 subscriptions.

Campus Life

There are 100 active organizations on campus, including a drama/theater group, newspaper, radio station, and choral group. No national or local **fraternities** or **sororities**.

Amherst is a member of the NCAA (Division III). **Intercollegiate sports** include baseball (m), basketball, cross-country running, field hockey (w), football (m), golf, ice hockey, lacrosse, soccer, softball (w), squash, swimming and diving, tennis, track and field, volleyball (w).

Campus Safety

Student safety services include late-night transport/escort service, 24-hour emergency telephone alarm devices, 24-hour patrols by trained security personnel, student patrols, and electronically operated dormitory entrances.

Applying

Amherst requires an essay, SAT and SAT Subject Tests or ACT, a high school transcript, and 3 recommendations. Application deadline: 1/1; 2/15 priority date for financial aid. Early and deferred admission are possible.

Amherst seeks talented students who have demonstrated their passion for learning along with a willingness to be involved in the world around them. With its dynamic, dedicated faculty, Amherst is a lively intellectual and diverse community in which students are active members. Small classes, experiential learning opportunities, and a wide variety of extracurricular offerings provide multiple avenues for exploration. An open curriculum, with majors ranging from neuroscience to law, jurisprudence, and social thought, allows students substantial freedom to pursue their goals. Membership in the Five College Consortium provides students with additional course offerings and broader social and student organization networks.

Getting Accepted
7,745 applied
15% were accepted
439 enrolled (38% of accepted)
79% from top tenth of their h.s. class
Mean SAT critical reading score: 708
Mean SAT math score: 707
Mean ACT score: 31
94% had SAT critical reading scores over 600
91% had SAT math scores over 600
92% had SAT writing scores over 600
99% had ACT scores over 24
63% had SAT critical reading scores over 700
60% had SAT math scores over 700
60% had SAT writing scores over 700
72% had ACT scores over 30
64 National Merit Scholars
36 valedictorians

Graduation and After
85% graduated in 4 years
9% graduated in 5 years
1% graduated in 6 years
63% had job offers within 6 months
59 organizations recruited on campus

Financial Matters
$37,640 tuition and fees (2008–09)
$9790 room and board
100% average percent of need met
$35,055 average financial aid amount received
  per undergraduate (2007–08 estimated)

ASBURY COLLEGE

SMALL-TOWN SETTING ■ PRIVATE ■ INDEPENDENT RELIGIOUS ■ COED
WILMORE, KENTUCKY

Web site: www.asbury.edu
Contact: 1 Macklem Drive, Wilmore, KY 40390
Telephone: 859-858-3511 Ext. 2142 or toll-free 800-888-1818
Fax: 859-858-3921
E-mail: admissions@asbury.edu

Getting Accepted

1,563 applied
56% were accepted
313 enrolled (36% of accepted)
31% from top tenth of their h.s. class
3.57 average high school GPA
Mean SAT critical reading score: 594
Mean SAT math score: 564
Mean ACT score: 24
53% had SAT critical reading scores over 600
39% had SAT math scores over 600
51% had ACT scores over 24
15% had SAT critical reading scores over 700
6% had SAT math scores over 700
9% had ACT scores over 30

Graduation and After

60% graduated in 4 years
10% graduated in 5 years
1% graduated in 6 years
45 organizations recruited on campus

Financial Matters

$22,413 tuition and fees (2009–10)
$5414 room and board
80% average percent of need met
$15,957 average financial aid amount received
per undergraduate (2007–08 estimated)

Academics

Asbury awards associate, bachelor's, and master's **degrees**. **Challenging opportunities** include advanced placement credit, double majors, and a senior project. Special programs include summer session for credit, study-abroad, and Army and Air Force ROTC.

The most frequently chosen **baccalaureate** fields are communication technologies, theology and religious vocations, and business/marketing. A complete listing of majors at Asbury appears in the Majors by College index beginning on page 469.

The **faculty** at Asbury has 80 full-time members, 73% with terminal degrees. The student-faculty ratio is 12:1.

Students of Asbury

The student body totals 1,550, of whom 1,446 are undergraduates. 60.2% are women and 39.8% are men. Students come from 44 states and territories and 11 other countries. 38% are from Kentucky. 1.1% are international students. 2.1% are African American, 0.3% American Indian, 1.6% Asian American, and 2.4% Hispanic American. 79% returned for their sophomore year.

Facilities and Resources

200 **computers/terminals** are available on campus for general student use. Students can access the following: computer help desk, free student e-mail accounts, online (class) registration, online (class) schedules. Campuswide network is available. 100% of college-owned or -operated housing units are wired for high-speed Internet access. Wireless service is available via classrooms, computer labs, libraries, student centers. The **library** has 164,773 books and 545 subscriptions.

Campus Life

There are 35 active organizations on campus, including a drama/theater group, newspaper, radio station, television station, and choral group. No national or local **fraternities** or **sororities**.

Asbury is a member of the NAIA and NCCAA. **Intercollegiate sports** (some offering scholarships) include baseball (m), basketball, cross-country running, soccer, softball (w), swimming and diving, tennis, volleyball (w).

Campus Safety

Student safety services include late night security personnel, late-night transport/escort service, 24-hour emergency telephone alarm devices, and electronically operated dormitory entrances.

Applying

Asbury requires an essay, SAT or ACT, a high school transcript, 2 recommendations, and a minimum high school GPA of 2.5, and in some cases an interview. Application deadline: rolling admissions; 3/1 priority date for financial aid. Early and deferred admission are possible.

Auburn University

SMALL-TOWN SETTING ■ PUBLIC ■ STATE-SUPPORTED ■ COED
AUBURN UNIVERSITY, ALABAMA

Web site: www.auburn.edu
Contact: Ms. Cindy Singley, Director, University Recruitment, 202 Mary
  Martin Hall, Auburn, AL 36849-0001
Telephone: 334-844-4080 or toll-free 800-AUBURN9 (in-state)
E-mail: admissions@auburn.edu

Academics

Auburn awards bachelor's, master's, doctoral, and first-professional **degrees** and post-master's certificates. **Challenging opportunities** include advanced placement credit, accelerated degree programs, freshman honors college, an honors program, double majors, independent study, and a senior project. Special programs include cooperative education, internships, summer session for credit, study-abroad, and Army, Navy, and Air Force ROTC.

The most frequently chosen **baccalaureate** fields are business/marketing, engineering, and education. A complete listing of majors at Auburn appears in the Majors by College index beginning on page 469.

The **faculty** at Auburn has 1,176 full-time members. The student-faculty ratio is 18:1.

Students of Auburn

The student body totals 24,530, of whom 20,037 are undergraduates. 48.7% are women and 51.3% are men. Students come from 56 states and territories and 39 other countries. 65% are from Alabama. 0.6% are international students. 8.2% are African American, 0.6% American Indian, 1.7% Asian American, and 1.9% Hispanic American. 87% returned for their sophomore year.

Facilities and Resources

1,722 **computers/terminals** are available on campus for general student use. Students can access the following: computer help desk, free student e-mail accounts, online (class) grades, online (class) registration, pay Bursar online, course materials available online. Campuswide network is available. 100% of college-owned or -operated housing units are wired for high-speed Internet access. Wireless service is available via entire campus. The 3 **libraries** have 3,016,986 books and 29,355 subscriptions.

Campus Life

There are 300 active organizations on campus, including a drama/theater group, newspaper, radio station, television station, choral group, and marching band. 21% of eligible men and 31% of eligible women are members of national **fraternities** and national **sororities**.

Auburn is a member of the NCAA (Division I). **Intercollegiate sports** (some offering scholarships) include baseball (m), basketball, cross-country running, equestrian sports (w), football (m), golf, gymnastics (w), soccer (w), softball (w), swimming and diving, tennis, track and field, volleyball (w).

Campus Safety

Student safety services include late-night transport/escort service, 24-hour emergency telephone alarm devices, 24-hour patrols by trained security personnel, and electronically operated dormitory entrances.

Applying

Auburn requires an essay, SAT Subject Tests, SAT or ACT, a high school transcript, and a minimum high school GPA of 2.0, and in some cases a minimum high school GPA of 3.0. Application deadline: rolling admissions; 3/1 priority date for financial aid. Early and deferred admission are possible.

Getting Accepted

17,068 applied
71% were accepted
3,984 enrolled (33% of accepted)
31% from top tenth of their h.s. class
3.69 average high school GPA
Mean SAT critical reading score: 575
Mean SAT math score: 600
Mean SAT writing score: 570
Mean ACT score: 26
38% had SAT critical reading scores over 600
50% had SAT math scores over 600
36% had SAT writing scores over 600
72% had ACT scores over 24
7% had SAT critical reading scores over 700
11% had SAT math scores over 700
5% had SAT writing scores over 700
20% had ACT scores over 30
31 National Merit Scholars

Graduation and After

34% graduated in 4 years
24% graduated in 5 years
6% graduated in 6 years
75% had job offers within 6 months
550 organizations recruited on campus

Financial Matters

$5880 resident tuition and fees (2008–09)
$17,640 nonresident tuition and fees (2008–09)
$8260 room and board
44% average percent of need met
$7917 average financial aid amount received per undergraduate (2006–07)

At Augustana College, students find an array of opportunities in a rich liberal arts environment to challenge and prepare them for meaningful work in a complex world. Important features of the academic program include an interdisciplinary general education sequence for all students; intensive global learning experiences; a liberal arts background fostering skills in creative and critical thinking, combined with depth of study in the major field(s); programs that focus on one's purpose or path in life; and domestic and international internships. Close connections with faculty mentors and a dynamic culture of inquiry foster collaboration in research, the arts, and social service. Fifth in the nation for the number of Academic All-Americans, the College offers a wide variety of extracurricular and cocurricular activities, campus ministries, and residential life programs to engage students beyond the classroom.

Getting Accepted
3,413 applied
69% were accepted
641 enrolled (27% of accepted)
32% from top tenth of their h.s. class
Mean ACT score: 26
67% had ACT scores over 24
14% had ACT scores over 30

Graduation and After
69% graduated in 4 years
4% graduated in 5 years
1% graduated in 6 years
56% had job offers within 6 months
201 organizations recruited on campus

Financial Matters
$30,150 tuition and fees (2008–09)
$7650 room and board
83% average percent of need met
$17,681 average financial aid amount received per undergraduate (2006–07)

AUGUSTANA COLLEGE
SUBURBAN SETTING ■ PRIVATE ■ INDEPENDENT RELIGIOUS ■ COED
ROCK ISLAND, ILLINOIS

Web site: www.augustana.edu
Contact: Megan Cooley, Director of Admissions, 639 38th Street, Rock Island, IL 61201-2296
Telephone: 309-794-7341 or toll-free 800-798-8100
Fax: 309-794-7422
E-mail: admissions@augustana.edu

Academics
Augustana awards bachelor's **degrees**. **Challenging opportunities** include advanced placement credit, student-designed majors, an honors program, double majors, independent study, and a senior project. Special programs include internships, summer session for credit, and study-abroad.

The most frequently chosen **baccalaureate** fields are business/marketing, biological/life sciences, and health professions and related sciences. A complete listing of majors at Augustana appears in the Majors by College index beginning on page 469.

The **faculty** at Augustana has 181 full-time members, 85% with terminal degrees. The student-faculty ratio is 12:1.

Students of Augustana
The student body is made up of 2,546 undergraduates. 57.1% are women and 42.9% are men. Students come from 30 states and territories and 20 other countries. 87% are from Illinois. 1% are international students. 2% are African American, 0.4% American Indian, 2.4% Asian American, and 3.4% Hispanic American. 87% returned for their sophomore year.

Facilities and Resources
600 **computers/terminals** and 1,800 ports are available on campus for general student use. Students can access the following: campus intranet, computer help desk, free student e-mail accounts, online (class) grades, online (class) registration, online (class) schedules. Campuswide network is available. 100% of college-owned or -operated housing units are wired for high-speed Internet access. Wireless service is available via computer centers, libraries. The 3 **libraries** have 213,982 books and 3,251 subscriptions.

Campus Life
There are 116 active organizations on campus, including a drama/theater group, newspaper, radio station, and choral group. 16% of eligible men and 23% of eligible women are members of local **fraternities** and local **sororities**.

Augustana is a member of the NCAA (Division III). **Intercollegiate sports** include baseball (m), basketball, cross-country running, football (m), golf, soccer, softball (w), swimming and diving, tennis, track and field, volleyball (w), wrestling (m).

Campus Safety
Student safety services include late-night transport/escort service, 24-hour emergency telephone alarm devices, 24-hour patrols by trained security personnel, and electronically operated dormitory entrances.

Applying
Augustana requires a high school transcript, and in some cases an essay, Test optional for those who interview and submit a photocopy of a graded high school paper, and an interview. Application deadline: rolling admissions; 4/1 priority date for financial aid. Deferred admission is possible.

AUGUSTANA COLLEGE

URBAN SETTING ■ PRIVATE ■ INDEPENDENT RELIGIOUS ■ COED
SIOUX FALLS, SOUTH DAKOTA

Web site: www.augie.edu
Contact: Ms. Nancy Davidson, Vice President for Enrollment, 2001 S.
Summit Avenue, Sioux Falls, SD 57197
Telephone: 605-274-5516 or toll-free 800-727-2844 Ext. 5516 (in-state),
800-727-2844 (out-of-state)
Fax: 605-274-5518
E-mail: admission@augie.edu

Academics

Augustana awards bachelor's and master's **degrees. Challenging opportunities** include advanced placement credit, accelerated degree programs, student-designed majors, freshman honors college, an honors program, double majors, independent study, and a senior project. Special programs include cooperative education, internships, summer session for credit, off-campus study, and study-abroad.

The most frequently chosen **baccalaureate** fields are education, business/marketing, and health professions and related sciences. A complete listing of majors at Augustana appears in the Majors by College index beginning on page 469.

The **faculty** at Augustana has 119 full-time members, 78% with terminal degrees. The student-faculty ratio is 12:1.

Students of Augustana

The student body totals 1,754, of whom 1,733 are undergraduates. 63.9% are women and 36.1% are men. Students come from 28 states and territories and 14 other countries. 48% are from South Dakota. 2.5% are international students. 1.2% are African American, 0.3% American Indian, 1.2% Asian American, and 0.3% Hispanic American. 78% returned for their sophomore year.

Facilities and Resources

260 **computers/terminals** are available on campus for general student use. Students can access the following: computer help desk, free student e-mail accounts, online (class) grades, online (class) registration, online (class) schedules. Campuswide network is available. 100% of college-owned or -operated housing units are wired for high-speed Internet access. Wireless service is available via learning centers, libraries, student centers. The 2 **libraries** have 203,804 books and 5,533 subscriptions.

Campus Life

There are 60 active organizations on campus, including a drama/theater group, newspaper, radio station, and choral group. No national or local **fraternities** or **sororities**.

Augustana is a member of the NCAA (Division II). **Intercollegiate sports** (some offering scholarships) include baseball (m), basketball, cheerleading (w), cross-country running, football (m), golf, soccer (w), softball (w), tennis, track and field, volleyball (w), wrestling (m).

Campus Safety

Student safety services include late-night transport/escort service, 24-hour emergency telephone alarm devices, 24-hour patrols by trained security personnel, and electronically operated dormitory entrances.

Applying

Augustana requires an essay, SAT or ACT, a high school transcript, 1 recommendation, minimum ACT score of 20, and a minimum high school GPA of 2.75. It recommends an interview. Application deadline: 8/1; 3/1 priority date for financial aid. Deferred admission is possible.

Getting Accepted

1,186 applied
81% were accepted
438 enrolled (45% of accepted)
28% from top tenth of their h.s. class
3.62 average high school GPA
Mean SAT critical reading score: 567
Mean SAT math score: 572
Mean ACT score: 25
51% had SAT critical reading scores over 600
56% had SAT math scores over 600
66% had ACT scores over 24
13% had SAT critical reading scores over 700
6% had SAT math scores over 700
11% had ACT scores over 30
32 valedictorians

Graduation and After

49% graduated in 4 years
17% graduated in 5 years
1% graduated in 6 years
99% had job offers within 6 months
54 organizations recruited on campus

Financial Matters

$22,450 tuition and fees (2008–09)
$5920 room and board
91% average percent of need met
$17,439 average financial aid amount received per undergraduate (2007–08 estimated)

AUSTIN COLLEGE

SUBURBAN SETTING ■ PRIVATE ■ INDEPENDENT RELIGIOUS ■ COED
SHERMAN, TEXAS

Web site: www.austincollege.edu
Contact: Ms. Nan Davis, Vice President for Institutional Enrollment, 900
    North Grand Avenue, Suite 6N, Sherman, TX 75090-4400
Telephone: 903-813-3000 or toll-free 800-442-5363
Fax: 903-813-3198
E-mail: admission@austincollege.edu

Getting Accepted

1,525 applied
78% were accepted
319 enrolled (27% of accepted)
36% from top tenth of their h.s. class
3.45 average high school GPA
Mean SAT critical reading score: 610
Mean SAT math score: 620
Mean ACT score: 26
59% had SAT critical reading scores over 600
63% had SAT math scores over 600
46% had SAT writing scores over 600
66% had ACT scores over 24
13% had SAT critical reading scores over 700
11% had SAT math scores over 700
11% had SAT writing scores over 700
18% had ACT scores over 30
1 National Merit Scholar

Graduation and After

74% graduated in 4 years
3% graduated in 5 years
1% graduated in 6 years
36% had job offers within 6 months
34 organizations recruited on campus

Financial Matters

$27,875 tuition and fees (2009–10)
$9090 room and board
99% average percent of need met
$22,532 average financial aid amount received
  per undergraduate (2006–07)

Academics

Austin awards bachelor's and master's **degrees**. **Challenging opportunities** include advanced placement credit, student-designed majors, an honors program, double majors, independent study, and a senior project. Special programs include internships, summer session for credit, off-campus study, and study-abroad.

The most frequently chosen **baccalaureate** fields are social sciences, psychology, and business/marketing. A complete listing of majors at Austin appears in the Majors by College index beginning on page 469.

The **faculty** at Austin has 94 full-time members, 93% with terminal degrees. The student-faculty ratio is 12:1.

Students of Austin

The student body totals 1,298, of whom 1,263 are undergraduates. 55% are women and 45% are men. Students come from 30 states and territories and 27 other countries. 93% are from Texas. 2.2% are international students. 2.4% are African American, 1.3% American Indian, 15.8% Asian American, and 8.8% Hispanic American. 80% returned for their sophomore year.

Facilities and Resources

160 **computers/terminals** are available on campus for general student use. Students can access the following: campus intranet, computer help desk, free student e-mail accounts, online (class) grades, online (class) registration, online (class) schedules. Campuswide network is available. 100% of college-owned or -operated housing units are wired for high-speed Internet access. Wireless service is available via entire campus. The **library** has 240,944 books and 2,181 subscriptions.

Campus Life

There are 50 active organizations on campus, including a drama/theater group, newspaper, and choral group. 24% of eligible men and 27% of eligible women are members of local **fraternities** and local **sororities**.

Austin is a member of the NCAA (Division III). **Intercollegiate sports** include baseball (m), basketball, cheerleading, football (m), soccer, softball (w), swimming and diving, tennis, volleyball (w).

Campus Safety

Student safety services include late-night transport/escort service, 24-hour emergency telephone alarm devices, 24-hour patrols by trained security personnel, and electronically operated dormitory entrances.

Applying

Austin requires an essay, SAT or ACT, a high school transcript, and 2 recommendations, and in some cases an interview. It recommends an interview and a minimum high school GPA of 3.0. Application deadline: 5/1; 4/1 priority date for financial aid. Early and deferred admission are possible.

Azusa Pacific University

Small-town setting ■ Private ■ Independent Religious ■ Coed
Azusa, California

Web site: www.apu.edu
Contact: Ms. Lynnette Barnes, Processing Coordinator, 901 East Alosta
Avenue, PO Box 7000, Undergraduate Admissions—7221, Azusa, CA
91702-7000
Telephone: 626-815-6000 Ext. 3419 or toll-free 800-TALK-APU
Fax: 626-812-3096
E-mail: admissions@apu.edu

Academics
Azusa Pacific awards bachelor's, master's, doctoral, and first-professional **degrees. Challenging opportunities** include advanced placement credit, accelerated degree programs, freshman honors college, an honors program, double majors, independent study, and a senior project. Special programs include cooperative education, internships, summer session for credit, off-campus study, study-abroad, and Army ROTC.

The most frequently chosen **baccalaureate** fields are business/marketing, liberal arts/general studies, and communications/journalism. A complete listing of majors at Azusa Pacific appears in the Majors by College index beginning on page 469.

The **faculty** at Azusa Pacific has 315 full-time members. The student-faculty ratio is 13:1.

Students of Azusa Pacific
The student body totals 8,548, of whom 4,858 are undergraduates. 63.9% are women and 36.1% are men. Students come from 48 states and territories and 47 other countries. 81% are from California. 1.8% are international students. 4.8% are African American, 0.5% American Indian, 8.1% Asian American, and 15.1% Hispanic American. 82% returned for their sophomore year.

Facilities and Resources
300 **computers/terminals** are available on campus for general student use. Students can access the following: campus intranet, computer help desk, free student e-mail accounts, online (class) grades, online (class) registration. Campuswide network is available. Wireless service is available via entire campus. The 3 **libraries** have 185,708 books and 14,031 subscriptions.

Campus Life
There are 32 active organizations on campus, including a drama/theater group, newspaper, radio station, television station, choral group, and marching band. No national or local **fraternities** or **sororities**.

Azusa Pacific is a member of the NAIA. **Intercollegiate sports** (some offering scholarships) include baseball (m), basketball, cross-country running, football (m), golf (m), soccer, softball (w), tennis (m), track and field, volleyball.

Campus Safety
Student safety services include late-night transport/escort service, 24-hour emergency telephone alarm devices, 24-hour patrols by trained security personnel, student patrols, and electronically operated dormitory entrances.

Applying
Azusa Pacific requires an essay, SAT or ACT, a high school transcript, 2 recommendations, and a minimum high school GPA of 2.8, and in some cases an interview. Application deadline: 6/1; 7/1 for financial aid, with a 3/2 priority date. Early and deferred admission are possible.

Getting Accepted
4,441 applied
63% were accepted
1,093 enrolled (39% of accepted)
31% from top tenth of their h.s. class
3.63 average high school GPA
Mean SAT critical reading score: 541
Mean SAT math score: 542
Mean ACT score: 24
24% had SAT critical reading scores over 600
26% had SAT math scores over 600
50% had ACT scores over 24
2% had SAT critical reading scores over 700
4% had SAT math scores over 700
8% had ACT scores over 30

Graduation and After
52% graduated in 4 years
8% graduated in 5 years
5% graduated in 6 years
23 organizations recruited on campus

Financial Matters
$26,640 tuition and fees (2008–09)
$7742 room and board
67% average percent of need met
$12,246 average financial aid amount received
    per undergraduate (2006–07)

BABSON COLLEGE

SUBURBAN SETTING ■ PRIVATE ■ INDEPENDENT ■ COED
BABSON PARK, MASSACHUSETTS

Web site: www.babson.edu
Contact: Ms. Adrienne Ramsey, Senior Assistant Director of Undergraduate Admission, Lunder Undergraduate Admission Center, Babson Park, MA 02457-0310
Telephone: 781-239-5522 or toll-free 800-488-3696
Fax: 781-239-4135
E-mail: ugradadmission@babson.edu

Getting Accepted

4,318 applied
35% were accepted
469 enrolled (31% of accepted)
44% from top tenth of their h.s. class
Mean SAT critical reading score: 601
Mean SAT math score: 640
54% had SAT critical reading scores over 600
81% had SAT math scores over 600
59% had SAT writing scores over 600
88% had ACT scores over 24
10% had SAT critical reading scores over 700
22% had SAT math scores over 700
11% had SAT writing scores over 700
24% had ACT scores over 30

Graduation and After

84% graduated in 4 years
4% graduated in 5 years
1% graduated in 6 years
95.4% had job offers within 6 months
833 organizations recruited on campus

Financial Matters

$36,096 tuition and fees (2008–09)
$12,020 room and board
96% average percent of need met
$29,142 average financial aid amount received per undergraduate (2007–08 estimated)

Academics

Babson awards bachelor's and master's **degrees** and post-master's certificates. **Challenging opportunities** include advanced placement credit, student-designed majors, freshman honors college, an honors program, independent study, and a senior project. Special programs include internships, summer session for credit, off-campus study, study-abroad, and Army, Navy, and Air Force ROTC.

The most frequently chosen **baccalaureate** field is business/marketing. A complete listing of majors at Babson appears in the Majors by College index beginning on page 469.

The **faculty** at Babson has 157 full-time members, 89% with terminal degrees. The student-faculty ratio is 14:1.

Students of Babson

The student body totals 3,439, of whom 1,851 are undergraduates. 41.7% are women and 58.3% are men. Students come from 44 states and territories and 64 other countries. 30% are from Massachusetts. 20.2% are international students. 4.3% are African American, 0.4% American Indian, 12.5% Asian American, and 8.6% Hispanic American. 97% returned for their sophomore year.

Facilities and Resources

290 **computers/terminals** are available on campus for general student use. Students can access the following: campus intranet, computer help desk, free student e-mail accounts, online (class) grades, online (class) registration, online (class) schedules, network drives and folders. Campuswide network is available. The 2 **libraries** have 131,436 books and 626 subscriptions.

Campus Life

There are 74 active organizations on campus, including a drama/theater group, newspaper, radio station, and choral group. 14% of eligible men and 16% of eligible women are members of national **fraternities** and national **sororities**.

Babson is a member of the NCAA (Division III). **Intercollegiate sports** include baseball (m), basketball, cross-country running, field hockey (w), golf (m), ice hockey (m), lacrosse, skiing (downhill), soccer, softball (w), swimming and diving, tennis, track and field, volleyball (w).

Campus Safety

Student safety services include late-night transport/escort service, 24-hour emergency telephone alarm devices, 24-hour patrols by trained security personnel, and electronically operated dormitory entrances.

Applying

Babson requires an essay, SAT or ACT, a high school transcript, and 2 recommendations. It recommends an interview. Application deadline: 1/15; 2/15 for financial aid, with a 2/15 priority date. Deferred admission is possible.

Baldwin-Wallace College

Suburban setting ■ Private ■ Independent Religious ■ Coed
Berea, Ohio

Web site: www.bw.edu
Contact: Patricia Skrha, Director of Undergraduate Admission, Bonds
    Administration Building, 275 Eastland Road, Berea, OH 44017
Telephone: 440-826-2222 or toll-free 877-BWAPPLY (in-state)
Fax: 440-826-3830
E-mail: admission@bw.edu

Academics

B-W awards bachelor's and master's **degrees. Challenging opportunities** include advanced placement credit, accelerated degree programs, student-designed majors, an honors program, double majors, independent study, and a senior project. Special programs include internships, summer session for credit, off-campus study, study-abroad, and Air Force ROTC.

The most frequently chosen **baccalaureate** fields are business/marketing, education, and visual and performing arts. A complete listing of majors at B-W appears in the Majors by College index beginning on page 469.

The **faculty** at B-W has 164 full-time members, 80% with terminal degrees.

Students of B-W

The student body totals 4,382, of whom 3,681 are undergraduates. 57.4% are women and 42.6% are men. Students come from 36 states and territories and 13 other countries. 88% are from Ohio. 1.3% are international students. 7% are African American, 0.2% American Indian, 1.1% Asian American, and 2.6% Hispanic American. 83% returned for their sophomore year.

Facilities and Resources

465 **computers/terminals** and 100 ports are available on campus for general student use. Students can access the following: campus intranet, computer help desk, free student e-mail accounts, online (class) grades, online (class) registration, online (class) schedules. Campuswide network is available. 100% of college-owned or -operated housing units are wired for high-speed Internet access. Wireless service is available via entire campus. The 3 **libraries** have 200,000 books and 22,000 subscriptions.

Campus Life

There are 136 active organizations on campus, including a drama/theater group, newspaper, radio station, television station, choral group, and marching band. 11% of eligible men and 15% of eligible women are members of national **fraternities** and national **sororities.**

B-W is a member of the NCAA (Division III). **Intercollegiate sports** include baseball (m), basketball, cross-country running, football (m), golf, soccer, softball (w), swimming and diving, tennis, track and field, volleyball (w), wrestling (m).

Campus Safety

Student safety services include late-night transport/escort service, 24-hour emergency telephone alarm devices, 24-hour patrols by trained security personnel, student patrols, and electronically operated dormitory entrances.

Applying

B-W requires an essay, a high school transcript, 1 recommendation, and a minimum high school GPA of 2.75, and in some cases SAT or ACT. It recommends an interview and a minimum high school GPA of 3.2. Application deadline: 3/1; 9/1 for financial aid, with a 5/1 priority date. Deferred admission is possible.

Getting Accepted
3,321 applied
67% were accepted
738 enrolled (33% of accepted)
28% from top tenth of their h.s. class
3.46 average high school GPA
Mean SAT critical reading score: 555
Mean SAT math score: 545
Mean SAT writing score: 545
Mean ACT score: 24
32% had SAT critical reading scores over 600
27% had SAT math scores over 600
21% had SAT writing scores over 600
52% had ACT scores over 24
5% had SAT critical reading scores over 700
2% had SAT math scores over 700
2% had SAT writing scores over 700
7% had ACT scores over 30
16 valedictorians

Graduation and After
56% graduated in 4 years
16% graduated in 5 years
1% graduated in 6 years
105 organizations recruited on campus

Financial Matters
$23,524 tuition and fees (2008–09)
$7728 room and board
91% average percent of need met
$18,444 average financial aid amount received
    per undergraduate (2007–08 estimated)

Bard College

RURAL SETTING ■ PRIVATE ■ INDEPENDENT ■ COED
ANNANDALE-ON-HUDSON, NEW YORK

Web site: www.bard.edu
Contact: Ms. Mary Backlund, Director of Admissions, PO Box 5000, 51
    Ravine Road, Annandale-on-Hudson, NY 12504-5000
Telephone: 845-758-7472
Fax: 845-758-5208
E-mail: admission@bard.edu

Getting Accepted
5,459 applied
25% were accepted
517 enrolled (38% of accepted)
63% from top tenth of their h.s. class
3.5 average high school GPA
Mean SAT critical reading score: 680
Mean SAT math score: 650
73% had SAT math scores over 600
83% had SAT writing scores over 600
22% had SAT math scores over 700
36% had SAT writing scores over 700

Graduation and After
68% graduated in 4 years
7% graduated in 5 years
30 organizations recruited on campus

Financial Matters
$38,374 tuition and fees (2008–09)
$10,866 room and board
90% average percent of need met
$26,224 average financial aid amount received
    per undergraduate (2007–08 estimated)

Academics
Bard awards associate, bachelor's, master's, and doctoral **degrees**. **Challenging opportunities** include advanced placement credit, student-designed majors, double majors, independent study, and a senior project. Special programs include internships, off-campus study, and study-abroad.

The most frequently chosen **baccalaureate** fields are visual and performing arts, English, and social sciences. A complete listing of majors at Bard appears in the Majors by College index beginning on page 469.

The **faculty** at Bard has 141 full-time members, 96% with terminal degrees. The student-faculty ratio is 9:1.

Students of Bard
The student body totals 2,148, of whom 1,873 are undergraduates. 57.5% are women and 42.5% are men. Students come from 50 states and territories and 49 other countries. 30% are from New York. 11.6% are international students. 2.3% are African American, 0.7% American Indian, 2.9% Asian American, and 3.5% Hispanic American. 83% returned for their sophomore year.

Facilities and Resources
425 **computers/terminals** are available on campus for general student use. Students can access the following: campus intranet, computer help desk, free student e-mail accounts, online (class) grades, online (class) registration, online (class) schedules. Campuswide network is available. 100% of college-owned or -operated housing units are wired for high-speed Internet access. Wireless service is available via classrooms, computer centers, dorm rooms, libraries, student centers. The 4 **libraries** have 412,050 books and 15,450 subscriptions.

Campus Life
There are 120 active organizations on campus, including a drama/theater group, newspaper, radio station, and choral group. No national or local **fraternities** or **sororities**.

Bard is a member of the NCAA (Division III) and NAIA. **Intercollegiate sports** include basketball, cross-country running, soccer, squash (m), tennis, track and field, volleyball.

Campus Safety
Student safety services include late-night transport/escort service, 24-hour emergency telephone alarm devices, 24-hour patrols by trained security personnel, student patrols, and electronically operated dormitory entrances.

Applying
Bard requires an essay, a high school transcript, 3 recommendations, and a minimum high school GPA of 3.0, and in some cases an interview. It recommends an interview. Application deadline: 1/15; 2/15 for financial aid, with a 2/1 priority date. Early and deferred admission are possible.

BARD COLLEGE AT SIMON'S ROCK

RURAL SETTING ■ PRIVATE ■ INDEPENDENT ■ COED
GREAT BARRINGTON, MASSACHUSETTS

Web site: simons-rock.edu
Contact: Barbara Shultis, Assistant to the Director of Admissions, 84 Alford Road, Great Barrington, MA 01230
Telephone: 413-528-7312 or toll-free 800-235-7186
Fax: 413-528-7334
E-mail: admit@simons-rock.edu

Academics

Simon's Rock awards associate and bachelor's **degrees. Challenging opportunities** include student-designed majors, double majors, independent study, and a senior project. Special programs include internships, off-campus study, and study-abroad.

The most frequently chosen **baccalaureate** fields are area and ethnic studies, visual and performing arts, and English. A complete listing of majors at Simon's Rock appears in the Majors by College index beginning on page 469.

The **faculty** at Simon's Rock has 37 full-time members, 95% with terminal degrees. The student-faculty ratio is 8:1.

Students of Simon's Rock

The student body is made up of 408 undergraduates. 57.6% are women and 42.4% are men. Students come from 41 states and territories and 11 other countries. 18% are from Massachusetts. 4.3% are international students. 6.7% are African American, 0.8% American Indian, 4.3% Asian American, and 5.9% Hispanic American. 82% returned for their sophomore year.

Facilities and Resources

50 **computers/terminals** are available on campus for general student use. Students can access the following: campus intranet, computer help desk, free student e-mail accounts. Campuswide network is available. 100% of college-owned or -operated housing units are wired for high-speed Internet access. Wireless service is available via classrooms, computer centers, computer labs, dorm rooms, learning centers, libraries, student centers. The **library** has 73,514 books and 417 subscriptions.

Campus Life

There are 21 active organizations on campus, including a drama/theater group, newspaper, radio station, and choral group. No national or local **fraternities** or **sororities**.

Intercollegiate sports include basketball, cheerleading, cross-country running, fencing, racquetball, soccer, swimming and diving.

Campus Safety

Student safety services include 24-hour weekend patrols by trained security personnel, late-night transport/escort service, 24-hour emergency telephone alarm devices, and electronically operated dormitory entrances.

Applying

Simon's Rock requires an essay, a high school transcript, an interview, 2 recommendations, parent application, and a minimum high school GPA of 2.0, and in some cases SAT or ACT and PSAT. It recommends a minimum high school GPA of 3.0. Application deadline: 5/31; 4/15 priority date for financial aid. Deferred admission is possible.

Getting Accepted

236 applied
84% were accepted
182 enrolled (91% of accepted)
60% from top tenth of their h.s. class
Mean SAT critical reading score: 663
Mean SAT math score: 614
Mean SAT writing score: 630
Mean ACT score: 27
61% had SAT critical reading scores over 600
43% had SAT math scores over 600
88% had ACT scores over 24
20% had SAT critical reading scores over 700
13% had SAT math scores over 700
25% had ACT scores over 30

Graduation and After

69% graduated in 4 years
17% graduated in 5 years
2% graduated in 6 years

Financial Matters

$37,130 tuition and fees (2008–09)
$9730 room and board
65% average percent of need met
$19,500 average financial aid amount received per undergraduate (2007–08 estimated)

Barnard is a small, selective liberal arts college for women, located in New York City. Its superb faculty is composed of leading scholars who serve as dedicated, accessible teachers. Barnard's unique partnership with Columbia University, situated just across the street, provides students a vast selection of additional course offerings, extracurricular activities, NCAA Division I Ivy League athletic competition, and a fully coeducational social life. Barnard's metropolitan location grants students access to thousands of internships in addition to excellent cultural, intellectual, and social resources.

Getting Accepted
4,274 applied
28% were accepted
576 enrolled (47% of accepted)
74% from top tenth of their h.s. class
3.88 average high school GPA
Mean SAT critical reading score: 684
Mean SAT math score: 655
Mean SAT writing score: 696
Mean ACT score: 30
90% had SAT critical reading scores over 600
82% had SAT math scores over 600
92% had SAT writing scores over 600
96% had ACT scores over 24
47% had SAT critical reading scores over 700
28% had SAT math scores over 700
56% had SAT writing scores over 700
56% had ACT scores over 30
5 National Merit Scholars
55 class presidents
65 valedictorians

Graduation and After
82% graduated in 4 years
6% graduated in 5 years
1% graduated in 6 years
64% had job offers within 6 months
45 organizations recruited on campus

Financial Matters
$37,538 tuition and fees (2008–09)
$11,926 room and board
100% average percent of need met
$32,153 average financial aid amount received per undergraduate (2007–08 estimated)

BARNARD COLLEGE
URBAN SETTING ■ PRIVATE ■ INDEPENDENT ■ WOMEN ONLY
NEW YORK, NEW YORK

Web site: www.barnard.edu
Contact: Ms. Jennifer Gill Fondiller, Dean of Admissions, 3009 Broadway, New York, NY 10027
Telephone: 212-854-2014
Fax: 212-854-6220
E-mail: admissions@barnard.edu

Academics
Barnard awards bachelor's **degrees**. **Challenging opportunities** include advanced placement credit, accelerated degree programs, student-designed majors, double majors, independent study, and a senior project. Special programs include internships, off-campus study, and study-abroad.

The most frequently chosen **baccalaureate** fields are social sciences, psychology, and English. A complete listing of majors at Barnard appears in the Majors by College index beginning on page 469.

The **faculty** at Barnard has 204 full-time members, 90% with terminal degrees. The student-faculty ratio is 9:1.

Students of Barnard
The student body is made up of 2,359 undergraduates. Students come from 48 states and territories and 35 other countries. 30% are from New York. 4% are international students. 4.6% are African American, 0.2% American Indian, 15.9% Asian American, and 8.7% Hispanic American. 95% returned for their sophomore year.

Facilities and Resources
210 **computers/terminals** are available on campus for general student use. Students can access the following: campus intranet, computer help desk, free student e-mail accounts, online (class) grades, online (class) registration, online (class) schedules. Campuswide network is available. 100% of college-owned or -operated housing units are wired for high-speed Internet access. Wireless service is available via computer centers, computer labs, dorm rooms, libraries, student centers. The **library** has 205,920 books and 465 subscriptions.

Campus Life
There are 100 active organizations on campus, including a drama/theater group, newspaper, radio station, television station, choral group, and marching band. No national or local **sororities**.

Barnard is a member of the NCAA (Division I). **Intercollegiate sports** include archery, basketball, crew, cross-country running, fencing, field hockey, golf, lacrosse, soccer, softball, swimming and diving, tennis, track and field, volleyball.

Campus Safety
Student safety services include gated campus with permanent security posts, late-night transport/escort service, 24-hour emergency telephone alarm devices, and 24-hour patrols by trained security personnel.

Applying
Barnard requires an essay, SAT with writing and two subject tests or ACT with writing, a high school transcript, 3 recommendations, and Common Application with Barnard supplement. It recommends an interview. Application deadline: 1/1; 2/1 for financial aid. Early and deferred admission are possible.

BATES COLLEGE

SMALL-TOWN SETTING ■ PRIVATE ■ INDEPENDENT ■ COED
LEWISTON, MAINE

Web site: www.bates.edu
Contact: Mr. Wylie Mitchell, Dean of Admissions, Andrews Road, Lewiston, ME 04240-6028
Telephone: 207-786-6000
Fax: 207-786-6025
E-mail: admissions@bates.edu

Academics

Bates awards bachelor's **degrees**. **Challenging opportunities** include advanced placement credit, accelerated degree programs, student-designed majors, an honors program, double majors, independent study, and a senior project. Special programs include cooperative education, internships, off-campus study, and study-abroad.

The most frequently chosen **baccalaureate** fields are social sciences, English, and psychology. A complete listing of majors at Bates appears in the Majors by College index beginning on page 469.

The **faculty** at Bates has 166 full-time members, 90% with terminal degrees. The student-faculty ratio is 10:1.

Students of Bates

The student body is made up of 1,776 undergraduates. 53.9% are women and 46.1% are men. Students come from 46 states and territories and 65 other countries. 11% are from Maine. 5.5% are international students. 3.9% are African American, 0.3% American Indian, 6% Asian American, and 3.5% Hispanic American. 96% returned for their sophomore year.

Facilities and Resources

521 **computers/terminals** and 2,075 ports are available on campus for general student use. Students can access the following: computer help desk, free student e-mail accounts, online (class) grades, online (class) registration, online (class) schedules, course web pages, course evaluation, financial records. Campuswide network is available. 100% of college-owned or -operated housing units are wired for high-speed Internet access. Wireless service is available via classrooms, computer labs, dorm rooms, learning centers, libraries, student centers. The 2 **libraries** have 620,000 books and 27,000 subscriptions.

Campus Life

There are 99 active organizations on campus, including a drama/theater group, newspaper, radio station, and choral group. No national or local **fraternities** or **sororities**.

Bates is a member of the NCAA (Division III). **Intercollegiate sports** include baseball (m), basketball, crew, cross-country running, field hockey (w), football (m), golf, lacrosse, skiing (cross-country), skiing (downhill), soccer, softball (w), squash, swimming and diving, tennis, track and field, volleyball (w).

Campus Safety

Student safety services include late-night transport/escort service, 24-hour emergency telephone alarm devices, 24-hour patrols by trained security personnel, student patrols, and electronically operated dormitory entrances.

Applying

Bates requires an essay, a high school transcript, and 3 recommendations. It recommends an interview. Application deadline: 1/1; 2/1 for financial aid. Early and deferred admission are possible.

Getting Accepted

5,098 applied
29% were accepted
521 enrolled (35% of accepted)
53% from top tenth of their h.s. class
86% had SAT critical reading scores over 600
87% had SAT math scores over 600
85% had SAT writing scores over 600
36% had SAT critical reading scores over 700
33% had SAT math scores over 700
42% had SAT writing scores over 700

Graduation and After

85% graduated in 4 years
4% graduated in 5 years
1% graduated in 6 years
304 organizations recruited on campus

Financial Matters

$49,350 comprehensive fee (2008–09)
100% average percent of need met
$30,341 average financial aid amount received per undergraduate (2007–08 estimated)

Baylor University

Urban setting ■ Private ■ Independent Religious ■ Coed
Waco, Texas

Web site: www.baylor.edu
Contact: Ms. Jennifer Carron, Director of Admissions, PO Box 97056, Waco, TX 76798
Telephone: 254-710-3435 or toll-free 800-BAYLORU
Fax: 254-710-3436
E-mail: admissions@baylor.edu

Getting Accepted

25,501 applied
51% were accepted
3,062 enrolled (23% of accepted)
41% from top tenth of their h.s. class
Mean SAT critical reading score: 596
Mean SAT math score: 614
Mean SAT writing score: 584
Mean ACT score: 25
50% had SAT critical reading scores over 600
57% had SAT math scores over 600
42% had SAT writing scores over 600
67% had ACT scores over 24
12% had SAT critical reading scores over 700
15% had SAT math scores over 700
9% had SAT writing scores over 700
13% had ACT scores over 30
72 National Merit Scholars

Graduation and After

51% graduated in 4 years
20% graduated in 5 years
2% graduated in 6 years
194 organizations recruited on campus

Financial Matters

$27,910 tuition and fees (2009–10)
$8569 room and board
65% average percent of need met
$17,250 average financial aid amount received per undergraduate (2007–08 estimated)

Academics

Baylor awards bachelor's, master's, doctoral, and first-professional **degrees** and post-master's certificates. **Challenging opportunities** include advanced placement credit, accelerated degree programs, student-designed majors, an honors program, double majors, and a senior project. Special programs include internships, summer session for credit, study-abroad, and Air Force ROTC.

The most frequently chosen **baccalaureate** fields are business/marketing, health professions and related sciences, and communications/journalism. A complete listing of majors at Baylor appears in the Majors by College index beginning on page 469.

The **faculty** at Baylor has 823 full-time members, 80% with terminal degrees. The student-faculty ratio is 15:1.

Students of Baylor

The student body totals 14,541, of whom 12,162 are undergraduates. 58.2% are women and 41.8% are men. Students come from 51 states and territories and 71 other countries. 82% are from Texas. 1.8% are international students. 7.5% are African American, 0.8% American Indian, 6.8% Asian American, and 10.6% Hispanic American. 86% returned for their sophomore year.

Facilities and Resources

1,668 **computers/terminals** are available on campus for general student use. Students can access the following: campus intranet, computer help desk, free student e-mail accounts, online (class) grades, online (class) registration, online (class) schedules. Campuswide network is available. 99% of college-owned or -operated housing units are wired for high-speed Internet access. Wireless service is available via entire campus. The 9 **libraries** have 2,252,780 books and 8,429 subscriptions.

Campus Life

There are 289 active organizations on campus, including a drama/theater group, newspaper, radio station, television station, choral group, and marching band. 13% of eligible men and 18% of eligible women are members of national **fraternities**, national **sororities**, local fraternities, and local sororities.

Baylor is a member of the NCAA (Division I). **Intercollegiate sports** (some offering scholarships) include baseball (m), basketball, cross-country running, equestrian sports (w), football (m), golf, soccer (w), softball (w), tennis, track and field, volleyball (w).

Campus Safety

Student safety services include bicycle patrols, late-night transport/escort service, 24-hour emergency telephone alarm devices, 24-hour patrols by trained security personnel, and electronically operated dormitory entrances.

Applying

Baylor requires SAT or ACT, ACT essay, and a high school transcript, and in some cases an essay, 2 recommendations, and a minimum high school GPA of 2.5. It recommends an interview. Application deadline: 2/1; 2/15 priority date for financial aid. Early admission is possible.

BELMONT UNIVERSITY

URBAN SETTING ■ PRIVATE ■ INDEPENDENT RELIGIOUS ■ COED
NASHVILLE, TENNESSEE

Web site: www.belmont.edu
Contact: Dr. Kathryn Baugher, Dean of Enrollment Services, 1900 Belmont Boulevard, Nashville, TN 37212-3757
Telephone: 615-460-6785 or toll-free 800-56E-NROL
Fax: 615-460-5434
E-mail: buadmission@mail.belmont.edu

SPONSOR

Academics

Belmont awards bachelor's, master's, and doctoral **degrees** and post-master's certificates. **Challenging opportunities** include advanced placement credit, accelerated degree programs, student-designed majors, an honors program, double majors, independent study, and a senior project. Special programs include cooperative education, internships, summer session for credit, off-campus study, study-abroad, and Army and Navy ROTC.

The most frequently chosen **baccalaureate** fields are visual and performing arts, business/marketing, and health professions and related sciences. A complete listing of majors at Belmont appears in the Majors by College index beginning on page 469.

The **faculty** at Belmont has 266 full-time members, 78% with terminal degrees. The student-faculty ratio is 12:1.

Students of Belmont

The student body totals 4,991, of whom 4,174 are undergraduates. 57.8% are women and 42.2% are men. Students come from 49 states and territories and 20 other countries. 56% are from Tennessee. 1% are international students. 3.7% are African American, 0.5% American Indian, 2.3% Asian American, and 2% Hispanic American. 81% returned for their sophomore year.

Facilities and Resources

400 **computers/terminals** are available on campus for general student use. Students can access the following: campus intranet, free student e-mail accounts, online (class) grades, online (class) registration, online (class) schedules, individual student information via BANNER Web. Campuswide network is available. 100% of college-owned or -operated housing units are wired for high-speed Internet access. Wireless service is available via entire campus. The **library** has 220,637 books and 1,072 subscriptions.

Campus Life

There are 80 active organizations on campus, including a drama/theater group, newspaper, radio station, television station, choral group, and marching band. 6% of eligible men and 8% of eligible women are members of national **fraternities** and national **sororities**.

Belmont is a member of the NCAA (Division I). **Intercollegiate sports** (some offering scholarships) include baseball (m), basketball, cross-country running, golf, soccer, softball (w), tennis, track and field, volleyball (w).

Campus Safety

Student safety services include bicycle patrol, late-night transport/escort service, 24-hour emergency telephone alarm devices, 24-hour patrols by trained security personnel, and electronically operated dormitory entrances.

Applying

Belmont requires an essay, SAT or ACT, a high school transcript, 2 recommendations, resume of activities, and a minimum high school GPA of 3.0, and in some cases an interview. Application deadline: 8/1; 3/1 priority date for financial aid. Early and deferred admission are possible.

Belmont University brings together the best of liberal arts and professional education in a Christian community of learning and service. Located in Nashville on the former Belle Monte estate, Belmont offers a campus rich in heritage with the conveniences and advantages of one of the fastest-growing cities in the nation. Belmont students benefit from an education marked by personal attention from professors; special academic opportunities, such as the Belmont Undergraduate Research Symposium, the Engaged Scholars program, studies abroad, and the honors program; and outstanding internship opportunities in many areas, including business, health care, education, communication arts, and the music industry.

Getting Accepted
3,064 applied
63% were accepted
932 enrolled (49% of accepted)
36% from top tenth of their h.s. class
3.52 average high school GPA
Mean SAT critical reading score: 584
Mean SAT math score: 581
Mean ACT score: 26
42% had SAT critical reading scores over 600
42% had SAT math scores over 600
86% had ACT scores over 24
6% had SAT critical reading scores over 700
6% had SAT math scores over 700
27% had ACT scores over 30
31 valedictorians

Graduation and After
50% graduated in 4 years
15% graduated in 5 years
2% graduated in 6 years
80% had job offers within 6 months
180 organizations recruited on campus

Financial Matters
$21,110 tuition and fees (2008–09)
$10,000 room and board
79% average percent of need met
$7474 average financial aid amount received per undergraduate (2007–08 estimated)

BELOIT COLLEGE

SMALL-TOWN SETTING ■ PRIVATE ■ INDEPENDENT ■ COED
BELOIT, WISCONSIN

Web site: www.beloit.edu
Contact: Mr. James S. Zielinski, Director of Admissions, 700 College Street, Beloit, WI 53511-5596
Telephone: 608-363-2500 or toll-free 800-9-BELOIT
Fax: 608-363-2075
E-mail: admiss@beloit.edu

Getting Accepted

2,248 applied
63% were accepted
339 enrolled (24% of accepted)
40% from top tenth of their h.s. class
3.4 average high school GPA
Mean SAT critical reading score: 630
Mean SAT math score: 610
Mean ACT score: 27
67% had SAT critical reading scores over 600
61% had SAT math scores over 600
84% had ACT scores over 24
26% had SAT critical reading scores over 700
22% had SAT math scores over 700
24% had ACT scores over 30
2 National Merit Scholars
10 valedictorians

Graduation and After

74% graduated in 4 years
5% graduated in 5 years
1% graduated in 6 years
72% had job offers within 6 months

Financial Matters

$31,540 tuition and fees (2008–09)
$6696 room and board
96% average percent of need met
$24,506 average financial aid amount received per undergraduate (2007–08 estimated)

Academics

Beloit awards bachelor's **degrees**. **Challenging opportunities** include advanced placement credit, student-designed majors, double majors, independent study, and a senior project. Special programs include internships, summer session for credit, off-campus study, and study-abroad.

The most frequently chosen **baccalaureate** fields are social sciences, foreign languages and literature, and English. A complete listing of majors at Beloit appears in the Majors by College index beginning on page 469.

The **faculty** at Beloit has 124 full-time members, 96% with terminal degrees. The student-faculty ratio is 11:1.

Students of Beloit

The student body is made up of 1,388 undergraduates. 56.6% are women and 43.4% are men. Students come from 49 states and territories and 32 other countries. 22% are from Wisconsin. 5.2% are international students. 4% are African American, 0.5% American Indian, 3.2% Asian American, and 3.5% Hispanic American. 89% returned for their sophomore year.

Facilities and Resources

270 **computers/terminals** are available on campus for general student use. Students can access the following: campus intranet, computer help desk, free student e-mail accounts, online (class) schedules. Campuswide network is available. 100% of college-owned or -operated housing units are wired for high-speed Internet access. Wireless service is available via classrooms, computer centers, computer labs, dorm rooms, libraries, student centers. The **library** has 673,771 books and 25,352 subscriptions.

Campus Life

There are 69 active organizations on campus, including a drama/theater group, newspaper, radio station, television station, and choral group. 15% of eligible men and 5% of eligible women are members of national **fraternities**, national **sororities**, local fraternities, and local sororities.

Beloit is a member of the NCAA (Division III). **Intercollegiate sports** include baseball (m), basketball, cross-country running, football (m), golf, soccer, softball (w), swimming and diving, tennis, track and field, volleyball (w).

Campus Safety

Student safety services include late-night transport/escort service, 24-hour emergency telephone alarm devices, 24-hour patrols by trained security personnel, and electronically operated dormitory entrances.

Applying

Beloit requires an essay, SAT or ACT, a high school transcript, and 1 recommendation, and in some cases an interview. It recommends an interview. Application deadline: 1/15; 3/1 priority date for financial aid. Early and deferred admission are possible.

BENEDICTINE UNIVERSITY

SUBURBAN SETTING ■ PRIVATE ■ INDEPENDENT RELIGIOUS ■ COED
LISLE, ILLINOIS

Web site: www.ben.edu
Contact: Ms. Kari Gibbons, Dean of Enrollment, 5700 College Road, Lisle,
   IL 60532-0900
Telephone: 630-829-6300 or toll-free 888-829-6363 (out-of-state)
Fax: 630-829-6301
E-mail: admissions@ben.edu

Academics

Benedictine awards associate, bachelor's, master's, and doctoral **degrees** and post-bachelor's certificates. **Challenging opportunities** include advanced placement credit, accelerated degree programs, an honors program, double majors, independent study, and a senior project. Special programs include internships, summer session for credit, off-campus study, study-abroad, and Army ROTC.

The most frequently chosen **baccalaureate** fields are business/marketing, health professions and related sciences, and psychology. A complete listing of majors at Benedictine appears in the Majors by College index beginning on page 469.

The **faculty** at Benedictine has 102 full-time members, 85% with terminal degrees. The student-faculty ratio is 13:1.

Students of Benedictine

The student body totals 5,279, of whom 3,282 are undergraduates. 57.4% are women and 42.6% are men. Students come from 25 states and territories and 13 other countries. 100% are from Illinois. 1.2% are international students. 10% are African American, 0.3% American Indian, 13.3% Asian American, and 6.3% Hispanic American. 78% returned for their sophomore year.

Facilities and Resources

200 **computers/terminals** are available on campus for general student use. Students can access the following: computer help desk, free student e-mail accounts, online (class) grades, online (class) registration, online (class) schedules. Campuswide network is available. 100% of college-owned or -operated housing units are wired for high-speed Internet access. Wireless service is available via computer centers, dorm rooms, libraries, student centers. The **library** has 138,000 books and 23,906 subscriptions.

Campus Life

There are 46 active organizations on campus, including a drama/theater group, newspaper, television station, and choral group. No national or local **fraternities** or **sororities**.

Benedictine is a member of the NCAA (Division III). **Intercollegiate sports** include baseball (m), basketball, cross-country running, football (m), golf, soccer, softball (w), swimming and diving, tennis (w), track and field, volleyball (w).

Campus Safety

Student safety services include late-night transport/escort service, 24-hour emergency telephone alarm devices, 24-hour patrols by trained security personnel, and electronically operated dormitory entrances.

Applying

Benedictine requires an essay, SAT or ACT, and a high school transcript, and in some cases an interview. It recommends rank in upper 50% of high school class, minimum ACT score of 21. Application deadline: rolling admissions. Deferred admission is possible.

Getting Accepted

1,566 applied
80% were accepted
435 enrolled (35% of accepted)
21% from top tenth of their h.s. class
3.35 average high school GPA
Mean ACT score: 23
41% had ACT scores over 24
5% had ACT scores over 30
77 National Merit Scholars
2 class presidents

Graduation and After

46% graduated in 4 years
11% graduated in 5 years
3% graduated in 6 years

Financial Matters

$22,310 tuition and fees (2008–09)
$7300 room and board
85% average percent of need met
$11,980 average financial aid amount received
   per undergraduate (2005–06)

BENNINGTON COLLEGE

SMALL-TOWN SETTING ■ PRIVATE ■ INDEPENDENT ■ COED
BENNINGTON, VERMONT

Web site: www.bennington.edu
Contact: Mr. Ken Himmelman, Dean of Admissions and Financial Aid, One College Drive, Bennington, VT 05201-6003
Telephone: 802-440-4312 or toll-free 800-833-6845
Fax: 802-440-4320
E-mail: admissions@bennington.edu

Getting Accepted
1,057 applied
62% were accepted
190 enrolled (29% of accepted)
31% from top tenth of their h.s. class
3.4 average high school GPA
Mean SAT critical reading score: 657
Mean SAT math score: 603
Mean SAT writing score: 702
Mean ACT score: 27

Graduation and After
46% graduated in 4 years
14% graduated in 5 years
1% graduated in 6 years
74% had job offers within 6 months

Financial Matters
$38,270 tuition and fees (2008–09)
$10,680 room and board
81% average percent of need met
$29,528 average financial aid amount received per undergraduate (2007–08 estimated)

Academics
Bennington awards bachelor's and master's **degrees** and post-bachelor's certificates. **Challenging opportunities** include accelerated degree programs, student-designed majors, double majors, independent study, and a senior project. Special programs include internships and study-abroad.

The most frequently chosen **baccalaureate** fields are visual and performing arts, English, and foreign languages and literature. A complete listing of majors at Bennington appears in the Majors by College index beginning on page 469.

The **faculty** at Bennington has 62 full-time members, 73% with terminal degrees. The student-faculty ratio is 9:1.

Students of Bennington
The student body totals 759, of whom 618 are undergraduates. 66% are women and 34% are men. Students come from 41 states and territories and 12 other countries. 4% are from Vermont. 3.9% are international students. 1.8% are African American, 0.3% American Indian, 1.9% Asian American, and 2.8% Hispanic American. 89% returned for their sophomore year.

Facilities and Resources
100 **computers/terminals** and 25 ports are available on campus for general student use. Students can access the following: campus intranet, computer help desk, free student e-mail accounts, online (class) schedules. Campuswide network is available. 100% of college-owned or -operated housing units are wired for high-speed Internet access. Wireless service is available via entire campus. The 2 **libraries** have 121,500 books and 26,801 subscriptions.

Campus Life
There are 21 active organizations on campus, including a drama/theater group, newspaper, and choral group. No national or local **fraternities** or **sororities**.

This institution has no intercollegiate sports.

Campus Safety
Student safety services include prevention/awareness program, late-night transport/escort service, 24-hour emergency telephone alarm devices, and 24-hour patrols by trained security personnel.

Applying
Bennington requires an essay, a high school transcript, 2 recommendations, and graded analytic paper. It recommends an interview. Application deadline: 1/5; 3/1 priority date for financial aid. Early and deferred admission are possible.

Bentley University

Suburban setting ■ Private ■ Independent ■ Coed

Waltham, Massachusetts

Web site: www.bentley.edu
Contact: Admissions Office, 175 Forest Street, Waltham, MA 02452
Telephone: 781-891-2244 or toll-free 800-523-2354
Fax: 781-891-3414
E-mail: ugadmission@bentley.edu

Academics

Bentley awards associate, bachelor's, master's, and doctoral **degrees** and post-bachelor's and post-master's certificates. **Challenging opportunities** include advanced placement credit, accelerated degree programs, student-designed majors, an honors program, double majors, independent study, and a senior project. Special programs include internships, summer session for credit, off-campus study, study-abroad, and Army and Air Force ROTC.

The most frequently chosen **baccalaureate** fields are business/marketing, computer and information sciences, and interdisciplinary studies. A complete listing of majors at Bentley appears in the Majors by College index beginning on page 469.

The **faculty** at Bentley has 285 full-time members, 82% with terminal degrees. The student-faculty ratio is 12:1.

Students of Bentley

The student body totals 5,664, of whom 4,259 are undergraduates. 40.5% are women and 59.5% are men. Students come from 44 states and territories and 78 other countries. 50% are from Massachusetts. 9% are international students. 3% are African American, 0.1% American Indian, 7.6% Asian American, and 4.7% Hispanic American. 93% returned for their sophomore year.

Facilities and Resources

4,789 **computers/terminals** and 13,752 ports are available on campus for general student use. Students can access the following: campus intranet, computer help desk, free student e-mail accounts, online (class) grades, online (class) registration, online (class) schedules, grade checking, online admission, Blackboard, resume review, student employment, interlibrary loan, free software downloads for popular Microsoft titles and many academic applications. Campuswide network is available. 100% of college-owned or -operated housing units are wired for high-speed Internet access. Wireless service is available via entire campus. The **library** has 177,000 books and 30,700 subscriptions.

Campus Life

There are 104 active organizations on campus, including a drama/theater group, newspaper, radio station, television station, and choral group. 12% of eligible men and 12% of eligible women are members of national **fraternities**, national **sororities**, and local fraternities.

Bentley is a member of the NCAA (Division II). **Intercollegiate sports** (some offering scholarships) include baseball (m), basketball, cross-country running, field hockey (w), football (m), golf (m), ice hockey (m), lacrosse, soccer, softball (w), swimming and diving, tennis, track and field, volleyball (w).

Campus Safety

Student safety services include security cameras, late-night transport/escort service, 24-hour emergency telephone alarm devices, 24-hour patrols by trained security personnel, and electronically operated dormitory entrances.

Applying

Bentley requires an essay, SAT or ACT, a high school transcript, and 2 recommendations. It recommends an interview. Application deadline: 1/15, 1/15 for nonresidents; 2/1 for financial aid. Early and deferred admission are possible.

Getting Accepted

7,238 applied
38% were accepted
974 enrolled (36% of accepted)
45% from top tenth of their h.s. class
Mean SAT critical reading score: 590
Mean SAT math score: 650
Mean SAT writing score: 600
Mean ACT score: 27
48% had SAT critical reading scores over 600
81% had SAT math scores over 600
53% had SAT writing scores over 600
85% had ACT scores over 24
4% had SAT critical reading scores over 700
19% had SAT math scores over 700
8% had SAT writing scores over 700
17% had ACT scores over 30

Graduation and After

74% graduated in 4 years
7% graduated in 5 years
2% graduated in 6 years
83% had job offers within 6 months
222 organizations recruited on campus

Financial Matters

$34,488 tuition and fees (2008–09)
$11,320 room and board
89% average percent of need met
$24,587 average financial aid amount received per undergraduate (2006–07)

BEREA COLLEGE

SMALL-TOWN SETTING ■ PRIVATE ■ INDEPENDENT ■ COED
BEREA, KENTUCKY

Web site: www.berea.edu
Contact: Mr. Joe Bagnoli, Director of Admissions, CPO 2344, Berea, KY 40404
Telephone: 859-985-3500 or toll-free 800-326-5948
Fax: 859-985-3512
E-mail: admissions@berea.edu

Getting Accepted

2,468 applied
22% were accepted
413 enrolled (78% of accepted)
25% from top tenth of their h.s. class
3.4 average high school GPA
Mean SAT critical reading score: 562
Mean SAT math score: 538
Mean SAT writing score: 531
Mean ACT score: 23
37% had SAT critical reading scores over 600
22% had SAT math scores over 600
28% had SAT writing scores over 600
45% had ACT scores over 24
8% had SAT critical reading scores over 700
3% had SAT math scores over 700
3% had SAT writing scores over 700
4% had ACT scores over 30

Graduation and After

44% graduated in 4 years
18% graduated in 5 years
1% graduated in 6 years
125 organizations recruited on campus

Financial Matters

$866 tuition and fees (2008–09)
$5768 room and board
95% average percent of need met
$29,504 average financial aid amount received per undergraduate (2007–08 estimated)

Academics

Berea awards bachelor's **degrees**. **Challenging opportunities** include advanced placement credit, student-designed majors, an honors program, double majors, independent study, and a senior project. Special programs include internships, summer session for credit, and study-abroad.

The most frequently chosen **baccalaureate** fields are business/marketing, social sciences, and visual and performing arts. A complete listing of majors at Berea appears in the Majors by College index beginning on page 469.

The **faculty** at Berea has 131 full-time members, 89% with terminal degrees. The student-faculty ratio is 10:1.

Students of Berea

The student body is made up of 1,549 undergraduates. 60% are women and 40% are men. Students come from 40 states and territories and 55 other countries. 44% are from Kentucky. 7.6% are international students. 16.4% are African American, 1.2% American Indian, 1.6% Asian American, and 2.2% Hispanic American. 78% returned for their sophomore year.

Facilities and Resources

7,000 ports are available on campus for general student use. Students can access the following: campus intranet, computer help desk, free student e-mail accounts, online (class) grades, online (class) registration, online (class) schedules. Campuswide network is available. 100% of college-owned or -operated housing units are wired for high-speed Internet access. Wireless service is available via classrooms, libraries, student centers. The 2 **libraries** have 386,252 books and 2,020 subscriptions.

Campus Life

There are 70 active organizations on campus, including a drama/theater group, newspaper, and choral group. No national or local **fraternities** or **sororities**.

Berea is a member of the NAIA. **Intercollegiate sports** include baseball (m), basketball, cross-country running, golf (m), soccer, softball (w), swimming and diving, tennis, track and field, volleyball (w).

Campus Safety

Student safety services include crime prevention programs, late-night transport/escort service, 24-hour emergency telephone alarm devices, 24-hour patrols by trained security personnel, and electronically operated dormitory entrances.

Applying

Berea requires an essay, SAT or ACT, a high school transcript, an interview, and financial aid application. It recommends 2 recommendations. Application deadline: 4/30; 8/1 for financial aid, with a 4/15 priority date.

BERNARD M. BARUCH COLLEGE OF THE CITY UNIVERSITY OF NEW YORK

URBAN SETTING ■ PUBLIC ■ STATE AND LOCALLY SUPPORTED ■ COED
NEW YORK, NEW YORK

Web site: www.baruch.cuny.edu
Contact: Ms. Marybeth Murphy, Assistant Vice President for Undergraduate
   Admissions and Financial Aid, Box H-0720, New York, NY 10010-5585
Telephone: 646-312-1400
E-mail: marybeth_murphy@baruch.cuny.edu

Academics
Baruch College awards bachelor's and master's **degrees** and post-master's certificates.
Challenging opportunities include advanced placement credit, accelerated degree
programs, student-designed majors, an honors program, double majors, independent
study, and a senior project. Special programs include internships, summer session for
credit, and study-abroad.

The most frequently chosen **baccalaureate** fields are business/marketing, com-
munications/journalism, and psychology. A complete listing of majors at Baruch College
appears in the Majors by College index beginning on page 469.

The **faculty** at Baruch College has 501 full-time members, 91% with terminal
degrees. The student-faculty ratio is 19:1.

Students of Baruch College
The student body totals 16,097, of whom 12,863 are undergraduates. 52.1% are women
and 47.9% are men. 97% are from New York. 12.6% are international students. 11.1%
are African American, 0.1% American Indian, 29.8% Asian American, and 16.5%
Hispanic American. 88% returned for their sophomore year.

Facilities and Resources
1,300 **computers/terminals** are available on campus for general student use. Students
can access the following: campus intranet, computer help desk, free student e-mail
accounts, online (class) grades, online (class) registration, online (class) schedules.
Campuswide network is available. Wireless service is available via classrooms, computer
centers, computer labs, libraries, student centers. The 2 **libraries** have 456,132 books
and 35,000 subscriptions.

Campus Life
There are 172 active organizations on campus, including a drama/theater group,
newspaper, radio station, and choral group. Baruch College has national **fraternities**,
national **sororities**, local fraternities, and local sororities.

Baruch College is a member of the NCAA (Division III). **Intercollegiate sports**
include baseball (m), basketball, cheerleading (w), cross-country running, soccer (m),
softball (w), swimming and diving, tennis, volleyball.

Campus Safety
Student safety services include controlled access by ID card, late-night transport/escort
service, 24-hour emergency telephone alarm devices, and 24-hour patrols by trained
security personnel.

Applying
Baruch College requires SAT or ACT, a high school transcript, 16 academic units, and a
minimum high school GPA of 2.5, and in some cases an interview. Application deadline:
2/1; 3/15 priority date for financial aid. Early admission is possible.

Getting Accepted
17,114 applied
26% were accepted
1,479 enrolled (34% of accepted)
3.0 average high school GPA
Mean SAT critical reading score: 530
Mean SAT math score: 590
20% had SAT critical reading scores over 600
47% had SAT math scores over 600
2% had SAT critical reading scores over 700
11% had SAT math scores over 700

Graduation and After
33% graduated in 4 years
22% graduated in 5 years
5% graduated in 6 years
75% had job offers within 6 months
300 organizations recruited on campus

Financial Matters
$4320 resident tuition and fees (2008–09)
$8960 nonresident tuition and fees (2008–09)
60% average percent of need met
$5120 average financial aid amount received
   per undergraduate (2007–08 estimated)

BERRY COLLEGE

SUBURBAN SETTING ■ PRIVATE ■ INDEPENDENT RELIGIOUS ■ COED
MOUNT BERRY, GEORGIA

Web site: www.berry.edu

Contact: Mr. Timothy Tarpley, Director of Operations, Enrollment
Management, PO Box 490159, 2277 Martha Berry Highway, NW, Mount
Berry, GA 30149-0159

Telephone: 706-236-2215 or toll-free 800-237-7942

Fax: 706-290-2178

E-mail: admissions@berry.edu

Getting Accepted

2,121 applied
70% were accepted
448 enrolled (30% of accepted)
34% from top tenth of their h.s. class
3.61 average high school GPA
Mean SAT critical reading score: 571
Mean SAT math score: 561
Mean SAT writing score: 559
Mean ACT score: 25
40% had SAT critical reading scores over 600
33% had SAT math scores over 600
34% had SAT writing scores over 600
68% had ACT scores over 24
5% had SAT critical reading scores over 700
2% had SAT math scores over 700
3% had SAT writing scores over 700
14% had ACT scores over 30
8 valedictorians

Graduation and After

50% graduated in 4 years
11% graduated in 5 years
61% had job offers within 6 months
153 organizations recruited on campus

Financial Matters

$22,370 tuition and fees (2008–09)
$7978 room and board
85% average percent of need met
$16,563 average financial aid amount received
per undergraduate (2007–08 estimated)

Academics

Berry awards bachelor's and master's **degrees** and post-master's certificates. **Challenging opportunities** include advanced placement credit, accelerated degree programs, student-designed majors, an honors program, double majors, independent study, and a senior project. Special programs include cooperative education, internships, summer session for credit, and study-abroad.

The most frequently chosen **baccalaureate** fields are business/marketing, social sciences, and communications/journalism. A complete listing of majors at Berry appears in the Majors by College index beginning on page 469.

The **faculty** at Berry has 144 full-time members, 90% with terminal degrees. The student-faculty ratio is 11:1.

Students of Berry

The student body totals 1,795, of whom 1,686 are undergraduates. 67.6% are women and 32.4% are men. Students come from 40 states and territories and 20 other countries. 83% are from Georgia. 2.2% are international students. 4.5% are African American, 0.2% American Indian, 1.6% Asian American, and 2.4% Hispanic American. 78% returned for their sophomore year.

Facilities and Resources

140 **computers/terminals** and 80 ports are available on campus for general student use. Students can access the following: campus intranet, computer help desk, free student e-mail accounts, online (class) grades, online (class) registration, online (class) schedules. Campuswide network is available. 100% of college-owned or -operated housing units are wired for high-speed Internet access. Wireless service is available via classrooms, computer centers, computer labs, dorm rooms, learning centers, libraries, student centers. The 2 **libraries** have 281,522 books and 2,088 subscriptions.

Campus Life

There are 80 active organizations on campus, including a drama/theater group, newspaper, television station, and choral group. No national or local **fraternities** or **sororities**.

Berry is a member of the NAIA. **Intercollegiate sports** include baseball (m), basketball, cheerleading, cross-country running, equestrian sports (w), golf, soccer, softball (w), swimming and diving, tennis, volleyball (w).

Campus Safety

Student safety services include lighted pathways, 24-hour emergency telephone alarm devices, 24-hour patrols by trained security personnel, and electronically operated dormitory entrances.

Applying

Berry requires SAT or ACT and a high school transcript. Application deadline: 7/24; 4/1 priority date for financial aid. Early and deferred admission are possible.

BETHEL UNIVERSITY
SUBURBAN SETTING ■ PRIVATE ■ INDEPENDENT RELIGIOUS ■ COED
ST. PAUL, MINNESOTA

Web site: www.bethel.edu
Contact: Admissions Office, 3900 Bethel Drive, St. Paul, MN 55112
Telephone: 651-638-6242 or toll-free 800-255-8706 Ext. 6242
Fax: 651-635-1490
E-mail: buadmissions-cas@bethel.edu

SPONSOR

> Bethel University provides academic excellence in a dynamic Christian environment. *U.S. News & World Report* has recognized Bethel as one of the top Midwestern universities. Outstanding faculty members, numerous extracurricular activities, service-learning experiences, and off-campus study opportunities make Bethel a great place to live and learn. Bethel is committed to providing a high-quality education that equips men and women for culturally sensitive leadership, scholarship, and service around the world.

Academics
Bethel awards associate, bachelor's, master's, and doctoral **degrees** and post-bachelor's and post-master's certificates. **Challenging opportunities** include advanced placement credit, accelerated degree programs, student-designed majors, an honors program, double majors, independent study, and a senior project. Special programs include internships, summer session for credit, off-campus study, study-abroad, and Army and Air Force ROTC.

The most frequently chosen **baccalaureate** fields are business/marketing, health professions and related sciences, and education. A complete listing of majors at Bethel appears in the Majors by College index beginning on page 469.

The **faculty** at Bethel has 207 full-time members, 76% with terminal degrees. The student-faculty ratio is 13:1.

Students of Bethel
The student body totals 4,335, of whom 3,392 are undergraduates. 62.6% are women and 37.4% are men. Students come from 38 states and territories and 20 other countries. 75% are from Minnesota. 0.4% are international students. 4.2% are African American, 0.2% American Indian, 2.4% Asian American, and 1.5% Hispanic American. 85% returned for their sophomore year.

Facilities and Resources
400 **computers/terminals** are available on campus for general student use. Students can access the following: campus intranet, computer help desk, free student e-mail accounts, online (class) grades, online (class) registration, online (class) schedules. Campuswide network is available. 100% of college-owned or -operated housing units are wired for high-speed Internet access. Wireless service is available via classrooms, computer centers, computer labs, dorm rooms, learning centers, libraries, student centers. The 2 **libraries** have 194,000 books and 38,080 subscriptions.

Campus Life
There are 74 active organizations on campus, including a drama/theater group, newspaper, radio station, and choral group. No national or local **fraternities** or **sororities**.

Bethel is a member of the NCAA (Division III). **Intercollegiate sports** include baseball (m), basketball, cross-country running, football (m), golf, ice hockey, soccer, softball (w), tennis, track and field, volleyball (w).

Campus Safety
Student safety services include late-night transport/escort service, 24-hour emergency telephone alarm devices, 24-hour patrols by trained security personnel, student patrols, and electronically operated dormitory entrances.

Applying
Bethel requires an essay, SAT or ACT, a high school transcript, and rank in upper 50% of high school class, minimum ACT score of 21 or SAT score of 920, and in some cases 2 recommendations. It recommends an interview. Application deadline: 4/15 priority date for financial aid. Early and deferred admission are possible.

Getting Accepted
1,945 applied
81% were accepted
642 enrolled (41% of accepted)
32% from top tenth of their h.s. class
3.52 average high school GPA
Mean SAT critical reading score: 575
Mean SAT math score: 583
Mean ACT score: 25
42% had SAT critical reading scores over 600
46% had SAT math scores over 600
58% had ACT scores over 24
14% had SAT critical reading scores over 700
7% had SAT math scores over 700
14% had ACT scores over 30
3 National Merit Scholars
31 valedictorians

Graduation and After
66% graduated in 4 years
9% graduated in 5 years
1% graduated in 6 years
70% had job offers within 6 months
180 organizations recruited on campus

Financial Matters
$25,860 tuition and fees (2008–09)
$7620 room and board
77% average percent of need met
$15,186 average financial aid amount received per undergraduate (2006–07)

Getting Accepted

2,470 applied
81% were accepted
838 enrolled (42% of accepted)
3.51 average high school GPA
Mean SAT critical reading score: 560
Mean SAT math score: 550
Mean SAT writing score: 560
Mean ACT score: 24
33% had SAT critical reading scores over 600
31% had SAT math scores over 600
54% had ACT scores over 24
5% had SAT critical reading scores over 700
4% had SAT math scores over 700
9% had ACT scores over 30

Graduation and After

49% graduated in 4 years
17% graduated in 5 years
3% graduated in 6 years
30% had job offers within 6 months
1241 organizations recruited on campus

Financial Matters

$26,579 tuition and fees (2008–09)
$8120 room and board
70% average percent of need met
$15,200 average financial aid amount received per undergraduate

BIOLA UNIVERSITY

SUBURBAN SETTING ■ PRIVATE ■ INDEPENDENT RELIGIOUS ■ COED
LA MIRADA, CALIFORNIA

Web site: www.biola.edu
Contact: Mr. Andre Stephens, Director of Enrollment Management, 13800 Biola Avenue, La Mirada, CA 90639
Telephone: 562-903-4752 or toll-free 800-652-4652
Fax: 562-903-4709
E-mail: admissions@biola.edu

Academics

Biola awards bachelor's, master's, doctoral, and first-professional **degrees** and post-master's certificates. **Challenging opportunities** include advanced placement credit, accelerated degree programs, an honors program, double majors, independent study, and a senior project. Special programs include cooperative education, internships, summer session for credit, off-campus study, study-abroad, and Army and Air Force ROTC.

The most frequently chosen **baccalaureate** fields are business/marketing, theology and religious vocations, and psychology. A complete listing of majors at Biola appears in the Majors by College index beginning on page 469.

The **faculty** at Biola has 221 full-time members, 78% with terminal degrees. The student-faculty ratio is 16:1.

Students of Biola

The student body totals 5,893, of whom 4,002 are undergraduates. 60.6% are women and 39.4% are men. Students come from 49 states and territories and 42 other countries. 78% are from California. 2.2% are international students. 3.7% are African American, 0.9% American Indian, 10.6% Asian American, and 11.9% Hispanic American. 94% returned for their sophomore year.

Facilities and Resources

165 **computers/terminals** are available on campus for general student use. Students can access the following: campus intranet, computer help desk, free student e-mail accounts, online (class) grades, online (class) registration, online (class) schedules. Campuswide network is available. 100% of college-owned or -operated housing units are wired for high-speed Internet access. Wireless service is available via computer centers, computer labs, dorm rooms, libraries, student centers. The **library** has 301,956 books and 17,876 subscriptions.

Campus Life

There are 33 active organizations on campus, including a drama/theater group, newspaper, radio station, television station, and choral group. No national or local **fraternities** or **sororities**.

Biola is a member of the NAIA. **Intercollegiate sports** (some offering scholarships) include baseball (m), basketball, cheerleading (w), cross-country running, golf, soccer, softball (w), swimming and diving, tennis, track and field, volleyball (w).

Campus Safety

Student safety services include access gates to roads through the middle of campus, late-night transport/escort service, 24-hour emergency telephone alarm devices, 24-hour patrols by trained security personnel, student patrols, and electronically operated dormitory entrances.

Applying

Biola requires an essay, SAT or ACT, a high school transcript, and 2 recommendations, and in some cases an interview. It recommends an interview and a minimum high school GPA of 3.0. Application deadline: 3/1. Early and deferred admission are possible.

BIRMINGHAM-SOUTHERN COLLEGE

URBAN SETTING ■ PRIVATE ■ INDEPENDENT RELIGIOUS ■ COED
BIRMINGHAM, ALABAMA

Web site: www.bsc.edu
Contact: Ms. Sheri E. Salmon, Dean of Enrollment Management, Box 549008, Birmingham, AL 35254
Telephone: 205-226-4696 or toll-free 800-523-5793
Fax: 205-226-3074
E-mail: admitme@bsc.edu

SPONSOR

Academics

Birmingham-Southern awards bachelor's and master's **degrees**. **Challenging opportunities** include advanced placement credit, student-designed majors, an honors program, double majors, independent study, and a senior project. Special programs include internships, summer session for credit, off-campus study, study-abroad, and Army and Air Force ROTC.

The most frequently chosen **baccalaureate** fields are business/marketing, English, and biological/life sciences. A complete listing of majors at Birmingham-Southern appears in the Majors by College index beginning on page 469.

The **faculty** at Birmingham-Southern has 104 full-time members, 94% with terminal degrees. The student-faculty ratio is 12:1.

Students of Birmingham-Southern

The student body totals 1,458, of whom 1,412 are undergraduates. 50.7% are women and 49.3% are men. Students come from 33 states and territories and 3 other countries. 66% are from Alabama. 0.2% are international students. 8.4% are African American, 0.4% American Indian, 3.2% Asian American, and 1.3% Hispanic American. 75% returned for their sophomore year.

Facilities and Resources

156 **computers/terminals** are available on campus for general student use. Students can access the following: campus intranet, computer help desk, free student e-mail accounts, online (class) grades, online (class) registration, online (class) schedules. Campuswide network is available. 100% of college-owned or -operated housing units are wired for high-speed Internet access. Wireless service is available via dorm rooms, libraries, student centers. The **library** has 215,565 books and 540 subscriptions.

Campus Life

Active organizations on campus include a drama/theater group, newspaper, and choral group. 41% of eligible men and 49% of eligible women are members of national **fraternities** and national **sororities**.

Birmingham-Southern is a member of the NCAA (Division III). **Intercollegiate sports** include baseball (m), basketball, cheerleading, cross-country running, football (m), golf, lacrosse, riflery (w), soccer, softball (w), table tennis, tennis, track and field, volleyball (w).

Campus Safety

Student safety services include vehicle safety inspection, late-night transport/escort service, 24-hour emergency telephone alarm devices, 24-hour patrols by trained security personnel, and electronically operated dormitory entrances.

Applying

Birmingham-Southern requires an essay, SAT or ACT, a high school transcript, 1 recommendation, and a minimum high school GPA of 2.0, and in some cases an interview. It recommends an interview. Application deadline: rolling admissions; 3/1 priority date for financial aid. Deferred admission is possible.

Getting Accepted
2,101 applied
69% were accepted
451 enrolled (31% of accepted)
32% from top tenth of their h.s. class
3.4 average high school GPA
45% had SAT critical reading scores over 600
40% had SAT math scores over 600
68% had ACT scores over 24
9% had SAT critical reading scores over 700
10% had SAT math scores over 700
18% had ACT scores over 30
7 National Merit Scholars
28 valedictorians

Graduation and After
53% graduated in 4 years
10% graduated in 5 years
3% graduated in 6 years
45% had job offers within 6 months
12 organizations recruited on campus

Financial Matters
$25,586 tuition and fees (2008–09)
$9105 room and board
87% average percent of need met
$22,166 average financial aid amount received per undergraduate (2006–07)

Boston College is a university with international stature strengthened by the more than 450-year tradition of Jesuit education, which emphasizes rigorous academic development grounded in the arts and sciences and a commitment to the development of the whole person. Through opportunities to participate in honors programs, research with faculty members, independent study, study abroad, and service learning, students are challenged to fulfill their potential as scholars. With artistic, cultural, service, social, religious, and athletic opportunities that abound on campus and throughout the city of Boston, students are challenged to fulfill their potential as caring, thoughtful individuals and future leaders in society.

Getting Accepted
30,845 applied
26% were accepted
2,167 enrolled (27% of accepted)
80% from top tenth of their h.s. class
Mean SAT critical reading score: 655
Mean SAT math score: 685
Mean SAT writing score: 665
Mean ACT score: 30
81% had SAT critical reading scores over 600
87% had SAT math scores over 600
85% had SAT writing scores over 600
94% had ACT scores over 24
29% had SAT critical reading scores over 700
42% had SAT math scores over 700
37% had SAT writing scores over 700
62% had ACT scores over 30
11 National Merit Scholars
56 valedictorians

Graduation and After
88% graduated in 4 years
2% graduated in 5 years
1% graduated in 6 years
64.5% had job offers within 6 months
315 organizations recruited on campus

Financial Matters
$37,950 tuition and fees (2008–09)
$12,395 room and board
100% average percent of need met
$26,101 average financial aid amount received per undergraduate (2006–07)

BOSTON COLLEGE
SUBURBAN SETTING ■ PRIVATE ■ INDEPENDENT RELIGIOUS ■ COED
CHESTNUT HILL, MASSACHUSETTS

Web site: www.bc.edu
Contact: Office of Undergraduate Admissions, 140 Commonwealth Avenue, Devlin 208, Chestnut Hill, MA 02467-3809
Telephone: 617-552-3100 or toll-free 800-360-2522
Fax: 617-552-0798
E-mail: ugadmis@bc.edu

Academics
BC awards bachelor's, master's, doctoral, and first-professional **degrees** and post-master's certificates (also offers continuing education program with significant enrollment not reflected in profile). **Challenging opportunities** include advanced placement credit, accelerated degree programs, student-designed majors, an honors program, double majors, independent study, and a senior project. Special programs include internships, summer session for credit, off-campus study, study-abroad, and Army, Navy, and Air Force ROTC.

The most frequently chosen **baccalaureate** fields are business/marketing, social sciences, and communications/journalism. A complete listing of majors at BC appears in the Majors by College index beginning on page 469.

The **faculty** at BC has 679 full-time members, 98% with terminal degrees. The student-faculty ratio is 13:1.

Students of BC
The student body totals 13,903, of whom 9,060 are undergraduates. 51.8% are women and 48.2% are men. Students come from 54 states and territories and 58 other countries. 29% are from Massachusetts. 2.5% are international students. 5.5% are African American, 0.3% American Indian, 9.5% Asian American, and 7.6% Hispanic American. 96% returned for their sophomore year.

Facilities and Resources
1,000 **computers/terminals** are available on campus for general student use. Students can access the following: campus intranet, computer help desk, free student e-mail accounts, online (class) grades, online (class) registration, online (class) schedules. Campuswide network is available. 100% of college-owned or -operated housing units are wired for high-speed Internet access. Wireless service is available via entire campus. The 8 **libraries** have 2,720,645 books and 31,664 subscriptions.

Campus Life
There are 223 active organizations on campus, including a drama/theater group, newspaper, radio station, television station, choral group, and marching band. No national or local **fraternities** or **sororities**.

BC is a member of the NCAA (Division I). **Intercollegiate sports** (some offering scholarships) include baseball (m), basketball, crew (w), cross-country running, fencing, field hockey (w), football (m), golf, ice hockey, lacrosse (w), sailing, skiing (downhill), soccer, softball (w), swimming and diving, tennis, track and field, volleyball (w).

Campus Safety
Student safety services include late-night transport/escort service, 24-hour emergency telephone alarm devices, 24-hour patrols by trained security personnel, and electronically operated dormitory entrances.

Applying
BC requires an essay, SAT and SAT Subject Tests or ACT, a high school transcript, and 2 recommendations. Application deadline: 1/1; 2/1 priority date for financial aid. Early and deferred admission are possible.

Boston University

Urban Setting ▪ Private ▪ Independent ▪ Coed
Boston, Massachusetts

Web site: www.bu.edu
Contact: Ms. Kelly Walter, Director of Undergraduate Admissions, 121 Bay
  State Road, Boston, MA 02215
Telephone: 617-353-2300
Fax: 617-353-9695
E-mail: admissions@bu.edu

Academics

BU awards bachelor's, master's, doctoral, and first-professional **degrees** and post-bachelor's, post-master's, and first-professional certificates. **Challenging opportunities** include advanced placement credit, accelerated degree programs, student-designed majors, an honors program, double majors, independent study, and a senior project. Special programs include cooperative education, internships, summer session for credit, off-campus study, study-abroad, and Army, Navy, and Air Force ROTC.

The most frequently chosen **baccalaureate** fields are business/marketing, social sciences, and communications/journalism. A complete listing of majors at BU appears in the Majors by College index beginning on page 469.

The **faculty** at BU has 1,502 full-time members, 78% with terminal degrees. The student-faculty ratio is 14:1.

Students of BU

The student body totals 32,053, of whom 18,733 are undergraduates. 59.4% are women and 40.6% are men. Students come from 53 states and territories and 100 other countries. 23% are from Massachusetts. 6.4% are international students. 2.8% are African American, 0.3% American Indian, 13.2% Asian American, and 6.7% Hispanic American. 91% returned for their sophomore year.

Facilities and Resources

750 **computers/terminals** are available on campus for general student use. Students can access the following: campus intranet, computer help desk, free student e-mail accounts, online (class) registration, research and educational networks. Campuswide network is available. 95% of college-owned or -operated housing units are wired for high-speed Internet access. Wireless service is available via entire campus. The 19 **libraries** have 2,427,253 books and 33,983 subscriptions.

Campus Life

There are 455 active organizations on campus, including a drama/theater group, newspaper, radio station, television station, choral group, and marching band. 3% of eligible men and 5% of eligible women are members of national **fraternities** and national **sororities**.

BU is a member of the NCAA (Division I). **Intercollegiate sports** (some offering scholarships) include basketball, crew, cross-country running, field hockey (w), golf, ice hockey, lacrosse (w), soccer, softball (w), swimming and diving, tennis, track and field, wrestling (m).

Campus Safety

Student safety services include security personnel at residence hall entrances, self-defense education, well-lit sidewalks, late-night transport/escort service, 24-hour emergency telephone alarm devices, 24-hour patrols by trained security personnel, and electronically operated dormitory entrances.

Applying

BU requires an essay, SAT and SAT Subject Tests or ACT, a high school transcript, and 2 recommendations, and in some cases an interview and audition, portfolio. It recommends a minimum high school GPA of 3.0. Application deadline: 1/1; 2/15 priority date for financial aid. Early and deferred admission are possible.

Getting Accepted
33,930 applied
59% were accepted
4,163 enrolled (21% of accepted)
51% from top tenth of their h.s. class
3.45 average high school GPA
Mean SAT critical reading score: 626
Mean SAT math score: 643
Mean SAT writing score: 631
Mean ACT score: 28
67% had SAT critical reading scores over 600
75% had SAT math scores over 600
71% had SAT writing scores over 600
93% had ACT scores over 24
17% had SAT critical reading scores over 700
22% had SAT math scores over 700
17% had SAT writing scores over 700
26% had ACT scores over 30
108 valedictorians

Graduation and After
76% graduated in 4 years
5% graduated in 5 years
1% graduated in 6 years
70% had job offers within 6 months
400 organizations recruited on campus

Financial Matters
$37,050 tuition and fees (2008–09)
$11,418 room and board
90% average percent of need met
$29,723 average financial aid amount received
  per undergraduate (2007–08 estimated)

BOWDOIN COLLEGE

SMALL-TOWN SETTING ■ PRIVATE ■ INDEPENDENT ■ COED
BRUNSWICK, MAINE

Web site: www.bowdoin.edu
Contact: Peter T. Wiley, Associate Dean of Admissions, 5000 College Station,
Brunswick, ME 04011-8411
Telephone: 207-725-3190
Fax: 207-725-3101
E-mail: admissions@bowdoin.edu

Getting Accepted

6,033 applied
19% were accepted
488 enrolled (44% of accepted)
82% from top tenth of their h.s. class
Mean SAT critical reading score: 700
Mean SAT math score: 700
Mean SAT writing score: 710
Mean ACT score: 31
93% had SAT critical reading scores over 600
90% had SAT math scores over 600
89% had SAT writing scores over 600
96% had ACT scores over 24
54% had SAT critical reading scores over 700
51% had SAT math scores over 700
55% had SAT writing scores over 700
69% had ACT scores over 30
33 National Merit Scholars
49 valedictorians

Graduation and After

84% graduated in 4 years
6% graduated in 5 years
1% graduated in 6 years
80% had job offers within 6 months
65 organizations recruited on campus

Financial Matters

$38,190 tuition and fees (2008–09)
$10,380 room and board
100% average percent of need met
$31,382 average financial aid amount received
per undergraduate (2007–08 estimated)

Academics

Bowdoin awards bachelor's **degrees** (SAT or ACT considered if submitted. Test scores
are required for home-schooled applicants). **Challenging opportunities** include
advanced placement credit, accelerated degree programs, student-designed majors,
double majors, and independent study. Special programs include off-campus study and
study-abroad.

The most frequently chosen **baccalaureate** fields are social sciences, foreign
languages and literature, and biological/life sciences. A complete listing of majors at
Bowdoin appears in the Majors by College index beginning on page 469.

The **faculty** at Bowdoin has 174 full-time members, 98% with terminal degrees. The
student-faculty ratio is 9:1.

Students of Bowdoin

The student body is made up of 1,723 undergraduates. 51.2% are women and 48.8% are
men. Students come from 51 states and territories and 26 other countries. 13% are from
Maine. 3% are international students. 6.3% are African American, 0.6% American
Indian, 11.6% Asian American, and 9% Hispanic American. 97% returned for their
sophomore year.

Facilities and Resources

450 **computers/terminals** and 5,500 ports are available on campus for general student
use. Students can access the following: campus intranet, computer help desk, free student
e-mail accounts, online (class) grades, online (class) schedules, training classes on variety
of desktop and academic software. Campuswide network is available. 100% of college-
owned or -operated housing units are wired for high-speed Internet access. Wireless
service is available via entire campus. The 7 **libraries** have 1,021,673 books and 18,851
subscriptions.

Campus Life

There are 109 active organizations on campus, including a drama/theater group,
newspaper, radio station, television station, and choral group. No national or local
fraternities or **sororities**.

Bowdoin is a member of the NCAA (Division III). **Intercollegiate sports** include
baseball (m), basketball, cross-country running, field hockey (w), football (m), golf, ice
hockey, lacrosse, rugby (w), sailing, skiing (cross-country), soccer, softball (w), squash,
swimming and diving, tennis, track and field, volleyball (w).

Campus Safety

Student safety services include self-defense education, whistle program, safe ride service
(daytime), late-night transport/escort service, 24-hour emergency telephone alarm
devices, 24-hour patrols by trained security personnel, and electronically operated
dormitory entrances.

Applying

Bowdoin requires an essay, a high school transcript, and 3 recommendations. It recommends an interview. Application deadline: 1/1; 2/15 for financial aid. Early and deferred
admission are possible.

Bradley University

SUBURBAN SETTING ■ PRIVATE ■ INDEPENDENT ■ COED
PEORIA, ILLINOIS

Web site: www.bradley.edu
Contact: Mr. Rodney San Jose, Director of Admissions, 1501 West Bradley
   Avenue, 100 Swords Hall, Peoria, IL 61625-0002
Telephone: 309-677-1000 or toll-free 800-447-6460
Fax: 309-677-2797
E-mail: admissions@bradley.edu

Academics
Bradley awards bachelor's, master's, and doctoral **degrees**. **Challenging opportunities**
include advanced placement credit, accelerated degree programs, student-designed
majors, an honors program, double majors, independent study, and a senior project.
Special programs include cooperative education, internships, summer session for credit,
off-campus study, study-abroad, and Army ROTC.

The most frequently chosen **baccalaureate** fields are business/marketing,
engineering, and communications/journalism. A complete listing of majors at Bradley
appears in the Majors by College index beginning on page 469.

The **faculty** at Bradley has 337 full-time members, 83% with terminal degrees. The
student-faculty ratio is 13:1.

Students of Bradley
The student body totals 5,872, of whom 5,074 are undergraduates. 53.9% are women
and 46.1% are men. Students come from 39 states and territories and 30 other countries.
89% are from Illinois. 0.6% are international students. 7.2% are African American, 0.5%
American Indian, 3.9% Asian American, and 3.5% Hispanic American. 89% returned for
their sophomore year.

Facilities and Resources
2,000 **computers/terminals** are available on campus for general student use. Students
can access the following: computer help desk, free student e-mail accounts, online (class)
grades, online (class) registration, online (class) schedules. Campuswide network is available. 100% of college-owned or -operated housing units are wired for high-speed
Internet access. Wireless service is available via entire campus. The **library** has 510,297
books and 29,776 subscriptions.

Campus Life
There are 220 active organizations on campus, including a drama/theater group,
newspaper, radio station, television station, and choral group. 33% of eligible men and
27% of eligible women are members of national **fraternities** and national **sororities**.

Bradley is a member of the NCAA (Division I). **Intercollegiate sports** (some
offering scholarships) include baseball (m), basketball, cheerleading, cross-country
running, golf, soccer (m), softball (w), tennis, track and field (w), volleyball (w).

Campus Safety
Student safety services include bicycle patrol, late-night transport/escort service, 24-hour
emergency telephone alarm devices, 24-hour patrols by trained security personnel, and
electronically operated dormitory entrances.

Applying
Bradley requires an essay, SAT or ACT, a high school transcript, and 1 recommendation.
It recommends an interview, 3 recommendations, and a minimum high school GPA of
3.0. Application deadline: rolling admissions; 3/1 priority date for financial aid. Early and
deferred admission are possible.

Getting Accepted
5,932 applied
64% were accepted
1,032 enrolled (27% of accepted)
29% from top tenth of their h.s. class
3.59 average high school GPA
Mean SAT critical reading score: 563
Mean SAT math score: 578
Mean SAT writing score: 547
Mean ACT score: 25
37% had SAT critical reading scores over 600
52% had SAT math scores over 600
64% had ACT scores over 24
10% had SAT critical reading scores over 700
11% had SAT math scores over 700
12% had ACT scores over 30
5 National Merit Scholars
32 valedictorians

Graduation and After
62% graduated in 4 years
9% graduated in 5 years
1% graduated in 6 years
75% had job offers within 6 months

Financial Matters
$22,814 tuition and fees (2008–09)
$7350 room and board
71% average percent of need met
**$14,018 average financial aid amount received
   per undergraduate (2006–07)**

BRANDEIS UNIVERSITY

SUBURBAN SETTING ■ PRIVATE ■ INDEPENDENT ■ COED
WALTHAM, MASSACHUSETTS

Web site: www.brandeis.edu
Contact: Mr. Gil J. Villanueva, Dean of Admissions, 415 South Street,
    Waltham, MA 02254-9110
Telephone: 781-736-3500 or toll-free 800-622-0622 (out-of-state)
Fax: 781-736-3536
E-mail: admissions@brandeis.edu

Getting Accepted
7,724 applied
33% were accepted
754 enrolled (30% of accepted)
82% from top tenth of their h.s. class
3.85 average high school GPA
89% had SAT critical reading scores over 600
91% had SAT math scores over 600
88% had SAT writing scores over 600
98% had ACT scores over 24
38% had SAT critical reading scores over 700
43% had SAT math scores over 700
43% had SAT writing scores over 700
61% had ACT scores over 30
32 National Merit Scholars

Graduation and After
86% graduated in 4 years
3% graduated in 5 years
1% graduated in 6 years

Financial Matters
$37,294 tuition and fees (2008–09)
$10,354 room and board
84% average percent of need met
$27,315 average financial aid amount received
   per undergraduate (2007–08 estimated)

Academics
Brandeis awards bachelor's, master's, and doctoral **degrees** and post-bachelor's certificates. **Challenging opportunities** include advanced placement credit, student-designed majors, an honors program, double majors, independent study, and a senior project. Special programs include internships, summer session for credit, off-campus study, study-abroad, and Army and Air Force ROTC.

   The most frequently chosen **baccalaureate** fields are social sciences, area and ethnic studies, and biological/life sciences. A complete listing of majors at Brandeis appears in the Majors by College index beginning on page 469.

Students of Brandeis
The student body totals 5,327, of whom 3,196 are undergraduates. 56.2% are women and 43.8% are men. Students come from 47 states and territories and 54 other countries. 26% are from Massachusetts. 7.6% are international students. 4.2% are African American, 0.3% American Indian, 9.7% Asian American, and 5.1% Hispanic American. 93% returned for their sophomore year.

Facilities and Resources
104 **computers/terminals** are available on campus for general student use. Students can access the following: computer help desk, free student e-mail accounts, online (class) grades, online (class) registration, online (class) schedules, educational software. Campuswide network is available. Wireless service is available via entire campus. The 3 **libraries** have 1,207,217 books and 35,125 subscriptions.

Campus Life
There are 200 active organizations on campus, including a drama/theater group, newspaper, radio station, television station, and choral group. No national or local **fraternities** or **sororities**.

   Brandeis is a member of the NCAA (Division III). **Intercollegiate sports** include baseball (m), basketball, cross-country running, fencing, soccer (w), softball (w), tennis, track and field, volleyball (w).

Campus Safety
Student safety services include late-night transport/escort service, 24-hour emergency telephone alarm devices, 24-hour patrols by trained security personnel, and electronically operated dormitory entrances.

Applying
Brandeis requires an essay, SAT or ACT, a high school transcript, and 2 recommendations. It recommends an interview. Application deadline: 1/15; 2/1 priority date for financial aid. Deferred admission is possible.

BRIGHAM YOUNG UNIVERSITY

SUBURBAN SETTING ■ PRIVATE ■ INDEPENDENT RELIGIOUS ■ COED
PROVO, UTAH

Web site: www.byu.edu
Contact: Mr. Tom Gourley, Dean of Admissions and Records, A-153 Abraham
    Smoot Building, Provo, UT 84602
Telephone: 801-422-2507
Fax: 801-422-0005
E-mail: admissions@byu.edu

Academics

BYU awards bachelor's, master's, doctoral, and first-professional **degrees. Challenging
opportunities** include advanced placement credit, accelerated degree programs,
freshman honors college, an honors program, double majors, independent study, and a
senior project. Special programs include cooperative education, internships, summer
session for credit, off-campus study, study-abroad, and Army and Air Force ROTC.

The most frequently chosen **baccalaureate** fields are business/marketing, biologi-
cal/life sciences, and education. A complete listing of majors at BYU appears in the
Majors by College index beginning on page 469.

The **faculty** at BYU has 1,326 full-time members, 84% with terminal degrees. The
student-faculty ratio is 20:1.

Students of BYU

The student body totals 34,244, of whom 30,912 are undergraduates. 49.2% are women
and 50.8% are men. Students come from 56 states and territories and 125 other
countries. 33% are from Utah. 2.3% are international students. 0.5% are African
American, 0.6% American Indian, 4.1% Asian American, and 4.1% Hispanic American.
83% returned for their sophomore year.

Facilities and Resources

2,000 **computers/terminals** are available on campus for general student use. Students
can access the following: campus intranet, computer help desk, online (class) grades,
online (class) registration, online (class) schedules. Campuswide network is available.
The 3 **libraries** have 3,539,032 books and 27,161 subscriptions.

Campus Life

There are 390 active organizations on campus, including a drama/theater group,
newspaper, radio station, television station, choral group, and marching band. No
national or local **fraternities** or **sororities**.

BYU is a member of the NCAA (Division I). **Intercollegiate sports** (some offering
scholarships) include baseball (m), basketball, cheerleading, cross-country running,
football (m), golf, gymnastics (w), racquetball, soccer (w), softball (w), swimming and
diving, tennis, track and field, volleyball.

Campus Safety

Student safety services include late-night transport/escort service, 24-hour emergency
telephone alarm devices, 24-hour patrols by trained security personnel, and electronically operated dormitory entrances.

Applying

BYU requires an essay, ACT, a high school transcript, an interview, and 1 recommendation. Application deadline: 2/1; 4/15 priority date for financial aid. Early and
deferred admission are possible.

Getting Accepted

10,081 applied
69% were accepted
4,665 enrolled (67% of accepted)
49% from top tenth of their h.s. class
3.76 average high school GPA
Mean SAT critical reading score: 614
Mean SAT math score: 630
Mean SAT writing score: 593
Mean ACT score: 28
59% had SAT critical reading scores over 600
65% had SAT math scores over 600
89% had ACT scores over 24
16% had SAT critical reading scores over 700
18% had SAT math scores over 700
29% had ACT scores over 30

Graduation and After

31% graduated in 4 years
22% graduated in 5 years
27% graduated in 6 years
75% had job offers within 6 months
450 organizations recruited on campus

Financial Matters

34% average percent of need met
$4464 average financial aid amount received
    per undergraduate (2006–07)

Brown is a university/college with renowned faculty members who teach students in the undergraduate college, the graduate school, and the medical school. The unique, nonrestrictive curriculum allows students freedom in selecting their courses, and they may choose their concentration from eighty-three areas, complete a double major, or pursue an independent concentration. The 140-acre campus is set in a residential neighborhood (National Historic District) and features state-of-the-art computing facilities and an athletic complex. A real sense of community exists on campus, as every student has an academic adviser, and there are several peer counselors in the residence halls.

Getting Accepted
19,097 applied
14% were accepted
1,479 enrolled (55% of accepted)
92% from top tenth of their h.s. class
Mean SAT critical reading score: 705
Mean SAT math score: 713
Mean SAT writing score: 703
Mean ACT score: 30
90% had SAT critical reading scores over 600
94% had SAT math scores over 600
90% had SAT writing scores over 600
96% had ACT scores over 24
61% had SAT critical reading scores over 700
66% had SAT math scores over 700
62% had SAT writing scores over 700
63% had ACT scores over 30
141 valedictorians

Graduation and After
84% graduated in 4 years
9% graduated in 5 years
2% graduated in 6 years
60% had job offers within 6 months
400 organizations recruited on campus

Financial Matters
$37,718 tuition and fees (2008–09)
$10,022 room and board
100% average percent of need met
$30,588 average financial aid amount received per undergraduate (2007–08 estimated)

BROWN UNIVERSITY
URBAN SETTING ■ PRIVATE ■ INDEPENDENT ■ COED
PROVIDENCE, RHODE ISLAND

Web site: www.brown.edu
Contact: Mr. James Miller, Dean of Admission, Box 1876, Providence, RI 02912
Telephone: 401-863-2378
Fax: 401-863-9300
E-mail: admission_undergraduate@brown.edu

Academics
Brown awards bachelor's, master's, doctoral, and first-professional **degrees**. **Challenging opportunities** include advanced placement credit, accelerated degree programs, student-designed majors, an honors program, double majors, independent study, and a senior project. Special programs include internships, summer session for credit, off-campus study, study-abroad, and Army ROTC.

The most frequently chosen **baccalaureate** fields are social sciences, biological/life sciences, and physical sciences. A complete listing of majors at Brown appears in the Majors by College index beginning on page 469.

The **faculty** at Brown has 661 full-time members, 95% with terminal degrees. The student-faculty ratio is 9:1.

Students of Brown
The student body totals 8,167, of whom 6,008 are undergraduates. 52.4% are women and 47.6% are men. Students come from 52 states and territories and 81 other countries. 4% are from Rhode Island. 7% are international students. 6.8% are African American, 0.7% American Indian, 15.3% Asian American, and 8.4% Hispanic American. 98% returned for their sophomore year.

Facilities and Resources
500 **computers/terminals** are available on campus for general student use. Students can access the following: computer help desk, free student e-mail accounts, online (class) registration, online (class) schedules. Campuswide network is available. 100% of college-owned or -operated housing units are wired for high-speed Internet access. Wireless service is available via entire campus. The 6 **libraries** have 3,000,000 books and 17,000 subscriptions.

Campus Life
There are 240 active organizations on campus, including a drama/theater group, newspaper, radio station, television station, choral group, and marching band. 12% of eligible men and 2% of eligible women are members of national **fraternities** and national **sororities**.

Brown is a member of the NCAA (Division I). **Intercollegiate sports** include baseball (m), basketball, crew, cross-country running, equestrian sports (w), fencing, field hockey (w), football (m), golf, gymnastics (w), ice hockey, lacrosse, skiing (downhill) (w), soccer, softball (w), squash, swimming and diving, tennis, track and field, volleyball (w), water polo, wrestling (m).

Campus Safety
Student safety services include late-night transport/escort service, 24-hour emergency telephone alarm devices, 24-hour patrols by trained security personnel, and electronically operated dormitory entrances.

Applying
Brown requires an essay, SAT and SAT Subject Tests or ACT, a high school transcript, and 2 recommendations, and in some cases 3 recommendations. Application deadline: 1/1; 2/1 for financial aid. Early and deferred admission are possible.

Bryan College

Small-town setting ■ Private ■ Independent Religious ■ Coed
Dayton, Tennessee

Web site: www.bryan.edu
Contact: Michael Sapienza, Vice President for Enrollment Management, PO Box 7000, Dayton, TN 37321-7000
Telephone: 423-775-2041 or toll-free 800-277-9522
Fax: 423-775-7199
E-mail: admissions@bryan.edu

Academics

Bryan awards associate, bachelor's, and master's **degrees**. **Challenging opportunities** include advanced placement credit, an honors program, double majors, independent study, and a senior project. Special programs include internships, summer session for credit, and study-abroad.

The most frequently chosen **baccalaureate** fields are business/marketing, communications/journalism, and education. A complete listing of majors at Bryan appears in the Majors by College index beginning on page 469.

The **faculty** at Bryan has 35 full-time members, 80% with terminal degrees. The student-faculty ratio is 13:1.

Students of Bryan

The student body totals 1,079, of whom 1,036 are undergraduates. Students come from 33 states and territories and 7 other countries. 39% are from Tennessee. 1.9% are international students. 5.4% are African American, 0.4% American Indian, 0.2% Asian American, and 1.6% Hispanic American. 77% returned for their sophomore year.

Facilities and Resources

74 **computers/terminals** are available on campus for general student use. Students can access the following: campus intranet, computer help desk, free student e-mail accounts, online (class) grades, online (class) schedules. Campuswide network is available. The **library** has 98,413 books and 4,212 subscriptions.

Campus Life

There are 7 active organizations on campus, including a drama/theater group, newspaper, and choral group. No national or local **fraternities** or **sororities**.

Bryan is a member of the NAIA and NCCAA. **Intercollegiate sports** (some offering scholarships) include baseball (m), basketball, cross-country running, soccer, track and field, volleyball (w).

Campus Safety

Student safety services include police patrols, late-night transport/escort service, student patrols, and electronically operated dormitory entrances.

Applying

Bryan requires an essay, SAT or ACT, a high school transcript, 3 recommendations, and a minimum high school GPA of 2.0, and in some cases an interview. Application deadline: rolling admissions; 2/15 priority date for financial aid. Early and deferred admission are possible.

Getting Accepted
532 applied
72% were accepted
3.6 average high school GPA
Mean ACT score: 24
54% had SAT critical reading scores over 600
33% had SAT math scores over 600
42% had SAT writing scores over 600
58% had ACT scores over 24
17% had SAT critical reading scores over 700
4% had SAT math scores over 700
7% had SAT writing scores over 700
10% had ACT scores over 30

Graduation and After
75% had job offers within 6 months
18 organizations recruited on campus

Financial Matters
$17,860 tuition and fees (2009–10)
$5354 room and board
67% average percent of need met
$12,203 average financial aid amount received per undergraduate (2007–08 estimated)

BRYN MAWR COLLEGE

SUBURBAN SETTING ■ PRIVATE ■ INDEPENDENT
■ UNDERGRADUATE: WOMEN ONLY; GRADUATE: COED
BRYN MAWR, PENNSYLVANIA

Web site: www.brynmawr.edu
Contact: Ms. Jody Sanford Sweeney, Director of Admissions, 101 North
    Merion Avenue, Bryn Mawr, PA 19010
Telephone: 610-526-5152 or toll-free 800-BMC-1885 (out-of-state)
Fax: 610-526-7471
E-mail: admissions@brynmawr.edu

Getting Accepted

2,150 applied
49% were accepted
366 enrolled (35% of accepted)
65% from top tenth of their h.s. class
Mean SAT critical reading score: 667
Mean SAT math score: 636
Mean SAT writing score: 664
Mean ACT score: 29
83% had SAT critical reading scores over 600
68% had SAT math scores over 600
83% had SAT writing scores over 600
95% had ACT scores over 24
39% had SAT critical reading scores over 700
21% had SAT math scores over 700
31% had SAT writing scores over 700
44% had ACT scores over 30
6 National Merit Scholars
9 valedictorians

Graduation and After

81% graduated in 4 years
3% graduated in 5 years
2% graduated in 6 years

Financial Matters

$38,034 tuition and fees (2009–10)
$12,000 room and board
100% average percent of need met
$31,610 average financial aid amount received
    per undergraduate (2007–08 estimated)

Academics

Bryn Mawr awards bachelor's, master's, and doctoral **degrees** and post-bachelor's certificates. **Challenging opportunities** include advanced placement credit, accelerated degree programs, student-designed majors, double majors, independent study, and a senior project. Special programs include internships, summer session for credit, off-campus study, study-abroad, and Air Force ROTC.

The most frequently chosen **baccalaureate** fields are social sciences, foreign languages and literature, and physical sciences. A complete listing of majors at Bryn Mawr appears in the Majors by College index beginning on page 469.

The **faculty** at Bryn Mawr has 158 full-time members, 94% with terminal degrees. The student-faculty ratio is 8:1.

Students of Bryn Mawr

The student body totals 1,745, of whom 1,287 are undergraduates. 100% are women. Students come from 48 states and territories and 58 other countries. 16% are from Pennsylvania. 7% are international students. 5.9% are African American, 0.2% American Indian, 11.7% Asian American, and 3.7% Hispanic American. 90% returned for their sophomore year.

Facilities and Resources

200 **computers/terminals** and 1,500 ports are available on campus for general student use. Students can access the following: online (class) registration. Campuswide network is available.

Campus Life

There are 100 active organizations on campus, including a drama/theater group, newspaper, and choral group. No national or local **sororities**.

Bryn Mawr is a member of the NCAA (Division III). **Intercollegiate sports** include badminton, basketball, crew, cross-country running, field hockey, lacrosse, soccer, swimming and diving, tennis, track and field, volleyball.

Campus Safety

Student safety services include shuttle bus service, awareness programs, bicycle registration, security Website, late-night transport/escort service, 24-hour emergency telephone alarm devices, 24-hour patrols by trained security personnel, and electronically operated dormitory entrances.

Applying

Bryn Mawr requires an essay, SAT and SAT Subject Tests or ACT, a high school transcript, and 3 recommendations. It recommends an interview. Application deadline: 1/15; 3/1 for financial aid. Early and deferred admission are possible.

BUCKNELL UNIVERSITY

SMALL-TOWN SETTING ▪ PRIVATE ▪ INDEPENDENT ▪ COED
LEWISBURG, PENNSYLVANIA

Web site: www.bucknell.edu
Contact: Mr. Kurt M. Thiede, Vice President, Enrollment Management and
Dean of Admissions, Lewisburg, PA 17837
Telephone: 570-577-1101
Fax: 570-577-3538
E-mail: admissions@bucknell.edu

SPONSOR

Academics

Bucknell awards bachelor's and master's **degrees. Challenging opportunities** include
advanced placement credit, student-designed majors, an honors program, double majors,
independent study, and a senior project. Special programs include internships, summer
session for credit, off-campus study, study-abroad, and Army ROTC.

The most frequently chosen **baccalaureate** fields are social sciences, engineering,
and business/marketing. A complete listing of majors at Bucknell appears in the Majors
by College index beginning on page 469.

The **faculty** at Bucknell has 334 full-time members, 95% with terminal degrees. The
student-faculty ratio is 11:1.

Students of Bucknell

The student body totals 3,719, of whom 3,583 are undergraduates. 52.7% are women
and 47.3% are men. Students come from 49 states and territories and 55 other countries.
25% are from Pennsylvania. 3.3% are international students. 3% are African American,
0.3% American Indian, 6% Asian American, and 3.5% Hispanic American. 95%
returned for their sophomore year.

Facilities and Resources

970 **computers/terminals** are available on campus for general student use. Students can
access the following: campus intranet, computer help desk, free student e-mail accounts,
online (class) grades, online (class) registration, online (class) schedules. Campuswide
network is available. 100% of college-owned or -operated housing units are wired for
high-speed Internet access. Wireless service is available via entire campus. The 3
libraries have 826,648 books and 36,737 subscriptions.

Campus Life

There are 135 active organizations on campus, including a drama/theater group,
newspaper, radio station, and choral group. 54% of eligible men and 53% of eligible
women are members of national **fraternities** and national **sororities**.

Bucknell is a member of the NCAA (Division I). **Intercollegiate sports** (some
offering scholarships) include baseball (m), basketball, crew (w), cross-country running,
field hockey (w), football (m), golf, lacrosse, soccer, softball (w), swimming and diving,
tennis, track and field, volleyball (w), water polo, wrestling (m).

Campus Safety

Student safety services include well-lit pathways, self-defense education, safety/security
orientation, late-night transport/escort service, 24-hour emergency telephone alarm
devices, 24-hour patrols by trained security personnel, and student patrols.

Applying

Bucknell requires an essay, SAT or ACT, a high school transcript, and 1 recommendation. Application deadline: 1/15; 1/1 for financial aid. Deferred admission is possible.

Getting Accepted
8,024 applied
30% were accepted
957 enrolled (40% of accepted)
69% from top tenth of their h.s. class
3.51 average high school GPA
Mean SAT critical reading score: 637
Mean SAT math score: 672
Mean ACT score: 29
76% had SAT critical reading scores over 600
89% had SAT math scores over 600
95% had ACT scores over 24
19% had SAT critical reading scores over 700
36% had SAT math scores over 700
42% had ACT scores over 30
12 National Merit Scholars
22 valedictorians

Graduation and After
85% graduated in 4 years
4% graduated in 5 years
67% had job offers within 6 months
593 organizations recruited on campus

Financial Matters
$40,816 tuition and fees (2009–10)
$9504 room and board
100% average percent of need met
$24,200 average financial aid amount received
    per undergraduate (2007–08 estimated)

BUTLER UNIVERSITY

URBAN SETTING ■ PRIVATE ■ INDEPENDENT ■ COED
INDIANAPOLIS, INDIANA

Web site: www.butler.edu
Contact: Mr. Scott McIntyre, Director of Admissions, 4600 Sunset Avenue,
Indianapolis, IN 46208-3485
Telephone: 317-940-8100 or toll-free 888-940-8100
Fax: 317-940-8150
E-mail: admission@butler.edu

At Butler University, students are actively engaged in the learning experience from the minute they step on campus. With small class sizes, students receive direct access to faculty members, personalized attention, and hands-on learning opportunities. Participation in research is an opportunity rarely offered to undergraduates; at Butler, students not only have the chance to participate in research with faculty members, but they also originate research projects and develop them into professional presentations and publications. Butler students receive research grants through the Butler Summer Institute and present their projects at the Undergraduate Research Conference, hosted by Butler every April.

Getting Accepted
5,923 applied
72% were accepted
934 enrolled (22% of accepted)
51% from top tenth of their h.s. class
3.75 average high school GPA
Mean SAT critical reading score: 587
Mean SAT math score: 600
Mean SAT writing score: 574
Mean ACT score: 27
45% had SAT critical reading scores over 600
53% had SAT math scores over 600
39% had SAT writing scores over 600
83% had ACT scores over 24
10% had SAT critical reading scores over 700
7% had SAT math scores over 700
6% had SAT writing scores over 700
23% had ACT scores over 30
2 National Merit Scholars
45 valedictorians

Graduation and After
52% graduated in 4 years
8% graduated in 5 years
14% graduated in 6 years
68% had job offers within 6 months
200 organizations recruited on campus

Financial Matters
$28,266 tuition and fees (2008–09)
$9410 room and board
$18,987 average financial aid amount received per undergraduate (2007–08 estimated)

Academics

Butler awards associate, bachelor's, master's, and first-professional **degrees. Challenging opportunities** include advanced placement credit, student-designed majors, an honors program, double majors, independent study, and a senior project. Special programs include cooperative education, internships, summer session for credit, off-campus study, study-abroad, and Army and Air Force ROTC.

The most frequently chosen **baccalaureate** fields are health professions and related sciences, business/marketing, and education. A complete listing of majors at Butler appears in the Majors by College index beginning on page 469.

The **faculty** at Butler has 304 full-time members, 82% with terminal degrees. The student-faculty ratio is 11:1.

Students of Butler

The student body totals 4,438, of whom 3,639 are undergraduates. 61% are women and 39% are men. Students come from 44 states and territories and 69 other countries. 59% are from Indiana. 3.2% are international students. 3.7% are African American, 0.2% American Indian, 2.3% Asian American, and 2.2% Hispanic American. 89% returned for their sophomore year.

Facilities and Resources

450 **computers/terminals** are available on campus for general student use. Students can access the following: campus intranet, computer help desk, free student e-mail accounts, online (class) grades, online (class) registration, online (class) schedules. Campuswide network is available. 100% of college-owned or -operated housing units are wired for high-speed Internet access. Wireless service is available via entire campus. The 2 **libraries** have 361,690 books and 25,965 subscriptions.

Campus Life

There are 135 active organizations on campus, including a drama/theater group, newspaper, television station, choral group, and marching band. 25% of eligible men and 27% of eligible women are members of national **fraternities** and national **sororities**.

Butler is a member of the NCAA (Division I). **Intercollegiate sports** (some offering scholarships) include baseball (m), basketball, cross-country running, football (m), golf, soccer, softball (w), swimming and diving (w), tennis, track and field, volleyball (w).

Campus Safety

Student safety services include late-night transport/escort service, 24-hour emergency telephone alarm devices, 24-hour patrols by trained security personnel, and electronically operated dormitory entrances.

Applying

Butler requires an essay, SAT or ACT, and a high school transcript, and in some cases an interview and audition. Application deadline: rolling admissions; 3/1 priority date for financial aid. Deferred admission is possible.

California Institute of Technology

SUBURBAN SETTING ■ PRIVATE ■ INDEPENDENT ■ COED
PASADENA, CALIFORNIA

Web site: www.caltech.edu
Contact: Mr. Rick T. Bischoff, Director of Admissions, 1200 East California
Boulevard, Pasadena, CA 91125-0001
Telephone: 626-395-6341
Fax: 626-683-3026
E-mail: rbisch@caltech.edu

Academics

Caltech awards bachelor's, master's, and doctoral **degrees**. **Challenging opportunities** include student-designed majors, double majors, and independent study. Special programs include cooperative education, off-campus study, study-abroad, and Army and Air Force ROTC.

The most frequently chosen **baccalaureate** fields are engineering, physical sciences, and mathematics. A complete listing of majors at Caltech appears in the Majors by College index beginning on page 469.

The **faculty** at Caltech has 291 full-time members, 98% with terminal degrees. The student-faculty ratio is 3:1.

Students of Caltech

The student body totals 2,133, of whom 913 are undergraduates. 30.6% are women and 69.4% are men. Students come from 49 states and territories and 32 other countries. 31% are from California. 9.4% are international students. 0.8% are African American, 0.3% American Indian, 37.9% Asian American, and 5.4% Hispanic American. 98% returned for their sophomore year.

Facilities and Resources

600 **computers/terminals** are available on campus for general student use. Students can access the following: computer help desk, free student e-mail accounts, online (class) grades, online (class) registration, online (class) schedules. Campuswide network is available. 100% of college-owned or -operated housing units are wired for high-speed Internet access. Wireless service is available via entire campus. The 11 **libraries** have 3,165,000 books and 3,500 subscriptions.

Campus Life

There are 150 active organizations on campus, including a drama/theater group, newspaper, and choral group. No national or local **fraternities** or **sororities**.

Caltech is a member of the NCAA (Division III). **Intercollegiate sports** include baseball (m), basketball, cross-country running, fencing, soccer (m), swimming and diving, tennis, track and field, volleyball (w), water polo.

Campus Safety

Student safety services include late-night transport/escort service, 24-hour emergency telephone alarm devices, and 24-hour patrols by trained security personnel.

Applying

Caltech requires an essay, SAT Subject Tests, SAT or ACT, a high school transcript, and 2 recommendations. Application deadline: 1/1; 1/15 priority date for financial aid. Early and deferred admission are possible.

Getting Accepted
3,597 applied
17% were accepted
231 enrolled (38% of accepted)
99% from top tenth of their h.s. class
97% had SAT critical reading scores over 600
100% had SAT math scores over 600
100% had ACT scores over 24
80% had SAT critical reading scores over 700
100% had SAT math scores over 700
99% had ACT scores over 30

Graduation and After
82% graduated in 4 years
7% graduated in 5 years
1% graduated in 6 years
109 organizations recruited on campus

Financial Matters
$34,437 tuition and fees (2008–09)
$10,146 room and board
100% average percent of need met
$29,533 average financial aid amount received per undergraduate (2007–08 estimated)

CALIFORNIA POLYTECHNIC STATE UNIVERSITY, SAN LUIS OBISPO

SMALL-TOWN SETTING ■ PUBLIC ■ STATE-SUPPORTED ■ COED
SAN LUIS OBISPO, CALIFORNIA

Web site: www.calpoly.edu

Contact: Mr. James Maraviglia, Assistant Vice President of Admissions, Recruitment, and Financial Aid, 1 Grand Avenue, San Luis Obispo, CA 93407

Telephone: 805-756-2311

Fax: 805-756-5911

E-mail: admissions@calpoly.edu

Getting Accepted
33,352 applied
34% were accepted
3,501 enrolled (31% of accepted)
47% from top tenth of their h.s. class
3.78 average high school GPA
Mean SAT critical reading score: 570
Mean SAT math score: 613
Mean ACT score: 25
43% had SAT critical reading scores over 600
65% had SAT math scores over 600
76% had ACT scores over 24
5% had SAT critical reading scores over 700
17% had SAT math scores over 700
17% had ACT scores over 30

Graduation and After
24% graduated in 4 years
38% graduated in 5 years
10% graduated in 6 years
90% had job offers within 6 months
630 organizations recruited on campus

Financial Matters
$5043 resident tuition and fees (2008–09)
$20,256 nonresident tuition and fees (2008–09)
$9256 room and board
63% average percent of need met
$7724 average financial aid amount received per undergraduate (2006–07)

Academics

Cal Poly awards bachelor's, master's, and doctoral **degrees**. **Challenging opportunities** include advanced placement credit, an honors program, double majors, independent study, and a senior project. Special programs include cooperative education, internships, summer session for credit, off-campus study, study-abroad, and Army ROTC.

The most frequently chosen **baccalaureate** fields are engineering, business/marketing, and agriculture. A complete listing of majors at Cal Poly appears in the Majors by College index beginning on page 469.

The **faculty** at Cal Poly has 824 full-time members, 82% with terminal degrees. The student-faculty ratio is 19:1.

Students of Cal Poly

The student body totals 19,471, of whom 18,516 are undergraduates. 43.6% are women and 56.4% are men. Students come from 46 states and territories and 39 other countries. 96% are from California. 0.8% are international students. 1.1% are African American, 0.8% American Indian, 11.1% Asian American, and 11.4% Hispanic American. 89% returned for their sophomore year.

Facilities and Resources

Students can access the following: campus intranet, free student e-mail accounts, online (class) grades, online (class) registration, online (class) schedules. Campuswide network is available. Wireless service is available via classrooms, computer centers, computer labs, learning centers, libraries, student centers. The 2 **libraries** have 763,651 books and 5,529 subscriptions.

Campus Life

There are 400 active organizations on campus, including a drama/theater group, newspaper, radio station, television station, choral group, and marching band. 10% of eligible men and 13% of eligible women are members of national **fraternities**, national **sororities**, local fraternities, and local sororities.

Cal Poly is a member of the NCAA (Division I). **Intercollegiate sports** (some offering scholarships) include baseball (m), basketball, cross-country running, football (m), golf, soccer, softball (w), swimming and diving, tennis, track and field, volleyball (w), wrestling (m).

Campus Safety

Student safety services include late-night transport/escort service, 24-hour emergency telephone alarm devices, 24-hour patrols by trained security personnel, student patrols, and electronically operated dormitory entrances.

Applying

Cal Poly requires SAT or ACT and a high school transcript. Application deadline: 11/30; 6/30 for financial aid, with a 3/1 priority date. Early admission is possible.

CALVIN COLLEGE

SUBURBAN SETTING ■ PRIVATE ■ INDEPENDENT RELIGIOUS ■ COED
GRAND RAPIDS, MICHIGAN

SPONSOR

Web site: www.calvin.edu
Contact: Mr. Dale Kuiper, Director of Admissions and Financial Aid, 3201
  Burton Street, SE, Grand Rapids, MI 49546
Telephone: 616-526-6106 or toll-free 800-688-0122
Fax: 616-526-6777
E-mail: admissions@calvin.edu

Academics

Calvin awards bachelor's and master's **degrees** and post-bachelor's certificates. **Challenging opportunities** include advanced placement credit, accelerated degree programs, student-designed majors, an honors program, double majors, independent study, and a senior project. Special programs include internships, summer session for credit, off-campus study, study-abroad, and Army ROTC.

The most frequently chosen **baccalaureate** fields are business/marketing, education, and health professions and related sciences. A complete listing of majors at Calvin appears in the Majors by College index beginning on page 469.

The **faculty** at Calvin has 320 full-time members, 81% with terminal degrees. The student-faculty ratio is 11:1.

Students of Calvin

The student body totals 4,171, of whom 4,104 are undergraduates. 54.3% are women and 45.7% are men. Students come from 48 states and territories and 54 other countries. 57% are from Michigan. 7.5% are international students. 1.5% are African American, 0.3% American Indian, 3.1% Asian American, and 1.4% Hispanic American. 86% returned for their sophomore year.

Facilities and Resources

800 **computers/terminals** are available on campus for general student use. Students can access the following: computer help desk, free student e-mail accounts, online (class) grades, online (class) registration, online (class) schedules. Campuswide network is available. 100% of college-owned or -operated housing units are wired for high-speed Internet access. Wireless service is available via classrooms, computer centers, computer labs, dorm rooms, libraries, student centers. The 2 **libraries** have 1,041,679 books and 15,697 subscriptions.

Campus Life

There are 65 active organizations on campus, including a drama/theater group, newspaper, television station, and choral group. No national or local **fraternities** or **sororities**.

Calvin is a member of the NCAA (Division III). **Intercollegiate sports** include baseball (m), basketball, cross-country running, golf, soccer, softball (w), swimming and diving, tennis, track and field, volleyball (w).

Campus Safety

Student safety services include crime prevention programs, crime alert bulletins, late-night transport/escort service, 24-hour emergency telephone alarm devices, 24-hour patrols by trained security personnel, student patrols, and electronically operated dormitory entrances.

Applying

Calvin requires an essay, SAT or ACT, a high school transcript, 1 recommendation, and a minimum high school GPA of 2.5. It recommends an interview. Application deadline: 8/15; 2/15 priority date for financial aid. Deferred admission is possible.

Calvin College, one of the largest Christian colleges in North America, is internationally recognized as a center of liberal arts education and faith-shaped thinking. The College was founded in 1876 by the Christian Reformed Church. Today, students from a variety of faith traditions choose Calvin for its distinctive blend of strong Christian foundations coupled with rigorous academic inquiry. Occupying 400 wooded acres, Calvin's graceful campus offers remarkable resources: state-of-the-art science and communications facilities, elegant performance spaces, an excellent library, a flourishing 100-acre ecosystem preserve, and a new $55-million athletic complex. Grand Rapids, Michigan (population: 600,000), hosts a professional ballet, opera, and symphony; a botanical and sculpture garden; four sport franchises; and every other urban amenity.

Getting Accepted
2,169 applied
94% were accepted
936 enrolled (46% of accepted)
27% from top tenth of their h.s. class
3.58 average high school GPA
Mean SAT critical reading score: 594
Mean SAT math score: 605
Mean ACT score: 26
52% had SAT critical reading scores over 600
52% had SAT math scores over 600
71% had ACT scores over 24
12% had SAT critical reading scores over 700
17% had SAT math scores over 700
18% had ACT scores over 30
14 National Merit Scholars
36 valedictorians

Graduation and After
56% graduated in 4 years
18% graduated in 5 years
2% graduated in 6 years
85% had job offers within 6 months
130 organizations recruited on campus

Financial Matters
$23,165 tuition and fees (2008–09)
$7970 room and board
82% average percent of need met
$16,220 average financial aid amount received
  per undergraduate (2007–08 estimated)

CANISIUS COLLEGE

URBAN SETTING ■ PRIVATE ■ INDEPENDENT RELIGIOUS ■ COED
BUFFALO, NEW YORK

Web site: www.canisius.edu
Contact: Ms. Ann Marie Moscovic, Director of Admissions, 2001 Main Street,
  Buffalo, NY 14208-1098
Telephone: 716-888-2200 or toll-free 800-843-1517
Fax: 716-888-3230
E-mail: admissions@canisius.edu

With more than seventy majors and special programs, small classes taught by caring faculty members, state-of-the-art living and learning facilities, and an unlimited range of learning opportunities outside the classroom, Canisius has everything a student could want in a challenging college experience. Thousands of Canisius graduates are leaders in their professions, including doctors, lawyers, scientists, business executives, and teachers. Canisius is all about giving students the best possible start to their careers and their future. It is how and where leaders are made.

Getting Accepted
3,847 applied
76% were accepted
807 enrolled (28% of accepted)
27% from top tenth of their h.s. class
3.5 average high school GPA
Mean SAT critical reading score: 557
Mean SAT math score: 572
Mean ACT score: 25
29% had SAT critical reading scores over 600
38% had SAT math scores over 600
65% had ACT scores over 24
5% had SAT critical reading scores over 700
5% had SAT math scores over 700
12% had ACT scores over 30

Graduation and After
55% graduated in 4 years
11% graduated in 5 years
2% graduated in 6 years
64.5% had job offers within 6 months
30 organizations recruited on campus

Financial Matters
$28,157 tuition and fees (2008–09)
$10,150 room and board
79% average percent of need met
$21,447 average financial aid amount received
  per undergraduate (2007–08 estimated)

Academics

Canisius awards associate, bachelor's, and master's **degrees** and post-master's certificates. **Challenging opportunities** include advanced placement credit, an honors program, double majors, independent study, and a senior project. Special programs include cooperative education, internships, summer session for credit, off-campus study, study-abroad, and Army ROTC.

The most frequently chosen **baccalaureate** fields are business/marketing, education, and psychology. A complete listing of majors at Canisius appears in the Majors by College index beginning on page 469.

The **faculty** at Canisius has 226 full-time members, 92% with terminal degrees. The student-faculty ratio is 11:1.

Students of Canisius

The student body totals 4,916, of whom 3,346 are undergraduates. 55.1% are women and 44.9% are men. Students come from 32 states and territories and 19 other countries. 92% are from New York. 3.2% are international students. 6% are African American, 0.4% American Indian, 1.4% Asian American, and 2.7% Hispanic American. 83% returned for their sophomore year.

Facilities and Resources

500 **computers/terminals** are available on campus for general student use. Students can access the following: computer help desk, free student e-mail accounts, online (class) grades, online (class) registration, online (class) schedules, online accounts. Campuswide network is available. 100% of college-owned or -operated housing units are wired for high-speed Internet access. Wireless service is available via entire campus. The 2 **libraries** have 379,498 books and 24,000 subscriptions.

Campus Life

There are 100 active organizations on campus, including a drama/theater group, newspaper, radio station, television station, and choral group. 1% of eligible men and 1% of eligible women are members of national **fraternities** and national **sororities**.

Canisius is a member of the NCAA (Division I). **Intercollegiate sports** (some offering scholarships) include baseball (m), basketball, cross-country running, golf (m), ice hockey (m), lacrosse, soccer, softball (w), swimming and diving, volleyball (w).

Campus Safety

Student safety services include crime prevention programs, closed-circuit television monitors, late-night transport/escort service, 24-hour emergency telephone alarm devices, 24-hour patrols by trained security personnel, and electronically operated dormitory entrances.

Applying

Canisius requires SAT or ACT, a high school transcript, and a minimum high school GPA of 2.0, and in some cases an interview. It recommends an essay, an interview, and 1 recommendation. Application deadline: 5/1; 2/15 priority date for financial aid. Early and deferred admission are possible.

CARLETON COLLEGE

SMALL-TOWN SETTING ■ PRIVATE ■ INDEPENDENT ■ COED
NORTHFIELD, MINNESOTA

Web site: www.carleton.edu
Contact: 100 South College Street, Northfield, MN 55057
Telephone: 507-222-4190 or toll-free 800-995-2275
Fax: 507-646-4526
E-mail: admissions@carleton.edu

Academics

Carleton awards bachelor's **degrees**. **Challenging opportunities** include advanced placement credit, accelerated degree programs, student-designed majors, double majors, independent study, and a senior project. Special programs include internships, off-campus study, and study-abroad.

The most frequently chosen **baccalaureate** fields are social sciences, physical sciences, and biological/life sciences. A complete listing of majors at Carleton appears in the Majors by College index beginning on page 469.

The **faculty** at Carleton has 215 full-time members, 96% with terminal degrees. The student-faculty ratio is 9:1.

Students of Carleton

The student body is made up of 2,000 undergraduates. 52.2% are women and 47.8% are men. Students come from 51 states and territories and 44 other countries. 26% are from Minnesota. 6.1% are international students. 5% are African American, 0.9% American Indian, 9.7% Asian American, and 5.3% Hispanic American. 95% returned for their sophomore year.

Facilities and Resources

300 **computers/terminals** and 220 ports are available on campus for general student use. Students can access the following: campus intranet, computer help desk, free student e-mail accounts, online (class) grades, online (class) registration, online (class) schedules. Campuswide network is available. 100% of college-owned or -operated housing units are wired for high-speed Internet access. Wireless service is available via classrooms, computer labs, dorm rooms, libraries. The 2 **libraries** have 1,113,497 books and 10,964 subscriptions.

Campus Life

There are 132 active organizations on campus, including a drama/theater group, newspaper, radio station, and choral group. No national or local **fraternities** or **sororities**.

Carleton is a member of the NCAA (Division III). **Intercollegiate sports** include baseball (m), basketball, cross-country running, football (m), golf, soccer, softball (w), swimming and diving, tennis, track and field, volleyball (w).

Campus Safety

Student safety services include late-night transport/escort service, 24-hour emergency telephone alarm devices, 24-hour patrols by trained security personnel, student patrols, and electronically operated dormitory entrances.

Applying

Carleton requires an essay, SAT or ACT, a high school transcript, 2 recommendations, and common application supplement. It recommends SAT Subject Tests and an interview. Application deadline: 1/15; 2/15 for financial aid, with a 2/15 priority date. Early and deferred admission are possible.

Getting Accepted
4,956 applied
27% were accepted
489 enrolled (36% of accepted)
74% from top tenth of their h.s. class
92% had SAT critical reading scores over 600
91% had SAT math scores over 600
95% had SAT writing scores over 600
95% had ACT scores over 24
56% had SAT critical reading scores over 700
53% had SAT math scores over 700
68% had SAT writing scores over 700
68% had ACT scores over 30
88 National Merit Scholars
42 valedictorians

Graduation and After
90% graduated in 4 years
3% graduated in 5 years
1% graduated in 6 years
57% had job offers within 6 months
60 organizations recruited on campus

Financial Matters
$38,046 tuition and fees (2008–09)
$9993 room and board
100% average percent of need met
$29,601 average financial aid amount received per undergraduate (2006–07)

Carnegie Mellon University has rapidly evolved into a powerful internationally recognized institution, with top-ranked business and liberal arts programs that are equally matched by world-class fine arts, technology, sciences, and computer science programs. Approximately 9,000 undergraduate and graduate students receive an education characterized by its focus on creating and implementing solutions to solve real problems, interdisciplinary collaboration, and innovation. A small student-faculty ratio provides an opportunity for close interaction between students and professors. Carnegie Mellon students learn to view life through a wide variety of lenses and leave prepared to make an important and lasting impact on society.

Getting Accepted
22,356 applied
28% were accepted
1,416 enrolled (23% of accepted)
73% from top tenth of their h.s. class
3.58 average high school GPA
Mean SAT critical reading score: 666
Mean SAT math score: 730
Mean SAT writing score: 663
Mean ACT score: 30
84% had SAT critical reading scores over 600
97% had SAT math scores over 600
85% had SAT writing scores over 600
97% had ACT scores over 24
35% had SAT critical reading scores over 700
74% had SAT math scores over 700
32% had SAT writing scores over 700
66% had ACT scores over 30

Graduation and After
70% graduated in 4 years
14% graduated in 5 years
2% graduated in 6 years
68% had job offers within 6 months
856 organizations recruited on campus

Financial Matters
$39,564 tuition and fees (2008–09)
$10,050 room and board
81% average percent of need met
$24,724 average financial aid amount received per undergraduate (2007–08 estimated)

CARNEGIE MELLON UNIVERSITY
URBAN SETTING ■ PRIVATE ■ INDEPENDENT ■ COED
PITTSBURGH, PENNSYLVANIA

Web site: www.cmu.edu
Contact: Mr. Michael Steidel, Director of Admissions, 5000 Forbes Avenue, Pittsburgh, PA 15213
Telephone: 412-268-2082
Fax: 412-268-7838
E-mail: undergraduate-admissions@andrew.cmu.edu

Academics
Carnegie Mellon awards bachelor's, master's, and doctoral **degrees** and post-master's certificates. **Challenging opportunities** include advanced placement credit, student-designed majors, freshman honors college, double majors, independent study, and a senior project. Special programs include cooperative education, internships, summer session for credit, off-campus study, study-abroad, and Army, Navy, and Air Force ROTC.

The most frequently chosen **baccalaureate** fields are engineering, business/marketing, and visual and performing arts. A complete listing of majors at Carnegie Mellon appears in the Majors by College index beginning on page 469.

The **faculty** at Carnegie Mellon has 830 full-time members, 98% with terminal degrees. The student-faculty ratio is 11:1.

Students of Carnegie Mellon
The student body totals 10,493, of whom 5,849 are undergraduates. 39.3% are women and 60.7% are men. Students come from 52 states and territories and 49 other countries. 23% are from Pennsylvania. 14.3% are international students. 5% are African American, 0.4% American Indian, 24% Asian American, and 4.6% Hispanic American. 95% returned for their sophomore year.

Facilities and Resources
402 **computers/terminals** are available on campus for general student use. Students can access the following: online (class) registration. Campuswide network is available. The 3 **libraries** have 1,084,013 books and 28,769 subscriptions.

Campus Life
There are 100 active organizations on campus, including a drama/theater group, newspaper, radio station, television station, choral group, and marching band. 12% of eligible men and 9% of eligible women are members of national **fraternities**, national **sororities**, and local sororities.

Carnegie Mellon is a member of the NCAA (Division III). **Intercollegiate sports** include basketball, cheerleading, cross-country running, football (m), golf (m), soccer, swimming and diving, tennis, track and field, volleyball (w).

Campus Safety
Student safety services include late-night transport/escort service, 24-hour emergency telephone alarm devices, 24-hour patrols by trained security personnel, and electronically operated dormitory entrances.

Applying
Carnegie Mellon requires an essay, SAT or ACT, a high school transcript, and 1 recommendation, and in some cases SAT and SAT Subject Tests or ACT and portfolio, audition. It recommends an interview. Application deadline: 1/1; 5/1 for financial aid, with a 2/15 priority date. Early and deferred admission are possible.

CARROLL COLLEGE

SMALL-TOWN SETTING ■ PRIVATE ■ INDEPENDENT RELIGIOUS ■ COED
HELENA, MONTANA

Web site: www.carroll.edu
Contact: Ms. Cynthia Thornquist, Director of Admissions and Enrollment
    Operations, 1601 North Benton Avenue, Helena, MT 59625-0002
Telephone: or toll-free 800-992-3648
Fax: 406-447-4533
E-mail: enroll@carroll.edu

Academics

Carroll awards associate and bachelor's **degrees. Challenging opportunities** include advanced placement credit, accelerated degree programs, student-designed majors, freshman honors college, an honors program, double majors, independent study, and a senior project. Special programs include cooperative education, internships, summer session for credit, study-abroad, and Army ROTC.

The most frequently chosen **baccalaureate** fields are business/marketing, health professions and related sciences, and biological/life sciences. A complete listing of majors at Carroll appears in the Majors by College index beginning on page 469.

The **faculty** at Carroll has 84 full-time members, 67% with terminal degrees.

Students of Carroll

The student body is made up of 1,409 undergraduates. 56.4% are women and 43.6% are men. Students come from 28 states and territories and 13 other countries. 60% are from Montana. 1.2% are international students. 0.5% are African American, 0.7% American Indian, 1.1% Asian American, and 2.1% Hispanic American. 80% returned for their sophomore year.

Facilities and Resources

91 **computers/terminals** are available on campus for general student use. Students can access the following: campus intranet, computer help desk, free student e-mail accounts, online (class) grades, online (class) registration, online (class) schedules, online book order. Campuswide network is available. The 2 **libraries** have 89,003 books and 2,721 subscriptions.

Campus Life

There are 35 active organizations on campus, including a drama/theater group, newspaper, radio station, and choral group. No national or local **fraternities** or **sororities**.

Carroll is a member of the NAIA. **Intercollegiate sports** (some offering scholarships) include basketball, cheerleading, cross-country running, football (m), golf, soccer (w), volleyball (w).

Campus Safety

Student safety services include late-night transport/escort service and electronically operated dormitory entrances.

Applying

Carroll requires an essay, SAT or ACT, a high school transcript, 1 recommendation, and a minimum high school GPA of 2.0, and in some cases SAT Subject Tests and an interview. It recommends an interview and a minimum high school GPA of 3.0. Application deadline: 6/1. Deferred admission is possible.

Getting Accepted

1,174 applied
76% were accepted
345 enrolled (39% of accepted)
26% from top tenth of their h.s. class
3.47 average high school GPA
Mean SAT critical reading score: 548
Mean SAT math score: 553
Mean SAT writing score: 535
Mean ACT score: 24
27% had SAT critical reading scores over 600
32% had SAT math scores over 600
21% had SAT writing scores over 600
52% had ACT scores over 24
2% had SAT critical reading scores over 700
3% had SAT math scores over 700
3% had SAT writing scores over 700
7% had ACT scores over 30

Graduation and After

46% graduated in 4 years
15% graduated in 5 years
1% graduated in 6 years

Financial Matters

$22,592 tuition and fees (2009–10)
$7118 room and board
80% average percent of need met
$15,113 average financial aid amount received
    per undergraduate (2005–06)

CARROLL UNIVERSITY

SUBURBAN SETTING ■ PRIVATE ■ INDEPENDENT RELIGIOUS ■ COED
WAUKESHA, WISCONSIN

Web site: www.cc.edu
Contact: Mr. James Wiseman, Vice President of Enrollment, 100 North East
    Avenue, Waukesha, WI 53186-5593
Telephone: 262-524-7221 or toll-free 800-CARROLL
Fax: 262-524-7139
E-mail: cc.info@ccadmin.cc.edu

Getting Accepted
2,906 applied
73% were accepted
690 enrolled (33% of accepted)
18% from top tenth of their h.s. class
3.3 average high school GPA
Mean ACT score: 23
44% had ACT scores over 24
4% had ACT scores over 30

Graduation and After
40% graduated in 4 years
16% graduated in 5 years
2% graduated in 6 years
3 organizations recruited on campus

Financial Matters
$21,926 tuition and fees (2008–09)
$6694 room and board
100% average percent of need met
$16,047 average financial aid amount received
    per undergraduate (2007–08 estimated)

Academics
Carroll awards bachelor's, master's, and first-professional **degrees. Challenging opportunities** include advanced placement credit, student-designed majors, an honors program, double majors, independent study, and a senior project. Special programs include internships, summer session for credit, study-abroad, and Army and Air Force ROTC.

The most frequently chosen **baccalaureate** fields are health professions and related sciences, business/marketing, and psychology. A complete listing of majors at Carroll appears in the Majors by College index beginning on page 469.

The **faculty** at Carroll has 121 full-time members, 63% with terminal degrees. The student-faculty ratio is 16:1.

Students of Carroll
The student body totals 3,316, of whom 3,030 are undergraduates. 66.8% are women and 33.2% are men. Students come from 25 states and territories and 33 other countries. 76% are from Wisconsin. 1% are international students. 2.8% are African American, 0.3% American Indian, 1.6% Asian American, and 3.6% Hispanic American. 74% returned for their sophomore year.

Facilities and Resources
250 **computers/terminals** are available on campus for general student use. Students can access the following: campus intranet, computer help desk, free student e-mail accounts, online (class) grades, online (class) registration, online (class) schedules. Campuswide network is available. 95% of college-owned or -operated housing units are wired for high-speed Internet access. Wireless service is available via classrooms, computer centers, computer labs, libraries. The **library** has 150,000 books and 18,000 subscriptions.

Campus Life
There are 40 active organizations on campus, including a drama/theater group, newspaper, radio station, and choral group. 10% of eligible men and 11% of eligible women are members of national **sororities** and local **fraternities**.

Carroll is a member of the NCAA (Division III). **Intercollegiate sports** include baseball (m), basketball, cross-country running, football (m), golf, soccer, swimming and diving, tennis, track and field, volleyball (w).

Campus Safety
Student safety services include late-night transport/escort service, 24-hour emergency telephone alarm devices, 24-hour patrols by trained security personnel, student patrols, and electronically operated dormitory entrances.

Applying
Carroll requires SAT or ACT, a high school transcript, 1 recommendation, and a minimum high school GPA of 2.0, and in some cases an essay. It recommends ACT and an interview. Application deadline: rolling admissions. Deferred admission is possible.

Carson-Newman College

Small-town setting ■ Private ■ Independent Religious ■ Coed
Jefferson City, Tennessee

Web site: www.cn.edu
Contact: Melanie Redding, Director of Admissions, 1646 Russell Avenue, PO Box 557, Jefferson City, TN 37760
Telephone: 865-471-3223 or toll-free 800-678-9061
Fax: 865-471-3502
E-mail: cnadmiss@cn.edu

Academics

Carson-Newman awards associate, bachelor's, and master's **degrees**. **Challenging opportunities** include advanced placement credit, accelerated degree programs, student-designed majors, an honors program, and a senior project. Special programs include internships, summer session for credit, off-campus study, study-abroad, and Army and Air Force ROTC.

The most frequently chosen **baccalaureate** fields are health professions and related sciences, business/marketing, and communications/journalism. A complete listing of majors at Carson-Newman appears in the Majors by College index beginning on page 469.

The **faculty** at Carson-Newman has 132 full-time members, 76% with terminal degrees. The student-faculty ratio is 13:1.

Students of Carson-Newman

The student body totals 2,032, of whom 1,823 are undergraduates. 57.7% are women and 42.3% are men. Students come from 37 states and territories and 22 other countries. 69% are from Tennessee. 3.3% are international students. 8% are African American, 0.3% American Indian, 0.6% Asian American, and 1% Hispanic American. 67% returned for their sophomore year.

Facilities and Resources

200 **computers/terminals** are available on campus for general student use. Campuswide network is available. The 2 **libraries** have 218,371 books and 3,966 subscriptions.

Campus Life

There are 63 active organizations on campus, including a drama/theater group, newspaper, choral group, and marching band. 5% of eligible men and 5% of eligible women are members of national **fraternities**, national **sororities**, local fraternities, and local sororities.

Carson-Newman is a member of the NCAA (Division II). **Intercollegiate sports** (some offering scholarships) include baseball (m), basketball, cross-country running, football (m), golf (m), soccer, softball (w), tennis, track and field, volleyball (w), wrestling (m).

Campus Safety

Student safety services include late-night transport/escort service, 24-hour emergency telephone alarm devices, 24-hour patrols by trained security personnel, and electronically operated dormitory entrances.

Applying

Carson-Newman requires SAT or ACT, a high school transcript, medical history, and a minimum high school GPA of 2.25, and in some cases an essay and an interview. It recommends an interview. Application deadline: 8/1; 4/1 priority date for financial aid. Deferred admission is possible.

Getting Accepted

2,815 applied
71% were accepted
444 enrolled (22% of accepted)
27% from top tenth of their h.s. class
3.35 average high school GPA
37% had ACT scores over 24
7% had ACT scores over 30

Graduation and After

42% graduated in 4 years
8% graduated in 5 years
2% graduated in 6 years
24 organizations recruited on campus

Financial Matters

$17,800 tuition and fees (2008–09)
$5790 room and board
80% average percent of need met
$14,894 average financial aid amount received per undergraduate (2007–08 estimated)

Case Western Reserve University

URBAN SETTING ■ PRIVATE ■ INDEPENDENT ■ COED
CLEVELAND, OHIO

Web site: www.case.edu
Contact: Ms. Rae Ann DiBaggio, Co-Director of Undergraduate Admission,
10900 Euclid Avenue, Cleveland, OH 44106
Telephone: 216-368-4450
Fax: 216-368-5111
E-mail: admission@case.edu

Getting Accepted
7,351 applied
73% were accepted
1,026 enrolled (19% of accepted)
63% from top tenth of their h.s. class
Mean SAT critical reading score: 639
Mean SAT math score: 670
Mean SAT writing score: 630
Mean ACT score: 29
73% had SAT critical reading scores over 600
84% had SAT math scores over 600
68% had SAT writing scores over 600
89% had ACT scores over 24
24% had SAT critical reading scores over 700
41% had SAT math scores over 700
20% had SAT writing scores over 700
48% had ACT scores over 30
43 National Merit Scholars
51 valedictorians

Graduation and After
58% graduated in 4 years
20% graduated in 5 years
2% graduated in 6 years
80% had job offers within 6 months
180 organizations recruited on campus

Financial Matters
$35,202 tuition and fees (2008–09)
$10,450 room and board
90% average percent of need met
$33,565 average financial aid amount received per undergraduate (2007–08 estimated)

Academics

Case awards bachelor's, master's, doctoral, and first-professional **degrees** and post-bachelor's certificates. **Challenging opportunities** include advanced placement credit, accelerated degree programs, student-designed majors, an honors program, double majors, independent study, and a senior project. Special programs include cooperative education, internships, summer session for credit, off-campus study, study-abroad, and Army and Air Force ROTC.

The most frequently chosen **baccalaureate** fields are engineering, social sciences, and biological/life sciences. A complete listing of majors at Case appears in the Majors by College index beginning on page 469.

The **faculty** at Case has 737 full-time members, 90% with terminal degrees. The student-faculty ratio is 10:1.

Students of Case

The student body totals 9,814, of whom 4,356 are undergraduates. 43.2% are women and 56.8% are men. Students come from 50 states and territories and 24 other countries. 54% are from Ohio. 3.4% are international students. 5.9% are African American, 0.2% American Indian, 16.7% Asian American, and 2.2% Hispanic American. 92% returned for their sophomore year.

Facilities and Resources

415 **computers/terminals** and 1,000 ports are available on campus for general student use. Students can access the following: campus intranet, computer help desk, free student e-mail accounts, online (class) grades, online (class) registration, online (class) schedules, software library, online reference databases, electronic books and journals. Campuswide network is available. 100% of college-owned or -operated housing units are wired for high-speed Internet access. Wireless service is available via entire campus. The 7 **libraries** have 2,518,324 books and 54,252 subscriptions.

Campus Life

There are 190 active organizations on campus, including a drama/theater group, newspaper, radio station, choral group, and marching band. 30% of eligible men and 29% of eligible women are members of national **fraternities**, national **sororities**, and local sororities.

Case is a member of the NCAA (Division III). **Intercollegiate sports** include baseball (m), basketball, cross-country running, football (m), soccer, softball (w), swimming and diving, tennis, track and field, volleyball (w), wrestling (m).

Campus Safety

Student safety services include crime prevention programs, late-night transport/escort service, 24-hour emergency telephone alarm devices, 24-hour patrols by trained security personnel, student patrols, and electronically operated dormitory entrances.

Applying

Case requires an essay, SAT or ACT, a high school transcript, and 1 recommendation. It recommends an interview. Application deadline: 1/15; 2/15 priority date for financial aid. Early and deferred admission are possible.

CEDARVILLE UNIVERSITY

RURAL SETTING ■ PRIVATE ■ INDEPENDENT RELIGIOUS ■ COED
CEDARVILLE, OHIO

Web site: www.cedarville.edu
Contact: Mr. Scott Van Loo, Director of Admissions, 251 North Main Street, Cedarville, OH 45314-0601
Telephone: 937-766-7700 or toll-free 800-CEDARVILLE
Fax: 937-766-7575
E-mail: admiss@cedarville.edu

Academics

Cedarville awards bachelor's and master's **degrees. Challenging opportunities** include advanced placement credit, accelerated degree programs, an honors program, double majors, independent study, and a senior project. Special programs include internships, summer session for credit, off-campus study, study-abroad, and Army and Air Force ROTC.

The most frequently chosen **baccalaureate** fields are business/marketing, education, and health professions and related sciences. A complete listing of majors at Cedarville appears in the Majors by College index beginning on page 469.

The **faculty** at Cedarville has 190 full-time members, 61% with terminal degrees. The student-faculty ratio is 15:1.

Students of Cedarville

The student body totals 3,077, of whom 2,996 are undergraduates. 54.4% are women and 45.6% are men. Students come from 50 states and territories and 21 other countries. 36% are from Ohio. 0.7% are international students. 1.5% are African American, 0.3% American Indian, 1.3% Asian American, and 2.2% Hispanic American. 84% returned for their sophomore year.

Facilities and Resources

2,600 **computers/terminals** are available on campus for general student use. Students can access the following: online (class) registration, over 150 software packages. Campuswide network is available. Wireless service is available via entire campus. The **library** has 181,053 books and 21,050 subscriptions.

Campus Life

There are 61 active organizations on campus, including a drama/theater group, newspaper, radio station, and choral group. No national or local **fraternities** or **sororities**.

Cedarville is a member of the NAIA and NCCAA. **Intercollegiate sports** (some offering scholarships) include baseball (m), basketball, cross-country running, golf (m), soccer, softball (w), tennis, track and field, volleyball (w).

Campus Safety

Student safety services include late-night transport/escort service, 24-hour emergency telephone alarm devices, 24-hour patrols by trained security personnel, student patrols, and electronically operated dormitory entrances.

Applying

Cedarville requires an essay, SAT or ACT, a high school transcript, 2 recommendations, clear testimony of faith in Jesus Christ and evidence of consistent Christian lifestyle, and a minimum high school GPA of 3.0, and in some cases an interview. It recommends SAT and SAT Subject Tests or ACT. Application deadline: rolling admissions; 3/1 priority date for financial aid. Early and deferred admission are possible.

Getting Accepted

2,990 applied
74% were accepted
774 enrolled (35% of accepted)
32% from top tenth of their h.s. class
3.61 average high school GPA
Mean SAT critical reading score: 594
Mean SAT math score: 582
Mean SAT writing score: 579
Mean ACT score: 26
49% had SAT critical reading scores over 600
43% had SAT math scores over 600
43% had SAT writing scores over 600
71% had ACT scores over 24
10% had SAT critical reading scores over 700
8% had SAT math scores over 700
9% had SAT writing scores over 700
19% had ACT scores over 30
10 National Merit Scholars
50 valedictorians

Graduation and After

54% graduated in 4 years
12% graduated in 5 years
1% graduated in 6 years

Financial Matters

$22,304 tuition and fees (2009–10)
$5006 room and board
41% average percent of need met
$18,834 average financial aid amount received per undergraduate (2006–07)

CENTRAL COLLEGE

SMALL-TOWN SETTING ■ PRIVATE ■ INDEPENDENT RELIGIOUS ■ COED
PELLA, IOWA

Web site: www.central.edu
Contact: 812 University Street, Pella, IA 50219-1999
Telephone: 641-628-7600 or toll-free 877-462-3687 (in-state), 877-462-3689 (out-of-state)
Fax: 641-628-5316
E-mail: admissions@central.edu

Academics

Central awards bachelor's **degrees**. **Challenging opportunities** include student-designed majors, an honors program, double majors, independent study, and a senior project. Special programs include internships, summer session for credit, off-campus study, and study-abroad.

The most frequently chosen **baccalaureate** fields are business/marketing, parks and recreation, and social sciences. A complete listing of majors at Central appears in the Majors by College index beginning on page 469.

The **faculty** at Central has 89 full-time members, 91% with terminal degrees. The student-faculty ratio is 14:1.

Students of Central

The student body is made up of 1,558 undergraduates. 53.5% are women and 46.5% are men. Students come from 35 states and territories and 5 other countries. 83% are from Iowa. 1.3% are international students. 1.7% are African American, 0.3% American Indian, 1.5% Asian American, and 2.1% Hispanic American. 80% returned for their sophomore year.

Facilities and Resources

400 **computers/terminals** and 1,600 ports are available on campus for general student use. Students can access the following: campus intranet, computer help desk, free student e-mail accounts, online (class) grades, online (class) registration, online (class) schedules. Campuswide network is available. 100% of college-owned or -operated housing units are wired for high-speed Internet access. Wireless service is available via entire campus. The **library** has 197,672 books and 634 subscriptions.

Campus Life

There are 72 active organizations on campus, including a drama/theater group, newspaper, radio station, television station, and choral group. 6% of eligible men and 6% of eligible women are members of local **fraternities** and local **sororities**.

Central is a member of the NCAA (Division III). **Intercollegiate sports** include baseball (m), basketball, cross-country running, football (m), golf, soccer, softball (w), tennis, track and field, volleyball (w), wrestling (m).

Campus Safety

Student safety services include late-night transport/escort service, 24-hour emergency telephone alarm devices, student patrols, and electronically operated dormitory entrances.

Applying

Central requires SAT or ACT and a high school transcript, and in some cases an essay, an interview, and 3 recommendations. It recommends an interview and a minimum high school GPA of 2.5. Application deadline: rolling admissions; 3/15 priority date for financial aid. Deferred admission is possible.

Centre College

SMALL-TOWN SETTING ■ PRIVATE ■ INDEPENDENT RELIGIOUS ■ COED
DANVILLE, KENTUCKY

Web site: www.centre.edu
Contact: Mr. Bob Nesmith, Director of Admission, 600 West Walnut Street,
   Danville, KY 40422-1394
Telephone: 859-238-5350 or toll-free 800-423-6236
Fax: 859-238-5373
E-mail: admission@centre.edu

Academics

Centre awards bachelor's **degrees**. **Challenging opportunities** include advanced placement credit, student-designed majors, double majors, independent study, and a senior project. Special programs include internships, off-campus study, study-abroad, and Army and Air Force ROTC.

The most frequently chosen **baccalaureate** fields are social sciences, biological/life sciences, and English. A complete listing of majors at Centre appears in the Majors by College index beginning on page 469.

The **faculty** at Centre has 101 full-time members, 95% with terminal degrees. The student-faculty ratio is 11:1.

Students of Centre

The student body is made up of 1,197 undergraduates. 54.1% are women and 45.9% are men. Students come from 39 states and territories and 12 other countries. 62% are from Kentucky. 1.5% are international students. 3.6% are African American, 0.2% American Indian, 2.2% Asian American, and 2.1% Hispanic American. 91% returned for their sophomore year.

Facilities and Resources

190 **computers/terminals** are available on campus for general student use. Students can access the following: campus intranet, computer help desk, free student e-mail accounts, online (class) grades, online (class) registration, online (class) schedules. Campuswide network is available. 100% of college-owned or -operated housing units are wired for high-speed Internet access. Wireless service is available via classrooms, computer centers, computer labs, dorm rooms, learning centers, libraries, student centers. The **library** has 278,200 books and 20,780 subscriptions.

Campus Life

There are 65 active organizations on campus, including a drama/theater group, newspaper, radio station, television station, and choral group. 34% of eligible men and 40% of eligible women are members of national **fraternities** and national **sororities**.

Centre is a member of the NCAA (Division III). **Intercollegiate sports** include baseball (m), basketball, cheerleading (w), cross-country running, field hockey (w), football (m), golf, soccer, softball (w), swimming and diving, tennis, track and field, volleyball (w).

Campus Safety

Student safety services include late-night transport/escort service, 24-hour emergency telephone alarm devices, 24-hour patrols by trained security personnel, and electronically operated dormitory entrances.

Applying

Centre requires an essay, SAT or ACT, a high school transcript, and 1 recommendation. It recommends an interview. Application deadline: 2/1; 3/1 for financial aid. Early and deferred admission are possible.

Getting Accepted

2,176 applied
63% were accepted
336 enrolled (25% of accepted)
53% from top tenth of their h.s. class
3.54 average high school GPA
61% had SAT critical reading scores over 600
63% had SAT math scores over 600
92% had ACT scores over 24
25% had SAT critical reading scores over 700
15% had SAT math scores over 700
29% had ACT scores over 30
4 National Merit Scholars
14 class presidents
28 valedictorians

Graduation and After

81% graduated in 4 years
1% graduated in 5 years
60% had job offers within 6 months
12 organizations recruited on campus

Financial Matters

$37,000 comprehensive fee (2008–09)
88% average percent of need met
$21,616 average financial aid amount received per undergraduate (2007–08 estimated)

In addition to the traditional type of academic advising and counseling available at most universities, all Chapman freshmen are assigned an executive-style personal coach to help them improve their motivation and effectiveness and achieve their goals. Thirty-minute weekly coaching sessions are focused on providing personal development, assistance with planning and organization, and, most importantly, motivation and encouragement. Coaches work with students to develop and review long-term and short-term goals; evaluate current academic performance and connect with their goals; clearly identify reasons for success, or lack of success, during the prior week; share positive feedback for successful activities; directly address ineffective activities; and create strategies, define action plans, and set deadlines for the coming week. This type of personal coaching in the university context provides an invaluable safety net, helping to improve academic preparedness and performance as well as maximize utilization of all of Chapman's services and programs, resulting in a "win-win" situation for everyone.

Getting Accepted
5,356 applied
50% were accepted
965 enrolled (36% of accepted)
51% from top tenth of their h.s. class
3.67 average high school GPA
Mean SAT critical reading score: 607
Mean SAT math score: 618
Mean SAT writing score: 615
Mean ACT score: 27
56% had SAT critical reading scores over 600
63% had SAT math scores over 600
62% had SAT writing scores over 600
86% had ACT scores over 24
11% had SAT critical reading scores over 700
13% had SAT math scores over 700
12% had SAT writing scores over 700
19% had ACT scores over 30
26 National Merit Scholars
10 class presidents
21 valedictorians

Graduation and After
49% graduated in 4 years
13% graduated in 5 years
5% graduated in 6 years

Financial Matters
$36,764 tuition and fees (2009–10)
$12,832 room and board
100% average percent of need met
$21,566 average financial aid amount received per undergraduate (2006–07)

CHAPMAN UNIVERSITY
SUBURBAN SETTING ■ PRIVATE ■ INDEPENDENT RELIGIOUS ■ COED
ORANGE, CALIFORNIA

Web site: www.chapman.edu
Contact: Mr. Michael Drummy, Assistant Vice Chancellor and Chief Admission Officer, One University Drive, Orange, CA 92866
Telephone: 714-997-6711 or toll-free 888-CUAPPLY
Fax: 714-997-6713
E-mail: admit@chapman.edu

Academics
Chapman awards bachelor's, master's, doctoral, and first-professional **degrees** and post-bachelor's certificates. **Challenging opportunities** include advanced placement credit, student-designed majors, an honors program, double majors, independent study, and a senior project. Special programs include internships, summer session for credit, off-campus study, study-abroad, and Army and Air Force ROTC.

The most frequently chosen **baccalaureate** fields are business/marketing, visual and performing arts, and communications/journalism. A complete listing of majors at Chapman appears in the Majors by College index beginning on page 469.

The **faculty** at Chapman has 333 full-time members, 89% with terminal degrees. The student-faculty ratio is 14:1.

Students of Chapman
The student body totals 6,128, of whom 4,293 are undergraduates. 58% are women and 42% are men. Students come from 47 states and territories and 32 other countries. 75% are from California. 2.3% are international students. 2.5% are African American, 0.7% American Indian, 8.6% Asian American, and 10.3% Hispanic American. 86% returned for their sophomore year.

Facilities and Resources
453 **computers/terminals** are available on campus for general student use. Students can access the following: campus intranet, computer help desk, free student e-mail accounts, online (class) grades, online (class) registration, online (class) schedules. Campuswide network is available. 100% of college-owned or -operated housing units are wired for high-speed Internet access. Wireless service is available via entire campus. The 2 **libraries** have 238,260 books and 35,884 subscriptions.

Campus Life
There are 79 active organizations on campus, including a drama/theater group, newspaper, radio station, and choral group. 26% of eligible men and 30% of eligible women are members of national **fraternities** and national **sororities**.

Chapman is a member of the NCAA (Division III). **Intercollegiate sports** include baseball (m), basketball, crew (w), cross-country running, football (m), golf (m), soccer, softball (w), swimming and diving (w), tennis, track and field (w), volleyball (w), water polo.

Campus Safety
Student safety services include full safety education program, late-night transport/escort service, 24-hour emergency telephone alarm devices, 24-hour patrols by trained security personnel, and electronically operated dormitory entrances.

Applying
Chapman requires an essay, SAT or ACT, a high school transcript, and 1 recommendation. It recommends SAT Subject Tests and an interview. Application deadline: 1/15; 3/2 priority date for financial aid.

CHRISTENDOM COLLEGE

RURAL SETTING ■ PRIVATE ■ INDEPENDENT RELIGIOUS ■ COED
FRONT ROYAL, VIRGINIA

Web site: www.christendom.edu
Contact: 134 Christendom Drive, Front Royal, VA 22630-5103
Telephone: 540-636-2900 Ext. 290 or toll-free 800-877-5456 Ext. 290
Fax: 540-636-1655
E-mail: tmcfadden@christendom.edu

Academics
Christendom awards associate, bachelor's, and master's **degrees. Challenging opportunities** include advanced placement credit, accelerated degree programs, double majors, independent study, and a senior project. Special programs include cooperative education, internships, summer session for credit, and study-abroad.

The most frequently chosen **baccalaureate** fields are history, theology and religious vocations, and English. A complete listing of majors at Christendom appears in the Majors by College index beginning on page 469.

The **faculty** at Christendom has 20 full-time members, 65% with terminal degrees. The student-faculty ratio is 14:1.

Students of Christendom
The student body totals 474, of whom 421 are undergraduates. 53.7% are women and 46.3% are men. Students come from 45 states and territories and 6 other countries. 25% are from Virginia. 3.6% are international students. 0.5% are African American, 0.2% American Indian, 2.1% Asian American, and 1.9% Hispanic American. 91% returned for their sophomore year.

Facilities and Resources
60 **computers/terminals** are available on campus for general student use. Students can access the following: computer help desk, free student e-mail accounts. Wireless service is available via student centers. The **library** has 64,265 books and 262 subscriptions.

Campus Life
There are 15 active organizations on campus, including a drama/theater group, newspaper, and choral group. No national or local **fraternities** or **sororities**.

Intercollegiate sports include baseball (m), basketball, golf, soccer, volleyball (w).

Campus Safety
Student safety services include night patrols by trained security personnel, late-night transport/escort service, and 24-hour emergency telephone alarm devices.

Applying
Christendom requires an essay, SAT or ACT, a high school transcript, and 2 recommendations. It recommends an interview and a minimum high school GPA of 3.0. Application deadline: 3/1; 4/1 priority date for financial aid. Early admission is possible.

Getting Accepted
271 applied
88% were accepted
123 enrolled (51% of accepted)
40% from top tenth of their h.s. class
3.6 average high school GPA
65% had SAT critical reading scores over 600
38% had SAT math scores over 600
59% had SAT writing scores over 600
27% had SAT critical reading scores over 700
5% had SAT math scores over 700
22% had SAT writing scores over 700
2 National Merit Scholars
2 class presidents
2 valedictorians

Graduation and After
74% graduated in 4 years
1% graduated in 5 years
2% graduated in 6 years
76% had job offers within 6 months
6 organizations recruited on campus

Financial Matters
$18,756 tuition and fees (2008–09)
$6688 room and board
90% average percent of need met
$14,235 average financial aid amount received per undergraduate (2007–08 estimated)

CHRISTIAN BROTHERS UNIVERSITY

URBAN SETTING ■ PRIVATE ■ INDEPENDENT RELIGIOUS ■ COED
MEMPHIS, TENNESSEE

Web site: www.cbu.edu
Contact: Ms. Tracey Dysart-Ford, Dean of Admissions, 650 East Parkway
South, Memphis, TN 38104
Telephone: 901-321-3205 or toll-free 800-288-7576
Fax: 901-321-3202
E-mail: admissions@cbu.edu

Getting Accepted

1,634 applied
59% were accepted
308 enrolled (32% of accepted)
40% from top tenth of their h.s. class
3.66 average high school GPA
Mean SAT critical reading score: 534
Mean SAT math score: 545
Mean ACT score: 25
22% had SAT critical reading scores over 600
34% had SAT math scores over 600
58% had ACT scores over 24
6% had SAT critical reading scores over 700
5% had SAT math scores over 700
12% had ACT scores over 30
8 valedictorians

Graduation and After

40% graduated in 4 years
16% graduated in 5 years
3% graduated in 6 years
92% had job offers within 6 months
246 organizations recruited on campus

Financial Matters

$22,600 tuition and fees (2008–09)
$5880 room and board
84% average percent of need met
$17,365 average financial aid amount received
per undergraduate (2007–08 estimated)

Academics

CBU awards bachelor's and master's **degrees** and post-bachelor's certificates. **Challenging opportunities** include advanced placement credit, accelerated degree programs, an honors program, double majors, independent study, and a senior project. Special programs include cooperative education, internships, summer session for credit, off-campus study, study-abroad, and Army, Navy, and Air Force ROTC.

The most frequently chosen **baccalaureate** fields are business/marketing, psychology, and engineering. A complete listing of majors at CBU appears in the Majors by College index beginning on page 469.

The **faculty** at CBU has 96 full-time members, 89% with terminal degrees. The student-faculty ratio is 13:1.

Students of CBU

The student body totals 1,869, of whom 1,420 are undergraduates. 54.7% are women and 45.3% are men. Students come from 29 states and territories and 18 other countries. 77% are from Tennessee. 2% are international students. 32% are African American, 0.3% American Indian, 5% Asian American, and 2.9% Hispanic American. 81% returned for their sophomore year.

Facilities and Resources

310 **computers/terminals** are available on campus for general student use. Students can access the following: campus intranet, computer help desk, free student e-mail accounts, online (class) grades, online (class) registration, online (class) schedules, online class listings, course assignments. Campuswide network is available. 100% of college-owned or -operated housing units are wired for high-speed Internet access. Wireless service is available via classrooms, computer centers, computer labs, libraries. The **library** has 182,060 books and 384 subscriptions.

Campus Life

There are 37 active organizations on campus, including a drama/theater group and choral group. 24% of eligible men and 22% of eligible women are members of national **fraternities**, national **sororities**, and local sororities.

CBU is a member of the NCAA (Division II). **Intercollegiate sports** (some offering scholarships) include baseball (m), basketball, cross-country running, golf, soccer, softball (w), tennis, volleyball (w).

Campus Safety

Student safety services include late-night transport/escort service, 24-hour emergency telephone alarm devices, 24-hour patrols by trained security personnel, student patrols, and electronically operated dormitory entrances.

Applying

CBU requires an essay, SAT or ACT, a high school transcript, and a minimum high school GPA of 2.0, and in some cases 2 recommendations. It recommends an interview. Application deadline: 8/1; 2/15 priority date for financial aid. Early and deferred admission are possible.

CLAREMONT MCKENNA COLLEGE

SMALL-TOWN SETTING ■ PRIVATE ■ INDEPENDENT ■ COED
CLAREMONT, CALIFORNIA

Web site: www.claremontmckenna.edu
Contact: Mr. Richard C. Vos, Vice President/Dean of Admission and
   Financial Aid, 890 Columbia Avenue, Claremont, CA 91711
Telephone: 909-621-8088
Fax: 909-621-8516
E-mail: admission@claremontmckenna.edu

Academics

CMC awards bachelor's and master's **degrees**. **Challenging opportunities** include advanced placement credit, accelerated degree programs, student-designed majors, an honors program, double majors, independent study, and a senior project. Special programs include internships, off-campus study, study-abroad, and Army and Air Force ROTC.

The most frequently chosen **baccalaureate** fields are social sciences, business/marketing, and psychology. A complete listing of majors at CMC appears in the Majors by College index beginning on page 469.

The **faculty** at CMC has 122 full-time members, 99% with terminal degrees. The student-faculty ratio is 8:1.

Students of CMC

The student body is made up of 1,212 undergraduates. 46% are women and 54% are men. Students come from 47 states and territories and 24 other countries. 46% are from California. 5.8% are international students. 3.8% are African American, 0.2% American Indian, 12.4% Asian American, and 11.3% Hispanic American. 97% returned for their sophomore year.

Facilities and Resources

153 **computers/terminals** are available on campus for general student use. Students can access the following: campus intranet, computer help desk, free student e-mail accounts, online (class) grades, online (class) schedules. Campuswide network is available. 100% of college-owned or -operated housing units are wired for high-speed Internet access. Wireless service is available via entire campus. The 4 **libraries** have 2,028,793 books and 6,028 subscriptions.

Campus Life

There are 280 active organizations on campus, including a drama/theater group, newspaper, radio station, television station, and choral group. No national or local **fraternities** or **sororities**.

CMC is a member of the NCAA (Division III). **Intercollegiate sports** include baseball (m), basketball, cross-country running, football (m), golf (m), lacrosse (w), soccer, softball (w), swimming and diving, tennis, track and field, volleyball (w), water polo.

Campus Safety

Student safety services include late-night transport/escort service, 24-hour emergency telephone alarm devices, 24-hour patrols by trained security personnel, student patrols, and electronically operated dormitory entrances.

Applying

CMC requires an essay, SAT or ACT, a high school transcript, and 3 recommendations, and in some cases SAT Subject Tests. It recommends an interview. Application deadline: 1/2. Early and deferred admission are possible.

Getting Accepted

3,670 applied
22% were accepted
320 enrolled (40% of accepted)
85% from top tenth of their h.s. class
Mean SAT critical reading score: 700
Mean SAT math score: 710
92% had SAT critical reading scores over 600
91% had SAT math scores over 600
52% had SAT critical reading scores over 700
55% had SAT math scores over 700
29 National Merit Scholars
29 class presidents
26 valedictorians

Graduation and After

90% graduated in 4 years
4% graduated in 5 years
100% had job offers within 6 months
135 organizations recruited on campus

Financial Matters

$36,825 tuition and fees (2008–09)
$11,930 room and board
100% average percent of need met
$28,191 average financial aid amount received
   per undergraduate (2006–07)

CLARKE COLLEGE

URBAN SETTING ■ PRIVATE ■ INDEPENDENT RELIGIOUS ■ COED
DUBUQUE, IOWA

Web site: www.clarke.edu
Contact: Mr. Andy Shroeder, Director of Admissions, 1550 Clarke Drive,
  Dubuque, IA 52001-3198
Telephone: 563-588-6316 or toll-free 800-383-2345
Fax: 563-588-6789
E-mail: admissions@clarke.edu

Getting Accepted

947 applied
62% were accepted
136 enrolled (23% of accepted)
19% from top tenth of their h.s. class
3.37 average high school GPA
Mean SAT critical reading score: 488
Mean SAT math score: 512
Mean SAT writing score: 452
Mean ACT score: 23
46% had ACT scores over 24
4% had ACT scores over 30

Graduation and After

49% graduated in 4 years
14% graduated in 5 years
1% graduated in 6 years
70% had job offers within 6 months
78 organizations recruited on campus

Financial Matters

$23,520 tuition and fees (2009–10)
$6840 room and board
85% average percent of need met
$18,369 average financial aid amount received
  per undergraduate

Academics

Clarke awards associate, bachelor's, master's, and doctoral **degrees**. **Challenging opportunities** include advanced placement credit, accelerated degree programs, student-designed majors, an honors program, double majors, independent study, and a senior project. Special programs include cooperative education, internships, summer session for credit, off-campus study, study-abroad, and Army ROTC.

The most frequently chosen **baccalaureate** fields are health professions and related sciences, business/marketing, and education. A complete listing of majors at Clarke appears in the Majors by College index beginning on page 469.

The **faculty** at Clarke has 72 full-time members, 64% with terminal degrees. The student-faculty ratio is 11:1.

Students of Clarke

The student body totals 1,156, of whom 956 are undergraduates. 68.7% are women and 31.3% are men. Students come from 30 states and territories and 5 other countries. 62% are from Iowa. 1.8% are international students. 1.2% are African American, 0.3% Asian American, and 1.7% Hispanic American. 80% returned for their sophomore year.

Facilities and Resources

237 **computers/terminals** are available on campus for general student use. Students can access the following: campus intranet, free student e-mail accounts, online (class) grades, online (class) registration, online (class) schedules. Campuswide network is available. Wireless service is available via learning centers, libraries, student centers. The **library** has 120,000 books and 9,600 subscriptions.

Campus Life

There are 63 active organizations on campus, including a drama/theater group, newspaper, radio station, and choral group. No national or local **fraternities** or **sororities**.

Clarke is a member of the NAIA. **Intercollegiate sports** (some offering scholarships) include baseball (m), basketball, cheerleading (w), cross-country running, golf, soccer, softball (w), tennis (w), track and field, volleyball.

Campus Safety

Student safety services include late-night transport/escort service, 24-hour emergency telephone alarm devices, 24-hour patrols by trained security personnel, and electronically operated dormitory entrances.

Applying

Clarke requires SAT or ACT, a high school transcript, rank in upper 50% of high school class, minimum ACT score of 21 or SAT score of 1000, and a minimum high school GPA of 2.0, and in some cases an interview. Application deadline: rolling admissions; 4/15 priority date for financial aid. Deferred admission is possible.

CLARKSON UNIVERSITY

SMALL-TOWN SETTING ■ PRIVATE ■ INDEPENDENT ■ COED
POTSDAM, NEW YORK

SPONSOR

Web site: www.clarkson.edu
Contact: Mr. Brian Grant, Director of Admission, Holcroft House, Potsdam, NY 13699-5605
Telephone: 315-268-6480 or toll-free 800-527-6577
Fax: 315-268-7647
E-mail: admission@clarkson.edu

Academics

Clarkson awards bachelor's, master's, doctoral, and first-professional **degrees. Challenging opportunities** include advanced placement credit, accelerated degree programs, student-designed majors, an honors program, double majors, independent study, and a senior project. Special programs include cooperative education, internships, summer session for credit, off-campus study, study-abroad, and Army and Air Force ROTC.

The most frequently chosen **baccalaureate** fields are engineering, business/marketing, and biological/life sciences. A complete listing of majors at Clarkson appears in the Majors by College index beginning on page 469.

The **faculty** at Clarkson has 186 full-time members, 94% with terminal degrees. The student-faculty ratio is 15:1.

Students of Clarkson

The student body totals 3,045, of whom 2,593 are undergraduates. 27% are women and 73% are men. Students come from 42 states and territories and 25 other countries. 81% are from New York. 3.6% are international students. 2.8% are African American, 0.5% American Indian, 3% Asian American, and 2.6% Hispanic American. 83% returned for their sophomore year.

Facilities and Resources

400 **computers/terminals** and 10,000 ports are available on campus for general student use. Students can access the following: campus intranet, computer help desk, free student e-mail accounts, online (class) grades, online (class) registration, online (class) schedules. Campuswide network is available. 100% of college-owned or -operated housing units are wired for high-speed Internet access. Wireless service is available via classrooms, computer centers, computer labs, learning centers, libraries, student centers. The 2 **libraries** have 309,235 books and 3,396 subscriptions.

Campus Life

There are 56 active organizations on campus, including a drama/theater group, newspaper, radio station, television station, and choral group. 12% of eligible men and 13% of eligible women are members of national **fraternities**, national **sororities**, and local fraternities.

Clarkson is a member of the NCAA (Division III). **Intercollegiate sports** (some offering scholarships) include baseball (m), basketball, cross-country running, golf (m), ice hockey, lacrosse, skiing (cross-country), skiing (downhill), soccer, swimming and diving, volleyball (w).

Campus Safety

Student safety services include late-night transport/escort service, 24-hour emergency telephone alarm devices, 24-hour patrols by trained security personnel, and electronically operated dormitory entrances.

Applying

Clarkson requires SAT or ACT, a high school transcript, and 2 recommendations. It recommends SAT Subject Tests and an interview. Application deadline: 1/15; 2/15 priority date for financial aid. Early and deferred admission are possible.

Clarkson is New York State's highest-ranked small research institution, with majors in business, engineering, health sciences, liberal arts, and science. Located in upstate New York's Northern Adirondack region near the St. Lawrence River Valley, the 3,100-student campus combines high-powered academics with a friendly, personal atmosphere. Students enjoy easy access to Clarkson's faculty members, state-of-the-art learning facilities, and outstanding outdoor recreational opportunities. Rigorous academic programs emphasize interactive learning and a collaborative approach in project-based problem solving. Students develop technical expertise; skills in innovation, communication, and teamwork; and versatility vital in today's knowledge-based economy. For more than 100 years, Clarkson has been launching leaders. One in six Clarkson alumni is a president, vice president, or owner of a company.

Getting Accepted
3,204 applied
79% were accepted
735 enrolled (29% of accepted)
38% from top tenth of their h.s. class
3.48 average high school GPA
Mean SAT critical reading score: 556
Mean SAT math score: 613
Mean SAT writing score: 540
Mean ACT score: 26
31% had SAT critical reading scores over 600
60% had SAT math scores over 600
21% had SAT writing scores over 600
72% had ACT scores over 24
4% had SAT critical reading scores over 700
13% had SAT math scores over 700
3% had SAT writing scores over 700
18% had ACT scores over 30
19 valedictorians

Graduation and After
58% graduated in 4 years
12% graduated in 5 years
2% graduated in 6 years
34% had job offers within 6 months
91 organizations recruited on campus

Financial Matters
$32,910 tuition and fees (2009–10)
$11,118 room and board
87% average percent of need met
$22,572 average financial aid amount received per undergraduate (2007–08 estimated)

CLARK UNIVERSITY

URBAN SETTING ■ PRIVATE ■ INDEPENDENT ■ COED
WORCESTER, MASSACHUSETTS

Web site: www.clarku.edu
Contact: Mr. Harold Wingood, Dean of Admissions, Admissions House, 950
Main Street, Worcester, MA 01610
Telephone: 508-793-7431 or toll-free 800-GO-CLARK
Fax: 508-793-8821
E-mail: admissions@clarku.edu

Getting Accepted

5,299 applied
56% were accepted
591 enrolled (20% of accepted)
39% from top tenth of their h.s. class
3.48 average high school GPA
Mean SAT critical reading score: 604
Mean SAT math score: 596
Mean ACT score: 26
56% had SAT critical reading scores over 600
49% had SAT math scores over 600
82% had ACT scores over 24
15% had SAT critical reading scores over 700
9% had SAT math scores over 700
17% had ACT scores over 30

Graduation and After

67% graduated in 4 years
5% graduated in 5 years
1% graduated in 6 years
80 organizations recruited on campus

Financial Matters

$35,220 tuition and fees (2009–10)
$6750 room and board
94% average percent of need met
$24,581 average financial aid amount received
per undergraduate (2007–08 estimated)

Academics

Clark awards bachelor's, master's, and doctoral **degrees** and post-bachelor's and post-master's certificates. **Challenging opportunities** include advanced placement credit, accelerated degree programs, student-designed majors, an honors program, double majors, independent study, and a senior project. Special programs include internships, summer session for credit, off-campus study, study-abroad, and Army, Navy, and Air Force ROTC.

The most frequently chosen **baccalaureate** fields are social sciences, psychology, and biological/life sciences. A complete listing of majors at Clark appears in the Majors by College index beginning on page 469.

The **faculty** at Clark has 184 full-time members, 97% with terminal degrees. The student-faculty ratio is 10:1.

Students of Clark

The student body totals 3,330, of whom 2,380 are undergraduates. 59.8% are women and 40.2% are men. Students come from 44 states and territories and 72 other countries. 36% are from Massachusetts. 8.4% are international students. 2.1% are African American, 0.3% American Indian, 4.1% Asian American, and 2.3% Hispanic American. 88% returned for their sophomore year.

Facilities and Resources

96 **computers/terminals** and 4,000 ports are available on campus for general student use. Students can access the following: campus intranet, computer help desk, free student e-mail accounts, online (class) grades, online (class) registration, online (class) schedules, online course support. Campuswide network is available. 100% of college-owned or -operated housing units are wired for high-speed Internet access. Wireless service is available via classrooms, computer centers, computer labs, learning centers, libraries, student centers. The 5 **libraries** have 289,658 books and 1,383 subscriptions.

Campus Life

There are 80 active organizations on campus, including a drama/theater group, newspaper, radio station, television station, choral group, and marching band. No national or local **fraternities** or **sororities**.

Clark is a member of the NCAA (Division III). **Intercollegiate sports** include baseball (m), basketball, crew, cross-country running, field hockey (w), lacrosse (m), soccer, softball (w), swimming and diving, tennis, volleyball (w).

Campus Safety

Student safety services include late-night transport/escort service, 24-hour emergency telephone alarm devices, 24-hour patrols by trained security personnel, student patrols, and electronically operated dormitory entrances.

Applying

Clark requires an essay, SAT or ACT, a high school transcript, and 2 recommendations. It recommends an interview. Application deadline: 1/15; 2/1 for financial aid, with a 2/1 priority date. Early and deferred admission are possible.

CLEMSON UNIVERSITY

SMALL-TOWN SETTING ■ PUBLIC ■ STATE-SUPPORTED ■ COED
CLEMSON, SOUTH CAROLINA

SPONSOR

Web site: www.clemson.edu
Contact: Ms. Audrey R. Bodell, Associate Director of Admissions, PO Box 345124, 105 Sikes Hall, Clemson, SC 29634
Telephone: 864-656-2287
Fax: 864-656-2464
E-mail: cuadmissions@clemson.edu

Academics

Clemson awards bachelor's, master's, and doctoral **degrees** and post-master's certificates. **Challenging opportunities** include advanced placement credit, an honors program, double majors, independent study, and a senior project. Special programs include cooperative education, internships, summer session for credit, study-abroad, and Army and Air Force ROTC.

The most frequently chosen **baccalaureate** fields are business/marketing, engineering, and education. A complete listing of majors at Clemson appears in the Majors by College index beginning on page 469.

The **faculty** at Clemson has 1,106 full-time members. The student-faculty ratio is 14:1.

Students of Clemson

The student body totals 18,317, of whom 14,713 are undergraduates. 45.8% are women and 54.2% are men. Students come from 53 states and territories and 84 other countries. 71% are from South Carolina. 0.9% are international students. 7.2% are African American, 0.3% American Indian, 1.6% Asian American, and 1.3% Hispanic American. 92% returned for their sophomore year.

Facilities and Resources

1,250 **computers/terminals** are available on campus for general student use. Students can access the following: online (class) registration. Campuswide network is available. 100% of college-owned or -operated housing units are wired for high-speed Internet access. Wireless service is available via entire campus. The 2 **libraries** have 1,233,478 books and 5,587 subscriptions.

Campus Life

There are 350 active organizations on campus, including a drama/theater group, newspaper, radio station, television station, choral group, and marching band. 17% of eligible men and 23% of eligible women are members of national **fraternities** and national **sororities**.

Clemson is a member of the NCAA (Division I). **Intercollegiate sports** (some offering scholarships) include baseball (m), basketball, cheerleading, crew (w), cross-country running, football (m), golf (m), soccer, swimming and diving, tennis, track and field, volleyball (w).

Campus Safety

Student safety services include late-night transport/escort service, 24-hour emergency telephone alarm devices, 24-hour patrols by trained security personnel, and electronically operated dormitory entrances.

Applying

Clemson requires SAT or ACT and a high school transcript. It recommends an essay. Application deadline: 5/1; 4/1 priority date for financial aid.

Getting Accepted
14,504 applied
58% were accepted
2,923 enrolled (35% of accepted)
54% from top tenth of their h.s. class
3.89 average high school GPA
51% had SAT critical reading scores over 600
71% had SAT math scores over 600
86% had ACT scores over 24
9% had SAT critical reading scores over 700
17% had SAT math scores over 700
27% had ACT scores over 30
26 National Merit Scholars
94 valedictorians

Graduation and After
50% graduated in 4 years
26% graduated in 5 years
3% graduated in 6 years
45% had job offers within 6 months
212 organizations recruited on campus

Financial Matters
$11,108 resident tuition and fees (2008–09)
$24,130 nonresident tuition and fees (2008–09)
$6556 room and board
61% average percent of need met
$10,057 average financial aid amount received per undergraduate (2007–08 estimated)

COE COLLEGE

URBAN SETTING ■ PRIVATE ■ INDEPENDENT RELIGIOUS ■ COED
CEDAR RAPIDS, IOWA

Web site: www.coe.edu
Contact: Mr. John Grundig, Dean of Admission, 1220 1st Avenue, NE, Cedar Rapids, IA 52402-5070
Telephone: 319-399-8500 or toll-free 877-225-5263
Fax: 319-399-8816
E-mail: admission@coe.edu

Getting Accepted
1,647 applied
68% were accepted
276 enrolled (25% of accepted)
34% from top tenth of their h.s. class
3.68 average high school GPA
Mean SAT critical reading score: 607
Mean SAT math score: 598
Mean ACT score: 25
70% had SAT critical reading scores over 600
78% had SAT math scores over 600
67% had ACT scores over 24
23% had SAT critical reading scores over 700
22% had SAT math scores over 700
13% had ACT scores over 30
8 valedictorians

Graduation and After
98% had job offers within 6 months
83 organizations recruited on campus

Financial Matters
$34,610 comprehensive fee (2008–09)
94% average percent of need met
$23,422 average financial aid amount received per undergraduate (2007–08 estimated)

Academics

Coe awards bachelor's and master's **degrees**. **Challenging opportunities** include advanced placement credit, accelerated degree programs, student-designed majors, an honors program, double majors, independent study, and a senior project. Special programs include internships, summer session for credit, off-campus study, study-abroad, and Army and Air Force ROTC.

The most frequently chosen **baccalaureate** fields are social sciences, business/marketing, and psychology. A complete listing of majors at Coe appears in the Majors by College index beginning on page 469.

The **faculty** at Coe has 77 full-time members, 94% with terminal degrees. The student-faculty ratio is 10:1.

Students of Coe

The student body totals 1,300, of whom 1,275 are undergraduates. 54.4% are women and 45.6% are men. Students come from 43 states and territories and 18 other countries. 64% are from Iowa. 4.4% are international students. 2.4% are African American, 0.5% American Indian, 1% Asian American, and 1.8% Hispanic American. 82% returned for their sophomore year.

Facilities and Resources

275 **computers/terminals** are available on campus for general student use. Students can access the following: online (class) registration. Campuswide network is available. The 2 **libraries** have 218,881 books and 1,576 subscriptions.

Campus Life

There are 60 active organizations on campus, including a drama/theater group, newspaper, radio station, and choral group. 26% of eligible men and 19% of eligible women are members of national **fraternities** and national **sororities**.

Coe is a member of the NCAA (Division III). **Intercollegiate sports** include baseball (m), basketball, cheerleading (w), cross-country running, football (m), golf, soccer, softball (w), swimming and diving, tennis, track and field, volleyball (w), wrestling (m).

Campus Safety

Student safety services include late-night transport/escort service, 24-hour emergency telephone alarm devices, 24-hour patrols by trained security personnel, and electronically operated dormitory entrances.

Applying

Coe requires an essay, SAT or ACT, a high school transcript, and 1 recommendation. It recommends an interview and a minimum high school GPA of 3.0. Application deadline: 3/1; 3/1 priority date for financial aid. Early and deferred admission are possible.

COLBY COLLEGE

SMALL-TOWN SETTING ■ PRIVATE ■ INDEPENDENT ■ COED
WATERVILLE, MAINE

Web site: www.colby.edu
Contact: Mr. Steve Thomas, Director of Admissions, Office of Admissions
and Financial Aid, 4800 Mayflower Hill, Waterville, ME 04901-8848
Telephone: 207-859-4800 or toll-free 800-723-3032
Fax: 207-859-4828
E-mail: admissions@colby.edu

Academics

Colby awards bachelor's **degrees. Challenging opportunities** include advanced placement credit, student-designed majors, an honors program, double majors, independent study, and a senior project. Special programs include internships, off-campus study, study-abroad, and Army ROTC.

The most frequently chosen **baccalaureate** fields are social sciences, area and ethnic studies, and biological/life sciences. A complete listing of majors at Colby appears in the Majors by College index beginning on page 469.

The **faculty** at Colby has 164 full-time members, 93% with terminal degrees. The student-faculty ratio is 10:1.

Students of Colby

The student body is made up of 1,846 undergraduates. 54.1% are women and 45.9% are men. Students come from 48 states and territories and 59 other countries. 11% are from Maine. 5.4% are international students. 2.2% are African American, 0.5% American Indian, 8.1% Asian American, and 2.7% Hispanic American. 96% returned for their sophomore year.

Facilities and Resources

350 **computers/terminals** are available on campus for general student use. Students can access the following: campus intranet, computer help desk, free student e-mail accounts, online (class) grades, online (class) registration, online (class) schedules, Portal. Campuswide network is available. 100% of college-owned or -operated housing units are wired for high-speed Internet access. Wireless service is available via classrooms, computer centers, computer labs, dorm rooms, learning centers, libraries, student centers. The 3 **libraries** have 814,952 books and 10,177 subscriptions.

Campus Life

There are 98 active organizations on campus, including a drama/theater group, newspaper, radio station, and choral group. No national or local **fraternities** or **sororities**.

Colby is a member of the NCAA (Division III). **Intercollegiate sports** include baseball (m), basketball, crew, cross-country running, field hockey (w), football, golf, ice hockey, lacrosse, skiing (cross-country), skiing (downhill), soccer, softball (w), squash, swimming and diving, tennis, track and field, volleyball (w).

Campus Safety

Student safety services include campus lighting, student emergency response team, self-defense class, property id program, party monitors, late-night transport/escort service, 24-hour emergency telephone alarm devices, 24-hour patrols by trained security personnel, and electronically operated dormitory entrances.

Applying

Colby requires an essay, a high school transcript, and 2 recommendations, and in some cases SAT Subject Tests and SAT or ACT. It recommends an interview. Application deadline: 1/1; 2/1 for financial aid. Early and deferred admission are possible.

Getting Accepted

4,835 applied
31% were accepted
482 enrolled (32% of accepted)
61% from top tenth of their h.s. class
Mean SAT critical reading score: 676
Mean SAT math score: 677
Mean SAT writing score: 669
Mean ACT score: 30
90% had SAT critical reading scores over 600
92% had SAT math scores over 600
85% had SAT writing scores over 600
99% had ACT scores over 24
39% had SAT critical reading scores over 700
38% had SAT math scores over 700
38% had SAT writing scores over 700
52% had ACT scores over 30
3 National Merit Scholars
14 valedictorians

Graduation and After

84% graduated in 4 years
6% graduated in 5 years
1% graduated in 6 years
65% had job offers within 6 months
45 organizations recruited on campus

Financial Matters

$48,520 comprehensive fee (2008–09)
100% average percent of need met
$29,960 average financial aid amount received per undergraduate (2007–08 estimated)

COLGATE UNIVERSITY

RURAL SETTING ■ PRIVATE ■ INDEPENDENT ■ COED
HAMILTON, NEW YORK

Web site: www.colgate.edu
Contact: Mr. Gary L. Ross, Dean of Admission, 13 Oak Drive, Hamilton, NY 13346-1383
Telephone: 315-228-7401
Fax: 315-228-7544
E-mail: admission@mail.colgate.edu

Getting Accepted

9,416 applied
24% were accepted
738 enrolled (33% of accepted)
65% from top tenth of their h.s. class
3.7 average high school GPA
Mean SAT critical reading score: 669
Mean SAT math score: 682
Mean ACT score: 30
84% had SAT critical reading scores over 600
87% had SAT math scores over 600
97% had ACT scores over 24
39% had SAT critical reading scores over 700
46% had SAT math scores over 700
62% had ACT scores over 30
32 valedictorians

Graduation and After

87% graduated in 4 years
4% graduated in 5 years
1% graduated in 6 years
80% had job offers within 6 months
132 organizations recruited on campus

Financial Matters

$39,545 tuition and fees (2008–09)
$9625 room and board
100% average percent of need met
$34,659 average financial aid amount received per undergraduate (2007–08 estimated)

Academics

Colgate awards bachelor's and master's **degrees**. **Challenging opportunities** include advanced placement credit, student-designed majors, an honors program, double majors, independent study, and a senior project. Special programs include internships, off-campus study, study-abroad, and Army ROTC.

The most frequently chosen **baccalaureate** fields are social sciences, English, and history. A complete listing of majors at Colgate appears in the Majors by College index beginning on page 469.

The **faculty** at Colgate has 263 full-time members, 98% with terminal degrees. The student-faculty ratio is 10:1.

Students of Colgate

The student body totals 2,844, of whom 2,836 are undergraduates. 51.7% are women and 48.3% are men. Students come from 40 states and territories and 33 other countries. 28% are from New York. 4.8% are international students. 5.6% are African American, 0.6% American Indian, 5.9% Asian American, and 6.2% Hispanic American. 94% returned for their sophomore year.

Facilities and Resources

Students can access the following: campus intranet, computer help desk, free student e-mail accounts, online (class) registration, online (class) schedules, software applications. Campuswide network is available. 100% of college-owned or -operated housing units are wired for high-speed Internet access. The 2 **libraries** have 1,172,551 books and 29,632 subscriptions.

Campus Life

There are 180 active organizations on campus, including a drama/theater group, newspaper, radio station, television station, and choral group. 30% of eligible men and 20% of eligible women are members of national **fraternities**, national **sororities**, and local fraternities.

Colgate is a member of the NCAA (Division I). **Intercollegiate sports** (some offering scholarships) include basketball, crew, cross-country running, field hockey (w), football (m), golf (m), ice hockey, lacrosse, soccer, softball (w), swimming and diving, tennis, track and field, volleyball (w).

Campus Safety

Student safety services include late-night transport/escort service, 24-hour emergency telephone alarm devices, 24-hour patrols by trained security personnel, student patrols, and electronically operated dormitory entrances.

Applying

Colgate requires an essay, SAT or ACT, a high school transcript, and 3 recommendations. Application deadline: 1/15; 1/15 for financial aid. Deferred admission is possible.

College of Charleston

Urban setting ■ Public ■ State-supported ■ Coed
Charleston, South Carolina

Web site: www.cofc.edu
Contact: Ms. Suzette Stille, Director of Undergraduate Admissions, 66 George Street, Charleston, SC 29424-0001
Telephone: 843-953-5670 or toll-free 843-953-5670 (in-state)
Fax: 843-953-6322
E-mail: admissions@cofc.edu

Academics

C of C awards bachelor's and master's **degrees** and post-bachelor's certificates (also offers graduate degree programs through University of Charleston, South Carolina). **Challenging opportunities** include advanced placement credit, accelerated degree programs, an honors program, double majors, independent study, and a senior project. Special programs include cooperative education, internships, summer session for credit, off-campus study, study-abroad, and Air Force ROTC.

The most frequently chosen **baccalaureate** fields are business/marketing, communications/journalism, and social sciences. A complete listing of majors at C of C appears in the Majors by College index beginning on page 469.

The **faculty** at C of C has 523 full-time members, 87% with terminal degrees. The student-faculty ratio is 13:1.

Students of C of C

The student body totals 11,367, of whom 9,784 are undergraduates. 63.4% are women and 36.6% are men. Students come from 50 states and territories and 66 other countries. 66% are from South Carolina. 1.3% are international students. 5.7% are African American, 0.3% American Indian, 1.8% Asian American, and 2.1% Hispanic American. 80% returned for their sophomore year.

Facilities and Resources

578 **computers/terminals** are available on campus for general student use. Students can access the following: computer help desk, free student e-mail accounts, online (class) registration, online (class) schedules. Campuswide network is available. 100% of college-owned or -operated housing units are wired for high-speed Internet access. Wireless service is available via entire campus. The 2 **libraries** have 762,034 books and 3,075 subscriptions.

Campus Life

There are 144 active organizations on campus, including a drama/theater group, newspaper, radio station, and choral group. 11% of eligible men and 16% of eligible women are members of national **fraternities**, national **sororities**, local fraternities, and local sororities.

C of C is a member of the NCAA (Division I). **Intercollegiate sports** (some offering scholarships) include baseball (m), basketball, cheerleading, cross-country running, equestrian sports (w), golf, sailing, soccer, softball (w), swimming and diving, tennis, track and field (w), volleyball (w).

Campus Safety

Student safety services include late-night transport/escort service, 24-hour emergency telephone alarm devices, 24-hour patrols by trained security personnel, student patrols, and electronically operated dormitory entrances.

Applying

C of C requires an essay, SAT or ACT, and a high school transcript. It recommends an interview. Application deadline: 4/1; 3/15 priority date for financial aid. Deferred admission is possible.

Getting Accepted
9,964 applied
64% were accepted
1,956 enrolled (31% of accepted)
26% from top tenth of their h.s. class
3.85 average high school GPA
Mean SAT critical reading score: 612
Mean SAT math score: 609
Mean ACT score: 25
60% had SAT critical reading scores over 600
59% had SAT math scores over 600
66% had ACT scores over 24
9% had SAT critical reading scores over 700
7% had SAT math scores over 700
6% had ACT scores over 30

Graduation and After
47% graduated in 4 years
14% graduated in 5 years
3% graduated in 6 years
94.3% had job offers within 6 months
271 organizations recruited on campus

Financial Matters
$8400 resident tuition and fees (2008–09)
$20,418 nonresident tuition and fees (2008–09)
$8999 room and board
66% average percent of need met
$11,492 average financial aid amount received per undergraduate (2007–08 estimated)

THE COLLEGE OF IDAHO

SUBURBAN SETTING ■ PRIVATE ■ INDEPENDENT ■ COED
CALDWELL, IDAHO

Web site: www.collegeofidaho.edu
Contact: 2112 Cleveland Boulevard, Caldwell, ID 83605-4494
Telephone: 208-459-5689 or toll-free 800-244-3246
Fax: 208-459-5151
E-mail: admission@collegeofidaho.edu

Getting Accepted
1,275 applied
59% were accepted
272 enrolled (36% of accepted)
29% from top tenth of their h.s. class
3.63 average high school GPA
Mean SAT critical reading score: 543
Mean SAT math score: 551
Mean SAT writing score: 514
Mean ACT score: 25
32% had SAT critical reading scores over 600
35% had SAT math scores over 600
19% had SAT writing scores over 600
61% had ACT scores over 24
8% had SAT critical reading scores over 700
5% had SAT math scores over 700
15% had ACT scores over 30

Graduation and After
50% graduated in 4 years
12% graduated in 5 years
6% graduated in 6 years
13 organizations recruited on campus

Financial Matters
$20,070 tuition and fees (2009–10)
$7478 room and board
89% average percent of need met
$15,382 average financial aid amount received
   per undergraduate (2007–08 estimated)

Academics
The C of I awards bachelor's and master's **degrees. Challenging opportunities** include advanced placement credit, student-designed majors, an honors program, double majors, independent study, and a senior project. Special programs include cooperative education, internships, off-campus study, study-abroad, and Army ROTC.

The most frequently chosen **baccalaureate** fields are biological/life sciences, psychology, and business/marketing. A complete listing of majors at The C of I appears in the Majors by College index beginning on page 469.

The **faculty** at The C of I has 65 full-time members, 82% with terminal degrees. The student-faculty ratio is 11:1.

Students of The C of I
The student body totals 944, of whom 928 are undergraduates. 59.5% are women and 40.5% are men. Students come from 26 states and territories and 28 other countries. 75% are from Idaho. 5.7% are international students. 1.2% are African American, 0.3% American Indian, 2.3% Asian American, and 7.8% Hispanic American. 80% returned for their sophomore year.

Facilities and Resources
242 **computers/terminals** are available on campus for general student use. Students can access the following: campus intranet, computer help desk, free student e-mail accounts, online (class) grades, online (class) registration, online (class) schedules, online course syllabi, course assignments, course discussion, online yearly catalog, College You_Tube. Campuswide network is available. 100% of college-owned or -operated housing units are wired for high-speed Internet access. Wireless service is available via entire campus. The **library** has 154,437 books and 1,758 subscriptions.

Campus Life
There are 55 active organizations on campus, including a drama/theater group, newspaper, radio station, and choral group. 21% of eligible men and 20% of eligible women are members of national **fraternities**, national **sororities**, local fraternities, and local sororities.

The C of I is a member of the NAIA. **Intercollegiate sports** (some offering scholarships) include baseball (m), basketball, cross-country running, golf, skiing (cross-country), skiing (downhill), soccer, softball (w), swimming and diving, tennis (w), track and field, volleyball (w).

Campus Safety
Student safety services include late-night transport/escort service, 24-hour emergency telephone alarm devices, 24-hour patrols by trained security personnel, student patrols, and electronically operated dormitory entrances.

Applying
The C of I requires an essay, SAT and SAT Subject Tests or ACT, a high school transcript, and 1 recommendation. It recommends an interview and extracurricular activities. Application deadline: 8/1; 2/15 priority date for financial aid. Early and deferred admission are possible.

THE COLLEGE OF NEW JERSEY

SUBURBAN SETTING ■ PUBLIC ■ STATE-SUPPORTED ■ COED
EWING, NEW JERSEY

SPONSOR

Web site: www.tcnj.edu
Contact: Ms. Lisa Angeloni, Dean of Admissions, PO Box 7718, Ewing, NJ 08628
Telephone: 609-771-2131 or toll-free 800-624-0967
Fax: 609-637-5174
E-mail: admiss@tcnj.edu

Academics

TCNJ awards bachelor's and master's **degrees** and post-bachelor's and post-master's certificates. **Challenging opportunities** include advanced placement credit, student-designed majors, an honors program, double majors, independent study, and a senior project. Special programs include internships, summer session for credit, off-campus study, study-abroad, and Army and Air Force ROTC.

The most frequently chosen **baccalaureate** fields are education, business/marketing, and English. A complete listing of majors at TCNJ appears in the Majors by College index beginning on page 469.

The **faculty** at TCNJ has 343 full-time members, 87% with terminal degrees. The student-faculty ratio is 13:1.

Students of TCNJ

The student body totals 6,949, of whom 6,244 are undergraduates. 58.6% are women and 41.4% are men. Students come from 21 states and territories and 11 other countries. 95% are from New Jersey. 0.2% are international students. 6.7% are African American, 0.1% American Indian, 6.2% Asian American, and 8.7% Hispanic American. 95% returned for their sophomore year.

Facilities and Resources

782 **computers/terminals** are available on campus for general student use. Students can access the following: campus intranet, computer help desk, free student e-mail accounts, online (class) grades, online (class) registration, online (class) schedules. Campuswide network is available. 100% of college-owned or -operated housing units are wired for high-speed Internet access. Wireless service is available via classrooms, computer labs, learning centers, libraries, student centers. The **library** has 674,051 books and 133,506 subscriptions.

Campus Life

There are 198 active organizations on campus, including a drama/theater group, newspaper, radio station, television station, and choral group. 13% of eligible men and 13% of eligible women are members of national **fraternities**, national **sororities**, local fraternities, and local sororities.

TCNJ is a member of the NCAA (Division III). **Intercollegiate sports** include baseball (m), basketball, cross-country running, field hockey (w), football (m), golf (m), lacrosse (w), soccer, softball (w), swimming and diving, tennis, track and field, wrestling (m).

Campus Safety

Student safety services include late-night transport/escort service, 24-hour emergency telephone alarm devices, 24-hour patrols by trained security personnel, student patrols, and electronically operated dormitory entrances.

Applying

TCNJ requires an essay, SAT, and a high school transcript, and in some cases an interview and art portfolio or music audition. It recommends 3 recommendations and a minimum high school GPA of 3.5. Application deadline: 2/15; 10/1 for financial aid, with a 3/1 priority date. Early and deferred admission are possible.

The College of New Jersey (TCNJ) is a highly selective institution that has earned national recognition for its commitment to excellence in undergraduate education. Founded in 1855, TCNJ's combination of small classes, close interaction with faculty members, and innovative academic programs offered on a picturesque, residential campus with state-of-the art facilities has made TCNJ the standard-bearer for undergraduate, public higher education. TCNJ currently is ranked as one of the seventy-five "Most Competitive" schools in the nation by *Barron's Profiles of American Colleges* and is rated the number one public master's institution in the northern region of the country by *U.S. News & World Report.* TCNJ was also awarded, in 2006, a Phi Beta Kappa chapter—an honor shared by less than 10 percent of colleges and universities nationally. TCNJ provides a wealth of opportunities that enable its 5,900 undergraduate students to enjoy a complete college experience. More than 150 campus organizations enable students to explore diverse interests. Additionally, TCNJ has maintained one of the most successful varsity athletic programs in the nation, garnering thirty-eight NCAA Division III national championships and thirty-two runner-up finishes.

Getting Accepted
9,692 applied
42% were accepted
1,295 enrolled (31% of accepted)
66% from top tenth of their h.s. class
Mean SAT critical reading score: 636
Mean SAT math score: 616
Mean SAT writing score: 607
60% had SAT critical reading scores over 600
71% had SAT math scores over 600
64% had SAT writing scores over 600
13% had SAT critical reading scores over 700
24% had SAT math scores over 700
16% had SAT writing scores over 700
36 class presidents

Graduation and After
68% graduated in 4 years
15% graduated in 5 years
3% graduated in 6 years
90% had job offers within 6 months
400 organizations recruited on campus

Financial Matters
$12,308 resident tuition and fees (2008–09)
$20,415 nonresident tuition and fees (2008–09)
$9612 room and board
55% average percent of need met
$9207 average financial aid amount received per undergraduate (2007–08 estimated)

Getting Accepted

1,677 applied
76% were accepted
537 enrolled (42% of accepted)
43% from top tenth of their h.s. class
3.75 average high school GPA
Mean SAT critical reading score: 582
Mean SAT math score: 586
Mean ACT score: 25
35% had SAT critical reading scores over 600
38% had SAT math scores over 600
67% had ACT scores over 24
12% had SAT critical reading scores over 700
9% had SAT math scores over 700
11% had ACT scores over 30

Graduation and After

75% graduated in 4 years
4% graduated in 5 years
72% had job offers within 6 months
118 organizations recruited on campus

Financial Matters

$28,628 tuition and fees (2008–09)
$7959 room and board
86% average percent of need met
$18,940 average financial aid amount received
per undergraduate (2006–07)

COLLEGE OF SAINT BENEDICT
COORDINATE WITH SAINT JOHN'S UNIVERSITY (MN)
SMALL-TOWN SETTING ■ PRIVATE ■ INDEPENDENT RELIGIOUS ■ WOMEN ONLY
SAINT JOSEPH, MINNESOTA

Web site: www.csbsju.edu
Contact: Ms. Karen Backes, Associate Dean of Admissions, 37 South College
    Avenue, St. Joseph, MN 56374
Telephone: 320-363-2196 or toll-free 800-544-1489
Fax: 320-363-2750
E-mail: admissions@csbsju.edu

Academics

CSB awards bachelor's **degrees** (coordinate with Saint John's University for men).
Challenging opportunities include advanced placement credit, accelerated degree
programs, student-designed majors, an honors program, double majors, independent
study, and a senior project. Special programs include internships, off-campus study,
study-abroad, and Army ROTC.

The most frequently chosen **baccalaureate** fields are English, health professions and
related sciences, and psychology. A complete listing of majors at CSB appears in the
Majors by College index beginning on page 469.

The **faculty** at CSB has 160 full-time members, 83% with terminal degrees. The
student-faculty ratio is 12:1.

Students of CSB

The student body is made up of 2,087 undergraduates. Students come from 34 states and
territories and 20 other countries. 84% are from Minnesota. 4.7% are international
students. 0.8% are African American, 0.3% American Indian, 2.8% Asian American, and
1.8% Hispanic American. 90% returned for their sophomore year.

Facilities and Resources

643 **computers/terminals** and 3,000 ports are available on campus for general student
use. Students can access the following: computer help desk, free student e-mail accounts,
online (class) grades, online (class) registration, online (class) schedules, online student
accounts. Campuswide network is available. 100% of college-owned or -operated
housing units are wired for high-speed Internet access. Wireless service is available via
classrooms, computer centers, computer labs, dorm rooms, learning centers, libraries,
student centers. The 4 **libraries** have 481,338 books and 5,315 subscriptions.

Campus Life

There are 90 active organizations on campus, including a drama/theater group,
newspaper, radio station, and choral group. No national or local **sororities**.

CSB is a member of the NCAA (Division III). **Intercollegiate sports** include
basketball, cross-country running, golf, ice hockey, skiing (cross-country), soccer,
softball, swimming and diving, tennis, track and field, volleyball.

Campus Safety

Student safety services include well-lit pathways, late-night transport/escort service,
24-hour emergency telephone alarm devices, 24-hour patrols by trained security
personnel, student patrols, and electronically operated dormitory entrances.

Applying

CSB requires an essay, SAT or ACT, a high school transcript, and 1 recommendation. It
recommends an interview and a minimum high school GPA of 3.0. Application deadline:
rolling admissions; 3/15 priority date for financial aid. Deferred admission is possible.

COLLEGE OF ST. CATHERINE

Urban setting ■ Private ■ Independent Religious
■ Undergraduate: Women Only; Graduate: Coed
St. Paul, Minnesota

Web site: www.stkate.edu
Contact: Ms. Cory Piper-Hauswirth, Associate Director of Admission and Financial Aid, 2004 Randolph Avenue, F-02, St. Paul, MN 55105
Telephone: 651-690-6047 or toll-free 800-656-5283 (in-state)
Fax: 651-690-8824
E-mail: stkate@stkate.edu

Academics

CSC awards associate, bachelor's, master's, and doctoral **degrees** and post-bachelor's certificates. **Challenging opportunities** include advanced placement credit, student-designed majors, an honors program, double majors, independent study, and a senior project. Special programs include internships, summer session for credit, off-campus study, study-abroad, and Army and Air Force ROTC.

The most frequently chosen **baccalaureate** fields are health professions and related sciences, business/marketing, and education. A complete listing of majors at CSC appears in the Majors by College index beginning on page 469.

The **faculty** at CSC has 261 full-time members. The student-faculty ratio is 11:1.

Students of CSC

The student body totals 5,246, of whom 3,831 are undergraduates. 96.1% are women and 3.9% are men. Students come from 37 states and territories and 16 other countries. 90% are from Minnesota. 1.6% are international students. 10.6% are African American, 0.5% American Indian, 7.3% Asian American, and 2.7% Hispanic American. 80% returned for their sophomore year.

Facilities and Resources

350 **computers/terminals** are available on campus for general student use. Students can access the following: transcript. Campuswide network is available. The 3 **libraries** have 263,495 books and 1,141 subscriptions.

Campus Life

There are 42 active organizations on campus, including a drama/theater group, newspaper, and choral group. 8% of eligible undergraduates are members of local **sororities**.

CSC is a member of the NCAA (Division III). **Intercollegiate sports** include basketball, cross-country running, ice hockey, soccer, softball, swimming and diving, tennis, track and field, volleyball.

Campus Safety

Student safety services include late-night transport/escort service, 24-hour emergency telephone alarm devices, 24-hour patrols by trained security personnel, student patrols, and electronically operated dormitory entrances.

Applying

CSC requires SAT or ACT, a high school transcript, and 1 recommendation, and in some cases an essay and an interview. It recommends an interview. Application deadline: rolling admissions; 4/15 priority date for financial aid. Deferred admission is possible.

Getting Accepted

1,632 applied
81% were accepted
437 enrolled (33% of accepted)
34% from top tenth of their h.s. class
3.64 average high school GPA
Mean ACT score: 23
55% had ACT scores over 24
4% had ACT scores over 30
4 National Merit Scholars
8 valedictorians

Graduation and After

82% had job offers within 6 months

Financial Matters

$27,414 tuition and fees (2008–09)
$7090 room and board
72% average percent of need met
$23,534 average financial aid amount received per undergraduate (2006–07)

THE COLLEGE OF ST. SCHOLASTICA

SUBURBAN SETTING ■ PRIVATE ■ INDEPENDENT RELIGIOUS ■ COED
DULUTH, MINNESOTA

Web site: www.css.edu
Contact: Mr. Eric Berg, Vice President for Enrollment Management, 1200
 Kenwood Avenue, Duluth, MN 55811-4199
Telephone: 218-723-6053 or toll-free 800-249-6412
Fax: 218-723-5991
E-mail: admissions@css.edu

Getting Accepted
1,899 applied
83% were accepted
537 enrolled (34% of accepted)
22% from top tenth of their h.s. class
3.44 average high school GPA
Mean SAT critical reading score: 518
Mean SAT math score: 556
Mean SAT writing score: 515
Mean ACT score: 23
22% had SAT critical reading scores over 600
32% had SAT math scores over 600
8% had SAT writing scores over 600
43% had ACT scores over 24
5% had SAT math scores over 700
4% had ACT scores over 30
8 valedictorians

Graduation and After
57% graduated in 4 years
5% graduated in 5 years
4% graduated in 6 years
71% had job offers within 6 months

Financial Matters
$26,489 tuition and fees (2008–09)
$6972 room and board
77% average percent of need met
$19,592 average financial aid amount received
 per undergraduate (2007–08 estimated)

Academics
St. Scholastica awards bachelor's, master's, and doctoral **degrees** and post-bachelor's and post-master's certificates. **Challenging opportunities** include advanced placement credit, accelerated degree programs, student-designed majors, an honors program, double majors, independent study, and a senior project. Special programs include internships, summer session for credit, off-campus study, study-abroad, and Air Force ROTC.

The most frequently chosen **baccalaureate** fields are health professions and related sciences, business/marketing, and biological/life sciences. A complete listing of majors at St. Scholastica appears in the Majors by College index beginning on page 469.

The **faculty** at St. Scholastica has 161 full-time members, 58% with terminal degrees. The student-faculty ratio is 14:1.

Students of St. Scholastica
The student body totals 3,593, of whom 2,769 are undergraduates. 69.5% are women and 30.5% are men. Students come from 28 states and territories and 34 other countries. 85% are from Minnesota. 3.5% are international students. 2.1% are African American, 2.9% American Indian, 1.9% Asian American, and 1.4% Hispanic American. 83% returned for their sophomore year.

Facilities and Resources
222 **computers/terminals** are available on campus for general student use. Students can access the following: campus intranet, computer help desk, free student e-mail accounts, online (class) grades, online (class) registration, online (class) schedules, student account information and transcripts online. Campuswide network is available. 100% of college-owned or -operated housing units are wired for high-speed Internet access. Wireless service is available via classrooms, computer centers, computer labs, dorm rooms, learning centers, libraries, student centers. The **library** has 114,769 books and 21,656 subscriptions.

Campus Life
There are 68 active organizations on campus, including a drama/theater group, newspaper, television station, and choral group. No national or local **fraternities** or **sororities**.

St. Scholastica is a member of the NCAA (Division III). **Intercollegiate sports** include baseball (m), basketball, cross-country running, football (m), ice hockey (m), soccer, softball (w), tennis, track and field, volleyball (w).

Campus Safety
Student safety services include student door monitor at night, late-night transport/escort service, 24-hour emergency telephone alarm devices, 24-hour patrols by trained security personnel, and electronically operated dormitory entrances.

Applying
St. Scholastica requires SAT or ACT and a high school transcript, and in some cases an interview and a minimum high school GPA of 2.0. It recommends an interview. Application deadline: rolling admissions; 3/15 priority date for financial aid. Early and deferred admission are possible.

THE COLLEGE OF SAINT THOMAS MORE

URBAN SETTING ■ PRIVATE ■ INDEPENDENT RELIGIOUS ■ COED
FORT WORTH, TEXAS

Web site: www.cstm.edu
Contact: Dr. James A. Patrick, 3020 Lubbock Avenue, Fort Worth, TX
76109-2323
Telephone: 817-928-8459 or toll-free 800-583-6489 (out-of-state)
Fax: 817-924-3206
E-mail: more-info@cstm.edu

Academics

CSTM awards associate and bachelor's **degrees**. Special programs include cooperative education, summer session for credit, study-abroad, and Army ROTC.

The most frequently chosen **baccalaureate** field is liberal arts/general studies. A complete listing of majors at CSTM appears in the Majors by College index beginning on page 469.

The **faculty** at CSTM has 3 full-time members, 67% with terminal degrees. The student-faculty ratio is 5:1.

Students of CSTM

The student body is made up of 53 undergraduates. 45.3% are women and 54.7% are men. Students come from 5 states and territories. 76% are from Texas. 2.6% are African American and 7.9% Hispanic American. 89% returned for their sophomore year.

Facilities and Resources

7 **computers/terminals** are available on campus for general student use. The **library** has 13,739 books and 50 subscriptions.

Campus Life

There are 3 active organizations on campus. No national or local **fraternities** or **sororities**.

This institution has no intercollegiate sports.

Campus Safety

Student safety services include late-night transport/escort service, 24-hour patrols by trained security personnel, and student patrols.

Applying

CSTM requires an essay, a high school transcript, 1 recommendation, and a minimum high school GPA of 2.0. It recommends an interview. Application deadline: rolling admissions; 4/15 priority date for financial aid. Early and deferred admission are possible.

Getting Accepted
12 applied
83% were accepted
4 enrolled (40% of accepted)
3.2 average high school GPA

Financial Matters
$12,000 tuition and fees (2008–09)
85% average percent of need met
$8560 average financial aid amount received
per undergraduate (2005–06)

COLLEGE OF THE ATLANTIC
SMALL-TOWN SETTING ■ PRIVATE ■ INDEPENDENT ■ COED
BAR HARBOR, MAINE

Web site: www.coa.edu
Contact: Ms. Sarah Baker, Dean of Admission, 105 Eden Street, Bar Harbor, ME 04609-1198
Telephone: 207-288-5015 Ext. 233 or toll-free 800-528-0025
Fax: 207-288-4126
E-mail: inquiry@coa.edu

The College of the Atlantic (COA) is an intellectually challenging, resolutely different college located between the ocean and Acadia National Park on Mount Desert Island, Maine. COA is small, with no departments and no majors; its courses are interdisciplinary and value centered. The College looks for students seeking a rigorous academic experience distinctive from what is usually offered by more traditionally structured colleges and universities. COA's mission is to foster independent thought, challenge conventional wisdom, deal with pressing environmental and social change, and be passionately engaged in transforming the world into a better place.

Academics
COA awards bachelor's and master's **degrees**. **Challenging opportunities** include advanced placement credit, accelerated degree programs, student-designed majors, independent study, and a senior project. Special programs include cooperative education, internships, off-campus study, and study-abroad.

The most frequently chosen **baccalaureate** field is liberal arts/general studies. A complete listing of majors at COA appears in the Majors by College index beginning on page 469.

The **faculty** at COA has 24 full-time members, 79% with terminal degrees. The student-faculty ratio is 11:1.

Students of COA
The student body totals 327, of whom 324 are undergraduates. 64.2% are women and 35.8% are men. Students come from 37 states and territories and 35 other countries. 18% are from Maine. 13.6% are international students. 0.3% are African American, 1.2% Asian American, and 0.9% Hispanic American. 82% returned for their sophomore year.

Facilities and Resources
38 **computers/terminals** and 50 ports are available on campus for general student use. Students can access the following: computer help desk, free student e-mail accounts, online (class) schedules. Campuswide network is available. 100% of college-owned or -operated housing units are wired for high-speed Internet access. Wireless service is available via entire campus. The **library** has 50,000 books and 30,000 subscriptions.

Campus Life
There are 12 active organizations on campus, including a drama/theater group, newspaper, and choral group. No national or local **fraternities** or **sororities**.

This institution has no intercollegiate sports.

Campus Safety
Student safety services include late-night transport/escort service, 24-hour emergency telephone alarm devices, and 24-hour patrols by trained security personnel.

Applying
COA requires an essay, a high school transcript, and 3 recommendations, and in some cases an interview. It recommends SAT or ACT, an interview, and a minimum high school GPA of 3.0. Application deadline: 2/15; 2/15 priority date for financial aid. Early and deferred admission are possible.

Getting Accepted
314 applied
69% were accepted
70 enrolled (32% of accepted)
31% from top tenth of their h.s. class
3.49 average high school GPA
Mean SAT critical reading score: 638
Mean SAT math score: 572
Mean SAT writing score: 614
Mean ACT score: 27
79% had SAT critical reading scores over 600
46% had SAT math scores over 600
58% had SAT writing scores over 600
91% had ACT scores over 24
21% had SAT critical reading scores over 700
10% had SAT math scores over 700
22% had SAT writing scores over 700

Graduation and After
45% graduated in 4 years
17% graduated in 5 years
80% had job offers within 6 months
10 organizations recruited on campus

Financial Matters
$33,060 tuition and fees (2009–10)
$8490 room and board
97% average percent of need met
$27,041 average financial aid amount received per undergraduate (2007–08 estimated)

COLLEGE OF THE HOLY CROSS

SUBURBAN SETTING ■ PRIVATE ■ INDEPENDENT RELIGIOUS ■ COED
WORCESTER, MASSACHUSETTS

SPONSOR

Web site: www.holycross.edu
Contact: 105 Fenwick Hall, 1 College Street, Worcester, MA 01610-2395
Telephone: 508-793-2443 or toll-free 800-442-2421
Fax: 508-793-3888
E-mail: admissions@holycross.edu

Academics

Holy Cross awards bachelor's **degrees** (standardized tests are optional for admission to the College of Holy Cross). **Challenging opportunities** include advanced placement credit, accelerated degree programs, student-designed majors, an honors program, double majors, independent study, and a senior project. Special programs include internships, off-campus study, study-abroad, and Army, Navy, and Air Force ROTC.

The most frequently chosen **baccalaureate** fields are social sciences, English, and psychology. A complete listing of majors at Holy Cross appears in the Majors by College index beginning on page 469.

The **faculty** at Holy Cross has 259 full-time members, 92% with terminal degrees. The student-faculty ratio is 10:1.

Students of Holy Cross

The student body is made up of 2,898 undergraduates. 56.1% are women and 43.9% are men. Students come from 46 states and territories and 15 other countries. 38% are from Massachusetts. 1.3% are international students. 4.4% are African American, 0.4% American Indian, 5.6% Asian American, and 6.4% Hispanic American. 95% returned for their sophomore year.

Facilities and Resources

485 **computers/terminals** are available on campus for general student use. Students can access the following: computer help desk, free student e-mail accounts, online (class) registration. Campuswide network is available. 100% of college-owned or -operated housing units are wired for high-speed Internet access. Wireless service is available via classrooms, computer centers, computer labs, dorm rooms, libraries, student centers. The 6 **libraries** have 624,981 books and 9,668 subscriptions.

Campus Life

There are 104 active organizations on campus, including a drama/theater group, newspaper, radio station, choral group, and marching band. No national or local **fraternities** or **sororities**.

Holy Cross is a member of the NCAA (Division I). **Intercollegiate sports** (some offering scholarships) include baseball (m), basketball, crew, cross-country running, field hockey (w), football (m), golf, ice hockey, lacrosse, soccer, softball (w), swimming and diving, tennis, track and field, volleyball (w).

Campus Safety

Student safety services include late-night transport/escort service, 24-hour emergency telephone alarm devices, 24-hour patrols by trained security personnel, and electronically operated dormitory entrances.

Applying

Holy Cross requires an essay, a high school transcript, and 2 recommendations. It recommends an interview. Application deadline: 1/15; 2/1 for financial aid. Early and deferred admission are possible.

Established in 1843, the College of the Holy Cross is renowned for its mentoring-based liberal arts education in the Jesuit tradition. With a total enrollment of 2,700 and a student-faculty ratio of 10:1, students are assured of highly personalized instruction. Professors of the exclusively undergraduate college conduct all their own classes and laboratories, and students have full access to state-of-the-art equipment and information technology. A storied sports tradition and diverse extracurricular activities round out the Holy Cross experience. Integrating faith and knowledge with an emphasis on public service, Holy Cross prepares its students for success in all aspects of life.

Getting Accepted
7,227 applied
34% were accepted
737 enrolled (30% of accepted)
61% from top tenth of their h.s. class
Mean SAT critical reading score: 629
Mean SAT math score: 641
72% had SAT critical reading scores over 600
77% had SAT math scores over 600
18% had SAT critical reading scores over 700
21% had SAT math scores over 700
2 National Merit Scholars
8 valedictorians

Graduation and After
92% graduated in 4 years
2% graduated in 5 years
64% had job offers within 6 months
48 organizations recruited on campus

Financial Matters
$38,722 tuition and fees (2009–10)
$10,620 room and board
100% average percent of need met
$27,856 average financial aid amount received per undergraduate (2007–08 estimated)

THE COLLEGE OF WILLIAM AND MARY

SMALL-TOWN SETTING ■ PUBLIC ■ STATE-SUPPORTED ■ COED
WILLIAMSBURG, VIRGINIA

Web site: www.wm.edu
Contact: Henry Broaddus, Dean of Admissions, PO Box 8795, Williamsburg, VA 23187-8795
Telephone: 757-221-4223
Fax: 757-221-1242
E-mail: admission@wm.edu

Getting Accepted
11,636 applied
34% were accepted
1,387 enrolled (35% of accepted)
79% from top tenth of their h.s. class
4.0 average high school GPA
84% had SAT critical reading scores over 600
83% had SAT math scores over 600
81% had SAT writing scores over 600
92% had ACT scores over 24
41% had SAT critical reading scores over 700
35% had SAT math scores over 700
36% had SAT writing scores over 700
58% had ACT scores over 30

Graduation and After
84% graduated in 4 years
7% graduated in 5 years
1% graduated in 6 years
47% had job offers within 6 months
222 organizations recruited on campus

Financial Matters
$10,246 resident tuition and fees (2008–09)
$29,116 nonresident tuition and fees (2008–09)
$7910 room and board
86% average percent of need met
$13,302 average financial aid amount received per undergraduate (2007–08 estimated)

Academics

William and Mary awards bachelor's, master's, doctoral, and first-professional **degrees** and post-master's certificates. **Challenging opportunities** include advanced placement credit, accelerated degree programs, student-designed majors, an honors program, double majors, independent study, and a senior project. Special programs include internships, summer session for credit, study-abroad, and Army ROTC.

The most frequently chosen **baccalaureate** fields are social sciences, business/marketing, and interdisciplinary studies. A complete listing of majors at William and Mary appears in the Majors by College index beginning on page 469.

The **faculty** at William and Mary has 628 full-time members, 89% with terminal degrees. The student-faculty ratio is 11:1.

Students of William and Mary

The student body totals 7,892, of whom 5,850 are undergraduates. 54.7% are women and 45.3% are men. Students come from 50 states and territories and 43 other countries. 59% are from Virginia. 2.4% are international students. 7.2% are African American, 0.8% American Indian, 8.1% Asian American, and 5.7% Hispanic American. 94% returned for their sophomore year.

Facilities and Resources

350 **computers/terminals** and 6,000 ports are available on campus for general student use. Students can access the following: campus intranet, computer help desk, free student e-mail accounts, online (class) grades, online (class) registration, online (class) schedules. Campuswide network is available. 100% of college-owned or -operated housing units are wired for high-speed Internet access. Wireless service is available via entire campus. The 9 **libraries** have 1,841,752 books and 18,000 subscriptions.

Campus Life

There are 517 active organizations on campus, including a drama/theater group, newspaper, radio station, television station, and choral group. 25% of eligible men and 27% of eligible women are members of national **fraternities** and national **sororities**.

William and Mary is a member of the NCAA (Division I). **Intercollegiate sports** (some offering scholarships) include baseball (m), basketball, cross-country running, field hockey (w), football (m), golf, gymnastics, lacrosse (w), soccer, swimming and diving, tennis, track and field, volleyball (w).

Campus Safety

Student safety services include late-night transport/escort service, 24-hour emergency telephone alarm devices, 24-hour patrols by trained security personnel, student patrols, and electronically operated dormitory entrances.

Applying

William and Mary requires an essay, SAT or ACT, a high school transcript, and 1 recommendation. It recommends SAT Subject Tests and 2 recommendations. Application deadline: 1/1; 2/15 priority date for financial aid. Early and deferred admission are possible.

The College of Wooster

Small-town setting ■ Private ■ Independent Religious ■ Coed
Wooster, Ohio

SPONSOR

Web site: www.wooster.edu
Contact: Ms. Mary Karen Vellines, Vice President for Enrollment, 847
   College Avenue, Wooster, OH 44691
Telephone: 330-263-2270 Ext. 2118 or toll-free 800-877-9905
Fax: 330-263-2621
E-mail: admissions@wooster.edu

Academics

Wooster awards bachelor's **degrees**. **Challenging opportunities** include advanced placement credit, student-designed majors, double majors, independent study, and a senior project. Special programs include cooperative education, internships, summer session for credit, off-campus study, and study-abroad.

The most frequently chosen **baccalaureate** fields are social sciences, history, and biological/life sciences. A complete listing of majors at Wooster appears in the Majors by College index beginning on page 469.

The **faculty** at Wooster has 143 full-time members, 97% with terminal degrees. The student-faculty ratio is 12:1.

Students of Wooster

The student body is made up of 1,777 undergraduates. 51.5% are women and 48.5% are men. Students come from 46 states and territories and 30 other countries. 44% are from Ohio. 5.4% are international students. 3.9% are African American, 0.5% American Indian, 2.6% Asian American, and 2.1% Hispanic American. 86% returned for their sophomore year.

Facilities and Resources

500 **computers/terminals** and 1,500 ports are available on campus for general student use. Students can access the following: campus intranet, computer help desk, free student e-mail accounts, online (class) grades, online (class) registration. Campuswide network is available. Wireless service is available via classrooms, computer centers, computer labs, learning centers, libraries, student centers. The 4 **libraries** have 581,518 books.

Campus Life

There are 102 active organizations on campus, including a drama/theater group, newspaper, radio station, choral group, and marching band. 9% of eligible men and 10% of eligible women are members of local **fraternities**, local **sororities**, and coed fraternity.

Wooster is a member of the NCAA (Division III). **Intercollegiate sports** include baseball (m), basketball, cross-country running, field hockey (w), football (m), golf (m), lacrosse, soccer, softball (w), swimming and diving, tennis, track and field, volleyball (w).

Campus Safety

Student safety services include late-night transport/escort service, 24-hour emergency telephone alarm devices, 24-hour patrols by trained security personnel, student patrols, and electronically operated dormitory entrances.

Applying

Wooster requires an essay, SAT or ACT, a high school transcript, and 2 recommendations. It recommends an interview. Application deadline: 2/15; 9/1 for financial aid, with a 2/15 priority date. Early and deferred admission are possible.

The College of Wooster is the nation's premier liberal arts college for undergraduate research. Wooster offers an excellent, comprehensive liberal education, culminating in a rigorous, in-depth project of inquiry or creative expression. By working in partnership with a faculty member to conceive, organize, and complete a significant project on a topic of the student's own choosing, every Wooster student develops abilities valued by employers and graduate schools alike: initiative, self-confidence, independent judgment, creative problem solving, and strong written and oral communication skills. Wooster is a diverse, supportive, unpretentious community of learners in which students can be themselves, discover and pursue their passions, and forge lifelong bonds with faculty, coaches, staff, and fellow students. These bonds enrich their college experiences and sustain the college's tradition of excellence.

Getting Accepted
3,168 applied
74% were accepted
543 enrolled (23% of accepted)
3.55 average high school GPA
Mean SAT critical reading score: 609
Mean SAT math score: 608
Mean ACT score: 26
51% had SAT critical reading scores over 600
47% had SAT math scores over 600
48% had SAT writing scores over 600
71% had ACT scores over 24
15% had SAT critical reading scores over 700
12% had SAT math scores over 700
13% had SAT writing scores over 700
24% had ACT scores over 30

Graduation and After
64% graduated in 4 years
7% graduated in 5 years
1% graduated in 6 years
90% had job offers within 6 months
32 organizations recruited on campus

Financial Matters
$33,770 tuition and fees (2008–09)
$8650 room and board
95% average percent of need met
$24,981 average financial aid amount received
   per undergraduate (2006–07 estimated)

COLORADO CHRISTIAN UNIVERSITY

SUBURBAN SETTING ■ PRIVATE ■ INDEPENDENT RELIGIOUS ■ COED
LAKEWOOD, COLORADO

Web site: www.ccu.edu
Contact: Mr. Jeff Cazer, Associate, 180 South Garrison Street, Lakewood, CO 80226
Telephone: 303-963-3200 or toll-free 800-44-FAITH
Fax: 303-963-3201
E-mail: admission@ccu.edu

Getting Accepted
772 applied
65% were accepted
225 enrolled (45% of accepted)
25% from top tenth of their h.s. class
3.45 average high school GPA
Mean SAT critical reading score: 555
Mean SAT math score: 528
Mean ACT score: 23
27% had SAT critical reading scores over 600
24% had SAT math scores over 600
46% had ACT scores over 24
6% had SAT critical reading scores over 700
3% had SAT math scores over 700
9% had ACT scores over 30

Financial Matters
$20,280 tuition and fees (2008–09)
$8050 room and board
54% average percent of need met
$8931 average financial aid amount received per undergraduate

Academics
CCU awards associate, bachelor's, and master's **degrees. Challenging opportunities** include advanced placement credit, accelerated degree programs, student-designed majors, an honors program, double majors, independent study, and a senior project. Special programs include cooperative education, internships, summer session for credit, off-campus study, study-abroad, and Army ROTC.

The most frequently chosen **baccalaureate** fields are business/marketing, computer and information sciences, and education. A complete listing of majors at CCU appears in the Majors by College index beginning on page 469.

The **faculty** at CCU has 43 full-time members, 70% with terminal degrees. The student-faculty ratio is 21:1.

Students of CCU
The student body totals 2,221, of whom 1,897 are undergraduates. 60.7% are women and 39.3% are men. Students come from 45 states and territories and 9 other countries. 44% are from Colorado. 0.5% are international students. 3.9% are African American, 1.1% American Indian, 1.3% Asian American, and 8.6% Hispanic American.

Facilities and Resources
141 **computers/terminals** are available on campus for general student use. Students can access the following: online (class) registration. Campuswide network is available. The 2 **libraries** have 71,565 books and 1,192 subscriptions.

Campus Life
There are 26 active organizations on campus, including a drama/theater group, newspaper, and choral group. No national or local **fraternities** or **sororities**.

CCU is a member of the NCAA (Division II). **Intercollegiate sports** (some offering scholarships) include basketball, cross-country running, golf (m), soccer, tennis, volleyball (w).

Campus Safety
Student safety services include 24-hour emergency telephone alarm devices, 24-hour patrols by trained security personnel, and student patrols.

Applying
CCU requires an essay, SAT or ACT, a high school transcript, an interview, and 2 recommendations, and in some cases an interview, 3 recommendations, and a minimum high school GPA of 2.8. Application deadline: 8/21; 3/15 priority date for financial aid. Deferred admission is possible.

THE COLORADO COLLEGE

URBAN SETTING ■ PRIVATE ■ INDEPENDENT ■ COED
COLORADO SPRINGS, COLORADO

Web site: www.coloradocollege.edu
Contact: Mr. Matt Bonser, Associate Director of Admission, 900 Block North
    Cascade, West, Colorado Springs, CO 80903-3294
Telephone: 719-389-6344 or toll-free 800-542-7214
Fax: 719-389-6816
E-mail: admission@coloradocollege.edu

Academics

CC awards bachelor's and master's **degrees** (master's degree in education only). **Challenging opportunities** include advanced placement credit, student-designed majors, double majors, independent study, and a senior project. Special programs include internships, summer session for credit, off-campus study, study-abroad, and Army ROTC.

The most frequently chosen **baccalaureate** fields are social sciences, biological/life sciences, and history. A complete listing of majors at CC appears in the Majors by College index beginning on page 469.

The **faculty** at CC has 175 full-time members, 84% with terminal degrees. The student-faculty ratio is 10:1.

Students of CC

The student body totals 2,026, of whom 1,996 are undergraduates. 54.3% are women and 45.7% are men. Students come from 49 states and territories and 35 other countries. 26% are from Colorado. 3.9% are international students. 2.2% are African American, 0.8% American Indian, 5.9% Asian American, and 6.9% Hispanic American. 90% returned for their sophomore year.

Facilities and Resources

208 **computers/terminals** are available on campus for general student use. Students can access the following: campus intranet, computer help desk, free student e-mail accounts, online (class) grades, online (class) registration, online (class) schedules. Campuswide network is available. 100% of college-owned or -operated housing units are wired for high-speed Internet access. Wireless service is available via entire campus. The 2 **libraries** have 540,276 books and 26,233 subscriptions.

Campus Life

There are 143 active organizations on campus, including a drama/theater group, newspaper, and choral group. 6% of eligible men and 13% of eligible women are members of national **fraternities** and national **sororities**.

CC is a member of the NCAA (Division III). **Intercollegiate sports** (some offering scholarships) include basketball, cross-country running, football (m), ice hockey (m), lacrosse, soccer, softball (w), swimming and diving, tennis, track and field, volleyball (w).

Campus Safety

Student safety services include whistle program, student escort service, good campus lighting, late-night transport/escort service, 24-hour emergency telephone alarm devices, 24-hour patrols by trained security personnel, and electronically operated dormitory entrances.

Applying

CC requires an essay, SAT or ACT, a high school transcript, and 2 recommendations. It recommends an interview. Application deadline: 1/15; 2/15 for financial aid, with a 2/15 priority date. Deferred admission is possible.

Getting Accepted

5,342 applied
26% were accepted
550 enrolled (40% of accepted)
66% from top tenth of their h.s. class
Mean SAT critical reading score: 660
Mean SAT math score: 660
Mean SAT writing score: 660
Mean ACT score: 29
85% had SAT critical reading scores over 600
81% had SAT math scores over 600
81% had SAT writing scores over 600
96% had ACT scores over 24
29% had SAT critical reading scores over 700
27% had SAT math scores over 700
28% had SAT writing scores over 700
50% had ACT scores over 30
18 valedictorians

Graduation and After

78% graduated in 4 years
8% graduated in 5 years
1% graduated in 6 years
43 organizations recruited on campus

Financial Matters

$36,044 tuition and fees (2008–09)
$9096 room and board
92% average percent of need met
$31,635 average financial aid amount received
    per undergraduate (2007–08 estimated)

Colorado School of Mines

Small-town setting ■ Public ■ State-supported ■ Coed
Golden, Colorado

Web site: www.mines.edu
Contact: Mrs. Joanne Lambert, Assistant Director of Enrollment
Management, Student Center, 1600 Maple Street, Golden, CO 80401
Telephone: 303-273-3256 or toll-free 800-446-9488 Ext. 3220 (out-of-state)
Fax: 303-273-3509
E-mail: admit@mines.edu

Getting Accepted

6,797 applied
61% were accepted
851 enrolled (20% of accepted)
52% from top tenth of their h.s. class
3.7 average high school GPA
Mean SAT critical reading score: 602
Mean SAT math score: 655
Mean ACT score: 28
52% had SAT critical reading scores over 600
80% had SAT math scores over 600
90% had ACT scores over 24
12% had SAT critical reading scores over 700
28% had SAT math scores over 700
32% had ACT scores over 30
64 valedictorians

Graduation and After

39% graduated in 4 years
25% graduated in 5 years
4% graduated in 6 years
95% had job offers within 6 months
206 organizations recruited on campus

Financial Matters

$11,238 resident tuition and fees (2008–09)
$25,248 nonresident tuition and fees
(2008–09)
$7626 room and board
93% average percent of need met
$15,500 average financial aid amount received
per undergraduate (2007–08 estimated)

Academics

CSM awards bachelor's, master's, doctoral, and first-professional **degrees**. **Challenging opportunities** include advanced placement credit, accelerated degree programs, an honors program, double majors, independent study, and a senior project. Special programs include cooperative education, internships, summer session for credit, study-abroad, and Army ROTC.

The most frequently chosen **baccalaureate** fields are engineering, mathematics, and social sciences. A complete listing of majors at CSM appears in the Majors by College index beginning on page 469.

The **faculty** at CSM has 250 full-time members, 83% with terminal degrees. The student-faculty ratio is 14:1.

Students of CSM

The student body totals 4,488, of whom 3,456 are undergraduates. 24% are women and 76% are men. Students come from 46 states and territories and 44 other countries. 80% are from Colorado. 6.6% are international students. 1.5% are African American, 0.8% American Indian, 5.2% Asian American, and 6.5% Hispanic American. 85% returned for their sophomore year.

Facilities and Resources

400 **computers/terminals** are available on campus for general student use. Students can access the following: campus intranet, computer help desk, free student e-mail accounts, online (class) grades, online (class) registration, online (class) schedules. Campuswide network is available. 100% of college-owned or -operated housing units are wired for high-speed Internet access. Wireless service is available via entire campus. The **library** has 412,560 books and 26,399 subscriptions.

Campus Life

There are 148 active organizations on campus, including a drama/theater group, newspaper, radio station, choral group, and marching band. 11% of eligible men and 15% of eligible women are members of national **fraternities** and national **sororities**.

CSM is a member of the NCAA (Division II). **Intercollegiate sports** (some offering scholarships) include baseball (m), basketball, cross-country running, football (m), golf (m), soccer, softball (w), swimming and diving, track and field, volleyball (w), wrestling (m).

Campus Safety

Student safety services include late-night transport/escort service, 24-hour emergency telephone alarm devices, 24-hour patrols by trained security personnel, and electronically operated dormitory entrances.

Applying

CSM requires SAT or ACT and a high school transcript, and in some cases an essay, an interview, and 2 recommendations. It recommends rank in upper one-third of high school class and a minimum high school GPA of 3.7. Application deadline: 5/1; 3/1 priority date for financial aid. Deferred admission is possible.

Colorado State University

URBAN SETTING ■ PUBLIC ■ STATE-SUPPORTED ■ COED
FORT COLLINS, COLORADO

Web site: www.colostate.edu
Contact: Mr. Jim Rawlins, Executive Director of Admissions, Spruce Hall,
Fort Collins, CO 80523-0015
Telephone: 970-491-6909
Fax: 970-491-7799
E-mail: admissions@colostate.edu

SPONSOR

Academics
Colorado State awards bachelor's, master's, doctoral, and first-professional **degrees**. **Challenging opportunities** include advanced placement credit, accelerated degree programs, an honors program, double majors, independent study, and a senior project. Special programs include cooperative education, internships, summer session for credit, off-campus study, study-abroad, and Army and Air Force ROTC.

The most frequently chosen **baccalaureate** fields are business/marketing, family and consumer sciences, and biological/life sciences. A complete listing of majors at Colorado State appears in the Majors by College index beginning on page 469.

The **faculty** at Colorado State has 925 full-time members, 100% with terminal degrees. The student-faculty ratio is 17:1.

Students of Colorado State
The student body totals 27,800, of whom 21,783 are undergraduates. 51.8% are women and 48.2% are men. Students come from 53 states and territories and 49 other countries. 84% are from Colorado. 1.8% are international students. 2.3% are African American, 1.5% American Indian, 3% Asian American, and 6.3% Hispanic American. 82% returned for their sophomore year.

Facilities and Resources
2,700 **computers/terminals** and 3,200 ports are available on campus for general student use. Students can access the following: campus intranet, computer help desk, free student e-mail accounts, online (class) grades, online (class) registration, online (class) schedules, personalized portal services including transcripts and financials (billing, financial aid). Campuswide network is available. 100% of college-owned or -operated housing units are wired for high-speed Internet access. Wireless service is available via classrooms, computer centers, computer labs, dorm rooms, libraries, student centers. The 4 **libraries** have 2,045,603 books and 36,133 subscriptions.

Campus Life
There are 295 active organizations on campus, including a drama/theater group, newspaper, radio station, television station, choral group, and marching band. 6% of eligible men and 7% of eligible women are members of national **fraternities**, national sororities, local fraternities, and local sororities.

Colorado State is a member of the NCAA (Division I). **Intercollegiate sports** (some offering scholarships) include basketball, cross-country running, football (m), golf, softball (w), swimming and diving (w), tennis (w), track and field, volleyball (w), water polo (w).

Campus Safety
Student safety services include late-night transport/escort service, 24-hour emergency telephone alarm devices, 24-hour patrols by trained security personnel, student patrols, and electronically operated dormitory entrances.

Applying
Colorado State requires an essay, SAT or ACT, a high school transcript, and 1 recommendation. Application deadline: 7/1; 3/1 priority date for financial aid. Deferred admission is possible.

Getting Accepted
12,494 applied
86% were accepted
4,404 enrolled (41% of accepted)
20% from top tenth of their h.s. class
3.53 average high school GPA
Mean SAT critical reading score: 555
Mean SAT math score: 566
Mean SAT writing score: 540
Mean ACT score: 24
31% had SAT critical reading scores over 600
37% had SAT math scores over 600
24% had SAT writing scores over 600
55% had ACT scores over 24
5% had SAT critical reading scores over 700
5% had SAT math scores over 700
3% had SAT writing scores over 700
7% had ACT scores over 30
17 National Merit Scholars

Graduation and After
35% graduated in 4 years
23% graduated in 5 years
5% graduated in 6 years
590 organizations recruited on campus

Financial Matters
$5874 resident tuition and fees (2008–09)
$21,590 nonresident tuition and fees (2008–09)
$8134 room and board
76% average percent of need met
$8685 average financial aid amount received per undergraduate (2006–07)

Getting Accepted
21,343 applied
11% were accepted
1,333 enrolled (59% of accepted)
92% had SAT critical reading scores over 600
94% had SAT math scores over 600
91% had SAT writing scores over 600
98% had ACT scores over 24
60% had SAT critical reading scores over 700
63% had SAT math scores over 700
58% had SAT writing scores over 700
65% had ACT scores over 30

Graduation and After
85% graduated in 4 years
7% graduated in 5 years
2% graduated in 6 years

Financial Matters
$38,552 tuition and fees (2008–09)
$9980 room and board

COLUMBIA UNIVERSITY
PRIVATE ■ INDEPENDENT ■ COED
NEW YORK, NEW YORK

Web site: www.columbia.edu
Contact: Ms. Jessica Marinaccio, Dean of Undergraduate Admissions, 116th Street and Broadway, New York, NY 10027

Academics
Columbia University awards bachelor's, master's, and doctoral **degrees**. A senior project is a **challenging opportunity.**

The most frequently chosen **baccalaureate** fields are engineering, social sciences, and English. A complete listing of majors at Columbia University appears in the Majors by College index beginning on page 469.

The **faculty** at Columbia University has 790 full-time members. The student-faculty ratio is 6:1.

Students of Columbia University
The student body is made up of 5,602 undergraduates. 46.5% are women and 53.5% are men. Students come from 53 states and territories and 66 other countries. 25% are from New York. 8.9% are international students. 8.9% are African American, 0.7% American Indian, 18.2% Asian American, and 10.1% Hispanic American. 97% returned for their sophomore year.

Facilities and Resources
400 **computers/terminals** are available on campus for general student use. Students can access the following: campus intranet, computer help desk, free student e-mail accounts, online (class) grades, online (class) registration, online (class) schedules. Campuswide network is available.

Campus Life
There are 300 active organizations on campus, including a drama/theater group, newspaper, radio station, television station, choral group, and marching band. 19% of eligible men and 25% of eligible women are members of national **fraternities** and national **sororities**.

Columbia University is a member of the NCAA (Division I). **Intercollegiate sports** include archery (w), baseball (m), basketball, crew, cross-country running, fencing, field hockey (w), football (m), golf (m), lacrosse (w), softball (w), swimming and diving, track and field, wrestling (m).

Applying
Columbia University requires an essay, SAT and SAT Subject Tests or ACT, a high school transcript, and 3 recommendations. Application deadline: 1/2. Early and deferred admission are possible.

CONCORDIA COLLEGE

SUBURBAN SETTING ■ PRIVATE ■ INDEPENDENT RELIGIOUS ■ COED
MOORHEAD, MINNESOTA

Web site: www.concordiacollege.edu
Contact: Mr. Scott E. Ellingson, Director of Admissions, 901 8th Street
   South, Moorhead, MN 56562
Telephone: 218-299-3004 or toll-free 800-699-9897
Fax: 218-299-3947
E-mail: admissions@cord.edu

Academics

Concordia awards bachelor's and master's **degrees**. **Challenging opportunities** include advanced placement credit, an honors program, double majors, independent study, and a senior project. Special programs include cooperative education, internships, summer session for credit, off-campus study, study-abroad, and Army and Air Force ROTC.

The most frequently chosen **baccalaureate** fields are education, business/marketing, and communications/journalism. A complete listing of majors at Concordia appears in the Majors by College index beginning on page 469.

The **faculty** at Concordia has 190 full-time members, 77% with terminal degrees. The student-faculty ratio is 13:1.

Students of Concordia

The student body totals 2,823, of whom 2,810 are undergraduates. 61.3% are women and 38.7% are men. Students come from 41 states and territories and 37 other countries. 3.8% are international students. 1% are African American, 0.3% American Indian, 1.6% Asian American, and 0.8% Hispanic American. 83% returned for their sophomore year.

Facilities and Resources

570 **computers/terminals** and 87 ports are available on campus for general student use. Students can access the following: computer help desk, free student e-mail accounts, online (class) grades, online (class) schedules, online degree audit. Campuswide network is available. 100% of college-owned or -operated housing units are wired for high-speed Internet access. Wireless service is available via entire campus. The **library** has 340,006 books and 3,329 subscriptions.

Campus Life

There are 80 active organizations on campus, including a drama/theater group, newspaper, radio station, television station, and choral group. Concordia has local **sororities** and local coed fraternity.

Concordia is a member of the NCAA (Division III). **Intercollegiate sports** include baseball (m), basketball, cross-country running, football (m), golf, ice hockey, soccer, softball (w), swimming and diving (w), tennis, track and field, volleyball (w), wrestling (m).

Campus Safety

Student safety services include well-lit campus, 24-hour locked wing doors, late-night transport/escort service, 24-hour emergency telephone alarm devices, 24-hour patrols by trained security personnel, and student patrols.

Applying

Concordia requires SAT or ACT, a high school transcript, 2 recommendations, and references. Application deadline: rolling admissions. Early and deferred admission are possible.

Getting Accepted

2,885 applied
78% were accepted
776 enrolled (34% of accepted)
33% from top tenth of their h.s. class
3.6 average high school GPA
Mean ACT score: 25
41% had SAT critical reading scores over 600
49% had SAT math scores over 600
38% had SAT writing scores over 600
64% had ACT scores over 24
12% had SAT critical reading scores over 700
13% had SAT math scores over 700
9% had SAT writing scores over 700
14% had ACT scores over 30
7 National Merit Scholars

Graduation and After

60% graduated in 4 years
5% graduated in 5 years
75% had job offers within 6 months
75 organizations recruited on campus

Financial Matters

$25,710 tuition and fees (2009–10)
$6825 room and board
85% average percent of need met
$16,001 average financial aid amount received
   per undergraduate (2006–07)

CONNECTICUT COLLEGE

SUBURBAN SETTING ■ PRIVATE ■ INDEPENDENT ■ COED
NEW LONDON, CONNECTICUT

Web site: www.conncoll.edu
Contact: Ms. Martha Merrill, Dean of Admissions and Financial Aid, 270
  Mohegan Avenue, New London, CT 06320-4196
Telephone: 860-439-2200
Fax: 860-439-4301
E-mail: admission@conncoll.edu

Getting Accepted
4,716 applied
37% were accepted
493 enrolled (29% of accepted)
60% from top tenth of their h.s. class
79% had SAT critical reading scores over 600
79% had SAT math scores over 600
81% had SAT writing scores over 600
88% had ACT scores over 24
28% had SAT critical reading scores over 700
21% had SAT math scores over 700
33% had SAT writing scores over 700
19% had ACT scores over 30

Graduation and After
83% graduated in 4 years
4% graduated in 5 years

Financial Matters
$49,385 comprehensive fee (2008–09)
100% average percent of need met
$29,758 average financial aid amount received
  per undergraduate (2007–08 estimated)

Academics
Connecticut awards bachelor's and master's **degrees**. **Challenging opportunities**
include advanced placement credit, student-designed majors, double majors,
independent study, and a senior project. Special programs include internships, summer
session for credit, off-campus study, and study-abroad.

The most frequently chosen **baccalaureate** fields are social sciences, visual and
performing arts, and biological/life sciences. A complete listing of majors at Connecticut
appears in the Majors by College index beginning on page 469.

The **faculty** at Connecticut has 169 full-time members, 93% with terminal degrees.
The student-faculty ratio is 9:1.

Students of Connecticut
The student body totals 1,852, of whom 1,845 are undergraduates. 59.6% are women
and 40.4% are men. Students come from 46 states and territories and 74 other countries.
81% are from Connecticut. 4.5% are international students. 4.1% are African American,
0.1% American Indian, 4.6% Asian American, and 5.6% Hispanic American. 90%
returned for their sophomore year.

Facilities and Resources
Students can access the following: campus intranet, computer help desk, free student
e-mail accounts, online (class) grades, online (class) registration, online (class) schedules.
Campuswide network is available. 100% of college-owned or -operated housing units are
wired for high-speed Internet access. Wireless service is available via entire campus. The
2 **libraries** have 496,817 books and 2,279 subscriptions.

Campus Life
There are 60 active organizations on campus, including a drama/theater group,
newspaper, radio station, and choral group. No national or local **fraternities** or **sororities**.

Connecticut is a member of the NCAA (Division III). **Intercollegiate sports** include
basketball, crew, cross-country running, field hockey (w), ice hockey, lacrosse, sailing,
soccer, squash, swimming and diving, tennis, track and field, volleyball, water polo.

Campus Safety
Student safety services include late-night transport/escort service, 24-hour emergency
telephone alarm devices, 24-hour patrols by trained security personnel, and electronically operated dormitory entrances.

Applying
Connecticut requires an essay, ACT or any 2 SAT Subject Tests required, a high school
transcript, and a minimum high school GPA of 2.0. It recommends an interview.
Application deadline: 1/1; 2/1 for financial aid. Deferred admission is possible.

CONVERSE COLLEGE

URBAN SETTING ■ PRIVATE ■ INDEPENDENT
■ UNDERGRADUATE: WOMEN ONLY; GRADUATE: COED
SPARTANBURG, SOUTH CAROLINA

Web site: www.converse.edu
Contact: Mr. Aaron Meis, Dean of Admission, 580 East Main Street,
Spartanburg, SC 29302
Telephone: 864-596-9040 Ext. 9746 or toll-free 800-766-1125
Fax: 864-596-9225
E-mail: admissions@converse.edu

Academics
Converse awards bachelor's and master's **degrees** and post-master's certificates. **Challenging opportunities** include advanced placement credit, student-designed majors, an honors program, double majors, independent study, and a senior project. Special programs include cooperative education, internships, summer session for credit, off-campus study, study-abroad, and Army ROTC.

The most frequently chosen **baccalaureate** fields are visual and performing arts, education, and business/marketing. A complete listing of majors at Converse appears in the Majors by College index beginning on page 469.

The **faculty** at Converse has 87 full-time members, 89% with terminal degrees.

Students of Converse
The student body totals 1,881, of whom 737 are undergraduates. 99.5% are women and 0.5% are men. Students come from 30 states and territories and 8 other countries. 77% are from South Carolina. 2.7% are international students. 11.9% are African American, 0.7% American Indian, 1.4% Asian American, and 2.4% Hispanic American. 72% returned for their sophomore year.

Facilities and Resources
72 **computers/terminals** are available on campus for general student use. Students can access the following: online (class) registration. Campuswide network is available. The **library** has 150,817 books and 19,808 subscriptions.

Campus Life
There are 30 active organizations on campus, including a drama/theater group, newspaper, and choral group. No national or local **sororities**.

Converse is a member of the NCAA (Division II). **Intercollegiate sports** (some offering scholarships) include basketball, cheerleading, cross-country running, soccer, tennis, volleyball.

Campus Safety
Student safety services include late-night transport/escort service, 24-hour emergency telephone alarm devices, 24-hour patrols by trained security personnel, and electronically operated dormitory entrances.

Applying
Converse requires SAT or ACT, a high school transcript, and 1 recommendation. It recommends an essay, an interview, and a minimum high school GPA of 3.0. Application deadline: 3/1 priority date for financial aid. Early and deferred admission are possible.

Getting Accepted
1,361 applied
47% were accepted
156 enrolled (24% of accepted)
30% from top tenth of their h.s. class
3.85 average high school GPA
Mean SAT critical reading score: 560
Mean SAT math score: 540
Mean ACT score: 23
26% had SAT critical reading scores over 600
22% had SAT math scores over 600
19% had SAT writing scores over 600
40% had ACT scores over 24
6% had SAT critical reading scores over 700
1% had SAT math scores over 700
2% had ACT scores over 30

Graduation and After
63% graduated in 4 years
1% graduated in 5 years
80% had job offers within 6 months
100 organizations recruited on campus

Financial Matters
$24,500 tuition and fees (2008–09)
$7550 room and board
88% average percent of need met
$20,513 average financial aid amount received per undergraduate (2007–08 estimated)

Getting Accepted

3,055 applied
9% were accepted
238 enrolled (84% of accepted)
93% from top tenth of their h.s. class
3.6 average high school GPA
Mean SAT critical reading score: 663
Mean SAT math score: 695
Mean ACT score: 31
85% had SAT critical reading scores over 600
86% had SAT math scores over 600
33% had SAT critical reading scores over 700
58% had SAT math scores over 700
12 valedictorians

Graduation and After

68% graduated in 4 years
17% graduated in 5 years
3% graduated in 6 years
98% had job offers within 6 months
120 organizations recruited on campus

Financial Matters

$34,600 tuition and fees (2008–09)
$13,700 room and board
93% average percent of need met
$30,000 average financial aid amount received per undergraduate (2006–07)

COOPER UNION FOR THE ADVANCEMENT OF SCIENCE AND ART

URBAN SETTING ▪ PRIVATE ▪ INDEPENDENT ▪ COED
NEW YORK, NEW YORK

Web site: www.cooper.edu
Contact: Mr. Mitchell L. Lipton, Dean of Admissions and Records and Registrar, 30 Cooper Square, New York, NY 10003
Telephone: 212-353-4120
Fax: 212-353-4342
E-mail: admissions@cooper.edu

Academics

Cooper Union awards bachelor's and master's **degrees** (also offers master's program primarily made up of currently-enrolled students). **Challenging opportunities** include advanced placement credit, student-designed majors, an honors program, independent study, and a senior project. Special programs include internships, summer session for credit, off-campus study, and study-abroad.

The most frequently chosen **baccalaureate** fields are engineering, visual and performing arts, and architecture. A complete listing of majors at Cooper Union appears in the Majors by College index beginning on page 469.

The **faculty** at Cooper Union has 52 full-time members, 87% with terminal degrees. The student-faculty ratio is 8:1.

Students of Cooper Union

The student body totals 969, of whom 917 are undergraduates. 38.5% are women and 61.5% are men. Students come from 41 states and territories and 27 other countries. 60% are from New York. 16.4% are international students. 5% are African American, 0.7% American Indian, 17.1% Asian American, and 7.1% Hispanic American. 92% returned for their sophomore year.

Facilities and Resources

400 **computers/terminals** are available on campus for general student use. Students can access the following: computer help desk, free student e-mail accounts, online (class) grades, online (class) schedules. Campuswide network is available. 100% of college-owned or -operated housing units are wired for high-speed Internet access. Wireless service is available via classrooms, computer labs, learning centers. The **library** has 107,348 books and 2,471 subscriptions.

Campus Life

There are 90 active organizations on campus, including a drama/theater group, newspaper, and choral group. 10% of eligible men and 5% of eligible women are members of national **fraternities** and national **sororities**.

Intercollegiate sports include badminton, basketball (m), cross-country running, football (m), soccer (m), table tennis, tennis, volleyball.

Campus Safety

Student safety services include security guards, 24-hour emergency telephone alarm devices, 24-hour patrols by trained security personnel, and electronically operated dormitory entrances.

Applying

Cooper Union requires an essay, SAT or ACT, a high school transcript, and a minimum high school GPA of 2.0, and in some cases SAT and SAT Subject Tests or ACT, an interview, 3 recommendations, portfolio, home examination, and a minimum high school GPA of 3.5. It recommends a minimum high school GPA of 3.0. Application deadline: 1/1; 6/1 for financial aid, with a 4/15 priority date. Early and deferred admission are possible.

CORNELL COLLEGE

SMALL-TOWN SETTING ■ PRIVATE ■ INDEPENDENT RELIGIOUS ■ COED
MOUNT VERNON, IOWA

SPONSOR

Web site: www.cornellcollege.edu
Contact: Todd White, Director of Admission, 600 First Street Southwest,
Mount Vernon, IA 52314-1098
Telephone: 319-895-4167 or toll-free 800-747-1112
Fax: 319-895-4451
E-mail: twhite@cornellcollege.edu

Academics
Cornell College awards bachelor's **degrees**. **Challenging opportunities** include
advanced placement credit, student-designed majors, double majors, independent study,
and a senior project. Special programs include internships, off-campus study, and study-
abroad.

The most frequently chosen **baccalaureate** fields are social sciences, biological/life
sciences, and visual and performing arts. A complete listing of majors at Cornell College
appears in the Majors by College index beginning on page 469.

The **faculty** at Cornell College has 83 full-time members, 95% with terminal
degrees. The student-faculty ratio is 11:1.

Students of Cornell College
The student body is made up of 1,083 undergraduates. 50.8% are women and 49.2% are
men. Students come from 46 states and territories and 20 other countries. 29% are from
Iowa. 3.1% are international students. 3% are African American, 0.6% American Indian,
1.6% Asian American, and 2.8% Hispanic American. 85% returned for their sophomore
year.

Facilities and Resources
176 **computers/terminals** are available on campus for general student use. Students can
access the following: campus intranet, computer help desk, free student e-mail accounts,
online (class) grades, online (class) registration, online (class) schedules. Campuswide
network is available. 100% of college-owned or -operated housing units are wired for
high-speed Internet access. Wireless service is available via classrooms, computer
centers, computer labs, learning centers, libraries, student centers. The 2 **libraries** have
194,131 books and 490 subscriptions.

Campus Life
There are 76 active organizations on campus, including a drama/theater group,
newspaper, radio station, and choral group. 35% of eligible men and 27% of eligible
women are members of local **fraternities** and local **sororities**.

Cornell College is a member of the NCAA (Division III). **Intercollegiate sports**
include baseball (m), basketball, cross-country running, football (m), golf, soccer, softball
(w), tennis, track and field, volleyball (w), wrestling (m).

Campus Safety
Student safety services include 24-hour emergency telephone alarm devices and 24-hour
patrols by trained security personnel.

Applying
Cornell College requires an essay, SAT or ACT, a high school transcript, and 1 recommendation. It recommends SAT Subject Tests and an interview. Application deadline:
2/1; 3/1 for financial aid. Early and deferred admission are possible.

Few colleges are as truly distinctive
as Cornell, recognized as one of the
nation's finest colleges. Cornell offers
students "one extraordinary opportunity after another—in the
classroom, on campus, and in the
world." During each of nine blocks,
students immerse themselves in a
single subject through the One-
Course-At-A-Time (OCAAT) academic,
or block, calendar. The flexibility of
OCAAT creates numerous off-campus
study opportunities. A standardized
schedule enables Cornell students to
pursue extracurricular interests with
the same passion as they do their
course work. This attractively diverse
college community typically receives
applicants from all fifty states and
more than forty countries. The College's beautiful hilltop campus is
listed in its entirety on the National
Register of Historic Places.

Getting Accepted
2,659 applied
45% were accepted
316 enrolled (26% of accepted)
29% from top tenth of their h.s. class
3.44 average high school GPA
Mean SAT critical reading score: 607
Mean SAT math score: 614
Mean ACT score: 27
54% had SAT critical reading scores over 600
57% had SAT math scores over 600
75% had ACT scores over 24
14% had SAT critical reading scores over 700
13% had SAT math scores over 700
21% had ACT scores over 30
13 valedictorians

Graduation and After
61% graduated in 4 years
3% graduated in 5 years
52% had job offers within 6 months
5 organizations recruited on campus

Financial Matters
$27,850 tuition and fees (2008–09)
$7220 room and board
89% average percent of need met
$22,665 average financial aid amount received
per undergraduate (2007–08 estimated)

Cornell University, an Ivy League university and public land-grant institution located in the Finger Lakes region of New York State, is home to 13,500 undergraduates pursuing studies in more than ninety majors and interdisciplinary programs found in the University's seven small to midsized undergraduate colleges: Arts & Sciences; Agriculture & Life Sciences; Architecture, Art, & Planning; Engineering; Hotel Administration; Human Ecology; and Industrial & Labor Relations. Students come from all fifty states and more than 120 countries. Cornell's special features include a world-renowned faculty; an outstanding undergraduate research program; twenty libraries; superb research and teaching facilities; a large, diverse study-abroad program; more than 800 student organizations; thirty-six varsity sports; and a graduation rate of 92 percent.

Getting Accepted
33,073 applied
21% were accepted
3,139 enrolled (46% of accepted)
88% from top tenth of their h.s. class
86% had SAT critical reading scores over 600
93% had SAT math scores over 600
97% had ACT scores over 24
41% had SAT critical reading scores over 700
64% had SAT math scores over 700
69% had ACT scores over 30
47 National Merit Scholars

Graduation and After
87% graduated in 4 years
5% graduated in 5 years
1% graduated in 6 years
48% had job offers within 6 months
455 organizations recruited on campus

Financial Matters
$37,954 tuition and fees (2009–10)
$12,110 room and board
100% average percent of need met
$28,577 average financial aid amount received per undergraduate (2007–08 estimated)

CORNELL UNIVERSITY
SMALL-TOWN SETTING ■ PRIVATE ■ INDEPENDENT ■ COED
ITHACA, NEW YORK

Web site: www.cornell.edu
Contact: Mr. Jason Locke, Director of Undergraduate Admissions, 410 Thurston Avenue, Ithaca, NY 14850
Telephone: 607-255-1446
Fax: 607-255-0659
E-mail: admissions@cornell.edu

Academics
Cornell awards bachelor's, master's, doctoral, and first-professional **degrees**. **Challenging opportunities** include advanced placement credit, accelerated degree programs, student-designed majors, an honors program, double majors, independent study, and a senior project. Special programs include cooperative education, internships, summer session for credit, off-campus study, study-abroad, and Army and Air Force ROTC.

The most frequently chosen **baccalaureate** fields are engineering, agriculture, and business/marketing. A complete listing of majors at Cornell appears in the Majors by College index beginning on page 469.

The **faculty** at Cornell has 1,720 full-time members, 92% with terminal degrees. The student-faculty ratio is 9:1.

Students of Cornell
The student body totals 20,273, of whom 13,846 are undergraduates. 49.3% are women and 50.7% are men. Students come from 54 states and territories and 77 other countries. 37% are from New York. 8.2% are international students. 5.1% are African American, 0.5% American Indian, 16.6% Asian American, and 5.6% Hispanic American. 96% returned for their sophomore year.

Facilities and Resources
2,650 **computers/terminals** and 1,000 ports are available on campus for general student use. Students can access the following: campus intranet, computer help desk, free student e-mail accounts, online (class) grades, online (class) registration. Campuswide network is available. 100% of college-owned or -operated housing units are wired for high-speed Internet access. Wireless service is available via entire campus. The 19 **libraries** have 8,141,781 books and 89,000 subscriptions.

Campus Life
There are 841 active organizations on campus, including a drama/theater group, newspaper, radio station, television station, choral group, and marching band. 32% of eligible men and 23% of eligible women are members of national **fraternities**, national **sororities**, and local fraternities.

Cornell is a member of the NCAA (Division I). **Intercollegiate sports** include baseball (m), basketball, crew, cross-country running, equestrian sports (w), fencing (w), field hockey (w), football (m), golf (m), gymnastics (w), ice hockey, lacrosse, soccer, softball (w), squash, swimming and diving, tennis, track and field, volleyball (w), wrestling (m).

Campus Safety
Student safety services include escort service, late-night transport/escort service, 24-hour emergency telephone alarm devices, 24-hour patrols by trained security personnel, and electronically operated dormitory entrances.

Applying
Cornell requires an essay, SAT or ACT, a high school transcript, and 2 recommendations, and in some cases SAT Subject Tests and an interview. Application deadline: 1/2; 2/11 for financial aid. Early and deferred admission are possible.

CORNERSTONE UNIVERSITY

SUBURBAN SETTING ■ PRIVATE ■ INDEPENDENT RELIGIOUS ■ COED
GRAND RAPIDS, MICHIGAN

Web site: www.cornerstone.edu
Contact: Office of Admissions, 1001 East Beltline Avenue, NE, Grand Rapids, MI 49525
Telephone: 616-222-1426 or toll-free 800-787-9778
Fax: 616-222-1400
E-mail: admissions@cornerstone.edu

Academics

Cornerstone awards associate, bachelor's, master's, and first-professional **degrees. Challenging opportunities** include advanced placement credit, accelerated degree programs, an honors program, double majors, independent study, and a senior project. Special programs include internships, summer session for credit, off-campus study, study-abroad, and Army ROTC.

The most frequently chosen **baccalaureate** fields are business/marketing, education, and theology and religious vocations. A complete listing of majors at Cornerstone appears in the Majors by College index beginning on page 469.

The **faculty** at Cornerstone has 62 full-time members, 50% with terminal degrees. The student-faculty ratio is 12:1.

Students of Cornerstone

The student body totals 2,440, of whom 1,797 are undergraduates. 58.9% are women and 41.1% are men. Students come from 35 states and territories and 7 other countries. 88% are from Michigan. 0.6% are international students. 11% are African American, 0.3% American Indian, 1.3% Asian American, and 3.7% Hispanic American. 69% returned for their sophomore year.

Facilities and Resources

531 **computers/terminals** are available on campus for general student use. Students can access the following: campus intranet, computer help desk, free student e-mail accounts, online (class) grades, online (class) registration, online (class) schedules. Campuswide network is available. 100% of college-owned or -operated housing units are wired for high-speed Internet access. Wireless service is available via entire campus. The **library** has 160,815 books and 2,587 subscriptions.

Campus Life

There are 13 active organizations on campus, including a drama/theater group, newspaper, and choral group. No national or local **fraternities** or **sororities**.

Cornerstone is a member of the NAIA. **Intercollegiate sports** (some offering scholarships) include basketball, cross-country running, golf, soccer, softball (w), track and field, volleyball (w).

Campus Safety

Student safety services include late-night transport/escort service, 24-hour emergency telephone alarm devices, 24-hour patrols by trained security personnel, student patrols, and electronically operated dormitory entrances.

Applying

Cornerstone requires an essay, SAT or ACT, a high school transcript, 1 recommendation, pastoral letter, and a minimum high school GPA of 2.5. It recommends an interview. Application deadline: rolling admissions; 3/1 for financial aid. Deferred admission is possible.

Getting Accepted

939 applied
75% were accepted
205 enrolled (29% of accepted)
3.3 average high school GPA
Mean ACT score: 23
31% had SAT critical reading scores over 600
14% had SAT math scores over 600
35% had ACT scores over 24
4% had SAT critical reading scores over 700
3% had ACT scores over 30

Graduation and After

25% graduated in 4 years
13% graduated in 5 years
4% graduated in 6 years
87% had job offers within 6 months
75 organizations recruited on campus

Financial Matters

$19,530 tuition and fees (2008–09)
$6500 room and board
84% average percent of need met
$16,272 average financial aid amount received per undergraduate (2007–08 estimated)

COVENANT COLLEGE

SUBURBAN SETTING ■ PRIVATE ■ INDEPENDENT RELIGIOUS ■ COED
LOOKOUT MOUNTAIN, GEORGIA

Web site: www.covenant.edu
Contact: Mr. David Gambrell, Assistant Director of Admissions, 14049 Scenic Highway, Lookout Mountain, GA 30750
Telephone: 706-419-1158 or toll-free 888-451-2683
Fax: 706-419-0893
E-mail: admissions@covenant.edu

Getting Accepted
996 applied
64% were accepted
267 enrolled (42% of accepted)
30% from top tenth of their h.s. class
3.7 average high school GPA
Mean SAT critical reading score: 591
Mean SAT math score: 562
Mean SAT writing score: 579
Mean ACT score: 25
50% had SAT critical reading scores over 600
38% had SAT math scores over 600
40% had SAT writing scores over 600
59% had ACT scores over 24
13% had SAT critical reading scores over 700
4% had SAT math scores over 700
8% had SAT writing scores over 700
13% had ACT scores over 30

Graduation and After
54% graduated in 4 years
9% graduated in 5 years
1% graduated in 6 years

Financial Matters
$24,320 tuition and fees (2008–09)
$6900 room and board
80% average percent of need met
$17,104 average financial aid amount received per undergraduate (2006–07)

Academics

Covenant awards associate, bachelor's, and master's **degrees** (master's degree in education only). **Challenging opportunities** include advanced placement credit, student-designed majors, double majors, independent study, and a senior project. Special programs include internships, summer session for credit, off-campus study, and study-abroad.

The most frequently chosen **baccalaureate** fields are social sciences, interdisciplinary studies, and education. A complete listing of majors at Covenant appears in the Majors by College index beginning on page 469.

The **faculty** at Covenant has 63 full-time members, 86% with terminal degrees. The student-faculty ratio is 14:1.

Students of Covenant

The student body totals 1,073, of whom 1,006 are undergraduates. 55.8% are women and 44.2% are men. Students come from 44 states and territories and 15 other countries. 25% are from Georgia. 1.5% are international students. 2.9% are African American, 0.2% American Indian, 1.8% Asian American, and 1.8% Hispanic American. 75% returned for their sophomore year.

Facilities and Resources

133 **computers/terminals** are available on campus for general student use. Students can access the following: computer help desk, free student e-mail accounts, online (class) registration, online student information system. Campuswide network is available. 100% of college-owned or -operated housing units are wired for high-speed Internet access. Wireless service is available via classrooms, computer labs, dorm rooms, libraries. The **library** has 90,000 books and 1,600 subscriptions.

Campus Life

There are 40 active organizations on campus, including a drama/theater group, newspaper, radio station, and choral group. No national or local **fraternities** or **sororities**.

Covenant is a member of the NAIA. **Intercollegiate sports** (some offering scholarships) include baseball (m), basketball, cross-country running, golf, soccer, softball (w), tennis (w), volleyball (w).

Campus Safety

Student safety services include night security guards.

Applying

Covenant requires an essay, SAT or ACT, a high school transcript, an interview, 2 recommendations, and a minimum high school GPA of 2.5. Application deadline: rolling admissions. Early and deferred admission are possible.

Creighton University

Urban setting ■ Private ■ Independent Religious ■ Coed
Omaha, Nebraska

Web site: www.creighton.edu
Contact: Ms. Mary Chase, Assistant Vice President for Enrollment
Management and Director of Admissions and Scholarships, 2500 California
Plaza, Omaha, NE 68178-0001
Telephone: 402-280-3105 or toll-free 800-282-5835
Fax: 402-280-2685
E-mail: admissions@creighton.edu

Academics

Creighton awards associate, bachelor's, master's, doctoral, and first-professional **degrees** and post-bachelor's certificates. **Challenging opportunities** include advanced placement credit, accelerated degree programs, freshman honors college, an honors program, double majors, independent study, and a senior project. Special programs include internships, summer session for credit, off-campus study, study-abroad, and Army and Air Force ROTC.

The most frequently chosen **baccalaureate** fields are health professions and related sciences, business/marketing, and biological/life sciences. A complete listing of majors at Creighton appears in the Majors by College index beginning on page 469.

The **faculty** at Creighton has 508 full-time members, 85% with terminal degrees. The student-faculty ratio is 11:1.

Students of Creighton

The student body totals 7,051, of whom 4,087 are undergraduates. 59.4% are women and 40.6% are men. Students come from 51 states and territories and 33 other countries. 35% are from Nebraska. 1.4% are international students. 3.6% are African American, 1.2% American Indian, 9.1% Asian American, and 3.7% Hispanic American. 87% returned for their sophomore year.

Facilities and Resources

Students can access the following: campus intranet, computer help desk, free student e-mail accounts, online (class) grades, online (class) registration, online (class) schedules, financial aid information. Campuswide network is available. 100% of college-owned or -operated housing units are wired for high-speed Internet access. Wireless service is available via entire campus. The 3 **libraries** have 925,385 books and 42,374 subscriptions.

Campus Life

There are 160 active organizations on campus, including a drama/theater group, newspaper, and choral group. 23% of eligible men and 21% of eligible women are members of national **fraternities**, national **sororities**, local fraternities, and local sororities.

Creighton is a member of the NCAA (Division I). **Intercollegiate sports** (some offering scholarships) include baseball (m), basketball, crew (w), cross-country running, golf, soccer, softball (w), tennis, volleyball (w).

Campus Safety

Student safety services include late-night transport/escort service, 24-hour emergency telephone alarm devices, 24-hour patrols by trained security personnel, student patrols, and electronically operated dormitory entrances.

Applying

Creighton requires an essay, SAT or ACT, a high school transcript, 1 recommendation, and a minimum high school GPA of 2.75. Application deadline: 2/15; 5/15 priority date for financial aid. Deferred admission is possible.

Getting Accepted

4,740 applied
82% were accepted
992 enrolled (26% of accepted)
42% from top tenth of their h.s. class
3.75 average high school GPA
Mean SAT critical reading score: 570
Mean SAT math score: 597
Mean SAT writing score: 563
Mean ACT score: 26
37% had SAT critical reading scores over 600
51% had SAT math scores over 600
35% had SAT writing scores over 600
79% had ACT scores over 24
9% had SAT critical reading scores over 700
11% had SAT math scores over 700
6% had SAT writing scores over 700
19% had ACT scores over 30
10 National Merit Scholars
25 class presidents
68 valedictorians

Graduation and After

67% graduated in 4 years
8% graduated in 5 years
1% graduated in 6 years
96% had job offers within 6 months
200 organizations recruited on campus

Financial Matters

$28,542 tuition and fees (2008–09)
$8516 room and board
88% average percent of need met
$26,932 average financial aid amount received per undergraduate (2007–08 estimated)

DARTMOUTH COLLEGE

SMALL-TOWN SETTING ■ PRIVATE ■ INDEPENDENT ■ COED
HANOVER, NEW HAMPSHIRE

Web site: www.dartmouth.edu
Contact: Maria Laskaris, Dean of Admissions and Financial Aid, 6016
McNutt Hall, Hanover, NH 03755
Telephone: 603-646-2875
E-mail: admissions.office@dartmouth.edu

Getting Accepted
16,538 applied
13% were accepted
1,096 enrolled (49% of accepted)
91% from top tenth of their h.s. class
Mean SAT critical reading score: 712
Mean SAT math score: 720
Mean SAT writing score: 714
Mean ACT score: 31
91% had SAT critical reading scores over 600
93% had SAT math scores over 600
91% had SAT writing scores over 600
96% had ACT scores over 24
65% had SAT critical reading scores over 700
67% had SAT math scores over 700
68% had SAT writing scores over 700
73% had ACT scores over 30
224 National Merit Scholars
78 class presidents
142 valedictorians

Graduation and After
86% graduated in 4 years
8% graduated in 5 years
1% graduated in 6 years
215 organizations recruited on campus

Financial Matters
$38,445 tuition and fees (2009–10)
$10,779 room and board
100% average percent of need met
$31,802 average financial aid amount received
per undergraduate (2006–07)

Academics

Dartmouth awards bachelor's, master's, doctoral, and first-professional **degrees**. **Challenging opportunities** include advanced placement credit, student-designed majors, an honors program, double majors, independent study, and a senior project. Special programs include internships, summer session for credit, off-campus study, study-abroad, and Army ROTC.

The most frequently chosen **baccalaureate** fields are social sciences, history, and psychology. A complete listing of majors at Dartmouth appears in the Majors by College index beginning on page 469.

The **faculty** at Dartmouth has 492 full-time members, 93% with terminal degrees. The student-faculty ratio is 8:1.

Students of Dartmouth

The student body totals 5,848, of whom 4,147 are undergraduates. 49.6% are women and 50.4% are men. Students come from 54 states and territories and 47 other countries. 4% are from New Hampshire. 6.9% are international students. 7.9% are African American, 3.6% American Indian, 13.5% Asian American, and 6.7% Hispanic American. 98% returned for their sophomore year.

Facilities and Resources

200 **computers/terminals** are available on campus for general student use. Students can access the following: campus intranet, computer help desk, free student e-mail accounts, online (class) grades, online (class) registration, online (class) schedules. Campuswide network is available. 100% of college-owned or -operated housing units are wired for high-speed Internet access. Wireless service is available via entire campus.

Campus Life

There are 250 active organizations on campus, including a drama/theater group, newspaper, radio station, television station, choral group, and marching band. 59% of eligible men and 55% of eligible women are members of national **fraternities**, national **sororities**, local fraternities, and local sororities.

Dartmouth is a member of the NCAA (Division I). **Intercollegiate sports** include baseball (m), basketball, crew, cross-country running, equestrian sports, field hockey (w), football (m), golf, ice hockey, lacrosse, sailing, skiing (cross-country), skiing (downhill), soccer, softball (w), squash, swimming and diving, tennis, track and field, volleyball (w).

Campus Safety

Student safety services include late-night transport/escort service, 24-hour emergency telephone alarm devices, 24-hour patrols by trained security personnel, student patrols, and electronically operated dormitory entrances.

Applying

Dartmouth requires an essay, SAT Subject Tests, SAT or ACT, a high school transcript, 2 recommendations, and peer evaluation. It recommends an interview. Application deadline: 1/1; 2/1 for financial aid. Early and deferred admission are possible.

DAVIDSON COLLEGE

SMALL-TOWN SETTING ■ PRIVATE ■ INDEPENDENT RELIGIOUS ■ COED
DAVIDSON, NORTH CAROLINA

Web site: www.davidson.edu
Contact: Mr. Christopher J. Gruber, Vice President and Dean of Admission
and Financial Aid, Box 7156, Davidson, NC 28035-7156
Telephone: 704-894-2230 or toll-free 800-768-0380
Fax: 704-894-2016
E-mail: admission@davidson.edu

Academics

Davidson awards bachelor's **degrees**. **Challenging opportunities** include advanced
placement credit, student-designed majors, an honors program, double majors,
independent study, and a senior project. Special programs include off-campus study,
study-abroad, and Army and Air Force ROTC.

The most frequently chosen **baccalaureate** fields are social sciences, English, and
foreign languages and literature. A complete listing of majors at Davidson appears in the
Majors by College index beginning on page 469.

The **faculty** at Davidson has 168 full-time members, 97% with terminal degrees.
The student-faculty ratio is 10:1.

Students of Davidson

The student body is made up of 1,668 undergraduates. 51% are women and 49% are
men. Students come from 51 states and territories and 36 other countries. 20% are from
North Carolina. 3.8% are international students. 5.7% are African American, 0.5%
American Indian, 4% Asian American, and 4.2% Hispanic American. 96% returned for
their sophomore year.

Facilities and Resources

142 **computers/terminals** are available on campus for general student use. Students can
access the following: campus intranet, computer help desk, free student e-mail accounts,
online (class) registration, online (class) schedules. Campuswide network is available.
100% of college-owned or -operated housing units are wired for high-speed Internet
access. Wireless service is available via entire campus. The 2 **libraries** have 631,294
books and 4,846 subscriptions.

Campus Life

There are 162 active organizations on campus, including a drama/theater group,
newspaper, radio station, and choral group. 43% of eligible men are members of national
fraternities.

Davidson is a member of the NCAA (Division I). **Intercollegiate sports** (some
offering scholarships) include baseball (m), basketball, cross-country running, field
hockey (w), football (m), golf (m), lacrosse (w), soccer, swimming and diving, tennis,
track and field, volleyball (w), wrestling (m).

Campus Safety

Student safety services include late-night transport/escort service, 24-hour emergency
telephone alarm devices, 24-hour patrols by trained security personnel, and electronically operated dormitory entrances.

Applying

Davidson requires an essay, SAT or ACT, a high school transcript, and 3 recommendations. It recommends SAT Subject Tests and an interview. Application deadline: 1/2; 2/15
priority date for financial aid. Early and deferred admission are possible.

Getting Accepted

4,412 applied
26% were accepted
480 enrolled (42% of accepted)
81% from top tenth of their h.s. class
3.85 average high school GPA
Mean SAT critical reading score: 678
Mean SAT math score: 681
Mean SAT writing score: 679
Mean ACT score: 30
88% had SAT critical reading scores over 600
90% had SAT math scores over 600
89% had SAT writing scores over 600
97% had ACT scores over 24
40% had SAT critical reading scores over 700
41% had SAT math scores over 700
46% had SAT writing scores over 700
61% had ACT scores over 30

Graduation and After

92% graduated in 4 years
2% graduated in 5 years
1% graduated in 6 years
64% had job offers within 6 months
955 organizations recruited on campus

Financial Matters

$33,479 tuition and fees (2008–09)
$9471 room and board
100% average percent of need met
$19,548 average financial aid amount received
  per undergraduate (2006–07)

Denison University, a four-year, highly selective, national, residential liberal arts college for men and women, located in Granville, Ohio, is known for its intellectual rigor, curricular innovation, and unique faculty-student learning partnerships. Students may choose from forty-nine courses of study and twelve preprofessional programs or design their own programs of study while living on the beautiful 900-acre hillside campus. Founded in 1831, Denison has 30,000 alumni and an endowment of $700 million.

Getting Accepted
5,305 applied
38% were accepted
605 enrolled (30% of accepted)
50% from top tenth of their h.s. class
3.6 average high school GPA
69% had SAT critical reading scores over 600
65% had SAT math scores over 600
87% had ACT scores over 24
22% had SAT critical reading scores over 700
17% had SAT math scores over 700
26% had ACT scores over 30
16 National Merit Scholars
27 class presidents
35 valedictorians

Graduation and After
77% graduated in 4 years
4% graduated in 5 years
1% graduated in 6 years
65% had job offers within 6 months
35 organizations recruited on campus

Financial Matters
$35,300 tuition and fees (2008–09)
$8610 room and board
98% average percent of need met
$27,693 average financial aid amount received per undergraduate (2007–08 estimated)

DENISON UNIVERSITY
SMALL-TOWN SETTING ■ PRIVATE ■ INDEPENDENT ■ COED
GRANVILLE, OHIO

Web site: www.denison.edu
Contact: Mr. Perry Robinson, Director of Admissions, Box H, Granville, OH 43023
Telephone: 740-587-6276 or toll-free 800-DENISON
Fax: 740-587-6306
E-mail: admissions@denison.edu

Academics
Denison awards bachelor's **degrees**. **Challenging opportunities** include advanced placement credit, student-designed majors, an honors program, double majors, independent study, and a senior project. Special programs include cooperative education, internships, off-campus study, study-abroad, and Army ROTC.

The most frequently chosen **baccalaureate** fields are social sciences, biological/life sciences, and communications/journalism. A complete listing of majors at Denison appears in the Majors by College index beginning on page 469.

The **faculty** at Denison has 195 full-time members, 97% with terminal degrees. The student-faculty ratio is 10:1.

Students of Denison
The student body is made up of 2,200 undergraduates. 55.7% are women and 44.3% are men. Students come from 50 states and territories and 27 other countries. 65% are from Ohio. 4.7% are international students. 5.4% are African American, 0.4% American Indian, 2.5% Asian American, and 2.6% Hispanic American. 88% returned for their sophomore year.

Facilities and Resources
587 **computers/terminals** are available on campus for general student use. Campuswide network is available. The **library** has 767,118 books and 6,616 subscriptions.

Campus Life
There are 147 active organizations on campus, including a drama/theater group, newspaper, radio station, television station, and choral group. 20% of eligible men and 29% of eligible women are members of national **fraternities** and national **sororities**.

Denison is a member of the NCAA (Division III). **Intercollegiate sports** include baseball (m), basketball, cross-country running, field hockey (w), football (m), golf (m), lacrosse, soccer, softball (w), swimming and diving, tennis, track and field, volleyball (w).

Campus Safety
Student safety services include security lighting, escort service, late-night transport/escort service, 24-hour emergency telephone alarm devices, 24-hour patrols by trained security personnel, student patrols, and electronically operated dormitory entrances.

Applying
Denison requires an essay, a high school transcript, and 2 recommendations, and in some cases SAT or ACT. It recommends an interview. Application deadline: 1/15; 2/15 priority date for financial aid. Early and deferred admission are possible.

DePauw University

SMALL-TOWN SETTING ■ PRIVATE ■ INDEPENDENT RELIGIOUS ■ COED
GREENCASTLE, INDIANA

Web site: www.depauw.edu
Contact: Brett Kennedy, Senior Associate Director of Admission, 101 East
  Seminary Street, Greencastle, IN 46135-0037
Telephone: 765-658-4006 or toll-free 800-447-2495
Fax: 765-658-4007
E-mail: admission@depauw.edu

Academics

DePauw awards bachelor's **degrees**. **Challenging opportunities** include advanced
placement credit, student-designed majors, an honors program, double majors,
independent study, and a senior project. Special programs include internships, off-
campus study, study-abroad, and Army and Air Force ROTC. A complete listing of
majors at DePauw appears in the Majors by College index beginning on page 469.

The **faculty** at DePauw has 217 full-time members, 98% with terminal degrees. The
student-faculty ratio is 10:1.

Students of DePauw

The student body is made up of 2,298 undergraduates. 56.8% are women and 43.2% are
men. Students come from 43 states and territories and 32 other countries. 45% are from
Indiana. 5.2% are international students. 6.2% are African American, 0.2% American
Indian, 3.1% Asian American, and 3.6% Hispanic American. 88% returned for their
sophomore year.

Facilities and Resources

424 **computers/terminals** are available on campus for general student use. Students can
access the following: online (class) registration. Campuswide network is available. The 4
libraries have 333,346 books and 2,030 subscriptions.

Campus Life

There are 90 active organizations on campus, including a drama/theater group,
newspaper, radio station, television station, and choral group. 78% of eligible men and
68% of eligible women are members of national **fraternities** and national **sororities**.

DePauw is a member of the NCAA (Division III). **Intercollegiate sports** include
baseball (m), basketball, cross-country running, field hockey (w), football (m), golf,
soccer, softball (w), swimming and diving, tennis, track and field, volleyball (w).

Campus Safety

Student safety services include late-night transport/escort service, 24-hour emergency
telephone alarm devices, 24-hour patrols by trained security personnel, student patrols,
and electronically operated dormitory entrances.

Applying

DePauw requires an essay, SAT or ACT, a high school transcript, and 1 recommendation. It recommends an interview. Application deadline: 2/1; 2/15 for financial aid.
Early and deferred admission are possible.

Getting Accepted
4,064 applied
65% were accepted
600 enrolled (23% of accepted)
51% from top tenth of their h.s. class
3.6 average high school GPA
53% had SAT critical reading scores over 600
63% had SAT math scores over 600
49% had SAT writing scores over 600
86% had ACT scores over 24
13% had SAT critical reading scores over 700
18% had SAT math scores over 700
11% had SAT writing scores over 700
24% had ACT scores over 30

Graduation and After
83% graduated in 4 years
2% graduated in 5 years
90% had job offers within 6 months
35 organizations recruited on campus

Financial Matters
$31,825 tuition and fees (2008–09)
$8400 room and board
92% average percent of need met
$24,579 average financial aid amount received
  per undergraduate (2007–08 estimated)

DICKINSON COLLEGE

SUBURBAN SETTING ■ PRIVATE ■ INDEPENDENT ■ COED
CARLISLE, PENNSYLVANIA

Web site: www.dickinson.edu
Contact: Stephanie Balmer, Dean of Admissions and Financial Aid, PO Box
1773, Carlisle, PA 17013-2896
Telephone: toll-free 800-644-1773
Fax: 717-245-1442
E-mail: admit@dickinson.edu

Getting Accepted
5,282 applied
44% were accepted
613 enrolled (26% of accepted)
50% from top tenth of their h.s. class
Mean SAT critical reading score: 644
Mean SAT math score: 649
Mean ACT score: 28
77% had SAT critical reading scores over 600
75% had SAT math scores over 600
28% had SAT critical reading scores over 700
24% had SAT math scores over 700

Graduation and After
80% graduated in 4 years
3% graduated in 5 years
69% had job offers within 6 months
31 organizations recruited on campus

Financial Matters
$38,234 tuition and fees (2008–09)
$9600 room and board
96% average percent of need met
$28,455 average financial aid amount received
per undergraduate (2007–08 estimated)

Academics

Dickinson awards bachelor's **degrees**. **Challenging opportunities** include advanced placement credit, accelerated degree programs, student-designed majors, double majors, independent study, and a senior project. Special programs include internships, summer session for credit, off-campus study, study-abroad, and Army ROTC.

The most frequently chosen **baccalaureate** fields are social sciences, business/marketing, and area and ethnic studies. A complete listing of majors at Dickinson appears in the Majors by College index beginning on page 469.

The **faculty** at Dickinson has 194 full-time members, 92% with terminal degrees. The student-faculty ratio is 10:1.

Students of Dickinson

The student body is made up of 2,388 undergraduates. 55% are women and 45% are men. Students come from 41 states and territories and 40 other countries. 27% are from Pennsylvania. 5.8% are international students. 4.5% are African American, 0.4% American Indian, 4.6% Asian American, and 5.2% Hispanic American. 92% returned for their sophomore year.

Facilities and Resources

600 **computers/terminals** and 5,000 ports are available on campus for general student use. Students can access the following: campus intranet, computer help desk, free student e-mail accounts, online (class) grades, online (class) registration, online (class) schedules. Campuswide network is available. 100% of college-owned or -operated housing units are wired for high-speed Internet access. Wireless service is available via classrooms, computer centers, computer labs, libraries, student centers. The 4 **libraries** have 580,763 books and 2,451 subscriptions.

Campus Life

There are 130 active organizations on campus, including a drama/theater group, newspaper, radio station, and choral group. 21% of eligible men and 24% of eligible women are members of national **fraternities**, national **sororities**, local fraternities, and local sororities.

Dickinson is a member of the NCAA (Division III). **Intercollegiate sports** include baseball (m), basketball, cross-country running, field hockey (w), football (m), golf, lacrosse, soccer, softball (w), swimming and diving, tennis, track and field, volleyball (w).

Campus Safety

Student safety services include late-night transport/escort service, 24-hour emergency telephone alarm devices, 24-hour patrols by trained security personnel, student patrols, and electronically operated dormitory entrances.

Applying

Dickinson requires an essay, a high school transcript, and 2 recommendations. It recommends SAT or ACT, an interview, and a minimum high school GPA of 3.0. Application deadline: 2/1; 2/1 for financial aid, with a 11/15 priority date. Deferred admission is possible.

DOMINICAN UNIVERSITY

SUBURBAN SETTING ■ PRIVATE ■ INDEPENDENT RELIGIOUS ■ COED
RIVER FOREST, ILLINOIS

Web site: www.dom.edu
Contact: Mr. Glenn Hamilton, Assistant Vice President, Enrollment
   Management, 7900 West Division Street, River Forest, IL 60305
Telephone: 708-524-6800 or toll-free 800-828-8475
Fax: 708-524-6864
E-mail: domadmis@dom.edu

SPONSOR

Academics

Dominican awards bachelor's and master's **degrees** and post-bachelor's and post-master's certificates. **Challenging opportunities** include advanced placement credit, accelerated degree programs, student-designed majors, an honors program, double majors, independent study, and a senior project. Special programs include internships, summer session for credit, off-campus study, and study-abroad.

The most frequently chosen **baccalaureate** fields are business/marketing, social sciences, and psychology. A complete listing of majors at Dominican appears in the Majors by College index beginning on page 469.

The **faculty** at Dominican has 132 full-time members, 86% with terminal degrees. The student-faculty ratio is 11:1.

Students of Dominican

The student body totals 3,413, of whom 1,709 are undergraduates. 68.9% are women and 31.1% are men. Students come from 28 states and territories and 21 other countries. 92% are from Illinois. 2.3% are international students. 7.3% are African American, 0.1% American Indian, 2.6% Asian American, and 23.5% Hispanic American. 79% returned for their sophomore year.

Facilities and Resources

625 **computers/terminals** are available on campus for general student use. Students can access the following: campus intranet, computer help desk, free student e-mail accounts, online (class) grades, online (class) registration, online (class) schedules, online student account information, online financial aid information. Campuswide network is available. 100% of college-owned or -operated housing units are wired for high-speed Internet access. Wireless service is available via computer centers, learning centers, libraries, student centers. The **library** has 348,474 books and 30,249 subscriptions.

Campus Life

There are 30 active organizations on campus, including a drama/theater group, newspaper, and choral group. No national or local **fraternities** or **sororities**.

Dominican is a member of the NCAA (Division III). **Intercollegiate sports** include baseball (m), basketball, cross-country running, golf (m), soccer, softball (w), tennis, volleyball (w).

Campus Safety

Student safety services include door alarms, late-night transport/escort service, 24-hour emergency telephone alarm devices, 24-hour patrols by trained security personnel, student patrols, and electronically operated dormitory entrances.

Applying

Dominican requires an essay, SAT or ACT, a high school transcript, and a minimum high school GPA of 2.75, and in some cases an interview and 2 recommendations. It recommends an interview. Application deadline: rolling admissions; 6/1 priority date for financial aid. Deferred admission is possible.

Dominican University, located just 10 miles from downtown Chicago, offers a comprehensive liberal arts education with a dynamic curriculum and inspiring faculty members. Students choose from fifty majors and participate in a series of four interdisciplinary seminars with their classmates to explore such topics as "Diversity, Culture, and Community" or "Virtues and Values." As a Catholic institution, Dominican is known for its rigorous and engaging academics, its enduring commitment to social justice programs, and the diversity of its students, faculty, and staff. This relationship-centered community encourages students to achieve amazing things—personally and professionally.

Getting Accepted
1,723 applied
71% were accepted
417 enrolled (34% of accepted)
18% from top tenth of their h.s. class
3.36 average high school GPA
Mean ACT score: 22
14% had SAT critical reading scores over 600
22% had SAT math scores over 600
18% had SAT writing scores over 600
33% had ACT scores over 24
2% had SAT critical reading scores over 700
4% had SAT math scores over 700
4% had ACT scores over 30
1 National Merit Scholar
2 valedictorians

Graduation and After
57% graduated in 4 years
9% graduated in 5 years
3% graduated in 6 years
95% had job offers within 6 months
13 organizations recruited on campus

Financial Matters
$23,800 tuition and fees (2008–09)
$7350 room and board
79% average percent of need met
$17,570 average financial aid amount received
   per undergraduate (2007–08 estimated)

DRAKE UNIVERSITY

SUBURBAN SETTING ■ PRIVATE ■ INDEPENDENT ■ COED
DES MOINES, IOWA

Web site: www.drake.edu
Contact: Ms. Laura Linn, Director of Admission, 2507 University Avenue, Des Moines, IA 50311
Telephone: 515-271-3181 Ext. 3182 or toll-free 800-44DRAKE Ext. 3181
Fax: 515-271-2831
E-mail: admission@drake.edu

A Drake education offers a unique mix of advantages for future success. Drake is large enough to offer more than seventy undergraduate academic programs, 160 organizations, and a community of students from around the world. Yet Drake's exceptional faculty and academic and extracurricular options are highly accessible to students beginning their first years of college. Drake's location in Des Moines, Iowa's capital, offers numerous professional internships; nearly 80 percent of Drake students graduate having one or more internships. Drake is affordable; more than 98 percent of its students receive financial assistance. It is a great value, too—nearly all Drake graduates (approximately 99 percent in 2007) obtain career positions or enter graduate school within six months after receiving their degrees.

Getting Accepted

4,786 applied
69% were accepted
902 enrolled (27% of accepted)
41% from top tenth of their h.s. class
3.67 average high school GPA
Mean SAT critical reading score: 580
Mean SAT math score: 606
Mean ACT score: 27
46% had SAT critical reading scores over 600
54% had SAT math scores over 600
80% had ACT scores over 24
7% had SAT critical reading scores over 700
18% had SAT math scores over 700
24% had ACT scores over 30
7 National Merit Scholars

Graduation and After

59% graduated in 4 years
10% graduated in 5 years
2% graduated in 6 years
73.4% had job offers within 6 months
216 organizations recruited on campus

Financial Matters

$26,622 tuition and fees (2009–10)
$7800 room and board
84% average percent of need met
$19,827 average financial aid amount received per undergraduate (2007–08 estimated)

Academics

Drake awards bachelor's, master's, doctoral, and first-professional **degrees** and post-bachelor's, post-master's, and first-professional certificates. **Challenging opportunities** include advanced placement credit, accelerated degree programs, student-designed majors, an honors program, double majors, independent study, and a senior project. Special programs include cooperative education, internships, summer session for credit, off-campus study, study-abroad, and Army and Air Force ROTC.

The most frequently chosen **baccalaureate** fields are business/marketing, communications/journalism, and education. A complete listing of majors at Drake appears in the Majors by College index beginning on page 469.

The **faculty** at Drake has 270 full-time members, 95% with terminal degrees. The student-faculty ratio is 14:1.

Students of Drake

The student body totals 5,668, of whom 3,516 are undergraduates. 57.2% are women and 42.8% are men. Students come from 41 states and territories and 46 other countries. 38% are from Iowa. 7.2% are international students. 3.1% are African American, 0.1% American Indian, 4.2% Asian American, and 1.9% Hispanic American. 86% returned for their sophomore year.

Facilities and Resources

1,000 **computers/terminals** are available on campus for general student use. Students can access the following: campus intranet, computer help desk, free student e-mail accounts, online (class) grades, online (class) registration, online (class) schedules. Campuswide network is available. 100% of college-owned or -operated housing units are wired for high-speed Internet access. Wireless service is available via classrooms, computer centers, computer labs, dorm rooms, libraries, student centers. The 3 **libraries** have 525,093 books and 28,499 subscriptions.

Campus Life

There are 160 active organizations on campus, including a drama/theater group, newspaper, radio station, television station, choral group, and marching band. 12% of eligible men and 15% of eligible women are members of national **fraternities** and national **sororities**.

Drake is a member of the NCAA (Division I). **Intercollegiate sports** (some offering scholarships) include basketball, cheerleading, crew (w), cross-country running, football (m), golf, soccer, softball (w), tennis, track and field, volleyball (w).

Campus Safety

Student safety services include 24-hour desk attendants in residence halls, late-night transport/escort service, 24-hour emergency telephone alarm devices, and 24-hour patrols by trained security personnel.

Applying

Drake requires an essay, SAT or ACT, and a high school transcript. It recommends an interview. Application deadline: 3/1; 3/1 priority date for financial aid. Early and deferred admission are possible.

DREW UNIVERSITY

SUBURBAN SETTING ■ PRIVATE ■ INDEPENDENT RELIGIOUS ■ COED
MADISON, NEW JERSEY

Web site: www.drew.edu
Contact: Ms. Mary Beth Carey, Dean of Admissions and Financial Assistance,
36 Madison Avenue, Madison, NJ 07940-1493
Telephone: 973-408-3739
Fax: 973-408-3068
E-mail: cadm@drew.edu

Academics

Drew awards bachelor's, master's, doctoral, and first-professional **degrees** and post-bachelor's certificates. **Challenging opportunities** include advanced placement credit, accelerated degree programs, student-designed majors, an honors program, double majors, independent study, and a senior project. Special programs include internships, summer session for credit, off-campus study, and study-abroad.

The most frequently chosen **baccalaureate** fields are social sciences, psychology, and visual and performing arts. A complete listing of majors at Drew appears in the Majors by College index beginning on page 469.

The **faculty** at Drew has 158 full-time members, 95% with terminal degrees. The student-faculty ratio is 11:1.

Students of Drew

The student body totals 2,640, of whom 1,676 are undergraduates. 60.7% are women and 39.3% are men. Students come from 45 states and territories and 16 other countries. 59% are from New Jersey. 2% are international students. 6.1% are African American, 0.3% American Indian, 4.8% Asian American, and 7.4% Hispanic American. 83% returned for their sophomore year.

Facilities and Resources

200 **computers/terminals** are available on campus for general student use. Students can access the following: online (class) registration. Campuswide network is available. The **library** has 581,734 books.

Campus Life

There are 80 active organizations on campus, including a drama/theater group, newspaper, radio station, television station, and choral group. No national or local **fraternities** or **sororities**.

Drew is a member of the NCAA (Division III). **Intercollegiate sports** include baseball (m), basketball, cross-country running, equestrian sports, fencing, field hockey (w), lacrosse, soccer, softball (w), swimming and diving, tennis.

Campus Safety

Student safety services include late-night transport/escort service, 24-hour emergency telephone alarm devices, 24-hour patrols by trained security personnel, and electronically operated dormitory entrances.

Applying

Drew requires an essay, a high school transcript, and 1 recommendation. It recommends an interview. Application deadline: 2/15; 2/15 for financial aid. Early and deferred admission are possible.

Getting Accepted

3,816 applied
77% were accepted
456 enrolled (16% of accepted)
28% from top tenth of their h.s. class
3.35 average high school GPA
Mean SAT critical reading score: 585
Mean SAT math score: 570
Mean SAT writing score: 590
Mean ACT score: 23
46% had SAT critical reading scores over 600
36% had SAT math scores over 600
46% had SAT writing scores over 600
48% had ACT scores over 24
12% had SAT critical reading scores over 700
6% had SAT math scores over 700
10% had SAT writing scores over 700
9% had ACT scores over 30

Graduation and After

68.1% had job offers within 6 months
43 organizations recruited on campus

Financial Matters

$36,470 tuition and fees (2008–09)
$9978 room and board
81% average percent of need met
$25,488 average financial aid amount received per undergraduate (2006–07)

DREXEL UNIVERSITY
URBAN SETTING ■ PRIVATE ■ INDEPENDENT ■ COED
PHILADELPHIA, PENNSYLVANIA

Web site: www.drexel.edu
Contact: Ms. Joan MacDonald, Vice President of Enrollment Management, 3141 Chestnut Street, Philadelphia, PA 19104-2875
Telephone: 215-895-2400 or toll-free 800-2-DREXEL
Fax: 215-895-5939
E-mail: enroll@drexel.edu

Getting Accepted
16,867 applied
72% were accepted
2,396 enrolled (20% of accepted)
3.5 average high school GPA

Graduation and After
50% had job offers within 6 months
265 organizations recruited on campus

Financial Matters
$30,440 tuition and fees (2008–09)
$12,135 room and board
59% average percent of need met
$15,076 average financial aid amount received per undergraduate (2005–06)

Academics
Drexel awards associate, bachelor's, master's, doctoral, and first-professional **degrees** and post-bachelor's, post-master's, and first-professional certificates. **Challenging opportunities** include advanced placement credit, accelerated degree programs, freshman honors college, an honors program, double majors, independent study, and a senior project. Special programs include cooperative education, internships, summer session for credit, study-abroad, and Army and Air Force ROTC.

The most frequently chosen **baccalaureate** fields are business/marketing, engineering, and health professions and related sciences. A complete listing of majors at Drexel appears in the Majors by College index beginning on page 469.

The student-faculty ratio is 10:1.

Students of Drexel
The student body totals 20,682, of whom 13,194 are undergraduates. 43.6% are women and 56.4% are men. Students come from 50 states and territories and 93 other countries. 52% are from Pennsylvania. 6.6% are international students. 8.4% are African American, 0.3% American Indian, 12.4% Asian American, and 3% Hispanic American.

Facilities and Resources
6,500 **computers/terminals** are available on campus for general student use. Students can access the following: online (class) registration. Campuswide network is available. Wireless service is available via entire campus. The **library** has 570,335 books and 8,321 subscriptions.

Campus Life
Active organizations on campus include a drama/theater group, newspaper, radio station, television station, and choral group. Drexel has national **fraternities**, national **sororities**, and local fraternities.

Drexel is a member of the NCAA (Division I). **Intercollegiate sports** (some offering scholarships) include basketball, crew, field hockey (w), golf (m), lacrosse, soccer, softball (w), swimming and diving, tennis, wrestling (m).

Campus Safety
Student safety services include late-night transport/escort service, 24-hour emergency telephone alarm devices, 24-hour patrols by trained security personnel, and electronically operated dormitory entrances.

Applying
Drexel requires SAT or ACT, a high school transcript, and a minimum high school GPA of 2.0, and in some cases an essay. It recommends SAT, an interview, and 2 recommendations. Application deadline: 3/1; 3/15 for financial aid. Deferred admission is possible.

DRURY UNIVERSITY

URBAN SETTING ■ PRIVATE ■ INDEPENDENT ■ COED
SPRINGFIELD, MISSOURI

Web site: www.drury.edu
Contact: Mr. Chip Parker, Director of Admission, 900 North Benton, Bay
    Hall, Springfield, MO 65802
Telephone: 417-873-7205 or toll-free 800-922-2274
Fax: 417-866-3873
E-mail: druryad@drury.edu

Academics

Drury awards bachelor's and master's **degrees** (also offers evening program with
significant enrollment not reflected in profile). **Challenging opportunities** include
advanced placement credit, accelerated degree programs, student-designed majors, an
honors program, double majors, independent study, and a senior project. Special
programs include cooperative education, internships, summer session for credit, off-
campus study, study-abroad, and Army ROTC.

    The most frequently chosen **baccalaureate** fields are business/marketing, biologi-
cal/life sciences, and communications/journalism. A complete listing of majors at Drury
appears in the Majors by College index beginning on page 469.

    The **faculty** at Drury has 127 full-time members, 91% with terminal degrees. The
student-faculty ratio is 12:1.

Students of Drury

The student body totals 2,060, of whom 1,555 are undergraduates. 52.7% are women
and 47.3% are men. Students come from 30 states and territories and 29 other countries.
83% are from Missouri. 5.7% are international students. 2.3% are African American,
0.7% American Indian, 2.1% Asian American, and 1.9% Hispanic American. 82%
returned for their sophomore year.

Facilities and Resources

323 **computers/terminals** are available on campus for general student use. Students can
access the following: campus intranet, computer help desk, free student e-mail accounts,
online (class) grades, online (class) registration, online (class) schedules, digital imaging
lab, online bill payment/student information. Campuswide network is available. 30% of
college-owned or -operated housing units are wired for high-speed Internet access.
Wireless service is available via entire campus. The 2 **libraries** have 169,968 books and
690 subscriptions.

Campus Life

There are 52 active organizations on campus, including a drama/theater group,
newspaper, radio station, television station, and choral group. 26% of eligible men and
27% of eligible women are members of national **fraternities** and national **sororities**.

    Drury is a member of the NCAA (Division II). **Intercollegiate sports** (some
offering scholarships) include baseball (m), basketball, cheerleading, cross-country
running, golf, soccer, softball (w), swimming and diving, tennis, track and field, volleyball
(w).

Campus Safety

Student safety services include security cameras in parking areas, late-night transport/
escort service, 24-hour emergency telephone alarm devices, 24-hour patrols by trained
security personnel, student patrols, and electronically operated dormitory entrances.

Applying

Drury requires an essay, SAT or ACT, a high school transcript, 1 recommendation,
minimum ACT score of 21, and a minimum high school GPA of 2.7. It recommends an
interview. Application deadline: 8/1; 3/15 priority date for financial aid. Deferred
admission is possible.

Getting Accepted

1,108 applied
72% were accepted
334 enrolled (42% of accepted)
35% from top tenth of their h.s. class
3.83 average high school GPA
Mean SAT critical reading score: 560
Mean SAT math score: 567
Mean SAT writing score: 562
Mean ACT score: 25
60% had ACT scores over 24
12% had ACT scores over 30
31 valedictorians

Graduation and After

50% graduated in 4 years
12% graduated in 5 years
2% graduated in 6 years
28 organizations recruited on campus

Financial Matters

$18,264 tuition and fees (2008–09)
$6384 room and board
84% average percent of need met
$7642 average financial aid amount received
    per undergraduate (2007–08 estimated)

DUKE UNIVERSITY

SUBURBAN SETTING ■ PRIVATE ■ INDEPENDENT RELIGIOUS ■ COED
DURHAM, NORTH CAROLINA

Web site: www.duke.edu
Contact: Mr. Christoph Guttentag, Director of Admissions, 2138 Campus
    Drive, Durham, NC 27708
Telephone: 919-684-3214
Fax: 919-684-8941
E-mail: askduke@admiss.duke.edu

Getting Accepted

17,748 applied
23% were accepted
1,700 enrolled (42% of accepted)
90% from top tenth of their h.s. class
92% had SAT critical reading scores over 600
94% had SAT math scores over 600
91% had SAT writing scores over 600
96% had ACT scores over 24
60% had SAT critical reading scores over 700
68% had SAT math scores over 700
57% had SAT writing scores over 700
72% had ACT scores over 30
197 valedictorians

Graduation and After

47% had job offers within 6 months
280 organizations recruited on campus

Financial Matters

$37,388 tuition and fees (2008–09)
$9689 room and board
100% average percent of need met
$31,014 average financial aid amount received
    per undergraduate (2007–08 estimated)

Academics

Duke awards bachelor's, master's, doctoral, and first-professional **degrees** and post-bachelor's and post-master's certificates. **Challenging opportunities** include advanced placement credit, accelerated degree programs, student-designed majors, an honors program, double majors, independent study, and a senior project. Special programs include internships, summer session for credit, off-campus study, study-abroad, and Army, Navy, and Air Force ROTC.

The most frequently chosen **baccalaureate** fields are social sciences, engineering, and psychology. A complete listing of majors at Duke appears in the Majors by College index beginning on page 469.

The **faculty** at Duke has 990 full-time members, 96% with terminal degrees. The student-faculty ratio is 8:1.

Students of Duke

The student body totals 13,598, of whom 6,394 are undergraduates. 49% are women and 51% are men. Students come from 53 states and territories and 89 other countries. 13% are from North Carolina. 5.8% are international students. 10% are African American, 0.2% American Indian, 19.5% Asian American, and 6.2% Hispanic American. 97% returned for their sophomore year.

Facilities and Resources

450 **computers/terminals** are available on campus for general student use. Students can access the following: campus intranet, computer help desk, free student e-mail accounts, online (class) registration. Campuswide network is available. 100% of college-owned or -operated housing units are wired for high-speed Internet access. Wireless service is available via entire campus. The 15 **libraries** have 5,560,966 books and 31,892 subscriptions.

Campus Life

There are 400 active organizations on campus, including a drama/theater group, newspaper, radio station, television station, choral group, and marching band. 29% of eligible men and 42% of eligible women are members of national **fraternities** and national **sororities**.

Duke is a member of the NCAA (Division I). **Intercollegiate sports** (some offering scholarships) include baseball (m), basketball, crew (w), cross-country running, fencing, field hockey (w), football (m), golf, lacrosse, soccer, swimming and diving, tennis, track and field, volleyball (w), wrestling (m).

Campus Safety

Student safety services include late-night transport/escort service, 24-hour emergency telephone alarm devices, 24-hour patrols by trained security personnel, and electronically operated dormitory entrances.

Applying

Duke requires an essay, SAT and SAT Subject Tests or ACT, and a high school transcript, and in some cases audition tape for dance, drama, or music; slides of work for art. It recommends an interview. Application deadline: 1/2; 2/1 for financial aid. Early and deferred admission are possible.

Duquesne University

URBAN SETTING ■ PRIVATE ■ INDEPENDENT RELIGIOUS ■ COED
PITTSBURGH, PENNSYLVANIA

Web site: www.duq.edu
Contact: Mr. Paul-James Cukanna, Associate Vice President for Enrollment Management and Director of Admissions, 1st Floor Administration Building, 600 Forbes Avenue, Pittsburgh, PA 15282-0201
Telephone: 412-396-5002 or toll-free 800-456-0590
Fax: 412-396-6223
E-mail: admissions@duq.edu

Academics

Duquesne awards bachelor's, master's, doctoral, and first-professional **degrees** and post-bachelor's and post-master's certificates. **Challenging opportunities** include advanced placement credit, accelerated degree programs, student-designed majors, freshman honors college, an honors program, double majors, independent study, and a senior project. Special programs include internships, summer session for credit, off-campus study, study-abroad, and Army, Navy, and Air Force ROTC.

The most frequently chosen **baccalaureate** fields are business/marketing, health professions and related sciences, and education. A complete listing of majors at Duquesne appears in the Majors by College index beginning on page 469.

The **faculty** at Duquesne has 463 full-time members, 83% with terminal degrees. The student-faculty ratio is 15:1.

Students of Duquesne

The student body totals 10,106, of whom 5,656 are undergraduates. 57.7% are women and 42.3% are men. Students come from 48 states and territories and 47 other countries. 80% are from Pennsylvania. 2.1% are international students. 3.5% are African American, 0.2% American Indian, 1.7% Asian American, and 1.5% Hispanic American. 88% returned for their sophomore year.

Facilities and Resources

1,000 **computers/terminals** are available on campus for general student use. Students can access the following: campus intranet, computer help desk, free student e-mail accounts, online (class) grades, online (class) registration, online (class) schedules. Campuswide network is available. 100% of college-owned or -operated housing units are wired for high-speed Internet access. Wireless service is available via classrooms, computer centers, computer labs, learning centers, libraries, student centers. The 2 **libraries** have 700,245 books and 30,980 subscriptions.

Campus Life

There are 150 active organizations on campus, including a drama/theater group, newspaper, radio station, television station, choral group, and marching band. 12% of eligible men and 9% of eligible women are members of national **fraternities**, national **sororities**, and local fraternities.

Duquesne is a member of the NCAA (Division I). **Intercollegiate sports** (some offering scholarships) include baseball (m), basketball (m), crew (w), cross-country running, football (m), golf (m), lacrosse (w), soccer, swimming and diving, tennis, track and field, volleyball (w), wrestling (m).

Campus Safety

Student safety services include 24-hour front desk personnel, 24-hour video monitors at residence hall entrances, surveillance cameras throughout the campus, late-night transport/escort service, 24-hour emergency telephone alarm devices, 24-hour patrols by trained security personnel, and electronically operated dormitory entrances.

Applying

Duquesne requires an essay, SAT or ACT, a high school transcript, and 1 recommendation. It recommends an interview and a minimum high school GPA of 3.0. Application deadline: 7/1; 5/1 for financial aid. Early and deferred admission are possible.

Getting Accepted

5,715 applied
76% were accepted
1,438 enrolled (33% of accepted)
23% from top tenth of their h.s. class
3.59 average high school GPA
Mean SAT critical reading score: 560
Mean SAT math score: 568
Mean SAT writing score: 553
Mean ACT score: 24
29% had SAT critical reading scores over 600
33% had SAT math scores over 600
29% had SAT writing scores over 600
56% had ACT scores over 24
4% had SAT critical reading scores over 700
4% had SAT math scores over 700
4% had SAT writing scores over 700
6% had ACT scores over 30
25 valedictorians

Graduation and After

58% graduated in 4 years
12% graduated in 5 years
2% graduated in 6 years
69% had job offers within 6 months
154 organizations recruited on campus

Financial Matters

$25,480 tuition and fees (2008–09)
$8888 room and board
89% average percent of need met
$15,204 average financial aid amount received per undergraduate (2006–07)

Earlham College

SMALL-TOWN SETTING ■ PRIVATE ■ INDEPENDENT RELIGIOUS ■ COED
RICHMOND, INDIANA

Web site: www.earlham.edu
Contact: Mr. Jeff Rickey, Dean of Admissions and Financial Aid, 801 National Road West, Richmond, IN 47374
Telephone: 765-983-1600 or toll-free 800-327-5426
Fax: 765-983-1560
E-mail: admission@earlham.edu

Getting Accepted

1,825 applied
75% were accepted
324 enrolled (24% of accepted)
32% from top tenth of their h.s. class
3.5 average high school GPA
Mean SAT critical reading score: 610
Mean SAT math score: 585
Mean SAT writing score: 610
Mean ACT score: 26
59% had SAT critical reading scores over 600
50% had SAT math scores over 600
58% had SAT writing scores over 600
75% had ACT scores over 24
21% had SAT critical reading scores over 700
10% had SAT math scores over 700
19% had SAT writing scores over 700
25% had ACT scores over 30
6 National Merit Scholars
13 class presidents
8 valedictorians

Graduation and After

58% graduated in 4 years
12% graduated in 5 years
3% graduated in 6 years
66% had job offers within 6 months
15 organizations recruited on campus

Financial Matters

$34,030 tuition and fees (2008–09)
$6814 room and board
93% average percent of need met
$22,596 average financial aid amount received per undergraduate (2006–07)

Academics

Earlham awards bachelor's, master's, and first-professional **degrees**. **Challenging opportunities** include advanced placement credit, accelerated degree programs, student-designed majors, double majors, independent study, and a senior project. Special programs include internships, off-campus study, and study-abroad.

The most frequently chosen **baccalaureate** fields are biological/life sciences, social sciences, and interdisciplinary studies. A complete listing of majors at Earlham appears in the Majors by College index beginning on page 469.

The **faculty** at Earlham has 94 full-time members, 96% with terminal degrees. The student-faculty ratio is 12:1.

Students of Earlham

The student body totals 1,308, of whom 1,184 are undergraduates. 55.9% are women and 44.1% are men. Students come from 44 states and territories and 71 other countries. 32% are from Indiana. 12.7% are international students. 5.7% are African American, 0.3% American Indian, 2.5% Asian American, and 2.5% Hispanic American. 85% returned for their sophomore year.

Facilities and Resources

175 **computers/terminals** and 30 ports are available on campus for general student use. Students can access the following: campus intranet, computer help desk, free student e-mail accounts, online (class) grades, online (class) registration, online (class) schedules. Campuswide network is available. 100% of college-owned or -operated housing units are wired for high-speed Internet access. Wireless service is available via classrooms, computer centers, computer labs, learning centers, libraries, student centers. The 3 **libraries** have 406,316 books and 22,439 subscriptions.

Campus Life

There are 70 active organizations on campus, including a drama/theater group, newspaper, radio station, and choral group. No national or local **fraternities** or **sororities**.

Earlham is a member of the NCAA (Division III). **Intercollegiate sports** include baseball (m), basketball, cross-country running, field hockey (w), football (m), soccer, tennis, track and field, volleyball (w).

Campus Safety

Student safety services include late-night transport/escort service, 24-hour emergency telephone alarm devices, 24-hour patrols by trained security personnel, student patrols, and electronically operated dormitory entrances.

Applying

Earlham requires an essay, SAT or ACT, a high school transcript, 2 recommendations, and a minimum high school GPA of 3.0. It recommends an interview. Application deadline: 2/15; 3/1 for financial aid. Early and deferred admission are possible.

ELIZABETHTOWN COLLEGE

SMALL-TOWN SETTING ■ PRIVATE ■ INDEPENDENT RELIGIOUS ■ COED
ELIZABETHTOWN, PENNSYLVANIA

Web site: www.etown.edu
Contact: Ms. Debra Murray, Director of Admissions, One Alpha Drive,
Elizabethtown, PA 17022
Telephone: 717-361-1400
Fax: 717-361-1365
E-mail: admissions@etown.edu

SPONSOR

Academics

E-town awards associate, bachelor's, and master's **degrees** and post-bachelor's certificates. **Challenging opportunities** include advanced placement credit, an honors program, double majors, independent study, and a senior project. Special programs include internships, summer session for credit, off-campus study, and study-abroad.

The most frequently chosen **baccalaureate** fields are business/marketing, education, and health professions and related sciences. A complete listing of majors at E-town appears in the Majors by College index beginning on page 469.

The **faculty** at E-town has 129 full-time members, 89% with terminal degrees. The student-faculty ratio is 11:1.

Students of E-town

The student body totals 2,311, of whom 2,258 are undergraduates. 65.1% are women and 34.9% are men. Students come from 26 states and territories and 13 other countries. 72% are from Pennsylvania. 1.6% are international students. 3.3% are African American, 0.2% American Indian, 2.1% Asian American, and 2.7% Hispanic American. 76% returned for their sophomore year.

Facilities and Resources

200 **computers/terminals** and 200 ports are available on campus for general student use. Students can access the following: campus intranet, computer help desk, free student e-mail accounts, online (class) grades, online (class) registration, online (class) schedules, file space, personal web page, financial aid, student billing. Campuswide network is available. 100% of college-owned or -operated housing units are wired for high-speed Internet access. Wireless service is available via classrooms, computer labs, learning centers, libraries, student centers. The **library** has 228,686 books and 23,380 subscriptions.

Campus Life

There are 80 active organizations on campus, including a drama/theater group, newspaper, radio station, television station, and choral group. No national or local **fraternities** or **sororities**.

E-town is a member of the NCAA (Division III). **Intercollegiate sports** include baseball (m), basketball, cross-country running, field hockey (w), golf (m), lacrosse, soccer, softball (w), swimming and diving, tennis, track and field, volleyball (w), wrestling (m).

Campus Safety

Student safety services include self-defense workshops, crime prevention program, late-night transport/escort service, 24-hour emergency telephone alarm devices, 24-hour patrols by trained security personnel, student patrols, and electronically operated dormitory entrances.

Applying

E-town requires an essay, SAT or ACT, a high school transcript, 2 recommendations, and a minimum high school GPA of 2.0, and in some cases an interview. It recommends an interview and a minimum high school GPA of 3.0. Application deadline: 3/1; 3/15 priority date for financial aid. Early and deferred admission are possible.

Getting Accepted

3,315 applied
65% were accepted
599 enrolled (28% of accepted)
36% from top tenth of their h.s. class
Mean SAT critical reading score: 570
Mean SAT math score: 578
Mean ACT score: 24
37% had SAT critical reading scores over 600
43% had SAT math scores over 600
74% had ACT scores over 24
4% had SAT critical reading scores over 700
5% had SAT math scores over 700
9% had ACT scores over 30
2 National Merit Scholars
23 valedictorians

Graduation and After

64% graduated in 4 years
4% graduated in 5 years
26 organizations recruited on campus

Financial Matters

$30,650 tuition and fees (2008–09)
$7950 room and board
82% average percent of need met
$19,988 average financial aid amount received per undergraduate (2007–08 estimated)

ELMIRA COLLEGE

SMALL-TOWN SETTING ■ PRIVATE ■ INDEPENDENT ■ COED
ELMIRA, NEW YORK

Web site: www.elmira.edu
Contact: Mr. Gary Fallis, Dean of Admissions, Office of Admissions, Elmira, NY 14901
Telephone: 607-735-1724 or toll-free 800-935-6472
Fax: 607-735-1718
E-mail: admissions@elmira.edu

Getting Accepted

1,966 applied
64% were accepted
323 enrolled (26% of accepted)
28% from top tenth of their h.s. class
3.5 average high school GPA
26% had SAT critical reading scores over 600
24% had SAT math scores over 600
61% had ACT scores over 24
4% had SAT critical reading scores over 700
4% had SAT math scores over 700
4% had ACT scores over 30
33 class presidents
26 valedictorians

Graduation and After

97% had job offers within 6 months
55 organizations recruited on campus

Financial Matters

$33,250 tuition and fees (2008–09)
$10,100 room and board
79% average percent of need met
$24,234 average financial aid amount received per undergraduate (2007–08 estimated)

Academics

Elmira awards bachelor's and master's **degrees**. **Challenging opportunities** include advanced placement credit, accelerated degree programs, student-designed majors, double majors, and independent study. Special programs include internships, summer session for credit, off-campus study, study-abroad, and Army and Air Force ROTC.

The most frequently chosen **baccalaureate** fields are education, business/marketing, and health professions and related sciences. A complete listing of majors at Elmira appears in the Majors by College index beginning on page 469.

The **faculty** at Elmira has 82 full-time members, 100% with terminal degrees. The student-faculty ratio is 12:1.

Students of Elmira

The student body totals 1,853, of whom 1,484 are undergraduates. 71% are women and 29% are men. Students come from 35 states and territories and 23 other countries. 49% are from New York. 4.2% are international students. 1.8% are African American, 0.1% American Indian, 0.8% Asian American, and 1.3% Hispanic American.

Facilities and Resources

105 **computers/terminals** are available on campus for general student use. Campuswide network is available. The **library** has 391,038 books and 859 subscriptions.

Campus Life

There are 80 active organizations on campus, including a drama/theater group, newspaper, radio station, and choral group. No national or local **fraternities** or **sororities**.

Elmira is a member of the NCAA (Division III). **Intercollegiate sports** include basketball, cheerleading (w), field hockey (w), golf, ice hockey, lacrosse, soccer, softball (w), tennis, volleyball (w).

Campus Safety

Student safety services include 24-hour locked residence hall entrances, late-night transport/escort service, and 24-hour patrols by trained security personnel.

Applying

Elmira requires an essay, SAT or ACT, a high school transcript, 2 recommendations, and a minimum high school GPA of 2.0, and in some cases an interview. It recommends an interview. Application deadline: 4/15; 2/1 priority date for financial aid. Early and deferred admission are possible.

ELON UNIVERSITY

SUBURBAN SETTING ■ PRIVATE ■ INDEPENDENT RELIGIOUS ■ COED
ELON, NORTH CAROLINA

Web site: www.elon.edu
Contact: Ms. Melinda Wood, Associate Director of Admissions and Director
of Applications, 100 Campus Box, Elon, NC 27244
Telephone: 336-278-3566 or toll-free 800-334-8448
Fax: 336-278-7699
E-mail: admissions@elon.edu

Academics

Elon awards bachelor's, master's, doctoral, and first-professional **degrees**. **Challenging opportunities** include advanced placement credit, accelerated degree programs, student-designed majors, an honors program, double majors, independent study, and a senior project. Special programs include internships, summer session for credit, off-campus study, study-abroad, and Army and Air Force ROTC.

The most frequently chosen **baccalaureate** fields are business/marketing, communications/journalism, and social sciences. A complete listing of majors at Elon appears in the Majors by College index beginning on page 469.

The **faculty** at Elon has 333 full-time members, 86% with terminal degrees. The student-faculty ratio is 14:1.

Students of Elon

The student body totals 5,628, of whom 4,992 are undergraduates. 58.8% are women and 41.2% are men. Students come from 43 states and territories and 51 other countries. 29% are from North Carolina. 2.4% are international students. 5.8% are African American, 0.1% American Indian, 1.3% Asian American, and 2.4% Hispanic American. 90% returned for their sophomore year.

Facilities and Resources

850 **computers/terminals** are available on campus for general student use. Students can access the following: computer help desk, free student e-mail accounts, online (class) grades, online (class) registration, online (class) schedules. Campuswide network is available. Wireless service is available via entire campus. The **library** has 290,938 books and 8,805 subscriptions.

Campus Life

There are 150 active organizations on campus, including a drama/theater group, newspaper, radio station, television station, choral group, and marching band. 19% of eligible men and 34% of eligible women are members of national **fraternities** and national **sororities**.

Elon is a member of the NCAA (Division I). **Intercollegiate sports** (some offering scholarships) include baseball (m), basketball, cheerleading, cross-country running, football (m), golf, soccer, softball (w), tennis, track and field (w), volleyball (w).

Campus Safety

Student safety services include late-night transport/escort service, 24-hour emergency telephone alarm devices, 24-hour patrols by trained security personnel, and electronically operated dormitory entrances.

Applying

Elon requires an essay, SAT or ACT, a high school transcript, and a minimum high school GPA of 2.7, and in some cases an interview. Application deadline: 1/10; 3/15 priority date for financial aid. Early and deferred admission are possible.

Getting Accepted

9,434 applied
42% were accepted
1,291 enrolled (32% of accepted)
33% from top tenth of their h.s. class
4.0 average high school GPA
Mean SAT critical reading score: 610
Mean SAT math score: 615
Mean SAT writing score: 615
Mean ACT score: 27
61% had SAT critical reading scores over 600
63% had SAT math scores over 600
63% had SAT writing scores over 600
82% had ACT scores over 24
10% had SAT critical reading scores over 700
12% had SAT math scores over 700
11% had SAT writing scores over 700
13% had ACT scores over 30

Graduation and After

72% graduated in 4 years
6% graduated in 5 years
1% graduated in 6 years
95% had job offers within 6 months
150 organizations recruited on campus

Financial Matters

$24,076 tuition and fees (2008–09)
$7770 room and board
68% average percent of need met
$13,400 average financial aid amount received
per undergraduate (2007–08 estimated)

EMBRY-RIDDLE AERONAUTICAL UNIVERSITY

SUBURBAN SETTING ■ PRIVATE ■ INDEPENDENT ■ COED
PRESCOTT, ARIZONA

Web site: www.embryriddle.edu
Contact: Debra Cates, Interim Director of Admissions, 3700 Willow Creek
   Road, Prescott, AZ 86301-3720
Telephone: 928-777-6600 or toll-free 800-888-3728
Fax: 928-777-6606
E-mail: pradmit@erau.edu

Getting Accepted
1,148 applied
86% were accepted
418 enrolled (42% of accepted)
25% from top tenth of their h.s. class
3.45 average high school GPA
Mean SAT critical reading score: 535
Mean SAT math score: 570
Mean ACT score: 25
28% had SAT critical reading scores over 600
40% had SAT math scores over 600
57% had ACT scores over 24
5% had SAT critical reading scores over 700
7% had SAT math scores over 700
14% had ACT scores over 30

Graduation and After
31% graduated in 4 years
20% graduated in 5 years
4% graduated in 6 years

Financial Matters
$27,750 tuition and fees (2009–10)
$8008 room and board
$16,151 average financial aid amount received
   per undergraduate (2007–08 estimated)

Academics
Embry-Riddle awards bachelor's and master's **degrees. Challenging opportunities** include advanced placement credit, accelerated degree programs, student-designed majors, an honors program, double majors, independent study, and a senior project. Special programs include cooperative education, internships, summer session for credit, study-abroad, and Army and Air Force ROTC.

The most frequently chosen **baccalaureate** fields are transportation and materials moving, engineering, and social sciences. A complete listing of majors at Embry-Riddle appears in the Majors by College index beginning on page 469.

The **faculty** at Embry-Riddle has 98 full-time members, 70% with terminal degrees. The student-faculty ratio is 15:1.

Students of Embry-Riddle
The student body totals 1,719, of whom 1,688 are undergraduates. 17.7% are women and 82.3% are men. Students come from 50 states and territories and 24 other countries. 21% are from Arizona. 4.3% are international students. 2.2% are African American, 1.4% American Indian, 7.3% Asian American, and 8.4% Hispanic American. 79% returned for their sophomore year.

Facilities and Resources
470 **computers/terminals** are available on campus for general student use. Students can access the following: campus intranet, computer help desk, free student e-mail accounts, online (class) grades, online (class) registration, online (class) schedules. Campuswide network is available. Wireless service is available via entire campus. The **library** has 40,505 books and 668 subscriptions.

Campus Life
There are 85 active organizations on campus, including a newspaper, radio station, and television station. 85% of eligible men and 93% of eligible women are members of national **fraternities** and national **sororities**.

Embry-Riddle is a member of the NAIA. **Intercollegiate sports** (some offering scholarships) include volleyball (w), wrestling (m).

Campus Safety
Student safety services include late-night transport/escort service, 24-hour emergency telephone alarm devices, 24-hour patrols by trained security personnel, and student patrols.

Applying
Embry-Riddle requires SAT and SAT Subject Tests or ACT, a high school transcript, and a minimum high school GPA of 2.0, and in some cases medical examination for flight students and a minimum high school GPA of 3.0. It recommends an essay, an interview, and 1 recommendation. Application deadline: rolling admissions. Deferred admission is possible.

EMERSON COLLEGE

URBAN SETTING ■ PRIVATE ■ INDEPENDENT ■ COED
BOSTON, MASSACHUSETTS

Web site: www.emerson.edu
Contact: Ms. Sara Ramirez, Director of Undergraduate Admission, 120
Boylston Street, Boston, MA 02116-4624
Telephone: 617-824-8600
Fax: 617-824-8609
E-mail: admission@emerson.edu

SPONSOR

Academics

Emerson awards bachelor's, master's, and doctoral **degrees**. **Challenging opportunities** include advanced placement credit, student-designed majors, an honors program, double majors, independent study, and a senior project. Special programs include internships, summer session for credit, off-campus study, and study-abroad.

The most frequently chosen **baccalaureate** fields are communications/journalism, visual and performing arts, and English. A complete listing of majors at Emerson appears in the Majors by College index beginning on page 469.

The **faculty** at Emerson has 162 full-time members, 72% with terminal degrees. The student-faculty ratio is 14:1.

Students of Emerson

The student body totals 4,536, of whom 3,644 are undergraduates. 58.6% are women and 41.4% are men. Students come from 44 states and territories and 50 other countries. 25% are from Massachusetts. 2.8% are international students. 2.6% are African American, 0.6% American Indian, 4.7% Asian American, and 7.5% Hispanic American. 90% returned for their sophomore year.

Facilities and Resources

480 **computers/terminals** are available on campus for general student use. Students can access the following: computer help desk, free student e-mail accounts, online (class) registration, online (class) schedules. Campuswide network is available. 100% of college-owned or -operated housing units are wired for high-speed Internet access. Wireless service is available via classrooms, computer centers, computer labs, dorm rooms, learning centers, libraries, student centers. The 2 **libraries** have 179,380 books and 31,258 subscriptions.

Campus Life

There are 60 active organizations on campus, including a drama/theater group, newspaper, radio station, television station, and choral group. 3% of eligible men and 3% of eligible women are members of national **fraternities**, national **sororities**, local fraternities, and local sororities.

Emerson is a member of the NCAA (Division III). **Intercollegiate sports** include baseball (m), basketball, cross-country running, golf, lacrosse, soccer, softball (w), tennis, track and field (w), volleyball.

Campus Safety

Student safety services include late-night transport/escort service, 24-hour emergency telephone alarm devices, 24-hour patrols by trained security personnel, and electronically operated dormitory entrances.

Applying

Emerson requires an essay, SAT or ACT, a high school transcript, and 1 recommendation, and in some cases an interview and Performing Arts applicants must submit a theatrical resume and either audition or interview, or submit a portfolio or an essay. Film applicants must submit a sample of creative work.. Application deadline: 1/5; 3/1 priority date for financial aid. Early and deferred admission are possible.

Boston is considered one of the country's most popular college towns, and Emerson is located right on Boston Common in the heart of the city's Theatre District. The campus is home to WERS-FM, the historic 1,200-seat Cutler Majestic Theatre, and award-winning literary journal, *Ploughshares*. Emerson's 3,100 students come from across the United States and more than forty countries. There are more than sixty student organizations and performance groups, fifteen NCAA intercollegiate teams, and several student publications and honor societies. The College also sponsors programs in Los Angeles; Washington, DC; the Netherlands; Taiwan; summer film study in the Czech Republic; and course cross-registration with the six-member Boston ProArts Consortium.

Getting Accepted
6,944 applied
37% were accepted
774 enrolled (30% of accepted)
39% from top tenth of their h.s. class
3.62 average high school GPA
Mean SAT critical reading score: 629
Mean SAT math score: 593
Mean SAT writing score: 626
Mean ACT score: 27
69% had SAT critical reading scores over 600
49% had SAT math scores over 600
67% had SAT writing scores over 600
88% had ACT scores over 24
17% had SAT critical reading scores over 700
6% had SAT math scores over 700
16% had SAT writing scores over 700
21% had ACT scores over 30

Graduation and After
72% graduated in 4 years
3% graduated in 5 years
1% graduated in 6 years
80% had job offers within 6 months
100 organizations recruited on campus

Financial Matters
$28,884 tuition and fees (2008–09)
$11,832 room and board
73% average percent of need met
$15,646 average financial aid amount received
per undergraduate (2007–08 estimated)

Getting Accepted

17,446 applied
27% were accepted
1,278 enrolled (28% of accepted)
85% from top tenth of their h.s. class
3.82 average high school GPA
Mean SAT critical reading score: 662
Mean SAT math score: 695
Mean SAT writing score: 669
Mean ACT score: 30
93% had SAT critical reading scores over 600
95% had SAT math scores over 600
91% had SAT writing scores over 600
99% had ACT scores over 24
45% had SAT critical reading scores over 700
61% had SAT math scores over 700
50% had SAT writing scores over 700
75% had ACT scores over 30
76 National Merit Scholars

Graduation and After

82% graduated in 4 years
4% graduated in 5 years
1% graduated in 6 years
271 organizations recruited on campus

Financial Matters

$36,336 tuition and fees (2008–09)
$10,572 room and board
100% average percent of need met
$29,143 average financial aid amount received per undergraduate (2006–07)

EMORY UNIVERSITY

SUBURBAN SETTING ■ PRIVATE ■ INDEPENDENT RELIGIOUS ● COED
ATLANTA, GEORGIA

Web site: www.emory.edu
Contact: Ms. Jean Jordan, Dean of Admission, 200 Boisfeuillet Jones Center, Atlanta, GA 30322-1100
Telephone: 404-727-6036 or toll-free 800-727-6036
Fax: 404-727-4303
E-mail: admiss@emory.edu

Academics

Emory awards bachelor's, master's, doctoral, and first-professional **degrees** (enrollment figures include Emory University, Oxford College; application data for main campus only). **Challenging opportunities** include advanced placement credit, accelerated degree programs, an honors program, double majors, independent study, and a senior project. Special programs include cooperative education, internships, summer session for credit, off-campus study, study-abroad, and Army, Navy, and Air Force ROTC.

The most frequently chosen **baccalaureate** fields are social sciences, business/marketing, and psychology. A complete listing of majors at Emory appears in the Majors by College index beginning on page 469.

The **faculty** at Emory has 1,255 full-time members, 99% with terminal degrees. The student-faculty ratio is 7:1.

Students of Emory

The student body totals 10,921, of whom 5,214 are undergraduates. 55.2% are women and 44.8% are men. Students come from 49 states and territories and 70 other countries. 30% are from Georgia. 95% returned for their sophomore year.

Facilities and Resources

600 **computers/terminals** and 300 ports are available on campus for general student use. Students can access the following: campus intranet, computer help desk, free student e-mail accounts, online (class) grades, online (class) registration, online (class) schedules. Campuswide network is available. 100% of college-owned or -operated housing units are wired for high-speed Internet access. Wireless service is available via entire campus. The 8 **libraries** have 3,377,140 books and 54,295 subscriptions.

Campus Life

There are 220 active organizations on campus, including a drama/theater group, newspaper, radio station, television station, and choral group. 28% of eligible men and 30% of eligible women are members of national **fraternities** and national **sororities**.

Emory is a member of the NCAA (Division III). **Intercollegiate sports** include baseball (m), basketball, cross-country running, golf (m), soccer, softball (w), swimming and diving, tennis, track and field, volleyball (w).

Campus Safety

Student safety services include late-night transport/escort service, 24-hour emergency telephone alarm devices, 24-hour patrols by trained security personnel, and student patrols.

Applying

Emory requires an essay, SAT or ACT, a high school transcript, and 1 recommendation. It recommends SAT Subject Tests and a minimum high school GPA of 3.0. Application deadline: 1/15; 3/1 for financial aid, with a 2/15 priority date. Early and deferred admission are possible.

Erskine College

RURAL SETTING ■ PRIVATE ■ INDEPENDENT RELIGIOUS ■ COED
DUE WEST, SOUTH CAROLINA

Web site: www.erskine.edu
Contact: PO Box 176, Due West, SC 29639
Telephone: 864-379-8838 or toll-free 800-241-8721
Fax: 864-379-8759
E-mail: ocain@erskine.edu

Academics

Erskine awards bachelor's, master's, doctoral, and first-professional **degrees. Challenging opportunities** include advanced placement credit, double majors, independent study, and a senior project. Special programs include internships, summer session for credit, off-campus study, and study-abroad.

The most frequently chosen **baccalaureate** fields are biological/life sciences, business/marketing, and education. A complete listing of majors at Erskine appears in the Majors by College index beginning on page 469.

The **faculty** at Erskine has 42 full-time members, 86% with terminal degrees. The student-faculty ratio is 11:1.

Students of Erskine

The student body totals 864, of whom 566 are undergraduates. 54.2% are women and 45.8% are men. Students come from 17 states and territories and 7 other countries. 75% are from South Carolina. 1.9% are international students. 5.7% are African American, 0.2% Asian American, and 0.4% Hispanic American. 77% returned for their sophomore year.

Facilities and Resources

Campuswide network is available. Wireless service is available via classrooms, dorm rooms, libraries, student centers. The **library** has 236,323 books and 1,219 subscriptions.

Campus Life

There are 51 active organizations on campus, including a drama/theater group, newspaper, radio station, and choral group. No national or local **fraternities** or **sororities**.

Erskine is a member of the NCAA (Division II). **Intercollegiate sports** (some offering scholarships) include baseball (m), basketball, cross-country running, golf, lacrosse (w), soccer, softball (w), tennis, volleyball (w).

Campus Safety

Student safety services include late-night transport/escort service, 24-hour patrols by trained security personnel, and electronically operated dormitory entrances.

Applying

Erskine requires an essay, SAT or ACT, and a high school transcript. It recommends an interview. Application deadline: rolling admissions; 4/1 priority date for financial aid. Deferred admission is possible.

Getting Accepted

895 applied
59% were accepted
163 enrolled (31% of accepted)
32% from top tenth of their h.s. class
3.48 average high school GPA
Mean SAT critical reading score: 540
Mean SAT math score: 548
Mean SAT writing score: 531
Mean ACT score: 24
26% had SAT critical reading scores over 600
28% had SAT math scores over 600
21% had SAT writing scores over 600
52% had ACT scores over 24
6% had SAT critical reading scores over 700
5% had SAT math scores over 700
6% had SAT writing scores over 700
17% had ACT scores over 30

Graduation and After

53% graduated in 4 years
4% graduated in 5 years
1% graduated in 6 years
70% had job offers within 6 months
46 organizations recruited on campus

Financial Matters

$23,165 tuition and fees (2008–09)
$7961 room and board
87% average percent of need met
$19,100 average financial aid amount received
    per undergraduate (2005–06)

Eugene Lang College offers students of diverse backgrounds the opportunity to design their own paths of study within one of twelve interdisciplinary liberal arts concentrations in the social sciences, arts, and humanities. Students discuss and debate issues in small seminar courses that are never larger than 20 students. They enrich their programs with internships in a wide variety of areas, such as media and publishing, community service, and education. As part of a larger urban university, students can pursue a dual degree at one of The New School's five other divisions. The Greenwich Village location, with all of the intellectual and cultural treasures of New York City, provides a distinct resource for academics and campus life.

Getting Accepted
1,984 applied
55% were accepted
301 enrolled (27% of accepted)
29% from top tenth of their h.s. class
3.3 average high school GPA
54% had SAT critical reading scores over 600
33% had SAT math scores over 600
59% had SAT writing scores over 600
72% had ACT scores over 24
13% had SAT critical reading scores over 700
4% had SAT math scores over 700
16% had SAT writing scores over 700
10% had ACT scores over 30

Graduation and After
36% graduated in 4 years
10% graduated in 5 years
4% graduated in 6 years
30 organizations recruited on campus

Financial Matters
$33,060 tuition and fees (2008–09)
$15,260 room and board
80% average percent of need met
$19,478 average financial aid amount received per undergraduate (2006–07)

EUGENE LANG COLLEGE THE NEW SCHOOL FOR LIBERAL ARTS

URBAN SETTING ■ PRIVATE ■ INDEPENDENT ■ COED
NEW YORK, NEW YORK

Web site: www.lang.edu
Contact: Nicole Curvin, Director of Admissions, 65 West 11th Street, New York, NY 10011-8601
Telephone: 212-229-5665 or toll-free 877-528-3321
Fax: 212-229-5355
E-mail: lang@newschool.edu

Academics
Eugene Lang awards bachelor's **degrees**. **Challenging opportunities** include advanced placement credit, accelerated degree programs, student-designed majors, double majors, independent study, and a senior project. Special programs include internships, summer session for credit, off-campus study, and study-abroad.

The most frequently chosen **baccalaureate** field is liberal arts/general studies. A complete listing of majors at Eugene Lang appears in the Majors by College index beginning on page 469.

The **faculty** at Eugene Lang has 72 full-time members, 72% with terminal degrees. The student-faculty ratio is 14:1.

Students of Eugene Lang
The student body is made up of 1,347 undergraduates. 67.8% are women and 32.2% are men. Students come from 50 states and territories and 30 other countries. 29% are from New York. 4.1% are international students. 4.4% are African American, 0.7% American Indian, 5.6% Asian American, and 7.3% Hispanic American. 73% returned for their sophomore year.

Facilities and Resources
1,200 **computers/terminals** are available on campus for general student use. Students can access the following: computer help desk, free student e-mail accounts, online (class) grades, online (class) registration, online (class) schedules, online portal. Campuswide network is available. 94% of college-owned or -operated housing units are wired for high-speed Internet access. Wireless service is available via entire campus. The 3 **libraries** have 1,710,809 books and 42,051 subscriptions.

Campus Life
There are 25 active organizations on campus, including a drama/theater group, newspaper, radio station, and choral group. No national or local **fraternities** or **sororities**.

This institution has no intercollegiate sports.

Campus Safety
Student safety services include 24-hour desk attendants in residence halls, 24-hour emergency telephone alarm devices, and electronically operated dormitory entrances.

Applying
Eugene Lang requires an essay, SAT or ACT, a high school transcript, an interview, and 2 recommendations. It recommends a minimum high school GPA of 3.0. Application deadline: 2/1. Deferred admission is possible.

FAIRFIELD UNIVERSITY

SUBURBAN SETTING ■ PRIVATE ■ INDEPENDENT RELIGIOUS ■ COED
FAIRFIELD, CONNECTICUT

Web site: www.fairfield.edu
Contact: Ms. Karen Pellegrino, Director of Admission, 1073 North Benson
Road, Fairfield, CT 06824-5195
Telephone: 203-254-4100
Fax: 203-254-4199
E-mail: admis@mail.fairfield.edu

Academics

Fairfield awards associate, bachelor's, and master's **degrees** and post-master's certificates. **Challenging opportunities** include advanced placement credit, student-designed majors, an honors program, double majors, independent study, and a senior project. Special programs include internships, summer session for credit, study-abroad, and Army and Air Force ROTC.

The most frequently chosen **baccalaureate** fields are business/marketing, social sciences, and communications/journalism. A complete listing of majors at Fairfield appears in the Majors by College index beginning on page 469.

The **faculty** at Fairfield has 251 full-time members, 93% with terminal degrees. The student-faculty ratio is 12:1.

Students of Fairfield

The student body totals 5,128, of whom 4,084 are undergraduates. 58.3% are women and 41.7% are men. Students come from 33 states and territories and 24 other countries. 24% are from Connecticut. 0.7% are international students. 3.2% are African American, 0.4% American Indian, 3.7% Asian American, and 7.6% Hispanic American. 90% returned for their sophomore year.

Facilities and Resources

220 **computers/terminals** and 150 ports are available on campus for general student use. Students can access the following: campus intranet, computer help desk, free student e-mail accounts, online (class) grades, online (class) registration, online (class) schedules. Campuswide network is available. 100% of college-owned or -operated housing units are wired for high-speed Internet access. Wireless service is available via classrooms, dorm rooms, libraries, student centers. The **library** has 351,091 books and 31,424 subscriptions.

Campus Life

There are 110 active organizations on campus, including a drama/theater group, newspaper, radio station, television station, and choral group. No national or local **fraternities** or **sororities**.

Fairfield is a member of the NCAA (Division I). **Intercollegiate sports** (some offering scholarships) include baseball (m), basketball, crew, cross-country running, field hockey (w), golf, lacrosse, soccer, softball (w), swimming and diving, tennis, volleyball (w).

Campus Safety

Student safety services include bicycle patrols, late-night transport/escort service, 24-hour emergency telephone alarm devices, 24-hour patrols by trained security personnel, and electronically operated dormitory entrances.

Applying

Fairfield requires an essay, SAT or ACT, a high school transcript, 1 recommendation, and rank in upper 20% of high school class. It recommends an interview. Application deadline: 1/15; 2/15 for financial aid, with a 2/15 priority date. Early and deferred admission are possible.

Getting Accepted

8,732 applied
59% were accepted
899 enrolled (17% of accepted)
38% from top tenth of their h.s. class
3.41 average high school GPA
34% had SAT critical reading scores over 600
44% had SAT math scores over 600
44% had SAT writing scores over 600
67% had ACT scores over 24
4% had SAT critical reading scores over 700
6% had SAT math scores over 700
6% had SAT writing scores over 700
10% had ACT scores over 30
10 National Merit Scholars
47 class presidents

Graduation and After

75% graduated in 4 years
3% graduated in 5 years
1% graduated in 6 years
70% had job offers within 6 months
160 organizations recruited on campus

Financial Matters

$36,075 tuition and fees (2008–09)
$10,850 room and board
81% average percent of need met
$21,509 average financial aid amount received
per undergraduate (2007–08 estimated)

FLORIDA INSTITUTE OF TECHNOLOGY

SMALL-TOWN SETTING ■ PRIVATE ■ INDEPENDENT ■ COED
MELBOURNE, FLORIDA

Web site: www.fit.edu
Contact: Michael J. Perry, Director of Undergraduate Admission, 150 West
University Boulevard, Melbourne, FL 32901-6975
Telephone: 321-674-8030 or toll-free 800-888-4348
Fax: 321-723-9468
E-mail: admission@fit.edu

Getting Accepted

3,168 applied
82% were accepted
637 enrolled (25% of accepted)
23% from top tenth of their h.s. class
3.41 average high school GPA
Mean SAT critical reading score: 559
Mean SAT math score: 588
Mean ACT score: 25
31% had SAT critical reading scores over 600
46% had SAT math scores over 600
62% had ACT scores over 24
7% had SAT critical reading scores over 700
8% had SAT math scores over 700
16% had ACT scores over 30
12 valedictorians

Graduation and After

42% graduated in 4 years
15% graduated in 5 years
2% graduated in 6 years
98% had job offers within 6 months
227 organizations recruited on campus

Financial Matters

$30,440 tuition and fees (2008–09)
$10,250 room and board
82% average percent of need met
$24,617 average financial aid amount received
per undergraduate (2007–08 estimated)

Academics

Florida Tech awards associate, bachelor's, master's, and doctoral **degrees** and post-master's certificates. **Challenging opportunities** include advanced placement credit, accelerated degree programs, double majors, independent study, and a senior project. Special programs include cooperative education, internships, summer session for credit, study-abroad, and Army ROTC.

The most frequently chosen **baccalaureate** fields are engineering, transportation and materials moving, and biological/life sciences. A complete listing of majors at Florida Tech appears in the Majors by College index beginning on page 469.

The **faculty** at Florida Tech has 234 full-time members, 89% with terminal degrees. The student-faculty ratio is 9:1.

Students of Florida Tech

The student body totals 6,400, of whom 3,685 are undergraduates. 38.6% are women and 61.4% are men. Students come from 56 states and territories and 87 other countries. 55% are from Florida. 17.1% are international students. 7.8% are African American, 0.6% American Indian, 2.9% Asian American, and 6% Hispanic American. 73% returned for their sophomore year.

Facilities and Resources

400 **computers/terminals** and 50 ports are available on campus for general student use. Students can access the following: computer help desk, free student e-mail accounts, online (class) grades, online (class) registration, online (class) schedules. Campuswide network is available. 100% of college-owned or -operated housing units are wired for high-speed Internet access. Wireless service is available via classrooms, computer centers, computer labs, learning centers, libraries, student centers. The **library** has 295,624 books and 28,597 subscriptions.

Campus Life

There are 94 active organizations on campus, including a drama/theater group, newspaper, radio station, television station, and choral group. 18% of eligible men and 13% of eligible women are members of national **fraternities**, national **sororities**, and local sororities.

Florida Tech is a member of the NCAA (Division II). **Intercollegiate sports** (some offering scholarships) include baseball (m), basketball, crew (w), cross-country running, golf, soccer, softball (w), tennis, volleyball (w).

Campus Safety

Student safety services include self-defense education, late-night transport/escort service, 24-hour emergency telephone alarm devices, and 24-hour patrols by trained security personnel.

Applying

Florida Tech requires SAT or ACT, a high school transcript, and a minimum high school GPA of 2.6. It recommends a minimum high school GPA of 3.3. Application deadline: rolling admissions; 3/1 priority date for financial aid. Early and deferred admission are possible.

FLORIDA INTERNATIONAL UNIVERSITY

URBAN SETTING ■ PUBLIC ■ STATE-SUPPORTED ■ COED
MIAMI, FLORIDA

Web site: www.fiu.edu
Contact: Ms. Valerire Peterson, Associate Director of Admissions, 11200 SW
Eighth Street, PC 140, Miami, FL 33199
Telephone: 305-348-3675
Fax: 305-348-3648
E-mail: admiss@fiu.edu

Academics

FIU awards bachelor's, master's, doctoral, and first-professional **degrees** and post-bachelor's certificates. **Challenging opportunities** include advanced placement credit, accelerated degree programs, freshman honors college, an honors program, double majors, independent study, and a senior project. Special programs include cooperative education, internships, summer session for credit, off-campus study, study-abroad, and Army and Air Force ROTC.

The most frequently chosen **baccalaureate** fields are business/marketing, education, and health professions and related sciences. A complete listing of majors at FIU appears in the Majors by College index beginning on page 469.

The **faculty** at FIU has 854 full-time members, 88% with terminal degrees.

Students of FIU

The student body is made up of 31,589 undergraduates. 56.2% are women and 43.8% are men. Students come from 52 states and territories. 98% are from Florida. 4% are international students. 12.3% are African American, 0.2% American Indian, 3.7% Asian American, and 64.1% Hispanic American. 81% returned for their sophomore year.

Facilities and Resources

Students can access the following: free student e-mail accounts, online (class) grades, online (class) registration, online (class) schedules, online financial aid and cashier's information. Campuswide network is available. 100% of college-owned or -operated housing units are wired for high-speed Internet access. Wireless service is available via classrooms, computer centers, computer labs, libraries, student centers. The 3 **libraries** have 1,973,612 books and 40,813 subscriptions.

Campus Life

There are 190 active organizations on campus, including a drama/theater group, newspaper, radio station, choral group, and marching band. FIU has national **fraternities** and national **sororities**.

FIU is a member of the NCAA (Division I). **Intercollegiate sports** (some offering scholarships) include baseball (m), basketball, cross-country running, football (m), golf (w), soccer, softball (w), tennis (w), track and field, volleyball (w).

Campus Safety

Student safety services include late-night transport/escort service, 24-hour emergency telephone alarm devices, 24-hour patrols by trained security personnel, and electronically operated dormitory entrances.

Applying

FIU requires SAT or ACT, SAT Essay (starting fall 2009), a high school transcript, Test Scores, and a minimum high school GPA of 3.0, and in some cases 1 recommendation. It recommends SAT Subject Tests and SAT and SAT Subject Tests or ACT. Application deadline: 5/1; 5/15 for financial aid, with a 3/1 priority date.

Getting Accepted

14,627 applied
38% were accepted
2,991 enrolled (54% of accepted)
3.6 average high school GPA
Mean SAT critical reading score: 546
Mean SAT math score: 544
Mean ACT score: 23
22% had SAT critical reading scores over 600
20% had SAT math scores over 600
35% had ACT scores over 24
2% had SAT critical reading scores over 700
1% had SAT math scores over 700
1% had ACT scores over 30

Graduation and After

70% had job offers within 6 months
600 organizations recruited on campus

Financial Matters

$3900 resident tuition and fees (2008–09)
$16,299 nonresident tuition and fees (2008–09)
$11,120 room and board
46% average percent of need met
$1904 average financial aid amount received per undergraduate (2007–08 estimated)

FLORIDA STATE UNIVERSITY

SUBURBAN SETTING ■ PUBLIC ■ STATE-SUPPORTED ■ COED
TALLAHASSEE, FLORIDA

Web site: www.fsu.edu
Contact: Ms. Janice Finney, Director of Admissions, PO Box 3062400,
Tallahassee, FL 32306-2400
Telephone: 850-644-6200
Fax: 850-644-0197
E-mail: admissions@admin.fsu.edu

Getting Accepted

24,343 applied
55% were accepted
6,124 enrolled (46% of accepted)
26% from top tenth of their h.s. class
3.63 average high school GPA
Mean SAT critical reading score: 589
Mean SAT math score: 595
Mean SAT writing score: 565
Mean ACT score: 26
44% had SAT critical reading scores over 600
48% had SAT math scores over 600
32% had SAT writing scores over 600
75% had ACT scores over 24
6% had SAT critical reading scores over 700
6% had SAT math scores over 700
4% had SAT writing scores over 700
8% had ACT scores over 30
15 National Merit Scholars

Graduation and After

78% had job offers within 6 months
1044 organizations recruited on campus

Financial Matters

$4196 resident tuition and fees (2008–09)
$18,641 nonresident tuition and fees
(2008–09)
$8178 room and board
74% average percent of need met
$9531 average financial aid amount received
per undergraduate (2007–08 estimated)

Academics

Florida State awards associate, bachelor's, master's, doctoral, and first-professional **degrees** and post-bachelor's and post-master's certificates. **Challenging opportunities** include advanced placement credit, accelerated degree programs, an honors program, double majors, independent study, and a senior project. Special programs include cooperative education, internships, summer session for credit, off-campus study, study-abroad, and Army, Navy, and Air Force ROTC.

The most frequently chosen **baccalaureate** fields are business/marketing, social sciences, and family and consumer sciences. A complete listing of majors at Florida State appears in the Majors by College index beginning on page 469.

The **faculty** at Florida State has 1,353 full-time members, 92% with terminal degrees. The student-faculty ratio is 24:1.

Students of Florida State

The student body totals 40,555, of whom 31,595 are undergraduates. 55.5% are women and 44.5% are men. Students come from 51 states and territories and 118 other countries. 88% are from Florida. 0.4% are international students. 11.1% are African American, 0.6% American Indian, 3.3% Asian American, and 11.3% Hispanic American. 88% returned for their sophomore year.

Facilities and Resources

3,771 **computers/terminals** are available on campus for general student use. Students can access the following: campus intranet, computer help desk, free student e-mail accounts, online (class) grades, online (class) registration, online (class) schedules, course home pages, course search, online fee payment. Campuswide network is available. Wireless service is available via entire campus. The 9 **libraries** have 2,945,078 books and 58,093 subscriptions.

Campus Life

There are 266 active organizations on campus, including a drama/theater group, newspaper, radio station, television station, choral group, and marching band. 13% of eligible men and 15% of eligible women are members of national **fraternities**, national **sororities**, local fraternities, and local sororities.

Florida State is a member of the NCAA (Division I). **Intercollegiate sports** (some offering scholarships) include baseball (m), basketball, cheerleading, cross-country running, football (m), golf, soccer (w), softball (w), swimming and diving, tennis, track and field, volleyball (w).

Campus Safety

Student safety services include late-night transport/escort service, 24-hour emergency telephone alarm devices, 24-hour patrols by trained security personnel, and electronically operated dormitory entrances.

Applying

Florida State requires an essay, SAT or ACT, and a high school transcript, and in some cases audition. It recommends a minimum high school GPA of 3.0. Application deadline: 2/14. Early admission is possible.

FORDHAM UNIVERSITY

URBAN SETTING ■ PRIVATE ■ INDEPENDENT RELIGIOUS ■ COED
NEW YORK, NEW YORK

SPONSOR

Web site: www.fordham.edu
Contact: Mr. Peter Farrell, Director of Admission, Duane Library, 441 East
Fordham Road, New York, NY 10458
Telephone: 718-817-4000 or toll-free 800-FORDHAM
Fax: 718-367-9404
E-mail: enroll@fordham.edu

Academics

Fordham awards bachelor's, master's, doctoral, and first-professional **degrees** and post-master's certificates (branch locations at Rose Hill and Lincoln Center). **Challenging opportunities** include advanced placement credit, accelerated degree programs, student-designed majors, an honors program, double majors, independent study, and a senior project. Special programs include internships, summer session for credit, off-campus study, study-abroad, and Army, Navy, and Air Force ROTC. A complete listing of majors at Fordham appears in the Majors by College index beginning on page 469.

The **faculty** at Fordham has 686 full-time members, 96% with terminal degrees. The student-faculty ratio is 12:1.

Students of Fordham

The student body totals 14,448, of whom 7,652 are undergraduates. 57% are women and 43% are men. Students come from 53 states and territories and 48 other countries. 55% are from New York. 1.9% are international students. 5.6% are African American, 0.3% American Indian, 6.4% Asian American, and 12.3% Hispanic American. 90% returned for their sophomore year.

Facilities and Resources

1,400 **computers/terminals** are available on campus for general student use. Students can access the following: online (class) registration. Campuswide network is available. Wireless service is available via entire campus. The 4 **libraries** have 2,421,980 books and 32,300 subscriptions.

Campus Life

There are 133 active organizations on campus, including a drama/theater group, newspaper, radio station, choral group, and marching band. No national or local **fraternities** or **sororities**.

Fordham is a member of the NCAA (Division I). **Intercollegiate sports** (some offering scholarships) include baseball (m), basketball, crew (w), cross-country running, football (m), golf (m), soccer, softball (w), squash (m), swimming and diving, tennis, track and field, volleyball (w), water polo (m).

Campus Safety

Student safety services include security at each campus entrance and at residence halls, late-night transport/escort service, 24-hour emergency telephone alarm devices, 24-hour patrols by trained security personnel, student patrols, and electronically operated dormitory entrances.

Applying

Fordham requires an essay, SAT or ACT, a high school transcript, and 1 recommendation. It recommends SAT Subject Tests. Application deadline: 1/15; 2/1 for financial aid, with a 2/1 priority date. Early and deferred admission are possible.

Getting Accepted
22,035 applied
42% were accepted
1,784 enrolled (19% of accepted)
43% from top tenth of their h.s. class
3.68 average high school GPA
62% had SAT critical reading scores over 600
58% had SAT math scores over 600
61% had SAT writing scores over 600
86% had ACT scores over 24
14% had SAT critical reading scores over 700
11% had SAT math scores over 700
13% had SAT writing scores over 700
19% had ACT scores over 30

Graduation and After
76% graduated in 4 years
4% graduated in 5 years

Financial Matters
$35,257 tuition and fees (2008–09)
$12,980 room and board
79% average percent of need met
$25,258 average financial aid amount received per undergraduate (2007–08 estimated)

Getting Accepted

1,273 applied
81% were accepted
442 enrolled (43% of accepted)
33% from top tenth of their h.s. class
3.60 average high school GPA
Mean SAT critical reading score: 602
Mean SAT math score: 577
Mean ACT score: 25
50% had SAT critical reading scores over 600
41% had SAT math scores over 600
54% had ACT scores over 24
14% had SAT critical reading scores over 700
6% had SAT math scores over 700
14% had ACT scores over 30
9 valedictorians

Graduation and After

55% graduated in 4 years
10% graduated in 5 years
3% graduated in 6 years
84% had job offers within 6 months
158 organizations recruited on campus

Financial Matters

$19,100 tuition and fees (2008–09)
$6600 room and board
59% average percent of need met
$11,511 average financial aid amount received
 per undergraduate (2007–08 estimated)

FRANCISCAN UNIVERSITY OF STEUBENVILLE

SUBURBAN SETTING ■ PRIVATE ■ INDEPENDENT RELIGIOUS ■ COED
STEUBENVILLE, OHIO

Web site: www.franciscan.edu
Contact: Mrs. Margaret Weber, Director of Admissions, 1235 University
 Boulevard, Steubenville, OH 43952-1763
Telephone: 740-283-6226 or toll-free 800-783-6220
Fax: 740-284-5456
E-mail: admissions@franciscan.edu

Academics

Franciscan awards associate, bachelor's, and master's **degrees. Challenging opportunities** include advanced placement credit, accelerated degree programs, an honors program, double majors, independent study, and a senior project. Special programs include internships, summer session for credit, study-abroad, and Army ROTC.

The most frequently chosen **baccalaureate** fields are theology and religious vocations, health professions and related sciences, and business/marketing. A complete listing of majors at Franciscan appears in the Majors by College index beginning on page 469.

The **faculty** at Franciscan has 115 full-time members, 72% with terminal degrees. The student-faculty ratio is 15:1.

Students of Franciscan

The student body totals 2,434, of whom 2,033 are undergraduates. 59.8% are women and 40.2% are men. Students come from 51 states and territories and 13 other countries. 22% are from Ohio. 1.1% are international students. 0.5% are African American, 0.5% American Indian, 1.4% Asian American, and 1.3% Hispanic American. 88% returned for their sophomore year.

Facilities and Resources

126 **computers/terminals** are available on campus for general student use. Students can access the following: campus intranet, computer help desk, free student e-mail accounts, online (class) grades, online (class) registration, online (class) schedules. Campuswide network is available. The **library** has 236,689 books and 392 subscriptions.

Campus Life

There are 35 active organizations on campus, including a drama/theater group, newspaper, radio station, and choral group. 1% of eligible women are members of national **sororities**.

Franciscan is a member of the NCAA. **Intercollegiate sports** include baseball (m), basketball, cross-country running, rugby (m), soccer, softball (w), track and field, volleyball (w).

Campus Safety

Student safety services include late-night transport/escort service, 24-hour emergency telephone alarm devices, 24-hour patrols by trained security personnel, and student patrols.

Applying

Franciscan requires an essay, SAT or ACT, a high school transcript, and a minimum high school GPA of 2.4. It recommends an interview. Application deadline: rolling admissions; 4/15 priority date for financial aid. Early and deferred admission are possible.

Franklin & Marshall College

Suburban setting ■ Private ■ Independent ■ Coed
Lancaster, Pennsylvania

Web site: www.fandm.edu
Contact: Sara Harberson, Vice President for Enrollment Management, PO Box 3003, Lancaster, PA 17604-3003
Telephone: 717-291-3953
Fax: 717-291-4389
E-mail: admission@fandm.edu

Academics
F&M awards bachelor's **degrees. Challenging opportunities** include advanced placement credit, accelerated degree programs, student-designed majors, an honors program, double majors, independent study, and a senior project. Special programs include internships, summer session for credit, off-campus study, and study-abroad.

The most frequently chosen **baccalaureate** fields are social sciences, health professions and related sciences, and interdisciplinary studies. A complete listing of majors at F&M appears in the Majors by College index beginning on page 469.

The **faculty** at F&M has 192 full-time members, 95% with terminal degrees. The student-faculty ratio is 10:1.

Students of F&M
The student body is made up of 2,164 undergraduates. 51.7% are women and 48.3% are men. Students come from 39 states and territories and 47 other countries. 33% are from Pennsylvania. 8.7% are international students. 3.7% are African American, 0.2% American Indian, 4.2% Asian American, and 4.2% Hispanic American. 94% returned for their sophomore year.

Facilities and Resources
125 **computers/terminals** are available on campus for general student use. Students can access the following: campus intranet, computer help desk, free student e-mail accounts, online (class) grades, online (class) registration, online (class) schedules, online degree audit, unofficial transcripts, course material. Campuswide network is available. 100% of college-owned or -operated housing units are wired for high-speed Internet access. Wireless service is available via entire campus. The 2 **libraries** have 513,942 books and 2,202 subscriptions.

Campus Life
There are 120 active organizations on campus, including a drama/theater group, newspaper, radio station, television station, and choral group. 26% of eligible men and 12% of eligible women are members of national **fraternities** and national **sororities**.

F&M is a member of the NCAA (Division III). **Intercollegiate sports** include baseball (m), basketball (m), crew (w), cross-country running, field hockey (w), football (m), golf, lacrosse, soccer, softball (w), squash, swimming and diving, tennis, track and field, volleyball (w), wrestling (m).

Campus Safety
Student safety services include residence hall security, campus security connected to city police and fire company, late-night transport/escort service, 24-hour emergency telephone alarm devices, 24-hour patrols by trained security personnel, and electronically operated dormitory entrances.

Applying
F&M requires an essay, a high school transcript, and 2 recommendations. It recommends SAT or ACT and an interview. Application deadline: 2/1; 3/1 for financial aid, with a 2/1 priority date. Early and deferred admission are possible.

Getting Accepted
5,632 applied
36% were accepted
588 enrolled (29% of accepted)
62% from top tenth of their h.s. class
3.47 average high school GPA
Mean SAT critical reading score: 624
Mean SAT math score: 642
79% had SAT critical reading scores over 600
91% had SAT math scores over 600
22% had SAT critical reading scores over 700
28% had SAT math scores over 700

Graduation and After
73% graduated in 4 years
6% graduated in 5 years
1% graduated in 6 years
63% had job offers within 6 months
24 organizations recruited on campus

Financial Matters
$38,630 tuition and fees (2008–09)
$9870 room and board
96% average percent of need met
$28,513 average financial aid amount received per undergraduate (2007–08 estimated)

FURMAN UNIVERSITY

SUBURBAN SETTING ■ PRIVATE ■ INDEPENDENT ■ COED
GREENVILLE, SOUTH CAROLINA

Web site: www.furman.edu
Contact: Mr. Brad Pochard, Director of Admissions, 3300 Poinsett Highway, Greenville, SC 29613
Telephone: 864-294-2034
Fax: 864-294-2018
E-mail: admissions@furman.edu

Getting Accepted
4,414 applied
57% were accepted
761 enrolled (30% of accepted)
59% from top tenth of their h.s. class
3.52 average high school GPA
73% had SAT critical reading scores over 600
72% had SAT math scores over 600
68% had SAT writing scores over 600
91% had ACT scores over 24
20% had SAT critical reading scores over 700
18% had SAT math scores over 700
21% had SAT writing scores over 700
31% had ACT scores over 30
35 National Merit Scholars
30 valedictorians

Graduation and After
80% graduated in 4 years
4% graduated in 5 years
54% had job offers within 6 months
69 organizations recruited on campus

Financial Matters
$34,588 tuition and fees (2008–09)
$8966 room and board
85% average percent of need met
$24,109 average financial aid amount received per undergraduate (2007–08 estimated)

Academics

Furman awards bachelor's and master's **degrees** and post-bachelor's certificates. **Challenging opportunities** include advanced placement credit, accelerated degree programs, student-designed majors, double majors, independent study, and a senior project. Special programs include internships, summer session for credit, study-abroad, and Army ROTC.

The most frequently chosen **baccalaureate** fields are social sciences, business/marketing, and foreign languages and literature. A complete listing of majors at Furman appears in the Majors by College index beginning on page 469.

The **faculty** at Furman has 231 full-time members, 96% with terminal degrees. The student-faculty ratio is 11:1.

Students of Furman

The student body totals 2,977, of whom 2,801 are undergraduates. 57% are women and 43% are men. Students come from 46 states and territories and 46 other countries. 30% are from South Carolina. 2% are international students. 7.2% are African American, 0.2% American Indian, 2.5% Asian American, and 1.6% Hispanic American. 92% returned for their sophomore year.

Facilities and Resources

425 **computers/terminals** and 3,000 ports are available on campus for general student use. Students can access the following: campus intranet, computer help desk, free student e-mail accounts, online (class) grades, online (class) registration, online (class) schedules. Campuswide network is available. 100% of college-owned or -operated housing units are wired for high-speed Internet access. Wireless service is available via classrooms, computer centers, computer labs, learning centers, libraries, student centers. The 3 **libraries** have 453,211 books and 2,052 subscriptions.

Campus Life

There are 140 active organizations on campus, including a drama/theater group, newspaper, radio station, television station, choral group, and marching band. 33% of eligible men and 44% of eligible women are members of national **fraternities** and national **sororities**.

Furman is a member of the NCAA (Division I). **Intercollegiate sports** (some offering scholarships) include baseball (m), basketball, cheerleading, cross-country running, football (m), golf, soccer, softball (w), tennis, track and field, volleyball (w).

Campus Safety

Student safety services include late-night transport/escort service, 24-hour emergency telephone alarm devices, 24-hour patrols by trained security personnel, student patrols, and electronically operated dormitory entrances.

Applying

Furman requires an essay and a high school transcript, and in some cases an interview. It recommends SAT or ACT. Application deadline: 1/15; 1/15 for financial aid. Early admission is possible.

George Fox University

SMALL-TOWN SETTING ■ PRIVATE ■ INDEPENDENT RELIGIOUS ■ COED
NEWBERG, OREGON

Web site: www.georgefox.edu
Contact: Mr. Ryan Dougherty, Director of Undergraduate Admissions, 414
    North Meridian Street, Newberg, OR 97132
Telephone: 503-554-2240 or toll-free 800-765-4369
Fax: 503-554-3110
E-mail: admissions@georgefox.edu

Academics

George Fox awards bachelor's, master's, doctoral, and first-professional **degrees** and post-bachelor's and post-master's certificates. **Challenging opportunities** include advanced placement credit, accelerated degree programs, student-designed majors, an honors program, double majors, independent study, and a senior project. Special programs include internships, summer session for credit, off-campus study, study-abroad, and Air Force ROTC.

The most frequently chosen **baccalaureate** fields are business/marketing, interdisciplinary studies, and visual and performing arts. A complete listing of majors at George Fox appears in the Majors by College index beginning on page 469.

The **faculty** at George Fox has 162 full-time members, 67% with terminal degrees. The student-faculty ratio is 11:1.

Students of George Fox

The student body totals 3,383, of whom 1,980 are undergraduates. 61.3% are women and 38.7% are men. Students come from 26 states and territories and 9 other countries. 70% are from Oregon. 4.3% are international students. 2% are African American, 2.2% American Indian, 5.4% Asian American, and 4.3% Hispanic American. 76% returned for their sophomore year.

Facilities and Resources

140 **computers/terminals** and 200 ports are available on campus for general student use. Students can access the following: campus intranet, computer help desk, free student e-mail accounts, online (class) grades, online (class) registration, online (class) schedules. Campuswide network is available. 100% of college-owned or -operated housing units are wired for high-speed Internet access. Wireless service is available via entire campus. The **library** has 218,240 books and 6,369 subscriptions.

Campus Life

There are 20 active organizations on campus, including a drama/theater group, newspaper, radio station, and choral group. No national or local **fraternities** or **sororities**.

George Fox is a member of the NCAA (Division III). **Intercollegiate sports** include baseball (m), basketball, cross-country running, golf, soccer, softball (w), tennis, track and field, volleyball (w).

Campus Safety

Student safety services include late-night transport/escort service, 24-hour emergency telephone alarm devices, 24-hour patrols by trained security personnel, and electronically operated dormitory entrances.

Applying

George Fox requires an essay, SAT or ACT, a high school transcript, and 2 recommendations, and in some cases an interview. It recommends an interview and a minimum high school GPA of 2.6. Application deadline: 2/1; 2/1 priority date for financial aid. Deferred admission is possible.

Getting Accepted

1,212 applied
83% were accepted
398 enrolled (40% of accepted)
32% from top tenth of their h.s. class
3.65 average high school GPA
Mean SAT critical reading score: 555
Mean SAT math score: 540
Mean ACT score: 24
34% had SAT critical reading scores over 600
28% had SAT math scores over 600
25% had SAT writing scores over 600
49% had ACT scores over 24
8% had SAT critical reading scores over 700
5% had SAT math scores over 700
5% had SAT writing scores over 700
8% had ACT scores over 30
5 National Merit Scholars

Graduation and After

53% graduated in 4 years
8% graduated in 5 years
200 organizations recruited on campus

Financial Matters

$25,190 tuition and fees (2008–09)
$8000 room and board
86% average percent of need met
$21,552 average financial aid amount received
    per undergraduate (2007–08 estimated)

GEORGETOWN COLLEGE

SUBURBAN SETTING ■ PRIVATE ■ INDEPENDENT RELIGIOUS ■ COED
GEORGETOWN, KENTUCKY

Web site: www.georgetowncollege.edu
Contact: 400 East College Street, Georgetown, KY 40324
Telephone: 502-863-8009 or toll-free 800-788-9985
Fax: 502-868-7733
E-mail: admissions@georgetowncollege.edu

Getting Accepted
1,376 applied
84% were accepted
379 enrolled (33% of accepted)
29% from top tenth of their h.s. class
3.47 average high school GPA
Mean SAT critical reading score: 530
Mean SAT math score: 515
Mean ACT score: 24
21% had SAT critical reading scores over 600
18% had SAT math scores over 600
52% had ACT scores over 24
7% had SAT critical reading scores over 700
8% had ACT scores over 30
19 valedictorians

Graduation and After
46% graduated in 4 years
11% graduated in 5 years
1% graduated in 6 years
83% had job offers within 6 months
61 organizations recruited on campus

Financial Matters
$24,150 tuition and fees (2008–09)
$6700 room and board
87% average percent of need met
$21,039 average financial aid amount received
    per undergraduate (2007–08 estimated)

Academics
Georgetown College awards bachelor's and master's **degrees. Challenging opportunities** include advanced placement credit, student-designed majors, an honors program, double majors, independent study, and a senior project. Special programs include cooperative education, internships, summer session for credit, off-campus study, study-abroad, and Army and Air Force ROTC.

The most frequently chosen **baccalaureate** fields are business/marketing, communications/journalism, and psychology. A complete listing of majors at Georgetown College appears in the Majors by College index beginning on page 469.

The **faculty** at Georgetown College has 111 full-time members, 93% with terminal degrees. The student-faculty ratio is 12:1.

Students of Georgetown College
The student body totals 1,856, of whom 1,338 are undergraduates. 56.8% are women and 43.2% are men. Students come from 31 states and territories and 8 other countries. 85% are from Kentucky. 1.1% are international students. 6.7% are African American, 0.5% Asian American, and 1.3% Hispanic American. 79% returned for their sophomore year.

Facilities and Resources
175 **computers/terminals** are available on campus for general student use. Students can access the following: campus intranet, computer help desk, free student e-mail accounts, online (class) grades, online (class) registration, online (class) schedules. Campuswide network is available. 100% of college-owned or -operated housing units are wired for high-speed Internet access. Wireless service is available via classrooms, computer centers, computer labs, dorm rooms, learning centers, libraries. The **library** has 174,300 books and 458 subscriptions.

Campus Life
There are 97 active organizations on campus, including a drama/theater group, newspaper, radio station, and choral group. 33% of eligible men and 48% of eligible women are members of national **fraternities**, national **sororities**, and local fraternities.

Georgetown College is a member of the NAIA. **Intercollegiate sports** (some offering scholarships) include baseball (m), basketball, cheerleading (w), cross-country running, football (m), golf, soccer, softball (w), tennis, track and field, volleyball (w).

Campus Safety
Student safety services include late-night transport/escort service and 24-hour patrols by trained security personnel.

Applying
Georgetown College requires SAT or ACT, a high school transcript, and a minimum high school GPA of 2.5, and in some cases an essay and an interview. It recommends ACT. Application deadline: 8/1; 2/15 priority date for financial aid. Deferred admission is possible.

Georgetown University

URBAN SETTING ■ PRIVATE ■ INDEPENDENT RELIGIOUS ■ COED
WASHINGTON, DISTRICT OF COLUMBIA

Web site: www.georgetown.edu
Contact: Mr. Charles A. Deacon, Dean of Undergraduate Admissions, 37th
and O Street, NW, Washington, DC 20057
Telephone: 202-687-3600
Fax: 202-687-5084

Academics

Georgetown awards bachelor's, master's, doctoral, and first-professional **degrees. Challenging opportunities** include advanced placement credit, student-designed majors, an honors program, double majors, independent study, and a senior project. Special programs include internships, summer session for credit, off-campus study, study-abroad, and Army, Navy, and Air Force ROTC.

The most frequently chosen **baccalaureate** fields are social sciences, business/marketing, and English. A complete listing of majors at Georgetown appears in the Majors by College index beginning on page 469.

The **faculty** at Georgetown has 845 full-time members, 89% with terminal degrees.

Students of Georgetown

The student body totals 15,318, of whom 7,092 are undergraduates. 54% are women and 46% are men. Students come from 55 states and territories and 102 other countries. 2% are from District of Columbia. 6.7% are international students. 6.6% are African American, 0.1% American Indian, 9.1% Asian American, and 6.3% Hispanic American. 96% returned for their sophomore year.

Facilities and Resources

400 **computers/terminals** are available on campus for general student use. Students can access the following: online (class) registration, online grade reports. Campuswide network is available. Wireless service is available via classrooms, computer centers, computer labs, dorm rooms, learning centers, libraries, student centers. The 7 **libraries** have 2,472,239 books and 31,099 subscriptions.

Campus Life

There are 138 active organizations on campus, including a drama/theater group, newspaper, radio station, television station, and choral group. No national or local **fraternities** or **sororities**.

Georgetown is a member of the NCAA (Division I). **Intercollegiate sports** (some offering scholarships) include baseball (m), basketball, crew, cross-country running, field hockey (w), football (m), golf (m), lacrosse, sailing, soccer, swimming and diving, tennis, track and field, volleyball (w).

Campus Safety

Student safety services include student guards at residence halls and academic facilities, late-night transport/escort service, 24-hour emergency telephone alarm devices, 24-hour patrols by trained security personnel, and electronically operated dormitory entrances.

Applying

Georgetown requires an essay, SAT or ACT, a high school transcript, an interview, and 2 recommendations. It recommends SAT Subject Tests. Application deadline: 1/10; 2/1 for financial aid. Deferred admission is possible.

Getting Accepted
18,676 applied
19% were accepted
1,571 enrolled (45% of accepted)
89% had SAT critical reading scores over 600
91% had SAT math scores over 600
54% had SAT critical reading scores over 700
56% had SAT math scores over 700

Financial Matters
$38,122 tuition and fees (2008–09)
$12,153 room and board
100% average percent of need met
$29,600 average financial aid amount received
per undergraduate (2007–08 estimated)

THE GEORGE WASHINGTON UNIVERSITY

URBAN SETTING ■ PRIVATE ■ INDEPENDENT ■ COED
WASHINGTON, DISTRICT OF COLUMBIA

Web site: www.gwu.edu
Contact: Dr. Kathryn M. Napper, Director of Admission, Office of Undergraduate Admissions, Washington, DC 20052
Telephone: 202-994-6040 or toll-free 800-447-3765 (in-state)
Fax: 202-994-0325
E-mail: gwadm@gwis2.circ.gwu.edu

Getting Accepted

19,430 applied
37% were accepted
2,461 enrolled (34% of accepted)
67% from top tenth of their h.s. class
73% had SAT critical reading scores over 600
78% had SAT math scores over 600
75% had SAT writing scores over 600
92% had ACT scores over 24
19% had SAT critical reading scores over 700
21% had SAT math scores over 700
22% had SAT writing scores over 700
25% had ACT scores over 30

Graduation and After

76% graduated in 4 years
4% graduated in 5 years
1% graduated in 6 years
383 organizations recruited on campus

Financial Matters

$41,655 tuition and fees (2009–10)
$10,120 room and board
90% average percent of need met
$33,809 average financial aid amount received per undergraduate (2006–07)

Academics

GW awards associate, bachelor's, master's, doctoral, and first-professional **degrees** and post-bachelor's and post-master's certificates. **Challenging opportunities** include advanced placement credit, accelerated degree programs, student-designed majors, an honors program, double majors, independent study, and a senior project. Special programs include cooperative education, internships, summer session for credit, off-campus study, study-abroad, and Army, Navy, and Air Force ROTC.

The most frequently chosen **baccalaureate** fields are social sciences, business/marketing, and psychology. A complete listing of majors at GW appears in the Majors by College index beginning on page 469.

The **faculty** at GW has 861 full-time members, 91% with terminal degrees. The student-faculty ratio is 13:1.

Students of GW

The student body totals 25,116, of whom 10,590 are undergraduates. 55.6% are women and 44.4% are men. Students come from 55 states and territories and 101 other countries. 2% are from District of Columbia. 5.4% are international students. 6.9% are African American, 0.3% American Indian, 10.2% Asian American, and 6.6% Hispanic American. 91% returned for their sophomore year.

Facilities and Resources

550 **computers/terminals** are available on campus for general student use. Campuswide network is available. The 3 **libraries** have 1,984,094 books and 15,365 subscriptions.

Campus Life

There are 208 active organizations on campus, including a drama/theater group, newspaper, radio station, television station, choral group, and marching band. 22% of eligible men and 21% of eligible women are members of national **fraternities** and national **sororities**.

GW is a member of the NCAA (Division I). **Intercollegiate sports** (some offering scholarships) include baseball (m), basketball, crew, cross-country running, golf (m), gymnastics (w), soccer, swimming and diving, tennis, volleyball (w), water polo (m).

Campus Safety

Student safety services include late-night transport/escort service, 24-hour emergency telephone alarm devices, 24-hour patrols by trained security personnel, and electronically operated dormitory entrances.

Applying

GW requires an essay, SAT or ACT, a high school transcript, and 2 recommendations. It recommends an interview. Application deadline: 1/10; 2/1 for financial aid, with a 2/1 priority date. Early and deferred admission are possible.

Georgia Institute of Technology

Urban setting ■ Public ■ State-supported ■ Coed, Primarily Men
Atlanta, Georgia

Web site: www.gatech.edu
Contact: Mr. Rick A. Clark Jr., Director of Admissions (Undergraduate),
Georgia Institute of Technology, Office of Undergraduate Admission,
Atlanta, GA 30332-0320
Telephone: 404-894-4154
Fax: 404-894-9511
E-mail: admission@gatech.edu

Academics

Georgia Tech awards bachelor's, master's, and doctoral **degrees**. **Challenging opportunities** include advanced placement credit, accelerated degree programs, student-designed majors, an honors program, double majors, independent study, and a senior project. Special programs include cooperative education, internships, summer session for credit, off-campus study, study-abroad, and Army, Navy, and Air Force ROTC.

The most frequently chosen **baccalaureate** fields are engineering, business/marketing, and computer and information sciences. A complete listing of majors at Georgia Tech appears in the Majors by College index beginning on page 469.

The **faculty** at Georgia Tech has 887 full-time members, 98% with terminal degrees. The student-faculty ratio is 14:1.

Students of Georgia Tech

The student body totals 19,413, of whom 12,973 are undergraduates. 29.9% are women and 70.1% are men. Students come from 52 states and territories and 70 other countries. 73% are from Georgia. 5.1% are international students. 6.8% are African American, 0.3% American Indian, 16.8% Asian American, and 4.7% Hispanic American. 93% returned for their sophomore year.

Facilities and Resources

2,018 **computers/terminals** are available on campus for general student use. Students can access the following: campus intranet, computer help desk, free student e-mail accounts, online (class) grades, online (class) registration, online (class) schedules. Campuswide network is available. 100% of college-owned or -operated housing units are wired for high-speed Internet access. Wireless service is available via classrooms, computer centers, computer labs, dorm rooms, learning centers, libraries, student centers. The 2 **libraries** have 2,524,671 books and 44,875 subscriptions.

Campus Life

There are 425 active organizations on campus, including a drama/theater group, newspaper, radio station, television station, choral group, and marching band. 24% of eligible men and 32% of eligible women are members of national **fraternities**, national **sororities**, and local sororities.

Georgia Tech is a member of the NCAA (Division I). **Intercollegiate sports** (some offering scholarships) include baseball (m), basketball, cheerleading, cross-country running, football (m), golf (m), ice hockey (m), softball (w), swimming and diving, tennis, track and field, volleyball (w).

Campus Safety

Student safety services include self defense education, lighted pathways and walks, video cameras, late-night transport/escort service, 24-hour emergency telephone alarm devices, 24-hour patrols by trained security personnel, and electronically operated dormitory entrances.

Applying

Georgia Tech requires an essay, SAT or ACT, and a high school transcript. Application deadline: 1/15; 3/1 for financial aid, with a 3/1 priority date. Early admission is possible.

Getting Accepted

10,258 applied
61% were accepted
2,640 enrolled (42% of accepted)
58% from top tenth of their h.s. class
3.75 average high school GPA
Mean SAT critical reading score: 636
Mean SAT math score: 691
Mean SAT writing score: 629
Mean ACT score: 29
74% had SAT critical reading scores over 600
95% had SAT math scores over 600
70% had SAT writing scores over 600
96% had ACT scores over 24
19% had SAT critical reading scores over 700
47% had SAT math scores over 700
17% had SAT writing scores over 700
38% had ACT scores over 30
105 National Merit Scholars

Graduation and After

31% graduated in 4 years
38% graduated in 5 years
7% graduated in 6 years
85% had job offers within 6 months
550 organizations recruited on campus

Financial Matters

$6040 resident tuition and fees (2008–09)
$25,182 nonresident tuition and fees (2008–09)
$7694 room and board
67% average percent of need met
$10,475 average financial aid amount received per undergraduate (2007–08 estimated)

Undergraduate education is a strong focus at Georgia State, with small classes and opportunities for students to work with faculty members in a research setting. There are a total of 1,046 faculty members in more than 250 fields of study. Students can live in University housing and participate in over 200 different student organizations. Georgia State is located in the heart of Atlanta, an exciting metropolis that offers a variety of job and internship opportunities. Students can walk to such places as the State Capitol, Georgia Aquarium, and CNN Center or take the rapid transit system to explore all that Atlanta has to offer.

Getting Accepted
10,301 applied
55% were accepted
2,803 enrolled (49% of accepted)
3.31 average high school GPA
Mean SAT critical reading score: 544
Mean SAT math score: 543
Mean ACT score: 23
24% had SAT critical reading scores over 600
24% had SAT math scores over 600
34% had ACT scores over 24
3% had SAT critical reading scores over 700
2% had SAT math scores over 700
4% had ACT scores over 30

Graduation and After
16% graduated in 4 years
19% graduated in 5 years
8% graduated in 6 years
121 organizations recruited on campus

Financial Matters
$6056 resident tuition and fees (2008–09)
$20,624 nonresident tuition and fees (2008–09)
$9330 room and board
28% average percent of need met
$9754 average financial aid amount received per undergraduate (2006–07)

GEORGIA STATE UNIVERSITY
URBAN SETTING ■ PUBLIC ■ STATE-SUPPORTED ■ COED
ATLANTA, GEORGIA

Web site: www.gsu.edu
Contact: Daniel Niccum, Associate Director of Admissions, PO Box 4009, Atlanta, GA 30302-4009
Telephone: 404-651-4110
Fax: 404-651-4811
E-mail: dniccum@gsu.edu

Academics
Georgia State awards bachelor's, master's, doctoral, and first-professional **degrees** and post-bachelor's, post-master's, and first-professional certificates. **Challenging opportunities** include advanced placement credit, accelerated degree programs, an honors program, double majors, and independent study. Special programs include cooperative education, internships, summer session for credit, off-campus study, study-abroad, and Army, Navy, and Air Force ROTC.

The most frequently chosen **baccalaureate** fields are business/marketing, social sciences, and psychology. A complete listing of majors at Georgia State appears in the Majors by College index beginning on page 469.

The **faculty** at Georgia State has 1,120 full-time members, 84% with terminal degrees. The student-faculty ratio is 17:1.

Students of Georgia State
The student body totals 28,238, of whom 20,846 are undergraduates. 60.4% are women and 39.6% are men. Students come from 49 states and territories. 94% are from Georgia. 2.7% are international students. 28.7% are African American, 0.2% American Indian, 10.4% Asian American, and 5.2% Hispanic American. 83% returned for their sophomore year.

Facilities and Resources
1,000 **computers/terminals** are available on campus for general student use. Students can access the following: computer help desk, free student e-mail accounts, online (class) grades, online (class) registration, online (class) schedules. Campuswide network is available. 100% of college-owned or -operated housing units are wired for high-speed Internet access. Wireless service is available via classrooms, computer labs, dorm rooms, learning centers, libraries, student centers. The 2 **libraries** have 2,226,711 books and 7,398 subscriptions.

Campus Life
There are 270 active organizations on campus, including a drama/theater group, newspaper, radio station, television station, and choral group. 3% of eligible men and 4% of eligible women are members of national **fraternities** and national **sororities**.

Georgia State is a member of the NCAA (Division I). **Intercollegiate sports** (some offering scholarships) include baseball (m), basketball, cross-country running, golf, soccer, softball (w), tennis, track and field, volleyball (w).

Campus Safety
Student safety services include late-night transport/escort service, 24-hour emergency telephone alarm devices, 24-hour patrols by trained security personnel, and electronically operated dormitory entrances.

Applying
Georgia State requires SAT or ACT, a high school transcript, college prep high school curriculum, and a minimum high school GPA of 2.8, and in some cases SAT Subject Tests and an interview. Application deadline: 3/1; 4/1 priority date for financial aid. Deferred admission is possible.

GETTYSBURG COLLEGE

SMALL-TOWN SETTING ■ PRIVATE ■ INDEPENDENT RELIGIOUS ■ COED
GETTYSBURG, PENNSYLVANIA

SPONSOR

Web site: www.gettysburg.edu
Contact: Ms. Gail Sweezey, Director of Admissions, 300 North Washington
  Street, Gettysburg, PA 17325
Telephone: 717-337-6100 or toll-free 800-431-0803
Fax: 717-337-6145
E-mail: admiss@gettysburg.edu

Academics

Gettysburg awards bachelor's **degrees**. **Challenging opportunities** include advanced placement credit, student-designed majors, double majors, independent study, and a senior project. Special programs include internships, off-campus study, study-abroad, and Army ROTC.

The most frequently chosen **baccalaureate** fields are social sciences, biological/life sciences, and business/marketing. A complete listing of majors at Gettysburg appears in the Majors by College index beginning on page 469.

The **faculty** at Gettysburg has 204 full-time members, 91% with terminal degrees. The student-faculty ratio is 11:1.

Students of Gettysburg

The student body is made up of 2,457 undergraduates. 52.7% are women and 47.3% are men. Students come from 40 states and territories and 35 other countries. 26% are from Pennsylvania. 2.1% are international students. 4.8% are African American, 1.5% Asian American, and 3.1% Hispanic American. 90% returned for their sophomore year.

Facilities and Resources

Students can access the following: campus intranet, computer help desk, free student e-mail accounts, online (class) grades, online (class) registration, online (class) schedules. Campuswide network is available. 100% of college-owned or -operated housing units are wired for high-speed Internet access. Wireless service is available via entire campus. The **library** has 393,163 books and 4,778 subscriptions.

Campus Life

There are 130 active organizations on campus, including a drama/theater group, newspaper, radio station, television station, choral group, and marching band. 40% of eligible men and 26% of eligible women are members of national **fraternities** and national **sororities**.

Gettysburg is a member of the NCAA (Division III). **Intercollegiate sports** include baseball (m), basketball, cheerleading, cross-country running, field hockey (w), football (m), golf, lacrosse, soccer, softball (w), swimming and diving, tennis, track and field, volleyball (w), wrestling (m).

Campus Safety

Student safety services include late-night transport/escort service, 24-hour emergency telephone alarm devices, 24-hour patrols by trained security personnel, and electronically operated dormitory entrances.

Applying

Gettysburg requires an essay, SAT or ACT, a high school transcript, and 2 recommendations. It recommends SAT Subject Tests, an interview, extracurricular activities, and a minimum high school GPA of 3.0. Application deadline: 2/1; 2/15 for financial aid. Early and deferred admission are possible.

Gettysburg College is a highly motivated community of determined students, faculty members, and administrators who come together to build in each other a passion for the responsibility of citizenship and the opportunity of leadership. With a strong liberal arts and sciences philosophy at its core, the Gettysburg curriculum instills in students a capacity for integrative and critical thinking from a global perspective. Students expand upon their classroom experiences by conducting collaborative research with esteemed faculty members in the campus' state-of-the-art facilities, immersing themselves in foreign cultures through Gettysburg's extensive array of off-campus study programs, and pursuing internships with some of the nation's most influential corporations and organizations. Students' active involvement in clubs, athletics, and community service creates a vibrant atmosphere on Gettysburg's residential campus. Gettysburg College challenges students to do great work, thereby preparing them to lead energetic, engaged, and enlightened lives.

Getting Accepted
5,790 applied
38% were accepted
714 enrolled (33% of accepted)
66% from top tenth of their h.s. class
Mean SAT critical reading score: 648
Mean SAT math score: 647
82% had SAT critical reading scores over 600
75% had SAT math scores over 600
19% had SAT critical reading scores over 700
10% had SAT math scores over 700

Graduation and After
77% graduated in 4 years
5% graduated in 5 years
1% graduated in 6 years
78% had job offers within 6 months
93 organizations recruited on campus

Financial Matters
$37,600 tuition and fees (2008–09)
$9100 room and board
100% average percent of need met
$27,610 average financial aid amount received
  per undergraduate (2007–08 estimated)

GONZAGA UNIVERSITY

Urban setting ■ Private ■ Independent Religious ■ Coed
Spokane, Washington

Web site: www.gonzaga.edu
Contact: Ms. Julie McCulloh, Dean of Admission, 502 East Boone Avenue,
   Spokane, WA 99258-0102
Telephone: 509-323-6591 or toll-free 800-322-2584 Ext. 6572
Fax: 509-323-5780
E-mail: admissions@gonzaga.edu

Getting Accepted
5,026 applied
78% were accepted
1,107 enrolled (28% of accepted)
36% from top tenth of their h.s. class
3.66 average high school GPA
42% had SAT critical reading scores over 600
49% had SAT math scores over 600
79% had ACT scores over 24
6% had SAT critical reading scores over 700
7% had SAT math scores over 700
18% had ACT scores over 30

Graduation and After
67% graduated in 4 years
10% graduated in 5 years
3% graduated in 6 years
37% had job offers within 6 months
137 organizations recruited on campus

Financial Matters
$28,262 tuition and fees (2008–09)
$7860 room and board
84% average percent of need met
$19,207 average financial aid amount received
   per undergraduate (2006–07)

Academics

Gonzaga awards bachelor's, master's, doctoral, and first-professional **degrees** and post-master's certificates. **Challenging opportunities** include advanced placement credit, accelerated degree programs, an honors program, double majors, independent study, and a senior project. Special programs include internships, summer session for credit, off-campus study, study-abroad, and Army ROTC.

The most frequently chosen **baccalaureate** fields are business/marketing, engineering, and social sciences. A complete listing of majors at Gonzaga appears in the Majors by College index beginning on page 469.

The **faculty** at Gonzaga has 371 full-time members, 84% with terminal degrees. The student-faculty ratio is 11:1.

Students of Gonzaga

The student body totals 7,272, of whom 4,517 are undergraduates. 53.6% are women and 46.4% are men. Students come from 53 states and territories and 40 other countries. 49% are from Washington. 2% are international students. 1.4% are African American, 0.8% American Indian, 5.4% Asian American, and 4.3% Hispanic American. 92% returned for their sophomore year.

Facilities and Resources

625 **computers/terminals** are available on campus for general student use. Students can access the following: computer help desk, free student e-mail accounts, online (class) grades, online (class) registration, online (class) schedules. Campuswide network is available. Wireless service is available via classrooms, computer centers, computer labs, dorm rooms, libraries, student centers. The 2 **libraries** have 305,517 books and 32,106 subscriptions.

Campus Life

There are 69 active organizations on campus, including a drama/theater group, newspaper, radio station, television station, and choral group. No national or local **fraternities** or **sororities**.

Gonzaga is a member of the NCAA (Division I). **Intercollegiate sports** (some offering scholarships) include baseball (m), basketball, cross-country running, golf, soccer, tennis, track and field, volleyball (w).

Campus Safety

Student safety services include late-night transport/escort service, 24-hour emergency telephone alarm devices, 24-hour patrols by trained security personnel, and electronically operated dormitory entrances.

Applying

Gonzaga requires an essay, SAT or ACT, a high school transcript, 1 recommendation, and a minimum high school GPA of 3.0. It recommends an interview. Application deadline: 2/1; 2/1 priority date for financial aid. Deferred admission is possible.

Gordon College

SUBURBAN SETTING ■ PRIVATE ■ INDEPENDENT RELIGIOUS ■ COED
WENHAM, MASSACHUSETTS

Web site: www.gordon.edu
Contact: 255 Grapevine Road, Wenham, MA 01984-1899
Telephone: 978-867-4218 or toll-free 866-464-6736
Fax: 978-867-4682
E-mail: admissions@gordon.edu

Academics

Gordon awards bachelor's and master's **degrees**. **Challenging opportunities** include advanced placement credit, student-designed majors, an honors program, double majors, independent study, and a senior project. Special programs include cooperative education, internships, off-campus study, study-abroad, and Army and Air Force ROTC.

The most frequently chosen **baccalaureate** fields are education, English, and social sciences. A complete listing of majors at Gordon appears in the Majors by College index beginning on page 469.

The **faculty** at Gordon has 98 full-time members, 82% with terminal degrees. The student-faculty ratio is 15:1.

Students of Gordon

The student body totals 1,718, of whom 1,590 are undergraduates. 62.9% are women and 37.1% are men. Students come from 44 states and territories and 23 other countries. 29% are from Massachusetts. 2.9% are international students. 1.6% are African American, 0.3% American Indian, 1.6% Asian American, and 3.3% Hispanic American. 85% returned for their sophomore year.

Facilities and Resources

141 **computers/terminals** are available on campus for general student use. Students can access the following: campus intranet, computer help desk, free student e-mail accounts, online (class) registration, online (class) schedules. Campuswide network is available. 100% of college-owned or -operated housing units are wired for high-speed Internet access. Wireless service is available via classrooms, learning centers, libraries, student centers. The **library** has 142,688 books and 8,555 subscriptions.

Campus Life

There are 35 active organizations on campus, including a drama/theater group, newspaper, and choral group. No national or local **fraternities** or **sororities**.

Gordon is a member of the NCAA (Division III). **Intercollegiate sports** include baseball (m), basketball, cheerleading, cross-country running, field hockey (w), lacrosse, soccer, softball (w), swimming and diving, tennis, track and field, volleyball (w).

Campus Safety

Student safety services include late-night transport/escort service, 24-hour emergency telephone alarm devices, 24-hour patrols by trained security personnel, and electronically operated dormitory entrances.

Applying

Gordon requires an essay, SAT or ACT, a high school transcript, an interview, 2 recommendations, and pastoral recommendation, statement of Christian faith. It recommends SAT Subject Tests and a minimum high school GPA of 3.0. Application deadline: rolling admissions; 3/1 priority date for financial aid. Early and deferred admission are possible.

Getting Accepted

1,570 applied
71% were accepted
421 enrolled (38% of accepted)
33% from top tenth of their h.s. class
3.61 average high school GPA
Mean SAT critical reading score: 591
Mean SAT math score: 568
Mean SAT writing score: 590
Mean ACT score: 26
49% had SAT critical reading scores over 600
35% had SAT math scores over 600
47% had SAT writing scores over 600
13% had SAT critical reading scores over 700
5% had SAT math scores over 700
8% had SAT writing scores over 700
5 National Merit Scholars

Graduation and After

66% graduated in 4 years
7% graduated in 5 years
1% graduated in 6 years
73 organizations recruited on campus

Financial Matters

$27,294 tuition and fees (2008–09)
$7424 room and board
70% average percent of need met
$14,540 average financial aid amount received per undergraduate (2005–06)

GOSHEN COLLEGE

SMALL-TOWN SETTING ■ PRIVATE ■ INDEPENDENT RELIGIOUS ■ COED
GOSHEN, INDIANA

Web site: www.goshen.edu
Contact: Ms. Lynn Jackson, Vice President for Enrollment Management,
    1700 South Main Street, Goshen, IN 46526-4794
Telephone: 574-535-7535 or toll-free 800-348-7422
Fax: 574-535-7609
E-mail: lynnj@goshen.edu

Getting Accepted
586 applied
76% were accepted
202 enrolled (46% of accepted)
31% from top tenth of their h.s. class
3.49 average high school GPA
Mean SAT critical reading score: 569
Mean SAT math score: 569
Mean SAT writing score: 557
Mean ACT score: 26
39% had SAT critical reading scores over 600
42% had SAT math scores over 600
37% had SAT writing scores over 600
68% had ACT scores over 24
12% had SAT critical reading scores over 700
9% had SAT math scores over 700
7% had SAT writing scores over 700
21% had ACT scores over 30
4 National Merit Scholars
14 valedictorians

Graduation and After
49% graduated in 4 years
11% graduated in 5 years
1% graduated in 6 years
35 organizations recruited on campus

Financial Matters
$22,300 tuition and fees (2008–09)
$7450 room and board
87% average percent of need met
$16,555 average financial aid amount received
  per undergraduate (2005–06)

Academics
Goshen awards bachelor's and master's **degrees**. **Challenging opportunities** include advanced placement credit, accelerated degree programs, student-designed majors, freshman honors college, an honors program, double majors, independent study, and a senior project. Special programs include internships, summer session for credit, off-campus study, and study-abroad.

The most frequently chosen **baccalaureate** fields are health professions and related sciences, business/marketing, and biological/life sciences. A complete listing of majors at Goshen appears in the Majors by College index beginning on page 469.

The **faculty** at Goshen has 71 full-time members, 63% with terminal degrees. The student-faculty ratio is 10:1.

Students of Goshen
The student body is made up of 955 undergraduates. 59.6% are women and 40.4% are men. Students come from 35 states and territories and 37 other countries. 46% are from Indiana. 5.8% are international students. 3.4% are African American, 0.3% American Indian, 2.1% Asian American, and 5.7% Hispanic American. 84% returned for their sophomore year.

Facilities and Resources
160 **computers/terminals** and 2,000 ports are available on campus for general student use. Students can access the following: campus intranet, computer help desk, free student e-mail accounts, online (class) grades, online (class) registration, online (class) schedules. Campuswide network is available. 100% of college-owned or -operated housing units are wired for high-speed Internet access. Wireless service is available via classrooms, computer centers, computer labs, learning centers, libraries, student centers. The 3 **libraries** have 136,550 books and 496 subscriptions.

Campus Life
There are 26 active organizations on campus, including a drama/theater group, newspaper, radio station, television station, and choral group. No national or local **fraternities** or **sororities**.

Goshen is a member of the NAIA. **Intercollegiate sports** (some offering scholarships) include baseball (m), basketball, cross-country running, golf (m), soccer, softball (w), tennis, track and field, volleyball (w).

Campus Safety
Student safety services include late-night transport/escort service, 24-hour emergency telephone alarm devices, and 24-hour patrols by trained security personnel.

Applying
Goshen requires an essay, SAT or ACT, a high school transcript, 2 recommendations, and a minimum high school GPA of 2.0. It recommends an interview, rank in upper 50% of high school class, minimum SAT score math and verbal of 1000 or ACT score of 22, and a minimum high school GPA of 2.6. Application deadline: 8/15; 2/15 priority date for financial aid. Deferred admission is possible.

GOUCHER COLLEGE

SUBURBAN SETTING ■ PRIVATE ■ INDEPENDENT ■ COED
BALTIMORE, MARYLAND

SPONSOR

Web site: www.goucher.edu
Contact: 1021 Dulaney Valley Road, Baltimore, MD 21204-2794
Telephone: 410-337-6100 or toll-free 800-468-2437
Fax: 410-337-6354
E-mail: admissions@goucher.edu

Academics

Goucher awards bachelor's and master's **degrees** and post-bachelor's certificates. **Challenging opportunities** include advanced placement credit, student-designed majors, double majors, independent study, and a senior project. Special programs include internships, off-campus study, study-abroad, and Army ROTC.

The most frequently chosen **baccalaureate** fields are social sciences, psychology, and visual and performing arts. A complete listing of majors at Goucher appears in the Majors by College index beginning on page 469.

The **faculty** at Goucher has 130 full-time members, 89% with terminal degrees. The student-faculty ratio is 9:1.

Students of Goucher

The student body totals 2,319, of whom 1,447 are undergraduates. 68.3% are women and 31.7% are men. Students come from 43 states and territories and 27 other countries. 30% are from Maryland. 0.9% are international students. 6.4% are African American, 0.3% American Indian, 2.9% Asian American, and 3.8% Hispanic American. 83% returned for their sophomore year.

Facilities and Resources

150 **computers/terminals** are available on campus for general student use. Students can access the following: campus intranet, computer help desk, free student e-mail accounts, online (class) grades, online (class) registration, online (class) schedules, transcripts, financial aid information, billing, ePortfolios, academic progress reports, study abroad plan. Campuswide network is available. 40% of college-owned or -operated housing units are wired for high-speed Internet access. Wireless service is available via entire campus. The **library** has 303,286 books and 41,432 subscriptions.

Campus Life

There are 54 active organizations on campus, including a drama/theater group, newspaper, radio station, television station, and choral group. No national or local **fraternities** or **sororities**.

Goucher is a member of the NCAA (Division III). **Intercollegiate sports** include basketball, cross-country running, equestrian sports, field hockey (w), gymnastics, lacrosse, soccer, swimming and diving, tennis, track and field, volleyball (w).

Campus Safety

Student safety services include late-night transport/escort service, 24-hour emergency telephone alarm devices, 24-hour patrols by trained security personnel, and electronically operated dormitory entrances.

Applying

Goucher requires an essay, a high school transcript, and a minimum high school GPA of 2.0. It recommends an interview, 3 recommendations, and a minimum high school GPA of 2.8. Application deadline: 2/1; 2/15 priority date for financial aid. Early and deferred admission are possible.

Goucher College is a small, private, coeducational liberal arts and sciences college in Baltimore, Maryland, with an international emphasis and an academic program that partners classroom learning with real, hands-on experience. Since it was founded in 1885, Goucher has provided a truly global kind of education that puts learning in perspective with the events and developments of the entire world, encouraging students to test what they have learned against their experiences in service-learning, study-abroad, and internship programs throughout the nation and around the globe. Goucher is a small college with a big view of the world—an educational community without boundaries.

Getting Accepted
4,077 applied
64% were accepted
360 enrolled (14% of accepted)
3.17 average high school GPA
Mean SAT critical reading score: 587
Mean SAT math score: 552
Mean SAT writing score: 583
49% had SAT critical reading scores over 600
36% had SAT math scores over 600
47% had SAT writing scores over 600
72% had ACT scores over 24
12% had SAT critical reading scores over 700
3% had SAT math scores over 700
10% had SAT writing scores over 700
13% had ACT scores over 30

Graduation and After
57% graduated in 4 years
6% graduated in 5 years
1% graduated in 6 years
80% had job offers within 6 months

Financial Matters
$32,636 tuition and fees (2008–09)
$10,104 room and board
82% average percent of need met
$19,917 average financial aid amount received per undergraduate (2005–06)

GRINNELL COLLEGE

SMALL-TOWN SETTING ■ PRIVATE ■ INDEPENDENT ■ COED
GRINNELL, IOWA

Web site: www.grinnell.edu
Contact: Mr. Seth Allen, Dean for Admission and Financial Aid, 1103 Park Street, Grinnell, IA 50112
Telephone: 641-269-3600 or toll-free 800-247-0113
Fax: 641-269-4800
E-mail: askgrin@grinnell.edu

Getting Accepted
3,217 applied
43% were accepted
464 enrolled (34% of accepted)
64% from top tenth of their h.s. class
80% had SAT critical reading scores over 600
84% had SAT math scores over 600
96% had ACT scores over 24
43% had SAT critical reading scores over 700
32% had SAT math scores over 700
63% had ACT scores over 30
9 class presidents
33 valedictorians

Graduation and After
81% graduated in 4 years
4% graduated in 5 years
1% graduated in 6 years
73% had job offers within 6 months
27 organizations recruited on campus

Financial Matters
$35,428 tuition and fees (2008–09)
$8272 room and board
100% average percent of need met
$28,190 average financial aid amount received per undergraduate (2007–08 estimated)

Academics
Grinnell awards bachelor's **degrees. Challenging opportunities** include advanced placement credit, accelerated degree programs, student-designed majors, double majors, and independent study. Special programs include internships, off-campus study, and study-abroad.

The most frequently chosen **baccalaureate** fields are social sciences, foreign languages and literature, and biological/life sciences. A complete listing of majors at Grinnell appears in the Majors by College index beginning on page 469.

The **faculty** at Grinnell has 158 full-time members, 95% with terminal degrees. The student-faculty ratio is 9:1.

Students of Grinnell
The student body is made up of 1,678 undergraduates. 53.3% are women and 46.7% are men. Students come from 51 states and territories and 51 other countries. 12% are from Iowa. 10.9% are international students. 5.1% are African American, 0.4% American Indian, 7.6% Asian American, and 6.1% Hispanic American. 94% returned for their sophomore year.

Facilities and Resources
Students can access the following: campus intranet, computer help desk, free student e-mail accounts, online (class) grades, online (class) schedules. Campuswide network is available. 100% of college-owned or -operated housing units are wired for high-speed Internet access. Wireless service is available via entire campus. The 3 **libraries** have 1,200,430 books and 26,692 subscriptions.

Campus Life
There are 240 active organizations on campus, including a drama/theater group, newspaper, radio station, and choral group. No national or local **fraternities** or **sororities**.

Grinnell is a member of the NCAA (Division III). **Intercollegiate sports** include baseball (m), basketball, cross-country running, football (m), golf, soccer, softball (w), swimming and diving, tennis, track and field, volleyball (w).

Campus Safety
Student safety services include late-night transport/escort service, 24-hour emergency telephone alarm devices, 24-hour patrols by trained security personnel, student patrols, and electronically operated dormitory entrances.

Applying
Grinnell requires an essay, SAT or ACT, a high school transcript, and 3 recommendations. It recommends an interview. Application deadline: 1/2; 2/1 for financial aid. Early and deferred admission are possible.

GROVE CITY COLLEGE

SMALL-TOWN SETTING ■ PRIVATE ■ INDEPENDENT RELIGIOUS ■ COED
GROVE CITY, PENNSYLVANIA

Web site: www.gcc.edu
Contact: Mr. Jeffrey Mincey, Director of Admissions, 100 Campus Drive,
   Grove City, PA 16127-2104
Telephone: 724-458-2100
Fax: 724-458-3395
E-mail: admissions@gcc.edu

SPONSOR

Academics

Grove City awards bachelor's **degrees**. **Challenging opportunities** include advanced placement credit, student-designed majors, double majors, independent study, and a senior project. Special programs include internships, summer session for credit, study-abroad, and Army ROTC.

The most frequently chosen **baccalaureate** fields are business/marketing, education, and biological/life sciences. A complete listing of majors at Grove City appears in the Majors by College index beginning on page 469.

The **faculty** at Grove City has 140 full-time members, 83% with terminal degrees. The student-faculty ratio is 15:1.

Students of Grove City

The student body is made up of 2,499 undergraduates. 49.6% are women and 50.4% are men. Students come from 44 states and territories and 8 other countries. 48% are from Pennsylvania. 0.6% are international students. 0.7% are African American, 0.1% American Indian, 2.4% Asian American, and 1.2% Hispanic American. 92% returned for their sophomore year.

Facilities and Resources

50 **computers/terminals** are available on campus for general student use. Students can access the following: campus intranet, computer help desk, free student e-mail accounts, online (class) grades, online (class) registration, online (class) schedules. Campuswide network is available. 100% of college-owned or -operated housing units are wired for high-speed Internet access. Wireless service is available via classrooms, learning centers, student centers. The **library** has 135,093 books and 300 subscriptions.

Campus Life

There are 123 active organizations on campus, including a drama/theater group, newspaper, radio station, television station, choral group, and marching band. 16% of eligible men and 21% of eligible women are members of local **fraternities** and local **sororities**.

Grove City is a member of the NCAA (Division III). **Intercollegiate sports** include baseball (m), basketball, cheerleading (w), cross-country running, football (m), golf, soccer, softball (w), swimming and diving, tennis, track and field, volleyball (w), water polo (w).

Campus Safety

Student safety services include monitored women's residence hall entrances, late-night transport/escort service, 24-hour emergency telephone alarm devices, 24-hour patrols by trained security personnel, student patrols, and electronically operated dormitory entrances.

Applying

Grove City requires an essay, SAT or ACT, a high school transcript, and 2 recommendations. It recommends an interview. Application deadline: 2/1; 4/15 for financial aid. Early and deferred admission are possible.

Getting Accepted

1,847 applied
56% were accepted
621 enrolled (60% of accepted)
52% from top tenth of their h.s. class
3.74 average high school GPA
Mean SAT critical reading score: 633
Mean SAT math score: 634
Mean SAT writing score: 616
Mean ACT score: 28
72% had SAT critical reading scores over 600
72% had SAT math scores over 600
91% had ACT scores over 24
26% had SAT critical reading scores over 700
19% had SAT math scores over 700
31% had ACT scores over 30
27 National Merit Scholars
16 class presidents
58 valedictorians

Graduation and After

80% graduated in 4 years
5% graduated in 5 years
90% had job offers within 6 months
209 organizations recruited on campus

Financial Matters

$12,074 tuition and fees (2008–09)
$6440 room and board
58% average percent of need met
$5845 average financial aid amount received per undergraduate (2007–08 estimated)

Gustavus Adolphus College

Small-Town Setting ■ Private ■ Independent Religious ■ Coed
St. Peter, Minnesota

Web site: www.gustavus.edu
Contact: Mr. Mark Anderson, Vice President for Admission and Student
Financial Aid, 800 West College Avenue, St. Peter, MN 56082-1498
Telephone: 507-933-7676 or toll-free 800-GUSTAVU(S)
Fax: 507-933-7474
E-mail: admission@gac.edu

Getting Accepted
3,128 applied
75% were accepted
606 enrolled (26% of accepted)
34% from top tenth of their h.s. class
3.64 average high school GPA
Mean SAT math score: 629
Mean ACT score: 26
69% had SAT math scores over 600
80% had ACT scores over 24
19% had SAT math scores over 700
17% had ACT scores over 30

Graduation and After
79% graduated in 4 years
1% graduated in 5 years
54% had job offers within 6 months
106 organizations recruited on campus

Financial Matters
$29,990 tuition and fees (2008–09)
$7460 room and board
89% average percent of need met
$18,100 average financial aid amount received
per undergraduate (2005–06)

Academics

Gustavus awards bachelor's **degrees. Challenging opportunities** include advanced placement credit, accelerated degree programs, student-designed majors, an honors program, double majors, independent study, and a senior project. Special programs include cooperative education, internships, summer session for credit, off-campus study, study-abroad, and Army ROTC.

The most frequently chosen **baccalaureate** fields are social sciences, business/marketing, and psychology. A complete listing of majors at Gustavus appears in the Majors by College index beginning on page 469.

The **faculty** at Gustavus has 200 full-time members, 85% with terminal degrees. The student-faculty ratio is 13:1.

Students of Gustavus

The student body is made up of 2,578 undergraduates. 57.1% are women and 42.9% are men. Students come from 40 states and territories and 15 other countries. 83% are from Minnesota. 1.6% are international students. 1.8% are African American, 0.3% American Indian, 5.1% Asian American, and 1.8% Hispanic American. 91% returned for their sophomore year.

Facilities and Resources

440 **computers/terminals** and 5,000 ports are available on campus for general student use. Students can access the following: computer help desk, free student e-mail accounts, online (class) grades, online (class) registration, online (class) schedules. Campuswide network is available. 100% of college-owned or -operated housing units are wired for high-speed Internet access. Wireless service is available via entire campus. The 2 **libraries** have 343,448 books and 22,931 subscriptions.

Campus Life

There are 100 active organizations on campus, including a drama/theater group, newspaper, radio station, television station, and choral group. 14% of eligible men and 16% of eligible women are members of national **fraternities**, national **sororities**, local fraternities, and local sororities.

Gustavus is a member of the NCAA (Division III). **Intercollegiate sports** include baseball (m), basketball, cross-country running, football (m), golf, gymnastics (w), ice hockey, skiing (cross-country), soccer, softball (w), swimming and diving, tennis, track and field, volleyball (w).

Campus Safety

Student safety services include late-night transport/escort service, 24-hour emergency telephone alarm devices, 24-hour patrols by trained security personnel, and electronically operated dormitory entrances.

Applying

Gustavus requires an essay, a high school transcript, and 1 recommendation. It recommends SAT or ACT and an interview. Application deadline: 4/1; 4/1 for financial aid, with a 2/15 priority date. Early and deferred admission are possible.

HAMILTON COLLEGE

SMALL-TOWN SETTING ■ PRIVATE ■ INDEPENDENT ■ COED
CLINTON, NEW YORK

SPONSOR

Web site: www.hamilton.edu
Contact: Ms. Monica Inzer, Dean of Admission and Financial Aid, 198 College Hill Road, Clinton, NY 13323
Telephone: 315-859-4421 or toll-free 800-843-2655
Fax: 315-859-4457
E-mail: admission@hamilton.edu

Academics

Hamilton awards bachelor's **degrees. Challenging opportunities** include advanced placement credit, accelerated degree programs, student-designed majors, double majors, independent study, and a senior project. Special programs include internships, off-campus study, study-abroad, and Army and Air Force ROTC.

The most frequently chosen **baccalaureate** fields are social sciences, foreign languages and literature, and physical sciences. A complete listing of majors at Hamilton appears in the Majors by College index beginning on page 469.

The **faculty** at Hamilton has 174 full-time members, 97% with terminal degrees. The student-faculty ratio is 10:1.

Students of Hamilton

The student body is made up of 1,872 undergraduates. 51.9% are women and 48.1% are men. Students come from 50 states and territories and 44 other countries. 30% are from New York. 5.3% are international students. 3.9% are African American, 0.9% American Indian, 7.1% Asian American, and 4.6% Hispanic American. 96% returned for their sophomore year.

Facilities and Resources

625 **computers/terminals** and 6,000 ports are available on campus for general student use. Students can access the following: campus intranet, computer help desk, free student e-mail accounts, online (class) grades, online (class) registration. Campuswide network is available. 100% of college-owned or -operated housing units are wired for high-speed Internet access. Wireless service is available via entire campus. The 4 **libraries** have 3,800 subscriptions.

Campus Life

Active organizations on campus include a drama/theater group, newspaper, radio station, television station, and choral group. 34% of eligible men and 18% of eligible women are members of national **fraternities**, national **sororities**, and local sororities.

Hamilton is a member of the NCAA (Division III). **Intercollegiate sports** include baseball (m), basketball, crew, cross-country running, field hockey (w), football (m), golf (m), ice hockey, lacrosse, soccer, softball (w), squash, swimming and diving, tennis, track and field, volleyball (w).

Campus Safety

Student safety services include student safety program, late-night transport/escort service, 24-hour emergency telephone alarm devices, 24-hour patrols by trained security personnel, and electronically operated dormitory entrances.

Applying

Hamilton requires an essay, SAT and SAT Subject Tests or ACT, a high school transcript, 1 recommendation, and sample of expository prose. It recommends an interview. Application deadline: 1/1; 2/8 for financial aid. Deferred admission is possible.

Students come to Hamilton to find their voice. As a national leader for teaching students to write effectively, learn from each other, and think for themselves, Hamilton produces graduates who have the knowledge, skills, and confidence to make their voices heard on issues of importance to them and their communities. A key component of the Hamilton experience is the College's open yet rigorous liberal arts curriculum. In place of distribution requirements that are common at most colleges, Hamilton gives students the freedom to choose the courses that reflect their unique interests and plans. A distinguished faculty then helps students fulfill those plans.

Getting Accepted

5,073 applied
28% were accepted
462 enrolled (32% of accepted)
76% from top tenth of their h.s. class
Mean SAT critical reading score: 681
Mean SAT math score: 686
92% had SAT critical reading scores over 600
93% had SAT math scores over 600
44% had SAT critical reading scores over 700
44% had SAT math scores over 700
26 class presidents
18 valedictorians

Graduation and After

86% graduated in 4 years
5% graduated in 5 years
1% graduated in 6 years

Financial Matters

$38,600 tuition and fees (2008–09)
$9810 room and board
100% average percent of need met
$31,003 average financial aid amount received per undergraduate (2007–08 estimated)

URBAN SETTING ■ PRIVATE ■ INDEPENDENT RELIGIOUS ■ COED
ST. PAUL, MINNESOTA

Web site: www.hamline.edu
Contact: Mr. Milyon Trulove, Director of Admission, 1536 Hewitt Avenue, C1930, St. Paul, MN 55104-2458
Telephone: 651-523-2207 or toll-free 800-753-9753
Fax: 651-523-2458
E-mail: cla-admis@hamline.edu

Getting Accepted

2,234 applied
80% were accepted
452 enrolled (25% of accepted)
16% from top tenth of their h.s. class
3.33 average high school GPA
48% had SAT critical reading scores over 600
29% had SAT math scores over 600
30% had SAT writing scores over 600
54% had ACT scores over 24
9% had SAT critical reading scores over 700
7% had SAT math scores over 700
9% had SAT writing scores over 700
9% had ACT scores over 30
5 National Merit Scholars
9 valedictorians

Graduation and After

64% graduated in 4 years
6% graduated in 5 years
2% graduated in 6 years
80% had job offers within 6 months
64 organizations recruited on campus

Financial Matters

$28,152 tuition and fees (2008–09)
$7784 room and board
80% average percent of need met
$18,598 average financial aid amount received per undergraduate (2006–07)

Academics

Hamline awards bachelor's, master's, doctoral, and first-professional **degrees** and post-bachelor's certificates. **Challenging opportunities** include advanced placement credit, student-designed majors, an honors program, double majors, independent study, and a senior project. Special programs include internships, summer session for credit, off-campus study, study-abroad, and Air Force ROTC.

The most frequently chosen **baccalaureate** fields are social sciences, business/marketing, and psychology. A complete listing of majors at Hamline appears in the Majors by College index beginning on page 469.

The **faculty** at Hamline has 193 full-time members, 90% with terminal degrees. The student-faculty ratio is 13:1.

Students of Hamline

The student body totals 4,876, of whom 2,053 are undergraduates. 55.6% are women and 44.4% are men. Students come from 35 states and territories and 62 other countries. 84% are from Minnesota. 3.5% are international students. 5.8% are African American, 0.7% American Indian, 5.2% Asian American, and 2.6% Hispanic American. 80% returned for their sophomore year.

Facilities and Resources

150 **computers/terminals** are available on campus for general student use. Students can access the following: computer help desk, free student e-mail accounts, online (class) grades, online (class) registration, online (class) schedules. Campuswide network is available. 100% of college-owned or -operated housing units are wired for high-speed Internet access. Wireless service is available via entire campus. The 2 **libraries** have 239,643 books and 1,738 subscriptions.

Campus Life

There are 89 active organizations on campus, including a drama/theater group, newspaper, radio station, television station, and choral group. 3% of eligible men and 2% of eligible women are members of national **fraternities**, national **sororities**, and international dining club.

Hamline is a member of the NCAA (Division III). **Intercollegiate sports** include baseball (m), basketball, cross-country running, football (m), gymnastics (w), ice hockey, soccer, softball (w), swimming and diving, tennis, track and field, volleyball (w).

Campus Safety

Student safety services include late-night transport/escort service, 24-hour emergency telephone alarm devices, 24-hour patrols by trained security personnel, student patrols, and electronically operated dormitory entrances.

Applying

Hamline requires an essay, SAT or ACT, a high school transcript, and 1 recommendation. It recommends an interview and activity resume. Application deadline: rolling admissions; 3/1 priority date for financial aid. Early and deferred admission are possible.

Hampshire College

SMALL-TOWN SETTING ■ PRIVATE ■ INDEPENDENT ■ COED
AMHERST, MASSACHUSETTS

Web site: www.hampshire.edu
Contact: Ms. Karen S. Parker, Director of Admissions, 893 West Street,
Amherst, MA 01002
Telephone: 413-559-5471 or toll-free 877-937-4267 (out-of-state)
Fax: 413-559-5631
E-mail: admissions@hampshire.edu

Academics

Hampshire awards bachelor's **degrees. Challenging opportunities** include advanced placement credit, accelerated degree programs, student-designed majors, independent study, and a senior project. Special programs include internships, off-campus study, study-abroad, and Army ROTC.

The most frequently chosen **baccalaureate** fields are visual and performing arts, social sciences, and English. A complete listing of majors at Hampshire appears in the Majors by College index beginning on page 469.

The **faculty** at Hampshire has 98 full-time members, 86% with terminal degrees. The student-faculty ratio is 11:1.

Students of Hampshire

The student body is made up of 1,428 undergraduates. 58% are women and 42% are men. Students come from 46 states and territories and 31 other countries. 18% are from Massachusetts. 4.7% are international students. 4.5% are African American, 1% American Indian, 3.6% Asian American, and 6.2% Hispanic American. 79% returned for their sophomore year.

Facilities and Resources

215 **computers/terminals** are available on campus for general student use. Students can access the following: campus intranet, computer help desk, free student e-mail accounts, online (class) registration, online (class) schedules. Campuswide network is available. 100% of college-owned or -operated housing units are wired for high-speed Internet access. Wireless service is available via entire campus. The **library** has 134,695 books and 28,558 subscriptions.

Campus Life

There are 107 active organizations on campus, including a drama/theater group, newspaper, radio station, and choral group. No national or local **fraternities** or **sororities**.

This institution has no intercollegiate sports.

Campus Safety

Student safety services include late-night transport/escort service, 24-hour emergency telephone alarm devices, 24-hour patrols by trained security personnel, and student patrols.

Applying

Hampshire requires an essay, a high school transcript, and 2 recommendations. It recommends an interview. Application deadline: 1/15; 2/1 priority date for financial aid. Early and deferred admission are possible.

Getting Accepted

2,842 applied
53% were accepted
389 enrolled (26% of accepted)
25% from top tenth of their h.s. class
3.45 average high school GPA
Mean SAT critical reading score: 660
Mean SAT math score: 600
Mean ACT score: 27
83% had SAT critical reading scores over 600
55% had SAT math scores over 600
73% had SAT writing scores over 600
90% had ACT scores over 24
28% had SAT critical reading scores over 700
13% had SAT math scores over 700
26% had SAT writing scores over 700
22% had ACT scores over 30
1 National Merit Scholar
206 class presidents
9 valedictorians

Graduation and After

53% graduated in 4 years
12% graduated in 5 years
2% graduated in 6 years
65% had job offers within 6 months
534 organizations recruited on campus

Financial Matters

$38,549 tuition and fees (2008–09)
$10,080 room and board
99% average percent of need met
$29,875 average financial aid amount received
per undergraduate (2007–08 estimated)

HANOVER COLLEGE
RURAL SETTING ■ PRIVATE ■ INDEPENDENT RELIGIOUS ■ COED
HANOVER, INDIANA

Getting Accepted
2,180 applied
67% were accepted
328 enrolled (22% of accepted)
31% from top tenth of their h.s. class
3.61 average high school GPA
Mean SAT critical reading score: 568
Mean SAT math score: 566
Mean ACT score: 25
38% had SAT critical reading scores over 600
29% had SAT math scores over 600
24% had SAT writing scores over 600
66% had ACT scores over 24
9% had SAT critical reading scores over 700
4% had SAT math scores over 700
3% had SAT writing scores over 700
16% had ACT scores over 30
10 valedictorians

Graduation and After
55% graduated in 4 years
4% graduated in 5 years
34 organizations recruited on campus

Financial Matters
$25,220 tuition and fees (2008–09)
$7500 room and board
87% average percent of need met
$18,447 average financial aid amount received
per undergraduate (2006–07)

Web site: www.hanover.edu
Contact: Mr. Chris Gage, Director of Admission, Box 108, Hanover, IN
47243-0108
Telephone: 812-866-7021 or toll-free 800-213-2178
Fax: 812-866-7098
E-mail: admission@hanover.edu

Academics
Hanover awards bachelor's **degrees**. **Challenging opportunities** include advanced placement credit, student-designed majors, double majors, independent study, and a senior project. Special programs include internships, off-campus study, and study-abroad.

The most frequently chosen **baccalaureate** fields are social sciences, psychology, and visual and performing arts. A complete listing of majors at Hanover appears in the Majors by College index beginning on page 469.

The **faculty** at Hanover has 91 full-time members, 99% with terminal degrees. The student-faculty ratio is 10:1.

Students of Hanover
The student body is made up of 926 undergraduates. 54.8% are women and 45.2% are men. Students come from 25 states and territories and 13 other countries. 65% are from Indiana. 3% are international students. 1.3% are African American, 0.7% American Indian, 2.1% Asian American, and 1.2% Hispanic American. 83% returned for their sophomore year.

Facilities and Resources
112 **computers/terminals** are available on campus for general student use. Students can access the following: campus intranet, computer help desk, free student e-mail accounts, online (class) grades, online (class) registration, online (class) schedules. Campuswide network is available. 100% of college-owned or -operated housing units are wired for high-speed Internet access. Wireless service is available via entire campus. The **library** has 224,478 books and 1,035 subscriptions.

Campus Life
There are 46 active organizations on campus, including a drama/theater group, newspaper, radio station, television station, choral group, and marching band. 45% of eligible men and 49% of eligible women are members of national **fraternities** and national **sororities**.

Hanover is a member of the NCAA (Division III). **Intercollegiate sports** include baseball (m), basketball, cross-country running, football (m), golf, soccer, softball (w), tennis, track and field, volleyball (w).

Campus Safety
Student safety services include late-night transport/escort service, 24-hour emergency telephone alarm devices, 24-hour patrols by trained security personnel, and electronically operated dormitory entrances.

Applying
Hanover requires an essay, SAT or ACT, a high school transcript, and 1 recommendation. It recommends an interview. Application deadline: 3/1; 3/1 priority date for financial aid. Early and deferred admission are possible.

HARDING UNIVERSITY

SMALL-TOWN SETTING ■ PRIVATE ■ INDEPENDENT RELIGIOUS ■ COED
SEARCY, ARKANSAS

SPONSOR

Web site: www.harding.edu
Contact: Mr. Glenn Dillard, Assistant Vice President for Enrollment
    Management, Box 12255, Searcy, AR 72149-2255
Telephone: 501-279-4407 or toll-free 800-477-4407
Fax: 501-279-4129
E-mail: admissions@harding.edu

Academics

Harding awards bachelor's, master's, doctoral, and first-professional **degrees** and post-master's certificates. **Challenging opportunities** include advanced placement credit, accelerated degree programs, freshman honors college, an honors program, double majors, independent study, and a senior project. Special programs include cooperative education, internships, summer session for credit, study-abroad, and Army ROTC.

The most frequently chosen **baccalaureate** fields are business/marketing, education, and health professions and related sciences. A complete listing of majors at Harding appears in the Majors by College index beginning on page 469.

The **faculty** at Harding has 240 full-time members, 65% with terminal degrees. The student-faculty ratio is 17:1.

Students of Harding

The student body totals 6,447, of whom 4,168 are undergraduates. 54.3% are women and 45.7% are men. Students come from 48 states and territories and 48 other countries. 29% are from Arkansas. 5.1% are international students. 4.3% are African American, 0.8% American Indian, 0.6% Asian American, and 2.2% Hispanic American. 82% returned for their sophomore year.

Facilities and Resources

465 **computers/terminals** and 2,400 ports are available on campus for general student use. Students can access the following: campus intranet, computer help desk, free student e-mail accounts, online (class) grades, online (class) registration, online (class) schedules. Campuswide network is available. 100% of college-owned or -operated housing units are wired for high-speed Internet access. The 2 **libraries** have 237,892 books and 22,180 subscriptions.

Campus Life

There are 52 active organizations on campus, including a drama/theater group, newspaper, radio station, television station, choral group, and marching band. 35% of eligible men and 33% of eligible women are members of local **fraternities** and local **sororities**.

Harding is a member of the NCAA (Division II). **Intercollegiate sports** (some offering scholarships) include baseball (m), basketball, cheerleading (w), cross-country running, football (m), golf, soccer, tennis, track and field, ultimate Frisbee, volleyball (w).

Campus Safety

Student safety services include late-night transport/escort service, 24-hour emergency telephone alarm devices, 24-hour patrols by trained security personnel, and electronically operated dormitory entrances.

Applying

Harding requires SAT or ACT, a high school transcript, and 2 recommendations. Application deadline: 4/15 priority date for financial aid. Early and deferred admission are possible.

Located in the beautiful foothills of the Ozark Mountains, Harding is one of America's more highly regarded private universities. At Harding, students build lifetime friendships and, upon graduation, are highly recruited. Harding's Christian environment and challenging academic program develop students who can compete and succeed. Whether on the main campus or in the international studies program in Australia, Chile, England, France/Switzerland, Greece, Italy, or Zambia, Africa, students find Harding to be a caring and serving family. From Missouri flood relief to working with orphans in Haiti or farmers in Kenya, hundreds of Harding students serve others worldwide each year.

Getting Accepted
1,874 applied
74% were accepted
986 enrolled (71% of accepted)
29% from top tenth of their h.s. class
3.57 average high school GPA
Mean SAT critical reading score: 570
Mean SAT math score: 568
Mean SAT writing score: 550
Mean ACT score: 25
42% had SAT critical reading scores over 600
42% had SAT math scores over 600
31% had SAT writing scores over 600
59% had ACT scores over 24
11% had SAT critical reading scores over 700
8% had SAT math scores over 700
7% had SAT writing scores over 700
14% had ACT scores over 30
10 National Merit Scholars
31 valedictorians

Graduation and After
38% graduated in 4 years
19% graduated in 5 years
4% graduated in 6 years
92% had job offers within 6 months
255 organizations recruited on campus

Financial Matters
$13,130 tuition and fees (2008–09)
$5700 room and board
70% average percent of need met
$9959 average financial aid amount received
    per undergraduate (2006–07)

HARVARD UNIVERSITY

URBAN SETTING ■ PRIVATE ■ INDEPENDENT ■ COED
CAMBRIDGE, MASSACHUSETTS

Web site: www.harvard.edu
Contact: Byerly Hall, 8 Garden Street, Cambridge, MA 02138
Telephone: 617-495-1551
E-mail: college@harvard.edu

Getting Accepted
27,462 applied
8% were accepted
1,666 enrolled (77% of accepted)
95% from top tenth of their h.s. class

Graduation and After
88% graduated in 4 years
8% graduated in 5 years
1% graduated in 6 years
212 organizations recruited on campus

Financial Matters
$36,173 tuition and fees (2008–09)
$11,042 room and board
100% average percent of need met
$35,831 average financial aid amount received
    per undergraduate (2007–08 estimated)

Academics

Harvard awards bachelor's, master's, doctoral, and first-professional **degrees** and post-master's and first-professional certificates. **Challenging opportunities** include advanced placement credit, accelerated degree programs, student-designed majors, an honors program, double majors, independent study, and a senior project. Special programs include internships, summer session for credit, off-campus study, study-abroad, and Army, Navy, and Air Force ROTC.

The most frequently chosen **baccalaureate** fields are social sciences, biological/life sciences, and history. A complete listing of majors at Harvard appears in the Majors by College index beginning on page 469.

The **faculty** at Harvard has 1,833 full-time members, 99% with terminal degrees. The student-faculty ratio is 7:1.

Students of Harvard

The student body totals 19,230, of whom 6,678 are undergraduates. 50.4% are women and 49.6% are men. Students come from 54 states and territories and 108 other countries. 16% are from Massachusetts. 10.2% are international students. 7.8% are African American, 0.7% American Indian, 16.9% Asian American, and 6.6% Hispanic American. 97% returned for their sophomore year.

Facilities and Resources

605 **computers/terminals** are available on campus for general student use. Students can access the following: computer help desk, free student e-mail accounts, online (class) grades, online (class) registration, online (class) schedules. Campuswide network is available. 100% of college-owned or -operated housing units are wired for high-speed Internet access. Wireless service is available via entire campus. The 81 **libraries** have 15,965,675 books and 110,463 subscriptions.

Campus Life

There are 400 active organizations on campus, including a drama/theater group, newspaper, radio station, television station, choral group, and marching band. Harvard has a "House" system.

Harvard is a member of the NCAA (Division I). **Intercollegiate sports** include baseball (m), basketball, crew, cross-country running, fencing, field hockey (w), football (m), golf, ice hockey, lacrosse, sailing, skiing (cross-country), skiing (downhill), soccer, softball (w), squash, swimming and diving, tennis, track and field, volleyball, water polo, wrestling (m).

Campus Safety

Student safety services include required and optional safety courses, late-night transport/escort service, 24-hour emergency telephone alarm devices, 24-hour patrols by trained security personnel, and electronically operated dormitory entrances.

Applying

Harvard requires an essay, SAT Subject Tests, SAT or ACT, a high school transcript, an interview, and 2 recommendations. Application deadline: 1/1; 2/1 priority date for financial aid. Deferred admission is possible.

HARVEY MUDD COLLEGE

SUBURBAN SETTING ■ PRIVATE ■ INDEPENDENT ■ COED
CLAREMONT, CALIFORNIA

Web site: www.hmc.edu
Contact: Mr. Peter Osgood, Director of Admissions, 301 Platt Boulevard,
    Claremont, CA 91711
Telephone: 909-621-8011
Fax: 909-607-7046
E-mail: admission@hmc.edu

Academics

Harvey Mudd awards bachelor's **degrees**. **Challenging opportunities** include advanced placement credit, student-designed majors, double majors, and a senior project. Special programs include internships, off-campus study, study-abroad, and Army and Air Force ROTC.

The most frequently chosen **baccalaureate** fields are engineering, physical sciences, and mathematics. A complete listing of majors at Harvey Mudd appears in the Majors by College index beginning on page 469.

The **faculty** at Harvey Mudd has 84 full-time members, 100% with terminal degrees. The student-faculty ratio is 9:1.

Students of Harvey Mudd

The student body is made up of 738 undergraduates. 35.6% are women and 64.4% are men. Students come from 48 states and territories and 16 other countries. 45% are from California. 3.4% are international students. 1.8% are African American, 0.9% American Indian, 20.6% Asian American, and 7.7% Hispanic American. 95% returned for their sophomore year.

Facilities and Resources

360 **computers/terminals** and 1,500 ports are available on campus for general student use. Students can access the following: campus intranet, computer help desk, free student e-mail accounts, online (class) grades, online (class) registration, online (class) schedules. Campuswide network is available. 100% of college-owned or -operated housing units are wired for high-speed Internet access. Wireless service is available via entire campus. The 2 **libraries** have 3,203,500 books and 16,308 subscriptions.

Campus Life

There are 80 active organizations on campus, including a drama/theater group, newspaper, radio station, and choral group. No national or local **fraternities** or **sororities**.

Harvey Mudd is a member of the NCAA (Division III). **Intercollegiate sports** include baseball (m), basketball, cross-country running, football (m), golf (m), lacrosse (w), soccer, softball (w), swimming and diving, tennis, track and field, volleyball (w), water polo.

Campus Safety

Student safety services include late-night transport/escort service, 24-hour emergency telephone alarm devices, and 24-hour patrols by trained security personnel.

Applying

Harvey Mudd requires an essay, SAT or ACT, SAT Subject Test in Math 2C and second exam of choice (Math 1C is not accepted), a high school transcript, and 3 recommendations. It recommends an interview. Application deadline: 1/2; 2/1 for financial aid. Early and deferred admission are possible.

Getting Accepted
2,190 applied
36% were accepted
202 enrolled (26% of accepted)
95% from top tenth of their h.s. class
Mean SAT critical reading score: 713
Mean SAT math score: 764
Mean SAT writing score: 718
Mean ACT score: 33
96% had SAT critical reading scores over 600
100% had SAT math scores over 600
98% had SAT writing scores over 600
100% had ACT scores over 24
65% had SAT critical reading scores over 700
94% had SAT math scores over 700
63% had SAT writing scores over 700
100% had ACT scores over 30
61 National Merit Scholars
32 valedictorians

Graduation and After
83% graduated in 4 years
5% graduated in 5 years
2% graduated in 6 years
110 organizations recruited on campus

Financial Matters
$36,635 tuition and fees (2008–09)
$11,971 room and board
100% average percent of need met
$29,603 average financial aid amount received
    per undergraduate (2007–08 estimated)

Haverford is a liberal arts college of 1,200 students located 10 miles outside of Philadelphia. The Haverford experience is shaped by an atmosphere of intellectual vitality and student engagement, as well as tremendous opportunities for research and independent scholarship. Aspects such as a student-run Honor Code, a sense of Quaker heritage, and a cooperative program with Bryn Mawr College, Swarthmore College, and the University of Pennsylvania mark Haverford as unique. Students thrive in part because classes are small and extracurricular commitment is expected and because the community is passionate about learning, understanding, and making sound and thoughtful judgments.

Getting Accepted
3,311 applied
27% were accepted
327 enrolled (37% of accepted)
91% from top tenth of their h.s. class
Mean SAT critical reading score: 710
Mean SAT math score: 700
Mean SAT writing score: 700
90% had SAT critical reading scores over 600
88% had SAT math scores over 600
90% had SAT writing scores over 600
52% had SAT critical reading scores over 700
51% had SAT math scores over 700
53% had SAT writing scores over 700

Graduation and After
91% graduated in 4 years
3% graduated in 5 years
46% had job offers within 6 months
276 organizations recruited on campus

Financial Matters
$37,525 tuition and fees (2008–09)
$11,450 room and board
100% average percent of need met
$29,072 average financial aid amount received per undergraduate (2007–08 estimated)

HAVERFORD COLLEGE
SUBURBAN SETTING ■ PRIVATE ■ INDEPENDENT ■ COED
HAVERFORD, PENNSYLVANIA

Web site: www.haverford.edu
Contact: Mr. Jess Lord, Dean of Admissions and Financial Aid, 370 Lancaster Avenue, Haverford, PA 19041-1392
Telephone: 610-896-1350
Fax: 610-896-1338
E-mail: admitme@haverford.edu

Academics
Haverford awards bachelor's **degrees**. **Challenging opportunities** include advanced placement credit, student-designed majors, double majors, independent study, and a senior project. Special programs include internships, off-campus study, and study-abroad.

The most frequently chosen **baccalaureate** fields are social sciences, biological/life sciences, and physical sciences. A complete listing of majors at Haverford appears in the Majors by College index beginning on page 469.

The **faculty** at Haverford has 115 full-time members, 96% with terminal degrees. The student-faculty ratio is 8:1.

Students of Haverford
The student body is made up of 1,169 undergraduates. 53.1% are women and 46.9% are men. Students come from 45 states and territories and 38 other countries. 14% are from Pennsylvania. 3.3% are international students. 8.4% are African American, 0.6% American Indian, 10.4% Asian American, and 8.8% Hispanic American. 96% returned for their sophomore year.

Facilities and Resources
300 **computers/terminals** and 1,600 ports are available on campus for general student use. Students can access the following: campus intranet, computer help desk, free student e-mail accounts, online (class) grades, online (class) registration, online (class) schedules. Campuswide network is available. 100% of college-owned or -operated housing units are wired for high-speed Internet access. Wireless service is available via classrooms, computer centers, computer labs, dorm rooms, learning centers, libraries, student centers. The 5 **libraries** have 773,401 books.

Campus Life
There are 100 active organizations on campus, including a drama/theater group, newspaper, radio station, and choral group. No national or local **fraternities** or **sororities**.

Haverford is a member of the NCAA (Division III). **Intercollegiate sports** include baseball (m), basketball, cross-country running, fencing, field hockey (w), lacrosse, soccer, softball (w), squash, tennis, track and field, volleyball (w).

Campus Safety
Student safety services include late-night transport/escort service, 24-hour emergency telephone alarm devices, 24-hour patrols by trained security personnel, and electronically operated dormitory entrances.

Applying
Haverford requires an essay, SAT Reasoning Test or ACT and two SAT Subject Tests, and 2 recommendations. It recommends an interview. Application deadline: 1/15; 2/1 for financial aid. Early and deferred admission are possible.

Hendrix College

SUBURBAN SETTING ■ PRIVATE ■ INDEPENDENT RELIGIOUS ■ COED
CONWAY, ARKANSAS

SPONSOR

Web site: www.hendrix.edu
Contact: Ms. Laura E. Martin, Director of Admission, 1600 Washington
Avenue, Conway, AR 72032
Telephone: 501-450-1362 or toll-free 800-277-9017
Fax: 501-450-3843
E-mail: martinl@hendrix.edu

Academics

Hendrix awards bachelor's and master's **degrees**. **Challenging opportunities** include advanced placement credit, student-designed majors, an honors program, double majors, independent study, and a senior project. Special programs include cooperative education, internships, off-campus study, study-abroad, and Army ROTC.

The most frequently chosen **baccalaureate** fields are social sciences, English, and biological/life sciences. A complete listing of majors at Hendrix appears in the Majors by College index beginning on page 469.

The **faculty** at Hendrix has 103 full-time members, 94% with terminal degrees. The student-faculty ratio is 12:1.

Students of Hendrix

The student body totals 1,350, of whom 1,342 are undergraduates. 55.1% are women and 44.9% are men. Students come from 33 states and territories and 14 other countries. 49% are from Arkansas. 2.2% are international students. 3.7% are African American, 0.7% American Indian, 3.1% Asian American, and 3.6% Hispanic American. 85% returned for their sophomore year.

Facilities and Resources

75 **computers/terminals** are available on campus for general student use. Students can access the following: campus intranet, computer help desk, free student e-mail accounts, online (class) grades, online (class) registration, online (class) schedules. Campuswide network is available. 100% of college-owned or -operated housing units are wired for high-speed Internet access. Wireless service is available via entire campus. The **library** has 223,074 books and 47,802 subscriptions.

Campus Life

There are 65 active organizations on campus, including a drama/theater group, newspaper, radio station, and choral group. No national or local **fraternities** or **sororities**.

Hendrix is a member of the NCAA (Division III). **Intercollegiate sports** include baseball (m), basketball, cross-country running, field hockey (w), golf, lacrosse (m), soccer, softball (w), swimming and diving, tennis, track and field, volleyball (w).

Campus Safety

Student safety services include late-night transport/escort service, 24-hour emergency telephone alarm devices, 24-hour patrols by trained security personnel, and electronically operated dormitory entrances.

Applying

Hendrix requires an essay, SAT or ACT, and a high school transcript, and in some cases an interview. It recommends 1 recommendation. Application deadline: 8/1; 2/15 priority date for financial aid. Deferred admission is possible.

A private liberal arts college, Hendrix prepares students for the country's finest postgraduate programs by combining classroom knowledge with hands-on learning. Students receive transcript credit for experiences—such as undergraduate research, study abroad, volunteer service, or internships—through the curricular initiative *Your Hendrix Odyssey: Engaging in Active Learning.* The College enrolls 1,350 students, who are taught by a faculty of 103 full-time professors, 96 percent of whom have Ph.D.'s or appropriate terminal degrees. More than 80 percent of Hendrix students live on campus, fostering an intimate community for students and faculty members to interact. Hendrix is located in Conway, a suburb of Little Rock.

Getting Accepted
1,695 applied
79% were accepted
433 enrolled (32% of accepted)
41% from top tenth of their h.s. class
3.76 average high school GPA
Mean SAT critical reading score: 629
Mean SAT math score: 602
Mean ACT score: 28
69% had SAT critical reading scores over 600
54% had SAT math scores over 600
87% had ACT scores over 24
21% had SAT critical reading scores over 700
11% had SAT math scores over 700
35% had ACT scores over 30
8 National Merit Scholars
21 valedictorians

Graduation and After
62% graduated in 4 years
5% graduated in 5 years
2% graduated in 6 years
62% had job offers within 6 months
72 organizations recruited on campus

Financial Matters
$26,080 tuition and fees (2008–09)
$7950 room and board
83% average percent of need met
$19,017 average financial aid amount received per undergraduate (2007–08 estimated)

HILLSDALE COLLEGE

SMALL-TOWN SETTING ■ PRIVATE ■ INDEPENDENT ■ COED
HILLSDALE, MICHIGAN

Web site: www.hillsdale.edu
Contact: Mr. Jeffrey S. Lantis, Director of Admissions, 33 East College
  Street, Hillsdale, MI 49242-1298
Telephone: 517-607-2327
Fax: 517-607-2223
E-mail: admissions@hillsdale.edu

Getting Accepted
1,502 applied
64% were accepted
385 enrolled (40% of accepted)
50% from top tenth of their h.s. class
3.72 average high school GPA
Mean SAT critical reading score: 680
Mean SAT math score: 620
Mean SAT writing score: 640
Mean ACT score: 28
85% had SAT critical reading scores over 600
69% had SAT math scores over 600
86% had ACT scores over 24
40% had SAT critical reading scores over 700
18% had SAT math scores over 700
31% had ACT scores over 30
13 National Merit Scholars
47 class presidents
38 valedictorians

Graduation and After
70% graduated in 4 years
5% graduated in 5 years
1% graduated in 6 years
100% had job offers within 6 months
48 organizations recruited on campus

Financial Matters
$19,920 tuition and fees (2008–09)
$7750 room and board
80% average percent of need met
$15,000 average financial aid amount received
  per undergraduate (2006–07)

Academics
Hillsdale awards bachelor's **degrees**. **Challenging opportunities** include advanced placement credit, accelerated degree programs, an honors program, double majors, independent study, and a senior project. Special programs include internships, summer session for credit, off-campus study, and study-abroad.

The most frequently chosen **baccalaureate** fields are business/marketing, history, and social sciences. A complete listing of majors at Hillsdale appears in the Majors by College index beginning on page 469.

The **faculty** at Hillsdale has 117 full-time members, 79% with terminal degrees. The student-faculty ratio is 10:1.

Students of Hillsdale
The student body is made up of 1,378 undergraduates. 52.2% are women and 47.8% are men. Students come from 48 states and territories and 7 other countries. 37% are from Michigan. 88% returned for their sophomore year.

Facilities and Resources
200 **computers/terminals** are available on campus for general student use. Students can access the following: computer help desk, free student e-mail accounts, online (class) grades, online (class) registration, online (class) schedules. Campuswide network is available. 100% of college-owned or -operated housing units are wired for high-speed Internet access. Wireless service is available via entire campus. The 4 **libraries** have 240,000 books and 1,650 subscriptions.

Campus Life
There are 45 active organizations on campus, including a drama/theater group, newspaper, and choral group. 35% of eligible men and 45% of eligible women are members of national **fraternities** and national **sororities**.

Hillsdale is a member of the NCAA (Division II). **Intercollegiate sports** (some offering scholarships) include baseball (m), basketball, equestrian sports (w), football (m), ice hockey (m), lacrosse (m), riflery, soccer (w), softball (w), swimming and diving (w), track and field, volleyball (w).

Campus Safety
Student safety services include late-night transport/escort service, 24-hour emergency telephone alarm devices, 24-hour patrols by trained security personnel, and electronically operated dormitory entrances.

Applying
Hillsdale requires an essay, SAT or ACT, a high school transcript, and 2 recommendations, and in some cases an interview. It recommends SAT Subject Tests, an interview, and a minimum high school GPA of 3.3. Application deadline: 2/15, 2/15 for nonresidents; 4/1 for financial aid, with a 2/1 priority date. Early and deferred admission are possible.

Hiram College

RURAL SETTING ■ PRIVATE ■ INDEPENDENT RELIGIOUS ■ COED
HIRAM, OHIO

Web site: www.hiram.edu
Contact: Mr. Sherman C. Dean II, Director of Admission, PO Box 96,
   Hiram, OH 44234
Telephone: 330-569-5169 or toll-free 800-362-5280
Fax: 330-569-5944
E-mail: admission@hiram.edu

Academics

Hiram awards bachelor's and master's **degrees**. **Challenging opportunities** include advanced placement credit, student-designed majors, double majors, independent study, and a senior project. Special programs include internships, summer session for credit, off-campus study, and study-abroad.

The most frequently chosen **baccalaureate** fields are business/marketing, social sciences, and biological/life sciences. A complete listing of majors at Hiram appears in the Majors by College index beginning on page 469.

The **faculty** at Hiram has 74 full-time members, 92% with terminal degrees. The student-faculty ratio is 12:1.

Students of Hiram

The student body totals 1,360, of whom 1,335 are undergraduates. 54.2% are women and 45.8% are men. Students come from 29 states and territories and 19 other countries. 87% are from Ohio. 5.4% are international students. 10.7% are African American, 0.5% American Indian, 1.1% Asian American, and 1.6% Hispanic American. 80% returned for their sophomore year.

Facilities and Resources

100 **computers/terminals** and 2,500 ports are available on campus for general student use. Students can access the following: campus intranet, computer help desk, free student e-mail accounts, online (class) grades, online (class) registration, online (class) schedules. Campuswide network is available. Wireless service is available via entire campus. The **library** has 187,451 books and 3,993 subscriptions.

Campus Life

There are 70 active organizations on campus, including a drama/theater group, newspaper, radio station, and choral group. 8% of eligible men and 12% of eligible women are members of local **fraternities** and local **sororities**.

Hiram is a member of the NCAA (Division III). **Intercollegiate sports** include baseball (m), basketball, cross-country running, football (m), golf, soccer, softball (w), swimming and diving, tennis, track and field, ultimate Frisbee, volleyball.

Campus Safety

Student safety services include late-night transport/escort service, 24-hour emergency telephone alarm devices, 24-hour patrols by trained security personnel, and electronically operated dormitory entrances.

Applying

Hiram requires an essay, SAT or ACT, and a high school transcript, and in some cases an interview. It recommends an interview and 3 recommendations. Application deadline: 4/1; 2/15 priority date for financial aid. Early and deferred admission are possible.

Getting Accepted

1,513 applied
75% were accepted
339 enrolled (30% of accepted)
18% from top tenth of their h.s. class
3.30 average high school GPA
Mean SAT critical reading score: 553
Mean SAT math score: 549
Mean ACT score: 24
31% had SAT critical reading scores over 600
22% had SAT math scores over 600
38% had ACT scores over 24
6% had SAT critical reading scores over 700
2% had SAT math scores over 700
8% had ACT scores over 30
11 valedictorians

Graduation and After

61% had job offers within 6 months
70 organizations recruited on campus

Financial Matters

$25,160 tuition and fees (2008–09)
$8380 room and board
95% average percent of need met
$21,218 average financial aid amount received
   per undergraduate

Hobart and William Smith Colleges

Small-town setting ■ Private ■ Independent ■ Coed
Geneva, New York

Web site: www.hws.edu

Contact: Don W. Emmons, Dean of Admissions and Vice President of Enrollment, 629 South Main Street, Geneva, NY 14456-3397

Telephone: 315-781-3622 or toll-free 800-245-0100

Fax: 315-781-5471

E-mail: emmons@hws.edu

Getting Accepted
4,165 applied
55% were accepted
619 enrolled (27% of accepted)
38% from top tenth of their h.s. class
3.39 average high school GPA
Mean SAT critical reading score: 600
Mean SAT math score: 605
50% had SAT critical reading scores over 600
54% had SAT math scores over 600
10% had SAT critical reading scores over 700
12% had SAT math scores over 700

Graduation and After
68% graduated in 4 years
4% graduated in 5 years
90% had job offers within 6 months
35 organizations recruited on campus

Financial Matters
$38,860 tuition and fees (2008–09)
$9686 room and board
80% average percent of need met
$25,054 average financial aid amount received per undergraduate (2006–07)

Academics

HWS awards bachelor's and master's **degrees** and post-bachelor's certificates. **Challenging opportunities** include advanced placement credit, accelerated degree programs, student-designed majors, an honors program, double majors, independent study, and a senior project. Special programs include internships, off-campus study, and study-abroad.

The most frequently chosen **baccalaureate** fields are social sciences, English, and history. A complete listing of majors at HWS appears in the Majors by College index beginning on page 469.

The **faculty** at HWS has 183 full-time members. The student-faculty ratio is 11:1.

Students of HWS

The student body totals 2,009, of whom 2,001 are undergraduates. 54.3% are women and 45.7% are men. Students come from 48 states and territories and 13 other countries. 42% are from New York. 1.8% are international students. 4.2% are African American, 0.4% American Indian, 2.9% Asian American, and 3.4% Hispanic American. 85% returned for their sophomore year.

Facilities and Resources

250 **computers/terminals** are available on campus for general student use. Students can access the following: campus intranet, computer help desk, free student e-mail accounts, online (class) grades, online (class) registration, online (class) schedules. Campuswide network is available. 100% of college-owned or -operated housing units are wired for high-speed Internet access. Wireless service is available via entire campus. The 2 **libraries** have 380,419 books and 2,469 subscriptions.

Campus Life

There are 80 active organizations on campus, including a drama/theater group, newspaper, radio station, and choral group. 15% of eligible men are members of national **fraternities**.

HWS is a member of the NCAA (Division III). **Intercollegiate sports** include basketball, crew, cross-country running, field hockey (w), football (m), golf, ice hockey (m), lacrosse, sailing, soccer, squash, swimming and diving (w), tennis.

Campus Safety

Student safety services include late-night transport/escort service, 24-hour emergency telephone alarm devices, 24-hour patrols by trained security personnel, and electronically operated dormitory entrances.

Applying

HWS requires an essay, a high school transcript, and 1 recommendation, and in some cases SAT or ACT. It recommends an interview. Application deadline: 2/1; 3/15 for financial aid, with a 2/15 priority date. Early and deferred admission are possible.

HOPE COLLEGE

SUBURBAN SETTING ■ PRIVATE ■ INDEPENDENT RELIGIOUS ■ COED
HOLLAND, MICHIGAN

Web site: www.hope.edu
Contact: Hope College Admissions, 69 East 10th Street, P.O. Box 9000, Holland, MI 49422-9000
Telephone: 616-395-7850 or toll-free 800-968-7850
Fax: 616-395-7130
E-mail: admissions@hope.edu

Academics

Hope awards bachelor's **degrees. Challenging opportunities** include advanced placement credit, student-designed majors, double majors, independent study, and a senior project. Special programs include internships, summer session for credit, off-campus study, study-abroad, and Army ROTC.

The most frequently chosen **baccalaureate** fields are education, business/marketing, and social sciences. A complete listing of majors at Hope appears in the Majors by College index beginning on page 469.

The **faculty** at Hope has 230 full-time members, 72% with terminal degrees. The student-faculty ratio is 11:1.

Students of Hope

The student body is made up of 3,238 undergraduates. 59.8% are women and 40.2% are men. Students come from 43 states and territories and 30 other countries. 70% are from Michigan. 1.5% are international students. 2.2% are African American, 0.3% American Indian, 2.3% Asian American, and 3.2% Hispanic American. 90% returned for their sophomore year.

Facilities and Resources

300 **computers/terminals** and 5,000 ports are available on campus for general student use. Students can access the following: campus intranet, computer help desk, free student e-mail accounts, online (class) grades, online (class) registration, online (class) schedules. Campuswide network is available. 100% of college-owned or -operated housing units are wired for high-speed Internet access. Wireless service is available via entire campus. The 2 **libraries** have 368,864 books and 5,771 subscriptions.

Campus Life

There are 67 active organizations on campus, including a drama/theater group, newspaper, radio station, television station, and choral group. 11% of eligible men and 11% of eligible women are members of national **fraternities**, national **sororities**, local fraternities, and local sororities.

Hope is a member of the NCAA (Division III). **Intercollegiate sports** include baseball (m), basketball, cheerleading, cross-country running, football (m), golf, soccer, softball (w), swimming and diving, tennis, track and field, volleyball (w).

Campus Safety

Student safety services include late-night transport/escort service, 24-hour emergency telephone alarm devices, 24-hour patrols by trained security personnel, and electronically operated dormitory entrances.

Applying

Hope requires an essay, SAT or ACT, and a high school transcript, and in some cases 1 recommendation. It recommends an interview. Application deadline: rolling admissions; 3/1 priority date for financial aid. Early and deferred admission are possible.

Getting Accepted

2,846 applied
82% were accepted
808 enrolled (35% of accepted)
38% from top tenth of their h.s. class
3.77 average high school GPA
Mean ACT score: 26
51% had SAT critical reading scores over 600
53% had SAT math scores over 600
74% had ACT scores over 24
15% had SAT critical reading scores over 700
14% had SAT math scores over 700
18% had ACT scores over 30
10 National Merit Scholars

Graduation and After

63% graduated in 4 years
10% graduated in 5 years
1% graduated in 6 years
89.6% had job offers within 6 months

Financial Matters

$24,920 tuition and fees (2008–09)
$7650 room and board
86% average percent of need met
$20,239 average financial aid amount received per undergraduate (2007–08 estimated)

Houghton College

RURAL SETTING ■ PRIVATE ■ INDEPENDENT RELIGIOUS ■ COED
HOUGHTON, NEW YORK

Web site: www.houghton.edu
Contact: Mr. Matthew Reitnour, Director of Admission, PO Box 128, Houghton, NY 14744
Telephone: 585-567-9353 or toll-free 800-777-2556
Fax: 585-567-9522
E-mail: admission@houghton.edu

Getting Accepted

972 applied
83% were accepted
328 enrolled (41% of accepted)
40% from top tenth of their h.s. class
3.54 average high school GPA
Mean SAT critical reading score: 593
Mean SAT math score: 573
Mean SAT writing score: 574
Mean ACT score: 26
47% had SAT critical reading scores over 600
38% had SAT math scores over 600
41% had SAT writing scores over 600
70% had ACT scores over 24
13% had SAT critical reading scores over 700
6% had SAT math scores over 700
10% had SAT writing scores over 700
21% had ACT scores over 30
5 National Merit Scholars
14 valedictorians

Graduation and After

65% graduated in 4 years
6% graduated in 5 years
1% graduated in 6 years
63% had job offers within 6 months
45 organizations recruited on campus

Financial Matters

$22,990 tuition and fees (2008–09)
$6930 room and board
74% average percent of need met
$16,899 average financial aid amount received per undergraduate (2007–08 estimated)

Academics

Houghton awards associate, bachelor's, and master's **degrees. Challenging opportunities** include advanced placement credit, an honors program, double majors, independent study, and a senior project. Special programs include internships, summer session for credit, off-campus study, study-abroad, and Army ROTC.

The most frequently chosen **baccalaureate** fields are business/marketing, education, and biological/life sciences. A complete listing of majors at Houghton appears in the Majors by College index beginning on page 469.

The **faculty** at Houghton has 88 full-time members, 85% with terminal degrees. The student-faculty ratio is 12:1.

Students of Houghton

The student body totals 1,419, of whom 1,381 are undergraduates. 63.8% are women and 36.2% are men. Students come from 42 states and territories and 22 other countries. 63% are from New York. 3.9% are international students. 2.3% are African American, 0.8% American Indian, 1.3% Asian American, and 1.1% Hispanic American. 85% returned for their sophomore year.

Facilities and Resources

15 **computers/terminals** and 820 ports are available on campus for general student use. Students can access the following: computer help desk, free student e-mail accounts, online (class) grades, online (class) registration, online (class) schedules. Campuswide network is available. 100% of college-owned or -operated housing units are wired for high-speed Internet access. Wireless service is available via entire campus. The 2 **libraries** have 240,330 books and 30,059 subscriptions.

Campus Life

There are 50 active organizations on campus, including a drama/theater group, newspaper, and choral group. No national or local **fraternities** or **sororities**.

Houghton is a member of the NAIA. **Intercollegiate sports** (some offering scholarships) include basketball, cross-country running, field hockey (w), soccer, track and field, volleyball (w).

Campus Safety

Student safety services include phone connection to security patrols, late-night transport/escort service, 24-hour patrols by trained security personnel, and electronically operated dormitory entrances.

Applying

Houghton requires an essay, SAT or ACT, a high school transcript, and 1 recommendation. It recommends an interview and a minimum high school GPA of 2.5. Application deadline: rolling admissions; 3/1 priority date for financial aid. Deferred admission is possible.

ILLINOIS COLLEGE

SMALL-TOWN SETTING ■ PRIVATE ■ INDEPENDENT RELIGIOUS ■ COED
JACKSONVILLE, ILLINOIS

Web site: www.ic.edu
Contact: Mr. Rick Bystry, Associate Director of Admission, 1101 West College, Jacksonville, IL 62650
Telephone: 217-245-3030 or toll-free 866-464-5265
Fax: 217-245-3034
E-mail: admissions@ic.edu

Academics

IC awards bachelor's **degrees**. **Challenging opportunities** include advanced placement credit, accelerated degree programs, student-designed majors, double majors, independent study, and a senior project. Special programs include internships, summer session for credit, and study-abroad.

The most frequently chosen **baccalaureate** fields are biological/life sciences, interdisciplinary studies, and social sciences. A complete listing of majors at IC appears in the Majors by College index beginning on page 469.

The **faculty** at IC has 73 full-time members, 81% with terminal degrees. The student-faculty ratio is 11:1.

Students of IC

The student body is made up of 898 undergraduates. 52.4% are women and 47.6% are men. Students come from 22 states and territories and 15 other countries. 92% are from Illinois. 2.2% are international students. 3.9% are African American, 0.2% American Indian, 0.5% Asian American, and 1.8% Hispanic American. 78% returned for their sophomore year.

Facilities and Resources

110 **computers/terminals** are available on campus for general student use. Students can access the following: computer help desk, free student e-mail accounts, online (class) grades, online (class) registration, online (class) schedules. Campuswide network is available. 30% of college-owned or -operated housing units are wired for high-speed Internet access. Wireless service is available via entire campus. The 2 **libraries** have 163,810 books and 10,234 subscriptions.

Campus Life

There are 81 active organizations on campus, including a drama/theater group, newspaper, television station, and choral group. 22% of eligible men and 18% of eligible women are members of local **fraternities** and local **sororities**.

IC is a member of the NCAA (Division III). **Intercollegiate sports** include baseball (m), cheerleading (w), cross-country running, football (m), golf, soccer, softball (w), swimming and diving, tennis, track and field, volleyball (w).

Campus Safety

Student safety services include late-night transport/escort service, 24-hour emergency telephone alarm devices, 24-hour patrols by trained security personnel, and electronically operated dormitory entrances.

Applying

IC requires SAT or ACT, a high school transcript, and 1 recommendation, and in some cases an essay. It recommends an essay, an interview, and a minimum high school GPA of 2.5. Application deadline: rolling admissions; 3/1 priority date for financial aid. Early and deferred admission are possible.

Getting Accepted

927 applied
67% were accepted
166 enrolled (27% of accepted)
33% from top tenth of their h.s. class
3.46 average high school GPA
Mean SAT critical reading score: 542
Mean SAT math score: 542
Mean SAT writing score: 544
Mean ACT score: 24
58% had ACT scores over 24
6% had ACT scores over 30
13 valedictorians

Graduation and After

51% graduated in 4 years
11% graduated in 5 years
1% graduated in 6 years
97% had job offers within 6 months

Financial Matters

$20,300 tuition and fees (2008–09)
$7600 room and board
91% average percent of need met
$13,907 average financial aid amount received per undergraduate (2007–08 estimated)

ILLINOIS INSTITUTE OF TECHNOLOGY

URBAN SETTING ■ PRIVATE ■ INDEPENDENT ■ COED
CHICAGO, ILLINOIS

Web site: www.iit.edu
Contact: Mr. Gerald Doyle, Vice Provost, Undergraduate Admissions and Financial Aid, Office of Undergraduate Admission, Perlstein 101, 10 West 33rd Street, Chicago, IL 60616
Telephone: 312-567-3025 or toll-free 800-448-2329 (out-of-state)
Fax: 312-567-6939
E-mail: admission@iit.edu

Getting Accepted

3,092 applied
57% were accepted
530 enrolled (30% of accepted)
42% from top tenth of their h.s. class
3.84 average high school GPA
Mean SAT critical reading score: 581
Mean SAT math score: 653
Mean SAT writing score: 575
Mean ACT score: 27
47% had SAT critical reading scores over 600
80% had SAT math scores over 600
40% had SAT writing scores over 600
82% had ACT scores over 24
9% had SAT critical reading scores over 700
27% had SAT math scores over 700
8% had SAT writing scores over 700
29% had ACT scores over 30
13 valedictorians

Graduation and After

38% graduated in 4 years
24% graduated in 5 years
3% graduated in 6 years
305 organizations recruited on campus

Financial Matters

$27,513 tuition and fees (2008–09)
$9233 room and board
85% average percent of need met
$22,542 average financial aid amount received per undergraduate (2006–07)

Academics

IIT awards bachelor's, master's, doctoral, and first-professional **degrees**. **Challenging opportunities** include advanced placement credit, double majors, independent study, and a senior project. Special programs include cooperative education, summer session for credit, study-abroad, and Army, Navy, and Air Force ROTC.

The most frequently chosen **baccalaureate** fields are engineering, architecture, and computer and information sciences. A complete listing of majors at IIT appears in the Majors by College index beginning on page 469.

The **faculty** at IIT has 370 full-time members, 90% with terminal degrees. The student-faculty ratio is 9:1.

Students of IIT

The student body totals 7,613, of whom 2,639 are undergraduates. 28.3% are women and 71.7% are men. Students come from 48 states and territories and 68 other countries. 68% are from Illinois. 16.5% are international students. 4.3% are African American, 0.6% American Indian, 12.5% Asian American, and 7.3% Hispanic American. 88% returned for their sophomore year.

Facilities and Resources

500 **computers/terminals** are available on campus for general student use. Students can access the following: campus intranet, computer help desk, free student e-mail accounts, online (class) grades, online (class) registration, online (class) schedules. Campuswide network is available. 100% of college-owned or -operated housing units are wired for high-speed Internet access. Wireless service is available via classrooms, computer centers, computer labs, dorm rooms, learning centers, libraries, student centers. The 6 **libraries** have 1,726,856 books and 33,535 subscriptions.

Campus Life

There are 100 active organizations on campus, including a drama/theater group, newspaper, radio station, and choral group. 12% of eligible men and 17% of eligible women are members of national **fraternities**, national **sororities**, and local sororities.

IIT is a member of the NAIA. **Intercollegiate sports** (some offering scholarships) include baseball (m), basketball, cross-country running, soccer, swimming and diving, volleyball (w).

Campus Safety

Student safety services include late-night transport/escort service, 24-hour emergency telephone alarm devices, 24-hour patrols by trained security personnel, and electronically operated dormitory entrances.

Applying

IIT requires an essay, a high school transcript, and 1 recommendation, and in some cases SAT or ACT. It recommends an interview. Application deadline: rolling admissions; 4/15 priority date for financial aid. Early and deferred admission are possible.

Illinois Wesleyan University

Suburban setting ■ Private ■ Independent ■ Coed
Bloomington, Illinois

Web site: www.iwu.edu
Contact: Mr. Tony Bankston, Dean of Admissions, PO Box 2900,
 Bloomington, IL 61702-2900
Telephone: 309-556-3031 or toll-free 800-332-2498
Fax: 309-556-3820
E-mail: iwuadmit@iwu.edu

Academics
IWU awards bachelor's **degrees**. **Challenging opportunities** include advanced placement credit, student-designed majors, an honors program, double majors, independent study, and a senior project. Special programs include internships, off-campus study, study-abroad, and Army ROTC.

The most frequently chosen **baccalaureate** fields are business/marketing, social sciences, and visual and performing arts. A complete listing of majors at IWU appears in the Majors by College index beginning on page 469.

The **faculty** at IWU has 161 full-time members, 94% with terminal degrees. The student-faculty ratio is 11:1.

Students of IWU
The student body is made up of 2,125 undergraduates. 58.5% are women and 41.5% are men. Students come from 39 states and territories and 22 other countries. 87% are from Illinois. 3.6% are international students. 5.6% are African American, 0.4% American Indian, 4.4% Asian American, and 2.9% Hispanic American. 90% returned for their sophomore year.

Facilities and Resources
400 **computers/terminals** and 75 ports are available on campus for general student use. Students can access the following: campus intranet, computer help desk, free student e-mail accounts, online (class) grades, online (class) registration, online (class) schedules. Campuswide network is available. 100% of college-owned or -operated housing units are wired for high-speed Internet access. Wireless service is available via entire campus. The **library** has 330,300 books and 32,080 subscriptions.

Campus Life
There are 160 active organizations on campus, including a drama/theater group, newspaper, radio station, television station, and choral group. 35% of eligible men and 32% of eligible women are members of national **fraternities**, national **sororities**, and local sororities.

IWU is a member of the NCAA (Division III). **Intercollegiate sports** include baseball (m), basketball, cross-country running, football (m), golf, soccer, softball (w), swimming and diving, tennis, track and field, volleyball (w).

Campus Safety
Student safety services include emergency response team, late-night transport/escort service, 24-hour emergency telephone alarm devices, 24-hour patrols by trained security personnel, and electronically operated dormitory entrances.

Applying
IWU requires an essay, SAT or ACT, a high school transcript, 1 recommendation, and a minimum high school GPA of 2.0. It recommends an interview, 2 recommendations, and a minimum high school GPA of 3.0. Application deadline: rolling admissions; 3/1 for financial aid, with a 3/1 priority date. Early and deferred admission are possible.

Getting Accepted
3,136 applied
52% were accepted
562 enrolled (34% of accepted)
45% from top tenth of their h.s. class
3.7 average high school GPA
56% had SAT critical reading scores over 600
74% had SAT math scores over 600
91% had ACT scores over 24
21% had SAT critical reading scores over 700
33% had SAT math scores over 700
32% had ACT scores over 30
10 National Merit Scholars
16 valedictorians

Graduation and After
78% graduated in 4 years
5% graduated in 5 years
56% had job offers within 6 months
163 organizations recruited on campus

Financial Matters
$32,434 tuition and fees (2008–09)
$7350 room and board
90% average percent of need met
$22,351 average financial aid amount received
 per undergraduate (2007–08 estimated)

Iowa State University of Science and Technology

SUBURBAN SETTING ■ PUBLIC ■ STATE-SUPPORTED ■ COED
AMES, IOWA

Web site: www.iastate.edu
Contact: Mr. Phil Caffrey, Associate Director for Freshman Admissions, 100 Enrollment Services Center, Ames, IA 50011-2010
Telephone: 515-294-5836 or toll-free 800-262-3810
Fax: 515-294-2592
E-mail: admissions@iastate.edu

Getting Accepted
12,549 applied
87% were accepted
4,546 enrolled (42% of accepted)
27% from top tenth of their h.s. class
3.49 average high school GPA
Mean ACT score: 25
41% had SAT critical reading scores over 600
58% had SAT math scores over 600
61% had ACT scores over 24
14% had SAT critical reading scores over 700
21% had SAT math scores over 700
12% had ACT scores over 30
32 National Merit Scholars

Graduation and After
34% graduated in 4 years
29% graduated in 5 years
5% graduated in 6 years
78% had job offers within 6 months

Financial Matters
$6651 resident tuition and fees (2009–10)
$17,871 nonresident tuition and fees (2009–10)
$7277 room and board
82% average percent of need met
$9798 average financial aid amount received per undergraduate (2007–08 estimated)

Academics
Iowa State awards bachelor's, master's, doctoral, and first-professional **degrees** and post-master's certificates. **Challenging opportunities** include advanced placement credit, accelerated degree programs, student-designed majors, freshman honors college, an honors program, double majors, independent study, and a senior project. Special programs include cooperative education, internships, summer session for credit, off-campus study, study-abroad, and Army, Navy, and Air Force ROTC.

The most frequently chosen **baccalaureate** fields are business/marketing, engineering, and agriculture. A complete listing of majors at Iowa State appears in the Majors by College index beginning on page 469.

The **faculty** at Iowa State has 1,411 full-time members, 92% with terminal degrees. The student-faculty ratio is 16:1.

Students of Iowa State
The student body totals 26,856, of whom 21,607 are undergraduates. 43.7% are women and 56.3% are men. Students come from 55 states and territories and 107 other countries. 77% are from Iowa. 4.6% are international students. 2.8% are African American, 0.3% American Indian, 3.2% Asian American, and 2.8% Hispanic American. 84% returned for their sophomore year.

Facilities and Resources
2,400 **computers/terminals** are available on campus for general student use. Students can access the following: campus intranet, computer help desk, free student e-mail accounts, online (class) grades, online (class) registration, online (class) schedules, network services. Campuswide network is available. 100% of college-owned or -operated housing units are wired for high-speed Internet access. Wireless service is available via entire campus. The 2 **libraries** have 2,529,921 books and 66,195 subscriptions.

Campus Life
There are 749 active organizations on campus, including a drama/theater group, newspaper, radio station, television station, choral group, and marching band. 11% of eligible men and 10% of eligible women are members of national **fraternities**, national **sororities**, and local fraternities.

Iowa State is a member of the NCAA (Division I). **Intercollegiate sports** (some offering scholarships) include basketball, cross-country running, football (m), golf, gymnastics (w), soccer (w), softball (w), swimming and diving, tennis (w), track and field, volleyball (w), wrestling (m).

Campus Safety
Student safety services include crime prevention programs, threat assessment team, motor vehicle help van, late-night transport/escort service, 24-hour emergency telephone alarm devices, 24-hour patrols by trained security personnel, student patrols, and electronically operated dormitory entrances.

Applying
Iowa State requires SAT or ACT, a high school transcript, and rank in upper 50% of high school class. Application deadline: 7/1; 3/1 priority date for financial aid. Early and deferred admission are possible.

Ithaca College

SMALL-TOWN SETTING ■ PRIVATE ■ INDEPENDENT ■ COED
ITHACA, NEW YORK

SPONSOR

Web site: www.ithaca.edu

Contact: Gerard Turbide, Director of Admission, 953 Danby Road, Ithaca, NY 14850-7000

Telephone: 607-274-3124 or toll-free 800-429-4274

Fax: 607-274-1900

E-mail: admission@ithaca.edu

Academics

Ithaca awards bachelor's, master's, and doctoral **degrees. Challenging opportunities** include advanced placement credit, accelerated degree programs, student-designed majors, freshman honors college, an honors program, double majors, independent study, and a senior project. Special programs include internships, summer session for credit, off-campus study, study-abroad, and Army and Air Force ROTC.

The most frequently chosen **baccalaureate** fields are visual and performing arts, communications/journalism, and business/marketing. A complete listing of majors at Ithaca appears in the Majors by College index beginning on page 469.

The **faculty** at Ithaca has 463 full-time members, 92% with terminal degrees. The student-faculty ratio is 12:1.

Students of Ithaca

The student body totals 6,448, of whom 6,031 are undergraduates. 56% are women and 44% are men. Students come from 51 states and territories and 75 other countries. 45% are from New York. 1.7% are international students. 3% are African American, 0.4% American Indian, 3.9% Asian American, and 4.1% Hispanic American. 84% returned for their sophomore year.

Facilities and Resources

640 **computers/terminals** and 20 ports are available on campus for general student use. Students can access the following: campus intranet, computer help desk, free student e-mail accounts, online (class) grades, online (class) registration, online (class) schedules. Campuswide network is available. 100% of college-owned or -operated housing units are wired for high-speed Internet access. Wireless service is available via classrooms, computer centers, computer labs, dorm rooms, libraries, student centers. The **library** has 366,970 books and 28,314 subscriptions.

Campus Life

There are 172 active organizations on campus, including a drama/theater group, newspaper, radio station, television station, and choral group. 1% of eligible men and 1% of eligible women are members of national **fraternities** and national **sororities**.

Ithaca is a member of the NCAA (Division III). **Intercollegiate sports** include baseball (m), basketball, crew, cross-country running, field hockey (w), football (m), gymnastics (w), lacrosse, soccer, softball (w), swimming and diving, tennis, track and field, volleyball (w), wrestling (m).

Campus Safety

Student safety services include patrols by trained security personnel 11 p.m. to 7 a.m, late-night transport/escort service, 24-hour emergency telephone alarm devices, student patrols, and electronically operated dormitory entrances.

Applying

Ithaca requires an essay, SAT or ACT, a high school transcript, and 1 recommendation, and in some cases audition. It recommends a minimum high school GPA of 3.0. Application deadline: 2/1; 2/1 priority date for financial aid. Early and deferred admission are possible.

Located in the heart of New York State's Finger Lakes region, Ithaca College is a nationally recognized, private residential college of 6,400 students and 463 full-time faculty members. Ithaca offers the perfect blend of liberal arts and professional programs, and its intimate student-faculty ratio of 12:1 ensures a first-rate education on a first-name basis. More than 100 degree programs are found in the College's five schools—business, communications, health sciences and human performance, humanities and sciences, and music—and interdisciplinary division. An Ithaca education emphasizes hands-on learning, social responsibility, and close student-faculty relationships. The College's broad, flexible curriculum prepares students to follow their passions in life.

Getting Accepted
12,233 applied
66% were accepted
1,441 enrolled (18% of accepted)
35% from top tenth of their h.s. class
Mean SAT critical reading score: 591
Mean SAT math score: 592
Mean SAT writing score: 590
47% had SAT critical reading scores over 600
47% had SAT math scores over 600
46% had SAT writing scores over 600
8% had SAT critical reading scores over 700
6% had SAT math scores over 700
9% had SAT writing scores over 700
4 National Merit Scholars
19 valedictorians

Graduation and After
71% graduated in 4 years
6% graduated in 5 years
1368 organizations recruited on campus

Financial Matters
$30,606 tuition and fees (2008–09)
$11,162 room and board
86% average percent of need met
$23,786 average financial aid amount received per undergraduate (2007–08 estimated)

Getting Accepted

19,245 applied
65% were accepted
3,957 enrolled (32% of accepted)
29% from top tenth of their h.s. class
3.7 average high school GPA
Mean SAT critical reading score: 568
Mean SAT math score: 581
Mean ACT score: 24
29% had SAT critical reading scores over 600
36% had SAT math scores over 600
59% had ACT scores over 24
3% had SAT critical reading scores over 700
3% had SAT math scores over 700
6% had ACT scores over 30

Graduation and After

67% graduated in 4 years
14% graduated in 5 years
2% graduated in 6 years
234 organizations recruited on campus

Financial Matters

$6964 resident tuition and fees (2008–09)
$18,458 nonresident tuition and fees
  (2008–09)
$7458 room and board
50% average percent of need met
$8116 average financial aid amount received
  per undergraduate (2007–08 estimated)

JAMES MADISON UNIVERSITY

SMALL-TOWN SETTING ■ PUBLIC ■ STATE-SUPPORTED ■ COED
HARRISONBURG, VIRGINIA

Web site: www.jmu.edu
Contact: Office of Admissions, Harrisonburg, VA 22807
Telephone: 540-568-5681
Fax: 540-568-3332
E-mail: admissions@jmu.edu

Academics

JMU awards bachelor's, master's, and doctoral **degrees** and post-master's certificates (also offers specialist in education degree). **Challenging opportunities** include advanced placement credit, accelerated degree programs, freshman honors college, an honors program, double majors, independent study, and a senior project. Special programs include internships, summer session for credit, study-abroad, and Army and Air Force ROTC.

The most frequently chosen **baccalaureate** fields are business/marketing, health professions and related sciences, and social sciences. A complete listing of majors at JMU appears in the Majors by College index beginning on page 469.

The **faculty** at JMU has 897 full-time members, 78% with terminal degrees. The student-faculty ratio is 16:1.

Students of JMU

The student body totals 18,454, of whom 16,916 are undergraduates. 59.5% are women and 40.5% are men. Students come from 47 states and territories and 60 other countries. 71% are from Virginia. 1% are international students. 4% are African American, 0.3% American Indian, 4.9% Asian American, and 2.4% Hispanic American. 91% returned for their sophomore year.

Facilities and Resources

600 **computers/terminals** and 7,000 ports are available on campus for general student use. Students can access the following: campus intranet, computer help desk, free student e-mail accounts, online (class) grades, online (class) registration, online (class) schedules. Campuswide network is available. 100% of college-owned or -operated housing units are wired for high-speed Internet access. Wireless service is available via classrooms, dorm rooms, learning centers, libraries, student centers. The 3 **libraries** have 788,639 books and 17,078 subscriptions.

Campus Life

There are 332 active organizations on campus, including a drama/theater group, newspaper, radio station, choral group, and marching band. 10% of eligible men and 12% of eligible women are members of national **fraternities** and national **sororities**.

JMU is a member of the NCAA (Division I). **Intercollegiate sports** (some offering scholarships) include baseball (m), basketball, cheerleading, cross-country running (w), field hockey (w), football (m), golf, lacrosse (w), soccer, softball (w), swimming and diving (w), tennis, track and field (w), volleyball (w).

Campus Safety

Student safety services include lighted pathways, late-night transport/escort service, 24-hour emergency telephone alarm devices, 24-hour patrols by trained security personnel, student patrols, and electronically operated dormitory entrances.

Applying

JMU requires SAT or ACT and a high school transcript. It recommends a minimum high school GPA of 3.0. Application deadline: 1/15; 3/1 priority date for financial aid. Deferred admission is possible.

JOHN BROWN UNIVERSITY

SMALL-TOWN SETTING ■ PRIVATE ■ INDEPENDENT RELIGIOUS ■ COED
SILOAM SPRINGS, ARKANSAS

Web site: www.jbu.edu
Contact: Mr. Don Crandall, Vice President for Enrollment Management, 200 West University Street, Siloam Springs, AR 72761-2121
Telephone: 479-524-7150 or toll-free 877-JBU-INFO
Fax: 479-524-4196
E-mail: dcrandal@jbu.edu

Academics

JBU awards associate, bachelor's, and master's **degrees. Challenging opportunities** include advanced placement credit, freshman honors college, an honors program, double majors, independent study, and a senior project. Special programs include internships, study-abroad, and Army and Air Force ROTC.

The most frequently chosen **baccalaureate** fields are business/marketing, visual and performing arts, and theology and religious vocations. A complete listing of majors at JBU appears in the Majors by College index beginning on page 469.

The **faculty** at JBU has 81 full-time members, 75% with terminal degrees. The student-faculty ratio is 13:1.

Students of JBU

The student body totals 2,017, of whom 1,709 are undergraduates. 54.6% are women and 45.4% are men. Students come from 41 states and territories and 52 other countries. 26% are from Arkansas. 7% are international students. 3.6% are African American, 1.8% American Indian, 1.5% Asian American, and 3.5% Hispanic American. 80% returned for their sophomore year.

Facilities and Resources

100 **computers/terminals** are available on campus for general student use. Students can access the following: campus intranet, computer help desk, free student e-mail accounts, online (class) grades, online (class) registration, online (class) schedules. Campuswide network is available. 100% of college-owned or -operated housing units are wired for high-speed Internet access. Wireless service is available via classrooms, dorm rooms, learning centers, libraries, student centers. The 7 **libraries** have 102,031 books and 751 subscriptions.

Campus Life

There are 20 active organizations on campus, including a drama/theater group, newspaper, and choral group. No national or local **fraternities** or **sororities**.

JBU is a member of the NAIA. **Intercollegiate sports** (some offering scholarships) include basketball, golf (m), soccer, tennis, volleyball (w).

Campus Safety

Student safety services include late-night transport/escort service, 24-hour emergency telephone alarm devices, and 24-hour patrols by trained security personnel.

Applying

JBU requires an essay, SAT or ACT, a high school transcript, 2 recommendations, and a minimum high school GPA of 2.5. It recommends an interview. Application deadline: rolling admissions; 3/1 priority date for financial aid. Deferred admission is possible.

Getting Accepted

896 applied
74% were accepted
310 enrolled (47% of accepted)
40% from top tenth of their h.s. class
3.62 average high school GPA
Mean SAT critical reading score: 590
Mean SAT math score: 580
Mean ACT score: 25
42% had SAT critical reading scores over 600
33% had SAT math scores over 600
66% had ACT scores over 24
13% had SAT critical reading scores over 700
6% had SAT math scores over 700
22% had ACT scores over 30

Graduation and After

58% graduated in 4 years
10% graduated in 5 years
1% graduated in 6 years
97% had job offers within 6 months
52 organizations recruited on campus

Financial Matters

$18,066 tuition and fees (2008–09)
$6580 room and board
50% average percent of need met
$13,310 average financial aid amount received per undergraduate (2006–07)

John Carroll University

Suburban setting ■ Private ■ Independent Religious ■ Coed
University Heights, Ohio

Web site: www.jcu.edu
Contact: Mr. Thomas P. Fanning, Director of Admission, 20700 North Park Blvd, University Heights, OH 44118
Telephone: 216-397-4246
Fax: 216-397-4981
E-mail: tfanning@jcu.edu

Getting Accepted
3,481 applied
80% were accepted
792 enrolled (29% of accepted)
20% from top tenth of their h.s. class
3.34 average high school GPA
Mean SAT critical reading score: 533
Mean SAT math score: 539
Mean SAT writing score: 530
Mean ACT score: 24
23% had SAT critical reading scores over 600
23% had SAT math scores over 600
22% had SAT writing scores over 600
35% had ACT scores over 24
1% had SAT critical reading scores over 700
2% had SAT math scores over 700
1% had SAT writing scores over 700
4% had ACT scores over 30
19 valedictorians

Graduation and After
77% graduated in 4 years
4% graduated in 5 years
1% graduated in 6 years
64% had job offers within 6 months
332 organizations recruited on campus

Financial Matters
$28,840 tuition and fees (2009–10)
$8330 room and board
82% average percent of need met
$20,158 average financial aid amount received per undergraduate (2007–08 estimated)

Academics

John Carroll awards bachelor's and master's **degrees**. **Challenging opportunities** include advanced placement credit, accelerated degree programs, student-designed majors, an honors program, double majors, independent study, and a senior project. Special programs include cooperative education, internships, summer session for credit, off-campus study, study-abroad, and Army ROTC.

The most frequently chosen **baccalaureate** fields are business/marketing, psychology, and social sciences. A complete listing of majors at John Carroll appears in the Majors by College index beginning on page 469.

The **faculty** at John Carroll has 210 full-time members, 89% with terminal degrees. The student-faculty ratio is 15:1.

Students of John Carroll

The student body totals 3,826, of whom 3,117 are undergraduates. 51% are women and 49% are men. Students come from 34 states and territories and 7 other countries. 72% are from Ohio. 6% are African American, 0.3% American Indian, 2.1% Asian American, and 2.7% Hispanic American. 82% returned for their sophomore year.

Facilities and Resources

210 **computers/terminals** are available on campus for general student use. Students can access the following: campus intranet, computer help desk, free student e-mail accounts, online (class) grades, online (class) registration, online (class) schedules. Campuswide network is available. 100% of college-owned or -operated housing units are wired for high-speed Internet access. Wireless service is available via entire campus. The **library** has 620,000 books and 2,198 subscriptions.

Campus Life

There are 90 active organizations on campus, including a drama/theater group, newspaper, radio station, television station, and choral group. 9% of eligible men and 14% of eligible women are members of national **fraternities** and national **sororities**.

John Carroll is a member of the NCAA (Division III). **Intercollegiate sports** include baseball (m), basketball, cross-country running, football (m), golf, soccer, softball (w), swimming and diving, tennis, track and field, volleyball (w), wrestling (m).

Campus Safety

Student safety services include late-night transport/escort service, 24-hour emergency telephone alarm devices, and 24-hour patrols by trained security personnel.

Applying

John Carroll requires an essay, SAT or ACT, a high school transcript, and 1 recommendation, and in some cases an interview. Application deadline: 2/1; 3/15 for financial aid, with a 2/15 priority date. Deferred admission is possible.

THE JOHNS HOPKINS UNIVERSITY

URBAN SETTING ■ PRIVATE ■ INDEPENDENT ■ COED
BALTIMORE, MARYLAND

Web site: www.jhu.edu
Contact: Dr. John Latting, Dean of Undergraduate Admissions, Mason Hall,
3400 North Charles Street, Baltimore, MD 21218-2699
Telephone: 410-516-8341
Fax: 410-516-6025
E-mail: gotojhu@jhu.edu

Academics

Johns Hopkins awards bachelor's, master's, doctoral, and first-professional **degrees** and post-bachelor's and post-master's certificates. **Challenging opportunities** include advanced placement credit, student-designed majors, an honors program, double majors, independent study, and a senior project. Special programs include internships, summer session for credit, off-campus study, study-abroad, and Army and Air Force ROTC.

The most frequently chosen **baccalaureate** fields are health professions and related sciences, engineering, and social sciences. A complete listing of majors at Johns Hopkins appears in the Majors by College index beginning on page 469.

The student-faculty ratio is 12:1.

Students of Johns Hopkins

The student body totals 6,437, of whom 4,744 are undergraduates. 47.8% are women and 52.2% are men. Students come from 52 states and territories and 51 other countries. 15% are from Maryland. 6.1% are international students. 6.7% are African American, 0.6% American Indian, 23.7% Asian American, and 6.8% Hispanic American. 98% returned for their sophomore year.

Facilities and Resources

140 **computers/terminals** and 1,000 ports are available on campus for general student use. Students can access the following: campus intranet, computer help desk, free student e-mail accounts, online (class) grades, online (class) registration, online (class) schedules. Campuswide network is available. 100% of college-owned or -operated housing units are wired for high-speed Internet access. Wireless service is available via entire campus. The 7 **libraries** have 2,900,000 books and 55,000 subscriptions.

Campus Life

There are 180 active organizations on campus, including a drama/theater group, newspaper, radio station, and choral group. 24% of eligible men and 23% of eligible women are members of national **fraternities** and national **sororities**.

Johns Hopkins is a member of the NCAA (Division III). **Intercollegiate sports** (some offering scholarships) include baseball (m), basketball, crew, cross-country running, fencing, field hockey (w), football (m), lacrosse, soccer, swimming and diving, tennis, track and field, volleyball (w), water polo (m), wrestling (m).

Campus Safety

Student safety services include late-night transport/escort service, 24-hour emergency telephone alarm devices, 24-hour patrols by trained security personnel, student patrols, and electronically operated dormitory entrances.

Applying

Johns Hopkins requires an essay, SAT or ACT, and a high school transcript. It recommends SAT Subject Tests and an interview. Application deadline: 1/1; 3/1 for financial aid, with a 3/1 priority date. Early and deferred admission are possible.

Getting Accepted

16,011 applied
25% were accepted
1,236 enrolled (30% of accepted)
84% from top tenth of their h.s. class
3.71 average high school GPA
88% had SAT critical reading scores over 600
92% had SAT math scores over 600
88% had SAT writing scores over 600
96% had ACT scores over 24
45% had SAT critical reading scores over 700
60% had SAT math scores over 700
48% had SAT writing scores over 700
69% had ACT scores over 30

Graduation and After

81% graduated in 4 years
8% graduated in 5 years
2% graduated in 6 years
45% had job offers within 6 months
251 organizations recruited on campus

Financial Matters

$37,700 tuition and fees (2008–09)
$11,578 room and board
93% average percent of need met
$28,765 average financial aid amount received per undergraduate (2007–08 estimated)

JUNIATA COLLEGE

SMALL-TOWN SETTING ■ PRIVATE ■ INDEPENDENT RELIGIOUS ■ COED
HUNTINGDON, PENNSYLVANIA

Web site: www.juniata.edu
Contact: Terry Bollman-Dalansky, Director of Admissions, 1700 Moore
Street, Huntingdon, PA 16652
Telephone: 814-641-3424 or toll-free 877-JUNIATA
Fax: 814-641-3100
E-mail: admissions@juniata.edu

Getting Accepted

2,349 applied
69% were accepted
453 enrolled (28% of accepted)
44% from top tenth of their h.s. class
3.75 average high school GPA
Mean SAT critical reading score: 590
Mean SAT math score: 594
45% had SAT critical reading scores over 600
50% had SAT math scores over 600
10% had SAT critical reading scores over 700
7% had SAT math scores over 700
14 National Merit Scholars
11 valedictorians

Graduation and After

76% graduated in 4 years
3% graduated in 5 years
1% graduated in 6 years
63% had job offers within 6 months
70 organizations recruited on campus

Financial Matters

$30,280 tuition and fees (2008–09)
$8420 room and board
84% average percent of need met
$22,439 average financial aid amount received
per undergraduate (2007–08 estimated)

Academics

Juniata awards bachelor's **degrees. Challenging opportunities** include advanced placement credit, accelerated degree programs, student-designed majors, freshman honors college, an honors program, double majors, independent study, and a senior project. Special programs include internships, summer session for credit, and off-campus study.

The most frequently chosen **baccalaureate** fields are biological/life sciences, business/marketing, and social sciences. A complete listing of majors at Juniata appears in the Majors by College index beginning on page 469.

The **faculty** at Juniata has 103 full-time members, 86% with terminal degrees. The student-faculty ratio is 12:1.

Students of Juniata

The student body is made up of 1,523 undergraduates. 55.7% are women and 44.3% are men. Students come from 37 states and territories and 29 other countries. 72% are from Pennsylvania. 6.4% are international students. 1.3% are African American, 0.1% American Indian, 2.1% Asian American, and 1.6% Hispanic American. 84% returned for their sophomore year.

Facilities and Resources

360 **computers/terminals** and 600 ports are available on campus for general student use. Students can access the following: online (class) registration. Campuswide network is available. 100% of college-owned or -operated housing units are wired for high-speed Internet access. Wireless service is available via classrooms, computer centers, computer labs, dorm rooms, learning centers, libraries, student centers. The **library** has 350,000 books and 1,000 subscriptions.

Campus Life

There are 80 active organizations on campus, including a drama/theater group, newspaper, radio station, television station, and choral group. No national or local **fraternities** or **sororities.**

Juniata is a member of the NCAA (Division III). **Intercollegiate sports** include baseball (m), basketball, cross-country running, field hockey (w), football (m), soccer, softball (w), swimming and diving (w), tennis, track and field, volleyball.

Campus Safety

Student safety services include fire safety training, adopt-an-officer program, security website, weather/terror alerts, travel forecast, crime statistics, late-night transport/escort service, 24-hour emergency telephone alarm devices, 24-hour patrols by trained security personnel, and student patrols.

Applying

Juniata requires an essay, a high school transcript, 1 recommendation, and a minimum high school GPA of 3.0. It recommends SAT or ACT and an interview. Application deadline: 3/15; 3/1 for financial aid, with a 3/1 priority date. Early and deferred admission are possible.

KALAMAZOO COLLEGE

SUBURBAN SETTING ■ PRIVATE ■ INDEPENDENT RELIGIOUS ■ COED
KALAMAZOO, MICHIGAN

Web site: www.kzoo.edu
Contact: Mrs. Linda Wirgau, Records Manager, Mandelle Hall, 1200
Academy Street, Kalamazoo, MI 49006-3295
Telephone: 269-337-7166 or toll-free 800-253-3602
Fax: 269-337-7190
E-mail: admissions@kzoo.edu

Academics

Kalamazoo awards bachelor's **degrees**. **Challenging opportunities** include advanced placement credit, double majors, independent study, and a senior project. Special programs include internships, off-campus study, study-abroad, and Army ROTC.

The most frequently chosen **baccalaureate** fields are social sciences, biological/life sciences, and psychology. A complete listing of majors at Kalamazoo appears in the Majors by College index beginning on page 469.

The **faculty** at Kalamazoo has 93 full-time members, 86% with terminal degrees. The student-faculty ratio is 14:1.

Students of Kalamazoo

The student body is made up of 1,387 undergraduates. 56.6% are women and 43.4% are men. Students come from 38 states and territories and 13 other countries. 69% are from Michigan. 1.8% are international students. 4% are African American, 0.3% American Indian, 5.5% Asian American, and 3.2% Hispanic American. 92% returned for their sophomore year.

Facilities and Resources

130 **computers/terminals** are available on campus for general student use. Students can access the following: campus intranet, computer help desk, free student e-mail accounts, online (class) grades, online (class) registration, online (class) schedules. Campuswide network is available. 100% of college-owned or -operated housing units are wired for high-speed Internet access. Wireless service is available via classrooms, computer centers, computer labs, libraries, student centers. The 2 **libraries** have 342,939 books and 1,495 subscriptions.

Campus Life

There are 50 active organizations on campus, including a drama/theater group, newspaper, radio station, and choral group. No national or local **fraternities** or **sororities**.

Kalamazoo is a member of the NCAA (Division III). **Intercollegiate sports** include baseball (m), basketball, cross-country running, football (m), golf, soccer, softball (w), swimming and diving, tennis, volleyball (w).

Campus Safety

Student safety services include late-night transport/escort service, 24-hour emergency telephone alarm devices, 24-hour patrols by trained security personnel, and electronically operated dormitory entrances.

Applying

Kalamazoo requires an essay, SAT or ACT, a high school transcript, and 2 recommendations. It recommends an interview and a minimum high school GPA of 3.0. Application deadline: 2/1; 2/15 priority date for financial aid. Deferred admission is possible.

Getting Accepted

2,059 applied
70% were accepted
364 enrolled (25% of accepted)
42% from top tenth of their h.s. class
3.63 average high school GPA
73% had SAT critical reading scores over 600
62% had SAT math scores over 600
64% had SAT writing scores over 600
89% had ACT scores over 24
29% had SAT critical reading scores over 700
11% had SAT math scores over 700
15% had SAT writing scores over 700
28% had ACT scores over 30
11 National Merit Scholars
13 class presidents
16 valedictorians

Graduation and After

71% graduated in 4 years
3% graduated in 5 years
1% graduated in 6 years
14 organizations recruited on campus

Financial Matters

$30,723 tuition and fees (2008–09)
$7443 room and board
$22,820 average financial aid amount received
per undergraduate (2006–07)

KENYON COLLEGE

RURAL SETTING ■ PRIVATE ■ INDEPENDENT ■ COED
GAMBIER, OHIO

Web site: www.kenyon.edu
Contact: Ms. Jennifer Delahunty, Dean of Admissions, Ransom Hall,
  Gambier, OH 43022
Telephone: 740-427-5778 or toll-free 800-848-2468
Fax: 740-427-5770
E-mail: admissions@kenyon.edu

Getting Accepted
4,509 applied
31% were accepted
456 enrolled (32% of accepted)
61% from top tenth of their h.s. class
3.85 average high school GPA
Mean SAT critical reading score: 678
Mean SAT math score: 653
Mean SAT writing score: 672
Mean ACT score: 30
88% had SAT critical reading scores over 600
83% had SAT math scores over 600
87% had SAT writing scores over 600
97% had ACT scores over 24
39% had SAT critical reading scores over 700
26% had SAT math scores over 700
37% had SAT writing scores over 700
54% had ACT scores over 30
26 National Merit Scholars
11 valedictorians

Graduation and After
85% graduated in 4 years
2% graduated in 5 years
19 organizations recruited on campus

Financial Matters
$40,980 tuition and fees (2009–10)
$7260 room and board
98% average percent of need met
$28,589 average financial aid amount received
  per undergraduate (2007–08 estimated)

Academics
Kenyon awards bachelor's **degrees**. **Challenging opportunities** include advanced placement credit, accelerated degree programs, student-designed majors, an honors program, double majors, independent study, and a senior project. Special programs include internships, off-campus study, and study-abroad.

The most frequently chosen **baccalaureate** fields are social sciences, English, and visual and performing arts. A complete listing of majors at Kenyon appears in the Majors by College index beginning on page 469.

The **faculty** at Kenyon has 152 full-time members, 98% with terminal degrees. The student-faculty ratio is 10:1.

Students of Kenyon
The student body is made up of 1,644 undergraduates. 52.9% are women and 47.1% are men. Students come from 47 states and territories and 30 other countries. 18% are from Ohio. 4% are international students. 3.7% are African American, 0.7% American Indian, 5.3% Asian American, and 2.8% Hispanic American. 94% returned for their sophomore year.

Facilities and Resources
300 **computers/terminals** are available on campus for general student use. Students can access the following: campus intranet, computer help desk, free student e-mail accounts, online (class) grades, online (class) registration, online (class) schedules, commercial databases. Campuswide network is available. 99% of college-owned or -operated housing units are wired for high-speed Internet access. Wireless service is available via entire campus. The 2 **libraries** have 1,140,890 books and 10,958 subscriptions.

Campus Life
There are 135 active organizations on campus, including a drama/theater group, newspaper, radio station, and choral group. 27% of eligible men and 8% of eligible women are members of national **fraternities**, local fraternities, and local **sororities**.

Kenyon is a member of the NCAA (Division III). **Intercollegiate sports** include baseball (m), basketball, cross-country running, field hockey (w), football (m), golf (m), lacrosse, soccer, softball (w), swimming and diving, tennis, track and field, volleyball (w).

Campus Safety
Student safety services include late-night transport/escort service, 24-hour emergency telephone alarm devices, 24-hour patrols by trained security personnel, and student patrols.

Applying
Kenyon requires an essay, SAT or ACT, a high school transcript, and counselor recommendation. It recommends an interview, 2 recommendations, and a minimum high school GPA of 3.5. Application deadline: 1/15; 2/15 priority date for financial aid. Early and deferred admission are possible.

KETTERING UNIVERSITY

URBAN SETTING ■ PRIVATE ■ INDEPENDENT ■ COED, PRIMARILY MEN
FLINT, MICHIGAN

SPONSOR

Web site: www.kettering.edu
Contact: Ms. Barbara Sosin, Director of Admissions, 1700 West Third
  Avenue, Flint, MI 48504-4898
Telephone: 810-762-7865 or toll-free 800-955-4464 Ext. 7865 (in-state),
  800-955-4464 (out-of-state)
Fax: 810-762-9837
E-mail: admissions@kettering.edu

Academics

Kettering awards bachelor's and master's **degrees**. **Challenging opportunities** include advanced placement credit, accelerated degree programs, double majors, independent study, and a senior project. Special programs include cooperative education, internships, and study-abroad.

The most frequently chosen **baccalaureate** fields are engineering, business/ marketing, and computer and information sciences. A complete listing of majors at Kettering appears in the Majors by College index beginning on page 469.

The **faculty** at Kettering has 120 full-time members, 87% with terminal degrees. The student-faculty ratio is 10:1.

Students of Kettering

The student body totals 2,600, of whom 2,134 are undergraduates. 16.7% are women and 83.3% are men. Students come from 48 states and territories and 14 other countries. 70% are from Michigan. 1% are international students. 5% are African American, 0.5% American Indian, 4.2% Asian American, and 2.5% Hispanic American. 94% returned for their sophomore year.

Facilities and Resources

450 **computers/terminals** and 800 ports are available on campus for general student use. Students can access the following: campus intranet, computer help desk, free student e-mail accounts, online (class) grades, online (class) registration, online (class) schedules. Campuswide network is available. 100% of college-owned or -operated housing units are wired for high-speed Internet access. Wireless service is available via classrooms, computer centers, computer labs, learning centers, libraries, student centers. The 2 **libraries** have 130,000 books and 400 subscriptions.

Campus Life

There are 40 active organizations on campus, including a drama/theater group, newspaper, and radio station. 29% of eligible men and 33% of eligible women are members of national **fraternities** and national **sororities**.

This institution has no intercollegiate sports.

Campus Safety

Student safety services include late-night transport/escort service, 24-hour emergency telephone alarm devices, 24-hour patrols by trained security personnel, and electronically operated dormitory entrances.

Applying

Kettering requires SAT or ACT and a high school transcript, and in some cases an essay. It recommends an interview and a minimum high school GPA of 3.0. Application deadline: rolling admissions; 2/14 priority date for financial aid. Deferred admission is possible.

Getting Accepted

2,529 applied
67% were accepted
441 enrolled (26% of accepted)
33% from top tenth of their h.s. class
3.58 average high school GPA
Mean SAT critical reading score: 586
Mean SAT math score: 631
Mean ACT score: 26
47% had SAT critical reading scores over 600
74% had SAT math scores over 600
83% had ACT scores over 24
10% had SAT critical reading scores over 700
12% had SAT math scores over 700
19% had ACT scores over 30
13 valedictorians

Graduation and After

7% graduated in 4 years
44% graduated in 5 years
10% graduated in 6 years
97% had job offers within 6 months
113 organizations recruited on campus

Financial Matters

$26,936 tuition and fees (2008–09)
$6182 room and board
52% average percent of need met
$13,586 average financial aid amount received per undergraduate (2005–06)

THE KING'S COLLEGE

URBAN SETTING ■ PRIVATE ■ INDEPENDENT RELIGIOUS ■ COED
NEW YORK, NEW YORK

Web site: www.tkc.edu
Contact: Empire State Building, 350 Fifth Avenue, Lower Lobby, New York, NY 10118
Telephone: 212-659-7217 or toll-free 888-969-7200 Ext. 3610
Fax: 212-659-3611
E-mail: bparker@tkc.edu

Getting Accepted
166 applied
75% were accepted
44 enrolled (35% of accepted)
41% from top tenth of their h.s. class
3.83 average high school GPA
Mean SAT critical reading score: 650
Mean SAT math score: 580
Mean SAT writing score: 630
Mean ACT score: 26
69% had SAT critical reading scores over 600
37% had SAT math scores over 600
69% had SAT writing scores over 600
86% had ACT scores over 24
23% had SAT critical reading scores over 700
3% had SAT math scores over 700
14% had SAT writing scores over 700
18% had ACT scores over 30

Financial Matters
$22,850 tuition and fees (2008–09)
$8750 room only

Academics

The King's College awards bachelor's **degrees**. **Challenging opportunities** include advanced placement credit, independent study, and a senior project. Special programs include summer session for credit and study-abroad.

The most frequently chosen **baccalaureate** fields are interdisciplinary studies, education, and business/marketing. A complete listing of majors at The King's College appears in the Majors by College index beginning on page 469.

The **faculty** at The King's College has 12 full-time members, 100% with terminal degrees. The student-faculty ratio is 13:1.

Students of The King's College

The student body is made up of 216 undergraduates. 62.5% are women and 37.5% are men. Students come from 39 states and territories and 11 other countries. 18% are from New York. 6% are international students. 2.3% are African American, 2.3% Asian American, and 3.3% Hispanic American. 64% returned for their sophomore year.

Facilities and Resources

20 **computers/terminals** are available on campus for general student use. Students can access the following: computer help desk, free student e-mail accounts, online (class) grades, online (class) registration, online (class) schedules. Campuswide network is available. 100% of college-owned or -operated housing units are wired for high-speed Internet access. Wireless service is available via entire campus. The **library** has 12,000 books and 75 subscriptions.

Campus Life

Active organizations on campus include a drama/theater group and newspaper. No national or local **fraternities** or **sororities**.

This institution has no intercollegiate sports.

Campus Safety

Student safety services include late-night transport/escort service and 24-hour emergency telephone alarm devices.

Applying

The King's College requires an essay, SAT or ACT, a high school transcript, and an interview. It recommends a minimum high school GPA of 3.0. Application deadline: 2/1. Deferred admission is possible.

KNOX COLLEGE

SMALL-TOWN SETTING ■ PRIVATE ■ INDEPENDENT ■ COED
GALESBURG, ILLINOIS

Web site: www.knox.edu
Contact: Mr. Paul Steenis, Dean of Admissions, Box K-148, Galesburg, IL
  61401
Telephone: 309-341-7100 or toll-free 800-678-KNOX
Fax: 309-341-7070
E-mail: admission@knox.edu

Academics

Knox awards bachelor's **degrees. Challenging opportunities** include advanced placement credit, student-designed majors, an honors program, double majors, independent study, and a senior project. Special programs include internships, off-campus study, and study-abroad.

The most frequently chosen **baccalaureate** fields are social sciences, English, and biological/life sciences. A complete listing of majors at Knox appears in the Majors by College index beginning on page 469.

The **faculty** at Knox has 103 full-time members, 92% with terminal degrees. The student-faculty ratio is 12:1.

Students of Knox

The student body is made up of 1,379 undergraduates. 58.4% are women and 41.6% are men. Students come from 47 states and territories and 35 other countries. 53% are from Illinois. 6.9% are international students. 4.7% are African American, 0.6% American Indian, 7% Asian American, and 4.8% Hispanic American. 88% returned for their sophomore year.

Facilities and Resources

338 **computers/terminals** are available on campus for general student use. Students can access the following: campus intranet, computer help desk, free student e-mail accounts, online (class) grades, online (class) registration, online (class) schedules, software applications. Campuswide network is available. 100% of college-owned or -operated housing units are wired for high-speed Internet access. Wireless service is available via entire campus. The 3 **libraries** have 324,807 books and 1,556 subscriptions.

Campus Life

There are 102 active organizations on campus, including a drama/theater group, newspaper, radio station, and choral group. 26% of eligible men and 15% of eligible women are members of national **fraternities** and national **sororities**.

Knox is a member of the NCAA (Division III). **Intercollegiate sports** include baseball (m), basketball, cross-country running, football (m), golf, soccer, softball (w), swimming and diving, tennis, track and field, volleyball (w), wrestling (m).

Campus Safety

Student safety services include late-night transport/escort service, 24-hour emergency telephone alarm devices, and 24-hour patrols by trained security personnel.

Applying

Knox requires an essay, a high school transcript, and 2 recommendations. It recommends SAT or ACT and an interview. Application deadline: 2/1; 2/1 priority date for financial aid. Early and deferred admission are possible.

Getting Accepted

2,750 applied
66% were accepted
367 enrolled (20% of accepted)
44% from top tenth of their h.s. class
3.43 average high school GPA
Mean SAT critical reading score: 640
Mean SAT math score: 622
Mean SAT writing score: 618
Mean ACT score: 29
75% had SAT critical reading scores over 600
67% had SAT math scores over 600
56% had SAT writing scores over 600
95% had ACT scores over 24
26% had SAT critical reading scores over 700
13% had SAT math scores over 700
17% had SAT writing scores over 700
37% had ACT scores over 30
6 National Merit Scholars

Graduation and After

64% graduated in 4 years
8% graduated in 5 years
2% graduated in 6 years
55.94% had job offers within 6 months
79 organizations recruited on campus

Financial Matters

$31,911 tuition and fees (2009–10)
$7164 room and board
94% average percent of need met
$23,820 average financial aid amount received
  per undergraduate (2007–08 estimated)

LAFAYETTE COLLEGE

SUBURBAN SETTING ■ PRIVATE ■ INDEPENDENT RELIGIOUS ■ COED
EASTON, PENNSYLVANIA

Web site: www.lafayette.edu
Contact: Ms. Carol Rowlands, Director of Admissions, Easton, PA
    18042-1798
Telephone: 610-330-5100
Fax: 610-330-5355
E-mail: admissions@lafayette.edu

Lafayette has achieved a unique niche in American higher education: liberal arts, sciences, and engineering programs in a most academically competitive small-college setting. Strictly undergraduate focused, Lafayette offers small classes, interdisciplinary first-year seminars, and student-faculty collaborative research on a residential campus located in eastern Pennsylvania, close to New York and Philadelphia.

Getting Accepted

6,357 applied
37% were accepted
601 enrolled (25% of accepted)
66% from top tenth of their h.s. class
3.44 average high school GPA
Mean SAT critical reading score: 625
Mean SAT math score: 665
Mean SAT writing score: 625
Mean ACT score: 28
66% had SAT critical reading scores over 600
80% had SAT math scores over 600
88% had ACT scores over 24
12% had SAT critical reading scores over 700
24% had SAT math scores over 700
20% had ACT scores over 30
6 National Merit Scholars

Graduation and After

86% graduated in 4 years
2% graduated in 5 years
1% graduated in 6 years

Financial Matters

$37,520 tuition and fees (2009–10)
$11,799 room and board
99% average percent of need met
$22,888 average financial aid amount received
   per undergraduate

Academics

Lafayette awards bachelor's **degrees. Challenging opportunities** include advanced placement credit, accelerated degree programs, student-designed majors, and an honors program. Special programs include internships, summer session for credit, off-campus study, and Army ROTC.

The most frequently chosen **baccalaureate** fields are social sciences, engineering, and English. A complete listing of majors at Lafayette appears in the Majors by College index beginning on page 469.

The **faculty** at Lafayette has 199 full-time members, 100% with terminal degrees. The student-faculty ratio is 11:1.

Students of Lafayette

The student body is made up of 2,382 undergraduates. 46% are women and 54% are men. Students come from 38 states and territories and 41 other countries. 30% are from Pennsylvania. 6.5% are international students. 5.1% are African American, 0.1% American Indian, 3.8% Asian American, and 5.1% Hispanic American. 94% returned for their sophomore year.

Facilities and Resources

600 **computers/terminals** and 600 ports are available on campus for general student use. Students can access the following: online (class) registration. Campuswide network is available.

Campus Life

There are 250 active organizations on campus, including a drama/theater group, newspaper, radio station, and choral group. 25% of eligible men and 45% of eligible women are members of national **fraternities,** national **sororities,** and social dorms.

Lafayette is a member of the NCAA (Division I). **Intercollegiate sports** include baseball (m), basketball, cross-country running, fencing, field hockey (w), football (m), golf (m), lacrosse, soccer, softball (w), swimming and diving, tennis, track and field, volleyball (w).

Campus Safety

Student safety services include late-night transport/escort service, 24-hour emergency telephone alarm devices, 24-hour patrols by trained security personnel, student patrols, and electronically operated dormitory entrances.

Applying

Lafayette requires an essay, SAT or ACT, a high school transcript, and 1 recommendation. It recommends SAT Subject Tests and an interview. Application deadline: 1/1; 3/15 for financial aid, with a 2/1 priority date. Early and deferred admission are possible.

LAKE FOREST COLLEGE

SUBURBAN SETTING ■ PRIVATE ■ INDEPENDENT ■ COED
LAKE FOREST, ILLINOIS

Web site: www.lakeforest.edu
Contact: Mr. William Motzer, Vice President for Admissions and Career
  Services, 555 North Sheridan Road, Lake Forest, IL 60045-2338
Telephone: 847-735-5000 or toll-free 800-828-4751
Fax: 847-735-6271
E-mail: admissions@lakeforest.edu

Academics

Lake Forest awards bachelor's and master's **degrees**. **Challenging opportunities** include advanced placement credit, student-designed majors, double majors, independent study, and a senior project. Special programs include internships, summer session for credit, off-campus study, and study-abroad.

The most frequently chosen **baccalaureate** fields are social sciences, communications/journalism, and visual and performing arts. A complete listing of majors at Lake Forest appears in the Majors by College index beginning on page 469.

The **faculty** at Lake Forest has 94 full-time members, 98% with terminal degrees. The student-faculty ratio is 12:1.

Students of Lake Forest

The student body totals 1,400, of whom 1,381 are undergraduates. 58.9% are women and 41.1% are men. Students come from 44 states and territories and 69 other countries. 48% are from Illinois. 9.9% are international students. 5.2% are African American, 0.3% American Indian, 4.1% Asian American, and 5.5% Hispanic American. 74% returned for their sophomore year.

Facilities and Resources

190 **computers/terminals** and 1,200 ports are available on campus for general student use. Students can access the following: campus intranet, computer help desk, free student e-mail accounts, online (class) grades, online (class) schedules, file storage. Campuswide network is available. 100% of college-owned or -operated housing units are wired for high-speed Internet access. Wireless service is available via classrooms, computer centers, computer labs, dorm rooms, learning centers, libraries, student centers. The **library** has 276,117 books and 2,364 subscriptions.

Campus Life

There are 70 active organizations on campus, including a drama/theater group, newspaper, radio station, and choral group. 7% of eligible men and 24% of eligible women are members of national **fraternities** and national **sororities**.

Lake Forest is a member of the NCAA (Division III). **Intercollegiate sports** include basketball, cross-country running, football (m), ice hockey, soccer, softball (w), swimming and diving, tennis, volleyball (w).

Campus Safety

Student safety services include late-night transport/escort service, 24-hour emergency telephone alarm devices, 24-hour patrols by trained security personnel, student patrols, and electronically operated dormitory entrances.

Applying

Lake Forest requires an essay, a high school transcript, 2 recommendations, and graded paper, and in some cases SAT or ACT. It recommends an interview. Application deadline: rolling admissions; 3/1 priority date for financial aid. Early and deferred admission are possible.

Getting Accepted

2,551 applied
59% were accepted
379 enrolled (25% of accepted)
36% from top tenth of their h.s. class
3.51 average high school GPA
Mean SAT critical reading score: 580
Mean SAT math score: 589
Mean SAT writing score: 576
Mean ACT score: 26

Graduation and After

59% graduated in 4 years
7% graduated in 5 years
74% had job offers within 6 months
30 organizations recruited on campus

Financial Matters

$32,520 tuition and fees (2008–09)
$7724 room and board
88% average percent of need met
$24,723 average financial aid amount received
  per undergraduate (2007–08 estimated)

LAWRENCE TECHNOLOGICAL UNIVERSITY

SUBURBAN SETTING ■ PRIVATE ■ INDEPENDENT ■ COED
SOUTHFIELD, MICHIGAN

Web site: www.ltu.edu
Contact: 21000 West Ten Mile Road, Southfield, MI 48075
Telephone: 248-204-3160 or toll-free 800-225-5588
Fax: 248-204-3188
E-mail: admissions@ltu.edu

Lawrence Technological University is a private, fully accredited university focused on providing superior education through cutting-edge technology, small class sizes, and innovative programs. Located in Southfield, Michigan, Lawrence Tech offers more than eighty degrees through Colleges of Architecture and Design, Arts and Sciences, Engineering, and Management. Undergraduate, master's, and doctoral programs are conveniently offered for full- or part-time students, with day, evening, weekend, and online courses. Lawrence Tech's 102-acre campus offers a full range of residential, housing, and recreational facilities. Ranked among the country's top fifty "unwired" universities, Lawrence Tech provides all undergraduates high-end laptop or tablet computers customized with the software they need to succeed.

Getting Accepted
1,498 applied
51% were accepted
308 enrolled (41% of accepted)
20% from top tenth of their h.s. class
3.23 average high school GPA
Mean ACT score: 24
54% had ACT scores over 24
9% had ACT scores over 30

Graduation and After
24% graduated in 4 years
15% graduated in 5 years
7% graduated in 6 years
84% had job offers within 6 months
550 organizations recruited on campus

Financial Matters
$21,979 tuition and fees (2008–09)
$8071 room and board
69% average percent of need met
$14,891 average financial aid amount received per undergraduate (2005–06)

Academics

Lawrence Tech awards associate, bachelor's, master's, and doctoral **degrees** and post-bachelor's certificates. **Challenging opportunities** include advanced placement credit, an honors program, double majors, independent study, and a senior project. Special programs include cooperative education, internships, summer session for credit, off-campus study, study-abroad, and Army, Navy, and Air Force ROTC.

The most frequently chosen **baccalaureate** fields are engineering, architecture, and computer and information sciences. A complete listing of majors at Lawrence Tech appears in the Majors by College index beginning on page 469.

The **faculty** at Lawrence Tech has 125 full-time members, 72% with terminal degrees. The student-faculty ratio is 12:1.

Students of Lawrence Tech

The student body totals 4,417, of whom 3,019 are undergraduates. 20.3% are women and 79.7% are men. Students come from 27 states and territories and 11 other countries. 97% are from Michigan. 8.3% are international students. 11.2% are African American, 0.3% American Indian, 2.9% Asian American, and 1.9% Hispanic American. 72% returned for their sophomore year.

Facilities and Resources

60 **computers/terminals** are available on campus for general student use. Students can access the following: campus intranet, computer help desk, free student e-mail accounts, online (class) grades, online (class) registration, online (class) schedules, degree audit, Blackboard, SCT Banner (student information). Campuswide network is available. 100% of college-owned or -operated housing units are wired for high-speed Internet access. Wireless service is available via entire campus. The 2 **libraries** have 129,721 books and 62,000 subscriptions.

Campus Life

There are 52 active organizations on campus, including a drama/theater group and newspaper. 10% of eligible men and 5% of eligible women are members of national **fraternities**, national **sororities**, local fraternities, and local sororities.

This institution has no intercollegiate sports.

Campus Safety

Student safety services include late-night transport/escort service, 24-hour emergency telephone alarm devices, 24-hour patrols by trained security personnel, and electronically operated dormitory entrances.

Applying

Lawrence Tech requires ACT (preferred), a high school transcript, and a minimum high school GPA of 2.5, and in some cases an essay, an interview, 1 recommendation, and a minimum high school GPA of 2.75. Application deadline: 8/15; 4/1 priority date for financial aid. Early and deferred admission are possible.

LAWRENCE UNIVERSITY

SMALL-TOWN SETTING ■ PRIVATE ■ INDEPENDENT ■ COED
APPLETON, WISCONSIN

Web site: www.lawrence.edu
Contact: Mr. Steven T. Syverson, Vice President for Enrollment Management,
PO Box 599, Appleton, WI 54912-0599
Telephone: 920-832-6500 or toll-free 800-227-0982
Fax: 920-832-6782
E-mail: excel@lawrence.edu

Academics

Lawrence awards bachelor's **degrees**. **Challenging opportunities** include advanced placement credit, student-designed majors, double majors, independent study, and a senior project. Special programs include internships, off-campus study, and study-abroad.

The most frequently chosen **baccalaureate** fields are visual and performing arts, social sciences, and interdisciplinary studies. A complete listing of majors at Lawrence appears in the Majors by College index beginning on page 469.

The **faculty** at Lawrence has 155 full-time members, 96% with terminal degrees. The student-faculty ratio is 9:1.

Students of Lawrence

The student body is made up of 1,503 undergraduates. 53.9% are women and 46.1% are men. Students come from 47 states and territories and 48 other countries. 36% are from Wisconsin. 7.6% are international students. 2.3% are African American, 0.3% American Indian, 2.5% Asian American, and 1.8% Hispanic American. 90% returned for their sophomore year.

Facilities and Resources

354 **computers/terminals** and 1,055 ports are available on campus for general student use. Students can access the following: campus intranet, computer help desk, free student e-mail accounts, online (class) grades, online (class) registration, online (class) schedules, online transcripts, financial aid, financial account information. Campuswide network is available. 100% of college-owned or -operated housing units are wired for high-speed Internet access. Wireless service is available via classrooms, computer centers, computer labs, dorm rooms, learning centers, libraries, student centers. The **library** has 659,425 books and 34,122 subscriptions.

Campus Life

There are 100 active organizations on campus, including a drama/theater group, newspaper, radio station, and choral group. 22% of eligible men and 12% of eligible women are members of national **fraternities** and national **sororities**.

Lawrence is a member of the NCAA (Division III). **Intercollegiate sports** include baseball (m), basketball, cross-country running, fencing, football (m), golf (m), ice hockey (m), soccer, softball (w), swimming and diving, tennis, track and field, volleyball (w), wrestling (m).

Campus Safety

Student safety services include evening patrols by trained security personnel, late-night transport/escort service, 24-hour emergency telephone alarm devices, student patrols, and electronically operated dormitory entrances.

Applying

Lawrence requires an essay, a high school transcript, 2 recommendations, and audition for music program. It recommends SAT or ACT (test scores will be considered at student's request), an interview, and a minimum high school GPA of 3.0. Application deadline: 1/15; 3/15 priority date for financial aid. Early and deferred admission are possible.

Getting Accepted

2,618 applied
59% were accepted
382 enrolled (25% of accepted)
41% from top tenth of their h.s. class
3.67 average high school GPA
79% had SAT critical reading scores over 600
79% had SAT math scores over 600
82% had SAT writing scores over 600
95% had ACT scores over 24
38% had SAT critical reading scores over 700
29% had SAT math scores over 700
25% had SAT writing scores over 700
51% had ACT scores over 30
14 National Merit Scholars
20 valedictorians

Graduation and After

58% graduated in 4 years
15% graduated in 5 years
2% graduated in 6 years
62% had job offers within 6 months
11 organizations recruited on campus

Financial Matters

$33,264 tuition and fees (2008–09)
$6975 room and board
94% average percent of need met
$25,800 average financial aid amount received
per undergraduate (2007–08 estimated)

Lebanon Valley College (LVC) is ranked number 1 in the North by *U.S. News & World Report* in the "Great Schools, Great Prices" category. More than 1,600 full-time students at this excellent regional liberal arts college enjoy a 14:1 student-faculty ratio and outstanding NCAA Division III athletic programs. Lebanon Valley College provides guaranteed scholarships of up to 50 percent off tuition to students in the top 30 percent of their high school class, guaranteed four-year on-campus housing, and guaranteed graduation in four years. More than 70 percent of entering freshmen are in the top 30 percent of their high school class. *U.S. News* ranks Lebanon Valley College among the top 2 percent of colleges for average freshman retention rate and the top 3 percent for average graduation rate in its category. For the last ten years, the National Science Foundation has recognized LVC as being among the top 15 percent of "Private, Predominantly Undergraduate Institutions" in the nation for producing the most Ph.D.'s in biology, biochemistry, and chemistry.

Getting Accepted
1,885 applied
73% were accepted
396 enrolled (29% of accepted)
38% from top tenth of their h.s. class
Mean SAT critical reading score: 539
Mean SAT math score: 563
Mean SAT writing score: 540
26% had SAT critical reading scores over 600
35% had SAT math scores over 600
28% had SAT writing scores over 600
49% had ACT scores over 24
2% had SAT critical reading scores over 700
5% had SAT math scores over 700
1% had SAT writing scores over 700
9% had ACT scores over 30
9 class presidents
8 valedictorians

Graduation and After
63% graduated in 4 years
5% graduated in 5 years
64% had job offers within 6 months
23 organizations recruited on campus

Financial Matters
$29,350 tuition and fees (2008–09)
$7760 room and board
86% average percent of need met
$20,458 average financial aid amount received per undergraduate (2007–08 estimated)

LEBANON VALLEY COLLEGE
SMALL-TOWN SETTING ■ PRIVATE ■ INDEPENDENT RELIGIOUS ■ COED
ANNVILLE, PENNSYLVANIA

Web site: www.lvc.edu
Contact: Ms. Susan Jones, Director of Admission, 101 North College Avenue, Annville, PA 17003
Telephone: toll-free 866-LVC-4ADM
Fax: 717-867-6026
E-mail: admission@lvc.edu

Academics
LVC awards associate, bachelor's, master's, and doctoral **degrees** and post-bachelor's certificates. **Challenging opportunities** include advanced placement credit, student-designed majors, double majors, and independent study. Special programs include internships, summer session for credit, off-campus study, and study-abroad.

The most frequently chosen **baccalaureate** fields are education, business/marketing, and social sciences. A complete listing of majors at LVC appears in the Majors by College index beginning on page 469.

The **faculty** at LVC has 99 full-time members, 86% with terminal degrees. The student-faculty ratio is 13:1.

Students of LVC
The student body totals 1,965, of whom 1,747 are undergraduates. 55.2% are women and 44.8% are men. Students come from 21 states and territories and 4 other countries. 78% are from Pennsylvania. 0.3% are international students. 1.4% are African American, 0.2% American Indian, 1.8% Asian American, and 2.4% Hispanic American. 81% returned for their sophomore year.

Facilities and Resources
187 **computers/terminals** are available on campus for general student use. Students can access the following: campus intranet, computer help desk, free student e-mail accounts, online (class) grades, online (class) registration, online (class) schedules. Campuswide network is available. 100% of college-owned or -operated housing units are wired for high-speed Internet access. Wireless service is available via classrooms, computer centers, computer labs, dorm rooms, learning centers, libraries, student centers. The **library** has 192,239 books and 3,100 subscriptions.

Campus Life
There are 79 active organizations on campus, including a drama/theater group, newspaper, radio station, choral group, and marching band. 11% of eligible men and 15% of eligible women are members of national **fraternities**, national **sororities**, local fraternities, and local sororities.

LVC is a member of the NCAA (Division III). **Intercollegiate sports** include baseball (m), basketball, cross-country running, field hockey (w), football (m), golf (m), ice hockey (m), lacrosse, soccer, softball (w), swimming and diving, tennis, track and field, volleyball (w).

Campus Safety
Student safety services include dormitory entrances locked at midnight, late-night transport/escort service, 24-hour emergency telephone alarm devices, 24-hour patrols by trained security personnel, and electronically operated dormitory entrances.

Applying
LVC requires a high school transcript, and in some cases an essay and audition for music majors. It recommends an interview and 2 recommendations. Application deadline: rolling admissions; 3/1 priority date for financial aid.

LEHIGH UNIVERSITY

SUBURBAN SETTING ■ PRIVATE ■ INDEPENDENT ■ COED
BETHLEHEM, PENNSYLVANIA

Web site: www.lehigh.edu
Contact: J. Bruce Gardiner, Director of Admissions, 27 Memorial Drive West,
   Bethlehem, PA 18015
Telephone: 610-758-3100
Fax: 610-758-4361
E-mail: admissions@lehigh.edu

Academics

Lehigh awards bachelor's, master's, and doctoral **degrees** and post-bachelor's and post-master's certificates. **Challenging opportunities** include advanced placement credit, accelerated degree programs, an honors program, double majors, independent study, and a senior project. Special programs include cooperative education, internships, summer session for credit, off-campus study, study-abroad, and Army ROTC.

The most frequently chosen **baccalaureate** fields are business/marketing, engineering, and social sciences. A complete listing of majors at Lehigh appears in the Majors by College index beginning on page 469.

The **faculty** at Lehigh has 443 full-time members, 99% with terminal degrees. The student-faculty ratio is 9:1.

Students of Lehigh

The student body totals 6,994, of whom 4,876 are undergraduates. 41.7% are women and 58.3% are men. Students come from 52 states and territories and 49 other countries. 25% are from Pennsylvania. 3.2% are international students. 3.4% are African American, 6.2% Asian American, and 4.9% Hispanic American. 94% returned for their sophomore year.

Facilities and Resources

588 **computers/terminals** are available on campus for general student use. Students can access the following: campus intranet, computer help desk, free student e-mail accounts, online (class) grades, online (class) registration, online (class) schedules. Campuswide network is available. 100% of college-owned or -operated housing units are wired for high-speed Internet access. Wireless service is available via classrooms, computer centers, computer labs, dorm rooms, learning centers, libraries, student centers. The 2 **libraries** have 1,182,975 books and 49,500 subscriptions.

Campus Life

There are 150 active organizations on campus, including a drama/theater group, newspaper, radio station, choral group, and marching band. 31% of eligible men and 34% of eligible women are members of national **fraternities** and national **sororities**.

Lehigh is a member of the NCAA (Division I). **Intercollegiate sports** (some offering scholarships) include baseball (m), basketball, crew (w), cross-country running, field hockey (w), football (m), golf, lacrosse, soccer, softball (w), swimming and diving, tennis, track and field, volleyball (w), wrestling (m).

Campus Safety

Student safety services include late-night transport/escort service, 24-hour emergency telephone alarm devices, 24-hour patrols by trained security personnel, student patrols, and electronically operated dormitory entrances.

Applying

Lehigh requires an essay, SAT or ACT, a high school transcript, 2 recommendations, and graded writing sample. It recommends an interview. Application deadline: 1/1; 2/1 for financial aid. Early and deferred admission are possible.

Getting Accepted

12,941 applied
28% were accepted
1,205 enrolled (33% of accepted)
93% from top tenth of their h.s. class
Mean SAT critical reading score: 633
Mean SAT math score: 675
74% had SAT critical reading scores over 600
88% had SAT math scores over 600
17% had SAT critical reading scores over 700
40% had SAT math scores over 700

Graduation and After

72% graduated in 4 years
11% graduated in 5 years
2% graduated in 6 years
60% had job offers within 6 months
282 organizations recruited on campus

Financial Matters

$37,550 tuition and fees (2008–09)
$9770 room and board
97% average percent of need met
$29,498 average financial aid amount received
   per undergraduate (2007–08 estimated)

LeTourneau University

Suburban setting ■ Private ■ Independent Religious ■ Coed
Longview, Texas

Web site: www.letu.edu
Contact: Mr. James Townsend, Director of Admissions, PO Box 7001,
   Longview, TX 75607-7001
Telephone: 903-233-3400 or toll-free 800-759-8811
Fax: 903-233-3411
E-mail: admissions@letu.edu

Getting Accepted

970 applied
66% were accepted
341 enrolled (53% of accepted)
30% from top tenth of their h.s. class
3.58 average high school GPA
48% had SAT critical reading scores over 600
56% had SAT math scores over 600
33% had SAT writing scores over 600
67% had ACT scores over 24
10% had SAT critical reading scores over 700
9% had SAT math scores over 700
6% had SAT writing scores over 700
23% had ACT scores over 30

Graduation and After

31% graduated in 4 years
16% graduated in 5 years
5% graduated in 6 years
92% had job offers within 6 months

Financial Matters

$19,140 tuition and fees (2008–09)
$7500 room and board
61% average percent of need met
$9566 average financial aid amount received
   per undergraduate (2007–08 estimated)

Academics

LeTourneau awards associate, bachelor's, and master's **degrees**. **Challenging opportunities** include advanced placement credit, accelerated degree programs, an honors program, double majors, independent study, and a senior project. Special programs include cooperative education, internships, summer session for credit, off-campus study, and study-abroad.

The most frequently chosen **baccalaureate** fields are engineering, transportation and materials moving, and business/marketing. A complete listing of majors at LeTourneau appears in the Majors by College index beginning on page 469.

The **faculty** at LeTourneau has 74 full-time members, 74% with terminal degrees. The student-faculty ratio is 19:1.

Students of LeTourneau

The student body totals 3,662, of whom 3,371 are undergraduates. 55.7% are women and 44.3% are men. Students come from 50 states and territories and 27 other countries. 48% are from Texas. 0.8% are international students. 19.7% are African American, 0.3% American Indian, 1% Asian American, and 8.3% Hispanic American. 75% returned for their sophomore year.

Facilities and Resources

191 **computers/terminals** are available on campus for general student use. Students can access the following: online (class) registration. Campuswide network is available. The **library** has 84,779 books and 383 subscriptions.

Campus Life

There are 22 active organizations on campus, including a drama/theater group, newspaper, and choral group. LeTourneau has 3 societies for men, 1 society for women.

LeTourneau is a member of the NCAA (Division III) and NCCAA. **Intercollegiate sports** include baseball (m), basketball, cross-country running, golf, soccer, softball (w), tennis, volleyball (w).

Campus Safety

Student safety services include late-night transport/escort service, 24-hour emergency telephone alarm devices, 24-hour patrols by trained security personnel, and electronically operated dormitory entrances.

Applying

LeTourneau requires SAT or ACT. Application deadline: rolling admissions; 2/1 priority date for financial aid. Deferred admission is possible.

Lewis & Clark College

Suburban setting ■ Private ■ Independent ■ Coed
Portland, Oregon

Web site: www.lclark.edu
Contact: Mr. Michael Sexton, Dean of Admissions, 0615 SW Palatine Hill Road, Portland, OR 97219
Telephone: 503-768-7040 or toll-free 800-444-4111
Fax: 503-768-7055
E-mail: admissions@lclark.edu

Academics

L & C awards bachelor's, master's, doctoral, and first-professional **degrees** and post-master's certificates. **Challenging opportunities** include advanced placement credit, accelerated degree programs, student-designed majors, an honors program, double majors, independent study, and a senior project. Special programs include internships, summer session for credit, off-campus study, and study-abroad.

The most frequently chosen **baccalaureate** fields are social sciences, psychology, and foreign languages and literature. A complete listing of majors at L & C appears in the Majors by College index beginning on page 469.

The **faculty** at L & C has 222 full-time members, 97% with terminal degrees. The student-faculty ratio is 12:1.

Students of L & C

The student body totals 3,565, of whom 1,999 are undergraduates. 60.8% are women and 39.2% are men. Students come from 47 states and territories and 55 other countries. 19% are from Oregon. 7.8% are international students. 2% are African American, 0.8% American Indian, 5.8% Asian American, and 4.5% Hispanic American. 86% returned for their sophomore year.

Facilities and Resources

158 **computers/terminals** are available on campus for general student use. Students can access the following: campus intranet, computer help desk, free student e-mail accounts, online (class) grades, online (class) registration, online (class) schedules. Campuswide network is available. 100% of college-owned or -operated housing units are wired for high-speed Internet access. Wireless service is available via classrooms, computer centers, computer labs, dorm rooms, learning centers, libraries, student centers. The 2 **libraries** have 312,679 books and 3,603 subscriptions.

Campus Life

There are 70 active organizations on campus, including a drama/theater group, newspaper, radio station, television station, and choral group. No national or local **fraternities** or **sororities**.

L & C is a member of the NCAA (Division III). **Intercollegiate sports** include baseball (m), basketball, crew, cross-country running, football (m), golf, soccer (w), softball (w), swimming and diving, tennis, track and field, volleyball (w).

Campus Safety

Student safety services include late-night transport/escort service, 24-hour emergency telephone alarm devices, 24-hour patrols by trained security personnel, student patrols, and electronically operated dormitory entrances.

Applying

L & C requires an essay, SAT, ACT, or academic portfolio, a high school transcript, and a minimum high school GPA of 2.0, and in some cases 4 recommendations. "Portfolio path" applicants must submit samples of graded work. It recommends an interview and a minimum high school GPA of 3.0. Application deadline: 2/1; 3/1 priority date for financial aid. Early and deferred admission are possible.

Getting Accepted

5,551 applied
58% were accepted
533 enrolled (17% of accepted)
43% from top tenth of their h.s. class
3.72 average high school GPA
88% had SAT critical reading scores over 600
72% had SAT math scores over 600
78% had SAT writing scores over 600
96% had ACT scores over 24
33% had SAT critical reading scores over 700
17% had SAT math scores over 700
25% had SAT writing scores over 700
35% had ACT scores over 30
6 National Merit Scholars
31 valedictorians

Graduation and After

64% graduated in 4 years
6% graduated in 5 years
1% graduated in 6 years
59 organizations recruited on campus

Financial Matters

$33,726 tuition and fees (2008–09)
$8820 room and board
84% average percent of need met
$23,801 average financial aid amount received per undergraduate (2007–08 estimated)

LINCOLN MEMORIAL UNIVERSITY
SMALL-TOWN SETTING ■ PRIVATE ■ INDEPENDENT ■ COED
HARROGATE, TENNESSEE

Web site: www.lmunet.edu
Contact: 6965 Cumberland Gap Parkway, Harrogate, TN 37752-1901
Telephone: 423-869-6280 or toll-free 800-325-0900
Fax: 423-869-6250
E-mail: admissions@lmunet.edu

Getting Accepted
1,080 applied
78% were accepted
287 enrolled (34% of accepted)
3.36 average high school GPA
Mean SAT critical reading score: 484
Mean SAT math score: 495
Mean ACT score: 21
10% had SAT critical reading scores over 600
18% had SAT math scores over 600
23% had ACT scores over 24
4% had SAT math scores over 700
4% had ACT scores over 30

Graduation and After
23% graduated in 4 years
8% graduated in 5 years
15% graduated in 6 years

Financial Matters
$15,700 tuition and fees (2009–10)
$5680 room and board
90% average percent of need met
$9800 average financial aid amount received
  per undergraduate

Academics
LMU awards associate, bachelor's, master's, and first-professional **degrees** and post-master's certificates. **Challenging opportunities** include advanced placement credit, accelerated degree programs, an honors program, double majors, and independent study. Special programs include internships and summer session for credit.

The most frequently chosen **baccalaureate** fields are health professions and related sciences, business/marketing, and education. A complete listing of majors at LMU appears in the Majors by College index beginning on page 469.

The **faculty** at LMU has 141 full-time members. The student-faculty ratio is 13:1.

Students of LMU
The student body totals 3,365, of whom 1,429 are undergraduates. 69.3% are women and 30.7% are men. Students come from 33 states and territories and 19 other countries. 70% are from Tennessee. 4% are international students. 4.5% are African American, 0.7% Asian American, and 1% Hispanic American. 60% returned for their sophomore year.

Facilities and Resources
Students can access the following: campus intranet, computer help desk, free student e-mail accounts, online (class) grades, online (class) registration, online (class) schedules. Campuswide network is available. 100% of college-owned or -operated housing units are wired for high-speed Internet access. The **library** has 199,892 books and 334 subscriptions.

Campus Life
There are 40 active organizations on campus, including a drama/theater group, radio station, television station, and choral group. 2% of eligible men and 6% of eligible women are members of local **fraternities** and local **sororities**.

LMU is a member of the NCAA (Division II). **Intercollegiate sports** (some offering scholarships) include baseball (m), basketball, cross-country running, golf, soccer, softball (w), tennis, volleyball (w).

Campus Safety
Student safety services include 24-hour emergency telephone alarm devices and 24-hour patrols by trained security personnel.

Applying
LMU requires SAT or ACT, a high school transcript, immunization records, financial aid application, and a minimum high school GPA of 2.3. Application deadline: rolling admissions; 4/1 priority date for financial aid.

LINFIELD COLLEGE

SMALL-TOWN SETTING ■ PRIVATE ■ INDEPENDENT RELIGIOUS ■ COED
MCMINNVILLE, OREGON

Web site: www.linfield.edu
Contact: Ms. Lisa Knodle-Bragiel, Director of Admission, 900 SE Baker
    Street, McMinnville, OR 97128
Telephone: 503-883-2213 or toll-free 800-640-2287
Fax: 503-883-2472
E-mail: admission@linfield.edu

SPONSOR

Academics

Linfield awards bachelor's **degrees** and post-bachelor's certificates. **Challenging opportunities** include advanced placement credit, student-designed majors, double majors, independent study, and a senior project. Special programs include internships, summer session for credit, off-campus study, study-abroad, and Air Force ROTC.

The most frequently chosen **baccalaureate** fields are business/marketing, education, and social sciences. A complete listing of majors at Linfield appears in the Majors by College index beginning on page 469.

The **faculty** at Linfield has 108 full-time members, 94% with terminal degrees. The student-faculty ratio is 13:1.

Students of Linfield

The student body is made up of 1,720 undergraduates. 55.8% are women and 44.2% are men. Students come from 27 states and territories and 24 other countries. 55% are from Oregon. 4.8% are international students. 1.5% are African American, 1.5% American Indian, 8.4% Asian American, and 4.7% Hispanic American. 81% returned for their sophomore year.

Facilities and Resources

250 **computers/terminals** are available on campus for general student use. Students can access the following: computer help desk, free student e-mail accounts, online (class) grades, online (class) registration, online (class) schedules. Campuswide network is available. 95% of college-owned or -operated housing units are wired for high-speed Internet access. Wireless service is available via classrooms, computer centers, computer labs, dorm rooms, learning centers, libraries, student centers. The **library** has 184,931 books and 958 subscriptions.

Campus Life

Active organizations on campus include a drama/theater group, newspaper, radio station, and choral group. 10% of eligible men and 18% of eligible women are members of national **fraternities**, national **sororities**, local fraternities, and local sororities.

Linfield is a member of the NCAA (Division III). **Intercollegiate sports** include baseball (m), basketball, cross-country running, football (m), golf, lacrosse (w), soccer, softball (w), swimming and diving, tennis, track and field, volleyball (w).

Campus Safety

Student safety services include late-night transport/escort service, 24-hour emergency telephone alarm devices, 24-hour patrols by trained security personnel, and electronically operated dormitory entrances.

Applying

Linfield requires an essay, SAT or ACT, a high school transcript, and 1 recommendation. It recommends an interview. Application deadline: 2/15; 2/1 priority date for financial aid. Deferred admission is possible.

Getting Accepted

2,066 applied
79% were accepted
478 enrolled (29% of accepted)
33% from top tenth of their h.s. class
3.55 average high school GPA
Mean SAT critical reading score: 550
Mean SAT math score: 559
Mean SAT writing score: 545
Mean ACT score: 24
31% had SAT critical reading scores over 600
33% had SAT math scores over 600
24% had SAT writing scores over 600
61% had ACT scores over 24
5% had SAT critical reading scores over 700
4% had SAT math scores over 700
3% had SAT writing scores over 700
10% had ACT scores over 30
1 National Merit Scholar
9 class presidents
21 valedictorians

Graduation and After

61% graduated in 4 years
9% graduated in 5 years
2% graduated in 6 years
85% had job offers within 6 months
10 organizations recruited on campus

Financial Matters

$27,414 tuition and fees (2008–09)
$7860 room and board
82% average percent of need met
$20,059 average financial aid amount received
    per undergraduate (2007–08 estimated)

Getting Accepted

2,028 applied
75% were accepted
658 enrolled (43% of accepted)
24% from top tenth of their h.s. class
3.39 average high school GPA
Mean SAT critical reading score: 548
Mean SAT math score: 552
Mean ACT score: 24
35% had SAT critical reading scores over 600
32% had SAT math scores over 600
25% had SAT writing scores over 600
54% had ACT scores over 24
5% had SAT critical reading scores over 700
4% had SAT math scores over 700
3% had SAT writing scores over 700
12% had ACT scores over 30

Graduation and After

97% had job offers within 6 months
100 organizations recruited on campus

Financial Matters

$18,580 tuition and fees (2008–09)
$7400 room and board
68% average percent of need met
$15,765 average financial aid amount received
  per undergraduate (2007–08 estimated)

LIPSCOMB UNIVERSITY

SUBURBAN SETTING ■ PRIVATE ■ INDEPENDENT RELIGIOUS ■ COED
NASHVILLE, TENNESSEE

Web site: www.lipscomb.edu
Contact: Office of Admissions, One University Park Drive, Nashville, TN
  37204-3951
Telephone: 615-966-1776 or toll-free 877-582-4766
Fax: 615-966-1804
E-mail: admissions@lipscomb.edu

Academics

Lipscomb awards bachelor's, master's, and first-professional **degrees** and post-bachelor's certificates. **Challenging opportunities** include advanced placement credit, accelerated degree programs, an honors program, double majors, independent study, and a senior project. Special programs include internships, summer session for credit, study-abroad, and Army and Air Force ROTC.

The most frequently chosen **baccalaureate** fields are business/marketing, education, and health professions and related sciences. A complete listing of majors at Lipscomb appears in the Majors by College index beginning on page 469.

The **faculty** at Lipscomb has 117 full-time members, 88% with terminal degrees. The student-faculty ratio is 15:1.

Students of Lipscomb

The student body totals 3,054, of whom 2,420 are undergraduates. 56.9% are women and 43.1% are men. Students come from 42 states and territories and 24 other countries. 66% are from Tennessee. 2.6% are international students. 5.2% are African American, 0.4% American Indian, 1.9% Asian American, and 2.3% Hispanic American. 77% returned for their sophomore year.

Facilities and Resources

203 **computers/terminals** are available on campus for general student use. Students can access the following: computer help desk, free student e-mail accounts, online (class) grades, online (class) registration, online (class) schedules. Campuswide network is available. 100% of college-owned or -operated housing units are wired for high-speed Internet access. Wireless service is available via entire campus. The 2 **libraries** have 258,965 books and 809 subscriptions.

Campus Life

There are 60 active organizations on campus, including a drama/theater group, newspaper, radio station, television station, and choral group. 13% of eligible men and 19% of eligible women are members of local **fraternities** and local **sororities**.

Lipscomb is a member of the NCAA (Division I). **Intercollegiate sports** (some offering scholarships) include baseball (m), basketball, cross-country running, golf, soccer, softball (w), tennis, volleyball (w).

Campus Safety

Student safety services include late-night transport/escort service, 24-hour emergency telephone alarm devices, 24-hour patrols by trained security personnel, and electronically operated dormitory entrances.

Applying

Lipscomb requires SAT or ACT, a high school transcript, an interview, 1 recommendation, TOEFL for students whose first language is not English, and a minimum high school GPA of 2.25. It recommends an essay. Application deadline: rolling admissions; 3/1 priority date for financial aid. Early and deferred admission are possible.

List College, The Jewish Theological Seminary

SPONSOR

Urban setting ■ Private ■ Independent Religious ■ Coed
New York, New York

Web site: www.jtsa.edu
Contact: Mr. Sergio Lineberge, List College Admissions Coordinator, 3080 Broadway, New York, NY 10027
Telephone: 212-678-8820
Fax: 212-280-6022
E-mail: lcadmissions@jtsa.edu

Academics

List College awards bachelor's, master's, doctoral, and first-professional **degrees** (double bachelor's degree with Barnard College, Columbia University, joint bachelor's degree with Columbia University). **Challenging opportunities** include advanced placement credit, student-designed majors, freshman honors college, an honors program, double majors, and a senior project. Special programs include internships, summer session for credit, off-campus study, study-abroad, and Army, Navy, and Air Force ROTC. A complete listing of majors at List College appears in the Majors by College index beginning on page 469.

The **faculty** at List College has 63 full-time members, 94% with terminal degrees. The student-faculty ratio is 5:1.

Students of List College

The student body totals 566, of whom 190 are undergraduates. 56.8% are women and 43.2% are men. Students come from 24 states and territories and 3 other countries. 19% are from New York. 1.1% are Hispanic American. 100% returned for their sophomore year.

Facilities and Resources

50 **computers/terminals** are available on campus for general student use. Students can access the following: computer help desk, free student e-mail accounts, online (class) registration. Campuswide network is available. 100% of college-owned or -operated housing units are wired for high-speed Internet access. Wireless service is available via classrooms, computer labs, dorm rooms, learning centers, libraries, student centers. The **library** has 380,000 books and 720 subscriptions.

Campus Life

Active organizations on campus include a drama/theater group, newspaper, radio station, and choral group. No national or local **fraternities** or **sororities**.

This institution has no intercollegiate sports.

Campus Safety

Student safety services include late-night transport/escort service, 24-hour emergency telephone alarm devices, 24-hour patrols by trained security personnel, and electronically operated dormitory entrances.

Applying

List College requires an essay, SAT or ACT, a high school transcript, and 2 recommendations. It recommends an interview and a minimum high school GPA of 3.0. Application deadline: 2/15; 3/1 for financial aid, with a 2/1 priority date. Early and deferred admission are possible.

Getting Accepted
124 applied
60% were accepted
46 enrolled (62% of accepted)
3.7 average high school GPA
Mean SAT critical reading score: 668
Mean SAT math score: 656
Mean SAT writing score: 701
Mean ACT score: 29
95% had SAT critical reading scores over 600
89% had SAT math scores over 600
92% had SAT writing scores over 600
100% had ACT scores over 24
42% had SAT critical reading scores over 700
28% had SAT math scores over 700
61% had SAT writing scores over 700
61% had ACT scores over 30

Graduation and After
91% graduated in 4 years
67% had job offers within 6 months

Financial Matters
$15,000 tuition and fees (2008–09)
$9200 room only
92% average percent of need met
$18,639 average financial aid amount received per undergraduate (2007–08 estimated)

Getting Accepted

15,093 applied
73% were accepted
4,596 enrolled (41% of accepted)
26% from top tenth of their h.s. class
3.49 average high school GPA
Mean SAT critical reading score: 579
Mean SAT math score: 596
Mean SAT writing score: 551
Mean ACT score: 25
44% had SAT critical reading scores over 600
51% had SAT math scores over 600
31% had SAT writing scores over 600
67% had ACT scores over 24
9% had SAT critical reading scores over 700
10% had SAT math scores over 700
5% had SAT writing scores over 700
13% had ACT scores over 30
35 National Merit Scholars
282 valedictorians

Graduation and After

28% graduated in 4 years
26% graduated in 5 years
7% graduated in 6 years
895 organizations recruited on campus

Financial Matters

$5086 resident tuition and fees (2008–09)
$13,800 nonresident tuition and fees
(2008–09)
$7238 room and board
58% average percent of need met
$8011 average financial aid amount received
per undergraduate (2006–07)

LOUISIANA STATE UNIVERSITY AND AGRICULTURAL AND MECHANICAL COLLEGE

URBAN SETTING ■ PUBLIC ■ STATE-SUPPORTED ■ COED
BATON ROUGE, LOUISIANA

Web site: www.lsu.edu
Contact: 110 Thomas Boyd Hall, Baton Rouge, LA 70803
Telephone: 225-578-1175
Fax: 225-578-4433
E-mail: admissions@lsu.edu

Academics

LSU awards bachelor's, master's, doctoral, and first-professional **degrees** and post-master's certificates. **Challenging opportunities** include advanced placement credit, accelerated degree programs, student-designed majors, freshman honors college, an honors program, double majors, independent study, and a senior project. Special programs include cooperative education, internships, summer session for credit, off-campus study, study-abroad, and Army, Navy, and Air Force ROTC.

The most frequently chosen **baccalaureate** fields are business/marketing, education, and social sciences. A complete listing of majors at LSU appears in the Majors by College index beginning on page 469.

The **faculty** at LSU has 1,324 full-time members, 85% with terminal degrees. The student-faculty ratio is 21:1.

Students of LSU

The student body totals 28,628, of whom 23,393 are undergraduates. 51.4% are women and 48.6% are men. Students come from 49 states and territories and 74 other countries. 85% are from Louisiana. 1.5% are international students. 8.9% are African American, 0.5% American Indian, 3.3% Asian American, and 3.2% Hispanic American. 85% returned for their sophomore year.

Facilities and Resources

7,000 **computers/terminals** and 8,500 ports are available on campus for general student use. Students can access the following: computer help desk, free student e-mail accounts, online (class) grades, online (class) registration, online (class) schedules, free software for download, personal Web sites, storage, discounts on hardware, virtual computer lab. Campuswide network is available. 100% of college-owned or -operated housing units are wired for high-speed Internet access. Wireless service is available via entire campus. The 5 **libraries** have 4,082,803 books and 104,545 subscriptions.

Campus Life

There are 300 active organizations on campus, including a drama/theater group, newspaper, radio station, television station, choral group, and marching band. 11% of eligible men and 18% of eligible women are members of national **fraternities** and national **sororities**.

LSU is a member of the NCAA (Division I). **Intercollegiate sports** (some offering scholarships) include baseball (m), basketball, cheerleading, cross-country running, football (m), golf, gymnastics (w), soccer (w), softball (w), swimming and diving, tennis, track and field, volleyball (w).

Campus Safety

Student safety services include self-defense education, crime prevention programs, late-night transport/escort service, 24-hour emergency telephone alarm devices, 24-hour patrols by trained security personnel, and electronically operated dormitory entrances.

Applying

LSU requires SAT or ACT, a high school transcript, minimum ACT score of 22 or SAT score of 1030 and a minimum SAT reading score of 430 (ACT 18) and minimum SAT math score of 450 (ACT 19), and a minimum high school GPA of 3.0, and in some cases an essay and an interview. Application deadline: 4/15; 3/1 priority date for financial aid. Early and deferred admission are possible.

LOYOLA COLLEGE IN MARYLAND

URBAN SETTING ■ PRIVATE ■ INDEPENDENT RELIGIOUS ■ COED
BALTIMORE, MARYLAND

Web site: www.loyola.edu
Contact: 4501 North Charles Street, Baltimore, MD 21210
Telephone: 410-617-2251 or toll-free 800-221-9107 Ext. 2252 (in-state)
Fax: 410-617-2176

SPONSOR

Academics

Loyola awards bachelor's, master's, and doctoral **degrees** and post-master's certificates. **Challenging opportunities** include advanced placement credit, accelerated degree programs, an honors program, double majors, independent study, and a senior project. Special programs include internships, summer session for credit, off-campus study, study-abroad, and Army and Air Force ROTC.

The most frequently chosen **baccalaureate** fields are business/marketing, communications/journalism, and social sciences. A complete listing of majors at Loyola appears in the Majors by College index beginning on page 469.

The **faculty** at Loyola has 334 full-time members, 79% with terminal degrees. The student-faculty ratio is 12:1.

Students of Loyola

The student body totals 6,080, of whom 3,716 are undergraduates. 58.4% are women and 41.6% are men. 19% are from Maryland. 0.8% are international students. 4.3% are African American, 0.2% American Indian, 3.4% Asian American, and 3.8% Hispanic American. 91% returned for their sophomore year.

Facilities and Resources

Students can access the following: campus intranet, computer help desk, free student e-mail accounts, online (class) grades, online (class) registration, online (class) schedules. Campuswide network is available. 100% of college-owned or -operated housing units are wired for high-speed Internet access. Wireless service is available via entire campus. The **library** has 293,639 books and 2,126 subscriptions.

Campus Life

There are 172 active organizations on campus, including a drama/theater group, newspaper, radio station, and choral group. No national or local **fraternities** or **sororities**.

Loyola is a member of the NCAA (Division I). **Intercollegiate sports** (some offering scholarships) include basketball, crew, cross-country running, golf (m), lacrosse, soccer, swimming and diving, tennis, track and field, volleyball (w).

Campus Safety

Student safety services include late-night transport/escort service, 24-hour emergency telephone alarm devices, 24-hour patrols by trained security personnel, and electronically operated dormitory entrances.

Applying

Loyola requires an essay, SAT or ACT, and a high school transcript. Application deadline: 1/15, 1/15 for nonresidents; 2/15 for financial aid. Early and deferred admission are possible.

Traditional academic standards are central to Jesuit education. Loyola's curriculum is rigorous, and the faculty's expectations for students are high. The aim is to challenge students and to try to develop their skills and abilities. Hard work is required for a good education, and Loyola is interested in admitting students who have been ambitious in their course selection in high school and who have shown that they can do well in academic work.

Getting Accepted
7,623 applied
69% were accepted
1,068 enrolled (20% of accepted)
30% from top tenth of their h.s. class
3.46 average high school GPA
47% had SAT critical reading scores over 600
53% had SAT math scores over 600
77% had ACT scores over 24
7% had SAT critical reading scores over 700
9% had SAT math scores over 700
13% had ACT scores over 30

Graduation and After
77% graduated in 4 years
5% graduated in 5 years
1% graduated in 6 years
62% had job offers within 6 months
150 organizations recruited on campus

Financial Matters
$36,240 tuition and fees (2008–09)
$7790 room only
96% average percent of need met
$23,705 average financial aid amount received per undergraduate (2007–08 estimated)

Loyola Marymount University

Suburban setting ■ Private ■ Independent Religious ■ Coed
Los Angeles, California

Web site: www.lmu.edu
Contact: Mr. Matthew Fissinger, Director of Admissions, 1 LMU Drive Suite 100, Los Angeles, CA 90045-8350
Telephone: 310-338-2750 or toll-free 800-LMU-INFO
E-mail: admissions@lmu.edu

Getting Accepted
9,086 applied
50% were accepted
1,261 enrolled (28% of accepted)
33% from top tenth of their h.s. class
3.66 average high school GPA
Mean SAT critical reading score: 582
Mean SAT math score: 591
Mean ACT score: 26
41% had SAT critical reading scores over 600
48% had SAT math scores over 600
73% had ACT scores over 24
6% had SAT critical reading scores over 700
7% had SAT math scores over 700
14% had ACT scores over 30

Graduation and After
71% graduated in 4 years
7% graduated in 5 years
2% graduated in 6 years
60% had job offers within 6 months
305 organizations recruited on campus

Financial Matters
$34,462 tuition and fees (2008–09)
$11,810 room and board
80% average percent of need met
$14,617 average financial aid amount received per undergraduate (2007–08 estimated)

Academics

Loyola Marymount awards bachelor's, master's, doctoral, and first-professional **degrees** and post-bachelor's, post-master's, and first-professional certificates. **Challenging opportunities** include advanced placement credit, accelerated degree programs, student-designed majors, an honors program, double majors, independent study, and a senior project. Special programs include cooperative education, internships, summer session for credit, study-abroad, and Army and Air Force ROTC.

The most frequently chosen **baccalaureate** fields are business/marketing, visual and performing arts, and social sciences. A complete listing of majors at Loyola Marymount appears in the Majors by College index beginning on page 469.

The **faculty** at Loyola Marymount has 498 full-time members, 100% with terminal degrees. The student-faculty ratio is 11:1.

Students of Loyola Marymount

The student body totals 9,011, of whom 5,676 are undergraduates. 56.7% are women and 43.3% are men. Students come from 52 states and territories and 33 other countries. 75% are from California. 2.3% are international students. 8.2% are African American, 0.6% American Indian, 12.3% Asian American, and 20.2% Hispanic American. 88% returned for their sophomore year.

Facilities and Resources

56 **computers/terminals** are available on campus for general student use. Students can access the following: campus intranet, computer help desk, free student e-mail accounts, online (class) grades, online (class) registration, online (class) schedules. Campuswide network is available. 100% of college-owned or -operated housing units are wired for high-speed Internet access. Wireless service is available via entire campus. The **library** has 566,000 books and 19,500 subscriptions.

Campus Life

There are 146 active organizations on campus, including a drama/theater group, newspaper, radio station, television station, and choral group. 13% of eligible men and 23% of eligible women are members of national **fraternities** and national **sororities**.

Loyola Marymount is a member of the NCAA (Division I). **Intercollegiate sports** (some offering scholarships) include baseball (m), basketball, cheerleading, crew, cross-country running, golf (m), soccer, softball (w), swimming and diving (w), tennis, track and field, volleyball (w), water polo.

Campus Safety

Student safety services include late-night transport/escort service, 24-hour emergency telephone alarm devices, 24-hour patrols by trained security personnel, and electronically operated dormitory entrances.

Applying

Loyola Marymount requires an essay, SAT or ACT, a high school transcript, and 2 recommendations. It recommends an interview. Application deadline: 1/15; 7/30 for financial aid, with a 2/15 priority date. Early and deferred admission are possible.

LOYOLA UNIVERSITY CHICAGO

URBAN SETTING ■ PRIVATE ■ INDEPENDENT RELIGIOUS ■ COED
CHICAGO, ILLINOIS

Web site: www.luc.edu
Contact: 820 North Michigan Avenue, Suite 613, Chicago, IL 60611-9810
Telephone: 773-508-3075 or toll-free 800-262-2373
Fax: 312-915-7216
E-mail: admission@luc.edu

Academics

Loyola Chicago awards bachelor's, master's, doctoral, and first-professional **degrees** and post-bachelor's and post-master's certificates (also offers adult part-time program with significant enrollment not reflected in profile). **Challenging opportunities** include advanced placement credit, accelerated degree programs, an honors program, double majors, independent study, and a senior project. Special programs include internships, summer session for credit, off-campus study, study-abroad, and Army, Navy, and Air Force ROTC.

The most frequently chosen **baccalaureate** fields are business/marketing, social sciences, and health professions and related sciences. A complete listing of majors at Loyola Chicago appears in the Majors by College index beginning on page 469.

The **faculty** at Loyola Chicago has 597 full-time members, 97% with terminal degrees. The student-faculty ratio is 15:1.

Students of Loyola Chicago

The student body totals 15,670, of whom 10,124 are undergraduates. 64.5% are women and 35.5% are men. Students come from 50 states and territories and 96 other countries. 65% are from Illinois. 1% are international students. 4.5% are African American, 0.2% American Indian, 11.8% Asian American, and 9.8% Hispanic American. 84% returned for their sophomore year.

Facilities and Resources

800 **computers/terminals** are available on campus for general student use. Students can access the following: campus intranet, computer help desk, free student e-mail accounts, online (class) grades, online (class) registration, online (class) schedules. Campuswide network is available. 43% of college-owned or -operated housing units are wired for high-speed Internet access. Wireless service is available via entire campus. The 8 **libraries** have 1,366,338 books and 50,531 subscriptions.

Campus Life

There are 160 active organizations on campus, including a drama/theater group, newspaper, radio station, and choral group. 3% of eligible men and 6% of eligible women are members of national **fraternities** and national **sororities**.

Loyola Chicago is a member of the NCAA (Division I). **Intercollegiate sports** (some offering scholarships) include basketball, cheerleading, cross-country running, golf, soccer, softball (w), track and field, volleyball.

Campus Safety

Student safety services include late-night transport/escort service, 24-hour emergency telephone alarm devices, 24-hour patrols by trained security personnel, and electronically operated dormitory entrances.

Applying

Loyola Chicago requires an essay, SAT or ACT, a high school transcript, and a minimum high school GPA of 2.0. It recommends an interview. Application deadline: 4/1.

Getting Accepted
17,287 applied
74% were accepted
2,176 enrolled (17% of accepted)
34% from top tenth of their h.s. class
3.57 average high school GPA
Mean SAT critical reading score: 596
Mean SAT math score: 582
Mean SAT writing score: 583
Mean ACT score: 26
51% had SAT critical reading scores over 600
42% had SAT math scores over 600
42% had SAT writing scores over 600
79% had ACT scores over 24
10% had SAT critical reading scores over 700
6% had SAT math scores over 700
7% had SAT writing scores over 700
19% had ACT scores over 30
19 National Merit Scholars
42 valedictorians

Graduation and After
51% graduated in 4 years
13% graduated in 5 years
3% graduated in 6 years
467 organizations recruited on campus

Financial Matters
$30,656 tuition and fees (2009–10)
$10,885 room and board
83% average percent of need met
$24,221 average financial aid amount received per undergraduate (2007–08 estimated)

Loyola University New Orleans

Urban setting ■ Private ■ Independent Religious ■ Coed
New Orleans, Louisiana

Web site: www.loyno.edu
Contact: 6363 Saint Charles Avenue, Box 18, New Orleans, LA 70118-6195
Telephone: 504-865-3240 or toll-free 800-4-LOYOLA
Fax: 504-865-3383
E-mail: liberto@loyno.edu

Loyola's unique combination of high-quality academic programs and outstanding faculty members, an ideal size that fosters a positive learning environment and individual attention, and the centuries-old Jesuit tradition of educating the whole person distinguishes it from other institutions. Loyola provides big-school experiences with small-school relationships. The University consistently ranks among the top regional colleges and universities in the South and is one of the top sixty in the U.S. Loyola's students have been awarded British Marshall, Fulbright, Goldwater, Mellon, Mitchell, and Rhodes scholarships and have been included as *USA Today's* top students. A unique and expanded service-learning program offers Loyola students the opportunity to become engaged in the creation of a city and a region while strengthening their professional skills at the same time. Loyola students are actively involved in restoring local and national businesses, researching environmental impacts along the Gulf Coast, documenting oral histories, and exploring the importance of musical origins. Now more than ever, Loyola's students are offered an education like no other in the United States.

Getting Accepted
3,651 applied
63% were accepted
700 enrolled (30% of accepted)
30% from top tenth of their h.s. class
3.74 average high school GPA
46% had SAT critical reading scores over 600
46% had SAT math scores over 600
70% had ACT scores over 24
6% had SAT critical reading scores over 700
6% had SAT math scores over 700
13% had ACT scores over 30
11 valedictorians

Graduation and After
57% graduated in 4 years
9% graduated in 5 years
2% graduated in 6 years
61.7% had job offers within 6 months
225 organizations recruited on campus

Financial Matters
$29,706 tuition and fees (2009–10)
$9826 room and board
83% average percent of need met
$22,253 average financial aid amount received per undergraduate (2007–08 estimated)

Academics

Loyola New Orleans awards bachelor's, master's, and first-professional **degrees** and post-bachelor's, post-master's, and first-professional certificates. **Challenging opportunities** include advanced placement credit, accelerated degree programs, student-designed majors, an honors program, double majors, independent study, and a senior project. Special programs include internships, summer session for credit, off-campus study, study-abroad, and Army, Navy, and Air Force ROTC.

The most frequently chosen **baccalaureate** fields are business/marketing, communications/journalism, and social sciences. A complete listing of majors at Loyola New Orleans appears in the Majors by College index beginning on page 469.

The **faculty** at Loyola New Orleans has 255 full-time members, 91% with terminal degrees. The student-faculty ratio is 11:1.

Students of Loyola New Orleans

The student body totals 4,474, of whom 2,658 are undergraduates. 57% are women and 43% are men. Students come from 48 states and territories and 33 other countries. 51% are from Louisiana. 2.8% are international students. 13% are African American, 0.7% American Indian, 4.3% Asian American, and 11.3% Hispanic American. 73% returned for their sophomore year.

Facilities and Resources

525 **computers/terminals** and 2,500 ports are available on campus for general student use. Students can access the following: campus intranet, computer help desk, free student e-mail accounts, online (class) grades, online (class) registration, online (class) schedules. Campuswide network is available. 100% of college-owned or -operated housing units are wired for high-speed Internet access. Wireless service is available via entire campus. The 2 **libraries** have 612,163 books and 40,662 subscriptions.

Campus Life

There are 140 active organizations on campus, including a drama/theater group, newspaper, radio station, and choral group. 9% of eligible men and 13% of eligible women are members of national **fraternities**, national **sororities**, and local fraternities.

Loyola New Orleans is a member of the NAIA. **Intercollegiate sports** (some offering scholarships) include baseball (m), basketball, cross-country running, racquetball, soccer, softball, swimming and diving, track and field, volleyball (w).

Campus Safety

Student safety services include self-defense education, bicycle patrols, closed circuit TV monitors, door alarms, crime prevention programs, late-night transport/escort service, 24-hour emergency telephone alarm devices, 24-hour patrols by trained security personnel, and electronically operated dormitory entrances.

Applying

Loyola New Orleans requires an essay, SAT or ACT, a high school transcript, and 1 recommendation, and in some cases an interview. It recommends an interview. Application deadline: rolling admissions; 6/1 for financial aid, with a 2/15 priority date. Early admission is possible.

Luther College

SMALL-TOWN SETTING ■ PRIVATE ■ INDEPENDENT RELIGIOUS ■ COED
DECORAH, IOWA

Web site: www.luther.edu
Contact: Kirk Neubauer, Director of Recruiting Services, 700 College Drive, Decorah, IA 52101
Telephone: 563-387-1287 or toll-free 800-458-8437
Fax: 563-387-2159
E-mail: admissions@luther.edu

Academics

Luther awards bachelor's **degrees**. **Challenging opportunities** include advanced placement credit, student-designed majors, an honors program, double majors, independent study, and a senior project. Special programs include internships, summer session for credit, off-campus study, and study-abroad.

The most frequently chosen **baccalaureate** fields are visual and performing arts, business/marketing, and social sciences. A complete listing of majors at Luther appears in the Majors by College index beginning on page 469.

The **faculty** at Luther has 178 full-time members, 90% with terminal degrees. The student-faculty ratio is 12:1.

Students of Luther

The student body is made up of 2,423 undergraduates. 57.7% are women and 42.3% are men. Students come from 40 states and territories and 44 other countries. 35% are from Iowa. 4.1% are international students. 1.1% are African American, 0.1% American Indian, 2.1% Asian American, and 1.9% Hispanic American. 85% returned for their sophomore year.

Facilities and Resources

500 **computers/terminals** are available on campus for general student use. Students can access the following: campus intranet, computer help desk, free student e-mail accounts, online (class) grades, online (class) registration, online (class) schedules. Campuswide network is available. 100% of college-owned or -operated housing units are wired for high-speed Internet access. Wireless service is available via entire campus. The **library** has 327,019 books and 831 subscriptions.

Campus Life

There are 139 active organizations on campus, including a drama/theater group, newspaper, radio station, and choral group. 3% of eligible men and 4% of eligible women are members of local **fraternities** and local **sororities**.

Luther is a member of the NCAA (Division III). **Intercollegiate sports** include baseball (m), basketball, cross-country running, football (m), golf, soccer, softball (w), swimming and diving, tennis, track and field, volleyball (w), wrestling (m).

Campus Safety

Student safety services include late-night transport/escort service, 24-hour emergency telephone alarm devices, 24-hour patrols by trained security personnel, and electronically operated dormitory entrances.

Applying

Luther requires an essay, SAT or ACT, a high school transcript, and 1 recommendation. It recommends an interview. Application deadline: 3/1 priority date for financial aid. Deferred admission is possible.

Getting Accepted

2,053 applied
80% were accepted
630 enrolled (38% of accepted)
39% from top tenth of their h.s. class
3.66 average high school GPA
Mean SAT critical reading score: 564
Mean SAT math score: 587
Mean SAT writing score: 565
Mean ACT score: 26
40% had SAT critical reading scores over 600
48% had SAT math scores over 600
41% had SAT writing scores over 600
73% had ACT scores over 24
7% had SAT critical reading scores over 700
14% had SAT math scores over 700
9% had SAT writing scores over 700
20% had ACT scores over 30
10 National Merit Scholars
51 valedictorians

Graduation and After

61% graduated in 4 years
10% graduated in 5 years
1% graduated in 6 years
98% had job offers within 6 months
212 organizations recruited on campus

Financial Matters

$32,290 tuition and fees (2009–10)
$5380 room and board
88% average percent of need met
$22,935 average financial aid amount received per undergraduate (2007–08 estimated)

Lycoming College

SMALL-TOWN SETTING ■ PRIVATE ■ INDEPENDENT RELIGIOUS ■ COED
WILLIAMSPORT, PENNSYLVANIA

Web site: www.lycoming.edu
Contact: Mr. James Spencer, Vice President of Admissions and Financial Aid,
    700 College Place, Williamsport, PA 17701
Telephone: 570-321-4026 or toll-free 800-345-3920 Ext. 4026
Fax: 570-321-4317
E-mail: admissions@lycoming.edu

Getting Accepted
1,601 applied
69% were accepted
19% from top tenth of their h.s. class
Mean SAT critical reading score: 528
Mean SAT math score: 524
Mean SAT writing score: 515
Mean ACT score: 24
22% had SAT critical reading scores over 600
19% had SAT math scores over 600
19% had SAT writing scores over 600
51% had ACT scores over 24
3% had SAT critical reading scores over 700
1% had SAT math scores over 700
2% had SAT writing scores over 700
7% had ACT scores over 30
12 class presidents
6 valedictorians

Graduation and After
61% graduated in 4 years
8% graduated in 5 years
98% had job offers within 6 months
40 organizations recruited on campus

Financial Matters
$28,784 tuition and fees (2008–09)
$7672 room and board
79% average percent of need met
$20,288 average financial aid amount received
    per undergraduate (2007–08 estimated)

Academics
Lycoming awards bachelor's **degrees**. **Challenging opportunities** include advanced placement credit, accelerated degree programs, student-designed majors, an honors program, double majors, independent study, and a senior project. Special programs include internships, summer session for credit, off-campus study, study-abroad, and Army ROTC.

The most frequently chosen **baccalaureate** fields are social sciences, business/marketing, and psychology. A complete listing of majors at Lycoming appears in the Majors by College index beginning on page 469.

The **faculty** at Lycoming has 82 full-time members. The student-faculty ratio is 14:1.

Students of Lycoming
The student body is made up of 1,431 undergraduates. Students come from 28 states and territories and 7 other countries. 65% are from Pennsylvania. 1.1% are international students. 2.8% are African American, 0.3% American Indian, 0.7% Asian American, and 1.9% Hispanic American. 79% returned for their sophomore year.

Facilities and Resources
140 **computers/terminals** are available on campus for general student use. Students can access the following: campus intranet, computer help desk, free student e-mail accounts, online (class) grades, online (class) registration, online (class) schedules. Campuswide network is available. 100% of college-owned or -operated housing units are wired for high-speed Internet access. Wireless service is available via entire campus. The 2 **libraries** have 210,617 books and 4,347 subscriptions.

Campus Life
There are 76 active organizations on campus, including a drama/theater group, newspaper, radio station, and choral group. 14% of eligible men and 17% of eligible women are members of national **fraternities**, national **sororities**, and local sororities.

Lycoming is a member of the NCAA (Division III). **Intercollegiate sports** include basketball, cross-country running, football (m), golf, lacrosse, soccer, softball (w), swimming and diving, tennis, volleyball (w), wrestling (m).

Campus Safety
Student safety services include late-night transport/escort service, 24-hour emergency telephone alarm devices, 24-hour patrols by trained security personnel, student patrols, and electronically operated dormitory entrances.

Applying
Lycoming requires an essay, SAT or ACT, a high school transcript, and 2 recommendations. It recommends an interview and a minimum high school GPA of 2.3. Application deadline: 5/1; 3/1 priority date for financial aid. Deferred admission is possible.

Lyon College

SMALL-TOWN SETTING ■ PRIVATE ■ INDEPENDENT RELIGIOUS ■ COED
BATESVILLE, ARKANSAS

Web site: www.lyon.edu
Contact: PO Box 2317, Batesville, AR 72503-2317
Telephone: 870-307-7250 or toll-free 800-423-2542
Fax: 870-793-1791
E-mail: admissions@lyon.edu

Academics

Lyon awards bachelor's **degrees**. **Challenging opportunities** include advanced placement credit, accelerated degree programs, student-designed majors, double majors, independent study, and a senior project. Special programs include internships, summer session for credit, and study-abroad.

The most frequently chosen **baccalaureate** fields are business/marketing, social sciences, and biological/life sciences. A complete listing of majors at Lyon appears in the Majors by College index beginning on page 469.

The **faculty** at Lyon has 44 full-time members, 93% with terminal degrees. The student-faculty ratio is 9:1.

Students of Lyon

The student body is made up of 458 undergraduates. 54.4% are women and 45.6% are men. Students come from 23 states and territories and 5 other countries. 70% are from Arkansas. 1.3% are international students. 3.7% are African American, 2% American Indian, 1.3% Asian American, and 2.2% Hispanic American. 70% returned for their sophomore year.

Facilities and Resources

101 **computers/terminals** are available on campus for general student use. Students can access the following: campus intranet, computer help desk, free student e-mail accounts, online (class) grades, online (class) registration, online (class) schedules. Campuswide network is available. 100% of college-owned or -operated housing units are wired for high-speed Internet access. Wireless service is available via entire campus. The **library** has 203,257 books and 434 subscriptions.

Campus Life

There are 44 active organizations on campus, including a drama/theater group, newspaper, and choral group. 12% of eligible men and 14% of eligible women are members of national **fraternities** and national **sororities**.

Lyon is a member of the NAIA. **Intercollegiate sports** (some offering scholarships) include baseball (m), basketball, cross-country running, golf, soccer, softball (w), volleyball (w).

Campus Safety

Student safety services include late-night transport/escort service and 24-hour patrols by trained security personnel.

Applying

Lyon requires SAT or ACT, a high school transcript, and a minimum high school GPA of 2.5, and in some cases an essay and 2 recommendations. Application deadline: rolling admissions; 3/15 priority date for financial aid. Early and deferred admission are possible.

Getting Accepted

847 applied
67% were accepted
109 enrolled (19% of accepted)
27% from top tenth of their h.s. class
3.54 average high school GPA
Mean SAT critical reading score: 569
Mean SAT math score: 570
Mean ACT score: 25
46% had SAT critical reading scores over 600
41% had SAT math scores over 600
55% had ACT scores over 24
5% had SAT math scores over 700
12% had ACT scores over 30
4 valedictorians

Graduation and After

56% graduated in 4 years
5% graduated in 5 years
3% graduated in 6 years
35% had job offers within 6 months
34 organizations recruited on campus

Financial Matters

$19,034 tuition and fees (2008–09)
$6990 room and board
80% average percent of need met
$14,548 average financial aid amount received per undergraduate (2007–08 estimated)

MACALESTER COLLEGE

URBAN SETTING ■ PRIVATE ■ INDEPENDENT RELIGIOUS ■ COED
ST. PAUL, MINNESOTA

Web site: www.macalester.edu
Contact: Mr. Lorne T. Robinson, Dean of Admissions and Financial Aid,
1600 Grand Avenue, St. Paul, MN 55105-1899
Telephone: 651-696-6357 or toll-free 800-231-7974
Fax: 651-696-6724
E-mail: admissions@macalester.edu

Getting Accepted

4,967 applied
41% were accepted
485 enrolled (24% of accepted)
68% from top tenth of their h.s. class
Mean SAT critical reading score: 681
Mean SAT math score: 662
Mean SAT writing score: 663
Mean ACT score: 30
87% had SAT critical reading scores over 600
85% had SAT math scores over 600
83% had SAT writing scores over 600
96% had ACT scores over 24
47% had SAT critical reading scores over 700
31% had SAT math scores over 700
37% had SAT writing scores over 700
55% had ACT scores over 30
39 National Merit Scholars
45 valedictorians

Graduation and After

83% graduated in 4 years
4% graduated in 5 years
64% had job offers within 6 months
100 organizations recruited on campus

Financial Matters

$36,704 tuition and fees (2008–09)
$8472 room and board
100% average percent of need met
$28,508 average financial aid amount received
per undergraduate (2007–08 estimated)

Academics

Macalester awards bachelor's **degrees**. **Challenging opportunities** include student-designed majors, an honors program, double majors, independent study, and a senior project. Special programs include internships, off-campus study, study-abroad, and Navy and Air Force ROTC.

The most frequently chosen **baccalaureate** fields are social sciences, foreign languages and literature, and interdisciplinary studies. A complete listing of majors at Macalester appears in the Majors by College index beginning on page 469.

The **faculty** at Macalester has 157 full-time members, 94% with terminal degrees. The student-faculty ratio is 10:1.

Students of Macalester

The student body is made up of 1,920 undergraduates. 57.7% are women and 42.3% are men. Students come from 53 states and territories and 87 other countries. 22% are from Minnesota. 12.4% are international students. 4.6% are African American, 0.9% American Indian, 8.8% Asian American, and 3.8% Hispanic American. 94% returned for their sophomore year.

Facilities and Resources

400 **computers/terminals** and 2,500 ports are available on campus for general student use. Students can access the following: campus intranet, computer help desk, free student e-mail accounts, online (class) registration, online (class) schedules, Web space. Campuswide network is available. 100% of college-owned or -operated housing units are wired for high-speed Internet access. Wireless service is available via entire campus. The **library** has 448,968 books and 3,559 subscriptions.

Campus Life

There are 80 active organizations on campus, including a drama/theater group, newspaper, radio station, and choral group. No national or local **fraternities** or **sororities**.

Macalester is a member of the NCAA (Division III). **Intercollegiate sports** include baseball (m), basketball, cross-country running, football (m), golf, soccer, softball (w), swimming and diving, tennis, track and field, volleyball (w), water polo (w).

Campus Safety

Student safety services include late-night transport/escort service, 24-hour emergency telephone alarm devices, 24-hour patrols by trained security personnel, and electronically operated dormitory entrances.

Applying

Macalester requires an essay, SAT or ACT, a high school transcript, and 3 recommendations. It recommends an interview. Application deadline: 1/15; 2/8 priority date for financial aid. Early and deferred admission are possible.

MAHARISHI UNIVERSITY OF MANAGEMENT

SMALL-TOWN SETTING ■ PRIVATE ■ INDEPENDENT ■ COED
FAIRFIELD, IOWA

Web site: www.mum.edu
Contact: Ms. Barbara Rainbow, Associate Dean of Admissions, Office of
  Admissions, Fairfield, IA 52557
Telephone: 641-472-1110 or toll-free 800-369-6480
Fax: 641-472-1179
E-mail: admissions@mum.edu

Academics

MUM awards bachelor's, master's, and doctoral **degrees** and post-bachelor's certificates.
Challenging opportunities include advanced placement credit, student-designed
majors, an honors program, double majors, independent study, and a senior project.
Special programs include cooperative education, internships, and study-abroad.

The most frequently chosen **baccalaureate** fields are liberal arts/general studies,
natural resources/environmental science, and visual and performing arts. A complete
listing of majors at MUM appears in the Majors by College index beginning on page
469.

The **faculty** at MUM has 49 full-time members, 100% with terminal degrees. The
student-faculty ratio is 16:1.

Students of MUM

The student body totals 948, of whom 204 are undergraduates. 43.1% are women and
56.9% are men. Students come from 38 states and territories and 72 other countries.
47% are from Iowa. 17.1% are international students. 2% are African American, 3.5%
Asian American, and 6.5% Hispanic American. 61% returned for their sophomore year.

Facilities and Resources

20 **computers/terminals** are available on campus for general student use. Students can
access the following: campus intranet, computer help desk, free student e-mail accounts,
online (class) grades, online (class) schedules. Campuswide network is available. 100% of
college-owned or -operated housing units are wired for high-speed Internet access. The
library has 137,775 books and 11,146 subscriptions.

Campus Life

There are 15 active organizations on campus, including a drama/theater group,
newspaper, radio station, and choral group. No national or local **fraternities** or **sororities**.

This institution has no intercollegiate sports.

Campus Safety

Student safety services include late-night transport/escort service, 24-hour emergency
telephone alarm devices, 24-hour patrols by trained security personnel, and electronically operated dormitory entrances.

Applying

MUM requires an essay, a high school transcript, 2 recommendations, minimum SAT
score of 950 or ACT score of 19, and a minimum high school GPA of 2.5. It recommends SAT or ACT and an interview. Application deadline: 8/1. Early and deferred
admission are possible.

Getting Accepted
126 applied
41% were accepted
45 enrolled (87% of accepted)
1 National Merit Scholar

Graduation and After
41% graduated in 4 years
4% graduated in 5 years
75% had job offers within 6 months
20 organizations recruited on campus

Financial Matters
$24,430 tuition and fees (2008–09)
$6000 room and board
89% average percent of need met
$23,963 average financial aid amount received
  per undergraduate (2006–07)

Marietta College
Small-town setting ■ Private ■ Independent ■ Coed
Marietta, Ohio

Web site: www.marietta.edu
Contact: Mr. Jason Turley, Director of Admission, 215 Fifth Street, Marietta, OH 45750
Telephone: 740-376-4600 or toll-free 800-331-7896
Fax: 740-376-8888
E-mail: admit@marietta.edu

Academics
Marietta awards associate, bachelor's, and master's **degrees. Challenging opportunities** include advanced placement credit, accelerated degree programs, student-designed majors, an honors program, double majors, independent study, and a senior project. Special programs include internships, summer session for credit, off-campus study, and study-abroad.

The most frequently chosen **baccalaureate** fields are business/marketing, communications/journalism, and visual and performing arts. A complete listing of majors at Marietta appears in the Majors by College index beginning on page 469.

The **faculty** at Marietta has 103 full-time members, 80% with terminal degrees. The student-faculty ratio is 13:1.

Students of Marietta
The student body totals 1,602, of whom 1,485 are undergraduates. 50.2% are women and 49.8% are men. Students come from 29 states and territories and 18 other countries. 67% are from Ohio. 9.1% are international students. 3.5% are African American, 0.4% American Indian, 1.2% Asian American, and 1.5% Hispanic American. 73% returned for their sophomore year.

Facilities and Resources
350 **computers/terminals** are available on campus for general student use. Students can access the following: campus intranet, computer help desk, free student e-mail accounts, online (class) grades, online (class) registration, online (class) schedules. Campuswide network is available. 100% of college-owned or -operated housing units are wired for high-speed Internet access. Wireless service is available via classrooms, computer centers, computer labs, dorm rooms, learning centers, libraries, student centers. The **library** has 246,706 books and 28,188 subscriptions.

Campus Life
There are 100 active organizations on campus, including a drama/theater group, newspaper, radio station, television station, and choral group. 15% of eligible men and 23% of eligible women are members of national **fraternities** and national **sororities**.

Marietta is a member of the NCAA (Division III). **Intercollegiate sports** include baseball (m), basketball, crew, cross-country running, football (m), soccer, softball (w), tennis, track and field, volleyball (w).

Campus Safety
Student safety services include late-night transport/escort service, 24-hour emergency telephone alarm devices, 24-hour patrols by trained security personnel, student patrols, and electronically operated dormitory entrances.

Applying
Marietta requires an essay, SAT or ACT, a high school transcript, 1 recommendation, and a minimum high school GPA of 2.0. It recommends SAT Subject Tests, an interview, and a minimum high school GPA of 3.0. Application deadline: 5/1; 3/1 priority date for financial aid. Early and deferred admission are possible.

Founded in 1788, Marietta, Ohio, has the distinction of being the first permanent settlement of America's Northwest Territory. The College traces its beginning to 1797. Both the city and the College are rich in history, with stately homes, brick-paved streets, and antique stores. In 1860, Marietta College became only the sixteenth college in America to be awarded a chapter of Phi Beta Kappa. Students' academic life is enriched by the McDonough Leadership Program, the most comprehensive program in leadership studies in the country, whereby students may earn a minor, be actively involved in volunteer work, and participate in internships throughout the world.

Getting Accepted
2,440 applied
77% were accepted
385 enrolled (20% of accepted)
27% from top tenth of their h.s. class
3.41 average high school GPA
Mean SAT critical reading score: 544
Mean SAT math score: 538
Mean ACT score: 24
29% had SAT critical reading scores over 600
36% had SAT math scores over 600
48% had ACT scores over 24
1% had SAT critical reading scores over 700
4% had SAT math scores over 700
6% had ACT scores over 30

Graduation and After
49% graduated in 4 years
13% graduated in 5 years
3% graduated in 6 years
75% had job offers within 6 months
70 organizations recruited on campus

Financial Matters
$26,080 tuition and fees (2008–09)
$7764 room and board
93% average percent of need met
$22,222 average financial aid amount received per undergraduate (2007–08 estimated)

MARIST COLLEGE
SMALL-TOWN SETTING ■ PRIVATE ■ INDEPENDENT ■ COED
POUGHKEEPSIE, NEW YORK

Web site: www.marist.edu
Contact: Mr. Kenton Rinehart, Dean of Undergraduate Admissions, 3399 North Road, Poughkeepsie, NY 12601
Telephone: 845-575-3226 or toll-free 800-436-5483
Fax: 845-575-3215
E-mail: admission@marist.edu

Academics
Marist awards bachelor's and master's **degrees** and post-bachelor's certificates. **Challenging opportunities** include advanced placement credit, accelerated degree programs, an honors program, double majors, independent study, and a senior project. Special programs include cooperative education, internships, summer session for credit, off-campus study, study-abroad, and Army ROTC.

The most frequently chosen **baccalaureate** fields are business/marketing, communications/journalism, and education. A complete listing of majors at Marist appears in the Majors by College index beginning on page 469.

The **faculty** at Marist has 218 full-time members, 78% with terminal degrees. The student-faculty ratio is 15:1.

Students of Marist
The student body totals 5,727, of whom 4,851 are undergraduates. 57.3% are women and 42.7% are men. Students come from 39 states and territories and 9 other countries. 59% are from New York. 0.3% are international students. 3.3% are African American, 0.2% American Indian, 2.4% Asian American, and 5.3% Hispanic American. 91% returned for their sophomore year.

Facilities and Resources
646 **computers/terminals** and 1,000 ports are available on campus for general student use. Students can access the following: campus intranet, computer help desk, free student e-mail accounts, online (class) grades, online (class) registration, online (class) schedules, admissions application, billing, transcript, degree audit, online financial aid summary, online library database search. Campuswide network is available. 100% of college-owned or -operated housing units are wired for high-speed Internet access. Wireless service is available via entire campus. The **library** has 197,209 books and 22,755 subscriptions.

Campus Life
There are 84 active organizations on campus, including a drama/theater group, newspaper, radio station, television station, choral group, and marching band. 1% of eligible men and 3% of eligible women are members of national **fraternities** and local **sororities**.

Marist is a member of the NCAA (Division I). **Intercollegiate sports** (some offering scholarships) include baseball (m), basketball, crew, cross-country running, football (m), lacrosse, soccer, softball (w), swimming and diving, tennis, track and field, volleyball (w), water polo (w).

Campus Safety
Student safety services include night residence hall monitors, late-night transport/escort service, 24-hour emergency telephone alarm devices, 24-hour patrols by trained security personnel, student patrols, and electronically operated dormitory entrances.

Applying
Marist requires an essay, SAT or ACT, a high school transcript, and 2 recommendations. Application deadline: 2/15; 5/1 for financial aid, with a 2/15 priority date. Early and deferred admission are possible.

Getting Accepted
8,328 applied
42% were accepted
1,019 enrolled (29% of accepted)
29% from top tenth of their h.s. class
3.3 average high school GPA
Mean SAT critical reading score: 580
Mean SAT math score: 580
Mean SAT writing score: 570
Mean ACT score: 25
36% had SAT critical reading scores over 600
42% had SAT math scores over 600
36% had SAT writing scores over 600
60% had ACT scores over 24
2% had SAT critical reading scores over 700
5% had SAT math scores over 700
2% had SAT writing scores over 700
9% had ACT scores over 30
17 class presidents
4 valedictorians

Graduation and After
70% graduated in 4 years
9% graduated in 5 years
1% graduated in 6 years
84% had job offers within 6 months
227 organizations recruited on campus

Financial Matters
$25,596 tuition and fees (2008–09)
$10,730 room and board
67% average percent of need met
$19,790 average financial aid amount received per undergraduate (2007–08 estimated)

MARLBORO COLLEGE

RURAL SETTING ■ PRIVATE ■ INDEPENDENT ■ COED
MARLBORO, VERMONT

Web site: www.marlboro.edu
Contact: Ms. Amy VanTassel, Associate Director of Admission, PO Box A, South Road, Marlboro, VT 05344-0300
Telephone: toll-free 800-343-0049
Fax: 800-451-7555
E-mail: admissions@marlboro.edu

Getting Accepted
420 applied
44% were accepted
65 enrolled (35% of accepted)
3.3 average high school GPA
Mean SAT critical reading score: 648
Mean SAT math score: 558
Mean SAT writing score: 680
Mean ACT score: 26
74% had SAT critical reading scores over 600
34% had SAT math scores over 600
62% had ACT scores over 24
32% had SAT critical reading scores over 700
8% had SAT math scores over 700
24% had ACT scores over 30

Financial Matters
$32,180 tuition and fees (2008–09)
$9040 room and board
80% average percent of need met

Academics
Marlboro awards bachelor's, master's, and first-professional **degrees**. **Challenging opportunities** include advanced placement credit, accelerated degree programs, student-designed majors, double majors, independent study, and a senior project. Special programs include internships, off-campus study, and study-abroad. A complete listing of majors at Marlboro appears in the Majors by College index beginning on page 469.

The **faculty** at Marlboro has 40 full-time members, 75% with terminal degrees. The student-faculty ratio is 8:1.

Students of Marlboro
The student body totals 338, of whom 323 are undergraduates. 51.1% are women and 48.9% are men. Students come from 36 states and territories and 5 other countries. 20% are from Vermont. 1.3% are international students. 1% are African American, 0.3% American Indian, 3.5% Asian American, and 3.2% Hispanic American.

Facilities and Resources
47 **computers/terminals** are available on campus for general student use. Students can access the following: campus intranet, computer help desk, free student e-mail accounts. Campuswide network is available. Wireless service is available via classrooms, computer centers, computer labs, learning centers, libraries, student centers. The **library** has 71,000 books and 275 subscriptions.

Campus Life
There are 25 active organizations on campus, including a drama/theater group, newspaper, radio station, and choral group. No national or local **fraternities** or **sororities**.

Intercollegiate sports include rock climbing, soccer.

Campus Safety
Student safety services include 24-hour emergency telephone alarm devices.

Applying
Marlboro requires an essay, SAT or ACT, a high school transcript, 2 recommendations, and expository essay, and in some cases an interview. It recommends an interview. Application deadline: 3/1; 3/1 for financial aid. Early and deferred admission are possible.

MARQUETTE UNIVERSITY

URBAN SETTING ■ PRIVATE ■ INDEPENDENT RELIGIOUS ■ COED
MILWAUKEE, WISCONSIN

Web site: www.marquette.edu
Contact: Mr. Robert Blust, Dean of Undergraduate Admissions, PO Box 1881, Milwaukee, WI 53201-1881
Telephone: 414-288-7004 or toll-free 800-222-6544
Fax: 414-288-3764
E-mail: admissions@marquette.edu

Academics

Marquette awards bachelor's, master's, doctoral, and first-professional **degrees** and post-master's certificates. **Challenging opportunities** include advanced placement credit, an honors program, double majors, and a senior project. Special programs include cooperative education, internships, summer session for credit, off-campus study, study-abroad, and Army, Navy, and Air Force ROTC.

The most frequently chosen **baccalaureate** fields are business/marketing, communications/journalism, and social sciences. A complete listing of majors at Marquette appears in the Majors by College index beginning on page 469.

The **faculty** at Marquette has 609 full-time members, 89% with terminal degrees. The student-faculty ratio is 15:1.

Students of Marquette

The student body totals 11,516, of whom 7,955 are undergraduates. 53.7% are women and 46.3% are men. Students come from 51 states and territories and 47 other countries. 47% are from Wisconsin. 89% returned for their sophomore year.

Facilities and Resources

1,200 **computers/terminals** and 500 ports are available on campus for general student use. Students can access the following: campus intranet, computer help desk, free student e-mail accounts, online (class) grades, online (class) registration, online (class) schedules. Campuswide network is available. 100% of college-owned or -operated housing units are wired for high-speed Internet access. Wireless service is available via classrooms, computer centers, computer labs, dorm rooms, learning centers, libraries, student centers. The 2 **libraries** have 1,482,930 books and 23,039 subscriptions.

Campus Life

There are 180 active organizations on campus, including a drama/theater group, newspaper, radio station, television station, and choral group. 5% of eligible men and 7% of eligible women are members of national **fraternities** and national **sororities**.

Marquette is a member of the NCAA (Division I). **Intercollegiate sports** (some offering scholarships) include basketball, cheerleading, cross-country running, golf (m), soccer, tennis, track and field, volleyball (w).

Campus Safety

Student safety services include 24-hour desk attendants in residence halls, late-night transport/escort service, 24-hour emergency telephone alarm devices, 24-hour patrols by trained security personnel, and student patrols.

Applying

Marquette requires an essay, SAT or ACT, a high school transcript, 1 recommendation, and a minimum high school GPA of 2.5. It recommends a minimum high school GPA of 3.4. Application deadline: 12/1. Deferred admission is possible.

Getting Accepted

13,375 applied
67% were accepted
1,820 enrolled (20% of accepted)
34% from top tenth of their h.s. class
Mean SAT critical reading score: 588
Mean SAT math score: 609
Mean SAT writing score: 585
Mean ACT score: 26
44% had SAT critical reading scores over 600
60% had SAT math scores over 600
45% had SAT writing scores over 600
78% had ACT scores over 24
9% had SAT critical reading scores over 700
12% had SAT math scores over 700
8% had SAT writing scores over 700
20% had ACT scores over 30

Graduation and After

57% graduated in 4 years
17% graduated in 5 years
1% graduated in 6 years
226 organizations recruited on campus

Financial Matters

$28,128 tuition and fees (2008–09)
71% average percent of need met
$30,356 average financial aid amount received per undergraduate (2007–08 estimated)

MARYVILLE COLLEGE

SUBURBAN SETTING ■ PRIVATE ■ INDEPENDENT RELIGIOUS ■ COED
MARYVILLE, TENNESSEE

Web site: www.maryvillecollege.edu
Contact: Ms. Linda L. Moore, Administrative Assistant of Admissions, 502 East Lamar Alexander Parkway, Maryville, TN 37804-5907
Telephone: 865-981-8092 or toll-free 800-597-2687
Fax: 865-981-8005
E-mail: admissions@maryvillecollege.edu

Getting Accepted
1,621 applied
75% were accepted
297 enrolled (24% of accepted)
34% from top tenth of their h.s. class
3.59 average high school GPA
Mean SAT critical reading score: 548
Mean SAT math score: 549
Mean SAT writing score: 533
Mean ACT score: 25
39% had SAT critical reading scores over 600
36% had SAT math scores over 600
31% had SAT writing scores over 600
60% had ACT scores over 24
8% had SAT critical reading scores over 700
4% had SAT math scores over 700
5% had SAT writing scores over 700
10% had ACT scores over 30
6 valedictorians

Graduation and After
73% had job offers within 6 months
19 organizations recruited on campus

Financial Matters
$26,947 tuition and fees (2008–09)
$8240 room and board
92% average percent of need met
$20,380 average financial aid amount received per undergraduate (2005–06)

Academics

MC awards bachelor's **degrees**. **Challenging opportunities** include advanced placement credit, student-designed majors, an honors program, double majors, independent study, and a senior project. Special programs include internships, summer session for credit, off-campus study, and study-abroad.

The most frequently chosen **baccalaureate** fields are business/marketing, education, and psychology. A complete listing of majors at MC appears in the Majors by College index beginning on page 469.

The **faculty** at MC has 79 full-time members, 85% with terminal degrees. The student-faculty ratio is 12:1.

Students of MC

The student body is made up of 1,114 undergraduates. 55.5% are women and 44.5% are men. Students come from 30 states and territories and 20 other countries. 80% are from Tennessee. 4% are international students. 5.3% are African American, 0.3% American Indian, 1.1% Asian American, and 1.9% Hispanic American. 67% returned for their sophomore year.

Facilities and Resources

265 **computers/terminals** are available on campus for general student use. Students can access the following: campus intranet, computer help desk, free student e-mail accounts, online (class) registration. Campuswide network is available. 100% of college-owned or -operated housing units are wired for high-speed Internet access. Wireless service is available via classrooms, computer centers, computer labs, dorm rooms, learning centers, libraries, student centers. The 2 **libraries** have 131,838 books and 14,531 subscriptions.

Campus Life

There are 55 active organizations on campus, including a drama/theater group, newspaper, and choral group. No national or local **fraternities** or **sororities**.

MC is a member of the NCAA (Division III). **Intercollegiate sports** include baseball (m), basketball, cheerleading, cross-country running, equestrian sports, football (m), soccer, softball (w), tennis, volleyball (w), wrestling (m).

Campus Safety

Student safety services include late-night transport/escort service, 24-hour emergency telephone alarm devices, 24-hour patrols by trained security personnel, and electronically operated dormitory entrances.

Applying

MC requires SAT or ACT, a high school transcript, and a minimum high school GPA of 2.5, and in some cases an essay and an interview. It recommends a minimum high school GPA of 3.0. Application deadline: 3/1; 3/1 priority date for financial aid. Early and deferred admission are possible.

MARYVILLE UNIVERSITY OF SAINT LOUIS

SUBURBAN SETTING ■ PRIVATE ■ INDEPENDENT ■ COED
ST. LOUIS, MISSOURI

Web site: www.maryville.edu
Contact: Ms. Shani Lenore, Assistant Vice President of Enrollment, 650
   Maryville University Drive, St. Louis, MO 63141-7299
Telephone: 314-529-9350 or toll-free 800-627-9855
Fax: 314-529-9927
E-mail: admissions@maryville.edu

Academics

Maryville awards bachelor's, master's, and doctoral **degrees. Challenging opportunities** include advanced placement credit, accelerated degree programs, student-designed majors, freshman honors college, an honors program, double majors, independent study, and a senior project. Special programs include cooperative education, internships, summer session for credit, off-campus study, study-abroad, and Army ROTC.

The most frequently chosen **baccalaureate** fields are health professions and related sciences, business/marketing, and psychology. A complete listing of majors at Maryville appears in the Majors by College index beginning on page 469.

The **faculty** at Maryville has 113 full-time members, 86% with terminal degrees. The student-faculty ratio is 12:1.

Students of Maryville

The student body totals 3,517, of whom 2,898 are undergraduates. 75.5% are women and 24.5% are men. Students come from 24 states and territories and 10 other countries. 87% are from Missouri. 0.5% are international students. 6.3% are African American, 0.4% American Indian, 1.8% Asian American, and 1.5% Hispanic American. 80% returned for their sophomore year.

Facilities and Resources

489 **computers/terminals** are available on campus for general student use. Students can access the following: campus intranet, computer help desk, free student e-mail accounts, online (class) grades, online (class) registration, online (class) schedules, specialized software, university catalog. Campuswide network is available. 100% of college-owned or -operated housing units are wired for high-speed Internet access. Wireless service is available via entire campus. The **library** has 156,073 books and 15,923 subscriptions.

Campus Life

There are 45 active organizations on campus, including a drama/theater group, newspaper, and choral group. No national or local **fraternities** or **sororities**.

Maryville is a member of the NCAA (Division III). **Intercollegiate sports** include baseball (m), basketball, cross-country running, golf, soccer, softball (w), tennis, volleyball (w).

Campus Safety

Student safety services include video security system in residence halls, self-defense and education programs, late-night transport/escort service, 24-hour emergency telephone alarm devices, 24-hour patrols by trained security personnel, and electronically operated dormitory entrances.

Applying

Maryville requires SAT or ACT, a high school transcript, and a minimum high school GPA of 2.5, and in some cases an essay, an interview, and audition, portfolio. Application deadline: 8/15; 3/1 priority date for financial aid. Deferred admission is possible.

Getting Accepted

1,637 applied
54% were accepted
355 enrolled (40% of accepted)
25% from top tenth of their h.s. class
3.58 average high school GPA
Mean ACT score: 24
54% had ACT scores over 24
8% had ACT scores over 30
3 valedictorians

Graduation and After

48% graduated in 4 years
8% graduated in 5 years
90% had job offers within 6 months
109 organizations recruited on campus

Financial Matters

$21,145 tuition and fees (2009–10)
$8300 room and board
65% average percent of need met
$15,055 average financial aid amount received
   per undergraduate (2007–08 estimated)

MASSACHUSETTS INSTITUTE OF TECHNOLOGY

URBAN SETTING ■ PRIVATE ■ INDEPENDENT ■ COED
CAMBRIDGE, MASSACHUSETTS

Web site: web.mit.edu
Contact: Admissions Counselors, Building 3-108, 77 Massachusetts Avenue, Cambridge, MA 02139-4307
Telephone: 617-253-3400
Fax: 617-258-8304
E-mail: admissions@mit.edu

Getting Accepted
12,445 applied
12% were accepted
1,067 enrolled (69% of accepted)
97% from top tenth of their h.s. class
Mean SAT critical reading score: 705
Mean SAT math score: 753
Mean SAT writing score: 699
Mean ACT score: 32
94% had SAT critical reading scores over 600
99% had SAT math scores over 600
100% had ACT scores over 24
59% had SAT critical reading scores over 700
87% had SAT math scores over 700
87% had ACT scores over 30
252 valedictorians

Graduation and After
83% graduated in 4 years
7% graduated in 5 years
2% graduated in 6 years
42% had job offers within 6 months
427 organizations recruited on campus

Financial Matters
$36,390 tuition and fees (2008–09)
$10,860 room and board
100% average percent of need met
$29,116 average financial aid amount received per undergraduate (2006–07)

Academics

MIT awards bachelor's, master's, and doctoral **degrees. Challenging opportunities** include advanced placement credit and a senior project. Special programs include cooperative education, internships, off-campus study, study-abroad, and Army, Navy, and Air Force ROTC.

The most frequently chosen **baccalaureate** fields are engineering, computer and information sciences, and physical sciences. A complete listing of majors at MIT appears in the Majors by College index beginning on page 469.

The **faculty** at MIT has 1,362 full-time members, 91% with terminal degrees. The student-faculty ratio is 6:1.

Students of MIT

The student body totals 10,220, of whom 4,172 are undergraduates. 44.5% are women and 55.5% are men. Students come from 55 states and territories and 89 other countries. 10% are from Massachusetts. 8.2% are international students. 7.1% are African American, 1.3% American Indian, 25.9% Asian American, and 11.8% Hispanic American. 98% returned for their sophomore year.

Facilities and Resources

1,100 **computers/terminals** are available on campus for general student use. Students can access the following: campus intranet, computer help desk, free student e-mail accounts, online (class) grades, online (class) registration, online (class) schedules. Campuswide network is available. 85% of college-owned or -operated housing units are wired for high-speed Internet access. Wireless service is available via entire campus. The 12 **libraries** have 964,656 books and 22,991 subscriptions.

Campus Life

There are 415 active organizations on campus, including a drama/theater group, newspaper, radio station, television station, choral group, and marching band. MIT has national **fraternities**, national **sororities**, and local fraternities.

MIT is a member of the NCAA (Division III). **Intercollegiate sports** include baseball (m), basketball, crew, cross-country running, fencing, field hockey (w), football (m), golf (m), gymnastics, ice hockey (w), lacrosse, riflery, sailing, skiing (cross-country), skiing (downhill), soccer, softball (w), squash (m), swimming and diving, tennis, track and field, volleyball, water polo (m), wrestling (m).

Campus Safety

Student safety services include late-night transport/escort service, 24-hour emergency telephone alarm devices, 24-hour patrols by trained security personnel, and electronically operated dormitory entrances.

Applying

MIT requires an essay, SAT Subject Tests, a high school transcript, and 2 recommendations, and in some cases SAT or ACT. It recommends an interview. Application deadline: 1/1; 2/15 for financial aid, with a 2/15 priority date. Deferred admission is possible.

The Master's College and Seminary

Suburban setting ■ Private ■ Independent Religious ■ Coed
Santa Clarita, California

Web site: www.masters.edu
Contact: Ms. Hollie Gorsh, Director of Admissions, 21726 Placerita Canyon Road, Santa Clarita, CA 91321
Telephone: 661-259-3540 Ext. 3369 or toll-free 800-568-6248
Fax: 661-288-1037
E-mail: admissions@masters.edu

Academics

Master's awards bachelor's, master's, doctoral, and first-professional **degrees** and first-professional certificates. **Challenging opportunities** include advanced placement credit, accelerated degree programs, double majors, independent study, and a senior project. Special programs include cooperative education, internships, summer session for credit, and study-abroad.

The most frequently chosen **baccalaureate** fields are business/marketing, liberal arts/general studies, and communications/journalism. A complete listing of majors at Master's appears in the Majors by College index beginning on page 469.

The **faculty** at Master's has 70 full-time members, 76% with terminal degrees. The student-faculty ratio is 10:1.

Students of Master's

The student body totals 1,439, of whom 1,039 are undergraduates. 51% are women and 49% are men. Students come from 39 states and territories and 36 other countries. 64% are from California. 5% are international students. 2.1% are African American, 0.8% American Indian, 5.3% Asian American, and 7.5% Hispanic American. 90% returned for their sophomore year.

Facilities and Resources

57 **computers/terminals** are available on campus for general student use. Students can access the following: free student e-mail accounts, online (class) grades, online (class) registration, online (class) schedules. Campuswide network is available. Wireless service is available via entire campus. The 2 **libraries** have 170,136 books and 36,469 subscriptions.

Campus Life

There are 15 active organizations on campus, including a drama/theater group and choral group. No national or local **fraternities** or **sororities**.

Master's is a member of the NAIA and NCCAA. **Intercollegiate sports** (some offering scholarships) include baseball (m), basketball, cross-country running, golf (m), soccer, tennis (w), track and field, volleyball (w).

Campus Safety

Student safety services include 24-hour patrols by trained security personnel.

Applying

Master's requires an essay, SAT or ACT, a high school transcript, 2 recommendations, ACT or SAT, and a minimum high school GPA of 2.75. It recommends an interview. Application deadline: 3/2 priority date for financial aid. Early and deferred admission are possible.

Getting Accepted

428 applied
84% were accepted
192 enrolled (54% of accepted)
33% from top tenth of their h.s. class
3.65 average high school GPA
Mean SAT critical reading score: 562
Mean SAT math score: 545
Mean ACT score: 24
37% had SAT critical reading scores over 600
29% had SAT math scores over 600
55% had ACT scores over 24
7% had SAT critical reading scores over 700
5% had SAT math scores over 700
10% had ACT scores over 30

Graduation and After

48% graduated in 4 years
6% graduated in 5 years
3% graduated in 6 years
27 organizations recruited on campus

Financial Matters

$24,650 tuition and fees (2009–10)
$8000 room and board
72% average percent of need met
$17,317 average financial aid amount received per undergraduate (2007–08 estimated)

McDaniel College

SUBURBAN SETTING ■ PRIVATE ■ INDEPENDENT ■ COED
WESTMINSTER, MARYLAND

Web site: www.mcdaniel.edu
Contact: Ms. Florence Hines, Vice President for Enrollment Management
   and Dean of Admissions, 2 College Hill, Westminster, MD 21157-4390
Telephone: 410-857-2230 or toll-free 800-638-5005
Fax: 410-857-2757
E-mail: admissions@mcdaniel.edu

Getting Accepted
2,651 applied
77% were accepted
421 enrolled (21% of accepted)
28% from top tenth of their h.s. class
3.44 average high school GPA
Mean SAT critical reading score: 572
Mean SAT math score: 572
Mean ACT score: 25
34% had SAT critical reading scores over 600
31% had SAT math scores over 600
50% had ACT scores over 24
8% had SAT critical reading scores over 700
5% had SAT math scores over 700
12% had ACT scores over 30
6 National Merit Scholars
5 class presidents
6 valedictorians

Graduation and After
65 organizations recruited on campus

Financial Matters
$30,780 tuition and fees (2008–09)
$6150 room and board
95% average percent of need met
$23,339 average financial aid amount received
   per undergraduate (2007–08 estimated)

Academics

McDaniel awards bachelor's and master's **degrees** and post-bachelor's certificates. **Challenging opportunities** include advanced placement credit, student-designed majors, an honors program, double majors, independent study, and a senior project. Special programs include internships, summer session for credit, off-campus study, study-abroad, and Army ROTC.

The most frequently chosen **baccalaureate** fields are social sciences, psychology, and visual and performing arts. A complete listing of majors at McDaniel appears in the Majors by College index beginning on page 469.

The **faculty** at McDaniel has 135 full-time members, 88% with terminal degrees. The student-faculty ratio is 12:1.

Students of McDaniel

The student body totals 3,896, of whom 1,772 are undergraduates. 55% are women and 45% are men. Students come from 35 states and territories and 18 other countries. 68% are from Maryland. 0.2% are international students. 5.4% are African American, 0.6% American Indian, 2.9% Asian American, and 2.2% Hispanic American. 87% returned for their sophomore year.

Facilities and Resources

340 **computers/terminals** and 1,350 ports are available on campus for general student use. Students can access the following: campus intranet, computer help desk, free student e-mail accounts, online (class) grades, online (class) registration, online (class) schedules. Campuswide network is available. 100% of college-owned or -operated housing units are wired for high-speed Internet access. Wireless service is available via classrooms, computer labs, dorm rooms, learning centers, libraries, student centers. The **library** has 434,525 books and 30,159 subscriptions.

Campus Life

There are 132 active organizations on campus, including a drama/theater group, newspaper, radio station, television station, and choral group. 12% of eligible men and 11% of eligible women are members of national **fraternities**, national **sororities**, local fraternities, and local sororities.

McDaniel is a member of the NCAA (Division III). **Intercollegiate sports** include baseball (m), basketball, cross-country running, field hockey (w), football (m), golf, lacrosse, soccer, softball (w), swimming and diving, tennis, track and field, volleyball (w), wrestling (m).

Campus Safety

Student safety services include late-night transport/escort service, 24-hour emergency telephone alarm devices, 24-hour patrols by trained security personnel, and electronically operated dormitory entrances.

Applying

McDaniel requires an essay, a high school transcript, 2 recommendations, and a minimum high school GPA of 2.5, and in some cases SAT or ACT and an interview. It recommends an interview. Application deadline: 2/1; 3/1 priority date for financial aid. Early and deferred admission are possible.

McGill University

URBAN SETTING ■ PUBLIC ■ COED
MONTRÉAL, QUEBEC

Web site: www.mcgill.ca
Contact: Enrollment Services, 845 Sherbrooke Street West, James
  Administration Building, Room 205, Montreal, QC H3A 2T5 Canada
Telephone: 514-398-3910
Fax: 514-398-4193
E-mail: admissions@mcgill.ca

Academics

McGill awards bachelor's, master's, doctoral, and first-professional **degrees** and post-bachelor's certificates. **Challenging opportunities** include advanced placement credit, accelerated degree programs, an honors program, double majors, independent study, and a senior project. Special programs include cooperative education, internships, summer session for credit, off-campus study, and study-abroad.

The most frequently chosen **baccalaureate** fields are social sciences, business/marketing, and biological/life sciences. A complete listing of majors at McGill appears in the Majors by College index beginning on page 469.

The **faculty** at McGill has 1,689 full-time members, 95% with terminal degrees. The student-faculty ratio is 16:1.

Students of McGill

The student body totals 31,664, of whom 22,523 are undergraduates. 58.9% are women and 41.1% are men. Students come from 13 states and territories and 118 other countries. 63% are from Quebec. 16.9% are international students. 93% returned for their sophomore year.

Facilities and Resources

3,730 **computers/terminals** are available on campus for general student use. Students can access the following: campus intranet, computer help desk, free student e-mail accounts, online (class) grades, online (class) registration, online (class) schedules. Campuswide network is available. 100% of college-owned or -operated housing units are wired for high-speed Internet access. Wireless service is available via entire campus. The 14 **libraries** have 4,236,684 books and 49,433 subscriptions.

Campus Life

There are 250 active organizations on campus, including a drama/theater group, newspaper, radio station, and choral group. No national or local **fraternities** or **sororities**.

Intercollegiate sports include badminton, baseball (m), basketball, cheerleading, crew, cross-country running, fencing, field hockey (w), football (m), golf, ice hockey, lacrosse, rugby, sailing, skiing (cross-country), skiing (downhill), soccer, squash, swimming and diving, tennis, track and field, ultimate Frisbee, volleyball, wrestling.

Campus Safety

Student safety services include late-night transport/escort service, 24-hour emergency telephone alarm devices, 24-hour patrols by trained security personnel, student patrols, and electronically operated dormitory entrances.

Applying

McGill requires a high school transcript and a minimum high school GPA of 3.3, and in some cases SAT and SAT Subject Tests or ACT, an interview, and audition for music program, portfolio for architecture program. Application deadline: 1/15; 6/30 for financial aid, with a 6/1 priority date. Deferred admission is possible.

Getting Accepted

21,242 applied
54% were accepted
4,998 enrolled (44% of accepted)
3.52 average high school GPA
Mean SAT critical reading score: 690
Mean SAT math score: 680
Mean SAT writing score: 690
Mean ACT score: 30
91% had SAT critical reading scores over 600
93% had SAT math scores over 600
92% had SAT writing scores over 600
99% had ACT scores over 24
44% had SAT critical reading scores over 700
43% had SAT math scores over 700
48% had SAT writing scores over 700
60% had ACT scores over 30

Graduation and After

67% graduated in 4 years
16% graduated in 5 years
2% graduated in 6 years
3000 organizations recruited on campus

Financial Matters

$1868 resident tuition and fees (2008–09)
$5378 nonresident tuition and fees (2008–09)
$12,948 room and board
$3371 average financial aid amount received
  per undergraduate (2007–08)

McKendree University

SMALL-TOWN SETTING ■ PRIVATE ■ INDEPENDENT RELIGIOUS ■ COED
LEBANON, ILLINOIS

Web site: www.mckendree.edu
Contact: Chris Hall, Vice President for Admissions and Financial Aid, 701 College Road, Lebanon, IL 62254
Telephone: 618-537-6833 or toll-free 800-232-7228 Ext. 6831
Fax: 618-537-6496
E-mail: inquiry@mckendree.edu

Getting Accepted
1,347 applied
67% were accepted
308 enrolled (34% of accepted)
18% from top tenth of their h.s. class
3.5 average high school GPA
Mean ACT score: 24
18% had SAT critical reading scores over 600
14% had SAT math scores over 600
40% had ACT scores over 24
5% had ACT scores over 30
6 valedictorians

Graduation and After
47% graduated in 4 years
19% graduated in 5 years
4% graduated in 6 years
96% had job offers within 6 months
100 organizations recruited on campus

Financial Matters
$21,270 tuition and fees (2008–09)
$7850 room and board
82% average percent of need met
$15,561 average financial aid amount received per undergraduate (2007–08 estimated)

Academics

McKendree awards bachelor's and master's **degrees. Challenging opportunities** include advanced placement credit, accelerated degree programs, student-designed majors, an honors program, double majors, independent study, and a senior project. Special programs include internships, summer session for credit, off-campus study, study-abroad, and Army and Air Force ROTC.

The most frequently chosen **baccalaureate** fields are business/marketing, education, and health professions and related sciences. A complete listing of majors at McKendree appears in the Majors by College index beginning on page 469.

The **faculty** at McKendree has 94 full-time members, 78% with terminal degrees. The student-faculty ratio is 13:1.

Students of McKendree

The student body totals 3,327, of whom 2,308 are undergraduates. 56.4% are women and 43.6% are men. Students come from 22 states and territories and 14 other countries. 75% are from Illinois. 1.8% are international students. 12.8% are African American, 0.4% American Indian, 1.3% Asian American, and 2.3% Hispanic American. 70% returned for their sophomore year.

Facilities and Resources

140 **computers/terminals** are available on campus for general student use. Students can access the following: campus intranet, computer help desk, free student e-mail accounts, online (class) grades, online (class) registration, online (class) schedules. Campuswide network is available. 100% of college-owned or -operated housing units are wired for high-speed Internet access. Wireless service is available via entire campus. The **library** has 109,000 books and 450 subscriptions.

Campus Life

There are 54 active organizations on campus, including a drama/theater group, newspaper, radio station, choral group, and marching band. 7% of eligible men and 10% of eligible women are members of national **fraternities**, local fraternities, and local **sororities**.

McKendree is a member of the NAIA. **Intercollegiate sports** (some offering scholarships) include baseball (m), basketball, bowling, cheerleading, cross-country running, football (m), golf, ice hockey (m), soccer, softball (w), tennis, track and field, volleyball (w), wrestling (m).

Campus Safety

Student safety services include late-night transport/escort service, 24-hour emergency telephone alarm devices, 24-hour patrols by trained security personnel, student patrols, and electronically operated dormitory entrances.

Applying

McKendree requires an essay, SAT or ACT, a high school transcript, 1 recommendation, rank in upper 50% of high school class, minimum ACT score of 20, and a minimum high school GPA of 2.5, and in some cases an interview. Application deadline: rolling admissions; 5/31 priority date for financial aid. Deferred admission is possible.

MERCER UNIVERSITY

SUBURBAN SETTING ■ PRIVATE ■ INDEPENDENT RELIGIOUS ■ COED
MACON, GEORGIA

Web site: www.mercer.edu
Contact: Mr. Emory Dunn, Director of Freshman Admissions, 1400 Coleman
  Avenue, Macon, GA 31207-0003
Telephone: 478-301-2312 or toll-free 800-840-8577
Fax: 478-301-2828
E-mail: dunn_e@mercer.edu

Academics

Mercer awards bachelor's, master's, doctoral, and first-professional **degrees** and post-master's certificates. **Challenging opportunities** include advanced placement credit, accelerated degree programs, student-designed majors, an honors program, double majors, independent study, and a senior project. Special programs include cooperative education, internships, summer session for credit, off-campus study, study-abroad, and Army ROTC.

The most frequently chosen **baccalaureate** fields are business/marketing, engineering, and social sciences. A complete listing of majors at Mercer appears in the Majors by College index beginning on page 469.

The **faculty** at Mercer has 354 full-time members, 88% with terminal degrees. The student-faculty ratio is 13:1.

Students of Mercer

The student body totals 5,464, of whom 2,245 are undergraduates. 53.8% are women and 46.2% are men. Students come from 41 states and territories and 39 other countries. 79% are from Georgia. 2.9% are international students. 16.7% are African American, 0.2% American Indian, 6.2% Asian American, and 2.9% Hispanic American. 78% returned for their sophomore year.

Facilities and Resources

500 **computers/terminals** and 2,500 ports are available on campus for general student use. Students can access the following: campus intranet, computer help desk, free student e-mail accounts, online (class) grades, online (class) registration, online (class) schedules. Campuswide network is available. 100% of college-owned or -operated housing units are wired for high-speed Internet access. Wireless service is available via classrooms, computer centers, computer labs, learning centers, libraries, student centers. The 4 **libraries** have 692,225 books and 28,163 subscriptions.

Campus Life

There are 104 active organizations on campus, including a drama/theater group, newspaper, radio station, television station, and choral group. 24% of eligible men and 28% of eligible women are members of national **fraternities**, national **sororities**, and local sororities.

Mercer is a member of the NCAA (Division I). **Intercollegiate sports** (some offering scholarships) include baseball (m), basketball, cross-country running, golf, riflery (m), soccer, softball (w), tennis, volleyball (w).

Campus Safety

Student safety services include patrols by police officers, late-night transport/escort service, 24-hour emergency telephone alarm devices, 24-hour patrols by trained security personnel, student patrols, and electronically operated dormitory entrances.

Applying

Mercer requires SAT or ACT, a high school transcript, and a minimum high school GPA of 3.0, and in some cases an interview and 2 recommendations. It recommends an interview and counselor's evaluation. Application deadline: 7/1; 4/1 priority date for financial aid. Early and deferred admission are possible.

Getting Accepted

4,678 applied
67% were accepted
593 enrolled (19% of accepted)
42% from top tenth of their h.s. class
3.68 average high school GPA
Mean SAT critical reading score: 589
Mean SAT math score: 596
Mean SAT writing score: 575
Mean ACT score: 25
46% had SAT critical reading scores over 600
47% had SAT math scores over 600
38% had SAT writing scores over 600
70% had ACT scores over 24
9% had SAT critical reading scores over 700
8% had SAT math scores over 700
6% had SAT writing scores over 700
15% had ACT scores over 30

Graduation and After

41% graduated in 4 years
12% graduated in 5 years
5% graduated in 6 years

Financial Matters

$28,700 tuition and fees (2008–09)
$8450 room and board
88% average percent of need met
$26,214 average financial aid amount received
  per undergraduate (2007–08 estimated)

Messiah College provides an education that is both rigorously academic and unapologetically Christian. The learning process is characterized by a lively student-faculty interaction that actively integrates academic content and faith issues. Messiah offers a strategically located campus, impressive academic and residence life facilities, and more than sixty majors and sixty minors in the applied and liberal arts and sciences. Students pursue extracurricular interests in twenty-two intercollegiate sports, ministries, service-learning areas, music ensembles, and scores of other activities. A multifaceted internship program provides career experience for students before they graduate. After graduation, 99 percent of graduates report employment/voluntary service or enrollment in graduate school within six months.

Getting Accepted
2,844 applied
70% were accepted
678 enrolled (34% of accepted)
33% from top tenth of their h.s. class
3.71 average high school GPA
Mean SAT critical reading score: 579
Mean SAT math score: 579
Mean SAT writing score: 581
Mean ACT score: 25
43% had SAT critical reading scores over 600
41% had SAT math scores over 600
44% had SAT writing scores over 600
57% had ACT scores over 24
9% had SAT critical reading scores over 700
9% had SAT math scores over 700
8% had SAT writing scores over 700
10% had ACT scores over 30
2 National Merit Scholars
20 valedictorians

Graduation and After
68% graduated in 4 years
7% graduated in 5 years
1% graduated in 6 years
95% had job offers within 6 months
470 organizations recruited on campus

Financial Matters
$25,670 tuition and fees (2008–09)
$7610 room and board
70% average percent of need met
$15,442 average financial aid amount received per undergraduate (2007–08 estimated)

MESSIAH COLLEGE
SMALL-TOWN SETTING ■ PRIVATE ■ INDEPENDENT RELIGIOUS ■ COED
GRANTHAM, PENNSYLVANIA

Web site: www.messiah.edu
Contact: Mr. John Chopka, Vice President for Enrollment Management, PO Box 3005, One College Avenue, Grantham, PA 17027
Telephone: 717-691-6000 or toll-free 800-233-4220
Fax: 717-791-2307
E-mail: admiss@messiah.edu

Academics
Messiah awards bachelor's **degrees. Challenging opportunities** include advanced placement credit, accelerated degree programs, student-designed majors, freshman honors college, an honors program, double majors, independent study, and a senior project. Special programs include internships, summer session for credit, off-campus study, and study-abroad.

The most frequently chosen **baccalaureate** fields are education, business/marketing, and health professions and related sciences. A complete listing of majors at Messiah appears in the Majors by College index beginning on page 469.

The **faculty** at Messiah has 173 full-time members, 83% with terminal degrees. The student-faculty ratio is 13:1.

Students of Messiah
The student body is made up of 2,802 undergraduates. 63.3% are women and 36.7% are men. Students come from 40 states and territories and 35 other countries. 57% are from Pennsylvania. 2.6% are international students. 1.8% are African American, 0.1% American Indian, 1.7% Asian American, and 1.2% Hispanic American. 83% returned for their sophomore year.

Facilities and Resources
571 **computers/terminals** are available on campus for general student use. Students can access the following: campus intranet, computer help desk, free student e-mail accounts, online (class) grades, online (class) registration, online (class) schedules, access to software. Campuswide network is available. 100% of college-owned or -operated housing units are wired for high-speed Internet access. Wireless service is available via entire campus. The **library** has 259,252 books and 27,936 subscriptions.

Campus Life
There are 66 active organizations on campus, including a drama/theater group, newspaper, radio station, and choral group. No national or local **fraternities** or **sororities**.

Messiah is a member of the NCAA (Division III). **Intercollegiate sports** include baseball (m), basketball, cross-country running, field hockey (w), golf (m), lacrosse, soccer, softball (w), swimming and diving, tennis, track and field, volleyball (w), wrestling (m).

Campus Safety
Student safety services include bicycle patrols, security lighting, self-defense classes, prevention/awareness programs, late-night transport/escort service, 24-hour emergency telephone alarm devices, 24-hour patrols by trained security personnel, student patrols, and electronically operated dormitory entrances.

Applying
Messiah requires an essay, a high school transcript, and 1 recommendation, and in some cases SAT or ACT. It recommends SAT or ACT and an interview. Application deadline: rolling admissions; 4/1 priority date for financial aid. Deferred admission is possible.

MIAMI UNIVERSITY

SMALL-TOWN SETTING ■ PUBLIC ■ STATE-RELATED ■ COED
OXFORD, OHIO

Web site: www.muohio.edu
Contact: 301 South Campus Avenue, Oxford, OH 45056
Telephone: 513-529-5040
Fax: 513-529-1550
E-mail: admission@muohio.edu

Academics

Miami awards associate, bachelor's, master's, and doctoral **degrees** and post-master's certificates. **Challenging opportunities** include advanced placement credit, student-designed majors, an honors program, double majors, independent study, and a senior project. Special programs include cooperative education, internships, summer session for credit, off-campus study, study-abroad, and Army, Navy, and Air Force ROTC.

The most frequently chosen **baccalaureate** fields are business/marketing, social sciences, and education. A complete listing of majors at Miami appears in the Majors by College index beginning on page 469.

The **faculty** at Miami has 867 full-time members, 87% with terminal degrees. The student-faculty ratio is 16:1.

Students of Miami

The student body totals 17,191, of whom 14,785 are undergraduates. 53.5% are women and 46.5% are men. Students come from 51 states and territories and 46 other countries. 70% are from Ohio. 2.3% are international students. 3.6% are African American, 0.6% American Indian, 2.8% Asian American, and 2% Hispanic American. 90% returned for their sophomore year.

Facilities and Resources

1,200 **computers/terminals** are available on campus for general student use. Students can access the following: campus intranet, computer help desk, free student e-mail accounts, online (class) grades, online (class) registration, online (class) schedules. Campuswide network is available. Wireless service is available via entire campus. The 4 **libraries** have 2,697,078 books and 14,089 subscriptions.

Campus Life

There are 350 active organizations on campus, including a drama/theater group, newspaper, radio station, television station, choral group, and marching band. 20% of eligible men and 26% of eligible women are members of national **fraternities** and national **sororities**.

Miami is a member of the NCAA (Division I). **Intercollegiate sports** (some offering scholarships) include baseball (m), basketball, cross-country running, field hockey (w), football (m), golf (m), ice hockey (m), soccer (w), softball (w), swimming and diving, tennis (w), track and field, volleyball (w).

Campus Safety

Student safety services include late-night transport/escort service, 24-hour emergency telephone alarm devices, 24-hour patrols by trained security personnel, student patrols, and electronically operated dormitory entrances.

Applying

Miami requires an essay, SAT or ACT, a high school transcript, and 1 recommendation. It recommends an essay. Application deadline: 2/1; 2/15 priority date for financial aid. Deferred admission is possible.

Getting Accepted

15,009 applied
80% were accepted
3,609 enrolled (30% of accepted)
37% from top tenth of their h.s. class
3.66 average high school GPA
Mean SAT critical reading score: 586
Mean SAT math score: 609
Mean ACT score: 26
44% had SAT critical reading scores over 600
58% had SAT math scores over 600
80% had ACT scores over 24
8% had SAT critical reading scores over 700
11% had SAT math scores over 700
19% had ACT scores over 30
48 National Merit Scholars
38 class presidents

Graduation and After

68% graduated in 4 years
11% graduated in 5 years
1% graduated in 6 years
424 organizations recruited on campus

Financial Matters

$11,887 resident tuition and fees (2008–09)
$25,771 nonresident tuition and fees (2008–09)
$8998 room and board
66% average percent of need met
$10,299 average financial aid amount received per undergraduate (2007–08 estimated)

On a Big Ten campus known and loved for its beauty, Michigan State University's modern facilities, historic buildings, and parklike setting provide a unique environment of tradition and innovation. A diverse and talented student body, a dynamic faculty, and a dedicated staff all create a friendly and stimulating academic community that balances intellectual challenge and support for student success. Undergraduate education comes first at MSU, with 200 undergraduate majors, a nationally recognized Honors College, and other highly regarded living-learning programs. Michigan State has the top-ranked public study-abroad program in the nation, with more than 200 programs on all seven continents. An MSU education attracts students who are interested in combining a high-quality liberal arts education with extraordinary opportunities for hands-on experiences through internships, undergraduate research, outreach, and public service.

Getting Accepted
25,589 applied
70% were accepted
7,555 enrolled (42% of accepted)
31% from top tenth of their h.s. class
3.61 average high school GPA
Mean SAT critical reading score: 547
Mean SAT math score: 596
Mean SAT writing score: 544
Mean ACT score: 25
35% had SAT critical reading scores over 600
51% had SAT math scores over 600
28% had SAT writing scores over 600
67% had ACT scores over 24
8% had SAT critical reading scores over 700
13% had SAT math scores over 700
6% had SAT writing scores over 700
12% had ACT scores over 30
45 National Merit Scholars

Graduation and After
44% graduated in 4 years
27% graduated in 5 years
4% graduated in 6 years
600 organizations recruited on campus

Financial Matters
$10,214 resident tuition and fees (2008–09)
$25,672 nonresident tuition and fees (2008–09)
$7026 room and board
73% average percent of need met
$10,004 average financial aid amount received per undergraduate (2007–08 estimated)

MICHIGAN STATE UNIVERSITY
SUBURBAN SETTING ■ PUBLIC ■ STATE-SUPPORTED ■ COED
EAST LANSING, MICHIGAN

Web site: www.msu.edu
Contact: James Cotter, Acting Director of Admissions, 250 Administration Building, East Lansing, MI 48824
Telephone: 517-355-8332
Fax: 517-353-1647
E-mail: admis@msu.edu

Academics
Michigan State awards bachelor's, master's, doctoral, and first-professional **degrees** and post-master's certificates. **Challenging opportunities** include advanced placement credit, accelerated degree programs, student-designed majors, freshman honors college, an honors program, double majors, independent study, and a senior project. Special programs include cooperative education, internships, summer session for credit, off-campus study, study-abroad, and Army and Air Force ROTC.

The most frequently chosen **baccalaureate** fields are business/marketing, communications/journalism, and social sciences. A complete listing of majors at Michigan State appears in the Majors by College index beginning on page 469.

The **faculty** at Michigan State has 2,616 full-time members, 93% with terminal degrees. The student-faculty ratio is 16:1.

Students of Michigan State
The student body totals 46,648, of whom 36,337 are undergraduates. 53% are women and 47% are men. Students come from 55 states and territories and 89 other countries. 92% are from Michigan. 6% are international students. 8% are African American, 0.7% American Indian, 5.1% Asian American, and 2.9% Hispanic American. 91% returned for their sophomore year.

Facilities and Resources
2,100 **computers/terminals** are available on campus for general student use. Students can access the following: campus intranet, computer help desk, free student e-mail accounts, online (class) grades, online (class) registration, online (class) schedules. Campuswide network is available. 100% of college-owned or -operated housing units are wired for high-speed Internet access. Wireless service is available via classrooms, computer centers, computer labs, learning centers, libraries, student centers. The 15 **libraries** have 4,915,621 books and 74,177 subscriptions.

Campus Life
There are 500 active organizations on campus, including a drama/theater group, newspaper, radio station, television station, choral group, and marching band. 8% of eligible men and 7% of eligible women are members of national **fraternities** and national **sororities**.

Michigan State is a member of the NCAA (Division I). **Intercollegiate sports** (some offering scholarships) include baseball (m), basketball, cheerleading, crew (w), cross-country running, field hockey (w), football (m), golf, gymnastics (w), ice hockey (m), soccer, softball (w), swimming and diving, tennis, track and field, volleyball (w), wrestling (m).

Campus Safety
Student safety services include self-defense workshops, late-night transport/escort service, 24-hour emergency telephone alarm devices, and 24-hour patrols by trained security personnel.

Applying
Michigan State requires an essay, SAT or ACT, and a high school transcript. Application deadline: rolling admissions. Deferred admission is possible.

Michigan Technological University

Small-town setting ■ Public ■ State-supported ■ Coed
Houghton, Michigan

Web site: www.mtu.edu
Contact: Ms. Allison Carter, Director of Admissions, 1400 Townsend Drive, Houghton, MI 49931-1295
Telephone: 906-487-2335 or toll-free 888-MTU-1885
Fax: 906-487-2125
E-mail: mtu4u@mtu.edu

Academics

Michigan Tech awards associate, bachelor's, master's, and doctoral **degrees** and post-bachelor's certificates. **Challenging opportunities** include advanced placement credit, student-designed majors, an honors program, double majors, independent study, and a senior project. Special programs include cooperative education, internships, summer session for credit, off-campus study, study-abroad, and Army and Air Force ROTC.

The most frequently chosen **baccalaureate** fields are engineering, business/marketing, and computer and information sciences. A complete listing of majors at Michigan Tech appears in the Majors by College index beginning on page 469.

The **faculty** at Michigan Tech has 362 full-time members, 86% with terminal degrees. The student-faculty ratio is 11:1.

Students of Michigan Tech

The student body totals 7,018, of whom 6,034 are undergraduates. 23.4% are women and 76.6% are men. Students come from 47 states and territories and 73 other countries. 77% are from Michigan. 6.7% are international students. 1.6% are African American, 0.7% American Indian, 1.1% Asian American, and 1.1% Hispanic American. 82% returned for their sophomore year.

Facilities and Resources

1,555 **computers/terminals** are available on campus for general student use. Students can access the following: online (class) registration. Campuswide network is available. The **library** has 799,775 books and 2,777 subscriptions.

Campus Life

There are 145 active organizations on campus, including a drama/theater group, newspaper, radio station, and choral group. 7% of eligible men and 12% of eligible women are members of national **fraternities**, national **sororities**, local fraternities, and local sororities.

Michigan Tech is a member of the NCAA (Division II). **Intercollegiate sports** (some offering scholarships) include basketball, cross-country running, football (m), ice hockey (m), skiing (cross-country), tennis, track and field, volleyball (w).

Campus Safety

Student safety services include late-night transport/escort service, 24-hour emergency telephone alarm devices, 24-hour patrols by trained security personnel, and electronically operated dormitory entrances.

Applying

Michigan Tech requires SAT or ACT and a high school transcript. It recommends an interview and a minimum high school GPA of 2.75. Application deadline: rolling admissions; 2/16 priority date for financial aid. Deferred admission is possible.

Getting Accepted

5,049 applied
75% were accepted
1,365 enrolled (36% of accepted)
28% from top tenth of their h.s. class
3.52 average high school GPA
49% had SAT critical reading scores over 600
65% had SAT math scores over 600
34% had SAT writing scores over 600
69% had ACT scores over 24
11% had SAT critical reading scores over 700
25% had SAT math scores over 700
4% had SAT writing scores over 700
17% had ACT scores over 30

Graduation and After

26% graduated in 4 years
32% graduated in 5 years
7% graduated in 6 years
85% had job offers within 6 months
290 organizations recruited on campus

Financial Matters

$10,761 resident tuition and fees (2008–09)
$22,521 nonresident tuition and fees (2008–09)
$7738 room and board
74% average percent of need met
$9572 average financial aid amount received per undergraduate (2007–08 estimated)

MIDDLEBURY COLLEGE

SMALL-TOWN SETTING ■ PRIVATE ■ INDEPENDENT ■ COED
MIDDLEBURY, VERMONT

Web site: www.middlebury.edu
Contact: Mr. Robert Clagett, Dean of Admissions, Emma Willard House,
  Middlebury, VT 05753-6002
Telephone: 802-443-3000
Fax: 802-443-2056
E-mail: admissions@middlebury.edu

Getting Accepted

7,823 applied
17% were accepted
576 enrolled (44% of accepted)
86% from top tenth of their h.s. class

Graduation and After

88% graduated in 4 years
5% graduated in 5 years
50% had job offers within 6 months
70 organizations recruited on campus

Financial Matters

$49,210 comprehensive fee (2008–09)
100% average percent of need met
$30,439 average financial aid amount received
  per undergraduate (2006–07)

Academics

Middlebury awards bachelor's, master's, and doctoral **degrees**. **Challenging opportunities** include advanced placement credit, accelerated degree programs, student-designed majors, an honors program, double majors, and independent study. Special programs include internships, summer session for credit, off-campus study, study-abroad, and Army ROTC.

The most frequently chosen **baccalaureate** fields are social sciences, English, and visual and performing arts. A complete listing of majors at Middlebury appears in the Majors by College index beginning on page 469.

The **faculty** at Middlebury has 249 full-time members, 94% with terminal degrees. The student-faculty ratio is 9:1.

Students of Middlebury

The student body is made up of 2,455 undergraduates. 50.9% are women and 49.1% are men. Students come from 52 states and territories and 75 other countries. 6% are from Vermont. 11.1% are international students. 3.3% are African American, 0.7% American Indian, 9% Asian American, and 6.3% Hispanic American. 95% returned for their sophomore year.

Facilities and Resources

494 **computers/terminals** are available on campus for general student use. Students can access the following: computer help desk, free student e-mail accounts, online (class) registration, online (class) schedules, help-line, personal Web pages, file servers. Campuswide network is available. Wireless service is available via entire campus. The 4 **libraries** have 853,000 books and 2,908 subscriptions.

Campus Life

There are 95 active organizations on campus, including a drama/theater group, newspaper, radio station, and choral group. No national or local **fraternities** or **sororities**.

Middlebury is a member of the NCAA (Division III). **Intercollegiate sports** include baseball (m), basketball, cross-country running, field hockey (w), football (m), golf, ice hockey, lacrosse, skiing (cross-country), skiing (downhill), soccer, softball (w), squash (w), swimming and diving, tennis, track and field, volleyball (w).

Campus Safety

Student safety services include late-night transport/escort service, 24-hour patrols by trained security personnel, student patrols, and electronically operated dormitory entrances.

Applying

Middlebury requires an essay, three tests to include: a writing test, a quantitative test, and an area of the applicant's choice, a high school transcript, and 3 recommendations. It recommends an interview. Application deadline: 1/1; 1/1 for financial aid, with a 11/15 priority date. Early and deferred admission are possible.

Milligan College

SUBURBAN SETTING ■ PRIVATE ■ INDEPENDENT RELIGIOUS ■ COED
MILLIGAN COLLEGE, TENNESSEE

Web site: www.milligan.edu
Contact: Ms. Tracy Brinn, Director of Enrollment Management, PO Box 210, Milligan College, TN 37682
Telephone: 423-461-8730 or toll-free 800-262-8337 (in-state)
Fax: 423-461-8982
E-mail: admissions@milligan.edu

Academics

Milligan awards bachelor's and master's **degrees**. **Challenging opportunities** include advanced placement credit, double majors, independent study, and a senior project. Special programs include cooperative education, internships, summer session for credit, off-campus study, study-abroad, and Army ROTC.

The most frequently chosen **baccalaureate** fields are education, business/marketing, and health professions and related sciences. A complete listing of majors at Milligan appears in the Majors by College index beginning on page 469.

The **faculty** at Milligan has 66 full-time members, 80% with terminal degrees. The student-faculty ratio is 12:1.

Students of Milligan

The student body totals 1,070, of whom 845 are undergraduates. 61.5% are women and 38.5% are men. Students come from 18 states and territories and 11 other countries. 46% are from Tennessee. 2% are international students. 5.5% are African American, 0.4% American Indian, 1.3% Asian American, and 1.9% Hispanic American. 71% returned for their sophomore year.

Facilities and Resources

97 **computers/terminals** are available on campus for general student use. Students can access the following: campus intranet, computer help desk, free student e-mail accounts, online (class) grades, online (class) registration, online (class) schedules. Campuswide network is available. 100% of college-owned or -operated housing units are wired for high-speed Internet access. Wireless service is available via classrooms, computer centers, computer labs, dorm rooms, libraries, student centers. The **library** has 145,605 books and 11,097 subscriptions.

Campus Life

There are 31 active organizations on campus, including a drama/theater group, newspaper, radio station, and choral group. No national or local **fraternities** or **sororities**.

Milligan is a member of the NAIA. **Intercollegiate sports** (some offering scholarships) include baseball (m), basketball, cross-country running, golf (m), soccer, softball (w), swimming and diving, tennis, volleyball (w).

Campus Safety

Student safety services include late-night transport/escort service and 24-hour patrols by trained security personnel.

Applying

Milligan requires an essay, SAT or ACT, a high school transcript, 2 recommendations, and a minimum high school GPA of 2.0, and in some cases an interview. It recommends a minimum high school GPA of 3.0. Application deadline: 8/1; 3/1 priority date for financial aid. Deferred admission is possible.

Getting Accepted

580 applied
74% were accepted
200 enrolled (46% of accepted)
25% from top tenth of their h.s. class
3.54 average high school GPA
Mean SAT critical reading score: 551
Mean SAT math score: 532
Mean SAT writing score: 528
Mean ACT score: 23
26% had SAT critical reading scores over 600
28% had SAT math scores over 600
22% had SAT writing scores over 600
40% had ACT scores over 24
3% had SAT critical reading scores over 700
2% had SAT math scores over 700
4% had ACT scores over 30

Graduation and After

35 organizations recruited on campus

Financial Matters

$20,560 tuition and fees (2008–09)
$5650 room and board
55% average percent of need met
$13,266 average financial aid amount received per undergraduate (2006–07)

MILLSAPS COLLEGE

URBAN SETTING ■ PRIVATE ■ INDEPENDENT RELIGIOUS ■ COED
JACKSON, MISSISSIPPI

Web site: www.millsaps.edu
Contact: Mr. Mathew Cox, Dean of Enrollment Management, 1701 North
  State Street, Jackson, MS 39210-0001
Telephone: 601-974-1050 or toll-free 800-352-1050
Fax: 601-974-1059
E-mail: admissions@millsaps.edu

Getting Accepted

1,266 applied
77% were accepted
271 enrolled (28% of accepted)
3.46 average high school GPA
Mean SAT critical reading score: 601
Mean SAT math score: 589
58% had SAT critical reading scores over 600
47% had SAT math scores over 600
72% had ACT scores over 24
14% had SAT critical reading scores over 700
10% had SAT math scores over 700
22% had ACT scores over 30
5 National Merit Scholars
3 valedictorians

Graduation and After

63% graduated in 4 years
4% graduated in 5 years
1% graduated in 6 years
104 organizations recruited on campus

Financial Matters

$24,754 tuition and fees (2008–09)
$8800 room and board
83% average percent of need met
$18,892 average financial aid amount received
  per undergraduate (2006–07)

Academics

Millsaps awards bachelor's and master's **degrees**. **Challenging opportunities** include advanced placement credit, accelerated degree programs, student-designed majors, an honors program, double majors, independent study, and a senior project. Special programs include internships, summer session for credit, off-campus study, study-abroad, and Army ROTC.

The most frequently chosen **baccalaureate** fields are business/marketing, social sciences, and psychology. A complete listing of majors at Millsaps appears in the Majors by College index beginning on page 469.

The **faculty** at Millsaps has 97 full-time members, 94% with terminal degrees. The student-faculty ratio is 10:1.

Students of Millsaps

The student body totals 1,118, of whom 1,013 are undergraduates. 51.3% are women and 48.7% are men. Students come from 33 states and territories and 17 other countries. 44% are from Mississippi. 1.4% are international students. 11.1% are African American, 0.3% American Indian, 4.3% Asian American, and 1.7% Hispanic American. 79% returned for their sophomore year.

Facilities and Resources

150 **computers/terminals** are available on campus for general student use. Students can access the following: campus intranet, computer help desk, free student e-mail accounts, online (class) grades, online (class) registration, online (class) schedules, online transcripts. Campuswide network is available. 100% of college-owned or -operated housing units are wired for high-speed Internet access. Wireless service is available via entire campus. The **library** has 195,586 books and 860 subscriptions.

Campus Life

There are 70 active organizations on campus, including a drama/theater group, newspaper, and choral group. 40% of eligible men and 56% of eligible women are members of national **fraternities** and national **sororities**.

Millsaps is a member of the NCAA (Division III). **Intercollegiate sports** include baseball (m), basketball, cheerleading, cross-country running, football (m), golf, soccer, softball (w), tennis, volleyball (w).

Campus Safety

Student safety services include self-defense education, lighted pathways, late-night transport/escort service, 24-hour emergency telephone alarm devices, 24-hour patrols by trained security personnel, student patrols, and electronically operated dormitory entrances.

Applying

Millsaps requires an essay, SAT or ACT, a high school transcript, 1 recommendation, and a minimum high school GPA of 2.5, and in some cases an interview. Application deadline: rolling admissions, rolling admissions for nonresidents; 3/1 priority date for financial aid. Deferred admission is possible.

MILLS COLLEGE

URBAN SETTING ■ PRIVATE ■ INDEPENDENT
■ UNDERGRADUATE: WOMEN ONLY; GRADUATE: COED
OAKLAND, CALIFORNIA

SPONSOR

Web site: www.mills.edu
Contact: Ms. Giulietta Aquino, Vice President of Enrollment Management,
5000 MacArthur Boulevard, Oakland, CA 94613-1301
Telephone: 510-430-2135 or toll-free 800-87-MILLS
Fax: 510-430-3314
E-mail: admission@mills.edu

Academics

Mills awards bachelor's, master's, and doctoral **degrees** and post-bachelor's certificates. **Challenging opportunities** include advanced placement credit, student-designed majors, an honors program, double majors, independent study, and a senior project. Special programs include internships, off-campus study, and study-abroad.

The most frequently chosen **baccalaureate** fields are social sciences, visual and performing arts, and psychology. A complete listing of majors at Mills appears in the Majors by College index beginning on page 469.

The **faculty** at Mills has 96 full-time members, 89% with terminal degrees. The student-faculty ratio is 11:1.

Students of Mills

The student body totals 1,476, of whom 969 are undergraduates. 100% are women. Students come from 49 states and territories and 15 other countries. 80% are from California. 2.6% are international students. 9.3% are African American, 0.7% American Indian, 7.5% Asian American, and 13.9% Hispanic American. 74% returned for their sophomore year.

Facilities and Resources

336 **computers/terminals** and 8 ports are available on campus for general student use. Students can access the following: campus intranet, computer help desk, free student e-mail accounts, online (class) grades, online (class) registration, online (class) schedules, online degree audit. Campuswide network is available. 100% of college-owned or -operated housing units are wired for high-speed Internet access. Wireless service is available via entire campus. The 2 **libraries** have 243,317 books and 24,721 subscriptions.

Campus Life

There are 30 active organizations on campus, including a drama/theater group, newspaper, and choral group. No national or local **sororities**.

Mills is a member of the NCAA (Division III) and NAIA. **Intercollegiate sports** include crew, cross-country running, soccer, swimming and diving, tennis, track and field, volleyball.

Campus Safety

Student safety services include late-night transport/escort service, 24-hour emergency telephone alarm devices, 24-hour patrols by trained security personnel, and electronically operated dormitory entrances.

Applying

Mills requires SAT or ACT, a high school transcript, 2 recommendations, and essay or graded paper. It recommends SAT Subject Tests and an interview. Application deadline: 5/1; 2/15 for financial aid, with a 2/15 priority date. Deferred admission is possible.

Mills College offers women the opportunity to study and grow in a dynamic environment that supports intellectual exploration and a thoughtful approach to life. Working closely with renowned faculty members and diverse students in intimate, collaborative classes, Mills women explore, debate, and challenge conventional thinking—both inside and outside the classroom. Students work with faculty members on meaningful real-world projects and engage with distinguished professors, thinkers, writers, and artists. Set on a lush 135-acre parklike campus, Mills provides a beautiful home with convenient access to the thriving cultural, artistic, social, and professional worlds of the metropolitan San Francisco Bay Area.

Getting Accepted

1,416 applied
55% were accepted
202 enrolled (26% of accepted)
43% from top tenth of their h.s. class
3.65 average high school GPA
Mean SAT critical reading score: 588
Mean SAT math score: 543
Mean SAT writing score: 571
Mean ACT score: 24
51% had SAT critical reading scores over 600
25% had SAT math scores over 600
33% had SAT writing scores over 600
50% had ACT scores over 24
11% had SAT critical reading scores over 700
4% had SAT math scores over 700
6% had SAT writing scores over 700
8% had ACT scores over 30
2 National Merit Scholars
8 class presidents
3 valedictorians

Graduation and After

54% graduated in 4 years
7% graduated in 5 years
1% graduated in 6 years
70% had job offers within 6 months
150 organizations recruited on campus

Financial Matters

$35,190 tuition and fees (2008–09)
$10,550 room and board
83% average percent of need met
$24,002 average financial aid amount received per undergraduate (2005–06)

MILWAUKEE SCHOOL OF ENGINEERING

URBAN SETTING ■ PRIVATE ■ INDEPENDENT ■ COED, PRIMARILY MEN
MILWAUKEE, WISCONSIN

Web site: www.msoe.edu
Contact: Dana-Marie Grennier, Director of Admissions, 1025 North Broadway, Milwaukee, WI 53202-3109
Telephone: 414-277-6761 or toll-free 800-332-6763
Fax: 414-277-7475
E-mail: grennier@msoe.edu

Getting Accepted

2,279 applied
70% were accepted
645 enrolled (40% of accepted)
3.47 average high school GPA
Mean SAT critical reading score: 580
Mean SAT math score: 620
Mean ACT score: 26
41% had SAT critical reading scores over 600
64% had SAT math scores over 600
70% had ACT scores over 24
9% had SAT critical reading scores over 700
19% had SAT math scores over 700
15% had ACT scores over 30

Graduation and After

39% graduated in 4 years
14% graduated in 5 years
2% graduated in 6 years
98% had job offers within 6 months
107 organizations recruited on campus

Financial Matters

$28,665 tuition and fees (2009–10)
$7164 room and board
72% average percent of need met
$16,915 average financial aid amount received per undergraduate (2006–07)

Academics

MSOE awards bachelor's and master's **degrees**. **Challenging opportunities** include advanced placement credit, double majors, independent study, and a senior project. Special programs include internships, summer session for credit, study-abroad, and Army, Navy, and Air Force ROTC.

The most frequently chosen **baccalaureate** fields are engineering, business/marketing, and health professions and related sciences. A complete listing of majors at MSOE appears in the Majors by College index beginning on page 469.

The **faculty** at MSOE has 130 full-time members, 72% with terminal degrees. The student-faculty ratio is 14:1.

Students of MSOE

The student body totals 2,622, of whom 2,418 are undergraduates. 17.8% are women and 82.2% are men. Students come from 32 states and territories and 15 other countries. 73% are from Wisconsin. 2.4% are international students. 3.5% are African American, 0.5% American Indian, 3% Asian American, and 2.5% Hispanic American. 74% returned for their sophomore year.

Facilities and Resources

125 **computers/terminals** and 2,000 ports are available on campus for general student use. Students can access the following: campus intranet, computer help desk, free student e-mail accounts, online (class) grades, online (class) registration, online (class) schedules. Campuswide network is available. 100% of college-owned or -operated housing units are wired for high-speed Internet access. Wireless service is available via entire campus. The **library** has 79,275 books and 378 subscriptions.

Campus Life

There are 63 active organizations on campus, including a drama/theater group, radio station, and choral group. 43% of eligible men and 35% of eligible women are members of national **fraternities**, national **sororities**, local fraternities, and local sororities.

MSOE is a member of the NCAA (Division III). **Intercollegiate sports** include baseball (m), basketball, cheerleading, crew (m), cross-country running, golf, ice hockey (m), soccer, softball (w), tennis, track and field, volleyball, wrestling (m).

Campus Safety

Student safety services include late-night transport/escort service, 24-hour emergency telephone alarm devices, 24-hour patrols by trained security personnel, and electronically operated dormitory entrances.

Applying

MSOE requires SAT or ACT, a high school transcript, and a minimum high school GPA of 2.5, and in some cases an essay and an interview. Application deadline: rolling admissions; 3/15 priority date for financial aid. Deferred admission is possible.

MISSISSIPPI COLLEGE

SUBURBAN SETTING ■ PRIVATE ■ INDEPENDENT RELIGIOUS ■ COED
CLINTON, MISSISSIPPI

Web site: www.mc.edu
Contact: Mr. Chad Phillips, Director of Admissions, PO Box 4026, 200 South Capitol Street, Clinton, MS 39058
Telephone: 601-925-3800 or toll-free 800-738-1236
Fax: 601-925-3804
E-mail: enrollment-services@mc.edu

Academics

MC awards bachelor's, master's, doctoral, and first-professional **degrees** and post-bachelor's certificates. **Challenging opportunities** include advanced placement credit, accelerated degree programs, an honors program, double majors, independent study, and a senior project. Special programs include cooperative education, internships, summer session for credit, study-abroad, and Army ROTC.

The most frequently chosen **baccalaureate** fields are business/marketing, education, and health professions and related sciences. A complete listing of majors at MC appears in the Majors by College index beginning on page 469.

The **faculty** at MC has 172 full-time members, 80% with terminal degrees. The student-faculty ratio is 17:1.

Students of MC

The student body totals 4,741, of whom 3,039 are undergraduates. 61.6% are women and 38.4% are men. 82% are from Mississippi. 3.1% are international students. 24.5% are African American, 0.5% American Indian, 1.1% Asian American, and 0.8% Hispanic American. 69% returned for their sophomore year.

Facilities and Resources

340 **computers/terminals** are available on campus for general student use. Students can access the following: campus intranet, computer help desk, free student e-mail accounts, online (class) grades, online (class) registration, online (class) schedules. Campuswide network is available. 100% of college-owned or -operated housing units are wired for high-speed Internet access. Wireless service is available via classrooms, computer centers, computer labs, dorm rooms, learning centers, libraries, student centers. The 2 **libraries** have 376,719 books.

Campus Life

There are 26 active organizations on campus, including a drama/theater group, newspaper, radio station, choral group, and marching band. MC has local **fraternities** and local **sororities**.

MC is a member of the NCAA (Division III). **Intercollegiate sports** include baseball (m), basketball, cheerleading (w), cross-country running, equestrian sports (w), football (m), golf (m), soccer, softball (w), table tennis, tennis, track and field, volleyball (w).

Campus Safety

Student safety services include late-night transport/escort service, 24-hour emergency telephone alarm devices, 24-hour patrols by trained security personnel, and electronically operated dormitory entrances.

Applying

MC requires SAT or ACT, a high school transcript, and 1 recommendation. It recommends an interview and a minimum high school GPA of 2.0. Application deadline: rolling admissions; 3/1 priority date for financial aid. Early and deferred admission are possible.

Getting Accepted

1,728 applied
62% were accepted
533 enrolled (50% of accepted)
27% from top tenth of their h.s. class
3.37 average high school GPA
Mean SAT critical reading score: 540
Mean SAT math score: 540
Mean ACT score: 23
33% had SAT critical reading scores over 600
28% had SAT math scores over 600
40% had ACT scores over 24
9% had SAT critical reading scores over 700
5% had SAT math scores over 700
8% had ACT scores over 30

Graduation and After

42% graduated in 4 years
14% graduated in 5 years
3% graduated in 6 years

Financial Matters

$13,290 tuition and fees (2008–09)
$5800 room and board
71% average percent of need met
$14,463 average financial aid amount received per undergraduate (2007–08 estimated)

MISSOURI STATE UNIVERSITY

SUBURBAN SETTING ■ PUBLIC ■ STATE-SUPPORTED ■ COED
SPRINGFIELD, MISSOURI

Web site: www.missouristate.edu
Contact: Ms. Jill Duncan, Associate Director of Admissions, 901 South National, Springfield, MO 65804
Telephone: 417-836-5517 or toll-free 800-492-7900
Fax: 417-836-6334
E-mail: info@missouristate.edu

Getting Accepted

7,677 applied
75% were accepted
2,649 enrolled (46% of accepted)
21% from top tenth of their h.s. class
3.44 average high school GPA
49% had ACT scores over 24
8% had ACT scores over 30

Graduation and After

27% graduated in 4 years
22% graduated in 5 years
6% graduated in 6 years
72% had job offers within 6 months
475 organizations recruited on campus

Financial Matters

$6256 resident tuition and fees (2008–09)
$11,536 nonresident tuition and fees (2008–09)
55% average percent of need met
$6579 average financial aid amount received per undergraduate (2007–08 estimated)

Academics

Missouri State awards bachelor's, master's, and doctoral **degrees** and post-bachelor's and post-master's certificates. **Challenging opportunities** include advanced placement credit, accelerated degree programs, student-designed majors, freshman honors college, an honors program, double majors, independent study, and a senior project. Special programs include cooperative education, internships, summer session for credit, off-campus study, study-abroad, and Army ROTC.

The most frequently chosen **baccalaureate** fields are business/marketing, education, and social sciences. A complete listing of majors at Missouri State appears in the Majors by College index beginning on page 469.

The **faculty** at Missouri State has 718 full-time members, 79% with terminal degrees. The student-faculty ratio is 19:1.

Students of Missouri State

The student body totals 19,348, of whom 16,255 are undergraduates. 55.8% are women and 44.2% are men. Students come from 47 states and territories and 81 other countries. 94% are from Missouri. 1.9% are international students. 2.9% are African American, 0.9% American Indian, 1.6% Asian American, and 1.9% Hispanic American. 74% returned for their sophomore year.

Facilities and Resources

1,800 **computers/terminals** are available on campus for general student use. Students can access the following: campus intranet, computer help desk, free student e-mail accounts, online (class) grades, online (class) registration, online (class) schedules. Campuswide network is available. Wireless service is available via classrooms, computer centers, computer labs, libraries. The 4 **libraries** have 1,699,860 books and 4,238 subscriptions.

Campus Life

There are 260 active organizations on campus, including a drama/theater group, newspaper, radio station, television station, choral group, and marching band. Missouri State has national **fraternities** and national **sororities**.

Missouri State is a member of the NCAA (Division I). **Intercollegiate sports** (some offering scholarships) include baseball (m), basketball, cross-country running (w), field hockey (w), football (m), golf, soccer, softball (w), swimming and diving, track and field (w), volleyball (w).

Campus Safety

Student safety services include on-campus police substation, late-night transport/escort service, 24-hour emergency telephone alarm devices, 24-hour patrols by trained security personnel, and electronically operated dormitory entrances.

Applying

Missouri State requires SAT or ACT and a high school transcript, and in some cases an essay and an interview. Application deadline: 7/20; 3/31 priority date for financial aid. Deferred admission is possible.

Missouri University of Science and Technology

Small-town setting ■ Public ■ State-supported ■ Coed, Primarily Men
Rolla, Missouri

Web site: www.mst.edu
Contact: Admissions Office, 300 W. 13th Street, 106 Parker Hall, Rolla, MO
Telephone: 573-341-4165 or toll-free 800-522-0938
Fax: 573-341-4082
E-mail: admissions@mst.edu

Academics

Missouri S&T awards bachelor's, master's, and doctoral **degrees** and post-bachelor's certificates. **Challenging opportunities** include advanced placement credit, accelerated degree programs, freshman honors college, an honors program, double majors, independent study, and a senior project. Special programs include cooperative education, internships, summer session for credit, off-campus study, study-abroad, and Army, Navy, and Air Force ROTC.

The most frequently chosen **baccalaureate** fields are engineering, computer and information sciences, and business/marketing. A complete listing of majors at Missouri S&T appears in the Majors by College index beginning on page 469.

The **faculty** at Missouri S&T has 363 full-time members, 88% with terminal degrees. The student-faculty ratio is 15:1.

Students of Missouri S&T

The student body totals 6,371, of whom 4,912 are undergraduates. 22.4% are women and 77.6% are men. Students come from 47 states and territories and 26 other countries. 80% are from Missouri. 2.9% are international students. 4.9% are African American, 0.6% American Indian, 2.6% Asian American, and 2% Hispanic American. 87% returned for their sophomore year.

Facilities and Resources

980 **computers/terminals** and 25 ports are available on campus for general student use. Students can access the following: campus intranet, computer help desk, free student e-mail accounts, online (class) grades, online (class) registration, online (class) schedules. Campuswide network is available. 100% of college-owned or -operated housing units are wired for high-speed Internet access. Wireless service is available via entire campus. The **library** has 477,201 books and 2,593 subscriptions.

Campus Life

There are 202 active organizations on campus, including a drama/theater group, newspaper, radio station, choral group, and marching band. 25% of eligible men and 24% of eligible women are members of national **fraternities**, national **sororities**, and local sororities.

Missouri S&T is a member of the NCAA (Division II). **Intercollegiate sports** (some offering scholarships) include baseball (m), basketball, cross-country running, football (m), soccer, softball (w), swimming and diving (m), track and field, volleyball (w).

Campus Safety

Student safety services include crime prevention programs, late-night transport/escort service, 24-hour emergency telephone alarm devices, 24-hour patrols by trained security personnel, student patrols, and electronically operated dormitory entrances.

Applying

Missouri S&T requires SAT or ACT and a high school transcript. Application deadline: 7/1; 3/1 priority date for financial aid. Early and deferred admission are possible.

Getting Accepted

2,379 applied
92% were accepted
1,046 enrolled (48% of accepted)
39% from top tenth of their h.s. class
3.70 average high school GPA
Mean SAT critical reading score: 600
Mean SAT math score: 660
Mean ACT score: 27
56% had SAT critical reading scores over 600
79% had SAT math scores over 600
84% had ACT scores over 24
14% had SAT critical reading scores over 700
28% had SAT math scores over 700
33% had ACT scores over 30
9 National Merit Scholars

Graduation and After

22% graduated in 4 years
31% graduated in 5 years
8% graduated in 6 years
74% had job offers within 6 months
673 organizations recruited on campus

Financial Matters

$8498 resident tuition and fees (2008–09)
$19,589 nonresident tuition and fees (2008–09)
$7035 room and board
46% average percent of need met
$8675 average financial aid amount received per undergraduate (2006–07)

MORAVIAN COLLEGE

SUBURBAN SETTING ■ PRIVATE ■ INDEPENDENT RELIGIOUS ■ COED
BETHLEHEM, PENNSYLVANIA

Web site: www.moravian.edu
Contact: Mr. James Mackin, Director of Admission, 1200 Main Street,
Bethlehem, PA 18018
Telephone: 610-861-1320 or toll-free 800-441-3191
Fax: 610-625-7930
E-mail: admissions@moravian.edu

Getting Accepted

2,189 applied
64% were accepted
401 enrolled (29% of accepted)
29% from top tenth of their h.s. class
Mean SAT critical reading score: 553
Mean SAT math score: 561
Mean SAT writing score: 545
26% had SAT critical reading scores over 600
31% had SAT math scores over 600
24% had SAT writing scores over 600
3% had SAT critical reading scores over 700
5% had SAT math scores over 700
4% had SAT writing scores over 700
2 class presidents
1 valedictorian

Graduation and After

70% graduated in 4 years
5% graduated in 5 years
61% had job offers within 6 months
30 organizations recruited on campus

Financial Matters

$30,062 tuition and fees (2008–09)
$8312 room and board
75% average percent of need met
$18,154 average financial aid amount received
per undergraduate (2006–07)

Academics

Moravian awards bachelor's and master's **degrees** and post-bachelor's certificates. **Challenging opportunities** include advanced placement credit, student-designed majors, an honors program, double majors, independent study, and a senior project. Special programs include internships, summer session for credit, off-campus study, study-abroad, and Army ROTC.

The most frequently chosen **baccalaureate** fields are business/marketing, social sciences, and psychology. A complete listing of majors at Moravian appears in the Majors by College index beginning on page 469.

The **faculty** at Moravian has 118 full-time members, 92% with terminal degrees. The student-faculty ratio is 11:1.

Students of Moravian

The student body totals 1,917, of whom 1,784 are undergraduates. 58.2% are women and 41.8% are men. Students come from 20 states and territories and 15 other countries. 57% are from Pennsylvania. 1.1% are international students. 1.8% are African American, 0.2% American Indian, 1.8% Asian American, and 3.1% Hispanic American. 86% returned for their sophomore year.

Facilities and Resources

263 **computers/terminals** and 150 ports are available on campus for general student use. Students can access the following: campus intranet, computer help desk, free student e-mail accounts, online (class) grades, online (class) schedules. Campuswide network is available. 100% of college-owned or -operated housing units are wired for high-speed Internet access. Wireless service is available via classrooms, computer centers, computer labs, learning centers, libraries, student centers. The **library** has 260,363 books and 3,274 subscriptions.

Campus Life

There are 77 active organizations on campus, including a drama/theater group, newspaper, radio station, choral group, and marching band. 14% of eligible men and 22% of eligible women are members of national **fraternities** and national **sororities**.

Moravian is a member of the NCAA (Division III). **Intercollegiate sports** include baseball (m), basketball, cross-country running, field hockey (w), football (m), golf (m), lacrosse, soccer, softball (w), tennis, track and field, volleyball (w).

Campus Safety

Student safety services include late-night transport/escort service, 24-hour emergency telephone alarm devices, 24-hour patrols by trained security personnel, and electronically operated dormitory entrances.

Applying

Moravian requires an essay, SAT or ACT, a high school transcript, and 3 recommendations. It recommends an interview. Application deadline: 3/1; 2/14 priority date for financial aid. Early and deferred admission are possible.

MOREHOUSE COLLEGE

URBAN SETTING ■ PRIVATE ■ INDEPENDENT ■ MEN ONLY
ATLANTA, GEORGIA

Web site: www.morehouse.edu
Contact: Mr. Terrance Dixon, Associate Dean for Admissions and Recruitment, 830 Westview Drive, SW, Atlanta, GA 30314
Telephone: 404-215-2632 or toll-free 800-851-1254
Fax: 404-524-5635
E-mail: janderso@morehouse.edu

Academics

Morehouse awards bachelor's **degrees. Challenging opportunities** include advanced placement credit, an honors program, double majors, and a senior project. Special programs include cooperative education, internships, summer session for credit, off-campus study, study-abroad, and Army, Navy, and Air Force ROTC.

The most frequently chosen **baccalaureate** fields are business/marketing, social sciences, and biological/life sciences. A complete listing of majors at Morehouse appears in the Majors by College index beginning on page 469.

The **faculty** at Morehouse has 161 full-time members, 87% with terminal degrees. The student-faculty ratio is 15:1.

Students of Morehouse

The student body is made up of 2,810 undergraduates. Students come from 41 states and territories and 15 other countries. 31% are from Georgia. 2.6% are international students. 95.3% are African American and 0.3% Hispanic American. 83% returned for their sophomore year.

Facilities and Resources

355 **computers/terminals** are available on campus for general student use. Students can access the following: online (class) registration, online (class) schedules. Campuswide network is available. The 2 **libraries** have 280,022 books and 30,083 subscriptions.

Campus Life

There are 34 active organizations on campus, including a drama/theater group, newspaper, choral group, and marching band. 1% of eligible undergraduates are members of national **fraternities**.

Morehouse is a member of the NCAA (Division II). **Intercollegiate sports** (some offering scholarships) include basketball, cross-country running, football, tennis, track and field.

Campus Safety

Student safety services include late-night transport/escort service, 24-hour emergency telephone alarm devices, 24-hour patrols by trained security personnel, and electronically operated dormitory entrances.

Applying

Morehouse requires an essay, SAT Subject Tests, SAT or ACT, a high school transcript, and a minimum high school GPA of 2.8. It recommends an interview and a minimum high school GPA of 3.0. Application deadline: 2/15; 4/1 priority date for financial aid. Early and deferred admission are possible.

Getting Accepted

2,369 applied
59% were accepted
677 enrolled (48% of accepted)
14% from top tenth of their h.s. class
3.2 average high school GPA
Mean SAT critical reading score: 520
Mean SAT math score: 521
Mean ACT score: 21
16% had SAT critical reading scores over 600
14% had SAT math scores over 600
30% had ACT scores over 24
1% had SAT critical reading scores over 700
1% had SAT math scores over 700
2% had ACT scores over 30

Graduation and After

55% had job offers within 6 months
60 organizations recruited on campus

Financial Matters

$20,358 tuition and fees (2008–09)
$10,424 room and board
25% average percent of need met
$11,079 average financial aid amount received per undergraduate

MOUNT ALLISON UNIVERSITY

SMALL-TOWN SETTING ■ PUBLIC ■ COED
SACKVILLE, NEW BRUNSWICK

Web site: www.mta.ca
Contact: Mr. Matt Sheridan-Jonah, Manager of Admissions, 65 York Street, Sackville, NB Canada
Telephone: 506-364-3294
Fax: 506-364-2272
E-mail: admissions@mta.ca

Getting Accepted

1,591 applied
88% were accepted
696 enrolled (50% of accepted)
64% from top tenth of their h.s. class
3.36 average high school GPA

Graduation and After

60% graduated in 4 years
4% graduated in 5 years
1% graduated in 6 years
15% had job offers within 6 months

Financial Matters

$6987 resident tuition and fees (2008–09)
$7174 room and board

Academics

Mount Allison awards bachelor's and master's **degrees. Challenging opportunities** include advanced placement credit, student-designed majors, an honors program, double majors, independent study, and a senior project. Special programs include internships, summer session for credit, off-campus study, and study-abroad.

The most frequently chosen **baccalaureate** fields are social sciences, business/marketing, and psychology. A complete listing of majors at Mount Allison appears in the Majors by College index beginning on page 469.

The **faculty** at Mount Allison has 133 full-time members, 80% with terminal degrees. The student-faculty ratio is 15:1.

Students of Mount Allison

The student body totals 2,170, of whom 2,163 are undergraduates. 58.3% are women and 41.7% are men. Students come from 15 states and territories and 38 other countries. 40% are from New Brunswick. 76% returned for their sophomore year.

Facilities and Resources

100 **computers/terminals** and 120 ports are available on campus for general student use. Students can access the following: computer help desk, free student e-mail accounts, online (class) registration, online (class) schedules, online student account/Websis. Campuswide network is available. 100% of college-owned or -operated housing units are wired for high-speed Internet access. Wireless service is available via entire campus. The 4 **libraries** have 400,000 books and 1,700 subscriptions.

Campus Life

There are 100 active organizations on campus, including a drama/theater group, newspaper, radio station, and choral group. No national or local **fraternities** or **sororities**.

Intercollegiate sports include basketball, football (m), ice hockey (w), rugby, soccer, swimming and diving.

Campus Safety

Student safety services include late-night transport/escort service and 24-hour emergency telephone alarm devices.

Applying

Mount Allison requires a high school transcript and a minimum high school GPA of 3.0, and in some cases an essay and an interview. It recommends 2 recommendations. Application deadline: rolling admissions. Deferred admission is possible.

Mount Holyoke College

Small-town setting ■ Private ■ Independent ■ Women Only
South Hadley, Massachusetts

Web site: www.mtholyoke.edu
Contact: Ms. Diane Anci, Dean of Admission, 50 College Street, South
   Hadley, MA 01075
Telephone: 413-538-2023
Fax: 413-538-2409
E-mail: admission@mtholyoke.edu

Academics

Mount Holyoke awards bachelor's and master's **degrees** and post-bachelor's certificates. **Challenging opportunities** include advanced placement credit, student-designed majors, an honors program, double majors, independent study, and a senior project. Special programs include cooperative education, internships, off-campus study, study-abroad, and Army and Air Force ROTC.

The most frequently chosen **baccalaureate** fields are social sciences, biological/life sciences, and English. A complete listing of majors at Mount Holyoke appears in the Majors by College index beginning on page 469.

The **faculty** at Mount Holyoke has 208 full-time members, 94% with terminal degrees. The student-faculty ratio is 10:1.

Students of Mount Holyoke

The student body totals 2,241, of whom 2,240 are undergraduates. Students come from 48 states and territories and 67 other countries. 26% are from Massachusetts. 17.2% are international students. 5.1% are African American, 0.5% American Indian, 11.7% Asian American, and 5.1% Hispanic American. 92% returned for their sophomore year.

Facilities and Resources

586 **computers/terminals** and 500 ports are available on campus for general student use. Students can access the following: campus intranet, computer help desk, free student e-mail accounts, online (class) grades, online (class) registration, online (class) schedules, personal Web pages. Campuswide network is available. 100% of college-owned or -operated housing units are wired for high-speed Internet access. Wireless service is available via entire campus. The 3 **libraries** have 1,116,118 books and 4,119 subscriptions.

Campus Life

There are 150 active organizations on campus, including a drama/theater group, newspaper, radio station, and choral group. No national or local **sororities**.

Mount Holyoke is a member of the NCAA (Division III). **Intercollegiate sports** include basketball, crew, cross-country running, equestrian sports, field hockey, golf, lacrosse, soccer, squash, swimming and diving, tennis, track and field, volleyball.

Campus Safety

Student safety services include police officers on-campus, late-night transport/escort service, 24-hour emergency telephone alarm devices, 24-hour patrols by trained security personnel, student patrols, and electronically operated dormitory entrances.

Applying

Mount Holyoke requires an essay, a high school transcript, and 2 recommendations, and in some cases SAT Subject Tests. It recommends an interview. Application deadline: 1/15; 3/1 for financial aid, with a 2/15 priority date. Early and deferred admission are possible.

Getting Accepted

3,127 applied
53% were accepted
518 enrolled (31% of accepted)
62% from top tenth of their h.s. class
3.65 average high school GPA
83% had SAT critical reading scores over 600
73% had SAT math scores over 600
89% had SAT writing scores over 600
98% had ACT scores over 24
35% had SAT critical reading scores over 700
25% had SAT math scores over 700
31% had SAT writing scores over 700
40% had ACT scores over 30
23 National Merit Scholars
24 valedictorians

Graduation and After

79% graduated in 4 years
3% graduated in 5 years
57 organizations recruited on campus

Financial Matters

$37,646 tuition and fees (2008–09)
$11,020 room and board
100% average percent of need met
$31,077 average financial aid amount received
   per undergraduate (2007–08 estimated)

Mount Saint Vincent University

Suburban setting ■ Public ■ Coed, Primarily Women
Halifax, Nova Scotia

Web site: www.msvu.ca
Contact: Ms. Heidi Tattrie, Assistant Registrar/Admissions, 166 Bedford
Highway, Halifax, NS B3M2J6 Canada
Telephone: 902-457-6117
Fax: 902-457-6498
E-mail: admissions@msvu.ca

Getting Accepted
584 applied
60% were accepted

Graduation and After
972 organizations recruited on campus

Financial Matters
$6355 resident tuition and fees (2008–09)
$6960 room and board

Academics

MSVU awards bachelor's, master's, and first-professional **degrees** and post-bachelor's certificates. **Challenging opportunities** include an honors program, double majors, independent study, and a senior project. Special programs include cooperative education, internships, summer session for credit, off-campus study, and study-abroad.

The most frequently chosen **baccalaureate** fields are education, business/marketing, and communications/journalism. A complete listing of majors at MSVU appears in the Majors by College index beginning on page 469.

The **faculty** at MSVU has 149 full-time members, 79% with terminal degrees. The student-faculty ratio is 13:1.

Students of MSVU

The student body totals 2,946. Students come from 13 states and territories and 40 other countries. 90% are from Nova Scotia. 79% returned for their sophomore year.

Facilities and Resources

Students can access the following: online (class) registration. Campuswide network is available. The 4 **libraries** have 356,763 books and 3,570 subscriptions.

Campus Life

There are 18 active organizations on campus, including a newspaper and choral group. No national or local **fraternities** or **sororities**.

Intercollegiate sports include badminton, basketball, soccer, volleyball (w).

Campus Safety

Student safety services include late-night transport/escort service, 24-hour emergency telephone alarm devices, 24-hour patrols by trained security personnel, and electronically operated dormitory entrances.

Applying

MSVU requires a high school transcript and a minimum high school GPA of 2.0, and in some cases an essay, an interview, 2 recommendations, and a minimum high school GPA of 3.0. Application deadline: 3/15, 5/30 for nonresidents; 11/3 for financial aid. Deferred admission is possible.

MUHLENBERG COLLEGE
SUBURBAN SETTING ■ PRIVATE ■ INDEPENDENT RELIGIOUS ■ COED
ALLENTOWN, PENNSYLVANIA

SPONSOR

Web site: www.muhlenberg.edu
Contact: Mr. Christopher Hooker-Haring, Director of Undergraduate
    Admissions, 2400 Chew Street, Allentown, PA 18104
Telephone: 484-664-3245
Fax: 484-664-3234
E-mail: adm@muhlenberg.edu

Academics
Muhlenberg awards associate and bachelor's **degrees**. **Challenging opportunities**
include advanced placement credit, accelerated degree programs, student-designed
majors, an honors program, double majors, independent study, and a senior project.
Special programs include internships, summer session for credit, off-campus study,
study-abroad, and Army ROTC.

The most frequently chosen **baccalaureate** fields are business/marketing, visual and
performing arts, and social sciences. A complete listing of majors at Muhlenberg appears
in the Majors by College index beginning on page 469.

The **faculty** at Muhlenberg has 161 full-time members, 89% with terminal degrees.
The student-faculty ratio is 12:1.

Students of Muhlenberg
The student body is made up of 2,492 undergraduates. 58.5% are women and 41.5% are
men. Students come from 34 states and territories and 5 other countries. 25% are from
Pennsylvania. 0.2% are international students. 2.1% are African American, 0.1%
American Indian, 2.2% Asian American, and 3.7% Hispanic American. 92% returned for
their sophomore year.

Facilities and Resources
486 **computers/terminals** and 100 ports are available on campus for general student
use. Students can access the following: campus intranet, computer help desk, free student
e-mail accounts, online (class) grades, online (class) registration, online (class) schedules.
Campuswide network is available. 100% of college-owned or -operated housing units are
wired for high-speed Internet access. Wireless service is available via classrooms, dorm
rooms, libraries, student centers. The **library** has 409,798 books and 583 subscriptions.

Campus Life
There are 109 active organizations on campus, including a drama/theater group,
newspaper, radio station, television station, and choral group. 14% of eligible men and
17% of eligible women are members of national **fraternities** and national **sororities**.

Muhlenberg is a member of the NCAA (Division III). **Intercollegiate sports** include
baseball (m), basketball, cheerleading, cross-country running, field hockey (w), football
(m), golf, lacrosse, soccer, softball (w), tennis, track and field, volleyball (w), wrestling
(m).

Campus Safety
Student safety services include late-night transport/escort service, 24-hour emergency
telephone alarm devices, 24-hour patrols by trained security personnel, and electronically operated dormitory entrances.

Applying
Muhlenberg requires an essay, a high school transcript, and 2 recommendations, and in
some cases SAT or ACT, an interview, and graded paper. It recommends an interview.
Application deadline: 2/15; 2/15 for financial aid. Early and deferred admission are possible.

Located in a beautiful campus setting
on the outskirts of a small city,
Muhlenberg offers its students an
active, highly participatory
educational experience within the
context of a friendly and very supportive community. Local internships,
field study, study abroad, and a
Washington semester all supplement
the traditional classroom experience.
Every year, large numbers of
Muhlenberg students go on to law
and medical school as well as into a
variety of competitive entry-level
career positions. They take with them
an ability to analyze and think criti-
cally as well as an ability to express
themselves effectively in person and
in writing. These are the most prized
outcomes of a Muhlenberg education.

Getting Accepted
4,703 applied
37% were accepted
597 enrolled (34% of accepted)
47% from top tenth of their h.s. class
3.41 average high school GPA
Mean SAT critical reading score: 602
Mean SAT math score: 612
Mean SAT writing score: 612
Mean ACT score: 26
55% had SAT critical reading scores over 600
61% had SAT math scores over 600
79% had ACT scores over 24
10% had SAT critical reading scores over 700
12% had SAT math scores over 700
16% had ACT scores over 30
26 class presidents
4 valedictorians

Graduation and After
78% graduated in 4 years
4% graduated in 5 years
1% graduated in 6 years
70% had job offers within 6 months
466 organizations recruited on campus

Financial Matters
$35,375 tuition and fees (2008–09)
$8060 room and board
92% average percent of need met
$21,496 average financial aid amount received
    per undergraduate (2007–08 estimated)

MURRAY STATE UNIVERSITY

SMALL-TOWN SETTING ■ PUBLIC ■ STATE-SUPPORTED ■ COED
MURRAY, KENTUCKY

Web site: www.murraystate.edu
Contact: Ms. Stacy Bell, Undergraduate Admissions Specialist, 113 Sparks
  Hall, Murray, KY 42701-0009
Telephone: 270-809-3035 or toll-free 800-272-4678
Fax: 270-809-3050
E-mail: admissions@murraystate.edu

Getting Accepted
2,972 applied
88% were accepted
1,478 enrolled (56% of accepted)
27% from top tenth of their h.s. class
3.53 average high school GPA
Mean ACT score: 23
42% had ACT scores over 24
4% had ACT scores over 30
56 valedictorians

Graduation and After
33% graduated in 4 years
14% graduated in 5 years
3% graduated in 6 years
337 organizations recruited on campus

Financial Matters
$5748 resident tuition and fees (2008–09)
$8242 nonresident tuition and fees (2008–09)
$6004 room and board
87% average percent of need met
$4220 average financial aid amount received
  per undergraduate (2007–08 estimated)

Academics
Murray State awards bachelor's and master's **degrees** and post-master's certificates. **Challenging opportunities** include advanced placement credit, freshman honors college, an honors program, double majors, independent study, and a senior project. Special programs include cooperative education, internships, summer session for credit, off-campus study, study-abroad, and Army ROTC.

The most frequently chosen **baccalaureate** fields are education, business/marketing, and health professions and related sciences. A complete listing of majors at Murray State appears in the Majors by College index beginning on page 469.

The **faculty** at Murray State has 398 full-time members, 79% with terminal degrees. The student-faculty ratio is 16:1.

Students of Murray State
The student body totals 10,014, of whom 8,171 are undergraduates. 57.6% are women and 42.4% are men. Students come from 43 states and territories and 46 other countries. 73% are from Kentucky. 1.8% are international students. 6.3% are African American, 0.4% American Indian, 0.9% Asian American, and 0.9% Hispanic American. 72% returned for their sophomore year.

Facilities and Resources
1,800 **computers/terminals** are available on campus for general student use. Students can access the following: campus intranet, computer help desk, free student e-mail accounts, online (class) grades, online (class) schedules, billing accounts. Campuswide network is available. 100% of college-owned or -operated housing units are wired for high-speed Internet access. Wireless service is available via entire campus. The 2 **libraries** have 518,450 books and 1,381 subscriptions.

Campus Life
There are 175 active organizations on campus, including a drama/theater group, newspaper, radio station, television station, choral group, and marching band. 16% of eligible men and 12% of eligible women are members of national **fraternities**, national **sororities**, local fraternities, and local sororities.

Murray State is a member of the NCAA (Division I). **Intercollegiate sports** (some offering scholarships) include baseball (m), basketball, cheerleading, crew (w), cross-country running, football (m), golf, riflery, soccer (w), softball (w), tennis, track and field, volleyball (w).

Campus Safety
Student safety services include late-night transport/escort service, 24-hour emergency telephone alarm devices, 24-hour patrols by trained security personnel, student patrols, and electronically operated dormitory entrances.

Applying
Murray State requires ACT, a high school transcript, and a minimum high school GPA of 3.0. Application deadline: 4/1 priority date for financial aid.

Nebraska Wesleyan University

Suburban setting ■ Private ■ Independent Religious ■ Coed
Lincoln, Nebraska

Web site: www.nebrwesleyan.edu
Contact: 5000 Saint Paul Avenue, Lincoln, NE 68504
Telephone: 402-465-2218 or toll-free 800-541-3818
Fax: 402-465-2177
E-mail: admissions@nebrwesleyan.edu

Academics

Nebraska Wesleyan awards bachelor's and master's **degrees** and post-bachelor's and post-master's certificates. **Challenging opportunities** include advanced placement credit, accelerated degree programs, double majors, independent study, and a senior project. Special programs include internships, summer session for credit, off-campus study, study-abroad, and Army and Air Force ROTC.

The most frequently chosen **baccalaureate** fields are business/marketing, health professions and related sciences, and biological/life sciences. A complete listing of majors at Nebraska Wesleyan appears in the Majors by College index beginning on page 469.

The **faculty** at Nebraska Wesleyan has 105 full-time members, 85% with terminal degrees. The student-faculty ratio is 13:1.

Students of Nebraska Wesleyan

The student body totals 2,086, of whom 1,870 are undergraduates. 57.6% are women and 42.4% are men. Students come from 25 states and territories and 14 other countries. 89% are from Nebraska. 0.2% are international students. 1.9% are African American, 0.1% American Indian, 1.7% Asian American, and 1.5% Hispanic American. 83% returned for their sophomore year.

Facilities and Resources

360 **computers/terminals** are available on campus for general student use. Students can access the following: computer help desk, free student e-mail accounts, online (class) grades, online (class) registration, online (class) schedules. Campuswide network is available. 100% of college-owned or -operated housing units are wired for high-speed Internet access. Wireless service is available via classrooms, computer centers, computer labs, learning centers, libraries, student centers. The **library** has 251,909 books and 597 subscriptions.

Campus Life

There are 65 active organizations on campus, including a drama/theater group, newspaper, and choral group. 14% of eligible men and 19% of eligible women are members of national **fraternities**, national **sororities**, local fraternities, and local sororities.

Nebraska Wesleyan is a member of the NCAA (Division III) and NAIA. **Intercollegiate sports** include baseball (m), basketball, cheerleading (w), cross-country running, football (m), golf, soccer, softball (w), tennis, track and field, volleyball (w).

Campus Safety

Student safety services include late-night transport/escort service, 24-hour emergency telephone alarm devices, and electronically operated dormitory entrances.

Applying

Nebraska Wesleyan requires SAT or ACT, a high school transcript, and a minimum high school GPA of 2.0, and in some cases an essay and resume of activities. It recommends an interview. Application deadline: 8/15. Deferred admission is possible.

Getting Accepted

1,519 applied
80% were accepted
383 enrolled (32% of accepted)
26% from top tenth of their h.s. class
Mean ACT score: 25
63% had ACT scores over 24
10% had ACT scores over 30
27 valedictorians

Graduation and After

47% graduated in 4 years
17% graduated in 5 years
1% graduated in 6 years
70 organizations recruited on campus

Financial Matters

$21,392 tuition and fees (2008–09)
$5710 room and board
72% average percent of need met
$14,913 average financial aid amount received
per undergraduate (2007–08 estimated)

Getting Accepted

1,221 applied
58% were accepted
222 enrolled (31% of accepted)
39% from top tenth of their h.s. class
3.91 average high school GPA
Mean SAT critical reading score: 678
Mean SAT math score: 632
Mean SAT writing score: 648
Mean ACT score: 29
88% had SAT critical reading scores over 600
70% had SAT math scores over 600
77% had SAT writing scores over 600
96% had ACT scores over 24
39% had SAT critical reading scores over 700
17% had SAT math scores over 700
24% had SAT writing scores over 700
41% had ACT scores over 30
10 National Merit Scholars
4 valedictorians

Graduation and After

45% graduated in 4 years
16% graduated in 5 years
3% graduated in 6 years
27% had job offers within 6 months
50 organizations recruited on campus

Financial Matters

$4127 resident tuition and fees (2008–09)
$23,766 nonresident tuition and fees (2008–09)
$7464 room and board
96% average percent of need met
$12,116 average financial aid amount received per undergraduate (2007–08 estimated)

NEW COLLEGE OF FLORIDA

SUBURBAN SETTING ■ PUBLIC ■ STATE-SUPPORTED ■ COED
SARASOTA, FLORIDA

Web site: www.ncf.edu
Contact: Office of Admissions, 5800 Bay Shore Road, Sarasota, FL 34243-2109
Telephone: 941-487-5000
Fax: 941-487-5010
E-mail: admissions@ncf.edu

Academics

New College awards bachelor's **degrees**. **Challenging opportunities** include student-designed majors, an honors program, double majors, independent study, and a senior project. Special programs include internships, off-campus study, and study-abroad.

The most frequently chosen **baccalaureate** field is liberal arts/general studies. A complete listing of majors at New College appears in the Majors by College index beginning on page 469.

The **faculty** at New College has 73 full-time members, 99% with terminal degrees. The student-faculty ratio is 10:1.

Students of New College

The student body is made up of 785 undergraduates. 61.7% are women and 38.3% are men. Students come from 40 states and territories and 17 other countries. 77% are from Florida. 0.3% are international students. 1.8% are African American, 1% American Indian, 2.7% Asian American, and 10.1% Hispanic American. 82% returned for their sophomore year.

Facilities and Resources

41 **computers/terminals** are available on campus for general student use. Students can access the following: campus intranet, computer help desk, free student e-mail accounts, online (class) grades, online (class) registration, online (class) schedules. Campuswide network is available. 100% of college-owned or -operated housing units are wired for high-speed Internet access. Wireless service is available via classrooms, libraries, student centers. The **library** has 274,059 books and 953 subscriptions.

Campus Life

There are 43 active organizations on campus, including a drama/theater group, newspaper, radio station, and choral group. No national or local **fraternities** or **sororities**.

Intercollegiate sports include sailing.

Campus Safety

Student safety services include late-night transport/escort service, 24-hour emergency telephone alarm devices, and 24-hour patrols by trained security personnel.

Applying

New College requires an essay, SAT or ACT, a high school transcript, and 1 recommendation, and in some cases an interview. It recommends a minimum high school GPA of 3.0. Application deadline: 2/15; 2/15 priority date for financial aid. Early and deferred admission are possible.

NEW JERSEY INSTITUTE OF TECHNOLOGY

URBAN SETTING ■ PUBLIC ■ STATE-SUPPORTED ■ COED
NEWARK, NEW JERSEY

Web site: www.njit.edu
Contact: Mr. Stephen Eck, Director of University Admissions, University
Heights, Newark, NJ 07102
Telephone: 973-596-3306 or toll-free 800-925-NJIT
Fax: 973-596-3461
E-mail: admissions@njit.edu

SPONSOR

Academics

NJIT awards bachelor's, master's, and doctoral **degrees** and post-bachelor's certificates. **Challenging opportunities** include advanced placement credit, accelerated degree programs, freshman honors college, an honors program, double majors, independent study, and a senior project. Special programs include cooperative education, internships, summer session for credit, off-campus study, study-abroad, and Air Force ROTC.

The most frequently chosen **baccalaureate** fields are engineering, computer and information sciences, and engineering technologies. A complete listing of majors at NJIT appears in the Majors by College index beginning on page 469.

The **faculty** at NJIT has 396 full-time members, 100% with terminal degrees. The student-faculty ratio is 14:1.

Students of NJIT

The student body totals 8,398, of whom 5,576 are undergraduates. 20.8% are women and 79.2% are men. Students come from 30 states and territories and 95 other countries. 96% are from New Jersey. 4.8% are international students. 10% are African American, 0.8% American Indian, 20.7% Asian American, and 19.2% Hispanic American. 83% returned for their sophomore year.

Facilities and Resources

1,938 **computers/terminals** are available on campus for general student use. Students can access the following: computer help desk, free student e-mail accounts, online (class) grades, online (class) registration, online (class) schedules. Campuswide network is available. 100% of college-owned or -operated housing units are wired for high-speed Internet access. Wireless service is available via entire campus. The 2 **libraries** have 160,000 books and 1,100 subscriptions.

Campus Life

There are 70 active organizations on campus, including a drama/theater group, newspaper, radio station, and marching band. 8% of eligible men and 4% of eligible women are members of national **fraternities**, national **sororities**, local fraternities, and local sororities.

NJIT is a member of the NCAA (Division I). **Intercollegiate sports** (some offering scholarships) include baseball (m), basketball, cross-country running, fencing, soccer, swimming and diving, tennis, track and field, volleyball.

Campus Safety

Student safety services include bicycle patrols, late-night transport/escort service, 24-hour emergency telephone alarm devices, 24-hour patrols by trained security personnel, and electronically operated dormitory entrances.

Applying

NJIT requires SAT or ACT and a high school transcript, and in some cases an essay and an interview. It recommends 1 recommendation. Application deadline: 4/1; 5/15 for financial aid, with a 3/15 priority date. Early and deferred admission are possible.

Recognized by *U.S. News & World Report* as a top-tier national research university offering bachelor's, master's, and doctoral degrees, New Jersey Institute of Technology (NJIT) has been a leader in the field of engineering education for almost ninety years. NJIT's Newark College of Engineering is one of the largest professional engineering schools in the United States; among its more than 40,000 alumni are pioneers and leaders in such fields as aerospace, telecommunications, plastics, electronics, and environmental engineering.

Getting Accepted
3,429 applied
69% were accepted
907 enrolled (38% of accepted)
25% from top tenth of their h.s. class
Mean SAT critical reading score: 538
Mean SAT math score: 604
Mean SAT writing score: 530
22% had SAT critical reading scores over 600
52% had SAT math scores over 600
20% had SAT writing scores over 600
3% had SAT critical reading scores over 700
11% had SAT math scores over 700
2% had SAT writing scores over 700

Graduation and After
17% graduated in 4 years
30% graduated in 5 years
11% graduated in 6 years
80% had job offers within 6 months
400 organizations recruited on campus

Financial Matters
$12,482 resident tuition and fees (2008–09)
$21,942 nonresident tuition and fees (2008–09)
$9596 room and board
81% average percent of need met
$10,089 average financial aid amount received per undergraduate (2006–07)

New Mexico Institute of Mining and Technology

SMALL-TOWN SETTING ■ PUBLIC ■ STATE-SUPPORTED ■ COED
SOCORRO, NEW MEXICO

Web site: www.nmt.edu
Contact: Mr. Mike Kloeppel, Director of Admissions, 801 Leroy Place, Socorro, NM 87801
Telephone: 575-835-5424 or toll-free 800-428-TECH
Fax: 575-835-5989
E-mail: admission@admin.nmt.edu

Getting Accepted
763 applied
55% were accepted
240 enrolled (57% of accepted)
31% from top tenth of their h.s. class
3.6 average high school GPA
Mean SAT critical reading score: 593
Mean SAT math score: 615
Mean ACT score: 26
52% had SAT critical reading scores over 600
58% had SAT math scores over 600
70% had ACT scores over 24
15% had SAT critical reading scores over 700
17% had SAT math scores over 700
20% had ACT scores over 30

Graduation and After
16% graduated in 4 years
22% graduated in 5 years
5% graduated in 6 years
75% had job offers within 6 months
22 organizations recruited on campus

Financial Matters
$4352 resident tuition and fees (2008–09)
$12,544 nonresident tuition and fees (2008–09)
$5320 room and board
94% average percent of need met
$9429 average financial aid amount received per undergraduate (2007–08 estimated)

Academics
New Mexico Tech awards associate, bachelor's, master's, and doctoral **degrees**. **Challenging opportunities** include advanced placement credit, accelerated degree programs, student-designed majors, double majors, independent study, and a senior project. Special programs include cooperative education, internships, and summer session for credit.

The most frequently chosen **baccalaureate** fields are engineering, physical sciences, and computer and information sciences. A complete listing of majors at New Mexico Tech appears in the Majors by College index beginning on page 469.

The **faculty** at New Mexico Tech has 119 full-time members, 97% with terminal degrees. The student-faculty ratio is 11:1.

Students of New Mexico Tech
The student body totals 1,882, of whom 1,327 are undergraduates. 33% are women and 67% are men. Students come from 24 states and territories and 29 other countries. 87% are from New Mexico. 1.9% are international students. 1.1% are African American, 2.6% American Indian, 3% Asian American, and 24.8% Hispanic American. 73% returned for their sophomore year.

Facilities and Resources
225 **computers/terminals** are available on campus for general student use. Students can access the following: computer help desk, free student e-mail accounts, online (class) registration, online (class) schedules. Campuswide network is available. Wireless service is available via computer centers, learning centers, student centers. The 2 **libraries** have 321,829 books and 884 subscriptions.

Campus Life
There are 55 active organizations on campus, including a drama/theater group, newspaper, radio station, and choral group. No national or local **fraternities** or **sororities**.

This institution has no intercollegiate sports.

Campus Safety
Student safety services include late-night transport/escort service, 24-hour emergency telephone alarm devices, and 24-hour patrols by trained security personnel.

Applying
New Mexico Tech requires SAT or ACT, a high school transcript, and a minimum high school GPA of 2.5, and in some cases 2 recommendations. It recommends ACT and an interview. Application deadline: 8/1; 6/1 priority date for financial aid. Deferred admission is possible.

NEW YORK SCHOOL OF INTERIOR DESIGN

URBAN SETTING ■ PRIVATE ■ INDEPENDENT ■ COED, PRIMARILY WOMEN
NEW YORK, NEW YORK

SPONSOR

Web site: www.nysid.edu
Contact: Cassandra Ramirez, Admissions Associate, 170 East 70th Street, New York, NY 10021-5110
Telephone: 212-472-1500 Ext. 204 or toll-free 800-336-9743 Ext. 204
Fax: 212-472-1867
E-mail: admissions@nysid.edu

Academics

NYSID awards associate, bachelor's, and master's **degrees. Challenging opportunities** include advanced placement credit, independent study, and a senior project. Special programs include internships and summer session for credit. A complete listing of majors at NYSID appears in the Majors by College index beginning on page 469.

The **faculty** at NYSID has 2 full-time members. The student-faculty ratio is 10:1.

Students of NYSID

The student body totals 721, of whom 705 are undergraduates. 90.5% are women and 9.5% are men. 72% are from New York. 0.3% are international students. 3.4% are African American, 0.1% American Indian, 9.8% Asian American, and 6.7% Hispanic American. 25% returned for their sophomore year.

Facilities and Resources

135 **computers/terminals** are available on campus for general student use. Students can access the following: free student e-mail accounts, online (class) grades, online (class) registration, online (class) schedules. Campuswide network is available.

Campus Life

No national or local **fraternities** or **sororities**.
This institution has no intercollegiate sports.

Campus Safety

Student safety services include security during school hours.

Applying

NYSID requires an essay, a high school transcript, 2 recommendations, portfolio, and a minimum high school GPA of 2.8, and in some cases SAT or ACT. Application deadline: 3/1; 5/1 priority date for financial aid. Deferred admission is possible.

Manhattan, with its world-famous museums, showrooms, and architectural landmarks, is home to the New York School of Interior Design (NYSID). NYSID is a college that dedicates all of its resources to the study of interior design. Facilities include a lighting lab, a computer-aided design (CAD) lab, and an extensive reference library. NYSID graduates have gone on to find work in the best design and architectural firms in New York City and around the world. The Bachelor of Fine Arts degree program is accredited by CIDA, the Council for Interior Design Accreditation.

Getting Accepted
93 applied
46% were accepted
15 enrolled (35% of accepted)
3.49 average high school GPA
9% had SAT math scores over 600

Graduation and After
65% had job offers within 6 months

Financial Matters
$20,840 tuition and fees (2009–10)
50% average percent of need met
$6500 average financial aid amount received per undergraduate (2006–07)

Getting Accepted
37,245 applied
32% were accepted
4,496 enrolled (38% of accepted)
68% from top tenth of their h.s. class
3.6 average high school GPA
Mean SAT critical reading score: 664
Mean SAT math score: 672
Mean SAT writing score: 669
Mean ACT score: 30
85% had SAT critical reading scores over 600
85% had SAT math scores over 600
85% had SAT writing scores over 600
99% had ACT scores over 24
32% had SAT critical reading scores over 700
37% had SAT math scores over 700
37% had SAT writing scores over 700
45% had ACT scores over 30

Graduation and After
77% graduated in 4 years
5% graduated in 5 years
2% graduated in 6 years
92% had job offers within 6 months
686 organizations recruited on campus

Financial Matters
$37,372 tuition and fees (2008–09)
$12,910 room and board
65% average percent of need met
$22,207 average financial aid amount received
per undergraduate (2007–08 estimated)

NEW YORK UNIVERSITY
URBAN SETTING ■ PRIVATE ■ INDEPENDENT ■ COED
NEW YORK, NEW YORK

Web site: www.nyu.edu
Contact: Ms. Barbara Hall, Associate Provost for Admissions and Financial
Aid, 22 Washington Square North, New York, NY 10011
Telephone: 212-998-4500
Fax: 212-995-4902
E-mail: nyuadmit@uccvm.nyu.edu

Academics
NYU awards associate, bachelor's, master's, doctoral, and first-professional **degrees** and
post-bachelor's, post-master's, and first-professional certificates. **Challenging opportunities** include advanced placement credit, student-designed majors, an honors
program, double majors, independent study, and a senior project. Special programs
include internships, summer session for credit, off-campus study, study-abroad, and
Army and Navy ROTC.

The most frequently chosen **baccalaureate** fields are business/marketing, visual and
performing arts, and social sciences. A complete listing of majors at NYU appears in the
Majors by College index beginning on page 469.

The **faculty** at NYU has 2,227 full-time members, 90% with terminal degrees. The
student-faculty ratio is 12:1.

Students of NYU
The student body totals 42,189, of whom 21,269 are undergraduates. 61.5% are women
and 38.5% are men. Students come from 52 states and territories and 99 other countries.
36% are from New York. 6.3% are international students. 4.3% are African American,
0.2% American Indian, 19.2% Asian American, and 7.6% Hispanic American. 92%
returned for their sophomore year.

Facilities and Resources
4,500 **computers/terminals** are available on campus for general student use. Students
can access the following: computer help desk, free student e-mail accounts, online (class)
registration, online (class) schedules. Campuswide network is available. 100% of college-
owned or -operated housing units are wired for high-speed Internet access. Wireless
service is available via computer labs, learning centers, libraries, student centers. The 12
libraries have 5,235,527 books and 48,958 subscriptions.

Campus Life
There are 407 active organizations on campus, including a drama/theater group,
newspaper, radio station, television station, choral group, and marching band. 1% of
eligible men and 2% of eligible women are members of national **fraternities**, national
sororities, and local sororities.

NYU is a member of the NCAA (Division III). **Intercollegiate sports** include
basketball, cheerleading, cross-country running, fencing, golf (m), soccer, swimming and
diving, tennis, track and field, volleyball, wrestling (m).

Campus Safety
Student safety services include 24-hour security in residence halls, late-night transport/
escort service, 24-hour emergency telephone alarm devices, 24-hour patrols by trained
security personnel, student patrols, and electronically operated dormitory entrances.

Applying
NYU requires an essay, SAT or ACT, a high school transcript, and 2 recommendations,
and in some cases SAT Subject Tests and audition, portfolio. Application deadline: 1/1;
2/15 priority date for financial aid. Deferred admission is possible.

North Carolina State University

URBAN SETTING ■ PUBLIC ■ STATE-SUPPORTED ■ COED
RALEIGH, NORTH CAROLINA

Web site: www.ncsu.edu
Contact: Mr. Thomas Griffin, Director of Undergraduate Admissions, Box 7103, Raleigh, NC 27695
Telephone: 919-515-2434
Fax: 919-515-5039
E-mail: undergrad_admissions@ncsu.edu

Academics

NC State awards associate, bachelor's, master's, doctoral, and first-professional **degrees** and post-bachelor's and first-professional certificates. **Challenging opportunities** include advanced placement credit, accelerated degree programs, student-designed majors, an honors program, double majors, independent study, and a senior project. Special programs include cooperative education, internships, summer session for credit, off-campus study, study-abroad, and Army, Navy, and Air Force ROTC.

The most frequently chosen **baccalaureate** fields are engineering, business/marketing, and biological/life sciences. A complete listing of majors at NC State appears in the Majors by College index beginning on page 469.

The **faculty** at NC State has 1,760 full-time members, 89% with terminal degrees. The student-faculty ratio is 16:1.

Students of NC State

The student body totals 32,872, of whom 24,741 are undergraduates. 43.8% are women and 56.2% are men. Students come from 52 states and territories and 65 other countries. 93% are from North Carolina. 1.6% are international students. 8.9% are African American, 0.5% American Indian, 5.1% Asian American, and 2.6% Hispanic American. 90% returned for their sophomore year.

Facilities and Resources

3,000 **computers/terminals** and 500 ports are available on campus for general student use. Students can access the following: campus intranet, computer help desk, free student e-mail accounts, online (class) grades, online (class) registration, online (class) schedules, course materials, online homework submission, online testing/quizzes, financial aid/cashier's office account balances, wiki space, blogging service, Web space, online storage space, on-site OS and virus removal, online/hybrid courses. Campuswide network is available. 100% of college-owned or -operated housing units are wired for high-speed Internet access. Wireless service is available via classrooms, computer centers, computer labs, dorm rooms, learning centers, libraries, student centers. The 7 **libraries** have 3,687,733 books and 49,480 subscriptions.

Campus Life

There are 300 active organizations on campus, including a drama/theater group, newspaper, radio station, television station, choral group, and marching band. 9% of eligible men and 12% of eligible women are members of national **fraternities**, national **sororities**, and local sororities.

NC State is a member of the NCAA (Division I). **Intercollegiate sports** (some offering scholarships) include baseball (m), basketball, cheerleading, cross-country running, fencing, football (m), golf, gymnastics (w), riflery, soccer, softball (w), swimming and diving, tennis, track and field, volleyball (w), wrestling (m).

Campus Safety

Student safety services include late-night transport/escort service, 24-hour emergency telephone alarm devices, 24-hour patrols by trained security personnel, student patrols, and electronically operated dormitory entrances.

Applying

NC State requires SAT or ACT and a high school transcript, and in some cases an interview. It recommends an essay and SAT Subject Tests. Application deadline: 2/1; 3/1 priority date for financial aid. Deferred admission is possible.

Getting Accepted

17,652 applied
59% were accepted
4,804 enrolled (46% of accepted)
40% from top tenth of their h.s. class
Mean SAT critical reading score: 569
Mean SAT math score: 607
Mean SAT writing score: 560
Mean ACT score: 25
36% had SAT critical reading scores over 600
56% had SAT math scores over 600
30% had SAT writing scores over 600
63% had ACT scores over 24
5% had SAT critical reading scores over 700
12% had SAT math scores over 700
4% had SAT writing scores over 700
11% had ACT scores over 30
3 National Merit Scholars
67 valedictorians

Graduation and After

37% graduated in 4 years
28% graduated in 5 years
5% graduated in 6 years
60% had job offers within 6 months
340 organizations recruited on campus

Financial Matters

$5274 resident tuition and fees (2008–09)
$17,572 nonresident tuition and fees (2008–09)
$7982 room and board
81% average percent of need met
$9540 average financial aid amount received per undergraduate (2007–08 estimated)

NORTH CENTRAL COLLEGE

SUBURBAN SETTING ■ PRIVATE ■ INDEPENDENT RELIGIOUS ■ COED
NAPERVILLE, ILLINOIS

Web site: www.noctrl.edu
Contact: Ms. Martha Stolze, Director of Freshman Admission, 30 North
  Brainard Street, PO Box 3063, Naperville, IL 60566-7063
Telephone: 630-637-5800 or toll-free 800-411-1861
Fax: 630-637-5819
E-mail: admissions@noctrl.edu

North Central College, nestled in the heart of Naperville, Illinois—*Money* magazine's "Second Best Place to Live" in the nation—is just 29 miles from downtown Chicago. The College is committed to undergraduate teaching and to sustaining its strong campus life tradition. The curriculum is grounded in a liberal arts foundation, with an emphasis on leadership, ethics, and values. North Central College offers more than fifty-five academic areas of concentration in business, communication, education, liberal arts, and science as well as preprofessional programs. Cocurricular opportunities include nationally recognized Division III intercollegiate athletics, a student radio station, a Model UN team, a community conflict-resolution program, forensics, and community service.

Getting Accepted
2,574 applied
68% were accepted
528 enrolled (30% of accepted)
3.50 average high school GPA
Mean ACT score: 24
55% had ACT scores over 24
10% had ACT scores over 30
1 National Merit Scholar
8 valedictorians

Graduation and After
52% graduated in 4 years
10% graduated in 5 years
1% graduated in 6 years
63% had job offers within 6 months
25 organizations recruited on campus

Financial Matters
$25,938 tuition and fees (2008–09)
$8217 room and board
77% average percent of need met
$18,164 average financial aid amount received
  per undergraduate (2007–08 estimated)

Academics
North Central awards bachelor's and master's **degrees** and post-bachelor's certificates. **Challenging opportunities** include advanced placement credit, accelerated degree programs, student-designed majors, an honors program, double majors, independent study, and a senior project. Special programs include internships, summer session for credit, off-campus study, study-abroad, and Army and Air Force ROTC.

The most frequently chosen **baccalaureate** fields are business/marketing, education, and social sciences. A complete listing of majors at North Central appears in the Majors by College index beginning on page 469.

The **faculty** at North Central has 119 full-time members, 87% with terminal degrees. The student-faculty ratio is 16:1.

Students of North Central
The student body totals 2,726, of whom 2,388 are undergraduates. 54.7% are women and 45.3% are men. Students come from 28 states and territories and 28 other countries. 92% are from Illinois. 0.9% are international students. 3.4% are African American, 0.2% American Indian, 3.2% Asian American, and 4.6% Hispanic American. 79% returned for their sophomore year.

Facilities and Resources
325 **computers/terminals** and 15 ports are available on campus for general student use. Students can access the following: campus intranet, computer help desk, free student e-mail accounts, online (class) grades, online (class) registration, online (class) schedules, software packages. Campuswide network is available. 100% of college-owned or -operated housing units are wired for high-speed Internet access. Wireless service is available via computer centers, computer labs, dorm rooms, learning centers, libraries, student centers. The **library** has 152,785 books and 3,092 subscriptions.

Campus Life
There are 59 active organizations on campus, including a drama/theater group, newspaper, radio station, and choral group. No national or local **fraternities** or **sororities**.

North Central is a member of the NCAA (Division III). **Intercollegiate sports** include baseball (m), basketball, cheerleading (w), cross-country running, football (m), golf, lacrosse (w), soccer, softball (w), swimming and diving, tennis, track and field, volleyball (w), wrestling (m).

Campus Safety
Student safety services include late-night transport/escort service, 24-hour emergency telephone alarm devices, and 24-hour patrols by trained security personnel.

Applying
North Central requires SAT or ACT, a high school transcript, and a minimum high school GPA of 2.5, and in some cases an interview. It recommends an essay, ACT, and 1 recommendation. Application deadline: rolling admissions. Deferred admission is possible.

NORTHWESTERN COLLEGE

RURAL SETTING ■ PRIVATE ■ INDEPENDENT RELIGIOUS ■ COED
ORANGE CITY, IOWA

Web site: www.nwciowa.edu
Contact: Mr. Mark Bloemendaal, Director of Admissions, 101 7th Street SW,
    Orange City, IA 51041-1996
Telephone: 712-737-7130 or toll-free 800-747-4757
Fax: 712-707-7164
E-mail: admissions@nwciowa.edu

Academics

Northwestern College awards bachelor's **degrees**. **Challenging opportunities** include advanced placement credit, student-designed majors, an honors program, double majors, independent study, and a senior project. Special programs include cooperative education, internships, summer session for credit, off-campus study, and study-abroad.

The most frequently chosen **baccalaureate** fields are business/marketing, education, and biological/life sciences. A complete listing of majors at Northwestern College appears in the Majors by College index beginning on page 469.

The **faculty** at Northwestern College has 82 full-time members, 79% with terminal degrees. The student-faculty ratio is 15:1.

Students of Northwestern College

The student body is made up of 1,315 undergraduates. 60.7% are women and 39.3% are men. Students come from 30 states and territories and 20 other countries. 54% are from Iowa. 2.6% are international students. 0.9% are African American, 0.2% American Indian, 0.9% Asian American, and 1.4% Hispanic American. 76% returned for their sophomore year.

Facilities and Resources

250 **computers/terminals** are available on campus for general student use. Students can access the following: campus intranet, computer help desk, free student e-mail accounts, online (class) grades, online (class) registration, online (class) schedules, online degree audits. Campuswide network is available. Wireless service is available via classrooms, computer centers, computer labs, learning centers, libraries, student centers. The 2 **libraries** have 125,000 books and 615 subscriptions.

Campus Life

There are 30 active organizations on campus, including a drama/theater group, newspaper, television station, and choral group. No national or local **fraternities** or **sororities**.

Northwestern College is a member of the NAIA. **Intercollegiate sports** (some offering scholarships) include baseball (m), basketball, cross-country running, football (m), golf, soccer, softball (w), track and field, volleyball (w), wrestling (m).

Campus Safety

Student safety services include 24-hour emergency telephone alarm devices and electronically operated dormitory entrances.

Applying

Northwestern College requires an essay, SAT or ACT, a high school transcript, 1 recommendation, and a minimum high school GPA of 2.0. It recommends an interview and a minimum high school GPA of 2.5. Application deadline: rolling admissions; 4/1 priority date for financial aid. Early and deferred admission are possible.

Getting Accepted
1,311 applied
79% were accepted
324 enrolled (31% of accepted)
31% from top tenth of their h.s. class
3.54 average high school GPA
Mean ACT score: 24
61% had ACT scores over 24
9% had ACT scores over 30
30 valedictorians

Graduation and After
53% graduated in 4 years
7% graduated in 5 years
1% graduated in 6 years
93% had job offers within 6 months
35 organizations recruited on campus

Financial Matters
$22,950 tuition and fees (2008–09)
$6580 room and board
87% average percent of need met
$16,330 average financial aid amount received
    per undergraduate (2007–08 estimated)

Getting Accepted

1,109 applied
93% were accepted
502 enrolled (49% of accepted)
28% from top tenth of their h.s. class
3.57 average high school GPA
Mean SAT critical reading score: 565
Mean SAT math score: 560
Mean ACT score: 24
40% had SAT critical reading scores over 600
46% had SAT math scores over 600
58% had ACT scores over 24
17% had SAT critical reading scores over 700
14% had SAT math scores over 700
11% had ACT scores over 30
15 valedictorians

Graduation and After

47% graduated in 4 years
11% graduated in 5 years
3% graduated in 6 years
65% had job offers within 6 months
90 organizations recruited on campus

Financial Matters

$22,420 tuition and fees (2008–09)
$7050 room and board
73% average percent of need met
$14,555 average financial aid amount received per undergraduate (2006–07)

NORTHWESTERN COLLEGE

SUBURBAN SETTING ■ PRIVATE ■ INDEPENDENT RELIGIOUS ■ COED
ST. PAUL, MINNESOTA

Web site: www.nwc.edu
Contact: Mr. Kenneth K. Faffler, Director of Admissions, Officer of Admissions, 3003 Snelling Avenue North, 212 Nazareth Hall, St. Paul, MN 55113-1598
Telephone: 651-631-5111 or toll-free 800-827-6827
Fax: 651-631-5680
E-mail: admissions@nwc.edu

Academics

Northwestern College awards associate, bachelor's, and master's **degrees. Challenging opportunities** include advanced placement credit, student-designed majors, an honors program, double majors, independent study, and a senior project. Special programs include internships, summer session for credit, off-campus study, study-abroad, and Army and Air Force ROTC.

The most frequently chosen **baccalaureate** fields are education, theology and religious vocations, and communications/journalism. A complete listing of majors at Northwestern College appears in the Majors by College index beginning on page 469.

The **faculty** at Northwestern College has 96 full-time members, 61% with terminal degrees.

Students of Northwestern College

The student body totals 1,925, of whom 1,845 are undergraduates. 58.8% are women and 41.2% are men. Students come from 35 states and territories and 21 other countries. 68% are from Minnesota. 0.3% are international students. 2.7% are African American, 0.6% American Indian, 4.4% Asian American, and 2% Hispanic American. 83% returned for their sophomore year.

Facilities and Resources

100 **computers/terminals** and 12 ports are available on campus for general student use. Students can access the following: campus intranet, computer help desk, free student e-mail accounts, online (class) grades, online (class) registration, online (class) schedules. Campuswide network is available. 100% of college-owned or -operated housing units are wired for high-speed Internet access. Wireless service is available via classrooms, computer labs, dorm rooms, learning centers, libraries, student centers. The **library** has 117,745 books and 1,131 subscriptions.

Campus Life

There are 25 active organizations on campus, including a drama/theater group, newspaper, radio station, and choral group. No national or local **fraternities** or **sororities**.

Northwestern College is a member of the NCAA (Division III) and NCCAA. **Intercollegiate sports** include baseball (m), basketball, cheerleading (w), cross-country running, football (m), golf (m), soccer, softball (w), tennis, track and field, volleyball (w).

Campus Safety

Student safety services include late-night transport/escort service, 24-hour patrols by trained security personnel, and electronically operated dormitory entrances.

Applying

Northwestern College requires an essay, SAT or ACT, a high school transcript, 2 recommendations, lifestyle agreement, statement of Christian faith, and a minimum high school GPA of 2.0, and in some cases an interview. It recommends a minimum high school GPA of 3.0. Application deadline: 8/1; 5/1 for financial aid, with a 3/1 priority date. Early and deferred admission are possible.

NORTHWESTERN UNIVERSITY

SUBURBAN SETTING ■ PRIVATE ■ INDEPENDENT ■ COED
EVANSTON, ILLINOIS

Web site: www.northwestern.edu
Contact: Mr. Christopher Watson, Dean of Undergraduate Admission, PO
   Box 3060, Evanston, IL 60204-3060
Telephone: 847-491-7271
E-mail: ug-admission@northwestern.edu

Academics

Northwestern awards bachelor's, master's, doctoral, and first-professional **degrees** and post-master's certificates. **Challenging opportunities** include advanced placement credit, accelerated degree programs, student-designed majors, an honors program, double majors, independent study, and a senior project. Special programs include cooperative education, internships, summer session for credit, study-abroad, and Army, Navy, and Air Force ROTC.

The most frequently chosen **baccalaureate** fields are social sciences, communications/journalism, and engineering. A complete listing of majors at Northwestern appears in the Majors by College index beginning on page 469.

The **faculty** at Northwestern has 1,010 full-time members, 100% with terminal degrees. The student-faculty ratio is 7:1.

Students of Northwestern

The student body totals 18,028, of whom 8,284 are undergraduates. 52.8% are women and 47.2% are men. Students come from 51 states and territories and 42 other countries. 25% are from Illinois. 5% are international students. 5.9% are African American, 0.1% American Indian, 17.1% Asian American, and 6.7% Hispanic American. 96% returned for their sophomore year.

Facilities and Resources

678 **computers/terminals** are available on campus for general student use. Students can access the following: campus intranet, computer help desk, free student e-mail accounts, online (class) grades, online (class) registration, online (class) schedules. Campuswide network is available. 100% of college-owned or -operated housing units are wired for high-speed Internet access. The 7 **libraries** have 4,687,828 books and 45,259 subscriptions.

Campus Life

There are 415 active organizations on campus, including a drama/theater group, newspaper, radio station, television station, choral group, and marching band. 37% of eligible men and 42% of eligible women are members of national **fraternities** and national **sororities**.

Northwestern is a member of the NCAA (Division I). **Intercollegiate sports** (some offering scholarships) include baseball (m), basketball, cheerleading, cross-country running (w), fencing (w), field hockey (w), football (m), golf, lacrosse (w), soccer, softball (w), swimming and diving, tennis, volleyball (w), wrestling (m).

Campus Safety

Student safety services include late-night transport/escort service, 24-hour emergency telephone alarm devices, 24-hour patrols by trained security personnel, and electronically operated dormitory entrances.

Applying

Northwestern requires an essay, SAT or ACT, a high school transcript, and 1 recommendation, and in some cases SAT Subject Tests and audition for music program. It recommends SAT Subject Tests. Application deadline: 1/1; 2/15 for financial aid. Early and deferred admission are possible.

Getting Accepted
21,930 applied
27% were accepted
1,981 enrolled (34% of accepted)
85% from top tenth of their h.s. class
94% had SAT critical reading scores over 600
95% had SAT math scores over 600
93% had SAT writing scores over 600
96% had ACT scores over 24
61% had SAT critical reading scores over 700
66% had SAT math scores over 700
57% had SAT writing scores over 700
76% had ACT scores over 30
249 National Merit Scholars
132 valedictorians

Graduation and After
86% graduated in 4 years
6% graduated in 5 years
1% graduated in 6 years
624 organizations recruited on campus

Financial Matters
$37,125 tuition and fees (2008–09)
$11,295 room and board
100% average percent of need met
$27,936 average financial aid amount received per undergraduate (2007–08 estimated)

OBERLIN COLLEGE

SMALL-TOWN SETTING ■ PRIVATE ■ INDEPENDENT ■ COED
OBERLIN, OHIO

Web site: www.oberlin.edu
Contact: Ms. Debra Chermonte, Dean of Admissions and Financial Aid,
    Admissions Office, Carnegie Building, Oberlin, OH 44074-1090
Telephone: 440-775-8411 or toll-free 800-622-OBIE
Fax: 440-775-6905
E-mail: college.admissions@oberlin.edu

Oberlin is a four-year, highly selective liberal arts college and home to America's oldest continuously operating music conservatory. From its founding, Oberlin has been a community of thinkers, scholars, scientists, musicians, athletes, activists, and artists—all of whom seek to make the world a better place. Oberlin invented coeducation in 1837 and made interracial education central to its mission in 1835. More Oberlin graduates have gone on to earn Ph.D.'s than those at any other American college. Oberlin alumni, who include 3 Nobel laureates and 7 MacArthur genius award recipients, are leaders in law, scientific and scholarly research, medicine, the arts, theology, communication, business, and government.

Getting Accepted

7,006 applied
33% were accepted
766 enrolled (33% of accepted)
69% from top tenth of their h.s. class
3.6 average high school GPA
Mean SAT critical reading score: 700
Mean SAT math score: 674
Mean SAT writing score: 690
Mean ACT score: 30
89% had SAT critical reading scores over 600
84% had SAT math scores over 600
87% had SAT writing scores over 600
94% had ACT scores over 24
54% had SAT critical reading scores over 700
34% had SAT math scores over 700
47% had SAT writing scores over 700
53% had ACT scores over 30
47 National Merit Scholars
38 valedictorians

Graduation and After

69% graduated in 4 years
12% graduated in 5 years
1% graduated in 6 years
90% had job offers within 6 months
32 organizations recruited on campus

Financial Matters

$38,280 tuition and fees (2008–09)
$9870 room and board
100% average percent of need met
$25,047 average financial aid amount received
   per undergraduate (2007–08 estimated)

Academics

Oberlin awards bachelor's and master's **degrees** and post-bachelor's certificates. **Challenging opportunities** include advanced placement credit, student-designed majors, an honors program, double majors, independent study, and a senior project. Special programs include internships, off-campus study, and study-abroad. A complete listing of majors at Oberlin appears in the Majors by College index beginning on page 469.

The **faculty** at Oberlin has 285 members, 96% with terminal degrees. The student-faculty ratio is 9:1.

Students of Oberlin

The student body totals 2,865, of whom 2,839 are undergraduates. 55.2% are women and 44.8% are men. Students come from 50 states and territories and 44 other countries. 9% are from Ohio. 6% are international students. 6.4% are African American, 0.6% American Indian, 7.1% Asian American, and 5.1% Hispanic American. 94% returned for their sophomore year.

Facilities and Resources

340 **computers/terminals** are available on campus for general student use. Students can access the following: campus intranet, computer help desk, free student e-mail accounts, online (class) registration, online (class) schedules. Campuswide network is available. 100% of college-owned or -operated housing units are wired for high-speed Internet access. Wireless service is available via classrooms, computer centers, computer labs, dorm rooms, learning centers, libraries, student centers. The 4 **libraries** have 1,541,260 books and 4,560 subscriptions.

Campus Life

There are 120 active organizations on campus, including a drama/theater group, newspaper, radio station, choral group, and marching band. No national or local **fraternities** or **sororities**.

Oberlin is a member of the NCAA (Division III). **Intercollegiate sports** include baseball (m), basketball, cross-country running, field hockey (w), football (m), golf, lacrosse, soccer, swimming and diving, tennis, track and field, volleyball (w).

Campus Safety

Student safety services include crime prevention programs, late-night transport/escort service, 24-hour emergency telephone alarm devices, 24-hour patrols by trained security personnel, student patrols, and electronically operated dormitory entrances.

Applying

Oberlin requires an essay, SAT or ACT, a high school transcript, and 2 recommendations, and in some cases an interview. It recommends SAT Subject Tests. Application deadline: 1/15; 2/15 priority date for financial aid. Early and deferred admission are possible.

OCCIDENTAL COLLEGE
URBAN SETTING ■ PRIVATE ■ INDEPENDENT ■ COED
LOS ANGELES, CALIFORNIA

Web site: www.oxy.edu
Contact: Mr. Vince Cuseo, Dean of Admission, 1600 Campus Road, Los Angeles, CA 90041
Telephone: 323-259-2700 or toll-free 800-825-5262
Fax: 323-341-4875
E-mail: admission@oxy.edu

Academics
Occidental awards bachelor's and master's **degrees**. **Challenging opportunities** include advanced placement credit, student-designed majors, an honors program, double majors, independent study, and a senior project. Special programs include internships, summer session for credit, off-campus study, study-abroad, and Army and Air Force ROTC.

The most frequently chosen **baccalaureate** fields are social sciences, visual and performing arts, and physical sciences. A complete listing of majors at Occidental appears in the Majors by College index beginning on page 469.

The **faculty** at Occidental has 163 full-time members, 93% with terminal degrees. The student-faculty ratio is 9:1.

Students of Occidental
The student body totals 1,868, of whom 1,846 are undergraduates. 55.6% are women and 44.4% are men. Students come from 47 states and territories and 23 other countries. 46% are from California. 2.3% are international students. 5.9% are African American, 0.9% American Indian, 14.9% Asian American, and 14.1% Hispanic American. 94% returned for their sophomore year.

Facilities and Resources
440 **computers/terminals** are available on campus for general student use. Students can access the following: computer help desk, free student e-mail accounts, online (class) grades, online (class) registration, online (class) schedules. Campuswide network is available. Wireless service is available via classrooms, computer centers, computer labs, dorm rooms, libraries, student centers. The 3 **libraries** have 497,161 books and 903 subscriptions.

Campus Life
There are 112 active organizations on campus, including a drama/theater group, newspaper, radio station, and choral group. 6% of eligible men and 13% of eligible women are members of national **fraternities**, national **sororities**, and local sororities.

Occidental is a member of the NCAA (Division III). **Intercollegiate sports** include baseball (m), basketball, cross-country running, football (m), golf, lacrosse (w), soccer, softball (w), swimming and diving, tennis, track and field, volleyball (w), water polo.

Campus Safety
Student safety services include lighted pathways and sidewalks; whistle alert program, late-night transport/escort service, 24-hour emergency telephone alarm devices, 24-hour patrols by trained security personnel, and electronically operated dormitory entrances.

Applying
Occidental requires an essay, SAT or ACT, a high school transcript, and 2 recommendations. It recommends SAT Subject Tests and an interview. Application deadline: 1/10; 2/1 for financial aid, with a 2/1 priority date. Early and deferred admission are possible.

Getting Accepted
5,790 applied
39% were accepted
467 enrolled (20% of accepted)
65% from top tenth of their h.s. class
3.58 average high school GPA
Mean SAT critical reading score: 670
Mean SAT math score: 660
Mean SAT writing score: 670
Mean ACT score: 29
74% had SAT critical reading scores over 600
77% had SAT math scores over 600
71% had SAT writing scores over 600
87% had ACT scores over 24
26% had SAT critical reading scores over 700
20% had SAT math scores over 700
21% had SAT writing scores over 700
51% had ACT scores over 30
6 National Merit Scholars
15 valedictorians

Graduation and After
82% graduated in 4 years
3% graduated in 5 years
1% graduated in 6 years
47 organizations recruited on campus

Financial Matters
$38,922 tuition and fees (2009–10)
$10,780 room and board
100% average percent of need met
$32,991 average financial aid amount received per undergraduate (2007–08 estimated)

SPONSOR

It is not just the rigorous core curriculum, the small class discussions, and the motivating professors that make Oglethorpe different. It is the location—near the center of one of the country's most exciting, dynamic, and international cities, Atlanta. A distinctive honors program and the dynamic Rich Foundation Urban Leadership Program are gaining much recognition from city leaders as Oglethorpe helps connect students to the rich resources of Atlanta. Internships are available in every major and are very popular among the students.

Getting Accepted
4,150 applied
43% were accepted
245 enrolled (14% of accepted)
3.52 average high school GPA
48% had SAT critical reading scores over 600
32% had SAT math scores over 600
38% had SAT writing scores over 600
74% had ACT scores over 24
10% had SAT critical reading scores over 700
2% had SAT math scores over 700
5% had SAT writing scores over 700
7% had ACT scores over 30

Graduation and After
49% graduated in 4 years
8% graduated in 5 years
1% graduated in 6 years
70% had job offers within 6 months

Financial Matters
$25,580 tuition and fees (2008–09)
$9500 room and board
76% average percent of need met
$20,578 average financial aid amount received per undergraduate (2007–08 estimated)

OGLETHORPE UNIVERSITY
SUBURBAN SETTING ■ PRIVATE ■ INDEPENDENT ■ COED
ATLANTA, GEORGIA

Web site: www.oglethorpe.edu
Contact: Ms. Lucy Leusch, Vice President for Enrollment and Financial Aid, 4484 Peachtree Road, NE, Atlanta, GA 30319
Telephone: 404-364-8307 or toll-free 800-428-4484
Fax: 404-364-8491
E-mail: admission@oglethorpe.edu

Academics
Oglethorpe awards bachelor's and master's **degrees**. **Challenging opportunities** include advanced placement credit, accelerated degree programs, student-designed majors, an honors program, double majors, independent study, and a senior project. Special programs include cooperative education, internships, summer session for credit, off-campus study, and study-abroad.

The most frequently chosen **baccalaureate** fields are business/marketing, English, and social sciences. A complete listing of majors at Oglethorpe appears in the Majors by College index beginning on page 469.

The **faculty** at Oglethorpe has 48 full-time members, 96% with terminal degrees. The student-faculty ratio is 13:1.

Students of Oglethorpe
The student body totals 1,053, of whom 999 are undergraduates. 59.3% are women and 40.7% are men. Students come from 35 states and territories and 20 other countries. 71% are from Georgia. 5.1% are international students. 22.1% are African American, 0.6% American Indian, 4.2% Asian American, and 3.7% Hispanic American. 80% returned for their sophomore year.

Facilities and Resources
100 **computers/terminals** are available on campus for general student use. Students can access the following: campus intranet, computer help desk, free student e-mail accounts, online (class) grades, online (class) registration, online (class) schedules. Campuswide network is available. 100% of college-owned or -operated housing units are wired for high-speed Internet access. Wireless service is available via classrooms, computer centers, computer labs, learning centers, libraries, student centers. The **library** has 150,000 books and 710 subscriptions.

Campus Life
There are 52 active organizations on campus, including a drama/theater group, newspaper, radio station, and choral group. 33% of eligible men and 25% of eligible women are members of national **fraternities** and national **sororities**.

Oglethorpe is a member of the NCAA (Division III). **Intercollegiate sports** include baseball (m), basketball, cross-country running, golf, soccer, tennis, track and field, volleyball (w).

Campus Safety
Student safety services include late-night transport/escort service, 24-hour emergency telephone alarm devices, 24-hour patrols by trained security personnel, and electronically operated dormitory entrances.

Applying
Oglethorpe requires an essay, SAT or ACT, a high school transcript, and 1 recommendation, and in some cases an interview. It recommends an interview and a minimum high school GPA of 2.5. Application deadline: rolling admissions; 3/1 priority date for financial aid. Early and deferred admission are possible.

Ohio Northern University

Small-town setting ■ Private ■ Independent Religious ■ Coed
Ada, Ohio

SPONSOR

Web site: www.onu.edu
Contact: Ms. Deborah Miller, Director of Admission, 525 South Main, Ada, OH 45810-1599
Telephone: 419-772-2260 or toll-free 888-408-4ONU
Fax: 419-772-2821
E-mail: admissions-ug@onu.edu

Academics

Ohio Northern awards bachelor's, master's, doctoral, and first-professional **degrees** and post-bachelor's certificates. **Challenging opportunities** include advanced placement credit, an honors program, double majors, independent study, and a senior project. Special programs include cooperative education, internships, summer session for credit, off-campus study, study-abroad, and Army and Air Force ROTC.

The most frequently chosen **baccalaureate** fields are business/marketing, engineering, and biological/life sciences. A complete listing of majors at Ohio Northern appears in the Majors by College index beginning on page 469.

The **faculty** at Ohio Northern has 235 full-time members, 79% with terminal degrees. The student-faculty ratio is 13:1.

Students of Ohio Northern

The student body totals 3,721, of whom 2,744 are undergraduates. 47.3% are women and 52.7% are men. Students come from 48 states and territories and 18 other countries. 86% are from Ohio. 2.5% are international students. 3.6% are African American, 0.4% American Indian, 1.7% Asian American, and 1.5% Hispanic American. 86% returned for their sophomore year.

Facilities and Resources

533 **computers/terminals** and 3,000 ports are available on campus for general student use. Students can access the following: campus intranet, computer help desk, free student e-mail accounts, online (class) grades, online (class) registration, online (class) schedules. Campuswide network is available. 100% of college-owned or -operated housing units are wired for high-speed Internet access. Wireless service is available via entire campus.

Campus Life

There are 200 active organizations on campus, including a drama/theater group, newspaper, radio station, television station, choral group, and marching band. 15% of eligible men and 20% of eligible women are members of national **fraternities** and national **sororities**.

Ohio Northern is a member of the NCAA (Division III). **Intercollegiate sports** include baseball (m), basketball, cross-country running, football (m), golf, soccer, softball (w), swimming and diving, tennis, track and field, volleyball (w), wrestling (m).

Campus Safety

Student safety services include late-night transport/escort service, 24-hour emergency telephone alarm devices, 24-hour patrols by trained security personnel, and electronically operated dormitory entrances.

Applying

Ohio Northern requires SAT or ACT and a high school transcript. It recommends an essay, an interview, 2 recommendations, and a minimum high school GPA of 2.5. Application deadline: 8/15; 4/15 priority date for financial aid. Deferred admission is possible.

Student-focused, high-quality academic programs with national recognition; smaller classes; excellent facilities; and outstanding, supportive faculty members are just a few of the features that set Ohio Northern University (ONU) apart from other universities in the Midwest. ONU offers a unique blend of the arts and sciences along with professional programs rich in cross-learning opportunities. Students come to ONU as highly motivated scholars who reflect the values of service and leadership. They are supported by individual attention from a close-knit community where they are prepared to lead successful lives in a changing world.

Getting Accepted
3,032 applied
88% were accepted
749 enrolled (28% of accepted)
41% from top tenth of their h.s. class
3.62 average high school GPA
Mean SAT critical reading score: 562
Mean SAT math score: 591
Mean SAT writing score: 561
Mean ACT score: 25
33% had SAT critical reading scores over 600
51% had SAT math scores over 600
68% had ACT scores over 24
7% had SAT critical reading scores over 700
8% had SAT math scores over 700
15% had ACT scores over 30

Graduation and After
50% graduated in 4 years
16% graduated in 5 years
3% graduated in 6 years
94% had job offers within 6 months
459 organizations recruited on campus

Financial Matters
$31,866 tuition and fees (2009–10)
$8280 room and board
87% average percent of need met
$23,919 average financial aid amount received per undergraduate (2007–08 estimated)

Getting Accepted

21,508 applied
59% were accepted
6,168 enrolled (49% of accepted)
52% from top tenth of their h.s. class
52% had SAT critical reading scores over 600
66% had SAT math scores over 600
47% had SAT writing scores over 600
87% had ACT scores over 24
11% had SAT critical reading scores over 700
19% had SAT math scores over 700
9% had SAT writing scores over 700
23% had ACT scores over 30

Financial Matters

$8679 resident tuition and fees (2008–09)
$21,918 nonresident tuition and fees (2008–09)
$7755 room and board
65% average percent of need met
$10,225 average financial aid amount received per undergraduate (2007–08 estimated)

THE OHIO STATE UNIVERSITY

URBAN SETTING ■ PUBLIC ■ STATE-SUPPORTED ■ COED
COLUMBUS, OHIO

Web site: www.osu.edu
Contact: Admissions Office, 110 Enarson Hall, 154 West 12th Avenue, Columbus, OH 43210
Telephone: 614-292-3980
Fax: 614-292-4818
E-mail: professional@osu.edu

Academics

Ohio State awards associate, bachelor's, master's, doctoral, and first-professional **degrees** and post-bachelor's and post-master's certificates. **Challenging opportunities** include advanced placement credit, accelerated degree programs, student-designed majors, freshman honors college, an honors program, double majors, independent study, and a senior project. Special programs include cooperative education, internships, summer session for credit, off-campus study, study-abroad, and Army, Navy, and Air Force ROTC. A complete listing of majors at Ohio State appears in the Majors by College index beginning on page 469.

The **faculty** at Ohio State has 3,118 full-time members, 99% with terminal degrees. The student-faculty ratio is 13:1.

Students of Ohio State

The student body totals 52,568, of whom 39,209 are undergraduates. 46.7% are women and 53.3% are men. Students come from 53 states and territories and 76 other countries. 89% are from Ohio. 2.4% are international students. 6.9% are African American, 0.4% American Indian, 5.2% Asian American, and 2.6% Hispanic American. 92% returned for their sophomore year.

Facilities and Resources

800 **computers/terminals** are available on campus for general student use. Students can access the following: online (class) registration. Campuswide network is available. The 13 **libraries** have 5,881,219 books and 43,086 subscriptions.

Campus Life

There are 750 active organizations on campus, including a drama/theater group, newspaper, radio station, television station, choral group, and marching band. 6% of eligible men and 6% of eligible women are members of national **fraternities**, national **sororities**, local fraternities, and local sororities.

Ohio State is a member of the NCAA (Division I). **Intercollegiate sports** (some offering scholarships) include baseball (m), basketball, cheerleading, cross-country running, fencing, field hockey (w), football (m), golf, gymnastics, ice hockey, lacrosse, riflery, soccer, softball (w), swimming and diving, tennis, track and field, volleyball, wrestling (m).

Campus Safety

Student safety services include dorm entrances locked after 9 p.m., lighted pathways and sidewalks, self-defense education, late-night transport/escort service, 24-hour emergency telephone alarm devices, 24-hour patrols by trained security personnel, student patrols, and electronically operated dormitory entrances.

Applying

Ohio State requires an essay, SAT or ACT, and a high school transcript. Application deadline: 2/1; 2/15 priority date for financial aid.

OHIO WESLEYAN UNIVERSITY

SMALL-TOWN SETTING ■ PRIVATE ■ INDEPENDENT RELIGIOUS ■ COED
DELAWARE, OHIO

Web site: www.owu.edu
Contact: Ms. Carol DelPropost, Assistant Vice President of Admission and
    Financial Aid, 61 South Sandusky Street, Delaware, OH 43015
Telephone: 740-368-3059 or toll-free 800-922-8953
Fax: 740-368-3314
E-mail: cjdelpro@owu.edu

Academics

Ohio Wesleyan awards bachelor's **degrees**. **Challenging opportunities** include advanced placement credit, student-designed majors, freshman honors college, an honors program, double majors, independent study, and a senior project. Special programs include internships, summer session for credit, off-campus study, study-abroad, and Army and Air Force ROTC.

The most frequently chosen **baccalaureate** fields are social sciences, biological/life sciences, and business/marketing. A complete listing of majors at Ohio Wesleyan appears in the Majors by College index beginning on page 469.

The **faculty** at Ohio Wesleyan has 135 full-time members, 96% with terminal degrees. The student-faculty ratio is 12:1.

Students of Ohio Wesleyan

The student body is made up of 1,960 undergraduates. 53.2% are women and 46.8% are men. Students come from 45 states and territories and 45 other countries. 55% are from Ohio. 9.2% are international students. 4.6% are African American, 0.6% American Indian, 1.7% Asian American, and 1.1% Hispanic American. 79% returned for their sophomore year.

Facilities and Resources

320 **computers/terminals** are available on campus for general student use. Campuswide network is available. The 4 **libraries** have 441,912 books and 1,073 subscriptions.

Campus Life

There are 85 active organizations on campus, including a drama/theater group, newspaper, radio station, and choral group. 28% of eligible men and 26% of eligible women are members of national **fraternities** and national **sororities**.

Ohio Wesleyan is a member of the NCAA (Division III). **Intercollegiate sports** include baseball (m), basketball, cross-country running, field hockey (w), football (m), golf (m), lacrosse, soccer, softball (w), swimming and diving, tennis, track and field, volleyball (w).

Campus Safety

Student safety services include late-night transport/escort service, 24-hour emergency telephone alarm devices, 24-hour patrols by trained security personnel, and electronically operated dormitory entrances.

Applying

Ohio Wesleyan requires an essay, SAT or ACT, a high school transcript, 1 recommendation, and a minimum high school GPA of 2.5. It recommends an interview and 2 recommendations. Application deadline: 3/1; 5/1 for financial aid, with a 3/1 priority date. Early and deferred admission are possible.

Ohio Wesleyan is a liberal arts university that transforms lives. Students form lifelong relationships with each other and their professors as they pursue a rigorous academic program. Internships, research, service learning, and mission trips encourage students to push personal boundaries and develop a wider perspective. Ohio Wesleyan helps students discover and follow their passions and prepares them to change the world.

Getting Accepted

4,338 applied
63% were accepted
570 enrolled (21% of accepted)
30% from top tenth of their h.s. class
3.43 average high school GPA
Mean SAT critical reading score: 609
Mean SAT math score: 616
Mean ACT score: 27
44% had SAT critical reading scores over 600
48% had SAT math scores over 600
83% had ACT scores over 24
11% had SAT critical reading scores over 700
13% had SAT math scores over 700
19% had ACT scores over 30
17 National Merit Scholars
22 valedictorians

Graduation and After

58% graduated in 4 years
5% graduated in 5 years
95% had job offers within 6 months
37 organizations recruited on campus

Financial Matters

$33,700 tuition and fees (2008–09)
$8270 room and board
83% average percent of need met
$25,579 average financial aid amount received per undergraduate (2007–08 estimated)

OKLAHOMA BAPTIST UNIVERSITY

SMALL-TOWN SETTING ■ PRIVATE ■ INDEPENDENT RELIGIOUS ■ COED
SHAWNEE, OKLAHOMA

Web site: www.okbu.edu
Contact: Mr. Trent Argo, Dean of Enrollment Management, Box 61174,
Shawnee, OK 74804
Telephone: 405-878-2033 or toll-free 800-654-3285
Fax: 405-878-2046
E-mail: admissions@mail.okbu.edu

Academics

OBU awards bachelor's and master's **degrees. Challenging opportunities** include advanced placement credit, student-designed majors, an honors program, double majors, and independent study. Special programs include cooperative education, internships, summer session for credit, off-campus study, study-abroad, and Air Force ROTC. A complete listing of majors at OBU appears in the Majors by College index beginning on page 469.

Students of OBU

The student body totals 1,618, of whom 1,593 are undergraduates.

Facilities and Resources

Campuswide network is available. The **library** has 230,000 books and 1,800 subscriptions.

Campus Life

Active organizations on campus include a drama/theater group, newspaper, television station, and choral group. OBU has local **fraternities** and local **sororities**.

OBU is a member of the NAIA. **Intercollegiate sports** (some offering scholarships) include baseball (m), basketball, cross-country running, golf, soccer, softball (w), tennis, track and field.

Campus Safety

Student safety services include late-night transport/escort service, 24-hour emergency telephone alarm devices, 24-hour patrols by trained security personnel, and electronically operated dormitory entrances.

Applying

OBU requires SAT or ACT, a high school transcript, and a minimum high school GPA of 2.5, and in some cases an essay and an interview. Application deadline: rolling admissions; 3/1 priority date for financial aid. Early and deferred admission are possible.

OKLAHOMA CITY UNIVERSITY

URBAN SETTING ■ PRIVATE ■ INDEPENDENT RELIGIOUS ■ COED
OKLAHOMA CITY, OKLAHOMA

Web site: www.okcu.edu
Contact: Ms. Michelle Lockhart, Associate Director, Undergraduate
  Admissions, 2501 North Blackwelder, Oklahoma City, OK 73106
Telephone: 405-208-5340 or toll-free 800-633-7242
Fax: 405-208-5916
E-mail: mlockhart@okcu.edu

Academics

OCU awards bachelor's, master's, and first-professional **degrees. Challenging opportunities** include advanced placement credit, accelerated degree programs, student-designed majors, an honors program, double majors, independent study, and a senior project. Special programs include cooperative education, internships, summer session for credit, off-campus study, study-abroad, and Army and Air Force ROTC.

The most frequently chosen **baccalaureate** fields are liberal arts/general studies, visual and performing arts, and health professions and related sciences. A complete listing of majors at OCU appears in the Majors by College index beginning on page 469.

The **faculty** at OCU has 198 full-time members, 78% with terminal degrees. The student-faculty ratio is 11:1.

Students of OCU

The student body totals 3,897, of whom 2,190 are undergraduates. 61.6% are women and 38.4% are men. Students come from 48 states and territories and 34 other countries. 61% are from Oklahoma. 16.1% are international students. 9% are African American, 4.6% American Indian, 3.7% Asian American, and 4.7% Hispanic American. 78% returned for their sophomore year.

Facilities and Resources

402 **computers/terminals** are available on campus for general student use. Students can access the following: campus intranet, computer help desk, free student e-mail accounts, online (class) grades, online (class) registration, online (class) schedules. Campuswide network is available. 100% of college-owned or -operated housing units are wired for high-speed Internet access. Wireless service is available via entire campus. The 2 **libraries** have 520,953 books and 14,000 subscriptions.

Campus Life

There are 42 active organizations on campus, including a drama/theater group, newspaper, television station, and choral group. 15% of eligible men and 17% of eligible women are members of national **fraternities** and national **sororities**.

OCU is a member of the NAIA. **Intercollegiate sports** (some offering scholarships) include baseball (m), basketball, cheerleading, crew, golf, soccer, softball (w), track and field, wrestling.

Campus Safety

Student safety services include Operation ID, late-night transport/escort service, 24-hour emergency telephone alarm devices, 24-hour patrols by trained security personnel, and student patrols.

Applying

OCU requires an essay, SAT or ACT, a high school transcript, 2 recommendations, and a minimum high school GPA of 3.0, and in some cases an interview and audition for music and dance programs. It recommends an interview. Application deadline: 8/21; 3/1 priority date for financial aid. Deferred admission is possible.

Getting Accepted

1,065 applied
79% were accepted
376 enrolled (45% of accepted)
39% from top tenth of their h.s. class
3.53 average high school GPA
Mean SAT critical reading score: 547
Mean SAT math score: 534
Mean ACT score: 25
29% had SAT critical reading scores over 600
23% had SAT math scores over 600
60% had ACT scores over 24
4% had SAT critical reading scores over 700
2% had SAT math scores over 700
12% had ACT scores over 30
3 National Merit Scholars
34 valedictorians

Graduation and After

37% graduated in 4 years
12% graduated in 5 years
2% graduated in 6 years
16 organizations recruited on campus

Financial Matters

$23,400 tuition and fees (2008–09)
$9200 room and board
79% average percent of need met
$11,702 average financial aid amount received
  per undergraduate

OKLAHOMA STATE UNIVERSITY

SMALL-TOWN SETTING ■ PUBLIC ■ STATE-SUPPORTED ■ COED
STILLWATER, OKLAHOMA

Web site: osu.okstate.edu
Contact: 219 Student Union, Stillwater, OK 74078
Telephone: 405-744-4371 or toll-free 800-233-5019 Ext. 1 (in-state),
    800-852-1255 (out-of-state)
Fax: 405-744-5285
E-mail: karen.lucas@okstate.edu

Getting Accepted

6,406 applied
89% were accepted
3,073 enrolled (54% of accepted)
27% from top tenth of their h.s. class
3.51 average high school GPA
Mean SAT critical reading score: 540
Mean SAT math score: 557
Mean ACT score: 25
27% had SAT critical reading scores over 600
34% had SAT math scores over 600
58% had ACT scores over 24
5% had SAT critical reading scores over 700
5% had SAT math scores over 700
12% had ACT scores over 30
18 National Merit Scholars

Graduation and After

30% graduated in 4 years
24% graduated in 5 years
6% graduated in 6 years

Financial Matters

$6202 resident tuition and fees (2008–09)
$16,556 nonresident tuition and fees
    (2008–09)
$7402 room and board
73% average percent of need met
$9650 average financial aid amount received
    per undergraduate (2006–07)

Academics

Oklahoma State awards bachelor's, master's, doctoral, and first-professional **degrees** and post-bachelor's and post-master's certificates. **Challenging opportunities** include advanced placement credit, accelerated degree programs, student-designed majors, freshman honors college, an honors program, double majors, independent study, and a senior project. Special programs include internships, summer session for credit, off-campus study, study-abroad, and Army and Air Force ROTC.

The most frequently chosen **baccalaureate** fields are business/marketing, agriculture, and family and consumer sciences. A complete listing of majors at Oklahoma State appears in the Majors by College index beginning on page 469.

The **faculty** at Oklahoma State has 991 full-time members, 91% with terminal degrees. The student-faculty ratio is 18:1.

Students of Oklahoma State

The student body totals 22,768, of whom 17,986 are undergraduates. 48.4% are women and 51.6% are men. Students come from 49 states and territories and 79 other countries. 84% are from Oklahoma. 2.5% are international students. 4.3% are African American, 9.7% American Indian, 1.6% Asian American, and 2.7% Hispanic American. 77% returned for their sophomore year.

Facilities and Resources

Students can access the following: campus intranet, computer help desk, free student e-mail accounts, online (class) grades, online (class) registration, online (class) schedules. Campuswide network is available. 100% of college-owned or -operated housing units are wired for high-speed Internet access. Wireless service is available via computer centers, computer labs, libraries, student centers.

Campus Life

There are 360 active organizations on campus, including a drama/theater group, newspaper, radio station, television station, choral group, and marching band. 14% of eligible men and 18% of eligible women are members of national **fraternities** and national **sororities**.

Oklahoma State is a member of the NCAA (Division I). **Intercollegiate sports** (some offering scholarships) include baseball (m), basketball, cross-country running, equestrian sports (w), football (m), golf, soccer (w), softball (w), tennis, track and field, wrestling (m).

Campus Safety

Student safety services include 24-hour emergency telephone alarm devices, 24-hour patrols by trained security personnel, student patrols, and electronically operated dormitory entrances.

Applying

Oklahoma State requires SAT or ACT, a high school transcript, class rank, and a minimum high school GPA of 3.0, and in some cases an essay and an interview. Application deadline: rolling admissions. Deferred admission is possible.

Pacific Lutheran University

Suburban setting ■ Private ■ Independent Religious ■ Coed
Tacoma, Washington

Web site: www.plu.edu
Contact: Dr. Laura Majovski, Vice President for Admissions and Student Life, Tacoma, WA 98447
Telephone: 253-535-7151 or toll-free 800-274-6758
Fax: 253-536-5136
E-mail: admission@plu.edu

Academics

Pacific Lutheran awards bachelor's and master's **degrees** and post-bachelor's and post-master's certificates. **Challenging opportunities** include advanced placement credit, student-designed majors, double majors, independent study, and a senior project. Special programs include cooperative education, internships, summer session for credit, study-abroad, and Army ROTC.

The most frequently chosen **baccalaureate** fields are business/marketing, social sciences, and health professions and related sciences. A complete listing of majors at Pacific Lutheran appears in the Majors by College index beginning on page 469.

The **faculty** at Pacific Lutheran has 240 full-time members, 83% with terminal degrees. The student-faculty ratio is 14:1.

Students of Pacific Lutheran

The student body totals 3,661, of whom 3,349 are undergraduates. 63.2% are women and 36.8% are men. Students come from 40 states and territories and 21 other countries. 79% are from Washington. 5.8% are international students. 2.2% are African American, 1.3% American Indian, 6.6% Asian American, and 2.1% Hispanic American. 84% returned for their sophomore year.

Facilities and Resources

390 **computers/terminals** and 1,200 ports are available on campus for general student use. Students can access the following: campus intranet, computer help desk, free student e-mail accounts, online (class) grades, online (class) registration, online (class) schedules. Campuswide network is available. 100% of college-owned or -operated housing units are wired for high-speed Internet access. The **library** has 350,750 books and 3,433 subscriptions.

Campus Life

There are 64 active organizations on campus, including a drama/theater group, newspaper, radio station, television station, and choral group. No national or local **fraternities** or **sororities**.

Pacific Lutheran is a member of the NCAA (Division III). **Intercollegiate sports** include baseball (m), basketball, cheerleading, crew, cross-country running, football (m), golf, soccer, softball (w), swimming and diving, tennis, track and field, volleyball (w).

Campus Safety

Student safety services include late-night transport/escort service, 24-hour emergency telephone alarm devices, 24-hour patrols by trained security personnel, and student patrols.

Applying

Pacific Lutheran requires an essay, SAT or ACT, a high school transcript, and 1 recommendation, and in some cases an interview. It recommends a minimum high school GPA of 2.5. Application deadline: rolling admissions; 3/1 priority date for financial aid. Early and deferred admission are possible.

Getting Accepted

2,236 applied
76% were accepted
715 enrolled (42% of accepted)
36% from top tenth of their h.s. class
3.61 average high school GPA
Mean SAT critical reading score: 558
Mean SAT math score: 548
Mean SAT writing score: 539
Mean ACT score: 25
36% had SAT critical reading scores over 600
30% had SAT math scores over 600
26% had SAT writing scores over 600
62% had ACT scores over 24
6% had SAT critical reading scores over 700
4% had SAT math scores over 700
4% had SAT writing scores over 700
16% had ACT scores over 30

Graduation and After

50% graduated in 4 years
14% graduated in 5 years
2% graduated in 6 years
75% had job offers within 6 months
80 organizations recruited on campus

Financial Matters

$26,800 tuition and fees (2008–09)
$8200 room and board
86% average percent of need met
$24,551 average financial aid amount received per undergraduate (2007–08 estimated)

PACIFIC UNIVERSITY

SMALL-TOWN SETTING ■ PRIVATE ■ INDEPENDENT ■ COED
FOREST GROVE, OREGON

Web site: www.pacificu.edu
Contact: Ms. Karen Dunston, Director of Undergraduate Admission, 2043 College Way, Forest Grove, OR 97116-1797
Telephone: 503-352-2218 or toll-free 877-722-8648
Fax: 503-352-2975
E-mail: admissions@pacificu.edu

Getting Accepted

1,516 applied
78% were accepted
345 enrolled (29% of accepted)
39% from top tenth of their h.s. class
3.62 average high school GPA
55% had ACT scores over 24
6% had ACT scores over 30

Graduation and After

61% graduated in 4 years
5% graduated in 5 years
1% graduated in 6 years
50% had job offers within 6 months
300 organizations recruited on campus

Financial Matters

$28,670 tuition and fees (2008–09)
$7516 room and board
78% average percent of need met
$22,706 average financial aid amount received per undergraduate (2007–08 estimated)

Academics

Pacific awards bachelor's, master's, doctoral, and first-professional **degrees. Challenging opportunities** include advanced placement credit, double majors, and independent study. Special programs include cooperative education, internships, summer session for credit, off-campus study, study-abroad, and Army and Air Force ROTC.

The most frequently chosen **baccalaureate** fields are business/marketing, parks and recreation, and social sciences. A complete listing of majors at Pacific appears in the Majors by College index beginning on page 469.

The **faculty** at Pacific has 205 full-time members, 83% with terminal degrees. The student-faculty ratio is 11:1.

Students of Pacific

The student body totals 3,167, of whom 1,481 are undergraduates. 64.2% are women and 35.8% are men. Students come from 36 states and territories. 51% are from Oregon. 0.4% are international students. 1.2% are African American, 0.8% American Indian, 23.3% Asian American, and 4.5% Hispanic American. 76% returned for their sophomore year.

Facilities and Resources

315 **computers/terminals** and 5,900 ports are available on campus for general student use. Students can access the following: campus intranet, computer help desk, free student e-mail accounts, online (class) grades, online (class) schedules, Web space, printing, student and academic information, WebCT, computer peripherals. Campuswide network is available. 100% of college-owned or -operated housing units are wired for high-speed Internet access. Wireless service is available via entire campus. The **library** has 206,198 books and 20,908 subscriptions.

Campus Life

There are 59 active organizations on campus, including a drama/theater group, newspaper, radio station, and choral group. 9% of eligible men and 11% of eligible women are members of local **fraternities** and local **sororities**.

Pacific is a member of the NCAA (Division III) and NAIA. **Intercollegiate sports** include baseball (m), basketball, cross-country running, golf, lacrosse (w), soccer, softball (w), swimming and diving, tennis, track and field, volleyball (w), wrestling.

Campus Safety

Student safety services include late-night transport/escort service, 24-hour emergency telephone alarm devices, 24-hour patrols by trained security personnel, and electronically operated dormitory entrances.

Applying

Pacific requires an essay, SAT or ACT, a high school transcript, 1 recommendation, and a minimum high school GPA of 3.0. It recommends an interview. Application deadline: 8/15; 3/1 priority date for financial aid. Deferred admission is possible.

Peabody Conservatory of Music of The Johns Hopkins University

Urban Setting ■ Private ■ Independent ■ Coed
Baltimore, Maryland

Web site: www.peabody.jhu.edu
Contact: Mr. David Lane, Director of Admissions, Peabody Conservatory Admissions Office, One East Mount Vernon Place, Baltimore, MD 21202-2397
Telephone: 410-659-8110 or toll-free 800-368-2521 (out-of-state)

Academics

Peabody Conservatory awards bachelor's, master's, and doctoral **degrees** and post-bachelor's certificates. **Challenging opportunities** include advanced placement credit, accelerated degree programs, an honors program, double majors, and independent study. Special programs include internships and off-campus study.

The most frequently chosen **baccalaureate** field is visual and performing arts. A complete listing of majors at Peabody Conservatory appears in the Majors by College index beginning on page 469.

The **faculty** at Peabody Conservatory has 165 members, 23% with terminal degrees. The student-faculty ratio is 4:1.

Students of Peabody Conservatory

The student body totals 670, of whom 333 are undergraduates. 47.7% are women and 52.3% are men. Students come from 37 states and territories and 19 other countries. 30% are from Maryland. 15.6% are international students. 3.6% are African American, 0.3% American Indian, 13.8% Asian American, and 4.8% Hispanic American.

Facilities and Resources

40 **computers/terminals** are available on campus for general student use. Students can access the following: campus intranet, computer help desk, free student e-mail accounts, online (class) grades, online (class) registration, online (class) schedules, word processing, music processing. Campuswide network is available. 100% of college-owned or -operated housing units are wired for high-speed Internet access. Wireless service is available via entire campus. The **library** has 95,000 books and 225 subscriptions.

Campus Life

There are 84 active organizations on campus, including a choral group. No national or local **fraternities** or **sororities**.

This institution has no intercollegiate sports.

Campus Safety

Student safety services include late-night transport/escort service, 24-hour emergency telephone alarm devices, 24-hour patrols by trained security personnel, and electronically operated dormitory entrances.

Applying

Peabody Conservatory requires an essay, a high school transcript, an interview, 3 recommendations, and audition, and in some cases SAT or ACT. It recommends a minimum high school GPA of 3.0. Application deadline: 12/1; 3/1 priority date for financial aid.

Getting Accepted
685 applied
46% were accepted
83 enrolled (26% of accepted)
Mean SAT critical reading score: 591
Mean SAT math score: 584
57% had SAT math scores over 600
55% had SAT writing scores over 600
22% had SAT math scores over 700
15% had SAT writing scores over 700

Graduation and After
54% graduated in 4 years
8% graduated in 5 years
20% had job offers within 6 months
13 organizations recruited on campus

Financial Matters
$34,250 tuition and fees (2009–10)
$11,100 room and board
34% average percent of need met
$8999 average financial aid amount received per undergraduate (2005–06)

PENN STATE UNIVERSITY PARK

SMALL-TOWN SETTING ■ PUBLIC ■ STATE-RELATED ■ COED
UNIVERSITY PARK, PENNSYLVANIA

Web site: www.psu.edu
Contact: Anne L. Rohrbach, Director for Undergraduate Admissions, 201
Shields Building, Box 3000, University Park, PA 16804-3000
Telephone: 814-865-4700
Fax: 814-863-7590
E-mail: admissions@psu.edu

Getting Accepted

39,089 applied
51% were accepted
7,241 enrolled (36% of accepted)
43% from top tenth of their h.s. class
3.57 average high school GPA
Mean SAT critical reading score: **578**
Mean SAT math score: **614**
42% had SAT critical reading scores over 600
62% had SAT math scores over 600
7% had SAT critical reading scores over 700
15% had SAT math scores over 700

Graduation and After

60% graduated in 4 years
22% graduated in 5 years
3% graduated in 6 years
82.4% had job offers within 6 months
800 organizations recruited on campus

Financial Matters

$13,706 resident tuition and fees (2008–09)
$24,940 nonresident tuition and fees (2008–09)
$7670 room and board
67% average percent of need met
$9035 average financial aid amount received per undergraduate (2006–07)

Academics

Penn State awards associate, bachelor's, master's, doctoral, and first-professional **degrees** and post-bachelor's certificates. **Challenging opportunities** include advanced placement credit, accelerated degree programs, student-designed majors, freshman honors college, an honors program, double majors, independent study, and a senior project. Special programs include cooperative education, internships, summer session for credit, off-campus study, study-abroad, and Army, Navy, and Air Force ROTC.

The most frequently chosen **baccalaureate** fields are business/marketing, engineering, and communications/journalism. A complete listing of majors at Penn State appears in the Majors by College index beginning on page 469.

The **faculty** at Penn State has 2,392 full-time members, 77% with terminal degrees. The student-faculty ratio is 17:1.

Students of Penn State

The student body totals 44,406, of whom 37,988 are undergraduates. 44.9% are women and 55.1% are men. Students come from 54 states and territories and 86 other countries. 75% are from Pennsylvania. 3.2% are international students. 4.1% are African American, 0.1% American Indian, 5.6% Asian American, and 3.6% Hispanic American. 92% returned for their sophomore year.

Facilities and Resources

4,800 **computers/terminals** and 21,281 ports are available on campus for general student use. Students can access the following: campus intranet, computer help desk, free student e-mail accounts, online (class) grades, online (class) registration, online (class) schedules. Campuswide network is available. Wireless service is available via entire campus. The 15 **libraries** have 5,069,854 books and 71,230 subscriptions.

Campus Life

There are 700 active organizations on campus, including a drama/theater group, newspaper, radio station, television station, choral group, and marching band. 12% of eligible men and 11% of eligible women are members of national **fraternities** and national **sororities**.

Penn State is a member of the NCAA (Division I). **Intercollegiate sports** (some offering scholarships) include baseball (m), basketball, cheerleading, cross-country running, fencing, field hockey (w), football (m), golf, gymnastics, lacrosse, soccer, softball (w), swimming and diving, tennis, track and field, volleyball, wrestling (m).

Campus Safety

Student safety services include late-night transport/escort service, 24-hour emergency telephone alarm devices, 24-hour patrols by trained security personnel, student patrols, and electronically operated dormitory entrances.

Applying

Penn State requires SAT or ACT and a high school transcript, and in some cases an interview. It recommends an essay. Application deadline: rolling admissions; 2/15 priority date for financial aid. Early and deferred admission are possible.

PEPPERDINE UNIVERSITY

SMALL-TOWN SETTING ■ PRIVATE ■ INDEPENDENT RELIGIOUS ■ COED
MALIBU, CALIFORNIA

Web site: www.pepperdine.edu
Contact: Mrs. Kristin Paredes-Collins, Director of Admissions and
Enrollment Management. Seaver College, 24255 Pacific Coast Highway,
Malibu, CA 90263-4392
Telephone: 310-506-4392
Fax: 310-506-4861
E-mail: kristin.paredes@pepperdine.edu

Academics

Pepperdine awards bachelor's, master's, doctoral, and first-professional **degrees**. **Challenging opportunities** include advanced placement credit, student-designed majors, an honors program, double majors, independent study, and a senior project. Special programs include internships, summer session for credit, study-abroad, and Army and Air Force ROTC.

The most frequently chosen **baccalaureate** fields are business/marketing, communications/journalism, and social sciences. A complete listing of majors at Pepperdine appears in the Majors by College index beginning on page 469.

The **faculty** at Pepperdine has 367 full-time members, 89% with terminal degrees. The student-faculty ratio is 14:1.

Students of Pepperdine

The student body totals 7,614, of whom 3,404 are undergraduates. 54.3% are women and 45.7% are men. Students come from 50 states and territories and 64 other countries. 50% are from California. 6.2% are international students. 7.1% are African American, 1.4% American Indian, 9% Asian American, and 10.1% Hispanic American. 91% returned for their sophomore year.

Facilities and Resources

292 **computers/terminals** are available on campus for general student use. Students can access the following: campus intranet, computer help desk, free student e-mail accounts, online (class) grades, online (class) registration. Campuswide network is available. 100% of college-owned or -operated housing units are wired for high-speed Internet access. Wireless service is available via entire campus.

Campus Life

Active organizations on campus include a drama/theater group, newspaper, radio station, television station, and choral group. 18% of eligible men and 31% of eligible women are members of national **fraternities** and national **sororities**.

Pepperdine is a member of the NCAA (Division I). **Intercollegiate sports** (some offering scholarships) include baseball (m), basketball, cheerleading, cross-country running, golf, soccer (w), swimming and diving (w), tennis, volleyball, water polo (m).

Campus Safety

Student safety services include front gate security, 24-hour security in residence halls, controlled access, crime prevention programs, late-night transport/escort service, 24-hour emergency telephone alarm devices, 24-hour patrols by trained security personnel, and student patrols.

Applying

Pepperdine requires an essay, SAT or ACT, a high school transcript, and 2 recommendations. It recommends an interview. Application deadline: 1/15; 2/15 for financial aid, with a 2/15 priority date.

Getting Accepted

6,910 applied
34% were accepted
782 enrolled (33% of accepted)
40% from top tenth of their h.s. class
3.69 average high school GPA
Mean SAT critical reading score: 610
Mean SAT math score: 621
Mean SAT writing score: 605
Mean ACT score: 26
59% had SAT critical reading scores over 600
63% had SAT math scores over 600
54% had SAT writing scores over 600
85% had ACT scores over 24
16% had SAT critical reading scores over 700
19% had SAT math scores over 700
12% had SAT writing scores over 700
33% had ACT scores over 30

Graduation and After

74% graduated in 4 years
6% graduated in 5 years
1% graduated in 6 years
90% had job offers within 6 months
276 organizations recruited on campus

Financial Matters

$36,770 tuition and fees (2008–09)
$10,480 room and board
87% average percent of need met
$32,908 average financial aid amount received per undergraduate (2007–08 estimated)

PITZER COLLEGE

SUBURBAN SETTING ■ PRIVATE ■ INDEPENDENT ■ COED
CLAREMONT, CALIFORNIA

Web site: www.pitzer.edu
Contact: Angel Perez, Director of Admission, 1050 North Mills Avenue,
 Claremont, CA 91711-6101
Telephone: 909-621-8129 or toll-free 800-748-9371
Fax: 909-621-8770
E-mail: admission@pitzer.edu

Pitzer College, a liberal arts and sciences college, offers students membership in a closely knit academic community and access to the resources of a midsized university through its partnership with The Claremont Colleges. Pitzer's distinctive curriculum encourages students to discover the relationships among different academic subjects (interdisciplinary learning), gives students a chance to see issues and events from different cultural perspectives (intercultural understanding), and shows students how to take responsibility for making the world a better place (social responsibility). Pitzer College believes that students should have the freedom and responsibility for selecting what courses to take. Therefore, required general education courses are few.

Academics

Pitzer awards bachelor's **degrees**. **Challenging opportunities** include advanced placement credit, student-designed majors, an honors program, double majors, independent study, and a senior project. Special programs include cooperative education, internships, summer session for credit, off-campus study, study-abroad, and Army and Air Force ROTC.

The most frequently chosen **baccalaureate** fields are social sciences, psychology, and visual and performing arts. A complete listing of majors at Pitzer appears in the Majors by College index beginning on page 469.

The **faculty** at Pitzer has 71 full-time members, 100% with terminal degrees. The student-faculty ratio is 12:1.

Students of Pitzer

The student body is made up of 1,025 undergraduates. 59.4% are women and 40.6% are men. Students come from 42 states and territories and 13 other countries. 55% are from California. 3% are international students. 6% are African American, 0.5% American Indian, 9.2% Asian American, and 15.2% Hispanic American. 92% returned for their sophomore year.

Facilities and Resources

100 **computers/terminals** are available on campus for general student use. Students can access the following: campus intranet, computer help desk, free student e-mail accounts. Campuswide network is available. 100% of college-owned or -operated housing units are wired for high-speed Internet access. Wireless service is available via entire campus. The 4 **libraries** have 2,500,000 books and 16,000 subscriptions.

Campus Life

There are 75 active organizations on campus, including a drama/theater group, radio station, and choral group. No national or local **fraternities** or **sororities**.

Pitzer is a member of the NCAA (Division III). **Intercollegiate sports** include baseball (m), basketball, cross-country running, football (m), golf (m), lacrosse (w), soccer, softball (w), swimming and diving, tennis, track and field, volleyball (w), water polo.

Campus Safety

Student safety services include late-night transport/escort service, 24-hour emergency telephone alarm devices, 24-hour patrols by trained security personnel, and electronically operated dormitory entrances.

Applying

Pitzer requires an essay, a high school transcript, 3 recommendations, and a minimum high school GPA of 2.0, and in some cases SAT or ACT. It recommends an interview. Application deadline: 1/1; 2/1 for financial aid. Deferred admission is possible.

Getting Accepted
4,031 applied
22% were accepted
264 enrolled (29% of accepted)
51% from top tenth of their h.s. class
3.72 average high school GPA
71% had SAT critical reading scores over 600
69% had SAT math scores over 600
77% had ACT scores over 24
24% had SAT critical reading scores over 700
19% had SAT math scores over 700
34% had ACT scores over 30

Graduation and After
64% graduated in 4 years
5% graduated in 5 years
1% graduated in 6 years

Financial Matters
$37,870 tuition and fees (2008–09)
$10,930 room and board
100% average percent of need met
$31,956 average financial aid amount received per undergraduate (2007–08 estimated)

Point Loma Nazarene University

Suburban setting ■ Private ■ Independent Religious ■ Coed
San Diego, California

Web site: www.pointloma.edu
Contact: Eric Groves, Director of Admissions, 3900 Lomaland Drive, San Diego, CA 92106
Telephone: 619-849-2273 or toll-free 800-733-7770
Fax: 619-849-2601
E-mail: admissions@pointloma.edu

Academics

Point Loma awards bachelor's and master's **degrees** and post-master's certificates. **Challenging opportunities** include advanced placement credit, an honors program, double majors, independent study, and a senior project. Special programs include internships, summer session for credit, off-campus study, study-abroad, and Army, Navy, and Air Force ROTC.

The most frequently chosen **baccalaureate** fields are business/marketing, health professions and related sciences, and psychology. A complete listing of majors at Point Loma appears in the Majors by College index beginning on page 469.

The **faculty** at Point Loma has 169 full-time members, 78% with terminal degrees. The student-faculty ratio is 14:1.

Students of Point Loma

The student body totals 3,490, of whom 2,394 are undergraduates. 61.2% are women and 38.8% are men. Students come from 40 states and territories and 13 other countries. 79% are from California. 0.3% are international students. 2.2% are African American, 0.7% American Indian, 6.3% Asian American, and 11.4% Hispanic American. 83% returned for their sophomore year.

Facilities and Resources

270 **computers/terminals** are available on campus for general student use. Students can access the following: computer help desk, free student e-mail accounts, online (class) grades, online (class) registration, online (class) schedules. Campuswide network is available. 100% of college-owned or -operated housing units are wired for high-speed Internet access. Wireless service is available via entire campus.

Campus Life

There are 30 active organizations on campus, including a drama/theater group, newspaper, radio station, television station, and choral group. Point Loma has national **sororities**, local **fraternities**, and local sororities.

Point Loma is a member of the NAIA. **Intercollegiate sports** (some offering scholarships) include baseball (m), basketball, cross-country running, golf (m), soccer, softball (w), tennis, track and field, volleyball (w).

Campus Safety

Student safety services include late-night transport/escort service, 24-hour patrols by trained security personnel, and student patrols.

Applying

Point Loma requires an essay, SAT or ACT, a high school transcript, 2 recommendations, and a minimum high school GPA of 2.8, and in some cases an interview. It recommends SAT. Application deadline: 3/1; 3/2 priority date for financial aid.

Getting Accepted
1,810 applied
78% were accepted
538 enrolled (38% of accepted)
38% from top tenth of their h.s. class
3.68 average high school GPA
Mean SAT critical reading score: 563
Mean SAT math score: 562
Mean ACT score: 24
31% had SAT critical reading scores over 600
35% had SAT math scores over 600
55% had ACT scores over 24
5% had SAT critical reading scores over 700
5% had SAT math scores over 700
9% had ACT scores over 30

Graduation and After
59% graduated in 4 years
9% graduated in 5 years
1% graduated in 6 years
197 organizations recruited on campus

Financial Matters
$25,840 tuition and fees (2009–10)
$8170 room and board
61% average percent of need met
$13,943 average financial aid amount received per undergraduate (2006–07)

POLYTECHNIC INSTITUTE OF NYU

URBAN SETTING ■ PRIVATE ■ INDEPENDENT ■ COED
BROOKLYN, NEW YORK

Web site: www.poly.edu
Contact: Joy Colelli, Dean of Admissions and New Students, Six Metrotech Center, Brooklyn, NY 11201-2990
Telephone: 718-260-5917 or toll-free 800-POLYTECH
Fax: 718-260-3446
E-mail: uadmit@poly.edu

Getting Accepted

1,854 applied
55% were accepted
292 enrolled (29% of accepted)
31% from top tenth of their h.s. class
3.3 average high school GPA
Mean SAT critical reading score: 570
Mean SAT math score: 645
32% had SAT critical reading scores over 600
69% had SAT math scores over 600
4% had SAT critical reading scores over 700
20% had SAT math scores over 700
25 National Merit Scholars
2 valedictorians

Graduation and After

38% graduated in 4 years
11% graduated in 5 years
4% graduated in 6 years
90% had job offers within 6 months
200 organizations recruited on campus

Financial Matters

$32,644 tuition and fees (2008–09)
$8721 room and board
89% average percent of need met
$19,711 average financial aid amount received per undergraduate (2007–08 estimated)

Academics

Polytechnic awards bachelor's, master's, and doctoral **degrees** and post-bachelor's certificates. **Challenging opportunities** include advanced placement credit, accelerated degree programs, an honors program, double majors, and a senior project. Special programs include cooperative education, internships, summer session for credit, study-abroad, and Army and Air Force ROTC.

The most frequently chosen **baccalaureate** fields are engineering, computer and information sciences, and business/marketing. A complete listing of majors at Polytechnic appears in the Majors by College index beginning on page 469.

The **faculty** at Polytechnic has 138 full-time members, 91% with terminal degrees. The student-faculty ratio is 17:1.

Students of Polytechnic

The student body totals 3,983, of whom 1,541 are undergraduates. 18.7% are women and 81.3% are men. Students come from 24 states and territories and 45 other countries. 92% are from New York. 14.5% are international students. 12.6% are African American, 0.1% American Indian, 28.7% Asian American, and 12.1% Hispanic American. 84% returned for their sophomore year.

Facilities and Resources

1,334 **computers/terminals** are available on campus for general student use. Students can access the following: campus intranet, computer help desk, free student e-mail accounts, online (class) grades, online (class) registration, online (class) schedules. Campuswide network is available. 100% of college-owned or -operated housing units are wired for high-speed Internet access. Wireless service is available via entire campus. The 2 **libraries** have 150,000 books and 1,621 subscriptions.

Campus Life

There are 45 active organizations on campus, including a newspaper. 6% of eligible men and 3% of eligible women are members of national **fraternities**, national **sororities**, local fraternities, local sororities, and a coed fraternity.

Polytechnic is a member of the NCAA (Division III). **Intercollegiate sports** include baseball (m), basketball, cross-country running, soccer, softball (w), tennis, track and field, volleyball.

Campus Safety

Student safety services include 24-hour patrols by trained security personnel and electronically operated dormitory entrances.

Applying

Polytechnic requires an essay, SAT or ACT, a high school transcript, and 2 recommendations. It recommends SAT Subject Tests and an interview. Application deadline: 2/1. Early and deferred admission are possible.

POMONA COLLEGE

SUBURBAN SETTING ■ PRIVATE ■ INDEPENDENT ■ COED
CLAREMONT, CALIFORNIA

Web site: www.pomona.edu
Contact: Mr. Bruce Poch, Vice President and Dean of Admissions, 333 North College Way, Claremont, CA 91711
Telephone: 909-621-8134
Fax: 909-621-8952
E-mail: admissions@pomona.edu

Academics

Pomona awards bachelor's **degrees**. **Challenging opportunities** include advanced placement credit, student-designed majors, double majors, independent study, and a senior project. Special programs include internships, off-campus study, study-abroad, and Army and Air Force ROTC.

The most frequently chosen **baccalaureate** fields are social sciences, interdisciplinary studies, and psychology. A complete listing of majors at Pomona appears in the Majors by College index beginning on page 469.

The **faculty** at Pomona has 178 full-time members, 99% with terminal degrees. The student-faculty ratio is 8:1.

Students of Pomona

The student body is made up of 1,532 undergraduates. 50.3% are women and 49.7% are men. 33% are from California. 4.1% are international students. 8.2% are African American, 0.5% American Indian, 14.3% Asian American, and 11.2% Hispanic American. 97% returned for their sophomore year.

Facilities and Resources

180 **computers/terminals** are available on campus for general student use. Students can access the following: computer help desk, free student e-mail accounts, online (class) grades, online (class) schedules. Campuswide network is available. 100% of college-owned or -operated housing units are wired for high-speed Internet access. Wireless service is available via classrooms, computer centers, computer labs, dorm rooms, learning centers, libraries, student centers. The 4 **libraries** have 2,500,000 books.

Campus Life

There are 280 active organizations on campus, including a drama/theater group, newspaper, radio station, television station, and choral group. 9% of eligible men are members of local **fraternities**.

Pomona is a member of the NCAA (Division III). **Intercollegiate sports** include baseball (m), basketball, cross-country running, football (m), golf, lacrosse (w), soccer, softball (w), swimming and diving, tennis, track and field, volleyball (w), water polo.

Campus Safety

Student safety services include late-night transport/escort service, 24-hour emergency telephone alarm devices, 24-hour patrols by trained security personnel, and electronically operated dormitory entrances.

Applying

Pomona requires an essay, SAT and SAT Subject Tests or ACT, a high school transcript, and 2 recommendations. It recommends an interview, portfolio or tapes for art and performing arts programs, and a minimum high school GPA of 3.0. Application deadline: 1/2; 2/1 for financial aid. Early and deferred admission are possible.

Getting Accepted
6,293 applied
16% were accepted
382 enrolled (39% of accepted)
Mean SAT critical reading score: 740
Mean SAT math score: 750
Mean SAT writing score: 730
Mean ACT score: 33
95% had SAT critical reading scores over 600
96% had SAT math scores over 600
96% had SAT writing scores over 600
97% had ACT scores over 24
76% had SAT critical reading scores over 700
74% had SAT math scores over 700
69% had SAT writing scores over 700
80% had ACT scores over 30
24 National Merit Scholars

Graduation and After
90% graduated in 4 years
4% graduated in 5 years
150 organizations recruited on campus

Financial Matters
$35,625 tuition and fees (2008–09)
$12,220 room and board
100% average percent of need met
$34,000 average financial aid amount received per undergraduate (2007–08 estimated)

PRESBYTERIAN COLLEGE
SMALL-TOWN SETTING ■ PRIVATE ■ INDEPENDENT RELIGIOUS ■ COED
CLINTON, SOUTH CAROLINA

Web site: www.presby.edu
Contact: Mrs. Leni Patterson, Dean of Admissions and Financial Aid, 503 South Broad Street, Clinton, SC 29325
Telephone: 864-833-8229 or toll-free 800-476-7272
Fax: 864-833-8481
E-mail: lpatters@presby.edu

Getting Accepted
1,403 applied
69% were accepted
324 enrolled (34% of accepted)
35% from top tenth of their h.s. class
3.39 average high school GPA
Mean SAT critical reading score: 567
Mean SAT math score: 579
Mean ACT score: 25
37% had SAT critical reading scores over 600
42% had SAT math scores over 600
10% had SAT critical reading scores over 700
8% had SAT math scores over 700

Graduation and After
63% graduated in 4 years
7% graduated in 5 years
2% graduated in 6 years
64% had job offers within 6 months
92 organizations recruited on campus

Financial Matters
$28,880 tuition and fees (2009–10)
$8345 room and board
82% average percent of need met
$25,712 average financial aid amount received per undergraduate (2007–08 estimated)

Academics
Presbyterian awards bachelor's **degrees**. **Challenging opportunities** include advanced placement credit, accelerated degree programs, an honors program, double majors, independent study, and a senior project. Special programs include internships, summer session for credit, off-campus study, study-abroad, and Army ROTC.

The most frequently chosen **baccalaureate** fields are business/marketing, biological/life sciences, and history. A complete listing of majors at Presbyterian appears in the Majors by College index beginning on page 469.

The **faculty** at Presbyterian has 89 full-time members, 90% with terminal degrees. The student-faculty ratio is 12:1.

Students of Presbyterian
The student body is made up of 1,174 undergraduates. 49.3% are women and 50.7% are men. Students come from 29 states and territories and 9 other countries. 64% are from South Carolina. 1.2% are international students. 7.8% are African American, 0.4% American Indian, 0.7% Asian American, and 1% Hispanic American. 84% returned for their sophomore year.

Facilities and Resources
86 **computers/terminals** and 275 ports are available on campus for general student use. Students can access the following: campus intranet, free student e-mail accounts, online (class) grades, online (class) registration, online (class) schedules. Campuswide network is available. 100% of college-owned or -operated housing units are wired for high-speed Internet access. Wireless service is available via entire campus. The **library** has 142,055 books and 4,166 subscriptions.

Campus Life
There are 60 active organizations on campus, including a drama/theater group, newspaper, radio station, and choral group. 70% of eligible men and 70% of eligible women are members of national **fraternities** and national **sororities**.

Presbyterian is a member of the NCAA (Division I). **Intercollegiate sports** (some offering scholarships) include baseball (m), basketball, cheerleading, cross-country running, football (m), golf, lacrosse, soccer, softball (w), tennis, volleyball (w).

Campus Safety
Student safety services include late-night transport/escort service, 24-hour emergency telephone alarm devices, 24-hour patrols by trained security personnel, and electronically operated dormitory entrances.

Applying
Presbyterian requires an essay, SAT or ACT, a high school transcript, 1 recommendation, and a minimum high school GPA of 2.5. It recommends an interview. Application deadline: 2/1; 3/15 priority date for financial aid. Early and deferred admission are possible.

PRINCETON UNIVERSITY

SUBURBAN SETTING ■ PRIVATE ■ INDEPENDENT ■ COED
PRINCETON, NEW JERSEY

Web site: www.princeton.edu
Contact: Ms. Janet Rapelye, Dean of Admission, PO Box 430, Princeton, NJ
   08542-0430
Telephone: 609-258-3060
Fax: 609-258-6743
E-mail: uaoffice@princeton.edu

SPONSOR

Academics

Princeton awards bachelor's, master's, and doctoral **degrees**. **Challenging opportunities** include advanced placement credit, student-designed majors, independent study, and a senior project. Special programs include off-campus study, study-abroad, and Army and Air Force ROTC.

The most frequently chosen **baccalaureate** fields are social sciences, engineering, and biological/life sciences. A complete listing of majors at Princeton appears in the Majors by College index beginning on page 469.

The **faculty** at Princeton has 843 full-time members, 93% with terminal degrees. The student-faculty ratio is 5:1.

Students of Princeton

The student body totals 7,497, of whom 4,981 are undergraduates. 47.5% are women and 52.5% are men. Students come from 54 states and territories and 100 other countries. 16% are from New Jersey. 10% are international students. 8.5% are African American, 0.7% American Indian, 15% Asian American, and 7.6% Hispanic American. 98% returned for their sophomore year.

Facilities and Resources

500 **computers/terminals** and 17,000 ports are available on campus for general student use. Students can access the following: campus intranet, computer help desk, free student e-mail accounts, online (class) grades, online (class) registration, online (class) schedules, academic applications and courseware, printing, network file space, Web site hosting, media lab, broadcast center. Campuswide network is available. 100% of college-owned or -operated housing units are wired for high-speed Internet access. Wireless service is available via entire campus. The 11 **libraries** have 6,778,675 books and 165,412 subscriptions.

Campus Life

There are 250 active organizations on campus, including a drama/theater group, newspaper, radio station, choral group, and marching band. No national or local **fraternities** or **sororities**.

Princeton is a member of the NCAA (Division I). **Intercollegiate sports** include baseball (m), basketball, crew, cross-country running, fencing, field hockey (w), football (m), golf, ice hockey, lacrosse, soccer, softball (w), squash, swimming and diving, tennis, track and field, volleyball, water polo, wrestling (m).

Campus Safety

Student safety services include late-night transport/escort service, 24-hour emergency telephone alarm devices, 24-hour patrols by trained security personnel, student patrols, and electronically operated dormitory entrances.

Applying

Princeton requires an essay, SAT Subject Tests, SAT or ACT, a high school transcript, and 3 recommendations. It recommends an interview. Application deadline: 1/1; 2/1 priority date for financial aid. Deferred admission is possible.

Getting Accepted
21,370 applied
10% were accepted
1,243 enrolled (59% of accepted)
97% from top tenth of their h.s. class
3.86 average high school GPA
Mean SAT critical reading score: 715
Mean SAT math score: 723
Mean SAT writing score: 716
97% had SAT critical reading scores over 600
98% had SAT math scores over 600
98% had SAT writing scores over 600
100% had ACT scores over 24
73% had SAT critical reading scores over 700
77% had SAT math scores over 700
75% had SAT writing scores over 700
85% had ACT scores over 30

Graduation and After
90% graduated in 4 years
5% graduated in 5 years
1% graduated in 6 years
1387 organizations recruited on campus

Financial Matters
$34,290 tuition and fees (2008–09)
$11,405 room and board
100% average percent of need met
$30,242 average financial aid amount received per undergraduate (2006–07)

PROVIDENCE COLLEGE
SUBURBAN SETTING ■ PRIVATE ■ INDEPENDENT RELIGIOUS ■ COED
PROVIDENCE, RHODE ISLAND

Web site: www.providence.edu
Contact: River Avenue and Eaton Street, Providence, RI 02918
Telephone: 401-865-2535 or toll-free 800-721-6444
Fax: 401-865-2826
E-mail: pcadmiss@providence.edu

Providence College (PC) is the only liberal arts college in the U.S. that was founded and administered by the Dominican Friars, a Catholic teaching order whose heritage spans nearly 800 years. The College not only is concerned with the rigors of intellectual life but also recognizes the importance of students' experiences outside the classroom, including service to others. Scholarship, service, and the exuberant PC spirit—these are the qualities that shape the character of Providence College. The 105-acre campus of Providence College, situated in Rhode Island's vibrant capital city, is removed from the traffic and noise of the metropolitan area but still remains close to the many cultural and educational offerings of Providence, a city that is enjoying a lively urban renaissance. The city is located only an hour from Boston and 3½ hours from New York City. Interstate bus, train, and air transportation are conveniently available.

Getting Accepted
8,844 applied
45% were accepted
988 enrolled (25% of accepted)
44% from top tenth of their h.s. class
3.47 average high school GPA
Mean SAT critical reading score: 578
Mean SAT math score: 589
Mean SAT writing score: 600
Mean ACT score: 26
41% had SAT critical reading scores over 600
49% had SAT math scores over 600
53% had SAT writing scores over 600
71% had ACT scores over 24
5% had SAT critical reading scores over 700
8% had SAT math scores over 700
12% had SAT writing scores over 700
13% had ACT scores over 30
12 National Merit Scholars
39 class presidents
18 valedictorians

Graduation and After
84% graduated in 4 years
1% graduated in 5 years
110 organizations recruited on campus

Financial Matters
$31,394 tuition and fees (2008–09)
$10,810 room and board
83% average percent of need met
$19,185 average financial aid amount received
   per undergraduate (2007–08 estimated)

Academics
PC awards associate, bachelor's, and master's **degrees. Challenging opportunities** include advanced placement credit, student-designed majors, an honors program, double majors, independent study, and a senior project. Special programs include cooperative education, internships, summer session for credit, study-abroad, and Army ROTC.

The most frequently chosen **baccalaureate** fields are business/marketing, social sciences, and education. A complete listing of majors at PC appears in the Majors by College index beginning on page 469.

The **faculty** at PC has 295 full-time members, 92% with terminal degrees. The student-faculty ratio is 12:1.

Students of PC
The student body totals 4,673, of whom 3,938 are undergraduates. 56.2% are women and 43.8% are men. Students come from 38 states and territories and 19 other countries. 13% are from Rhode Island. 1.3% are international students. 2.4% are African American, 0.3% American Indian, 2.6% Asian American, and 3.5% Hispanic American. 92% returned for their sophomore year.

Facilities and Resources
278 **computers/terminals** and 5,000 ports are available on campus for general student use. Students can access the following: campus intranet, computer help desk, free student e-mail accounts, online (class) grades, online (class) registration, online (class) schedules. Campuswide network is available. 100% of college-owned or -operated housing units are wired for high-speed Internet access. Wireless service is available via classrooms, computer centers, computer labs, learning centers, libraries, student centers. The **library** has 424,229 books and 43,632 subscriptions.

Campus Life
There are 112 active organizations on campus, including a drama/theater group, newspaper, radio station, television station, and choral group. No national or local **fraternities** or **sororities**.

PC is a member of the NCAA (Division I). **Intercollegiate sports** (some offering scholarships) include basketball, cheerleading (w), cross-country running, field hockey (w), ice hockey, lacrosse (m), soccer, softball (w), swimming and diving, tennis (w), track and field, volleyball (w).

Campus Safety
Student safety services include late-night transport/escort service, 24-hour emergency telephone alarm devices, 24-hour patrols by trained security personnel, student patrols, and electronically operated dormitory entrances.

Applying
PC requires an essay, a high school transcript, and 2 recommendations. Application deadline: 1/15; 2/1 for financial aid. Early and deferred admission are possible.

PURDUE UNIVERSITY

SUBURBAN SETTING ■ PUBLIC ■ STATE-SUPPORTED ■ COED
WEST LAFAYETTE, INDIANA

Web site: www.purdue.edu
Contact: Ms. Pamela T. Home, Assistant Vice President for Enrollment Management and Dean of Admissions, 475 Stadium Mall Drive, Schleman Hall, West Lafayette, IN 47907-2050
Telephone: 765-494-1776
Fax: 765-494-0544
E-mail: admissions@purdue.edu

Academics

Purdue awards associate, bachelor's, master's, doctoral, and first-professional **degrees**. **Challenging opportunities** include advanced placement credit, accelerated degree programs, freshman honors college, an honors program, double majors, independent study, and a senior project. Special programs include cooperative education, internships, summer session for credit, study-abroad, and Army, Navy, and Air Force ROTC.

The most frequently chosen **baccalaureate** fields are engineering, business/marketing, and engineering technologies. A complete listing of majors at Purdue appears in the Majors by College index beginning on page 469.

The **faculty** at Purdue has 2,110 full-time members, 98% with terminal degrees. The student-faculty ratio is 14:1.

Students of Purdue

The student body totals 40,090, of whom 31,761 are undergraduates. 42.2% are women and 57.8% are men. Students come from 54 states and territories and 128 other countries. 74% are from Indiana. 7.4% are international students. 3.4% are African American, 0.5% American Indian, 5.5% Asian American, and 2.9% Hispanic American. 86% returned for their sophomore year.

Facilities and Resources

5,783 **computers/terminals** are available on campus for general student use. Students can access the following: computer help desk, free student e-mail accounts, online (class) grades, online (class) registration, online (class) schedules. Campuswide network is available. 97% of college-owned or -operated housing units are wired for high-speed Internet access. Wireless service is available via entire campus. The 14 **libraries** have 2,504,803 books and 40,073 subscriptions.

Campus Life

There are 850 active organizations on campus, including a drama/theater group, newspaper, radio station, television station, choral group, and marching band. 16% of eligible men and 17% of eligible women are members of national **fraternities** and national **sororities**.

Purdue is a member of the NCAA (Division I). **Intercollegiate sports** (some offering scholarships) include baseball (m), basketball, cross-country running, football (m), golf, soccer (w), softball (w), swimming and diving, tennis, track and field, volleyball (w), wrestling (m).

Campus Safety

Student safety services include late-night transport/escort service, 24-hour emergency telephone alarm devices, 24-hour patrols by trained security personnel, student patrols, and electronically operated dormitory entrances.

Applying

Purdue requires SAT or ACT and a high school transcript. Application deadline: 3/1; 3/1 priority date for financial aid. Early and deferred admission are possible.

Getting Accepted

29,952 applied
72% were accepted
6,840 enrolled (32% of accepted)
30% from top tenth of their h.s. class
3.6 average high school GPA
Mean SAT critical reading score: 554
Mean SAT math score: 598
Mean SAT writing score: 544
Mean ACT score: 26
30% had SAT critical reading scores over 600
50% had SAT math scores over 600
26% had SAT writing scores over 600
70% had ACT scores over 24
5% had SAT critical reading scores over 700
14% had SAT math scores over 700
4% had SAT writing scores over 700
20% had ACT scores over 30
66 National Merit Scholars
267 valedictorians

Graduation and After

41% graduated in 4 years
26% graduated in 5 years
5% graduated in 6 years
73.4% had job offers within 6 months
717 organizations recruited on campus

Financial Matters

$7750 resident tuition and fees (2008–09)
$23,224 nonresident tuition and fees (2008–09)
$7930 room and board
93% average percent of need met
$12,807 average financial aid amount received per undergraduate (2007–08 estimated)

QUEEN'S UNIVERSITY AT KINGSTON
Urban setting ■ Public ■ Coed
Kingston, Ontario

Web site: www.queensu.ca
Contact: Ms. Wendy Smith, Admission Coordinator, -Gordon Hall, 74 Union Street, Kingston, ON K7L 3N6 Canada
Telephone: 613-533-2218
Fax: 613-533-6810
E-mail: admission@queensu.ca

Getting Accepted
23,196 applied
3,608 enrolled
48% had SAT critical reading scores over 600
63% had SAT math scores over 600
15% had SAT critical reading scores over 700
22% had SAT math scores over 700

Graduation and After
73% graduated in 4 years
12% graduated in 5 years
2% graduated in 6 years
95% had job offers within 6 months
442 organizations recruited on campus

Financial Matters
$5843 resident tuition and fees (2009–10)
$10,110 room and board

Academics
Queen's awards bachelor's, master's, doctoral, and first-professional **degrees**. **Challenging opportunities** include advanced placement credit, accelerated degree programs, student-designed majors, an honors program, and double majors. Special programs include cooperative education, internships, summer session for credit, and study-abroad.

The most frequently chosen **baccalaureate** fields are education, biological/life sciences, and engineering. A complete listing of majors at Queen's appears in the Majors by College index beginning on page 469.

The **faculty** at Queen's has 1,087 full-time members, 96% with terminal degrees. The student-faculty ratio is 15:1.

Students of Queen's
The student body totals 21,717, of whom 16,774 are undergraduates. 60% are women and 40% are men. Students come from 55 states and territories and 99 other countries. 80% are from Ontario. 95% returned for their sophomore year.

Facilities and Resources
455 **computers/terminals** are available on campus for general student use. Students can access the following: computer help desk, free student e-mail accounts, online (class) grades, online (class) registration, online (class) schedules. Campuswide network is available. 100% of college-owned or -operated housing units are wired for high-speed Internet access. Wireless service is available via computer centers, computer labs, learning centers, libraries, student centers. The 5 **libraries** have 3,509,317 books and 16,109 subscriptions.

Campus Life
There are 270 active organizations on campus, including a drama/theater group, newspaper, radio station, choral group, and marching band. No national or local **fraternities** or **sororities**.

Queen's is a member of the Canadian Interuniversity Athletic Union. **Intercollegiate sports** include basketball, crew, cross-country running, fencing, field hockey (w), football (m), ice hockey, lacrosse (w), rugby, soccer, squash, swimming and diving, track and field, ultimate Frisbee (m), volleyball, water polo, wrestling.

Campus Safety
Student safety services include late-night transport/escort service, 24-hour emergency telephone alarm devices, 24-hour patrols by trained security personnel, student patrols, and electronically operated dormitory entrances.

Applying
Queen's requires an essay, SAT or ACT, a high school transcript, and a minimum high school GPA of 2.7, and in some cases 1 recommendation. Application deadline: 2/1; 7/1 priority date for financial aid. Deferred admission is possible.

QUINCY UNIVERSITY

SMALL-TOWN SETTING ■ PRIVATE ■ INDEPENDENT RELIGIOUS ■ COED
QUINCY, ILLINOIS

Web site: www.quincy.edu
Contact: Mrs. Syndi Peck, Director of Admissions, Admissions Office,
   Quincy, IL 62301
Telephone: 217-228-5210 or toll-free 800-688-4295
E-mail: admissions@quincy.edu

Academics

Quincy awards associate, bachelor's, and master's **degrees**. **Challenging opportunities**
include advanced placement credit, accelerated degree programs, student-designed
majors, an honors program, double majors, independent study, and a senior project.
Special programs include internships, summer session for credit, and study-abroad.

The most frequently chosen **baccalaureate** fields are business/marketing, education,
and health professions and related sciences. A complete listing of majors at Quincy
appears in the Majors by College index beginning on page 469.

The **faculty** at Quincy has 49 full-time members, 76% with terminal degrees.

Students of Quincy

The student body totals 1,424, of whom 1,144 are undergraduates. 54.5% are women
and 45.5% are men. Students come from 26 states and territories and 3 other countries.
75% are from Illinois. 0.3% are international students. 9.2% are African American, 0.3%
American Indian, 1.2% Asian American, and 3.1% Hispanic American. 69% returned for
their sophomore year.

Facilities and Resources

190 **computers/terminals** are available on campus for general student use. Students can
access the following: campus intranet, computer help desk, free student e-mail accounts,
online (class) grades, online (class) registration, online (class) schedules. Campuswide
network is available. 100% of college-owned or -operated housing units are wired for
high-speed Internet access. Wireless service is available via classrooms, computer
centers, computer labs, dorm rooms, learning centers, libraries, student centers. The
library has 204,557 books and 365 subscriptions.

Campus Life

There are 41 active organizations on campus, including a drama/theater group,
newspaper, radio station, and choral group. 5% of eligible men and 12% of eligible
women are members of national **fraternities** and national **sororities**.

Quincy is a member of the NCAA (Division II). **Intercollegiate sports** (some
offering scholarships) include baseball (m), basketball, football (m), golf, soccer, softball
(w), tennis, volleyball.

Campus Safety

Student safety services include late-night transport/escort service, 24-hour emergency
telephone alarm devices, 24-hour patrols by trained security personnel, student patrols,
and electronically operated dormitory entrances.

Applying

Quincy requires an essay, SAT or ACT, a high school transcript, and a minimum high
school GPA of 2.0, and in some cases 1 recommendation. It recommends an interview.
Application deadline: rolling admissions; 3/15 priority date for financial aid. Early and
deferred admission are possible.

Getting Accepted

978 applied
90% were accepted
246 enrolled (28% of accepted)
11% from top tenth of their h.s. class
3.2 average high school GPA
Mean SAT critical reading score: 486
Mean SAT math score: 501
Mean ACT score: 22
6% had SAT critical reading scores over 600
17% had SAT math scores over 600
29% had ACT scores over 24
4% had ACT scores over 30

Graduation and After

38% graduated in 4 years
13% graduated in 5 years
1% graduated in 6 years
61% had job offers within 6 months
45 organizations recruited on campus

Financial Matters

$20,790 tuition and fees (2008–09)
$7900 room and board
78% average percent of need met
$18,744 average financial aid amount received
   per undergraduate (2007–08 estimated)

Quinnipiac University's stunning 500-acre campus and its location adjacent to Sleeping Giant State Park give students 1,700 acres of trails for hiking, with views of the area and Long Island Sound. Hamden and nearby New Haven offer music, theater, museums, restaurants, shopping, and entertainment. Accessible to New York City and Boston via Metro-North and Amtrak, a broad spectrum of possibilities awaits. Through study abroad, whether at the Quinnipiac program in Ireland or in a variety of other countries, the possibilities are endless. Students are enthusiastic, bright, and involved in leadership development, the honors program, service learning, and technology. The recreation center and aerobic studios, with a suspended indoor track, support an active student lifestyle. Students support the Bobcats in twenty-one Division I teams for men and women. The new TD Banknorth Sports Center, with twin 3,000-plus-seat arenas for basketball and ice hockey, opened as the first project on the nearby 250-acre "York Hill" section of the campus, soon to offer additional residence halls, a new student center, and a multilevel parking garage.

Getting Accepted
14,994 applied
45% were accepted
1,484 enrolled (22% of accepted)
26% from top tenth of their h.s. class
3.4 average high school GPA
Mean SAT critical reading score: 555
Mean SAT math score: 575
Mean SAT writing score: 590
Mean ACT score: 26
23% had SAT critical reading scores over 600
31% had SAT math scores over 600
80% had ACT scores over 24
2% had SAT critical reading scores over 700
3% had SAT math scores over 700
19% had ACT scores over 30

Graduation and After
69% graduated in 4 years
3% graduated in 5 years
2% graduated in 6 years
84% had job offers within 6 months
220 organizations recruited on campus

Financial Matters
$32,400 tuition and fees (2009–10)
$12,380 room and board
65% average percent of need met
$16,914 average financial aid amount received per undergraduate (2007–08 estimated)

QUINNIPIAC UNIVERSITY
SUBURBAN SETTING ■ PRIVATE ■ INDEPENDENT ■ COED
HAMDEN, CONNECTICUT

Web site: www.quinnipiac.edu
Contact: Ms. Joan Isaac Mohr, Vice President and Dean of Admissions, 275 Mount Carmel Avenue, Hamden, CT 06518
Telephone: 203-582-8600 or toll-free 800-462-1944 (out-of-state)
Fax: 203-582-8906
E-mail: admissions@quinnipiac.edu

Academics
Quinnipiac awards bachelor's, master's, doctoral, and first-professional **degrees** and post-bachelor's certificates. **Challenging opportunities** include advanced placement credit, student-designed majors, an honors program, double majors, independent study, and a senior project. Special programs include internships, summer session for credit, study-abroad, and Army and Air Force ROTC.

The most frequently chosen **baccalaureate** fields are business/marketing, health professions and related sciences, and communications/journalism. A complete listing of majors at Quinnipiac appears in the Majors by College index beginning on page 469.

The **faculty** at Quinnipiac has 304 full-time members, 85% with terminal degrees. The student-faculty ratio is 15:1.

Students of Quinnipiac
The student body totals 7,434, of whom 5,891 are undergraduates. 61.6% are women and 38.4% are men. Students come from 28 states and territories and 18 other countries. 30% are from Connecticut. 1.3% are international students. 3% are African American, 0.2% American Indian, 2.4% Asian American, and 5.1% Hispanic American. 90% returned for their sophomore year.

Facilities and Resources
600 **computers/terminals** and 2,500 ports are available on campus for general student use. Students can access the following: campus intranet, computer help desk, free student e-mail accounts, online (class) grades, online (class) registration, online (class) schedules, e-commerce 'Q' card for local merchants, food service, dorm card access. Campuswide network is available. 100% of college-owned or -operated housing units are wired for high-speed Internet access. Wireless service is available via entire campus. The 2 **libraries** have 285,000 books and 5,500 subscriptions.

Campus Life
There are 80 active organizations on campus, including a drama/theater group, newspaper, radio station, television station, and choral group. 5% of eligible men and 7% of eligible women are members of national **fraternities**, national **sororities**, and local sororities.

Quinnipiac is a member of the NCAA (Division I). **Intercollegiate sports** (some offering scholarships) include baseball (m), basketball, cross-country running, field hockey (w), golf (m), ice hockey, lacrosse, soccer, softball (w), tennis, track and field, volleyball (w).

Campus Safety
Student safety services include late-night transport/escort service, 24-hour emergency telephone alarm devices, 24-hour patrols by trained security personnel, and electronically operated dormitory entrances.

Applying
Quinnipiac requires an essay, SAT or ACT, a high school transcript, and 1 recommendation, and in some cases a minimum high school GPA of 3.0. It recommends an interview and a minimum high school GPA of 3.0. Application deadline: 2/1, 2/1 for nonresidents; 3/1 priority date for financial aid. Deferred admission is possible.

RANDOLPH COLLEGE

SUBURBAN SETTING ■ PRIVATE ■ INDEPENDENT RELIGIOUS ■ COED
LYNCHBURG, VIRGINIA

SPONSOR

Web site: www.randolphcollege.edu
Contact: Mr. Jim Duffy, Senior Associate Director of Admissions, 2500 Rivermont Avenue, Lynchburg, VA 24503-1526
Telephone: 434-947-8100 or toll-free 800-745-7692
Fax: 434-947-8996
E-mail: admissions@randolphcollege.edu

Academics

Randolph awards bachelor's and master's **degrees**. **Challenging opportunities** include advanced placement credit, accelerated degree programs, student-designed majors, an honors program, double majors, independent study, and a senior project. Special programs include internships, off-campus study, and study-abroad.

The most frequently chosen **baccalaureate** fields are social sciences, visual and performing arts, and biological/life sciences. A complete listing of majors at Randolph appears in the Majors by College index beginning on page 469.

The **faculty** at Randolph has 75 full-time members, 92% with terminal degrees. The student-faculty ratio is 8:1.

Students of Randolph

The student body totals 656, of whom 649 are undergraduates. 88.1% are women and 11.9% are men. Students come from 44 states and territories and 44 other countries. 48% are from Virginia. 12.3% are international students. 8.9% are African American, 0.6% American Indian, 3.2% Asian American, and 5.9% Hispanic American. 78% returned for their sophomore year.

Facilities and Resources

154 **computers/terminals** and 10 ports are available on campus for general student use. Students can access the following: campus intranet, computer help desk, free student e-mail accounts, online (class) grades, online (class) registration, online (class) schedules. Campuswide network is available. 100% of college-owned or -operated housing units are wired for high-speed Internet access. Wireless service is available via classrooms, computer centers, learning centers, libraries, student centers. The **library** has 197,332 books and 618 subscriptions.

Campus Life

There are 41 active organizations on campus, including a drama/theater group, newspaper, radio station, and choral group. No national or local **fraternities** or **sororities**.

Randolph is a member of the NCAA (Division III). **Intercollegiate sports** include basketball, cross-country running, equestrian sports, lacrosse, soccer, softball (w), swimming and diving (w), tennis, volleyball (w).

Campus Safety

Student safety services include late-night transport/escort service, 24-hour emergency telephone alarm devices, and 24-hour patrols by trained security personnel.

Applying

Randolph requires an essay, SAT or ACT, a high school transcript, and 2 recommendations. It recommends an interview. Application deadline: 3/1; 3/1 priority date for financial aid. Early and deferred admission are possible.

At Randolph College, students become world-wise in a community based on honesty, individualized education, intellects, passions, and involvement. Each student can achieve the skills necessary to live meaningfully in a world that grows more complex and connected every day, through original research conducted with faculty members, leadership positions held in campus organizations, and volunteer work in the Lynchburg community. The class size is small (70 percent of classes have 15 or fewer students), enabling Randolph College students easy access to their professors, which fosters an exciting and engaging atmosphere of academic excellence. Contemporary facilities and advanced technology afford students a competitive edge for career prospects and/or advanced study. Randolph College challenges and empowers each student to engage in the world, take charge of their education throughout their lives, and lead lives of integrity and honor.

Getting Accepted
1,222 applied
83% were accepted
178 enrolled (17% of accepted)
30% from top tenth of their h.s. class
3.4 average high school GPA
Mean SAT critical reading score: 570
Mean SAT math score: 550
Mean ACT score: 24
40% had SAT critical reading scores over 600
29% had SAT math scores over 600
8% had SAT critical reading scores over 700
5% had SAT math scores over 700
2 National Merit Scholars
3 class presidents
10 valedictorians

Graduation and After
65% graduated in 4 years
60% had job offers within 6 months
12 organizations recruited on campus

Financial Matters
$27,380 tuition and fees (2008–09)
$9350 room and board
88% average percent of need met
$23,600 average financial aid amount received per undergraduate (2007–08 estimated)

REED COLLEGE
URBAN SETTING ■ PRIVATE ■ INDEPENDENT ■ COED
PORTLAND, OREGON

Web site: www.reed.edu
Contact: Mr. Paul Marthers, Dean of Admission, 3203 Southeast Woodstock Boulevard, Portland, OR 97202-8199
Telephone: 503-777-7511 or toll-free 800-547-4750 (out-of-state)
Fax: 503-777-7553
E-mail: admission@reed.edu

Reed's uniqueness lies in the uncompromising rigor of its academic program and the self-discipline and intellectual curiosity of its students. Ranked first among national liberal arts colleges in the percentage of graduates earning Ph.D. degrees and second in the number of Rhodes Scholars, Reed has long been known as an intellectually dynamic school that fosters independent thought and a lifelong love of learning. The Reed campus features Tudor Gothic brick buildings, state-of-the-art research facilities, and plentiful green space—while Portland offers all the advantages of a major city. Reed graduates are leaders in the fields of science and technology, entrepreneurship, social reform, and academia and carry on the school's tradition of scholarship, service, ingenuity, and responsibility.

Academics
Reed awards bachelor's and master's **degrees**. **Challenging opportunities** include advanced placement credit, double majors, independent study, and a senior project. Special programs include cooperative education, internships, off-campus study, and study-abroad.

The most frequently chosen **baccalaureate** fields are social sciences, English, and biological/life sciences. A complete listing of majors at Reed appears in the Majors by College index beginning on page 469.

The **faculty** at Reed has 128 full-time members, 89% with terminal degrees. The student-faculty ratio is 10:1.

Students of Reed
The student body totals 1,471, of whom 1,442 are undergraduates. 56.3% are women and 43.7% are men. Students come from 51 states and territories and 41 other countries. 14% are from Oregon. 5.7% are international students. 3.1% are African American, 1.2% American Indian, 9.3% Asian American, and 7.1% Hispanic American. 89% returned for their sophomore year.

Facilities and Resources
424 **computers/terminals** are available on campus for general student use. Students can access the following: campus intranet, computer help desk, free student e-mail accounts, online (class) registration, online (class) schedules. Campuswide network is available. 100% of college-owned or -operated housing units are wired for high-speed Internet access. Wireless service is available via entire campus. The **library** has 592,335 books and 6,705 subscriptions.

Campus Life
There are 130 active organizations on campus, including a drama/theater group, newspaper, radio station, and choral group. No national or local **fraternities** or **sororities**.

This institution has no intercollegiate sports.

Campus Safety
Student safety services include 24-hour emergency dispatch, late-night transport/escort service, 24-hour emergency telephone alarm devices, 24-hour patrols by trained security personnel, student patrols, and electronically operated dormitory entrances.

Applying
Reed requires an essay, SAT or ACT, a high school transcript, and 2 recommendations. It recommends SAT Subject Tests and an interview. Application deadline: 1/15; 1/15 for financial aid, with a 1/15 priority date. Early and deferred admission are possible.

Getting Accepted
3,485 applied
32% were accepted
330 enrolled (29% of accepted)
65% from top tenth of their h.s. class
3.9 average high school GPA
Mean SAT critical reading score: 712
Mean SAT math score: 669
Mean SAT writing score: 687
Mean ACT score: 30
93% had SAT critical reading scores over 600
86% had SAT math scores over 600
90% had SAT writing scores over 600
100% had ACT scores over 24
64% had SAT critical reading scores over 700
35% had SAT math scores over 700
47% had SAT writing scores over 700
66% had ACT scores over 30
7 National Merit Scholars
14 valedictorians

Graduation and After
60% graduated in 4 years
16% graduated in 5 years
1% graduated in 6 years
63% had job offers within 6 months
54 organizations recruited on campus

Financial Matters
$38,190 tuition and fees (2008–09)
$9920 room and board
100% average percent of need met
$32,154 average financial aid amount received per undergraduate (2007–08 estimated)

REGIS UNIVERSITY

SUBURBAN SETTING ■ PRIVATE ■ INDEPENDENT RELIGIOUS ■ COED
DENVER, COLORADO

Web site: www.regis.edu
Contact: Mr. Vic Davolt, Director of Admission, 3333 Regis Boulevard, Denver, CO 80221-1099
Telephone: 303-458-4905 or toll-free 800-388-2366 Ext. 4900
Fax: 303-964-5534
E-mail: regisadm@regis.edu

Academics

Regis awards bachelor's, master's, doctoral, and first-professional **degrees**. **Challenging opportunities** include advanced placement credit, accelerated degree programs, student-designed majors, freshman honors college, an honors program, double majors, independent study, and a senior project. Special programs include cooperative education, internships, summer session for credit, off-campus study, study-abroad, and Army and Air Force ROTC.

The most frequently chosen **baccalaureate** fields are business/marketing, interdisciplinary studies, and social sciences. A complete listing of majors at Regis appears in the Majors by College index beginning on page 469.

The **faculty** at Regis has 226 full-time members, 55% with terminal degrees.

Students of Regis

The student body totals 15,740, of whom 7,900 are undergraduates. 62.6% are women and 37.4% are men. Students come from 40 states and territories. 71% are from Colorado. 0.9% are international students. 5.3% are African American, 1% American Indian, 3.6% Asian American, and 9.9% Hispanic American. 84% returned for their sophomore year.

Facilities and Resources

300 **computers/terminals** and 72 ports are available on campus for general student use. Students can access the following: campus intranet, computer help desk, free student e-mail accounts, online (class) grades, online (class) registration, online (class) schedules. Campuswide network is available. 100% of college-owned or -operated housing units are wired for high-speed Internet access. Wireless service is available via entire campus. The **library** has 350,000 books and 20,800 subscriptions.

Campus Life

There are 30 active organizations on campus, including a drama/theater group, newspaper, radio station, and choral group. No national or local **fraternities** or **sororities**.

Regis is a member of the NCAA (Division II). **Intercollegiate sports** (some offering scholarships) include baseball (m), basketball, golf, lacrosse (w), soccer, softball (w), volleyball (w).

Campus Safety

Student safety services include late-night transport/escort service, 24-hour emergency telephone alarm devices, 24-hour patrols by trained security personnel, student patrols, and electronically operated dormitory entrances.

Applying

Regis requires an essay, SAT or ACT, a high school transcript, 1 recommendation, and a minimum high school GPA of 2.5, and in some cases an interview and 2 recommendations. It recommends SAT Subject Tests. Application deadline: rolling admissions, rolling admissions for nonresidents; 3/1 priority date for financial aid.

Getting Accepted

13,912 applied
25% were accepted
549 enrolled (16% of accepted)
25% from top tenth of their h.s. class
3.5 average high school GPA
Mean SAT critical reading score: 544
Mean SAT math score: 542
Mean ACT score: 23
26% had SAT critical reading scores over 600
28% had SAT math scores over 600
42% had ACT scores over 24
4% had SAT critical reading scores over 700
3% had SAT math scores over 700
6% had ACT scores over 30

Graduation and After

45% graduated in 4 years
10% graduated in 5 years
2% graduated in 6 years
83 organizations recruited on campus

Financial Matters

$28,700 tuition and fees (2008–09)
$8982 room and board
75% average percent of need met
$17,572 average financial aid amount received per undergraduate (2005–06)

RENSSELAER POLYTECHNIC INSTITUTE

SUBURBAN SETTING ■ PRIVATE ■ INDEPENDENT ■ COED
TROY, NEW YORK

Getting Accepted
11,249 applied
44% were accepted
1,356 enrolled (27% of accepted)
64% from top tenth of their h.s. class
Mean SAT critical reading score: 645
Mean SAT math score: 695
Mean SAT writing score: 630
Mean ACT score: 27
77% had SAT critical reading scores over 600
96% had SAT math scores over 600
69% had SAT writing scores over 600
82% had ACT scores over 24
23% had SAT critical reading scores over 700
52% had SAT math scores over 700
17% had SAT writing scores over 700
23% had ACT scores over 30
25 National Merit Scholars
50 valedictorians

Graduation and After
64% graduated in 4 years
17% graduated in 5 years
1% graduated in 6 years
63% had job offers within 6 months
182 organizations recruited on campus

Financial Matters
$37,990 tuition and fees (2008–09)
$10,730 room and board
87% average percent of need met
$27,810 average financial aid amount received
per undergraduate (2007–08 estimated)

Web site: www.rpi.edu
Contact: Mr. James Nondorf, Vice President for Enrollment, 110 8th Street, Troy, NY 12180
Telephone: 518-276-6216 or toll-free 800-448-6562
Fax: 518-276-4072
E-mail: admissions@rpi.edu

Academics
Rensselaer awards bachelor's, master's, and doctoral **degrees. Challenging opportunities** include advanced placement credit, accelerated degree programs, student-designed majors, an honors program, double majors, independent study, and a senior project. Special programs include cooperative education, internships, summer session for credit, off-campus study, study-abroad, and Army, Navy, and Air Force ROTC.

The most frequently chosen **baccalaureate** fields are engineering, computer and information sciences, and business/marketing. A complete listing of majors at Rensselaer appears in the Majors by College index beginning on page 469.

The **faculty** at Rensselaer has 401 full-time members, 99% with terminal degrees. The student-faculty ratio is 14:1.

Students of Rensselaer
The student body totals 7,521, of whom 5,394 are undergraduates. 27.9% are women and 72.1% are men. Students come from 49 states and territories and 34 other countries. 41% are from New York. 2.2% are international students. 4% are African American, 0.5% American Indian, 10.7% Asian American, and 6% Hispanic American. 95% returned for their sophomore year.

Facilities and Resources
1,081 **computers/terminals** and 10,000 ports are available on campus for general student use. Students can access the following: campus intranet, computer help desk, free student e-mail accounts, online (class) registration, online (class) schedules, billing. Campuswide network is available. 100% of college-owned or -operated housing units are wired for high-speed Internet access. Wireless service is available via classrooms, computer centers, computer labs, dorm rooms, learning centers, libraries, student centers. The 2 **libraries** have 309,171 books and 10,210 subscriptions.

Campus Life
There are 164 active organizations on campus, including a drama/theater group, newspaper, radio station, television station, and choral group. 25% of eligible men and 18% of eligible women are members of national **fraternities**, national **sororities**, local fraternities, and local sororities.

Rensselaer is a member of the NCAA (Division III). **Intercollegiate sports** (some offering scholarships) include baseball (m), basketball, cross-country running, field hockey (w), football (m), golf (m), ice hockey, lacrosse, soccer, softball (w), swimming and diving, tennis, track and field, volleyball (w).

Campus Safety
Student safety services include campus foot patrols at night, late-night transport/escort service, 24-hour emergency telephone alarm devices, 24-hour patrols by trained security personnel, and electronically operated dormitory entrances.

Applying
Rensselaer requires an essay, SAT or ACT, a high school transcript, and 1 recommendation, and in some cases SAT and SAT Subject Tests or ACT, an interview, and portfolio for Electronic Arts is required; portfolio for architecture highly recommended. Application deadline: 1/15; 2/15 priority date for financial aid. Early and deferred admission are possible.

RHODES COLLEGE

SUBURBAN SETTING ■ PRIVATE ■ INDEPENDENT RELIGIOUS ■ COED
MEMPHIS, TENNESSEE

Web site: www.rhodes.edu
Contact: Mr. David J. Wottle, Dean of Admissions and Financial Aid, 2000
   North Parkway, Memphis, TN 38112-1690
Telephone: 901-843-3700 or toll-free 800-844-5969 (out-of-state)
Fax: 901-843-3631
E-mail: adminfo@rhodes.edu

Academics

Rhodes awards bachelor's and master's **degrees** (master's degree in accounting only).
Challenging opportunities include advanced placement credit, student-designed
majors, an honors program, double majors, independent study, and a senior project.
Special programs include internships, off-campus study, study-abroad, and Army and Air
Force ROTC.

The most frequently chosen **baccalaureate** fields are social sciences, biological/life
sciences, and psychology. A complete listing of majors at Rhodes appears in the Majors
by College index beginning on page 469.

The **faculty** at Rhodes has 158 full-time members, 94% with terminal degrees. The
student-faculty ratio is 10:1.

Students of Rhodes

The student body totals 1,673, of whom 1,664 are undergraduates. 57.6% are women
and 42.4% are men. Students come from 46 states and territories and 13 other countries.
26% are from Tennessee. 2% are international students. 7.2% are African American,
0.4% American Indian, 4.6% Asian American, and 2% Hispanic American. 85%
returned for their sophomore year.

Facilities and Resources

220 **computers/terminals** are available on campus for general student use. Students can
access the following: computer help desk, free student e-mail accounts, online (class)
grades, online (class) registration, online (class) schedules. Campuswide network is available. 100% of college-owned or -operated housing units are wired for high-speed
Internet access. Wireless service is available via entire campus. The **library** has 281,099
books and 873 subscriptions.

Campus Life

There are 44 active organizations on campus, including a drama/theater group,
newspaper, radio station, television station, and choral group. 45% of eligible men and
53% of eligible women are members of national **fraternities** and national **sororities**.

Rhodes is a member of the NCAA (Division III). **Intercollegiate sports** include
baseball (m), basketball, cross-country running, field hockey (w), football (m), golf,
soccer, softball (w), swimming and diving, tennis, track and field, volleyball (w).

Campus Safety

Student safety services include 24-hour monitored security cameras in parking areas,
fenced campus with monitored access at night, late-night transport/escort service,
24-hour emergency telephone alarm devices, 24-hour patrols by trained security
personnel, and student patrols.

Applying

Rhodes requires an essay, SAT or ACT, a high school transcript, and 2 recommendations. It recommends an interview. Application deadline: 1/15; 3/1 for financial aid, with
a 3/1 priority date. Early and deferred admission are possible.

Getting Accepted

3,747 applied
50% were accepted
477 enrolled (26% of accepted)
55% from top tenth of their h.s. class
3.73 average high school GPA
67% had SAT critical reading scores over 600
66% had SAT math scores over 600
92% had ACT scores over 24
20% had SAT critical reading scores over 700
19% had SAT math scores over 700
31% had ACT scores over 30

Graduation and After

69% graduated in 4 years
3% graduated in 5 years
67 organizations recruited on campus

Financial Matters

$32,446 tuition and fees (2008–09)
$7842 room and board
82% average percent of need met
$22,891 average financial aid amount received
   per undergraduate (2007–08 estimated)

Rice University is a comprehensive research university distinguished by its nationally renowned faculty, academic resources, residential college system, and collaborative culture. Rice offers a 5:1 student-faculty ratio, a median class size of 14, and an endowment of $4.7 billion. All undergraduates have access to research, study-abroad, and experiential learning opportunities. Rice is connected to downtown Houston by a light-rail system that is free to Rice students; the excitement of the nation's fourth-largest city adds to the fun and excitement of daily life for all. Rice practices need-blind admission, meets 100 percent of students' demonstrated need, and has eliminated loans from the financial aid packages of its neediest families. Merit scholarships are also available. Rice has a commitment to diversity on multiple levels, from ethnicity (39 percent of its students are members of minority groups) to socioeconomic diversity (20 percent of its students come from families earning under $60,000 per year) to geographic diversity (students come from all fifty states and forty-six other countries).

Getting Accepted
8,968 applied
25% were accepted
742 enrolled (33% of accepted)
83% from top tenth of their h.s. class
88% had SAT critical reading scores over 600
92% had SAT math scores over 600
84% had SAT writing scores over 600
96% had ACT scores over 24
53% had SAT critical reading scores over 700
64% had SAT math scores over 700
48% had SAT writing scores over 700
71% had ACT scores over 30

Graduation and After
78% graduated in 4 years
11% graduated in 5 years
2% graduated in 6 years
51% had job offers within 6 months
173 organizations recruited on campus

Financial Matters
$30,479 tuition and fees (2008–09)
$10,750 room and board
100% average percent of need met
$23,529 average financial aid amount received per undergraduate (2007–08 estimated)

RICE UNIVERSITY
URBAN SETTING ■ PRIVATE ■ INDEPENDENT ■ COED
HOUSTON, TEXAS

Web site: www.rice.edu
Contact: Office of Admission, Office of Admission, PO Box 1892, MS 17, Houston, TX 77251-1892
Telephone: 713-348-RICE or toll-free 800-527-OWLS
E-mail: admi@rice.edu

Academics
Rice awards bachelor's, master's, and doctoral **degrees**. **Challenging opportunities** include advanced placement credit, accelerated degree programs, student-designed majors, an honors program, double majors, independent study, and a senior project. Special programs include internships, summer session for credit, off-campus study, study-abroad, and Army, Navy, and Air Force ROTC.

The most frequently chosen **baccalaureate** fields are social sciences, engineering, and biological/life sciences. A complete listing of majors at Rice appears in the Majors by College index beginning on page 469.

The student-faculty ratio is 5:1.

Students of Rice
The student body totals 5,243, of whom 3,051 are undergraduates. 48.3% are women and 51.7% are men. Students come from 57 states and territories and 44 other countries. 55% are from Texas. 5.1% are international students. 6.8% are African American, 0.5% American Indian, 19.2% Asian American, and 12.2% Hispanic American. 97% returned for their sophomore year.

Facilities and Resources
523 **computers/terminals** are available on campus for general student use. Students can access the following: online (class) registration. Campuswide network is available. The **library** has 2,474,352 books and 13,486 subscriptions.

Campus Life
There are 204 active organizations on campus, including a drama/theater group, newspaper, radio station, television station, choral group, and marching band. No national or local **fraternities** or **sororities**.

Rice is a member of the NCAA (Division I). **Intercollegiate sports** (some offering scholarships) include baseball (m), basketball, cross-country running, football (m), golf (m), soccer (w), swimming and diving (w), tennis, track and field, volleyball (w).

Campus Safety
Student safety services include late-night transport/escort service, 24-hour emergency telephone alarm devices, 24-hour patrols by trained security personnel, and electronically operated dormitory entrances.

Applying
Rice requires an essay, SAT and SAT Subject Tests or ACT, a high school transcript, and 2 recommendations, and in some cases portfolio required for architecture students; audition required for music students. It recommends an interview. Application deadline: 1/2; 3/1 priority date for financial aid. Deferred admission is possible.

RIPON COLLEGE

SMALL-TOWN SETTING ■ PRIVATE ■ INDEPENDENT ■ COED
RIPON, WISCONSIN

SPONSOR

Web site: www.ripon.edu
Contact: Office of Admission, 300 Seward Street, PO Box 248, Ripon, WI 54971
Telephone: 920-748-8114 or toll-free 800-947-4766
Fax: 920-748-8335
E-mail: adminfo@ripon.edu

Academics

Ripon awards bachelor's **degrees. Challenging opportunities** include advanced placement credit, accelerated degree programs, student-designed majors, double majors, and a senior project. Special programs include internships, off-campus study, study-abroad, and Army ROTC.

The most frequently chosen **baccalaureate** fields are business/marketing, social sciences, and history. A complete listing of majors at Ripon appears in the Majors by College index beginning on page 469.

The **faculty** at Ripon has 56 full-time members, 95% with terminal degrees. The student-faculty ratio is 15:1.

Students of Ripon

The student body is made up of 1,057 undergraduates. 52.4% are women and 47.6% are men. Students come from 32 states and territories and 14 other countries. 76% are from Wisconsin. 2.1% are international students. 1.8% are African American, 0.8% American Indian, 0.9% Asian American, and 2.9% Hispanic American. 85% returned for their sophomore year.

Facilities and Resources

150 **computers/terminals** are available on campus for general student use. Students can access the following: campus intranet, computer help desk, free student e-mail accounts. Campuswide network is available. 100% of college-owned or -operated housing units are wired for high-speed Internet access. Wireless service is available via classrooms, libraries, student centers. The **library** has 173,355 books and 372 subscriptions.

Campus Life

There are 45 active organizations on campus, including a drama/theater group, newspaper, radio station, and choral group. 33% of eligible men and 23% of eligible women are members of national **fraternities**, national **sororities**, local fraternities, and local sororities.

Ripon is a member of the NCAA (Division III). **Intercollegiate sports** include baseball (m), basketball, cheerleading (w), cross-country running, football (m), golf, soccer, softball (w), swimming and diving, tennis, track and field, volleyball (w).

Campus Safety

Student safety services include late-night transport/escort service, 24-hour emergency telephone alarm devices, 24-hour patrols by trained security personnel, student patrols, and electronically operated dormitory entrances.

Applying

Ripon requires an essay, SAT or ACT, a high school transcript, 1 recommendation, and a minimum high school GPA of 2.0, and in some cases an interview. It recommends an interview. Application deadline: rolling admissions; 3/1 priority date for financial aid. Deferred admission is possible.

Getting Accepted
1,081 applied
79% were accepted
283 enrolled (33% of accepted)
26% from top tenth of their h.s. class
3.36 average high school GPA
Mean SAT critical reading score: 524
Mean SAT math score: 565
Mean ACT score: 24
27% had SAT critical reading scores over 600
40% had SAT math scores over 600
54% had ACT scores over 24
9% had SAT critical reading scores over 700
9% had SAT math scores over 700
11% had ACT scores over 30
6 National Merit Scholars
20 valedictorians

Graduation and After
56% graduated in 4 years
12% graduated in 5 years
2% graduated in 6 years
97% had job offers within 6 months
16 organizations recruited on campus

Financial Matters
$24,245 tuition and fees (2008–09)
$6770 room and board
93% average percent of need met
$20,438 average financial aid amount received per undergraduate (2007–08 estimated)

ROCHESTER INSTITUTE OF TECHNOLOGY

SUBURBAN SETTING ■ PRIVATE ■ INDEPENDENT ■ COED
ROCHESTER, NEW YORK

Web site: www.rit.edu
Contact: Dr. Daniel Shelley, Assistant Vice President, 60 Lomb Memorial
   Drive, Rochester, NY 14623-5604
Telephone: 585-475-6631
Fax: 585-475-7424
E-mail: admissions@rit.edu

RIT is among the world's leading career-oriented, technological universities. Students find an incredible array of academic programs and learning opportunities, along with diverse, talented, and accessible faculty members and sophisticated facilities to enrich their experience. More than 200 academic programs and eighty minors are offered in business, engineering, engineering technology, art and design, science, mathematics, computing, information sciences, liberal arts, photography, and hospitality. Students also find an unusual emphasis on experiential learning through cooperative education, internships, research projects, and study abroad programs. The RIT campus is a vibrant, connected community that is home to ambitious and creative students from more than ninety-five countries. The result is a unique blend of rigor and imagination, of specialization and perspective, of intellect and practice that defines the RIT experience.

Getting Accepted
12,725 applied
60% were accepted
2,625 enrolled (34% of accepted)
26% from top tenth of their h.s. class
3.7 average high school GPA
43% had SAT critical reading scores over 600
59% had SAT math scores over 600
33% had SAT writing scores over 600
70% had ACT scores over 24
8% had SAT critical reading scores over 700
15% had SAT math scores over 700
5% had SAT writing scores over 700
18% had ACT scores over 30
57 valedictorians

Graduation and After
95% had job offers within 6 months
1200 organizations recruited on campus

Financial Matters
$28,035 tuition and fees (2008–09)
$9381 room and board
88% average percent of need met
$18,600 average financial aid amount received
   per undergraduate (2006–07)

Academics

RIT awards associate, bachelor's, master's, and doctoral **degrees** and post-bachelor's and post-master's certificates. **Challenging opportunities** include advanced placement credit, accelerated degree programs, student-designed majors, an honors program, double majors, independent study, and a senior project. Special programs include cooperative education, internships, summer session for credit, off-campus study, study-abroad, and Army, Navy, and Air Force ROTC.

The most frequently chosen **baccalaureate** fields are engineering, computer and information sciences, and visual and performing arts. A complete listing of majors at RIT appears in the Majors by College index beginning on page 469.

The **faculty** at RIT has 851 full-time members. The student-faculty ratio is 14:1.

Students of RIT

The student body totals 16,494, of whom 13,861 are undergraduates. 33.7% are women and 66.3% are men. Students come from 54 states and territories and 95 other countries. 57% are from New York. 11.1% are international students. 4.7% are African American, 0.5% American Indian, 4.9% Asian American, and 3.7% Hispanic American. 88% returned for their sophomore year.

Facilities and Resources

2,500 **computers/terminals** are available on campus for general student use. Students can access the following: campus intranet, computer help desk, free student e-mail accounts, online (class) grades, online (class) registration, student account information. Campuswide network is available. 100% of college-owned or -operated housing units are wired for high-speed Internet access. Wireless service is available via classrooms, computer centers, computer labs, learning centers, libraries, student centers. The **library** has 452,355 books and 23,325 subscriptions.

Campus Life

There are 175 active organizations on campus, including a drama/theater group, newspaper, radio station, and choral group. 5% of eligible men and 5% of eligible women are members of national **fraternities**, national **sororities**, local fraternities, and local sororities.

RIT is a member of the NCAA (Division III). **Intercollegiate sports** include baseball (m), basketball, crew, cross-country running, ice hockey, lacrosse, soccer, softball (w), swimming and diving, tennis, track and field, volleyball (w), wrestling (m).

Campus Safety

Student safety services include late-night transport/escort service, 24-hour emergency telephone alarm devices, 24-hour patrols by trained security personnel, and student patrols.

Applying

RIT requires an essay, SAT or ACT, and a high school transcript, and in some cases portfolio. It recommends an interview, 1 recommendation, and a minimum high school GPA of 3.0. Application deadline: 2/1; 3/1 priority date for financial aid. Early and deferred admission are possible.

ROLLINS COLLEGE

SUBURBAN SETTING ■ PRIVATE ■ INDEPENDENT ■ COED
WINTER PARK, FLORIDA

Web site: www.rollins.edu
Contact: Mr. David Erdmann, Dean of Admission and Enrollment, 1000 Holt
  Avenue, Box 2720, Winter Park, FL 32789-4499
Telephone: 407-646-2161
Fax: 407-646-1502
E-mail: admission@rollins.edu

Academics

Rollins awards bachelor's and master's **degrees**. **Challenging opportunities** include advanced placement credit, accelerated degree programs, student-designed majors, an honors program, double majors, independent study, and a senior project. Special programs include internships, off-campus study, and study-abroad.

The most frequently chosen **baccalaureate** fields are social sciences, business/marketing, and visual and performing arts. A complete listing of majors at Rollins appears in the Majors by College index beginning on page 469.

The **faculty** at Rollins has 194 full-time members, 94% with terminal degrees. The student-faculty ratio is 10:1.

Students of Rollins

The student body totals 2,511, of whom 1,785 are undergraduates. 56.5% are women and 43.5% are men. Students come from 42 states and territories and 43 other countries. 53% are from Florida. 4.3% are international students. 3.9% are African American, 0.7% American Indian, 3.6% Asian American, and 10% Hispanic American. 87% returned for their sophomore year.

Facilities and Resources

240 **computers/terminals** and 155 ports are available on campus for general student use. Students can access the following: campus intranet, computer help desk, free student e-mail accounts, online (class) grades, online (class) registration, online (class) schedules. Campuswide network is available. 100% of college-owned or -operated housing units are wired for high-speed Internet access. Wireless service is available via entire campus. The **library** has 306,243 books and 36,989 subscriptions.

Campus Life

There are 112 active organizations on campus, including a drama/theater group, newspaper, radio station, television station, and choral group. 75% of eligible men and 75% of eligible women are members of national **fraternities**, national **sororities**, local fraternities, and local sororities.

Rollins is a member of the NCAA (Division II). **Intercollegiate sports** (some offering scholarships) include baseball (m), basketball, crew, cross-country running, golf, lacrosse, sailing, soccer, softball (w), swimming and diving, tennis, volleyball (w).

Campus Safety

Student safety services include late-night transport/escort service, 24-hour emergency telephone alarm devices, 24-hour patrols by trained security personnel, and electronically operated dormitory entrances.

Applying

Rollins requires an essay, a high school transcript, and 1 recommendation, and in some cases SAT or ACT. It recommends an interview and a minimum high school GPA of 2.0. Application deadline: 2/15; 3/1 for financial aid, with a 3/1 priority date. Early and deferred admission are possible.

Getting Accepted

3,485 applied
53% were accepted
464 enrolled (25% of accepted)
43% from top tenth of their h.s. class
3.4 average high school GPA
Mean SAT critical reading score: **608**
Mean SAT math score: **608**
Mean ACT score: **26**
52% had SAT critical reading scores over 600
50% had SAT math scores over 600
80% had ACT scores over 24
12% had SAT critical reading scores over 700
8% had SAT math scores over 700
18% had ACT scores over 30

Graduation and After

60% graduated in 4 years
8% graduated in 5 years
1% graduated in 6 years
60% had job offers within 6 months
7 organizations recruited on campus

Financial Matters

$34,520 tuition and fees (2008–09)
$10,780 room and board
87% average percent of need met
$30,003 average financial aid amount received
  per undergraduate (2007–08 estimated)

ROSE-HULMAN INSTITUTE OF TECHNOLOGY

SUBURBAN SETTING ■ PRIVATE ■ INDEPENDENT ■ COED, PRIMARILY MEN
TERRE HAUTE, INDIANA

Web site: www.rose-hulman.edu
Contact: Mr. James Goecker, Dean of Admissions and Financial Aid, 5500 Wabash Avenue, CM 1, Terre Haute, IN 47803-3920
Telephone: 812-877-8894 or toll-free 800-248-7448
Fax: 812-877-8941
E-mail: admissions@rose-hulman.edu

Getting Accepted
3,165 applied
70% were accepted
482 enrolled (22% of accepted)
57% from top tenth of their h.s. class
Mean SAT critical reading score: 609
Mean SAT math score: 669
Mean SAT writing score: 579
Mean ACT score: 29
54% had SAT critical reading scores over 600
85% had SAT math scores over 600
40% had SAT writing scores over 600
93% had ACT scores over 24
16% had SAT critical reading scores over 700
36% had SAT math scores over 700
6% had SAT writing scores over 700
44% had ACT scores over 30
20 National Merit Scholars
22 valedictorians

Graduation and After
66% graduated in 4 years
12% graduated in 5 years
1% graduated in 6 years
99% had job offers within 6 months
356 organizations recruited on campus

Financial Matters
$32,826 tuition and fees (2008–09)
$8868 room and board
87% average percent of need met
$30,370 average financial aid amount received per undergraduate (2007–08 estimated)

Academics

Rose-Hulman awards bachelor's and master's **degrees. Challenging opportunities** include advanced placement credit, accelerated degree programs, double majors, independent study, and a senior project. Special programs include cooperative education, internships, summer session for credit, off-campus study, study-abroad, and Army and Air Force ROTC.

The most frequently chosen **baccalaureate** fields are engineering, computer and information sciences, and biological/life sciences. A complete listing of majors at Rose-Hulman appears in the Majors by College index beginning on page 469.

The **faculty** at Rose-Hulman has 164 full-time members, 99% with terminal degrees. The student-faculty ratio is 11:1.

Students of Rose-Hulman

The student body totals 1,923, of whom 1,832 are undergraduates. 19.9% are women and 80.1% are men. Students come from 50 states and territories and 20 other countries. 42% are from Indiana. 1.9% are international students. 2.2% are African American, 0.3% American Indian, 4.6% Asian American, and 1.9% Hispanic American. 90% returned for their sophomore year.

Facilities and Resources

45 **computers/terminals** and 8,000 ports are available on campus for general student use. Students can access the following: campus intranet, computer help desk, free student e-mail accounts, online (class) grades, online (class) registration, online (class) schedules. Campuswide network is available. 100% of college-owned or -operated housing units are wired for high-speed Internet access. Wireless service is available via classrooms, computer centers, computer labs, learning centers, libraries, student centers. The **library** has 80,301 books and 23,498 subscriptions.

Campus Life

There are 80 active organizations on campus, including a drama/theater group, newspaper, radio station, and choral group. 36% of eligible men and 40% of eligible women are members of national **fraternities** and national **sororities**.

Rose-Hulman is a member of the NCAA (Division III). **Intercollegiate sports** include baseball (m), basketball, cheerleading, cross-country running, football (m), golf, riflery, soccer, softball (w), swimming and diving, tennis, track and field, volleyball (w), wrestling (m).

Campus Safety

Student safety services include late-night transport/escort service, 24-hour emergency telephone alarm devices, 24-hour patrols by trained security personnel, and electronically operated dormitory entrances.

Applying

Rose-Hulman requires SAT or ACT, a high school transcript, 1 recommendation, and curricular. It recommends an essay and an interview. Application deadline: 3/1; 3/1 priority date for financial aid. Deferred admission is possible.

RUTGERS, THE STATE UNIVERSITY OF NEW JERSEY, NEWARK

URBAN SETTING ■ PUBLIC ■ STATE-SUPPORTED ■ COED
NEWARK, NEW JERSEY

Web site: www.newark.rutgers.edu
Contact: Mr. Jason Hand, Director of Admissions, 249 University Avenue, Newark, NJ 07102-1896
Telephone: 973-353-5205
Fax: 973-353-1440
E-mail: admissions@ugadm.rutgers.edu

Academics

Rutgers-Newark awards bachelor's, master's, doctoral, and first-professional **degrees**. **Challenging opportunities** include advanced placement credit, accelerated degree programs, student-designed majors, freshman honors college, an honors program, double majors, independent study, and a senior project. Special programs include cooperative education, summer session for credit, off-campus study, study-abroad, and Army and Air Force ROTC.

The most frequently chosen **baccalaureate** fields are business/marketing, health professions and related sciences, and security and protective services. A complete listing of majors at Rutgers-Newark appears in the Majors by College index beginning on page 469.

The **faculty** at Rutgers-Newark has 404 full-time members, 99% with terminal degrees. The student-faculty ratio is 12:1.

Students of Rutgers-Newark

The student body totals 10,553, of whom 6,685 are undergraduates. 55.3% are women and 44.7% are men. Students come from 25 states and territories and 65 other countries. 97% are from New Jersey. 1.9% are international students. 20.1% are African American, 0.2% American Indian, 23.9% Asian American, and 19.4% Hispanic American.

Facilities and Resources

708 **computers/terminals** are available on campus for general student use. Students can access the following: online grade reports. Campuswide network is available. The 5 **libraries** have 941,103 books and 6,408 subscriptions.

Campus Life

Active organizations on campus include a drama/theater group, newspaper, radio station, and choral group. No national or local **fraternities** or **sororities**.

This institution has no intercollegiate sports.

Applying

Rutgers-Newark requires SAT or ACT and a high school transcript. Application deadline: rolling admissions; 3/15 priority date for financial aid.

Getting Accepted
13,085 applied
49% were accepted
989 enrolled (15% of accepted)
24% from top tenth of their h.s. class
24% had SAT critical reading scores over 600
28% had SAT math scores over 600
4% had SAT critical reading scores over 700
5% had SAT math scores over 700

Graduation and After
395 organizations recruited on campus

Financial Matters
$11,083 resident tuition and fees (2008–09)
$21,031 nonresident tuition and fees (2008–09)
$10,639 room and board
80% average percent of need met
$10,851 average financial aid amount received per undergraduate (2006–07)

RUTGERS, THE STATE UNIVERSITY OF NEW JERSEY, NEW BRUNSWICK

URBAN SETTING ■ PUBLIC ■ STATE-SUPPORTED ■ COED
NEW BRUNSWICK, NEW JERSEY

Web site: www.rutgers.edu
Contact: Ms. Diane Williams Harris, Associate Director of University Undergraduate Admissions, 65 Davidson Road, Room 202, Piscataway, NJ 08854-8097
Telephone: 732-932-4636
Fax: 732-445-0237
E-mail: admissions@ugadm.rutgers.edu

Getting Accepted

28,208 applied
56% were accepted
5,519 enrolled (35% of accepted)
40% from top tenth of their h.s. class
42% had SAT critical reading scores over 600
58% had SAT math scores over 600
9% had SAT critical reading scores over 700
17% had SAT math scores over 700

Graduation and After

80% had job offers within 6 months
500 organizations recruited on campus

Financial Matters

$11,540 resident tuition and fees (2008–09)
$21,488 nonresident tuition and fees (2008–09)
$10,232 room and board
69% average percent of need met
$12,305 average financial aid amount received per undergraduate (2006–07)

Academics

Rutgers-New Brunswick awards bachelor's, master's, doctoral, and first-professional **degrees** and post-master's certificates. **Challenging opportunities** include advanced placement credit, accelerated degree programs, student-designed majors, an honors program, double majors, independent study, and a senior project. Special programs include cooperative education, study-abroad, and Army and Air Force ROTC.

The most frequently chosen **baccalaureate** fields are social sciences, biological/life sciences, and communications/journalism. A complete listing of majors at Rutgers-New Brunswick appears in the Majors by College index beginning on page 469.

The **faculty** at Rutgers-New Brunswick has 1,533 full-time members, 99% with terminal degrees. The student-faculty ratio is 14:1.

Students of Rutgers-New Brunswick

The student body totals 34,804, of whom 26,829 are undergraduates. 49.1% are women and 50.9% are men. Students come from 48 states and territories and 112 other countries. 93% are from New Jersey. 1.7% are international students. 9.2% are African American, 0.2% American Indian, 24.5% Asian American, and 8.5% Hispanic American.

Facilities and Resources

1,450 **computers/terminals** are available on campus for general student use. Students can access the following: online grade reports. Campuswide network is available. The 15 **libraries** have 4,737,147 books and 17,182 subscriptions.

Campus Life

Active organizations on campus include a drama/theater group, newspaper, radio station, television station, choral group, and marching band. Rutgers-New Brunswick has national **fraternities** and national **sororities**.

Rutgers-New Brunswick is a member of the NCAA (Division I). **Intercollegiate sports** include baseball (m), basketball, crew, cross-country running, fencing, football (m), golf, gymnastics (w), lacrosse, soccer, softball (w), swimming and diving, tennis, track and field, volleyball (w), wrestling (m).

Applying

Rutgers-New Brunswick requires SAT or ACT and a high school transcript. Application deadline: rolling admissions; 3/15 priority date for financial aid.

SAINT FRANCIS UNIVERSITY

RURAL SETTING ■ PRIVATE ■ INDEPENDENT RELIGIOUS ■ COED
LORETTO, PENNSYLVANIA

Web site: www.francis.edu
Contact: Robert Beener, Associate Dean for Enrollment Management, PO Box 600, 117 Evergreen Drive, Loretto, PA 15940-0600
Telephone: 814-472-3100 or toll-free 800-342-5732
Fax: 814-472-3335
E-mail: rbeener@francis.edu

SPONSOR

Academics

Saint Francis awards associate, bachelor's, master's, and doctoral **degrees**. **Challenging opportunities** include advanced placement credit, accelerated degree programs, student-designed majors, freshman honors college, an honors program, double majors, and a senior project. Special programs include internships, summer session for credit, off-campus study, study-abroad, and Army ROTC.

The most frequently chosen **baccalaureate** fields are business/marketing, health professions and related sciences, and education. A complete listing of majors at Saint Francis appears in the Majors by College index beginning on page 469.

The **faculty** at Saint Francis has 105 full-time members, 75% with terminal degrees. The student-faculty ratio is 19:1.

Students of Saint Francis

The student body totals 2,210, of whom 1,612 are undergraduates. 59.8% are women and 40.2% are men. Students come from 33 states and territories and 9 other countries. 78% are from Pennsylvania. 0.1% are international students. 5% are African American, 0.2% American Indian, 1.2% Asian American, and 1.2% Hispanic American. 84% returned for their sophomore year.

Facilities and Resources

60 **computers/terminals** are available on campus for general student use. Students can access the following: campus intranet, computer help desk, free student e-mail accounts, online (class) grades, online (class) registration, online (class) schedules. Campuswide network is available. 95% of college-owned or -operated housing units are wired for high-speed Internet access. Wireless service is available via entire campus. The **library** has 124,000 books and 16,400 subscriptions.

Campus Life

There are 75 active organizations on campus, including a drama/theater group, newspaper, radio station, television station, and choral group. 17% of eligible men and 13% of eligible women are members of national **fraternities**, national **sororities**, and local sororities.

Saint Francis is a member of the NCAA (Division I). **Intercollegiate sports** (some offering scholarships) include basketball, cross-country running, field hockey (w), football (m), golf, lacrosse (w), soccer, softball (w), swimming and diving, tennis, track and field, volleyball.

Campus Safety

Student safety services include late-night transport/escort service, 24-hour emergency telephone alarm devices, 24-hour patrols by trained security personnel, and electronically operated dormitory entrances.

Applying

Saint Francis requires an essay, SAT or ACT, a high school transcript, 1 recommendation, and 3 letters of recommendation for health science applicants, and in some cases an interview. It recommends an interview. Application deadline: rolling admissions. Deferred admission is possible.

Founded in 1847, Saint Francis is the oldest Franciscan university in the United States. Saint Francis has been helping students to use their minds to reach higher and go further than they ever dreamed. Graduates have gone on to become teachers, journalists, physical therapists, politicians, engineers, doctors, accountants, chemists, and environmentalists. Nationally ranked programs, a solid and diverse liberal arts curriculum, and a 99-percent placement rate are a few of the outstanding features students experience at Saint Francis. Saint Francis has consistently fostered the ability to be forward thinking, while maintaining the values on which the University is based.

Getting Accepted

1,533 applied
75% were accepted
408 enrolled (35% of accepted)
24% from top tenth of their h.s. class
3.43 average high school GPA
Mean SAT critical reading score: 522
Mean SAT math score: 534
Mean ACT score: 24
17% had SAT critical reading scores over 600
24% had SAT math scores over 600
60% had ACT scores over 24
1% had SAT critical reading scores over 700
3% had SAT math scores over 700
5% had ACT scores over 30
14 class presidents
9 valedictorians

Graduation and After

45% graduated in 4 years
1% graduated in 5 years
9% graduated in 6 years
96% had job offers within 6 months
175 organizations recruited on campus

Financial Matters

$24,840 tuition and fees (2008–09)
$8422 room and board
76% average percent of need met
$17,459 average financial aid amount received per undergraduate (2007–08 estimated)

Getting Accepted
460 applied
81% were accepted
154 enrolled (41% of accepted)
34% from top tenth of their h.s. class
91% had SAT critical reading scores over 600
73% had SAT math scores over 600
52% had SAT critical reading scores over 700
18% had SAT math scores over 700
7 National Merit Scholars

Graduation and After
60% graduated in 4 years
12% graduated in 5 years
1% graduated in 6 years
50% had job offers within 6 months
10 organizations recruited on campus

Financial Matters
$39,154 tuition and fees (2008–09)
$9284 room and board
97% average percent of need met
$26,029 average financial aid amount received per undergraduate (2006–07)

St. John's College
SMALL-TOWN SETTING ■ PRIVATE ■ INDEPENDENT ■ COED
ANNAPOLIS, MARYLAND

Web site: www.stjohnscollege.edu
Contact: Mr. John Christensen, Director of Admissions, PO Box 2800, 60 College Avenue, Annapolis, MD 21404
Telephone: 410-626-2522 or toll-free 800-727-9238
Fax: 410-269-7916
E-mail: admissions@sjca.edu

Academics
St. John's awards bachelor's and master's **degrees**. A senior project is a **challenging opportunity**. Internships is a special program.

The most frequently chosen **baccalaureate** field is liberal arts/general studies. A complete listing of majors at St. John's appears in the Majors by College index beginning on page 469.

The **faculty** at St. John's has 76 full-time members, 78% with terminal degrees. The student-faculty ratio is 8:1.

Students of St. John's
The student body totals 562, of whom 489 are undergraduates. 47.2% are women and 52.8% are men. Students come from 45 states and territories and 17 other countries. 15% are from Maryland. 2.2% are international students. 0.8% are African American, 0.2% American Indian, 1.6% Asian American, and 4.7% Hispanic American. 78% returned for their sophomore year.

Facilities and Resources
16 **computers/terminals** and 12 ports are available on campus for general student use. Students can access the following: computer help desk, free student e-mail accounts. Campuswide network is available. 100% of college-owned or -operated housing units are wired for high-speed Internet access. Wireless service is available via computer labs, dorm rooms, libraries. The 2 **libraries** have 113,343 books and 123 subscriptions.

Campus Life
There are 38 active organizations on campus, including a drama/theater group, newspaper, and choral group. No national or local **fraternities** or **sororities**.

This institution has no intercollegiate sports.

Campus Safety
Student safety services include late-night transport/escort service, 24-hour emergency telephone alarm devices, 24-hour patrols by trained security personnel, and electronically operated dormitory entrances.

Applying
St. John's requires an essay, a high school transcript, and 2 recommendations, and in some cases SAT or ACT. It recommends SAT or ACT and an interview. Application deadline: rolling admissions; 2/15 priority date for financial aid. Early and deferred admission are possible.

St. John's College

SUBURBAN SETTING ■ PRIVATE ■ INDEPENDENT ■ COED
SANTA FE, NEW MEXICO

SPONSOR

Web site: www.stjohnscollege.edu
Contact: Mr. Larry Clendenin, Director of Admissions, 1160 Camino Cruz Blanca, Santa Fe, NM 87505
Telephone: 505-984-6060 or toll-free 800-331-5232
Fax: 505-984-6162
E-mail: admissions@sjcsf.edu

Academics

St. John's awards bachelor's and master's **degrees**. A senior project is a **challenging opportunity**. Special programs include internships, summer session for credit, and off-campus study.

The most frequently chosen **baccalaureate** field is liberal arts/general studies. A complete listing of majors at St. John's appears in the Majors by College index beginning on page 469.

The **faculty** at St. John's has 68 full-time members, 82% with terminal degrees. The student-faculty ratio is 7:1.

Students of St. John's

The student body totals 511, of whom 431 are undergraduates. 38.7% are women and 61.3% are men. Students come from 51 states and territories and 12 other countries. 7% are from New Mexico. 3.7% are international students. 0.5% are African American, 1.2% American Indian, 3.5% Asian American, and 4.6% Hispanic American. 78% returned for their sophomore year.

Facilities and Resources

25 **computers/terminals** and 375 ports are available on campus for general student use. Students can access the following: computer help desk, free student e-mail accounts. Campuswide network is available. 100% of college-owned or -operated housing units are wired for high-speed Internet access. Wireless service is available via classrooms, computer labs, learning centers, student centers. The **library** has 65,104 books and 116 subscriptions.

Campus Life

There are 32 active organizations on campus, including a drama/theater group, newspaper, and choral group. No national or local **fraternities** or **sororities**.

Intercollegiate sports include fencing.

Campus Safety

Student safety services include late-night transport/escort service, 24-hour emergency telephone alarm devices, 24-hour patrols by trained security personnel, and student patrols.

Applying

St. John's requires an essay, a high school transcript, and 2 recommendations, and in some cases SAT and an interview. It recommends an interview and 3 recommendations. Application deadline: rolling admissions; 2/15 for financial aid. Early and deferred admission are possible.

Great works of poetry, philosophy, history, mathematics, natural science and scientific method, religion, theology, and music are the daily study of students and faculty members at St.John's College. The College's pedagogy directs the mind by questions and by practice in the means of answering those questions. The intention is that each individual mind become responsible for its own inquiry, imagination, judgment, and understanding. The means of study include reading, conversation—both formal and informal, mathematical demonstration, writing, translation, direct observation of natural and laboratory appearances, development of hands-on laboratory skills, and practice in the rudimentary skills of music.

Getting Accepted
323 applied
81% were accepted
110 enrolled (42% of accepted)
27% from top tenth of their h.s. class
Mean SAT critical reading score: 680
Mean SAT math score: 630
Mean SAT writing score: 640
Mean ACT score: 28
86% had SAT critical reading scores over 600
74% had SAT math scores over 600
80% had ACT scores over 24
48% had SAT critical reading scores over 700
18% had SAT math scores over 700
29% had ACT scores over 30

Graduation and After
41% graduated in 4 years
13% graduated in 5 years
2% graduated in 6 years
29% had job offers within 6 months
10 organizations recruited on campus

Financial Matters
$40,392 tuition and fees (2009–10)
$9562 room and board
94% average percent of need met
$24,858 average financial aid amount received per undergraduate (2006–07)

Getting Accepted

1,527 applied
74% were accepted
515 enrolled (46% of accepted)
23% from top tenth of their h.s. class
3.57 average high school GPA
Mean SAT critical reading score: 568
Mean SAT math score: 597
Mean ACT score: 25
37% had SAT critical reading scores over 600
48% had SAT math scores over 600
72% had ACT scores over 24
11% had SAT critical reading scores over 700
9% had SAT math scores over 700
18% had ACT scores over 30
1 National Merit Scholar

Graduation and After

72% graduated in 4 years
7% graduated in 5 years
2% graduated in 6 years
72% had job offers within 6 months
118 organizations recruited on campus

Financial Matters

$28,628 tuition and fees (2008–09)
$7248 room and board
88% average percent of need met
$20,628 average financial aid amount received
per undergraduate (2007–08 estimated)

SAINT JOHN'S UNIVERSITY
COORDINATE WITH COLLEGE OF SAINT BENEDICT

RURAL SETTING ■ PRIVATE ■ INDEPENDENT RELIGIOUS ■ MEN ONLY
COLLEGEVILLE, MINNESOTA

Web site: www.csbsju.edu
Contact: Mr. Matt Beirne, Director of Admission, PO Box 7155, Collegeville, MN 56321-7155
Telephone: 320-363-2196 or toll-free 800-544-1489
Fax: 320-363-2750
E-mail: admissions@csbsju.edu

Academics

St. John's awards bachelor's, master's, and first-professional **degrees** (coordinate with College of Saint Benedict for women). **Challenging opportunities** include advanced placement credit, accelerated degree programs, student-designed majors, an honors program, double majors, independent study, and a senior project. Special programs include internships, off-campus study, study-abroad, and Army ROTC.

The most frequently chosen **baccalaureate** fields are business/marketing, social sciences, and English. A complete listing of majors at St. John's appears in the Majors by College index beginning on page 469.

The **faculty** at St. John's has 148 full-time members, 82% with terminal degrees. The student-faculty ratio is 12:1.

Students of St. John's

The student body totals 2,080, of whom 1,952 are undergraduates. Students come from 32 states and territories and 22 other countries. 83% are from Minnesota. 4.8% are international students. 1% are African American, 0.2% American Indian, 2% Asian American, and 1.1% Hispanic American. 89% returned for their sophomore year.

Facilities and Resources

643 **computers/terminals** and 3,000 ports are available on campus for general student use. Students can access the following: computer help desk, free student e-mail accounts, online (class) grades, online (class) registration, online (class) schedules, online student accounts. Campuswide network is available. 100% of college-owned or -operated housing units are wired for high-speed Internet access. Wireless service is available via classrooms, computer centers, computer labs, dorm rooms, learning centers, libraries, student centers. The 4 **libraries** have 481,338 books and 5,315 subscriptions.

Campus Life

There are 90 active organizations on campus, including a drama/theater group, newspaper, radio station, and choral group. No national or local **fraternities**.

St. John's is a member of the NCAA (Division III). **Intercollegiate sports** include baseball, basketball, cross-country running, football, golf, ice hockey, skiing (cross-country), soccer, swimming and diving, tennis, track and field, wrestling.

Campus Safety

Student safety services include well-lit pathways, 911 center on campus, closed circuit TV monitors, late-night transport/escort service, 24-hour emergency telephone alarm devices, 24-hour patrols by trained security personnel, and student patrols.

Applying

St. John's requires an essay, SAT or ACT, a high school transcript, and 1 recommendation. It recommends an interview and a minimum high school GPA of 3.0. Application deadline: rolling admissions; 3/15 priority date for financial aid. Deferred admission is possible.

Saint Joseph's University

Suburban setting ■ Private ■ Independent Religious ■ Coed
Philadelphia, Pennsylvania

Web site: www.sju.edu
Contact: Admissions Department, 5600 City Avenue, Philadelphia, PA
19131-1395
Telephone: 610-660-1300 or toll-free 888-BEAHAWK (in-state)
Fax: 610-660-1314
E-mail: admit@sju.edu

SPONSOR

Academics

St. Joseph's awards associate, bachelor's, master's, and doctoral **degrees** and post-bachelor's and post-master's certificates. **Challenging opportunities** include advanced placement credit, accelerated degree programs, student-designed majors, an honors program, double majors, independent study, and a senior project. Special programs include cooperative education, internships, summer session for credit, off-campus study, study-abroad, and Army, Navy, and Air Force ROTC.

The most frequently chosen **baccalaureate** fields are business/marketing, social sciences, and education. A complete listing of majors at St. Joseph's appears in the Majors by College index beginning on page 469.

The **faculty** at St. Joseph's has 290 full-time members, 90% with terminal degrees. The student-faculty ratio is 13:1.

Students of St. Joseph's

The student body totals 7,900, of whom 5,331 are undergraduates. 52.6% are women and 47.4% are men. Students come from 38 states and territories and 38 other countries. 49% are from Pennsylvania. 1.9% are international students. 7.6% are African American, 0.2% American Indian, 2.6% Asian American, and 3.5% Hispanic American. 88% returned for their sophomore year.

Facilities and Resources

670 **computers/terminals** are available on campus for general student use. Students can access the following: campus intranet, computer help desk, free student e-mail accounts, online (class) grades, online (class) registration, online (class) schedules. Campuswide network is available. 100% of college-owned or -operated housing units are wired for high-speed Internet access. Wireless service is available via entire campus. The 2 **libraries** have 352,000 books and 16,600 subscriptions.

Campus Life

There are 97 active organizations on campus, including a drama/theater group, newspaper, radio station, and choral group. 8% of eligible men and 13% of eligible women are members of national **fraternities** and national **sororities**.

St. Joseph's is a member of the NCAA (Division I). **Intercollegiate sports** (some offering scholarships) include baseball (m), basketball, cross-country running, field hockey (w), golf (m), lacrosse, soccer, softball (w), tennis, track and field.

Campus Safety

Student safety services include 24-hour shuttle/escort service, bicycle patrols, late-night transport/escort service, 24-hour emergency telephone alarm devices, 24-hour patrols by trained security personnel, and electronically operated dormitory entrances.

Applying

St. Joseph's requires an essay, SAT or ACT, a high school transcript, and 1 recommendation. Application deadline: 2/1; 2/15 priority date for financial aid. Deferred admission is possible.

Getting Accepted
7,012 applied
86% were accepted
1,478 enrolled (25% of accepted)
19% from top tenth of their h.s. class
3.4 average high school GPA
Mean SAT critical reading score: 551
Mean SAT math score: 563
Mean ACT score: 24
29% had SAT critical reading scores over 600
33% had SAT math scores over 600
29% had SAT writing scores over 600
45% had ACT scores over 24
3% had SAT critical reading scores over 700
3% had SAT math scores over 700
3% had SAT writing scores over 700
2% had ACT scores over 30

Graduation and After
73% graduated in 4 years
5% graduated in 5 years
95% had job offers within 6 months
760 organizations recruited on campus

Financial Matters
$32,860 tuition and fees (2008–09)
$11,180 room and board
86% average percent of need met
$17,132 average financial aid amount received per undergraduate (2007–08 estimated)

St. Lawrence University

SMALL-TOWN SETTING ■ PRIVATE ■ INDEPENDENT ■ COED
CANTON, NEW YORK

Web site: www.stlawu.edu
Contact: Ms. Terry Cowdrey, Dean of Admissions and Financial Aid, Payson
   Hall, Canton, NY 13617-1455
Telephone: 315-229-5261 or toll-free 800-285-1856
Fax: 315-229-5818
E-mail: admissions@stlawu.edu

With more than thirty majors and minors from which to choose, St.Lawrence students can sample from a variety of disciplines and specialize in those areas that are most intriguing to them. The diverse options for cocurricular activities, including thirty-two varsity sports, encourage students to further develop their abilities and interests outside the classroom. The University's location provides students with a residential community as well as easy access to the Adirondack Mountains, Ottawa, and Montreal. St.Lawrence alumni successfully pursue careers and graduate study, consistently achieving placement rates higher than 95 percent within one year of graduation.

Academics
St. Lawrence awards bachelor's and master's **degrees** and post-master's certificates. **Challenging opportunities** include advanced placement credit, student-designed majors, double majors, independent study, and a senior project. Special programs include internships, summer session for credit, off-campus study, study-abroad, and Army and Air Force ROTC.

The most frequently chosen **baccalaureate** fields are social sciences, psychology, and visual and performing arts. A complete listing of majors at St. Lawrence appears in the Majors by College index beginning on page 469.

The **faculty** at St. Lawrence has 173 full-time members, 97% with terminal degrees. The student-faculty ratio is 11:1.

Students of St. Lawrence
The student body totals 2,325, of whom 2,206 are undergraduates. 54.7% are women and 45.3% are men. Students come from 42 states and territories and 49 other countries. 44% are from New York. 5.2% are international students. 3.1% are African American, 0.5% American Indian, 1.8% Asian American, and 3.2% Hispanic American. 88% returned for their sophomore year.

Facilities and Resources
608 **computers/terminals** are available on campus for general student use. Students can access the following: computer help desk, free student e-mail accounts, online (class) grades, online (class) registration, online (class) schedules. Campuswide network is available. 100% of college-owned or -operated housing units are wired for high-speed Internet access. Wireless service is available via entire campus. The 2 libraries have 594,276 books and 1,207 subscriptions.

Campus Life
There are 100 active organizations on campus, including a drama/theater group, newspaper, radio station, and choral group. 2% of eligible men and 20% of eligible women are members of national **fraternities**, national **sororities**, and local sororities.

St. Lawrence is a member of the NCAA (Division III). **Intercollegiate sports** (some offering scholarships) include baseball (m), basketball, crew, cross-country running, equestrian sports, field hockey (w), football (m), golf, ice hockey, lacrosse, skiing (cross-country), skiing (downhill), soccer, softball (w), squash, swimming and diving, tennis, track and field, volleyball (w).

Campus Safety
Student safety services include late-night transport/escort service, 24-hour emergency telephone alarm devices, 24-hour patrols by trained security personnel, student patrols, and electronically operated dormitory entrances.

Applying
St. Lawrence requires an essay, a high school transcript, and 2 recommendations. It recommends an interview and a minimum high school GPA of 2.0. Application deadline: 2/1; 2/15 for financial aid. Early and deferred admission are possible.

Getting Accepted
5,419 applied
34% were accepted
616 enrolled (34% of accepted)
44% from top tenth of their h.s. class
3.55 average high school GPA
Mean SAT critical reading score: 600
Mean SAT math score: 610
Mean SAT writing score: 600
Mean ACT score: 27
56% had SAT critical reading scores over 600
61% had SAT math scores over 600
54% had SAT writing scores over 600
89% had ACT scores over 24
8% had SAT critical reading scores over 700
6% had SAT math scores over 700
8% had SAT writing scores over 700
23% had ACT scores over 30
14 valedictorians

Graduation and After
72% graduated in 4 years
3% graduated in 5 years
67.5% had job offers within 6 months
18 organizations recruited on campus

Financial Matters
$37,905 tuition and fees (2008–09)
$9645 room and board
94% average percent of need met
$32,471 average financial aid amount received per undergraduate (2006–07)

St. Louis College of Pharmacy

Urban setting ■ Private ■ Independent ■ Coed
St. Louis, Missouri

Web site: www.stlcop.edu
Contact: Connie Horrall, Administrative Assistant, 4588 Parkview Place, St. Louis, MO 63110-1088
Telephone: 314-446-8328 or toll-free 800-278-5267 (in-state)
Fax: 314-446-8310
E-mail: chorrall@stlcop.edu

Academics

StLCoP awards first-professional **degrees**. Advanced placement credit is a **challenging opportunity**. Special programs include internships, summer session for credit, and Army and Air Force ROTC.

The most frequently chosen **baccalaureate** field is health professions and related sciences. A complete listing of majors at StLCoP appears in the Majors by College index beginning on page 469.

The **faculty** at StLCoP has 77 full-time members, 94% with terminal degrees. The student-faculty ratio is 18:1.

Students of StLCoP

The student body totals 1,191, of whom 645 are undergraduates. 57.5% are women and 42.5% are men. Students come from 23 states and territories and 3 other countries. 50% are from Missouri. 0.9% are international students. 2% are African American, 19.1% Asian American, and 0.8% Hispanic American. 89% returned for their sophomore year.

Facilities and Resources

6 **computers/terminals** are available on campus for general student use. Students can access the following: campus intranet, computer help desk, free student e-mail accounts, online (class) grades, online (class) registration, online (class) schedules. Campuswide network is available. 100% of college-owned or -operated housing units are wired for high-speed Internet access. Wireless service is available via entire campus. The **library** has 69,820 books and 155 subscriptions.

Campus Life

There are 15 active organizations on campus, including a drama/theater group, newspaper, and choral group. 70% of eligible men and 65% of eligible women are members of national **fraternities** and national **sororities**.

StLCoP is a member of the NAIA. **Intercollegiate sports** include basketball, cross-country running, volleyball (w).

Campus Safety

Student safety services include late-night transport/escort service, 24-hour emergency telephone alarm devices, 24-hour patrols by trained security personnel, and electronically operated dormitory entrances.

Applying

StLCoP requires an essay, SAT or ACT, a high school transcript, 2 recommendations, and a minimum high school GPA of 3.0, and in some cases an interview. Application deadline: 2/1; 3/15 priority date for financial aid.

Getting Accepted

599 applied
49% were accepted
237 enrolled (81% of accepted)
34% from top tenth of their h.s. class
3.88 average high school GPA
Mean ACT score: 28
100% had ACT scores over 24
17% had ACT scores over 30
24 valedictorians

Graduation and After

100% had job offers within 6 months

Financial Matters

$21,925 tuition and fees (2009–10)
$8154 room and board
51% average percent of need met
$13,028 average financial aid amount received per undergraduate (2007–08 estimated)

Every student who comes to Saint Louis University (SLU) is embraced as a Billiken. Being a Billiken means being a student at a Jesuit Catholic university ranked among the top research institutions in the nation. It means experiencing challenging academics, compassionate service opportunities, an active campus life, and a welcoming city. It means encountering a diverse student body of more than 12,700 students from all fifty states and nearly eighty countries. It means working with faculty members who want to help students pursue their dreams. Like SLU's distinctive mascot, a Billiken embraces the entire SLU experience as a student, volunteer, leader, and collaborator.

Getting Accepted
10,022 applied
72% were accepted
1,645 enrolled (23% of accepted)
36% from top tenth of their h.s. class
3.68 average high school GPA
Mean ACT score: 26
44% had SAT critical reading scores over 600
52% had SAT math scores over 600
76% had ACT scores over 24
10% had SAT critical reading scores over 700
12% had SAT math scores over 700
25% had ACT scores over 30

Graduation and After
62% graduated in 4 years
11% graduated in 5 years
1% graduated in 6 years
61% had job offers within 6 months
310 organizations recruited on campus

Financial Matters
$30,728 tuition and fees (2008–09)
$8760 room and board
62% average percent of need met
$18,773 average financial aid amount received per undergraduate (2006–07)

SAINT LOUIS UNIVERSITY
URBAN SETTING ■ PRIVATE ■ INDEPENDENT RELIGIOUS ■ COED
ST. LOUIS, MISSOURI

Web site: www.slu.edu
Contact: Director, 221 North Grand Boulevard, DuBourg Hall, Room 100, St. Louis, MO 63103-2097
Telephone: 314-977-2500 or toll-free 800-758-3678 (out-of-state)
Fax: 314-977-7136
E-mail: admitme@slu.edu

Academics
SLU awards bachelor's, master's, doctoral, and first-professional **degrees** and post-bachelor's and post-master's certificates. **Challenging opportunities** include advanced placement credit, accelerated degree programs, student-designed majors, freshman honors college, an honors program, double majors, independent study, and a senior project. Special programs include cooperative education, internships, summer session for credit, off-campus study, study-abroad, and Army and Air Force ROTC.

The most frequently chosen **baccalaureate** fields are business/marketing, health professions and related sciences, and social sciences. A complete listing of majors at SLU appears in the Majors by College index beginning on page 469.

The **faculty** at SLU has 633 full-time members, 90% with terminal degrees. The student-faculty ratio is 12:1.

Students of SLU
The student body totals 12,733, of whom 7,814 are undergraduates. 58.9% are women and 41.1% are men. Students come from 43 states and territories and 57 other countries. 43% are from Missouri. 5.2% are international students. 8.4% are African American, 0.3% American Indian, 6.2% Asian American, and 3.1% Hispanic American. 84% returned for their sophomore year.

Facilities and Resources
300 **computers/terminals** and 4,725 ports are available on campus for general student use. Students can access the following: campus intranet, computer help desk, free student e-mail accounts, online (class) grades, online (class) registration, online (class) schedules. Campuswide network is available. 100% of college-owned or -operated housing units are wired for high-speed Internet access. Wireless service is available via entire campus. The 3 **libraries** have 1,946,490 books and 16,067 subscriptions.

Campus Life
There are 170 active organizations on campus, including a drama/theater group, newspaper, radio station, television station, and choral group. 18% of eligible men and 23% of eligible women are members of national **fraternities** and national **sororities**.

SLU is a member of the NCAA (Division I). **Intercollegiate sports** (some offering scholarships) include baseball (m), basketball, cross-country running, field hockey (w), soccer, softball (w), swimming and diving, tennis, track and field, volleyball (w).

Campus Safety
Student safety services include crime prevention program, bicycle patrols, pamphlets, posters, films, late-night transport/escort service, 24-hour emergency telephone alarm devices, 24-hour patrols by trained security personnel, and electronically operated dormitory entrances.

Applying
SLU requires an essay, SAT or ACT, a high school transcript, secondary school report form, and a minimum high school GPA of 2.5. It recommends an interview and 2 recommendations. Application deadline: 8/1, 8/1 for nonresidents; 3/1 priority date for financial aid. Deferred admission is possible.

SAINT MARY'S COLLEGE

SUBURBAN SETTING ■ PRIVATE ■ INDEPENDENT RELIGIOUS ■ WOMEN ONLY
NOTRE DAME, INDIANA

SPONSOR

Web site: www.saintmarys.edu
Contact: Mona Bowe, Director of Admission, Notre Dame, IN 46556
Telephone: 574-284-4587 or toll-free 800-551-7621
Fax: 574-284-4841
E-mail: admission@saintmarys.edu

Academics

Saint Mary's awards bachelor's **degrees**. **Challenging opportunities** include advanced placement credit, accelerated degree programs, student-designed majors, double majors, independent study, and a senior project. Special programs include cooperative education, internships, summer session for credit, off-campus study, study-abroad, and Army, Navy, and Air Force ROTC.

The most frequently chosen **baccalaureate** fields are business/marketing, communications/journalism, and social sciences. A complete listing of majors at Saint Mary's appears in the Majors by College index beginning on page 469.

The **faculty** at Saint Mary's has 136 full-time members, 90% with terminal degrees. The student-faculty ratio is 10:1.

Students of Saint Mary's

The student body is made up of 1,628 undergraduates. Students come from 43 states and territories and 5 other countries. 27% are from Indiana. 0.4% are international students. 1.4% are African American, 0.4% American Indian, 2% Asian American, and 6.3% Hispanic American. 79% returned for their sophomore year.

Facilities and Resources

236 **computers/terminals** and 1,456 ports are available on campus for general student use. Students can access the following: computer help desk, free student e-mail accounts, online (class) grades, online (class) registration, online (class) schedules. Campuswide network is available. 100% of college-owned or -operated housing units are wired for high-speed Internet access. Wireless service is available via classrooms, computer centers, computer labs, dorm rooms, learning centers, libraries, student centers. The **library** has 268,569 books and 938 subscriptions.

Campus Life

There are 74 active organizations on campus, including a drama/theater group, newspaper, radio station, television station, choral group, and marching band. No national or local **sororities**.

Saint Mary's is a member of the NCAA (Division III). **Intercollegiate sports** include basketball, cross-country running, golf, soccer, softball, swimming and diving, tennis, volleyball.

Campus Safety

Student safety services include late-night transport/escort service, 24-hour emergency telephone alarm devices, 24-hour patrols by trained security personnel, and electronically operated dormitory entrances.

Applying

Saint Mary's requires an essay, SAT or ACT, a high school transcript, and 1 recommendation. It recommends an interview. Application deadline: 2/15; 3/1 priority date for financial aid. Early and deferred admission are possible.

Founded in 1844 and still sponsored by the Congregation of the Sisters of the Holy Cross, Saint Mary's College has preserved the best of its rich heritage as it pioneers new approaches to educating today's women. At Saint Mary's, students obtain a solid liberal arts foundation as well as excellent preparation for career opportunities or graduate and professional programs. Students also enjoy "the best of both worlds" through academic and social co-exchange programs with the University of Notre Dame. With 1,600 students from forty-two states and seven countries, Saint Mary's brings together women from a wide range of geographical areas, social backgrounds, and educational experiences.

Getting Accepted

1,422 applied
80% were accepted
455 enrolled (40% of accepted)
35% from top tenth of their h.s. class
3.73 average high school GPA
Mean SAT critical reading score: 569
Mean SAT math score: 569
Mean SAT writing score: 572
Mean ACT score: 25
37% had SAT critical reading scores over 600
36% had SAT math scores over 600
43% had SAT writing scores over 600
70% had ACT scores over 24
4% had SAT critical reading scores over 700
3% had SAT math scores over 700
6% had SAT writing scores over 700
9% had ACT scores over 30
1 National Merit Scholar
13 class presidents
15 valedictorians

Graduation and After

71% graduated in 4 years
4% graduated in 5 years
1% graduated in 6 years
67% had job offers within 6 months
42 organizations recruited on campus

Financial Matters

$28,212 tuition and fees (2008–09)
$8938 room and board
74% average percent of need met
$18,104 average financial aid amount received per undergraduate (2007–08 estimated)

Getting Accepted
3,638 applied
81% were accepted
675 enrolled (23% of accepted)
3.33 average high school GPA
Mean SAT critical reading score: 530
Mean SAT math score: 540
24% had SAT critical reading scores over 600
23% had SAT math scores over 600
3% had SAT critical reading scores over 700
3% had SAT math scores over 700

Graduation and After
58% graduated in 4 years
5% graduated in 5 years
1% graduated in 6 years
40% had job offers within 6 months
90 organizations recruited on campus

Financial Matters
$33,250 tuition and fees (2008–09)
$11,680 room and board
50% average percent of need met
$23,378 average financial aid amount received
    per undergraduate (2007–08 estimated)

SAINT MARY'S COLLEGE OF CALIFORNIA
SUBURBAN SETTING ■ PRIVATE ■ INDEPENDENT RELIGIOUS ■ COED
MORAGA, CALIFORNIA

Web site: www.stmarys-ca.edu
Contact: Ms. Dorothy Jones, Dean of Admissions, PO Box 4800, Moraga, CA 94556-4800
Telephone: 925-631-4224 or toll-free 800-800-4SMC
Fax: 925-376-7193
E-mail: smcadmit@stmarys-ca.edu

Academics
SMC awards bachelor's, master's, and doctoral **degrees**. **Challenging opportunities** include advanced placement credit, student-designed majors, an honors program, double majors, independent study, and a senior project. Special programs include internships, off-campus study, study-abroad, and Army and Air Force ROTC.

The most frequently chosen **baccalaureate** fields are business/marketing, social sciences, and communications/journalism. A complete listing of majors at SMC appears in the Majors by College index beginning on page 469.

The **faculty** at SMC has 208 full-time members, 92% with terminal degrees. The student-faculty ratio is 11:1.

Students of SMC
The student body totals 3,840, of whom 2,621 are undergraduates. 62.5% are women and 37.5% are men. Students come from 40 states and territories and 30 other countries. 87% are from California. 2.1% are international students. 5.7% are African American, 1.1% American Indian, 10.8% Asian American, and 20.8% Hispanic American. 81% returned for their sophomore year.

Facilities and Resources
325 **computers/terminals** and 1,800 ports are available on campus for general student use. Students can access the following: campus intranet, computer help desk, free student e-mail accounts, online (class) grades, online (class) registration, online (class) schedules, student accounts. Campuswide network is available. 100% of college-owned or -operated housing units are wired for high-speed Internet access. Wireless service is available via classrooms, computer centers, computer labs, learning centers, libraries, student centers. The **library** has 227,104 books and 40,355 subscriptions.

Campus Life
There are 40 active organizations on campus, including a drama/theater group, newspaper, radio station, television station, and choral group. No national or local **fraternities** or **sororities**.

SMC is a member of the NCAA (Division I). **Intercollegiate sports** (some offering scholarships) include baseball (m), basketball, crew (w), cross-country running, golf (m), lacrosse (w), soccer, softball (w), tennis, volleyball (w).

Campus Safety
Student safety services include late-night transport/escort service, 24-hour emergency telephone alarm devices, and 24-hour patrols by trained security personnel.

Applying
SMC requires an essay, SAT or ACT, a high school transcript, 1 recommendation, and a minimum high school GPA of 2.0, and in some cases an interview and a minimum high school GPA of 3.0. It recommends a minimum high school GPA of 3.0. Application deadline: 2/1; 2/15 priority date for financial aid. Deferred admission is possible.

St. Mary's College of Maryland

RURAL SETTING ■ PUBLIC ■ STATE-SUPPORTED ■ COED
St. Mary's City, Maryland

Web site: www.smcm.edu
Contact: Mr. Richard Edgar, Director of Admissions, 18952 East Fisher Road, St. Mary's City, MD 20686-3001
Telephone: 240-895-5000 or toll-free 800-492-7181
Fax: 240-895-5001
E-mail: admissions@smcm.edu

SPONSOR

Academics

St. Mary's awards bachelor's and master's **degrees. Challenging opportunities** include advanced placement credit, student-designed majors, freshman honors college, an honors program, double majors, independent study, and a senior project. Special programs include cooperative education, internships, summer session for credit, off-campus study, and study-abroad.

The most frequently chosen **baccalaureate** fields are social sciences, psychology, and English. A complete listing of majors at St. Mary's appears in the Majors by College index beginning on page 469.

The **faculty** at St. Mary's has 144 full-time members, 98% with terminal degrees. The student-faculty ratio is 12:1.

Students of St. Mary's

The student body totals 2,065, of whom 2,035 are undergraduates. 58% are women and 42% are men. Students come from 38 states and territories and 41 other countries. 83% are from Maryland. 2.2% are international students. 8.1% are African American, 0.7% American Indian, 3.9% Asian American, and 4.5% Hispanic American. 90% returned for their sophomore year.

Facilities and Resources

387 **computers/terminals** and 500 ports are available on campus for general student use. Students can access the following: campus intranet, computer help desk, free student e-mail accounts, online (class) grades, online (class) registration, online (class) schedules, Blackboard. Campuswide network is available. 100% of college-owned or -operated housing units are wired for high-speed Internet access. Wireless service is available via classrooms, computer centers, computer labs, learning centers, libraries, student centers. The **library** has 161,866 books and 845 subscriptions.

Campus Life

There are 116 active organizations on campus, including a drama/theater group, newspaper, radio station, television station, and choral group. No national or local **fraternities** or **sororities**.

St. Mary's is a member of the NCAA (Division III). **Intercollegiate sports** include baseball (m), basketball, field hockey (w), lacrosse, sailing, soccer, swimming and diving, tennis, volleyball (w).

Campus Safety

Student safety services include late-night transport/escort service, 24-hour emergency telephone alarm devices, 24-hour patrols by trained security personnel, student patrols, and electronically operated dormitory entrances.

Applying

St. Mary's requires an essay, SAT or ACT, a high school transcript, resume of co-curricular activities, and a minimum high school GPA of 2.0. It recommends an interview and 2 recommendations. Application deadline: 1/1; 3/1 for financial aid. Early admission is possible.

St. Mary's College of Maryland, with its distinctive identity as Maryland's "Public Honors College," is one of the finest liberal arts and sciences colleges in the country. The lively academic atmosphere and stunning beauty of the riverfront campus create a challenging and memorable college experience. More than 50 percent of the graduates of St. Mary's College of Maryland continue their studies in graduate or professional schools. Suite-style residences were completed in 2007, and the new athletic and recreation center opened in 2005.

Getting Accepted
2,723 applied
52% were accepted
458 enrolled (32% of accepted)
47% from top tenth of their h.s. class
3.56 average high school GPA
Mean SAT critical reading score: 620
Mean SAT math score: 610
Mean SAT writing score: 620
69% had SAT critical reading scores over 600
60% had SAT math scores over 600
63% had SAT writing scores over 600
19% had SAT critical reading scores over 700
10% had SAT math scores over 700
18% had SAT writing scores over 700
3 National Merit Scholars
17 valedictorians

Graduation and After
67% graduated in 4 years
7% graduated in 5 years
1% graduated in 6 years
40 organizations recruited on campus

Financial Matters
$12,604 resident tuition and fees (2008–09)
$23,454 nonresident tuition and fees (2008–09)
$9225 room and board
62% average percent of need met
$6250 average financial aid amount received per undergraduate (2006–07)

Getting Accepted
2,116 applied
81% were accepted
532 enrolled (31% of accepted)
22% from top tenth of their h.s. class
3.52 average high school GPA
Mean ACT score: 24
52% had ACT scores over 24
6% had ACT scores over 30
14 valedictorians

Graduation and After
69% graduated in 4 years
4% graduated in 5 years
75 organizations recruited on campus

Financial Matters
$25,926 tuition and fees (2008–09)
$6781 room and board
88% average percent of need met
$17,025 average financial aid amount received per undergraduate (2006–07)

St. Norbert College
Suburban setting ■ Private ■ Independent Religious ■ Coed
De Pere, Wisconsin

Web site: www.snc.edu
Contact: Ms. Bridget O'Connor, Vice President for Enrollment Management and Communications, 100 Grant Street, De Pere, WI 54115-2099
Telephone: 920-403-3005 or toll-free 800-236-4878
Fax: 920-403-4072
E-mail: admit@snc.edu

Academics
St. Norbert awards bachelor's and master's **degrees. Challenging opportunities** include advanced placement credit, student-designed majors, an honors program, double majors, independent study, and a senior project. Special programs include internships, summer session for credit, off-campus study, study-abroad, and Army ROTC.

The most frequently chosen **baccalaureate** fields are business/marketing, education, and social sciences. A complete listing of majors at St. Norbert appears in the Majors by College index beginning on page 469.

The **faculty** at St. Norbert has 132 full-time members, 86% with terminal degrees. The student-faculty ratio is 14:1.

Students of St. Norbert
The student body totals 2,137, of whom 2,084 are undergraduates. 56% are women and 44% are men. Students come from 33 states and territories and 28 other countries. 71% are from Wisconsin. 3.2% are international students. 0.6% are African American, 0.8% American Indian, 0.9% Asian American, and 1.5% Hispanic American. 84% returned for their sophomore year.

Facilities and Resources
233 **computers/terminals** are available on campus for general student use. Students can access the following: campus intranet, computer help desk, free student e-mail accounts, online (class) grades, online (class) registration, online (class) schedules. Campuswide network is available. 100% of college-owned or -operated housing units are wired for high-speed Internet access. Wireless service is available via classrooms, libraries. The **library** has 229,958 books and 485 subscriptions.

Campus Life
There are 67 active organizations on campus, including a drama/theater group, newspaper, radio station, television station, and choral group. 7% of eligible men and 7% of eligible women are members of national **fraternities**, national **sororities**, and local sororities.

St. Norbert is a member of the NCAA (Division III). **Intercollegiate sports** include baseball (m), basketball, cross-country running, football (m), golf, ice hockey (m), soccer, softball (w), swimming and diving (w), tennis, track and field, volleyball (w).

Campus Safety
Student safety services include crime prevention programs, late-night transport/escort service, 24-hour emergency telephone alarm devices, 24-hour patrols by trained security personnel, student patrols, and electronically operated dormitory entrances.

Applying
St. Norbert requires SAT or ACT, a high school transcript, and 1 recommendation, and in some cases an interview. It recommends an essay. Application deadline: rolling admissions; 3/1 priority date for financial aid. Deferred admission is possible.

St. Olaf College

SMALL-TOWN SETTING ■ PRIVATE ■ INDEPENDENT RELIGIOUS ■ COED
NORTHFIELD, MINNESOTA

Web site: www.stolaf.edu
Contact: Derek Gueldenzoph, Dean of Admissions, 1520 St. Olaf Avenue,
    Northfield, MN 55057
Telephone: 507-786-3025 or toll-free 800-800-3025
Fax: 507-786-3832
E-mail: admissions@stolaf.edu

Academics

St. Olaf awards bachelor's **degrees. Challenging opportunities** include advanced
placement credit, student-designed majors, double majors, independent study, and a
senior project. Special programs include internships, summer session for credit, off-
campus study, and study-abroad.

The most frequently chosen **baccalaureate** fields are biological/life sciences, social
sciences, and visual and performing arts. A complete listing of majors at St. Olaf appears
in the Majors by College index beginning on page 469.

The **faculty** at St. Olaf has 194 full-time members, 91% with terminal degrees. The
student-faculty ratio is 13:1.

Students of St. Olaf

The student body is made up of 3,073 undergraduates. 55.1% are women and 44.9% are
men. Students come from 50 states and territories and 30 other countries. 55% are from
Minnesota. 2% are international students. 1.3% are African American, 0.2% American
Indian, 5.1% Asian American, and 1.6% Hispanic American. 92% returned for their
sophomore year.

Facilities and Resources

969 **computers/terminals** and 2,600 ports are available on campus for general student
use. Students can access the following: campus intranet, computer help desk, free student
e-mail accounts, online (class) grades, online (class) registration, online (class) schedules.
Campuswide network is available. 100% of college-owned or -operated housing units are
wired for high-speed Internet access. Wireless service is available via entire campus. The
3 **libraries** have 741,478 books and 5,935 subscriptions.

Campus Life

There are 137 active organizations on campus, including a drama/theater group,
newspaper, radio station, television station, and choral group. No national or local
fraternities or **sororities.**

St. Olaf is a member of the NCAA (Division III). **Intercollegiate sports** include
baseball (m), basketball, cross-country running, football (m), golf, ice hockey, skiing
(cross-country), skiing (downhill), soccer, softball (w), swimming and diving, tennis, track
and field, volleyball (w), wrestling (m).

Campus Safety

Student safety services include lighted pathways and sidewalks, first-year only dorms,
quiet halls, late-night transport/escort service, 24-hour emergency telephone alarm
devices, 24-hour patrols by trained security personnel, and electronically operated
dormitory entrances.

Applying

St. Olaf requires an essay, SAT or ACT, a high school transcript, and 2 recommendations. It recommends an interview. Application deadline: 1/15; 4/15 for financial aid,
with a 1/15 priority date. Deferred admission is possible.

Getting Accepted

3,964 applied
59% were accepted
813 enrolled (35% of accepted)
59% from top tenth of their h.s. class
3.65 average high school GPA
Mean SAT critical reading score: 646
Mean SAT math score: 647
Mean ACT score: 29
74% had SAT critical reading scores over 600
74% had SAT math scores over 600
92% had ACT scores over 24
29% had SAT critical reading scores over 700
30% had SAT math scores over 700
43% had ACT scores over 30
36 National Merit Scholars
2 class presidents
65 valedictorians

Graduation and After

83% graduated in 4 years
3% graduated in 5 years
1% graduated in 6 years
64.7% had job offers within 6 months
570 organizations recruited on campus

Financial Matters

$35,500 tuition and fees (2009–10)
$8200 room and board
100% average percent of need met
$22,743 average financial aid amount received
    per undergraduate (2007–08 estimated)

Salem College

URBAN SETTING ■ PRIVATE ■ INDEPENDENT RELIGIOUS
■ UNDERGRADUATE: WOMEN ONLY; GRADUATE: COED
WINSTON-SALEM, NORTH CAROLINA

Web site: www.salem.edu
Contact: Katherine Knapp Watts, Dean of Admissions and Financial Aid,
  Single Sisters House, 601 South Church Street, Winston Salem, NC 27101
Telephone: 336-721-2621 or toll-free 800-327-2536
Fax: 336-917-5572
E-mail: admissions@salem.edu

Getting Accepted

429 applied
59% were accepted
125 enrolled (50% of accepted)
36% from top tenth of their h.s. class
3.7 average high school GPA
Mean SAT critical reading score: 558
Mean SAT math score: 537
Mean ACT score: 25
26% had SAT critical reading scores over 600
21% had SAT math scores over 600
66% had ACT scores over 24
6% had SAT critical reading scores over 700
3% had SAT math scores over 700
11% had ACT scores over 30
4 valedictorians

Graduation and After

50% graduated in 4 years
2% graduated in 5 years
1% graduated in 6 years
78% had job offers within 6 months

Financial Matters

$20,420 tuition and fees (2008–09)
$10,705 room and board
100% average percent of need met
$15,340 average financial aid amount received
  per undergraduate (2006–07)

Academics

Salem awards bachelor's and master's **degrees** (only students age 23 or over are eligible
to enroll part-time). **Challenging opportunities** include advanced placement credit,
student-designed majors, an honors program, double majors, independent study, and a
senior project. Special programs include internships, summer session for credit, and off-
campus study.

The most frequently chosen **baccalaureate** fields are social sciences, communica-
tions/journalism, and business/marketing. A complete listing of majors at Salem appears
in the Majors by College index beginning on page 469.

The **faculty** at Salem has 58 full-time members. The student-faculty ratio is 11:1.

Students of Salem

The student body totals 966, of whom 761 are undergraduates. 97.2% are women and
2.8% are men. Students come from 29 states and territories and 18 other countries. 77%
are from North Carolina. 76% returned for their sophomore year.

Facilities and Resources

54 **computers/terminals** are available on campus for general student use. Students can
access the following: campus intranet, computer help desk, free student e-mail accounts,
online (class) grades, online (class) schedules. Campuswide network is available. 100% of
college-owned or -operated housing units are wired for high-speed Internet access.
Wireless service is available via entire campus. The 2 **libraries** have 152,000 books and
679 subscriptions.

Campus Life

There are 41 active organizations on campus, including a drama/theater group,
newspaper, choral group, and marching band. No national or local **sororities**.

Salem is a member of the NCAA (Division III). **Intercollegiate sports** include
basketball, cross-country running, field hockey, soccer, swimming and diving, tennis,
volleyball.

Campus Safety

Student safety services include late-night transport/escort service, 24-hour emergency
telephone alarm devices, 24-hour patrols by trained security personnel, and electronically operated dormitory entrances.

Applying

Salem requires an essay, SAT or ACT, a high school transcript, and 2 recommendations.
It recommends an interview. Application deadline: rolling admissions; 3/1 priority date
for financial aid. Early and deferred admission are possible.

SAMFORD UNIVERSITY

SUBURBAN SETTING ■ PRIVATE ■ INDEPENDENT RELIGIOUS ■ COED
BIRMINGHAM, ALABAMA

SPONSOR

Web site: www.samford.edu
Contact: Brian E. Willett, Director of Admissions, 800 Lakeshore Drive,
Samford Hall, Birmingham, AL 35229-0002
Telephone: 205-726-2902 or toll-free 800-888-7218
Fax: 205-726-2171
E-mail: bewillet@samford.edu

Academics

Samford awards associate, bachelor's, master's, doctoral, and first-professional **degrees**
and post-master's certificates. **Challenging opportunities** include advanced placement
credit, accelerated degree programs, an honors program, double majors, independent
study, and a senior project. Special programs include cooperative education, internships,
summer session for credit, off-campus study, study-abroad, and Army and Air Force
ROTC.

The most frequently chosen **baccalaureate** fields are business/marketing, health
professions and related sciences, and visual and performing arts. A complete listing of
majors at Samford appears in the Majors by College index beginning on page 469.

The **faculty** at Samford has 290 full-time members, 83% with terminal degrees. The
student-faculty ratio is 11:1.

Students of Samford

The student body totals 4,469, of whom 2,848 are undergraduates. 64% are women and
36% are men. Students come from 39 states and territories and 15 other countries. 47%
are from Alabama. 0.7% are international students. 6.7% are African American, 0.4%
American Indian, 0.8% Asian American, and 1.3% Hispanic American. 84% returned for
their sophomore year.

Facilities and Resources

330 **computers/terminals** and 430 ports are available on campus for general student
use. Students can access the following: campus intranet, computer help desk, free student
e-mail accounts, online (class) grades, online (class) registration, online (class) schedules.
Campuswide network is available. 100% of college-owned or -operated housing units are
wired for high-speed Internet access. Wireless service is available via entire campus. The
6 **libraries** have 439,760 books and 3,724 subscriptions.

Campus Life

There are 119 active organizations on campus, including a drama/theater group,
newspaper, radio station, choral group, and marching band. 20% of eligible men and
31% of eligible women are members of national **fraternities** and national **sororities**.

Samford is a member of the NCAA (Division I). **Intercollegiate sports** (some
offering scholarships) include baseball (m), basketball, cross-country running, football
(m), golf, soccer (w), softball (w), tennis, track and field, volleyball (w).

Campus Safety

Student safety services include late-night transport/escort service, 24-hour emergency
telephone alarm devices, and 24-hour patrols by trained security personnel.

Applying

Samford requires an essay, SAT or ACT, 1 recommendation, and leadership resumé. It
recommends an interview. Application deadline: rolling admissions; 3/1 priority date for
financial aid. Early and deferred admission are possible.

Samford University is the largest
private accredited university in
Alabama, yet, with more than 4,500
students, it is an ideal size. More
than half of the undergraduates
reside on campus. Students from
forty-four states and territories and
thirty-three other countries enjoy a
beautiful setting characterized by
Georgian-Colonial architecture. The
institution takes seriously its
Christian heritage and is consistently
listed in rankings of Southeastern
institutions. Faculty members have
earned degrees from more than 180
colleges and universities, with more
than 80 percent holding the terminal
degree in their field. Excellent opportunities to "stretch" academically,
socially, physically, and spiritually are
provided, as are special opportunities
in computer competency, international
experiences, and externships.

Getting Accepted
2,153 applied
89% were accepted
708 enrolled (37% of accepted)
36% from top tenth of their h.s. class
3.61 average high school GPA
36% had SAT critical reading scores over 600
31% had SAT math scores over 600
58% had ACT scores over 24
8% had SAT critical reading scores over 700
3% had SAT math scores over 700
12% had ACT scores over 30
18 National Merit Scholars
22 class presidents
22 valedictorians

Graduation and After
59% graduated in 4 years
13% graduated in 5 years
4% graduated in 6 years
166 organizations recruited on campus

Financial Matters
$20,420 tuition and fees (2009–10)
$6624 room and board
68% average percent of need met
$12,542 average financial aid amount received
per undergraduate (2006–07)

SAN DIEGO STATE UNIVERSITY

URBAN SETTING ■ PUBLIC ■ STATE-SUPPORTED ■ COED
SAN DIEGO, CALIFORNIA

Web site: www.sdsu.edu
Contact: Ms. Beverly Arata, Director of Admissions, 5500 Campanile Drive, San Diego, CA 92182-0771
Telephone: 619-594-6336
E-mail: admissions@sdsu.edu

Getting Accepted
50,148 applied
31% were accepted
4,386 enrolled (28% of accepted)
3.47 average high school GPA
Mean SAT critical reading score: 513
Mean SAT math score: 536
Mean ACT score: 22
16% had SAT critical reading scores over 600
25% had SAT math scores over 600
40% had ACT scores over 24
1% had SAT critical reading scores over 700
2% had SAT math scores over 700
2% had ACT scores over 30

Graduation and After
24% graduated in 4 years
29% graduated in 5 years
53% had job offers within 6 months
645 organizations recruited on campus

Financial Matters
$3754 resident tuition and fees (2008–09)
$13,924 nonresident tuition and fees (2008–09)
$11,266 room and board
69% average percent of need met
$8540 average financial aid amount received per undergraduate (2007–08 estimated)

Academics
SDSU awards bachelor's, master's, and doctoral **degrees** and post-bachelor's and post-master's certificates. **Challenging opportunities** include advanced placement credit, student-designed majors, an honors program, double majors, independent study, and a senior project. Special programs include internships, summer session for credit, off-campus study, study-abroad, and Army, Navy, and Air Force ROTC.

The most frequently chosen **baccalaureate** fields are business/marketing, social sciences, and psychology. A complete listing of majors at SDSU appears in the Majors by College index beginning on page 469.

The **faculty** at SDSU has 806 full-time members. The student-faculty ratio is 20:1.

Students of SDSU
The student body totals 35,832, of whom 29,481 are undergraduates. 57.4% are women and 42.6% are men. Students come from 51 states and territories and 90 other countries. 94% are from California. 3% are international students. 4.1% are African American, 0.6% American Indian, 15.8% Asian American, and 23.9% Hispanic American. 81% returned for their sophomore year.

Facilities and Resources
400 **computers/terminals** are available on campus for general student use. Students can access the following: free student e-mail accounts, online (class) grades, online (class) registration, online (class) schedules. Campuswide network is available. Wireless service is available via entire campus. The **library** has 1,342,735 books and 8,245 subscriptions.

Campus Life
There are 253 active organizations on campus, including a drama/theater group, newspaper, radio station, television station, choral group, and marching band. 9% of eligible men and 9% of eligible women are members of national **fraternities**, national **sororities**, local fraternities, and local sororities.

SDSU is a member of the NCAA (Division I). **Intercollegiate sports** (some offering scholarships) include baseball (m), basketball, cross-country running (w), football (m), golf, soccer, softball (w), swimming and diving (w), tennis, track and field (w), volleyball, water polo (w).

Campus Safety
Student safety services include late-night transport/escort service, 24-hour emergency telephone alarm devices, 24-hour patrols by trained security personnel, and student patrols.

Applying
SDSU requires SAT or ACT, a high school transcript, 2.5 GPA for non-California residents, and a minimum high school GPA of 2.0. Application deadline: 11/30; 3/2 for financial aid.

SANTA CLARA UNIVERSITY

SUBURBAN SETTING ■ PRIVATE ■ INDEPENDENT RELIGIOUS ■ COED
SANTA CLARA, CALIFORNIA

Web site: www.scu.edu
Contact: Ms. Sandra Hayes, Dean of Undergraduate Admissions, 500 El
   Camino Real, Santa Clara, CA 95053
Telephone: 408-554-4700
Fax: 408-554-5255
E-mail: ugadmissions@scu.edu

Academics

Santa Clara awards bachelor's, master's, doctoral, and first-professional **degrees** and
post-bachelor's, post-master's, and first-professional certificates. **Challenging opportunities** include advanced placement credit, student-designed majors, an honors
program, double majors, independent study, and a senior project. Special programs
include cooperative education, internships, summer session for credit, study-abroad, and
Army and Air Force ROTC.

The most frequently chosen **baccalaureate** fields are business/marketing, social sciences, and engineering. A complete listing of majors at Santa Clara appears in the Majors
by College index beginning on page 469.

The **faculty** at Santa Clara has 515 full-time members, 88% with terminal degrees.
The student-faculty ratio is 12:1.

Students of Santa Clara

The student body totals 8,758, of whom 5,267 are undergraduates. 53.1% are women
and 46.9% are men. Students come from 37 states and territories and 16 other countries.
64% are from California. 2.9% are international students. 3.6% are African American,
0.3% American Indian, 15.7% Asian American, and 13.5% Hispanic American. 93%
returned for their sophomore year.

Facilities and Resources

800 **computers/terminals** and 6,000 ports are available on campus for general student
use. Students can access the following: campus intranet, computer help desk, free student
e-mail accounts, online (class) grades, online (class) registration, online (class) schedules.
Campuswide network is available. 100% of college-owned or -operated housing units are
wired for high-speed Internet access. Wireless service is available via entire campus. The
2 **libraries** have 797,312 books and 4,400 subscriptions.

Campus Life

There are 86 active organizations on campus, including a drama/theater group,
newspaper, radio station, and choral group. No national or local **fraternities** or **sororities**.

Santa Clara is a member of the NCAA (Division I). **Intercollegiate sports** (some
offering scholarships) include baseball (m), basketball, crew, cross-country running, golf,
soccer, tennis, track and field, volleyball (w), water polo.

Campus Safety

Student safety services include late-night transport/escort service, 24-hour emergency
telephone alarm devices, 24-hour patrols by trained security personnel, and electronically operated dormitory entrances.

Applying

Santa Clara requires an essay, SAT or ACT, a high school transcript, and 1 recommendation. Application deadline: 1/7; 2/1 priority date for financial aid. Deferred
admission is possible.

Getting Accepted
10,124 applied
58% were accepted
1,221 enrolled (21% of accepted)
40% from top tenth of their h.s. class
3.53 average high school GPA
Mean SAT critical reading score: 600
Mean SAT math score: 627
Mean ACT score: 27
54% had SAT critical reading scores over 600
67% had SAT math scores over 600
85% had ACT scores over 24
9% had SAT critical reading scores over 700
19% had SAT math scores over 700
27% had ACT scores over 30
7 National Merit Scholars

Graduation and After
78% graduated in 4 years
6% graduated in 5 years
1% graduated in 6 years
65% had job offers within 6 months
1082 organizations recruited on campus

Financial Matters
$34,950 tuition and fees (2008–09)
$11,070 room and board
70% average percent of need met
$21,337 average financial aid amount received
   per undergraduate (2007–08 estimated)

SPONSOR

Sarah Lawrence College

Suburban setting ■ Private ■ Independent ■ Coed
Bronxville, New York

Web site: www.sarahlawrence.edu
Contact: Mr. Stephen M. Schierloh, Acting Dean of Admission, 1 Mead Way, Bronxville, NY 10708-5999
Telephone: 914-395-2510 or toll-free 800-888-2858
Fax: 914-395-2515
E-mail: slcadmit@sarahlawrence.edu

Sarah Lawrence, a private, coeducational college of the liberal arts and sciences founded in 1926, is a lively community of students, scholars, and artists just 30 minutes from midtown Manhattan. In its distinctive seminar/conference system, each course consists of two parts: the seminar, limited to 15 students, and the conference, a private biweekly meeting with the seminar professor. In conference, student and teacher create a project that extends the seminar material and connects it to the student's academic goals. To prepare for this rigorous work, all first-year students enroll in a First-Year Studies Seminar. This seminar teacher becomes the student's don, or adviser, throughout his or her Sarah Lawrence years.

Getting Accepted
2,801 applied
44% were accepted
363 enrolled (29% of accepted)
37% from top tenth of their h.s. class
3.6 average high school GPA
6 National Merit Scholars
3 valedictorians

Graduation and After
70% graduated in 4 years
9% graduated in 5 years
1% graduated in 6 years

Financial Matters
$40,350 tuition and fees (2008–09)
$13,104 room and board
88% average percent of need met
$27,282 average financial aid amount received per undergraduate (2007–08 estimated)

Academics
Sarah Lawrence awards bachelor's and master's **degrees. Challenging opportunities** include advanced placement credit, student-designed majors, double majors, and independent study. Special programs include internships, off-campus study, and study-abroad.

The most frequently chosen **baccalaureate** field is liberal arts/general studies. A complete listing of majors at Sarah Lawrence appears in the Majors by College index beginning on page 469.

The **faculty** at Sarah Lawrence has 195 full-time members. The student-faculty ratio is 6:1.

Students of Sarah Lawrence
The student body totals 1,700, of whom 1,383 are undergraduates. 74.3% are women and 25.7% are men. Students come from 47 states and territories and 34 other countries. 23% are from New York. 2.5% are international students. 3.9% are African American, 0.6% American Indian, 5% Asian American, and 5% Hispanic American. 86% returned for their sophomore year.

Facilities and Resources
110 **computers/terminals** and 30 ports are available on campus for general student use. Students can access the following: campus intranet, computer help desk, free student e-mail accounts. Campuswide network is available. 100% of college-owned or -operated housing units are wired for high-speed Internet access. Wireless service is available via classrooms, computer centers, computer labs, libraries, student centers. The 3 **libraries** have 298,611 books and 917 subscriptions.

Campus Life
There are 30 active organizations on campus, including a drama/theater group, newspaper, radio station, and choral group. No national or local **fraternities** or **sororities**.

Intercollegiate sports include basketball (m), crew, equestrian sports, softball (w), swimming and diving (w), tennis, volleyball (w).

Campus Safety
Student safety services include late-night transport/escort service, 24-hour emergency telephone alarm devices, 24-hour patrols by trained security personnel, and electronically operated dormitory entrances.

Applying
Sarah Lawrence requires an essay, a high school transcript, and 3 recommendations. It recommends an interview and a minimum high school GPA of 3.0. Application deadline: 1/1; 2/1 for financial aid. Early and deferred admission are possible.

SCRIPPS COLLEGE

SUBURBAN SETTING ■ PRIVATE ■ INDEPENDENT ■ WOMEN ONLY
CLAREMONT, CALIFORNIA

Web site: www.scrippscollege.edu
Contact: Ms. Patricia F. Goldsmith, Vice President for Enrollment, Marketing, and Communications, 1030 Columbia Avenue, Claremont, CA 91711
Telephone: 909-621-8149 or toll-free 800-770-1333
Fax: 909-607-7508
E-mail: admission@scrippscollege.edu

Academics
Scripps awards bachelor's **degrees** and post-bachelor's certificates. **Challenging opportunities** include advanced placement credit, accelerated degree programs, student-designed majors, double majors, independent study, and a senior project. Special programs include internships, off-campus study, study-abroad, and Army and Air Force ROTC.

The most frequently chosen **baccalaureate** fields are social sciences, visual and performing arts, and area and ethnic studies. A complete listing of majors at Scripps appears in the Majors by College index beginning on page 469.

The **faculty** at Scripps has 81 full-time members, 99% with terminal degrees. The student-faculty ratio is 10:1.

Students of Scripps
The student body is made up of 954 undergraduates. Students come from 44 states and territories and 12 other countries. 42% are from California. 1.7% are international students. 3.7% are African American, 0.7% American Indian, 13.1% Asian American, and 7.4% Hispanic American. 95% returned for their sophomore year.

Facilities and Resources
72 **computers/terminals** are available on campus for general student use. Students can access the following: campus intranet, computer help desk, free student e-mail accounts, online (class) grades, online (class) schedules, 2 ports per dorm room. Campuswide network is available. 100% of college-owned or -operated housing units are wired for high-speed Internet access. Wireless service is available via classrooms, computer centers, computer labs, dorm rooms, libraries, student centers. The 4 **libraries** have 2,604,795 books and 46,862 subscriptions.

Campus Life
There are 200 active organizations on campus, including a drama/theater group, newspaper, radio station, and choral group. No national or local **sororities**.

Scripps is a member of the NCAA (Division III). **Intercollegiate sports** include basketball, cross-country running, golf, lacrosse, soccer, softball, swimming and diving, tennis, track and field, volleyball, water polo.

Campus Safety
Student safety services include late-night transport/escort service, 24-hour emergency telephone alarm devices, 24-hour patrols by trained security personnel, and electronically operated dormitory entrances.

Applying
Scripps requires an essay, SAT or ACT, a high school transcript, 3 recommendations, and graded writing sample. It recommends an interview and a minimum high school GPA of 3.0. Application deadline: 1/1; 2/1 priority date for financial aid. Early and deferred admission are possible.

Getting Accepted
1,931 applied
43% were accepted
252 enrolled (30% of accepted)
70% from top tenth of their h.s. class
Mean SAT critical reading score: 685
Mean SAT math score: 663
Mean SAT writing score: 686
Mean ACT score: 29
90% had SAT critical reading scores over 600
82% had SAT math scores over 600
91% had SAT writing scores over 600
90% had ACT scores over 24
43% had SAT critical reading scores over 700
33% had SAT math scores over 700
44% had SAT writing scores over 700
55% had ACT scores over 30
24 National Merit Scholars
21 valedictorians

Graduation and After
79% graduated in 4 years
3% graduated in 5 years
363 organizations recruited on campus

Financial Matters
$37,950 tuition and fees (2008–09)
$11,500 room and board
100% average percent of need met
$30,842 average financial aid amount received per undergraduate (2007–08 estimated)

SEATTLE PACIFIC UNIVERSITY

URBAN SETTING ■ PRIVATE ■ INDEPENDENT RELIGIOUS ■ COED
SEATTLE, WASHINGTON

Web site: www.spu.edu
Contact: Mr. Jobe Korb-Nice, Acting Director of Admissions, 3307 3rd
    Avenue, W, Seattle, WA 98119-1997
Telephone: 206-281-2021 or toll-free 800-366-3344
Fax: 206-281-2669
E-mail: admissions@spu.edu

Getting Accepted

2,049 applied
88% were accepted
713 enrolled (39% of accepted)
3.61 average high school GPA
Mean SAT critical reading score: 580
Mean SAT math score: 573
Mean SAT writing score: 568
Mean ACT score: 25
42% had SAT critical reading scores over 600
40% had SAT math scores over 600
33% had SAT writing scores over 600
67% had ACT scores over 24
8% had SAT critical reading scores over 700
6% had SAT math scores over 700
5% had SAT writing scores over 700
16% had ACT scores over 30

Graduation and After

50% graduated in 4 years
11% graduated in 5 years
3% graduated in 6 years
86% had job offers within 6 months
56 organizations recruited on campus

Financial Matters

$26,817 tuition and fees (2008–09)
$8454 room and board
82% average percent of need met
$20,988 average financial aid amount received
    per undergraduate (2007–08 estimated)

Academics

SPU awards bachelor's, master's, and doctoral **degrees** and post-master's certificates. **Challenging opportunities** include advanced placement credit, student-designed majors, an honors program, double majors, independent study, and a senior project. Special programs include internships, summer session for credit, off-campus study, study-abroad, and Army, Navy, and Air Force ROTC.

The most frequently chosen **baccalaureate** fields are business/marketing, social sciences, and family and consumer sciences. A complete listing of majors at SPU appears in the Majors by College index beginning on page 469.

The **faculty** at SPU has 190 full-time members, 85% with terminal degrees. The student-faculty ratio is 14:1.

Students of SPU

The student body totals 3,891, of whom 3,007 are undergraduates. 67.2% are women and 32.8% are men. Students come from 46 states and territories. 39% are from Washington. 0.8% are international students. 2.1% are African American, 1% American Indian, 7% Asian American, and 2.9% Hispanic American. 82% returned for their sophomore year.

Facilities and Resources

150 **computers/terminals** are available on campus for general student use. Students can access the following: campus intranet, computer help desk, free student e-mail accounts, online (class) grades, online (class) registration, online (class) schedules. Campuswide network is available. Wireless service is available via entire campus. The **library** has 191,807 books and 1,230 subscriptions.

Campus Life

There are 50 active organizations on campus, including a drama/theater group, newspaper, radio station, and choral group. No national or local **fraternities** or **sororities**.

SPU is a member of the NCAA (Division II). **Intercollegiate sports** (some offering scholarships) include basketball, crew, cross-country running, gymnastics (w), soccer, track and field, volleyball (w).

Campus Safety

Student safety services include closed-circuit TV monitors, late-night transport/escort service, 24-hour emergency telephone alarm devices, 24-hour patrols by trained security personnel, and student patrols.

Applying

SPU requires an essay, SAT or ACT, a high school transcript, 2 recommendations, and a minimum high school GPA of 2.5. It recommends an interview. Application deadline: 2/1; 4/1 priority date for financial aid. Early admission is possible.

SEATTLE UNIVERSITY

URBAN SETTING ■ PRIVATE ■ INDEPENDENT RELIGIOUS ■ COED
SEATTLE, WASHINGTON

SPONSOR

Web site: www.seattleu.edu
Contact: Mr. Michael K. McKeon, Dean of Admissions, Broadway and
    Madison, Seattle, WA 98122
Telephone: 206-296-2000 or toll-free 800-542-0833 (in-state), 800-426-7123
    (out-of-state)
Fax: 206-296-5656
E-mail: admissions@seattleu.edu

Academics

Seattle U awards bachelor's, master's, doctoral, and first-professional **degrees** and post-
bachelor's, post-master's, and first-professional certificates. **Challenging opportunities**
include advanced placement credit, accelerated degree programs, student-designed
majors, freshman honors college, an honors program, double majors, independent study,
and a senior project. Special programs include internships, summer session for credit,
off-campus study, study-abroad, and Army and Air Force ROTC.

The most frequently chosen **baccalaureate** fields are business/marketing, health
professions and related sciences, and social sciences. A complete listing of majors at
Seattle U appears in the Majors by College index beginning on page 469.

The **faculty** at Seattle U has 426 full-time members, 82% with terminal degrees.
The student-faculty ratio is 13:1.

Students of Seattle U

The student body totals 7,529, of whom 4,253 are undergraduates. 61.1% are women
and 38.9% are men. Students come from 47 states and territories and 76 other countries.
45% are from Washington. 7.6% are international students. 5.3% are African American,
1.3% American Indian, 20% Asian American, and 7.3% Hispanic American. 86%
returned for their sophomore year.

Facilities and Resources

401 **computers/terminals** are available on campus for general student use. Students can
access the following: online (class) registration. Campuswide network is available. The 2
libraries have 141,478 books and 2,701 subscriptions.

Campus Life

There are 78 active organizations on campus, including a drama/theater group,
newspaper, radio station, and choral group. No national or local **fraternities** or **sororities**.

Seattle U is a member of the NCAA (Division II) and NAIA. **Intercollegiate sports**
(some offering scholarships) include basketball, cross-country running, soccer, softball
(w), swimming and diving, track and field, volleyball (w).

Campus Safety

Student safety services include bicycle patrols, late-night transport/escort service,
24-hour emergency telephone alarm devices, 24-hour patrols by trained security
personnel, and electronically operated dormitory entrances.

Applying

Seattle U requires an essay, SAT or ACT, a high school transcript, 2 recommendations,
and a minimum high school GPA of 2.5. Application deadline: rolling admissions; 2/1
priority date for financial aid. Deferred admission is possible.

Getting Accepted
4,918 applied
64% were accepted
768 enrolled (25% of accepted)
32% from top tenth of their h.s. class
3.55 average high school GPA
43% had SAT critical reading scores over 600
41% had SAT math scores over 600
36% had SAT writing scores over 600
68% had ACT scores over 24
11% had SAT critical reading scores over 700
6% had SAT math scores over 700
6% had SAT writing scores over 700
11% had ACT scores over 30

Graduation and After
50% graduated in 4 years
16% graduated in 5 years
2% graduated in 6 years
220 organizations recruited on campus

Financial Matters
$28,260 tuition and fees (2008–09)
$8340 room and board
71% average percent of need met
$24,468 average financial aid amount received
    per undergraduate (2007–08 estimated)

Getting Accepted
2,488 applied
64% were accepted
410 enrolled (26% of accepted)
49% from top tenth of their h.s. class
3.62 average high school GPA
64% had SAT critical reading scores over 600
66% had SAT math scores over 600
92% had ACT scores over 24
19% had SAT critical reading scores over 700
17% had SAT math scores over 700
31% had ACT scores over 30
22 National Merit Scholars

Graduation and After
73% graduated in 4 years
4% graduated in 5 years
74% had job offers within 6 months
17 organizations recruited on campus

Financial Matters
$34,172 tuition and fees (2009–10)
$9760 room and board
95% average percent of need met
$22,471 average financial aid amount received per undergraduate (2007–08 estimated)

Sewanee: The University of the South
Small-town setting ■ Private ■ Independent Religious ■ Coed
Sewanee, Tennessee

Web site: www.sewanee.edu
Contact: Mr. David Lesesne, Dean of Admission, 735 University Avenue, Sewanee, TN 37383-1000
Telephone: 931-598-1238 or toll-free 800-522-2234
Fax: 931-598-3248
E-mail: admiss@sewanee.edu

Academics
Sewanee awards bachelor's, master's, doctoral, and first-professional **degrees** and post-bachelor's, post-master's, and first-professional certificates. **Challenging opportunities** include advanced placement credit, student-designed majors, double majors, independent study, and a senior project. Special programs include internships, summer session for credit, and study-abroad.

The most frequently chosen **baccalaureate** fields are social sciences, history, and English. A complete listing of majors at Sewanee appears in the Majors by College index beginning on page 469.

The **faculty** at Sewanee has 132 full-time members, 95% with terminal degrees. The student-faculty ratio is 10:1.

Students of Sewanee
The student body totals 1,562, of whom 1,483 are undergraduates. 52.6% are women and 47.4% are men. Students come from 41 states and territories and 22 other countries. 24% are from Tennessee. 1.6% are international students. 3.9% are African American, 1% American Indian, 2.8% Asian American, and 2.7% Hispanic American. 88% returned for their sophomore year.

Facilities and Resources
340 **computers/terminals** are available on campus for general student use. Students can access the following: campus intranet, computer help desk, free student e-mail accounts, online (class) grades, online (class) registration, online (class) schedules. Campuswide network is available. 100% of college-owned or -operated housing units are wired for high-speed Internet access. Wireless service is available via entire campus. The **library** has 648,459 books and 3,444 subscriptions.

Campus Life
There are 110 active organizations on campus, including a drama/theater group, newspaper, radio station, and choral group. 82% of eligible men and 88% of eligible women are members of national **fraternities** and local **sororities**.

Sewanee is a member of the NCAA (Division III). **Intercollegiate sports** include baseball (m), basketball, cross-country running, field hockey (w), football (m), golf, soccer, swimming and diving, tennis, track and field, volleyball (w).

Campus Safety
Student safety services include security lighting, late-night transport/escort service, 24-hour emergency telephone alarm devices, 24-hour patrols by trained security personnel, and electronically operated dormitory entrances.

Applying
Sewanee requires an essay, SAT or ACT, a high school transcript, and 2 recommendations. It recommends an interview. Application deadline: 2/1; 3/1 priority date for financial aid. Early and deferred admission are possible.

Siena College

SUBURBAN SETTING ■ PRIVATE ■ INDEPENDENT RELIGIOUS ■ COED
LOUDONVILLE, NEW YORK

Web site: www.siena.edu
Contact: Ms. Heather Renault, Director of Admissions, 515 Loudon Road,
   Loudonville, NY 12211-1462
Telephone: 518-783-2426 or toll-free 888-AT-SIENA
Fax: 518-783-2436
E-mail: admit@siena.edu

Academics

Siena awards bachelor's **degrees. Challenging opportunities** include advanced placement credit, accelerated degree programs, an honors program, double majors, independent study, and a senior project. Special programs include internships, summer session for credit, off-campus study, study-abroad, and Army and Air Force ROTC.

The most frequently chosen **baccalaureate** fields are business/marketing, psychology, and biological/life sciences. A complete listing of majors at Siena appears in the Majors by College index beginning on page 469.

The **faculty** at Siena has 187 full-time members, 92% with terminal degrees. The student-faculty ratio is 13:1.

Students of Siena

The student body is made up of 3,217 undergraduates. 55.4% are women and 44.6% are men. Students come from 30 states and territories and 6 other countries. 87% are from New York. 0.5% are international students. 2.2% are African American, 0.1% American Indian, 3.7% Asian American, and 3.5% Hispanic American. 87% returned for their sophomore year.

Facilities and Resources

462 **computers/terminals** are available on campus for general student use. Students can access the following: online (class) registration. Campuswide network is available. 100% of college-owned or -operated housing units are wired for high-speed Internet access. Wireless service is available via classrooms, computer labs, dorm rooms, libraries. The **library** has 337,411 books and 6,470 subscriptions.

Campus Life

There are 78 active organizations on campus, including a drama/theater group, newspaper, radio station, and television station. No national or local **fraternities** or **sororities**.

Siena is a member of the NCAA (Division I). **Intercollegiate sports** (some offering scholarships) include baseball (m), basketball, cross-country running, field hockey (w), golf, lacrosse, soccer, softball (w), swimming and diving (w), tennis, volleyball (w), water polo (w).

Campus Safety

Student safety services include call boxes in parking lots and on roadways, late-night transport/escort service, 24-hour emergency telephone alarm devices, 24-hour patrols by trained security personnel, and electronically operated dormitory entrances.

Applying

Siena requires an essay, SAT or ACT, a high school transcript, and 1 recommendation, and in some cases an interview. It recommends an interview. Application deadline: 3/1; 2/1 priority date for financial aid. Early and deferred admission are possible.

Getting Accepted

5,792 applied
54% were accepted
781 enrolled (25% of accepted)
21% from top tenth of their h.s. class
Mean SAT critical reading score: 552
Mean SAT math score: 573
Mean SAT writing score: 544
Mean ACT score: 25
24% had SAT critical reading scores over 600
40% had SAT math scores over 600
24% had SAT writing scores over 600
38% had ACT scores over 24
2% had SAT critical reading scores over 700
5% had SAT math scores over 700
3% had SAT writing scores over 700
2% had ACT scores over 30

Graduation and After

74% graduated in 4 years
4% graduated in 5 years
1% graduated in 6 years
71% had job offers within 6 months
125 organizations recruited on campus

Financial Matters

$23,950 tuition and fees (2008–09)
$9410 room and board
80% average percent of need met
$12,655 average financial aid amount received
   per undergraduate

Simpson College combines the best of a liberal arts education with outstanding career preparation and extracurricular programs. Activities range from an award-winning music program to nationally recognized NCAA Division III teams. Located just 12 miles from Des Moines, Simpson offers the comfort of a small town and the advantages of a metropolitan area. Outstanding facilities have been enhanced with multimillion-dollar expansions and renovations, including the Carver Science Center, named after Simpson's most distinguished alumnus, George Washington Carver. The 4-4-1 academic calendar includes a May Term that provides students with unique learning opportunities. Simpson's beautiful 85-acre, tree-lined campus offers a setting that nurtures creativity, energy, and productivity.

Getting Accepted
1,259 applied
88% were accepted
389 enrolled (35% of accepted)
28% from top tenth of their h.s. class
Mean ACT score: 24
59% had ACT scores over 24
7% had ACT scores over 30
23 valedictorians

Graduation and After
59% graduated in 4 years
8% graduated in 5 years
1% graduated in 6 years
78% had job offers within 6 months
93 organizations recruited on campus

Financial Matters
$24,771 tuition and fees (2008–09)
$6988 room and board
86% average percent of need met
$21,384 average financial aid amount received per undergraduate (2007–08 estimated)

SIMPSON COLLEGE
SMALL-TOWN SETTING ■ PRIVATE ■ INDEPENDENT RELIGIOUS ■ COED
INDIANOLA, IOWA

Web site: www.simpson.edu
Contact: Ms. Deborah Tierney, Vice President for Enrollment, 701 North C Street, Indianola, IA 50125
Telephone: 515-961-1624 or toll-free 800-362-2454 (in-state), 800-362-2454 Ext. 1624 (out-of-state)
Fax: 515-961-1870
E-mail: admiss@simpson.edu

Academics
Simpson awards bachelor's and master's **degrees** and post-bachelor's certificates. **Challenging opportunities** include advanced placement credit, accelerated degree programs, an honors program, double majors, independent study, and a senior project. Special programs include cooperative education, internships, summer session for credit, off-campus study, and study-abroad.

The most frequently chosen **baccalaureate** fields are business/marketing, social sciences, and communications/journalism. A complete listing of majors at Simpson appears in the Majors by College index beginning on page 469.

The **faculty** at Simpson has 101 full-time members, 84% with terminal degrees. The student-faculty ratio is 13:1.

Students of Simpson
The student body totals 2,054, of whom 2,035 are undergraduates. 58.7% are women and 41.3% are men. Students come from 21 states and territories and 16 other countries. 90% are from Iowa. 0.8% are international students. 1.8% are African American, 0.4% American Indian, 1.9% Asian American, and 1.4% Hispanic American. 79% returned for their sophomore year.

Facilities and Resources
327 **computers/terminals** are available on campus for general student use. Students can access the following: campus intranet, computer help desk, free student e-mail accounts, online (class) grades, online (class) schedules. Campuswide network is available. 100% of college-owned or -operated housing units are wired for high-speed Internet access. Wireless service is available via classrooms, computer centers, computer labs, learning centers, libraries, student centers. The 2 **libraries** have 161,529 books and 457 subscriptions.

Campus Life
There are 81 active organizations on campus, including a drama/theater group, newspaper, radio station, and choral group. 23% of eligible men and 19% of eligible women are members of national **fraternities**, national **sororities**, and local fraternities.

Simpson is a member of the NCAA (Division III). **Intercollegiate sports** include baseball (m), basketball, cheerleading, cross-country running, football (m), golf, soccer, softball (w), swimming and diving (w), tennis, track and field, volleyball (w), wrestling (m).

Campus Safety
Student safety services include late-night transport/escort service, 24-hour emergency telephone alarm devices, 24-hour patrols by trained security personnel, student patrols, and electronically operated dormitory entrances.

Applying
Simpson requires SAT or ACT, a high school transcript, 1 recommendation, and ACT/SAT score. It recommends an interview. Application deadline: 8/15. Deferred admission is possible.

SKIDMORE COLLEGE

SMALL-TOWN SETTING ■ PRIVATE ■ INDEPENDENT ■ COED
SARATOGA SPRINGS, NEW YORK

SPONSOR

Web site: www.skidmore.edu
Contact: Ms. Mary Lou Bates, Dean of Admissions and Financial Aid, 815
North Broadway, Saratoga Springs, NY 12866-1632
Telephone: 518-580-5570 or toll-free 800-867-6007
Fax: 518-580-5584
E-mail: admissions@skidmore.edu

Academics

Skidmore awards bachelor's and master's **degrees. Challenging opportunities** include advanced placement credit, accelerated degree programs, student-designed majors, an honors program, double majors, independent study, and a senior project. Special programs include internships, summer session for credit, off-campus study, study-abroad, and Army and Air Force ROTC.

The most frequently chosen **baccalaureate** fields are social sciences, visual and performing arts, and business/marketing. A complete listing of majors at Skidmore appears in the Majors by College index beginning on page 469.

The **faculty** at Skidmore has 249 full-time members, 80% with terminal degrees. The student-faculty ratio is 8:1.

Students of Skidmore

The student body totals 2,777, of whom 2,717 are undergraduates. 60.4% are women and 39.6% are men. Students come from 44 states and territories and 41 other countries. 33% are from New York. 3.2% are international students. 3.4% are African American, 0.6% American Indian, 8.7% Asian American, and 4.9% Hispanic American. 93% returned for their sophomore year.

Facilities and Resources

230 **computers/terminals** and 600 ports are available on campus for general student use. Students can access the following: campus intranet, computer help desk, free student e-mail accounts, online (class) grades, online (class) registration, online (class) schedules. Campuswide network is available. 100% of college-owned or -operated housing units are wired for high-speed Internet access. Wireless service is available via classrooms, computer centers, computer labs, learning centers, libraries, student centers. The 2 **libraries** have 376,682 books and 959 subscriptions.

Campus Life

There are 80 active organizations on campus, including a drama/theater group, newspaper, radio station, television station, and choral group. No national or local **fraternities** or **sororities.**

Skidmore is a member of the NCAA (Division III). **Intercollegiate sports** include baseball (m), basketball, crew, equestrian sports (w), field hockey (w), golf (m), ice hockey (m), lacrosse, soccer, softball (w), swimming and diving, tennis, volleyball (w).

Campus Safety

Student safety services include well-lit campus, late-night transport/escort service, 24-hour emergency telephone alarm devices, 24-hour patrols by trained security personnel, and electronically operated dormitory entrances.

Applying

Skidmore requires an essay, SAT or ACT, a high school transcript, and 2 recommendations. It recommends SAT Subject Tests and an interview. Application deadline: 1/15; 1/15 for financial aid. Early and deferred admission are possible.

Skidmore College, located on a beautiful 850-acre campus, is a liberal arts college where creative thought matters. An interdisciplinary liberal studies curriculum challenges students to explore broadly. A rich cocurricular program provides further opportunities for personal growth and leadership. Among the largest majors are business, studio art, English, psychology, government, and biology. Students from forty-four states and territories and twenty-three countries live and learn in Skidmore's lively intellectual climate and beautiful campus surroundings.

Getting Accepted
7,316 applied
30% were accepted
652 enrolled (30% of accepted)
37% from top tenth of their h.s. class
3.40 average high school GPA
Mean SAT critical reading score: 626
Mean SAT math score: 625
Mean SAT writing score: 635
Mean ACT score: 28
71% had SAT critical reading scores over 600
70% had SAT math scores over 600
72% had SAT writing scores over 600
94% had ACT scores over 24
18% had SAT critical reading scores over 700
13% had SAT math scores over 700
21% had SAT writing scores over 700
22% had ACT scores over 30

Graduation and After
78% graduated in 4 years
3% graduated in 5 years
95% had job offers within 6 months
12 organizations recruited on campus

Financial Matters
$38,888 tuition and fees (2008–09)
$10,378 room and board
94% average percent of need met
$27,280 average financial aid amount received per undergraduate (2007–08 estimated)

SMITH COLLEGE

SMALL-TOWN SETTING ■ PRIVATE ■ INDEPENDENT ■ WOMEN ONLY
NORTHAMPTON, MASSACHUSETTS

Web site: www.smith.edu
Contact: Ms. Debra Shaver, Director of Admissions, 7 College Lane,
    Northampton, MA 01063
Telephone: 413-585-2500 or toll-free 800-383-3232
Fax: 413-585-2527
E-mail: admission@smith.edu

Students choose Smith because of its outstanding academic reputation. From its founding in 1871, the College has been committed to providing women with countless opportunities for personal and intellectual growth. The open curriculum allows each student, with the assistance of a faculty adviser, to plan an individualized course of study outside the major. Superb facilities, a beautiful New England campus, and a diverse student body complement the rigorous academic schedule. Unique programs include the first engineering science major at a women's college and the guarantee of funding for summer internships that are related to career and academic goals.

Academics

Smith awards bachelor's, master's, and doctoral **degrees** and post-bachelor's and post-master's certificates. **Challenging opportunities** include advanced placement credit, accelerated degree programs, student-designed majors, an honors program, double majors, independent study, and a senior project. Special programs include internships, off-campus study, study-abroad, and Army and Air Force ROTC.

The most frequently chosen **baccalaureate** fields are social sciences, area and ethnic studies, and foreign languages and literature. A complete listing of majors at Smith appears in the Majors by College index beginning on page 469.

The **faculty** at Smith has 281 full-time members, 98% with terminal degrees. The student-faculty ratio is 9:1.

Getting Accepted
3,329 applied
52% were accepted
656 enrolled (38% of accepted)
63% from top tenth of their h.s. class
3.85 average high school GPA
75% had SAT critical reading scores over 600
59% had SAT math scores over 600
74% had SAT writing scores over 600
86% had ACT scores over 24
32% had SAT critical reading scores over 700
17% had SAT math scores over 700
27% had SAT writing scores over 700
29% had ACT scores over 30

Students of Smith

The student body totals 3,065, of whom 2,596 are undergraduates. Students come from 51 states and territories and 62 other countries. 23% are from Massachusetts. 6.8% are international students. 7.4% are African American, 0.7% American Indian, 12% Asian American, and 6.4% Hispanic American. 90% returned for their sophomore year.

Facilities and Resources

624 **computers/terminals** are available on campus for general student use. Students can access the following: campus intranet, computer help desk, free student e-mail accounts, online (class) grades, online (class) registration, online (class) schedules. Campuswide network is available. 100% of college-owned or -operated housing units are wired for high-speed Internet access. Wireless service is available via classrooms, computer centers, computer labs, dorm rooms, learning centers, libraries, student centers. The 4 **libraries** have 1,451,872 books and 37,414 subscriptions.

Graduation and After
83% graduated in 4 years
3% graduated in 5 years
63 organizations recruited on campus

Campus Life

There are 112 active organizations on campus, including a drama/theater group, newspaper, radio station, television station, and choral group. No national or local **sororities**.

Smith is a member of the NCAA (Division III). **Intercollegiate sports** include basketball, crew, cross-country running, equestrian sports, field hockey, lacrosse, skiing (downhill), soccer, softball, squash, swimming and diving, tennis, track and field, volleyball.

Financial Matters
$36,058 tuition and fees (2008–09)
$12,050 room and board
100% average percent of need met
$32,752 average financial aid amount received
    per undergraduate (2007–08 estimated)

Campus Safety

Student safety services include self-defense workshops, emergency telephones, programs in crime and sexual assault prevention, late-night transport/escort service, 24-hour emergency telephone alarm devices, and 24-hour patrols by trained security personnel.

Applying

Smith requires an essay, a high school transcript, and 3 recommendations, and in some cases SAT or ACT. It recommends an interview. Application deadline: 1/15; 2/15 for financial aid. Early and deferred admission are possible.

SOUTHERN METHODIST UNIVERSITY

SUBURBAN SETTING ■ PRIVATE ■ INDEPENDENT RELIGIOUS ■ COED
DALLAS, TEXAS

SPONSOR

Web site: www.smu.edu
Contact: Mr. Ron Moss, Director of Admission and Enrollment Management,
PO Box 750181, Dallas, TX 75275-0181
Telephone: 214-768-3417 or toll-free 800-323-0672
Fax: 214-768-0202
E-mail: enrol_serv@smu.edu

> SMU is a vibrant, diverse academic community in the heart of a dynamic city. Excellence is the standard and success is the goal through nearly eighty majors, access to expert faculty members in relatively small classes, and opportunities to pursue an honors curriculum, research, internships, study abroad, and community service.

Academics

SMU awards bachelor's, master's, doctoral, and first-professional **degrees** and post-bachelor's certificates. **Challenging opportunities** include advanced placement credit, accelerated degree programs, student-designed majors, an honors program, double majors, and independent study. Special programs include cooperative education, internships, summer session for credit, study-abroad, and Army and Air Force ROTC.

The most frequently chosen **baccalaureate** fields are business/marketing, social sciences, and communications/journalism. A complete listing of majors at SMU appears in the Majors by College index beginning on page 469.

The **faculty** at SMU has 656 full-time members, 84% with terminal degrees. The student-faculty ratio is 12:1.

Students of SMU

The student body totals 10,965, of whom 6,240 are undergraduates. 53.5% are women and 46.5% are men. Students come from 50 states and territories and 65 other countries. 58% are from Texas. 5.6% are international students. 4.8% are African American, 0.6% American Indian, 5.8% Asian American, and 7.8% Hispanic American. 89% returned for their sophomore year.

Facilities and Resources

758 **computers/terminals** are available on campus for general student use. Students can access the following: online (class) registration, online billing/payment processing. Campuswide network is available. Wireless service is available via classrooms, computer centers, computer labs, dorm rooms, learning centers, libraries, student centers. The 8 **libraries** have 2,848,971 books and 11,701 subscriptions.

Campus Life

There are 180 active organizations on campus, including a drama/theater group, newspaper, radio station, choral group, and marching band. 23% of eligible men and 31% of eligible women are members of national **fraternities** and national **sororities**.

SMU is a member of the NCAA (Division I). **Intercollegiate sports** (some offering scholarships) include basketball, crew (w), cross-country running (w), equestrian sports (w), football (m), golf, soccer, swimming and diving, tennis, track and field (w), volleyball (w).

Campus Safety

Student safety services include late-night transport/escort service, 24-hour emergency telephone alarm devices, 24-hour patrols by trained security personnel, and electronically operated dormitory entrances.

Applying

SMU requires an essay, SAT or ACT, a high school transcript, and 1 recommendation, and in some cases SAT Subject Tests. Application deadline: 1/15. Early and deferred admission are possible.

Getting Accepted
8,270 applied
50% were accepted
1,398 enrolled (34% of accepted)
42% from top tenth of their h.s. class
3.57 average high school GPA
Mean SAT critical reading score: 610
Mean SAT math score: 645
Mean SAT writing score: 610
Mean ACT score: 28
58% had SAT critical reading scores over 600
71% had SAT math scores over 600
59% had SAT writing scores over 600
88% had ACT scores over 24
13% had SAT critical reading scores over 700
19% had SAT math scores over 700
15% had SAT writing scores over 700
28% had ACT scores over 30

Graduation and After
59% graduated in 4 years
14% graduated in 5 years
2% graduated in 6 years

Financial Matters
$35,160 tuition and fees (2009–10)
$12,445 room and board
88% average percent of need met
$26,276 average financial aid amount received per undergraduate (2007–08 estimated)

SOUTHWEST BAPTIST UNIVERSITY

SMALL-TOWN SETTING ■ PRIVATE ■ INDEPENDENT RELIGIOUS ■ COED
BOLIVAR, MISSOURI

Web site: www.sbuniv.edu
Contact: Mr. Darren Crowder, Director of Admissions, 1600 University
   Avenue, Bolivar, MO 65613-2597
Telephone: 417-328-1817 or toll-free 800-526-5859
Fax: 417-328-1808
E-mail: dcrowder@sbuniv.edu

Getting Accepted
1,380 applied
74% were accepted
516 enrolled (51% of accepted)
23% from top tenth of their h.s. class
3.33 average high school GPA
Mean SAT critical reading score: 522
Mean SAT math score: 520
Mean ACT score: 23
25% had SAT critical reading scores over 600
29% had SAT math scores over 600
45% had ACT scores over 24
10% had SAT critical reading scores over 700
6% had SAT math scores over 700
11% had ACT scores over 30

Graduation and After
46% graduated in 4 years
7% graduated in 5 years
2% graduated in 6 years
70% had job offers within 6 months
77 organizations recruited on campus

Financial Matters
$16,530 tuition and fees (2009–10)
$5470 room and board
75% average percent of need met
$12,575 average financial aid amount received
   per undergraduate (2007–08 estimated)

Academics

SBU awards associate, bachelor's, master's, and doctoral **degrees** and post-master's certificates. **Challenging opportunities** include advanced placement credit, student-designed majors, an honors program, double majors, independent study, and a senior project. Special programs include cooperative education, internships, summer session for credit, off-campus study, study-abroad, and Army ROTC.

The most frequently chosen **baccalaureate** fields are education, business/marketing, and health professions and related sciences. A complete listing of majors at SBU appears in the Majors by College index beginning on page 469.

The **faculty** at SBU has 116 full-time members, 60% with terminal degrees. The student-faculty ratio is 14:1.

Students of SBU

The student body totals 3,656, of whom 2,803 are undergraduates. 65% are women and 35% are men. Students come from 37 states and territories and 16 other countries. 70% are from Missouri. 0.9% are international students. 4% are African American, 1% American Indian, 0.6% Asian American, and 1.3% Hispanic American. 72% returned for their sophomore year.

Facilities and Resources

261 **computers/terminals** are available on campus for general student use. Students can access the following: computer help desk, free student e-mail accounts, online (class) grades, online (class) registration, online (class) schedules. Campuswide network is available. 90% of college-owned or -operated housing units are wired for high-speed Internet access. Wireless service is available via entire campus. The 4 **libraries** have 185,703 books and 22,388 subscriptions.

Campus Life

There are 27 active organizations on campus, including a drama/theater group, newspaper, and choral group. No national or local **fraternities** or **sororities**.

SBU is a member of the NCAA (Division II). **Intercollegiate sports** (some offering scholarships) include baseball (m), basketball, cheerleading, cross-country running, football (m), golf (m), soccer, softball (w), tennis, track and field, volleyball (w).

Campus Safety

Student safety services include 24-hour emergency telephone alarm devices, 24-hour patrols by trained security personnel, and electronically operated dormitory entrances.

Applying

SBU requires SAT or ACT, a high school transcript, and a minimum high school GPA of 2.5, and in some cases 3 recommendations. It recommends an essay and an interview. Application deadline: rolling admissions; 3/15 priority date for financial aid.

SOUTHWESTERN UNIVERSITY

SUBURBAN SETTING ■ PRIVATE ■ INDEPENDENT RELIGIOUS ■ COED
GEORGETOWN, TEXAS

SPONSOR

Web site: www.southwestern.edu
Contact: Mr. Tom Oliver, Vice President for Enrollment Services, 1001 East
   University Avenue, Georgetown, TX 78626
Telephone: 512-863-1200 or toll-free 800-252-3166
Fax: 512-863-9601
E-mail: admission@southwestern.edu

Academics

Southwestern awards bachelor's **degrees**. **Challenging opportunities** include advanced placement credit, student-designed majors, an honors program, double majors, independent study, and a senior project. Special programs include internships, summer session for credit, off-campus study, and study-abroad.

The most frequently chosen **baccalaureate** fields are social sciences, business/marketing, and communications/journalism. A complete listing of majors at Southwestern appears in the Majors by College index beginning on page 469.

The **faculty** at Southwestern has 121 full-time members, 97% with terminal degrees. The student-faculty ratio is 10:1.

Students of Southwestern

The student body is made up of 1,270 undergraduates. 60.6% are women and 39.4% are men. Students come from 31 states and territories and 8 other countries. 94% are from Texas. 0.2% are international students. 3% are African American, 0.9% American Indian, 4.5% Asian American, and 14.9% Hispanic American. 84% returned for their sophomore year.

Facilities and Resources

410 **computers/terminals** are available on campus for general student use. Students can access the following: computer help desk, free student e-mail accounts, online (class) registration, online (class) schedules, transcripts. Campuswide network is available. Wireless service is available via entire campus. The **library** has 323,000 books and 2,598 subscriptions.

Campus Life

There are 105 active organizations on campus, including a drama/theater group, newspaper, and choral group. 29% of eligible men and 30% of eligible women are members of national **fraternities** and national **sororities**.

Southwestern is a member of the NCAA (Division III). **Intercollegiate sports** include baseball (m), basketball, cross-country running, golf, lacrosse (m), soccer, softball (w), swimming and diving, tennis, volleyball (w).

Campus Safety

Student safety services include late-night transport/escort service, 24-hour emergency telephone alarm devices, 24-hour patrols by trained security personnel, student patrols, and electronically operated dormitory entrances.

Applying

Southwestern requires an essay, SAT, a high school transcript, and 1 recommendation, and in some cases SAT and SAT Subject Tests or ACT and an interview. It recommends an interview. Application deadline: 3/1 for financial aid, with a 3/1 priority date. Deferred admission is possible.

Getting Accepted

1,923 applied
65% were accepted
349 enrolled (28% of accepted)
50% from top tenth of their h.s. class
Mean SAT critical reading score: 612
Mean SAT math score: 608
Mean ACT score: 27
58% had SAT critical reading scores over 600
57% had SAT math scores over 600
78% had ACT scores over 24
15% had SAT critical reading scores over 700
12% had SAT math scores over 700
22% had ACT scores over 30

Graduation and After

69% graduated in 4 years
6% graduated in 5 years
1% graduated in 6 years
53% had job offers within 6 months
31 organizations recruited on campus

Financial Matters

$27,940 tuition and fees (2008–09)
$8870 room and board
86% average percent of need met
$23,310 average financial aid amount received
   per undergraduate (2007–08 estimated)

STANFORD UNIVERSITY

SUBURBAN SETTING ■ PRIVATE ■ INDEPENDENT ■ COED
STANFORD, CALIFORNIA

Web site: www.stanford.edu
Contact: Rick Shaw, Dean of Undergraduate Admission and Financial Aid,
   Montag Hall, 355 Galvez Street, Stanford, CA 94305-3020
Telephone: 650-723-2091
Fax: 650-725-2846
E-mail: admission@stanford.edu

Getting Accepted
25,299 applied
9% were accepted
1,703 enrolled (71% of accepted)
92% from top tenth of their h.s. class
92% had SAT critical reading scores over 600
95% had SAT math scores over 600
93% had SAT writing scores over 600
99% had ACT scores over 24
57% had SAT critical reading scores over 700
66% had SAT math scores over 700
63% had SAT writing scores over 700
77% had ACT scores over 30

Graduation and After
79% graduated in 4 years
13% graduated in 5 years
2% graduated in 6 years
87% had job offers within 6 months
550 organizations recruited on campus

Financial Matters
$37,380 tuition and fees (2009–10)
$11,463 room and board
100% average percent of need met
$31,515 average financial aid amount received
   per undergraduate (2006–07)

Academics

Stanford awards bachelor's, master's, doctoral, and first-professional **degrees**. **Challenging opportunities** include advanced placement credit, student-designed majors, an honors program, double majors, independent study, and a senior project. Special programs include internships, summer session for credit, off-campus study, study-abroad, and Army, Navy, and Air Force ROTC.

The most frequently chosen **baccalaureate** fields are social sciences, interdisciplinary studies, and engineering. A complete listing of majors at Stanford appears in the Majors by College index beginning on page 469.

The **faculty** at Stanford has 984 full-time members, 98% with terminal degrees. The student-faculty ratio is 6:1.

Students of Stanford

The student body totals 17,833, of whom 6,532 are undergraduates. 48.9% are women and 51.1% are men. Students come from 52 states and territories and 88 other countries. 49% are from California. 7% are international students. 10% are African American, 2.7% American Indian, 23% Asian American, and 12.2% Hispanic American. 98% returned for their sophomore year.

Facilities and Resources

1,000 **computers/terminals** and 22,000 ports are available on campus for general student use. Students can access the following: campus intranet, computer help desk, free student e-mail accounts, online (class) grades, online (class) registration, online (class) schedules. Campuswide network is available. 100% of college-owned or -operated housing units are wired for high-speed Internet access. Wireless service is available via entire campus. The 19 **libraries** have 8,500,000 books and 75,000 subscriptions.

Campus Life

There are 600 active organizations on campus, including a drama/theater group, newspaper, radio station, television station, choral group, and marching band. Stanford has national **fraternities** and national **sororities**.

Stanford is a member of the NCAA (Division I) and NAIA. **Intercollegiate sports** (some offering scholarships) include baseball (m), basketball, crew, cross-country running, fencing, field hockey (w), football (m), golf, gymnastics, lacrosse (w), sailing, soccer, softball (w), squash (w), swimming and diving, tennis, track and field, volleyball, water polo, wrestling (m).

Campus Safety

Student safety services include late-night transport/escort service, 24-hour emergency telephone alarm devices, 24-hour patrols by trained security personnel, and electronically operated dormitory entrances.

Applying

Stanford requires an essay, SAT or ACT, a high school transcript, and 2 recommendations. It recommends SAT Subject Tests. Application deadline: 1/1; 2/15 priority date for financial aid. Deferred admission is possible.

STATE UNIVERSITY OF NEW YORK AT BINGHAMTON

SUBURBAN SETTING ■ PUBLIC ■ STATE-SUPPORTED ■ COED
BINGHAMTON, NEW YORK

Web site: www.binghamton.edu
Contact: Ms. Cheryl S. Brown, Director of Admissions, PO Box 6001,
   Binghamton, NY 13902-6001
Telephone: 607-777-2171
Fax: 607-777-4445
E-mail: admit@binghamton.edu

Academics

Binghamton awards bachelor's, master's, and doctoral **degrees** and post-master's certificates. **Challenging opportunities** include advanced placement credit, accelerated degree programs, student-designed majors, an honors program, double majors, independent study, and a senior project. Special programs include internships, summer session for credit, off-campus study, study-abroad, and Air Force ROTC.

The most frequently chosen **baccalaureate** fields are social sciences, business/ marketing, and psychology. A complete listing of majors at Binghamton appears in the Majors by College index beginning on page 469.

The **faculty** at Binghamton has 594 full-time members, 92% with terminal degrees. The student-faculty ratio is 20:1.

Students of Binghamton

The student body totals 14,898, of whom 11,821 are undergraduates. 47.6% are women and 52.4% are men. Students come from 40 states and territories and 102 other countries. 92% are from New York. 8.8% are international students. 5.4% are African American, 0.2% American Indian, 12.7% Asian American, and 7% Hispanic American. 90% returned for their sophomore year.

Facilities and Resources

992 **computers/terminals** are available on campus for general student use. Students can access the following: campus intranet, computer help desk, free student e-mail accounts, online (class) grades, online (class) registration, online (class) schedules, course management system, personal Web space. Campuswide network is available. 100% of college-owned or -operated housing units are wired for high-speed Internet access. Wireless service is available via entire campus. The 3 **libraries** have 2,387,358 books and 76,166 subscriptions.

Campus Life

There are 250 active organizations on campus, including a drama/theater group, newspaper, radio station, television station, and choral group. 5% of eligible men and 5% of eligible women are members of national **fraternities**, national **sororities**, local fraternities, and local sororities.

Binghamton is a member of the NCAA (Division I). **Intercollegiate sports** (some offering scholarships) include baseball (m), basketball, cheerleading, cross-country running, golf (m), lacrosse, soccer, softball (w), swimming and diving, tennis, track and field, volleyball (w), wrestling (m).

Campus Safety

Student safety services include safety awareness programs, well-lit campus, self-defense education, secured campus entrance 12 a.m. to 5 a.m. emergency telephones, late-night transport/escort service, 24-hour emergency telephone alarm devices, 24-hour patrols by trained security personnel, student patrols, and electronically operated dormitory entrances.

Applying

Binghamton requires an essay, SAT or ACT, and a high school transcript, and in some cases 1 recommendation and portfolio, audition. Application deadline: rolling admissions; 2/1 priority date for financial aid. Early and deferred admission are possible.

Getting Accepted

26,666 applied
40% were accepted
2,519 enrolled (24% of accepted)
48% from top tenth of their h.s. class
3.7 average high school GPA
Mean SAT critical reading score: 620
Mean SAT math score: 654
Mean ACT score: 28
66% had SAT critical reading scores over 600
83% had SAT math scores over 600
95% had ACT scores over 24
12% had SAT critical reading scores over 700
24% had SAT math scores over 700
24% had ACT scores over 30

Graduation and After

69% graduated in 4 years
10% graduated in 5 years
1% graduated in 6 years
136 organizations recruited on campus

Financial Matters

$6692 resident tuition and fees (2009–10)
$14,592 nonresident tuition and fees (2009–10)
$9774 room and board
79% average percent of need met
$12,403 average financial aid amount received per undergraduate (2007–08 estimated)

STATE UNIVERSITY OF NEW YORK COLLEGE AT GENESEO

SMALL-TOWN SETTING ■ PUBLIC ■ STATE-SUPPORTED ■ COED
GENESEO, NEW YORK

Web site: www.geneseo.edu
Contact: Kris Shay, Director of Admissions, 1 College Circle, Geneseo, NY 14454-1401
Telephone: 585-245-5571 or toll-free 866-245-5211
Fax: 585-245-5550
E-mail: admissions@geneseo.edu

Getting Accepted
10,588 applied
37% were accepted
1,081 enrolled (28% of accepted)
50% from top tenth of their h.s. class
Mean SAT critical reading score: 645
Mean SAT math score: 654
Mean ACT score: 29
80% had SAT critical reading scores over 600
87% had SAT math scores over 600
95% had ACT scores over 24
24% had SAT critical reading scores over 700
22% had SAT math scores over 700
39% had ACT scores over 30
15 valedictorians

Graduation and After
58% graduated in 4 years
17% graduated in 5 years
2% graduated in 6 years
45% had job offers within 6 months
57 organizations recruited on campus

Financial Matters
$6278 resident tuition and fees (2009–10)
$14,178 nonresident tuition and fees (2009–10)
$9070 room and board
85% average percent of need met
$7786 average financial aid amount received per undergraduate (2007–08 estimated)

Academics

Geneseo awards bachelor's and master's **degrees. Challenging opportunities** include advanced placement credit, an honors program, double majors, independent study, and a senior project. Special programs include internships, summer session for credit, off-campus study, study-abroad, and Army and Air Force ROTC.

The most frequently chosen **baccalaureate** fields are education, business/marketing, and social sciences. A complete listing of majors at Geneseo appears in the Majors by College index beginning on page 469.

The **faculty** at Geneseo has 251 full-time members, 87% with terminal degrees. The student-faculty ratio is 19:1.

Students of Geneseo

The student body totals 5,585, of whom 5,451 are undergraduates. 58% are women and 42% are men. Students come from 23 states and territories and 27 other countries. 98% are from New York. 2.6% are international students. 2.3% are African American, 0.4% American Indian, 5.8% Asian American, and 3.7% Hispanic American. 92% returned for their sophomore year.

Facilities and Resources

900 **computers/terminals** are available on campus for general student use. Students can access the following: campus intranet, computer help desk, free student e-mail accounts, online (class) grades, online (class) registration, online (class) schedules. Campuswide network is available. 100% of college-owned or -operated housing units are wired for high-speed Internet access. Wireless service is available via entire campus. The **library** has 647,100 books and 54,864 subscriptions.

Campus Life

There are 177 active organizations on campus, including a drama/theater group, newspaper, radio station, television station, and choral group. 8% of eligible men and 11% of eligible women are members of national **fraternities**, national **sororities**, local fraternities, and local sororities.

Geneseo is a member of the NCAA (Division III). **Intercollegiate sports** include basketball, cross-country running, equestrian sports (w), field hockey (w), ice hockey (m), lacrosse, racquetball, soccer, softball (w), swimming and diving, tennis (w), track and field, volleyball (w).

Campus Safety

Student safety services include late-night transport/escort service, 24-hour emergency telephone alarm devices, 24-hour patrols by trained security personnel, student patrols, and electronically operated dormitory entrances.

Applying

Geneseo requires an essay, SAT or ACT, and a high school transcript. It recommends an interview, 1 recommendation, and a minimum high school GPA of 3.5. Application deadline: 1/1; 2/15 for financial aid, with a 2/15 priority date. Early and deferred admission are possible.

STATE UNIVERSITY OF NEW YORK COLLEGE OF ENVIRONMENTAL SCIENCE AND FORESTRY

URBAN SETTING ■ PUBLIC ■ STATE-SUPPORTED ■ COED
SYRACUSE, NEW YORK

Web site: www.esf.edu
Contact: Ms. Susan Sanford, Director of Admissions, Office of Undergraduate Admissions, 106 Bray Hall, 1 Forestry Lane, Syracuse, NY 13210-2779
Telephone: 315-470-6600 or toll-free 800-777-7373
Fax: 315-470-6933
E-mail: esfinfo@esf.edu

SPONSOR

Academics

ESF awards associate, bachelor's, master's, and doctoral **degrees** and post-bachelor's certificates. **Challenging opportunities** include advanced placement credit, accelerated degree programs, freshman honors college, an honors program, double majors, independent study, and a senior project. Special programs include cooperative education, internships, off-campus study, study-abroad, and Army and Air Force ROTC.

The most frequently chosen **baccalaureate** fields are biological/life sciences, natural resources/environmental science, and engineering. A complete listing of majors at ESF appears in the Majors by College index beginning on page 469.

The **faculty** at ESF has 146 full-time members, 96% with terminal degrees. The student-faculty ratio is 12:1.

Students of ESF

The student body totals 2,201, of whom 1,633 are undergraduates. 40.3% are women and 59.7% are men. Students come from 30 states and territories and 6 other countries. 85% are from New York. 1.1% are international students. 0.8% are African American, 0.7% American Indian, 2.9% Asian American, and 3% Hispanic American. 89% returned for their sophomore year.

Facilities and Resources

150 **computers/terminals** are available on campus for general student use. Students can access the following: campus intranet, computer help desk, free student e-mail accounts, online (class) grades, online (class) registration, online (class) schedules. Campuswide network is available. 100% of college-owned or -operated housing units are wired for high-speed Internet access. Wireless service is available via classrooms, computer centers, computer labs, dorm rooms, libraries, student centers. The 2 **libraries** have 135,258 books and 2,000 subscriptions.

Campus Life

There are 300 active organizations on campus, including a drama/theater group, newspaper, radio station, choral group, and marching band. 33% of eligible men and 33% of eligible women are members of national **fraternities** and national **sororities**.

Intercollegiate sports include golf, soccer.

Campus Safety

Student safety services include late-night transport/escort service, 24-hour emergency telephone alarm devices, 24-hour patrols by trained security personnel, and electronically operated dormitory entrances.

Applying

ESF requires an essay, SAT or ACT, a high school transcript, supplemental application, and a minimum high school GPA of 3.3. It recommends an interview and 3 recommendations. Application deadline: 12/1; 3/1 priority date for financial aid. Early and deferred admission are possible.

Environmental problems make headlines every day. For students who want to understand the complex scientific and social issues behind the headlines and contribute to solving the problems, and for those who intend to make a living by helping to shape the environmental future for this century and beyond, the SUNY College of Environmental Science and Forestry can help achieve those goals. Students study with professors whose work improves and sustains the environment—from the Yucatan Peninsula to Alaska—and whose expertise is sought by governments and corporations. The size of the student population means students receive individual attention and personal assistance from faculty and staff members. The student-faculty ratio is 12:1 at the Syracuse campus. Several factors are considered for admission, including academic preparation, personal motivation, and reasons for wanting to study at the College.

Getting Accepted

1,568 applied
48% were accepted
310 enrolled (41% of accepted)
25% from top tenth of their h.s. class
3.75 average high school GPA
Mean SAT critical reading score: 570
Mean SAT math score: 589
Mean ACT score: 25
37% had SAT critical reading scores over 600
47% had SAT math scores over 600
71% had ACT scores over 24
4% had SAT critical reading scores over 700
4% had SAT math scores over 700
11% had ACT scores over 30

Graduation and After

55% graduated in 4 years
17% graduated in 5 years
1% graduated in 6 years
67% had job offers within 6 months
52 organizations recruited on campus

Financial Matters

$4970 resident tuition and fees (2009–10)
$12,870 nonresident tuition and fees (2009–10)
$11,920 room and board
100% average percent of need met
$12,800 average financial aid amount received per undergraduate (2007–08 estimated)

Getting Accepted
4,110 applied
54% were accepted
588 enrolled (27% of accepted)
35% from top tenth of their h.s. class
3.70 average high school GPA
Mean SAT critical reading score: 562
Mean SAT math score: 551
Mean SAT writing score: 531
Mean ACT score: 24
32% had SAT critical reading scores over 600
27% had SAT math scores over 600
20% had SAT writing scores over 600
44% had ACT scores over 24
5% had SAT critical reading scores over 700
2% had SAT math scores over 700
2% had SAT writing scores over 700
7% had ACT scores over 30
9 valedictorians

Graduation and After
55% graduated in 4 years
10% graduated in 5 years
1% graduated in 6 years
150 organizations recruited on campus

Financial Matters
$31,770 tuition and fees (2009–10)
$8934 room and board
83% average percent of need met
$22,727 average financial aid amount received
per undergraduate (2006–07)

STETSON UNIVERSITY
SMALL-TOWN SETTING ■ PRIVATE ■ INDEPENDENT ■ COED
DELAND, FLORIDA

Web site: www.stetson.edu
Contact: Ms. Deborah Thompson, Vice President for Enrollment
Management and Campus Life, Unit 8378, Griffith Hall, DeLand, FL
32723
Telephone: 386-822-7100 or toll-free 800-688-0101
Fax: 386-822-7112
E-mail: admissions@stetson.edu

Academics
Stetson awards bachelor's, master's, and first-professional **degrees** and post-master's and
first-professional certificates. **Challenging opportunities** include advanced placement
credit, accelerated degree programs, student-designed majors, an honors program,
double majors, independent study, and a senior project. Special programs include internships, summer session for credit, off-campus study, study-abroad, and Army ROTC.

The most frequently chosen **baccalaureate** fields are business/marketing, social sciences, and visual and performing arts. A complete listing of majors at Stetson appears in
the Majors by College index beginning on page 469.

The **faculty** at Stetson has 231 full-time members, 93% with terminal degrees. The
student-faculty ratio is 11:1.

Students of Stetson
The student body totals 3,696, of whom 2,222 are undergraduates. 57.1% are women
and 42.9% are men. Students come from 38 states and territories and 29 other countries.
82% are from Florida. 3.2% are international students. 5% are African American, 0.5%
American Indian, 2.3% Asian American, and 9.8% Hispanic American. 77% returned for
their sophomore year.

Facilities and Resources
458 **computers/terminals** are available on campus for general student use. Students can
access the following: campus intranet, computer help desk, free student e-mail accounts,
online (class) grades, online (class) registration, online (class) schedules. Campuswide
network is available. 100% of college-owned or -operated housing units are wired for
high-speed Internet access. Wireless service is available via entire campus. The 2
libraries have 393,753 books and 31,000 subscriptions.

Campus Life
There are 122 active organizations on campus, including a drama/theater group,
newspaper, radio station, and choral group. 27% of eligible men and 25% of eligible
women are members of national **fraternities** and national **sororities**.

Stetson is a member of the NCAA (Division I). **Intercollegiate sports** (some
offering scholarships) include baseball (m), basketball, crew, cross-country running, golf,
soccer, softball (w), tennis, volleyball (w).

Campus Safety
Student safety services include late-night transport/escort service, 24-hour emergency
telephone alarm devices, and 24-hour patrols by trained security personnel.

Applying
Stetson requires an essay, SAT or ACT, a high school transcript, and 1 recommendation.
It recommends an interview. Application deadline: 3/15; 3/15 priority date for financial
aid. Early and deferred admission are possible.

Stevens Institute of Technology

Urban setting ■ Private ■ Independent ■ Coed
Hoboken, New Jersey

Web site: www.stevens.edu
Contact: Mr. Daniel Gallagher, Dean of University Admissions, Castle Point on Hudson, Hoboken, NJ 07030
Telephone: 201-216-5197 or toll-free 800-458-5323
Fax: 201-216-8348
E-mail: admissions@stevens.edu

Academics

Stevens awards bachelor's, master's, and doctoral **degrees** and post-bachelor's certificates. **Challenging opportunities** include advanced placement credit, accelerated degree programs, an honors program, double majors, independent study, and a senior project. Special programs include cooperative education, internships, summer session for credit, off-campus study, study-abroad, and Army and Air Force ROTC.

The most frequently chosen **baccalaureate** fields are engineering, business/marketing, and computer and information sciences. A complete listing of majors at Stevens appears in the Majors by College index beginning on page 469.

The **faculty** at Stevens has 214 full-time members, 80% with terminal degrees. The student-faculty ratio is 8:1.

Students of Stevens

The student body totals 5,406, of whom 2,044 are undergraduates. 25.6% are women and 74.4% are men. Students come from 42 states and territories and 28 other countries. 65% are from New Jersey. 5.6% are international students. 3.8% are African American, 0.2% American Indian, 11.2% Asian American, and 9.3% Hispanic American. 89% returned for their sophomore year.

Facilities and Resources

175 **computers/terminals** and 3,693 ports are available on campus for general student use. Students can access the following: campus intranet, computer help desk, free student e-mail accounts, online (class) grades, online (class) registration, online (class) schedules, online account information, debit dining program, laundry status. Campuswide network is available. 100% of college-owned or -operated housing units are wired for high-speed Internet access. Wireless service is available via entire campus. The **library** has 115,234 books and 134 subscriptions.

Campus Life

There are 120 active organizations on campus, including a drama/theater group, newspaper, radio station, television station, and choral group. 30% of eligible men and 28% of eligible women are members of national **fraternities**, national **sororities**, and local sororities.

Stevens is a member of the NCAA (Division III). **Intercollegiate sports** include baseball (m), basketball, cross-country running, equestrian sports (w), fencing, field hockey (w), lacrosse, soccer, swimming and diving, tennis, track and field, volleyball, wrestling (m).

Campus Safety

Student safety services include late-night transport/escort service, 24-hour emergency telephone alarm devices, 24-hour patrols by trained security personnel, and electronically operated dormitory entrances.

Applying

Stevens requires an essay, SAT or ACT, a high school transcript, and an interview, and in some cases SAT Subject Tests. Application deadline: 2/1; 2/15 priority date for financial aid. Early and deferred admission are possible.

Getting Accepted

2,783 applied
51% were accepted
521 enrolled (37% of accepted)
47% from top tenth of their h.s. class
3.7 average high school GPA
52% had SAT critical reading scores over 600
83% had SAT math scores over 600
10% had SAT critical reading scores over 700
31% had SAT math scores over 700
6 valedictorians

Graduation and After

38% graduated in 4 years
33% graduated in 5 years
4% graduated in 6 years
90% had job offers within 6 months
350 organizations recruited on campus

Financial Matters

$36,500 tuition and fees (2008–09)
$11,200 room and board
85% average percent of need met
$21,139 average financial aid amount received per undergraduate (2005–06)

STONEHILL COLLEGE

SUBURBAN SETTING ■ PRIVATE ■ INDEPENDENT RELIGIOUS ■ COED
EASTON, MASSACHUSETTS

Getting Accepted
6,838 applied
45% were accepted
635 enrolled (21% of accepted)
57% from top tenth of their h.s. class
3.44 average high school GPA
Mean SAT critical reading score: 600
Mean SAT math score: 600
Mean ACT score: 26
54% had SAT critical reading scores over 600
55% had SAT math scores over 600
76% had ACT scores over 24
6% had SAT critical reading scores over 700
8% had SAT math scores over 700
15% had ACT scores over 30
15 class presidents
3 valedictorians

Graduation and After
79% graduated in 4 years
2% graduated in 5 years
1% graduated in 6 years
65% had job offers within 6 months
372 organizations recruited on campus

Financial Matters
$30,150 tuition and fees (2008–09)
$11,830 room and board
75% average percent of need met
$18,434 average financial aid amount received
per undergraduate (2007–08 estimated)

Web site: www.stonehill.edu
Contact: Mr. Brian P. Murphy, Dean of Admissions and Enrollment, 320
Washington Street, Easton, MA 02357-5610
Telephone: 508-565-1373
Fax: 508-565-1545
E-mail: admissions@stonehill.edu

Academics
Stonehill awards bachelor's **degrees**. **Challenging opportunities** include advanced placement credit, student-designed majors, an honors program, double majors, independent study, and a senior project. Special programs include internships, summer session for credit, off-campus study, study-abroad, and Army ROTC.

The most frequently chosen **baccalaureate** fields are business/marketing, social sciences, and psychology. A complete listing of majors at Stonehill appears in the Majors by College index beginning on page 469.

The **faculty** at Stonehill has 148 full-time members, 82% with terminal degrees. The student-faculty ratio is 13:1.

Students of Stonehill
The student body is made up of 2,426 undergraduates. 60.4% are women and 39.6% are men. Students come from 30 states and territories and 11 other countries. 54% are from Massachusetts. 0.5% are international students. 2.3% are African American, 0.2% American Indian, 1.4% Asian American, and 3.7% Hispanic American. 89% returned for their sophomore year.

Facilities and Resources
346 **computers/terminals** and 300 ports are available on campus for general student use. Students can access the following: campus intranet, computer help desk, free student e-mail accounts, online (class) grades, online (class) registration, online (class) schedules. Campuswide network is available. 100% of college-owned or -operated housing units are wired for high-speed Internet access. Wireless service is available via classrooms, computer centers, computer labs, dorm rooms, learning centers, libraries, student centers. The **library** has 210,000 books and 9,980 subscriptions.

Campus Life
There are 61 active organizations on campus, including a drama/theater group, newspaper, radio station, and choral group. No national or local **fraternities** or **sororities**.

Stonehill is a member of the NCAA (Division II). **Intercollegiate sports** (some offering scholarships) include baseball (m), basketball, cross-country running, equestrian sports (w), field hockey (w), football (m), ice hockey (m), lacrosse (w), soccer, softball (w), tennis, track and field, volleyball (w).

Campus Safety
Student safety services include late-night transport/escort service, 24-hour emergency telephone alarm devices, and 24-hour patrols by trained security personnel.

Applying
Stonehill requires an essay and a high school transcript, and in some cases an interview. It recommends campus visit. Application deadline: 1/15; 2/1 priority date for financial aid. Deferred admission is possible.

Stony Brook University, State University of New York

Small-town setting ■ Public ■ State-supported ■ Coed
Stony Brook, New York

Web site: www.sunysb.edu
Contact: Ms. Judith Burke-Berhanan, Admissions, Nicolls Road, Stony Brook, NY 11794
Telephone: 631-632-6868 or toll-free 800-872-7869 (out-of-state)
Fax: 631-632-9898
E-mail: enroll@stonybrook.edu

Academics
Stony Brook awards bachelor's, master's, doctoral, and first-professional **degrees** and post-bachelor's, post-master's, and first-professional certificates. **Challenging opportunities** include advanced placement credit, student-designed majors, freshman honors college, an honors program, double majors, independent study, and a senior project. Special programs include internships, summer session for credit, off-campus study, study-abroad, and Army and Air Force ROTC.

The most frequently chosen **baccalaureate** fields are health professions and related sciences, social sciences, and biological/life sciences. A complete listing of majors at Stony Brook appears in the Majors by College index beginning on page 469.

The **faculty** at Stony Brook has 938 full-time members, 97% with terminal degrees. The student-faculty ratio is 18:1.

Students of Stony Brook
The student body totals 23,994, of whom 15,924 are undergraduates. 49.4% are women and 50.6% are men. Students come from 46 states and territories and 106 other countries. 94% are from New York. 6.4% are international students. 7.3% are African American, 0.2% American Indian, 22.4% Asian American, and 8.4% Hispanic American. 88% returned for their sophomore year.

Facilities and Resources
2,600 **computers/terminals** are available on campus for general student use. Students can access the following: campus intranet, computer help desk, free student e-mail accounts, online (class) grades, online (class) registration, online (class) schedules. Campuswide network is available. Wireless service is available via computer labs, dorm rooms, libraries, student centers. The 7 **libraries** have 1,991,940 books and 59,198 subscriptions.

Campus Life
There are 160 active organizations on campus, including a drama/theater group, newspaper, radio station, television station, choral group, and marching band. 2% of eligible men and 3% of eligible women are members of national **fraternities**, national **sororities**, local fraternities, and local sororities.

Stony Brook is a member of the NCAA (Division I). **Intercollegiate sports** (some offering scholarships) include baseball (m), basketball, cross-country running, football (m), lacrosse, soccer, softball (w), swimming and diving, tennis, track and field, volleyball (w).

Campus Safety
Student safety services include late-night transport/escort service, 24-hour emergency telephone alarm devices, 24-hour patrols by trained security personnel, and electronically operated dormitory entrances.

Applying
Stony Brook requires an essay, SAT or ACT, a high school transcript, and a minimum high school GPA of 3.0, and in some cases audition. It recommends SAT Subject Tests, an interview, and 2 recommendations. Application deadline: 3/1; 3/1 priority date for financial aid. Deferred admission is possible.

Getting Accepted
25,590 applied
43% were accepted
2,894 enrolled (26% of accepted)
36% from top tenth of their h.s. class
3.6 average high school GPA
Mean SAT critical reading score: 563
Mean SAT math score: 614
Mean SAT writing score: 560
34% had SAT critical reading scores over 600
60% had SAT math scores over 600
32% had SAT writing scores over 600
4% had SAT critical reading scores over 700
13% had SAT math scores over 700
5% had SAT writing scores over 700
16 National Merit Scholars
10 valedictorians

Graduation and After
40% graduated in 4 years
17% graduated in 5 years
4% graduated in 6 years
524 organizations recruited on campus

Financial Matters
$6430 resident tuition and fees (2009–10)
$14,330 nonresident tuition and fees (2009–10)
$9132 room and board
64% average percent of need met
$8335 average financial aid amount received per undergraduate (2006–07)

SUSQUEHANNA UNIVERSITY

SUBURBAN SETTING ■ PRIVATE ■ INDEPENDENT RELIGIOUS ■ COED
SELINSGROVE, PENNSYLVANIA

Web site: www.susqu.edu
Contact: Mr. Chris Markle, Director of Admissions, 514 University Avenue,
Selinsgrove, PA 17870-1040
Telephone: 570-372-4260 or toll-free 800-326-9672
Fax: 570-372-2722
E-mail: suadmiss@susqu.edu

Susquehanna is a selective, national liberal arts college that prepares students for achievement, leadership, and service in a diverse and interconnected world. Its 2,000 undergraduates come from thirty states and twelve countries to Susquehanna's scenic Susquehanna River Valley campus in Selinsgrove, Pennsylvania, for excellent academics, mentoring, and experiential learning. The University, located 50 miles north of Harrisburg, is a 3-hour drive from New York City, Philadelphia, and Washington, D.C.

Getting Accepted
2,777 applied
73% were accepted
616 enrolled (31% of accepted)
25% from top tenth of their h.s. class
3.22 average high school GPA
1 National Merit Scholar
24 class presidents
8 valedictorians

Graduation and After
80% graduated in 4 years
2% graduated in 5 years
78% had job offers within 6 months
82 organizations recruited on campus

Financial Matters
$31,080 tuition and fees (2008–09)
$8400 room and board
83% average percent of need met
$17,743 average financial aid amount received per undergraduate

Academics

Susquehanna awards bachelor's **degrees** (also offers evening associate degree program limited to local adult students). **Challenging opportunities** include advanced placement credit, accelerated degree programs, student-designed majors, an honors program, double majors, independent study, and a senior project. Special programs include internships, summer session for credit, off-campus study, study-abroad, and Army ROTC.

The most frequently chosen **baccalaureate** fields are business/marketing, communications/journalism, and social sciences. A complete listing of majors at Susquehanna appears in the Majors by College index beginning on page 469.

The **faculty** at Susquehanna has 128 full-time members, 92% with terminal degrees. The student-faculty ratio is 13:1.

Students of Susquehanna

The student body is made up of 2,137 undergraduates. 53.9% are women and 46.1% are men. Students come from 30 states and territories and 12 other countries. 55% are from Pennsylvania. 1.3% are international students. 2.9% are African American, 0.1% American Indian, 1.6% Asian American, and 2.2% Hispanic American. 85% returned for their sophomore year.

Facilities and Resources

292 **computers/terminals** and 50 ports are available on campus for general student use. Students can access the following: campus intranet, computer help desk, free student e-mail accounts, online (class) grades, online (class) registration, online (class) schedules, class listings and assignments, online voting booth. Campuswide network is available. 100% of college-owned or -operated housing units are wired for high-speed Internet access. Wireless service is available via classrooms, computer centers, computer labs, dorm rooms, learning centers, libraries, student centers. The **library** has 256,475 books and 16,655 subscriptions.

Campus Life

There are 129 active organizations on campus, including a drama/theater group, newspaper, radio station, television station, and choral group. 19% of eligible men and 13% of eligible women are members of national **fraternities** and national **sororities**.

Susquehanna is a member of the NCAA (Division III). **Intercollegiate sports** include baseball (m), basketball, cross-country running, field hockey (w), football (m), golf, lacrosse, soccer, softball (w), swimming and diving, tennis, track and field, volleyball (w).

Campus Safety

Student safety services include late-night transport/escort service, 24-hour patrols by trained security personnel, and electronically operated dormitory entrances.

Applying

Susquehanna requires an essay, a high school transcript, 1 recommendation, and a minimum high school GPA of 2.5, and in some cases writing portfolio, auditions for music programs. It recommends SAT or ACT, an interview, and a minimum high school GPA of 3.0. Application deadline: 3/1; 3/1 priority date for financial aid. Early and deferred admission are possible.

SWARTHMORE COLLEGE

SUBURBAN SETTING ■ PRIVATE ■ INDEPENDENT ■ COED
SWARTHMORE, PENNSYLVANIA

Web site: www.swarthmore.edu
Contact: Mr. Jim Bock, Dean of Admissions and Financial Aid, 500 College
Avenue, Swarthmore, PA 19081
Telephone: 610-328-8300 or toll-free 800-667-3110
Fax: 610-328-8580
E-mail: admissions@swarthmore.edu

Academics

Swarthmore awards bachelor's **degrees**. **Challenging opportunities** include advanced placement credit, accelerated degree programs, student-designed majors, an honors program, double majors, independent study, and a senior project. Special programs include internships, off-campus study, study-abroad, and Army and Air Force ROTC.

The most frequently chosen **baccalaureate** fields are social sciences, biological/life sciences, and visual and performing arts. A complete listing of majors at Swarthmore appears in the Majors by College index beginning on page 469.

The **faculty** at Swarthmore has 169 full-time members, 100% with terminal degrees. The student-faculty ratio is 8:1.

Students of Swarthmore

The student body is made up of 1,490 undergraduates. 52.1% are women and 47.9% are men. Students come from 51 states and territories and 35 other countries. 13% are from Pennsylvania. 7% are international students. 9% are African American, 0.6% American Indian, 17.1% Asian American, and 11% Hispanic American. 96% returned for their sophomore year.

Facilities and Resources

206 **computers/terminals** and 3,300 ports are available on campus for general student use. Students can access the following: campus intranet, computer help desk, free student e-mail accounts, online (class) grades, online (class) registration, online (class) schedules. Campuswide network is available. 100% of college-owned or -operated housing units are wired for high-speed Internet access. Wireless service is available via entire campus. The 7 **libraries** have 868,563 books and 12,655 subscriptions.

Campus Life

There are 138 active organizations on campus, including a drama/theater group, newspaper, radio station, and choral group. 11% of eligible men are members of national **fraternities** and local fraternities.

Swarthmore is a member of the NCAA (Division III). **Intercollegiate sports** include badminton (w), baseball (m), basketball, cross-country running, field hockey (w), golf (m), lacrosse, soccer, softball (w), swimming and diving, tennis, track and field, volleyball (w).

Campus Safety

Student safety services include late-night transport/escort service, 24-hour emergency telephone alarm devices, 24-hour patrols by trained security personnel, and student patrols.

Applying

Swarthmore requires an essay, SAT and SAT Subject Tests or ACT, a high school transcript, and 3 recommendations. It recommends an interview. Application deadline: 1/2; 2/15 for financial aid, with a 2/15 priority date. Early and deferred admission are possible.

Getting Accepted

6,121 applied
16% were accepted
372 enrolled (39% of accepted)
87% from top tenth of their h.s. class
Mean SAT critical reading score: 723
Mean SAT math score: 710
Mean SAT writing score: 711
Mean ACT score: 30
96% had SAT critical reading scores over 600
91% had SAT math scores over 600
96% had SAT writing scores over 600
100% had ACT scores over 24
65% had SAT critical reading scores over 700
59% had SAT math scores over 700
62% had SAT writing scores over 700
66% had ACT scores over 30
15 National Merit Scholars
19 valedictorians

Graduation and After

88% graduated in 4 years
4% graduated in 5 years
1% graduated in 6 years
66% had job offers within 6 months
57 organizations recruited on campus

Financial Matters

$36,490 tuition and fees (2008–09)
$11,314 room and board
100% average percent of need met
$31,553 average financial aid amount received
per undergraduate (2007–08 estimated)

SWEET BRIAR COLLEGE
RURAL SETTING ■ PRIVATE ■ INDEPENDENT ■ WOMEN ONLY
SWEET BRIAR, VIRGINIA

Web site: www.sbc.edu
Contact: PO Box B, Sweet Briar, VA 24595
Telephone: 434-381-6142 or toll-free 800-381-6142
Fax: 434-381-6152
E-mail: admissions@sbc.edu

Getting Accepted
629 applied
83% were accepted
198 enrolled (38% of accepted)
28% from top tenth of their h.s. class
3.53 average high school GPA
Mean SAT critical reading score: 580
Mean SAT math score: 520
Mean ACT score: 24
40% had SAT critical reading scores over 600
26% had SAT math scores over 600
51% had ACT scores over 24
8% had SAT critical reading scores over 700
3% had SAT math scores over 700
7% had ACT scores over 30
1 class president
5 valedictorians

Graduation and After
68% graduated in 4 years
3% graduated in 5 years
1% graduated in 6 years
59% had job offers within 6 months
56 organizations recruited on campus

Financial Matters
$29,135 tuition and fees (2009–10)
$10,460 room and board
83% average percent of need met
$15,150 average financial aid amount received per undergraduate (2006–07)

Academics
Sweet Briar awards bachelor's and master's **degrees. Challenging opportunities** include advanced placement credit, accelerated degree programs, student-designed majors, an honors program, double majors, independent study, and a senior project. Special programs include internships, summer session for credit, off-campus study, and study-abroad.

The most frequently chosen **baccalaureate** fields are social sciences, biological/life sciences, and visual and performing arts. A complete listing of majors at Sweet Briar appears in the Majors by College index beginning on page 469.

The **faculty** at Sweet Briar has 65 full-time members, 100% with terminal degrees. The student-faculty ratio is 9:1.

Students of Sweet Briar
The student body totals 828, of whom 813 are undergraduates. Students come from 45 states and territories and 16 other countries. 51% are from Virginia. 1.2% are international students. 3.1% are African American, 0.9% American Indian, 1.1% Asian American, and 3.2% Hispanic American. 71% returned for their sophomore year.

Facilities and Resources
128 **computers/terminals** and 3,000 ports are available on campus for general student use. Students can access the following: campus intranet, computer help desk, free student e-mail accounts, online (class) grades, online (class) registration, online (class) schedules. Campuswide network is available. 90% of college-owned or -operated housing units are wired for high-speed Internet access. Wireless service is available via classrooms, computer centers, computer labs, libraries, student centers. The 4 **libraries** have 282,324 books and 56,272 subscriptions.

Campus Life
There are 61 active organizations on campus, including a drama/theater group, newspaper, radio station, television station, and choral group. No national or local **sororities.**

Sweet Briar is a member of the NCAA (Division III). **Intercollegiate sports** include field hockey, lacrosse, soccer, swimming and diving, tennis, volleyball.

Campus Safety
Student safety services include front gate security, late-night transport/escort service, 24-hour emergency telephone alarm devices, 24-hour patrols by trained security personnel, and electronically operated dormitory entrances.

Applying
Sweet Briar requires an essay, SAT or ACT, a high school transcript, and 2 recommendations, and in some cases portfolio with courses taken, list of texts covered, essay about homeschooling, campus visit, interview for homeschooled applicants. It recommends an interview. Application deadline: 2/1; 3/1 priority date for financial aid. Early and deferred admission are possible.

Syracuse University

Urban setting ■ Private ■ Independent ■ Coed
Syracuse, New York

Web site: www.syracuse.edu
Contact: Office of Admissions, 200 Crouse-Hinds Hall, South Crouse Avenue, Syracuse, NY 13244-2130
Telephone: 315-443-3611
E-mail: orange@syr.edu

SPONSOR

Academics
Syracuse awards associate, bachelor's, master's, doctoral, and first-professional **degrees** and post-bachelor's and post-master's certificates. **Challenging opportunities** include advanced placement credit, accelerated degree programs, student-designed majors, an honors program, double majors, independent study, and a senior project. Special programs include cooperative education, internships, summer session for credit, off-campus study, study-abroad, and Army and Air Force ROTC.

The most frequently chosen **baccalaureate** fields are business/marketing, communications/journalism, and social sciences. A complete listing of majors at Syracuse appears in the Majors by College index beginning on page 469.

The **faculty** at Syracuse has 943 full-time members, 87% with terminal degrees. The student-faculty ratio is 15:1.

Students of Syracuse
The student body totals 19,366, of whom 13,651 are undergraduates. 56.6% are women and 43.4% are men. Students come from 50 states and territories and 70 other countries. 46% are from New York. 4.8% are international students. 7.5% are African American, 0.9% American Indian, 9% Asian American, and 6.4% Hispanic American. 90% returned for their sophomore year.

Facilities and Resources
2,955 **computers/terminals** and 650 ports are available on campus for general student use. Students can access the following: campus intranet, computer help desk, free student e-mail accounts, online (class) grades, online (class) registration, online (class) schedules, online services, networked client and server computing. Campuswide network is available. 100% of college-owned or -operated housing units are wired for high-speed Internet access. Wireless service is available via classrooms, computer centers, computer labs, dorm rooms, learning centers, libraries, student centers. The 8 **libraries** have 3,160,240 books and 23,285 subscriptions.

Campus Life
There are 320 active organizations on campus, including a drama/theater group, newspaper, radio station, television station, choral group, and marching band. 19% of eligible men and 28% of eligible women are members of national **fraternities** and national **sororities**.

Syracuse is a member of the NCAA (Division I). **Intercollegiate sports** (some offering scholarships) include basketball, cheerleading, crew, cross-country running, field hockey (w), football (m), ice hockey (w), lacrosse, soccer, softball (w), swimming and diving, tennis (w), track and field, volleyball (w).

Campus Safety
Student safety services include crime prevention and neighborhood outreach programs, late-night transport/escort service, 24-hour emergency telephone alarm devices, 24-hour patrols by trained security personnel, and electronically operated dormitory entrances.

Applying
Syracuse requires an essay, SAT or ACT, a high school transcript, 2 recommendations, and audition for drama and music programs, portfolio for art and architecture programs. It recommends an interview. Application deadline: 1/1; 2/1 for financial aid. Early and deferred admission are possible.

Getting Accepted
22,079 applied
53% were accepted
3,186 enrolled (27% of accepted)
39% from top tenth of their h.s. class
3.6 average high school GPA
38% had SAT critical reading scores over 600
54% had SAT math scores over 600
43% had SAT writing scores over 600
5% had SAT critical reading scores over 700
12% had SAT math scores over 700
7% had SAT writing scores over 700

Graduation and After
71% graduated in 4 years
10% graduated in 5 years
1% graduated in 6 years
228 organizations recruited on campus

Financial Matters
$33,440 tuition and fees (2008–09)
$11,656 room and board
82% average percent of need met
$24,200 average financial aid amount received per undergraduate (2007–08 estimated)

TABOR COLLEGE

SMALL-TOWN SETTING ■ PRIVATE ■ INDEPENDENT RELIGIOUS ■ COED
HILLSBORO, KANSAS

Web site: www.tabor.edu
Contact: Mr. Rusty Allen, Dean of Enrollment Management, 400 South
    Jefferson, Hillsboro, KS 67063
Telephone: 620-947-3121 or toll-free 800-822-6799
Fax: 620-947-6276
E-mail: rustya@tabor.edu

Getting Accepted
241 applied
100% were accepted
120 enrolled (50% of accepted)
18% from top tenth of their h.s. class
3.36 average high school GPA
Mean SAT critical reading score: 506
Mean SAT math score: 518
Mean ACT score: 22
40% had ACT scores over 24
3% had ACT scores over 30
2 National Merit Scholars

Graduation and After
41% graduated in 4 years
3% graduated in 5 years
2% graduated in 6 years
79% had job offers within 6 months
105 organizations recruited on campus

Financial Matters
$18,710 tuition and fees (2008–09)
$6750 room and board
89% average percent of need met
$15,751 average financial aid amount received
    per undergraduate (2007–08 estimated)

Academics
Tabor awards associate, bachelor's, and master's **degrees**. **Challenging opportunities**
include advanced placement credit, accelerated degree programs, student-designed
majors, an honors program, double majors, independent study, and a senior project.
Special programs include cooperative education, internships, off-campus study, and
study-abroad.

The most frequently chosen **baccalaureate** fields are business/marketing, health
professions and related sciences, and theology and religious vocations. A complete listing
of majors at Tabor appears in the Majors by College index beginning on page 469.

The **faculty** at Tabor has 33 full-time members, 73% with terminal degrees. The
student-faculty ratio is 10:1.

Students of Tabor
The student body is made up of 574 undergraduates. 50.3% are women and 49.7% are
men. Students come from 27 states and territories and 6 other countries. 59% are from
Kansas. 1% are international students. 6.8% are African American, 0.9% American
Indian, 0.9% Asian American, and 4% Hispanic American. 65% returned for their
sophomore year.

Facilities and Resources
60 **computers/terminals** and 450 ports are available on campus for general student use.
Students can access the following: campus intranet, computer help desk, free student
e-mail accounts, online (class) grades, online (class) registration, online (class) schedules.
Campuswide network is available. 100% of college-owned or -operated housing units are
wired for high-speed Internet access. Wireless service is available via dorm rooms,
learning centers, libraries, student centers. The **library** has 80,099 books and 265
subscriptions.

Campus Life
There are 6 active organizations on campus, including a drama/theater group,
newspaper, and choral group. No national or local **fraternities** or **sororities**.

Tabor is a member of the NAIA. **Intercollegiate sports** (some offering scholarships)
include baseball (m), basketball, cheerleading, cross-country running, football (m), golf,
soccer, softball (w), tennis, track and field, volleyball (w).

Applying
Tabor requires an essay, SAT or ACT, a high school transcript, minimum ACT score of
18, and a minimum high school GPA of 2.5. It recommends an interview. Application
deadline: 8/1, 8/1 for nonresidents; 8/15 for financial aid, with a 3/1 priority date. Early
and deferred admission are possible.

TAYLOR UNIVERSITY

RURAL SETTING ■ PRIVATE ■ INDEPENDENT RELIGIOUS ■ COED
UPLAND, INDIANA

Web site: www.taylor.edu
Contact: Ms. Amy Barnett, Visit Coordinator, 236 West Reade Avenue,
   Upland, IN 46989-1001
Telephone: 765-998-5565 or toll-free 800-882-3456
Fax: 765-998-4925
E-mail: admissions@taylor.edu

Academics

Taylor awards associate, bachelor's, and master's **degrees. Challenging opportunities** include advanced placement credit, student-designed majors, an honors program, double majors, independent study, and a senior project. Special programs include cooperative education, internships, summer session for credit, off-campus study, and study-abroad.

The most frequently chosen **baccalaureate** fields are education, business/marketing, and psychology. A complete listing of majors at Taylor appears in the Majors by College index beginning on page 469.

The **faculty** at Taylor has 126 full-time members, 81% with terminal degrees. The student-faculty ratio is 13:1.

Students of Taylor

The student body is made up of 1,871 undergraduates. 54.8% are women and 45.2% are men. Students come from 44 states and territories and 31 other countries. 31% are from Indiana. 2.2% are international students. 2.1% are African American, 0.1% American Indian, 2.4% Asian American, and 1.9% Hispanic American. 84% returned for their sophomore year.

Facilities and Resources

339 **computers/terminals** are available on campus for general student use. Students can access the following: campus intranet, computer help desk, free student e-mail accounts, online (class) grades, online (class) registration, online (class) schedules. Campuswide network is available. 100% of college-owned or -operated housing units are wired for high-speed Internet access. Wireless service is available via entire campus. The **library** has 188,986 books and 30,449 subscriptions.

Campus Life

Active organizations on campus include a drama/theater group, newspaper, radio station, television station, and choral group. No national or local **fraternities** or **sororities**.

Taylor is a member of the NAIA. **Intercollegiate sports** (some offering scholarships) include baseball (m), basketball, cross-country running, football (m), golf (m), soccer, softball (w), tennis, track and field, volleyball (w).

Campus Safety

Student safety services include late-night transport/escort service, 24-hour patrols by trained security personnel, and student patrols.

Applying

Taylor requires an essay, SAT or ACT, a high school transcript, an interview, and 2 recommendations. It recommends a minimum high school GPA of 2.8. Application deadline: rolling admissions; 3/10 for financial aid. Deferred admission is possible.

Getting Accepted
1,557 applied
84% were accepted
465 enrolled (36% of accepted)
35% from top tenth of their h.s. class
3.54 average high school GPA
Mean SAT critical reading score: 587
Mean SAT math score: 584
Mean SAT writing score: 577
Mean ACT score: 26
51% had SAT critical reading scores over 600
50% had SAT math scores over 600
71% had ACT scores over 24
14% had SAT critical reading scores over 700
10% had SAT math scores over 700
27% had ACT scores over 30
10 National Merit Scholars
23 valedictorians

Graduation and After
70% graduated in 4 years
8% graduated in 5 years
67% had job offers within 6 months
81 organizations recruited on campus

Financial Matters
$24,546 tuition and fees (2008–09)
$6352 room and board
76% average percent of need met
$16,085 average financial aid amount received
   per undergraduate (2007–08 estimated)

TENNESSEE TECHNOLOGICAL UNIVERSITY

SMALL-TOWN SETTING ■ PUBLIC ■ STATE-SUPPORTED ■ COED
COOKEVILLE, TENNESSEE

Web site: www.tntech.edu
Contact: Ms. Vanessa Palmer, Interim Director of Admissions, PO Box 5006, Cookeville, TN 38505
Telephone: 931-372-3888 or toll-free 800-255-8881
Fax: 931-372-6250
E-mail: admissions@tntech.edu

Getting Accepted
3,790 applied
88% were accepted
1,661 enrolled (50% of accepted)
26% from top tenth of their h.s. class
3.24 average high school GPA
32% had SAT critical reading scores over 600
36% had SAT math scores over 600
40% had ACT scores over 24
4% had SAT critical reading scores over 700
30% had SAT math scores over 700
6% had ACT scores over 30
4 National Merit Scholars

Graduation and After
67% had job offers within 6 months
334 organizations recruited on campus

Financial Matters
$5244 resident tuition and fees (2008–09)
$16,136 nonresident tuition and fees (2008–09)
$7290 room and board
83% average percent of need met
$3401 average financial aid amount received per undergraduate (2007–08 estimated)

Academics
Tennessee Tech awards bachelor's, master's, and doctoral **degrees** and post-bachelor's certificates. **Challenging opportunities** include advanced placement credit, accelerated degree programs, an honors program, double majors, independent study, and a senior project. Special programs include cooperative education, internships, summer session for credit, off-campus study, study-abroad, and Army and Air Force ROTC.

The most frequently chosen **baccalaureate** fields are business/marketing, education, and engineering. A complete listing of majors at Tennessee Tech appears in the Majors by College index beginning on page 469.

The **faculty** at Tennessee Tech has 388 full-time members, 80% with terminal degrees. The student-faculty ratio is 18:1.

Students of Tennessee Tech
The student body totals 10,321, of whom 8,060 are undergraduates. 46.5% are women and 53.5% are men. Students come from 40 states and territories and 40 other countries. 96% are from Tennessee. 1.6% are international students. 3.6% are African American, 0.3% American Indian, 1.4% Asian American, and 1.2% Hispanic American. 73% returned for their sophomore year.

Facilities and Resources
800 **computers/terminals** are available on campus for general student use. Students can access the following: online (class) registration. Campuswide network is available. 100% of college-owned or -operated housing units are wired for high-speed Internet access. Wireless service is available via entire campus. The **library** has 640,056 books and 4,847 subscriptions.

Campus Life
There are 178 active organizations on campus, including a drama/theater group, newspaper, radio station, choral group, and marching band. 18% of eligible men and 12% of eligible women are members of national **fraternities** and national **sororities**.

Tennessee Tech is a member of the NCAA (Division I). **Intercollegiate sports** (some offering scholarships) include baseball (m), basketball, cheerleading, cross-country running, football (m), golf, riflery, soccer (w), softball (w), tennis, track and field (w), volleyball (w).

Campus Safety
Student safety services include student safety organization, lighted pathways, late-night transport/escort service, 24-hour emergency telephone alarm devices, and 24-hour patrols by trained security personnel.

Applying
Tennessee Tech requires SAT or ACT, a high school transcript, ACT composite score of 19, and a minimum high school GPA of 2.5. It recommends ACT and an interview. Application deadline: 8/1; 3/15 priority date for financial aid. Early and deferred admission are possible.

Texas A&M University

Suburban setting ■ Public ■ State-supported ■ Coed
College Station, Texas

Web site: www.tamu.edu
Contact: Mr. Scott McDonald, Director of Admissions, 217 John J. Koldus
  Building, College Station, TX 77843-1265
Telephone: 979-845-3741
Fax: 979-845-8737
E-mail: admissions@tamu.edu

Academics

Texas A&M awards bachelor's, master's, doctoral, and first-professional **degrees** and post-bachelor's certificates. **Challenging opportunities** include advanced placement credit, accelerated degree programs, an honors program, double majors, independent study, and a senior project. Special programs include cooperative education, internships, summer session for credit, off-campus study, study-abroad, and Army, Navy, and Air Force ROTC.

The most frequently chosen **baccalaureate** fields are business/marketing, agriculture, and engineering. A complete listing of majors at Texas A&M appears in the Majors by College index beginning on page 469.

The **faculty** at Texas A&M has 2,234 full-time members, 90% with terminal degrees. The student-faculty ratio is 19:1.

Students of Texas A&M

The student body totals 48,039, of whom 38,430 are undergraduates. 47.8% are women and 52.2% are men. Students come from 52 states and territories and 128 other countries. 97% are from Texas. 1.5% are international students. 3.2% are African American, 0.6% American Indian, 4.6% Asian American, and 13.5% Hispanic American. 92% returned for their sophomore year.

Facilities and Resources

1,483 **computers/terminals** and 5,000 ports are available on campus for general student use. Students can access the following: campus intranet, computer help desk, free student e-mail accounts, online (class) grades, online (class) registration, online (class) schedules. Campuswide network is available. 100% of college-owned or -operated housing units are wired for high-speed Internet access. Wireless service is available via classrooms, computer labs, libraries. The 7 **libraries** have 3,849,847 books and 61,717 subscriptions.

Campus Life

There are 700 active organizations on campus, including a drama/theater group, newspaper, radio station, television station, choral group, and marching band. 6% of eligible men and 12% of eligible women are members of national **fraternities**, national **sororities**, local fraternities, and local sororities.

Texas A&M is a member of the NCAA (Division I). **Intercollegiate sports** (some offering scholarships) include archery (w), baseball (m), basketball, cross-country running, equestrian sports (w), football (m), golf, soccer (w), softball (w), swimming and diving, tennis, track and field, volleyball (w).

Campus Safety

Student safety services include student escorts, late-night transport/escort service, 24-hour emergency telephone alarm devices, 24-hour patrols by trained security personnel, and electronically operated dormitory entrances.

Applying

Texas A&M requires an essay, SAT or ACT, and a high school transcript. Application deadline: 1/15.

Getting Accepted

20,887 applied
70% were accepted
8,093 enrolled (55% of accepted)
54% from top tenth of their h.s. class
Mean SAT critical reading score: 579
Mean SAT math score: 616
Mean SAT writing score: 561
Mean ACT score: 26
43% had SAT critical reading scores over 600
60% had SAT math scores over 600
32% had SAT writing scores over 600
73% had ACT scores over 24
9% had SAT critical reading scores over 700
15% had SAT math scores over 700
5% had SAT writing scores over 700
20% had ACT scores over 30
162 National Merit Scholars
228 valedictorians

Graduation and After

41% graduated in 4 years
32% graduated in 5 years
5% graduated in 6 years
1970 organizations recruited on campus

Financial Matters

$7844 resident tuition and fees (2008–09)
$22,184 nonresident tuition and fees (2008–09)
$8000 room and board
85% average percent of need met
$13,215 average financial aid amount received per undergraduate (2007–08 estimated)

SPONSOR

Texas Christian University

SUBURBAN SETTING ■ PRIVATE ■ INDEPENDENT RELIGIOUS ■ COED
FORT WORTH, TEXAS

Web site: www.tcu.edu
Contact: Mr. Wes Waggoner, Director of Freshman Admissions, TCU Box 297013, Fort Worth, TX 76129-0002
Telephone: 817-257-7490 or toll-free 800-828-3764
Fax: 817-257-7268
E-mail: frogmail@tcu.edu

TCU's mission—to educate individuals to think and act as ethical leaders and responsible citizens in the global community—influences every area of this person-centered, private university. TCU offers a world-class study-abroad program. Its degree programs offer internships as part of the education. The Freshman Experience provides the opportunities students need to succeed, from writing enhancement to Internet connections in every residence room. A Division I-A teaching and research university, TCU provides the personal attention crucial to every student's success. The final grade? TCU students earn more than degrees that can improve their lives. They learn to change their world.

Getting Accepted
12,212 applied
50% were accepted
1,630 enrolled (26% of accepted)
32% from top tenth of their h.s. class

Graduation and After
50% graduated in 4 years
18% graduated in 5 years
2% graduated in 6 years
390 organizations recruited on campus

Financial Matters
$28,298 tuition and fees (2009–10)
$9800 room and board
76% average percent of need met
$19,570 average financial aid amount received per undergraduate (2007–08 estimated)

Academics
TCU awards bachelor's, master's, and doctoral **degrees** and post-bachelor's certificates. **Challenging opportunities** include advanced placement credit, accelerated degree programs, an honors program, double majors, independent study, and a senior project. Special programs include internships, summer session for credit, off-campus study, study-abroad, and Army and Air Force ROTC.

The most frequently chosen **baccalaureate** fields are business/marketing, communications/journalism, and health professions and related sciences. A complete listing of majors at TCU appears in the Majors by College index beginning on page 469.

The **faculty** at TCU has 506 full-time members, 83% with terminal degrees. The student-faculty ratio is 14:1.

Students of TCU
The student body totals 8,696, of whom 7,471 are undergraduates. 59% are women and 41% are men. Students come from 50 states and territories and 80 other countries. 80% are from Texas. 5.1% are international students. 5.4% are African American, 0.5% American Indian, 2.9% Asian American, and 8.4% Hispanic American. 86% returned for their sophomore year.

Facilities and Resources
Students can access the following: campus intranet, computer help desk, free student e-mail accounts, online (class) grades, online (class) registration, online (class) schedules. Campuswide network is available. 100% of college-owned or -operated housing units are wired for high-speed Internet access. Wireless service is available via entire campus. The **library** has 1,421,763 books and 32,935 subscriptions.

Campus Life
There are 207 active organizations on campus, including a drama/theater group, newspaper, radio station, television station, choral group, and marching band. 37% of eligible men and 39% of eligible women are members of national **fraternities**, national **sororities**, local fraternities, local sororities, and local coed music fraternities.

TCU is a member of the NCAA (Division I). **Intercollegiate sports** (some offering scholarships) include baseball (m), basketball, cross-country running, equestrian sports (w), football (m), golf, riflery (w), soccer (w), swimming and diving, tennis, track and field, volleyball (w).

Campus Safety
Student safety services include emergency call boxes, video camera surveillance in parking lots, late-night transport/escort service, 24-hour emergency telephone alarm devices, 24-hour patrols by trained security personnel, student patrols, and electronically operated dormitory entrances.

Applying
TCU requires an essay, SAT or ACT, a high school transcript, 2 recommendations, and a minimum high school GPA of 2.0. It recommends an interview and a minimum high school GPA of 3.0. Application deadline: 2/15; 5/1 for financial aid, with a 5/1 priority date. Deferred admission is possible.

Texas Tech University

URBAN SETTING ■ PUBLIC ■ STATE-SUPPORTED ■ COED
LUBBOCK, TEXAS

Web site: www.ttu.edu
Contact: Box 45005, Lubbock, TX 79409-5005
Telephone: 806-742-1480
Fax: 806-742-0062
E-mail: admissions@ttu.edu

Academics

Texas Tech awards bachelor's, master's, doctoral, and first-professional **degrees** and post-bachelor's certificates. **Challenging opportunities** include advanced placement credit, accelerated degree programs, student-designed majors, freshman honors college, an honors program, double majors, independent study, and a senior project. Special programs include cooperative education, internships, summer session for credit, off-campus study, study-abroad, and Army and Air Force ROTC.

The most frequently chosen **baccalaureate** fields are business/marketing, family and consumer sciences, and engineering. A complete listing of majors at Texas Tech appears in the Majors by College index beginning on page 469.

The **faculty** at Texas Tech has 1,099 full-time members, 87% with terminal degrees. The student-faculty ratio is 19:1.

Students of Texas Tech

The student body totals 28,422, of whom 23,107 are undergraduates. 44.1% are women and 55.9% are men. Students come from 49 states and territories and 103 other countries. 96% are from Texas. 1% are international students. 4.3% are African American, 0.7% American Indian, 3.1% Asian American, and 13.8% Hispanic American. 80% returned for their sophomore year.

Facilities and Resources

3,000 **computers/terminals** are available on campus for general student use. Students can access the following: computer help desk, free student e-mail accounts, online (class) grades, online (class) registration, online (class) schedules, online degree plans, accounts, transcripts, schedules. Campuswide network is available. 100% of college-owned or -operated housing units are wired for high-speed Internet access. Wireless service is available via entire campus. The 4 **libraries** have 2,413,645 books and 42,372 subscriptions.

Campus Life

There are 440 active organizations on campus, including a drama/theater group, newspaper, choral group, and marching band. 15% of eligible men and 20% of eligible women are members of national **fraternities**, national **sororities**, local fraternities, and local sororities.

Texas Tech is a member of the NCAA (Division I). **Intercollegiate sports** (some offering scholarships) include baseball (m), basketball, cross-country running, football (m), golf, soccer (w), softball (w), tennis, track and field, volleyball (w).

Campus Safety

Student safety services include late-night transport/escort service, 24-hour emergency telephone alarm devices, 24-hour patrols by trained security personnel, and electronically operated dormitory entrances.

Applying

Texas Tech requires SAT or ACT and a high school transcript. It recommends an essay. Application deadline: 5/1; 4/15 priority date for financial aid. Early admission is possible.

Getting Accepted

16,143 applied
72% were accepted
4,385 enrolled (38% of accepted)
21% from top tenth of their h.s. class
Mean SAT critical reading score: 542
Mean SAT math score: 570
Mean ACT score: 24
23% had SAT critical reading scores over 600
36% had SAT math scores over 600
14% had SAT writing scores over 600
54% had ACT scores over 24
3% had SAT critical reading scores over 700
5% had SAT math scores over 700
1% had SAT writing scores over 700
8% had ACT scores over 30
11 National Merit Scholars
19 valedictorians

Graduation and After

30% graduated in 4 years
21% graduated in 5 years
6% graduated in 6 years
80% had job offers within 6 months
550 organizations recruited on campus

Financial Matters

$6783 resident tuition and fees (2008–09)
$15,213 nonresident tuition and fees (2008–09)
$7310 room and board
60% average percent of need met
$7823 average financial aid amount received per undergraduate (2006–07)

Thomas Aquinas College

RURAL SETTING ■ PRIVATE ■ INDEPENDENT RELIGIOUS ■ COED
SANTA PAULA, CALIFORNIA

Web site: www.thomasaquinas.edu
Contact: Mr. Jonathan P. Daly, Director of Admissions, 10000 North Ojai
Road, Santa Paula, CA 93060-9621
Telephone: 805-525-4417 Ext. 5901 or toll-free 800-634-9797
Fax: 805-525-5905
E-mail: admissions@thomasaqinas.edu

Getting Accepted

232 applied
64% were accepted
102 enrolled (68% of accepted)
75% from top tenth of their h.s. class
3.67 average high school GPA
Mean SAT critical reading score: 660
Mean SAT math score: 600
Mean SAT writing score: 630
Mean ACT score: 27
80% had SAT critical reading scores over 600
53% had SAT math scores over 600
76% had SAT writing scores over 600
81% had ACT scores over 24
37% had SAT critical reading scores over 700
3% had SAT math scores over 700
17% had SAT writing scores over 700
19% had ACT scores over 30

Graduation and After

67% graduated in 4 years
2% graduated in 5 years
97% had job offers within 6 months
10 organizations recruited on campus

Financial Matters

$22,400 tuition and fees (2009–10)
$7400 room and board
100% average percent of need met
$16,793 average financial aid amount received
per undergraduate (2007–08 estimated)

Academics

Thomas Aquinas awards bachelor's **degrees**. A senior project is a **challenging opportunity**. Cooperative education is a special program.

The most frequently chosen **baccalaureate** field is liberal arts/general studies. A complete listing of majors at Thomas Aquinas appears in the Majors by College index beginning on page 469.

The **faculty** at Thomas Aquinas has 27 full-time members, 56% with terminal degrees. The student-faculty ratio is 11:1.

Students of Thomas Aquinas

The student body is made up of 340 undergraduates. 51.8% are women and 48.2% are men. Students come from 42 states and territories and 7 other countries. 35% are from California. 7.4% are international students. 0.9% are American Indian, 2.9% Asian American, and 6.2% Hispanic American. 85% returned for their sophomore year.

Facilities and Resources

19 **computers/terminals** and 17 ports are available on campus for general student use. Students can access the following: free student e-mail accounts. Campuswide network is available. The **library** has 62,000 books and 72 subscriptions.

Campus Life

There are 5 active organizations on campus, including a drama/theater group and choral group. No national or local **fraternities** or **sororities**.

This institution has no intercollegiate sports.

Campus Safety

Student safety services include daily security daytime patrol and 24-hour emergency telephone alarm devices.

Applying

Thomas Aquinas requires an essay, SAT or ACT, a high school transcript, and 3 recommendations, and in some cases an interview. It recommends a minimum high school GPA of 3.0. Application deadline: rolling admissions; 3/2 for financial aid. Early and deferred admission are possible.

TOWSON UNIVERSITY

SUBURBAN SETTING ■ PUBLIC ■ STATE-SUPPORTED ■ COED
TOWSON, MARYLAND

Web site: www.towson.edu
Contact: Ms. Louise Shulack, Director of Admissions, 8000 York Road,
Towson, MD 21252
Telephone: 410-704-2113 or toll-free 888-4TOWSON
Fax: 410-704-3030
E-mail: admissions@towson.edu

Academics

Towson awards bachelor's, master's, and doctoral **degrees** and post-bachelor's and post-master's certificates. **Challenging opportunities** include advanced placement credit, accelerated degree programs, student-designed majors, freshman honors college, an honors program, double majors, independent study, and a senior project. Special programs include cooperative education, internships, summer session for credit, off-campus study, study-abroad, and Army and Air Force ROTC.

The most frequently chosen **baccalaureate** fields are business/marketing, education, and social sciences. A complete listing of majors at Towson appears in the Majors by College index beginning on page 469.

The **faculty** at Towson has 788 full-time members, 74% with terminal degrees. The student-faculty ratio is 18:1.

Students of Towson

The student body totals 21,111, of whom 17,272 are undergraduates. 59.7% are women and 40.3% are men. Students come from 47 states and territories and 93 other countries. 83% are from Maryland. 2.9% are international students. 11.8% are African American, 0.4% American Indian, 4.3% Asian American, and 2.7% Hispanic American. 82% returned for their sophomore year.

Facilities and Resources

1,200 **computers/terminals** are available on campus for general student use. Students can access the following: computer help desk, free student e-mail accounts, online (class) grades, online (class) registration, online (class) schedules. Campuswide network is available. 100% of college-owned or -operated housing units are wired for high-speed Internet access. Wireless service is available via entire campus. The **library** has 578,057 books and 4,653 subscriptions.

Campus Life

There are 198 active organizations on campus, including a drama/theater group, newspaper, radio station, television station, choral group, and marching band. 7% of eligible men and 7% of eligible women are members of national **fraternities** and national **sororities**.

Towson is a member of the NCAA (Division I). **Intercollegiate sports** (some offering scholarships) include baseball (m), basketball, cheerleading, cross-country running, field hockey (w), football (m), golf, gymnastics (w), lacrosse, soccer, softball (w), swimming and diving, tennis, track and field, volleyball.

Campus Safety

Student safety services include late-night transport/escort service, 24-hour emergency telephone alarm devices, 24-hour patrols by trained security personnel, and electronically operated dormitory entrances.

Applying

Towson requires SAT or ACT and a high school transcript, and in some cases an essay and an interview. It recommends 2 recommendations and a minimum high school GPA of 3.0. Application deadline: 2/15; 2/15 for financial aid, with a 1/31 priority date. Early and deferred admission are possible.

Getting Accepted

15,699 applied
61% were accepted
2,832 enrolled (29% of accepted)
21% from top tenth of their h.s. class
3.53 average high school GPA
Mean SAT critical reading score: 532
Mean SAT math score: 543
Mean SAT writing score: 543
18% had SAT critical reading scores over 600
23% had SAT math scores over 600
23% had SAT writing scores over 600
33% had ACT scores over 24
2% had SAT critical reading scores over 700
2% had SAT math scores over 700
2% had SAT writing scores over 700
1% had ACT scores over 30

Graduation and After

40% graduated in 4 years
22% graduated in 5 years
4% graduated in 6 years
49 organizations recruited on campus

Financial Matters

$7314 resident tuition and fees (2008–09)
$17,860 nonresident tuition and fees
(2008–09)
$8306 room and board
70% average percent of need met
$8849 average financial aid amount received
per undergraduate (2007–08 estimated)

TRANSYLVANIA UNIVERSITY

URBAN SETTING ■ PRIVATE ■ INDEPENDENT RELIGIOUS ■ COED
LEXINGTON, KENTUCKY

Web site: www.transy.edu
Contact: Mr. Bradley Goan, Director of Admissions, 300 North Broadway,
   Lexington, KY 40508-1797
Telephone: 859-233-4242 or toll-free 800-872-6798
Fax: 859-281-3642
E-mail: admissions@transy.edu

Founded in 1780 as the nation's sixteenth college, Transylvania consistently ranks among the nation's best liberal arts colleges and is considered an exceptional value in education. Students benefit from an innovative teacher-recognition program, the first in the nation to attract and reward outstanding teaching on a substantial scale. Small classes and individual attention from faculty members prepare students well for highly selective graduate and professional schools as well as for jobs in a highly competitive work-force. Transylvania's location in a historic district near downtown Lexington, Kentucky, provides oppor-tunities for internships, jobs, and cultural activities.

Academics

Transylvania awards bachelor's **degrees**. **Challenging opportunities** include advanced placement credit, student-designed majors, double majors, independent study, and a senior project. Special programs include internships, summer session for credit, off-campus study, study-abroad, and Army and Air Force ROTC.

The most frequently chosen **baccalaureate** fields are business/marketing, social sci-ences, and biological/life sciences. A complete listing of majors at Transylvania appears in the Majors by College index beginning on page 469.

The **faculty** at Transylvania has 85 full-time members, 93% with terminal degrees. The student-faculty ratio is 13:1.

Getting Accepted

1,365 applied
80% were accepted
349 enrolled (32% of accepted)
41% from top tenth of their h.s. class
3.56 average high school GPA
Mean SAT critical reading score: 593
Mean SAT math score: 587
Mean SAT writing score: 579
Mean ACT score: 26
50% had SAT critical reading scores over 600
45% had SAT math scores over 600
75% had ACT scores over 24
13% had SAT critical reading scores over 700
9% had SAT math scores over 700
22% had ACT scores over 30
7 National Merit Scholars
31 valedictorians

Students of Transylvania

The student body is made up of 1,153 undergraduates. Students come from 28 states and territories and 2 other countries. 83% are from Kentucky. 0.2% are international students. 3.2% are African American, 0.3% American Indian, 1.5% Asian American, and 1.3% Hispanic American. 84% returned for their sophomore year.

Facilities and Resources

250 **computers/terminals** and 250 ports are available on campus for general student use. Students can access the following: campus intranet, computer help desk, free student e-mail accounts, online (class) grades, online (class) schedules. Campuswide network is available. 100% of college-owned or -operated housing units are wired for high-speed Internet access. The **library** has 125,000 books and 500 subscriptions.

Graduation and After

61% graduated in 4 years
10% graduated in 5 years
1% graduated in 6 years
60% had job offers within 6 months
80 organizations recruited on campus

Campus Life

There are 61 active organizations on campus, including a drama/theater group, newspaper, radio station, and choral group. 53% of eligible men and 53% of eligible women are members of national **fraternities** and national **sororities**.

Transylvania is a member of the NCAA (Division III). **Intercollegiate sports** include baseball (m), basketball, cheerleading, cross-country running, field hockey (w), golf, soccer, softball (w), swimming and diving, tennis, track and field, volleyball (w).

Campus Safety

Student safety services include late-night transport/escort service, 24-hour emergency telephone alarm devices, 24-hour patrols by trained security personnel, and electroni-cally operated dormitory entrances.

Financial Matters

$23,810 tuition and fees (2008–09)
$7450 room and board
86% average percent of need met
$18,812 average financial aid amount received per undergraduate (2007–08 estimated)

Applying

Transylvania requires an essay, SAT or ACT, a high school transcript, 2 recommenda-tions, and a minimum high school GPA of 2.75, and in some cases an interview. It recommends an interview. Application deadline: 2/1; 3/1 priority date for financial aid. Early and deferred admission are possible.

TRINITY COLLEGE

URBAN SETTING ■ PRIVATE ■ INDEPENDENT ■ COED
HARTFORD, CONNECTICUT

Web site: www.trincoll.edu
Contact: Mr. Larry Dow, Dean of Admissions and Financial Aid, 300 Summit Street, Hartford, CT 06106-3100
Telephone: 860-297-2180
Fax: 860-297-2287
E-mail: admissions.office@trincoll.edu

Academics

Trinity College awards bachelor's and master's **degrees**. **Challenging opportunities** include advanced placement credit, accelerated degree programs, student-designed majors, an honors program, double majors, independent study, and a senior project. Special programs include internships, summer session for credit, off-campus study, study-abroad, and Army ROTC.

The most frequently chosen **baccalaureate** fields are social sciences, area and ethnic studies, and English. A complete listing of majors at Trinity College appears in the Majors by College index beginning on page 469.

The **faculty** at Trinity College has 173 full-time members, 92% with terminal degrees. The student-faculty ratio is 10:1.

Students of Trinity College

The student body totals 2,564, of whom 2,375 are undergraduates. 50.2% are women and 49.8% are men. Students come from 44 states and territories and 31 other countries. 18% are from Connecticut. 3.7% are international students. 6.7% are African American, 0.2% American Indian, 5.3% Asian American, and 6% Hispanic American. 90% returned for their sophomore year.

Facilities and Resources

249 **computers/terminals** and 3,000 ports are available on campus for general student use. Students can access the following: campus intranet, computer help desk, free student e-mail accounts, online (class) grades, online (class) registration, online (class) schedules, Web pages. Campuswide network is available. 100% of college-owned or -operated housing units are wired for high-speed Internet access. Wireless service is available via classrooms, computer centers, computer labs, learning centers, libraries, student centers. The 2 **libraries** have 1,008,701 books and 1,813 subscriptions.

Campus Life

There are 105 active organizations on campus, including a drama/theater group, newspaper, radio station, and choral group. 20% of eligible men and 16% of eligible women are members of national **fraternities**, national **sororities**, local fraternities, local sororities, and coed fraternities.

Trinity College is a member of the NCAA (Division III). **Intercollegiate sports** include baseball (m), basketball, crew, cross-country running, field hockey (w), football (m), golf (m), ice hockey, lacrosse, soccer, softball (w), squash, swimming and diving, tennis, track and field, volleyball (w), wrestling (m).

Campus Safety

Student safety services include late-night transport/escort service, 24-hour emergency telephone alarm devices, 24-hour patrols by trained security personnel, and electronically operated dormitory entrances.

Applying

Trinity College requires an essay, ACT or SAT and SAT Writing Test or three SAT subject tests, a high school transcript, and 3 recommendations. It recommends an interview. Application deadline: 1/1; 3/1 for financial aid, with a 2/1 priority date. Early and deferred admission are possible.

Getting Accepted

5,950 applied
34% were accepted
576 enrolled (28% of accepted)
61% from top tenth of their h.s. class
Mean SAT critical reading score: 643
Mean SAT math score: 645
Mean SAT writing score: 656
Mean ACT score: 28
76% had SAT critical reading scores over 600
79% had SAT math scores over 600
79% had SAT writing scores over 600
94% had ACT scores over 24
24% had SAT critical reading scores over 700
19% had SAT math scores over 700
33% had SAT writing scores over 700
19% had ACT scores over 30

Graduation and After

79% graduated in 4 years
6% graduated in 5 years
1% graduated in 6 years
77% had job offers within 6 months

Financial Matters

$38,724 tuition and fees (2008–09)
$9900 room and board
100% average percent of need met
$25,590 average financial aid amount received per undergraduate (2005–06)

TRINITY UNIVERSITY

URBAN SETTING ■ PRIVATE ■ INDEPENDENT RELIGIOUS ■ COED
SAN ANTONIO, TEXAS

Web site: www.trinity.edu
Contact: Mr. Christopher Ellertson, Dean of Admissions and Financial Aid, One Trinity Place, San Antonio, TX 78212-7200
Telephone: 210-999-7207 or toll-free 800-TRINITY
Fax: 210-999-8164
E-mail: admissions@trinity.edu

Getting Accepted

3,754 applied
58% were accepted
656 enrolled (30% of accepted)
50% from top tenth of their h.s. class
3.55 average high school GPA
Mean SAT critical reading score: 641
Mean SAT math score: 647
Mean ACT score: 29
73% had SAT critical reading scores over 600
81% had SAT math scores over 600
99% had ACT scores over 24
24% had SAT critical reading scores over 700
23% had SAT math scores over 700
50% had ACT scores over 30
11 National Merit Scholars

Graduation and After

70% graduated in 4 years
10% graduated in 5 years
1% graduated in 6 years

Financial Matters

$27,699 tuition and fees (2008–09)
$8822 room and board
93% average percent of need met
$21,149 average financial aid amount received per undergraduate (2007–08 estimated)

Academics

Trinity awards bachelor's and master's **degrees. Challenging opportunities** include advanced placement credit, accelerated degree programs, an honors program, double majors, independent study, and a senior project. Special programs include internships, summer session for credit, study-abroad, and Air Force ROTC.

The most frequently chosen **baccalaureate** fields are business/marketing, social sciences, and foreign languages and literature. A complete listing of majors at Trinity appears in the Majors by College index beginning on page 469.

The **faculty** at Trinity has 248 full-time members, 100% with terminal degrees. The student-faculty ratio is 10:1.

Students of Trinity

The student body totals 2,703, of whom 2,489 are undergraduates. 53.5% are women and 46.5% are men. Students come from 52 states and territories and 48 other countries. 71% are from Texas. 5.9% are international students. 3.8% are African American, 1% American Indian, 7% Asian American, and 10.9% Hispanic American. 90% returned for their sophomore year.

Facilities and Resources

450 **computers/terminals** are available on campus for general student use. Students can access the following: campus intranet, computer help desk, free student e-mail accounts, online (class) grades, online (class) registration, online (class) schedules. Campuswide network is available. 100% of college-owned or -operated housing units are wired for high-speed Internet access. Wireless service is available via entire campus. The **library** has 1,112,758 books and 2,118 subscriptions.

Campus Life

Active organizations on campus include a drama/theater group, newspaper, radio station, television station, and choral group. 14% of eligible men and 26% of eligible women are members of local **fraternities** and local **sororities**.

Trinity is a member of the NCAA (Division III). **Intercollegiate sports** include baseball (m), basketball, cross-country running, football (m), golf, soccer, softball (w), swimming and diving, tennis, track and field, volleyball (w).

Campus Safety

Student safety services include late-night transport/escort service, 24-hour emergency telephone alarm devices, 24-hour patrols by trained security personnel, and electronically operated dormitory entrances.

Applying

Trinity requires an essay, SAT or ACT, a high school transcript, and 2 recommendations. It recommends an interview. Application deadline: 2/1; 4/1 for financial aid, with a 2/1 priority date. Deferred admission is possible.

Truman State University

Small-town setting ■ Public ■ State-supported ■ Coed

Kirksville, Missouri

Web site: www.truman.edu

Contact: Melody Chambers, Director of Admissions, 205 McClain Hall, 100 East Normal Street, Kirksville, MO 63501-4221

Telephone: 660-785-4114 or toll-free 800-892-7792 (in-state)

Fax: 660-785-7456

E-mail: admissions@truman.edu

Academics

Truman State awards bachelor's and master's **degrees. Challenging opportunities** include advanced placement credit, student-designed majors, an honors program, double majors, independent study, and a senior project. Special programs include internships, summer session for credit, off-campus study, study-abroad, and Army ROTC.

The most frequently chosen **baccalaureate** fields are business/marketing, English, and psychology. A complete listing of majors at Truman State appears in the Majors by College index beginning on page 469.

The **faculty** at Truman State has 357 full-time members, 84% with terminal degrees. The student-faculty ratio is 16:1.

Students of Truman State

The student body totals 5,842, of whom 5,586 are undergraduates. 58.1% are women and 41.9% are men. Students come from 44 states and territories and 46 other countries. 79% are from Missouri. 5.2% are international students. 4.6% are African American, 0.8% American Indian, 2.2% Asian American, and 2.5% Hispanic American. 85% returned for their sophomore year.

Facilities and Resources

965 **computers/terminals** and 3,690 ports are available on campus for general student use. Students can access the following: computer help desk, free student e-mail accounts, online (class) grades, online (class) registration, online (class) schedules. Campuswide network is available. 100% of college-owned or -operated housing units are wired for high-speed Internet access. Wireless service is available via entire campus. The **library** has 497,022 books and 3,942 subscriptions.

Campus Life

There are 250 active organizations on campus, including a drama/theater group, newspaper, radio station, television station, choral group, and marching band. 23% of eligible men and 19% of eligible women are members of national **fraternities**, national **sororities**, and local sororities.

Truman State is a member of the NCAA (Division II). **Intercollegiate sports** (some offering scholarships) include baseball (m), basketball, cross-country running, football (m), golf, soccer, softball (w), swimming and diving, tennis, track and field, volleyball (w), wrestling (m).

Campus Safety

Student safety services include patrols by commissioned officers, late-night transport/escort service, 24-hour emergency telephone alarm devices, 24-hour patrols by trained security personnel, and student patrols.

Applying

Truman State requires an essay, SAT or ACT, a high school transcript. It recommends ACT, an interview, and a minimum high school GPA of 3.0. Application deadline: rolling admissions; 4/1 priority date for financial aid. Deferred admission is possible.

Getting Accepted

4,280 applied
79% were accepted
1,334 enrolled (40% of accepted)
50% from top tenth of their h.s. class
3.76 average high school GPA
Mean SAT critical reading score: 620
Mean SAT math score: 630
Mean ACT score: 27
62% had SAT critical reading scores over 600
63% had SAT math scores over 600
80% had ACT scores over 24
27% had SAT critical reading scores over 700
22% had SAT math scores over 700
26% had ACT scores over 30
23 National Merit Scholars
156 valedictorians

Graduation and After

45% graduated in 4 years
19% graduated in 5 years
4% graduated in 6 years
48.35% had job offers within 6 months
242 organizations recruited on campus

Financial Matters

$6685 resident tuition and fees (2008–09)
$11,536 nonresident tuition and fees (2008–09)
$5910 room and board
80% average percent of need met
$6848 average financial aid amount received per undergraduate (2006–07)

Getting Accepted
15,619 applied
26% were accepted
1,297 enrolled (33% of accepted)
85% from top tenth of their h.s. class
Mean SAT critical reading score: 702
Mean SAT math score: 709
Mean SAT writing score: 708
Mean ACT score: 31
94% had SAT critical reading scores over 600
95% had SAT math scores over 600
96% had SAT writing scores over 600
62% had SAT critical reading scores over 700
62% had SAT math scores over 700
65% had SAT writing scores over 700

Graduation and After
86% graduated in 4 years
5% graduated in 5 years
1% graduated in 6 years
225 organizations recruited on campus

Financial Matters
$38,840 tuition and fees (2008–09)
$10,518 room and board
100% average percent of need met
$27,828 average financial aid amount received
per undergraduate (2007–08 estimated)

TUFTS UNIVERSITY

SUBURBAN SETTING ■ PRIVATE ■ INDEPENDENT ■ COED
MEDFORD, MASSACHUSETTS

Web site: www.tufts.edu
Contact: Mr. Lee Coffin, Office of Undergraduate Admissions, Bendetson
Hall, Medford, MA 02155
Telephone: 617-627-3170
Fax: 617-627-3860
E-mail: admissions.inquiry@ase.tufts.edu

Academics

Tufts awards bachelor's, master's, doctoral, and first-professional **degrees** and post-master's certificates. **Challenging opportunities** include advanced placement credit, student-designed majors, an honors program, double majors, independent study, and a senior project. Special programs include internships, summer session for credit, off-campus study, study-abroad, and Army, Navy, and Air Force ROTC.

The most frequently chosen **baccalaureate** fields are social sciences, engineering, and visual and performing arts. A complete listing of majors at Tufts appears in the Majors by College index beginning on page 469.

The **faculty** at Tufts has 640 full-time members, 94% with terminal degrees. The student-faculty ratio is 7:1.

Students of Tufts

The student body totals 10,030, of whom 5,044 are undergraduates. 50.9% are women and 49.1% are men. Students come from 52 states and territories and 78 other countries. 25% are from Massachusetts. 5.9% are international students. 6.2% are African American, 0.3% American Indian, 13% Asian American, and 6.1% Hispanic American. 97% returned for their sophomore year.

Facilities and Resources

300 **computers/terminals** are available on campus for general student use. Students can access the following: computer help desk, free student e-mail accounts, online (class) registration, online (class) schedules. Campuswide network is available. 100% of college-owned or -operated housing units are wired for high-speed Internet access. Wireless service is available via classrooms, computer centers, computer labs, learning centers, libraries, student centers. The 2 **libraries** have 1,746,659 books and 4,341 subscriptions.

Campus Life

There are 200 active organizations on campus, including a drama/theater group, newspaper, radio station, television station, choral group, and marching band. 15% of eligible men and 4% of eligible women are members of national **fraternities** and national **sororities**.

Tufts is a member of the NCAA (Division III). **Intercollegiate sports** include baseball (m), basketball, crew, cross-country running, fencing (w), field hockey (w), football (m), golf (m), ice hockey (m), lacrosse, sailing, soccer, softball (w), squash, swimming and diving, tennis, track and field, volleyball (w).

Campus Safety

Student safety services include security lighting, call boxes to campus police, late-night transport/escort service, 24-hour emergency telephone alarm devices, 24-hour patrols by trained security personnel, and electronically operated dormitory entrances.

Applying

Tufts requires an essay, SAT and SAT Subject Tests or ACT, a high school transcript, and 1 recommendation. It recommends an interview. Application deadline: 1/1; 2/15 for financial aid. Early and deferred admission are possible.

Tulane University

Urban setting ■ Private ■ Independent ■ Coed
New Orleans, Louisiana

Web site: www.tulane.edu
Contact: Mr. Earl Retif, Vice President for Enrollment Management and University Registrar, Office of Admissions, 210 Gibson Hall, New Orleans, LA 70118
Telephone: 504-865-5731 or toll-free 800-873-9283
Fax: 504-862-8715
E-mail: undergrad.admission@tulane.edu

Academics

Tulane awards associate, bachelor's, master's, doctoral, and first-professional **degrees** and post-bachelor's certificates. **Challenging opportunities** include advanced placement credit, accelerated degree programs, student-designed majors, freshman honors college, an honors program, double majors, independent study, and a senior project. Special programs include cooperative education, internships, summer session for credit, off-campus study, study-abroad, and Army, Navy, and Air Force ROTC.

The most frequently chosen **baccalaureate** fields are business/marketing, social sciences, and psychology. A complete listing of majors at Tulane appears in the Majors by College index beginning on page 469.

The **faculty** at Tulane has 897 full-time members, 92% with terminal degrees. The student-faculty ratio is 9:1.

Students of Tulane

The student body totals 11,157, of whom 6,749 are undergraduates. 54.2% are women and 45.8% are men. Students come from 53 states and territories and 79 other countries. 33% are from Louisiana. 3% are international students. 8.7% are African American, 1.6% American Indian, 4.8% Asian American, and 4.1% Hispanic American. 87% returned for their sophomore year.

Facilities and Resources

556 **computers/terminals** are available on campus for general student use. Students can access the following: computer help desk, free student e-mail accounts, online (class) grades, online (class) registration, online (class) schedules. Campuswide network is available. 100% of college-owned or -operated housing units are wired for high-speed Internet access. Wireless service is available via entire campus. The 9 **libraries** have 3,106,645 books and 34,820 subscriptions.

Campus Life

There are 250 active organizations on campus, including a drama/theater group, newspaper, radio station, television station, choral group, and marching band. 20% of eligible men and 22% of eligible women are members of national **fraternities** and national **sororities**.

Tulane is a member of the NCAA (Division I). **Intercollegiate sports** (some offering scholarships) include baseball (m), basketball, cross-country running, football (m), golf (w), soccer (w), swimming and diving (w), tennis, track and field (w), volleyball (w).

Campus Safety

Student safety services include on and off-campus shuttle service, crime prevention programs, lighted pathways, late-night transport/escort service, 24-hour emergency telephone alarm devices, 24-hour patrols by trained security personnel, student patrols, and electronically operated dormitory entrances.

Applying

Tulane requires an essay, SAT or ACT, a high school transcript, and 1 recommendation. Application deadline: 1/15; 2/1 for financial aid, with a 2/1 priority date. Deferred admission is possible.

Getting Accepted
34,125 applied
27% were accepted
1,560 enrolled (17% of accepted)
59% from top tenth of their h.s. class
3.49 average high school GPA
Mean SAT critical reading score: 675
Mean SAT math score: 660
Mean SAT writing score: 680
Mean ACT score: 31
90% had SAT critical reading scores over 600
74% had SAT math scores over 600
86% had SAT writing scores over 600
97% had ACT scores over 24
43% had SAT critical reading scores over 700
24% had SAT math scores over 700
32% had SAT writing scores over 700
54% had ACT scores over 30

Graduation and After
59% graduated in 4 years
14% graduated in 5 years
2% graduated in 6 years
30% had job offers within 6 months
133 organizations recruited on campus

Financial Matters
$38,664 tuition and fees (2009–10)
$9296 room and board
93% average percent of need met
$30,721 average financial aid amount received per undergraduate (2006–07)

Union College

Suburban setting ■ Private ■ Independent Religious ■ Coed
Lincoln, Nebraska

Web site: www.ucollege.edu
Contact: Huda McClelland, Director of Admissions, 3800 South 48th Street, Lincoln, NE 68506
Telephone: 402-486-2504 or toll-free 800-228-4600 (out-of-state)
Fax: 402-486-2895
E-mail: ucenroll@ucollege.edu

Getting Accepted
169 enrolled
13% from top tenth of their h.s. class
3.43 average high school GPA
Mean ACT score: 23
44% had ACT scores over 24
7% had ACT scores over 30

Graduation and After
89% had job offers within 6 months
96 organizations recruited on campus

Financial Matters
$16,920 tuition and fees (2008–09)
$5610 room and board
71% average percent of need met
$12,234 average financial aid amount received per undergraduate (2005–06)

Academics

Union College awards associate, bachelor's, and master's **degrees**. **Challenging opportunities** include advanced placement credit, accelerated degree programs, student-designed majors, an honors program, double majors, independent study, and a senior project. Special programs include cooperative education, internships, summer session for credit, off-campus study, and study-abroad.

The most frequently chosen **baccalaureate** fields are health professions and related sciences, business/marketing, and education. A complete listing of majors at Union College appears in the Majors by College index beginning on page 469.

The **faculty** at Union College has 58 full-time members, 41% with terminal degrees. The student-faculty ratio is 13:1.

Students of Union College

The student body totals 914, of whom 843 are undergraduates. 56.9% are women and 43.1% are men. Students come from 46 states and territories and 23 other countries. 18% are from Nebraska. 9.2% are international students. 3% are African American, 1.4% American Indian, 3.2% Asian American, and 6.3% Hispanic American. 66% returned for their sophomore year.

Facilities and Resources

520 **computers/terminals** are available on campus for general student use. Campuswide network is available. The **library** has 147,813 books and 1,357 subscriptions.

Campus Life

Active organizations on campus include a drama/theater group, newspaper, and choral group. No national or local **fraternities** or **sororities**.

Intercollegiate sports include basketball, volleyball (w).

Campus Safety

Student safety services include late-night transport/escort service, 24-hour emergency telephone alarm devices, and student patrols.

Applying

Union College requires SAT or ACT, a high school transcript, 3 recommendations, and a minimum high school GPA of 2.5, and in some cases an essay and an interview. Application deadline: rolling admissions.

UNION COLLEGE

URBAN SETTING ■ PRIVATE ■ INDEPENDENT ■ COED
SCHENECTADY, NEW YORK

Web site: www.union.edu
Contact: Dean of Admissions, Grant Hall, Schenectady, NY 02308
Telephone: 518-388-6112 or toll-free 888-843-6688 (in-state)
Fax: 518-388-6986
E-mail: admissions@union.edu

Academics

Union College awards bachelor's **degrees**. **Challenging opportunities** include advanced placement credit, accelerated degree programs, student-designed majors, an honors program, double majors, independent study, and a senior project. Special programs include internships, summer session for credit, off-campus study, study-abroad, and Army, Navy, and Air Force ROTC.

The most frequently chosen **baccalaureate** fields are social sciences, engineering, and psychology. A complete listing of majors at Union College appears in the Majors by College index beginning on page 469.

The **faculty** at Union College has 197 full-time members, 95% with terminal degrees. The student-faculty ratio is 10:1.

Students of Union College

The student body is made up of 2,240 undergraduates. 48.8% are women and 51.2% are men. Students come from 40 states and territories and 33 other countries. 41% are from New York. 2.8% are international students. 3.7% are African American, 0.2% American Indian, 5.7% Asian American, and 4.5% Hispanic American. 93% returned for their sophomore year.

Facilities and Resources

504 **computers/terminals** and 3,032 ports are available on campus for general student use. Students can access the following: campus intranet, computer help desk, free student e-mail accounts, online (class) grades, online (class) registration, online (class) schedules, multimedia lab. Campuswide network is available. 100% of college-owned or -operated housing units are wired for high-speed Internet access. Wireless service is available via classrooms, computer centers, computer labs, dorm rooms, learning centers, libraries, student centers. The **library** has 624,475 books and 5,534 subscriptions.

Campus Life

There are 105 active organizations on campus, including a drama/theater group, newspaper, radio station, television station, and choral group. 29% of eligible men and 22% of eligible women are members of national **fraternities**, national **sororities**, local fraternities, local sororities, and theme houses.

Union College is a member of the NCAA (Division III). **Intercollegiate sports** include baseball (m), basketball, crew, cross-country running, field hockey (w), football (m), ice hockey, lacrosse, soccer, softball (w), swimming and diving, tennis, track and field, volleyball (w).

Campus Safety

Student safety services include awareness programs, bicycle patrol, shuttle service, late-night transport/escort service, 24-hour emergency telephone alarm devices, 24-hour patrols by trained security personnel, and electronically operated dormitory entrances.

Applying

Union College requires an essay, a high school transcript, and 2 recommendations, and in some cases SAT and SAT Subject Tests or ACT. It recommends an interview. Application deadline: 1/15; 2/1 for financial aid. Early and deferred admission are possible.

Union College, one of the oldest nondenominational colleges in America, is located in the small city of Schenectady, about 3 hours north of New York City. Its distinctive curriculum combines the traditional liberal arts with engineering study. Three basic tenets undergird a Union education: commitments to lifelong learning, the liberal arts, and close working relationships between students and faculty members. People from many different backgrounds come to Union, attracted by these values and the opportunities they imply: small classes, excellent access to superb facilities, a caring and committed faculty, and an academic program of depth and diversity.

Getting Accepted
5,271 applied
39% were accepted
580 enrolled (28% of accepted)
57% from top tenth of their h.s. class
3.5 average high school GPA
Mean SAT critical reading score: 620
Mean SAT math score: 650
Mean SAT writing score: 630
Mean ACT score: 28
67% had SAT critical reading scores over 600
78% had SAT math scores over 600
65% had SAT writing scores over 600
97% had ACT scores over 24
10% had SAT critical reading scores over 700
19% had SAT math scores over 700
11% had SAT writing scores over 700
32% had ACT scores over 30
9 valedictorians

Graduation and After
77% graduated in 4 years
6% graduated in 5 years
1% graduated in 6 years
55% had job offers within 6 months
108 organizations recruited on campus

Financial Matters
$48,552 comprehensive fee (2008–09)
97% average percent of need met
$28,800 average financial aid amount received per undergraduate (2006–07)

Union University enjoys a national reputation for integrating rigorous academics with an authentic Christian commitment. The University's acclaimed faculty members work closely with students, who pursue excellence in more than 100 fields of study. This personal approach is possible because of an 11:1 student-teacher ratio and the faculty's focus on classroom instruction. Union is nationally recognized for its community service programs. It also offers outstanding placement records for employment or graduate study and opportunities to study abroad. Students prepare for the changes, challenges, and opportunities of a competitive world as they strengthen their Christian faith. To find out more about Union University, students should visit http://www.uu.edu.

Getting Accepted
1,164 applied
82% were accepted
462 enrolled (48% of accepted)
39% from top tenth of their h.s. class
3.52 average high school GPA
Mean SAT critical reading score: 583
Mean SAT math score: 573
Mean ACT score: 25
51% had SAT critical reading scores over 600
38% had SAT math scores over 600
60% had ACT scores over 24
14% had SAT critical reading scores over 700
11% had SAT math scores over 700
21% had ACT scores over 30
10 National Merit Scholars
27 valedictorians

Graduation and After
64% graduated in 4 years
11% graduated in 5 years
1% graduated in 6 years
80% had job offers within 6 months
60 organizations recruited on campus

Financial Matters
$19,610 tuition and fees (2008–09)
$6500 room and board
$17,421 average financial aid amount received per undergraduate (2007–08 estimated)

UNION UNIVERSITY

SMALL-TOWN SETTING ■ PRIVATE ■ INDEPENDENT RELIGIOUS ■ COED
JACKSON, TENNESSEE

Web site: www.uu.edu
Contact: Mr. Robbie Graves, Director of Enrollment Services, 1050 Union University Drive, Jackson, TN 38305-3697
Telephone: 731-661-5590 or toll-free 800-33-UNION
Fax: 731-661-5017
E-mail: cgraves@uu.edu

Academics

Union awards associate, bachelor's, master's, doctoral, and first-professional **degrees** and post-master's certificates. **Challenging opportunities** include advanced placement credit, accelerated degree programs, an honors program, double majors, independent study, and a senior project. Special programs include cooperative education, internships, summer session for credit, off-campus study, and study-abroad.

The most frequently chosen **baccalaureate** fields are health professions and related sciences, interdisciplinary studies, and education. A complete listing of majors at Union appears in the Majors by College index beginning on page 469.

The **faculty** at Union has 177 full-time members, 83% with terminal degrees. The student-faculty ratio is 12:1.

Students of Union

The student body totals 3,700, of whom 2,574 are undergraduates. 59% are women and 41% are men. Students come from 44 states and territories and 36 other countries. 70% are from Tennessee. 2.4% are international students. 10.8% are African American, 0.1% American Indian, 1.4% Asian American, and 1.2% Hispanic American. 93% returned for their sophomore year.

Facilities and Resources

236 **computers/terminals** are available on campus for general student use. Students can access the following: campus intranet, computer help desk, free student e-mail accounts, online (class) grades, online (class) registration, online (class) schedules. Campuswide network is available. 100% of college-owned or -operated housing units are wired for high-speed Internet access. Wireless service is available via entire campus. The 2 **libraries** have 155,500 books and 20,324 subscriptions.

Campus Life

There are 52 active organizations on campus, including a drama/theater group, newspaper, and choral group. 6% of eligible men and 10% of eligible women are members of national **fraternities** and national **sororities**.

Union is a member of the NAIA and NCCAA. **Intercollegiate sports** (some offering scholarships) include baseball (m), basketball, cheerleading (w), cross-country running, golf (m), soccer, softball (w), track and field, volleyball (w).

Campus Safety

Student safety services include late-night transport/escort service, 24-hour emergency telephone alarm devices, 24-hour patrols by trained security personnel, and student patrols.

Applying

Union requires SAT or ACT, a high school transcript, and a minimum high school GPA of 2.5, and in some cases 3 recommendations. It recommends an essay, SAT Subject Tests, and an interview. Application deadline: rolling admissions; 3/1 priority date for financial aid. Early and deferred admission are possible.

UNITED STATES AIR FORCE ACADEMY

SUBURBAN SETTING ■ PUBLIC ■ FEDERALLY SUPPORTED ■ COED, PRIMARILY MEN
USAF ACADEMY, COLORADO

Web site: www.usafa.edu
Contact: Dr. Phillip Prosseda, Chief, Selections Division, HQ USAFA/RR,
   2304 Cadet Drive, Suite 2400, USAF Academy, CO 80840-5025
Telephone: 719-333-2520 or toll-free 800-443-9266
Fax: 719-333-3012
E-mail: rr_apps@usafa.af.mil

SPONSOR

> The Air Force Academy challenge requires a well-rounded academic, physical, and leadership background. Cadets must accept discipline, be competitive, and have a desire to serve others with a sense of duty and integrity. Applicants should prepare early to meet the admission requirements, competition, and demands they will face at the Academy.

Academics

USAFA awards bachelor's **degrees. Challenging opportunities** include advanced placement credit, student-designed majors, an honors program, double majors, independent study, and a senior project. Special programs include internships, summer session for credit, and study-abroad.

The most frequently chosen **baccalaureate** fields are engineering, social sciences, and business/marketing. A complete listing of majors at USAFA appears in the Majors by College index beginning on page 469.

The **faculty** at USAFA has 519 full-time members, 50% with terminal degrees. The student-faculty ratio is 9:1.

Students of USAFA

The student body is made up of 4,537 undergraduates. 19.2% are women and 80.8% are men. Students come from 51 states and territories and 14 other countries. 6% are from Colorado. 1.2% are international students. 4.7% are African American, 1.5% American Indian, 8.5% Asian American, and 7.4% Hispanic American. 93% returned for their sophomore year.

Facilities and Resources

500 **computers/terminals** are available on campus for general student use. Students can access the following: campus intranet, computer help desk, free student e-mail accounts, online (class) grades, online (class) registration, online (class) schedules. Campuswide network is available. Wireless service is available via classrooms, computer centers, computer labs, learning centers, libraries, student centers. The 2 **libraries** have 566,000 books and 38,000 subscriptions.

Campus Life

There are 77 active organizations on campus, including a drama/theater group, radio station, choral group, and marching band. No national or local **fraternities** or **sororities**.

USAFA is a member of the NCAA (Division I). **Intercollegiate sports** include baseball (m), basketball, cheerleading, cross-country running, fencing, football (m), golf (m), gymnastics, ice hockey (m), lacrosse (m), riflery, soccer, swimming and diving, tennis, track and field, volleyball (w), water polo (m), wrestling (m).

Campus Safety

Student safety services include self-defense education, well-lit campus, late-night transport/escort service, 24-hour emergency telephone alarm devices, and 24-hour patrols by trained security personnel.

Applying

USAFA requires an essay, SAT or ACT, a high school transcript, an interview, authorized nomination, and a minimum high school GPA of 2.0. It recommends 3 recommendations. Application deadline: 1/31.

Getting Accepted
9,001 applied
18% were accepted
1,286 enrolled (78% of accepted)
52% from top tenth of their h.s. class
3.86 average high school GPA
Mean SAT critical reading score: 629
Mean SAT math score: 663
Mean SAT writing score: 642
Mean ACT score: 29
77% had SAT critical reading scores over 600
88% had SAT math scores over 600
59% had SAT writing scores over 600
99% had ACT scores over 24
19% had SAT critical reading scores over 700
27% had SAT math scores over 700
11% had SAT writing scores over 700
50% had ACT scores over 30
82 National Merit Scholars
13 class presidents
38 valedictorians

Graduation and After
72% graduated in 4 years
2% graduated in 5 years
1% graduated in 6 years
100% had job offers within 6 months
1 organization recruited on campus

United States Coast Guard Academy

Suburban setting ■ Public ■ Federally supported ■ Coed
New London, Connecticut

Getting Accepted
1,370 applied
22% were accepted
271 enrolled (92% of accepted)
52% from top tenth of their h.s. class
3.74 average high school GPA
Mean SAT critical reading score: 617
Mean SAT math score: 639
Mean ACT score: 27
62% had SAT critical reading scores over 600
79% had SAT math scores over 600
91% had ACT scores over 24
13% had SAT critical reading scores over 700
17% had SAT math scores over 700
21% had ACT scores over 30
24 class presidents
10 valedictorians

Graduation and After
68% graduated in 4 years
2% graduated in 5 years
100% had job offers within 6 months
1 organization recruited on campus

Web site: www.uscga.edu
Contact: Capt. Susan Bibeau, Director of Admissions, 31 Mohegan Avenue, New London, CT 06320-4195
Telephone: 860-444-8500 or toll-free 800-883-8724
Fax: 860-701-6700
E-mail: admissions@uscga.edu

Academics

USCGA awards bachelor's **degrees. Challenging opportunities** include an honors program, double majors, independent study, and a senior project. Special programs include internships, summer session for credit, and off-campus study.

The most frequently chosen **baccalaureate** fields are engineering, social sciences, and business/marketing. A complete listing of majors at USCGA appears in the Majors by College index beginning on page 469.

The **faculty** at USCGA has 114 full-time members, 53% with terminal degrees. The student-faculty ratio is 8:1.

Students of USCGA

The student body is made up of 973 undergraduates. 27% are women and 73% are men. Students come from 51 states and territories and 10 other countries. 6% are from Connecticut. 1.2% are international students. 2.3% are African American, 0.2% American Indian, 4.6% Asian American, and 5.7% Hispanic American. 96% returned for their sophomore year.

Facilities and Resources

325 **computers/terminals** are available on campus for general student use. Students can access the following: campus intranet, computer help desk, free student e-mail accounts, online (class) grades, online (class) registration, online (class) schedules. Campuswide network is available. 100% of college-owned or -operated housing units are wired for high-speed Internet access. Wireless service is available via entire campus. The **library** has 155,000 books and 514 subscriptions.

Campus Life

Active organizations on campus include a drama/theater group, choral group, and marching band. No national or local **fraternities** or **sororities**.

USCGA is a member of the NCAA (Division III). **Intercollegiate sports** include baseball (m), basketball, crew, cross-country running, football (m), riflery, sailing, soccer, softball (w), swimming and diving, tennis (m), track and field, volleyball (w), wrestling (m).

Campus Safety

Student safety services include 24-hour patrols by trained security personnel and student patrols.

Applying

USCGA requires an essay, SAT or ACT, a high school transcript, 3 recommendations, and medical exam, physical fitness exam. It recommends an interview. Application deadline: 2/1.

UNITED STATES MERCHANT MARINE ACADEMY

SUBURBAN SETTING ■ PUBLIC ■ FEDERALLY SUPPORTED ■ COED
KINGS POINT, NEW YORK

SPONSOR

Web site: www.usmma.edu
Contact: Capt. Robert E. Johnson, Director of Admissions and Financial Aid,
300 Steamboat Road, Kings Point, NY 11024-1699
Telephone: 516-773-5391 or toll-free 866-546-4778
Fax: 516-773-5390
E-mail: admissions@usmma.edu

Academics
USMMA awards bachelor's and master's **degrees. Challenging opportunities** include
an honors program and a senior project. Internships is a special program.

The most frequently chosen **baccalaureate** fields are transportation and materials
moving and engineering. A complete listing of majors at USMMA appears in the Majors
by College index beginning on page 469.

The **faculty** at USMMA has 95 full-time members, 100% with terminal degrees.
The student-faculty ratio is 11:1.

Students of USMMA
The student body totals 1,003, of whom 985 are undergraduates. 12.1% are women and
87.9% are men. Students come from 50 states and territories and 7 other countries. 10%
are from New York. 2.7% are international students. 2.8% are African American, 0.7%
American Indian, 5% Asian American, and 4.9% Hispanic American. 92% returned for
their sophomore year.

Facilities and Resources
1,200 **computers/terminals** are available on campus for general student use. Students
can access the following: campus intranet, computer help desk, free student e-mail
accounts, engineering and economics software. Campuswide network is available. The
library has 187,191 books and 961 subscriptions.

Campus Life
There are 45 active organizations on campus, including a drama/theater group,
newspaper, choral group, and marching band. No national or local **fraternities** or
sororities.

USMMA is a member of the NCAA (Division III). **Intercollegiate sports** include
baseball (m), basketball, crew, cross-country running, football (m), golf, lacrosse (m),
sailing, soccer (m), softball (w), swimming and diving, tennis, track and field, volleyball
(w), wrestling (m).

Campus Safety
Student safety services include 24-hour patrols by trained security personnel.

Applying
USMMA requires an essay, SAT or ACT, a high school transcript, and 3 recommendations. It recommends an interview. Application deadline: 3/1.

The United States Merchant Marine Academy is a four-year federal service academy dedicated to educating and training young men and women as officers in America's maritime shipping industry (merchant marine) and U.S. Navy Reserve and as future leaders of the maritime and transportation industries. The Academy, in Kings Point, Long Island, offers accredited programs in marine transportation and marine engineering, leading to a B.S. degree, a U.S. merchant marine officer's license, and a Navy Reserve commission. Students spend three trimesters at sea aboard U.S. merchant ships during their sophomore and junior years as part of their training.

Getting Accepted
1,734 applied
18% were accepted
307 enrolled (100% of accepted)
18% from top tenth of their h.s. class
3.6 average high school GPA
Mean SAT critical reading score: 579
Mean SAT math score: 622
Mean ACT score: 27
43% had SAT critical reading scores over 600
72% had SAT math scores over 600
98% had ACT scores over 24
8% had SAT critical reading scores over 700
10% had SAT math scores over 700
9% had ACT scores over 30
15 National Merit Scholars
19 class presidents
9 valedictorians

Graduation and After
95% had job offers within 6 months
70 organizations recruited on campus

UNITED STATES MILITARY ACADEMY

SMALL-TOWN SETTING ■ PUBLIC ■ FEDERALLY SUPPORTED ■ COED
WEST POINT, NEW YORK

Web site: www.usma.edu
Contact: Col. Deborah J. McDonald, Director of Admissions, Building 606,
West Point, NY 10996
Telephone: 845-938-4041
E-mail: 8dad@sunams.usma.army.mil

> West Point is all about leadership. For more than 200 years, West Point has developed many of the nation's finest leaders. The academy builds leaders of character while developing the foundation for career success. West Point offers a premier undergraduate education, develops strong leadership skills, and provides unique and unforgettable life experiences. West Point's graduates are prepared for a career of professional excellence and service to the nation as officers in the United States Army. West Point is tough but well worth the challenge. One cadet may have said it best: "The person I have become is so much better than the person who first came here."

Getting Accepted
10,958 applied
14% were accepted
1,194 enrolled (77% of accepted)
50% from top tenth of their h.s. class
Mean SAT critical reading score: 630
Mean SAT math score: 648
Mean ACT score: 29
66% had SAT critical reading scores over 600
77% had SAT math scores over 600
97% had ACT scores over 24
20% had SAT critical reading scores over 700
25% had SAT math scores over 700
34% had ACT scores over 30
226 National Merit Scholars
225 class presidents
85 valedictorians

Graduation and After
100% had job offers within 6 months

Academics

West Point awards bachelor's **degrees**. **Challenging opportunities** include advanced placement credit and double majors. Special programs include summer session for credit and off-campus study.

The most frequently chosen **baccalaureate** fields are engineering, area and ethnic studies, and computer and information sciences. A complete listing of majors at West Point appears in the Majors by College index beginning on page 469.

The **faculty** at West Point has 604 full-time members, 63% with terminal degrees. The student-faculty ratio is 7:1.

Students of West Point

The student body is made up of 4,231 undergraduates. 14.9% are women and 85.1% are men. Students come from 53 states and territories and 25 other countries. 8% are from New York. 1.3% are international students. 6.1% are African American, 0.9% American Indian, 6.8% Asian American, and 6.6% Hispanic American.

Facilities and Resources

5,500 **computers/terminals** are available on campus for general student use. Students can access the following: online (class) registration. Campuswide network is available. The 2 **libraries** have 457,340 books and 2,220 subscriptions.

Campus Life

There are 120 active organizations on campus, including a drama/theater group, radio station, and choral group. No national or local **fraternities** or **sororities**.

West Point is a member of the NCAA (Division I). **Intercollegiate sports** include baseball (m), basketball, cross-country running, football (m), golf (m), gymnastics (m), ice hockey (m), lacrosse (m), soccer, softball (w), swimming and diving, tennis, track and field, volleyball (w), wrestling (m).

Campus Safety

Student safety services include late-night transport/escort service, 24-hour emergency telephone alarm devices, 24-hour patrols by trained security personnel, and student patrols.

Applying

West Point requires an essay, SAT or ACT, a high school transcript, 4 recommendations, and medical examination, authorized nomination. It recommends an interview. Application deadline: 2/28.

United States Naval Academy

SMALL-TOWN SETTING ■ PUBLIC ■ FEDERALLY SUPPORTED ■ COED, PRIMARILY MEN
ANNAPOLIS, MARYLAND

Web site: www.usna.edu
Contact: 117 Decatur Road, United States Naval Academy, Annapolis, MD 21402
Telephone: 410-293-4361
Fax: 410-293-4348
E-mail: webmail@usna.edu

Academics

Naval Academy awards bachelor's **degrees. Challenging opportunities** include advanced placement credit, an honors program, double majors, independent study, and a senior project. Special programs include summer session for credit and study-abroad.

The most frequently chosen **baccalaureate** fields are engineering, social sciences, and physical sciences. A complete listing of majors at Naval Academy appears in the Majors by College index beginning on page 469.

The **faculty** at Naval Academy has 526 full-time members, 67% with terminal degrees. The student-faculty ratio is 9:1.

Students of Naval Academy

The student body is made up of 4,489 undergraduates. 20.3% are women and 79.7% are men. Students come from 54 states and territories and 27 other countries. 4% are from Maryland. 1% are international students. 4.3% are African American, 0.5% American Indian, 3.4% Asian American, and 10.5% Hispanic American. 96% returned for their sophomore year.

Facilities and Resources

6,100 **computers/terminals** are available on campus for general student use. Students can access the following: campus intranet, computer help desk, free student e-mail accounts, online (class) grades, online (class) registration, online (class) schedules. Campuswide network is available. 100% of college-owned or -operated housing units are wired for high-speed Internet access. The **library** has 701,505 books and 1,979 subscriptions.

Campus Life

There are 75 active organizations on campus, including a drama/theater group, radio station, choral group, and marching band. No national or local **fraternities** or **sororities**.

Naval Academy is a member of the NCAA (Division I). **Intercollegiate sports** include baseball (m), basketball, crew, cross-country running, football (m), golf (m), gymnastics (m), lacrosse, riflery, sailing, soccer, squash (m), swimming and diving, tennis, track and field, volleyball (w), water polo (m), wrestling (m).

Campus Safety

Student safety services include campus gate security, 24-hour emergency telephone alarm devices, 24-hour patrols by trained security personnel, and student patrols.

Applying

Naval Academy requires an essay, SAT or ACT, a high school transcript, an interview, 2 recommendations, and authorized nomination. Application deadline: 1/31.

Getting Accepted
10,960 applied
12% were accepted
1,232 enrolled (98% of accepted)
56% from top tenth of their h.s. class
Mean SAT critical reading score: 639
Mean SAT math score: 661
63% had SAT critical reading scores over 600
77% had SAT math scores over 600
17% had SAT critical reading scores over 700
27% had SAT math scores over 700

Graduation and After
84% graduated in 4 years
100% had job offers within 6 months
2 organizations recruited on campus

Financial Matters
$0 comprehensive fee (2009–10)

UNIVERSITY AT BUFFALO, THE STATE UNIVERSITY OF NEW YORK

SUBURBAN SETTING ■ PUBLIC ■ STATE-SUPPORTED ■ COED
BUFFALO, NEW YORK

Web site: www.buffalo.edu
Contact: Ms. Patricia Armstrong, Director of Admissions, 12 Capen Hall, North Campus, Buffalo, NY 14260-1660
Telephone: 716-645-6900 or toll-free 888-UB-ADMIT
Fax: 716-645-6411
E-mail: ub-admissions@buffalo.edu

The University at Buffalo (UB) is New York's premier public research university. UB has distinguished itself by cultivating a vibrant academic environment where undergraduates work side by side with faculty members who are on the cutting edge of their fields. UB's diverse community of scholars is actively engaged in the pursuit and creation of knowledge, and UB's academic initiatives focused on collaborative and experiential learning encourage students to explore the possibilities offered by UB's extensive resources. From architecture to biophysics to media study, UB students are well positioned at the forefront of innovation and research.

Getting Accepted
19,784 applied
52% were accepted
3,390 enrolled (33% of accepted)
25% from top tenth of their h.s. class
3.4 average high school GPA
Mean SAT critical reading score: 553
Mean SAT math score: 595
Mean ACT score: 25
29% had SAT critical reading scores over 600
52% had SAT math scores over 600
71% had ACT scores over 24
4% had SAT critical reading scores over 700
9% had SAT math scores over 700
10% had ACT scores over 30
17 valedictorians

Graduation and After
40% graduated in 4 years
18% graduated in 5 years
7% graduated in 6 years
150 organizations recruited on campus

Financial Matters
$6595 resident tuition and fees (2008–09)
$13,675 nonresident tuition and fees (2008–09)
$9058 room and board
70% average percent of need met
$7368 average financial aid amount received per undergraduate (2006–07)

Academics

UB awards bachelor's, master's, doctoral, and first-professional **degrees** and post-master's and first-professional certificates. **Challenging opportunities** include advanced placement credit, accelerated degree programs, student-designed majors, freshman honors college, an honors program, double majors, independent study, and a senior project. Special programs include cooperative education, internships, summer session for credit, off-campus study, study-abroad, and Army ROTC.

The most frequently chosen **baccalaureate** fields are business/marketing, engineering, and psychology. A complete listing of majors at UB appears in the Majors by College index beginning on page 469.

The **faculty** at UB has 1,237 full-time members, 92% with terminal degrees. The student-faculty ratio is 16:1.

Students of UB

The student body totals 28,192, of whom 19,022 are undergraduates. 46.2% are women and 53.8% are men. Students come from 44 states and territories and 81 other countries. 96% are from New York. 11.5% are international students. 7% are African American, 0.3% American Indian, 9.3% Asian American, and 3.6% Hispanic American. 87% returned for their sophomore year.

Facilities and Resources

2,000 **computers/terminals** are available on campus for general student use. Students can access the following: campus intranet, computer help desk, free student e-mail accounts, online (class) grades, online (class) registration, online (class) schedules. Campuswide network is available. 100% of college-owned or -operated housing units are wired for high-speed Internet access. Wireless service is available via entire campus. The 8 **libraries** have 3,681,102 books and 71,234 subscriptions.

Campus Life

There are 212 active organizations on campus, including a drama/theater group, newspaper, radio station, television station, choral group, and marching band. 3% of eligible men and 4% of eligible women are members of national **fraternities**, national **sororities**, local fraternities, and local sororities.

UB is a member of the NCAA (Division I). **Intercollegiate sports** (some offering scholarships) include baseball (m), basketball, crew (w), cross-country running, football (m), soccer, softball (w), swimming and diving, tennis, track and field, volleyball (w), wrestling (m).

Campus Safety

Student safety services include self-defense and awareness programs, late-night transport/escort service, 24-hour emergency telephone alarm devices, 24-hour patrols by trained security personnel, student patrols, and electronically operated dormitory entrances.

Applying

UB requires an essay, SAT or ACT, a high school transcript, and 1 recommendation, and in some cases portfolio, audition. Application deadline: 3/1 priority date for financial aid. Early admission is possible.

THE UNIVERSITY OF ALABAMA IN HUNTSVILLE

SUBURBAN SETTING ■ PUBLIC ■ STATE-SUPPORTED ■ COED
HUNTSVILLE, ALABAMA

Web site: www.uah.edu
Contact: Ms. Sandra Patterson, Director of Admissions, Enrollment Services,
    301 Sparkman Drive, Huntsville, AL 35899
Telephone: 256-824-6070 or toll-free 800-UAH-CALL
Fax: 256-824-6073
E-mail: admitme@email.uah.edu

Academics

UAH awards bachelor's, master's, and doctoral **degrees** and post-bachelor's and post-master's certificates. **Challenging opportunities** include advanced placement credit, an honors program, double majors, independent study, and a senior project. Special programs include cooperative education, internships, summer session for credit, off-campus study, study-abroad, and Army ROTC.

The most frequently chosen **baccalaureate** fields are engineering, business/marketing, and health professions and related sciences. A complete listing of majors at UAH appears in the Majors by College index beginning on page 469.

The **faculty** at UAH has 302 full-time members, 91% with terminal degrees. The student-faculty ratio is 16:1.

Students of UAH

The student body totals 7,431, of whom 5,893 are undergraduates. 47.5% are women and 52.5% are men. Students come from 42 states and territories and 76 other countries. 87% are from Alabama. 3.5% are international students. 15.4% are African American, 1.6% American Indian, 2.8% Asian American, and 2.3% Hispanic American. 77% returned for their sophomore year.

Facilities and Resources

1,153 **computers/terminals** are available on campus for general student use. Students can access the following: campus intranet, computer help desk, free student e-mail accounts, online (class) grades, online (class) registration, online (class) schedules. Campuswide network is available. 100% of college-owned or -operated housing units are wired for high-speed Internet access. Wireless service is available via classrooms, computer centers, computer labs, learning centers, libraries, student centers. The **library** has 334,612 books and 926 subscriptions.

Campus Life

There are 60 active organizations on campus, including a drama/theater group, newspaper, and choral group. 6% of eligible men and 6% of eligible women are members of national **fraternities** and national **sororities**.

UAH is a member of the NCAA (Division II). **Intercollegiate sports** (some offering scholarships) include baseball (m), basketball, cheerleading, cross-country running, ice hockey (m), soccer, softball (w), tennis, track and field, volleyball (w).

Campus Safety

Student safety services include late-night transport/escort service, 24-hour emergency telephone alarm devices, 24-hour patrols by trained security personnel, and electronically operated dormitory entrances.

Applying

UAH requires SAT or ACT and a high school transcript. Application deadline: 8/15; 7/31 for financial aid, with a 4/1 priority date. Deferred admission is possible.

Getting Accepted

1,874 applied
89% were accepted
796 enrolled (48% of accepted)
23% from top tenth of their h.s. class
3.39 average high school GPA
Mean SAT critical reading score: 554
Mean SAT math score: 563
Mean ACT score: 24
36% had SAT critical reading scores over 600
36% had SAT math scores over 600
57% had ACT scores over 24
7% had SAT critical reading scores over 700
9% had SAT math scores over 700
11% had ACT scores over 30
5 National Merit Scholars
12 valedictorians

Graduation and After

17% graduated in 4 years
22% graduated in 5 years
9% graduated in 6 years
70% had job offers within 6 months
268 organizations recruited on campus

Financial Matters

$5952 resident tuition and fees (2008–09)
$13,092 nonresident tuition and fees (2008–09)
$6526 room and board
64% average percent of need met
$7137 average financial aid amount received per undergraduate (2007–08 estimated)

THE UNIVERSITY OF ARIZONA

URBAN SETTING ■ PUBLIC ■ STATE-SUPPORTED ■ COED
TUCSON, ARIZONA

Web site: www.arizona.edu
Contact: Paul Kohn, Dean of Admissions, PO Box 210040, Tucson, AZ 85721-0040
Telephone: 520-621-3705
Fax: 520-621-9799
E-mail: admissions@arizona.edu

Getting Accepted
22,544 applied
81% were accepted
6,709 enrolled (37% of accepted)
32% from top tenth of their h.s. class
3.28 average high school GPA
Mean SAT critical reading score: 540
Mean SAT math score: 560
Mean ACT score: 24
27% had SAT critical reading scores over 600
34% had SAT math scores over 600
50% had ACT scores over 24
4% had SAT critical reading scores over 700
6% had SAT math scores over 700
7% had ACT scores over 30
63 National Merit Scholars

Graduation and After
32% graduated in 4 years
20% graduated in 5 years
5% graduated in 6 years
94% had job offers within 6 months
297 organizations recruited on campus

Financial Matters
$5542 resident tuition and fees (2008–09)
$18,676 nonresident tuition and fees (2008–09)
$7812 room and board
65% average percent of need met
$8629 average financial aid amount received per undergraduate (2006–07)

Academics
Arizona awards bachelor's, master's, doctoral, and first-professional **degrees** and post-bachelor's certificates. **Challenging opportunities** include advanced placement credit, freshman honors college, an honors program, double majors, independent study, and a senior project. Special programs include internships, summer session for credit, off-campus study, study-abroad, and Army, Navy, and Air Force ROTC.

The most frequently chosen **baccalaureate** fields are business/marketing, social sciences, and biological/life sciences. A complete listing of majors at Arizona appears in the Majors by College index beginning on page 469.

The **faculty** at Arizona has 1,593 full-time members, 92% with terminal degrees. The student-faculty ratio is 19:1.

Students of Arizona
The student body totals 38,057, of whom 29,719 are undergraduates. 52.3% are women and 47.7% are men. Students come from 55 states and territories and 119 other countries. 71% are from Arizona. 3% are international students. 3.5% are African American, 2.5% American Indian, 6.7% Asian American, and 16.8% Hispanic American. 79% returned for their sophomore year.

Facilities and Resources
3,000 **computers/terminals** are available on campus for general student use. Students can access the following: campus intranet, computer help desk, free student e-mail accounts, online (class) grades, online (class) registration, online (class) schedules. Campuswide network is available. 100% of college-owned or -operated housing units are wired for high-speed Internet access. Wireless service is available via classrooms, computer centers, computer labs, dorm rooms, learning centers, libraries, student centers. The 6 **libraries** have 5,266,051 books and 62,468 subscriptions.

Campus Life
There are 346 active organizations on campus, including a drama/theater group, newspaper, radio station, television station, choral group, and marching band. 10% of eligible men and 11% of eligible women are members of national **fraternities**, national **sororities**, local fraternities, and local sororities.

Arizona is a member of the NCAA (Division I). **Intercollegiate sports** (some offering scholarships) include baseball (m), basketball, cross-country running, football (m), golf, gymnastics (w), soccer (w), softball (w), swimming and diving, tennis, track and field, volleyball (w).

Campus Safety
Student safety services include emergency telephones, late-night transport/escort service, 24-hour patrols by trained security personnel, and student patrols.

Applying
Arizona requires an essay and a high school transcript, and in some cases an interview and a minimum high school GPA of 3.0. It recommends SAT or ACT. Application deadline: 4/1. Early admission is possible.

UNIVERSITY OF ARKANSAS

SUBURBAN SETTING ■ PUBLIC ■ STATE-SUPPORTED ■ COED
FAYETTEVILLE, ARKANSAS

Web site: www.uark.edu

Contact: Karen Hodges, Director, 232 Silas H. Hunt Hall, Office of
Admissions, Fayetteville, AR 72701-1201

Telephone: 479-575-5346 or toll-free 800-377-5346 (in-state), 800-377-8632
(out-of-state)

Fax: 479-575-7515

E-mail: uofa@uark.edu

SPONSOR

Academics

Arkansas awards bachelor's, master's, doctoral, and first-professional **degrees** and post-bachelor's and post-master's certificates. **Challenging opportunities** include advanced placement credit, accelerated degree programs, freshman honors college, an honors program, double majors, independent study, and a senior project. Special programs include cooperative education, internships, summer session for credit, study-abroad, and Army and Air Force ROTC.

The most frequently chosen **baccalaureate** fields are business/marketing, engineering, and education. A complete listing of majors at Arkansas appears in the Majors by College index beginning on page 469.

The **faculty** at Arkansas has 899 full-time members, 89% with terminal degrees. The student-faculty ratio is 17:1.

Students of Arkansas

The student body totals 19,194, of whom 15,426 are undergraduates. 48.8% are women and 51.2% are men. Students come from 50 states and territories and 106 other countries. 74% are from Arkansas. 2.7% are international students. 4.8% are African American, 2.1% American Indian, 2.8% Asian American, and 3.3% Hispanic American. 81% returned for their sophomore year.

Facilities and Resources

2,457 **computers/terminals** are available on campus for general student use. Students can access the following: online (class) registration. Campuswide network is available. 100% of college-owned or -operated housing units are wired for high-speed Internet access. Wireless service is available via entire campus. The 6 **libraries** have 1,776,460 books and 18,576 subscriptions.

Campus Life

There are 340 active organizations on campus, including a drama/theater group, newspaper, radio station, television station, choral group, and marching band. 12% of eligible men and 15% of eligible women are members of national **fraternities** and national **sororities**.

Arkansas is a member of the NCAA (Division I). **Intercollegiate sports** (some offering scholarships) include baseball (m), basketball, cross-country running, football (m), golf, gymnastics (w), soccer (w), softball (w), swimming and diving (w), tennis, track and field, volleyball (w).

Campus Safety

Student safety services include RAD (Rape Aggression Defense program), late-night transport/escort service, 24-hour emergency telephone alarm devices, 24-hour patrols by trained security personnel, student patrols, and electronically operated dormitory entrances.

Applying

Arkansas requires SAT or ACT and a high school transcript. It recommends a minimum high school GPA of 3.0. Application deadline: 8/15; 3/15 priority date for financial aid. Early admission is possible.

Getting Accepted
12,045 applied
58% were accepted
3,011 enrolled (43% of accepted)
30% from top tenth of their h.s. class
3.59 average high school GPA
Mean SAT critical reading score: 566
Mean SAT math score: 582
Mean SAT writing score: 558
Mean ACT score: 26
37% had SAT critical reading scores over 600
45% had SAT math scores over 600
9% had SAT critical reading scores over 700
9% had SAT math scores over 700
45 National Merit Scholars

Graduation and After
32% graduated in 4 years
20% graduated in 5 years
5% graduated in 6 years
300 organizations recruited on campus

Financial Matters
$6400 resident tuition and fees (2008–09)
$15,278 nonresident tuition and fees (2008–09)
$7422 room and board
73% average percent of need met
$8528 average financial aid amount received per undergraduate (2007–08 estimated)

UNIVERSITY OF CALIFORNIA, BERKELEY

Urban setting ■ Public ■ State-supported ■ Coed
Berkeley, California

Web site: www.berkeley.edu
Contact: Berkeley, CA 94720-1500
Telephone: 510-642-2316
Fax: 510-642-7333
E-mail: ouars@uclink.berkeley.edu

Getting Accepted
48,263 applied
22% were accepted
98% from top tenth of their h.s. class
3.9 average high school GPA
72% had SAT critical reading scores over 600
83% had SAT math scores over 600
76% had SAT writing scores over 600
29% had SAT critical reading scores over 700
51% had SAT math scores over 700
34% had SAT writing scores over 700

Graduation and After
64% graduated in 4 years
23% graduated in 5 years
3% graduated in 6 years
300 organizations recruited on campus

Financial Matters
$7656 resident tuition and fees (2008–09)
$28,258 nonresident tuition and fees
   (2008–09)
$14,494 room and board
88% average percent of need met
$16,095 average financial aid amount received
   per undergraduate (2007–08 estimated)

Academics
Berkeley awards bachelor's, master's, doctoral, and first-professional **degrees** and post-bachelor's certificates. **Challenging opportunities** include advanced placement credit, accelerated degree programs, student-designed majors, an honors program, double majors, independent study, and a senior project. Special programs include internships, summer session for credit, off-campus study, study-abroad, and Army, Navy, and Air Force ROTC.

The most frequently chosen **baccalaureate** fields are social sciences, biological/life sciences, and engineering. A complete listing of majors at Berkeley appears in the Majors by College index beginning on page 469.

The student-faculty ratio is 15:1.

Students of Berkeley
The student body totals 35,409, of whom 25,151 are undergraduates. Students come from 50 states and territories and 80 other countries. 90% are from California. 4.3% are international students. 3.5% are African American, 0.5% American Indian, 41.6% Asian American, and 11.6% Hispanic American.

Facilities and Resources
Students can access the following: computer help desk, free student e-mail accounts, online (class) grades, online (class) registration, online (class) schedules. Campuswide network is available. The 31 **libraries** have 15,189,997 books and 192,030 subscriptions.

Campus Life
There are 400 active organizations on campus, including a drama/theater group, newspaper, radio station, television station, choral group, and marching band. 11% of eligible men and 10% of eligible women are members of national **fraternities**, national **sororities**, local fraternities, and local sororities.

Berkeley is a member of the NCAA (Division I). **Intercollegiate sports** include baseball (m), basketball, crew, cross-country running, field hockey (w), football (m), golf, gymnastics, lacrosse (w), rugby (m), soccer, softball (w), swimming and diving, tennis, track and field, volleyball (w), water polo.

Campus Safety
Student safety services include Office of Emergency Preparedness, late-night transport/escort service, 24-hour emergency telephone alarm devices, 24-hour patrols by trained security personnel, and electronically operated dormitory entrances.

Applying
Berkeley requires an essay, SAT and SAT Subject Tests or ACT, and a high school transcript. Application deadline: 11/30; 3/2 for financial aid, with a 3/2 priority date.

University of California, Davis

Suburban setting ■ Public ■ State-supported ■ Coed
Davis, California

Web site: www.ucdavis.edu
Contact: Pamela Burnett, Director of Undergraduate Admissions,
Undergraduate Admission and Outreach Services, 178 Mrak Hall, Davis,
CA 95616
Telephone: 530-752-1011
Fax: 530-752-1280
E-mail: undergraduateadmissions@ucdavis.edu

Academics

UC Davis awards bachelor's, master's, doctoral, and first-professional **degrees** and post-bachelor's and post-master's certificates. **Challenging opportunities** include advanced placement credit, student-designed majors, freshman honors college, an honors program, double majors, independent study, and a senior project. Special programs include internships, summer session for credit, study-abroad, and Army, Navy, and Air Force ROTC.

The most frequently chosen **baccalaureate** fields are biological/life sciences, social sciences, and psychology. A complete listing of majors at UC Davis appears in the Majors by College index beginning on page 469.

The **faculty** at UC Davis has 1,586 full-time members, 98% with terminal degrees. The student-faculty ratio is 19:1.

Students of UC Davis

The student body totals 30,568, of whom 24,209 are undergraduates. 56.3% are women and 43.7% are men. Students come from 49 states and territories and 105 other countries. 98% are from California. 2% are international students. 2.9% are African American, 0.6% American Indian, 40.4% Asian American, and 12.7% Hispanic American. 90% returned for their sophomore year.

Facilities and Resources

600 **computers/terminals** are available on campus for general student use. Students can access the following: campus intranet, computer help desk, free student e-mail accounts, online (class) grades, online (class) registration, online (class) schedules, software packages. Campuswide network is available. The 6 **libraries** have 3,650,774 books and 56,268 subscriptions.

Campus Life

There are 320 active organizations on campus, including a drama/theater group, newspaper, radio station, television station, choral group, and marching band. 9% of eligible men and 8% of eligible women are members of national **fraternities**, national **sororities**, and state fraternities and sororities.

UC Davis is a member of the NCAA (Division I). **Intercollegiate sports** (some offering scholarships) include baseball (m), basketball, crew (w), cross-country running, football (m), golf, gymnastics (w), lacrosse (w), soccer, softball (w), swimming and diving, tennis, track and field, volleyball (w), water polo, wrestling (m).

Campus Safety

Student safety services include rape prevention programs, late-night transport/escort service, 24-hour emergency telephone alarm devices, 24-hour patrols by trained security personnel, student patrols, and electronically operated dormitory entrances.

Applying

UC Davis requires an essay, SAT Subject Tests, SAT or ACT, a high school transcript, high school subject requirements, and a minimum high school GPA of 2.8. Application deadline: 11/30; 3/2 priority date for financial aid.

Getting Accepted

40,605 applied
53% were accepted
4,972 enrolled (23% of accepted)
96% from top tenth of their h.s. class
3.79 average high school GPA
Mean SAT critical reading score: 565
Mean SAT math score: 605
Mean SAT writing score: 572
Mean ACT score: 25
41% had SAT critical reading scores over 600
57% had SAT math scores over 600
43% had SAT writing scores over 600
61% had ACT scores over 24
8% had SAT critical reading scores over 700
16% had SAT math scores over 700
8% had SAT writing scores over 700
13% had ACT scores over 30

Graduation and After

47% graduated in 4 years
29% graduated in 5 years
5% graduated in 6 years
91% had job offers within 6 months

Financial Matters

$8124 resident tuition and fees (2008–09)
$27,744 nonresident tuition and fees
(2008–09)
$11,533 room and board
77% average percent of need met
$13,159 average financial aid amount received
per undergraduate (2007–08 estimated)

UNIVERSITY OF CALIFORNIA, IRVINE

SUBURBAN SETTING ■ PUBLIC ■ STATE-SUPPORTED ■ COED
IRVINE, CALIFORNIA

Web site: www.uci.edu
Contact: 204 Administration, Irvine, CA 92697-1075
Telephone: 949-824-6703

Getting Accepted
42,414 applied
49% were accepted
4,583 enrolled (22% of accepted)
96% from top tenth of their h.s. class
3.82 average high school GPA
Mean SAT critical reading score: 573
Mean SAT math score: 618
Mean SAT writing score: 576
40% had SAT critical reading scores over 600
63% had SAT math scores over 600
40% had SAT writing scores over 600
8% had SAT critical reading scores over 700
18% had SAT math scores over 700
6% had SAT writing scores over 700

Graduation and After
57% graduated in 4 years
21% graduated in 5 years
3% graduated in 6 years

Financial Matters
$8775 resident tuition and fees (2008–09)
$37,238 nonresident tuition and fees
  (2008–09)
$10,527 room and board
82% average percent of need met
$14,129 average financial aid amount received
  per undergraduate (2007–08 estimated)

Academics
UC Irvine awards bachelor's, master's, doctoral, and first-professional **degrees** and post-bachelor's certificates. **Challenging opportunities** include advanced placement credit, accelerated degree programs, an honors program, double majors, independent study, and a senior project. Special programs include internships, summer session for credit, off-campus study, study-abroad, and Army and Air Force ROTC.

The most frequently chosen **baccalaureate** fields are social sciences, biological/life sciences, and psychology. A complete listing of majors at UC Irvine appears in the Majors by College index beginning on page 469.

The **faculty** at UC Irvine has 1,520 full-time members, 98% with terminal degrees. The student-faculty ratio is 19:1.

Students of UC Irvine
The student body totals 26,984, of whom 22,122 are undergraduates. 52.5% are women and 47.5% are men. Students come from 52 states and territories and 114 other countries. 97% are from California. 2.7% are international students. 2.3% are African American, 0.4% American Indian, 52.3% Asian American, and 12.9% Hispanic American. 94% returned for their sophomore year.

Facilities and Resources
1,500 **computers/terminals** are available on campus for general student use. Students can access the following: campus intranet, computer help desk, free student e-mail accounts, online (class) grades, online (class) registration, online (class) schedules. Campuswide network is available. Wireless service is available via entire campus. The 4 **libraries** have 2,700,000 books and 47,000 subscriptions.

Campus Life
There are 394 active organizations on campus, including a drama/theater group, newspaper, radio station, and choral group. 9% of eligible men and 8% of eligible women are members of national **fraternities**, national **sororities**, local fraternities, and local sororities.

UC Irvine is a member of the NCAA (Division I). **Intercollegiate sports** (some offering scholarships) include baseball (m), basketball, crew, cross-country running, golf, sailing, soccer, swimming and diving, tennis, track and field, volleyball, water polo.

Applying
UC Irvine requires an essay, SAT and SAT Subject Tests or ACT, a high school transcript, and a minimum high school GPA of 2.8. Application deadline: 11/30; 5/1 for financial aid, with a 3/2 priority date.

UNIVERSITY OF CALIFORNIA, LOS ANGELES

URBAN SETTING ■ PUBLIC ■ STATE-SUPPORTED ■ COED
LOS ANGELES, CALIFORNIA

Web site: www.ucla.edu
Contact: Dr. Vu T. Tran, Director of Undergraduate Admissions, 405 Hilgard Avenue, Box 951436, Los Angeles, CA 90095-1436
Telephone: 310-825-3101
E-mail: ugadm@saonet.ucla.edu

Academics

UCLA awards bachelor's, master's, doctoral, and first-professional **degrees**. **Challenging opportunities** include advanced placement credit, accelerated degree programs, student-designed majors, freshman honors college, an honors program, double majors, independent study, and a senior project. Special programs include internships, summer session for credit, off-campus study, study-abroad, and Army, Navy, and Air Force ROTC.

The most frequently chosen **baccalaureate** fields are social sciences, biological/life sciences, and psychology. A complete listing of majors at UCLA appears in the Majors by College index beginning on page 469.

The **faculty** at UCLA has 1,948 full-time members, 98% with terminal degrees. The student-faculty ratio is 16:1.

Students of UCLA

The student body totals 39,650, of whom 26,536 are undergraduates. 55.4% are women and 44.6% are men. Students come from 49 states and territories and 66 other countries. 94% are from California. 4.5% are international students. 3.5% are African American, 0.4% American Indian, 38.2% Asian American, and 14.9% Hispanic American. 97% returned for their sophomore year.

Facilities and Resources

4,134 **computers/terminals** are available on campus for general student use. Students can access the following: campus intranet, computer help desk, free student e-mail accounts, online (class) grades, online (class) registration, online (class) schedules. Campuswide network is available. 100% of college-owned or -operated housing units are wired for high-speed Internet access. Wireless service is available via entire campus. The 14 **libraries** have 8,157,182 books and 77,509 subscriptions.

Campus Life

There are 870 active organizations on campus, including a drama/theater group, newspaper, radio station, television station, choral group, and marching band. 13% of eligible men and 13% of eligible women are members of national **fraternities**, national **sororities**, local fraternities, and local sororities.

UCLA is a member of the NCAA (Division I). **Intercollegiate sports** (some offering scholarships) include baseball (m), basketball, crew (w), cross-country running, football (m), golf, gymnastics (w), soccer, softball (w), swimming and diving (w), tennis, track and field, volleyball, water polo.

Campus Safety

Student safety services include late-night transport/escort service, 24-hour emergency telephone alarm devices, 24-hour patrols by trained security personnel, student patrols, and electronically operated dormitory entrances.

Applying

UCLA requires an essay, SAT Subject Tests, and SAT or ACT. Application deadline: 11/30.

Getting Accepted

55,437 applied
23% were accepted
4,735 enrolled (37% of accepted)
97% from top tenth of their h.s. class
Mean SAT critical reading score: 623
Mean SAT math score: 658
Mean SAT writing score: 637
Mean ACT score: 27
67% had SAT critical reading scores over 600
76% had SAT math scores over 600
71% had SAT writing scores over 600
80% had ACT scores over 24
20% had SAT critical reading scores over 700
40% had SAT math scores over 700
27% had SAT writing scores over 700
39% had ACT scores over 30

Graduation and After

65% graduated in 4 years
23% graduated in 5 years
2% graduated in 6 years
425 organizations recruited on campus

Financial Matters

$8310 resident tuition and fees (2008–09)
$28,331 nonresident tuition and fees (2008–09)
$12,891 room and board
82% average percent of need met
$14,899 average financial aid amount received per undergraduate (2007–08 estimated)

UNIVERSITY OF CALIFORNIA, RIVERSIDE

URBAN SETTING ■ PUBLIC ■ STATE-SUPPORTED ■ COED
RIVERSIDE, CALIFORNIA

Web site: www.ucr.edu
Contact: Emily Engelschall, Director, Undergraduate Recruitment, 1120 Hinderaker Hall, Riverside, CA 92521
Telephone: 951-827-4531
Fax: 951-827-6344
E-mail: discover@ucr.edu

Getting Accepted

21,453 applied
78% were accepted
4,423 enrolled (26% of accepted)
94% from top tenth of their h.s. class
3.44 average high school GPA
16% had SAT critical reading scores over 600
30% had SAT math scores over 600
17% had SAT writing scores over 600
30% had ACT scores over 24
2% had SAT critical reading scores over 700
6% had SAT math scores over 700
2% had SAT writing scores over 700
3% had ACT scores over 30

Graduation and After

39% graduated in 4 years
20% graduated in 5 years
5% graduated in 6 years
52% had job offers within 6 months
459 organizations recruited on campus

Financial Matters

$7845 resident tuition and fees (2008–09)
$27,867 nonresident tuition and fees (2008–09)
$10,850 room and board
81% average percent of need met
$14,311 average financial aid amount received per undergraduate (2007–08 estimated)

Academics

UC Riverside awards bachelor's, master's, doctoral, and first-professional **degrees** and post-bachelor's certificates. **Challenging opportunities** include advanced placement credit, accelerated degree programs, student-designed majors, an honors program, double majors, independent study, and a senior project. Special programs include cooperative education, internships, summer session for credit, off-campus study, study-abroad, and Army and Air Force ROTC.

The most frequently chosen **baccalaureate** fields are business/marketing, social sciences, and biological/life sciences. A complete listing of majors at UC Riverside appears in the Majors by College index beginning on page 469.

The **faculty** at UC Riverside has 817 full-time members, 98% with terminal degrees. The student-faculty ratio is 19:1.

Students of UC Riverside

The student body totals 18,079, of whom 15,708 are undergraduates. 52% are women and 48% are men. Students come from 32 states and territories and 31 other countries. 98% are from California. 1.7% are international students. 7.8% are African American, 0.4% American Indian, 40.2% Asian American, and 27.8% Hispanic American. 84% returned for their sophomore year.

Facilities and Resources

793 **computers/terminals** are available on campus for general student use. Students can access the following: campus intranet, computer help desk, free student e-mail accounts, online (class) grades, online (class) registration, online (class) schedules, online viewing of financial information. Campuswide network is available. Wireless service is available via entire campus. The 7 **libraries** have 2,435,296 books and 29,941 subscriptions.

Campus Life

There are 251 active organizations on campus, including a drama/theater group, newspaper, radio station, and choral group. 6% of eligible men and 6% of eligible women are members of national **fraternities**, national **sororities**, local fraternities, local sororities, and coed fraternities.

UC Riverside is a member of the NCAA (Division I). **Intercollegiate sports** (some offering scholarships) include baseball (m), basketball, cross-country running, golf, softball (w), tennis, track and field, volleyball (w).

Campus Safety

Student safety services include late-night transport/escort service, 24-hour emergency telephone alarm devices, 24-hour patrols by trained security personnel, student patrols, and electronically operated dormitory entrances.

Applying

UC Riverside requires an essay, SAT Subject Tests, SAT or ACT, a high school transcript, and a minimum high school GPA of 2.8. Application deadline: 11/30; 3/2 for financial aid, with a 3/2 priority date.

University of California, San Diego

SUBURBAN SETTING ■ PUBLIC ■ STATE-SUPPORTED ■ COED
LA JOLLA, CALIFORNIA

Web site: www.ucsd.edu
Contact: Ms. Mae Brown, Assistant Vice Chancellor, Admissions and
Relations with Schools, 9500 Gilman Drive, 0021, La Jolla, CA
92093-0021
Telephone: 858-534-4831
E-mail: admissionsinfo@ucsd.edu

Academics
UCSD awards bachelor's, master's, doctoral, and first-professional **degrees**. **Challenging opportunities** include advanced placement credit, accelerated degree programs, student-designed majors, freshman honors college, an honors program, double majors, independent study, and a senior project. Special programs include cooperative education, internships, summer session for credit, off-campus study, study-abroad, and Army ROTC.

The most frequently chosen **baccalaureate** fields are social sciences, biological/life sciences, and engineering. A complete listing of majors at UCSD appears in the Majors by College index beginning on page 469.

The **faculty** at UCSD has 1,166 members. The student-faculty ratio is 19:1.

Students of UCSD
The student body totals 27,520, of whom 22,518 are undergraduates. 52.1% are women and 47.9% are men. 97% are from California. 3.8% are international students. 1.5% are African American, 0.4% American Indian, 45.2% Asian American, and 12.2% Hispanic American. 93% returned for their sophomore year.

Facilities and Resources
1,500 **computers/terminals** are available on campus for general student use. Students can access the following: online (class) registration. Campuswide network is available.

Campus Life
Active organizations on campus include a drama/theater group, newspaper, radio station, television station, choral group, and marching band. 10% of eligible men and 10% of eligible women are members of national **fraternities** and national **sororities**.

UCSD is a member of the NCAA (Division II). **Intercollegiate sports** include baseball (m), basketball, crew, cross-country running, fencing, golf (m), soccer, softball (w), swimming and diving, tennis, track and field, volleyball, water polo.

Campus Safety
Student safety services include crime prevention programs, late-night transport/escort service, 24-hour emergency telephone alarm devices, 24-hour patrols by trained security personnel, and student patrols.

Applying
UCSD requires an essay, SAT or ACT, ACT Assessment with Writing or SAT Reasoning Test, plus two SAT Subject Tests, a high school transcript, and a minimum high school GPA of 2.8, and in some cases a minimum high school GPA of 3.4. Application deadline: 11/30; 3/2 priority date for financial aid.

Getting Accepted
47,365 applied
42% were accepted
4,702 enrolled (24% of accepted)
100% from top tenth of their h.s. class
3.94 average high school GPA
Mean SAT critical reading score: 597
Mean SAT math score: 646
Mean SAT writing score: 608
56% had SAT critical reading scores over 600
78% had SAT math scores over 600
61% had SAT writing scores over 600
79% had ACT scores over 24
11% had SAT critical reading scores over 700
29% had SAT math scores over 700
14% had SAT writing scores over 700
29% had ACT scores over 30
49 National Merit Scholars

Graduation and After
56% graduated in 4 years
24% graduated in 5 years
4% graduated in 6 years

Financial Matters
$8062 resident tuition and fees (2008–09)
$28,083 nonresident tuition and fees (2008–09)
$10,820 room and board
82% average percent of need met
$14,961 average financial aid amount received per undergraduate (2007–08 estimated)

UNIVERSITY OF CALIFORNIA, SANTA BARBARA

SUBURBAN SETTING ■ PUBLIC ■ STATE-SUPPORTED ■ COED
SANTA BARBARA, CALIFORNIA

Web site: www.ucsb.edu
Contact: Office of Admissions, 1210 Cheadle Hall, Santa Barbara, CA 93106-2014
Telephone: 805-893-2881
Fax: 805-893-2676
E-mail: admissions@sa.ucsb.edu

Getting Accepted
40,933 applied
54% were accepted
4,335 enrolled (19% of accepted)
96% from top tenth of their h.s. class
3.76 average high school GPA
Mean SAT critical reading score: 592
Mean SAT math score: 601
Mean SAT writing score: 584
Mean ACT score: 26
51% had SAT critical reading scores over 600
56% had SAT math scores over 600
48% had SAT writing scores over 600
74% had ACT scores over 24
11% had SAT critical reading scores over 700
13% had SAT math scores over 700
8% had SAT writing scores over 700
18% had ACT scores over 30

Graduation and After
61% graduated in 4 years
16% graduated in 5 years
3% graduated in 6 years
91% had job offers within 6 months

Financial Matters
$8573 resident tuition and fees (2008–09)
$29,181 nonresident tuition and fees (2008–09)
$12,485 room and board
80% average percent of need met
$14,216 average financial aid amount received per undergraduate (2006–07)

Academics

UCSB awards bachelor's, master's, and doctoral **degrees** and first-professional certificates. **Challenging opportunities** include advanced placement credit, accelerated degree programs, student-designed majors, an honors program, double majors, and independent study. Special programs include cooperative education, internships, summer session for credit, off-campus study, study-abroad, and Army ROTC.

The most frequently chosen **baccalaureate** fields are social sciences, business/marketing, and biological/life sciences. A complete listing of majors at UCSB appears in the Majors by College index beginning on page 469.

The **faculty** at UCSB has 917 full-time members, 100% with terminal degrees. The student-faculty ratio is 17:1.

Students of UCSB

The student body totals 21,410, of whom 18,415 are undergraduates. 55.2% are women and 44.8% are men. Students come from 51 states and territories and 72 other countries. 96% are from California. 1.2% are international students. 2.7% are African American, 0.7% American Indian, 16.4% Asian American, and 19.4% Hispanic American. 91% returned for their sophomore year.

Facilities and Resources

3,000 **computers/terminals** are available on campus for general student use. Campuswide network is available. The **library** has 3,301,449 books and 36,902 subscriptions.

Campus Life

There are 241 active organizations on campus, including a drama/theater group, newspaper, radio station, television station, and choral group. 4% of eligible men and 4% of eligible women are members of national **fraternities**, national **sororities**, local fraternities, and local sororities.

UCSB is a member of the NCAA (Division I). **Intercollegiate sports** (some offering scholarships) include baseball (m), basketball, cross-country running, golf (m), gymnastics, soccer, softball (w), swimming and diving, tennis, track and field, volleyball, water polo.

Campus Safety

Student safety services include late-night transport/escort service and 24-hour emergency telephone alarm devices.

Applying

UCSB requires an essay, SAT Subject Tests, SAT or ACT, and a high school transcript, and in some cases an interview. Application deadline: 11/30; 3/2 priority date for financial aid.

UNIVERSITY OF CALIFORNIA, SANTA CRUZ
SMALL-TOWN SETTING ■ PUBLIC ■ STATE-SUPPORTED ■ COED
SANTA CRUZ, CALIFORNIA

Web site: www.ucsc.edu
Contact: Admissions Office, Cook House, Santa Cruz, CA 95064
Telephone: 831-459-1372
Fax: 831-459-4452
E-mail: admissions@ucsc.edu

Academics
UCSC awards bachelor's, master's, and doctoral **degrees** and post-bachelor's certificates. **Challenging opportunities** include advanced placement credit, accelerated degree programs, student-designed majors, freshman honors college, an honors program, double majors, independent study, and a senior project. Special programs include cooperative education, internships, summer session for credit, off-campus study, study-abroad, and Army, Navy, and Air Force ROTC.

The most frequently chosen **baccalaureate** fields are social sciences, biological/life sciences, and visual and performing arts. A complete listing of majors at UCSC appears in the Majors by College index beginning on page 469.

The **faculty** at UCSC has 566 full-time members, 95% with terminal degrees. The student-faculty ratio is 19:1.

Students of UCSC
The student body totals 16,625, of whom 15,135 are undergraduates. 53.3% are women and 46.7% are men. Students come from 43 states and territories and 22 other countries. 97% are from California. 0.5% are international students. 2.6% are African American, 0.9% American Indian, 21.5% Asian American, and 17.1% Hispanic American. 88% returned for their sophomore year.

Facilities and Resources
320 **computers/terminals** are available on campus for general student use. Students can access the following: campus intranet, computer help desk, free student e-mail accounts, online (class) grades, online (class) registration, online (class) schedules. Campuswide network is available. 100% of college-owned or -operated housing units are wired for high-speed Internet access. Wireless service is available via entire campus. The **library** has 1,692,553 books and 25,486 subscriptions.

Campus Life
There are 136 active organizations on campus, including a drama/theater group, newspaper, radio station, television station, and choral group. 1% of eligible men and 1% of eligible women are members of national **fraternities**, national **sororities**, local fraternities, and local sororities.

UCSC is a member of the NCAA (Division III). **Intercollegiate sports** include basketball, cross-country running (w), golf (w), soccer, swimming and diving, tennis, volleyball, water polo.

Campus Safety
Student safety services include evening main gate security, campus police force and fire station, late-night transport/escort service, 24-hour emergency telephone alarm devices, 24-hour patrols by trained security personnel, and electronically operated dormitory entrances.

Applying
UCSC requires an essay, SAT or ACT, SAT Subject Tests required in two different areas: history/social science, English literature, mathematics, laboratory science, or language other than English, a high school transcript, and minimum high school GPA of 3.0 for California residents, 3.4 for non-residents. Application deadline: 11/30; 6/1 for financial aid, with a 3/17 priority date.

Getting Accepted
27,837 applied
73% were accepted
3,965 enrolled (19% of accepted)
96% from top tenth of their h.s. class
3.54 average high school GPA
Mean SAT critical reading score: 570
Mean SAT math score: 582
Mean SAT writing score: 568
Mean ACT score: 24
41% had SAT critical reading scores over 600
46% had SAT math scores over 600
39% had SAT writing scores over 600
60% had ACT scores over 24
7% had SAT critical reading scores over 700
8% had SAT math scores over 700
5% had SAT writing scores over 700
9% had ACT scores over 30

Graduation and After
50% graduated in 4 years
17% graduated in 5 years
4% graduated in 6 years

Financial Matters
$10,131 resident tuition and fees (2009–10)
$31,554 nonresident tuition and fees (2009–10)
$13,641 room and board
87% average percent of need met
$14,422 average financial aid amount received per undergraduate (2006–07)

University of Central Arkansas

Small-town setting ■ Public ■ State-supported ■ Coed
Conway, Arkansas

Getting Accepted
5,780 applied
49% were accepted
1,793 enrolled (64% of accepted)
3.3 average high school GPA
Mean ACT score: 23
45% had ACT scores over 24
11% had ACT scores over 30

Graduation and After
23% graduated in 4 years
22% graduated in 5 years
9% graduated in 6 years
60 organizations recruited on campus

Financial Matters
$6505 resident tuition and fees (2008–09)
$11,605 nonresident tuition and fees (2008–09)
$4740 room and board
51% average percent of need met
$8510 average financial aid amount received per undergraduate (2006–07)

Web site: www.uca.edu
Contact: Ms. Melissa Goff, Director of Institutional Research and Admissions, 201 Donaghey Avenue, Conway, AR 72035
Telephone: 501-450-5371 or toll-free 800-243-8245 (in-state)
Fax: 501-450-5228
E-mail: mgoff@uca.edu

Academics
UCA awards associate, bachelor's, master's, and doctoral **degrees** and post-bachelor's and post-master's certificates. **Challenging opportunities** include advanced placement credit, accelerated degree programs, freshman honors college, an honors program, double majors, independent study, and a senior project. Special programs include cooperative education, internships, summer session for credit, study-abroad, and Army ROTC.

The most frequently chosen **baccalaureate** fields are health professions and related sciences, business/marketing, and education. A complete listing of majors at UCA appears in the Majors by College index beginning on page 469.

The **faculty** at UCA has 510 full-time members, 69% with terminal degrees. The student-faculty ratio is 18:1.

Students of UCA
The student body totals 12,619, of whom 10,675 are undergraduates. 58.1% are women and 41.9% are men. Students come from 44 states and territories and 61 other countries. 94% are from Arkansas. 4% are international students. 14.8% are African American, 0.8% American Indian, 1.4% Asian American, and 1.7% Hispanic American. 71% returned for their sophomore year.

Facilities and Resources
643 **computers/terminals** are available on campus for general student use. Students can access the following: campus intranet, computer help desk, free student e-mail accounts, online (class) grades, online (class) registration, online (class) schedules. Campuswide network is available. 100% of college-owned or -operated housing units are wired for high-speed Internet access. Wireless service is available via entire campus. The **library** has 505,000 books and 2,000 subscriptions.

Campus Life
There are 158 active organizations on campus, including a drama/theater group, newspaper, radio station, television station, choral group, and marching band. 10% of eligible men and 10% of eligible women are members of national **fraternities** and national **sororities**.

UCA is a member of the NCAA (Division I). **Intercollegiate sports** (some offering scholarships) include baseball (m), basketball, cheerleading, cross-country running, football (m), golf, soccer, softball (w), tennis (w), track and field, volleyball (w).

Campus Safety
Student safety services include security personnel at entrances during evening hours, late-night transport/escort service, 24-hour emergency telephone alarm devices, 24-hour patrols by trained security personnel, student patrols, and electronically operated dormitory entrances.

Applying
UCA requires SAT or ACT and a high school transcript. Application deadline: rolling admissions; 7/1 for financial aid, with a 4/15 priority date. Early and deferred admission are possible.

University of Central Florida

Suburban setting ■ Public ■ State-supported ■ Coed
Orlando, Florida

Web site: www.ucf.edu
Contact: Dr. Gordon Chavis, Assistant Vice President, PO Box 160111,
Orlando, FL 32816-0111
Telephone: 407-823-3000
Fax: 407-823-5625
E-mail: admission@mail.ucf.edu

SPONSOR

> The University of Central Florida (UCF) is a public, multicampus research university dedicated to serving its surrounding communities with their diverse and expanding populations, technological corridors, and international partners. The mission of the University is to offer high-quality undergraduate and graduate education, student development, and continuing education; to conduct research and creative activities; and to provide services that address national and international issues in key areas, contribute to the global community, establish UCF as a major presence, and enhance the intellectual, cultural, environmental, and economic development of the metropolitan region.

Academics

UCF awards associate, bachelor's, master's, and doctoral **degrees** and post-bachelor's certificates. **Challenging opportunities** include advanced placement credit, freshman honors college, an honors program, double majors, and a senior project. Special programs include cooperative education, internships, summer session for credit, off-campus study, study-abroad, and Army and Air Force ROTC.

The most frequently chosen **baccalaureate** fields are business/marketing, education, and health professions and related sciences. A complete listing of majors at UCF appears in the Majors by College index beginning on page 469.

The **faculty** at UCF has 1,195 full-time members, 77% with terminal degrees. The student-faculty ratio is 30:1.

Students of UCF

The student body totals 50,254, of whom 42,910 are undergraduates. 54.7% are women and 45.3% are men. Students come from 51 states and territories and 132 other countries. 95% are from Florida. 1.3% are international students. 9% are African American, 0.4% American Indian, 5.4% Asian American, and 14.4% Hispanic American. 86% returned for their sophomore year.

Facilities and Resources

3,276 **computers/terminals** and 200 ports are available on campus for general student use. Students can access the following: campus intranet, computer help desk, free student e-mail accounts, online (class) grades, online (class) registration, online (class) schedules. Campuswide network is available. 100% of college-owned or -operated housing units are wired for high-speed Internet access. Wireless service is available via entire campus. The **library** has 1,587,161 books and 18,012 subscriptions.

Campus Life

There are 329 active organizations on campus, including a drama/theater group, newspaper, radio station, choral group, and marching band. 11% of eligible men and 9% of eligible women are members of national **fraternities**, national **sororities**, local fraternities, and local sororities.

UCF is a member of the NCAA (Division I). **Intercollegiate sports** (some offering scholarships) include baseball (m), basketball, cheerleading, crew (w), cross-country running, football (m), golf, soccer, tennis, track and field (w), volleyball (w).

Campus Safety

Student safety services include late-night transport/escort service, 24-hour emergency telephone alarm devices, 24-hour patrols by trained security personnel, and electronically operated dormitory entrances.

Applying

UCF requires SAT or ACT, a high school transcript, and a minimum high school GPA of 2.0. It recommends an essay. Application deadline: 3/1; 6/30 for financial aid, with a 3/1 priority date. Early admission is possible.

Getting Accepted
28,659 applied
48% were accepted
6,344 enrolled (46% of accepted)
35% from top tenth of their h.s. class
3.67 average high school GPA
39% had SAT critical reading scores over 600
49% had SAT math scores over 600
27% had SAT writing scores over 600
70% had ACT scores over 24
6% had SAT critical reading scores over 700
7% had SAT math scores over 700
3% had SAT writing scores over 700
7% had ACT scores over 30
63 National Merit Scholars
22 valedictorians

Graduation and After
33% graduated in 4 years
24% graduated in 5 years
6% graduated in 6 years
80% had job offers within 6 months
3666 organizations recruited on campus

Financial Matters
$3947 resident tuition and fees (2008–09)
$19,427 nonresident tuition and fees (2008–09)
$8492 room and board
56% average percent of need met
$6438 average financial aid amount received per undergraduate (2006–07)

Getting Accepted
12,376 applied
28% were accepted
1,306 enrolled (38% of accepted)
86% from top tenth of their h.s. class
Mean SAT critical reading score: 709
Mean SAT math score: 703
Mean ACT score: 31
91% had SAT critical reading scores over 600
89% had SAT math scores over 600
96% had ACT scores over 24
63% had SAT critical reading scores over 700
60% had SAT math scores over 700
68% had ACT scores over 30
143 National Merit Scholars

Graduation and After
86% graduated in 4 years
5% graduated in 5 years
1% graduated in 6 years

Financial Matters
$37,632 tuition and fees (2008–09)
$11,697 room and board

UNIVERSITY OF CHICAGO
URBAN SETTING ■ PRIVATE ■ INDEPENDENT ■ COED
CHICAGO, ILLINOIS

Web site: www.uchicago.edu
Contact: Mr. Theodore O'Neill, Dean of Admissions, Rosenwald Hall, 1101 East 58th Street, Suite 105, Chicago, IL 60637-1513
Telephone: 773-702-8650
Fax: 773-702-4199
E-mail: questions@phoenix.uchicago.edu

Academics
Chicago awards bachelor's, master's, doctoral, and first-professional **degrees**. **Challenging opportunities** include advanced placement credit, accelerated degree programs, student-designed majors, double majors, independent study, and a senior project. Special programs include internships, summer session for credit, off-campus study, study-abroad, and Army and Air Force ROTC.

The most frequently chosen **baccalaureate** fields are social sciences, biological/life sciences, and foreign languages and literature. A complete listing of majors at Chicago appears in the Majors by College index beginning on page 469.

The **faculty** at Chicago has 1,099 full-time members, 100% with terminal degrees. The student-faculty ratio is 6:1.

Students of Chicago
The student body totals 12,787, of whom 5,065 are undergraduates. 49.7% are women and 50.3% are men. Students come from 52 states and territories and 72 other countries. 22% are from Illinois. 8.8% are international students. 5.7% are African American, 0.3% American Indian, 13.8% Asian American, and 8.6% Hispanic American. 98% returned for their sophomore year.

Facilities and Resources
1,000 **computers/terminals** are available on campus for general student use. Students can access the following: online (class) registration. Campuswide network is available. Wireless service is available via entire campus. The 7 **libraries** have 7,000,000 books and 47,000 subscriptions.

Campus Life
There are 400 active organizations on campus, including a drama/theater group, newspaper, radio station, and choral group. Chicago has national **fraternities** and national **sororities**.

Chicago is a member of the NCAA (Division III). **Intercollegiate sports** include baseball (m), basketball, cross-country running, football (m), soccer, softball (w), swimming and diving, tennis, track and field, volleyball (w), wrestling (m).

Campus Safety
Student safety services include late-night transport/escort service, 24-hour emergency telephone alarm devices, 24-hour patrols by trained security personnel, student patrols, and electronically operated dormitory entrances.

Applying
Chicago requires an essay, SAT or ACT, a high school transcript, and 3 recommendations. It recommends an interview. Application deadline: 1/2; 2/1 priority date for financial aid. Early and deferred admission are possible.

University of Colorado at Boulder

Suburban setting ■ Public ■ State-supported ■ Coed
Boulder, Colorado

Web site: www.colorado.edu
Contact: Admissions Office, Regent Administrative Center 125, 552 UCB, Boulder, CO 80309
Telephone: 303-492-6301
Fax: 303-492-7115
E-mail: apply@colorado.edu

Academics

CU-Boulder awards bachelor's, master's, doctoral, and first-professional **degrees** and post-master's certificates. **Challenging opportunities** include advanced placement credit, accelerated degree programs, student-designed majors, freshman honors college, an honors program, double majors, independent study, and a senior project. Special programs include cooperative education, internships, summer session for credit, off-campus study, study-abroad, and Army, Navy, and Air Force ROTC.

The most frequently chosen **baccalaureate** fields are business/marketing, social sciences, and biological/life sciences. A complete listing of majors at CU-Boulder appears in the Majors by College index beginning on page 469.

The **faculty** at CU-Boulder has 1,389 full-time members, 89% with terminal degrees. The student-faculty ratio is 18:1.

Students of CU-Boulder

The student body totals 32,191, of whom 26,725 are undergraduates. 47.3% are women and 52.7% are men. Students come from 51 states and territories and 97 other countries. 67% are from Colorado. 1.6% are international students. 1.6% are African American, 0.8% American Indian, 6.1% Asian American, and 6.4% Hispanic American. 84% returned for their sophomore year.

Facilities and Resources

1,855 **computers/terminals** are available on campus for general student use. Students can access the following: campus intranet, computer help desk, free student e-mail accounts, online (class) grades, online (class) registration, online (class) schedules, standard and academic software, student government voting. Campuswide network is available. 100% of college-owned or -operated housing units are wired for high-speed Internet access. Wireless service is available via entire campus. The 6 **libraries** have 3,843,458 books and 50,350 subscriptions.

Campus Life

There are 800 active organizations on campus, including a drama/theater group, newspaper, radio station, television station, choral group, and marching band. 8% of eligible men and 13% of eligible women are members of national **fraternities**, national **sororities**, and local sororities.

CU-Boulder is a member of the NCAA (Division I). **Intercollegiate sports** (some offering scholarships) include basketball, cross-country running, football (m), golf, skiing (cross-country), skiing (downhill), soccer (w), tennis (w), track and field, volleyball (w).

Campus Safety

Student safety services include University police department, late-night transport/escort service, 24-hour emergency telephone alarm devices, 24-hour patrols by trained security personnel, student patrols, and electronically operated dormitory entrances.

Applying

CU-Boulder requires an essay, SAT or ACT, and a high school transcript, and in some cases audition for music program. It recommends 1 recommendation and a minimum high school GPA of 3.0. Application deadline: 2/15; 4/1 priority date for financial aid. Deferred admission is possible.

Getting Accepted

23,004 applied
78% were accepted
5,863 enrolled (33% of accepted)
27% from top tenth of their h.s. class
3.57 average high school GPA
Mean SAT critical reading score: 579
Mean SAT math score: 598
Mean ACT score: 26
41% had SAT critical reading scores over 600
50% had SAT math scores over 600
76% had ACT scores over 24
7% had SAT critical reading scores over 700
10% had SAT math scores over 700
17% had ACT scores over 30
8 National Merit Scholars
197 valedictorians

Graduation and After

41% graduated in 4 years
21% graduated in 5 years
5% graduated in 6 years
77% had job offers within 6 months
911 organizations recruited on campus

Financial Matters

$7287 resident tuition and fees (2008–09)
$26,765 nonresident tuition and fees (2008–09)
$9860 room and board
89% average percent of need met
$11,404 average financial aid amount received per undergraduate (2007–08 estimated)

UNIVERSITY OF CONNECTICUT

RURAL SETTING ▪ PUBLIC ▪ STATE-SUPPORTED ▪ COED
STORRS, CONNECTICUT

Web site: www.uconn.edu
Contact: Mr. Brian Usher, Associate Director of Admissions, 2131 Hillside Road, U-88, Storrs, CT 06269
Telephone: 860-486-3137
Fax: 860-486-1476
E-mail: beahusky@uconnvm.uconn.edu

Getting Accepted
21,058 applied
54% were accepted
3,604 enrolled (31% of accepted)
39% from top tenth of their h.s. class
Mean SAT critical reading score: 585
Mean SAT math score: 615
45% had SAT critical reading scores over 600
61% had SAT math scores over 600
48% had SAT writing scores over 600
78% had ACT scores over 24
7% had SAT critical reading scores over 700
13% had SAT math scores over 700
7% had SAT writing scores over 700
13% had ACT scores over 30
146 valedictorians

Graduation and After
56% graduated in 4 years
18% graduated in 5 years
2% graduated in 6 years
83% had job offers within 6 months
330 organizations recruited on campus

Financial Matters
$9338 resident tuition and fees (2008–09)
$24,050 nonresident tuition and fees (2008–09)
$9300 room and board
68% average percent of need met
$10,530 average financial aid amount received per undergraduate (2007–08 estimated)

Academics
UConn awards associate, bachelor's, master's, doctoral, and first-professional **degrees** and post-bachelor's and post-master's certificates. **Challenging opportunities** include advanced placement credit, accelerated degree programs, student-designed majors, an honors program, double majors, independent study, and a senior project. Special programs include cooperative education, internships, summer session for credit, off-campus study, study-abroad, and Army and Air Force ROTC.

The most frequently chosen **baccalaureate** fields are social sciences, business/ marketing, and health professions and related sciences. A complete listing of majors at UConn appears in the Majors by College index beginning on page 469.

The **faculty** at UConn has 1,030 full-time members, 93% with terminal degrees. The student-faculty ratio is 17:1.

Students of UConn
The student body totals 24,273, of whom 16,765 are undergraduates. 50.1% are women and 49.9% are men. Students come from 47 states and territories and 62 other countries. 77% are from Connecticut. 1.1% are international students. 5.1% are African American, 0.3% American Indian, 7.8% Asian American, and 5.2% Hispanic American. 93% returned for their sophomore year.

Facilities and Resources
1,318 **computers/terminals** are available on campus for general student use. Students can access the following: computer help desk, free student e-mail accounts, online (class) grades, online (class) registration, online (class) schedules. Campuswide network is available. 100% of college-owned or -operated housing units are wired for high-speed Internet access. Wireless service is available via classrooms, computer centers, computer labs, dorm rooms, learning centers, libraries, student centers. The 4 **libraries** have 2,987,772 books and 17,378 subscriptions.

Campus Life
There are 300 active organizations on campus, including a drama/theater group, newspaper, radio station, television station, choral group, and marching band. 8% of eligible men and 8% of eligible women are members of national **fraternities**, national **sororities**, local fraternities, and local sororities.

UConn is a member of the NCAA (Division I). **Intercollegiate sports** (some offering scholarships) include baseball (m), basketball, crew (w), cross-country running, field hockey (w), football (m), golf (m), ice hockey, lacrosse (w), soccer, softball (w), swimming and diving, tennis, track and field, volleyball (w).

Campus Safety
Student safety services include late-night transport/escort service and 24-hour emergency telephone alarm devices.

Applying
UConn requires an essay, SAT or ACT, and a high school transcript. It recommends 1 recommendation. Application deadline: 2/1; 3/1 priority date for financial aid. Deferred admission is possible.

University of Dallas

Suburban setting ■ Private ■ Independent Religious ■ Coed
Irving, Texas

Web site: www.udallas.edu
Contact: Sr. Mary Brian Bole, Assistant Dean of Enrollment Management,
    1845 East Northgate Drive, Irving, TX 75062-4799
Telephone: 972-721-5266 or toll-free 800-628-6999
Fax: 972-721-5017
E-mail: ugadmis@udallas.edu

Academics

Dallas awards bachelor's, master's, and doctoral **degrees** and post-bachelor's and post-master's certificates. **Challenging opportunities** include advanced placement credit, student-designed majors, double majors, independent study, and a senior project. Special programs include internships, summer session for credit, off-campus study, study-abroad, and Army and Air Force ROTC.

The most frequently chosen **baccalaureate** fields are business/marketing, English, and biological/life sciences. A complete listing of majors at Dallas appears in the Majors by College index beginning on page 469.

The **faculty** at Dallas has 125 full-time members, 88% with terminal degrees. The student-faculty ratio is 13:1.

Students of Dallas

The student body totals 2,972, of whom 1,233 are undergraduates. 54.3% are women and 45.7% are men. Students come from 44 states and territories and 11 other countries. 51% are from Texas. 79% returned for their sophomore year.

Facilities and Resources

125 **computers/terminals** are available on campus for general student use. Students can access the following: campus intranet, computer help desk, free student e-mail accounts, online (class) grades, online (class) registration, online (class) schedules. Campuswide network is available. 100% of college-owned or -operated housing units are wired for high-speed Internet access. Wireless service is available via computer centers, computer labs, dorm rooms, learning centers, libraries, student centers. The **library** has 223,350 books and 691 subscriptions.

Campus Life

There are 42 active organizations on campus, including a drama/theater group, newspaper, radio station, and choral group. No national or local **fraternities** or **sororities**.

Dallas is a member of the NCAA (Division III). **Intercollegiate sports** include baseball (m), basketball, cross-country running, golf (m), lacrosse (w), soccer, softball (w), tennis (w), track and field, volleyball (w), wrestling (m).

Campus Safety

Student safety services include late-night transport/escort service, 24-hour emergency telephone alarm devices, 24-hour patrols by trained security personnel, and electronically operated dormitory entrances.

Applying

Dallas requires an essay, SAT or ACT, a high school transcript, and 2 recommendations, and in some cases an interview. It recommends an interview. Application deadline: 8/1; 3/1 priority date for financial aid. Early and deferred admission are possible.

Getting Accepted

1,161 applied
75% were accepted
363 enrolled (42% of accepted)
33% from top tenth of their h.s. class
3.6 average high school GPA
Mean SAT critical reading score: 614
Mean SAT math score: 585
Mean SAT writing score: 596
Mean ACT score: 26
59% had SAT critical reading scores over 600
44% had SAT math scores over 600
52% had SAT writing scores over 600
76% had ACT scores over 24
21% had SAT critical reading scores over 700
10% had SAT math scores over 700
14% had SAT writing scores over 700
21% had ACT scores over 30
6 National Merit Scholars
9 valedictorians

Graduation and After

55% graduated in 4 years
7% graduated in 5 years
1% graduated in 6 years
60% had job offers within 6 months
40 organizations recruited on campus

Financial Matters

$24,770 tuition and fees (2008–09)
$7885 room and board
80% average percent of need met
$21,257 average financial aid amount received
    per undergraduate (2006–07)

University of Dayton

Suburban setting ■ Private ■ Independent Religious ■ Coed
Dayton, Ohio

Getting Accepted
11,610 applied
74% were accepted
1,984 enrolled (23% of accepted)
21% from top tenth of their h.s. class
3.52 average high school GPA
Mean SAT critical reading score: 570
Mean SAT math score: 590
Mean ACT score: 26
38% had SAT critical reading scores over 600
46% had SAT math scores over 600
72% had ACT scores over 24
7% had SAT critical reading scores over 700
10% had SAT math scores over 700
16% had ACT scores over 30
9 National Merit Scholars
20 valedictorians

Graduation and After
57% graduated in 4 years
16% graduated in 5 years
1% graduated in 6 years
50% had job offers within 6 months
164 organizations recruited on campus

Financial Matters
$27,330 tuition and fees (2008–09)
$7980 room and board
96% average percent of need met
$17,980 average financial aid amount received
    per undergraduate (2006–07)

Web site: www.udayton.edu
Contact: Mr. Robert Durkle, Assistant Vice President and Dean of Admission,
    300 College Park, Dayton, OH 45469-1300
Telephone: 937-229-4411 or toll-free 800-837-7433
Fax: 937-229-4729
E-mail: admission@udayton.edu

Academics
UD awards bachelor's, master's, doctoral, and first-professional **degrees** and post-master's certificates. **Challenging opportunities** include advanced placement credit, accelerated degree programs, student-designed majors, an honors program, double majors, independent study, and a senior project. Special programs include cooperative education, internships, summer session for credit, off-campus study, study-abroad, and Army and Air Force ROTC.

The most frequently chosen **baccalaureate** fields are business/marketing, engineering, and communications/journalism. A complete listing of majors at UD appears in the Majors by College index beginning on page 469.

The **faculty** at UD has 462 full-time members, 90% with terminal degrees. The student-faculty ratio is 16:1.

Students of UD
The student body totals 10,920, of whom 7,731 are undergraduates. 49.6% are women and 50.4% are men. Students come from 50 states and territories and 50 other countries. 62% are from Ohio. 1.6% are international students. 3.4% are African American, 0.3% American Indian, 1.1% Asian American, and 1.8% Hispanic American. 86% returned for their sophomore year.

Facilities and Resources
250 **computers/terminals** and 100 ports are available on campus for general student use. Students can access the following: campus intranet, computer help desk, free student e-mail accounts, online (class) grades, online (class) registration, online (class) schedules, applications, admission/enrollment status, virtual orientation, online digital resources, online courses, assistive technology, learning management system, multimedia labs, payment, cyber cafes, centrally-licensed, downloadable software and training. Campuswide network is available. 100% of college-owned or -operated housing units are wired for high-speed Internet access. Wireless service is available via entire campus. The 3 **libraries** have 920,035 books and 10,481 subscriptions.

Campus Life
There are 200 active organizations on campus, including a drama/theater group, newspaper, radio station, television station, choral group, and marching band. 13% of eligible men and 13% of eligible women are members of national **fraternities**, national **sororities**, local fraternities, and local sororities.

UD is a member of the NCAA (Division I). **Intercollegiate sports** (some offering scholarships) include baseball (m), basketball, cheerleading, crew (w), cross-country running, football (m), golf, soccer, softball (w), tennis, track and field (w), volleyball (w).

Campus Safety
Student safety services include late-night transport/escort service, 24-hour emergency telephone alarm devices, 24-hour patrols by trained security personnel, student patrols, and electronically operated dormitory entrances.

Applying
UD requires an essay, SAT or ACT, a high school transcript, and 1 recommendation, and in some cases audition required for music, music therapy, music education programs. It recommends an interview. Application deadline: rolling admissions; 3/31 priority date for financial aid. Deferred admission is possible.

UNIVERSITY OF DELAWARE
SMALL-TOWN SETTING ■ PUBLIC ■ STATE-RELATED ■ COED
NEWARK, DELAWARE

Web site: www.udel.edu
Contact: Mr. Lou Hirsh, Director of Admissions, 116 Hullihen Hall, Newark, DE 19716
Telephone: 302-831-8123
Fax: 302-831-6905
E-mail: admissions@udel.edu

Academics
Delaware awards associate, bachelor's, master's, and doctoral **degrees**. **Challenging opportunities** include advanced placement credit, accelerated degree programs, student-designed majors, an honors program, double majors, independent study, and a senior project. Special programs include cooperative education, internships, summer session for credit, study-abroad, and Army and Air Force ROTC.

The most frequently chosen **baccalaureate** fields are business/marketing, social sciences, and education. A complete listing of majors at Delaware appears in the Majors by College index beginning on page 469.

The **faculty** at Delaware has 1,165 full-time members, 85% with terminal degrees. The student-faculty ratio is 12:1.

Students of Delaware
The student body totals 19,832, of whom 16,384 are undergraduates. 57.7% are women and 42.3% are men. Students come from 52 states and territories and 100 other countries. 36% are from Delaware. 1.1% are international students. 5.3% are African American, 0.3% American Indian, 4.5% Asian American, and 5.3% Hispanic American. 91% returned for their sophomore year.

Facilities and Resources
908 **computers/terminals** are available on campus for general student use. Students can access the following: online (class) registration, e-mail, personal Web page. Campuswide network is available. The 6 **libraries** have 2,704,986 books and 12,532 subscriptions.

Campus Life
There are 200 active organizations on campus, including a drama/theater group, newspaper, radio station, television station, choral group, and marching band. 10% of eligible men and 14% of eligible women are members of national **fraternities**, national **sororities**, local fraternities, and local sororities.

Delaware is a member of the NCAA (Division I). **Intercollegiate sports** (some offering scholarships) include baseball (m), basketball, cheerleading, crew (w), cross-country running, field hockey (w), football (m), golf (m), lacrosse, soccer, softball (w), swimming and diving, tennis, track and field, volleyball (w).

Campus Safety
Student safety services include late-night transport/escort service, 24-hour emergency telephone alarm devices, 24-hour patrols by trained security personnel, student patrols, and electronically operated dormitory entrances.

Applying
Delaware requires an essay, SAT or ACT, a high school transcript, and 1 recommendation. It recommends SAT Subject Tests. Application deadline: 1/15; 3/15 for financial aid, with a 2/1 priority date. Early and deferred admission are possible.

Getting Accepted
22,491 applied
56% were accepted
3,422 enrolled (27% of accepted)
42% from top tenth of their h.s. class
3.6 average high school GPA
52% had SAT critical reading scores over 600
61% had SAT math scores over 600
53% had SAT writing scores over 600
80% had ACT scores over 24
11% had SAT critical reading scores over 700
13% had SAT math scores over 700
10% had SAT writing scores over 700
16% had ACT scores over 30

Graduation and After
67% graduated in 4 years
11% graduated in 5 years
77% had job offers within 6 months
442 organizations recruited on campus

Financial Matters
$8646 resident tuition and fees (2008–09)
$21,126 nonresident tuition and fees (2008–09)
$8478 room and board
79% average percent of need met
$9891 average financial aid amount received per undergraduate (2006–07)

UNIVERSITY OF DENVER

SUBURBAN SETTING ■ PRIVATE ■ INDEPENDENT ■ COED
DENVER, COLORADO

Web site: www.du.edu
Contact: Mr. Todd Rinehart, Assistant Vice Chancellor for Enrollment, University Park, Denver, CO 80208
Telephone: 303-871-2036 or toll-free 800-525-9495 (out-of-state)
Fax: 303-871-3301
E-mail: admission@du.edu

University of Denver (DU) students are bright and energetic leaders committed to personal achievement and community engagement. Although they come from diverse backgrounds and from all fifty states and seventy-eight countries, they share an appreciation for an active and culturally enriched lifestyle. As first-year students, they benefit from a mentoring seminar that immerses them in a rigorous academic culture. As juniors and seniors, many embark on DU-funded research projects and study-abroad experiences that prepare them for life as global citizens. Throughout their years at DU, they work with professors who are committed to empowering greatness through cross-disciplinary learning and innovative curricula.

Getting Accepted
7,144 applied
64% were accepted
1,134 enrolled (25% of accepted)
43% from top tenth of their h.s. class
3.66 average high school GPA
Mean SAT critical reading score: 588
Mean SAT math score: 605
Mean ACT score: 27
46% had SAT critical reading scores over 600
56% had SAT math scores over 600
82% had ACT scores over 24
8% had SAT critical reading scores over 700
12% had SAT math scores over 700
20% had ACT scores over 30

Graduation and After
58% graduated in 4 years
14% graduated in 5 years
2% graduated in 6 years
81% had job offers within 6 months
187 organizations recruited on campus

Financial Matters
$33,810 tuition and fees (2008–09)
$9670 room and board
72% average percent of need met
$22,017 average financial aid amount received per undergraduate (2006–07)

Academics

DU awards bachelor's, master's, doctoral, and first-professional **degrees** and post-bachelor's and post-master's certificates. **Challenging opportunities** include advanced placement credit, accelerated degree programs, student-designed majors, freshman honors college, an honors program, double majors, independent study, and a senior project. Special programs include cooperative education, internships, summer session for credit, study-abroad, and Army and Air Force ROTC.

The most frequently chosen **baccalaureate** fields are business/marketing, social sciences, and communications/journalism. A complete listing of majors at DU appears in the Majors by College index beginning on page 469.

The **faculty** at DU has 586 full-time members, 90% with terminal degrees. The student-faculty ratio is 10:1.

Students of DU

The student body totals 11,328, of whom 5,324 are undergraduates. 55.7% are women and 44.3% are men. Students come from 52 states and territories and 51 other countries. 52% are from Colorado. 5.2% are international students. 3.1% are African American, 1.4% American Indian, 5.5% Asian American, and 6.8% Hispanic American. 87% returned for their sophomore year.

Facilities and Resources

200 **computers/terminals** and 30,000 ports are available on campus for general student use. Students can access the following: campus intranet, computer help desk, free student e-mail accounts, online (class) grades, online (class) registration, online (class) schedules. Campuswide network is available. 95% of college-owned or -operated housing units are wired for high-speed Internet access. Wireless service is available via entire campus. The **library** has 1,325,641 books and 33,745 subscriptions.

Campus Life

There are 97 active organizations on campus, including a drama/theater group, newspaper, radio station, and choral group. 19% of eligible men and 11% of eligible women are members of national **fraternities** and national **sororities**.

DU is a member of the NCAA (Division I). **Intercollegiate sports** (some offering scholarships) include basketball, golf, gymnastics (w), ice hockey (m), lacrosse, skiing (cross-country), skiing (downhill), soccer, swimming and diving, tennis, volleyball (w).

Campus Safety

Student safety services include 24-hour locked residence hall entrances, late-night transport/escort service, 24-hour emergency telephone alarm devices, 24-hour patrols by trained security personnel, and electronically operated dormitory entrances.

Applying

DU requires an essay, SAT or ACT, a high school transcript, and 2 recommendations, and in some cases a minimum high school GPA of 2.0. It recommends an interview. Application deadline: 1/15; 3/1 priority date for financial aid. Early and deferred admission are possible.

UNIVERSITY OF EVANSVILLE

URBAN SETTING ■ PRIVATE ■ INDEPENDENT RELIGIOUS ■ COED
EVANSVILLE, INDIANA

Web site: www.evansville.edu
Contact: Don Vos, Dean of Admission, 1800 Lincoln Avenue, Evansville, IN 47722
Telephone: 812-488-2468 or toll-free 800-423-8633 Ext. 2468
Fax: 812-488-4076
E-mail: admission@evansville.edu

Academics

Evansville awards associate, bachelor's, master's, and doctoral **degrees**. **Challenging opportunities** include advanced placement credit, accelerated degree programs, student-designed majors, an honors program, double majors, independent study, and a senior project. Special programs include cooperative education, internships, summer session for credit, and study-abroad.

The most frequently chosen **baccalaureate** fields are engineering, business/marketing, and education. A complete listing of majors at Evansville appears in the Majors by College index beginning on page 469.

The **faculty** at Evansville has 176 full-time members, 85% with terminal degrees. The student-faculty ratio is 13:1.

Students of Evansville

The student body totals 2,789, of whom 2,632 are undergraduates. 59.5% are women and 40.5% are men. Students come from 39 states and territories and 52 other countries. 60% are from Indiana. 6.5% are international students. 2.6% are African American, 0.2% American Indian, 0.9% Asian American, and 1.8% Hispanic American. 81% returned for their sophomore year.

Facilities and Resources

385 **computers/terminals** and 3,000 ports are available on campus for general student use. Students can access the following: campus intranet, computer help desk, free student e-mail accounts, online (class) grades, online (class) registration, online (class) schedules. Campuswide network is available. 100% of college-owned or -operated housing units are wired for high-speed Internet access. Wireless service is available via entire campus. The **library** has 274,174 books and 845 subscriptions.

Campus Life

There are 160 active organizations on campus, including a drama/theater group, newspaper, radio station, and choral group. 28% of eligible men and 24% of eligible women are members of national **fraternities**, national **sororities**, and local sororities.

Evansville is a member of the NCAA (Division I). **Intercollegiate sports** (some offering scholarships) include baseball (m), basketball, cross-country running, golf, soccer, softball (w), swimming and diving, tennis (w), volleyball (w).

Campus Safety

Student safety services include late-night transport/escort service, 24-hour emergency telephone alarm devices, 24-hour patrols by trained security personnel, student patrols, and electronically operated dormitory entrances.

Applying

Evansville requires SAT or ACT, a high school transcript, and 1 recommendation, and in some cases an essay and an interview. It recommends an interview and a minimum high school GPA of 3.0. Application deadline: 2/1; 3/10 priority date for financial aid. Deferred admission is possible.

Getting Accepted

2,887 applied
88% were accepted
619 enrolled (24% of accepted)
31% from top tenth of their h.s. class
3.64 average high school GPA
Mean SAT critical reading score: 557
Mean SAT math score: 560
Mean SAT writing score: 541
Mean ACT score: 25
33% had SAT critical reading scores over 600
35% had SAT math scores over 600
24% had SAT writing scores over 600
65% had ACT scores over 24
6% had SAT critical reading scores over 700
3% had SAT math scores over 700
3% had SAT writing scores over 700
14% had ACT scores over 30
7 National Merit Scholars
41 valedictorians

Graduation and After

49% graduated in 4 years
13% graduated in 5 years
95% had job offers within 6 months
171 organizations recruited on campus

Financial Matters

$25,845 tuition and fees (2008–09)
$8230 room and board
86% average percent of need met
$20,659 average financial aid amount received per undergraduate (2007–08 estimated)

UNIVERSITY OF FLORIDA

SUBURBAN SETTING ■ PUBLIC ■ STATE-SUPPORTED ■ COED
GAINESVILLE, FLORIDA

Web site: www.ufl.edu
Contact: Office of Admissions, PO Box 114000, Gainesville, FL 32611-4000
Telephone: 352-392-1365
E-mail: zevans@ufl.edu

Getting Accepted

27,612 applied
39% were accepted
6,384 enrolled (59% of accepted)
3.9 average high school GPA
65% had SAT critical reading scores over 600
73% had SAT math scores over 600
86% had ACT scores over 24
17% had SAT critical reading scores over 700
25% had SAT math scores over 700
30% had ACT scores over 30
154 National Merit Scholars

Graduation and After

53% graduated in 4 years
23% graduated in 5 years
4% graduated in 6 years
1050 organizations recruited on campus

Financial Matters

$3778 resident tuition and fees (2008–09)
$19,821 nonresident tuition and fees (2008–09)
$7150 room and board
83% average percent of need met
$11,105 average financial aid amount received per undergraduate (2006–07)

Academics

UF awards bachelor's, master's, doctoral, and first-professional **degrees**. **Challenging opportunities** include advanced placement credit, accelerated degree programs, student-designed majors, an honors program, double majors, independent study, and a senior project. Special programs include cooperative education, internships, summer session for credit, off-campus study, study-abroad, and Army and Air Force ROTC.

The most frequently chosen **baccalaureate** fields are business/marketing, social sciences, and engineering. A complete listing of majors at UF appears in the Majors by College index beginning on page 469.

The **faculty** at UF has 1,937 full-time members, 85% with terminal degrees. The student-faculty ratio is 20:1.

Students of UF

The student body totals 51,474, of whom 34,654 are undergraduates. 54.2% are women and 45.8% are men. Students come from 52 states and territories and 139 other countries. 96% are from Florida. 0.9% are international students. 10.2% are African American, 0.5% American Indian, 8.2% Asian American, and 14.6% Hispanic American. 95% returned for their sophomore year.

Facilities and Resources

2,200 **computers/terminals** and 1,000 ports are available on campus for general student use. Students can access the following: campus intranet, computer help desk, free student e-mail accounts, online (class) grades, online (class) registration, online (class) schedules. Campuswide network is available. 100% of college-owned or -operated housing units are wired for high-speed Internet access. Wireless service is available via computer centers, computer labs, learning centers, libraries, student centers. The 9 **libraries** have 5,347,896 books and 25,342 subscriptions.

Campus Life

There are 800 active organizations on campus, including a drama/theater group, newspaper, radio station, television station, choral group, and marching band. 15% of eligible men and 15% of eligible women are members of national **fraternities**, national **sororities**, local fraternities, and local sororities.

UF is a member of the NCAA (Division I). **Intercollegiate sports** (some offering scholarships) include baseball (m), basketball, cross-country running, football (m), golf, gymnastics (w), lacrosse (w), soccer (w), softball (w), swimming and diving, tennis, track and field, volleyball (w).

Campus Safety

Student safety services include crime and rape prevention programs, late-night transport/escort service, 24-hour emergency telephone alarm devices, 24-hour patrols by trained security personnel, student patrols, and electronically operated dormitory entrances.

Applying

UF requires an essay, SAT or ACT, and a high school transcript. Application deadline: 11/1; 3/15 priority date for financial aid. Early admission is possible.

UNIVERSITY OF GEORGIA

SUBURBAN SETTING ■ PUBLIC ■ STATE-SUPPORTED ■ COED
ATHENS, GEORGIA

Web site: www.uga.edu
Contact: 212 Terrell Hall, 210 South Jackson Street, Athens, GA 30602
Telephone: 706-542-8776
Fax: 706-542-1466
E-mail: undergrad@admissions.uga.edu

Academics

Georgia awards bachelor's, master's, doctoral, and first-professional **degrees** and post-bachelor's, post-master's, and first-professional certificates. **Challenging opportunities** include advanced placement credit, accelerated degree programs, student-designed majors, an honors program, double majors, independent study, and a senior project. Special programs include cooperative education, internships, summer session for credit, off-campus study, study-abroad, and Army and Air Force ROTC.

The most frequently chosen **baccalaureate** fields are business/marketing, social sciences, and biological/life sciences. A complete listing of majors at Georgia appears in the Majors by College index beginning on page 469.

The **faculty** at Georgia has 1,761 full-time members, 95% with terminal degrees. The student-faculty ratio is 18:1.

Students of Georgia

The student body totals 34,180, of whom 25,467 are undergraduates. 57.8% are women and 42.2% are men. Students come from 54 states and territories and 127 other countries. 88% are from Georgia. 0.7% are international students. 6.7% are African American, 0.2% American Indian, 7% Asian American, and 2.4% Hispanic American. 93% returned for their sophomore year.

Facilities and Resources

3,100 **computers/terminals** are available on campus for general student use. Students can access the following: campus intranet, computer help desk, free student e-mail accounts, online (class) grades, online (class) registration, online (class) schedules. Campuswide network is available. 100% of college-owned or -operated housing units are wired for high-speed Internet access. Wireless service is available via classrooms, computer centers, computer labs, dorm rooms, learning centers, libraries, student centers. The 3 **libraries** have 4,559,220 books and 49,097 subscriptions.

Campus Life

There are 430 active organizations on campus, including a drama/theater group, newspaper, radio station, television station, choral group, and marching band. 20% of eligible men and 25% of eligible women are members of national **fraternities**, national **sororities**, local fraternities, and local sororities.

Georgia is a member of the NCAA (Division I). **Intercollegiate sports** (some offering scholarships) include baseball (m), basketball, cheerleading, cross-country running, equestrian sports (w), football (m), golf, gymnastics (w), soccer (w), softball (w), swimming and diving, tennis, track and field, volleyball (w).

Campus Safety

Student safety services include late-night transport/escort service, 24-hour emergency telephone alarm devices, 24-hour patrols by trained security personnel, and electronically operated dormitory entrances.

Applying

Georgia requires SAT or ACT, a high school transcript, and counselor evaluation. It recommends an essay, SAT Subject Tests, and a minimum high school GPA of 2.0. Application deadline: 1/15; 3/1 priority date for financial aid. Early and deferred admission are possible.

Getting Accepted

17,207 applied
56% were accepted
4,791 enrolled (50% of accepted)
52% from top tenth of their h.s. class
3.59 average high school GPA
Mean SAT critical reading score: 617
Mean SAT math score: 620
Mean SAT writing score: 610
Mean ACT score: 27
58% had SAT critical reading scores over 600
62% had SAT math scores over 600
57% had SAT writing scores over 600
84% had ACT scores over 24
11% had SAT critical reading scores over 700
14% had SAT math scores over 700
12% had SAT writing scores over 700
20% had ACT scores over 30
138 National Merit Scholars

Graduation and After

51% graduated in 4 years
24% graduated in 5 years
4% graduated in 6 years
65% had job offers within 6 months
1032 organizations recruited on campus

Financial Matters

$6030 resident tuition and fees (2008–09)
$22,342 nonresident tuition and fees (2008–09)
$7528 room and board
75% average percent of need met
$8170 average financial aid amount received per undergraduate (2007–08 estimated)

UNIVERSITY OF ILLINOIS AT CHICAGO

URBAN SETTING ■ PUBLIC ■ STATE-SUPPORTED ■ COED
CHICAGO, ILLINOIS

Web site: www.uic.edu
Contact: Mr. Thomas Glenn, Executive Director of Admissions, 1100 SSB, m/c 018, Chicago, IL 60607-7128
Telephone: 312-996-4350
Fax: 312-996-2953
E-mail: uic.admit@uic.edu

Getting Accepted
14,269 applied
60% were accepted
2,964 enrolled (35% of accepted)
25% from top tenth of their h.s. class
Mean ACT score: 24
53% had ACT scores over 24
8% had ACT scores over 30

Graduation and After
21% graduated in 4 years
22% graduated in 5 years
6% graduated in 6 years
520 organizations recruited on campus

Financial Matters
$11,716 resident tuition and fees (2008–09)
$23,836 nonresident tuition and fees (2008–09)
$8744 room and board
86% average percent of need met
$10,598 average financial aid amount received per undergraduate (2006–07)

Academics
UIC awards bachelor's, master's, doctoral, and first-professional **degrees** and post-bachelor's, post-master's, and first-professional certificates. **Challenging opportunities** include advanced placement credit, accelerated degree programs, student-designed majors, an honors program, double majors, independent study, and a senior project. Special programs include cooperative education, internships, summer session for credit, off-campus study, study-abroad, and Army, Navy, and Air Force ROTC.

The most frequently chosen **baccalaureate** fields are business/marketing, psychology, and biological/life sciences. A complete listing of majors at UIC appears in the Majors by College index beginning on page 469.

The **faculty** at UIC has 1,201 full-time members, 78% with terminal degrees. The student-faculty ratio is 16:1.

Students of UIC
The student body totals 25,835, of whom 15,665 are undergraduates. 52.9% are women and 47.1% are men. Students come from 42 states and territories and 49 other countries. 98% are from Illinois. 1.5% are international students. 8.5% are African American, 0.2% American Indian, 22.9% Asian American, and 16.9% Hispanic American. 78% returned for their sophomore year.

Facilities and Resources
800 **computers/terminals** and 3,200 ports are available on campus for general student use. Students can access the following: campus intranet, computer help desk, free student e-mail accounts, online (class) grades, online (class) registration, online (class) schedules. Campuswide network is available. 100% of college-owned or -operated housing units are wired for high-speed Internet access. Wireless service is available via classrooms, computer centers, computer labs, dorm rooms, libraries, student centers. The 4 **libraries** have 3,287,129 books and 44,614 subscriptions.

Campus Life
Active organizations on campus include a drama/theater group, newspaper, radio station, and choral group. 1% of eligible men and 1% of eligible women are members of national **fraternities**, national **sororities**, local fraternities, and local sororities.

UIC is a member of the NCAA (Division I). **Intercollegiate sports** (some offering scholarships) include baseball (m), basketball, cross-country running, gymnastics, soccer (m), softball (w), swimming and diving, tennis, track and field, volleyball (w).

Campus Safety
Student safety services include housing ID stickers, guest escort policy, 24-hour closed circuit videos for exits and entrances, security screen for first floor, late-night transport/escort service, 24-hour emergency telephone alarm devices, 24-hour patrols by trained security personnel, student patrols, and electronically operated dormitory entrances.

Applying
UIC requires SAT or ACT and a high school transcript. It recommends an essay. Application deadline: 1/31; 3/1 priority date for financial aid.

University of Illinois at Urbana–Champaign

Urban setting ■ Public ■ State-supported ■ Coed
Champaign, Illinois

Web site: www.uiuc.edu
Contact: Mrs. Stacey Kostell, Director of Admissions, 901 West Illinois, Urbana, IL 61801
Telephone: 217-333-0302
Fax: 217-244-4614
E-mail: ugradadmissions@uiuc.edu

Academics

UIUC awards bachelor's, master's, doctoral, and first-professional **degrees** and post-master's certificates. **Challenging opportunities** include advanced placement credit, accelerated degree programs, student-designed majors, an honors program, double majors, independent study, and a senior project. Special programs include cooperative education, internships, summer session for credit, off-campus study, study-abroad, and Army, Navy, and Air Force ROTC.

The most frequently chosen **baccalaureate** fields are business/marketing, engineering, and social sciences. A complete listing of majors at UIUC appears in the Majors by College index beginning on page 469.

The **faculty** at UIUC has 1,974 full-time members, 92% with terminal degrees. The student-faculty ratio is 17:1.

Students of UIUC

The student body totals 42,326, of whom 30,895 are undergraduates. 47% are women and 53% are men. Students come from 52 states and territories and 69 other countries. 93% are from Illinois. 5.6% are international students. 6.7% are African American, 0.3% American Indian, 12.8% Asian American, and 6.9% Hispanic American. 93% returned for their sophomore year.

Facilities and Resources

3,400 **computers/terminals** and 70,000 ports are available on campus for general student use. Students can access the following: computer help desk, free student e-mail accounts, online (class) grades, online (class) registration, online (class) schedules. Campuswide network is available. 100% of college-owned or -operated housing units are wired for high-speed Internet access. Wireless service is available via classrooms, computer centers, computer labs, dorm rooms, learning centers, libraries, student centers. The 37 **libraries** have 10,371,460 books and 63,413 subscriptions.

Campus Life

There are 981 active organizations on campus, including a drama/theater group, newspaper, radio station, television station, choral group, and marching band. 22% of eligible men and 23% of eligible women are members of national **fraternities**, national **sororities**, local fraternities, and local sororities.

UIUC is a member of the NCAA (Division I). **Intercollegiate sports** (some offering scholarships) include baseball (m), basketball, cheerleading, cross-country running, football (m), golf, gymnastics, soccer (w), softball (w), swimming and diving (w), tennis, track and field, volleyball (w), wrestling (m).

Campus Safety

Student safety services include safety training classes, ID cards with safety numbers, late-night transport/escort service, 24-hour emergency telephone alarm devices, 24-hour patrols by trained security personnel, student patrols, and electronically operated dormitory entrances.

Applying

UIUC requires an essay, SAT or ACT, ACT Writing Component, and a high school transcript, and in some cases an interview and audition, statement of professional interest. Application deadline: 1/2; 3/15 priority date for financial aid. Deferred admission is possible.

Getting Accepted

21,645 applied
71% were accepted
6,940 enrolled (45% of accepted)
55% from top tenth of their h.s. class
Mean SAT critical reading score: 607
Mean SAT math score: 680
Mean ACT score: 27
58% had SAT critical reading scores over 600
85% had SAT math scores over 600
89% had ACT scores over 24
16% had SAT critical reading scores over 700
47% had SAT math scores over 700
36% had ACT scores over 30
57 National Merit Scholars

Graduation and After

63% graduated in 4 years
17% graduated in 5 years
2% graduated in 6 years
50% had job offers within 6 months
6258 organizations recruited on campus

Financial Matters

$12,240 resident tuition and fees (2008–09)
$26,024 nonresident tuition and fees (2008–09)
$8764 room and board
72% average percent of need met
$10,288 average financial aid amount received per undergraduate (2006–07)

THE UNIVERSITY OF IOWA

SMALL-TOWN SETTING ■ PUBLIC ■ STATE-SUPPORTED ■ COED
IOWA CITY, IOWA

Web site: www.uiowa.edu
Contact: Mr. Michael Barron, Assistant Provost for Enrollment Services and Director of Admissions, 107 Calvin Hall, Iowa City, IA 52242
Telephone: 319-335-3847 or toll-free 800-553-4692
Fax: 319-335-1535
E-mail: admissions@uiowa.edu

Getting Accepted
15,582 applied
82% were accepted
4,246 enrolled (33% of accepted)
22% from top tenth of their h.s. class
3.56 average high school GPA
46% had SAT critical reading scores over 600
61% had SAT math scores over 600
69% had ACT scores over 24
14% had SAT critical reading scores over 700
19% had SAT math scores over 700
13% had ACT scores over 30
24 National Merit Scholars

Graduation and After
40% graduated in 4 years
22% graduated in 5 years
3% graduated in 6 years
578 organizations recruited on campus

Financial Matters
$6824 resident tuition and fees (2009–10)
$22,198 nonresident tuition and fees (2009–10)
97% average percent of need met
$7998 average financial aid amount received per undergraduate (2007–08 estimated)

Academics

Iowa awards bachelor's, master's, doctoral, and first-professional **degrees** and post-master's and first-professional certificates. **Challenging opportunities** include advanced placement credit, accelerated degree programs, student-designed majors, an honors program, double majors, independent study, and a senior project. Special programs include cooperative education, internships, summer session for credit, off-campus study, study-abroad, and Army and Air Force ROTC.

The most frequently chosen **baccalaureate** fields are business/marketing, communications/journalism, and social sciences. A complete listing of majors at Iowa appears in the Majors by College index beginning on page 469.

The **faculty** at Iowa has 1,588 full-time members, 97% with terminal degrees. The student-faculty ratio is 15:1.

Students of Iowa

The student body totals 29,747, of whom 20,823 are undergraduates. 51.7% are women and 48.3% are men. Students come from 56 states and territories and 67 other countries. 66% are from Iowa. 2.2% are international students. 2.2% are African American, 0.5% American Indian, 3.6% Asian American, and 2.8% Hispanic American. 83% returned for their sophomore year.

Facilities and Resources

1,200 **computers/terminals** are available on campus for general student use. Students can access the following: computer help desk, free student e-mail accounts, online (class) grades, online (class) registration, online (class) schedules, online degree process, financial aid summary, bills. Campuswide network is available. 95% of college-owned or -operated housing units are wired for high-speed Internet access. Wireless service is available via classrooms, computer labs, dorm rooms, learning centers, libraries, student centers. The 11 **libraries** have 4,134,268 books and 49,279 subscriptions.

Campus Life

There are 425 active organizations on campus, including a drama/theater group, newspaper, radio station, choral group, and marching band. 8% of eligible men and 13% of eligible women are members of national **fraternities** and national **sororities**.

Iowa is a member of the NCAA (Division I). **Intercollegiate sports** (some offering scholarships) include baseball (m), basketball, crew (w), cross-country running, field hockey (w), football (m), golf, gymnastics, soccer (w), softball (w), swimming and diving, tennis, track and field, volleyball (w), wrestling (m).

Campus Safety

Student safety services include late-night transport/escort service, 24-hour emergency telephone alarm devices, 24-hour patrols by trained security personnel, and electronically operated dormitory entrances.

Applying

Iowa requires SAT or ACT, a high school transcript, and must meet Regent Admission Index (RAI) requirement: residents 245 or above; nonresidents 255 or above. Application deadline: 4/1. Early and deferred admission are possible.

THE UNIVERSITY OF KANSAS

SUBURBAN SETTING ■ PUBLIC ■ STATE-SUPPORTED ■ COED
LAWRENCE, KANSAS

Web site: www.ku.edu
Contact: Ms. Lisa Pinamonti Kress, Director of Admissions and Scholarships,
   KU Visitor Center, 1502 Iowa Street, Lawrence, KS 66045-7576
Telephone: 785-864-3911 or toll-free 888-686-7323 (in-state)
Fax: 785-864-5006
E-mail: adm@ku.edu

Academics

KU awards bachelor's, master's, doctoral, and first-professional **degrees** and post-master's certificates (University of Kansas is a single institution with academic programs and facilities at two primary locations: Lawrence and Kansas City.). **Challenging opportunities** include advanced placement credit, accelerated degree programs, an honors program, double majors, independent study, and a senior project. Special programs include cooperative education, internships, summer session for credit, study-abroad, and Army, Navy, and Air Force ROTC.

The most frequently chosen **baccalaureate** fields are business/marketing, health professions and related sciences, and social sciences. A complete listing of majors at KU appears in the Majors by College index beginning on page 469.

The **faculty** at KU has 1,218 full-time members, 97% with terminal degrees. The student-faculty ratio is 19:1.

Students of KU

The student body totals 29,365, of whom 21,332 are undergraduates. 50.3% are women and 49.7% are men. Students come from 54 states and territories and 82 other countries. 77% are from Kansas. 3.4% are international students. 3.7% are African American, 1.1% American Indian, 4.3% Asian American, and 3.7% Hispanic American. 80% returned for their sophomore year.

Facilities and Resources

1,500 **computers/terminals** are available on campus for general student use. Students can access the following: campus intranet, computer help desk, free student e-mail accounts, online (class) grades, online (class) registration, online (class) schedules. Campuswide network is available. 100% of college-owned or -operated housing units are wired for high-speed Internet access. Wireless service is available via computer centers, computer labs, libraries, student centers. The 12 **libraries** have 3,543,454 books and 62,016 subscriptions.

Campus Life

There are 550 active organizations on campus, including a drama/theater group, newspaper, radio station, television station, choral group, and marching band. 12% of eligible men and 17% of eligible women are members of national **fraternities** and national **sororities**.

KU is a member of the NCAA (Division I). **Intercollegiate sports** (some offering scholarships) include baseball (m), basketball, crew (w), cross-country running, football (m), golf, soccer (w), softball (w), swimming and diving (w), tennis (w), track and field, volleyball (w).

Campus Safety

Student safety services include University police department, late-night transport/escort service, 24-hour emergency telephone alarm devices, 24-hour patrols by trained security personnel, and electronically operated dormitory entrances.

Applying

KU requires SAT or ACT, a high school transcript, Kansas Board of Regents admissions criteria with GPA of 2.0 resident, 2.5 nonresident; or upper third of high school class; or minimum ACT score 21 resident, 24 nonresident; or minimum SAT score 980 resident, 1090 nonresident, and a minimum high school GPA of 2.0, and in some cases a minimum high school GPA of 2.5. Application deadline: 4/1; 3/1 priority date for financial aid.

Getting Accepted

10,902 applied
92% were accepted
4,483 enrolled (45% of accepted)
27% from top tenth of their h.s. class
3.41 average high school GPA
Mean ACT score: 25
61% had ACT scores over 24
13% had ACT scores over 30
45 National Merit Scholars

Graduation and After

31% graduated in 4 years
23% graduated in 5 years
6% graduated in 6 years
500 organizations recruited on campus

Financial Matters

$7725 resident tuition and fees (2008–09)
$18,909 nonresident tuition and fees (2008–09)
$6474 room and board
64% average percent of need met
$8117 average financial aid amount received per undergraduate (2006–07)

University of Kentucky

Urban setting ■ Public ■ State-supported ■ Coed
Lexington, Kentucky

Web site: www.uky.edu
Contact: Ms. Michelle Nordin, Associate Director of Admissions, 100 W.D.
    Funkhouser Building, Lexington, KY 40506-0054
Telephone: 859-257-2000 or toll-free 800-432-0967 (in-state)
E-mail: admissio@uky.edu

Getting Accepted
10,619 applied
77% were accepted
3,865 enrolled (47% of accepted)
23% from top tenth of their h.s. class
3.48 average high school GPA
Mean SAT critical reading score: 550
Mean SAT math score: 565
Mean ACT score: 24
33% had SAT critical reading scores over 600
40% had SAT math scores over 600
62% had ACT scores over 24
6% had SAT critical reading scores over 700
9% had SAT math scores over 700
17% had ACT scores over 30
28 National Merit Scholars
157 valedictorians

Graduation and After
574 organizations recruited on campus

Financial Matters
$7736 resident tuition and fees (2008–09)
$15,884 nonresident tuition and fees
    (2008–09)
$8785 room and board
81% average percent of need met
$7861 average financial aid amount received
    per undergraduate (2005–06)

Academics
UK awards bachelor's, master's, doctoral, and first-professional **degrees** and post-master's certificates. **Challenging opportunities** include advanced placement credit, accelerated degree programs, student-designed majors, an honors program, double majors, and independent study. Special programs include cooperative education, internships, summer session for credit, off-campus study, study-abroad, and Army and Air Force ROTC.

The most frequently chosen **baccalaureate** fields are business/marketing, communications/journalism, and social sciences. A complete listing of majors at UK appears in the Majors by College index beginning on page 469.

The **faculty** at UK has 1,268 full-time members. The student-faculty ratio is 17:1.

Students of UK
The student body totals 25,856, of whom 18,770 are undergraduates. 51.2% are women and 48.8% are men. Students come from 52 states and territories and 63 other countries. 80% are from Kentucky. 0.8% are international students. 5.7% are African American, 0.2% American Indian, 2.1% Asian American, and 1.1% Hispanic American. 76% returned for their sophomore year.

Facilities and Resources
1,400 **computers/terminals** are available on campus for general student use. Students can access the following: online (class) registration, various software packages. Campuswide network is available. The 16 **libraries** have 3,092,616 books and 29,633 subscriptions.

Campus Life
There are 305 active organizations on campus, including a drama/theater group, newspaper, radio station, choral group, and marching band. 15% of eligible men and 19% of eligible women are members of national **fraternities** and national **sororities**.

UK is a member of the NCAA (Division I). **Intercollegiate sports** (some offering scholarships) include baseball (m), basketball, cross-country running, football (m), golf, gymnastics (w), riflery, soccer, softball (w), swimming and diving, tennis, track and field, volleyball (w).

Campus Safety
Student safety services include late-night transport/escort service, 24-hour emergency telephone alarm devices, 24-hour patrols by trained security personnel, and electronically operated dormitory entrances.

Applying
UK requires SAT or ACT, a high school transcript, and a minimum high school GPA of 2.0. Application deadline: 2/15; 2/15 priority date for financial aid. Early admission is possible.

UNIVERSITY OF MARYLAND, BALTIMORE COUNTY

SUBURBAN SETTING ■ PUBLIC ■ STATE-SUPPORTED ■ COED
BALTIMORE, MARYLAND

Web site: www.umbc.edu
Contact: Mr. Dale Bittinger, Director of Admissions, 1000 Hilltop Circle,
   Baltimore, MD 21250
Telephone: 410-455-2291 or toll-free 800-UMBC-4U2 (in-state),
   800-862-2402 (out-of-state)
Fax: 410-455-1094
E-mail: admissions@umbc.edu

Academics

UMBC awards bachelor's, master's, and doctoral **degrees** and post-bachelor's
certificates. **Challenging opportunities** include advanced placement credit, student-
designed majors, freshman honors college, an honors program, double majors,
independent study, and a senior project. Special programs include cooperative education,
internships, summer session for credit, off-campus study, study-abroad, and Army
ROTC.

The most frequently chosen **baccalaureate** fields are communication technologies,
social sciences, and biological/life sciences. A complete listing of majors at UMBC
appears in the Majors by College index beginning on page 469.

The **faculty** at UMBC has 483 full-time members, 87% with terminal degrees. The
student-faculty ratio is 18:1.

Students of UMBC

The student body totals 12,268, of whom 9,612 are undergraduates. 45.4% are women
and 54.6% are men. Students come from 43 states and territories and 75 other countries.
93% are from Maryland. 3.7% are international students. 16.7% are African American,
0.5% American Indian, 21.7% Asian American, and 4% Hispanic American. 87%
returned for their sophomore year.

Facilities and Resources

875 **computers/terminals** are available on campus for general student use. Students can
access the following: campus intranet, computer help desk, free student e-mail accounts,
online (class) grades, online (class) registration, online (class) schedules, student account
information. Campuswide network is available. 100% of college-owned or -operated
housing units are wired for high-speed Internet access. Wireless service is available via
classrooms, computer centers, computer labs, libraries, student centers. The 2 **libraries**
have 1,020,627 books and 4,204 subscriptions.

Campus Life

There are 250 active organizations on campus, including a drama/theater group,
newspaper, radio station, and choral group. 3% of eligible men and 4% of eligible
women are members of national **fraternities** and national **sororities**.

UMBC is a member of the NCAA (Division I). **Intercollegiate sports** (some
offering scholarships) include baseball (m), basketball, cross-country running, lacrosse,
soccer, softball (w), swimming and diving, tennis, track and field, volleyball (w).

Campus Safety

Student safety services include late-night transport/escort service, 24-hour emergency
telephone alarm devices, and 24-hour patrols by trained security personnel.

Applying

UMBC requires an essay, SAT or ACT, and a high school transcript. It recommends 2
recommendations and a minimum high school GPA of 3.0. Application deadline: 2/1;
2/14 priority date for financial aid. Early and deferred admission are possible.

Getting Accepted

5,820 applied
72% were accepted
1,569 enrolled (38% of accepted)
26% from top tenth of their h.s. class
3.57 average high school GPA
Mean SAT critical reading score: 579
Mean SAT math score: 612
Mean SAT writing score: 574
Mean ACT score: 25
40% had SAT critical reading scores over 600
57% had SAT math scores over 600
38% had SAT writing scores over 600
56% had ACT scores over 24
8% had SAT critical reading scores over 700
14% had SAT math scores over 700
8% had SAT writing scores over 700
12% had ACT scores over 30

Graduation and After

35% graduated in 4 years
19% graduated in 5 years
7% graduated in 6 years
69% had job offers within 6 months
821 organizations recruited on campus

Financial Matters

$8780 resident tuition and fees (2008–09)
$17,512 nonresident tuition and fees
   (2008–09)
$8960 room and board
73% average percent of need met
$9527 average financial aid amount received
   per undergraduate (2006–07)

University of Maryland, College Park

Suburban setting ■ Public ■ State-supported ■ Coed
College Park, Maryland

Web site: www.maryland.edu
Contact: Ms. Barbara Gill, Director of Undergraduate Admissions, Mitchell Building, College Park, MD 20742-5235
Telephone: 301-314-8385 or toll-free 800-422-5867
Fax: 301-314-9693
E-mail: um-admit@uga.umd.edu

Getting Accepted
28,161 applied
39% were accepted
3,912 enrolled (36% of accepted)
73% from top tenth of their h.s. class
3.92 average high school GPA
66% had SAT critical reading scores over 600
76% had SAT math scores over 600
17% had SAT critical reading scores over 700
30% had SAT math scores over 700

Graduation and After
63% graduated in 4 years
17% graduated in 5 years
2% graduated in 6 years
792 organizations recruited on campus

Financial Matters
$8005 resident tuition and fees (2008–09)
$23,076 nonresident tuition and fees (2008–09)
$9109 room and board
54% average percent of need met
$8843 average financial aid amount received per undergraduate (2006–07)

Academics

Maryland, College Park awards bachelor's, master's, doctoral, and first-professional **degrees** and post-bachelor's and post-master's certificates. **Challenging opportunities** include advanced placement credit, accelerated degree programs, student-designed majors, an honors program, double majors, independent study, and a senior project. Special programs include cooperative education, internships, summer session for credit, off-campus study, study-abroad, and Army, Navy, and Air Force ROTC.

The most frequently chosen **baccalaureate** fields are social sciences, business/marketing, and engineering. A complete listing of majors at Maryland, College Park appears in the Majors by College index beginning on page 469.

The **faculty** at Maryland, College Park has 1,644 full-time members, 92% with terminal degrees. The student-faculty ratio is 18:1.

Students of Maryland, College Park

The student body totals 36,956, of whom 26,431 are undergraduates. 48% are women and 52% are men. Students come from 54 states and territories and 137 other countries. 76% are from Maryland. 2.1% are international students. 13.1% are African American, 0.3% American Indian, 14.6% Asian American, and 5.9% Hispanic American. 94% returned for their sophomore year.

Facilities and Resources

11,097 **computers/terminals** are available on campus for general student use. Students can access the following: campus intranet, computer help desk, free student e-mail accounts, online (class) grades, online (class) registration, online (class) schedules, student account information, financial aid summary. Campuswide network is available. 100% of college-owned or -operated housing units are wired for high-speed Internet access. Wireless service is available via entire campus. The 7 **libraries** have 3,716,860 books and 42,393 subscriptions.

Campus Life

There are 527 active organizations on campus, including a drama/theater group, newspaper, radio station, television station, choral group, and marching band. 13% of eligible men and 10% of eligible women are members of national **fraternities** and national **sororities**.

Maryland, College Park is a member of the NCAA (Division I). **Intercollegiate sports** (some offering scholarships) include baseball (m), basketball, cheerleading (w), cross-country running, field hockey (w), football (m), golf, gymnastics (w), lacrosse, soccer, softball (w), swimming and diving, tennis, track and field, volleyball (w), water polo (w), wrestling (m).

Campus Safety

Student safety services include campus police, video camera surveillance, late-night transport/escort service, 24-hour emergency telephone alarm devices, 24-hour patrols by trained security personnel, student patrols, and electronically operated dormitory entrances.

Applying

Maryland, College Park requires an essay, SAT or ACT, and a high school transcript, and in some cases resume of activities, auditions. It recommends 2 recommendations. Application deadline: 1/20; 2/15 priority date for financial aid. Early and deferred admission are possible.

UNIVERSITY OF MARY WASHINGTON

SMALL-TOWN SETTING ■ PUBLIC ■ STATE-SUPPORTED ■ COED
FREDERICKSBURG, VIRGINIA

Web site: www.umw.edu
Contact: Dr. Martin Wilder, Vice President for Enrollment and
Communications, 1301 College Avenue, Fredericksburg, VA 22401-5358
Telephone: 540-654-2000 or toll-free 800-468-5614
Fax: 540-654-1857
E-mail: admit@umw.edu

Academics

Mary Washington awards bachelor's and master's **degrees** and post-bachelor's
certificates. **Challenging opportunities** include advanced placement credit, accelerated
degree programs, student-designed majors, double majors, independent study, and a
senior project. Special programs include cooperative education, internships, summer
session for credit, and study-abroad.

The most frequently chosen **baccalaureate** fields are social sciences, business/
marketing, and English. A complete listing of majors at Mary Washington appears in the
Majors by College index beginning on page 469.

The **faculty** at Mary Washington has 246 full-time members, 98% with terminal
degrees. The student-faculty ratio is 15:1.

Students of Mary Washington

The student body totals 5,084, of whom 4,231 are undergraduates. 65.6% are women
and 34.4% are men. Students come from 44 states and territories and 24 other countries.
78% are from Virginia. 1.1% are international students. 3.9% are African American,
0.5% American Indian, 4.3% Asian American, and 3.8% Hispanic American. 83%
returned for their sophomore year.

Facilities and Resources

306 **computers/terminals** are available on campus for general student use. Students can
access the following: computer help desk, free student e-mail accounts, online (class)
grades, online (class) registration. Campuswide network is available. 100% of college-
owned or -operated housing units are wired for high-speed Internet access. Wireless
service is available via entire campus. The 2 **libraries** have 495,747 books and 9,087
subscriptions.

Campus Life

There are 116 active organizations on campus, including a drama/theater group,
newspaper, radio station, and choral group. No national or local **fraternities** or **sororities.**

Mary Washington is a member of the NCAA (Division III). **Intercollegiate sports**
include baseball (m), basketball, crew, cross-country running, equestrian sports, field
hockey (w), lacrosse, soccer, softball (w), swimming and diving, tennis, track and field,
volleyball (w).

Campus Safety

Student safety services include self-defense and safety classes, late-night transport/escort
service, 24-hour emergency telephone alarm devices, 24-hour patrols by trained security
personnel, student patrols, and electronically operated dormitory entrances.

Applying

Mary Washington requires an essay, SAT or ACT, and a high school transcript. It recommends SAT Subject Tests. Application deadline: 2/1; 3/1 priority date for financial aid.
Deferred admission is possible.

Getting Accepted

4,600 applied
71% were accepted
877 enrolled (27% of accepted)
3.59 average high school GPA
Mean SAT critical reading score: 601
Mean SAT math score: 577
Mean SAT writing score: 590
Mean ACT score: 26
55% had SAT critical reading scores over 600
40% had SAT math scores over 600
48% had SAT writing scores over 600
82% had ACT scores over 24
11% had SAT critical reading scores over 700
2% had SAT math scores over 700
8% had SAT writing scores over 700
10% had ACT scores over 30
4 National Merit Scholars

Graduation and After

69% graduated in 4 years
6% graduated in 5 years
73% had job offers within 6 months

Financial Matters

$7500 resident tuition and fees (2008–09)
$19,950 nonresident tuition and fees
(2008–09)
$7700 room and board
56% average percent of need met
$6600 average financial aid amount received
per undergraduate (2006–07)

University of Miami

Suburban setting ■ Private ■ Independent ■ Coed
Coral Gables, Florida

Web site: www.miami.edu
Contact: PO Box 248025, Ashe Building Room 132, 1252 Memorial Drive, Coral Gables, FL 33146-4616
Telephone: 305-284-4323
Fax: 305-284-2507
E-mail: egillis@miami.edu

Getting Accepted
21,774 applied
39% were accepted
2,010 enrolled (24% of accepted)
66% from top tenth of their h.s. class
Mean SAT critical reading score: 631
Mean SAT math score: 652
Mean SAT writing score: 622
Mean ACT score: 29
71% had SAT critical reading scores over 600
80% had SAT math scores over 600
66% had SAT writing scores over 600
94% had ACT scores over 24
20% had SAT critical reading scores over 700
27% had SAT math scores over 700
16% had SAT writing scores over 700
42% had ACT scores over 30
27 National Merit Scholars
61 valedictorians

Graduation and After
64% graduated in 4 years
11% graduated in 5 years
2% graduated in 6 years
673 organizations recruited on campus

Financial Matters
$34,834 tuition and fees (2008–09)
$10,254 room and board
81% average percent of need met
$27,182 average financial aid amount received per undergraduate (2007–08 estimated)

Academics

UM awards bachelor's, master's, doctoral, and first-professional **degrees** and post-bachelor's and post-master's certificates. **Challenging opportunities** include advanced placement credit, accelerated degree programs, student-designed majors, an honors program, double majors, independent study, and a senior project. Special programs include internships, summer session for credit, study-abroad, and Army and Air Force ROTC.

The most frequently chosen **baccalaureate** fields are business/marketing, biological/life sciences, and visual and performing arts. A complete listing of majors at UM appears in the Majors by College index beginning on page 469.

The **faculty** at UM has 947 full-time members, 85% with terminal degrees. The student-faculty ratio is 11:1.

Students of UM

The student body totals 15,323, of whom 10,422 are undergraduates. 52.9% are women and 47.1% are men. Students come from 54 states and territories and 102 other countries. 50% are from Florida. 6.9% are international students. 8% are African American, 0.3% American Indian, 5% Asian American, and 22.9% Hispanic American. 90% returned for their sophomore year.

Facilities and Resources

1,800 **computers/terminals** are available on campus for general student use. Students can access the following: computer help desk, free student e-mail accounts, online (class) grades, online (class) registration, online (class) schedules, online student account information. Campuswide network is available. 100% of college-owned or -operated housing units are wired for high-speed Internet access. The 8 **libraries** have 3,227,943 books and 62,621 subscriptions.

Campus Life

There are 275 active organizations on campus, including a drama/theater group, newspaper, radio station, television station, choral group, and marching band. 14% of eligible men and 14% of eligible women are members of national **fraternities** and national **sororities**.

UM is a member of the NCAA (Division I). **Intercollegiate sports** (some offering scholarships) include baseball (m), basketball, cheerleading, cross-country running, football (m), golf (w), soccer (w), swimming and diving (w), tennis, track and field, volleyball (w).

Campus Safety

Student safety services include crime prevention and safety workshops, residential college crime watch, late-night transport/escort service, 24-hour emergency telephone alarm devices, 24-hour patrols by trained security personnel, student patrols, and electronically operated dormitory entrances.

Applying

UM requires an essay, SAT or ACT, a high school transcript, and counselor evaluation, and in some cases SAT Subject Tests and SAT and SAT Subject Tests or ACT. Application deadline: 1/15; 2/1 priority date for financial aid. Early and deferred admission are possible.

University of Michigan

Suburban setting ■ Public ■ State-supported ■ Coed
Ann Arbor, Michigan

Web site: www.umich.edu
Contact: 1220 Student Activities Building, 515 East Jefferson, Ann Arbor, MI 48109-1316
Telephone: 734-764-7433
Fax: 734-936-0740
E-mail: ugadmiss@umich.edu

Academics

Michigan awards bachelor's, master's, doctoral, and first-professional **degrees** and post-bachelor's and post-master's certificates. **Challenging opportunities** include advanced placement credit, accelerated degree programs, student-designed majors, an honors program, double majors, independent study, and a senior project. Special programs include cooperative education, internships, summer session for credit, off-campus study, study-abroad, and Army and Air Force ROTC.

The most frequently chosen **baccalaureate** fields are social sciences, engineering, and psychology. A complete listing of majors at Michigan appears in the Majors by College index beginning on page 469.

The **faculty** at Michigan has 2,420 full-time members, 91% with terminal degrees. The student-faculty ratio is 15:1.

Students of Michigan

The student body totals 41,028, of whom 25,994 are undergraduates. 49.8% are women and 50.2% are men. Students come from 55 states and territories and 109 other countries. 65% are from Michigan. 5.3% are international students. 6.3% are African American, 0.8% American Indian, 11.9% Asian American, and 4.4% Hispanic American. 96% returned for their sophomore year.

Facilities and Resources

2,254 **computers/terminals** and 5,000 ports are available on campus for general student use. Students can access the following: computer help desk, free student e-mail accounts, online (class) grades, online (class) registration, online (class) schedules, personal webpages. Campuswide network is available. 100% of college-owned or -operated housing units are wired for high-speed Internet access. Wireless service is available via classrooms, computer centers, computer labs, libraries, student centers. The 25 **libraries** have 8,164,309 books and 74,022 subscriptions.

Campus Life

There are 1,008 active organizations on campus, including a drama/theater group, newspaper, radio station, television station, choral group, and marching band. 16% of eligible men and 18% of eligible women are members of national **fraternities**, national **sororities**, local fraternities, and local sororities.

Michigan is a member of the NCAA (Division I). **Intercollegiate sports** (some offering scholarships) include baseball (m), basketball, cheerleading, crew, cross-country running, field hockey (w), football (m), golf, gymnastics, ice hockey (m), soccer, softball (w), swimming and diving, tennis, track and field, volleyball (w), water polo, wrestling (m).

Campus Safety

Student safety services include bicycle patrols, late-night transport/escort service, 24-hour emergency telephone alarm devices, 24-hour patrols by trained security personnel, student patrols, and electronically operated dormitory entrances.

Applying

Michigan requires an essay, SAT or ACT, and a high school transcript, and in some cases SAT Subject Tests and an interview. Application deadline: 2/1; 4/30 for financial aid. Deferred admission is possible.

Getting Accepted
29,814 applied
42% were accepted
5,783 enrolled (46% of accepted)
92% from top tenth of their h.s. class
3.75 average high school GPA
72% had SAT critical reading scores over 600
86% had SAT math scores over 600
74% had SAT writing scores over 600
93% had ACT scores over 24
22% had SAT critical reading scores over 700
46% had SAT math scores over 700
28% had SAT writing scores over 700
44% had ACT scores over 30

Graduation and After
70% graduated in 4 years
15% graduated in 5 years
3% graduated in 6 years

Financial Matters
$11,927 resident tuition and fees (2008–09)
$34,419 nonresident tuition and fees (2008–09)
$8590 room and board
90% average percent of need met
$11,174 average financial aid amount received per undergraduate (2006–07)

University of Michigan–Dearborn

Suburban setting ■ Public ■ State-supported ■ Coed
Dearborn, Michigan

Getting Accepted

3,438 applied
66% were accepted
893 enrolled (39% of accepted)
25% from top tenth of their h.s. class
3.46 average high school GPA
Mean SAT writing score: 546
54% had ACT scores over 24
9% had ACT scores over 30
5 valedictorians

Graduation and After

14% graduated in 4 years
27% graduated in 5 years
12% graduated in 6 years
53% had job offers within 6 months
92 organizations recruited on campus

Financial Matters

$7769 resident tuition and fees (2008–09)
$16,989 nonresident tuition and fees (2008–09)
36% average percent of need met
$5311 average financial aid amount received per undergraduate (2006–07)

Web site: www.umd.umich.edu
Contact: Mr. Christopher Tremblay, Director of Admissions and Orientation, 4901 Evergreen Road, Dearborn, MI 48128-1491
Telephone: 313-593-5100
Fax: 313-436-9167
E-mail: admissions@umd.umich.edu

Academics

UM-D awards bachelor's and master's **degrees** and post-bachelor's certificates. **Challenging opportunities** include advanced placement credit, accelerated degree programs, student-designed majors, an honors program, double majors, independent study, and a senior project. Special programs include cooperative education, internships, summer session for credit, off-campus study, study-abroad, and Army, Navy, and Air Force ROTC.

The most frequently chosen **baccalaureate** fields are education, business/marketing, and engineering. A complete listing of majors at UM-D appears in the Majors by College index beginning on page 469.

The **faculty** at UM-D has 292 full-time members, 100% with terminal degrees. The student-faculty ratio is 16:1.

Students of UM-D

The student body totals 8,336, of whom 6,447 are undergraduates. 51.9% are women and 48.1% are men. Students come from 11 states and territories and 28 other countries. 98% are from Michigan. 1.2% are international students. 9.6% are African American, 0.7% American Indian, 5.9% Asian American, and 2.8% Hispanic American. 81% returned for their sophomore year.

Facilities and Resources

350 **computers/terminals** are available on campus for general student use. Campuswide network is available. The **library** has 340,897 books and 1,099 subscriptions.

Campus Life

Active organizations on campus include a drama/theater group, newspaper, radio station, and television station. 25% of eligible men and 25% of eligible women are members of national **fraternities** and national **sororities**.

UM-D is a member of the NAIA. **Intercollegiate sports** (some offering scholarships) include basketball, ice hockey (m), volleyball (w).

Campus Safety

Student safety services include late-night transport/escort service, 24-hour emergency telephone alarm devices, and 24-hour patrols by trained security personnel.

Applying

UM-D requires SAT or ACT, a high school transcript, and a minimum high school GPA of 3.0, and in some cases an interview. Application deadline: rolling admissions; 2/14 priority date for financial aid. Deferred admission is possible.

UNIVERSITY OF MINNESOTA, MORRIS

SMALL-TOWN SETTING ■ PUBLIC ■ STATE-SUPPORTED ■ COED
MORRIS, MINNESOTA

Web site: www.mrs.umn.edu
Contact: Ms. Jaime Moquin, Director of Admissions, 600 East 4th Street, Morris, MN 56267-2199
Telephone: 320-539-6035 or toll-free 800-992-8863
Fax: 320-589-1673
E-mail: admissions@morris.umn.edu

Academics

UMM awards bachelor's **degrees. Challenging opportunities** include advanced placement credit, accelerated degree programs, student-designed majors, freshman honors college, an honors program, double majors, independent study, and a senior project. Special programs include internships, summer session for credit, off-campus study, and study-abroad.

The most frequently chosen **baccalaureate** fields are social sciences, English, and biological/life sciences. A complete listing of majors at UMM appears in the Majors by College index beginning on page 469.

The **faculty** at UMM has 119 full-time members, 95% with terminal degrees. The student-faculty ratio is 12:1.

Students of UMM

The student body is made up of 1,740 undergraduates. 57.9% are women and 42.1% are men. Students come from 30 states and territories and 11 other countries. 87% are from Minnesota. 1.9% are international students. 2.3% are African American, 11.3% American Indian, 3.5% Asian American, and 1.7% Hispanic American. 86% returned for their sophomore year.

Facilities and Resources

124 **computers/terminals** are available on campus for general student use. Students can access the following: online (class) registration. Campuswide network is available. The 2 **libraries** have 191,469 books and 9,042 subscriptions.

Campus Life

There are 91 active organizations on campus, including a drama/theater group, newspaper, radio station, television station, and choral group. No national or local **fraternities** or **sororities**.

UMM is a member of the NCAA (Division III). **Intercollegiate sports** include baseball (m), basketball, cross-country running (w), football (m), golf, soccer (w), softball (w), swimming and diving (w), tennis, track and field, volleyball (w).

Campus Safety

Student safety services include late-night transport/escort service, 24-hour emergency telephone alarm devices, 24-hour patrols by trained security personnel, and electronically operated dormitory entrances.

Applying

UMM requires an essay, SAT or ACT, and a high school transcript, and in some cases an interview and 1 recommendation. It recommends a minimum high school GPA of 3.0. Application deadline: 3/15. Early and deferred admission are possible.

Getting Accepted

1,216 applied
80% were accepted
377 enrolled (39% of accepted)
28% from top tenth of their h.s. class
Mean SAT critical reading score: 618
Mean SAT math score: 617
Mean SAT writing score: 579
Mean ACT score: 24
66% had SAT critical reading scores over 600
66% had SAT math scores over 600
42% had SAT writing scores over 600
56% had ACT scores over 24
26% had SAT critical reading scores over 700
21% had SAT math scores over 700
19% had SAT writing scores over 700
11% had ACT scores over 30
27 class presidents
36 valedictorians

Graduation and After

80% had job offers within 6 months
90 organizations recruited on campus

Financial Matters

$10,006 resident tuition and fees (2008–09)
$10,006 nonresident tuition and fees (2008–09)
$6710 room and board
82% average percent of need met
$12,660 average financial aid amount received per undergraduate (2006–07)

University of Minnesota, Twin Cities Campus

Urban setting ■ Public ■ State-supported ■ Coed
Minneapolis, Minnesota

Web site: www.umn.edu/tc
Contact: Rachelle Hernandez, Associate Director of Admissions, 240 Williamson, Minneapolis, MN 55455-0213
Telephone: 612-625-2008 or toll-free 800-752-1000
Fax: 612-626-1693
E-mail: admissions@tc.umn.edu

Getting Accepted

29,159 applied
53% were accepted
5,106 enrolled (33% of accepted)
45% from top tenth of their h.s. class
55% had SAT critical reading scores over 600
70% had SAT math scores over 600
49% had SAT writing scores over 600
77% had ACT scores over 24
18% had SAT critical reading scores over 700
28% had SAT math scores over 700
12% had SAT writing scores over 700
21% had ACT scores over 30

Graduation and After

37% graduated in 4 years
21% graduated in 5 years
6% graduated in 6 years

Financial Matters

$10,273 resident tuition and fees (2008–09)
$21,903 nonresident tuition and fees (2008–09)
$7280 room and board
85% average percent of need met
$11,969 average financial aid amount received per undergraduate (2007–08 estimated)

Academics

U of M–Twin Cities awards bachelor's, master's, doctoral, and first-professional **degrees** and post-bachelor's, post-master's, and first-professional certificates. **Challenging opportunities** include advanced placement credit, accelerated degree programs, student-designed majors, freshman honors college, an honors program, double majors, independent study, and a senior project. Special programs include cooperative education, internships, summer session for credit, off-campus study, study-abroad, and Army, Navy, and Air Force ROTC.

The most frequently chosen **baccalaureate** fields are social sciences, engineering, and business/marketing. A complete listing of majors at U of M–Twin Cities appears in the Majors by College index beginning on page 469.

The **faculty** at U of M–Twin Cities has 1,933 full-time members, 81% with terminal degrees. The student-faculty ratio is 20:1.

Students of U of M–Twin Cities

The student body totals 51,140, of whom 32,557 are undergraduates. 53.1% are women and 46.9% are men. Students come from 51 states and territories and 77 other countries. 74% are from Minnesota. 3.1% are international students. 4.9% are African American, 1% American Indian, 9.8% Asian American, and 2.3% Hispanic American. 88% returned for their sophomore year.

Facilities and Resources

Students can access the following: online (class) registration, e-mail. Campuswide network is available. The 18 **libraries** have 5,700,000 books and 45,000 subscriptions.

Campus Life

There are 350 active organizations on campus, including a drama/theater group, newspaper, radio station, television station, choral group, and marching band. 3% of eligible men and 3% of eligible women are members of national **fraternities**, national **sororities**, and local sororities.

U of M–Twin Cities is a member of the NCAA (Division I). **Intercollegiate sports** (some offering scholarships) include baseball (m), basketball, cross-country running, football (m), golf, gymnastics, ice hockey, soccer (w), softball (w), swimming and diving, tennis, track and field, volleyball (w), wrestling (m).

Campus Safety

Student safety services include safety/security orientation, security lighting, late-night transport/escort service, 24-hour emergency telephone alarm devices, 24-hour patrols by trained security personnel, student patrols, and electronically operated dormitory entrances.

Applying

U of M–Twin Cities requires SAT or ACT and a high school transcript. It recommends a minimum high school GPA of 2.0. Application deadline: rolling admissions. Early and deferred admission are possible.

University of Missouri–Columbia

Suburban setting ■ Public ■ State-supported ■ Coed
Columbia, Missouri

Web site: www.missouri.edu
Contact: Ms. Barbara Rupp, Director of Admissions, 230 Jesse Hall, Columbia, MO 65211
Telephone: 573-882-7786 or toll-free 800-225-6075 (in-state)
Fax: 573-882-7887
E-mail: mu4u@missouri.edu

Academics

Missouri-Columbia awards bachelor's, master's, doctoral, and first-professional **degrees** and post-master's and first-professional certificates. **Challenging opportunities** include advanced placement credit, accelerated degree programs, student-designed majors, freshman honors college, an honors program, double majors, independent study, and a senior project. Special programs include cooperative education, internships, summer session for credit, off-campus study, study-abroad, and Army, Navy, and Air Force ROTC.

The most frequently chosen **baccalaureate** fields are business/marketing, communications/journalism, and social sciences. A complete listing of majors at Missouri-Columbia appears in the Majors by College index beginning on page 469.

The **faculty** at Missouri-Columbia has 1,270 full-time members, 91% with terminal degrees. The student-faculty ratio is 17:1.

Students of Missouri-Columbia

The student body totals 30,200, of whom 23,042 are undergraduates. 51.8% are women and 48.2% are men. Students come from 53 states and territories and 57 other countries. 85% are from Missouri. 1.8% are international students. 6.3% are African American, 0.6% American Indian, 2.5% Asian American, and 1.9% Hispanic American. 85% returned for their sophomore year.

Facilities and Resources

1,080 **computers/terminals** are available on campus for general student use. Students can access the following: computer help desk, free student e-mail accounts, online (class) registration, online (class) schedules, telephone registration. Campuswide network is available. Wireless service is available via entire campus. The 11 **libraries** have 3,339,765 books and 54,347 subscriptions.

Campus Life

There are 583 active organizations on campus, including a drama/theater group, newspaper, radio station, television station, choral group, and marching band. 20% of eligible men and 25% of eligible women are members of national **fraternities** and national **sororities.**

Missouri-Columbia is a member of the NCAA (Division I). **Intercollegiate sports** (some offering scholarships) include baseball (m), basketball, cross-country running, football (m), golf, gymnastics (w), soccer (w), softball (w), swimming and diving, tennis (w), track and field, volleyball (w), wrestling (m).

Campus Safety

Student safety services include late-night transport/escort service, 24-hour emergency telephone alarm devices, 24-hour patrols by trained security personnel, and electronically operated dormitory entrances.

Applying

Missouri-Columbia requires SAT or ACT, a high school transcript, and specific high school curriculum. It recommends ACT. Application deadline: rolling admissions; 3/1 priority date for financial aid. Deferred admission is possible.

Getting Accepted
14,491 applied
85% were accepted
5,782 enrolled (47% of accepted)
25% from top tenth of their h.s. class
Mean ACT score: 24
52% had SAT critical reading scores over 600
52% had SAT math scores over 600
68% had ACT scores over 24
13% had SAT critical reading scores over 700
10% had SAT math scores over 700
15% had ACT scores over 30
33 National Merit Scholars

Graduation and After
1400 organizations recruited on campus

Financial Matters
$8467 resident tuition and fees (2008–09)
$19,558 nonresident tuition and fees (2008–09)
$8100 room and board
88% average percent of need met
$12,880 average financial aid amount received per undergraduate (2007–08 estimated)

University of Missouri–Kansas City

Urban setting ■ Public ■ State-supported ■ Coed
Kansas City, Missouri

Web site: www.umkc.edu
Contact: Ms. Jennifer DeHaemers, Director of Admissions, Office of Admissions, 5100 Rockhill Road, Kansas City, MO 64110-2499
Telephone: 816-235-1111 or toll-free 800-775-8652 (out-of-state)
Fax: 816-235-5544
E-mail: admit@umkc.edu

Getting Accepted

3,276 applied
73% were accepted
1,007 enrolled (42% of accepted)
31% from top tenth of their h.s. class
3.34 average high school GPA
51% had SAT critical reading scores over 600
53% had SAT math scores over 600
53% had ACT scores over 24
10% had SAT critical reading scores over 700
21% had SAT math scores over 700
13% had ACT scores over 30

Graduation and After

19% graduated in 4 years
13% graduated in 5 years
11% graduated in 6 years
82% had job offers within 6 months
300 organizations recruited on campus

Financial Matters

$8273 resident tuition and fees (2008–09)
$19,364 nonresident tuition and fees (2008–09)
$7881 room and board
55% average percent of need met
$9318 average financial aid amount received per undergraduate (2007–08 estimated)

Academics

UMKC awards bachelor's, master's, doctoral, and first-professional **degrees** and post-master's and first-professional certificates. **Challenging opportunities** include advanced placement credit, accelerated degree programs, student-designed majors, an honors program, double majors, independent study, and a senior project. Special programs include cooperative education, internships, summer session for credit, off-campus study, study-abroad, and Army and Air Force ROTC.

The most frequently chosen **baccalaureate** fields are liberal arts/general studies, business/marketing, and health professions and related sciences. A complete listing of majors at UMKC appears in the Majors by College index beginning on page 469.

The **faculty** at UMKC has 698 full-time members, 76% with terminal degrees. The student-faculty ratio is 12:1.

Students of UMKC

The student body totals 14,499, of whom 9,274 are undergraduates. 58.8% are women and 41.2% are men. Students come from 42 states and territories and 58 other countries. 74% are from Missouri. 2.7% are international students. 14.9% are African American, 0.8% American Indian, 6.2% Asian American, and 4.4% Hispanic American. 71% returned for their sophomore year.

Facilities and Resources

728 **computers/terminals** are available on campus for general student use. Students can access the following: campus intranet, computer help desk, free student e-mail accounts, online (class) grades, online (class) registration, online (class) schedules. Campuswide network is available. 100% of college-owned or -operated housing units are wired for high-speed Internet access. Wireless service is available via classrooms, computer labs, dorm rooms, libraries. The 4 **libraries** have 1,751,450 books and 30,976 subscriptions.

Campus Life

There are 100 active organizations on campus, including a drama/theater group, newspaper, radio station, and choral group. 8% of eligible men and 6% of eligible women are members of national **fraternities**, national **sororities**, local fraternities, and local sororities.

UMKC is a member of the NCAA (Division I). **Intercollegiate sports** (some offering scholarships) include basketball, cheerleading (w), cross-country running, golf, riflery, soccer (m), softball (w), tennis, track and field, volleyball (w).

Campus Safety

Student safety services include late-night transport/escort service, 24-hour emergency telephone alarm devices, 24-hour patrols by trained security personnel, and electronically operated dormitory entrances.

Applying

UMKC requires SAT or ACT and a high school transcript, and in some cases an essay and an interview. Application deadline: rolling admissions; 3/1 priority date for financial aid. Deferred admission is possible.

UNIVERSITY OF NEBRASKA–LINCOLN

URBAN SETTING ■ PUBLIC ■ STATE-SUPPORTED ■ COED
LINCOLN, NEBRASKA

Web site: www.unl.edu
Contact: Pat McBride, Director, New Student Enrollment, 1410 Q Street, Lincoln, NE 68588-0256
Telephone: 402-472-2023 or toll-free 800-742-8800
Fax: 402-472-0670
E-mail: admissions@unl.edu

Academics

UNL awards associate, bachelor's, master's, doctoral, and first-professional **degrees** and post-bachelor's and post-master's certificates. **Challenging opportunities** include advanced placement credit, accelerated degree programs, student-designed majors, an honors program, double majors, independent study, and a senior project. Special programs include cooperative education, internships, summer session for credit, off-campus study, study-abroad, and Army, Navy, and Air Force ROTC.

The most frequently chosen **baccalaureate** fields are business/marketing, education, and engineering. A complete listing of majors at UNL appears in the Majors by College index beginning on page 469.

The **faculty** at UNL has 1,070 full-time members, 96% with terminal degrees. The student-faculty ratio is 20:1.

Students of UNL

The student body totals 23,573, of whom 18,526 are undergraduates. 45.7% are women and 54.3% are men. Students come from 51 states and territories and 82 other countries. 82% are from Nebraska. 2.9% are international students. 2.4% are African American, 0.7% American Indian, 2.6% Asian American, and 3.5% Hispanic American. 84% returned for their sophomore year.

Facilities and Resources

600 **computers/terminals** are available on campus for general student use. Students can access the following: campus intranet, computer help desk, free student e-mail accounts, online (class) grades, online (class) registration, online (class) schedules. Campuswide network is available. 100% of college-owned or -operated housing units are wired for high-speed Internet access. Wireless service is available via entire campus. The 8 **libraries** have 3,487,244 books and 29,245 subscriptions.

Campus Life

There are 335 active organizations on campus, including a drama/theater group, newspaper, radio station, choral group, and marching band. 14% of eligible men and 18% of eligible women are members of national **fraternities**, national **sororities**, local fraternities, and local sororities.

UNL is a member of the NCAA (Division I). **Intercollegiate sports** (some offering scholarships) include baseball (m), basketball, bowling (w), cross-country running, football (m), golf, gymnastics, riflery (w), soccer (w), softball (w), swimming and diving (w), tennis, track and field, volleyball (w), wrestling (m).

Campus Safety

Student safety services include late-night transport/escort service, 24-hour emergency telephone alarm devices, 24-hour patrols by trained security personnel, student patrols, and electronically operated dormitory entrances.

Applying

UNL requires SAT or ACT and a high school transcript, and in some cases rank in upper 50% of high school class. It recommends ACT. Application deadline: 5/1.

Getting Accepted

9,709 applied
63% were accepted
4,164 enrolled (68% of accepted)
24% from top tenth of their h.s. class
Mean SAT critical reading score: 580
Mean SAT math score: 600
Mean ACT score: 25
45% had SAT critical reading scores over 600
54% had SAT math scores over 600
60% had ACT scores over 24
15% had SAT critical reading scores over 700
18% had SAT math scores over 700
17% had ACT scores over 30
63 National Merit Scholars

Graduation and After

25% graduated in 4 years
31% graduated in 5 years
7% graduated in 6 years
368 organizations recruited on campus

Financial Matters

$6585 resident tuition and fees (2008–09)
$17,205 nonresident tuition and fees (2008–09)
$6882 room and board
85% average percent of need met
$10,356 average financial aid amount received per undergraduate (2006–07)

THE UNIVERSITY OF NORTH CAROLINA AT ASHEVILLE

SUBURBAN SETTING ▪ PUBLIC ▪ STATE-SUPPORTED ▪ COED
ASHEVILLE, NORTH CAROLINA

Web site: www.unca.edu
Contact: Ms. Leigh McBride, Associate Director of Admissions, University
Dining Hall, CPO # 1320, Asheville, NC 28804-8510
Telephone: 828-251-6481 or toll-free 800-531-9842
Fax: 828-251-6482
E-mail: admissions@unca.edu

Academics

UNC Asheville awards bachelor's and master's **degrees** and post-bachelor's certificates. **Challenging opportunities** include advanced placement credit, student-designed majors, an honors program, double majors, independent study, and a senior project. Special programs include internships, summer session for credit, off-campus study, and study-abroad.

The most frequently chosen **baccalaureate** fields are psychology, social sciences, and visual and performing arts. A complete listing of majors at UNC Asheville appears in the Majors by College index beginning on page 469.

The **faculty** at UNC Asheville has 207 full-time members, 86% with terminal degrees. The student-faculty ratio is 13:1.

Students of UNC Asheville

The student body totals 3,629, of whom 3,589 are undergraduates. 58% are women and 42% are men. Students come from 44 states and territories and 19 other countries. 87% are from North Carolina. 79% returned for their sophomore year.

Facilities and Resources

390 **computers/terminals** are available on campus for general student use. Students can access the following: online (class) registration, online grade reports. Campuswide network is available. 100% of college-owned or -operated housing units are wired for high-speed Internet access. Wireless service is available via classrooms, libraries, student centers. The **library** has 269,044 books and 6,943 subscriptions.

Campus Life

There are 82 active organizations on campus, including a drama/theater group, newspaper, radio station, and choral group. 2% of eligible men and 3% of eligible women are members of national **fraternities** and national **sororities**.

UNC Asheville is a member of the NCAA (Division I). **Intercollegiate sports** (some offering scholarships) include baseball (m), basketball, cheerleading, cross-country running, soccer, tennis, track and field, volleyball (w).

Campus Safety

Student safety services include dorm entrances secured at night, late-night transport/ escort service, 24-hour emergency telephone alarm devices, and 24-hour patrols by trained security personnel.

Applying

UNC Asheville requires an essay, SAT or ACT, a high school transcript, 1 recom- mendation, and Minimum Course Requirement, and in some cases an interview. Application deadline: 2/15; 3/1 priority date for financial aid. Deferred admission is pos- sible.

THE UNIVERSITY OF NORTH CAROLINA AT CHAPEL HILL

SUBURBAN SETTING ■ PUBLIC ■ STATE-SUPPORTED ■ COED
CHAPEL HILL, NORTH CAROLINA

Web site: www.unc.edu
Contact: Campus Box # 2200, Jackson Hall, Chapel Hill, NC 27599-2200
Telephone: 919-966-3621
Fax: 919-962-3045
E-mail: uadm@email.unc.edu

Academics

UNC Chapel Hill awards bachelor's, master's, doctoral, and first-professional **degrees** and post-bachelor's, post-master's, and first-professional certificates. **Challenging opportunities** include advanced placement credit, student-designed majors, freshman honors college, an honors program, double majors, independent study, and a senior project. Special programs include internships, summer session for credit, off-campus study, study-abroad, and Army, Navy, and Air Force ROTC.

The most frequently chosen **baccalaureate** fields are social sciences, communications/journalism, and psychology. A complete listing of majors at UNC Chapel Hill appears in the Majors by College index beginning on page 469.

The **faculty** at UNC Chapel Hill has 1,600 full-time members, 87% with terminal degrees. The student-faculty ratio is 14:1.

Students of UNC Chapel Hill

The student body totals 28,567, of whom 17,895 are undergraduates. 58.5% are women and 41.5% are men. Students come from 53 states and territories and 133 other countries. 84% are from North Carolina. 1.4% are international students. 10.9% are African American, 0.8% American Indian, 7.1% Asian American, and 4.9% Hispanic American. 97% returned for their sophomore year.

Facilities and Resources

600 **computers/terminals** are available on campus for general student use. Students can access the following: computer help desk, free student e-mail accounts, online (class) grades, online (class) registration, online (class) schedules. Campuswide network is available. 100% of college-owned or -operated housing units are wired for high-speed Internet access. Wireless service is available via entire campus. The 16 **libraries** have 6,526,824 books and 60,713 subscriptions.

Campus Life

There are 630 active organizations on campus, including a drama/theater group, newspaper, radio station, television station, choral group, and marching band. 15% of eligible men and 17% of eligible women are members of national **fraternities** and national **sororities**.

UNC Chapel Hill is a member of the NCAA (Division I). **Intercollegiate sports** (some offering scholarships) include baseball (m), basketball, crew (w), cross-country running, fencing, field hockey (w), football (m), golf, gymnastics (w), lacrosse, soccer, softball (w), swimming and diving, tennis, track and field, volleyball (w), wrestling (m).

Campus Safety

Student safety services include crime prevention programs, late-night transport/escort service, 24-hour emergency telephone alarm devices, 24-hour patrols by trained security personnel, student patrols, and electronically operated dormitory entrances.

Applying

UNC Chapel Hill requires an essay, SAT or ACT, a high school transcript, 1 recommendation, and counselor's statement. Application deadline: 1/15; 3/1 priority date for financial aid. Deferred admission is possible.

Getting Accepted
21,543 applied
34% were accepted
3,865 enrolled (53% of accepted)
79% from top tenth of their h.s. class
Mean SAT critical reading score: 643
Mean SAT math score: 658
Mean SAT writing score: 638
Mean ACT score: 28
75% had SAT critical reading scores over 600
82% had SAT math scores over 600
71% had SAT writing scores over 600
90% had ACT scores over 24
25% had SAT critical reading scores over 700
30% had SAT math scores over 700
24% had SAT writing scores over 700
38% had ACT scores over 30
166 National Merit Scholars
212 valedictorians

Graduation and After
73% graduated in 4 years
11% graduated in 5 years
2% graduated in 6 years
64.9% had job offers within 6 months
218 organizations recruited on campus

Financial Matters
$5397 resident tuition and fees (2008–09)
$22,295 nonresident tuition and fees (2008–09)
$7334 room and board
100% average percent of need met
$11,394 average financial aid amount received per undergraduate (2006–07)

THE UNIVERSITY OF NORTH CAROLINA WILMINGTON

URBAN SETTING ■ PUBLIC ■ STATE-SUPPORTED ■ COED
WILMINGTON, NORTH CAROLINA

Web site: www.uncw.edu
Contact: Dr. Terrence M. Curran, Associate Provost, 601 South College Road, Wilmington, NC 28403-3297
Telephone: 910-962-3876 or toll-free 800-228-5571 (out-of-state)
Fax: 910-962-3922
E-mail: admissions@uncw.edu

Getting Accepted
9,311 applied
59% were accepted
2,073 enrolled (38% of accepted)
23% from top tenth of their h.s. class
3.74 average high school GPA
Mean SAT critical reading score: 568
Mean SAT math score: 588
Mean SAT writing score: 568
25% had SAT critical reading scores over 600
40% had SAT math scores over 600
23% had SAT writing scores over 600
50% had ACT scores over 24
1% had SAT critical reading scores over 700
2% had SAT math scores over 700
1% had SAT writing scores over 700
4% had ACT scores over 30

Graduation and After
42% graduated in 4 years
20% graduated in 5 years
3% graduated in 6 years
58.4% had job offers within 6 months
422 organizations recruited on campus

Financial Matters
$4528 resident tuition and fees (2008–09)
$14,695 nonresident tuition and fees (2008–09)
$7370 room and board
88% average percent of need met
$6476 average financial aid amount received per undergraduate (2007–08 estimated)

Academics
UNCW awards bachelor's, master's, and doctoral **degrees** and post-bachelor's and post-master's certificates. **Challenging opportunities** include advanced placement credit, accelerated degree programs, an honors program, double majors, independent study, and a senior project. Special programs include cooperative education, internships, and summer session for credit.

The most frequently chosen **baccalaureate** fields are business/marketing, education, and biological/life sciences. A complete listing of majors at UNCW appears in the Majors by College index beginning on page 469.

The **faculty** at UNCW has 580 full-time members, 84% with terminal degrees. The student-faculty ratio is 16:1.

Students of UNCW
The student body totals 12,195, of whom 10,989 are undergraduates. 57.9% are women and 42.1% are men. Students come from 46 states and territories and 44 other countries. 85% are from North Carolina. 0.4% are international students. 5.2% are African American, 0.7% American Indian, 2% Asian American, and 3.2% Hispanic American. 85% returned for their sophomore year.

Facilities and Resources
1,170 **computers/terminals** are available on campus for general student use. Students can access the following: campus intranet, computer help desk, free student e-mail accounts, online (class) grades, online (class) registration, online (class) schedules. Campuswide network is available. 100% of college-owned or -operated housing units are wired for high-speed Internet access. Wireless service is available via entire campus. The **library** has 1,037,601 books and 30,000 subscriptions.

Campus Life
There are 180 active organizations on campus, including a drama/theater group, newspaper, radio station, television station, and choral group. 7% of eligible men and 9% of eligible women are members of national **fraternities**, national **sororities**, and local sororities.

UNCW is a member of the NCAA (Division I). **Intercollegiate sports** (some offering scholarships) include baseball (m), basketball, cheerleading, cross-country running, golf, soccer, softball (w), swimming and diving, tennis, track and field, volleyball (w).

Campus Safety
Student safety services include escort service, late-night transport/escort service, 24-hour emergency telephone alarm devices, 24-hour patrols by trained security personnel, and electronically operated dormitory entrances.

Applying
UNCW requires an essay, SAT or ACT, and a high school transcript. Application deadline: 2/1. Early and deferred admission are possible.

UNIVERSITY OF NORTH FLORIDA

URBAN SETTING ■ PUBLIC ■ STATE-SUPPORTED ■ COED
JACKSONVILLE, FLORIDA

Web site: www.unf.edu
Contact: Mr. John Yancey, Director of Admissions, 1 UNF Drive,
   Jacksonville, FL 32224
Telephone: 904-620-2624
Fax: 904-620-2014
E-mail: admissions@unf.edu

Academics

UNF awards associate, bachelor's, master's, and doctoral **degrees** and post-bachelor's
and post-master's certificates (doctoral degree in education only). **Challenging opportunities** include advanced placement credit, accelerated degree programs, student-
designed majors, an honors program, double majors, independent study, and a senior
project. Special programs include cooperative education, internships, summer session for
credit, off-campus study, study-abroad, and Navy ROTC.

The most frequently chosen **baccalaureate** fields are business/marketing, health
professions and related sciences, and education. A complete listing of majors at UNF
appears in the Majors by College index beginning on page 469.

The **faculty** at UNF has 492 full-time members, 78% with terminal degrees. The
student-faculty ratio is 21:1.

Students of UNF

The student body totals 15,280, of whom 13,387 are undergraduates. 56.6% are women
and 43.4% are men. Students come from 47 states and territories and 65 other countries.
97% are from Florida. 1.6% are international students. 10.2% are African American,
0.5% American Indian, 5.8% Asian American, and 6.8% Hispanic American. 77%
returned for their sophomore year.

Facilities and Resources

750 **computers/terminals** are available on campus for general student use. Students can
access the following: campus intranet, computer help desk, free student e-mail accounts,
online (class) grades, online (class) registration, online (class) schedules, applications
software. Campuswide network is available. 100% of college-owned or -operated
housing units are wired for high-speed Internet access. Wireless service is available via
entire campus. The **library** has 957,625 books and 3,979 subscriptions.

Campus Life

There are 140 active organizations on campus, including a drama/theater group,
newspaper, radio station, television station, and choral group. 8% of eligible men and 6%
of eligible women are members of national **fraternities** and national **sororities**.

UNF is a member of the NCAA (Division I). **Intercollegiate sports** (some offering
scholarships) include baseball (m), basketball, cheerleading, cross-country running, golf
(m), soccer, softball (w), swimming and diving (w), tennis, track and field, volleyball (w).

Campus Safety

Student safety services include electronic parking lot security, late-night transport/escort
service, 24-hour emergency telephone alarm devices, 24-hour patrols by trained security
personnel, student patrols, and electronically operated dormitory entrances.

Applying

UNF requires SAT or ACT, a high school transcript, and a minimum high school GPA
of 2.9, and in some cases an essay and an interview. It recommends a minimum high
school GPA of 3.0. Application deadline: 7/2; 4/1 priority date for financial aid. Deferred
admission is possible.

Getting Accepted

9,397 applied
64% were accepted
1,851 enrolled (31% of accepted)
20% from top tenth of their h.s. class
3.58 average high school GPA
Mean SAT critical reading score: 566
Mean SAT math score: 573
Mean ACT score: 23
34% had SAT critical reading scores over 600
36% had SAT math scores over 600
32% had ACT scores over 24
3% had SAT critical reading scores over 700
3% had SAT math scores over 700
1% had ACT scores over 30

Graduation and After

23% graduated in 4 years
18% graduated in 5 years
5% graduated in 6 years
324 organizations recruited on campus

Financial Matters

$3775 resident tuition and fees (2008–09)
$15,417 nonresident tuition and fees
   (2008–09)
$7366 room and board
89% average percent of need met
$1443 average financial aid amount received
   per undergraduate (2007–08 estimated)

University of Notre Dame

Suburban setting ■ Private ■ Independent Religious ■ Coed
Notre Dame, Indiana

Getting Accepted
13,945 applied
27% were accepted
2,000 enrolled (54% of accepted)
86% from top tenth of their h.s. class
Mean SAT critical reading score: 693
Mean SAT math score: 712
Mean SAT writing score: 681
Mean ACT score: 32
92% had SAT critical reading scores over 600
96% had SAT math scores over 600
85% had SAT writing scores over 600
98% had ACT scores over 24
50% had SAT critical reading scores over 700
64% had SAT math scores over 700
43% had SAT writing scores over 700
83% had ACT scores over 30

Financial Matters
$36,847 tuition and fees (2008–09)
$9828 room and board
99% average percent of need met
$30,285 average financial aid amount received
   per undergraduate (2007–08 estimated)

Web site: www.nd.edu
Contact: Office of Undergraduate Admissions, 220 Main Building, Notre Dame, IN 46556-5612
Telephone: 574-631-7505
Fax: 574-631-8865
E-mail: admissions@nd.edu

Academics

Notre Dame awards bachelor's, master's, doctoral, and first-professional **degrees**. **Challenging opportunities** include advanced placement credit, accelerated degree programs, student-designed majors, an honors program, double majors, independent study, and a senior project. Special programs include internships, summer session for credit, off-campus study, study-abroad, and Army, Navy, and Air Force ROTC.

The most frequently chosen **baccalaureate** fields are business/marketing, social sciences, and engineering. A complete listing of majors at Notre Dame appears in the Majors by College index beginning on page 469.

The **faculty** at Notre Dame has 813 full-time members. The student-faculty ratio is 12:1.

Students of Notre Dame

The student body totals 11,731, of whom 8,363 are undergraduates. 46.6% are women and 53.4% are men. Students come from 53 states and territories and 42 other countries. 8% are from Indiana. 2.7% are international students. 3.7% are African American, 0.6% American Indian, 7.1% Asian American, and 9.3% Hispanic American. 97% returned for their sophomore year.

Facilities and Resources

261 **computers/terminals** are available on campus for general student use. Students can access the following: computer help desk, free student e-mail accounts, online (class) grades, online (class) registration, online (class) schedules. Campuswide network is available. Wireless service is available via entire campus. The 9 **libraries** have 3,043,137 books and 42,029 subscriptions.

Campus Life

There are 299 active organizations on campus, including a drama/theater group, newspaper, radio station, choral group, and marching band. No national or local **fraternities** or **sororities**.

Notre Dame is a member of the NCAA (Division I). **Intercollegiate sports** (some offering scholarships) include baseball (m), basketball, crew (w), cross-country running, fencing, football (m), golf, ice hockey (m), lacrosse, soccer, softball (w), swimming and diving, tennis, track and field, volleyball (w).

Campus Safety

Student safety services include crime prevention and personal safety workshops, full-time trained police investigators, fire sprinklers in all residence halls, late-night transport/escort service, 24-hour emergency telephone alarm devices, 24-hour patrols by trained security personnel, student patrols, and electronically operated dormitory entrances.

Applying

Notre Dame requires an essay, SAT or ACT, a high school transcript, and 1 recommendation, and in some cases SAT Subject Tests. Application deadline: 12/31; 2/15 for financial aid, with a 2/15 priority date. Deferred admission is possible.

University of Oklahoma

Suburban setting ■ Public ■ State-supported ■ Coed
Norman, Oklahoma

Web site: www.ou.edu
Contact: Mr. Craig Hayes, Executive Director of Recruitment Services, 550 Parrington Oval, L-1, Norman, OK 73019-3032
Telephone: 405-325-2151 or toll-free 800-234-6868
Fax: 405-325-7478
E-mail: ou-pss@ou.edu

Academics

OU awards bachelor's, master's, doctoral, and first-professional **degrees** and post-bachelor's and post-master's certificates. **Challenging opportunities** include advanced placement credit, accelerated degree programs, student-designed majors, freshman honors college, an honors program, double majors, independent study, and a senior project. Special programs include cooperative education, internships, summer session for credit, off-campus study, study-abroad, and Army, Navy, and Air Force ROTC.

The most frequently chosen **baccalaureate** fields are business/marketing, social sciences, and communications/journalism. A complete listing of majors at OU appears in the Majors by College index beginning on page 469.

The **faculty** at OU has 1,131 full-time members, 86% with terminal degrees. The student-faculty ratio is 19:1.

Students of OU

The student body totals 26,185, of whom 19,592 are undergraduates. 50.2% are women and 49.8% are men. Students come from 50 states and territories and 78 other countries. 74% are from Oklahoma. 2% are international students. 5.6% are African American, 7.1% American Indian, 5.7% Asian American, and 4.2% Hispanic American. 83% returned for their sophomore year.

Facilities and Resources

3,600 **computers/terminals** and 2,200 ports are available on campus for general student use. Students can access the following: campus intranet, computer help desk, free student e-mail accounts, online (class) grades, online (class) registration, online (class) schedules. Campuswide network is available. 100% of college-owned or -operated housing units are wired for high-speed Internet access. Wireless service is available via classrooms, computer centers, computer labs, dorm rooms, learning centers, libraries, student centers. The 9 **libraries** have 4,730,967 books and 51,585 subscriptions.

Campus Life

There are 352 active organizations on campus, including a drama/theater group, newspaper, radio station, television station, choral group, and marching band. 19% of eligible men and 27% of eligible women are members of national **fraternities**, national **sororities**, local fraternities, and local sororities.

OU is a member of the NCAA (Division I). **Intercollegiate sports** (some offering scholarships) include baseball (m), basketball, cheerleading, crew (w), cross-country running, football (m), golf, gymnastics, soccer (w), softball (w), tennis, track and field, volleyball (w), wrestling (m).

Campus Safety

Student safety services include crime prevention programs, police bicycle patrols, self-defense classes, late-night transport/escort service, 24-hour emergency telephone alarm devices, 24-hour patrols by trained security personnel, student patrols, and electronically operated dormitory entrances.

Applying

OU requires SAT or ACT and 15 specified curricular units, and in some cases an essay and a high school transcript. Application deadline: 4/1.

Getting Accepted
9,764 applied
82% were accepted
3,803 enrolled (48% of accepted)
36% from top tenth of their h.s. class
3.62 average high school GPA
Mean SAT critical reading score: 583
Mean SAT math score: 599
Mean ACT score: 26
44% had SAT critical reading scores over 600
49% had SAT math scores over 600
77% had ACT scores over 24
12% had SAT critical reading scores over 700
12% had SAT math scores over 700
28% had ACT scores over 30
177 National Merit Scholars
319 valedictorians

Graduation and After
26% graduated in 4 years
27% graduated in 5 years
9% graduated in 6 years
1725 organizations recruited on campus

Financial Matters
$5245 resident tuition and fees (2008–09)
$13,229 nonresident tuition and fees (2008–09)
$7376 room and board
85% average percent of need met
$9811 average financial aid amount received per undergraduate (2006–07)

Getting Accepted
22,935 applied
17% were accepted
2,400 enrolled (62% of accepted)
99% from top tenth of their h.s. class
3.83 average high school GPA
Mean SAT critical reading score: 697
Mean SAT math score: 722
Mean SAT writing score: 709
Mean ACT score: 31
93% had SAT critical reading scores over 600
96% had SAT math scores over 600
95% had SAT writing scores over 600
98% had ACT scores over 24
52% had SAT critical reading scores over 700
70% had SAT math scores over 700
63% had SAT writing scores over 700
75% had ACT scores over 30

Graduation and After
88% graduated in 4 years
6% graduated in 5 years
1% graduated in 6 years
68% had job offers within 6 months
734 organizations recruited on campus

Financial Matters
$37,526 tuition and fees (2008–09)
$10,621 room and board
100% average percent of need met
$29,931 average financial aid amount received
per undergraduate (2006–07)

UNIVERSITY OF PENNSYLVANIA
URBAN SETTING ■ PRIVATE ■ INDEPENDENT ■ COED
PHILADELPHIA, PENNSYLVANIA

Web site: www.upenn.edu
Contact: 1 College Hall, Levy Park, Philadelphia, PA 19104
Telephone: 215-898-7507
E-mail: info@admissions.ugao.upenn.edu

Academics
Penn awards associate, bachelor's, master's, doctoral, and first-professional **degrees** and post-bachelor's, post-master's, and first-professional certificates (also offers evening program with significant enrollment not reflected in profile). **Challenging opportunities** include advanced placement credit, accelerated degree programs, student-designed majors, an honors program, double majors, independent study, and a senior project. Special programs include internships, summer session for credit, off-campus study, study-abroad, and Army, Navy, and Air Force ROTC.

The most frequently chosen **baccalaureate** fields are business/marketing, social sciences, and engineering. A complete listing of majors at Penn appears in the Majors by College index beginning on page 469.

The **faculty** at Penn has 1,406 full-time members, 100% with terminal degrees. The student-faculty ratio is 6:1.

Students of Penn
The student body totals 19,018, of whom 9,756 are undergraduates. 50.2% are women and 49.8% are men. 17% are from Pennsylvania. 9.9% are international students. 7.9% are African American, 0.5% American Indian, 17.8% Asian American, and 6% Hispanic American. 98% returned for their sophomore year.

Facilities and Resources
1,295 **computers/terminals** and 1,472 ports are available on campus for general student use. Students can access the following: campus intranet, computer help desk, free student e-mail accounts, online (class) grades, online (class) registration, online (class) schedules, billing information, financial aid application, status, academic records, student services. Campuswide network is available. 100% of college-owned or -operated housing units are wired for high-speed Internet access. Wireless service is available via entire campus. The 16 **libraries** have 5,756,742 books and 50,252 subscriptions.

Campus Life
There are 350 active organizations on campus, including a drama/theater group, newspaper, radio station, television station, choral group, and marching band. 24% of eligible men and 17% of eligible women are members of national **fraternities** and national **sororities**.

Penn is a member of the NCAA (Division I). **Intercollegiate sports** include baseball (m), basketball, crew, cross-country running, fencing, field hockey (w), football (m), golf, gymnastics (w), lacrosse, soccer, softball (w), squash, swimming and diving, tennis, track and field, volleyball (w), wrestling (m).

Campus Safety
Student safety services include late-night transport/escort service, 24-hour emergency telephone alarm devices, 24-hour patrols by trained security personnel, and electronically operated dormitory entrances.

Applying
Penn requires an essay, SAT and SAT Subject Tests or ACT, a high school transcript, and 2 recommendations. Application deadline: 1/1; 2/1 priority date for financial aid. Early and deferred admission are possible.

University of Pittsburgh

URBAN SETTING ■ PUBLIC ■ STATE-RELATED ■ COED
PITTSBURGH, PENNSYLVANIA

Web site: www.pitt.edu
Contact: Dr. Betsy A. Porter, Director of Office of Admissions and Financial
   Aid, 4227 Fifth Avenue, First Floor, Alumni Hall, Pittsburgh, PA 15260
Telephone: 412-624-7488
Fax: 412-648-8815
E-mail: oafa@pitt.edu

Academics

Pitt awards bachelor's, master's, doctoral, and first-professional **degrees** and post-bachelor's and post-master's certificates. **Challenging opportunities** include advanced placement credit, accelerated degree programs, student-designed majors, freshman honors college, an honors program, double majors, independent study, and a senior project. Special programs include cooperative education, internships, summer session for credit, off-campus study, study-abroad, and Army, Navy, and Air Force ROTC.

The most frequently chosen **baccalaureate** fields are business/marketing, social sciences, and English. A complete listing of majors at Pitt appears in the Majors by College index beginning on page 469.

The **faculty** at Pitt has 1,656 full-time members, 92% with terminal degrees. The student-faculty ratio is 16:1.

Students of Pitt

The student body totals 27,562, of whom 17,427 are undergraduates. 51.5% are women and 48.5% are men. Students come from 52 states and territories and 43 other countries. 83% are from Pennsylvania. 1.1% are international students. 8.4% are African American, 0.1% American Indian, 5.1% Asian American, and 1.2% Hispanic American. 91% returned for their sophomore year.

Facilities and Resources

1,150 **computers/terminals** and 1,150 ports are available on campus for general student use. Students can access the following: campus intranet, computer help desk, free student e-mail accounts, online (class) grades, online (class) schedules, online class listings, online tuition payment. Campuswide network is available. 100% of college-owned or -operated housing units are wired for high-speed Internet access. Wireless service is available via entire campus. The 25 **libraries** have 5,116,305 books and 48,637 subscriptions.

Campus Life

There are 300 active organizations on campus, including a drama/theater group, newspaper, radio station, television station, choral group, and marching band. 8% of eligible men and 8% of eligible women are members of national **fraternities** and national **sororities**.

Pitt is a member of the NCAA (Division I). **Intercollegiate sports** (some offering scholarships) include baseball (m), basketball, cross-country running, football (m), gymnastics (w), soccer, softball (w), swimming and diving, tennis (w), track and field, volleyball (w), wrestling (m).

Campus Safety

Student safety services include on-call van transportation, late-night transport/escort service, 24-hour emergency telephone alarm devices, 24-hour patrols by trained security personnel, and electronically operated dormitory entrances.

Applying

Pitt requires SAT or ACT and a high school transcript. It recommends an essay and an interview. Application deadline: rolling admissions; 3/1 priority date for financial aid. Early admission is possible.

Getting Accepted

20,685 applied
55% were accepted
3,524 enrolled (31% of accepted)
48% from top tenth of their h.s. class
3.95 average high school GPA
Mean SAT critical reading score: 624
Mean SAT math score: 638
Mean ACT score: 27
63% had SAT critical reading scores over 600
72% had SAT math scores over 600
87% had ACT scores over 24
20% had SAT critical reading scores over 700
21% had SAT math scores over 700
28% had ACT scores over 30
119 valedictorians

Graduation and After

55% graduated in 4 years
18% graduated in 5 years
2% graduated in 6 years

Financial Matters

$13,642 resident tuition and fees (2008–09)
$23,290 nonresident tuition and fees (2008–09)
$7750 room and board
78% average percent of need met
$10,197 average financial aid amount received per undergraduate (2007–08 estimated)

UNIVERSITY OF PORTLAND

URBAN SETTING ■ PRIVATE ■ INDEPENDENT RELIGIOUS ■ COED
PORTLAND, OREGON

Web site: www.up.edu
Contact: Mr. Jason McDonald, Dean of Admissions, 5000 North Willamette
Boulevard, Portland, OR 97203
Telephone: 503-943-7147 or toll-free 888-627-5601 (out-of-state)
Fax: 503-943-7315
E-mail: admissions@up.edu

Getting Accepted
6,156 applied
79% were accepted
794 enrolled (16% of accepted)
44% from top tenth of their h.s. class
3.66 average high school GPA
47% had SAT critical reading scores over 600
52% had SAT math scores over 600
13% had SAT critical reading scores over 700
10% had SAT math scores over 700

Graduation and After
60% graduated in 4 years
10% graduated in 5 years
1% graduated in 6 years
175 organizations recruited on campus

Financial Matters
$30,400 tuition and fees (2008–09)
$8756 room and board
94% average percent of need met
$21,821 average financial aid amount received
per undergraduate

Academics

U of P awards bachelor's, master's, and doctoral **degrees** and post-master's certificates.
Challenging opportunities include advanced placement credit, an honors program,
double majors, independent study, and a senior project. Special programs include internships, summer session for credit, off-campus study, study-abroad, and Army and Air
Force ROTC.

The most frequently chosen **baccalaureate** fields are health professions and related
sciences, business/marketing, and engineering. A complete listing of majors at U of P
appears in the Majors by College index beginning on page 469.

The **faculty** at U of P has 205 full-time members, 90% with terminal degrees. The
student-faculty ratio is 12:1.

Students of U of P

The student body totals 3,661, of whom 3,041 are undergraduates. 63% are women and
37% are men. Students come from 39 states and territories and 19 other countries. 42%
are from Oregon. 2% are international students. 1.2% are African American, 0.9%
American Indian, 10.4% Asian American, and 4.9% Hispanic American. 86% returned
for their sophomore year.

Facilities and Resources

575 **computers/terminals** and 1,950 ports are available on campus for general student
use. Students can access the following: campus intranet, computer help desk, free student
e-mail accounts, online (class) grades, online (class) registration, online (class) schedules.
Campuswide network is available. 90% of college-owned or -operated housing units are
wired for high-speed Internet access. Wireless service is available via classrooms, dorm
rooms, learning centers, libraries, student centers. The 2 **libraries** have 350,000 books
and 1,400 subscriptions.

Campus Life

There are 40 active organizations on campus, including a drama/theater group,
newspaper, radio station, and choral group. No national or local **fraternities** or **sororities**.

U of P is a member of the NCAA (Division I). **Intercollegiate sports** (some offering
scholarships) include baseball (m), basketball, cross-country running, golf, soccer, tennis,
track and field, volleyball (w).

Campus Safety

Student safety services include late-night transport/escort service, 24-hour patrols by
trained security personnel, student patrols, and electronically operated dormitory
entrances.

Applying

U of P requires an essay, SAT or ACT, a high school transcript, and 1 recommendation.
Application deadline: 6/1; 3/1 priority date for financial aid. Deferred admission is possible.

UNIVERSITY OF PUGET SOUND

SUBURBAN SETTING ■ PRIVATE ■ INDEPENDENT ■ COED
TACOMA, WASHINGTON

Web site: www.ups.edu
Contact: Dr. George Mills, Vice President for Enrollment, 1500 North
    Warner Street, Tacoma, WA 98416-1062
Telephone: 253-879-3211 or toll-free 800-396-7191
Fax: 253-879-3993
E-mail: admission@ups.edu

Academics

Puget Sound awards bachelor's, master's, and first-professional **degrees** and post-master's certificates. **Challenging opportunities** include advanced placement credit, student-designed majors, an honors program, double majors, independent study, and a senior project. Special programs include cooperative education, internships, summer session for credit, study-abroad, and Army ROTC.

The most frequently chosen **baccalaureate** fields are social sciences, business/marketing, and visual and performing arts. A complete listing of majors at Puget Sound appears in the Majors by College index beginning on page 469.

The **faculty** at Puget Sound has 224 full-time members, 88% with terminal degrees. The student-faculty ratio is 11:1.

Students of Puget Sound

The student body totals 2,799, of whom 2,539 are undergraduates. 58.5% are women and 41.5% are men. Students come from 47 states and territories and 19 other countries. 29% are from Washington. 0.3% are international students. 2.7% are African American, 1.3% American Indian, 9.1% Asian American, and 3.9% Hispanic American. 86% returned for their sophomore year.

Facilities and Resources

314 **computers/terminals** and 5,000 ports are available on campus for general student use. Students can access the following: campus intranet, computer help desk, free student e-mail accounts, online (class) grades, online (class) registration, online (class) schedules, financial aid, admission, student employment, library. Campuswide network is available. 100% of college-owned or -operated housing units are wired for high-speed Internet access. Wireless service is available via entire campus. The **library** has 364,662 books and 20,008 subscriptions.

Campus Life

There are 65 active organizations on campus, including a drama/theater group, newspaper, radio station, and choral group. 23% of eligible men and 22% of eligible women are members of national **fraternities** and national **sororities**.

Puget Sound is a member of the NCAA (Division III). **Intercollegiate sports** include baseball (m), basketball, cheerleading, crew, cross-country running, football (m), golf, lacrosse (w), soccer, softball (w), swimming and diving, tennis, track and field, volleyball (w).

Campus Safety

Student safety services include 24-hour locked residence hall entrances, late-night transport/escort service, 24-hour emergency telephone alarm devices, 24-hour patrols by trained security personnel, student patrols, and electronically operated dormitory entrances.

Applying

Puget Sound requires an essay, SAT or ACT, a high school transcript, 2 recommendations, and school report. It recommends an interview and a minimum high school GPA of 3.0. Application deadline: 2/1; 2/1 priority date for financial aid. Early and deferred admission are possible.

Getting Accepted

5,273 applied
66% were accepted
644 enrolled (18% of accepted)
40% from top tenth of their h.s. class
3.54 average high school GPA
Mean SAT critical reading score: 623
Mean SAT math score: 608
Mean SAT writing score: 607
Mean ACT score: 27
64% had SAT critical reading scores over 600
58% had SAT math scores over 600
58% had SAT writing scores over 600
86% had ACT scores over 24
21% had SAT critical reading scores over 700
11% had SAT math scores over 700
12% had SAT writing scores over 700
25% had ACT scores over 30
48 National Merit Scholars

Graduation and After

68% graduated in 4 years
8% graduated in 5 years
1% graduated in 6 years
63% had job offers within 6 months
68 organizations recruited on campus

Financial Matters

$33,975 tuition and fees (2008–09)
$8760 room and board
83% average percent of need met
$25,089 average financial aid amount received
    per undergraduate (2007–08 estimated)

At the University of Redlands, students explore connections, blurring the barriers often artificially imposed between academic disciplines, between the classroom and the real world, and between their own views and the way others see things. Academics are combined with a community-based residential life and a range of opportunities to gain firsthand experience through internships, international study, and original faculty-directed research. Students take ownership of their education with the active support of professors who are truly committed to student participation in the learning process; they coax, challenge, captivate, support, nourish, and actively engage students in an exchange of stimulating and provocative ideas.

Getting Accepted
3,443 applied
68% were accepted
574 enrolled (25% of accepted)
31% from top tenth of their h.s. class
3.54 average high school GPA
Mean SAT critical reading score: 574
Mean SAT math score: 575
Mean ACT score: 24
35% had SAT critical reading scores over 600
35% had SAT math scores over 600
55% had ACT scores over 24
7% had SAT critical reading scores over 700
3% had SAT math scores over 700
7% had ACT scores over 30

Graduation and After
62% graduated in 4 years
6% graduated in 5 years
1% graduated in 6 years
51% had job offers within 6 months
6 organizations recruited on campus

Financial Matters
$32,294 tuition and fees (2008–09)
$10,122 room and board
83% average percent of need met
$29,203 average financial aid amount received per undergraduate (2007–08 estimated)

UNIVERSITY OF REDLANDS
SMALL-TOWN SETTING ■ PRIVATE ■ INDEPENDENT ■ COED
REDLANDS, CALIFORNIA

Web site: www.redlands.edu
Contact: PO Box 3080, Redlands, CA 92373-0999
Telephone: 909-748-8159 or toll-free 800-455-5064
Fax: 909-335-4089
E-mail: admissions@redlands.edu

Academics
Redlands awards bachelor's, master's, and doctoral **degrees** and post-bachelor's and post-master's certificates. **Challenging opportunities** include advanced placement credit, student-designed majors, freshman honors college, an honors program, double majors, independent study, and a senior project. Special programs include internships, off-campus study, study-abroad, and Army and Air Force ROTC.

The most frequently chosen **baccalaureate** fields are business/marketing, liberal arts/general studies, and social sciences. A complete listing of majors at Redlands appears in the Majors by College index beginning on page 469.

The **faculty** at Redlands has 224 full-time members, 87% with terminal degrees. The student-faculty ratio is 13:1.

Students of Redlands
The student body totals 4,317, of whom 2,820 are undergraduates. 56% are women and 44% are men. Students come from 44 states and territories and 7 other countries. 73% are from California. 2.2% are international students. 3.9% are African American, 0.5% American Indian, 5.2% Asian American, and 13% Hispanic American. 85% returned for their sophomore year.

Facilities and Resources
804 **computers/terminals** and 920 ports are available on campus for general student use. Students can access the following: campus intranet, computer help desk, free student e-mail accounts, online (class) grades, online (class) registration, online (class) schedules. Campuswide network is available. 100% of college-owned or -operated housing units are wired for high-speed Internet access. Wireless service is available via entire campus. The **library** has 280,503 books and 18,953 subscriptions.

Campus Life
There are 105 active organizations on campus, including a drama/theater group, newspaper, radio station, and choral group. 10% of eligible men and 13% of eligible women are members of local **fraternities** and local **sororities**.

Redlands is a member of the NCAA (Division III). **Intercollegiate sports** include baseball (m), basketball, cross-country running, football (m), golf, lacrosse (w), soccer, softball (w), swimming and diving, tennis, track and field, volleyball (w), water polo.

Campus Safety
Student safety services include safety whistles, late-night transport/escort service, 24-hour emergency telephone alarm devices, 24-hour patrols by trained security personnel, student patrols, and electronically operated dormitory entrances.

Applying
Redlands requires an essay, SAT or ACT, a high school transcript, and 2 recommendations. It recommends an interview. Application deadline: 6/1; 2/15 priority date for financial aid. Deferred admission is possible.

University of Rhode Island

Small-town setting ■ Public ■ State-supported ■ Coed
Kingston, Rhode Island

Web site: www.uri.edu
Contact: Ms. Joanne Lynch, Assistant Dean of Admissions, Undergraduate
Admission Office, Newman Hall, 14 Upper College Road, Kingston, RI
02881
Telephone: 401-874-7110
Fax: 401-874-5523
E-mail: lynch@uri.edu

Academics

Rhode Island awards bachelor's, master's, doctoral, and first-professional **degrees** and post-bachelor's certificates. **Challenging opportunities** include advanced placement credit, an honors program, double majors, independent study, and a senior project. Special programs include cooperative education, internships, summer session for credit, off-campus study, study-abroad, and Army ROTC.

The most frequently chosen **baccalaureate** fields are business/marketing, communications/journalism, and health professions and related sciences. A complete listing of majors at Rhode Island appears in the Majors by College index beginning on page 469.

The **faculty** at Rhode Island has 683 full-time members, 89% with terminal degrees. The student-faculty ratio is 17:1.

Students of Rhode Island

The student body totals 15,904, of whom 12,793 are undergraduates. 56% are women and 44% are men. Students come from 55 states and territories and 64 other countries. 61% are from Rhode Island. 0.3% are international students. 4.9% are African American, 0.5% American Indian, 2.5% Asian American, and 5.2% Hispanic American. 80% returned for their sophomore year.

Facilities and Resources

552 **computers/terminals** are available on campus for general student use. Students can access the following: campus intranet, computer help desk, free student e-mail accounts, online (class) grades, online (class) registration, online (class) schedules. Campuswide network is available. 100% of college-owned or -operated housing units are wired for high-speed Internet access. Wireless service is available via entire campus. The 2 **libraries** have 1,205,138 books and 7,926 subscriptions.

Campus Life

There are 85 active organizations on campus, including a drama/theater group, newspaper, radio station, television station, choral group, and marching band. 14% of eligible men and 13% of eligible women are members of national **fraternities**, national **sororities**, and local sororities.

Rhode Island is a member of the NCAA (Division I). **Intercollegiate sports** (some offering scholarships) include baseball (m), basketball (m), crew (w), cross-country running, football (m), golf (m), soccer, softball (w), swimming and diving (w), tennis (w), track and field, volleyball (w).

Campus Safety

Student safety services include late-night transport/escort service, 24-hour emergency telephone alarm devices, 24-hour patrols by trained security personnel, student patrols, and electronically operated dormitory entrances.

Applying

Rhode Island requires an essay, SAT or ACT, and a high school transcript, and in some cases a minimum high school GPA of 3.0. It recommends an interview, 2 recommendations, and a minimum high school GPA of 3.0. Application deadline: 2/1; 3/1 priority date for financial aid. Early admission is possible.

Getting Accepted
15,887 applied
77% were accepted
3,042 enrolled (25% of accepted)
16% from top tenth of their h.s. class
3.09 average high school GPA
Mean SAT critical reading score: 531
Mean SAT math score: 546
18% had SAT critical reading scores over 600
24% had SAT math scores over 600
39% had ACT scores over 24
2% had SAT critical reading scores over 700
3% had SAT math scores over 700
2% had ACT scores over 30

Graduation and After
40% graduated in 4 years
15% graduated in 5 years
3% graduated in 6 years

Financial Matters
$8678 resident tuition and fees (2008–09)
$24,776 nonresident tuition and fees (2008–09)
$8826 room and board
63% average percent of need met
$13,343 average financial aid amount received per undergraduate (2007–08 estimated)

UNIVERSITY OF RICHMOND

SUBURBAN SETTING ■ PRIVATE ■ INDEPENDENT ■ COED
UNIVERSITY OF RICHMOND, VIRGINIA

Web site: www.richmond.edu
Contact: Ms. Pamela Spence, Dean of Admission, 28 Westhampton Way,
   University of Richmond, VA 23173
Telephone: 804-289-8640 or toll-free 800-700-1662
Fax: 804-287-6003
E-mail: admissions@richmond.edu

Getting Accepted
7,970 applied
32% were accepted
738 enrolled (29% of accepted)
58% from top tenth of their h.s. class
Mean SAT critical reading score: 627
Mean SAT math score: 638
Mean SAT writing score: 639
Mean ACT score: 28
72% had SAT critical reading scores over 600
74% had SAT math scores over 600
92% had ACT scores over 24
15% had SAT critical reading scores over 700
18% had SAT math scores over 700
33% had ACT scores over 30
5 National Merit Scholars
68 class presidents
19 valedictorians

Graduation and After
82% graduated in 4 years
5% graduated in 5 years
48.8% had job offers within 6 months
239 organizations recruited on campus

Financial Matters
$40,010 tuition and fees (2009–10)
$8480 room and board
100% average percent of need met
$30,646 average financial aid amount received
   per undergraduate (2007–08 estimated)

Academics
Richmond awards associate, bachelor's, master's, and first-professional **degrees** and post-bachelor's certificates. **Challenging opportunities** include advanced placement credit, accelerated degree programs, student-designed majors, double majors, independent study, and a senior project. Special programs include cooperative education, internships, summer session for credit, off-campus study, study-abroad, and Army ROTC.

The most frequently chosen **baccalaureate** fields are business/marketing, social sciences, and English. A complete listing of majors at Richmond appears in the Majors by College index beginning on page 469.

The **faculty** at Richmond has 322 full-time members, 84% with terminal degrees. The student-faculty ratio is 8:1.

Students of Richmond
The student body totals 3,445, of whom 2,795 are undergraduates. 51.1% are women and 48.9% are men. Students come from 48 states and territories and 72 other countries. 17% are from Virginia. 7.8% are international students. 5.9% are African American, 0.3% American Indian, 3.5% Asian American, and 2.9% Hispanic American. 91% returned for their sophomore year.

Facilities and Resources
700 **computers/terminals** are available on campus for general student use. Students can access the following: campus intranet, computer help desk, free student e-mail accounts, online (class) registration, online (class) schedules. Campuswide network is available. 100% of college-owned or -operated housing units are wired for high-speed Internet access. Wireless service is available via entire campus. The 3 **libraries** have 1,098,581 books and 43,747 subscriptions.

Campus Life
There are 275 active organizations on campus, including a drama/theater group, newspaper, radio station, and choral group. 28% of eligible men and 49% of eligible women are members of national **fraternities** and national **sororities**.

Richmond is a member of the NCAA (Division I). **Intercollegiate sports** (some offering scholarships) include baseball (m), basketball, cheerleading, cross-country running, field hockey (w), football (m), golf, lacrosse (w), soccer, swimming and diving (w), tennis, track and field.

Campus Safety
Student safety services include campus police, late-night transport/escort service, 24-hour emergency telephone alarm devices, 24-hour patrols by trained security personnel, and electronically operated dormitory entrances.

Applying
Richmond requires an essay, SAT or ACT, a high school transcript, 1 recommendation, signed character statement, and a minimum high school GPA of 2.0. Application deadline: 1/15; 2/15 for financial aid. Early and deferred admission are possible.

University of Rochester

Suburban setting ■ Private ■ Independent ■ Coed
Rochester, New York

SPONSOR

Web site: www.rochester.edu
Contact: Admissions Office, PO Box 270251, 300 Wilson Boulevard,
Rochester, NY 14627-0251
Telephone: 585-275-3221 or toll-free 888-822-2256
Fax: 585-461-4595
E-mail: admit@admissions.rochester.edu

Academics
Rochester awards bachelor's, master's, doctoral, and first-professional **degrees** and post-bachelor's, post-master's, and first-professional certificates. **Challenging opportunities** include advanced placement credit, accelerated degree programs, student-designed majors, an honors program, double majors, and independent study. Special programs include internships, summer session for credit, off-campus study, study-abroad, and Army, Navy, and Air Force ROTC.

The most frequently chosen **baccalaureate** fields are social sciences, biological/life sciences, and psychology. A complete listing of majors at Rochester appears in the Majors by College index beginning on page 469.

The **faculty** at Rochester has 521 full-time members, 89% with terminal degrees. The student-faculty ratio is 9:1.

Students of Rochester
The student body totals 9,712, of whom 5,355 are undergraduates. 51.7% are women and 48.3% are men. Students come from 52 states and territories and 40 other countries. 48% are from New York. 6.9% are international students. 4.3% are African American, 0.3% American Indian, 10% Asian American, and 3.6% Hispanic American. 93% returned for their sophomore year.

Facilities and Resources
450 **computers/terminals** and 4,000 ports are available on campus for general student use. Students can access the following: computer help desk, free student e-mail accounts, online (class) grades, online (class) registration, online (class) schedules. Campuswide network is available. 100% of college-owned or -operated housing units are wired for high-speed Internet access. Wireless service is available via classrooms, computer centers, computer labs, learning centers, libraries, student centers. The 6 **libraries** have 3,672,976 books and 24,240 subscriptions.

Campus Life
There are 211 active organizations on campus, including a drama/theater group, newspaper, radio station, television station, and choral group. 19% of eligible men and 20% of eligible women are members of national **fraternities** and national **sororities**.

Rochester is a member of the NCAA (Division III). **Intercollegiate sports** include baseball (m), basketball, crew (w), cross-country running, field hockey (w), football (m), golf (m), lacrosse (w), soccer, softball (w), squash (m), swimming and diving, tennis, track and field, volleyball (w).

Campus Safety
Student safety services include late-night transport/escort service, 24-hour emergency telephone alarm devices, 24-hour patrols by trained security personnel, and electronically operated dormitory entrances.

Applying
Rochester requires an essay, SAT or ACT, and a high school transcript, and in some cases SAT and SAT Subject Tests or ACT and audition is required for music programs at Eastman School of Music. It recommends SAT Subject Tests, an interview, and 2 recommendations. Application deadline: 1/1, 1/1 for nonresidents; 2/1 priority date for financial aid. Early and deferred admission are possible.

Founded in 1850, the University of Rochester is one of the most innovative private research universities in the country. Rochester offers the diversity of a major university while fostering more individual attention from faculty members. Programs are available in six divisions, including the College (Arts and Sciences and Engineering), Nursing, Education, Business, Medicine, and the Eastman School of Music. The open curriculum eliminates general education courses. Instead, students define a personal course plan based on their own interests, taking advantage of such distinctive opportunities as Take Five (a tuition-free fifth year of study); unique research, study-abroad, and internship options; and guaranteed bachelor's/master's or professional programs in medicine, engineering, business, and education.

Getting Accepted
11,633 applied
43% were accepted
1,282 enrolled (26% of accepted)
75% from top tenth of their h.s. class
3.7 average high school GPA
Mean SAT critical reading score: 634
Mean SAT math score: 670
Mean ACT score: 29
72% had SAT critical reading scores over 600
85% had SAT math scores over 600
72% had SAT writing scores over 600
88% had ACT scores over 24
22% had SAT critical reading scores over 700
41% had SAT math scores over 700
23% had SAT writing scores over 700
43% had ACT scores over 30
21 National Merit Scholars
43 valedictorians

Graduation and After
74% graduated in 4 years
9% graduated in 5 years
1% graduated in 6 years
62% had job offers within 6 months
143 organizations recruited on campus

Financial Matters
$37,250 tuition and fees (2008–09)
$10,810 room and board
86% average percent of need met
$28,668 average financial aid amount received per undergraduate (2007–08 estimated)

The University of St. Thomas, founded in 1885, is a Catholic, independent liberal arts university with more than 10,000 undergraduate and graduate students. The largest independent college or university in Minnesota, it has campuses in a quiet St. Paul neighborhood and in thriving downtown Minneapolis. St. Thomas offers more than ninety majors, including biology, business administration, computer science, engineering, journalism, and a number of preprofessional areas of study. St. Thomas ranked fifth (and highest among schools) in a newspaper-sponsored survey on "Which Minnesota nonprofit organizations have the most respected reputations?" St. Thomas emphasizes a values-centered, career-oriented education.

Getting Accepted
5,312 applied
74% were accepted
1,315 enrolled (34% of accepted)
21% from top tenth of their h.s. class
3.56 average high school GPA
47% had SAT critical reading scores over 600
50% had SAT math scores over 600
69% had ACT scores over 24
15% had SAT critical reading scores over 700
10% had SAT math scores over 700
10% had ACT scores over 30

Graduation and After
56% graduated in 4 years
14% graduated in 5 years
2% graduated in 6 years
85% had job offers within 6 months
60 organizations recruited on campus

Financial Matters
$27,822 tuition and fees (2008–09)
$7614 room and board
79% average percent of need met
$20,620 average financial aid amount received per undergraduate (2007–08 estimated)

UNIVERSITY OF ST. THOMAS
URBAN SETTING ■ PRIVATE ■ INDEPENDENT RELIGIOUS ■ COED
ST. PAUL, MINNESOTA

Web site: www.stthomas.edu
Contact: Ms. Marla Friederichs, Associate Vice President of Enrollment Management, Mail #32F-1, 2115 Summit Avenue, St. Paul, MN 55105-1096
Telephone: 651-962-6150 or toll-free 800-328-6819 Ext. 26150
Fax: 651-962-6160
E-mail: admissions@stthomas.edu

Academics
St. Thomas awards bachelor's, master's, doctoral, and first-professional **degrees** and post-bachelor's and post-master's certificates. **Challenging opportunities** include advanced placement credit, student-designed majors, an honors program, double majors, independent study, and a senior project. Special programs include internships, summer session for credit, off-campus study, study-abroad, and Army, Navy, and Air Force ROTC.

The most frequently chosen **baccalaureate** fields are business/marketing, social sciences, and communications/journalism. A complete listing of majors at St. Thomas appears in the Majors by College index beginning on page 469.

The **faculty** at St. Thomas has 394 full-time members. The student-faculty ratio is 15:1.

Students of St. Thomas
The student body totals 10,984, of whom 6,076 are undergraduates. 48.9% are women and 51.1% are men. Students come from 44 states and territories and 7 other countries. 83% are from Minnesota. 0.8% are international students. 3.3% are African American, 0.5% American Indian, 4.3% Asian American, and 2.5% Hispanic American. 88% returned for their sophomore year.

Facilities and Resources
1,549 **computers/terminals** are available on campus for general student use. Students can access the following: online (class) registration. Campuswide network is available. The 4 **libraries** have 510,355 books and 2,743 subscriptions.

Campus Life
There are 94 active organizations on campus, including a drama/theater group, newspaper, radio station, and choral group. No national or local **fraternities** or **sororities**.

St. Thomas is a member of the NCAA (Division III). **Intercollegiate sports** include baseball (m), basketball, cross-country running, football (m), golf, ice hockey, soccer, softball (w), swimming and diving, tennis, track and field, volleyball (w).

Campus Safety
Student safety services include late-night transport/escort service, 24-hour emergency telephone alarm devices, 24-hour patrols by trained security personnel, and electronically operated dormitory entrances.

Applying
St. Thomas requires an essay, SAT or ACT, and a high school transcript. It recommends an interview. Application deadline: rolling admissions. Deferred admission is possible.

University of St. Thomas

Urban setting ■ Private ■ Independent Religious ■ Coed
Houston, Texas

Web site: www.stthom.edu
Contact: 3800 Montrose Boulevard, Houston, TX 77006-4696
Telephone: 713-525-3500 or toll-free 800-856-8565
Fax: 713-525-3558
E-mail: admissions@stthom.edu

Academics

St. Thomas awards bachelor's, master's, doctoral, and first-professional **degrees**. **Challenging opportunities** include advanced placement credit, an honors program, double majors, independent study, and a senior project. Special programs include internships, summer session for credit, off-campus study, study-abroad, and Army ROTC.

The most frequently chosen **baccalaureate** fields are business/marketing, liberal arts/general studies, and social sciences. A complete listing of majors at St. Thomas appears in the Majors by College index beginning on page 469.

The **faculty** at St. Thomas has 135 full-time members, 91% with terminal degrees. The student-faculty ratio is 12:1.

Students of St. Thomas

The student body totals 3,246, of whom 1,750 are undergraduates. 59.5% are women and 40.5% are men. Students come from 23 states and territories and 60 other countries. 97% are from Texas. 5% are international students. 4.6% are African American, 0.5% American Indian, 11.1% Asian American, and 32.3% Hispanic American. 72% returned for their sophomore year.

Facilities and Resources

Students can access the following: computer help desk, free student e-mail accounts, online (class) grades, online (class) registration, online (class) schedules. Campuswide network is available. Wireless service is available via entire campus. The 2 **libraries** have 223,898 books and 19,351 subscriptions.

Campus Life

There are 69 active organizations on campus, including a drama/theater group, newspaper, and choral group. No national or local **fraternities** or **sororities**.

St. Thomas is a member of the NAIA. **Intercollegiate sports** include soccer (m), volleyball (m).

Campus Safety

Student safety services include late-night transport/escort service, 24-hour emergency telephone alarm devices, 24-hour patrols by trained security personnel, and electronically operated dormitory entrances.

Applying

St. Thomas requires an essay, SAT or ACT, a high school transcript, and a minimum high school GPA of 2.5. Application deadline: rolling admissions; 4/1 priority date for financial aid. Deferred admission is possible.

Getting Accepted

810 applied
81% were accepted
298 enrolled (46% of accepted)
Mean SAT critical reading score: 560
Mean SAT math score: 568
Mean SAT writing score: 554
Mean ACT score: 25
33% had SAT critical reading scores over 600
35% had SAT math scores over 600
30% had SAT writing scores over 600
59% had ACT scores over 24
6% had SAT critical reading scores over 700
5% had SAT math scores over 700
6% had SAT writing scores over 700
10% had ACT scores over 30
5 valedictorians

Graduation and After

24% graduated in 4 years
18% graduated in 5 years
6% graduated in 6 years
28 organizations recruited on campus

Financial Matters

$20,190 tuition and fees (2008–09)
$7700 room and board
79% average percent of need met
$20,620 average financial aid amount received per undergraduate (2007–08 estimated)

The breadth of programs and depth of facilities at the University of San Diego (USD) mean that students can easily find a course of study that ignites their intellectual fire. In the classroom, course work across disciplines encourages students to develop their critical-thinking skills. Small class size means the instructors know their students and can stimulate curious minds with anything from a spot on a research project to an after-class discussion on topic. In this environment, students begin a lifelong habit of appreciating and cultivating their individual gifts. To complement this instruction, USD's honors program provides a challenging curriculum for USD's uniquely motivated students. Honors students have numerous opportunities for individual counseling and discussions with honors faculty members. USD's 180-acre campus sits atop a mesa overlooking San Diego, Mission Bay, and the Pacific Ocean.

Getting Accepted
10,584 applied
52% were accepted
1,260 enrolled (23% of accepted)
39% from top tenth of their h.s. class
3.79 average high school GPA
Mean SAT critical reading score: 588
Mean SAT math score: 602
Mean SAT writing score: 596
Mean ACT score: 26
48% had SAT critical reading scores over 600
55% had SAT math scores over 600
53% had SAT writing scores over 600
83% had ACT scores over 24
7% had SAT critical reading scores over 700
8% had SAT math scores over 700
8% had SAT writing scores over 700
16% had ACT scores over 30
21 valedictorians

Graduation and After
64% graduated in 4 years
10% graduated in 5 years
1% graduated in 6 years
85% had job offers within 6 months
113 organizations recruited on campus

Financial Matters
$36,292 tuition and fees (2009–10)
$12,602 room and board
68% average percent of need met
$21,463 average financial aid amount received
  per undergraduate (2006–07)

UNIVERSITY OF SAN DIEGO
URBAN SETTING ■ PRIVATE ■ INDEPENDENT RELIGIOUS ■ COED
SAN DIEGO, CALIFORNIA

Web site: www.sandiego.edu
Contact: Mr. Stephen Pultz, Director of Admission, 5998 Alcala Park, San Diego, CA 92110
Telephone: 619-260-4506 or toll-free 800-248-4873
Fax: 619-260-6836
E-mail: admissions@sandiego.edu

Academics
USD awards bachelor's, master's, doctoral, and first-professional **degrees** and post-bachelor's, post-master's, and first-professional certificates. **Challenging opportunities** include advanced placement credit, an honors program, double majors, independent study, and a senior project. Special programs include internships, summer session for credit, study-abroad, and Army, Navy, and Air Force ROTC.

The most frequently chosen **baccalaureate** fields are business/marketing, social sciences, and communications/journalism. A complete listing of majors at USD appears in the Majors by College index beginning on page 469.

The **faculty** at USD has 369 full-time members, 94% with terminal degrees. The student-faculty ratio is 15:1.

Students of USD
The student body totals 7,882, of whom 5,119 are undergraduates. 58.3% are women and 41.7% are men. Students come from 52 states and territories and 42 other countries. 60% are from California. 3.1% are international students. 2.3% are African American, 1.4% American Indian, 9.8% Asian American, and 14.5% Hispanic American. 85% returned for their sophomore year.

Facilities and Resources
765 **computers/terminals** and 4,000 ports are available on campus for general student use. Students can access the following: campus intranet, computer help desk, free student e-mail accounts, online (class) grades, online (class) registration, online (class) schedules. Campuswide network is available. 100% of college-owned or -operated housing units are wired for high-speed Internet access. Wireless service is available via entire campus. The 2 **libraries** have 704,887 books and 38,488 subscriptions.

Campus Life
Active organizations on campus include a drama/theater group, newspaper, television station, and choral group. 17% of eligible men and 26% of eligible women are members of national **fraternities** and national **sororities**.

USD is a member of the NCAA (Division I). **Intercollegiate sports** (some offering scholarships) include baseball (m), basketball, crew, cross-country running, football (m), golf (m), soccer, softball (w), swimming and diving (w), tennis, track and field (w), volleyball (w).

Campus Safety
Student safety services include late-night transport/escort service, 24-hour emergency telephone alarm devices, 24-hour patrols by trained security personnel, student patrols, and electronically operated dormitory entrances.

Applying
USD requires an essay, SAT or ACT, a high school transcript, 1 recommendation, and SAT with Written test or ACT. Application deadline: 1/15; 2/20 priority date for financial aid. Deferred admission is possible.

THE UNIVERSITY OF SCRANTON
URBAN SETTING ■ PRIVATE ■ INDEPENDENT RELIGIOUS ■ COED
SCRANTON, PENNSYLVANIA

Web site: www.scranton.edu
Contact: Mr. Joseph Roback, Associate Vice President, Undergraduate
Admissions and Enrollment, St. Thomas Hall, Room 409, Scranton, PA
18510-4501
Telephone: 570-941-7540 or toll-free 888-SCRANTON
Fax: 570-941-4370
E-mail: admissions@scranton.edu

Academics
Scranton awards associate, bachelor's, master's, and doctoral **degrees** and post-
bachelor's and post-master's certificates. **Challenging opportunities** include advanced
placement credit, accelerated degree programs, student-designed majors, an honors
program, double majors, independent study, and a senior project. Special programs
include internships, summer session for credit, off-campus study, study-abroad, and
Army and Air Force ROTC.

The most frequently chosen **baccalaureate** fields are business/marketing, health
professions and related sciences, and education. A complete listing of majors at Scranton
appears in the Majors by College index beginning on page 469.

The **faculty** at Scranton has 258 full-time members, 84% with terminal degrees. The
student-faculty ratio is 11:1.

Students of Scranton
The student body totals 5,612, of whom 4,081 are undergraduates. 57.3% are women
and 42.7% are men. Students come from 25 states and territories and 18 other countries.
48% are from Pennsylvania. 0.4% are international students. 1.3% are African
American, 0.2% American Indian, 2.2% Asian American, and 4.7% Hispanic American.
90% returned for their sophomore year.

Facilities and Resources
927 **computers/terminals** are available on campus for general student use. Students can
access the following: computer help desk, free student e-mail accounts, online (class)
grades, online (class) registration, online (class) schedules. Campuswide network is available. 100% of college-owned or -operated housing units are wired for high-speed
Internet access. Wireless service is available via classrooms, computer centers, computer
labs, dorm rooms, learning centers, libraries, student centers. The 2 **libraries** have
481,542 books and 1,579 subscriptions.

Campus Life
There are 80 active organizations on campus, including a drama/theater group,
newspaper, radio station, television station, and choral group. No national or local
fraternities or **sororities**.

Scranton is a member of the NCAA (Division III). **Intercollegiate sports** include
baseball (m), basketball, cross-country running, field hockey (w), golf (m), ice hockey
(m), lacrosse (m), soccer, softball (w), swimming and diving, tennis, volleyball (w),
wrestling (m).

Campus Safety
Student safety services include late-night transport/escort service, 24-hour emergency
telephone alarm devices, 24-hour patrols by trained security personnel, student patrols,
and electronically operated dormitory entrances.

Applying
Scranton requires an essay, SAT or ACT, and a high school transcript, and in some cases
an interview. Application deadline: 3/1; 2/15 priority date for financial aid. Early and
deferred admission are possible.

Getting Accepted
7,609 applied
66% were accepted
1,027 enrolled (20% of accepted)
27% from top tenth of their h.s. class
3.36 average high school GPA
Mean SAT critical reading score: 555
Mean SAT math score: 566
25% had SAT critical reading scores over 600
33% had SAT math scores over 600
4% had SAT critical reading scores over 700
4% had SAT math scores over 700
14 valedictorians

Graduation and After
67% graduated in 4 years
10% graduated in 5 years
87 organizations recruited on campus

Financial Matters
$31,576 tuition and fees (2008–09)
$10,780 room and board
72% average percent of need met
$15,558 average financial aid amount received
per undergraduate

UNIVERSITY OF SOUTH CAROLINA
URBAN SETTING ■ PUBLIC ■ STATE-SUPPORTED ■ COED
COLUMBIA, SOUTH CAROLINA

Web site: www.sc.edu
Contact: Mr. Scott Verzyl, Director of Undergraduate Admissions, Columbia, SC 29208
Telephone: 803-777-7700 or toll-free 800-868-5872 (in-state)
Fax: 803-777-0101
E-mail: admissions-ugrad@sc.edu

The University of South Carolina offers a wealth of resources for its high-achieving students. The Honors College provides intensive study led by the University's top researchers and teachers. Competitive study-abroad grants are available, and assistance is provided for the pursuit of prestigious national awards such as Fulbright grants and Rotary and Truman scholarships. Fall freshman applicants who apply by the University's December 1 priority deadline receive consideration for attractive merit-based scholarships. The University has more than 350 degree programs, and many, such as the number one–ranked undergraduate international business program, receive prominent national accolades. Scholars flourish at the University of South Carolina.

Getting Accepted
17,018 applied
58% were accepted
3,859 enrolled (39% of accepted)
30% from top tenth of their h.s. class
3.9 average high school GPA
Mean SAT critical reading score: 586
Mean SAT math score: 605
Mean ACT score: 26
44% had SAT critical reading scores over 600
54% had SAT math scores over 600
78% had ACT scores over 24
7% had SAT critical reading scores over 700
9% had SAT math scores over 700
17% had ACT scores over 30
58 National Merit Scholars
82 valedictorians

Graduation and After
45% graduated in 4 years
19% graduated in 5 years
3% graduated in 6 years
17695 organizations recruited on campus

Financial Matters
$8838 resident tuition and fees (2008–09)
$22,908 nonresident tuition and fees (2008–09)
$7318 room and board
72% average percent of need met
$10,558 average financial aid amount received per undergraduate (2007–08 estimated)

Academics
South Carolina awards bachelor's, master's, doctoral, and first-professional **degrees** and post-bachelor's and post-master's certificates. **Challenging opportunities** include advanced placement credit, accelerated degree programs, student-designed majors, freshman honors college, an honors program, double majors, independent study, and a senior project. Special programs include cooperative education, internships, summer session for credit, study-abroad, and Army, Navy, and Air Force ROTC.

The most frequently chosen **baccalaureate** fields are business/marketing, social sciences, and communications/journalism. A complete listing of majors at South Carolina appears in the Majors by College index beginning on page 469.

The **faculty** at South Carolina has 1,201 full-time members, 83% with terminal degrees. The student-faculty ratio is 18:1.

Students of South Carolina
The student body totals 27,488, of whom 19,765 are undergraduates. 54.5% are women and 45.5% are men. Students come from 53 states and territories and 75 other countries. 74% are from South Carolina. 1.3% are international students. 11.6% are African American, 0.4% American Indian, 3% Asian American, and 2.2% Hispanic American. 87% returned for their sophomore year.

Facilities and Resources
2,800 **computers/terminals** are available on campus for general student use. Students can access the following: computer help desk, free student e-mail accounts, online (class) grades, online (class) registration, online (class) schedules. Campuswide network is available. 100% of college-owned or -operated housing units are wired for high-speed Internet access. Wireless service is available via entire campus. The 8 **libraries** have 3,579,504 books and 51,540 subscriptions.

Campus Life
There are 270 active organizations on campus, including a drama/theater group, newspaper, radio station, choral group, and marching band. 14% of eligible men and 15% of eligible women are members of national **fraternities** and national **sororities**.

South Carolina is a member of the NCAA (Division I). **Intercollegiate sports** (some offering scholarships) include baseball (m), basketball, cross-country running (w), equestrian sports (w), football (m), golf, soccer, softball (w), swimming and diving, tennis, track and field, volleyball (w).

Campus Safety
Student safety services include late-night transport/escort service, 24-hour emergency telephone alarm devices, 24-hour patrols by trained security personnel, student patrols, and electronically operated dormitory entrances.

Applying
South Carolina requires SAT or ACT, a high school transcript, and a minimum high school GPA of 2.0. Application deadline: 12/1; 4/1 priority date for financial aid.

University of Southern California

Urban setting ■ Private ■ Independent ■ Coed
Los Angeles, California

Web site: www.usc.edu
Contact: Timothy Brunold, Associate Dean and Director of Undergraduate Admission, University Park Campus, Los Angeles, CA 90089
Telephone: 213-740-1111
Fax: 213-821-0200
E-mail: admitusc@usc.edu

Academics

USC awards bachelor's, master's, doctoral, and first-professional **degrees** and post-bachelor's, post-master's, and first-professional certificates. **Challenging opportunities** include advanced placement credit, accelerated degree programs, student-designed majors, freshman honors college, an honors program, double majors, independent study, and a senior project. Special programs include cooperative education, internships, summer session for credit, off-campus study, study-abroad, and Army, Navy, and Air Force ROTC.

The most frequently chosen **baccalaureate** fields are business/marketing, social sciences, and visual and performing arts. A complete listing of majors at USC appears in the Majors by College index beginning on page 469.

The **faculty** at USC has 1,666 full-time members, 89% with terminal degrees. The student-faculty ratio is 9:1.

Students of USC

The student body totals 33,747, of whom 16,608 are undergraduates. 50.4% are women and 49.6% are men. Students come from 56 states and territories and 116 other countries. 63% are from California. 9.1% are international students. 5.4% are African American, 0.9% American Indian, 22.9% Asian American, and 12.1% Hispanic American. 97% returned for their sophomore year.

Facilities and Resources

2,700 **computers/terminals** and 6,000 ports are available on campus for general student use. Students can access the following: campus intranet, computer help desk, free student e-mail accounts, online (class) grades, online (class) registration, online (class) schedules, online degree progress, financial aid applications, document sharing, calendars, personal Web space, customizable Web portal, course management systems (including data and video). Campuswide network is available. 100% of college-owned or -operated housing units are wired for high-speed Internet access. Wireless service is available via entire campus. The 18 **libraries** have 4,373,395 books and 60,852 subscriptions.

Campus Life

There are 627 active organizations on campus, including a drama/theater group, newspaper, radio station, television station, choral group, and marching band. 17% of eligible men and 20% of eligible women are members of national **fraternities**, national **sororities**, local fraternities, and local sororities.

USC is a member of the NCAA (Division I). **Intercollegiate sports** (some offering scholarships) include baseball (m), basketball, crew (w), cross-country running, football (m), golf, soccer (w), swimming and diving, tennis, track and field, volleyball, water polo.

Campus Safety

Student safety services include late-night transport/escort service, 24-hour emergency telephone alarm devices, 24-hour patrols by trained security personnel, student patrols, and electronically operated dormitory entrances.

Applying

USC requires an essay, SAT or ACT, and a high school transcript. Application deadline: 1/10; 1/22 priority date for financial aid.

Getting Accepted
35,900 applied
22% were accepted
2,766 enrolled (35% of accepted)
87% from top tenth of their h.s. class
3.71 average high school GPA
85% had SAT critical reading scores over 600
91% had SAT math scores over 600
90% had SAT writing scores over 600
96% had ACT scores over 24
33% had SAT critical reading scores over 700
50% had SAT math scores over 700
44% had SAT writing scores over 700
63% had ACT scores over 30
244 National Merit Scholars

Graduation and After
69% graduated in 4 years
17% graduated in 5 years
2% graduated in 6 years
740 organizations recruited on campus

Financial Matters
$37,694 tuition and fees (2008–09)
$11,298 room and board
100% average percent of need met
$31,212 average financial aid amount received per undergraduate (2006–07)

THE UNIVERSITY OF TENNESSEE

URBAN SETTING ■ PUBLIC ■ STATE-SUPPORTED ■ COED
KNOXVILLE, TENNESSEE

Web site: www.tennessee.edu
Contact: Mr. Richard Bayer, Assistant Provost and Director, 320 Student
Services Building, 1331 Circle Park, Knoxville, TN 37996-0230
Telephone: 865-974-2184 or toll-free 800-221-8657 (in-state)
Fax: 865-974-6341
E-mail: admissions@tennessee.edu

Getting Accepted
13,894 applied
65% were accepted
4,215 enrolled (47% of accepted)
41% from top tenth of their h.s. class
3.66 average high school GPA
Mean SAT critical reading score: 579
Mean SAT math score: 590
Mean ACT score: 27
42% had SAT critical reading scores over 600
48% had SAT math scores over 600
84% had ACT scores over 24
7% had SAT critical reading scores over 700
8% had SAT math scores over 700
19% had ACT scores over 30
21 National Merit Scholars

Graduation and After
30% graduated in 4 years
25% graduated in 5 years
5% graduated in 6 years
75% had job offers within 6 months
500 organizations recruited on campus

Financial Matters
$6250 resident tuition and fees (2008–09)
**$18,908 nonresident tuition and fees
(2008–09)**
$6888 room and board
73% average percent of need met
**$9357 average financial aid amount received
per undergraduate (2007–08 estimated)**

Academics

Tennessee awards bachelor's, master's, doctoral, and first-professional **degrees** and post-bachelor's, post-master's, and first-professional certificates. **Challenging opportunities** include advanced placement credit, accelerated degree programs, student-designed majors, freshman honors college, an honors program, double majors, independent study, and a senior project. Special programs include cooperative education, internships, summer session for credit, off-campus study, study-abroad, and Army and Air Force ROTC.

The most frequently chosen **baccalaureate** fields are business/marketing, social sciences, and psychology. A complete listing of majors at Tennessee appears in the Majors by College index beginning on page 469.

The **faculty** at Tennessee has 1,562 full-time members, 83% with terminal degrees. The student-faculty ratio is 16:1.

Students of Tennessee

The student body totals 30,410, of whom 21,717 are undergraduates. 49.9% are women and 50.1% are men. Students come from 51 states and territories and 110 other countries. 87% are from Tennessee. 0.9% are international students. 8.2% are African American, 0.4% American Indian, 2.7% Asian American, and 1.7% Hispanic American. 84% returned for their sophomore year.

Facilities and Resources

600 **computers/terminals** are available on campus for general student use. Students can access the following: campus intranet, computer help desk, free student e-mail accounts, online (class) grades, online (class) registration, online (class) schedules, Blackboard Course Management System. Campuswide network is available. 100% of college-owned or -operated housing units are wired for high-speed Internet access. Wireless service is available via entire campus. The 7 **libraries** have 2,960,180 books and 27,000 subscriptions.

Campus Life

There are 350 active organizations on campus, including a drama/theater group, newspaper, radio station, television station, choral group, and marching band. 14% of eligible men and 14% of eligible women are members of national **fraternities** and national **sororities**.

Tennessee is a member of the NCAA (Division I). **Intercollegiate sports** (some offering scholarships) include baseball (m), basketball, cheerleading, crew (w), cross-country running, football (m), golf, soccer (w), softball (w), swimming and diving, tennis, track and field, volleyball (w).

Campus Safety

Student safety services include late-night transport/escort service, 24-hour emergency telephone alarm devices, and 24-hour patrols by trained security personnel.

Applying

Tennessee requires SAT or ACT, a high school transcript, specific high school units, and a minimum high school GPA of 2.0. It recommends an essay. Application deadline: 12/1; 3/1 priority date for financial aid. Early and deferred admission are possible.

THE UNIVERSITY OF TENNESSEE AT CHATTANOOGA

URBAN SETTING ■ PUBLIC ■ STATE-SUPPORTED ■ COED
CHATTANOOGA, TENNESSEE

Web site: www.utc.edu
Contact: Mr. Yancy Freeman, Director, Admissions and Recruitment, 615 McCallie Avenue, Guerry Hall, Chattanooga, TN 37403
Telephone: 423-755-4597 or toll-free 800-UTC-MOCS (in-state)
Fax: 423-425-4157
E-mail: yancy-freeman@utc.edu

Academics

UTC awards bachelor's, master's, doctoral, and first-professional **degrees** and post-bachelor's and post-master's certificates. **Challenging opportunities** include advanced placement credit, an honors program, double majors, independent study, and a senior project. Special programs include cooperative education, internships, summer session for credit, off-campus study, and study-abroad.

The most frequently chosen **baccalaureate** fields are business/marketing, family and consumer sciences, and psychology. A complete listing of majors at UTC appears in the Majors by College index beginning on page 469.

The **faculty** at UTC has 402 full-time members, 68% with terminal degrees. The student-faculty ratio is 14:1.

Students of UTC

The student body totals 9,807, of whom 8,405 are undergraduates. 56.2% are women and 43.8% are men. Students come from 40 states and territories and 40 other countries. 94% are from Tennessee. 0.8% are international students. 17.1% are African American, 0.5% American Indian, 2.3% Asian American, and 2% Hispanic American. 62% returned for their sophomore year.

Facilities and Resources

300 **computers/terminals** are available on campus for general student use. Students can access the following: campus intranet, computer help desk, free student e-mail accounts, online (class) grades, online (class) registration, online (class) schedules. Campuswide network is available. 100% of college-owned or -operated housing units are wired for high-speed Internet access. Wireless service is available via classrooms, computer labs, libraries. The **library** has 586,633 books and 1,822 subscriptions.

Campus Life

There are 130 active organizations on campus, including a drama/theater group, newspaper, radio station, choral group, and marching band. 5% of eligible men and 4% of eligible women are members of national **fraternities** and national **sororities**.

UTC is a member of the NCAA (Division I). **Intercollegiate sports** (some offering scholarships) include basketball, crew, cross-country running, football (m), golf, soccer, softball (w), tennis, track and field, volleyball (w), wrestling (m).

Campus Safety

Student safety services include late-night transport/escort service, 24-hour emergency telephone alarm devices, 24-hour patrols by trained security personnel, and electronically operated dormitory entrances.

Applying

UTC requires SAT or ACT and a high school transcript. It recommends an essay. Application deadline: 4/1 priority date for financial aid. Deferred admission is possible.

Getting Accepted
5,849 applied
79% were accepted
2,083 enrolled (45% of accepted)
3.22 average high school GPA
Mean ACT score: 22
32% had ACT scores over 24
3% had ACT scores over 30

Graduation and After
15% graduated in 4 years
19% graduated in 5 years
5% graduated in 6 years
66 organizations recruited on campus

Financial Matters
$5310 resident tuition and fees (2008–09)
$11,660 nonresident tuition and fees (2008–09)
$8100 room and board
81% average percent of need met
$9022 average financial aid amount received per undergraduate (2007–08 estimated)

The University of Texas at Austin

Urban setting ■ Public ■ State-supported ■ Coed
Austin, Texas

Web site: www.utexas.edu
Contact: Dr. Bruce Walker, Vice Provost and Director of Admissions, Office of Admissions, Freshman Admissions Center, PO Box 8058, Austin, TX 78713-8058
Telephone: 512-475-7440
Fax: 512-475-7475

Getting Accepted

29,501 applied
44% were accepted
6,718 enrolled (52% of accepted)
75% from top tenth of their h.s. class
Mean SAT critical reading score: 600
Mean SAT math score: 632
Mean SAT writing score: 599
Mean ACT score: 27
55% had SAT critical reading scores over 600
67% had SAT math scores over 600
53% had SAT writing scores over 600
76% had ACT scores over 24
15% had SAT critical reading scores over 700
25% had SAT math scores over 700
16% had SAT writing scores over 700
27% had ACT scores over 30
281 National Merit Scholars

Graduation and After

48% graduated in 4 years
25% graduated in 5 years
5% graduated in 6 years

Financial Matters

$8532 resident tuition and fees (2008–09)
$27,760 nonresident tuition and fees (2008–09)
$9246 room and board
90% average percent of need met
$10,900 average financial aid amount received per undergraduate (2006–07)

Academics

UT Austin awards bachelor's, master's, doctoral, and first-professional **degrees. Challenging opportunities** include advanced placement credit, accelerated degree programs, student-designed majors, an honors program, double majors, independent study, and a senior project. Special programs include cooperative education, internships, summer session for credit, off-campus study, study-abroad, and Army, Navy, and Air Force ROTC.

The most frequently chosen **baccalaureate** fields are communications/journalism, social sciences, and business/marketing. A complete listing of majors at UT Austin appears in the Majors by College index beginning on page 469.

The **faculty** at UT Austin has 2,687 full-time members, 88% with terminal degrees. The student-faculty ratio is 17:1.

Students of UT Austin

The student body totals 49,984, of whom 37,389 are undergraduates. 51.9% are women and 48.1% are men. Students come from 54 states and territories and 125 other countries. 96% are from Texas. 4.1% are international students. 4.8% are African American, 0.5% American Indian, 17.6% Asian American, and 18.1% Hispanic American. 91% returned for their sophomore year.

Facilities and Resources

500 **computers/terminals** and 9,000 ports are available on campus for general student use. Students can access the following: computer help desk, free student e-mail accounts, online (class) grades, online (class) registration, online (class) schedules. Campuswide network is available. 100% of college-owned or -operated housing units are wired for high-speed Internet access. Wireless service is available via libraries, student centers. The 12 **libraries** have 9,022,363 books.

Campus Life

There are 900 active organizations on campus, including a drama/theater group, newspaper, radio station, television station, choral group, and marching band. 9% of eligible men and 12% of eligible women are members of national **fraternities** and national **sororities**.

UT Austin is a member of the NCAA (Division I). **Intercollegiate sports** (some offering scholarships) include baseball (m), basketball, crew (w), cross-country running, football (m), golf, soccer (w), softball (w), swimming and diving, tennis, track and field, volleyball (w).

Campus Safety

Student safety services include late-night transport/escort service, 24-hour emergency telephone alarm devices, 24-hour patrols by trained security personnel, student patrols, and electronically operated dormitory entrances.

Applying

UT Austin requires an essay, SAT or ACT, and a high school transcript, and in some cases SAT Subject Tests. Application deadline: 12/15; 4/1 priority date for financial aid. Deferred admission is possible.

THE UNIVERSITY OF TEXAS AT DALLAS

SUBURBAN SETTING ■ PUBLIC ■ STATE-SUPPORTED ■ COED
RICHARDSON, TEXAS

Web site: www.utdallas.edu
Contact: Enrollment Services, 800 W. Campbell Road, Mail Station HH10, Richardson, TX 75083-0688
Telephone: 972-883-2270 or toll-free 800-889-2443
Fax: 972-883-2599
E-mail: interest@utdallas.edu

Academics

UT Dallas awards bachelor's, master's, doctoral, and first-professional **degrees** and post-bachelor's certificates. **Challenging opportunities** include advanced placement credit, accelerated degree programs, student-designed majors, freshman honors college, an honors program, double majors, independent study, and a senior project. Special programs include cooperative education, internships, summer session for credit, study-abroad, and Army and Air Force ROTC.

The most frequently chosen **baccalaureate** fields are business/marketing, interdisciplinary studies, and social sciences. A complete listing of majors at UT Dallas appears in the Majors by College index beginning on page 469.

The **faculty** at UT Dallas has 515 full-time members, 92% with terminal degrees. The student-faculty ratio is 19:1.

Students of UT Dallas

The student body totals 14,944, of whom 9,393 are undergraduates. 45.6% are women and 54.4% are men. Students come from 42 states and territories and 98 other countries. 96% are from Texas. 4.1% are international students. 7.6% are African American, 0.5% American Indian, 21.4% Asian American, and 11.4% Hispanic American. 83% returned for their sophomore year.

Facilities and Resources

630 **computers/terminals** are available on campus for general student use. Students can access the following: computer help desk, free student e-mail accounts, online (class) grades, online (class) registration, online (class) schedules. Campuswide network is available. 100% of college-owned or -operated housing units are wired for high-speed Internet access. Wireless service is available via classrooms, computer centers, dorm rooms, libraries, student centers. The 2 **libraries** have 1,863,527 books.

Campus Life

There are 130 active organizations on campus, including a drama/theater group, newspaper, and radio station. 5% of eligible men and 5% of eligible women are members of national **fraternities**, national **sororities**, and local sororities.

UT Dallas is a member of the NCAA (Division III). **Intercollegiate sports** include baseball (m), basketball, cross-country running, golf, soccer, softball (w), tennis, volleyball (w).

Campus Safety

Student safety services include late-night transport/escort service, 24-hour emergency telephone alarm devices, and 24-hour patrols by trained security personnel.

Applying

UT Dallas requires an essay, SAT or ACT, and a high school transcript, and in some cases Texas Higher Education Assessment and an interview. It recommends 3 recommendations. Application deadline: 7/1; 3/31 priority date for financial aid. Deferred admission is possible.

Getting Accepted

4,916 applied
54% were accepted
1,118 enrolled (42% of accepted)
40% from top tenth of their h.s. class
3.62 average high school GPA
Mean SAT critical reading score: 605
Mean SAT math score: 643
Mean ACT score: 27
54% had SAT critical reading scores over 600
73% had SAT math scores over 600
45% had SAT writing scores over 600
81% had ACT scores over 24
15% had SAT critical reading scores over 700
28% had SAT math scores over 700
11% had SAT writing scores over 700
29% had ACT scores over 30
46 National Merit Scholars
39 valedictorians

Graduation and After

36% graduated in 4 years
18% graduated in 5 years
5% graduated in 6 years
546 organizations recruited on campus

Financial Matters

$9850 resident tuition and fees (2008–09)
$21,000 nonresident tuition and fees (2008–09)
$6828 room and board
75% average percent of need met
$10,324 average financial aid amount received per undergraduate (2007–08 estimated)

UNIVERSITY OF THE PACIFIC

SUBURBAN SETTING ■ PRIVATE ■ INDEPENDENT ■ COED
STOCKTON, CALIFORNIA

Web site: www.pacific.edu
Contact: Mr. Rich Toledo, Director of Admissions, 3601 Pacific Avenue, Stockton, CA 95211
Telephone: 209-946-2211 or toll-free 800-959-2867
Fax: 209-946-2413
E-mail: admissions@pacific.edu

Getting Accepted
5,450 applied
69% were accepted
882 enrolled (23% of accepted)
39% from top tenth of their h.s. class
3.46 average high school GPA
Mean SAT critical reading score: 560
Mean SAT math score: 600
Mean ACT score: 25
36% had SAT critical reading scores over 600
52% had SAT math scores over 600
36% had SAT writing scores over 600
60% had ACT scores over 24
6% had SAT critical reading scores over 700
18% had SAT math scores over 700
5% had SAT writing scores over 700
12% had ACT scores over 30

Graduation and After
44% graduated in 4 years
18% graduated in 5 years
5% graduated in 6 years

Financial Matters
$30,880 tuition and fees (2008–09)
$10,118 room and board
$25,889 average financial aid amount received per undergraduate (2007–08 estimated)

Academics
Pacific awards bachelor's, master's, doctoral, and first-professional **degrees**. **Challenging opportunities** include advanced placement credit, accelerated degree programs, student-designed majors, an honors program, double majors, independent study, and a senior project. Special programs include cooperative education, internships, summer session for credit, and Air Force ROTC.

The most frequently chosen **baccalaureate** fields are biological/life sciences, business/marketing, and parks and recreation. A complete listing of majors at Pacific appears in the Majors by College index beginning on page 469.

The **faculty** at Pacific has 426 full-time members, 92% with terminal degrees. The student-faculty ratio is 13:1.

Students of Pacific
The student body totals 6,251, of whom 3,457 are undergraduates. 56.2% are women and 43.8% are men. Students come from 36 states and territories and 18 other countries. 87% are from California. 3.5% are international students. 3.6% are African American, 0.7% American Indian, 33.7% Asian American, and 10.8% Hispanic American. 82% returned for their sophomore year.

Facilities and Resources
350 **computers/terminals** are available on campus for general student use. Students can access the following: online (class) registration. Campuswide network is available.

Campus Life
There are 100 active organizations on campus, including a drama/theater group, newspaper, radio station, and choral group. 19% of eligible men and 18% of eligible women are members of national **fraternities**, national **sororities**, and local fraternities.

Pacific is a member of the NCAA (Division I). **Intercollegiate sports** (some offering scholarships) include baseball (m), basketball, cross-country running (w), field hockey (w), golf (m), soccer (w), softball (w), swimming and diving, tennis, volleyball, water polo.

Campus Safety
Student safety services include late-night transport/escort service, 24-hour emergency telephone alarm devices, 24-hour patrols by trained security personnel, and electronically operated dormitory entrances.

Applying
Pacific requires an essay, SAT or ACT, a high school transcript, 1 recommendation, and a minimum high school GPA of 2.5, and in some cases audition for music program. It recommends a minimum high school GPA of 3.0. Application deadline: 1/15; 2/15 priority date for financial aid.

University of the Sciences in Philadelphia

Urban Setting ■ Private ■ Independent ■ Coed

Philadelphia, Pennsylvania

Web site: www.usip.edu

Contact: Mr. Louis Hegyes, Director of Admission, 600 South 43rd Street, Philadelphia, PA 19104-4495

Telephone: 215-596-8810 or toll-free 888-996-8747 (in-state)

Fax: 215-596-8821

E-mail: admit@usp.edu

Academics

USP awards bachelor's, master's, doctoral, and first-professional **degrees** and post-bachelor's certificates. **Challenging opportunities** include advanced placement credit, an honors program, double majors, and a senior project. Special programs include cooperative education, internships, summer session for credit, off-campus study, study-abroad, and Army and Air Force ROTC.

The most frequently chosen **baccalaureate** fields are health professions and related sciences, biological/life sciences, and business/marketing. A complete listing of majors at USP appears in the Majors by College index beginning on page 469.

The **faculty** at USP has 157 full-time members, 78% with terminal degrees.

Students of USP

The student body totals 3,000, of whom 2,076 are undergraduates. 60.3% are women and 39.7% are men. Students come from 34 states and territories and 14 other countries. 50% are from Pennsylvania. 1.3% are international students. 4.9% are African American, 0.2% American Indian, 35.9% Asian American, and 2% Hispanic American. 86% returned for their sophomore year.

Facilities and Resources

190 **computers/terminals** are available on campus for general student use. Students can access the following: campus intranet, computer help desk, free student e-mail accounts, online (class) grades, online (class) registration, online (class) schedules. Campuswide network is available. 100% of college-owned or -operated housing units are wired for high-speed Internet access. Wireless service is available via classrooms, computer centers, computer labs, dorm rooms, learning centers, libraries, student centers. The 2 **libraries** have 87,125 books and 9,817 subscriptions.

Campus Life

There are 65 active organizations on campus, including a drama/theater group, newspaper, and choral group. USP has national **fraternities**, national **sororities**, local fraternities, and local sororities.

USP is a member of the NCAA (Division II) and NAIA. **Intercollegiate sports** (some offering scholarships) include baseball (m), basketball, cross-country running, golf, riflery, softball (w), tennis, volleyball (w).

Campus Safety

Student safety services include late-night transport/escort service, 24-hour emergency telephone alarm devices, 24-hour patrols by trained security personnel, and electronically operated dormitory entrances.

Applying

USP requires SAT or ACT and a high school transcript. It recommends SAT and a minimum high school GPA of 3.0. Application deadline: rolling admissions; 3/15 for financial aid, with a 3/15 priority date. Deferred admission is possible.

A private, coeducational institution of 2,500 students, University of the Sciences in Philadelphia (USP) is located in the University City section of historic Philadelphia—along with its neighbors Drexel University and the University of Pennsylvania. USP offers twenty-one majors in the pharmaceutical sciences, health sciences, and arts and sciences, with pharmacy, physical therapy, occupational therapy, physician assistant studies, biology, and premed being the most popular programs. All programs are direct-entry, whereby candidates are admitted directly into their program of choice. USP also follows a rolling admission policy, and candidates are urged to apply during the fall of their senior year in high school. USP is a member of NCAA Division II.

Getting Accepted

3,836 applied
58% were accepted
534 enrolled (24% of accepted)
39% from top tenth of their h.s. class
3.62 average high school GPA
Mean SAT critical reading score: 561
Mean SAT math score: 606
Mean ACT score: 25
29% had SAT critical reading scores over 600
56% had SAT math scores over 600
57% had ACT scores over 24
2% had SAT critical reading scores over 700
8% had SAT math scores over 700
9% had ACT scores over 30

Graduation and After

56% graduated in 4 years
7% graduated in 5 years
2% graduated in 6 years
95% had job offers within 6 months
225 organizations recruited on campus

Financial Matters

$28,506 tuition and fees (2008–09)
$11,146 room and board
52% average percent of need met
$11,801 average financial aid amount received per undergraduate (2006–07)

Getting Accepted

4,714 applied
46% were accepted
695 enrolled (32% of accepted)
64% from top tenth of their h.s. class
3.75 average high school GPA
Mean SAT critical reading score: 620
Mean SAT math score: 630
Mean ACT score: 28
59% had SAT critical reading scores over 600
63% had SAT math scores over 600
82% had ACT scores over 24
27% had SAT critical reading scores over 700
23% had SAT math scores over 700
33% had ACT scores over 30
76 National Merit Scholars
26 valedictorians

Graduation and After

48% graduated in 4 years
13% graduated in 5 years
2% graduated in 6 years
72% had job offers within 6 months
264 organizations recruited on campus

Financial Matters

$23,940 tuition and fees (2008–09)
$7776 room and board
87% average percent of need met
$22,586 average financial aid amount received
    per undergraduate (2005–06)

UNIVERSITY OF TULSA

URBAN SETTING ■ PRIVATE ■ INDEPENDENT RELIGIOUS ■ COED
TULSA, OKLAHOMA

Web site: www.utulsa.edu
Contact: Mr. Earl Johnson, Dean of Admission, 600 South College Avenue,
    Tulsa, OK 74104
Telephone: 918-631-2307 or toll-free 800-331-3050
Fax: 918-631-5003
E-mail: admission@utulsa.edu

Academics

TU awards bachelor's, master's, doctoral, and first-professional **degrees** and post-bachelor's and first-professional certificates. **Challenging opportunities** include advanced placement credit, accelerated degree programs, student-designed majors, an honors program, double majors, independent study, and a senior project. Special programs include internships, summer session for credit, study-abroad, and Air Force ROTC.

The most frequently chosen **baccalaureate** fields are business/marketing, engineering, and visual and performing arts. A complete listing of majors at TU appears in the Majors by College index beginning on page 469.

The **faculty** at TU has 317 full-time members, 96% with terminal degrees. The student-faculty ratio is 10:1.

Students of TU

The student body totals 4,192, of whom 3,049 are undergraduates. 47.9% are women and 52.1% are men. Students come from 47 states and territories and 50 other countries. 59% are from Oklahoma. 11.7% are international students. 6.3% are African American, 3.8% American Indian, 3.2% Asian American, and 4.4% Hispanic American. 88% returned for their sophomore year.

Facilities and Resources

900 **computers/terminals** are available on campus for general student use. Students can access the following: campus intranet, computer help desk, free student e-mail accounts, online (class) grades, online (class) registration, online (class) schedules. Campuswide network is available. 100% of college-owned or -operated housing units are wired for high-speed Internet access. Wireless service is available via entire campus. The 2 **libraries** have 1,124,126 books and 27,905 subscriptions.

Campus Life

There are 272 active organizations on campus, including a drama/theater group, newspaper, radio station, television station, choral group, and marching band. 21% of eligible men and 23% of eligible women are members of national **fraternities** and national **sororities**.

TU is a member of the NCAA (Division I). **Intercollegiate sports** (some offering scholarships) include basketball, crew (w), cross-country running, football (m), golf, soccer, softball (w), tennis, track and field, volleyball (w).

Campus Safety

Student safety services include late-night transport/escort service, 24-hour emergency telephone alarm devices, 24-hour patrols by trained security personnel, and electronically operated dormitory entrances.

Applying

TU requires an essay, SAT or ACT, a high school transcript, an interview, and 1 recommendation. It recommends a minimum high school GPA of 3.0. Application deadline: rolling admissions; 4/1 priority date for financial aid. Early and deferred admission are possible.

University of Utah

Urban setting ■ Public ■ State-supported ■ Coed
Salt Lake City, Utah

Web site: www.utah.edu
Contact: Mateo Remsburg, Director of High School Services, 201 Presidents Circle Room 206, Salt Lake City, UT 84112
Telephone: 801-581-8761 or toll-free 800-444-8638
Fax: 801-585-3257
E-mail: mremsburg@sa.utah.edu

Academics

U of U awards bachelor's, master's, doctoral, and first-professional **degrees** and post-bachelor's and post-master's certificates. **Challenging opportunities** include advanced placement credit, accelerated degree programs, student-designed majors, freshman honors college, an honors program, double majors, independent study, and a senior project. Special programs include cooperative education, internships, summer session for credit, off-campus study, study-abroad, and Army, Navy, and Air Force ROTC.

The most frequently chosen **baccalaureate** fields are social sciences, business/marketing, and communications/journalism. A complete listing of majors at U of U appears in the Majors by College index beginning on page 469.

The **faculty** at U of U has 1,276 full-time members, 82% with terminal degrees. The student-faculty ratio is 13:1.

Students of U of U

The student body totals 28,211, of whom 21,526 are undergraduates. 44.7% are women and 55.3% are men. Students come from 53 states and territories and 129 other countries. 83% are from Utah. 3% are international students. 1.1% are African American, 0.7% American Indian, 5.7% Asian American, and 5.2% Hispanic American. 83% returned for their sophomore year.

Facilities and Resources

8,000 **computers/terminals** are available on campus for general student use. Students can access the following: campus intranet, computer help desk, free student e-mail accounts, online (class) grades, online (class) registration, online (class) schedules, online classes. Campuswide network is available. Wireless service is available via entire campus. The 4 **libraries** have 4,147,086 books and 45,830 subscriptions.

Campus Life

There are 170 active organizations on campus, including a drama/theater group, newspaper, radio station, television station, choral group, and marching band. 2% of eligible men and 2% of eligible women are members of national **fraternities**, national **sororities**, local fraternities, and local sororities.

U of U is a member of the NCAA (Division I). **Intercollegiate sports** (some offering scholarships) include baseball (m), basketball, cheerleading, cross-country running (w), football (m), golf (m), gymnastics (w), skiing (cross-country), skiing (downhill), soccer (w), softball (w), swimming and diving, tennis, track and field (w), volleyball (w).

Campus Safety

Student safety services include late-night transport/escort service, 24-hour emergency telephone alarm devices, 24-hour patrols by trained security personnel, student patrols, and electronically operated dormitory entrances.

Applying

U of U requires SAT, ACT, SAT or ACT, a high school transcript, and a minimum high school GPA of 2.6, and in some cases an essay. It recommends a minimum high school GPA of 3.0. Application deadline: 4/1; 3/15 priority date for financial aid. Early admission is possible.

Getting Accepted

7,234 applied
81% were accepted
2,642 enrolled (45% of accepted)
29% from top tenth of their h.s. class
3.52 average high school GPA
Mean SAT critical reading score: 550
Mean SAT math score: 567
Mean ACT score: 24
34% had SAT critical reading scores over 600
40% had SAT math scores over 600
30% had SAT writing scores over 600
52% had ACT scores over 24
8% had SAT critical reading scores over 700
8% had SAT math scores over 700
6% had SAT writing scores over 700
12% had ACT scores over 30

Graduation and After

20% graduated in 4 years
19% graduated in 5 years
13% graduated in 6 years
80% had job offers within 6 months
190 organizations recruited on campus

Financial Matters

$5285 resident tuition and fees (2008–09)
$16,600 nonresident tuition and fees (2008–09)
$5972 room and board
58% average percent of need met
$8974 average financial aid amount received per undergraduate (2007–08 estimated)

University of Virginia

Suburban setting ■ Public ■ State-supported ■ Coed
Charlottesville, Virginia

Web site: www.virginia.edu
Contact: Dean of Admission, PO Box 400160, Charlottesville, VA 22904-4727
Telephone: 434-982-3200
Fax: 434-954-3587
E-mail: undergrad-admission@virginia.edu

Getting Accepted
18,363 applied
37% were accepted
3,256 enrolled (48% of accepted)
88% from top tenth of their h.s. class
Mean SAT critical reading score: 652
Mean SAT math score: 671
Mean SAT writing score: 661
Mean ACT score: 29
78% had SAT critical reading scores over 600
83% had SAT math scores over 600
80% had SAT writing scores over 600
32% had SAT critical reading scores over 700
40% had SAT math scores over 700
34% had SAT writing scores over 700
209 valedictorians

Graduation and After
85% graduated in 4 years
7% graduated in 5 years
1% graduated in 6 years
500 organizations recruited on campus

Financial Matters
$9300 resident tuition and fees (2008–09)
$29,382 nonresident tuition and fees
   (2008–09)
$7820 room and board
100% average percent of need met
$17,192 average financial aid amount received
   per undergraduate (2007–08 estimated)

Academics
UVA awards bachelor's, master's, doctoral, and first-professional **degrees** and post-master's certificates. **Challenging opportunities** include advanced placement credit, accelerated degree programs, student-designed majors, an honors program, double majors, independent study, and a senior project. Special programs include cooperative education, internships, summer session for credit, study-abroad, and Army, Navy, and Air Force ROTC.

The most frequently chosen **baccalaureate** fields are social sciences, engineering, and psychology. A complete listing of majors at UVA appears in the Majors by College index beginning on page 469.

The **faculty** at UVA has 1,267 full-time members, 91% with terminal degrees. The student-faculty ratio is 15:1.

Students of UVA
The student body totals 24,541, of whom 15,208 are undergraduates. 56.4% are women and 43.6% are men. Students come from 52 states and territories and 69 other countries. 69% are from Virginia. 4.9% are international students. 8.8% are African American, 0.2% American Indian, 11.4% Asian American, and 4.3% Hispanic American. 97% returned for their sophomore year.

Facilities and Resources
Students can access the following: campus intranet, computer help desk, free student e-mail accounts, online (class) grades, online (class) registration, online (class) schedules, online course management tool. Campuswide network is available. Wireless service is available via classrooms, computer centers, computer labs, dorm rooms, learning centers, libraries, student centers. The 15 **libraries** have 5,533,250 books.

Campus Life
There are 662 active organizations on campus, including a drama/theater group, newspaper, radio station, television station, choral group, and marching band. 30% of eligible men and 30% of eligible women are members of national **fraternities**, national **sororities**, local fraternities, and local sororities.

UVA is a member of the NCAA (Division I). **Intercollegiate sports** (some offering scholarships) include baseball (m), basketball, crew (w), cross-country running, field hockey (w), football (m), golf, lacrosse, soccer, softball (w), swimming and diving, tennis, track and field, volleyball (w), wrestling (m).

Campus Safety
Student safety services include late-night transport/escort service, 24-hour emergency telephone alarm devices, 24-hour patrols by trained security personnel, and electronically operated dormitory entrances.

Applying
UVA requires an essay, a high school transcript, and 1 recommendation. It recommends either SAT or ACT plus optional ACT writing test (ACT alone does not satisfy requirement); two SAT subject tests (student's choice). Application deadline: 1/2; 3/1 priority date for financial aid. Deferred admission is possible.

UNIVERSITY OF WASHINGTON
URBAN SETTING ■ PUBLIC ■ STATE-SUPPORTED ■ COED
SEATTLE, WASHINGTON

Web site: www.washington.edu
Contact: Admissions Office, 1410 NE Campus Parkway, Box 355852, Seattle, WA 98195-5852
Telephone: 206-543-9686
Fax: 206-685-3655

Academics
UW awards bachelor's, master's, doctoral, and first-professional **degrees** and first-professional certificates. **Challenging opportunities** include advanced placement credit, accelerated degree programs, student-designed majors, an honors program, double majors, independent study, and a senior project. Special programs include cooperative education, internships, summer session for credit, study-abroad, and Army, Navy, and Air Force ROTC.

The most frequently chosen **baccalaureate** fields are social sciences, biological/life sciences, and business/marketing. A complete listing of majors at UW appears in the Majors by College index beginning on page 469.

The **faculty** at UW has 2,640 full-time members, 89% with terminal degrees. The student-faculty ratio is 12:1.

Students of UW
The student body totals 40,218, of whom 28,570 are undergraduates. 51.9% are women and 48.1% are men. Students come from 52 states and territories and 105 other countries. 87% are from Washington. 3.8% are international students. 3.2% are African American, 1.3% American Indian, 26.1% Asian American, and 4.9% Hispanic American. 92% returned for their sophomore year.

Facilities and Resources
2,000 **computers/terminals** are available on campus for general student use. Students can access the following: computer help desk, free student e-mail accounts, online (class) grades, online (class) registration, online (class) schedules. Campuswide network is available. 100% of college-owned or -operated housing units are wired for high-speed Internet access. The 22 **libraries** have 5,820,229 books and 50,245 subscriptions.

Campus Life
There are 550 active organizations on campus, including a drama/theater group, newspaper, radio station, television station, choral group, and marching band. UW has national **fraternities** and national **sororities**.

UW is a member of the NCAA (Division I). **Intercollegiate sports** (some offering scholarships) include baseball (m), basketball, cheerleading, crew, cross-country running, football (m), golf, gymnastics (w), soccer, softball (w), swimming and diving, tennis, track and field, volleyball (w).

Campus Safety
Student safety services include late-night transport/escort service, 24-hour emergency telephone alarm devices, 24-hour patrols by trained security personnel, and electronically operated dormitory entrances.

Applying
UW requires an essay, SAT or ACT, and a minimum high school GPA of 2.0. Application deadline: 1/15; 2/28 priority date for financial aid. Early admission is possible.

Getting Accepted
17,877 applied
65% were accepted
5,325 enrolled (46% of accepted)
86% from top tenth of their h.s. class
3.69 average high school GPA
48% had SAT critical reading scores over 600
60% had SAT math scores over 600
42% had SAT writing scores over 600
74% had ACT scores over 24
12% had SAT critical reading scores over 700
16% had SAT math scores over 700
8% had SAT writing scores over 700
21% had ACT scores over 30
39 National Merit Scholars

Graduation and After
48% graduated in 4 years
23% graduated in 5 years
4% graduated in 6 years
450 organizations recruited on campus

Financial Matters
$6802 resident tuition and fees (2008–09)
$23,219 nonresident tuition and fees (2008–09)
$7488 room and board
85% average percent of need met
$13,000 average financial aid amount received per undergraduate (2007–08 estimated)

UNIVERSITY OF WISCONSIN–LA CROSSE

SUBURBAN SETTING ■ PUBLIC ■ STATE-SUPPORTED ■ COED
LA CROSSE, WISCONSIN

Web site: www.uwlax.edu
Contact: Ms. Kathryn Kiefer, Director of Admissions, 1725 State Street, La Crosse, WI
Telephone: 608-785-8939
Fax: 608-785-8940
E-mail: admissions@uwlax.edu

Getting Accepted
6,875 applied
66% were accepted
1,784 enrolled (39% of accepted)
32% from top tenth of their h.s. class
Mean ACT score: 25
27% had SAT critical reading scores over 600
33% had SAT math scores over 600
70% had ACT scores over 24
3% had SAT critical reading scores over 700
6% had SAT math scores over 700
5% had ACT scores over 30

Graduation and After
30% graduated in 4 years
30% graduated in 5 years
6% graduated in 6 years
97.98% had job offers within 6 months
95 organizations recruited on campus

Financial Matters
$6648 resident tuition and fees (2008–09)
$14,221 nonresident tuition and fees (2008–09)
$5420 room and board
74% average percent of need met
$4491 average financial aid amount received per undergraduate (2006–07)

Academics
UW-La Crosse awards associate, bachelor's, master's, and first-professional **degrees** and post-bachelor's certificates. **Challenging opportunities** include advanced placement credit, an honors program, double majors, independent study, and a senior project. Special programs include cooperative education, internships, summer session for credit, off-campus study, study-abroad, and Army ROTC.

The most frequently chosen **baccalaureate** fields are business/marketing, education, and biological/life sciences. A complete listing of majors at UW-La Crosse appears in the Majors by College index beginning on page 469.

The **faculty** at UW-La Crosse has 351 full-time members, 79% with terminal degrees.

Students of UW-La Crosse
The student body totals 9,900, of whom 8,634 are undergraduates. 57.9% are women and 42.1% are men. Students come from 37 states and territories and 35 other countries. 84% are from Wisconsin. 2.7% are international students. 1.1% are African American, 0.6% American Indian, 3.6% Asian American, and 1.5% Hispanic American. 87% returned for their sophomore year.

Facilities and Resources
600 **computers/terminals** and 100 ports are available on campus for general student use. Students can access the following: campus intranet, computer help desk, free student e-mail accounts, online (class) grades, online (class) registration, online (class) schedules. Campuswide network is available. 100% of college-owned or -operated housing units are wired for high-speed Internet access. Wireless service is available via classrooms, computer centers, computer labs, dorm rooms, learning centers, libraries, student centers. The **library** has 695,925 books and 1,052 subscriptions.

Campus Life
There are 185 active organizations on campus, including a drama/theater group, newspaper, radio station, television station, choral group, and marching band. 1% of eligible men and 1% of eligible women are members of national **fraternities** and national **sororities**.

UW-La Crosse is a member of the NCAA (Division III). **Intercollegiate sports** include baseball (m), basketball, cheerleading, cross-country running, football (m), gymnastics (w), soccer (w), softball (w), swimming and diving, tennis, track and field, volleyball (w), weight lifting, wrestling (m).

Campus Safety
Student safety services include late-night transport/escort service, 24-hour emergency telephone alarm devices, 24-hour patrols by trained security personnel, and electronically operated dormitory entrances.

Applying
UW-La Crosse requires SAT or ACT and a high school transcript, and in some cases an interview. It recommends an essay and ACT. Application deadline: rolling admissions, rolling admissions for nonresidents; 3/15 priority date for financial aid.

UNIVERSITY OF WISCONSIN–MADISON

URBAN SETTING ▪ PUBLIC ▪ STATE-SUPPORTED ▪ COED
MADISON, WISCONSIN

Web site: www.wisc.edu
Contact: Office of Undergraduate Admissions, 716 Langdon Street, Madison, WI 53706-1481
Telephone: 608-262-3961
Fax: 608-262-7706
E-mail: onwisconsin@admissions.wisc.edu

Academics

Wisconsin awards bachelor's, master's, doctoral, and first-professional **degrees** and post-master's and first-professional certificates. **Challenging opportunities** include advanced placement credit, accelerated degree programs, student-designed majors, an honors program, double majors, independent study, and a senior project. Special programs include cooperative education, internships, summer session for credit, study-abroad, and Army, Navy, and Air Force ROTC.

The most frequently chosen **baccalaureate** fields are social sciences, biological/life sciences, and business/marketing. A complete listing of majors at Wisconsin appears in the Majors by College index beginning on page 469.

The **faculty** at Wisconsin has 2,399 full-time members, 91% with terminal degrees. The student-faculty ratio is 14:1.

Students of Wisconsin

The student body totals 42,030, of whom 30,750 are undergraduates. 52.4% are women and 47.6% are men. 68% are from Wisconsin. 4.6% are international students. 2.9% are African American, 0.7% American Indian, 5.8% Asian American, and 3.6% Hispanic American. 94% returned for their sophomore year.

Facilities and Resources

Students can access the following: computer help desk, free student e-mail accounts, online (class) grades, online (class) registration, online (class) schedules. Campuswide network is available. 100% of college-owned or -operated housing units are wired for high-speed Internet access. Wireless service is available via entire campus.

Campus Life

There are 690 active organizations on campus, including a drama/theater group, newspaper, radio station, choral group, and marching band. 9% of eligible men and 8% of eligible women are members of national **fraternities** and national **sororities**.

Wisconsin is a member of the NCAA (Division I). **Intercollegiate sports** (some offering scholarships) include basketball, cheerleading, cross-country running, football (m), golf, ice hockey, soccer, softball (w), swimming and diving, tennis, track and field, volleyball (w), wrestling (m).

Campus Safety

Student safety services include free cab rides throughout the city, late-night transport/escort service, 24-hour emergency telephone alarm devices, 24-hour patrols by trained security personnel, and electronically operated dormitory entrances.

Applying

Wisconsin requires an essay, SAT or ACT, and a high school transcript. Application deadline: 2/1. Deferred admission is possible.

Getting Accepted

25,478 applied
53% were accepted
5,774 enrolled (43% of accepted)
58% from top tenth of their h.s. class
3.69 average high school GPA
Mean SAT critical reading score: 607
Mean SAT math score: 670
Mean ACT score: 28
58% had SAT critical reading scores over 600
83% had SAT math scores over 600
66% had SAT writing scores over 600
93% had ACT scores over 24
16% had SAT critical reading scores over 700
40% had SAT math scores over 700
17% had SAT writing scores over 700
35% had ACT scores over 30

Graduation and After

51% graduated in 4 years
29% graduated in 5 years
3% graduated in 6 years

Financial Matters

$7568 resident tuition and fees (2008–09)
$21,818 nonresident tuition and fees (2008–09)
$7700 room and board
84% average percent of need met
$10,005 average financial aid amount received per undergraduate (2006–07)

University of Wisconsin–River Falls

Suburban setting ■ Public ■ State-supported ■ Coed
River Falls, Wisconsin

Getting Accepted
3,183 applied
81% were accepted
1,296 enrolled (50% of accepted)
17% from top tenth of their h.s. class
3.34 average high school GPA
Mean ACT score: 22
28% had ACT scores over 24
1% had ACT scores over 30

Graduation and After
107 organizations recruited on campus

Financial Matters
$6220 resident tuition and fees (2008–09)
$13,793 nonresident tuition and fees (2008–09)
$5106 room and board
77% average percent of need met
$4429 average financial aid amount received per undergraduate

Web site: www.uwrf.edu
Contact: Dr. Alan Tuchtenhagen, Director of Admissions, 410 South Third Street, 112 South Hall, River Falls, WI 54022-5001
Telephone: 715-425-3500
Fax: 715-425-0676
E-mail: alan.j.tuchtenhagen@uwrf.edu

Academics
UW-River Falls awards bachelor's and master's **degrees** and post-master's certificates. **Challenging opportunities** include advanced placement credit, accelerated degree programs, student-designed majors, an honors program, double majors, independent study, and a senior project. Special programs include cooperative education, internships, summer session for credit, off-campus study, and study-abroad. A complete listing of majors at UW-River Falls appears in the Majors by College index beginning on page 469.

The **faculty** at UW-River Falls has 235 full-time members. The student-faculty ratio is 17:1.

Students of UW-River Falls
The student body totals 5,862, of whom 5,275 are undergraduates. 60.4% are women and 39.6% are men. Students come from 40 states and territories and 18 other countries. 58% are from Wisconsin. 76% returned for their sophomore year.

Facilities and Resources
387 **computers/terminals** are available on campus for general student use. Students can access the following: online (class) registration. Campuswide network is available. The **library** has 448,088 books and 1,660 subscriptions.

Campus Life
There are 120 active organizations on campus, including a drama/theater group, newspaper, radio station, television station, and choral group. 5% of eligible men and 3% of eligible women are members of national **fraternities** and national **sororities**.

UW-River Falls is a member of the NCAA (Division III). **Intercollegiate sports** include basketball, cross-country running, football (m), ice hockey, soccer (w), softball (w), swimming and diving, tennis (w), track and field (w), volleyball (w).

Campus Safety
Student safety services include late-night transport/escort service, 24-hour emergency telephone alarm devices, 24-hour patrols by trained security personnel, student patrols, and electronically operated dormitory entrances.

Applying
UW-River Falls requires ACT and a high school transcript. It recommends rank in upper 40% of high school class. Application deadline: rolling admissions; 3/15 priority date for financial aid. Deferred admission is possible.

URSINUS COLLEGE
SUBURBAN SETTING ■ PRIVATE ■ INDEPENDENT ■ COED
COLLEGEVILLE, PENNSYLVANIA

Web site: www.ursinus.edu
Contact: Mr. Robert McCullough, Dean of Admissions, Ursinus College, PO Box 1000, Main Street, Collegeville, PA 19426
Telephone: 610-409-3200
Fax: 610-409-3662
E-mail: admissions@ursinus.edu

Academics
Ursinus awards bachelor's **degrees**. **Challenging opportunities** include advanced placement credit, student-designed majors, an honors program, double majors, independent study, and a senior project. Special programs include internships, off-campus study, and study-abroad.

The most frequently chosen **baccalaureate** fields are social sciences, biological/life sciences, and psychology. A complete listing of majors at Ursinus appears in the Majors by College index beginning on page 469.

The **faculty** at Ursinus has 123 full-time members, 91% with terminal degrees. The student-faculty ratio is 12:1.

Students of Ursinus
The student body is made up of 1,680 undergraduates. 54.6% are women and 45.4% are men. Students come from 28 states and territories and 14 other countries. 58% are from Pennsylvania. 0.7% are international students. 6.4% are African American, 0.2% American Indian, 4% Asian American, and 2.6% Hispanic American. 88% returned for their sophomore year.

Facilities and Resources
1,655 **computers/terminals** and 1,100 ports are available on campus for general student use. Students can access the following: campus intranet, computer help desk, free student e-mail accounts, online (class) grades, online (class) registration, online (class) schedules. Campuswide network is available. 100% of college-owned or -operated housing units are wired for high-speed Internet access. Wireless service is available via entire campus. The 3 **libraries** have 420,000 books and 25,900 subscriptions.

Campus Life
There are 105 active organizations on campus, including a drama/theater group, newspaper, radio station, television station, and choral group. 26% of eligible men and 38% of eligible women are members of national **fraternities**, national **sororities**, local fraternities, and local sororities.

Ursinus is a member of the NCAA (Division III). **Intercollegiate sports** include baseball (m), basketball, cross-country running, field hockey (w), football (m), golf, gymnastics (w), lacrosse, soccer, softball (w), swimming and diving, tennis, track and field, volleyball (w), wrestling (m).

Campus Safety
Student safety services include student EMT Corps for first aid/emergency first response, late-night transport/escort service, 24-hour emergency telephone alarm devices, and 24-hour patrols by trained security personnel.

Applying
Ursinus requires an essay, a high school transcript, 2 recommendations, and graded paper, and in some cases SAT or ACT. It recommends an interview. Application deadline: 2/15; 2/15 for financial aid. Early and deferred admission are possible.

Getting Accepted
6,192 applied
55% were accepted
543 enrolled (16% of accepted)
48% from top tenth of their h.s. class
3.67 average high school GPA
Mean SAT critical reading score: 620
Mean SAT math score: 625
Mean SAT writing score: 610
Mean ACT score: 27
65% had SAT critical reading scores over 600
62% had SAT math scores over 600
58% had SAT writing scores over 600
81% had ACT scores over 24
19% had SAT critical reading scores over 700
12% had SAT math scores over 700
13% had SAT writing scores over 700
20% had ACT scores over 30
6 National Merit Scholars
13 class presidents
6 valedictorians

Graduation and After
72% graduated in 4 years
4% graduated in 5 years
60% had job offers within 6 months
50 organizations recruited on campus

Financial Matters
$36,910 tuition and fees (2008–09)
$8800 room and board
84% average percent of need met
$23,300 average financial aid amount received per undergraduate (2007–08 estimated)

VALPARAISO UNIVERSITY

SMALL-TOWN SETTING ■ PRIVATE ■ INDEPENDENT RELIGIOUS ■ COED
VALPARAISO, INDIANA

Web site: www.valpo.edu
Contact: Office of Admission, Kretzmann Hall, 1700 Chapel Drive,
Valparaiso, IN 46383-6493
Telephone: 219-464-5011 or toll-free 888-GO-VALPO
Fax: 219-464-6898
E-mail: undergrad.admissions@valpo.edu

Valparaiso University is home to 4,000 students seeking academic excellence in the Colleges of Arts and Sciences, Business Administration, Engineering, and Nursing and Christ College—The Honors College. Nestled in a safe, residential community of 31,000, the University offers more than seventy areas of study in the liberal arts as well as a law school and extensive graduate programs. Located 1 hour east of Chicago, "Valpo" is consistently ranked by *U.S. News & World Report* as a top regional university in the Midwest. A low student-faculty ratio encourages mentoring relationships, while the required interdisciplinary freshman curriculum, Valpo Core, fosters a true sense of community. Students who apply before November 1 are considered for Early Action.

Academics

Valparaiso awards associate, bachelor's, master's, doctoral, and first-professional **degrees** and post-bachelor's and post-master's certificates. **Challenging opportunities** include advanced placement credit, accelerated degree programs, student-designed majors, freshman honors college, an honors program, double majors, independent study, and a senior project. Special programs include cooperative education, internships, summer session for credit, off-campus study, study-abroad, and Air Force ROTC.

The most frequently chosen **baccalaureate** fields are business/marketing, social sciences, and engineering. A complete listing of majors at Valparaiso appears in the Majors by College index beginning on page 469.

The **faculty** at Valparaiso has 257 full-time members, 91% with terminal degrees. The student-faculty ratio is 12:1.

Students of Valparaiso

The student body totals 3,976, of whom 2,881 are undergraduates. 52.4% are women and 47.6% are men. Students come from 42 states and territories and 35 other countries. 40% are from Indiana. 2.9% are international students. 5.2% are African American, 0.3% American Indian, 1.7% Asian American, and 3.9% Hispanic American. 85% returned for their sophomore year.

Facilities and Resources

901 **computers/terminals** and 5,100 ports are available on campus for general student use. Students can access the following: campus intranet, computer help desk, free student e-mail accounts, online (class) grades, online (class) registration, online (class) schedules, Web academic information, degree audit. Campuswide network is available. 100% of college-owned or -operated housing units are wired for high-speed Internet access. Wireless service is available via classrooms, computer centers, computer labs, dorm rooms, learning centers, libraries, student centers. The 2 **libraries** have 506,437 books and 50,199 subscriptions.

Campus Life

There are 105 active organizations on campus, including a drama/theater group, newspaper, radio station, and choral group. 25% of eligible men and 20% of eligible women are members of national **fraternities** and local **sororities**.

Valparaiso is a member of the NCAA (Division I). **Intercollegiate sports** (some offering scholarships) include baseball (m), basketball, cross-country running, football (m), soccer, softball (w), swimming and diving, tennis, track and field, volleyball (w).

Campus Safety

Student safety services include late-night transport/escort service, 24-hour emergency telephone alarm devices, 24-hour patrols by trained security personnel, and electronically operated dormitory entrances.

Applying

Valparaiso requires an essay, SAT or ACT, and a high school transcript, and in some cases an interview. It recommends an interview and 2 recommendations. Application deadline: 8/15; 3/1 priority date for financial aid. Deferred admission is possible.

Getting Accepted
3,022 applied
92% were accepted
657 enrolled (24% of accepted)
31% from top tenth of their h.s. class
3.33 average high school GPA
Mean SAT critical reading score: 552
Mean SAT math score: 567
Mean SAT writing score: 536
Mean ACT score: 25
31% had SAT critical reading scores over 600
37% had SAT math scores over 600
22% had SAT writing scores over 600
66% had ACT scores over 24
6% had SAT critical reading scores over 700
9% had SAT math scores over 700
3% had SAT writing scores over 700
17% had ACT scores over 30
7 National Merit Scholars
18 valedictorians

Graduation and After
63% graduated in 4 years
10% graduated in 5 years
1% graduated in 6 years
47% had job offers within 6 months
170 organizations recruited on campus

Financial Matters
$26,950 tuition and fees (2008–09)
$7620 room and board
83% average percent of need met
$19,382 average financial aid amount received per undergraduate (2007–08 estimated)

Vanderbilt University

Urban setting ■ Private ■ Independent ■ Coed
Nashville, Tennessee

Web site: www.vanderbilt.edu
Contact: Mr. Douglas Christiansen, Dean of Undergraduate Admissions, 2305 West End Avenue, Nashville, TN 37203-1700
Telephone: 615-322-2561 or toll-free 800-288-0432
Fax: 615-343-7765
E-mail: admissions@vanderbilt.edu

Academics
Vanderbilt awards bachelor's, master's, doctoral, and first-professional **degrees**. **Challenging opportunities** include advanced placement credit, accelerated degree programs, student-designed majors, an honors program, double majors, independent study, and a senior project. Special programs include cooperative education, internships, summer session for credit, off-campus study, study-abroad, and Army, Navy, and Air Force ROTC.

The most frequently chosen **baccalaureate** fields are social sciences, engineering, and foreign languages and literature. A complete listing of majors at Vanderbilt appears in the Majors by College index beginning on page 469.

The **faculty** at Vanderbilt has 866 full-time members, 97% with terminal degrees. The student-faculty ratio is 9:1.

Students of Vanderbilt
The student body totals 12,093, of whom 6,637 are undergraduates. 52.1% are women and 47.9% are men. Students come from 54 states and territories and 36 other countries. 17% are from Tennessee. 3.3% are international students. 8.7% are African American, 0.5% American Indian, 7% Asian American, and 5.9% Hispanic American. 97% returned for their sophomore year.

Facilities and Resources
400 **computers/terminals** are available on campus for general student use. Students can access the following: productivity and educational software. Campuswide network is available. The 8 **libraries** have 1,812,869 books and 26,885 subscriptions.

Campus Life
There are 264 active organizations on campus, including a drama/theater group, newspaper, radio station, television station, choral group, and marching band. 34% of eligible men and 50% of eligible women are members of national **fraternities** and national **sororities**.

Vanderbilt is a member of the NCAA (Division I). **Intercollegiate sports** (some offering scholarships) include baseball (m), basketball, cross-country running, football (m), golf, lacrosse (w), soccer, tennis, track and field (w).

Campus Safety
Student safety services include late-night transport/escort service, 24-hour emergency telephone alarm devices, 24-hour patrols by trained security personnel, student patrols, and electronically operated dormitory entrances.

Applying
Vanderbilt requires an essay, SAT or ACT, a high school transcript, and 2 recommendations. Application deadline: 3/1; 2/1 priority date for financial aid. Early and deferred admission are possible.

Getting Accepted
16,944 applied
25% were accepted
1,569 enrolled (37% of accepted)
84% from top tenth of their h.s. class
3.72 average high school GPA
91% had SAT critical reading scores over 600
95% had SAT math scores over 600
90% had SAT writing scores over 600
99% had ACT scores over 24
47% had SAT critical reading scores over 700
66% had SAT math scores over 700
47% had SAT writing scores over 700
82% had ACT scores over 30

Graduation and After
84% graduated in 4 years
5% graduated in 5 years
1% graduated in 6 years
63% had job offers within 6 months
250 organizations recruited on campus

Financial Matters
$37,005 tuition and fees (2008–09)
$12,028 room and board
99% average percent of need met
$35,853 average financial aid amount received per undergraduate (2007–08 estimated)

Vassar College

Suburban setting ■ Private ■ Independent ■ Coed
Poughkeepsie, New York

Web site: www.vassar.edu
Contact: Dr. David M. Borus, Dean of Admission and Financial Aid, 124
    Raymond Avenue, Poughkeepsie, NY 12604
Telephone: 845-437-7300 or toll-free 800-827-7270
Fax: 845-437-7063
E-mail: admissions@vassar.edu

Getting Accepted
7,361 applied
25% were accepted
638 enrolled (35% of accepted)
70% from top tenth of their h.s. class
3.75 average high school GPA
Mean SAT critical reading score: 703
Mean SAT math score: 686
Mean SAT writing score: 697
Mean ACT score: 30
95% had SAT critical reading scores over 600
95% had SAT math scores over 600
93% had SAT writing scores over 600
100% had ACT scores over 24
57% had SAT critical reading scores over 700
43% had SAT math scores over 700
54% had SAT writing scores over 700
72% had ACT scores over 30
28 class presidents
30 valedictorians

Graduation and After
87% graduated in 4 years
3% graduated in 5 years
1% graduated in 6 years
51.8% had job offers within 6 months
29 organizations recruited on campus

Financial Matters
$40,210 tuition and fees (2008–09)
$9040 room and board
100% average percent of need met
$31,747 average financial aid amount received
    per undergraduate (2007–08 estimated)

Academics
Vassar awards bachelor's and master's **degrees**. **Challenging opportunities** include advanced placement credit, student-designed majors, double majors, independent study, and a senior project. Special programs include cooperative education, internships, off-campus study, and study-abroad.

The most frequently chosen **baccalaureate** fields are social sciences, visual and performing arts, and foreign languages and literature. A complete listing of majors at Vassar appears in the Majors by College index beginning on page 469.

The **faculty** at Vassar has 299 full-time members, 89% with terminal degrees. The student-faculty ratio is 8:1.

Students of Vassar
The student body is made up of 2,389 undergraduates. 58% are women and 42% are men. Students come from 51 states and territories and 50 other countries. 26% are from New York. 6.4% are international students. 5.1% are African American, 0.2% American Indian, 9.9% Asian American, and 6.7% Hispanic American. 96% returned for their sophomore year.

Facilities and Resources
300 **computers/terminals** are available on campus for general student use. Students can access the following: campus intranet, computer help desk, free student e-mail accounts, online (class) grades, online (class) registration, online (class) schedules, Ethernet. Campuswide network is available. 100% of college-owned or -operated housing units are wired for high-speed Internet access. Wireless service is available via entire campus. The 5 **libraries** have 948,415 books and 10,417 subscriptions.

Campus Life
There are 120 active organizations on campus, including a drama/theater group, newspaper, radio station, television station, and choral group. No national or local **fraternities** or **sororities**.

Vassar is a member of the NCAA (Division III). **Intercollegiate sports** include baseball (m), basketball, crew, cross-country running, fencing, field hockey (w), golf (w), lacrosse, soccer, squash, swimming and diving, tennis, volleyball.

Campus Safety
Student safety services include late-night transport/escort service, 24-hour emergency telephone alarm devices, 24-hour patrols by trained security personnel, student patrols, and electronically operated dormitory entrances.

Applying
Vassar requires an essay, SAT and SAT Subject Tests or ACT, a high school transcript, and 2 recommendations. Application deadline: 1/1; 2/1 for financial aid. Deferred admission is possible.

VILLANOVA UNIVERSITY

SUBURBAN SETTING ■ PRIVATE ■ INDEPENDENT RELIGIOUS ■ COED
VILLANOVA, PENNSYLVANIA

Web site: www.villanova.edu
Contact: Mr. Michael Gaynor, Director of University Admission, 800
   Lancaster Avenue, Villanova, PA 19085-1672
Telephone: 610-519-4000
Fax: 610-519-6450
E-mail: gotovu@villanova.edu

SPONSOR

Villanova, the oldest and largest Catholic university in Pennsylvania, offers over forty rigorous academic programs. Students of all faiths are welcome. Villanova's 254-acre campus houses sixty buildings including twenty-six residence halls, the Davis Center for Athletics, and an 800,000-volume library. Villanova is nationally recognized for excellence in learning technology and environmental sustainability efforts on campus. Study-abroad opportunities are extensive. Villanova tends to attract students interested in volunteerism and hosts the largest student-run Special Olympics in the United States. Programs are offered through the Colleges of Liberal Arts and Sciences, Engineering, Nursing, and the Villanova School of Business. After graduation, the median starting salary for Villanovans is $50,000.

Academics

Villanova awards associate, bachelor's, master's, doctoral, and first-professional **degrees**. **Challenging opportunities** include advanced placement credit, accelerated degree programs, an honors program, double majors, independent study, and a senior project. Special programs include cooperative education, internships, summer session for credit, off-campus study, study-abroad, and Army, Navy, and Air Force ROTC.

The most frequently chosen **baccalaureate** fields are business/marketing, engineering, and social sciences. A complete listing of majors at Villanova appears in the Majors by College index beginning on page 469.

The **faculty** at Villanova has 579 full-time members, 89% with terminal degrees. The student-faculty ratio is 11:1.

Students of Villanova

The student body totals 10,275, of whom 7,161 are undergraduates. 50.5% are women and 49.5% are men. Students come from 48 states and territories and 51 other countries. 25% are from Pennsylvania. 2.9% are international students. 4.5% are African American, 0.1% American Indian, 6.7% Asian American, and 6.3% Hispanic American. 95% returned for their sophomore year.

Facilities and Resources

6,609 **computers/terminals** and 20,000 ports are available on campus for general student use. Students can access the following: campus intranet, computer help desk, free student e-mail accounts, online (class) grades, online (class) registration, online (class) schedules, learning management system, Web-based laundry reservation, electronic portfolios, data vaulting, calendar system, basketball ticket lottery, printing. Campuswide network is available. 100% of college-owned or -operated housing units are wired for high-speed Internet access. Wireless service is available via classrooms, computer centers, computer labs, dorm rooms, learning centers, libraries, student centers. The 3 **libraries** have 720,500 books and 12,000 subscriptions.

Campus Life

There are 250 active organizations on campus, including a drama/theater group, newspaper, radio station, television station, choral group, and marching band. 18% of eligible men and 25% of eligible women are members of national **fraternities** and national **sororities**.

Villanova is a member of the NCAA (Division I). **Intercollegiate sports** (some offering scholarships) include baseball (m), basketball, cheerleading, crew (w), cross-country running, field hockey (w), football (m), golf (m), lacrosse, soccer, softball (w), swimming and diving, tennis, track and field, volleyball (w), water polo (w).

Campus Safety

Student safety services include late-night transport/escort service, 24-hour emergency telephone alarm devices, 24-hour patrols by trained security personnel, student patrols, and electronically operated dormitory entrances.

Applying

Villanova requires an essay, SAT or ACT, a high school transcript, 1 recommendation, and activities resume. Application deadline: 1/7, 1/7 for nonresidents; 2/7 priority date for financial aid. Deferred admission is possible.

Getting Accepted
15,102 applied
39% were accepted
1,604 enrolled (27% of accepted)
60% from top tenth of their h.s. class
3.86 average high school GPA
Mean SAT critical reading score: 629
Mean SAT math score: 659
Mean SAT writing score: 634
Mean ACT score: 29
71% had SAT critical reading scores over 600
82% had SAT math scores over 600
72% had SAT writing scores over 600
95% had ACT scores over 24
16% had SAT critical reading scores over 700
32% had SAT math scores over 700
21% had SAT writing scores over 700
56% had ACT scores over 30
21 valedictorians

Graduation and After
84% graduated in 4 years
4% graduated in 5 years
1% graduated in 6 years
72% had job offers within 6 months
265 organizations recruited on campus

Financial Matters
$37,655 tuition and fees (2009–10)
$10,070 room and board
79% average percent of need met
$23,433 average financial aid amount received
   per undergraduate (2007–08 estimated)

SPONSOR

Virginia Military Institute (VMI) offers a challenging curricular and cocurricular undergraduate experience, with the mission of producing educated and honorable men and women who will be leaders in all walks of life. Its 1,370 cadets pursue B.A. or B.S. degrees in fourteen disciplines in the general fields of engineering, science, and liberal arts. VMI combines a full college curriculum within a framework of military discipline that emphasizes the qualities of honor, integrity, and responsibility. Undergirding all aspects of cadet life is the VMI Honor Code, to which all cadets subscribe.

Getting Accepted
1,704 applied
54% were accepted
410 enrolled (44% of accepted)
14% from top tenth of their h.s. class
3.37 average high school GPA
31% had SAT critical reading scores over 600
31% had SAT math scores over 600
20% had SAT writing scores over 600
43% had ACT scores over 24
3% had SAT critical reading scores over 700
3% had SAT math scores over 700
1% had SAT writing scores over 700
4% had ACT scores over 30

Graduation and After
98% had job offers within 6 months
40 organizations recruited on campus

Financial Matters
$8401 resident tuition and fees (2008–09)
$25,299 nonresident tuition and fees (2008–09)
$6444 room and board
90% average percent of need met
$15,527 average financial aid amount received per undergraduate (2006–07)

VIRGINIA MILITARY INSTITUTE
SMALL-TOWN SETTING ■ PUBLIC ■ STATE-SUPPORTED ■ COED, PRIMARILY MEN
LEXINGTON, VIRGINIA

Web site: www.vmi.edu
Contact: Lt. Col. Tom Mortenson, Associate Director of Admissions, Admissions Office, Lexington, VA 24450
Telephone: 540-464-7211 or toll-free 800-767-4207
Fax: 540-464-7746
E-mail: admissions@vmi.edu

Academics
VMI awards bachelor's **degrees. Challenging opportunities** include advanced placement credit, accelerated degree programs, an honors program, double majors, independent study, and a senior project. Special programs include internships, summer session for credit, study-abroad, and Army, Navy, and Air Force ROTC. A complete listing of majors at VMI appears in the Majors by College index beginning on page 469.

The **faculty** at VMI has 117 full-time members, 98% with terminal degrees. The student-faculty ratio is 10:1.

Students of VMI
The student body is made up of 1,378 undergraduates. 8.1% are women and 91.9% are men. Students come from 45 states and territories and 9 other countries. 58% are from Virginia. 1.6% are international students. 5.5% are African American, 0.4% American Indian, 3.9% Asian American, and 3.4% Hispanic American.

Facilities and Resources
200 **computers/terminals** are available on campus for general student use. Campuswide network is available. The 2 **libraries** have 162,053 books and 785 subscriptions.

Campus Life
There are 47 active organizations on campus, including a drama/theater group, newspaper, choral group, and marching band. No national or local **fraternities** or **sororities**.

VMI is a member of the NCAA (Division I). **Intercollegiate sports** (some offering scholarships) include baseball (m), basketball (m), cross-country running, football (m), golf (m), lacrosse (m), riflery, soccer (m), swimming and diving, tennis (m), track and field, wrestling (m).

Campus Safety
Student safety services include 24-hour emergency telephone alarm devices, 24-hour patrols by trained security personnel, and student patrols.

Applying
VMI requires SAT or ACT and a high school transcript. It recommends an essay, an interview, and 2 recommendations. Application deadline: 3/1; 3/1 priority date for financial aid. Early admission is possible.

Virginia Polytechnic Institute and State University

SMALL-TOWN SETTING ■ PUBLIC ■ STATE-SUPPORTED ■ COED
BLACKSBURG, VIRGINIA

Web site: www.vt.edu
Contact: 201 Burruss Hall, Blacksburg, VA 24061
Telephone: 540-231-6267
Fax: 540-231-3242
E-mail: vtadmiss@vt.edu

Academics

Virginia Tech awards associate, bachelor's, master's, doctoral, and first-professional **degrees**. **Challenging opportunities** include advanced placement credit, accelerated degree programs, an honors program, double majors, independent study, and a senior project. Special programs include cooperative education, internships, summer session for credit, study-abroad, and Army, Navy, and Air Force ROTC.

The most frequently chosen **baccalaureate** fields are engineering, business/marketing, and family and consumer sciences. A complete listing of majors at Virginia Tech appears in the Majors by College index beginning on page 469.

The **faculty** at Virginia Tech has 1,369 full-time members, 88% with terminal degrees. The student-faculty ratio is 16:1.

Students of Virginia Tech

The student body totals 30,739, of whom 23,567 are undergraduates. 42.7% are women and 57.3% are men. 1.7% are international students. 3.9% are African American, 0.3% American Indian, 7.6% Asian American, and 2.8% Hispanic American. 91% returned for their sophomore year.

Facilities and Resources

8,000 **computers/terminals** are available on campus for general student use. Students can access the following: campus intranet, computer help desk, free student e-mail accounts, online (class) grades, online (class) registration, online (class) schedules. Campuswide network is available. Wireless service is available via entire campus. The 5 **libraries** have 2,268,619 books and 33,874 subscriptions.

Campus Life

There are 600 active organizations on campus, including a drama/theater group, newspaper, radio station, television station, choral group, and marching band. 13% of eligible men and 20% of eligible women are members of national **fraternities**, national **sororities**, and local fraternities.

Virginia Tech is a member of the NCAA (Division I). **Intercollegiate sports** (some offering scholarships) include baseball (m), basketball (m), cross-country running, football (m), golf (m), lacrosse (w), soccer, swimming and diving, tennis, track and field, ultimate Frisbee, volleyball (w).

Campus Safety

Student safety services include late-night transport/escort service, 24-hour emergency telephone alarm devices, 24-hour patrols by trained security personnel, student patrols, and electronically operated dormitory entrances.

Applying

Virginia Tech requires SAT or ACT and a high school transcript, and in some cases SAT and SAT Subject Tests or ACT. It recommends a minimum high school GPA of 3.0. Application deadline: 1/15; 3/11 priority date for financial aid. Early and deferred admission are possible.

Getting Accepted

20,615 applied
65% were accepted
5,460 enrolled (40% of accepted)
42% from top tenth of their h.s. class
3.86 average high school GPA
Mean SAT critical reading score: 596
Mean SAT math score: 628
45% had SAT critical reading scores over 600
62% had SAT math scores over 600
43% had SAT writing scores over 600
7% had SAT critical reading scores over 700
14% had SAT math scores over 700
6% had SAT writing scores over 700
98 valedictorians

Graduation and After

52% graduated in 4 years
23% graduated in 5 years
3% graduated in 6 years
58% had job offers within 6 months
400 organizations recruited on campus

Financial Matters

$8198 resident tuition and fees (2008–09)
$20,655 nonresident tuition and fees (2008–09)
$5476 room and board
69% average percent of need met
$10,013 average financial aid amount received per undergraduate (2006–07)

WABASH COLLEGE

SMALL-TOWN SETTING ■ PRIVATE ■ INDEPENDENT ■ MEN ONLY
CRAWFORDSVILLE, INDIANA

Web site: www.wabash.edu
Contact: Mr. Steve Klein, Dean of Admissions, PO Box 362, Crawfordsville, IN 47933-0352
Telephone: 765-361-6225 or toll-free 800-345-5385
Fax: 765-361-6437
E-mail: admissions@wabash.edu

As a college for men, Wabash helps students achieve their full potential—intellectually, athletically, emotionally, and artistically. Wabash prepares students for leadership in an ever-changing world. The College helps them learn to think clearly and openly and to explore a variety of interests. Independence and responsibility are emphasized and defined by the Gentlemen's Rule, which calls on students to conduct themselves as gentlemen at all times. With the guidance of professors who are accessible, a support staff that cares, and a nationwide network of alumni willing to offer assistance and encouragement, Wabash men frequently surpass even their own expectations.

Getting Accepted

1,365 applied
49% were accepted
253 enrolled (38% of accepted)
31% from top tenth of their h.s. class
3.6 average high school GPA
Mean SAT critical reading score: 562
Mean SAT math score: 598
Mean SAT writing score: 547
Mean ACT score: 25
37% had SAT critical reading scores over 600
47% had SAT math scores over 600
27% had SAT writing scores over 600
64% had ACT scores over 24
7% had SAT critical reading scores over 700
13% had SAT math scores over 700
6% had SAT writing scores over 700
15% had ACT scores over 30
5 valedictorians

Graduation and After

67% graduated in 4 years
3% graduated in 5 years
60% had job offers within 6 months
90 organizations recruited on campus

Financial Matters

$27,950 tuition and fees (2008–09)
$7400 room and board
100% average percent of need met
$24,261 average financial aid amount received per undergraduate (2007–08 estimated)

Academics

Wabash awards bachelor's **degrees**. **Challenging opportunities** include advanced placement credit, double majors, independent study, and a senior project. Special programs include internships, off-campus study, and study-abroad.

The most frequently chosen **baccalaureate** fields are social sciences, psychology, and history. A complete listing of majors at Wabash appears in the Majors by College index beginning on page 469.

The **faculty** at Wabash has 89 full-time members, 97% with terminal degrees. The student-faculty ratio is 10:1.

Students of Wabash

The student body is made up of 917 undergraduates. Students come from 35 states and territories and 14 other countries. 76% are from Indiana. 5.3% are international students. 5.9% are African American, 0.7% American Indian, 1.4% Asian American, and 4.8% Hispanic American. 86% returned for their sophomore year.

Facilities and Resources

350 **computers/terminals** are available on campus for general student use. Students can access the following: campus intranet, computer help desk, free student e-mail accounts, online (class) grades, online (class) schedules, online course management, degree audit, expenses. Campuswide network is available. 100% of college-owned or -operated housing units are wired for high-speed Internet access. Wireless service is available via entire campus. The **library** has 296,556 books and 24,569 subscriptions.

Campus Life

There are 64 active organizations on campus, including a drama/theater group, newspaper, radio station, and choral group. 60% of eligible undergraduates are members of national **fraternities**.

Wabash is a member of the NCAA (Division III). **Intercollegiate sports** include baseball, basketball, cross-country running, football, golf, soccer, swimming and diving, tennis, track and field, wrestling.

Campus Safety

Student safety services include late-night transport/escort service, 24-hour emergency telephone alarm devices, and 24-hour patrols by trained security personnel.

Applying

Wabash requires SAT or ACT and a high school transcript. It recommends an essay, an interview, and 1 recommendation. Application deadline: rolling admissions; 3/1 for financial aid, with a 2/15 priority date. Early and deferred admission are possible.

WAGNER COLLEGE

URBAN SETTING ■ PRIVATE ■ INDEPENDENT ■ COED
STATEN ISLAND, NEW YORK

Web site: www.wagner.edu
Contact: One Campus Road, Staten Island, NY 10301
Telephone: 718-420-4242 or toll-free 800-221-1010 (out-of-state)
Fax: 718-390-3105
E-mail: leigh-ann.nowicki@wagner.edu

Academics

Wagner awards bachelor's and master's **degrees** and post-bachelor's certificates. **Challenging opportunities** include an honors program, double majors, and a senior project. Special programs include internships, summer session for credit, off-campus study, study-abroad, and Army ROTC.

The most frequently chosen **baccalaureate** fields are visual and performing arts, business/marketing, and health professions and related sciences. A complete listing of majors at Wagner appears in the Majors by College index beginning on page 469.

The **faculty** at Wagner has 101 full-time members, 92% with terminal degrees. The student-faculty ratio is 14:1.

Students of Wagner

The student body totals 2,294, of whom 1,924 are undergraduates. 62.3% are women and 37.7% are men. Students come from 42 states and territories and 13 other countries. 48% are from New York. 0.9% are international students. 4.7% are African American, 0.3% American Indian, 2% Asian American, and 6.2% Hispanic American. 77% returned for their sophomore year.

Facilities and Resources

225 **computers/terminals** are available on campus for general student use. Students can access the following: campus intranet, computer help desk, free student e-mail accounts, online (class) grades, online (class) registration, online (class) schedules. Campuswide network is available. 100% of college-owned or -operated housing units are wired for high-speed Internet access. Wireless service is available via entire campus. The **library** has 170,527 books and 19,400 subscriptions.

Campus Life

There are 66 active organizations on campus, including a drama/theater group, newspaper, radio station, and choral group. 13% of eligible men and 15% of eligible women are members of national **fraternities**, national **sororities**, local fraternities, and local sororities.

Wagner is a member of the NCAA (Division I). **Intercollegiate sports** (some offering scholarships) include baseball (m), basketball, cross-country running, football (m), golf, lacrosse, soccer (w), softball (w), swimming and diving (w), tennis, track and field, water polo (w).

Campus Safety

Student safety services include late-night transport/escort service, 24-hour emergency telephone alarm devices, 24-hour patrols by trained security personnel, and electronically operated dormitory entrances.

Applying

Wagner requires an essay, SAT or ACT, a high school transcript, 2 recommendations, and a minimum high school GPA of 2.5, and in some cases an interview. It recommends an interview and a minimum high school GPA of 3.0. Application deadline: 2/15; 2/15 priority date for financial aid. Deferred admission is possible.

Getting Accepted

3,012 applied
61% were accepted
481 enrolled (26% of accepted)
17% from top tenth of their h.s. class
3.56 average high school GPA
Mean SAT critical reading score: 564
Mean SAT math score: 568
Mean SAT writing score: 569
Mean ACT score: 25
49% had SAT critical reading scores over 600
51% had SAT math scores over 600
46% had SAT writing scores over 600
88% had ACT scores over 24
7% had SAT critical reading scores over 700
7% had SAT math scores over 700
5% had SAT writing scores over 700
8% had ACT scores over 30

Graduation and After

62% graduated in 4 years
3% graduated in 5 years
2% graduated in 6 years
45% had job offers within 6 months
28 organizations recruited on campus

Financial Matters

$31,050 tuition and fees (2008–09)
$9250 room and board
72% average percent of need met
$18,072 average financial aid amount received per undergraduate (2007–08 estimated)

WAKE FOREST UNIVERSITY

SUBURBAN SETTING ■ PRIVATE ■ INDEPENDENT ■ COED
WINSTON-SALEM, NORTH CAROLINA

Web site: www.wfu.edu
Contact: Ms. Martha Allman, Director of Admissions, PO Box 7305,
   Winston-Salem, NC 27109
Telephone: 336-758-5201
Fax: 336-758-5201
E-mail: admissions@wfu.edu

Getting Accepted

9,050 applied
38% were accepted
1,201 enrolled (35% of accepted)
64% from top tenth of their h.s. class
82% had SAT critical reading scores over 600
87% had SAT math scores over 600
91% had ACT scores over 24
25% had SAT critical reading scores over 700
33% had SAT math scores over 700
42% had ACT scores over 30

Graduation and After

83% graduated in 4 years
5% graduated in 5 years
58% had job offers within 6 months
195 organizations recruited on campus

Financial Matters

$38,622 tuition and fees (2009–10)
$10,410 room and board
97% average percent of need met
$27,709 average financial aid amount received
   per undergraduate (2007–08 estimated)

Academics

Wake Forest awards bachelor's, master's, doctoral, and first-professional **degrees**. **Challenging opportunities** include advanced placement credit, an honors program, double majors, independent study, and a senior project. Special programs include internships, summer session for credit, off-campus study, study-abroad, and Army ROTC.

The most frequently chosen **baccalaureate** fields are social sciences, business/marketing, and psychology. A complete listing of majors at Wake Forest appears in the Majors by College index beginning on page 469.

The **faculty** at Wake Forest has 471 full-time members, 91% with terminal degrees. The student-faculty ratio is 10:1.

Students of Wake Forest

The student body totals 6,862, of whom 4,476 are undergraduates. 50.8% are women and 49.2% are men. Students come from 50 states and territories and 25 other countries. 25% are from North Carolina. 1.4% are international students. 7.1% are African American, 0.5% American Indian, 5.2% Asian American, and 3.1% Hispanic American. 93% returned for their sophomore year.

Facilities and Resources

150 **computers/terminals** and 3,128 ports are available on campus for general student use. Students can access the following: campus intranet, computer help desk, free student e-mail accounts, online (class) grades, online (class) registration, online (class) schedules, financial information online, drop-add, transcript requests. Campuswide network is available. 100% of college-owned or -operated housing units are wired for high-speed Internet access. Wireless service is available via entire campus. The 4 **libraries** have 923,123 books and 16,448 subscriptions.

Campus Life

There are 135 active organizations on campus, including a drama/theater group, newspaper, radio station, television station, choral group, and marching band. 33% of eligible men and 46% of eligible women are members of national **fraternities** and national **sororities**.

Wake Forest is a member of the NCAA (Division I). **Intercollegiate sports** (some offering scholarships) include baseball (m), basketball, cross-country running, field hockey (w), football (m), golf, soccer, tennis, track and field, volleyball (w).

Campus Safety

Student safety services include late-night transport/escort service, 24-hour emergency telephone alarm devices, 24-hour patrols by trained security personnel, and electronically operated dormitory entrances.

Applying

Wake Forest requires an essay, a high school transcript, and 1 recommendation. It recommends an interview. Application deadline: 1/15; 3/1 for financial aid, with a 2/1 priority date. Early and deferred admission are possible.

WARTBURG COLLEGE
SMALL-TOWN SETTING ■ PRIVATE ■ INDEPENDENT RELIGIOUS ■ COED
WAVERLY, IOWA

Web site: www.wartburg.edu
Contact: Mr. Todd Coleman, Assistant Vice President for Admissions, 100
    Wartburg Boulevard, PO Box 1003, Waverly, IA 50677-0903
Telephone: 319-352-8264 or toll-free 800-772-2085
Fax: 319-352-8579
E-mail: admissions@wartburg.edu

Academics
Wartburg awards bachelor's **degrees**. **Challenging opportunities** include advanced placement credit, accelerated degree programs, student-designed majors, an honors program, double majors, independent study, and a senior project. Special programs include internships, summer session for credit, off-campus study, and study-abroad.

The most frequently chosen **baccalaureate** fields are business/marketing, biological/life sciences, and communications/journalism. A complete listing of majors at Wartburg appears in the Majors by College index beginning on page 469.

The **faculty** at Wartburg has 110 full-time members, 87% with terminal degrees. The student-faculty ratio is 12:1.

Students of Wartburg
The student body is made up of 1,799 undergraduates. 52.9% are women and 47.1% are men. Students come from 27 states and territories and 40 other countries. 74% are from Iowa. 5.2% are international students. 3.8% are African American, 0.3% American Indian, 1.7% Asian American, and 1.4% Hispanic American. 76% returned for their sophomore year.

Facilities and Resources
250 **computers/terminals** are available on campus for general student use. Students can access the following: campus intranet, computer help desk, free student e-mail accounts, online (class) registration, online (class) schedules. Campuswide network is available. 100% of college-owned or -operated housing units are wired for high-speed Internet access. Wireless service is available via classrooms, libraries, student centers. The **library** has 198,978 books and 32,009 subscriptions.

Campus Life
There are 96 active organizations on campus, including a drama/theater group, newspaper, radio station, television station, and choral group. No national or local **fraternities** or **sororities**.

Wartburg is a member of the NCAA (Division III). **Intercollegiate sports** include baseball (m), basketball, cheerleading (w), cross-country running, football (m), golf, soccer, softball (w), tennis, track and field, volleyball (w), wrestling (m).

Campus Safety
Student safety services include late-night transport/escort service, 24-hour emergency telephone alarm devices, 24-hour patrols by trained security personnel, and electronically operated dormitory entrances.

Applying
Wartburg requires SAT or ACT, a high school transcript, and a minimum high school GPA of 2.0, and in some cases an interview. It recommends secondary school report. Application deadline: rolling admissions; 3/1 priority date for financial aid. Deferred admission is possible.

Getting Accepted
2,209 applied
74% were accepted
514 enrolled (31% of accepted)
30% from top tenth of their h.s. class
3.51 average high school GPA
Mean SAT critical reading score: 522
Mean SAT math score: 604
Mean SAT writing score: 545
Mean ACT score: 24
34% had SAT critical reading scores over 600
59% had SAT math scores over 600
35% had SAT writing scores over 600
55% had ACT scores over 24
9% had SAT critical reading scores over 700
15% had SAT math scores over 700
13% had SAT writing scores over 700
9% had ACT scores over 30

Graduation and After
58% graduated in 4 years
5% graduated in 5 years
98% had job offers within 6 months

Financial Matters
$26,160 tuition and fees (2008–09)
$7255 room and board
89% average percent of need met
$18,719 average financial aid amount received
    per undergraduate (2006–07)

WASHINGTON & JEFFERSON COLLEGE

SMALL-TOWN SETTING ▪ PRIVATE ▪ INDEPENDENT ▪ COED
WASHINGTON, PENNSYLVANIA

Web site: www.washjeff.edu
Contact: Mr. Alton E. Newell, Vice President for Enrollment Management,
    60 South Lincoln Street, Washington, PA 15301
Telephone: 724-223-6025 or toll-free 888-WANDJAY
Fax: 724-223-6534
E-mail: admission@washjeff.edu

Getting Accepted
6,826 applied
38% were accepted
399 enrolled (15% of accepted)
39% from top tenth of their h.s. class
3.39 average high school GPA
Mean SAT critical reading score: 560
Mean SAT math score: 580
Mean ACT score: 24
43% had SAT critical reading scores over 600
31% had SAT math scores over 600
53% had ACT scores over 24
5% had SAT critical reading scores over 700
3% had SAT math scores over 700
4% had ACT scores over 30
17 valedictorians

Graduation and After
67% graduated in 4 years
5% graduated in 5 years
1% graduated in 6 years
71% had job offers within 6 months
37 organizations recruited on campus

Financial Matters
$31,496 tuition and fees (2008–09)
$8488 room and board
81% average percent of need met
$21,882 average financial aid amount received
    per undergraduate (2007–08 estimated)

Academics

W & J awards bachelor's **degrees**. **Challenging opportunities** include advanced placement credit, accelerated degree programs, student-designed majors, an honors program, double majors, independent study, and a senior project. Special programs include internships, summer session for credit, off-campus study, study-abroad, and Army and Air Force ROTC.

The most frequently chosen **baccalaureate** fields are business/marketing, psychology, and English. A complete listing of majors at W & J appears in the Majors by College index beginning on page 469.

The **faculty** at W & J has 112 full-time members, 92% with terminal degrees. The student-faculty ratio is 12:1.

Students of W & J

The student body is made up of 1,519 undergraduates. 45.8% are women and 54.2% are men. Students come from 31 states and territories and 11 other countries. 75% are from Pennsylvania. 1.6% are international students. 2.7% are African American, 0.3% American Indian, 1.3% Asian American, and 1.3% Hispanic American. 87% returned for their sophomore year.

Facilities and Resources

450 **computers/terminals** and 2,000 ports are available on campus for general student use. Students can access the following: campus intranet, computer help desk, free student e-mail accounts, online (class) grades, online (class) registration, online (class) schedules. Campuswide network is available. 100% of college-owned or -operated housing units are wired for high-speed Internet access. Wireless service is available via entire campus. The **library** has 200,265 books and 23,631 subscriptions.

Campus Life

There are 70 active organizations on campus, including a drama/theater group, newspaper, radio station, and choral group. 40% of eligible men and 44% of eligible women are members of national **fraternities** and national **sororities**.

W & J is a member of the NCAA (Division III). **Intercollegiate sports** include baseball (m), basketball, cheerleading, cross-country running, field hockey (w), football (m), golf, lacrosse, soccer, softball (w), swimming and diving, tennis, track and field, volleyball (w), water polo, wrestling (m).

Campus Safety

Student safety services include late-night transport/escort service, 24-hour emergency telephone alarm devices, 24-hour patrols by trained security personnel, and electronically operated dormitory entrances.

Applying

W & J requires an essay, SAT or ACT, a high school transcript, and 1 recommendation, and in some cases an interview. It recommends an interview. Application deadline: 3/1; 3/1 priority date for financial aid. Early and deferred admission are possible.

WASHINGTON AND LEE UNIVERSITY

SMALL-TOWN SETTING ■ PRIVATE ■ INDEPENDENT ■ COED
LEXINGTON, VIRGINIA

Web site: www.wlu.edu
Contact: Mr. William M. Hartog, Dean of Admissions and Financial Aid, 204 West Washington Street, Lexington, VA 24450-2116
Telephone: 540-458-8710
Fax: 540-458-8062
E-mail: admissions@wlu.edu

Academics

W & L awards bachelor's, master's, and first-professional **degrees. Challenging opportunities** include advanced placement credit, student-designed majors, an honors program, double majors, independent study, and a senior project. Special programs include internships, off-campus study, study-abroad, and Army ROTC.

The most frequently chosen **baccalaureate** fields are business/marketing, social sciences, and biological/life sciences. A complete listing of majors at W & L appears in the Majors by College index beginning on page 469.

The **faculty** at W & L has 230 full-time members, 96% with terminal degrees. The student-faculty ratio is 8:1.

Students of W & L

The student body totals 2,155, of whom 1,752 are undergraduates. 49.7% are women and 50.3% are men. Students come from 47 states and territories and 33 other countries. 15% are from Virginia. 4.3% are international students. 3.8% are African American, 0.3% American Indian, 3.3% Asian American, and 1.7% Hispanic American. 94% returned for their sophomore year.

Facilities and Resources

297 **computers/terminals** are available on campus for general student use. Students can access the following: online (class) registration. Campuswide network is available. 100% of college-owned or -operated housing units are wired for high-speed Internet access. Wireless service is available via entire campus. The 3 **libraries** have 956,354 books and 10,362 subscriptions.

Campus Life

There are 127 active organizations on campus, including a drama/theater group, newspaper, radio station, television station, and choral group. 79% of eligible men and 77% of eligible women are members of national **fraternities** and national **sororities**.

W & L is a member of the NCAA (Division III). **Intercollegiate sports** include baseball (m), basketball, cross-country running, equestrian sports (w), field hockey (w), football (m), golf (m), lacrosse, soccer, swimming and diving, tennis, track and field, volleyball (w), wrestling (m).

Campus Safety

Student safety services include late-night transport/escort service, 24-hour emergency telephone alarm devices, 24-hour patrols by trained security personnel, and electronically operated dormitory entrances.

Applying

W & L requires SAT or ACT, 2 unrelated SAT Subject Tests, a high school transcript, and 3 recommendations. It recommends an essay and an interview. Application deadline: 1/15; 3/3 for financial aid. Deferred admission is possible.

Getting Accepted

6,386 applied
17% were accepted
454 enrolled (42% of accepted)
84% from top tenth of their h.s. class
Mean SAT critical reading score: 697
Mean SAT math score: 700
Mean SAT writing score: 693
Mean ACT score: 31
97% had SAT critical reading scores over 600
97% had SAT math scores over 600
100% had ACT scores over 24
49% had SAT critical reading scores over 700
53% had SAT math scores over 700
58% had ACT scores over 30
23 National Merit Scholars
37 class presidents
34 valedictorians

Graduation and After

89% graduated in 4 years
51 organizations recruited on campus

Financial Matters

$37,412 tuition and fees (2008–09)
$8428 room and board
99% average percent of need met
$30,933 average financial aid amount received per undergraduate (2007–08 estimated)

Getting Accepted
3,413 applied
69% were accepted
415 enrolled (18% of accepted)
29% from top tenth of their h.s. class
3.39 average high school GPA
Mean SAT critical reading score: 575
Mean SAT math score: 558
Mean ACT score: 24
36% had SAT critical reading scores over 600
31% had SAT math scores over 600
37% had SAT writing scores over 600
65% had ACT scores over 24
7% had SAT critical reading scores over 700
1% had SAT math scores over 700
4% had SAT writing scores over 700
5% had ACT scores over 30

Graduation and After
75% graduated in 4 years
4% graduated in 5 years
1% graduated in 6 years
80% had job offers within 6 months
65 organizations recruited on campus

Financial Matters
$34,005 tuition and fees (2008–09)
$7180 room and board
89% average percent of need met
$21,316 average financial aid amount received per undergraduate (2007–08 estimated)

WASHINGTON COLLEGE
SMALL-TOWN SETTING ■ PRIVATE ■ INDEPENDENT ■ COED
CHESTERTOWN, MARYLAND

Web site: www.washcoll.edu
Contact: Mr. Kevin Coveney, Vice President for Admissions and Enrollment Management, 300 Washington Avenue, Chesterton, MD 21620
Telephone: 410-778-7700 or toll-free 800-422-1782
Fax: 410-778-7287
E-mail: admissions_office@washcoll.edu

Academics
WC awards bachelor's and master's **degrees**. **Challenging opportunities** include advanced placement credit, student-designed majors, double majors, independent study, and a senior project. Special programs include internships, off-campus study, and study-abroad.

The most frequently chosen **baccalaureate** fields are social sciences, business/marketing, and psychology. A complete listing of majors at WC appears in the Majors by College index beginning on page 469.

The **faculty** at WC has 97 full-time members, 91% with terminal degrees. The student-faculty ratio is 11:1.

Students of WC
The student body totals 1,402, of whom 1,334 are undergraduates. 59.7% are women and 40.3% are men. Students come from 32 states and territories and 28 other countries. 51% are from Maryland. 4% are international students. 4.6% are African American, 0.4% American Indian, 1.2% Asian American, and 0.7% Hispanic American. 82% returned for their sophomore year.

Facilities and Resources
150 **computers/terminals** and 225 ports are available on campus for general student use. Students can access the following: campus intranet, computer help desk, free student e-mail accounts, online (class) grades, online (class) registration, online (class) schedules. Campuswide network is available. 100% of college-owned or -operated housing units are wired for high-speed Internet access. Wireless service is available via entire campus. The **library** has 218,350 books and 44,548 subscriptions.

Campus Life
There are 50 active organizations on campus, including a drama/theater group, newspaper, and choral group. 18% of eligible men and 20% of eligible women are members of national **fraternities** and national **sororities**.

WC is a member of the NCAA (Division III). **Intercollegiate sports** include baseball (m), basketball, crew, field hockey (w), lacrosse, sailing, soccer, softball (w), swimming and diving, tennis, volleyball (w).

Campus Safety
Student safety services include late-night transport/escort service, 24-hour emergency telephone alarm devices, 24-hour patrols by trained security personnel, student patrols, and electronically operated dormitory entrances.

Applying
WC requires an essay, SAT or ACT, a high school transcript, and 1 recommendation, and in some cases an interview. It recommends an interview. Application deadline: 3/1; 2/15 priority date for financial aid. Early and deferred admission are possible.

WASHINGTON UNIVERSITY IN ST. LOUIS
SUBURBAN SETTING ■ PRIVATE ■ INDEPENDENT ■ COED
ST. LOUIS, MISSOURI

Web site: www.wustl.edu
Contact: Ms. Julie Shimabukuro, Director of Admissions, Campus Box 1089, One Brookings Drive, St. Louis, MO 63130-4899
Telephone: 314-935-6000 or toll-free 800-638-0700
Fax: 314-935-4290
E-mail: admissions@wustl.edu

Academics
WUSTL awards bachelor's, master's, doctoral, and first-professional **degrees** and post-bachelor's and post-master's certificates. **Challenging opportunities** include advanced placement credit, accelerated degree programs, student-designed majors, double majors, and independent study. Special programs include cooperative education, internships, summer session for credit, off-campus study, study-abroad, and Army and Air Force ROTC.

The most frequently chosen **baccalaureate** fields are engineering, social sciences, and business/marketing. A complete listing of majors at WUSTL appears in the Majors by College index beginning on page 469.

The **faculty** at WUSTL has 907 full-time members, 98% with terminal degrees. The student-faculty ratio is 7:1.

Students of WUSTL
The student body totals 13,339, of whom 6,985 are undergraduates. 51.9% are women and 48.1% are men. Students come from 54 states and territories and 54 other countries. 10% are from Missouri. 4.5% are international students. 9.6% are African American, 0.1% American Indian, 12.9% Asian American, and 2.7% Hispanic American. 96% returned for their sophomore year.

Facilities and Resources
2,500 **computers/terminals** are available on campus for general student use. Students can access the following: campus intranet, computer help desk, free student e-mail accounts, online (class) grades, online (class) registration, online (class) schedules. Campuswide network is available. 90% of college-owned or -operated housing units are wired for high-speed Internet access. Wireless service is available via classrooms, computer centers, computer labs, dorm rooms, learning centers, libraries, student centers. The 14 **libraries** have 2,454,542 books and 67,057 subscriptions.

Campus Life
There are 200 active organizations on campus, including a drama/theater group, newspaper, radio station, television station, and choral group. 25% of eligible men and 25% of eligible women are members of national **fraternities** and national **sororities**.

WUSTL is a member of the NCAA (Division III). **Intercollegiate sports** include baseball (m), basketball, cross-country running, football (m), golf (w), soccer, softball (w), swimming and diving, tennis, track and field, volleyball (w).

Campus Safety
Student safety services include late-night transport/escort service, 24-hour emergency telephone alarm devices, 24-hour patrols by trained security personnel, student patrols, and electronically operated dormitory entrances.

Applying
WUSTL requires an essay, SAT or ACT, a high school transcript, and 2 recommendations. It recommends portfolio for art and architecture programs and a minimum high school GPA of 3.0. Application deadline: 1/15; 2/15 for financial aid. Early and deferred admission are possible.

Getting Accepted
22,005 applied
22% were accepted
1,426 enrolled (30% of accepted)
96% from top tenth of their h.s. class
98% had SAT critical reading scores over 600
99% had SAT math scores over 600
100% had ACT scores over 24
64% had SAT critical reading scores over 700
77% had SAT math scores over 700
92% had ACT scores over 30

Graduation and After
450 organizations recruited on campus

Financial Matters
$38,864 tuition and fees (2009–10)
$12,465 room and board
100% average percent of need met
$28,725 average financial aid amount received per undergraduate (2007–08 estimated)

WEBB INSTITUTE
SUBURBAN SETTING ■ PRIVATE ■ INDEPENDENT ■ COED
GLEN COVE, NEW YORK

Web site: www.webb-institute.edu
Contact: Crescent Beach Road, Glen Cove, NY 11542-1398
Telephone: 516-671-2213
Fax: 516-674-9838
E-mail: admissions@webb-institute.edu

Getting Accepted
95 applied
31% were accepted
23 enrolled (79% of accepted)
83% from top tenth of their h.s. class
3.9 average high school GPA
Mean SAT critical reading score: 670
Mean SAT math score: 710
Mean SAT writing score: 650
74% had SAT critical reading scores over 600
100% had SAT math scores over 600
82% had SAT writing scores over 600
35% had SAT critical reading scores over 700
52% had SAT math scores over 700
30% had SAT writing scores over 700
1 valedictorian

Graduation and After
57% graduated in 4 years
5% graduated in 5 years
100% had job offers within 6 months
12 organizations recruited on campus

Financial Matters
$0 tuition and fees (2008–09)
$9500 room and board
85% average percent of need met
$2797 average financial aid amount received
per undergraduate (2005–06)

Academics
Webb awards bachelor's **degrees**. **Challenging opportunities** include double majors, independent study, and a senior project. Special programs include cooperative education, internships, and off-campus study.

The most frequently chosen **baccalaureate** field is engineering. A complete listing of majors at Webb appears in the Majors by College index beginning on page 469.

The **faculty** at Webb has 11 full-time members, 64% with terminal degrees.

Students of Webb
The student body is made up of 91 undergraduates. 22% are women and 78% are men. Students come from 22 states and territories. 22% are from New York. 2.2% are Asian American and 2.2% Hispanic American. 96% returned for their sophomore year.

Facilities and Resources
110 **computers/terminals** are available on campus for general student use. Students can access the following: campus intranet, computer help desk, free student e-mail accounts. Campuswide network is available. 100% of college-owned or -operated housing units are wired for high-speed Internet access. Wireless service is available via entire campus. The **library** has 53,319 books and 270 subscriptions.

Campus Life
Active organizations on campus include a drama/theater group and choral group. Webb has The Webb Women.

Intercollegiate sports include basketball, cross-country running, sailing, soccer, tennis, volleyball.

Campus Safety
Student safety services include 24-hour emergency telephone alarm devices, 24-hour patrols by trained security personnel, and electronically operated dormitory entrances.

Applying
Webb requires SAT, SAT Subject Tests in math and either physics or chemistry, a high school transcript, an interview, 2 recommendations, proof of US citizenship or permanent residency status, and a minimum high school GPA of 3.5. Application deadline: 2/15; 7/1 priority date for financial aid.

WELLESLEY COLLEGE

SUBURBAN SETTING ■ PRIVATE ■ INDEPENDENT ■ WOMEN ONLY
WELLESLEY, MASSACHUSETTS

SPONSOR

Web site: www.wellesley.edu
Contact: Ms. Heather Ayres, Director of Admission, 240 Green Hall,
Wellesley, MA 02181
Telephone: 781-283-2253
Fax: 781-283-3678
E-mail: admission@wellesley.edu

Academics

Wellesley awards bachelor's **degrees** (double bachelor's degree with Massachusetts
Institute of Technology). **Challenging opportunities** include advanced placement
credit, student-designed majors, an honors program, double majors, independent study,
and a senior project. Special programs include internships, summer session for credit,
off-campus study, study-abroad, and Army and Air Force ROTC.

The most frequently chosen **baccalaureate** fields are social sciences, foreign
languages and literature, and area and ethnic studies. A complete listing of majors at
Wellesley appears in the Majors by College index beginning on page 469.

The **faculty** at Wellesley has 251 full-time members, 96% with terminal degrees.
The student-faculty ratio is 8:1.

Students of Wellesley

The student body is made up of 2,344 undergraduates. Students come from 53 states and
territories and 82 other countries. 14% are from Massachusetts. 7.7% are international
students. 6.4% are African American, 0.6% American Indian, 25.6% Asian American,
and 6.9% Hispanic American. 94% returned for their sophomore year.

Facilities and Resources

200 **computers/terminals** and 200 ports are available on campus for general student
use. Students can access the following: campus intranet, computer help desk, free student
e-mail accounts, online (class) registration, online (class) schedules, electronic bulletin
boards. Campuswide network is available. 100% of college-owned or -operated housing
units are wired for high-speed Internet access. Wireless service is available via computer
labs, learning centers, libraries, student centers. The 4 **libraries** have 873,897 books and
19,653 subscriptions.

Campus Life

There are 160 active organizations on campus, including a drama/theater group,
newspaper, radio station, television station, and choral group. No national or local
sororities.

Wellesley is a member of the NCAA (Division III). **Intercollegiate sports** include
basketball, crew, cross-country running, fencing, field hockey, golf, lacrosse, soccer,
softball, squash, swimming and diving, tennis, volleyball.

Campus Safety

Student safety services include late-night transport/escort service, 24-hour emergency
telephone alarm devices, 24-hour patrols by trained security personnel, and electronically operated dormitory entrances.

Applying

Wellesley requires an essay, SAT and SAT Subject Tests or ACT, a high school
transcript, 3 recommendations, and SAT & 2 SAT Subject Tests or ACT Writing;
Midyear Report, and in some cases an interview. It recommends an interview.
Application deadline: 1/15, 1/15 for nonresidents; 1/15 priority date for financial aid.
Early and deferred admission are possible.

Wellesley's mission as a liberal arts
and sciences college unites three
aspirations: to educate women, to
strive for academic excellence, and to
produce graduates whose lives and
careers exemplify an ideal of
engagement in the world. With a 9:1
student-faculty ratio, 1,000 course
offerings, and more than fifty-three
majors, Wellesley provides
exceptional opportunities for student-
faculty collaboration. The College's
outstanding resources enable it to
attract talented faculty members and
students, remain need-blind in
admission, and provide generous
financial aid awards. One of the most
diverse colleges in the United States,
Wellesley is a multicultural community located 12 miles from Boston.
Its graduates are leaders in the
laboratory, the classroom, the
courtroom, the boardroom, and their
communities—anywhere they
choose.

Getting Accepted
4,001 applied
36% were accepted
596 enrolled (41% of accepted)
76% from top tenth of their h.s. class
Mean SAT critical reading score: 678
Mean SAT math score: 689
Mean SAT writing score: 689
Mean ACT score: 30
91% had SAT critical reading scores over 600
87% had SAT math scores over 600
92% had SAT writing scores over 600
96% had ACT scores over 24
48% had SAT critical reading scores over 700
44% had SAT math scores over 700
50% had SAT writing scores over 700
59% had ACT scores over 30

Graduation and After
84% graduated in 4 years
6% graduated in 5 years
1% graduated in 6 years
67% had job offers within 6 months
100 organizations recruited on campus

Financial Matters
$36,640 tuition and fees (2008–09)
$11,336 room and board
100% average percent of need met
$31,530 average financial aid amount received
per undergraduate (2007–08 estimated)

WELLS COLLEGE

RURAL SETTING ■ PRIVATE ■ INDEPENDENT ■ COED, PRIMARILY WOMEN
AURORA, NEW YORK

Web site: www.wells.edu
Contact: Ms. Susan Raith Sloan, Director of Admission, 170 Main Street,
    Aurora, NY 13026
Telephone: 315-364-3264 or toll-free 800-952-9355
Fax: 315-364-3227
E-mail: admissions@wells.edu

Getting Accepted
1,117 applied
64% were accepted
155 enrolled (22% of accepted)
35% from top tenth of their h.s. class
3.5 average high school GPA
Mean SAT critical reading score: 560
Mean SAT math score: 545
Mean SAT writing score: 535
Mean ACT score: 24
33% had SAT critical reading scores over 600
27% had SAT math scores over 600
54% had ACT scores over 24
2% had SAT critical reading scores over 700
9% had ACT scores over 30

Graduation and After
47% graduated in 4 years
3% graduated in 5 years
1% graduated in 6 years
39% had job offers within 6 months
8 organizations recruited on campus

Financial Matters
$29,680 tuition and fees (2009–10)
$9000 room and board
91% average percent of need met
$18,890 average financial aid amount received
    per undergraduate (2007–08 estimated)

Academics

Wells awards bachelor's **degrees**. **Challenging opportunities** include advanced placement credit, accelerated degree programs, student-designed majors, double majors, independent study, and a senior project. Special programs include internships, off-campus study, study-abroad, and Army and Air Force ROTC.

The most frequently chosen **baccalaureate** fields are psychology, social sciences, and English. A complete listing of majors at Wells appears in the Majors by College index beginning on page 469.

The **faculty** at Wells has 44 full-time members, 84% with terminal degrees. The student-faculty ratio is 9:1.

Students of Wells

The student body is made up of 579 undergraduates. 69.6% are women and 30.4% are men. Students come from 28 states and territories. 68% are from New York. 1.4% are international students. 7.5% are African American, 0.9% American Indian, 2% Asian American, and 4.8% Hispanic American. 72% returned for their sophomore year.

Facilities and Resources

96 **computers/terminals** and 1,224 ports are available on campus for general student use. Students can access the following: campus intranet, computer help desk, free student e-mail accounts, online (class) grades, online (class) registration, online (class) schedules. Campuswide network is available. 100% of college-owned or -operated housing units are wired for high-speed Internet access. Wireless service is available via classrooms, learning centers, libraries, student centers. The **library** has 218,000 books and 350 subscriptions.

Campus Life

There are 40 active organizations on campus, including a drama/theater group, newspaper, and choral group. No national or local **fraternities** or **sororities**.

Wells is a member of the NCAA (Division III). **Intercollegiate sports** include basketball, cross-country running, field hockey (w), golf, lacrosse, soccer, softball (w), swimming and diving, tennis (w).

Campus Safety

Student safety services include late-night transport/escort service, 24-hour emergency telephone alarm devices, 24-hour patrols by trained security personnel, and electronically operated dormitory entrances.

Applying

Wells requires an essay, SAT or ACT, a high school transcript, and 2 recommendations. It recommends an interview. Application deadline: 3/1; 2/15 priority date for financial aid. Early and deferred admission are possible.

WESLEYAN COLLEGE

SUBURBAN SETTING ■ PRIVATE ■ INDEPENDENT RELIGIOUS
■ UNDERGRADUATE: WOMEN ONLY; GRADUATE: COED
MACON, GEORGIA

SPONSOR

Web site: www.wesleyancollege.edu
Contact: 4760 Forsyth Road, Macon, GA 31210-4462
Telephone: 478-757-3700 or toll-free 800-447-6610
Fax: 478-757-4030
E-mail: admissions@wesleyancollege.edu

Academics

Wesleyan College awards bachelor's and master's **degrees**. **Challenging opportunities** include advanced placement credit, student-designed majors, an honors program, double majors, independent study, and a senior project. Special programs include cooperative education, internships, summer session for credit, off-campus study, and study-abroad.

The most frequently chosen **baccalaureate** fields are business/marketing, psychology, and communications/journalism. A complete listing of majors at Wesleyan College appears in the Majors by College index beginning on page 469.

The **faculty** at Wesleyan College has 47 full-time members, 100% with terminal degrees. The student-faculty ratio is 8:1.

Students of Wesleyan College

The student body totals 739, of whom 624 are undergraduates. 97.8% are women and 2.2% are men. Students come from 21 states and territories and 25 other countries. 90% are from Georgia. 14.2% are international students. 32.9% are African American, 0.2% American Indian, 2.7% Asian American, and 2.3% Hispanic American. 68% returned for their sophomore year.

Facilities and Resources

16 **computers/terminals** are available on campus for general student use. Students can access the following: campus intranet, computer help desk, free student e-mail accounts, online (class) grades, online (class) registration, online (class) schedules, online payment. Campuswide network is available. 100% of college-owned or -operated housing units are wired for high-speed Internet access. Wireless service is available via classrooms, computer centers, computer labs, learning centers, libraries, student centers. The **library** has 144,210 books and 588 subscriptions.

Campus Life

There are 37 active organizations on campus, including a drama/theater group, newspaper, and choral group. No national or local **sororities**.

Wesleyan College is a member of the NCAA (Division III). **Intercollegiate sports** include basketball, cross-country running, equestrian sports, soccer, softball, tennis, volleyball.

Campus Safety

Student safety services include late-night transport/escort service, 24-hour emergency telephone alarm devices, 24-hour patrols by trained security personnel, and electronically operated dormitory entrances.

Applying

Wesleyan College requires SAT or ACT, a high school transcript, and 1 recommendation, and in some cases TOEFL required for some. It recommends an essay. Application deadline: rolling admissions; 4/1 priority date for financial aid. Early and deferred admission are possible.

Getting Accepted

536 applied
53% were accepted
90 enrolled (31% of accepted)
32% from top tenth of their h.s. class
3.47 average high school GPA
Mean SAT critical reading score: 555
Mean SAT math score: 530
Mean SAT writing score: 555
Mean ACT score: 24
31% had SAT critical reading scores over 600
26% had SAT math scores over 600
67% had ACT scores over 24
8% had SAT critical reading scores over 700
10% had SAT math scores over 700
6% had ACT scores over 30
3 class presidents

Graduation and After

45% graduated in 4 years
5% graduated in 5 years
5% graduated in 6 years
36% had job offers within 6 months
8 organizations recruited on campus

Financial Matters

$17,500 tuition and fees (2009–10)
$8000 room and board
79% average percent of need met
$10,758 average financial aid amount received per undergraduate (2006–07)

WESLEYAN UNIVERSITY

SMALL-TOWN SETTING ▪ PRIVATE ▪ INDEPENDENT ▪ COED
MIDDLETOWN, CONNECTICUT

Web site: www.wesleyan.edu
Contact: Ms. Nancy Meislahn, Dean of Admission and Financial Aid, Stewart M Reid House, 70 Wyllys Avenue, Middletown, CT 06459-0265
Telephone: 860-685-3000
Fax: 860-685-3001
E-mail: admissions@wesleyan.edu

Getting Accepted

8,250 applied
27% were accepted
715 enrolled (32% of accepted)
65% from top tenth of their h.s. class
3.95 average high school GPA
Mean SAT critical reading score: 700
Mean SAT math score: 700
Mean SAT writing score: 690
Mean ACT score: 30
87% had SAT critical reading scores over 600
90% had SAT math scores over 600
88% had SAT writing scores over 600
99% had ACT scores over 24
51% had SAT critical reading scores over 700
54% had SAT math scores over 700
52% had SAT writing scores over 700
78% had ACT scores over 30

Graduation and After

89% graduated in 4 years
4% graduated in 5 years
70% had job offers within 6 months
98 organizations recruited on campus

Financial Matters

$38,634 tuition and fees (2008–09)
$10,636 room and board
100% average percent of need met
$30,543 average financial aid amount received per undergraduate (2006–07)

Academics

Wesleyan awards bachelor's, master's, and doctoral **degrees** and post-master's certificates. **Challenging opportunities** include advanced placement credit, student-designed majors, an honors program, double majors, independent study, and a senior project. Special programs include summer session for credit, off-campus study, study-abroad, and Air Force ROTC.

The most frequently chosen **baccalaureate** fields are social sciences, area and ethnic studies, and English. A complete listing of majors at Wesleyan appears in the Majors by College index beginning on page 469.

The **faculty** at Wesleyan has 328 full-time members, 94% with terminal degrees. The student-faculty ratio is 9:1.

Students of Wesleyan

The student body totals 3,149, of whom 2,772 are undergraduates. 49% are women and 51% are men. Students come from 52 states and territories and 45 other countries. 8% are from Connecticut. 7% are international students. 7.4% are African American, 0.4% American Indian, 9.8% Asian American, and 8.3% Hispanic American. 95% returned for their sophomore year.

Facilities and Resources

190 **computers/terminals** are available on campus for general student use. Students can access the following: campus intranet, computer help desk, free student e-mail accounts, online (class) grades, online (class) registration, online (class) schedules, electronic portfolio, online course drop/add, Blackboard course management system. Campuswide network is available. 100% of college-owned or -operated housing units are wired for high-speed Internet access. Wireless service is available via entire campus. The 3 **libraries** have 1,661,056 books and 9,812 subscriptions.

Campus Life

There are 231 active organizations on campus, including a drama/theater group, newspaper, radio station, and choral group. 2% of eligible men and 1% of eligible women are members of national **fraternities**, national **sororities**, and local fraternities.

Wesleyan is a member of the NCAA (Division III). **Intercollegiate sports** include baseball (m), basketball, crew, cross-country running, field hockey (w), football (m), golf (m), ice hockey, lacrosse, soccer, softball (w), squash, swimming and diving, tennis, track and field, volleyball (w), wrestling (m).

Campus Safety

Student safety services include late-night transport/escort service, 24-hour emergency telephone alarm devices, 24-hour patrols by trained security personnel, student patrols, and electronically operated dormitory entrances.

Applying

Wesleyan requires an essay, SAT and SAT Subject Tests or ACT, a high school transcript, and 2 recommendations, and in some cases an interview. It recommends an interview. Application deadline: 1/1; 2/15 for financial aid. Early and deferred admission are possible.

WESTERN WASHINGTON UNIVERSITY
SMALL-TOWN SETTING ■ PUBLIC ■ STATE-SUPPORTED ■ COED
BELLINGHAM, WASHINGTON

Web site: www.wwu.edu
Contact: Ms. Karen Copetas, Director of Admissions, 516 High Street,
   Bellingham, WA 98225-9009
Telephone: 360-650-3440
Fax: 360-650-7369
E-mail: admit@wwu.edu

SPONSOR

Academics
Western awards bachelor's and master's **degrees** and post-bachelor's and post-master's certificates. **Challenging opportunities** include advanced placement credit, accelerated degree programs, student-designed majors, an honors program, double majors, independent study, and a senior project. Special programs include cooperative education, internships, summer session for credit, off-campus study, and study-abroad.

The most frequently chosen **baccalaureate** fields are business/marketing, social sciences, and English. A complete listing of majors at Western appears in the Majors by College index beginning on page 469.

The **faculty** at Western has 511 full-time members, 88% with terminal degrees. The student-faculty ratio is 19:1.

Students of Western
The student body totals 14,620, of whom 13,406 are undergraduates. 55.2% are women and 44.8% are men. Students come from 48 states and territories and 43 other countries. 92% are from Washington. 0.8% are international students. 2.9% are African American, 2.5% American Indian, 8.8% Asian American, and 4.4% Hispanic American. 84% returned for their sophomore year.

Facilities and Resources
2,408 **computers/terminals** are available on campus for general student use. Students can access the following: online (class) registration. Campuswide network is available. 99% of college-owned or -operated housing units are wired for high-speed Internet access. Wireless service is available via classrooms, computer centers, computer labs, dorm rooms, learning centers, libraries, student centers. The 2 **libraries** have 1,468,619 books and 7,778 subscriptions.

Campus Life
There are 140 active organizations on campus, including a drama/theater group, newspaper, radio station, television station, and choral group. No national or local **fraternities** or **sororities**.

Western is a member of the NCAA (Division II). **Intercollegiate sports** (some offering scholarships) include basketball, cheerleading, crew, cross-country running, football (m), golf, soccer, softball (w), track and field, volleyball (w).

Campus Safety
Student safety services include late-night transport/escort service, 24-hour emergency telephone alarm devices, 24-hour patrols by trained security personnel, student patrols, and electronically operated dormitory entrances.

Applying
Western requires SAT or ACT and a high school transcript. It recommends an essay. Application deadline: 3/1; 2/15 priority date for financial aid. Deferred admission is possible.

Getting Accepted
9,518 applied
71% were accepted
2,697 enrolled (40% of accepted)
26% from top tenth of their h.s. class
3.5 average high school GPA
Mean SAT critical reading score: 558
Mean SAT math score: 556
Mean SAT writing score: 541
Mean ACT score: 24
34% had SAT critical reading scores over 600
31% had SAT math scores over 600
57% had ACT scores over 24
6% had SAT critical reading scores over 700
3% had SAT math scores over 700
9% had ACT scores over 30

Graduation and After
34% graduated in 4 years
29% graduated in 5 years
6% graduated in 6 years
76% had job offers within 6 months
133 organizations recruited on campus

Financial Matters
$5535 resident tuition and fees (2008–09)
$17,166 nonresident tuition and fees (2008–09)
$7712 room and board
88% average percent of need met
$9709 average financial aid amount received per undergraduate (2007–08 estimated)

WESTMINSTER COLLEGE

SUBURBAN SETTING ■ PRIVATE ■ INDEPENDENT ■ COED
SALT LAKE CITY, UTAH

Web site: www.westminstercollege.edu
Contact: Darlene Dilley, Interim Director of Undergraduate Admissions, 1840 South 1300 East, Salt Lake City, UT 84105-3697
Telephone: 801-832-2200 or toll-free 800-748-4753 (out-of-state)
Fax: 801-832-3101
E-mail: admission@westminstercollege.edu

> Westminster is a nationally recognized, comprehensive liberal arts college. With a broad array of graduate and undergraduate programs, Westminster is distinguished by its unique environment for learning. Westminster prepares students for success through active and engaged learning, real-world experiences, and its vibrant campus community. Westminster's unique location, adjacent to the Rocky Mountains and to dynamic Salt Lake City, further enriches the college experience.

Getting Accepted
1,348 applied
81% were accepted
449 enrolled (41% of accepted)
26% from top tenth of their h.s. class
3.47 average high school GPA
Mean SAT critical reading score: 567
Mean SAT math score: 559
Mean ACT score: 24
34% had SAT critical reading scores over 600
33% had SAT math scores over 600
53% had ACT scores over 24
11% had SAT critical reading scores over 700
6% had SAT math scores over 700
8% had ACT scores over 30
12 National Merit Scholars
13 valedictorians

Graduation and After
43% graduated in 4 years
8% graduated in 5 years
4% graduated in 6 years
84% had job offers within 6 months
28 organizations recruited on campus

Financial Matters
$24,996 tuition and fees (2009–10)
$7006 room and board
88% average percent of need met
$15,651 average financial aid amount received per undergraduate (2005–06)

Academics

Westminster College awards bachelor's and master's **degrees** and post-bachelor's certificates. **Challenging opportunities** include advanced placement credit, accelerated degree programs, student-designed majors, an honors program, double majors, independent study, and a senior project. Special programs include cooperative education, internships, summer session for credit, off-campus study, study-abroad, and Army, Navy, and Air Force ROTC.

The most frequently chosen **baccalaureate** fields are business/marketing, health professions and related sciences, and education. A complete listing of majors at Westminster College appears in the Majors by College index beginning on page 469.

The **faculty** at Westminster College has 132 full-time members, 70% with terminal degrees. The student-faculty ratio is 11:1.

Students of Westminster College

The student body totals 2,863, of whom 2,131 are undergraduates. 55.6% are women and 44.4% are men. Students come from 38 states and territories and 27 other countries. 82% are from Utah. 1.8% are international students. 1.3% are African American, 0.5% American Indian, 3.1% Asian American, and 6.3% Hispanic American. 78% returned for their sophomore year.

Facilities and Resources

403 **computers/terminals** and 650 ports are available on campus for general student use. Students can access the following: campus intranet, computer help desk, free student e-mail accounts, online (class) grades, online (class) registration, online (class) schedules. Campuswide network is available. 100% of college-owned or -operated housing units are wired for high-speed Internet access. Wireless service is available via classrooms, computer centers, computer labs, learning centers, libraries, student centers. The 2 **libraries** have 181,319 books and 9,857 subscriptions.

Campus Life

There are 55 active organizations on campus, including a drama/theater group, newspaper, and choral group. 4% of eligible men and 6% of eligible women are members of local **fraternities** and local **sororities**.

Westminster College is a member of the NAIA. **Intercollegiate sports** (some offering scholarships) include basketball, cross-country running, golf, lacrosse, skiing (downhill), soccer, volleyball (w).

Campus Safety

Student safety services include late-night transport/escort service, 24-hour emergency telephone alarm devices, 24-hour patrols by trained security personnel, student patrols, and electronically operated dormitory entrances.

Applying

Westminster College requires an essay, SAT or ACT, a high school transcript, 1 recommendation, and a minimum high school GPA of 2.5. It recommends an interview. Application deadline: rolling admissions, rolling admissions for nonresidents; 4/15 priority date for financial aid. Deferred admission is possible.

Westmont College

Suburban Setting ■ Private ■ Independent Religious ■ Coed
Santa Barbara, California

Web site: www.westmont.edu
Contact: Mrs. Joyce Luy, Dean of Admission, 955 La Paz Road, Santa
  Barbara, CA 93108
Telephone: 805-565-6200 or toll-free 800-777-9011
Fax: 805-565-6234
E-mail: admissions@westmont.edu

Academics
Westmont awards bachelor's **degrees** and post-bachelor's certificates. **Challenging opportunities** include advanced placement credit, accelerated degree programs, student-designed majors, an honors program, double majors, and a senior project. Special programs include internships, summer session for credit, off-campus study, study-abroad, and Army and Air Force ROTC.

The most frequently chosen **baccalaureate** fields are business/marketing, English, and communications/journalism. A complete listing of majors at Westmont appears in the Majors by College index beginning on page 469.

The **faculty** at Westmont has 93 full-time members, 89% with terminal degrees. The student-faculty ratio is 12:1.

Students of Westmont
The student body is made up of 1,336 undergraduates. 61.3% are women and 38.7% are men. Students come from 41 states and territories and 8 other countries. 69% are from California. 0.7% are international students. 2.3% are African American, 2.3% American Indian, 8.9% Asian American, and 9.9% Hispanic American. 87% returned for their sophomore year.

Facilities and Resources
100 **computers/terminals** are available on campus for general student use. Students can access the following: campus intranet, free student e-mail accounts, online (class) schedules. Campuswide network is available. The **library** has 174,246 books and 380 subscriptions.

Campus Life
Active organizations on campus include a drama/theater group, newspaper, radio station, and choral group. No national or local **fraternities** or **sororities**.

Westmont is a member of the NAIA. **Intercollegiate sports** (some offering scholarships) include baseball (m), basketball, cross-country running, soccer, tennis, track and field, volleyball (w).

Campus Safety
Student safety services include late-night transport/escort service, 24-hour emergency telephone alarm devices, 24-hour patrols by trained security personnel, and electronically operated dormitory entrances.

Applying
Westmont requires an essay, SAT or ACT, a high school transcript, and 1 recommendation, and in some cases TOEFL and an interview. It recommends an interview. Application deadline: 2/20; 3/1 priority date for financial aid.

Getting Accepted
1,651 applied
73% were accepted
389 enrolled (32% of accepted)
45% from top tenth of their h.s. class
3.77 average high school GPA
Mean SAT critical reading score: 600
Mean SAT math score: 600
Mean SAT writing score: 600
Mean ACT score: 26
51% had SAT critical reading scores over 600
52% had SAT math scores over 600
51% had SAT writing scores over 600
78% had ACT scores over 24
12% had SAT critical reading scores over 700
10% had SAT math scores over 700
8% had SAT writing scores over 700
19% had ACT scores over 30

Graduation and After
65% graduated in 4 years
4% graduated in 5 years
1% graduated in 6 years
50 organizations recruited on campus

Financial Matters
$33,170 tuition and fees (2008–09)
$10,080 room and board
71% average percent of need met
$21,890 average financial aid amount received
  per undergraduate (2007–08 estimated)

WHEATON COLLEGE

SUBURBAN SETTING ■ PRIVATE ■ INDEPENDENT RELIGIOUS ■ COED
WHEATON, ILLINOIS

Web site: www.wheaton.edu
Contact: Ms. Shawn Leftwich, Director of Admissions, 501 College Avenue, Wheaton, IL 60187
Telephone: 630-752-5011 or toll-free 800-222-2419 (out-of-state)
Fax: 630-752-5285
E-mail: admissions@wheaton.edu

Getting Accepted
2,083 applied
62% were accepted
581 enrolled (45% of accepted)
59% from top tenth of their h.s. class
3.73 average high school GPA
Mean SAT critical reading score: 657
Mean SAT math score: 648
Mean SAT writing score: 651
Mean ACT score: 29
80% had SAT critical reading scores over 600
80% had SAT math scores over 600
76% had SAT writing scores over 600
95% had ACT scores over 24
30% had SAT critical reading scores over 700
25% had SAT math scores over 700
30% had SAT writing scores over 700
46% had ACT scores over 30
26 National Merit Scholars

Graduation and After
79% graduated in 4 years
5% graduated in 5 years
2% graduated in 6 years
53% had job offers within 6 months
202 organizations recruited on campus

Financial Matters
$25,500 tuition and fees (2008–09)
$7618 room and board
84% average percent of need met
$20,591 average financial aid amount received per undergraduate (2007–08 estimated)

Academics
Wheaton awards bachelor's, master's, and doctoral **degrees** and post-bachelor's certificates. **Challenging opportunities** include advanced placement credit, student-designed majors, double majors, independent study, and a senior project. Special programs include internships, summer session for credit, off-campus study, study-abroad, and Army ROTC.

The most frequently chosen **baccalaureate** fields are social sciences, theology and religious vocations, and business/marketing. A complete listing of majors at Wheaton appears in the Majors by College index beginning on page 469.

The **faculty** at Wheaton has 198 full-time members, 94% with terminal degrees. The student-faculty ratio is 12:1.

Students of Wheaton
The student body totals 2,915, of whom 2,366 are undergraduates. 49.9% are women and 50.1% are men. Students come from 52 states and territories and 18 other countries. 23% are from Illinois. 1.3% are international students. 3.3% are African American, 0.3% American Indian, 7.8% Asian American, and 3.7% Hispanic American. 96% returned for their sophomore year.

Facilities and Resources
125 **computers/terminals** and 4,200 ports are available on campus for general student use. Students can access the following: campus intranet, computer help desk, free student e-mail accounts, online (class) grades, online (class) registration, online (class) schedules, financial information, degree requirements evaluation. Campuswide network is available. 100% of college-owned or -operated housing units are wired for high-speed Internet access. Wireless service is available via computer centers, computer labs, dorm rooms, learning centers, libraries, student centers. The **library** has 465,822 books and 5,747 subscriptions.

Campus Life
There are 80 active organizations on campus, including a drama/theater group, newspaper, radio station, television station, and choral group. No national or local **fraternities** or **sororities**.

Wheaton is a member of the NCAA (Division III). **Intercollegiate sports** include baseball (m), basketball, cross-country running, football (m), golf, soccer, softball (w), swimming and diving, tennis, track and field, volleyball (w), water polo (w), wrestling (m).

Campus Safety
Student safety services include late-night transport/escort service, 24-hour emergency telephone alarm devices, 24-hour patrols by trained security personnel, student patrols, and electronically operated dormitory entrances.

Applying
Wheaton requires an essay, SAT or ACT, a high school transcript, and 2 recommendations. It recommends an interview. Application deadline: 1/10; 2/15 priority date for financial aid.

WHEATON COLLEGE

SMALL-TOWN SETTING ■ PRIVATE ■ INDEPENDENT ■ COED
NORTON, MASSACHUSETTS

Web site: www.wheatoncollege.edu
Contact: Ms. Gail Berson, Vice President For Enrollment and Dean of
Admission and Student Aid, 26 East Main Street, Norton, MA 02766
Telephone: 508-286-8251 or toll-free 800-394-6003
Fax: 508-286-8271
E-mail: admission@wheatoncollege.edu

Academics

Wheaton awards bachelor's **degrees**. **Challenging opportunities** include advanced placement credit, accelerated degree programs, student-designed majors, an honors program, double majors, independent study, and a senior project. Special programs include internships, off-campus study, study-abroad, and Army ROTC.

The most frequently chosen **baccalaureate** fields are social sciences, psychology, and area and ethnic studies. A complete listing of majors at Wheaton appears in the Majors by College index beginning on page 469.

The **faculty** at Wheaton has 141 full-time members, 92% with terminal degrees. The student-faculty ratio is 10:1.

Students of Wheaton

The student body is made up of 1,655 undergraduates. 62.1% are women and 37.9% are men. Students come from 43 states and territories and 36 other countries. 33% are from Massachusetts. 3.5% are international students. 4.8% are African American, 0.3% American Indian, 2.5% Asian American, and 3.3% Hispanic American. 83% returned for their sophomore year.

Facilities and Resources

356 **computers/terminals** and 2,100 ports are available on campus for general student use. Students can access the following: campus intranet, computer help desk, free student e-mail accounts, online (class) grades, online (class) registration, online (class) schedules. Campuswide network is available. 100% of college-owned or -operated housing units are wired for high-speed Internet access. Wireless service is available via entire campus. The **library** has 378,078 books and 14,282 subscriptions.

Campus Life

There are 60 active organizations on campus, including a drama/theater group, newspaper, radio station, and choral group. No national or local **fraternities** or **sororities**.

Wheaton is a member of the NCAA (Division III). **Intercollegiate sports** include baseball (m), basketball, cross-country running, field hockey (w), lacrosse, soccer, softball (w), swimming and diving, tennis, track and field, volleyball (w).

Campus Safety

Student safety services include late-night transport/escort service, 24-hour emergency telephone alarm devices, 24-hour patrols by trained security personnel, student patrols, and electronically operated dormitory entrances.

Applying

Wheaton requires an essay, a high school transcript, and 2 recommendations. It recommends an interview. Application deadline: 1/15; 2/1 for financial aid. Early and deferred admission are possible.

Getting Accepted
3,832 applied
43% were accepted
420 enrolled (25% of accepted)
56% from top tenth of their h.s. class
3.5 average high school GPA

Graduation and After
77% graduated in 4 years
4% graduated in 5 years
1% graduated in 6 years
50% had job offers within 6 months
22 organizations recruited on campus

Financial Matters
$38,860 tuition and fees (2008–09)
$9150 room and board
98% average percent of need met
$28,347 average financial aid amount received per undergraduate (2007–08 estimated)

WHITMAN COLLEGE

SMALL-TOWN SETTING ■ PRIVATE ■ INDEPENDENT ■ COED
WALLA WALLA, WASHINGTON

Web site: www.whitman.edu
Contact: Mr. Tony Cabasco, Dean of Admission and Financial Aid, 515 Boyer
    Avenue, Walla Walla, WA 99362-2083
Telephone: 509-527-5176 or toll-free 877-462-9448
Fax: 509-527-4967
E-mail: admission@whitman.edu

Getting Accepted
2,882 applied
49% were accepted
400 enrolled (29% of accepted)
61% from top tenth of their h.s. class
3.77 average high school GPA
Mean SAT critical reading score: 670
Mean SAT math score: 660
Mean SAT writing score: 670
Mean ACT score: 29
86% had SAT critical reading scores over 600
82% had SAT math scores over 600
80% had SAT writing scores over 600
93% had ACT scores over 24
39% had SAT critical reading scores over 700
32% had SAT math scores over 700
28% had SAT writing scores over 700
53% had ACT scores over 30

Graduation and After
80% graduated in 4 years
6% graduated in 5 years
1% graduated in 6 years
50 organizations recruited on campus

Financial Matters
$35,192 tuition and fees (2008–09)
$8812 room and board
98% average percent of need met
$28,779 average financial aid amount received
    per undergraduate (2007–08 estimated)

Academics

Whitman awards bachelor's **degrees**. **Challenging opportunities** include advanced placement credit, accelerated degree programs, student-designed majors, an honors program, double majors, independent study, and a senior project. Special programs include cooperative education, off-campus study, and study-abroad.

The most frequently chosen **baccalaureate** fields are social sciences, biological/life sciences, and visual and performing arts. A complete listing of majors at Whitman appears in the Majors by College index beginning on page 469.

The **faculty** at Whitman has 127 full-time members, 96% with terminal degrees. The student-faculty ratio is 10:1.

Students of Whitman

The student body is made up of 1,489 undergraduates. 56.3% are women and 43.7% are men. Students come from 42 states and territories and 32 other countries. 40% are from Washington. 3.8% are international students. 1.8% are African American, 1.1% American Indian, 10.3% Asian American, and 5% Hispanic American. 94% returned for their sophomore year.

Facilities and Resources

397 **computers/terminals** are available on campus for general student use. Students can access the following: computer help desk, free student e-mail accounts, online (class) grades, online (class) registration, online (class) schedules, course registration information. Campuswide network is available. 100% of college-owned or -operated housing units are wired for high-speed Internet access. Wireless service is available via classrooms, computer centers, computer labs, dorm rooms, learning centers, libraries, student centers. The 2 **libraries** have 395,841 books and 12,843 subscriptions.

Campus Life

There are 60 active organizations on campus, including a drama/theater group, newspaper, radio station, and choral group. 34% of eligible men and 29% of eligible women are members of national **fraternities** and national **sororities**.

Whitman is a member of the NCAA (Division III). **Intercollegiate sports** include baseball (m), basketball, cross-country running, golf, skiing (cross-country), skiing (downhill), soccer, swimming and diving, tennis, volleyball (w).

Campus Safety

Student safety services include late-night transport/escort service, 24-hour emergency telephone alarm devices, 24-hour patrols by trained security personnel, student patrols, and electronically operated dormitory entrances.

Applying

Whitman requires an essay, SAT or ACT, a high school transcript, and 1 recommendation. It recommends an interview. Application deadline: 1/15; 2/1 for financial aid, with a 11/15 priority date. Deferred admission is possible.

Whitworth University

Suburban setting ■ Private ■ Independent Religious ■ Coed
Spokane, Washington

Web site: www.whitworth.edu
Contact: Ms. Marianne Hansen, Director of Admission, 300 West, Hawthorne Road, Spokane, WA 99251
Telephone: 509-777-4348 or toll-free 800-533-4668 (out-of-state)
Fax: 509-777-3758
E-mail: admission@whitworth.edu

Academics

Whitworth awards bachelor's and master's **degrees**. **Challenging opportunities** include advanced placement credit, student-designed majors, double majors, independent study, and a senior project. Special programs include cooperative education, internships, summer session for credit, off-campus study, study-abroad, and Army ROTC.

The most frequently chosen **baccalaureate** fields are business/marketing, education, and social sciences. A complete listing of majors at Whitworth appears in the Majors by College index beginning on page 469.

The **faculty** at Whitworth has 123 full-time members, 77% with terminal degrees. The student-faculty ratio is 13:1.

Students of Whitworth

The student body totals 2,607, of whom 2,331 are undergraduates. 59.1% are women and 40.9% are men. Students come from 30 states and territories and 18 other countries. 64% are from Washington. 1% are international students. 2% are African American, 1.1% American Indian, 3.5% Asian American, and 2.5% Hispanic American. 87% returned for their sophomore year.

Facilities and Resources

300 **computers/terminals** are available on campus for general student use. Students can access the following: campus intranet, computer help desk, free student e-mail accounts, online (class) grades, online (class) registration, online (class) schedules. Campuswide network is available. Wireless service is available via classrooms, computer centers, computer labs, libraries, student centers. The 3 **libraries** have 17,982 books and 773 subscriptions.

Campus Life

There are 80 active organizations on campus, including a drama/theater group, newspaper, radio station, and choral group. No national or local **fraternities** or **sororities**.

Whitworth is a member of the NCAA (Division III). **Intercollegiate sports** include baseball (m), basketball, cross-country running, football (m), golf, soccer, softball (w), swimming and diving, tennis, track and field, volleyball (w).

Campus Safety

Student safety services include late-night transport/escort service, 24-hour emergency telephone alarm devices, and 24-hour patrols by trained security personnel.

Applying

Whitworth requires an essay and a high school transcript, and in some cases SAT or ACT and an interview. Application deadline: 3/1; 3/1 priority date for financial aid. Early and deferred admission are possible.

Getting Accepted
5,062 applied
49% were accepted
533 enrolled (21% of accepted)
3.69 average high school GPA
54% had SAT critical reading scores over 600
57% had SAT math scores over 600
46% had SAT writing scores over 600
84% had ACT scores over 24
12% had SAT critical reading scores over 700
9% had SAT math scores over 700
7% had SAT writing scores over 700
20% had ACT scores over 30

Graduation and After
58% graduated in 4 years
13% graduated in 5 years
3% graduated in 6 years
110 organizations recruited on campus

Financial Matters
$27,420 tuition and fees (2008–09)
$7700 room and board
81% average percent of need met
$18,549 average financial aid amount received per undergraduate (2007–08 estimated)

WILLAMETTE UNIVERSITY

URBAN SETTING ■ PRIVATE ■ INDEPENDENT RELIGIOUS ■ COED
SALEM, OREGON

Web site: www.willamette.edu
Contact: Susan Rauch, Vice President for Admission and Financial Aid, 900 State Street, Salem, OR 97301
Telephone: 877-LIBARTS or toll-free 877-542-2787
Fax: 503-375-5363
E-mail: libarts@willamette.edu

Getting Accepted

3,501 applied
76% were accepted
482 enrolled (18% of accepted)
43% from top tenth of their h.s. class
3.72 average high school GPA
Mean SAT critical reading score: 630
Mean SAT math score: 610
Mean SAT writing score: 610
Mean ACT score: 27
67% had SAT critical reading scores over 600
57% had SAT math scores over 600
55% had SAT writing scores over 600
86% had ACT scores over 24
17% had SAT critical reading scores over 700
9% had SAT math scores over 700
12% had SAT writing scores over 700
20% had ACT scores over 30
26 valedictorians

Graduation and After

60% graduated in 4 years
10% graduated in 5 years
1% graduated in 6 years
150 organizations recruited on campus

Financial Matters

$33,960 tuition and fees (2008–09)
$7950 room and board
91% average percent of need met
$27,209 average financial aid amount received per undergraduate (2007–08 estimated)

Academics

Willamette awards bachelor's, master's, and first-professional **degrees** and post-bachelor's and first-professional certificates. **Challenging opportunities** include advanced placement credit, accelerated degree programs, student-designed majors, double majors, independent study, and a senior project. Special programs include cooperative education, internships, off-campus study, study-abroad, and Air Force ROTC.

The most frequently chosen **baccalaureate** fields are social sciences, foreign languages and literature, and English. A complete listing of majors at Willamette appears in the Majors by College index beginning on page 469.

The **faculty** at Willamette has 207 full-time members, 96% with terminal degrees. The student-faculty ratio is 10:1.

Students of Willamette

The student body totals 2,716, of whom 1,864 are undergraduates. 56.7% are women and 43.3% are men. Students come from 43 states and territories and 7 other countries. 30% are from Oregon. 6.1% are international students. 2.1% are African American, 1% American Indian, 7.5% Asian American, and 4.5% Hispanic American. 86% returned for their sophomore year.

Facilities and Resources

400 **computers/terminals** are available on campus for general student use. Students can access the following: online (class) registration. Campuswide network is available. The 2 **libraries** have 317,000 books and 1,400 subscriptions.

Campus Life

There are 100 active organizations on campus, including a drama/theater group, newspaper, radio station, and choral group. 35% of eligible men and 29% of eligible women are members of national **fraternities** and national **sororities**.

Willamette is a member of the NCAA (Division III). **Intercollegiate sports** include baseball (m), basketball, crew, cross-country running, football (m), golf, soccer, softball (w), swimming and diving, tennis, track and field, volleyball (w).

Campus Safety

Student safety services include late-night transport/escort service, 24-hour emergency telephone alarm devices, 24-hour patrols by trained security personnel, student patrols, and electronically operated dormitory entrances.

Applying

Willamette requires an essay, SAT or ACT, a high school transcript, 1 recommendation, and a minimum high school GPA of 2.0, and in some cases an interview. It recommends an interview. Application deadline: 2/1; 2/1 priority date for financial aid. Deferred admission is possible.

William Jewell College

Small-town setting ■ Private ■ Independent Religious ■ Coed
Liberty, Missouri

Web site: www.jewell.edu
Contact: Ms. Bridget Gramling, Dean of Admission, 500 College Hill,
  Liberty, MO 64068
Telephone: 816-415-7511 or toll-free 888-2JEWELL
Fax: 816-415-5040
E-mail: gramblingb@william.jewell.edu

Academics

William Jewell awards bachelor's **degrees** (also offers evening program with significant enrollment not reflected in profile). **Challenging opportunities** include advanced placement credit, student-designed majors, an honors program, double majors, independent study, and a senior project. Special programs include cooperative education, internships, summer session for credit, off-campus study, and study-abroad.

The most frequently chosen **baccalaureate** fields are health professions and related sciences, business/marketing, and psychology. A complete listing of majors at William Jewell appears in the Majors by College index beginning on page 469.

The **faculty** at William Jewell has 76 full-time members, 86% with terminal degrees. The student-faculty ratio is 10:1.

Students of William Jewell

The student body is made up of 1,210 undergraduates. 60.4% are women and 39.6% are men. Students come from 33 states and territories. 70% are from Missouri. 0.2% are international students. 4.6% are African American, 1% American Indian, 1.3% Asian American, and 2.6% Hispanic American. 78% returned for their sophomore year.

Facilities and Resources

232 **computers/terminals** are available on campus for general student use. Students can access the following: campus intranet, computer help desk, free student e-mail accounts, online (class) grades, online (class) registration, online (class) schedules. Campuswide network is available. 100% of college-owned or -operated housing units are wired for high-speed Internet access. Wireless service is available via classrooms, learning centers, libraries, student centers. The **library** has 236,241 books and 527 subscriptions.

Campus Life

There are 60 active organizations on campus, including a drama/theater group, newspaper, radio station, and choral group. 37% of eligible men and 36% of eligible women are members of national **fraternities** and national **sororities**.

William Jewell is a member of the NAIA. **Intercollegiate sports** (some offering scholarships) include baseball (m), basketball, cheerleading, cross-country running, football (m), golf, soccer, softball (w), tennis, track and field, volleyball (w).

Campus Safety

Student safety services include late-night transport/escort service, 24-hour emergency telephone alarm devices, 24-hour patrols by trained security personnel, and electronically operated dormitory entrances.

Applying

William Jewell requires an essay, SAT or ACT, and a high school transcript, and in some cases an interview. It recommends an interview. Application deadline: 8/15; 3/1 priority date for financial aid. Deferred admission is possible.

Getting Accepted

1,585 applied
63% were accepted
265 enrolled (27% of accepted)
33% from top tenth of their h.s. class
3.68 average high school GPA
Mean ACT score: 25
50% had SAT critical reading scores over 600
44% had SAT math scores over 600
65% had ACT scores over 24
19% had SAT critical reading scores over 700
6% had SAT math scores over 700
15% had ACT scores over 30
16 valedictorians

Graduation and After

52% graduated in 4 years
9% graduated in 5 years
1% graduated in 6 years
76% had job offers within 6 months
136 organizations recruited on campus

Financial Matters

$24,600 tuition and fees (2009–10)
$6700 room and board
90% average percent of need met
$16,372 average financial aid amount received
  per undergraduate (2007–08 estimated)

Williams is a tightly knit residential community with a focus on the direct educational partnership between students and faculty members. The smallest classes offered—tutorials—pair 2 students with 1 professor. The College emphasizes the continuities between academic and extracurricular life while maintaining a firm commitment to excellence in teaching, artistic endeavor, and scholarly research. Williams admits both domestic and international students without regard to financial need and provides financial assistance to meet 100 percent of demonstrated need with zero loans. The College places a high priority on fostering a multicultural community—to promote an enriched exchange of ideas and to prepare its graduates for a world of increasing diversification.

Getting Accepted
7,552 applied
17% were accepted
540 enrolled (42% of accepted)
87% from top tenth of their h.s. class
93% had SAT critical reading scores over 600
91% had SAT math scores over 600
96% had ACT scores over 24
64% had SAT critical reading scores over 700
60% had SAT math scores over 700
69% had ACT scores over 30

Graduation and After
91% graduated in 4 years
4% graduated in 5 years
100 organizations recruited on campus

Financial Matters
$37,640 tuition and fees (2008–09)
$9890 room and board
100% average percent of need met
$34,879 average financial aid amount received per undergraduate (2007–08 estimated)

WILLIAMS COLLEGE
SMALL-TOWN SETTING ■ PRIVATE ■ INDEPENDENT ■ COED
WILLIAMSTOWN, MASSACHUSETTS

Web site: www.williams.edu
Contact: Mr. Richard L. Nesbitt, Director of Admission, 33 Stetson Court, Williamstown, MA 01267
Telephone: 413-597-2211
Fax: 413-597-4052
E-mail: admission@williams.edu

Academics
Williams awards bachelor's and master's **degrees**. **Challenging opportunities** include advanced placement credit, student-designed majors, double majors, independent study, and a senior project. Special programs include internships, off-campus study, and study-abroad.

The most frequently chosen **baccalaureate** fields are social sciences, visual and performing arts, and English. A complete listing of majors at Williams appears in the Majors by College index beginning on page 469.

The **faculty** at Williams has 267 full-time members, 96% with terminal degrees. The student-faculty ratio is 7:1.

Students of Williams
The student body totals 2,045, of whom 1,997 are undergraduates. 50% are women and 50% are men. Students come from 45 states and territories and 63 other countries. 14% are from Massachusetts. 7.2% are international students. 9.7% are African American, 0.6% American Indian, 11.3% Asian American, and 9.4% Hispanic American. 97% returned for their sophomore year.

Facilities and Resources
252 **computers/terminals** are available on campus for general student use. Students can access the following: computer help desk, free student e-mail accounts, online (class) grades, online (class) registration. Campuswide network is available. 100% of college-owned or -operated housing units are wired for high-speed Internet access. Wireless service is available via entire campus. The 11 **libraries** have 932,000 books and 12,063 subscriptions.

Campus Life
There are 110 active organizations on campus, including a drama/theater group, newspaper, radio station, and choral group. No national or local **fraternities** or **sororities**.

Williams is a member of the NCAA (Division III). **Intercollegiate sports** include baseball (m), basketball, crew, cross-country running, field hockey (w), football (m), golf (m), ice hockey, lacrosse, skiing (cross-country), skiing (downhill), soccer, softball (w), squash, swimming and diving, tennis, track and field, volleyball (w), wrestling (m).

Campus Safety
Student safety services include late-night transport/escort service, 24-hour emergency telephone alarm devices, 24-hour patrols by trained security personnel, student patrols, and electronically operated dormitory entrances.

Applying
Williams requires an essay, SAT and SAT Subject Tests or ACT, a high school transcript, and 2 recommendations. Application deadline: 1/1; 2/1 for financial aid. Early and deferred admission are possible.

WINONA STATE UNIVERSITY

SMALL-TOWN SETTING ■ PUBLIC ■ STATE-SUPPORTED ■ COED
WINONA, MINNESOTA

Web site: www.winona.edu
Contact: Carl Stange, Director of Admissions, PO Box 5838, Winona, MN 55987
Telephone: 507-457-5100 or toll-free 800-DIAL WSU
Fax: 507-457-5620
E-mail: admissions@winona.edu

Academics

Winona State awards associate, bachelor's, and master's **degrees** and post-master's certificates. **Challenging opportunities** include advanced placement credit, accelerated degree programs, student-designed majors, an honors program, double majors, independent study, and a senior project. Special programs include internships, summer session for credit, off-campus study, study-abroad, and Army ROTC. A complete listing of majors at Winona State appears in the Majors by College index beginning on page 469.

The **faculty** at Winona State has 367 full-time members, 78% with terminal degrees. The student-faculty ratio is 21:1.

Students of Winona State

The student body totals 8,220, of whom 7,608 are undergraduates. 62% are women and 38% are men. Students come from 21 states and territories and 48 other countries. 66% are from Minnesota. 4% are international students. 1.1% are African American, 0.3% American Indian, 1.8% Asian American, and 0.8% Hispanic American. 73% returned for their sophomore year.

Facilities and Resources

1,400 **computers/terminals** are available on campus for general student use. Students can access the following: campus intranet, computer help desk, free student e-mail accounts, online (class) grades, online (class) registration, online (class) schedules. Campuswide network is available. 100% of college-owned or -operated housing units are wired for high-speed Internet access. Wireless service is available via classrooms, computer centers, computer labs, learning centers, libraries, student centers. The **library** has 350,000 books and 1,000 subscriptions.

Campus Life

There are 130 active organizations on campus, including a drama/theater group, newspaper, radio station, choral group, and marching band. 3% of eligible men and 3% of eligible women are members of national **fraternities**, national **sororities**, local fraternities, and local sororities.

Winona State is a member of the NCAA (Division II). **Intercollegiate sports** (some offering scholarships) include baseball (m), basketball, cross-country running (w), football (m), golf, gymnastics (w), soccer (w), softball (w), tennis, track and field (w), volleyball (w).

Campus Safety

Student safety services include security cameras, late-night transport/escort service, 24-hour emergency telephone alarm devices, 24-hour patrols by trained security personnel, student patrols, and electronically operated dormitory entrances.

Applying

Winona State requires SAT or ACT, a high school transcript, and class rank, and in some cases an essay and an interview. Application deadline: rolling admissions. Early and deferred admission are possible.

Getting Accepted

5,359 applied
79% were accepted
1,727 enrolled (41% of accepted)
20% from top tenth of their h.s. class
3.3 average high school GPA
Mean ACT score: 23
59% had ACT scores over 24
3% had ACT scores over 30
2 National Merit Scholars
51 class presidents
28 valedictorians

Graduation and After

25% graduated in 4 years
48% graduated in 5 years
80% had job offers within 6 months
240 organizations recruited on campus

Financial Matters

$7627 resident tuition and fees (2008–09)
$12,231 nonresident tuition and fees (2008–09)
$6430 room and board
46% average percent of need met
$6400 average financial aid amount received per undergraduate (2006–07)

WISCONSIN LUTHERAN COLLEGE

SUBURBAN SETTING ■ PRIVATE ■ INDEPENDENT RELIGIOUS ■ COED
MILWAUKEE, WISCONSIN

Web site: www.wlc.edu
Contact: Ms. Amanda Delaney, Admissions, 8800 West Bluemound Road,
    Milwaukee, WI 53226-9942
Telephone: 414-443-8726 or toll-free 888-WIS LUTH
Fax: 414-443-8514
E-mail: amanda.delaney@wlc.edu

Getting Accepted

490 applied
82% were accepted
181 enrolled (45% of accepted)
21% from top tenth of their h.s. class
3.41 average high school GPA
Mean SAT critical reading score: 548
Mean SAT math score: 590
Mean ACT score: 24
38% had SAT critical reading scores over 600
57% had SAT math scores over 600
59% had ACT scores over 24
13% had SAT critical reading scores over 700
19% had SAT math scores over 700
12% had ACT scores over 30

Graduation and After

49% graduated in 4 years
15% graduated in 5 years
1% graduated in 6 years
63% had job offers within 6 months
10 organizations recruited on campus

Financial Matters

$20,560 tuition and fees (2008–09)
$6990 room and board
85% average percent of need met
$15,683 average financial aid amount received
    per undergraduate (2007–08 estimated)

Academics

Wisconsin Lutheran awards bachelor's **degrees**. **Challenging opportunities** include advanced placement credit, student-designed majors, double majors, independent study, and a senior project. Special programs include internships, summer session for credit, study-abroad, and Army, Navy, and Air Force ROTC.

The most frequently chosen **baccalaureate** fields are communications/journalism, psychology, and education. A complete listing of majors at Wisconsin Lutheran appears in the Majors by College index beginning on page 469.

The **faculty** at Wisconsin Lutheran has 58 full-time members, 67% with terminal degrees. The student-faculty ratio is 9:1.

Students of Wisconsin Lutheran

The student body is made up of 720 undergraduates. 56% are women and 44% are men. Students come from 29 states and territories and 8 other countries. 79% are from Wisconsin. 1.6% are international students. 2.3% are African American, 0.1% American Indian, 1.9% Asian American, and 1.9% Hispanic American. 72% returned for their sophomore year.

Facilities and Resources

Students can access the following: campus intranet, computer help desk, free student e-mail accounts, online (class) grades, online (class) registration, online (class) schedules. Campuswide network is available. 100% of college-owned or -operated housing units are wired for high-speed Internet access. Wireless service is available via entire campus.

Campus Life

There are 31 active organizations on campus, including a drama/theater group, newspaper, and choral group. No national or local **fraternities** or **sororities**.

Wisconsin Lutheran is a member of the NCAA (Division III). **Intercollegiate sports** include baseball (m), basketball, cross-country running, football (m), golf, soccer, softball (w), tennis (w), track and field, volleyball (w).

Campus Safety

Student safety services include closed-circuit TV monitors, late-night transport/escort service, 24-hour emergency telephone alarm devices, 24-hour patrols by trained security personnel, and electronically operated dormitory entrances.

Applying

Wisconsin Lutheran requires SAT or ACT, a high school transcript, minimum ACT score of 21, and a minimum high school GPA of 2.7, and in some cases an interview. It recommends 1 recommendation. Application deadline: 3/1 priority date for financial aid. Deferred admission is possible.

WITTENBERG UNIVERSITY

SUBURBAN SETTING ■ PRIVATE ■ INDEPENDENT RELIGIOUS ■ COED
SPRINGFIELD, OHIO

Web site: www.wittenberg.edu
Contact: Ms. Karen Hunt, Director of Admission, PO Box 720, Springfield, OH 45501-0720
Telephone: 877-206-0332 Ext. 6377 or toll-free 800-677-7558 Ext. 6314
Fax: 937-327-6379
E-mail: admission@wittenberg.edu

Academics

Wittenberg awards bachelor's and master's **degrees. Challenging opportunities** include advanced placement credit, student-designed majors, freshman honors college, an honors program, double majors, independent study, and a senior project. Special programs include cooperative education, internships, summer session for credit, off-campus study, study-abroad, and Army and Air Force ROTC.

The most frequently chosen **baccalaureate** fields are social sciences, biological/life sciences, and business/marketing. A complete listing of majors at Wittenberg appears in the Majors by College index beginning on page 469.

The **faculty** at Wittenberg has 142 full-time members, 92% with terminal degrees. The student-faculty ratio is 12:1.

Students of Wittenberg

The student body totals 1,976, of whom 1,967 are undergraduates. 56.3% are women and 43.7% are men. Students come from 40 states and territories and 26 other countries. 69% are from Ohio. 2.5% are international students. 4.3% are African American, 0.2% American Indian, 0.8% Asian American, and 1.1% Hispanic American. 73% returned for their sophomore year.

Facilities and Resources

Students can access the following: computer help desk, free student e-mail accounts, online (class) grades, online (class) registration, online (class) schedules. Campuswide network is available. The 2 **libraries** have 423,930 books and 14,551 subscriptions.

Campus Life

There are 129 active organizations on campus, including a drama/theater group, newspaper, radio station, and choral group. 27% of eligible men and 36% of eligible women are members of national **fraternities** and national **sororities**.

Wittenberg is a member of the NCAA (Division III). **Intercollegiate sports** include baseball (m), basketball, cross-country running, field hockey (w), football (m), golf, lacrosse, soccer, softball (w), swimming and diving, tennis, track and field, volleyball (w).

Campus Safety

Student safety services include crime prevention programs, late-night transport/escort service, 24-hour emergency telephone alarm devices, 24-hour patrols by trained security personnel, student patrols, and electronically operated dormitory entrances.

Applying

Wittenberg requires an essay, a high school transcript, and an interview. It recommends Tests optional. Application deadline: 3/1 priority date for financial aid. Early and deferred admission are possible.

Getting Accepted

3,344 applied
69% were accepted
510 enrolled (22% of accepted)
33% from top tenth of their h.s. class
3.46 average high school GPA
Mean SAT critical reading score: 582
Mean SAT math score: 587
Mean ACT score: 26
44% had SAT critical reading scores over 600
50% had SAT math scores over 600
70% had ACT scores over 24
10% had SAT critical reading scores over 700
6% had SAT math scores over 700
20% had ACT scores over 30

Graduation and After

56% graduated in 4 years
5% graduated in 5 years
1% graduated in 6 years

Financial Matters

$33,890 tuition and fees (2009–10)
$8772 room and board
85% average percent of need met
$23,022 average financial aid amount received per undergraduate (2006–07)

WOFFORD COLLEGE

URBAN SETTING ■ PRIVATE ■ INDEPENDENT RELIGIOUS ■ COED
SPARTANBURG, SOUTH CAROLINA

Web site: www.wofford.edu
Contact: Mrs. Jennifer B. Mauran, Director of Admissions, 429 North
    Church Street, Spartanburg, SC 29303-3663
Telephone: 864-597-4130
Fax: 864-597-4147
E-mail: admission@wofford.edu

Getting Accepted
2,278 applied
59% were accepted
415 enrolled (31% of accepted)
56% from top tenth of their h.s. class
3.49 average high school GPA
Mean SAT critical reading score: 613
Mean SAT math score: 624
Mean ACT score: 25
59% had SAT critical reading scores over 600
64% had SAT math scores over 600
61% had SAT writing scores over 600
64% had ACT scores over 24
13% had SAT critical reading scores over 700
16% had SAT math scores over 700
16% had SAT writing scores over 700
6% had ACT scores over 30
9 National Merit Scholars
19 valedictorians

Graduation and After
79% graduated in 4 years
3% graduated in 5 years
1% graduated in 6 years

Financial Matters
$29,465 tuition and fees (2008–09)
$8190 room and board
89% average percent of need met
$22,401 average financial aid amount received
    per undergraduate (2005–06)

Academics

Wofford awards bachelor's **degrees**. **Challenging opportunities** include advanced placement credit, accelerated degree programs, student-designed majors, double majors, independent study, and a senior project. Special programs include internships, summer session for credit, off-campus study, study-abroad, and Army ROTC.

The most frequently chosen **baccalaureate** fields are business/marketing, biological/life sciences, and social sciences. A complete listing of majors at Wofford appears in the Majors by College index beginning on page 469.

The **faculty** at Wofford has 113 full-time members, 94% with terminal degrees. The student-faculty ratio is 11:1.

Students of Wofford

The student body is made up of 1,389 undergraduates. 48.2% are women and 51.8% are men. Students come from 38 states and territories and 12 other countries. 60% are from South Carolina. 1% are international students. 5.7% are African American, 0.2% American Indian, 2.7% Asian American, and 1.7% Hispanic American. 91% returned for their sophomore year.

Facilities and Resources

250 **computers/terminals** are available on campus for general student use. Students can access the following: campus intranet, computer help desk, free student e-mail accounts, online (class) grades, online (class) registration, online (class) schedules. Campuswide network is available. 100% of college-owned or -operated housing units are wired for high-speed Internet access. Wireless service is available via classrooms, computer centers, computer labs, libraries, student centers. The **library** has 265,251 books and 36,192 subscriptions.

Campus Life

There are 105 active organizations on campus, including a drama/theater group, newspaper, radio station, and choral group. 45% of eligible men and 57% of eligible women are members of national **fraternities** and national **sororities**.

Wofford is a member of the NCAA (Division I). **Intercollegiate sports** (some offering scholarships) include baseball (m), basketball, cheerleading (w), cross-country running, football (m), golf, riflery, soccer, tennis, track and field, volleyball (w).

Campus Safety

Student safety services include late-night transport/escort service, 24-hour emergency telephone alarm devices, 24-hour patrols by trained security personnel, and electronically operated dormitory entrances.

Applying

Wofford requires an essay, SAT or ACT, and a high school transcript. It recommends an interview and 2 recommendations. Application deadline: 2/1; 3/15 priority date for financial aid. Early and deferred admission are possible.

WORCESTER POLYTECHNIC INSTITUTE

SUBURBAN SETTING ■ PRIVATE ■ INDEPENDENT ■ COED
WORCESTER, MASSACHUSETTS

SPONSOR

Web site: www.wpi.edu
Contact: Mr. Edward J. Connor, Director of Admissions, 100 Institute Road,
  Worcester, MA 01609-2280
Telephone: 508-831-5286
Fax: 508-831-5875
E-mail: admissions@wpi.edu

Academics

WPI awards bachelor's, master's, and doctoral **degrees** and post-bachelor's and post-master's certificates. **Challenging opportunities** include advanced placement credit, accelerated degree programs, student-designed majors, double majors, independent study, and a senior project. Special programs include cooperative education, internships, summer session for credit, off-campus study, study-abroad, and Army, Navy, and Air Force ROTC.

The most frequently chosen **baccalaureate** fields are engineering, biological/life sciences, and computer and information sciences. A complete listing of majors at WPI appears in the Majors by College index beginning on page 469.

The **faculty** at WPI has 251 full-time members, 94% with terminal degrees. The student-faculty ratio is 14:1.

Students of WPI

The student body totals 4,561, of whom 3,252 are undergraduates. 26.8% are women and 73.2% are men. Students come from 43 states and territories and 61 other countries. 55% are from Massachusetts. 8.4% are international students. 3% are African American, 0.4% American Indian, 6.2% Asian American, and 4.9% Hispanic American. 92% returned for their sophomore year.

Facilities and Resources

500 **computers/terminals** and 775 ports are available on campus for general student use. Students can access the following: campus intranet, computer help desk, free student e-mail accounts, online (class) grades, online (class) registration, online (class) schedules, online course content. Campuswide network is available. 100% of college-owned or -operated housing units are wired for high-speed Internet access. Wireless service is available via entire campus. The **library** has 272,022 books and 56,300 subscriptions.

Campus Life

There are 125 active organizations on campus, including a drama/theater group, newspaper, radio station, choral group, and marching band. 29% of eligible men and 34% of eligible women are members of national **fraternities** and national **sororities**.

WPI is a member of the NCAA (Division III). **Intercollegiate sports** include baseball (m), basketball, crew, cross-country running, field hockey (w), football (m), soccer, softball (w), swimming and diving, track and field, volleyball (w), wrestling (m).

Campus Safety

Student safety services include late-night transport/escort service, 24-hour emergency telephone alarm devices, 24-hour patrols by trained security personnel, student patrols, and electronically operated dormitory entrances.

Applying

WPI requires an essay, a high school transcript, and 2 recommendations, and in some cases SAT or ACT, TOEFL or IELTS, and an interview. Application deadline: 2/1; 2/1 for financial aid, with a 2/1 priority date. Early and deferred admission are possible.

Small classes, a flexible curriculum, hands-on project experience, and one-on-one interaction are hallmarks of the WPI education. Founded more than 140 years ago and located in Worcester, Massachusetts, WPI offers an innovative curriculum that has been widely recognized for its ability to prepare students for success. There are more than thirty-five areas of study in engineering, science, management, and the liberal arts. Exciting new programs are driven by real-world demand, such as robotics engineering (the first undergraduate program in the nation), interactive media and game development, and environmental studies and engineering.

Getting Accepted
5,706 applied
67% were accepted
907 enrolled (24% of accepted)
53% from top tenth of their h.s. class
3.7 average high school GPA
Mean SAT critical reading score: 604
Mean SAT math score: 672
Mean SAT writing score: 600
Mean ACT score: 28
55% had SAT critical reading scores over 600
88% had SAT math scores over 600
52% had SAT writing scores over 600
88% had ACT scores over 24
13% had SAT critical reading scores over 700
37% had SAT math scores over 700
10% had SAT writing scores over 700
35% had ACT scores over 30
8 National Merit Scholars
23 valedictorians

Graduation and After
71% graduated in 4 years
9% graduated in 5 years
1% graduated in 6 years

Financial Matters
$36,930 tuition and fees (2008–09)
$10,880 room and board
69% average percent of need met
$24,552 average financial aid amount received
  per undergraduate (2007–08 estimated)

XAVIER UNIVERSITY

URBAN SETTING ■ PRIVATE ■ INDEPENDENT RELIGIOUS ■ COED
CINCINNATI, OHIO

Web site: www.xu.edu
Contact: 3800 Victory Parkway, Cincinnati, OH 45207-5311
Telephone: 513-745-2941 or toll-free 800-344-4698
Fax: 513-745-4319
E-mail: xuadmit@xavier.edu

Getting Accepted
6,151 applied
76% were accepted
860 enrolled (18% of accepted)
27% from top tenth of their h.s. class
3.51 average high school GPA
Mean SAT critical reading score: 562
Mean SAT math score: 571
Mean SAT writing score: 549
Mean ACT score: 25
30% had SAT critical reading scores over 600
35% had SAT math scores over 600
28% had SAT writing scores over 600
62% had ACT scores over 24
6% had SAT critical reading scores over 700
5% had SAT math scores over 700
4% had SAT writing scores over 700
14% had ACT scores over 30
3 National Merit Scholars
10 valedictorians

Graduation and After
69% graduated in 4 years
8% graduated in 5 years
1% graduated in 6 years
400 organizations recruited on campus

Financial Matters
$28,570 tuition and fees (2009–10)
$9530 room and board
75% average percent of need met
$15,759 average financial aid amount received
per undergraduate (2007–08 estimated)

Academics

Xavier awards associate, bachelor's, master's, and doctoral **degrees** and post-bachelor's and post-master's certificates. **Challenging opportunities** include advanced placement credit, an honors program, double majors, independent study, and a senior project. Special programs include cooperative education, internships, summer session for credit, off-campus study, study-abroad, and Army and Air Force ROTC.

The most frequently chosen **baccalaureate** fields are business/marketing, liberal arts/general studies, and communications/journalism. A complete listing of majors at Xavier appears in the Majors by College index beginning on page 469.

The **faculty** at Xavier has 311 full-time members, 80% with terminal degrees. The student-faculty ratio is 12:1.

Students of Xavier

The student body totals 6,584, of whom 3,923 are undergraduates. 55.9% are women and 44.1% are men. Students come from 47 states and territories and 34 other countries. 61% are from Ohio. 2.7% are international students. 11.4% are African American, 0.3% American Indian, 2.4% Asian American, and 3.3% Hispanic American. 87% returned for their sophomore year.

Facilities and Resources

250 **computers/terminals** are available on campus for general student use. Students can access the following: computer help desk, free student e-mail accounts, online (class) grades, online (class) registration, online (class) schedules. Campuswide network is available. 99% of college-owned or -operated housing units are wired for high-speed Internet access. Wireless service is available via entire campus. The **library** has 363,140 books and 55,934 subscriptions.

Campus Life

There are 100 active organizations on campus, including a drama/theater group, newspaper, radio station, television station, and choral group. No national or local **fraternities** or **sororities**.

Xavier is a member of the NCAA (Division I). **Intercollegiate sports** (some offering scholarships) include baseball (m), basketball, cross-country running, golf, soccer, swimming and diving, tennis, track and field, volleyball (w).

Campus Safety

Student safety services include campus-wide shuttle service, late-night transport/escort service, 24-hour emergency telephone alarm devices, and 24-hour patrols by trained security personnel.

Applying

Xavier requires an essay, SAT or ACT, a high school transcript, and 1 recommendation. Application deadline: 2/1; 2/15 priority date for financial aid. Early and deferred admission are possible.

YALE UNIVERSITY
URBAN SETTING ■ PRIVATE ■ INDEPENDENT ■ COED
NEW HAVEN, CONNECTICUT

Web site: www.yale.edu
Contact: Admissions Director, PO Box 208234, New Haven, CT 06520
Telephone: 203-432-9300
Fax: 203-432-9392
E-mail: student.questions@yale.edu

Academics
Yale awards bachelor's, master's, doctoral, and first-professional **degrees** and post-master's certificates. **Challenging opportunities** include advanced placement credit, accelerated degree programs, student-designed majors, an honors program, double majors, independent study, and a senior project. Special programs include internships, summer session for credit, study-abroad, and Army and Air Force ROTC.

The most frequently chosen **baccalaureate** fields are social sciences, history, and interdisciplinary studies. A complete listing of majors at Yale appears in the Majors by College index beginning on page 469.

The **faculty** at Yale has 1,100 full-time members, 91% with terminal degrees. The student-faculty ratio is 6:1.

Students of Yale
The student body totals 11,445, of whom 5,277 are undergraduates. 49.9% are women and 50.1% are men. Students come from 52 states and territories and 74 other countries. 7% are from Connecticut. 8.6% are international students. 8.7% are African American, 0.9% American Indian, 13.7% Asian American, and 8.5% Hispanic American. 99% returned for their sophomore year.

Facilities and Resources
350 **computers/terminals** are available on campus for general student use. Students can access the following: campus intranet, computer help desk, free student e-mail accounts, online (class) grades, online (class) registration, online (class) schedules. Campuswide network is available. 100% of college-owned or -operated housing units are wired for high-speed Internet access. Wireless service is available via entire campus. The 23 **libraries** have 12,000,000 books and 85,000 subscriptions.

Campus Life
There are 350 active organizations on campus, including a drama/theater group, newspaper, radio station, television station, choral group, and marching band. 15% of eligible men and 10% of eligible women are members of national **fraternities** and national **sororities**.

Yale is a member of the NCAA (Division I). **Intercollegiate sports** include baseball (m), basketball, crew, cross-country running, fencing, field hockey (w), football (m), golf, gymnastics (w), ice hockey, lacrosse, sailing, soccer, softball (w), squash, swimming and diving, tennis, track and field, volleyball (w).

Campus Safety
Student safety services include late-night transport/escort service, 24-hour emergency telephone alarm devices, 24-hour patrols by trained security personnel, and electronically operated dormitory entrances.

Applying
Yale requires an essay, SAT and SAT Subject Tests or ACT, a high school transcript, and 3 recommendations. It recommends an interview. Application deadline: 12/31; 3/1 for financial aid, with a 3/1 priority date. Early and deferred admission are possible.

Getting Accepted
22,817 applied
9% were accepted
1,318 enrolled (68% of accepted)
97% from top tenth of their h.s. class
98% had SAT critical reading scores over 600
98% had SAT math scores over 600
98% had SAT writing scores over 600
77% had SAT critical reading scores over 700
77% had SAT math scores over 700
76% had SAT writing scores over 700

Graduation and After
87% graduated in 4 years
8% graduated in 5 years
1% graduated in 6 years
64% had job offers within 6 months

Financial Matters
$35,300 tuition and fees (2008–09)
$10,700 room and board
100% average percent of need met
$34,744 average financial aid amount received per undergraduate (2007–08 estimated)

INDEXES

SPECIALIZED INDEXES

William Jewell College

Brethren
Elizabethtown College
Juniata College

Christian (Unspecified)
Milligan College

Christian Church (Disciples of Christ)
Chapman University
Hiram College
Texas Christian University
Transylvania University

Church of the Nazarene
Point Loma Nazarene University

Churches of Christ
Harding University
Lipscomb University
Pepperdine University (CA)

Episcopal
Sewanee: The University of the South

Friends
Earlham College
George Fox University

Interdenominational
Berry College
Biola University
Bryan College (TN)
Colorado Christian University
Illinois College
John Brown University
Messiah College
Taylor University

Jewish
List College, The Jewish Theological Seminary

Latter-day Saints (Mormon)
Brigham Young University

Lutheran
Augustana College (IL)
Augustana College (SD)
Concordia College (MN)
Gettysburg College
Gustavus Adolphus College
Luther College
Muhlenberg College
Pacific Lutheran University
St. Olaf College
Susquehanna University
Valparaiso University
Wartburg College
Wisconsin Lutheran College
Wittenberg University

Mennonite
Goshen College
Tabor College

Methodist
Albion College
Albright College
American University
Baldwin-Wallace College
Birmingham-Southern College
Cornell College
DePauw University
Drew University
Duke University
Emory University
Hamline University
Hendrix College
Lebanon Valley College
Lycoming College
McKendree University
Millsaps College
Nebraska Wesleyan University
North Central College
Ohio Northern University
Ohio Wesleyan University
Oklahoma City University
Randolph College
Seattle Pacific University
Simpson College
Southern Methodist University
Southwestern University
University of Evansville
Wesleyan College
Willamette University
Wofford College

Moravian
Moravian College

Nondenominational
Asbury College
Azusa Pacific University
Cornerstone University
Gordon College (MA)
The King's College (NY)
LeTourneau University
The Master's College and Seminary (CA)
Northwestern College (MN)
Westmont College
Wheaton College (IL)

Presbyterian
Agnes Scott College
Alma College
Austin College
Carroll University
Centre College
Coe College

The College of Wooster
Covenant College
Davidson College
Erskine College
Grove City College
Hanover College
Lafayette College
Lyon College
Macalester College
Maryville College
Presbyterian College
Rhodes College
Trinity University
University of Tulsa
Whitworth University

Reformed Churches
Calvin College
Central College
Hope College
Northwestern College (IA)

Roman Catholic
Benedictine University
Boston College
Canisius College
Carroll College
Christendom College
Christian Brothers University
Clarke College
College of Saint Benedict
College of St. Catherine
The College of St. Scholastica
The College of Saint Thomas More
College of the Holy Cross
Creighton University
Dominican University
Duquesne University
Fairfield University
Fordham University
Franciscan University of Steubenville
Georgetown University
Gonzaga University
John Carroll University
Loyola College in Maryland
Loyola Marymount University
Loyola University Chicago
Loyola University New Orleans
Marquette University
Providence College
Quincy University
Regis University
Saint Francis University
Saint John's University (MN)
Saint Joseph's University
Saint Louis University
Saint Mary's College

Saint Mary's College of California
St. Norbert College
Santa Clara University
Seattle University
Siena College
Stonehill College
Thomas Aquinas College
University of Dallas
University of Dayton
University of Notre Dame
University of Portland
University of St. Thomas (MN)
University of St. Thomas (TX)
University of San Diego
The University of Scranton
Villanova University
Xavier University

United Church of Christ
Elon University

Wesleyan
Houghton College

PUBLIC COLLEGES
Auburn University
Bernard M. Baruch College of the City University of New York
California Polytechnic State University, San Luis Obispo
Clemson University
College of Charleston
The College of New Jersey
The College of William and Mary
Colorado School of Mines
Colorado State University
Florida International University
Florida State University
Georgia Institute of Technology
Georgia State University
Iowa State University of Science and Technology
James Madison University
Louisiana State University and Agricultural and Mechanical College
McGill University
Miami University
Michigan State University
Michigan Technological University
Missouri State University
Missouri University of Science and Technology
Mount Allison University
Mount Saint Vincent University
Murray State University
New College of Florida
New Jersey Institute of Technology
New Mexico Institute of Mining and Technology
North Carolina State University
The Ohio State University

Oklahoma State University
Penn State University Park
Purdue University
Queen's University at Kingston
Rutgers, The State University of New Jersey, Newark
Rutgers, The State University of New Jersey, New Brunswick
St. Mary's College of Maryland
San Diego State University
State University of New York at Binghamton
State University of New York College at Geneseo
State University of New York College of Environmental
    Science and Forestry
Stony Brook University, State University of New York
Tennessee Technological University
Texas A&M University
Texas Tech University
Towson University
Truman State University
United States Air Force Academy
United States Coast Guard Academy
United States Merchant Marine Academy
United States Military Academy
United States Naval Academy
University at Buffalo, the State University of New York
The University of Alabama in Huntsville
The University of Arizona
University of Arkansas
University of California, Berkeley
University of California, Davis
University of California, Irvine
University of California, Los Angeles
University of California, Riverside
University of California, San Diego
University of California, Santa Barbara
University of California, Santa Cruz
University of Central Arkansas
University of Central Florida
University of Colorado at Boulder
University of Connecticut
University of Delaware
University of Florida
University of Georgia

University of Illinois at Chicago
University of Illinois at Urbana–Champaign
The University of Iowa
The University of Kansas
University of Kentucky
University of Maryland, Baltimore County
University of Maryland, College Park
University of Mary Washington
University of Michigan
University of Michigan–Dearborn
University of Minnesota, Morris
University of Minnesota, Twin Cities Campus
University of Missouri–Columbia
University of Missouri–Kansas City
University of Nebraska–Lincoln
The University of North Carolina at Asheville
The University of North Carolina at Chapel Hill
The University of North Carolina Wilmington
University of North Florida
University of Oklahoma
University of Pittsburgh
University of Rhode Island
University of South Carolina
The University of Tennessee
The University of Tennessee at Chattanooga
The University of Texas at Austin
The University of Texas at Dallas
University of Utah
University of Virginia
University of Washington
University of Wisconsin–La Crosse
University of Wisconsin–Madison
University of Wisconsin–River Falls
Virginia Military Institute
Virginia Polytechnic Institute and State University
Western Washington University
Winona State University

HISPANIC-SERVING INSTITUTIONS
Florida International University
University of Miami
University of St. Thomas (TX)

Majors by College

Agnes Scott College
African studies; anthropology; architecture; art; astrophysics; biochemistry; biology/biological sciences; chemistry; classics and languages, literatures and linguistics; creative writing; dance; dramatic/theater arts; economics; economics related; engineering related; English; French; German; history; interdisciplinary studies; international relations and affairs; literature; mathematics; multi-/interdisciplinary studies related; music; neuroscience; nursing related; philosophy; physics; political science and government; psychology; religious studies; sociology; Spanish; women's studies.

Albany College of Pharmacy and Health Sciences
Clinical laboratory science/medical technology; cytotechnology; pharmacy; pharmacy, pharmaceutical sciences, and administration related.

Albion College
American studies; anthropology; art; biology/biological sciences; business administration and management; chemistry; computer science; dramatic/theater arts; economics; education; elementary education; English; environmental studies; French; geology/earth science; German; history; human services; international relations and affairs; mass communication/media; mathematics; modern languages; music; philosophy; physical education teaching and coaching; physics; political science and government; pre-law studies; pre-veterinary studies; premedical studies; psychology; public policy analysis; religious studies; secondary education; sociology; Spanish; women's studies.

Albright College
Accounting; American studies; apparel and textiles; art; art teacher education; biochemistry; biology/biological sciences; business administration and management; chemistry; communication/speech communication and rhetoric; computer science; criminology; design and visual communications; dramatic/theater arts; economics; elementary education; English; environmental science; finance; forestry; French; history; industrial and organizational psychology; information science/studies; interdisciplinary studies; international business/trade/commerce; kindergarten/preschool education; Latin American studies; marketing/marketing management; mathematics; multi-/interdisciplinary studies related; music; natural resources management and policy; philosophy; physics; physiological psychology/psychobiology; political science and government; pre-law studies; psychology; religious studies; secondary education; sociology; Spanish; special education; women's studies.

Alfred University
Accounting; art; art teacher education; athletic training; biological and physical sciences; biology/biological sciences; biomedical/medical engineering; business administration and management; business teacher education; ceramic arts and ceramics; ceramic sciences and engineering; chemistry; communication/speech communication and rhetoric; criminal justice/law enforcement administration; dramatic/theater arts; economics; electrical, electronics and communications engineering; elementary education; engineering related; English; environmental studies; finance; fine/studio arts; French; general studies; geology/earth science; German; gerontology; history; interdisciplinary studies; international/global studies; literature; marketing/marketing management; materials engineering; mathematics; mechanical engineering; modern languages; philosophy; physics; political science and government; psychology; public administration; science teacher education; secondary education; sociology; Spanish.

Allegheny College
Applied economics; art; art history, criticism and conservation; biochemistry; biology/biological sciences; business/managerial economics; chemistry; communication/speech communication and rhetoric; computer science; computer software engineering; creative writing; dramatic/theater arts; economics; education; English; environmental science; environmental studies; fine arts related; fine/studio arts; French; geological and earth sciences/geosciences related; geology/earth science; German; health/medical preparatory programs related; history; international relations and affairs; international/global studies; journalism; mass communication/media; mathematics; multi-/interdisciplinary studies related; music; music performance; neuroscience; philosophy; physics; political science and government; pre-dentistry studies; pre-law studies; pre-pharmacy studies; pre-veterinary studies; premedical studies; prenursing studies; psychology; religious studies; Spanish; technical and business writing; women's studies.

Allen College
Nursing (registered nurse training); radiologic technology/science.

Alma College
Accounting; anthropology; art; art teacher education; biochemistry; biological and physical sciences; biology teacher education; biology/biological sciences; business administration and management; chemistry; chemistry teacher education; communication and media related; computer science; computer teacher education; dance; design and visual communications; dramatic/theater arts; early childhood education; economics; education; elementary education; English; English/language arts teacher education; fine/studio arts; French; French language teacher education; German; German language teacher education; gerontology; graphic design; health science; health teacher education; history; history teacher education; humanities; international business/trade/commerce; kindergarten/preschool education; kinesiology and exercise science; liberal arts and sciences/liberal studies; marketing/marketing management; mathematics; mathematics teacher education; medical illustration; modern languages; music; music performance; music teacher education; philosophy; physical education teaching and coaching; physics; physics teacher education; political science and government; pre-dentistry studies; pre-law studies; pre-theology/pre-ministerial studies; pre-veterinary studies; premedical studies; psychology; psychology teacher education; public health; religious studies; science teacher education; secondary education; social science teacher education; social sciences; social studies teacher education; sociology; Spanish; Spanish language teacher education.

American University
American studies; anthropology; applied mathematics; art history, criticism and conservation; audio engineering; biochemistry; biology/biological sciences; business administration and management; chemistry; computer science; design and visual communications; dramatic/theater arts; economics; elementary education; environmental studies; European studies; fine/studio arts; foreign languages and literatures; French; French studies; German; German studies; graphic design; health science; history; interdisciplinary studies; intermedia/multimedia; international relations and affairs; Jewish/Judaic studies; journalism; Latin American studies; legal studies; liberal arts and sciences/liberal studies; literature; marine science/merchant marine officer; mass communication/media; mathematics; music; philosophy; physics; political science and government; psychology; public health education and promotion; public relations/image management; Russian; Russian studies; secondary education; sociology; Spanish; statistics; women's studies.

Amherst College
African American/Black studies; American studies; ancient/classical Greek; anthropology; art; Asian studies; astronomy; biology/biological

sciences; chemistry; classics and languages, literatures and linguistics; computer science; dance; dramatic/theater arts; economics; English; European studies; fine/studio arts; French; geology/earth science; German; history; interdisciplinary studies; Latin; legal studies; mathematics; music; neuroscience; philosophy; physics; political science and government; psychology; religious studies; Russian; sociology; Spanish; women's studies.

Asbury College

Accounting; ancient Near Eastern and biblical languages; applied mathematics; art teacher education; biblical studies; biochemistry; biology/biological sciences; business/commerce; chemistry; computational mathematics; creative writing; dramatic/theater arts; elementary education; English; equestrian studies; fine/studio arts; French; general studies; health and physical education; health/medical preparatory programs related; history; journalism; mathematics; mathematics and statistics related; middle school education; missionary studies and missiology; music; music teacher education; parks, recreation and leisure facilities management; philosophy; physical education teaching and coaching; physical sciences; political science and government; psychology; radio and television broadcasting technology; religious education; religious/sacred music; social sciences; social work; sociology; Spanish; speech and rhetoric; sport and fitness administration/management; youth ministry.

Auburn University

Accounting; adult and continuing education; aerospace, aeronautical and astronautical engineering; agricultural communication/journalism; agricultural economics; agricultural teacher education; agricultural/biological engineering and bioengineering; agriculture; agronomy and crop science; airline pilot and flight crew; animal sciences; anthropology; apparel and textiles; applied mathematics; aquaculture; architectural engineering; architecture; audiology and speech-language pathology; aviation/airway management; biochemistry; biology/biological sciences; biomedical sciences; botany/plant biology; broadcast journalism; business administration and management; business teacher education; business/managerial economics; chemical engineering; chemistry; child development; civil engineering; clinical laboratory science/medical technology; clinical/medical laboratory science and allied professions related; clinical/medical laboratory technology; commercial and advertising art; communication and journalism related; computer and information sciences; computer engineering; computer engineering related; computer hardware engineering; computer software engineering; criminology; design and visual communications; dramatic/theater arts; early childhood education; economics; electrical, electronics and communications engineering; elementary education; engineering; engineering related; English; English/language arts teacher education; environmental design/architecture; environmental science; family and consumer sciences/human sciences; finance; fine/studio arts; food science; foods, nutrition, and wellness; foreign languages and literatures; forest sciences and biology; French; French language teacher education; geography; geology/earth science; German; German language teacher education; graphic design; health teacher education; health/health-care administration; history; history teacher education; horticultural science; hospitality administration related; hotel/motel administration; human development and family studies; human resources management; industrial design; industrial engineering; interior architecture; interior design; international business/trade/commerce; journalism; logistics and materials management; management information systems; marine biology and biological oceanography; marketing/marketing management; mass communication/media; materials engineering; mathematics; mathematics teacher education; mechanical engineering; medical laboratory technology; medical microbiology and bacteriology; microbiology; molecular biology; music; music teacher education; nursing (registered nurse training); nutrition sciences; operations management; philosophy; physical education teaching and coaching; physics; physics teacher education; plant pathology/phytopathology; plant sciences; plant sciences related; political science and government; poultry science; pre-dentistry studies; pre-law studies; pre-pharmacy studies; pre-veterinary studies;

premedical studies; psychology; public administration; public relations/image management; radio and television; science teacher education; secondary education; social work; sociology; Spanish; Spanish language teacher education; special education; special education related; speech and rhetoric; speech therapy; textile sciences and engineering; trade and industrial teacher education; wildlife and wildlands science and management; zoology/animal biology.

Augustana College (IL)

Accounting; anthropology; art; art history, criticism and conservation; art teacher education; Asian studies; biochemistry; biology/biological sciences; business administration and management; chemistry; Chinese; classics and languages, literatures and linguistics; computer science; creative writing; dramatic/theater arts; economics; education; elementary education; engineering physics; engineering related; English; environmental studies; finance; fine/studio arts; French; geography; geology/earth science; German; history; Japanese; jazz/jazz studies; Latin; liberal arts and sciences/liberal studies; literature; marketing/marketing management; mass communication/media; mathematics; mathematics and computer science; music; music performance; music teacher education; occupational therapy; philosophy; physical education teaching and coaching; physics; piano and organ; political science and government; pre-dentistry studies; pre-law studies; pre-veterinary studies; premedical studies; psychology; public administration; religious studies; religious/sacred music; Scandinavian languages; science teacher education; secondary education; sociology; Spanish; speech and rhetoric; speech therapy; speech-language pathology; Swedish; violin, viola, guitar and other stringed instruments; voice and opera; wind/percussion instruments; women's studies.

Augustana College (SD)

Accounting; American Sign Language (ASL); art; art teacher education; athletic training; audiology and speech-language pathology; biology/biological sciences; business administration and management; business/corporate communications; chemical physics; chemistry; classics; clinical laboratory science/medical technology; communication/speech communication and rhetoric; computer science; dramatic/theater arts; economics; education (K-12); elementary education; engineering physics; English; foreign languages and literatures; French; German; health/health-care administration; history; international relations and affairs; journalism; kinesiology and exercise science; liberal arts and sciences/liberal studies; management information systems; mathematics; music; music teacher education; nursing (registered nurse training); philosophy; physical education teaching and coaching; physics; political science and government; pre-dentistry studies; pre-law studies; pre-veterinary studies; premedical studies; psychology; religious studies; secondary education; sign language interpretation and translation; social studies teacher education; social work; sociology; Spanish; special education; special education (hearing impaired); speech/theater education; sport and fitness administration/management.

Austin College

Art; biochemistry; biology/biological sciences; business administration and management; chemistry; classics and classical languages related; classics and languages, literatures and linguistics; communication/speech communication and rhetoric; computer science; economics; English; French; German; history; international economics; international relations and affairs; Latin; mathematics; multi-/interdisciplinary studies related; music; philosophy; physics; political science and government; psychology; religious studies; sociology; Spanish.

Azusa Pacific University

Accounting; applied art; athletic training; biblical studies; biochemistry; biology/biological sciences; business administration and management; chemistry; communication/speech communication and rhetoric; computer science; cultural studies; divinity/ministry; English; health science; history; international relations and affairs; liberal arts and sciences/liberal studies; management information systems; marketing/marketing management; mathematics; music; natural sciences; nursing (registered nurse training); philosophy; physical education teaching and coaching; physics; political science and government; pre-engineering; pre-law studies; psychology; religious studies; social sciences; social work; sociology; Spanish; theology; web page, digital/multimedia and information resources design.

Babson College
Accounting; accounting and business/management; accounting and finance; auditing; business administration and management; business administration, management and operations related; business/corporate communications; economics; entrepreneurial and small business related; entrepreneurship; finance; finance and financial management services related; international business/trade/commerce; international finance; investments and securities; management information systems; marketing related; marketing/marketing management; office management; operations management; operations research; pre-law studies; sales, distribution and marketing; small business administration.

Baldwin-Wallace College
Accounting; art; art history, criticism and conservation; athletic training; biology/biological sciences; business administration and management; chemistry; communication disorders; communication/speech communication and rhetoric; computer science; computer software and media applications related; computer systems analysis; computer systems networking and telecommunications; creative writing; criminal justice/safety; dramatic/theater arts and stagecraft related; early childhood education; economics; education; English; exercise physiology; film/cinema studies; finance; French; German; health and physical education; health professions related; history; human resources management; international/global studies; marketing/marketing management; mass communication/media; mathematics; middle school education; multi-/interdisciplinary studies related; music; music history, literature, and theory; music performance; music teacher education; music theory and composition; music therapy; musicology and ethnomusicology; neuroscience; philosophy; physical sciences related; physics; piano and organ; political science and government; psychology; public relations/image management; religious studies; sociology; Spanish; special education (specific learning disabilities); sport and fitness administration/management; visual and performing arts related; voice and opera.

Bard College
Acting; African studies; American government and politics; American history; American literature; American studies; ancient/classical Greek; anthropology; Arabic; archeology; area studies; art; art history, criticism and conservation; Asian history; Asian studies; biology/biological sciences; chemistry; Chinese; cinematography and film/video production; comparative literature; computer science; conducting; creative writing; dance; directing and theatrical production; dramatic/theater arts; economics; English; English literature (British and Commonwealth); environmental studies; European history; European studies; film/cinema studies; fine/studio arts; French; French studies; German; German studies; Hebrew; history; history and philosophy of science and technology; interdisciplinary studies; international relations and affairs; Italian; jazz/jazz studies; Jewish/Judaic studies; language interpretation and translation; Latin; Latin American studies; liberal arts and sciences/liberal studies; literature; mathematics; medieval and Renaissance studies; music; music history, literature, and theory; music performance; music theory and composition; Near and Middle Eastern studies; neuroscience; philosophy; photography; physics; piano and organ; playwriting and screenwriting; political science and government; pre-law studies; premedical studies; psychology; religious studies; Romance languages; Russian; Russian studies; Sanskrit and classical Indian languages; sociology; Spanish; Spanish and Iberian studies; theater literature, history and criticism; violin, viola, guitar and other stringed instruments; voice and opera.

Bard College at Simon's Rock
Acting; African American/Black studies; agricultural business and management; American literature; American native/native American

education; American studies; anthropology; applied mathematics; art history, criticism and conservation; Asian studies; biology/biological sciences; ceramic arts and ceramics; chemistry; Chinese; Chinese studies; cognitive psychology and psycholinguistics; computer and information sciences; computer graphics; computer science; creative writing; cultural studies; dance; developmental and child psychology; dramatic/theater arts; drawing; ecology; economics related; English composition; environmental studies; ethnic, cultural minority, and gender studies related; European studies; fine/studio arts; foreign languages and literatures; French; French studies; geography; geology/earth science; German; German studies; interdisciplinary studies; jazz/jazz studies; Latin; Latin American studies; liberal arts and sciences/liberal studies; literature; mathematics; metal and jewelry arts; music; music theory and composition; natural sciences; painting; philosophy; photography; physics; playwriting and screenwriting; political science and government; pre-law studies; premedical studies; printmaking; psychology; religious studies; sculpture; sociology; Spanish; Spanish and Iberian studies; theater design and technology; theater literature, history and criticism; Ukraine studies; visual and performing arts; visual and performing arts related; women's studies.

Barnard College
African studies; American studies; ancient/classical Greek; anthropology; architecture; art history, criticism and conservation; Asian studies; biochemistry; biology/biological sciences; chemistry; classics; comparative literature; computer and information sciences; dance; dramatic/theater arts; economics; education; English; environmental biology; environmental science; film/cinema studies; French; French studies; German; German studies; history; interdisciplinary studies; Italian; Jewish/Judaic studies; Latin; Latin American studies; mathematics; medieval and Renaissance studies; music; neuroscience; philosophy; physics; political science and government; psychology; religious studies; Russian; Slavic studies; sociology; Spanish; statistics; urban studies/affairs; visual and performing arts; women's studies.

Bates College
African American/Black studies; American studies; ancient studies; anthropology; art; Asian studies (East); biochemistry; biology/biological sciences; chemistry; Chinese; dramatic/theater arts; economics; engineering; English; environmental studies; French; geology/earth science; German; history; Japanese; mathematics; multi-/interdisciplinary studies related; music; neuroscience; philosophy; physics; political science and government; psychology; religious studies; Russian; sociology; Spanish; speech and rhetoric; women's studies.

Baylor University
Accounting; acting; airline pilot and flight crew; American studies; ancient Near Eastern and biblical languages; ancient/classical Greek; anthropology; applied mathematics; architecture; art; art history, criticism and conservation; art teacher education; Asian studies; athletic training; biochemistry; bioinformatics; biology/biological sciences; business administration and management; business statistics; business teacher education; business, management, and marketing related; business/commerce; business/managerial economics; chemistry; classics and languages, literatures and linguistics; clinical laboratory science/medical technology; communication disorders; communication/speech communication and rhetoric; computer science; computer teacher education; digital communication and media/multimedia; dramatic/theater arts; early childhood education; economics; education; education (specific subject areas) related; electrical, electronics and communications engineering; elementary education; engineering; English; English composition; English/language arts teacher education; entrepreneurship; environmental studies; exercise physiology; family and consumer sciences/human sciences; fashion merchandising; fashion/apparel design; finance; financial planning and services; fine/studio arts; foreign language teacher education; forestry; French; geological and earth sciences/geosciences related; geology/earth science; geophysics and seismology; German; health and physical education; health occupations teacher education; health teacher education; health/medical preparatory

programs related; history; human development and family studies; human nutrition; human resources management; humanities; information technology; insurance; interior design; international business/trade/commerce; international relations and affairs; journalism; kindergarten/preschool education; Latin; Latin American studies; linguistics and materials management; management information systems; marketing/marketing management; mathematics; mathematics teacher education; mechanical engineering; merchandising, sales, and marketing operations related (specialized); multi-/interdisciplinary studies related; music; music history, literature, and theory; music pedagogy; music performance; music teacher education; music theory and composition; neuroscience; nursing (registered nurse training); philosophy; physical education teaching and coaching; physics; political science and government; pre-dentistry studies; pre-law studies; premedical studies; prenursing studies; psychology; public administration; reading teacher education; real estate; religious studies; religious/sacred music; Russian; sales, distribution and marketing; science teacher education; secondary education; Slavic studies; social science teacher education; social studies teacher education; social work; sociology; Spanish; Spanish language teacher education; special education; special education (speech or language impaired); statistics; theater design and technology.

Belmont University
Accounting; advertising; ancient Near Eastern and biblical languages; applied mathematics; art; art teacher education; biblical studies; bilingual and multilingual education; biochemistry; biological and physical sciences; biology/biological sciences; broadcast journalism; business administration and management; business teacher education; business/managerial economics; chemistry; clinical laboratory science/medical technology; computer management; computer programming; computer science; consumer merchandising/retailing management; counselor education/school counseling and guidance; developmental and child psychology; divinity/ministry; dramatic/theater arts; economics; education; elementary education; engineering science; English; entrepreneurship; finance; fine/studio arts; health and physical education; health teacher education; health/health-care administration; history; information science/studies; international business/trade/commerce; journalism; marketing/marketing management; mass communication/media; mathematics; modern Greek; music; music history, literature, and theory; music management and merchandising; music teacher education; nursing (registered nurse training); parks, recreation and leisure; pastoral studies/counseling; philosophy; physical education teaching and coaching; physics; piano and organ; political science and government; psychology; public relations, advertising, and applied communication related; radio and television; religious/sacred music; social work; sociology; Spanish; special education; speech and rhetoric; voice and opera; western civilization.

Beloit College
Anthropology; art history, criticism and conservation; art teacher education; Asian studies; biochemistry; biology/biological sciences; business administration and management; business/managerial economics; cell biology and histology; chemistry; classics and languages, literatures and linguistics; comparative literature; computer science; creative writing; dramatic/theater arts; economics; education; elementary education; engineering; English; environmental biology; environmental studies; European studies; fine/studio arts; French; geology/earth science; German; history; interdisciplinary studies; international relations and affairs; Latin American studies; literature; mass communication/media; mathematics; modern languages; molecular biology; museum studies; music; music teacher education; philosophy; physics; political science and government; pre-dentistry studies; pre-law studies; premedical studies; psychology; religious studies; Romance languages; Russian; Russian studies; science teacher education; secondary education; sociobiology; sociology; Spanish; women's studies.

Benedictine University
Accounting; arts management; biochemistry; biology/biological sciences; business administration and management; business administration, management and operations related; business, management, and

marketing related; business/commerce; business/managerial economics; chemistry; clinical laboratory science/medical technology; communication and journalism related; communication/speech communication and rhetoric; comparative literature; computer science; diagnostic medical sonography and ultrasound technology; economics; education; elementary education; engineering science; English; environmental science; finance; fine/studio arts; health science; health/health-care administration; health/medical preparatory programs related; history; information science/studies; international business/trade/commerce; international relations and affairs; international/global studies; journalism related; marketing/marketing management; mathematics; molecular biology; music; nuclear medical technology; nursing (registered nurse training); nutrition sciences; organizational behavior; philosophy; physics; political science and government; pre-pharmacy studies; psychology; secondary education; social sciences; sociology; Spanish; special education; theology.

Bennington College
Acting; American government and politics; American history; American literature; American studies; animation, interactive technology, video graphics and special effects; anthropology; architecture; area, ethnic, cultural, and gender studies related; Asian studies; astronomy; biology/biological sciences; botany/plant biology; cell and molecular biology; ceramic arts and ceramics; chemistry; child development; Chinese; cinematography and film/video production; computer and information sciences; computer science; creative writing; dance; design and visual communications; directing and theatrical production; dramatic/theater arts; drawing; early childhood education; ecology; education; elementary education; English; English composition; English literature (British and Commonwealth); environmental biology; environmental science; environmental studies; European history; European studies; evolutionary biology; film/cinema studies; fine/studio arts; foreign languages and literatures; French; gay/lesbian studies; Germanic languages; history; humanities; intermedia/multimedia; international relations and affairs; international/global studies; Italian; Japanese; jazz/jazz studies; Jewish/Judaic studies; journalism; Latin American studies; liberal arts and sciences and humanities related; liberal arts and sciences/liberal studies; mathematics; mathematics and computer science; middle school education; music; music history, literature, and theory; music performance; music theory and composition; musicology and ethnomusicology; painting; peace studies and conflict resolution; philosophy; photography; physical sciences; physics; piano and organ; playwriting and screenwriting; political science and government; pre-law studies; premedical studies; printmaking; psychology; sculpture; secondary education; social psychology; social sciences; sociology; Spanish; theater design and technology; theater literature, history and criticism; violin, viola, guitar and other stringed instruments; visual and performing arts; voice and opera; women's studies; zoology/animal biology.

Bentley University
Accounting; accounting related; business administration and management; business, management, and marketing related; business/corporate communications; business/managerial economics; computer and information sciences; finance; history; interdisciplinary studies; liberal arts and sciences/liberal studies; marketing/marketing management; mass communication/media; mathematics; multi-/interdisciplinary studies related; philosophy.

Berea College
African American/Black studies; agriculture; applied mathematics related; art; art teacher education; Asian studies; biology/biological sciences; business administration and management; chemistry; computer and information sciences; dramatic/theater arts; economics; education; elementary/middle/secondary education administration; English; family and consumer sciences/human sciences; French; German; health and physical education; history; kinesiology and exercise science; manufacturing technology; mass communication/media; mathematics; middle school education; multi-/interdisciplinary studies related; music;

music teacher education; nursing (registered nurse training); philosophy; physics; political science and government; psychology; religious studies; sociology; Spanish; technology/industrial arts teacher education; women's studies.

Bernard M. Baruch College of the City University of New York

Accounting; actuarial science; advertising; arts management; business administration and management; business/managerial economics; creative writing; economics; education; English; finance; history; human resources management; information science/studies; interdisciplinary studies; international business/trade/commerce; journalism; literature; management information systems; marketing/marketing management; mathematics; music; natural sciences; operations research; philosophy; political science and government; psychology; public administration; public policy analysis; Romance languages; sociology; Spanish; statistics.

Berry College

Accounting; animal sciences; art; biology/biological sciences; chemistry; communication and journalism related; computer science; early childhood education; economics; engineering technology; English; environmental science; exercise physiology; finance; French; German; history; international relations and affairs; marketing/marketing management; mathematics; mathematics teacher education; middle school education; multi-/interdisciplinary studies related; music; music management and merchandising; music teacher education; nursing (registered nurse training); philosophy and religious studies related; physical education teaching and coaching; physics; political science and government; psychology; social sciences; Spanish; theater/theater arts management.

Bethel University

Accounting and finance; area, ethnic, cultural, and gender studies related; art; art history, criticism and conservation; art teacher education; athletic training; biblical studies; biological and biomedical sciences related; biology teacher education; biology/biological sciences; business administration and management; business teacher education; chemistry; chemistry teacher education; communication/speech communication and rhetoric; community health services counseling; computer and information sciences; dramatic/theater arts; economics; elementary education; engineering science; English; English as a second/foreign language (teaching); English/language arts teacher education; environmental science; environmental studies; fine/studio arts; French; French language teacher education; health and physical education; health teacher education; history; international relations and affairs; journalism; kinesiology and exercise science; liberal arts and sciences/liberal studies; mass communication/media; mathematics; mathematics teacher education; multi-/interdisciplinary studies related; music; music performance; music teacher education; nursing (registered nurse training); peace studies and conflict resolution; philosophy; physical education teaching and coaching; physics; physics teacher education; political science and government; psychology; religious/sacred music; social sciences; social studies teacher education; social work; Spanish; Spanish language teacher education; youth ministry.

Biola University

Anthropology; biblical studies; biochemistry; biology/biological sciences; chemistry; communication disorders; communication/speech communication and rhetoric; computer and information sciences; elementary education; engineering physics; English; fine arts related; foreign languages and literatures; history; humanities; journalism; kinesiology and exercise science; mathematics; missionary studies and missiology; music theory and composition; nursing (registered nurse training); philosophy; physical education teaching and coaching; physical sciences; political science and government; psychology; radio and television; religious education; religious/sacred music; social sciences; sociology; Spanish.

Birmingham-Southern College

Accounting; art; art history, criticism and conservation; art teacher education; Asian studies; biology/biological sciences; business

administration and management; chemistry; computer science; dance; dramatic/theater arts; drawing; economics; education; education (multiple levels); elementary education; English; environmental studies; film/video and photographic arts related; fine arts related; fine/studio arts; French; German; history; interdisciplinary studies; international business/trade/commerce; mathematics; music; music history, literature, and theory; music teacher education; music theory and composition; painting; philosophy; physics; piano and organ; political science and government; pre-dentistry studies; pre-law studies; premedical studies; printmaking; psychology; religious studies; sculpture; secondary education; sociology; Spanish; voice and opera.

Boston College

Accounting; ancient/classical Greek; art history, criticism and conservation; biochemistry; biology/biological sciences; business administration and management; business/managerial economics; chemistry; classics and languages, literatures and linguistics; communication/speech communication and rhetoric; computer and information sciences; computer science; dramatic/theater arts; economics; elementary education; English; film/cinema studies; finance; fine/studio arts; French; geology/earth science; geophysics and seismology; German; Hispanic American, Puerto Rican, and Mexican American/Chicano studies; history; human development and family studies; human resources management; interdisciplinary studies; Italian; kindergarten/preschool education; Latin; management information systems; marketing/marketing management; mathematics; music; nursing (registered nurse training); operations management; philosophy; physics; political science and government; psychology; Russian; Russian studies; secondary education; Slavic languages; sociology; Spanish; theology.

Boston University

Accounting; acting; aerospace, aeronautical and astronautical engineering; American studies; ancient/classical Greek; animal physiology; anthropology; archeology; area studies related; art history, criticism and conservation; art teacher education; Asian studies (East); astronomy; astrophysics; athletic training; bilingual and multilingual education; biochemistry; biological and biomedical sciences related; biology/biological sciences; biomedical/medical engineering; business administration and management; chemistry; chemistry teacher education; cinematography and film/video production; classics and languages, literatures and linguistics; clinical laboratory science/medical technology; commercial and advertising art; communication disorders; communication/speech communication and rhetoric; computer engineering; computer science; dental laboratory technology; drama and dance teacher education; drawing; ecology; economics; education; education (specific levels and methods) related; electrical, electronics and communications engineering; elementary education; engineering; engineering related; English; English/language arts teacher education; environmental studies; ethnic, cultural minority, and gender studies related; finance; foreign language teacher education; foreign languages and literatures; French; geography; geology/earth science; German; health science; history; hospitality administration; hotel/motel administration; industrial engineering; information science/studies; interdisciplinary studies; international business/trade/commerce; international finance; international relations and affairs; Italian; journalism; journalism related; kindergarten/preschool education; kinesiology and exercise science; Latin; Latin American studies; legal assistant/paralegal; linguistics; management information systems; marine biology and biological oceanography; marketing research; marketing/marketing management; mass communication/media; mathematics; mathematics and computer science; mathematics teacher education; mechanical engineering; modern Greek; molecular biology; music history, literature, and theory; music performance; music teacher education; music theory and composition; neuroscience; nutrition sciences; occupational therapy; operations management; organizational behavior; painting; parks, recreation and leisure; philosophy; physical education teaching and coaching; physical therapy; physics; piano and organ; political science and government; pre-dentistry studies; psychology; public relations/image management; radio and television; rehabilitation therapy; religious studies; Russian; Russian studies; science teacher education; sculpture; social sciences related; social studies teacher education; sociology; Spanish; special education; special education (hearing impaired); speech/theater education; theater design and technology; theater literature, history and criticism; urban studies/affairs; voice and opera.

Bowdoin College

African studies; ancient studies; anthropology; archeology; art; art history, criticism and conservation; Asian studies; biochemistry; biology/biological sciences; chemical physics; chemistry; classical, ancient Mediterranean and Near Eastern studies and archaeology; classics and languages, literatures and linguistics; computer science; econometrics and quantitative economics; economics; English; environmental studies; European studies (Central and Eastern); fine/studio arts; French; geochemistry; geology/earth science; geophysics and seismology; German; history; interdisciplinary studies; Latin American studies; mathematics; mathematics and computer science; music; neuroscience; philosophy; physics; political science and government; psychology; religious studies; Romance languages; Russian; sociology; Spanish; theater literature, history and criticism; women's studies.

Bradley University

Accounting; acting; acting/directing; actuarial science; advertising; animation, interactive technology, video graphics and special effects; art; art history, criticism and conservation; biochemistry; biology/biological sciences; business administration and management; business/managerial economics; cell and molecular biology; ceramic arts and ceramics; chemistry; civil engineering; civil engineering related; clinical laboratory science/medical technology; communication/speech communication and rhetoric; computer engineering; computer science; construction engineering; consumer merchandising/retailing management; criminal justice/law enforcement administration; dietetics; directing and theatrical production; dramatic/theater arts; drawing; early childhood education; economics; education (specific levels and methods) related; education (specific subject areas) related; electrical, electronics and communications engineering; elementary education; engineering physics; English; entrepreneurship; environmental science; family and consumer sciences/human sciences; family resource management; finance; fine/studio arts; French; German; graphic design; health professions related; health science; history; human resources management; humanities; industrial engineering; information science/studies; insurance; international business/trade/commerce; international relations and affairs; journalism; law and legal studies related; liberal arts and sciences/liberal studies; management information systems; manufacturing engineering; manufacturing technology; marketing/marketing management; mathematics; mechanical engineering; music; music management and merchandising; music performance; music teacher education; music theory and composition; nursing (registered nurse training); painting; philosophy; photography; photojournalism; physics; political science and government; printmaking; psychology; public relations/image management; radio and television; religious studies; sculpture; selling skills and sales; small business administration; social work; sociology; Spanish; special education (mentally retarded); special education (specific learning disabilities).

Brandeis University

African American/Black studies; American studies; anthropology; art history, criticism and conservation; Asian studies (East); biochemistry; biology/biological sciences; biophysics; chemistry; classics and languages, literatures and linguistics; comparative literature; computer science; creative writing; dramatic/theater arts; economics; education; English; environmental studies; European studies; film/cinema studies; fine/studio arts; French; German; health/health-care administration; Hebrew; history; international/global studies; Latin American studies; linguistics; mathematics; multi-/interdisciplinary studies related; music; Near and Middle Eastern studies; neuroscience; philosophy; physics; political science and government related; psychology; Russian; sociology; women's studies.

Brigham Young University

Accounting related; acting; actuarial science; advertising; agribusiness; agricultural business and management; agricultural economics; ancient/classical Greek; animation, interactive technology, video graphics and special effects; applied economics; astronomy; athletic training; ballet; biomedical sciences; biophysics; broadcast journalism; business family and consumer sciences/human sciences; cartography; ceramic arts and ceramics; child development; child-care and support services management; child-care provision; cinematography and film/video production; clinical laboratory science/medical technology; communication and journalism related; crafts, folk art and artisanry; dance related; directing and theatrical production; dramatic/theater arts and stagecraft related; drawing; early childhood education; education (specific levels and methods) related; education (specific subject areas) related; education related; English as a second/foreign language (teaching); English composition; entrepreneurship; environmental science; family and consumer economics related; family and consumer sciences/human sciences; family and consumer sciences/human sciences business services related; family resource management; film/cinema studies; film/video and photographic arts related; financial planning and services; fine/studio arts; food technology and processing; geography related; geological and earth sciences/geosciences related; graphic design; Hebrew; home furnishings and equipment installation; human development and family studies; human resources management; illustration; information technology; international finance; jazz/jazz studies; journalism; kinesiology and exercise science; Korean; language interpretation and translation; Latin teacher education; liberal arts and sciences and humanities related; liberal arts and sciences/liberal studies; linguistic and comparative language studies related; logistics and materials management; manufacturing engineering; microbiology; music history, literature, and theory; music pedagogy; music related; Norwegian; organizational communication; painting; parks, recreation, and leisure related; physics related; physiology; piano and organ; playwriting and screenwriting; prenursing studies; printmaking; psychology teacher education; public policy analysis; public relations, advertising, and applied communication related; radio, television, and digital communication related; science teacher education; sculpture; social psychology; social science teacher education; soil sciences related; special education; speech and rhetoric; speech teacher education; Swedish; theater design and technology; therapeutic recreation; veterinary/animal health technology; violin, viola, guitar and other stringed instruments; visual and performing arts related; voice and opera; work and family studies.

Brown University

African American/Black studies; American studies; anthropology; applied mathematics; archeology; architectural history and criticism; art; art history, criticism and conservation; Asian studies (East); Asian studies (South); behavioral sciences; biochemistry; biology/biological sciences; biomedical sciences; biomedical/medical engineering; biophysics; chemical engineering; chemistry; civil engineering; classics and languages, literatures and linguistics; cognitive psychology and psycholinguistics; comparative literature; computer engineering; computer science; creative writing; development economics and international development; dramatic/theater arts; economics; education; electrical, electronics and communications engineering; engineering; engineering physics; English; environmental science; environmental studies; film/cinema studies; fine/studio arts; French; French studies; geochemistry; geology/earth science; geophysics and seismology; German; German studies; Hispanic American, Puerto Rican, and Mexican American/Chicano studies; history; international relations and affairs; Italian; Italian studies; Jewish/Judaic studies; Latin American studies; linguistics; marine biology and biological oceanography; materials engineering; mathematics; mathematics and computer science; mechanical engineering; medieval and Renaissance studies; molecular biology; music; music related; musicology and ethnomusicology; Near and Middle Eastern studies; neuroscience; organizational behavior; philosophy; physics; political science and government; psychology; religious studies; Russian studies; sociology; Spanish; urban studies/affairs; visual and performing arts; women's studies.

Bryan College (TN)

Biblical studies; biology teacher education; biology/biological sciences; business administration and management; Christian studies; communication/speech communication and rhetoric; computer science; computer teacher education; dramatic/theater arts; elementary education; English; English/language arts teacher education; health and physical education; history; history teacher education; liberal arts and sciences and humanities related; liberal arts and sciences/liberal studies; mathematics; mathematics and computer science; mathematics teacher education; music; music teacher education; physical education teaching and coaching; psychology; psychology teacher education; religious education; Spanish; Spanish language teacher education.

Bryn Mawr College

Ancient/classical Greek; anthropology; archeology; art; art history, criticism and conservation; Asian studies (East); astronomy; biology/biological sciences; chemistry; classics and classical languages related; classics and languages, literatures and linguistics; comparative literature; economics; English; French; geology/earth science; German; history; Italian; Latin; mathematics; Middle/Near Eastern and Semitic languages related; music; philosophy; physics; political science and government; psychology; religious studies; Romance languages; Russian; sociology; Spanish; urban studies/affairs.

Bucknell University

Accounting; animal behavior and ethology; anthropology; area studies; art; art history, criticism and conservation; Asian studies (East); biochemistry; biology/biological sciences; biomedical/medical engineering; biopsychology; business administration and management; cell and molecular biology; chemical engineering; chemistry; civil engineering; classics and languages, literatures and linguistics; computer and information sciences; computer engineering; creative writing; dramatic/theater arts; early childhood education; econometrics and quantitative economics; economics; education; educational statistics and research methods; electrical, electronics and communications engineering; elementary education; English; environmental studies; fine/studio arts; French; geography; geology/earth science; German; history; humanities; interdisciplinary studies; international relations and affairs; kindergarten/preschool education; Latin American studies; mathematics; mechanical engineering; multi-/interdisciplinary studies related; music; music history, literature, and theory; music performance; music teacher education; music theory and composition; neuroscience; philosophy; physics; political science and government; psychology; religious studies; Russian; secondary education; sociology; Spanish; visual and performing arts; women's studies.

Butler University

Accounting; actuarial science; anthropology; arts management; biology/biological sciences; chemistry; classical, ancient Mediterranean and Near Eastern studies and archaeology; communication disorders; communication/speech communication and rhetoric; computer and information sciences; creative writing; criminology; dance; digital communication and media/multimedia; dramatic/theater arts; early childhood education; economics; elementary education; engineering physics; English; finance; French; German; history; international business/trade/commerce; international relations and affairs; journalism; kindergarten/preschool education; Latin; liberal arts and sciences/liberal studies; management information systems; marketing/marketing management; mathematics; middle school education; modern Greek; music; music history, literature, and theory; music management and merchandising; music performance; music teacher education; music theory and composition; pharmacy; philosophy; philosophy and religious studies related; physician assistant; physics; piano and organ; political science and government; psychology; radio and television; recording arts technology; religious studies; science, technology and society; secondary education; sociology; Spanish; speech and rhetoric; urban studies/affairs; violin, viola, guitar and other stringed instruments; voice and opera; wind/percussion instruments.

California Institute of Technology

Applied mathematics; astrophysics; biology/biological sciences; business/managerial economics; chemical engineering; chemistry; computational mathematics; computer engineering; computer science; economics; electrical, electronics and communications engineering; English; environmental/environmental health engineering; geochemistry; geology/earth science; geophysics and seismology; history; history of science and technology; materials science; mathematics; mechanical engineering; philosophy; physics; planetary astronomy and science; political science and government.

California Polytechnic State University, San Luis Obispo

Aerospace, aeronautical and astronautical engineering; agribusiness; agricultural mechanization; agricultural teacher education; agricultural/biological engineering and bioengineering; agronomy and crop science; animal sciences; architectural engineering; architecture; biochemistry; biology/biological sciences; biomedical/medical engineering; business administration and management; business administration, management and operations related; chemistry; city/urban, community and regional planning; civil engineering; civil engineering related; computer engineering; computer science; computer systems analysis; dairy science; dietetics; dramatic/theater arts; economics; electrical, electronics and communications engineering; engineering science; English; environmental/environmental health engineering; ethnic, cultural minority, and gender studies related; fine/studio arts; food science; foreign languages and literatures; forestry; geology/earth science; graphic communications; health and physical education; history; horticultural science; industrial engineering; journalism; kindergarten/preschool education; landscape architecture; liberal arts and sciences/liberal studies; materials engineering; mathematics; mechanical engineering; medical microbiology and bacteriology; music; natural resources and conservation related; ornamental horticulture; parks, recreation and leisure; philosophy; physics; political science and government; psychology; social sciences; soil science and agronomy; speech and rhetoric; statistics.

Calvin College

Accounting; art; art history, criticism and conservation; art teacher education; Asian studies; audiology and speech-language pathology; biblical studies; bilingual and multilingual education; biochemistry; biological and physical sciences; biology/biological sciences; biotechnology; business administration and management; business/corporate communications; chemical engineering; chemistry; civil engineering; classics and languages, literatures and linguistics; communication/speech communication and rhetoric; computer science; conducting; development economics and international development; digital communication and media/multimedia; dramatic/theater arts; economics; electrical, electronics and communications engineering; elementary education; engineering; English; English as a second/foreign language (teaching); environmental studies; film/cinema studies; fine/studio arts; French; geography; geology/earth science; German; Germanic languages related; history; interdisciplinary studies; international relations and affairs; kinesiology and exercise science; Latin; management information systems; mass communication/media; mathematics; mechanical engineering; modern Greek; music; music history, literature, and theory; music performance; music teacher education; music theory and composition; natural sciences; nursing (registered nurse training); occupational therapy; parks, recreation and leisure; philosophy; physical education teaching and coaching; physical sciences; physics; piano and organ; political science and government; pre-dentistry studies; pre-law studies; pre-veterinary studies; premedical studies; psychology; public administration; religious studies; religious/sacred music; science teacher education; secondary education; social sciences; social work; sociology; Spanish; special education; speech and rhetoric; sport and fitness administration/management; theology; therapeutic recreation; voice and opera.

Canisius College

Accounting; accounting technology and bookkeeping; anthropology; art history, criticism and conservation; athletic training; biochemistry; business/commerce; business/managerial economics; chemistry; communication/speech communication and rhetoric; computer science; criminal justice/law enforcement administration; economics; education (multiple levels); elementary education; English; entrepreneurship; environmental science; European studies; finance; French; German; health and physical education; history; international business/trade/commerce; international relations and affairs; management information systems; marketing/marketing management; mathematics; music; philosophy; physical education teaching and coaching; physics; political science and government; psychology; religious studies; secondary education; sociology; Spanish; special education; special education (early childhood); urban studies/affairs.

Carleton College

African studies; American studies; ancient/classical Greek; anthropology; art history, criticism and conservation; Asian studies; biology/biological sciences; chemistry; classics and languages, literatures and linguistics; computer science; dramatic/theater arts; economics; English; film/cinema studies; fine/studio arts; French; French studies; geology/earth science; German; history; interdisciplinary studies; international relations and affairs; Latin; Latin American studies; mathematics; music; philosophy; physics; political science and government; psychology; religious studies; Romance languages; Russian; Russian studies; sociology; Spanish; women's studies.

Carnegie Mellon University

Anthropology related; applied mathematics; architectural history and criticism; architectural technology; architecture; architecture related; art; astrophysics; behavioral sciences; biological and biomedical sciences related; biology/biological sciences; biomedical/medical engineering; biophysics; biopsychology; business administration and management; business/managerial economics; chemical engineering; chemical physics; chemistry; chemistry related; Chinese; civil engineering; cognitive science; communication and media related; computational mathematics; computer engineering related; computer science; creative writing; dramatic/theater arts; economics; engineering related; English; English as a second/foreign language (teaching); ethics; ethnic, cultural minority, and gender studies related; European history; European studies; foreign languages and literatures; French; German; history related; industrial design; information science/studies; international relations and affairs; Japanese; Latin American studies; liberal arts and sciences/liberal studies; logic; materials science; mathematical statistics and probability; mathematics and statistics related; mechanical engineering; music performance; music theory and composition; natural resources management and policy; operations research; philosophy; physics; physics related; piano and organ; political science and government; psychology; public policy analysis; science, technology and society; social sciences related; Spanish; statistics; systems science and theory; technical and business writing; violin, viola, guitar and other stringed instruments; voice and opera.

Carroll College

Accounting; applied mathematics; biology teacher education; biology/biological sciences; business administration and management; chemistry; chemistry teacher education; civil engineering; classics and languages, literatures and linguistics; communication/speech communication and rhetoric; community health services counseling; computer science; elementary education; English; English as a second/foreign language (teaching); English composition; English/language arts teacher education; environmental studies; ethics; French; health and physical education; health services/allied health/health sciences; history; history teacher education; international relations and affairs; mathematics; mathematics teacher education; multi-/interdisciplinary studies related; nursing (registered nurse training); philosophy; physical education teaching and coaching; political science and government; psychology; public administration; public relations/image management; social science teacher education; social studies teacher education; sociology; Spanish; Spanish language teacher education; speech teacher education; theology; visual and performing arts.

Carroll University

Accounting; actuarial science; animal behavior and ethology; applied mathematics; applied mathematics related; art; art teacher education; athletic training; biochemistry; biology teacher education; biology/biological sciences; business administration and management; chemistry; chemistry teacher education; clinical laboratory science/medical technology; commercial and advertising art; communication/speech communication and rhetoric; computer and information sciences; computer software engineering; creative writing; dramatic/theater arts; early childhood education; education; elementary education; engineering physics; English; English/language arts teacher education; environmental science; European studies; finance; fine/studio arts; foreign language teacher education; forensic science and technology; graphic communications; health and physical education; health teacher education; history; history teacher education; human resources management; information science/studies; international relations and affairs; journalism; kinesiology and exercise science; management information systems; marketing/marketing management; mathematics; mathematics teacher education; medical radiologic technology; middle school education; music; music teacher education; natural resources/conservation; nursing (registered nurse training); organizational behavior; organizational communication; parks, recreation and leisure facilities management; photography; physical education teaching and coaching; political science and government; pre-dentistry studies; pre-pharmacy studies; pre-veterinary studies; premedical studies; printing management; psychology; psychology teacher education; public relations, advertising, and applied communication related; public relations/image management; religious studies; science teacher education; small business administration; social science teacher education; social studies teacher education; sociology; Spanish; Spanish language teacher education; trade and industrial teacher education.

Carson-Newman College

Accounting; ancient Near Eastern and biblical languages; art; art teacher education; athletic training; biblical studies; biology/biological sciences; broadcast journalism; business administration and management; business teacher education; business/managerial economics; chemistry; child development; clinical laboratory science/medical technology; commercial and advertising art; computer science; consumer services and advocacy; creative writing; developmental and child psychology; dietetics; divinity/ministry; dramatic/theater arts; drawing; economics; education; elementary education; English; family and consumer economics related; family and consumer sciences/home economics teacher education; family and consumer sciences/human sciences; fashion merchandising; film/cinema studies; foods, nutrition, and wellness; French; history; hospital and health-care facilities administration; human services; information science/studies; interdisciplinary studies; interior design; international economics; journalism; kindergarten/preschool education; kinesiology and exercise science; liberal arts and sciences/liberal studies; literature; management information systems; marketing/marketing management; mass communication/media; mathematics; music; music teacher education; music theory and composition; nursing (registered nurse training); parks, recreation and leisure; philosophy; photography; physical education teaching and coaching; physics; physics related; piano and organ; political science and government; psychology; religious studies; secondary education; small business administration; sociology; Spanish; special education; speech and rhetoric; voice and opera.

Case Western Reserve University

Accounting; aerospace, aeronautical and astronautical engineering; American studies; anthropology; applied mathematics; art history, criticism and conservation; art teacher education; Asian studies; astronomy; biochemistry; biology/biological sciences; biomathematics and bioinformatics related; biomedical/medical engineering; business administration and management; chemical engineering; chemistry; civil engineering; classics and languages, literatures and linguistics; cognitive science; communication disorders; comparative literature; computer engineering; computer science; dietetics; dramatic/theater arts; economics; electrical, electronics and communications engineering;

engineering; engineering physics; English; environmental studies; evolutionary biology; French; French studies; geology/earth science; German; German studies; gerontology; history; history and philosophy of science and technology; human nutrition; international relations and affairs; international/global studies; Japanese studies; materials engineering; materials science; mathematics; mechanical engineering; music; music teacher education; natural sciences; nursing (registered nurse training); nutrition sciences; philosophy; political science and government; polymer/plastics engineering; psychology; religious studies; sociology; Spanish; statistics; systems engineering; women's studies.

Cedarville University

Accounting; American studies; athletic training; biblical studies; biology teacher education; biology/biological sciences; business administration and management; cell and molecular biology; chemistry; chemistry teacher education; clinical laboratory science/medical technology; communication and journalism related; communication/speech communication and rhetoric; communications technology; computer engineering; computer science; criminal justice/law enforcement administration; dramatic/theater arts; early childhood education; education related; electrical, electronics and communications engineering; English; English/language arts teacher education; environmental biology; finance; fine/studio arts; forensic science and technology; graphic design; health and physical education; health teacher education; health/medical preparatory programs related; history; history related; interdisciplinary studies; international business/trade/commerce; international relations and affairs; international/global studies; journalism; kinesiology and exercise science; management information systems; marketing/marketing management; mass communication/media; mathematics; mathematics teacher education; mechanical engineering; middle school education; missionary studies and missiology; music; music pedagogy; music performance; music teacher education; music theory and composition; nursing (registered nurse training); organizational communication; pastoral studies/counseling; philosophy; physical education teaching and coaching; physics; physics teacher education; political communication; political science and government; pre-dentistry studies; pre-law studies; pre-veterinary studies; premedical studies; psychology; psychology related; public administration; radio and television; religious education; religious/sacred music; science teacher education; social studies teacher education; social work; sociology; Spanish; Spanish language teacher education; special education; sport and fitness administration/management; technical and business writing; theater/theater arts management; theology; theology and religious vocations related; youth ministry.

Central College

Accounting; actuarial science; art; athletic training; biology/biological sciences; business administration and management; chemistry; communication/speech communication and rhetoric; computer science; dramatic/theater arts; economics; elementary education; English; environmental studies; French; general studies; German studies; history; information science/studies; interdisciplinary studies; international business/trade/commerce; international/global studies; kinesiology and exercise science; linguistics; mathematics; mathematics and computer science; music; music teacher education; natural sciences; philosophy; physics; political science and government; psychology; religious studies; social sciences; sociology; Spanish.

Centre College

Anthropology; art; art history, criticism and conservation; biochemistry; biology/biological sciences; chemistry; classics and languages, literatures and linguistics; computer science; dramatic/theater arts; economics; elementary education; English; French; German; history; international relations and affairs; mathematics; molecular biology; music; philosophy; physics; physiological psychology/psychobiology; political science and government; psychology; religious studies; sociology; Spanish.

Chapman University

Accounting; acting; advertising; American history; art; art history, criticism and conservation; athletic training; biochemistry; biology/

biological sciences; broadcast journalism; business administration and management; business/managerial economics; chemistry; cinematography and film/video production; communication/speech communication and rhetoric; computer and information sciences; computer science; conducting; creative writing; dance; dramatic/theater arts; English; European history; film/cinema studies; fine/studio arts; French; graphic design; health communication; health services administration; history; liberal arts and sciences/liberal studies; mathematics; music; music performance; music teacher education; music theory and composition; peace studies and conflict resolution; philosophy; playwriting and screenwriting; political science and government; pre-dentistry studies; pre-veterinary studies; premedical studies; psychology; public relations/image management; religious studies; social work; sociology; Spanish; voice and opera; wind/percussion instruments.

Christendom College

Classics and languages, literatures and linguistics; history; liberal arts and sciences/liberal studies; literature; philosophy; political science and government; theology.

Christian Brothers University

Biology teacher education; biomedical sciences; business administration and management; chemical engineering; chemistry; chemistry teacher education; civil engineering; computer science; education; electrical, electronics and communications engineering; elementary education; engineering physics; English; English/language arts teacher education; environmental/environmental health engineering; fine/studio arts; history; history teacher education; liberal arts and sciences/liberal studies; mathematics; mathematics teacher education; mechanical engineering; natural sciences; philosophy; physics; physics teacher education; psychology; public relations; religious studies.

Claremont McKenna College

Accounting; African American/Black studies; American government and politics; American studies; anthropology; archeology; area studies related; area, ethnic, cultural, and gender studies related; art; art history, criticism and conservation; Asian American studies; Asian studies; biochemistry; biology/biological sciences; biophysics; chemistry; Chinese; Chinese studies; classics and languages, literatures and linguistics; computer and information sciences; computer science; dance; dramatic/theater arts; East Asian languages related; economics; economics related; engineering; engineering related; engineering science; engineering/industrial management; English; environmental studies; ethnic, cultural minority, and gender studies related; European studies; European studies (Western); film/cinema studies; fine/studio arts; French; French studies; German; German studies; Germanic languages; Hispanic American, Puerto Rican, and Mexican American/Chicano studies; history; international business/trade/commerce; international economics; international relations and affairs; Italian; Japanese; Japanese studies; Korean studies; Latin; Latin American studies; legal studies; literature; mathematics; modern Greek; modern languages; music; music related; Near and Middle Eastern studies; Pacific area/Pacific rim studies; philosophy; philosophy and religious studies related; philosophy related; physics; physiological psychology/psychobiology; political science and government; political science and government related; pre-dentistry studies; pre-law studies; premedical studies; psychology; religious studies; religious studies related; Russian; Russian studies; sociology; South Asian languages; Spanish; visual and performing arts; visual and performing arts related; women's studies.

Clarke College

Accounting; advertising; art; art history, criticism and conservation; art teacher education; athletic training; biology/biological sciences; business administration and management; chemistry; dramatic/theater arts; economics; education; elementary education; English; fine/studio arts; history; information science/studies; international business/trade/commerce; kindergarten/preschool education; liberal arts and sciences/liberal studies; management information systems; marketing/marketing management; mass communication/media; mathematics; middle school education; music; music teacher education; nursing science; philosophy; physical education teaching and coaching; physical therapy; psychology; public relations/image management; religious studies; secondary education; social work; Spanish; sport and fitness administration/management.

Clarkson University

Accounting; aerospace, aeronautical and astronautical engineering; American literature; American studies; applied mathematics; biochemistry; biology/biological sciences; biophysics; biotechnology; business administration and management; cell biology and histology; chemical engineering; chemistry; civil engineering; communication/speech communication and rhetoric; computer and information sciences; computer engineering; computer science; computer software engineering; construction engineering; digital communication and media/multimedia; e-commerce; ecology; electrical, electronics and communications engineering; engineering; entrepreneurship; environmental health; environmental studies; environmental/environmental health engineering; finance; history; human resources management; humanities; industrial and organizational psychology; information resources management; interdisciplinary studies; international business/trade/commerce; liberal arts and sciences/liberal studies; logistics and materials management; management information systems; manufacturing engineering; marketing/marketing management; materials engineering; materials science; mathematics; mechanical engineering; molecular biology; nonprofit management; occupational health and industrial hygiene; operations management; physics; political science and government; pre-dentistry studies; pre-law studies; pre-veterinary studies; premedical studies; psychology; social sciences; sociology; statistics; structural engineering; technical and business writing; toxicology.

Clark University

Art history, criticism and conservation; Asian studies; biochemistry; biology/biological sciences; business administration and management; chemistry; classics and languages, literatures and linguistics; commercial and advertising art; comparative literature; computer science; cultural studies; development economics and international development; dramatic/theater arts; ecology; economics; education; elementary education; engineering; English; film/cinema studies; fine/studio arts; French; geography; geology/earth science; history; interdisciplinary studies; international relations and affairs; Jewish/Judaic studies; mass communication/media; mathematics; middle school education; modern languages; molecular biology; music; natural resources management and policy; neuroscience; peace studies and conflict resolution; philosophy; physics; political science and government; pre-dentistry studies; pre-law studies; pre-veterinary studies; premedical studies; psychology; secondary education; sociology; Spanish; women's studies.

Clemson University

Accounting; agricultural business and management; agricultural economics; agricultural mechanization; agricultural teacher education; agricultural/biological engineering and bioengineering; animal sciences; architecture; biochemistry; biology/biological sciences; biomedical/medical engineering; business administration and management; business, management, and marketing related; ceramic sciences and engineering; chemical engineering; chemistry; civil engineering; communication and journalism related; computer and information sciences; computer engineering; computer programming; computer science; construction management; counselor education/school counseling and guidance; early childhood education; economics; electrical, electronics and communications engineering; elementary education; engineering mechanics; engineering/industrial management; English; finance; fishing and fisheries sciences and management; food science; forest/forest resources management; genetics; geology/earth science; graphic communications; health professions related; health science; history; horticultural science; human resources development; industrial design; industrial engineering; information science/studies; international business/trade/commerce; international public health; landscape architecture; management information systems; marketing/marketing management; mass com-

munications; materials engineering; mathematics; mathematics teacher education; mechanical engineering; microbiology; modern languages; natural resources/conservation; nursing (registered nurse training); parks, recreation and leisure facilities management; philosophy; physics; political science and government; polymer chemistry; psychology; science teacher education; science technologies related; secondary education; sociology; special education; speech and rhetoric; textile sciences and engineering; turf and turfgrass management; visual and performing arts; visual and performing arts related; wildlife biology.

Coe College

Accounting; acting; African American/Black studies; American studies; architecture; area, ethnic, cultural, and gender studies related; art; art teacher education; Asian studies; athletic training; biochemistry; biological and physical sciences; biology/biological sciences; business administration and management; ceramic arts and ceramics; chemistry; classics and languages, literatures and linguistics; computer science; creative writing; directing and theatrical production; dramatic/theater arts; economics; education; elementary education; English; environmental studies; fine/studio arts; French; French studies; German; German studies; health and physical education related; history; interdisciplinary studies; liberal arts and sciences/liberal studies; literature; mathematics; molecular biology; music; music performance; music teacher education; music theory and composition; nursing (registered nurse training); painting; philosophy; photography; physical education teaching and coaching; physical sciences; physics; political science and government; pre-dentistry studies; pre-law studies; pre-veterinary studies; premedical studies; psychology; public relations/image management; religious studies; science teacher education; secondary education; sociology; Spanish; Spanish and Iberian studies; speech and rhetoric; theater design and technology.

Colby College

African American/Black studies; American studies; anthropology; art; art history, criticism and conservation; Asian studies (East); biochemistry; biology/biological sciences; cell biology and histology; chemistry; classics and languages, literatures and linguistics; computer science; creative writing; dramatic/theater arts; economics; English; environmental science; environmental studies; fine/studio arts; French; geology/earth science; German; history; interdisciplinary studies; international relations and affairs; international/global studies; Latin American studies; mathematics; molecular biology; music; neuroscience; philosophy; physics; political science and government; psychology; religious studies; Russian studies; science, technology and society; sociology; Spanish; women's studies.

Colgate University

African American/Black studies; African studies; American Indian/Native American studies; anthropology; art; art history, criticism and conservation; Asian studies; Asian studies (East); astronomy; astrophysics; biochemistry; biology/biological sciences; chemistry; Chinese; classics and languages, literatures and linguistics; dramatic/theater arts; economics; education; English; environmental biology; environmental studies; French; geography; geology/earth science; German; history; humanities; international relations and affairs; Japanese; Latin; Latin American studies; mathematics; modern Greek; molecular biology; music; natural sciences; neuroscience; peace studies and conflict resolution; philosophy; physical sciences; physics; political science and government; psychology; religious studies; Romance languages; Russian; Russian studies; social sciences; sociology; Spanish; women's studies.

College of Charleston

Accounting; anthropology; art history, criticism and conservation; arts management; astronomy and astrophysics related; athletic training; biochemistry; biology/biological sciences; business administration and management; chemistry; classics and languages, literatures and linguistics; communication/speech communication and rhetoric; computer and information sciences; computer and information sciences related; dramatic/theater arts; early childhood education; economics; elementary education; English; fine/studio arts; French; geology/earth science; German; historic preservation and conservation; history; hospitality administration; information science/studies; international business/trade/commerce; Latin American studies; marine biology and biological oceanography; mathematics; middle school education; music; philosophy; physical education teaching and coaching; physics; political science and government; pre-dentistry studies; premedical studies; psychology; religious studies; sociology; Spanish; special education; urban studies/affairs.

The College of Idaho
Accounting; anthropology; art; biology/biological sciences; business administration and management; chemistry; creative writing; dramatic/theater arts; economics; English; history; international business/trade/commerce; international economics; kinesiology and exercise science; mathematics; music; philosophy; physical education teaching and coaching; physics; political science and government; premedical studies; psychology; religious studies; sociology; Spanish; sport and fitness administration/management.

The College of New Jersey
Accounting; art; art teacher education; biology teacher education; biology/biological sciences; biomedical/medical engineering; business administration and management; business/managerial economics; chemistry; chemistry teacher education; commercial and advertising art; computer and information sciences; computer engineering; criminal justice/law enforcement administration; economics; education; electrical, electronics and communications engineering; elementary education; engineering science; English; English/language arts teacher education; finance; fine/studio arts; history; history teacher education; intermedia/multimedia; international business/trade/commerce; international relations and affairs; kindergarten/preschool education; mathematics; mathematics teacher education; mechanical engineering; multi-/interdisciplinary studies related; music; music teacher education; nursing (registered nurse training); philosophy; physical education teaching and coaching; physics; physics teacher education; political science and government; pre-law studies; premedical studies; psychology; secondary education; sociology; Spanish; Spanish language teacher education; special education; special education (hearing impaired); speech and rhetoric; statistics; technology/industrial arts teacher education; women's studies.

College of Saint Benedict
Accounting; art; biochemistry; biological and physical sciences; biology/biological sciences; business administration and management; chemistry; classics and languages, literatures and linguistics; clinical/medical laboratory assistant; computer science; dietetics; dramatic/theater arts; economics; education; elementary education; engineering physics; English; environmental studies; fine/studio arts; foods, nutrition, and wellness; forest sciences and biology; forestry; French; German; history; humanities; liberal arts and sciences/liberal studies; mathematics; mathematics and computer science; music; natural sciences; nursing (registered nurse training); nutrition sciences; occupational therapy; peace studies and conflict resolution; philosophy; physical therapy; physics; political science and government; pre-dentistry studies; pre-law studies; pre-pharmacy studies; pre-theology/pre-ministerial studies; pre-veterinary studies; premedical studies; psychology; religious education; secondary education; social sciences; social work; sociology; Spanish; speech and rhetoric; theology; women's studies.

College of St. Catherine
Accounting; American Sign Language (ASL); art; art history, criticism and conservation; art teacher education; biochemistry; biology teacher education; biology/biological sciences; business administration and management; chemistry; chemistry teacher education; clinical laboratory science/medical technology; computer and information sciences; creative writing; diagnostic medical sonography and ultrasound technology; dietetics; drama and dance teacher education; dramatic/theater arts; economics; education; elementary education; English; English/language

arts teacher education; family and consumer sciences/home economics teacher education; family and consumer sciences/human sciences; fashion merchandising; fashion/apparel design; fine/studio arts; foods, nutrition, and wellness; franchising; French; French language teacher education; health and physical education; health information/medical records technology; history; intercultural/multicultural and diversity studies; international business/trade/commerce; international economics; international relations and affairs; journalism; kindergarten/preschool education; liberal arts and sciences/liberal studies; literature; management information systems; marketing/marketing management; mass communication/media; mathematics; mathematics teacher education; medical radiologic technology; music; music teacher education; nursing (registered nurse training); occupational therapist assistant; occupational therapy; philosophy; physical education teaching and coaching; physical therapist assistant; physics; political science and government; pre-dentistry studies; pre-law studies; pre-veterinary studies; premedical studies; psychology; respiratory care therapy; secondary education; sign language interpretation and translation; social sciences; social studies teacher education; social work; sociology; Spanish; Spanish language teacher education; speech and rhetoric; speech teacher education; substance abuse/addiction counseling; theology; women's studies.

The College of St. Scholastica
Accounting; American native/native American education; applied economics; art; biochemistry; biology/biological sciences; business administration and management; chemistry; Christian studies; communication/speech communication and rhetoric; computer and information sciences; education (K-12); elementary education; English; exercise physiology; finance; health information/medical records administration; health services/allied health/health sciences; history; humanities; international business/trade/commerce; international/global studies; journalism; liberal arts and sciences/liberal studies; marketing/marketing management; mathematics; music performance; natural sciences; nursing (registered nurse training); organizational behavior; physical sciences related; psychology; public relations, advertising, and applied communication related; religious studies; school librarian/school library media; social sciences; social work.

The College of Saint Thomas More
Liberal arts and sciences/liberal studies.

College of the Atlantic
Art; biological and physical sciences; biology/biological sciences; botany/plant biology; ceramic arts and ceramics; computer graphics; drawing; economics; education; elementary education; English; environmental biology; environmental design/architecture; environmental education; environmental studies; evolutionary biology; human ecology; interdisciplinary studies; landscape architecture; legal studies; liberal arts and sciences/liberal studies; literature; marine biology and biological oceanography; maritime science; middle school education; museum studies; music; natural sciences; oceanography; philosophy; pre-veterinary studies; psychology; public policy analysis; science teacher education; secondary education; wildlife biology; zoology/animal biology.

College of the Holy Cross
Accounting; anthropology; art history, criticism and conservation; Asian studies; biology/biological sciences; chemistry; classics and languages, literatures and linguistics; comparative literature; computer science; dramatic/theater arts; economics; English; environmental studies; fine/studio arts; French; German; German studies; history; Italian; literature; mathematics; medieval and Renaissance studies; music; philosophy; physics; political science and government; premedical studies; psychology; religious studies; Russian; Russian studies; sociology; Spanish.

The College of William and Mary
Accounting; African American/Black studies; American studies; anthropology; art; art history, criticism and conservation; athletic training; biology/biological sciences; business administration and management; chemistry; Chinese studies; classics and languages, literatures and

linguistics; computer and information sciences; cultural studies; dramatic/theater arts; economics; English; environmental studies; finance; French; geology/earth science; German; history; interdisciplinary studies; international relations and affairs; Latin American studies; linguistics; marketing/marketing management; mathematics; medieval and Renaissance studies; modern languages; multi-/interdisciplinary studies related; music; neuroscience; philosophy; physics; political science and government; psychology; public policy analysis; religious studies; sociology; women's studies.

The College of Wooster

African American/Black studies; archeology; area, ethnic, cultural, and gender studies related; art history, criticism and conservation; biochemistry; biology/biological sciences; business/managerial economics; chemistry; classics and languages, literatures and linguistics; communication/speech communication and rhetoric; comparative literature; computer science; dramatic/theater arts; economics; English; fine/studio arts; French; geology/earth science; German; German studies; history; interdisciplinary studies; international relations and affairs; Latin; mass communication/media; mathematics; molecular biology; multi-/interdisciplinary studies related; music; music history, literature, and theory; music performance; music teacher education; music theory and composition; music therapy; philosophy; physics; physics related; political science and government; psychology; religious studies; Russian studies; sociology; Spanish; urban studies/affairs; women's studies.

Colorado Christian University

Accounting; art; biblical studies; biological and physical sciences; biology/biological sciences; business administration and management; communication/speech communication and rhetoric; computer and information sciences; dramatic/theater arts; English; fine/studio arts; health and physical education; history; international/global studies; liberal arts and sciences/liberal studies; management information systems; management science; mathematics; music; music performance; music related; music teacher education; political science and government; psychology; social sciences; youth ministry.

The Colorado College

Anthropology; art history, criticism and conservation; Asian studies; biochemistry; biology/biological sciences; chemistry; classics and languages, literatures and linguistics; comparative literature; computer and information sciences related; creative writing; dance; dramatic/theater arts; econometrics and quantitative economics; economics; economics related; English; environmental science; ethnic, cultural minority, and gender studies related; film/cinema studies; fine/studio arts; French; French studies; geology/earth science; German; health and physical education; Hispanic American, Puerto Rican, and Mexican American/Chicano studies; history; international economics; Italian; liberal arts and sciences and humanities related; mathematics; mathematics and computer science; multi-/interdisciplinary studies related; music; neuroscience; philosophy; physics; political science and government; psychology; regional studies; religious studies; Romance languages related; Russian; Russian studies; social sciences related; sociology; Spanish; women's studies.

Colorado School of Mines

Biomedical/medical engineering; chemical engineering; chemistry; economics; engineering; engineering physics; environmental/environmental health engineering; geological/geophysical engineering; mathematics; metallurgical engineering; mining and mineral engineering; petroleum engineering.

Colorado State University

Accounting; actuarial science; agribusiness; agricultural economics; agricultural teacher education; agronomy and crop science; American studies; animal sciences; anthropology; apparel and textile marketing management; applied horticulture; applied horticulture/horticultural business services related; applied mathematics; art history, criticism and conservation; art teacher education; Asian studies; athletic training/sports medicine; biochemistry; biology teacher education; biology/biological sciences; biomedical sciences; botany/plant biology; business administration and management; business teacher education; chemical engineering; chemistry; chemistry teacher education; civil engineering; communication/speech communication and rhetoric; computational mathematics; computer and information sciences; computer engineering; construction engineering technology; creative writing; criminal justice/safety; dance; dietetics; dramatic/theater arts; drawing; economics; education; electrical, electronics and communications engineering; engineering physics; engineering science; English; English/language arts teacher education; environmental/environmental health engineering; equestrian studies; family and consumer sciences/home economics teacher education; family and consumer sciences/human sciences; fashion/apparel design; fiber, textile and weaving arts; finance; fine/studio arts; fire services administration; fishing and fisheries sciences and management; floriculture/floristry management; foods, nutrition, and wellness; foreign languages and literatures; forest sciences and biology; French; French language teacher education; geology/earth science; German; German language teacher education; history; horticultural science; hotel/motel administration; human development and family studies; human nutrition; humanities; information science/studies; interior design; journalism; kinesiology and exercise science; landscape architecture; landscaping and groundskeeping; Latin American studies; liberal arts and sciences/liberal studies; management information systems; marketing/marketing management; mathematics; mathematics teacher education; mechanical engineering; metal and jewelry arts; microbiology; music; music performance; music teacher education; music theory and composition; music therapy; natural resource economics; natural resources management and policy; natural resources/conservation; natural sciences; nutrition science; painting; parks, recreation and leisure facilities management; philosophy; photography; physical sciences; physics; physics teacher education; plant nursery management; political science and government; pre-veterinary studies; printmaking; psychology; public relations/image management; radio and television; range science and management; real estate; restaurant/food services management; sales and marketing/marketing and distribution teacher education; science teacher education; sculpture; social sciences; social studies teacher education; social work; sociology; soil science and agronomy; Spanish; Spanish language teacher education; statistics; turf and turfgrass management; water, wetlands, and marine resources management; zoology/animal biology.

Columbia University

African American/Black studies; American studies; ancient studies; ancient/classical Greek; anthropology; applied mathematics; archeology; architecture; architecture related; art history, criticism and conservation; Asian American studies; Asian studies (East); astronomy; astrophysics; atomic/molecular physics; biochemistry; biology/biological sciences; biomedical/medical engineering; biophysics; biopsychology; chemical engineering; chemistry; civil engineering; classical, ancient Mediterranean and Near Eastern studies and archaeology; classics and languages, literatures and linguistics; comparative literature; computer engineering; computer science; creative writing; dance; dramatic/theater arts; East Asian languages; economics; education (K-12); electrical, electronics and communications engineering; engineering mechanics; engineering physics; engineering/industrial management; English; environmental biology; environmental studies; environmental/environmental health engineering; film/cinema studies; French; French studies; geochemistry; geology/earth science; German; German studies; Hispanic American, Puerto Rican, and Mexican American/Chicano studies; history; industrial engineering; Italian; Italian studies; Latin American studies; linguistics; materials science; mathematics; mechanical engineering; medieval and Renaissance studies; modern Greek; music; Near and Middle Eastern studies; operations research; philosophy; physics; political science and government; psychology; religious studies; Russian; Russian studies; Slavic languages; sociology; Spanish; statistics; urban studies/affairs; visual and performing arts; women's studies.

Concordia College (MN)

Accounting; advertising; art; art history, criticism and conservation; art teacher education; biology teacher education; biology/biological sciences; business administration and management; business/commerce; chemistry; chemistry teacher education; classics and classical languages related; clinical laboratory science/medical technology; communication/speech communication and rhetoric; computer science; dietetics; dramatic/theater arts; economics; education; elementary education; English; English/language arts teacher education; environmental studies; fine/studio arts; foods, nutrition, and wellness; French; French language teacher education; German; German language teacher education; health and physical education; health teacher education; health/health-care administration; history; humanities; international business/trade/commerce; international/global studies; journalism; kinesiology and exercise science; Latin; mass communication/media; mathematics; mathematics teacher education; music; music performance; music teacher education; music theory and composition; nursing (registered nurse training); philosophy; physical education teaching and coaching; physics; physics teacher education; political science and government; pre-dentistry studies; pre-law studies; pre-theology/pre-ministerial studies; pre-veterinary studies; premedical studies; psychology; public relations/image management; radio and television; religious studies; Russian studies; Scandinavian languages; science teacher education; secondary education; social studies teacher education; social work; sociology; Spanish; Spanish language teacher education; speech and rhetoric; voice and opera.

Connecticut College

African studies; American studies; anthropology; architecture; area, ethnic, cultural, and gender studies related; art; art history, criticism and conservation; Asian studies (East); astrophysics; biochemistry; biology/biological sciences; botany/plant biology; cell and molecular biology; chemistry; chemistry related; Chinese; classics and languages, literatures and linguistics; computer science; dance; dramatic/theater arts; ecology; economics; education (multiple levels); elementary education; engineering physics; English; environmental studies; ethnic, cultural minority, and gender studies related; European studies (Central and Eastern); family systems; film/cinema studies; French; German studies; Hispanic American, Puerto Rican, and Mexican American/Chicano studies; history; human development and family studies; human ecology; interdisciplinary studies; international relations and affairs; Italian; Italian studies; Japanese; Latin American studies; mathematics; medieval and Renaissance studies; molecular biology; multi-/interdisciplinary studies related; museum studies; music; music related; music teacher education; neuroscience; philosophy; physics teacher education; political science and government; psychology; religious studies; secondary education; Slavic languages; Slavic studies; social sciences related; sociology; Spanish; Spanish language teacher education; urban studies/affairs; women's studies.

Converse College

Accounting; applied art; art; art history, criticism and conservation; art teacher education; art therapy; biochemistry; biology/biological sciences; business administration and management; chemistry; computer science; dramatic/theater arts; economics; education; elementary education; English; fine/studio arts; French; history; interior design; international business/trade/commerce; kindergarten/preschool education; marketing/marketing management; mathematics; modern languages; music; music history, literature, and theory; music teacher education; music therapy; piano and organ; political science and government; psychology; religious studies; secondary education; sign language interpretation and translation; sociology; Spanish; special education; violin, viola, guitar and other stringed instruments; voice and opera.

Cooper Union for the Advancement of Science and Art

Architecture; chemical engineering; civil engineering; electrical, electronics and communications engineering; engineering; fine/studio arts; mechanical engineering; visual and performing arts.

Cornell College

Anthropology; architecture; art; art history, criticism and conservation; biochemistry; biology/biological sciences; chemistry; classics and languages, literatures and linguistics; computer science; cultural studies; dramatic/theater arts; economics; elementary education; English; environmental studies; ethnic, cultural minority, and gender studies related; French; geology/earth science; German; health and physical education related; history; interdisciplinary studies; international business/trade/commerce; international relations and affairs; kinesiology and exercise science; Latin; Latin American studies; liberal arts and sciences/liberal studies; mathematics; medieval and Renaissance studies; modern Greek; modern languages; multi-/interdisciplinary studies related; music; music teacher education; philosophy; physical education teaching and coaching; physics; political science and government; psychology; religious studies; Russian; secondary education; sociology; Spanish; speech and rhetoric; women's studies.

Cornell University

African American/Black studies; agribusiness; agricultural and horticultural plant breeding; agricultural business and management; agricultural economics; agricultural teacher education; agricultural/biological engineering and bioengineering; agriculture; agronomy and crop science; American studies; animal genetics; animal physiology; animal sciences; anthropology; archeology; architecture; art history, criticism and conservation; Asian studies; astronomy; atmospheric sciences and meteorology; biochemistry; biological and biomedical sciences related; biology teacher education; biology/biological sciences; biometry/biometrics; chemical engineering; chemistry; chemistry teacher education; city/urban, community and regional planning; civil engineering; classics and languages, literatures and linguistics; communication/speech communication and rhetoric; community organization and advocacy; comparative literature; computer science; consumer economics; dance; dramatic/theater arts; ecology; economics; education; educational psychology; electrical, electronics and communications engineering; engineering; engineering physics; English; entomology; environmental design/architecture; environmental science; environmental/environmental health engineering; family and consumer sciences/home economics teacher education; family and consumer sciences/human sciences; fiber, textile and weaving arts; film/cinema studies; fine/studio arts; food science; foods, nutrition, and wellness; French; gay/lesbian studies; geology/earth science; German; German studies; history; horticultural science; hotel/motel administration; human development and family studies; human services; information technology; interdisciplinary studies; international agriculture; Italian; labor and industrial relations; landscape architecture; liberal arts and sciences/liberal studies; linguistics; materials engineering; mathematics; mathematics teacher education; mechanical engineering; microbiology; multi-/interdisciplinary studies related; music; natural resource economics; natural resources/conservation; Near and Middle Eastern studies; nutrition sciences; operations research; ornamental horticulture; philosophy; physics; physics teacher education; plant pathology/phytopathology; plant sciences; political science and government; premedical studies; psychology; public policy analysis; religious studies; restaurant/food services management; Russian; Russian studies; science teacher education; science, technology and society; social sciences; social sciences related; sociology; Spanish; theater design and technology; women's studies.

Cornerstone University

Accounting; biblical studies; biology teacher education; biology/biological sciences; broadcast journalism; business administration and management; business administration, management and operations related; early childhood education; education; elementary education; English; English/language arts teacher education; environmental biology; history; history teacher education; interdisciplinary studies; kinesiology and exercise science; management information systems; marketing/marketing management; mass communication/media; mathematics teacher education; multi-/interdisciplinary studies related; music; music performance; music teacher education; pastoral studies/counseling; physical education teaching and coaching; pre-dentistry studies; pre-theology/pre-ministerial studies; pre-veterinary studies; premedical studies; psychology; science teacher education; secondary education; social science teacher education; social studies teacher education; social work; Spanish; speech and rhetoric.

Covenant College
Biblical studies; biological and physical sciences; biology/biological sciences; business/commerce; chemistry; computer and information sciences; dramatic/theater arts; elementary education; English; English/language arts teacher education; fine arts related; foreign languages and literatures; history; history teacher education; mathematics; mathematics teacher education; multi-/interdisciplinary studies related; music; music performance; philosophy; philosophy and religious studies related; physical sciences related; physics; psychology; science teacher education; social sciences related; sociology.

Creighton University
Accounting; American Indian/Native American studies; American studies; ancient/classical Greek; anthropology; applied mathematics; art; athletic training; atmospheric sciences and meteorology; biology/biological sciences; chemistry; classical, ancient Mediterranean and Near Eastern studies and archaeology; communication/speech communication and rhetoric; computer science; dramatic/theater arts; economics; elementary education; emergency medical technology (EMT paramedic); English; environmental studies; finance; French; German; graphic design; health/health-care administration; history; international business/trade/commerce; international relations and affairs; journalism; kinesiology and exercise science; Latin; management information systems; marketing/marketing management; mathematics; music; nursing (registered nurse training); organizational communication; philosophy; physics; political science and government; pre-law studies; psychology; social work; sociology; Spanish; speech and rhetoric; theological and ministerial studies related; theology.

Dartmouth College
African American/Black studies; African studies; American Indian/Native American studies; ancient/classical Greek; animal genetics; anthropology; Arabic; archeology; art history, criticism and conservation; Asian studies; astronomy; biochemistry; biology/biological sciences; chemistry; chemistry related; Chinese; classics and languages, literatures and linguistics; cognitive psychology and psycholinguistics; comparative literature; computer science; creative writing; dramatic/theater arts; East Asian languages related; ecology; economics; engineering; engineering physics; English; environmental studies; evolutionary biology; film/cinema studies; fine/studio arts; French; geography; geology/earth science; German; Hebrew; Hispanic American, Puerto Rican, and Mexican American/Chicano studies; history; Italian; Japanese; Latin; Latin American studies; linguistics; mathematics; molecular biology; multi-/interdisciplinary studies related; music; Near and Middle Eastern studies; philosophy; physics; political science and government; psychology; religious studies; Romance languages; Russian; Russian studies; sociology; Spanish; women's studies.

Davidson College
Anthropology; art; biology/biological sciences; chemistry; classics and languages, literatures and linguistics; dramatic/theater arts; economics; English; French; German; history; mathematics; multi-/interdisciplinary studies related; music; philosophy; physics; political science and government; psychology; religious studies; sociology; Spanish.

Denison University
African American/Black studies; anthropology; area studies; art; art history, criticism and conservation; Asian studies (East); biochemistry; biology/biological sciences; chemistry; classics and languages, literatures and linguistics; computer science; creative writing; dance; dramatic/theater arts; economics; English; environmental studies; film/cinema studies; fine/studio arts; French; geology/earth science; German; history;

international relations and affairs; Latin American studies; mass communication/media; mathematics; music; organizational behavior; philosophy; physical education teaching and coaching; physics; political science and government; psychology; religious studies; sociology; Spanish; speech and rhetoric; women's studies.

DePauw University
African American/Black studies; ancient/classical Greek; anthropology; art history, criticism and conservation; Asian studies (East); athletic training; biochemistry; biology/biological sciences; chemistry; classics and languages, literatures and linguistics; computer science; dramatic/theater arts; economics; elementary education; English; English composition; environmental studies; fine/studio arts; French; geology/earth science; German; history; interdisciplinary studies; kinesiology and exercise science; Latin; mass communication/media; mathematics; multi-/interdisciplinary studies related; music; music management and merchandising; music performance; music teacher education; music theory and composition; peace studies and conflict resolution; philosophy; physical education teaching and coaching; physics; political science and government; psychology; religious studies; Romance languages; Russian studies; sociology; Spanish; women's studies.

Dickinson College
African studies; American studies; anthropology; archeology; Asian studies (East); biochemistry; biology/biological sciences; chemistry; classics and languages, literatures and linguistics; computer and information sciences; dramatic/theater arts; economics; English; environmental science; environmental studies; fine/studio arts; French; geology/earth science; German; history; international business/trade/commerce; international relations and affairs; Italian studies; Jewish/Judaic studies; legal studies; mathematics; medieval and Renaissance studies; music; music related; Near and Middle Eastern studies; philosophy; physics; political science and government; psychology; public policy analysis; religious studies; Russian; sociology; Spanish; visual and performing arts related; women's studies.

Dominican University
Accounting; American studies; art history, criticism and conservation; biochemistry; biology/biological sciences; business administration and management; chemistry; commercial and advertising art; communication/speech communication and rhetoric; computer engineering; computer science; criminology; dietetics; dramatic/theater arts; economics; education (K-12); electrical, electronics and communications engineering; elementary education; English; environmental studies; fashion merchandising; fashion/apparel design; fine/studio arts; food science; foods, nutrition, and wellness; foodservice systems administration; French; gerontology; history; information science/studies; international business/trade/commerce; Italian; journalism; mass communication/media; mathematics; neuroscience; philosophy; photography; political science and government; pre-dentistry studies; pre-law studies; pre-veterinary studies; premedical studies; psychology; social sciences; sociology; Spanish; special products marketing; substance abuse/addiction counseling; theology.

Drake University
Accounting; accounting and finance; acting; actuarial science; advertising; anthropology; art; art history, criticism and conservation; astronomy; biochemistry; biology/biological sciences; broadcast journalism; business administration and management; business/commerce; chemistry; commercial and advertising art; computer science; directing and theatrical production; dramatic/theater arts; dramatic/theater arts and stagecraft related; drawing; elementary education; English; environmental science; environmental studies; ethics; finance; fine/studio arts; graphic design; history; international business/trade/commerce; international relations and affairs; jazz/jazz studies; journalism; marketing/marketing management; mass communication/media; mathematics; music; music management and merchandising; music performance; music teacher education; neuroscience; painting; pharmacy; pharmacy administration/pharmaceutics; philosophy; physics; piano and organ; political science and

government; pre-dentistry studies; pre-engineering; pre-law studies; pre-veterinary studies; premedical studies; printmaking; psychology; public relations/image management; radio and television; radio, television, and digital communication related; religious studies; religious/sacred music; sculpture; secondary education; sociology; speech and rhetoric; voice and opera.

Drew University
African studies; anthropology; art; art history, criticism and conservation; behavioral sciences; biochemistry; biology/biological sciences; chemistry; Chinese studies; classics and languages, literatures and linguistics; computer science; dramatic/theater arts; economics; English; French; German; history; mathematics; mathematics and computer science; music; neuroscience; philosophy; physics; political science and government; psychology; religious studies; Russian; sociology; Spanish; women's studies.

Drexel University
Accounting; architectural engineering; architecture; area studies related; biological and physical sciences; biology/biological sciences; biomedical/medical engineering; business, management, and marketing related; business/commerce; business/managerial economics; chemical engineering; chemistry; cinematography and film/video production; civil engineering; civil engineering related; commercial and advertising art; communication and journalism related; computer engineering; computer science; culinary arts; design and applied arts related; education (specific subject areas) related; electrical, electronics and communications engineering; engineering; English language and literature related; environmental studies; environmental/environmental health engineering; fashion/apparel design; finance; general studies; health/health-care administration; history; hospitality administration related; human resources management; humanities; industrial engineering; information science/studies; interior design; international business/trade/commerce; management information systems; marketing/marketing management; materials engineering; mathematics; mechanical engineering; music; nutrition sciences; photography; physics related; playwriting and screenwriting; psychology; social sciences; sociology; taxation; technical and business writing; web page, digital/multimedia and information resources design.

Drury University
Accounting; advertising; architecture; art history, criticism and conservation; arts management; biology/biological sciences; business administration and management; chemistry; communication/speech communication and rhetoric; computer and information sciences; computer science; creative writing; criminology; design and visual communications; dramatic/theater arts; economics; education; elementary education; engineering; English; environmental science; environmental studies; finance; fine/studio arts; French; German; history; kinesiology and exercise science; marketing/marketing management; mathematics; music; music performance; music teacher education; music theory and composition; occupational therapy; philosophy; physics; political science and government; pre-dentistry studies; pre-law studies; pre-pharmacy studies; pre-veterinary studies; premedical studies; psychology; public relations/image management; religious studies; secondary education; sociology; Spanish; sport and fitness administration/management.

Duke University
African American/Black studies; anatomy; ancient/classical Greek; anthropology; art; art history, criticism and conservation; Asian studies; biology/biological sciences; biomedical/medical engineering; Canadian studies; chemistry; civil engineering; classics and languages, literatures and linguistics; computer science; design and visual communications; dramatic/theater arts; economics; electrical, electronics and communications engineering; English; environmental studies; French; geology/earth science; German; history; international relations and affairs; Italian; Latin; linguistics; literature; materials science; mathematics; mechanical engineering; medieval and Renaissance studies; music; philosophy;

physics; political science and government; psychology; public policy analysis; religious studies; Russian; Slavic languages; sociology; Spanish; women's studies.

Duquesne University
Accounting; accounting related; ancient/classical Greek; art history, criticism and conservation; athletic training; biochemistry; biology/biological sciences; business administration, management and operations related; business, management, and marketing related; business/commerce; business/corporate communications; business/managerial economics; chemistry; chemistry related; classics and languages, literatures and linguistics; communication/speech communication and rhetoric; computer science; computer software and media applications related; dramatic/theater arts; early childhood education; economics; education; education (multiple levels); elementary education; English; English language and literature related; English/language arts teacher education; entrepreneurship; environmental science; finance; fine/studio arts; foreign languages and literatures; health/health-care administration; history; international business/trade/commerce; international relations and affairs; investments and securities; journalism; Latin; Latin teacher education; liberal arts and sciences and humanities related; logistics and materials management; management information systems; management science; marketing related; marketing/marketing management; mathematics; mathematics teacher education; music performance; music related; music teacher education; music therapy; nonprofit management; nursing (registered nurse training); occupational therapy; pharmacy, pharmaceutical sciences, and administration related; philosophy; physical therapy; physician assistant; physics; political science and government; premedical studies; psychology; public relations, advertising, and applied communication related; public relations/image management; secondary education; securities services administration; social studies teacher education; sociology; Spanish; Spanish language teacher education; special education; speech and rhetoric; speech-language pathology; theology; web page, digital/multimedia and information resources design; web/multimedia management and webmaster.

Earlham College
African American/Black studies; anthropology; art; biochemistry; biology/biological sciences; business administration and management; business/commerce; chemistry; classics and languages, literatures and linguistics; comparative literature; computer science; dramatic/theater arts; economics; English; environmental studies; French; geological and earth sciences/geosciences related; German; history; interdisciplinary studies; international relations and affairs; Japanese studies; Latin American studies; mathematics; multi-/interdisciplinary studies related; music; peace studies and conflict resolution; philosophy; physics; physiological psychology/psychobiology; political science and government; premedical studies; psychology; religious studies; sociology; Spanish; women's studies.

Elizabethtown College
Accounting; applied mathematics; applied mathematics related; biochemistry; biology/biological sciences; biotechnology; business administration and management; chemistry; communication and media related; computer engineering; computer science; criminal justice/safety; economics; elementary education; engineering; English; environmental biology; fine/studio arts; forest/forest resources management; French; German; health professions related; history; industrial engineering; information science/studies; international business/trade/commerce; Japanese; mathematics; music; music teacher education; music therapy; occupational therapy; philosophy; physics; political science and government; pre-dentistry studies; pre-law studies; pre-veterinary studies; premedical studies; psychology; religious studies; science teacher education; social sciences related; social work; Spanish; technical and business writing; theater/theater arts management.

Elmira College
Accounting; American studies; anthropology; art; art teacher education; audiology and speech-language pathology; biochemistry; biology teacher education; biology/biological sciences; business administration and

management; business/managerial economics; chemistry; chemistry teacher education; classics and languages, literatures and linguistics; clinical laboratory science/medical technology; criminal justice/law enforcement administration; dramatic/theater arts; economics; education; elementary education; English; English/language arts teacher education; environmental studies; European studies; fine/studio arts; foreign language teacher education; foreign languages and literatures; French; French language teacher education; history; history teacher education; human services; humanities; information science/studies; interdisciplinary studies; international business/trade/commerce; international relations and affairs; liberal arts and sciences/liberal studies; literature; marketing/ marketing management; mathematics; mathematics teacher education; mental health/rehabilitation; middle school education; modern languages; music; nursing (registered nurse training); nursing science; philosophy; political science and government; pre-dentistry studies; pre-law studies; pre-veterinary studies; premedical studies; psychology; religious studies; Romance languages; science teacher education; secondary education; social science teacher education; social sciences; social studies teacher education; social work; sociology; Spanish; Spanish language teacher education; speech teacher education.

Elon University

Accounting; anthropology; art; art history, criticism and conservation; athletic training; biology/biological sciences; broadcast journalism; business administration and management; business/corporate communications; chemical engineering; chemistry; clinical laboratory science/ medical technology; communication and media related; communication/ speech communication and rhetoric; computer and information sciences; computer science; dance; dramatic/theater arts; economics; education; elementary education; engineering; English; environmental studies; foreign languages and literatures; French; health teacher education; history; human services; journalism; mathematics; middle school education; music; music performance; music teacher education; parks, recreation and leisure; philosophy; physical education teaching and coaching; physics; political science and government; pre-dentistry studies; pre-law studies; pre-veterinary studies; premedical studies; psychology; public administration; religious studies; science teacher education; secondary education; sociology; Spanish; special education; sport and fitness administration/management; theater design and technology.

Embry-Riddle Aeronautical University (AZ)

Aeronautics/aviation/aerospace science and technology; aerospace, aeronautical and astronautical engineering; airline pilot and flight crew; atmospheric sciences and meteorology; business administration, management and operations related; computer engineering; electrical, electronics and communications engineering; international relations and affairs; multi-/interdisciplinary studies related; physics related; social sciences.

Emerson College

Acting; advertising; audiology and speech-language pathology; broadcast journalism; cinematography and film/video production; communication disorders; communication/speech communication and rhetoric; creative writing; drama and dance teacher education; dramatic/theater arts; film/ cinema studies; interdisciplinary studies; intermedia/multimedia; journalism; marketing/marketing management; mass communication/ media; playwriting and screenwriting; political communication; public relations/image management; publishing; radio and television; radio and television broadcasting technology; radio, television, and digital communication related; special education (speech or language impaired); speech and rhetoric; speech therapy; speech-language pathology; theater design and technology; visual and performing arts.

Emory University

Accounting; African American/Black studies; African studies; American studies; anthropology; art history, criticism and conservation; Asian American studies; Asian studies; banking and financial support services; biology/biological sciences; biomedical sciences; business administration and management; business/managerial economics; chemistry; Chinese;

classics; classics and languages, literatures and linguistics; comparative literature; computer science; creative writing; dance; dramatic/theater arts; economics; education; English; film/cinema studies; finance; fine/ studio arts; French; German; history; interdisciplinary studies; international relations and affairs; Italian; Japanese; Jewish/Judaic studies; journalism; Latin; Latin American studies; liberal arts and sciences/liberal studies; literature; marketing/marketing management; mathematics; medieval and Renaissance studies; modern Greek; music; neuroscience; nursing (registered nurse training); philosophy; physics; political science and government; psychology; religious studies; Russian; sociology; Spanish; women's studies.

Erskine College

American studies; art; athletic training; behavioral sciences; biblical studies; biology/biological sciences; business administration and management; chemistry; clinical laboratory science/medical technology; elementary education; English; French; history; kindergarten/preschool education; mathematics; music; philosophy; physical education teaching and coaching; physics; political science and government; psychology; religious education; religious studies; social studies teacher education; Spanish; special education; sport and fitness administration/management.

Eugene Lang College The New School for Liberal Arts

Anthropology; communication and media related; creative writing; cultural studies; dance; dramatic/theater arts; economics; education; English; foreign languages and literatures; history; humanities; journalism; liberal arts and sciences/liberal studies; literature; music history, literature, and theory; philosophy; political science and government; psychology; religious studies; social sciences; sociology; urban studies/affairs; women's studies.

Fairfield University

Accounting; American studies; art; art history, criticism and conservation; biochemistry; biology/biological sciences; business administration and management; chemistry; communication/speech communication and rhetoric; computer and information sciences; computer engineering; computer software engineering; dramatic/theater arts; economics; electrical, electronics and communications engineering; engineering mechanics; engineering physics; English; film/video and photographic arts related; finance; fine/studio arts; French; general studies; German; history; international business/trade/commerce; international relations and affairs; Italian; liberal arts and sciences/liberal studies; management information systems; marketing/marketing management; mathematics; mechanical engineering; music; nursing (registered nurse training); philosophy; physics; political science and government; psychology; religious studies; sociology; Spanish.

Florida Institute of Technology

Accounting; accounting and business/management; aeronautics/aviation/ aerospace science and technology; aerospace, aeronautical and astronautical engineering; air transportation related; analytical chemistry; applied mathematics; aquatic biology/limnology; astronomy and astrophysics related; aviation/airway management; biochemistry; biological and physical sciences; biology teacher education; biology/biological sciences; biomedical sciences; business administration and management; business administration, management and operations related; chemical engineering; chemistry; chemistry related; chemistry teacher education; civil engineering; clinical psychology; communication/speech communication and rhetoric; computer engineering; computer science; computer software engineering; computer teacher education; construction engineering technology; corrections and criminal justice related; e-commerce; earth sciences; ecology; electrical, electronics and communications engineering; engineering; environmental science; forensic psychology; general studies; health/health-care administration; history; humanities; information resources management; information science/studies; interdisciplinary studies; international business/trade/commerce; liberal arts and sciences/liberal studies; management information systems; management science; marine biology and biological oceanography; marketing/marketing management; mathematics; mathematics teacher education; mechanical engineering; meteorology; middle school education; military studies; molecular biology; multi-/interdisciplinary studies related; ocean engineering; oceanography; oceanography (chemical and physical); organizational behavior; physical sciences related; physics; physics related; physics teacher education; premedical studies; psychology; science teacher education.

Florida International University
Accounting; applied mathematics; architecture related; art history, criticism and conservation; art teacher education; Asian studies; biology/biological sciences; biomedical/medical engineering; broadcast journalism; business administration and management; chemical engineering; chemistry; civil engineering; communication/speech communication and rhetoric; computer and information sciences; computer engineering; computer science; construction engineering technology; criminal justice/safety; dance; dietetics; dramatic/theater arts; economics; electrical, electronics and communications engineering; elementary education; English; English/language arts teacher education; environmental control technologies related; environmental design/architecture; environmental studies; family and consumer sciences/home economics teacher education; finance; fine/studio arts; foreign language teacher education; French; geography; geology/earth science; German; health information/medical records administration; health science; health services/allied health/health sciences; health teacher education; health/health-care administration; history; hospitality administration; human resources management; humanities; information technology; insurance; interior design; international business/trade/commerce; international relations and affairs; Italian; kinesiology and exercise science; liberal arts and sciences/liberal studies; logistics and materials management; management information systems; marine biology and biological oceanography; marketing/marketing management; mathematics; mathematics teacher education; mechanical engineering; music; music teacher education; nursing (registered nurse training); occupational therapy; orthotics/prosthetics; parks, recreation and leisure facilities management; philosophy; physical education teaching and coaching; physics; political science and government; Portuguese; psychology; public administration; real estate; religious studies; science teacher education; social science teacher education; social work; sociology; Spanish; special education (emotionally disturbed); special education (mentally retarded); special education (specific learning disabilities); statistics; systems engineering; tourism and travel services management; trade and industrial teacher education; urban studies/affairs; women's studies.

Florida State University
Accounting; acting; advertising; American studies; anthropology; apparel and textile marketing management; apparel and textiles; applied economics; applied mathematics; art history, criticism and conservation; art teacher education; Asian studies; athletic training; atmospheric sciences and meteorology; bilingual and multilingual education; bilingual, multilingual, and multicultural education related; biochemistry; biology/biological sciences; biomathematics and bioinformatics related; biomedical/medical engineering; business administration and management; business/commerce; Caribbean studies; cell and molecular biology; chemical engineering; chemistry; chemistry related; child development; cinematography and film/video production; civil engineering; classics and languages, literatures and linguistics; commercial and advertising art; communication and media related; communication/speech communication and rhetoric; community health services counseling; computer engineering; computer programming; computer science; computer software and media applications related; computer software engineering; creative writing; criminal justice/safety; criminology; dance; dietetics; dramatic/theater arts; early childhood education; ecology; economics; electrical, electronics and communications engineering; elementary education; English; English/language arts teacher education; entrepreneurial and small business related; environmental biology; environmental studies; environmental/environmental health engineering; European studies (Central and Eastern); evolutionary biology; family and consumer economics related; family and consumer sciences/home

economics teacher education; family and consumer sciences/human sciences; fashion merchandising; fashion/apparel design; film/cinema studies; finance; fine/studio arts; foods, nutrition, and wellness; foreign language teacher education; French; geography; geology/earth science; German; graphic design; health teacher education; history; hospitality administration; hospitality administration related; housing and human environments; human development and family studies; human resources management; humanities; industrial engineering; information science/studies; interior design; international business/trade/commerce; international relations and affairs; Italian; jazz/jazz studies; kindergarten/preschool education; kinesiology and exercise science; Latin; Latin American studies; liberal arts and sciences/liberal studies; literature; marine biology and biological oceanography; mass communication/media; materials engineering; mathematics; mathematics teacher education; mechanical engineering; meteorology; middle school education; modern Greek; multicultural education; music; music history, literature, and theory; music pedagogy; music performance; music teacher education; music theory and composition; music therapy; neurobiology and neurophysiology; nursing (registered nurse training); nutrition sciences; parks, recreation and leisure facilities management; philosophy; physical education teaching and coaching; physical sciences; physical sciences related; physics; piano and organ; plant physiology; political science and government; pre-dentistry studies; pre-law studies; pre-pharmacy studies; pre-veterinary studies; premedical studies; psychology; public relations/image management; radio and television; radio, television, and digital communication related; religious studies; Russian; Russian studies; science teacher education; secondary education; social science teacher education; social sciences; social work; sociology; Spanish; special education (emotionally disturbed); special education (mentally retarded); special education (specific learning disabilities); special education (vision impaired); sport and fitness administration/management; statistics; textile science; theater design and technology; violin, viola, guitar and other stringed instruments; vocational rehabilitation counseling; voice and opera; wind/percussion instruments; women's studies; zoology/animal biology.

Fordham University
Accounting; accounting and computer science; African American/Black studies; African studies; American studies; anthropology; art; art history, criticism and conservation; bilingual and multilingual education; biological and physical sciences; biology/biological sciences; broadcast journalism; business administration and management; business/managerial economics; chemistry; classics and languages, literatures and linguistics; commercial and advertising art; comparative literature; computer and information sciences; computer management; computer science; creative writing; criminal justice/law enforcement administration; dance; dramatic/theater arts; economics; education; elementary education; engineering physics; English; entrepreneurship; European studies (Central and Eastern); film/cinema studies; finance; fine/studio arts; French; French studies; German; German studies; health/medical preparatory programs related; Hispanic American, Puerto Rican, and Mexican American/Chicano studies; history; human resources management; information science/studies; interdisciplinary studies; international business/trade/commerce; international economics; international relations and affairs; Italian; Italian studies; journalism; Latin; Latin American studies; liberal arts and sciences/liberal studies; literature; management information systems; management information systems and services related; marketing/marketing management; mass communication/media; mathematics; medieval and Renaissance studies; modern Greek; modern languages; music; music history, literature, and theory; natural sciences; Near and Middle Eastern studies; peace studies and conflict resolution; philosophy; photography; physical sciences; physics; playwriting and screenwriting; political science and government; pre-dentistry studies; pre-law studies; pre-pharmacy studies; pre-veterinary studies; premedical studies; psychology; public administration; radio and television; religious studies; Romance languages; Russian; Russian studies; secondary education; social sciences; social work; sociology; Spanish; Spanish and Iberian studies; theology; urban studies/affairs; women's studies.

Franciscan University of Steubenville

Accounting; anthropology; biology/biological sciences; business administration and management; chemistry; child development; classics and languages, literatures and linguistics; communication/speech communication and rhetoric; computer and information sciences; computer science; dramatic/theater arts; economics; elementary education; English; French; general studies; German; history; humanities; legal studies; mathematics; nursing (registered nurse training); philosophy; political science and government; psychiatric/mental health services technology; psychology; religious education; religious/sacred music; social work; sociology; Spanish; theology.

Franklin & Marshall College

African studies; American studies; ancient/classical Greek; animal behavior and ethology; anthropology; art history, criticism and conservation; astronomy; astrophysics; biochemistry; biology/biological sciences; business administration and management; chemistry; classics and languages, literatures and linguistics; creative writing; dance; dramatic/theater arts; economics; English; environmental science; environmental studies; fine/studio arts; French; geology/earth science; German; German studies; history; Latin; mathematics; multi-/interdisciplinary studies related; music; neuroscience; philosophy; physics; political science and government; psychology; religious studies; sociology; Spanish.

Furman University

Accounting; art; art history, criticism and conservation; Asian studies; biochemistry; biology/biological sciences; business administration and management; chemistry; classics; communication/speech communication and rhetoric; computer science; dramatic/theater arts; economics; education; elementary education; English; environmental studies; fine/studio arts; French; geology/earth science; German; history; information technology; kindergarten/preschool education; kinesiology and exercise science; Latin; mathematics; modern Greek; music; music teacher education; neuroscience; philosophy; physics; piano and organ; political science and government; pre-dentistry studies; pre-law studies; pre-veterinary studies; premedical studies; psychology; religious studies; religious/sacred music; secondary education; sociology; Spanish; special education; urban studies/affairs; voice and opera.

George Fox University

Accounting; art; athletic training; behavioral sciences; biblical studies; biology/biological sciences; business administration and management; chemistry; cinematography and film/video production; cognitive science; communication/speech communication and rhetoric; computer and information sciences; dramatic/theater arts; economics; electrical, electronics and communications engineering; elementary education; engineering; English; family and consumer sciences/human sciences; health and physical education; health teacher education; history; interdisciplinary studies; international/global studies; management information systems; mathematics; mechanical engineering; music; music teacher education; nursing (registered nurse training); organizational communication; pastoral counseling and specialized ministries related; philosophy; physical education teaching and coaching; political science and government; psychology; religious studies; social work; sociology; Spanish.

Georgetown College

Accounting; American studies; athletic training; biology/biological sciences; business administration and management; chemistry; communication and media related; computer and information sciences; dramatic/theater arts; ecology; economics; elementary education; English; European studies; fine/studio arts; French; German; history; kinesiology and exercise science; liberal arts and sciences/liberal studies; mathematics; middle school education; multi-/interdisciplinary studies related; music; music teacher education; philosophy; physics; political science and government; psychology; religious studies; sociology; Spanish.

Georgetown University

Accounting; American studies; anthropology; Arabic; art history, criticism and conservation; biochemistry; biology/biological sciences; business

administration and management; chemistry; Chinese; classics and languages, literatures and linguistics; comparative literature; computer science; economics; English; finance; fine/studio arts; French; German; health science; history; interdisciplinary studies; international business/trade/commerce; international economics; international relations and affairs; Italian; Japanese; liberal arts and sciences/liberal studies; linguistics; marketing/marketing management; mathematics; medieval and Renaissance studies; multi-/interdisciplinary studies related; nursing (registered nurse training); philosophy; physics; political science and government; Portuguese; psychology; Russian; science, technology and society; social sciences related; sociology; Spanish; theology; women's studies.

The George Washington University

Accounting; American studies; anthropology; applied mathematics; archeology; art; art history, criticism and conservation; Asian studies; Asian studies (East); audiology and speech-language pathology; biology/biological sciences; business administration and management; business/managerial economics; chemistry; Chinese; civil engineering; classics and languages, literatures and linguistics; clinical laboratory science/medical technology; clinical/medical laboratory technology; computer and information sciences; computer engineering; computer science; criminal justice/law enforcement administration; dance; diagnostic medical sonography and ultrasound technology; dramatic/theater arts; economics; electrical, electronics and communications engineering; emergency medical technology (EMT paramedic); engineering; English; environmental studies; environmental/environmental health engineering; European studies; finance; fine/studio arts; French; genetics related; geography; geology/earth science; German; history; human resources management; human services; humanities; industrial radiologic technology; interdisciplinary studies; international business/trade/commerce; international relations and affairs; Jewish/Judaic studies; journalism; kinesiology and exercise science; Latin American studies; liberal arts and sciences/liberal studies; marketing/marketing management; mass communication/media; mathematics; mechanical engineering; medical laboratory technology; music; Near and Middle Eastern studies; nuclear medical technology; pharmacology and toxicology related; philosophy; physician assistant; physics; political science and government; pre-dentistry studies; pre-law studies; premedical studies; psychology; public policy analysis; radio and television; radiologic technology/science; religious studies; Russian; Russian studies; sociology; Spanish; speech and rhetoric; statistics; systems engineering.

Georgia Institute of Technology

Aerospace, aeronautical and astronautical engineering; applied mathematics; applied mathematics related; architecture; architecture related; biochemistry; biology/biological sciences; biomedical/medical engineering; business administration and management; business/managerial economics; chemical engineering; chemistry; civil engineering; computer and information sciences; computer engineering; digital communication and media/multimedia; electrical, electronics and communications engineering; environmental/environmental health engineering; geological and earth sciences/geosciences related; history and philosophy of science and technology; industrial and organizational psychology; industrial design; industrial engineering; international relations and affairs; international/global studies; materials engineering; mechanical engineering; multi-/interdisciplinary studies related; nuclear engineering; physical sciences; physics; polymer chemistry; public policy analysis; science, technology and society; textile sciences and engineering.

Georgia State University

Accounting; actuarial science; African American/Black studies; anthropology; art; art teacher education; biology/biological sciences; business administration and management; business/managerial economics; chemistry; computer and information sciences; computer science; criminal justice/safety; early childhood education; economics; elementary education; English; facilities planning and management; film/cinema studies; finance; fine/studio arts; foods, nutrition, and wellness;

French; geography; geology/earth science; German; health and physical education; history; hotel/motel administration; human resources development; insurance; international business/trade/commerce; international economics; journalism; kinesiology and exercise science; marketing/marketing management; mathematics; multi-/interdisciplinary studies related; music management and merchandising; music performance; nursing (registered nurse' training); operations management; operations research; philosophy; physics; political science and government; psychology; public policy analysis; real estate; religious studies; respiratory care therapy; social work; sociology; Spanish; speech and rhetoric; urban studies/affairs; women's studies.

Gettysburg College

Accounting; African American/Black studies; American history; American studies; ancient/classical Greek; anthropology; area studies; area studies related; area, ethnic, cultural, and gender studies related; art; art history, criticism and conservation; Asian history; Asian studies (East); Asian studies (South); biochemistry; biological and physical sciences; biology/biological sciences; broadcast journalism; business administration and management; business administration, management and operations related; chemistry; classics and languages, literatures and linguistics; computer science; creative writing; dramatic/theater arts; economics; education; elementary education; engineering related; English; English composition; environmental science; environmental studies; European history; fine/studio arts; French; German; health science; Hispanic American, Puerto Rican, and Mexican American/Chicano studies; history; interdisciplinary studies; international business/trade/commerce; international economics; international relations and affairs; Italian; Japanese; Japanese studies; journalism; Latin; Latin American studies; liberal arts and sciences/liberal studies; literature; marine biology and biological oceanography; mathematics; middle school education; modern languages; molecular biology; music; music teacher education; nonprofit management; peace studies and conflict resolution; philosophy; physical education teaching and coaching; physics; political science and government; pre-dentistry studies; pre-law studies; pre-pharmacy studies; pre-veterinary studies; premedical studies; prenursing studies; psychology; religious studies; Romance languages; science teacher education; secondary education; social sciences; social sciences related; sociology; Spanish; visual and performing arts; western civilization; women's studies.

Gonzaga University

Accounting; art; Asian studies; biochemistry; biology/biological sciences; broadcast journalism; business administration and management; business/managerial economics; chemistry; civil engineering; computer engineering; computer science; criminal justice/law enforcement administration; dramatic/theater arts; economics; electrical, electronics and communications engineering; elementary education; engineering; English; finance; French; German; history; information science/studies; international business/trade/commerce; international relations and affairs; Italian; journalism; kinesiology and exercise science; liberal arts and sciences/liberal studies; literature; marketing/marketing management; mass communication/media; mathematics; mechanical engineering; music; music teacher education; nursing (registered nurse training); philosophy; physical education teaching and coaching; physics; political science and government; psychology; public relations/image management; religious studies; secondary education; sociology; Spanish; special education; speech and rhetoric; sport and fitness administration/management.

Gordon College (MA)

Accounting; art; biology/biological sciences; business administration and management; chemistry; Christian studies; communication/speech communication and rhetoric; computer science; economics; elementary education; English; foreign languages and literatures; French; German; history; international relations and affairs; kinesiology and exercise science; mathematics; middle school education; music; music performance; music teacher education; parks, recreation and leisure; philosophy; physics; political science and government; psychology; social work; sociology; Spanish; special education; youth ministry.

Goshen College

Accounting; art; biblical studies; bilingual and multilingual education; biology/biological sciences; broadcast journalism; business administration and management; chemistry; computer science; dramatic/theater arts; elementary education; English; English as a second/foreign language (teaching); environmental studies; history; journalism; mass communication/media; mathematics; nursing (registered nurse training); peace studies and conflict resolution; physical education teaching and coaching; physics; psychology; public relations/image management; sign language interpretation and translation; social work; sociology; Spanish; special education.

Goucher College

American studies; art; biology/biological sciences; business administration and management; chemistry; computer science; dance; dramatic/theater arts; economics; elementary education; English; French; history; interdisciplinary studies; international relations and affairs; mass communication/media; mathematics; music; peace studies and conflict resolution; philosophy; physics; political science and government; psychology; religious studies; Russian; sociology; Spanish; special education; women's studies.

Grinnell College

Anthropology; art; biochemistry; biology/biological sciences; chemistry; Chinese; classics and languages, literatures and linguistics; computer science; dramatic/theater arts; English; French; German; history; interdisciplinary studies; mathematics; music; philosophy; physics; political science and government; psychology; religious studies; Russian; sociology; Spanish.

Grove City College

Accounting; biochemistry; biology/biological sciences; business administration and management; business/managerial economics; chemistry; computer and information sciences; computer management; divinity/ministry; economics; electrical and electronic engineering technologies related; electrical, electronics and communications engineering; elementary education; English; entrepreneurship; finance; French; history; international business/trade/commerce; kindergarten/preschool education; literature; marketing/marketing management; mass communication/media; mathematics; mechanical engineering; mechanical engineering technologies related; modern languages; molecular biology; music; music management and merchandising; music performance; music teacher education; philosophy; physics; political science and government; pre-dentistry studies; pre-law studies; pre-veterinary studies; premedical studies; psychology; religious studies; science teacher education; secondary education; sociology; Spanish.

Gustavus Adolphus College

Accounting; anthropology; art; art history, criticism and conservation; art teacher education; athletic training; biochemistry; biology teacher education; biology/biological sciences; business administration and management; business/managerial economics; chemistry; chemistry teacher education; classics and languages, literatures and linguistics; computer science; criminal justice/law enforcement administration; dance; dramatic/theater arts; economics; education; elementary education; English; environmental studies; French; geography; geology/earth science; German; health and physical education related; health teacher education; history; interdisciplinary studies; international business/trade/commerce; Japanese; Japanese studies; Latin American studies; mass communication/media; mathematics; mathematics teacher education; music; music performance; music teacher education; natural resources/conservation; nursing (registered nurse training); philosophy; physical education teaching and coaching; physical therapy; physics; physics teacher education; political science and government; pre-dentistry studies; pre-law studies; pre-veterinary studies; premedical studies; psychology; religious studies; religious/sacred music; Russian; Russian studies; Scandinavian languages; Scandinavian studies; secondary education; social sciences; social studies teacher education; sociology; Spanish; speech and rhetoric; women's studies.

Hamilton College (NY)

African American/Black studies; American studies; ancient/classical Greek; anthropology; archeology; art history, criticism and conservation; Asian studies; biochemistry; biology/biological sciences; chemical physics; chemistry; Chinese; classics and languages, literatures and linguistics; communication/speech communication and rhetoric; comparative literature; computer and information sciences; creative writing; dance; dramatic/theater arts; economics; English; environmental studies; fine/studio arts; French; geology/earth science; German; history; international relations and affairs; Japanese; Latin; mathematics; molecular biology; multi-/interdisciplinary studies related; music; neuroscience; philosophy; physics; political science and government; psychology; public policy analysis; religious studies; Russian; Russian studies; sociology; Spanish; women's studies.

Hamline University

Anthropology; art; art history, criticism and conservation; Asian studies (East); athletic training; biochemistry; biology/biological sciences; business administration and management; chemistry; criminal justice/law enforcement administration; dramatic/theater arts; economics; education; education (K-12); elementary education; English; environmental studies; French; German; health and physical education; health teacher education; history; international business/trade/commerce; international relations and affairs; kinesiology and exercise science; Latin American studies; legal assistant/paralegal; legal studies; mass communication/media; mathematics; music; music teacher education; occupational therapy; peace studies and conflict resolution; philosophy; physical education teaching and coaching; physics; political science and government; pre-dentistry studies; pre-law studies; pre-veterinary studies; premedical studies; psychology; public administration; religious studies; Russian studies; science teacher education; secondary education; social sciences; sociology; Spanish; speech/theater education; urban studies/affairs; women's studies.

Hampshire College

Acting; African American/Black studies; American government and politics; American history; American Indian/Native American studies; American literature; American studies; animal sciences; animation, interactive technology, video graphics and special effects; anthropology; art; art history, criticism and conservation; artificial intelligence and robotics; Asian American studies; Asian history; Asian studies; behavioral sciences; biochemistry; biological and physical sciences; biology/biological sciences; biopsychology; botany/plant biology; business/commerce; chemistry; child development; cinematography and film/video production; cognitive psychology and psycholinguistics; cognitive science; communication/speech communication and rhetoric; community organization and advocacy; comparative literature; computer graphics; computer science; crafts, folk art and artisanry; creative writing; cultural resource management and policy analysis; cultural studies; dance; demography and population; design and visual communications; development economics and international development; developmental and child psychology; digital communication and media/multimedia; directing and theatrical production; dramatic/theater arts; drawing; early childhood education; East Asian languages; ecology; economics; education; elementary education; English; English composition; English literature (British and Commonwealth); environmental biology; environmental design/architecture; environmental science; environmental studies; ethics; European history; evolutionary biology; experimental psychology; film/cinema studies; fine/studio arts; foods, nutrition, and wellness; gay/lesbian studies; geology/earth science; Germanic languages; graphic design; Hispanic American, Puerto Rican, and Mexican American/Chicano studies; history; history and philosophy of science and technology; holocaust and related studies; human development and family studies; humanities; illustration; inorganic chemistry; intercultural/multicultural and diversity studies; intermedia/multimedia; international business/trade/commerce; international economics; international public health; international relations and affairs; international/global studies; Jewish/Judaic studies; labor studies; Latin American studies; legal studies; liberal arts and sciences/liberal studies; linguistics; linguistics of ASL and

other sign languages; mass communication/media; mathematics; mathematics and computer science; multicultural education; music; music performance; musicology and ethnomusicology; natural resources/conservation; natural sciences; neuroscience; nutrition sciences; organic chemistry; painting; peace studies and conflict resolution; philosophy; photography; physical sciences; physics; plant sciences; playwriting and screenwriting; political science and government; pre-dentistry studies; pre-law studies; pre-pharmacy studies; pre-veterinary studies; premedical studies; prenursing studies; psychology; public health education and promotion; religious studies; Romance languages; science, technology and society; sculpture; secondary education; social and philosophical foundations of education; social sciences; sociology; soil science and agronomy; theater literature, history and criticism; urban studies/affairs; visual and performing arts; women's studies; zoology/animal biology.

Hanover College

Anthropology; art; art history, criticism and conservation; biology/biological sciences; business administration and management; chemistry; classics and languages, literatures and linguistics; computer science; dramatic/theater arts; economics; English; French; geology/earth science; German; history; international/global studies; kinesiology and exercise science; mass communication/media; mathematics; medieval and Renaissance studies; music; philosophy; physical education teaching and coaching; physics; political science and government; psychology; sociology; Spanish; theology.

Harding University

Accounting; advertising; art teacher education; art therapy; athletic training; biblical studies; biochemistry; biology teacher education; biology/biological sciences; broadcast journalism; business administration and management; chemistry; Christian studies; clinical laboratory science/medical technology; communication disorders; computer engineering; computer science; corrections and criminal justice related; counselor education/school counseling and guidance; design and applied arts related; dietetics; digital communication and media/multimedia; divinity/ministry; dramatic/theater arts; early childhood education; economics; education (multiple levels); educational leadership and administration; electrical, electronics and communications engineering; elementary education; English; English/language arts teacher education; family and consumer sciences/home economics teacher education; family and consumer sciences/human sciences; fashion merchandising; finance; fine/studio arts; French; French language teacher education; general studies; graphic design; health teacher education; health/health-care administration; history; human development and family studies related; human resources management; humanities; information technology; interior design; international business/trade/commerce; international/global studies; kinesiology and exercise science; legal studies; marketing/marketing management; marriage and family therapy/counseling; mathematics; mathematics teacher education; mechanical engineering; middle school education; missionary studies and missiology; music; music teacher education; nursing (registered nurse training); painting; pastoral counseling and specialized ministries related; pastoral studies/counseling; photojournalism; physics; political science and government; pre-dentistry studies; pre-veterinary studies; premedical studies; psychology; public administration; public relations/image management; reading teacher education; religious education; sales, distribution and marketing; science teacher education; secondary education; social sciences; social studies teacher education; social work; Spanish; Spanish language teacher education; special education (early childhood); special education (specific learning disabilities); special education related; speech teacher education; speech-language pathology; sport and fitness administration/management; theology; youth ministry.

Harvard University

African American/Black studies; anthropology; applied mathematics; art history, criticism and conservation; Asian studies (East); astronomy and astrophysics related; atomic/molecular physics; biochemistry; biochemistry/biophysics and molecular biology; biology/biological sciences; cell and molecular biology; chemistry; classics and languages, literatures and linguistics; comparative literature; computer science; economics; engineering; English; English language and literature related; environmental studies; evolutionary biology; geology/earth science; German; history; history and philosophy of science and technology; history related; liberal arts and sciences/liberal studies; linguistics; mathematics; music; Near and Middle Eastern studies; neurobiology and neurophysiology; philosophy; physics; political science and government; psychology; religious studies; Romance languages; Sanskrit and classical Indian languages; Slavic languages; social sciences; sociology; statistics; visual and performing arts; women's studies.

Harvey Mudd College

Biology/biological sciences; chemistry; computer science; engineering; mathematics; physics.

Haverford College

African studies; anthropology; archeology; art; art history, criticism and conservation; Asian studies (East); astronomy; biochemistry; biology/biological sciences; biophysics; chemistry; classics and languages, literatures and linguistics; comparative literature; computer science; econometrics and quantitative economics; economics; education; English; French; geology/earth science; German; history; Italian; Latin; Latin American studies; mathematics; modern Greek; music; neuroscience; peace studies and conflict resolution; philosophy; physics; political science and government; pre-law studies; pre-veterinary studies; premedical studies; psychology; religious studies; Romance languages; Russian; sociology; Spanish; urban studies/affairs; women's studies.

Hendrix College

Accounting; American studies; anthropology; art; biochemistry/biophysics and molecular biology; biology/biological sciences; business/managerial economics; chemical physics; chemistry; computer science; dramatic/theater arts; early childhood education; economics; English; environmental studies; French; German; health services/allied health/health sciences; history; interdisciplinary studies; international relations and affairs; kinesiology and exercise science; mathematics; music; philosophy; philosophy and religious studies related; physics; political science and government; psychology; religious studies; sociology; Spanish.

Hillsdale College

Accounting; American studies; art; biology/biological sciences; business administration and management; chemistry; Christian studies; classics and languages, literatures and linguistics; communication/speech communication and rhetoric; comparative literature; computer science; dramatic/theater arts; early childhood education; economics; education; education (K-12); elementary education; English; European studies; finance; French; German; history; interdisciplinary studies; international relations and affairs; kindergarten/preschool education; marketing/marketing management; mathematics; mathematics related; music; philosophy; physical education teaching and coaching; physics; political science and government; pre-dentistry studies; pre-veterinary studies; premedical studies; psychology; religious studies; secondary education; sociology; Spanish.

Hiram College

Accounting and finance; art; biochemistry; biological and biomedical sciences related; biology/biological sciences; business administration and management; chemistry; computer science; creative writing; dramatic/theater arts; economics; education; English; environmental studies; fine/studio arts; French; history; mass communication/media; mathematics; music; neuroscience; nursing (registered nurse training); philosophy; physics; political science and government; psychology; religious studies; sociology; Spanish.

Hobart and William Smith Colleges

African American/Black studies; African studies; American studies; ancient/classical Greek; anthropology; architecture; art; art history, criticism and conservation; Asian studies; biochemistry; biology/biological sciences; chemistry; Chinese; classics and languages, literatures and linguistics; comparative literature; computer science; dance; dramatic/theater arts; economics; English; environmental studies; European studies; fine/studio arts; French; gay/lesbian studies; geology/earth science; history; interdisciplinary studies; international relations and affairs; Japanese; Latin; Latin American studies; liberal arts and sciences/liberal studies; mass communication/media; mathematics; medieval and Renaissance studies; modern languages; music; philosophy; physics; political science and government; pre-dentistry studies; pre-law studies; pre-veterinary studies; premedical studies; psychology; public policy analysis; religious studies; Russian; Russian studies; sociology; Spanish; urban studies/affairs; women's studies.

Hope College

Accounting; ancient Near Eastern and biblical languages; art history, criticism and conservation; art teacher education; athletic training; biology teacher education; biology/biological sciences; business administration and management; business/managerial economics; chemistry; chemistry teacher education; classics and languages, literatures and linguistics; communication/speech communication and rhetoric; computer science; dance; drama and dance teacher education; dramatic/theater arts; economics; education (specific subject areas) related; elementary education; engineering; engineering physics; English; English/language arts teacher education; environmental studies; fine/studio arts; French; French language teacher education; geology/earth science; geophysics and seismology; German; German language teacher education; history; history teacher education; humanities; interdisciplinary studies; international/global studies; Japanese; jazz/jazz studies; kinesiology and exercise science; Latin; Latin teacher education; mathematics; mathematics teacher education; multi-/interdisciplinary studies related; music; music performance; music teacher education; music theory and composition; nursing (registered nurse training); philosophy; physical education teaching and coaching; physics; physics teacher education; piano and organ; political science and government; psychology; religious studies; science teacher education; secondary education; social sciences; social studies teacher education; social work; sociology; Spanish; Spanish language teacher education; special education (emotionally disturbed); special education (specific learning disabilities); theology and religious vocations related; violin, viola, guitar and other stringed instruments; voice and opera.

Houghton College

Accounting; art; biblical studies; biochemistry; biological and physical sciences; biology/biological sciences; business administration and management; chemistry; clinical laboratory science/medical technology; computer science; creative writing; cultural studies; elementary education; English; English as a second/foreign language (teaching); environmental biology; French; health and physical education; history; humanities; information technology; international relations and affairs; liberal arts and sciences/liberal studies; literature; mathematics; music; music performance; music teacher education; music theory and composition; natural sciences; parks, recreation and leisure; pastoral studies/counseling; philosophy; physical education teaching and coaching; physics; piano and organ; political science and government; pre-dentistry studies; pre-law studies; pre-veterinary studies; premedical studies; psychology; religious education; religious studies; secondary education; sociology; Spanish; special education; theology; violin, viola, guitar and other stringed instruments; voice and opera; wind/percussion instruments.

Illinois College

Accounting; art; biology/biological sciences; business administration and management; business/managerial economics; chemistry; clinical laboratory science/medical technology; computer science; cytotechnology; dramatic/theater arts; early childhood education; economics; education; education (K-12); elementary education; English; environmental studies; finance; French; German; history; information science/studies; interdisciplinary studies; international relations and affairs; liberal arts and sciences/liberal studies; management information systems; mass communication/media; mathematics; music; occupational therapy; philosophy; physical education teaching and coaching; physics; political science and government; pre-dentistry studies; pre-law studies; pre-veterinary studies; premedical studies; psychology; religious studies; secondary education; sociology; Spanish; speech and rhetoric.

Illinois Institute of Technology

Aerospace, aeronautical and astronautical engineering; applied mathematics; architectural engineering; architecture; biochemistry; biochemistry/biophysics and molecular biology; biology/biological sciences; biomedical/medical engineering; biophysics; business administration and management; chemical engineering; chemistry; civil engineering; communication and journalism related; computer and information sciences; computer engineering; computer science; electrical, electronics and communications engineering; engineering/industrial management; information technology; journalism; liberal arts and sciences/liberal studies; materials engineering; mechanical engineering; pharmacy; physics; political science and government; psychology.

Illinois Wesleyan University

Accounting; acting; African studies; American studies; anthropology; area studies related; art; Asian studies; biology/biological sciences; business administration and management; chemistry; classics and languages, literatures and linguistics; computer science; dramatic/theater arts; economics; education; elementary education; environmental studies; European studies (Western); French; German; history; insurance; insurance/risk management; international business/trade/commerce; international relations and affairs; international/global studies; Latin American studies; liberal arts and sciences/liberal studies; mathematics; multi-/interdisciplinary studies related; music; music performance; music related; music teacher education; music theory and composition; nursing (registered nurse training); philosophy; physics; piano and organ; political science and government; psychology; religious studies; sociology; Spanish; theater design and technology; visual and performing arts related; voice and opera; women's studies.

Iowa State University of Science and Technology

Accounting; advertising; aerospace, aeronautical and astronautical engineering; agricultural business and management; agricultural mechanization; agricultural teacher education; agricultural/biological engineering and bioengineering; agriculture; agronomy and crop science; animal sciences; anthropology; apparel and textiles; applied horticulture; architecture; art; atmospheric sciences and meteorology; biochemistry; bioinformatics; biology/biological sciences; biophysics; botany/plant biology; business administration and management; chemical engineering; chemistry; city/urban, community and regional planning; civil engineering; commercial and advertising art; computer engineering; dairy science; design and visual communications; dietetics; dramatic/theater arts; ecology; economics; education; electrical, electronics and communications engineering; elementary education; engineering; engineering related; engineering science; English; entomology; entrepreneurship; environmental studies; family and community services; family and consumer economics related; family and consumer sciences/home economics teacher education; family and consumer sciences/human sciences; family resource management; farm and ranch management; fashion/apparel design; finance; fish/game management; food services technology; foods, nutrition, and wellness; foodservice systems administration; forestry; French; genetics; geology/earth science; German; graphic design; health and physical education; health teacher education; history; horticultural science; hotel/motel administration; industrial engineering; interdisciplinary studies; interior design; international agriculture; international business/trade/commerce; international relations and affairs; journalism; landscape architecture; liberal arts and sciences/liberal studies; linguistic and comparative language studies related; linguistics; logistics and materials management; management information systems; marketing/marketing management; mass communication/media; materials engineering; mathematics; mechanical engineering; medical illustration; microbiology; multi-/interdisciplinary studies related; music; music teacher education; natural resources management and policy; operations management; ornamental horticulture; philosophy; physics; plant protection and integrated pest

management; political science and government; pre-dentistry studies; pre-law studies; pre-veterinary studies; premedical studies; psychology; public administration; religious studies; Russian studies; secondary education; sociology; Spanish; special products marketing; speech and rhetoric; statistics; technical and business writing; trade and industrial teacher education; visual and performing arts; women's studies.

Ithaca College

Accounting; acting; anthropology; applied economics; applied mathematics; art; art history, criticism and conservation; art teacher education; arts management; athletic training; audiology and speech-language pathology; biochemistry; biology teacher education; biology/biological sciences; broadcast journalism; business administration and management; business/commerce; business/managerial economics; chemistry; chemistry teacher education; cinematography and film/video production; communication and journalism related; computer and information sciences; computer science; creative writing; dance; dramatic/theater arts; economics; education (K-12); education (multiple levels); educational/instructional media design; English; English/language arts teacher education; environmental studies; film/cinema studies; finance; fine/studio arts; foods, nutrition, and wellness; French; French language teacher education; German; German language teacher education; German studies; gerontology; health and physical education; health and physical education related; health teacher education; health/health-care administration; health/medical preparatory programs related; history; history teacher education; hospital and health-care facilities administration; industrial and organizational psychology; interdisciplinary studies; international business/trade/commerce; Italian; jazz/jazz studies; journalism; kinesiology and exercise science; labor and industrial relations; liberal arts and sciences/liberal studies; marketing research; marketing/marketing management; mass communication/media; mathematics; mathematics and computer science; mathematics teacher education; middle school education; multi-/interdisciplinary studies related; music; music performance; music teacher education; music theory and composition; occupational therapy; parks, recreation and leisure; philosophy; photography; physical education teaching and coaching; physical therapy; physics; physics teacher education; piano and organ; political science and government; pre-law studies; premedical studies; psychology; public health education and promotion; public relations/image management; radio and television; recording arts technology; rehabilitation therapy; science teacher education; secondary education; social sciences; social studies teacher education; sociology; Spanish; Spanish language teacher education; special education (speech or language impaired); speech and rhetoric; sport and fitness administration/management; telecommunications; theater design and technology; therapeutic recreation; visual and performing arts; voice and opera.

James Madison University

Accounting; anthropology; art; art history, criticism and conservation; athletic training; biology/biological sciences; biotechnology; business administration and management; business/managerial economics; chemistry; communication/speech communication and rhetoric; community health services counseling; computer and information sciences; dramatic/theater arts; economics; engineering; English; finance; finance and financial management services related; foods, nutrition, and wellness; foreign languages and literatures; geography; geology/earth science; health and physical education; health/health-care administration; history; hospitality administration; information science/studies; international business/trade/commerce; international relations and affairs; legal studies; liberal arts and sciences/liberal studies; marketing/marketing management; mathematics; music performance; nursing (registered nurse training); philosophy and religious studies related; physics; political science and government; psychology; public administration; science, technology and society; social sciences; social work; sociology; speech-language pathology; systems science and theory; technical and business writing.

John Brown University

Accounting; athletic training; biblical studies; biochemistry; biology/biological sciences; broadcast journalism; business administration and management; business teacher education; chemistry; computer graphics; construction engineering; construction management; divinity/ministry; early childhood education; education; electrical, electronics and communications engineering; elementary education; engineering; engineering technology; engineering/industrial management; English; English as a second/foreign language (teaching); English/language arts teacher education; environmental science; environmental studies; health teacher education; history; interdisciplinary studies; international business/trade/commerce; international relations and affairs; journalism; kindergarten/preschool education; kinesiology and exercise science; liberal arts and sciences/liberal studies; marketing/marketing management; mass communication/media; mathematics; mechanical engineering; middle school education; missionary studies and missiology; music; music teacher education; pastoral studies/counseling; psychology; public relations, advertising, and applied communication related; public relations/image management; radio and television; radio, television, and digital communication related; religious education; religious studies; secondary education; social sciences; social studies teacher education; Spanish; special education; theology; youth ministry.

John Carroll University

Accounting; art history, criticism and conservation; Asian studies; Asian studies (East); biological and physical sciences; biology/biological sciences; business administration and management; chemistry; classics and languages, literatures and linguistics; computer science; economics; education; education (K-12); elementary education; engineering physics; English; environmental studies; finance; French; German; gerontology; history; humanities; interdisciplinary studies; international economics; international relations and affairs; kindergarten/preschool education; Latin; literature; marketing/marketing management; mass communication/media; mathematics; modern Greek; neuroscience; philosophy; physical education teaching and coaching; physics; political science and government; pre-dentistry studies; pre-law studies; pre-veterinary studies; premedical studies; psychology; public administration; religious education; religious studies; secondary education; sociology; Spanish; special education.

The Johns Hopkins University

Anthropology; applied mathematics; archeology; art history, criticism and conservation; Asian studies (East); behavioral sciences; biological and physical sciences; biology/biological sciences; biomedical/medical engineering; biophysics; business/commerce; chemical engineering; chemistry; civil engineering; classics and languages, literatures and linguistics; cognitive psychology and psycholinguistics; computer and information sciences; computer engineering; creative writing; economics; electrical, electronics and communications engineering; electroneurodiagnostic/electroencephalographic technology; engineering; engineering mechanics; English; environmental science; environmental studies; environmental/environmental health engineering; film/cinema studies; French; geography; geology/earth science; German; history; history and philosophy of science and technology; industrial engineering; interdisciplinary studies; international relations and affairs; Italian; Latin American studies; liberal arts and sciences and humanities related; liberal arts and sciences/liberal studies; literature; materials engineering; materials science; mathematics; mechanical engineering; music; natural sciences; Near and Middle Eastern studies; neuroscience; nursing (registered nurse training); philosophy; physics; physiological psychology/psychobiology; political science and government; psychology; public health; social sciences; sociology; Spanish.

Juniata College

Accounting; anthropology; art history, criticism and conservation; biochemistry; biology teacher education; biology/biological sciences; botany/plant biology; business administration and management; business/commerce; cell biology and histology; chemistry; chemistry teacher education; communication/speech communication and rhetoric; computer and information sciences; criminology; digital communication and media/multimedia; dramatic/theater arts; early childhood education; ecology; economics; education; education (multiple levels); education

(specific subject areas) related; elementary education; engineering; engineering physics; English; English/language arts teacher education; entrepreneurship; environmental science; environmental studies; finance; fine/studio arts; foreign languages and literatures; French; French language teacher education; geology/earth science; German; German language teacher education; health communication; health/medical preparatory programs related; history; human resources management; humanities; information resources management; information technology; international business/trade/commerce; international relations and affairs; international/global studies; liberal arts and sciences/liberal studies; marine biology and biological oceanography; marketing/marketing management; mathematics; mathematics teacher education; microbiology; molecular biology; multi-/interdisciplinary studies related; museum studies; natural sciences; peace studies and conflict resolution; philosophy; philosophy and religious studies related; physical sciences; physics; physics teacher education; political science and government; pre-dentistry studies; pre-law studies; pre-pharmacy studies; pre-theology/pre-ministerial studies; pre-veterinary studies; premedical studies; prenursing studies; psychology; public administration; religious studies; Russian; science teacher education; secondary education; social studies teacher education; social work; sociology; Spanish; Spanish language teacher education; special education (early childhood); special education related; theater/theater arts management; wildlife and wildlands science and management; zoology/animal biology.

Kalamazoo College

Anthropology; art; art history, criticism and conservation; biology/biological sciences; business/managerial economics; chemistry; classics and languages, literatures and linguistics; computer science; dramatic/theater arts; English; French; German; health science; history; interdisciplinary studies; mathematics; music; philosophy; physics; political science and government; psychology; religious studies; sociology; Spanish.

Kenyon College

American studies; ancient/classical Greek; anthropology; art; art history, criticism and conservation; biochemistry; biology/biological sciences; chemistry; classics and languages, literatures and linguistics; dance; dramatic/theater arts; economics; English; French; German; history; international relations and affairs; Latin; mathematics; modern languages; molecular biology; music; neuroscience; philosophy; physics; political science and government; psychology; religious studies; sociology; Spanish; women's studies.

Kettering University

Applied mathematics; biochemistry; business administration, management and operations related; chemistry; chemistry related; computer engineering; computer science; electrical, electronics and communications engineering; engineering physics; industrial engineering; mechanical engineering; physics.

The King's College (NY)

Business administration and management; interdisciplinary studies.

Knox College

African American/Black studies; American studies; anthropology; art; art history, criticism and conservation; Asian studies; biochemistry; biology/biological sciences; chemistry; classics and languages, literatures and linguistics; computer and information sciences; creative writing; dramatic/theater arts; economics; education; English; environmental studies; foreign languages and literatures; French; German; history; international relations and affairs; mathematics; multi-/interdisciplinary studies related; music; neuroscience; philosophy; physics; political science and government; psychology; sociology; Spanish; women's studies.

Lafayette College

American studies; anthropology; art; art history, criticism and conservation; biochemistry; biology/biological sciences; business/managerial economics; chemical engineering; chemistry; civil engineering; computer science; economics; electrical, electronics and communications engineering; engineering; English; environmental/environmental health engineering; fine/studio arts; French; geology/earth science; German; history; international relations and affairs; mathematics; mechanical engineering; music; music history, literature, and theory; philosophy; physics; political science and government; psychology; religious studies; Russian studies; sociology; Spanish.

Lake Forest College

American studies; anthropology; area studies; art history, criticism and conservation; Asian studies; biology/biological sciences; business/managerial economics; chemistry; communication/speech communication and rhetoric; computer science; dramatic/theater arts; economics; education; elementary education; English; environmental studies; fine/studio arts; French; history; international relations and affairs; Latin American studies; mathematics; music; philosophy; physics; political science and government; psychology; secondary education; sociology; Spanish; theology.

Lawrence Technological University

Architecture; biochemistry; biomedical/medical engineering; business administration and management; chemical technology; chemistry; chemistry related; civil engineering; communication/speech communication and rhetoric; communications technology; computer engineering; computer science; construction engineering technology; construction management; design and visual communications; electrical and electronic engineering technologies related; electrical, electronic and communications engineering technology; electrical, electronics and communications engineering; engineering technology; English; environmental design/architecture; humanities; illustration; industrial engineering; industrial technology; information technology; interior architecture; international business/trade/commerce; manufacturing technology; mathematics; mathematics and computer science; mechanical engineering; mechanical engineering/mechanical technology; molecular biology; physics; physics related; psychology; radio and television.

Lawrence University

Ancient/classical Greek; anthropology; archeology; art history, criticism and conservation; art teacher education; Asian studies (East); biochemistry; biology/biological sciences; chemistry; Chinese; classics and classical languages related; classics and languages, literatures and linguistics; cognitive psychology and psycholinguistics; cognitive science; computer science; dramatic/theater arts; ecology; economics; English; environmental studies; ethnic, cultural minority, and gender studies related; fine/studio arts; French; geology/earth science; German; history; international economics; international relations and affairs; Japanese; Latin; linguistics; mathematics; mathematics and computer science; music; music pedagogy; music performance; music teacher education; music theory and composition; neuroscience; philosophy; physics; piano and organ; political science and government; pre-dentistry studies; pre-law studies; pre-veterinary studies; premedical studies; psychology; religious studies; Russian; Russian studies; secondary education; Slavic studies; social psychology; Spanish; violin, viola, guitar and other stringed instruments; voice and opera; wind/percussion instruments.

Lebanon Valley College

Accounting; actuarial science; American studies; biochemistry/biophysics and molecular biology; biology/biological sciences; business administration and management; chemistry; clinical/medical laboratory science and allied professions related; computer science; criminology; digital communication and media/multimedia; economics; elementary education; English; fine/studio arts; French; general studies; German; health services/allied health/health sciences; health/health-care administration; history; mathematics; multi-/interdisciplinary studies related; music management and merchandising; music performance; music teacher education; philosophy; physics; physiological psychology/psychobiology; political science and government; psychology; recording arts technology; religious studies; sociology; Spanish.

Lehigh University

Accounting; African American/Black studies; American studies; anthropology; architecture; art; art history, criticism and conservation; Asian studies; astronomy; astrophysics; biochemistry; biological and biomedical sciences related; biological and physical sciences; biology/biological sciences; biomedical/medical engineering; biopsychology; business administration and management; business/commerce; business/managerial economics; chemical engineering; chemistry; chemistry related; civil engineering; classics and languages, literatures and linguistics; cognitive science; communication and journalism related; computer and information sciences and support services related; computer engineering; computer science; design and applied arts related; design and visual communications; dramatic/theater arts; dramatic/theater arts and stagecraft related; ecology; education; electrical, electronics and communications engineering; engineering mechanics; engineering physics; engineering related; English; environmental science; environmental studies; environmental/environmental health engineering; finance; French; geological and earth sciences/geosciences related; German; history; industrial engineering; information science/studies; international relations and affairs; international/global studies; journalism; logistics and materials management; management information systems; marketing/marketing management; materials engineering; mathematics; mechanical engineering; molecular biology; music; music theory and composition; neuroscience; philosophy; physical and theoretical chemistry; physics; political science and government; pre-dentistry studies; premedical studies; psychology; religious studies; science technologies related; social sciences; social sciences related; sociology; Spanish; statistics; structural engineering; women's studies.

LeTourneau University

Accounting; airframe mechanics and aircraft maintenance technology; airline pilot and flight crew; avionics maintenance technology; biblical studies; biology/biological sciences; biomedical/medical engineering; business administration and management; chemistry; computer engineering; computer engineering technology; computer science; drafting and design technology; electrical, electronic and communications engineering technology; electrical, electronics and communications engineering; elementary education; engineering; engineering technology; English; finance; history; information science/studies; interdisciplinary studies; international business/trade/commerce; management information systems; marketing/marketing management; mathematics; mechanical engineering; mechanical engineering/mechanical technology; missionary studies and missiology; natural sciences; physical education teaching and coaching; pre-dentistry studies; pre-law studies; pre-veterinary studies; premedical studies; psychology; religious studies; secondary education; sport and fitness administration/management; welding technology.

Lewis & Clark College

Anthropology; art; Asian studies (East); biochemistry; biology/biological sciences; chemistry; communication/speech communication and rhetoric; computer science; dramatic/theater arts; economics; English; environmental studies; foreign languages and literatures; French; German; Hispanic American, Puerto Rican, and Mexican American/Chicano studies; history; international relations and affairs; mathematics; modern languages; music; philosophy; physics; political science and government; pre-engineering; psychology; religious studies; sociology; Spanish.

Lincoln Memorial University

Accounting; art; art teacher education; athletic training; biology teacher education; biology/biological sciences; business administration and management; business/managerial economics; chemistry; chemistry teacher education; clinical laboratory science/medical technology; computer and information sciences; criminal justice/law enforcement administration; economics; education; elementary education; English; environmental studies; finance; health and physical education; health teacher education; history; history teacher education; humanities; kindergarten/preschool education; kinesiology and exercise science; liberal arts and sciences/liberal studies; marketing/marketing management; mass communication/media; mathematics; mathematics teacher education; nursing (registered nurse training); physical education teaching and coaching; pre-law studies; pre-veterinary studies; premedical studies; psychology; science teacher education; secondary education; social work; veterinary sciences; veterinary technology; wildlife and wildlands science and management.

Linfield College
Accounting; anthropology; area, ethnic, cultural, and gender studies related; art; athletic training; biology/biological sciences; business/commerce; chemistry; communication/speech communication and rhetoric; computer science; creative writing; design and visual communications; dramatic/theater arts; economics; elementary education; English; environmental studies; finance; fine/studio arts; French; German; health and physical education; history; international business/trade/commerce; Japanese; kinesiology and exercise science; mass communication/media; mathematics; music; music performance; music theory and composition; nursing (registered nurse training); philosophy; physical sciences; physics; physics related; political science and government; psychology; religious studies; sociology; Spanish.

Lipscomb University
Accounting; American studies; apparel and textiles; architecture related; art teacher education; athletic training; biblical languages/literatures; biblical studies; biochemistry; biology teacher education; biology/biological sciences; business administration and management; business/managerial economics; chemistry; chemistry teacher education; commercial and advertising art; computer engineering; computer science; dietetics; drama and dance teacher education; dramatic/theater arts; education; elementary education; engineering mechanics; engineering related; engineering science; English; English as a second/foreign language (teaching); English/language arts teacher education; environmental studies; family and consumer sciences/human sciences; family systems; fashion merchandising; fine/studio arts; foodservice systems administration; French; French language teacher education; general studies; German; health/medical preparatory programs related; history; history teacher education; human resources management; information science/studies; information technology; international business/trade/commerce; journalism; kinesiology and exercise science; legal studies; management information systems; marketing/marketing management; mass communication/media; mathematics; mathematics teacher education; mechanical engineering; missionary studies and missiology; music performance; music teacher education; music theory and composition; nursing (registered nurse training); organizational communication; pastoral counseling and specialized ministries related; pharmacy; philosophy; physical education teaching and coaching; physics; physics teacher education; piano and organ; political science and government; pre-dentistry studies; pre-law studies; pre-pharmacy studies; pre-veterinary studies; premedical studies; prenursing studies; psychology; public administration; public relations/image management; social work; Spanish; Spanish language teacher education; speech and rhetoric; urban studies/affairs; voice and opera; youth ministry.

List College, The Jewish Theological Seminary
Ancient Near Eastern and biblical languages; biblical studies; Hebrew; history; Jewish/Judaic studies; literature; music; philosophy; religious education; religious studies; talmudic studies; women's studies.

Louisiana State University and Agricultural and Mechanical College
Accounting; adult and continuing education; agricultural business and management; animal sciences; anthropology; architecture; audiology and speech-language pathology; biochemistry; biology/biological sciences; biomedical/medical engineering; business administration and management; business/managerial economics; chemical engineering; chemistry; civil engineering; computer engineering; computer science; construction management; dietetics; dramatic/theater arts; early childhood education; economics; electrical, electronics and communications engineering; elementary education; English; environmental science; environmental/environmental health engineering; family and consumer

sciences/human sciences; fashion merchandising; finance; fine/studio arts; food science; forest/forest resources management; French; general studies; geography; geology/earth science; German; history; industrial engineering; interior architecture; international business/trade/commerce; international/global studies; landscape architecture; Latin; liberal arts and sciences/liberal studies; management science; marketing/marketing management; mass communication/media; mathematics; mechanical engineering; microbiology; music; music performance; music teacher education; natural resources management and policy; oceanography (chemical and physical); petroleum engineering; philosophy; physical education teaching and coaching; physics; plant sciences; political science and government; psychology; secondary education; sociology; Spanish; speech and rhetoric; sport and fitness administration/management; women's studies.

Loyola College in Maryland
Accounting; applied mathematics; art; biology/biological sciences; business/commerce; chemistry; classics and languages, literatures and linguistics; communication/speech communication and rhetoric; computer and information sciences; creative writing; economics; education; electrical, electronics and communications engineering; elementary education; engineering; English; finance; French; German; history; interdisciplinary studies; international business/trade/commerce; mathematics; philosophy; physics; political science and government; psychology; religious studies; sociology; Spanish; special education; speech-language pathology.

Loyola Marymount University
Accounting; African American/Black studies; animation, interactive technology, video graphics and special effects; applied mathematics; art history, criticism and conservation; Asian studies; biochemistry; biology/biological sciences; business administration and management; chemistry; cinematography and film/video production; civil engineering; communication/speech communication and rhetoric; computer and information sciences; dance; dramatic/theater arts; economics; electrical, electronics and communications engineering; English; European studies; fine/studio arts; French; Hispanic American, Puerto Rican, and Mexican American/Chicano studies; history; humanities; kinesiotherapy; liberal arts and sciences/liberal studies; mathematics; mechanical engineering; multi-/interdisciplinary studies related; music history, literature, and theory; natural sciences; philosophy; physics; playwriting and screenwriting; political science and government; psychology; radio and television; recording arts technology; sociology; Spanish; theology; urban studies/affairs; women's studies.

Loyola University Chicago
Accounting; advertising; African American/Black studies; ancient/classical Greek; anthropology; art history, criticism and conservation; behavioral sciences; bilingual and multilingual education; biochemistry; bioinformatics; biology/biological sciences; business administration and management; business/managerial economics; chemistry; classics and languages, literatures and linguistics; clinical laboratory science/medical technology; clinical nutrition; communication and media related; communication/speech communication and rhetoric; computer and information sciences; computer and information systems security; criminal justice/safety; design and visual communications; dramatic/theater arts; early childhood education; elementary education; English; entrepreneurial and small business related; environmental science; environmental studies; finance; fine/studio arts; forensic science and technology; French; general studies; German; health/health-care administration; history; human resources management; human services; international business/trade/commerce; international relations and affairs; Italian; journalism; Latin; legal professions and studies related; linguistics; marketing/marketing management; mathematics; mathematics and computer science; mathematics teacher education; music; nursing (registered nurse training); office management; operations management; organizational behavior; philosophy; physics; political science and government; psychology; psychology related; public administration;

religious education; secondary education; social work; sociology; Spanish; special education; statistics; theology; women's studies.

Loyola University New Orleans

Accounting; art; biology/biological sciences; business administration and management; business/managerial economics; chemistry; classics and languages, literatures and linguistics; commercial and advertising art; communication/speech communication and rhetoric; creative writing; criminal justice/safety; dramatic/theater arts; economics; English; finance; forensic science and technology; French; general studies; history; humanities; international business/trade/commerce; jazz/jazz studies; marketing/marketing management; mathematics; music; music management and merchandising; music performance; music teacher education; music theory and composition; nursing (registered nurse training); philosophy; physics; piano and organ; political science and government; psychology; religious education; religious studies; religious/sacred music; social sciences; sociology; Spanish; visual and performing arts.

Luther College

Accounting; African American/Black studies; ancient Near Eastern and biblical languages; anthropology; art; athletic training; biology/biological sciences; business administration and management; chemistry; communication/speech communication and rhetoric; computer science; dramatic/theater arts; economics; elementary education; English; environmental studies; French; German; health and physical education; history; interdisciplinary studies; international relations and affairs; management information systems; mathematics; music; nursing (registered nurse training); philosophy; physical education teaching and coaching; physics; political science and government; psychology; religious studies; Russian studies; Scandinavian studies; social work; sociology; Spanish; statistics; women's studies.

Lycoming College

Accounting; American studies; applied mathematics related; area studies related; art; art history, criticism and conservation; astronomy; biology/biological sciences; business administration and management; business/corporate communications; chemistry; classical, ancient Mediterranean and Near Eastern studies and archaeology; commercial and advertising art; communication and media related; creative writing; criminology; digital communication and media/multimedia; dramatic/theater arts; economics; English; finance; fine/studio arts; foreign languages and literatures; French; German; history; international finance; literature; mathematics; mathematics and statistics related; multi-/interdisciplinary studies related; music; philosophy; physics; political science and government; psychology; religious studies; sociology; Spanish.

Lyon College

Accounting; art; biochemistry; biology/biological sciences; business administration and management; chemistry; computer science; dramatic/theater arts; early childhood education; economics; English; history; mathematics; music; philosophy and religious studies related; political science and government; psychology; Spanish.

Macalester College

Anthropology; art history, criticism and conservation; Asian studies; biology/biological sciences; chemistry; classics and languages, literatures and linguistics; communication/speech communication and rhetoric; computer science; dramatic/theater arts; economics; English; environmental studies; fine/studio arts; French; geography; geology/earth science; German; history; humanities; international/global studies; Japanese; Latin American studies; linguistics; mathematics; music; neuroscience; philosophy; physics; political science and government; psychology; religious studies; Russian studies; sociology; Spanish; women's studies.

Maharishi University of Management

Ayurvedic medicine; business administration and management; cinematography and film/video production; computer science; elementary education; English; environmental studies; fine/studio arts; mathematics; secondary education.

Marietta College

Accounting; art; athletic training; biochemistry; biology/biological sciences; business administration and management; business/corporate communications; chemistry; commercial and advertising art; communication/speech communication and rhetoric; computer science; dramatic/theater arts; economics; education; elementary education; English; environmental science; environmental studies; fine/studio arts; geology/earth science; graphic design; history; human resources management; information science/studies; international business/trade/commerce; journalism; liberal arts and sciences/liberal studies; marketing/marketing management; mathematics; music; petroleum engineering; philosophy; physics; political science and government; psychology; public relations, advertising, and applied communication related; radio and television; secondary education; Spanish; speech and rhetoric.

Marist College

Accounting; advertising; American studies; applied mathematics; art; art history, criticism and conservation; athletic training; biochemistry; biology teacher education; biology/biological sciences; biomedical sciences; business administration and management; chemistry; chemistry teacher education; clinical laboratory science/medical technology; computational mathematics; computer programming; computer programming (vendor/product certification); computer science; criminal justice/law enforcement administration; digital communication and media/multimedia; dramatic/theater arts; economics; English; English/language arts teacher education; environmental studies; fashion merchandising; fashion/apparel design; fine/studio arts; French; French language teacher education; general studies; history; information science/studies; information technology; journalism; mathematics; mathematics teacher education; organizational communication; philosophy; political science and government; psychology; public relations/image management; radio and television; secondary education; social studies teacher education; social work; Spanish; Spanish language teacher education; special education.

Marlboro College

African studies; American studies; anthropology; applied mathematics; art; art history, criticism and conservation; Asian studies; Asian studies (East); astronomy; astrophysics; behavioral sciences; biblical studies; biochemistry; biology/biological sciences; botany/plant biology; cell biology and histology; ceramic arts and ceramics; chemistry; classics and languages, literatures and linguistics; comparative literature; computer science; creative writing; cultural studies; dance; developmental and child psychology; dramatic/theater arts; drawing; ecology; economics; English; environmental biology; environmental studies; European studies; European studies (Central and Eastern); experimental psychology; film/cinema studies; fine/studio arts; folklore; French; German; history; history of philosophy; humanities; interdisciplinary studies; international economics; international relations and affairs; Italian; Latin; Latin American studies; linguistics; literature; mathematics; medieval and Renaissance studies; modern Greek; modern languages; molecular biology; music; music history, literature, and theory; natural resources/conservation; natural sciences; philosophy; photography; physics; political science and government; Portuguese; pre-law studies; pre-veterinary studies; premedical studies; psychology; religious studies; Romance languages; Russian studies; sculpture; social sciences; sociology; Spanish; women's studies.

Marquette University

Accounting; advertising; African American/Black studies; anthropology; athletic training; audiology and speech-language pathology; biochemistry; biology/biological sciences; biomedical sciences; biomedical/medical engineering; broadcast journalism; business administration and management; business/managerial economics; chemistry; civil engineering; classics and languages, literatures and linguistics; clinical/medical laboratory technology; communication and journalism related; communication/speech communication and rhetoric; computational mathematics; computer engineering; computer science; creative writing; criminology; dental hygiene; dramatic/theater arts; economics; education;

education (specific subject areas) related; electrical, electronics and communications engineering; elementary education; engineering; engineering related; English; English/language arts teacher education; environmental/environmental health engineering; finance; foreign language teacher education; foreign languages related; French; German; history; history of philosophy; history related; human resources management; industrial engineering; information science/studies; intercultural/multicultural and diversity studies; interdisciplinary studies; international business/trade/commerce; international relations and affairs; international/global studies; journalism; kinesiology and exercise science; management information systems; marketing/marketing management; mass communication/media; mathematics; mathematics teacher education; mechanical engineering; middle school education; molecular biology; multi-/interdisciplinary studies related; nursing (registered nurse training); philosophy; physical therapy; physician assistant; physics; political science and government; pre-dentistry studies; pre-law studies; premedical studies; psychology; public relations/image management; religious studies; science teacher education; secondary education; social science teacher education; social studies teacher education; social work; sociology; Spanish; speech and rhetoric; statistics; women's studies.

Maryville College

American Sign Language (ASL); art history, criticism and conservation; art teacher education; atomic/molecular physics; biochemistry; biology teacher education; biology/biological sciences; business administration and management; chemistry; chemistry teacher education; computer and information sciences related; computer science; developmental and child psychology; dramatic/theater arts; economics; education; engineering; English; English as a second/foreign language (teaching); English/language arts teacher education; environmental studies; fine/studio arts; health and physical education; health teacher education; history; history teacher education; international business/trade/commerce; international relations and affairs; mathematics; mathematics and computer science; mathematics teacher education; multi-/interdisciplinary studies related; music performance; music teacher education; nursing (registered nurse training); parks, recreation and leisure; physical education teaching and coaching; physics teacher education; piano and organ; political science and government; psychology; religious studies; sign language interpretation and translation; social studies teacher education; sociology; Spanish; Spanish language teacher education; technical and business writing; voice and opera; wind/percussion instruments.

Maryville University of Saint Louis

Accounting; accounting related; actuarial science; applied mathematics; art teacher education; biochemistry; biological and physical sciences; biology teacher education; biology/biological sciences; biomedical sciences; business administration and management; business/commerce; chemistry; chemistry teacher education; clinical laboratory science/medical technology; computer science; criminology; e-commerce; elementary education; English; English/language arts teacher education; environmental science; environmental studies; fine/studio arts; graphic design; health science; health/medical preparatory programs related; history; history teacher education; industrial and organizational psychology; interdisciplinary studies; interior design; kindergarten/preschool education; legal assistant/paralegal; liberal arts and sciences/liberal studies; management information systems; marketing/marketing management; mass communication/media; mathematics; mathematics teacher education; middle school education; music therapy; nursing (registered nurse training); occupational therapy; philosophy and religious studies related; physical therapy; political science and government; pre-dentistry studies; pre-engineering; pre-law; premedical studies; psychology; public health; secondary education; social psychology; sociology; sport and fitness administration/management; vocational rehabilitation counseling.

Massachusetts Institute of Technology

Aerospace, aeronautical and astronautical engineering; anthropology; architecture; biology/biological sciences; biomedical/medical engineering; business/commerce; chemical engineering; chemistry; city/urban, community and regional planning; civil engineering; cognitive psychology and psycholinguistics; computer science; creative writing; economics; electrical, electronics and communications engineering; English; environmental/environmental health engineering; foreign languages and literatures; geology/earth science; history; liberal arts and sciences/liberal studies; linguistics; mass communication/media; materials engineering; mathematics; mathematics and computer science; mechanical engineering; music; neuroscience; nuclear engineering; ocean engineering; philosophy; physics; political science and government; science, technology and society.

The Master's College and Seminary (CA)

Accounting; actuarial science; American government and politics; ancient Near Eastern and biblical languages; applied mathematics; biblical studies; biological and physical sciences; biology/biological sciences; business administration and management; computer and information sciences; divinity/ministry; education; elementary education; English; environmental biology; family and consumer sciences/human sciences; finance; foods, nutrition, and wellness; health and physical education; history; kinesiology and exercise science; liberal arts and sciences/liberal studies; management information systems; mass communication/media; mathematics; middle school education; music; music management and merchandising; music teacher education; natural sciences; pastoral studies/counseling; physical education teaching and coaching; physical sciences; piano and organ; political science and government; pre-law studies; premedical studies; public relations/image management; radio and television; religious education; religious studies; religious/sacred music; science teacher education; secondary education; speech and rhetoric; theology; voice and opera.

McDaniel College

Art; art history, criticism and conservation; biochemistry; biology/biological sciences; business administration and management; chemistry; communication/speech communication and rhetoric; computer and information sciences; dramatic/theater arts; economics; English; environmental science; French; German; history; kinesiology and exercise science; mathematics; multi-/interdisciplinary studies related; music; philosophy; philosophy and religious studies related; physics; political science and government; psychology; religious studies; social work; sociology; Spanish.

McGill University

Accounting; accounting and finance; agronomy and crop science; analytical chemistry; anatomy; animal behavior and ethology; anthropology; applied horticulture; applied mathematics; aquatic biology/limnology; art history, criticism and conservation; Asian history; atmospheric physics and dynamics; atmospheric sciences and meteorology; auditing; bilingual and multilingual education; biochemistry; biological and physical sciences; biology/biological sciences; biomedical sciences; botany/plant biology; business/commerce; business/managerial economics; Canadian history; Caribbean studies; cell biology and anatomy; cell biology and histology; chemistry; civil engineering; cognitive science; computer engineering; computer software engineering; development economics and international development; dramatic/theater arts; e-commerce; East Asian languages; ecology; economics; elementary education; entrepreneurship; environmental biology; environmental science; European history; finance; French as a second/foreign language (teaching); genetics; geography; geography teacher education; geology/earth science; geophysics and seismology; German studies; health and physical education; health teacher education; Hispanic American, Puerto Rican, and Mexican American/Chicano studies; history; human nutrition; human resources management; humanities; hydrology and water resources science; inorganic chemistry; insurance; international business/trade/commerce; international finance; Italian studies; jazz/jazz studies; Jewish/Judaic studies; kinesiology and exercise science; labor and industrial relations; language interpretation and translation; legal studies; management science; marine biology and biological oceanography; marketing/marketing management; materials engineering; mathematical statistics and probability; mathematics; mathematics and computer science; mechanical engineering; medical microbiology and bacteriology; metallurgical engineering; microbiology; molecular biology; music; music history, literature, and theory; music pedagogy; music performance; music theory and composition; natural sciences; Near and Middle Eastern studies; neuroanatomy; nursing (registered nurse training); nutrition sciences; operations management; organic chemistry; organizational behavior; philosophy; physics; physiology; piano and organ; planetary astronomy and science; political science and government; psychology; regional studies; religious education; religious studies; religious/sacred music; social work; sociology; Spanish and Iberian studies; statistics; taxation; theology; transportation management; urban studies/affairs; violin, viola, guitar and other stringed instruments; voice and opera; wildlife biology; zoology/animal biology.

McKendree University
Accounting; art; art teacher education; athletic training; biology teacher education; biology/biological sciences; business administration and management; business teacher education; chemistry; clinical laboratory science/medical technology; computer science; criminal justice/law enforcement administration; economics; education (K-12); elementary education; English; English/language arts teacher education; finance; history; history teacher education; information science/studies; international relations and affairs; marketing/marketing management; mass communication/media; mathematics; mathematics teacher education; middle school education; music; music teacher education; nursing (registered nurse training); occupational therapy; organizational communication; philosophy; physical education teaching and coaching; political science and government; pre-dentistry studies; pre-law studies; pre-veterinary studies; premedical studies; psychology; public relations/image management; religious studies; sales, distribution and marketing; secondary education; social science teacher education; social sciences; social work; sociology; speech and rhetoric; speech/theater education.

Mercer University
African American/Black studies; art; biochemistry; biology/biological sciences; business administration, management and operations related; business/commerce; chemistry; Christian studies; classics and languages, literatures and linguistics; communication and journalism related; community organization and advocacy; computer science; criminal justice/safety; dramatic/theater arts; economics; education related; elementary education; engineering; English; environmental science; environmental studies; French; German; health/medical preparatory programs related; history; human services; information science/studies; international relations and affairs; journalism; Latin; liberal arts and sciences/liberal studies; mass communication/media; mathematics; middle school education; multi-/interdisciplinary studies related; music; music performance; music related; music teacher education; nursing (registered nurse training); philosophy; physics; political science and government; pre-dentistry studies; premedical studies; psychology; regional studies; sociology; Spanish.

Messiah College
Accounting; art history, criticism and conservation; art teacher education; athletic training; biblical studies; biochemistry; biology teacher education; biology/biological sciences; biopsychology; business administration and management; business, management, and marketing related; business/managerial economics; chemistry; chemistry teacher education; clinical nutrition; communication/speech communication and rhetoric; computer science; criminal justice/safety; dramatic/theater arts; early childhood education; economics; elementary education; engineering; English; English/language arts teacher education; entrepreneurship; environmental science; environmental studies; family and community services; fine/studio arts; French; French language teacher education; German; German language teacher education; history; human resources management; humanities; information science/studies; international business/trade/commerce; journalism; kinesiology and exercise science; marketing/marketing management; mathematics; mathematics teacher education; multi-/interdisciplinary studies related; music; music teacher education; nursing (registered nurse training); parks, recreation and

leisure; philosophy; physical education teaching and coaching; physics; political science and government; psychology; radio and television; religious education; religious studies; social studies teacher education; social work; sociology; Spanish; Spanish language teacher education; sport and fitness administration/management.

Miami University
Accounting; accounting technology and bookkeeping; African American/Black studies; American studies; anthropology; architectural history and criticism; art history, criticism and conservation; art teacher education; athletic training; biochemistry; biology teacher education; botany/plant biology; business administration and management; business/managerial economics; chemical engineering; chemical technology; chemistry; chemistry teacher education; city/urban, community and regional planning; classics and languages, literatures and linguistics; clinical laboratory science/medical technology; commercial and advertising art; communication/speech communication and rhetoric; computer and information sciences; computer engineering; computer science; computer systems analysis; computer technology/computer systems technology; criminal justice/police science; data processing and data processing technology; digital communication and media/multimedia; dramatic/theater arts; early childhood education; East Asian languages; economics; electrical, electronic and communications engineering technology; electrical, electronics and communications engineering; engineering; engineering physics; engineering technology; engineering/industrial management; English; English/language arts teacher education; environmental science; environmental studies; finance; fine/studio arts; foods, nutrition, and wellness; foreign language teacher education; French; French language teacher education; geography; geology/earth science; German; German language teacher education; gerontology; health and physical education; health teacher education; history; human development and family studies; interior architecture; international relations and affairs; Italian studies; journalism; kinesiology and exercise science; Latin American studies; Latin teacher education; liberal arts and sciences/liberal studies; linguistics; management information systems; manufacturing engineering; marketing/marketing management; mass communication/media; mathematics; mathematics teacher education; mechanical engineering; mechanical engineering/mechanical technology; medical microbiology and bacteriology; middle school education; multi-/interdisciplinary studies related; music; music performance; music teacher education; nursing (registered nurse training); office management; operations management; philosophy; physical education teaching and coaching; physics; physics teacher education; political science and government; psychology; public administration; public relations/image management; real estate; religious studies; Russian; science teacher education; secondary education; social studies teacher education; social work; sociology; Spanish; Spanish language teacher education; special education; speech and rhetoric; speech teacher education; speech-language pathology; sport and fitness administration/management; statistics; women's studies; wood science and wood products/pulp and paper technology; zoology/animal biology.

Michigan State University
Accounting; advertising; agricultural business and management; agricultural economics; agricultural/biological engineering and bioengineering; agriculture and agriculture operations related; animal sciences; anthropology; apparel and textiles; applied economics; applied mathematics; art; art history, criticism and conservation; art teacher education; astrophysics; audiology and speech-language pathology; biochemistry; biochemistry/biophysics and molecular biology; biological and physical sciences; biology/biological sciences; biomedical/medical engineering; botany/plant biology; business administration and management; chemical engineering; chemical physics; chemistry; chemistry teacher education; city/urban, community and regional planning; civil engineering; clinical laboratory science/medical technology; communication/speech communication and rhetoric; computational mathematics; computer and information sciences; computer engineering; construction management; criminal justice/safety; dietetics; dramatic/theater arts; East Asian languages related; economics;

electrical, electronics and communications engineering; elementary education; engineering; English; entomology; environmental biology; environmental science; family and community services; family and consumer sciences/home economics teacher education; family and consumer sciences/human sciences; fashion/apparel design; finance; food science; forestry; French; geography; geology/earth science; geophysics and seismology; German; history; horticultural science; hotel/motel administration; human resources management; humanities; interior design; international relations and affairs; international/global studies; jazz/jazz studies; journalism; landscape architecture; logistics and materials management; marketing/marketing management; materials science; mathematics; mechanical engineering; merchandising; microbiology; music; music pedagogy; music performance; music teacher education; music theory and composition; music therapy; nursing (registered nurse training); operations management; parks, recreation and leisure facilities management; philosophy; physical and theoretical chemistry; physical education teaching and coaching; physical sciences; physics; physiology; plant pathology/phytopathology; political science and government; psychology; public administration; religious studies; Russian; science, technology and society; social science teacher education; social sciences; social work; sociology; soil science and agronomy; Spanish; special education; statistics; telecommunications; veterinary technology; veterinary/animal health technology; zoology/animal biology.

Michigan Technological University
Accounting; actuarial science; applied mathematics; audio engineering; biochemistry; bioinformatics; biology teacher education; biology/biological sciences; biology/biotechnology laboratory technician; biomedical/medical engineering; business administration and management; business teacher education; business/managerial economics; chemical engineering; chemical physics; chemistry; civil engineering; civil engineering technology; clinical laboratory science/medical technology; communication/speech communication and rhetoric; computational mathematics; computer engineering; computer programming; computer science; computer software engineering; computer systems networking and telecommunications; computer teacher education; construction engineering; cytotechnology; digital communication and media/multimedia; ecology; economics; electrical, electronic and communications engineering technology; electrical, electronics and communications engineering; electromechanical technology; engineering; engineering mechanics; engineering physics; engineering technology; English; English/language arts teacher education; environmental science; environmental/environmental health engineering; finance; forestry; forestry technology; general studies; geological/geophysical engineering; geology/earth science; geophysics and seismology; histologic technology/histotechnologist; history; humanities; industrial engineering; information science/studies; liberal arts and sciences/liberal studies; management information systems; marine biology; marketing/marketing management; materials engineering; mathematics; mathematics teacher education; mechanical engineering; mechanical engineering/mechanical technology; medical microbiology and bacteriology; medicinal/pharmaceutical chemistry; metallurgical engineering; microbiology; molecular biochemistry; operations management; physical sciences; physics; predentistry studies; pre-law studies; pre-pharmacy studies; pre-veterinary studies; premedical studies; psychology; science teacher education; secondary education; social sciences; statistics; survey technology; system administration; technical and business writing; technology/industrial arts teacher education; theater design and technology; wildlife and wildlands science and management.

Middlebury College
American literature; American studies; art history, criticism and conservation; Asian studies (East); biochemistry; biology/biological sciences; chemistry; Chinese; cinematography and film/video production; classics and languages, literatures and linguistics; computer science; dance; dramatic/theater arts; economics; English; environmental studies; European studies; European studies (Central and Eastern); fine/studio arts; French; geography; geology/earth science; German; history; international relations and affairs; Italian; Japanese; Latin American studies;

liberal arts and sciences/liberal studies; mathematics; modern languages; molecular biology; music; neuroscience; philosophy; physics; political science and government; psychology; religious studies; Russian; Russian studies; sociology; Spanish; women's studies.

Milligan College
Accounting; biblical studies; biology/biological sciences; business administration and management; chemistry; communication and media related; computer and information sciences; computer science; early childhood education; education; English; English language and literature related; fine/studio arts; health and physical education; health science; history; humanities; mathematics; music; music related; music teacher education; nursing (registered nurse training); pastoral studies/counseling; psychology; public administration and social service professions related; sociology.

Millsaps College
Accounting; anthropology; applied mathematics; art history, criticism and conservation; biochemistry; biology/biological sciences; business administration and management; chemistry; classics and languages, literatures and linguistics; communication/speech communication and rhetoric; computer science; dramatic/theater arts; economics; education; English; European studies; fine/studio arts; French; geology/earth science; history; mathematics; multi-/interdisciplinary studies related; music; philosophy; philosophy and religious studies related; physics; political science and government; psychology; public administration; religious studies; sociology; Spanish.

Mills College
American studies; anthropology; art; art history, criticism and conservation; biochemistry; biology/biological sciences; business/managerial economics; chemistry; comparative literature; computer science; creative writing; cultural studies; dance; developmental and child psychology; economics; engineering; English; environmental science; environmental studies; fine/studio arts; French; French studies; Hispanic American, Puerto Rican, and Mexican American/Chicano studies; history; interdisciplinary studies; intermedia/multimedia; international relations and affairs; liberal arts and sciences/liberal studies; mathematics; music; philosophy; physiological psychology/psychobiology; political science and government; psychology; public policy analysis; sociology; Spanish; women's studies.

Milwaukee School of Engineering
Architectural engineering; biomedical/medical engineering; business administration and management; business/commerce; communication and journalism related; computer engineering; computer software engineering; construction management; electrical, electronic and communications engineering technology; electrical, electronics and communications engineering; engineering; industrial engineering; international business/trade/commerce; management information systems; mechanical engineering; mechanical engineering/mechanical technology; nursing (registered nurse training).

Mississippi College
Accounting; art; art history, criticism and conservation; art teacher education; biochemistry; biology/biological sciences; business administration and management; business teacher education; chemistry; Christian studies; communication and journalism related; communication/speech communication and rhetoric; computer and information sciences; computer science; criminal justice/law enforcement administration; education; elementary education; engineering physics; English; foreign languages and literatures; foreign languages related; French; graphic design; health and physical education; history; interior design; international/global studies; kinesiology and exercise science; language interpretation and translation; legal assistant/paralegal; liberal arts and sciences/liberal studies; marketing/marketing management; mass communication/media; mathematics; music; music performance; music teacher education; music theory and composition; nursing (registered nurse training); physics; piano and organ; political science and

government; pre-dentistry studies; pre-law studies; pre-pharmacy studies; pre-veterinary studies; premedical studies; psychology; public relations/image management; religious/sacred music; science teacher education; secondary education; social science teacher education; social sciences; social sciences related; social studies teacher education; social work; sociology; Spanish; special education; sport and fitness administration/management; voice and opera.

Missouri State University

Accounting; agribusiness; agricultural teacher education; agriculture; agronomy and crop science; ancient studies; animal sciences; anthropology; apparel and textiles; art; art history, criticism and conservation; art teacher education; athletic training; audiology and speech-language pathology; biology teacher education; biology/biological sciences; business administration and management; business administration, management and operations related; business teacher education; business/commerce; cartography; cell and molecular biology; chemistry; chemistry teacher education; city/urban, community and regional planning; clinical laboratory science/medical technology; communication/speech communication and rhetoric; computer science; construction management; criminology; dance; design and visual communications; dietetics; dramatic/theater arts; early childhood education; economics; education (specific subject areas) related; elementary education; engineering/industrial management; English; English/language arts teacher education; entrepreneurship; family and consumer sciences/home economics teacher education; finance; fine/studio arts; French; French language teacher education; geography; geology/earth science; German; German language teacher education; gerontology; history; history teacher education; horticultural science; hospitality administration; housing and human environments; human development and family studies; insurance; intermedia/multimedia; journalism; Latin; logistics and materials management; management information systems; marketing/marketing management; mass communication/media; mathematics; mathematics teacher education; middle school education; molecular biology; music; music performance; music teacher education; nursing (registered nurse training); parks, recreation and leisure; philosophy; physical education teaching and coaching; physical science technologies related; physics; physics teacher education; political science and government; psychology; public administration; radiologic technology/science; religious studies; respiratory care therapy; science teacher education; social work; sociology; Spanish; Spanish language teacher education; special education; technical and business writing; visual and performing arts; wildlife and wildlands science and management.

Missouri University of Science and Technology

Aerospace, aeronautical and astronautical engineering; agricultural/biological engineering and bioengineering; applied mathematics; architectural engineering; biology/biological sciences; business administration and management; business, management, and marketing related; ceramic sciences and engineering; chemical engineering; chemistry; civil engineering; computer and information sciences and support services related; computer engineering; computer science; economics; electrical, electronics and communications engineering; engineering; engineering/industrial management; English; environmental/environmental health engineering; geological/geophysical engineering; geology/earth science; geophysics and seismology; history; industrial engineering; information science/studies; mechanical engineering; metallurgical engineering; mining and mineral engineering; nuclear engineering; petroleum engineering; philosophy; physics; pre-dentistry studies; pre-law studies; pre-veterinary studies; premedical studies; prenursing studies; psychology; secondary education.

Moravian College

Accounting; art; art history, criticism and conservation; art teacher education; biochemistry; biology teacher education; biology/biological sciences; business administration and management; chemistry; chemistry teacher education; classics and languages, literatures and linguistics; clinical laboratory science/medical technology; clinical psychology; computer science; creative writing; criminal justice/law enforcement

administration; dramatic/theater arts; economics; education; elementary education; English; English language and literature related; environmental studies; experimental psychology; fine/studio arts; foreign language teacher education; French; French language teacher education; geology/earth science; German; German language teacher education; German studies; graphic design; history; history teacher education; industrial and organizational psychology; international business/trade/commerce; mathematics; mathematics teacher education; music; music performance; music teacher education; music theory and composition; natural resources management; nursing (registered nurse training); philosophy; physics; physics teacher education; political science and government; psychology; religious studies; religious/sacred music; science teacher education; secondary education; social psychology; social sciences; social studies teacher education; sociology; Spanish; Spanish language teacher education; theater literature, history and criticism.

Morehouse College

African American/Black studies; art; biology/biological sciences; business administration and management; chemistry; computer and information sciences; dramatic/theater arts; economics; education; engineering; English; French; general studies; health and physical education; history; international relations and affairs; mathematics; music; philosophy; physics; political science and government; psychology; religious studies; sociology; Spanish; urban studies/affairs.

Mount Allison University

Accounting; American studies; ancient/classical Greek; anthropology; applied mathematics; art history, criticism and conservation; biochemistry; biological and physical sciences; biology/biological sciences; biopsychology; business administration and management; business/commerce; business/managerial economics; Canadian studies; chemistry; classics and languages, literatures and linguistics; computer science; dramatic/theater arts; drawing; economics; English; environmental studies; fine/studio arts; French; geography; geology/earth science; German; history; humanities; interdisciplinary studies; international business/trade/commerce; international relations and affairs; Latin; liberal arts and sciences/liberal studies; literature; mathematics; mathematics and computer science; medieval and Renaissance studies; modern languages; music; music history, literature, and theory; music performance; natural sciences; philosophy; photography; physics; physiological psychology/psychobiology; piano and organ; political science and government; pre-dentistry studies; pre-law studies; pre-pharmacy studies; pre-theology/pre-ministerial studies; pre-veterinary studies; premedical studies; printmaking; psychology; religious studies; Romance languages; sculpture; sociology; Spanish; violin, viola, guitar and other stringed instruments; voice and opera; wind/percussion instruments.

Mount Holyoke College

African American/Black studies; American studies; ancient studies; ancient/classical Greek; anthropology; architecture related; area, ethnic, cultural, and gender studies related; art; art history, criticism and conservation; Asian studies; astronomy; biochemistry; biology/biological sciences; chemistry; classics and languages, literatures and linguistics; computer science; dance; dramatic/theater arts; economics; education related; engineering; English; environmental studies; European studies; film/cinema studies; fine/studio arts; French; geography; geology/earth science; German; German studies; history; international relations and affairs; Italian; Jewish/Judaic studies; Latin; Latin American studies; mathematics; medieval and Renaissance studies; modern Greek; multi-/interdisciplinary studies related; music; neuroscience; philosophy; physics; political science and government; psychology; religious studies; Romance languages; Romance languages related; Russian studies; social sciences related; sociology; Spanish; statistics; women's studies.

Mount Saint Vincent University

Accounting; adult development and aging; anthropology; applied mathematics; art teacher education; biological and physical sciences; biology/biological sciences; business administration and management; chemistry; child development; computer and information sciences;

computer systems analysis; developmental and child psychology; dietetics; economics; education; elementary education; English; family and consumer economics related; fine/studio arts; foods, nutrition, and wellness; French; German; gerontology; history; hospitality administration; hotel/motel administration; human ecology; humanities; information science/studies; interdisciplinary studies; kindergarten/preschool education; liberal arts and sciences/liberal studies; linguistics; literature; management information systems; marketing research; marketing/marketing management; mathematics; mathematics and computer science; modern languages; nutrition sciences; peace studies and conflict resolution; philosophy; political science and government; psychology; public relations/image management; reading teacher education; religious studies; secondary education; social sciences; sociology; Spanish; special products marketing; statistics; tourism and travel services management; tourism and travel services marketing; women's studies.

Muhlenberg College

Accounting; American studies; anthropology; art; biochemistry; biology/biological sciences; business administration and management; chemistry; dance; dramatic/theater arts; economics; economics related; English; environmental science; French; German; history; international relations and affairs; mathematics; music; natural sciences; neuroscience; philosophy; physical sciences; physics; political science and government; political science and government related; psychology; religious studies; Russian studies; social sciences; sociology; Spanish.

Murray State University

Accounting; administrative assistant and secretarial science; agricultural business and management; agricultural teacher education; apparel and textiles; art teacher education; audiology and speech-language pathology; biology teacher education; biology/biological sciences; business administration and management; business teacher education; business/commerce; chemical engineering; chemical technology; chemistry; chemistry teacher education; child-care provision; clinical laboratory science/medical technology; computer and information sciences; computer engineering technology; drafting and design technology; dramatic/theater arts; early childhood education; economics; electromechanical technology; elementary education; engineering physics; engineering technology; English; English as a second/foreign language (teaching); English/language arts teacher education; environmental engineering technology; executive assistant/executive secretary; family and consumer economics related; family and consumer sciences/home economics teacher education; finance; fine/studio arts; fishing and fisheries sciences and management; foods, nutrition, and wellness; foodservice systems administration; foreign language teacher education; French; French language teacher education; general studies; geography; geology/earth science; German; German language teacher education; graphic and printing equipment operation/production; health teacher education; history; history teacher education; human development and family studies; international business/trade/commerce; international relations and affairs; journalism; kinesiology and exercise science; library science; management information systems; manufacturing technology; marketing/marketing management; mass communication/media; mathematics; mathematics teacher education; mechanical drafting and CAD/CADD; mechanical engineering; mechanical engineering/mechanical technology; middle school education; military technologies; music; music teacher education; nursing (registered nurse training); occupational safety and health technology; office management; parks, recreation and leisure facilities management; perioperative/operating room and surgical nursing; philosophy; physical education teaching and coaching; physics; physics teacher education; political science and government; psychology; public administration; public relations, advertising, and applied communication related; public relations/image management; radio and television; reading teacher education; science teacher education; secondary education; social science teacher education; social studies teacher education; social work; sociology; Spanish; Spanish language teacher education; special education; speech and rhetoric; speech teacher education; speech therapy; technical and business writing; technology/industrial arts teacher

education; telecommunications; veterinary/animal health technology; wildlife and wildlands science and management.

Nebraska Wesleyan University

Accounting; art; athletic training; biochemistry; biochemistry/biophysics and molecular biology; biology/biological sciences; biopsychology; business administration and management; business, management, and marketing related; chemistry; communication/speech communication and rhetoric; computer science; dramatic/theater arts; dramatic/theater arts and stagecraft related; economics; elementary education; English; English/language arts teacher education; French; German; health and physical education; history; industrial and organizational psychology; information science/studies; interdisciplinary studies; international business/trade/commerce; international/global studies; kinesiology and exercise science; mathematics; middle school education; music; music performance; music teacher education; nursing administration; philosophy; physical education teaching and coaching; physics; political communication; political science and government; psychology; religious studies; science teacher education; social science teacher education; social work; sociology; Spanish; special education; speech and rhetoric; sport and fitness administration/management; women's studies.

New College of Florida

Anthropology; applied mathematics; art history, criticism and conservation; biochemistry; biology/biological sciences; chemistry; classics and classical languages related; comparative literature; economics; English; environmental studies; European studies; fine/studio arts; French; French studies; general studies; German; Germanic languages; history; humanities; international/global studies; Latin American studies; liberal arts and sciences/liberal studies; marine biology and biological oceanography; mathematics; medieval and Renaissance studies; music; music history, literature, and theory; natural sciences; neurobiology and neurophysiology; philosophy; physics; political science and government; psychology; public policy analysis; religious studies; Russian; social sciences; sociology; Spanish; urban studies/affairs.

New Jersey Institute of Technology

Actuarial science; architecture; bioinformatics; biology/biological sciences; biomedical/medical engineering; business administration and management; chemical engineering; chemistry; civil engineering; communication and media related; computer and information sciences; computer and information sciences and support services related; computer engineering; electrical, electronics and communications engineering; engineering science; engineering technologies related; engineering technology; environmental/environmental health engineering; geological/geophysical engineering; history; industrial design; industrial engineering; information technology; interior design; international business/trade/commerce; manufacturing engineering; mathematics; mechanical engineering; natural resources/conservation; nursing (registered nurse training); nursing science; physics related; science, technology and society; web page, digital/multimedia and information resources design.

New Mexico Institute of Mining and Technology

Biology/biological sciences; business administration and management; chemical engineering; chemistry; civil engineering; computer science; electrical, electronics and communications engineering; engineering mechanics; environmental studies; environmental/environmental health engineering; general studies; geology/earth science; geophysics and seismology; information technology; materials engineering; mathematics; mechanical engineering; mining and mineral engineering; petroleum engineering; physical sciences; physical sciences related; physics; psychology; technical and business writing.

New York School of Interior Design

Interior design.

New York University

Accounting; actuarial science; African American/Black studies; anthropology; archeology; area, ethnic, cultural, and gender studies related; art; art history, criticism and conservation; Asian studies (East); biochemistry; biology teacher education; biology/biological sciences; business administration and management; business, management, and marketing related; business/managerial economics; chemistry; chemistry teacher education; cinematography and film/video production; city/urban, community and regional planning; classics and languages, literatures and linguistics; communication/speech communication and rhetoric; comparative literature; computer and information sciences; computer programming; computer science; dance; dental hygiene; diagnostic medical sonography and ultrasound technology; digital communication and media/multimedia; dramatic/theater arts; economics; education; elementary education; engineering related; English; English/language arts teacher education; European studies; film/cinema studies; finance; fine/studio arts; foods, nutrition, and wellness; foreign language teacher education; French; French language teacher education; general studies; German; graphic communications; health information/medical records technology; health/health-care administration; Hebrew; history; hospitality administration; hotel/motel administration; human services; humanities; information science/studies; interdisciplinary studies; international business/trade/commerce; international relations and affairs; Italian; Jewish/Judaic studies; journalism; kindergarten/preschool education; Latin; Latin American studies; liberal arts and sciences/liberal studies; linguistics; management information systems; marketing/marketing management; mass communication/media; mathematics; mathematics and statistics related; mathematics teacher education; medieval and Renaissance studies; middle school education; modern Greek; music; music management and merchandising; music performance; music teacher education; music theory and composition; Near and Middle Eastern studies; neuroscience; nursing (registered nurse training); operations research; philosophy; photography; physical therapist assistant; physics; physics teacher education; piano and organ; playwriting and screenwriting; political science and government; Portuguese; pre-dentistry studies; premedical studies; psychology; radio and television; real estate; religious studies; Romance languages; Russian; secondary education; social sciences; social studies teacher education; social work; sociology; Spanish; special education; special education (speech or language impaired); sport and fitness administration/management; statistics; theater literature, history and criticism; tourism and travel services management; urban studies/affairs; voice and opera.

North Carolina State University

Accounting; aerospace, aeronautical and astronautical engineering; agribusiness; agricultural and extension education; agricultural and food products processing; agricultural business and management; agricultural economics; agricultural teacher education; agricultural/biological engineering and bioengineering; agriculture; American government and politics; animal sciences; anthropology; apparel and textile manufacturing; apparel and textile marketing management; applied mathematics; arts management; biochemistry; biology teacher education; biology/biological sciences; biomedical/medical engineering; botany/plant biology; business administration and management; chemical engineering; chemistry; chemistry teacher education; civil engineering; computer engineering; construction engineering; construction management; creative writing; criminology; design and applied arts related; design and visual communications; ecology; economics; education; electrical, electronics and communications engineering; engineering; English; English/language arts teacher education; environmental design/architecture; environmental science; environmental/environmental health engineering; film/cinema studies; finance; fishing and fisheries sciences and management; food science; foreign language teacher education; French; French language teacher education; geology/earth science; graphic design; health occupations teacher education; history; history teacher education; human resources management; hydrology and water resources science; industrial design; industrial engineering; information technology; landscaping and groundskeeping; liberal arts and sciences/liberal studies; marketing/marketing management; mass communication/media; materials

engineering; materials science; mathematics; mathematics teacher education; mechanical engineering; meteorology; microbiology; middle school education; nuclear engineering; oceanography (chemical and physical); paleontology; parks, recreation and leisure facilities management; parks, recreation, and leisure related; philosophy; physics; physics related; physics teacher education; plant protection and integrated pest management; political science and government; political science and government related; psychology; psychology related; public policy analysis; public relations/image management; religious studies; sales and marketing/marketing and distribution teacher education; science teacher education; science, technology and society; secondary education; social studies teacher education; social work; sociology; soil science and agronomy; Spanish; Spanish language teacher education; sport and fitness administration/management; statistics; technology/industrial arts teacher education; textile science; textile sciences and engineering; tourism and travel services management; turf and turfgrass management; wildlife and wildlands science and management; zoology/animal biology.

North Central College

Accounting; actuarial science; applied mathematics; art; art teacher education; Asian studies (East); athletic training; biochemistry; biological and physical sciences; biology/biological sciences; business administration and management; chemistry; classics and languages, literatures and linguistics; creative writing; dramatic/theater arts; dramatic/theater arts and stagecraft related; economics; education; elementary education; English; finance; French; German; graphic design; history; human resources management; humanities; international business/trade/commerce; Japanese; jazz/jazz studies; journalism; kinesiology and exercise science; liberal arts and sciences/liberal studies; management information systems; marketing/marketing management; mathematics; medical radiologic technology; multi-/interdisciplinary studies related; music; music teacher education; nuclear medical technology; organizational communication; philosophy; physical education teaching and coaching; physics; political science and government; pre-dentistry studies; pre-law studies; pre-veterinary studies; premedical studies; psychology; radio and television; religious studies; secondary education; small business administration; social sciences; sociology; Spanish; speech and rhetoric; sport and fitness administration/management.

Northwestern College (IA)

Accounting; actuarial science; art; art teacher education; athletic training; biology teacher education; biology/biological sciences; business administration and management; business teacher education; chemistry; cinematography and film/video production; clinical laboratory science/medical technology; computer science; dramatic/theater arts; economics; education (K-12); elementary education; English; environmental biology; graphic design; history; humanities; journalism; kinesiology and exercise science; mathematics; music; music teacher education; nursing (registered nurse training); philosophy; physical education teaching and coaching; political science and government; psychology; religious education; religious studies; secondary education; social work; sociology; Spanish; speech and rhetoric; speech/theater education.

Northwestern College (MN)

Accounting; animation, interactive technology, video graphics and special effects; art teacher education; biblical studies; biology/biological sciences; business administration and management; communication/speech communication and rhetoric; creative writing; criminal justice/safety; dramatic/theater arts; early childhood education; elementary education; engineering; English; English as a second/foreign language (teaching); English/language arts teacher education; finance; fine/studio arts; graphic design; health and physical education; history; international business/trade/commerce; journalism; kinesiology and exercise science; liberal arts and sciences/liberal studies; management information systems; marketing/marketing management; mathematics; mathematics teacher education; missionary studies and missiology; multi-/interdisciplinary studies related; music; music performance; music teacher education; music theory and composition; pastoral counseling and specialized ministries related; physical education teaching and coaching; piano and organ; pre-theology/pre-ministerial studies; psychology; public relations/image management; radio and television; social studies teacher education; technical and business writing; theological and ministerial studies related; violin, viola, guitar and other stringed instruments; voice and opera; youth ministry.

Northwestern University

African American/Black studies; African studies; American studies; anthropology; applied mathematics; area studies related; art; art history, criticism and conservation; Asian studies; astronomy; audiology and hearing sciences; audiology and speech-language pathology; biochemistry; biological and physical sciences; biology/biological sciences; biomedical/medical engineering; Caribbean studies; cell biology and histology; chemical engineering; chemistry; civil engineering; classics and languages, literatures and linguistics; cognitive psychology and psycholinguistics; communication and media related; communication disorders; communication/speech communication and rhetoric; community organization and advocacy; community psychology; comparative literature; computer and information sciences; computer engineering; computer science; counseling psychology; dance; dramatic/theater arts; East Asian languages related; ecology; economics; education; electrical, electronics and communications engineering; engineering; engineering related; engineering science; English; environmental science; environmental studies; environmental/environmental health engineering; film/cinema studies; French; general studies; geography; geology/earth science; German; history; humanities; industrial engineering; information science/studies; interdisciplinary studies; international relations and affairs; Italian; jazz/jazz studies; journalism; legal studies; liberal arts and sciences/liberal studies; linguistics; manufacturing engineering; materials engineering; materials science; mathematics; mathematics teacher education; mechanical engineering; molecular biology; multi-/interdisciplinary studies related; music; music history, literature, and theory; music performance; music related; music teacher education; music theory and composition; musicology and ethnomusicology; neuroscience; organizational behavior; philosophy; physics; piano and organ; political science and government; premedical studies; psychology; public policy analysis; radio and television; religious studies; science, technology and society; secondary education; Slavic languages; Slavic studies; social and philosophical foundations of education; social sciences related; sociology; South Asian languages; Spanish; special education (specific learning disabilities); speech and rhetoric; speech therapy; speech-language pathology; statistics; theater literature, history and criticism; urban studies/affairs; violin, viola, guitar and other stringed instruments; visual and performing arts; voice and opera; wind/percussion instruments; women's studies.

Oberlin College

African American/Black studies; anthropology; archeology; art; art history, criticism and conservation; Asian studies (East); biochemistry; biology/biological sciences; chemistry; classics and languages, literatures and linguistics; comparative literature; computer science; creative writing; dance; dramatic/theater arts; ecology; economics; English; environmental studies; fine/studio arts; French; geology/earth science; German; history; interdisciplinary studies; jazz/jazz studies; Jewish/Judaic studies; Latin; Latin American studies; legal studies; mathematics; modern Greek; music; music history, literature, and theory; music teacher education; music theory and composition; Near and Middle Eastern studies; neuroscience; philosophy; physics; physiological psychology/psychobiology; piano and organ; political science and government; psychology; religious studies; Romance languages; Russian; Russian studies; sociology; Spanish; violin, viola, guitar and other stringed instruments; voice and opera; wind/percussion instruments; women's studies.

Occidental College

American studies; art history, criticism and conservation; Asian studies; biochemistry; biology/biological sciences; business/managerial economics; chemistry; cognitive psychology and psycholinguistics; cognitive science; comparative literature; dramatic/theater arts; economics; English; fine/studio arts; French; geology/earth science; geo-

physics and seismology; history; international relations and affairs; kinesiology and exercise science; mathematics; music; philosophy; physics; physiological psychology/psychobiology; political science and government; psychology; public policy analysis; religious studies; sociology; Spanish; women's studies.

Oglethorpe University

Accounting; American studies; art; art history, criticism and conservation; biology/biological sciences; biopsychology; business administration and management; business/managerial economics; chemistry; communication/speech communication and rhetoric; economics; engineering; English; French; history; interdisciplinary studies; international relations and affairs; mass communication/media; mathematics; philosophy; physics; political science and government; pre-dentistry studies; pre-law studies; pre-veterinary studies; premedical studies; psychology; social work; sociology; Spanish; theater/theater arts management; urban studies/affairs.

Ohio Northern University

Accounting; art; art teacher education; athletic training; biochemistry; biology teacher education; biology/biological sciences; business administration and management; business/commerce; ceramic arts and ceramics; chemistry; chemistry related; chemistry teacher education; civil engineering; civil engineering related; clinical laboratory science/medical technology; commercial and advertising art; communication and journalism related; communication/speech communication and rhetoric; computer engineering; computer engineering related; computer science; creative writing; criminal justice/law enforcement administration; criminal justice/police science; criminal justice/safety; design and visual communications; dramatic/theater arts; early childhood education; education; education (multiple levels); education related; electrical, electronics and communications engineering; elementary education; engineering; engineering related; English; English/language arts teacher education; fine/studio arts; foreign language teacher education; French; French language teacher education; general studies; German language teacher education; Germanic languages related; graphic design; health and physical education; health and physical education related; health teacher education; history; history teacher education; industrial arts; industrial technology; international business/trade/commerce; international relations and affairs; journalism; kindergarten/preschool education; kinesiology and exercise science; management science; management sciences and quantitative methods related; mathematics; mathematics related; mathematics teacher education; mechanical engineering; medicinal and pharmaceutical chemistry; middle school education; molecular biology; music; music management and merchandising; music performance; music related; music teacher education; organizational communication; painting; pharmacy; pharmacy, pharmaceutical sciences, and administration related; philosophy; philosophy related; physical education teaching and coaching; physics; physics related; physics teacher education; political science and government; pre-dentistry studies; pre-law studies; pre-theology/pre-ministerial studies; pre-veterinary studies; premedical studies; printmaking; psychology; psychology related; radio and television; religious studies; religious studies related; science teacher education; sculpture; secondary education; social studies teacher education; sociology; Spanish; Spanish language teacher education; sport and fitness administration/management; statistics; statistics related; technical and business writing; theater/theater arts management; visual and performing arts; visual and performing arts related.

The Ohio State University

Accounting; actuarial science; aerospace, aeronautical and astronautical engineering; African American/Black studies; African studies; agricultural business and management; agricultural communication/journalism; agricultural economics; agricultural teacher education; agricultural/biological engineering and bioengineering; agronomy and crop science; animal sciences; anthropology; apparel and textiles; Arabic; architecture; art; art history, criticism and conservation; art teacher education; astronomy; athletic training; audiology and speech-language pathology;

aviation/airway management; biochemistry; biology/biological sciences; botany/plant biology; business administration and management; business family and consumer sciences/human sciences; chemical engineering; chemistry; Chinese; civil engineering; classics and languages, literatures and linguistics; clothing/textiles; communication/speech communication and rhetoric; comparative literature; computer and information sciences; computer engineering; computer science; construction management; criminology; dance; dental hygiene; design and visual communications; dietetics; dramatic/theater arts; ecology, evolution, systematics and population biology related; economics; electrical, electronics and communications engineering; engineering; engineering physics; English; entomology; environmental science; family and consumer sciences/home economics teacher education; family resource management; film/cinema studies; finance; fine/studio arts; fishing and fisheries sciences and management; food science; food/nutrition; foods, nutrition, and wellness; forestry; French; geography; geology/earth science; German; health and physical education; health information/medical records administration; health professions related; health science; Hebrew; history; hospitality administration; human development and family studies; human nutrition; human resources development; human resources management; humanities; industrial design; industrial engineering; information science/studies; insurance/risk management; interior design; international business/trade/commerce; international relations and affairs; international/global studies; Islamic studies; Italian; Japanese; jazz/jazz studies; Jewish/Judaic studies; journalism; Korean; landscape architecture; linguistics; literature; logistics and materials management; management information systems; marketing/marketing management; materials engineering; materials science; mathematics; mechanical engineering; medical dietician; medical pharmacology and pharmaceutical sciences; medieval and Renaissance studies; microbiology; middle school education; modern Greek; molecular genetics; music; music history, literature, and theory; music performance; music teacher education; music theory and composition; nursing (registered nurse training); nursing science; operations management; parks, recreation and leisure; pharmacy; philosophy; physical education teaching and coaching; physics; piano and organ; plant sciences; political science and government; Portuguese; pre-dentistry studies; psychology; radiologic technology/science; real estate; respiratory care therapy; restaurant/food services management; Russian; social work; sociology; Spanish; special education; technical teacher education; technology/industrial arts teacher education; turf and turfgrass management; voice and opera; welding technology; wildlife and wildlands science and management; women's studies; zoology/animal biology.

Ohio Wesleyan University

Accounting; African American/Black studies; ancient studies; animal genetics; anthropology; art history, criticism and conservation; art teacher education; art therapy; Asian studies (East); astronomy; astrophysics; biology teacher education; biology/biological sciences; botany/plant biology; broadcast journalism; business administration and management; business teacher education; business/managerial economics; chemistry; chemistry teacher education; classics and languages, literatures and linguistics; computer science; creative writing; cultural studies; drama and dance teacher education; dramatic/theater arts; early childhood education; economics; education; education (K-12); education (multiple levels); elementary education; engineering related; engineering science; English; environmental studies; fine/studio arts; foreign language teacher education; French; French language teacher education; general studies; genetics; geography; geology/earth science; German; German language teacher education; health teacher education; history; history teacher education; humanities; international business/trade/commerce; international relations and affairs; journalism; kindergarten/preschool education; Latin American studies; Latin teacher education; literature; mathematics; mathematics teacher education; medical microbiology and bacteriology; medieval and Renaissance studies; middle school education; multi-/interdisciplinary studies related; music; music performance; music teacher education; neuroscience; philosophy; physical education teaching and coaching; physics; physics teacher education; political science and government; pre-dentistry studies; pre-law studies; pre-theology/pre-ministerial studies; pre-veterinary studies; premedical studies; psychology;

psychology teacher education; public administration; religious studies; secondary education; social studies teacher education; sociology; Spanish; Spanish language teacher education; statistics; urban studies/affairs; women's studies; zoology/animal biology.

Oklahoma Baptist University

Accounting; anthropology; art; art teacher education; athletic training; biblical languages/literatures; biblical studies; biochemistry; biology/biological sciences; chemistry; Christian studies; communication/speech communication and rhetoric; computer and information sciences; computer science; divinity/ministry; dramatic/theater arts; early childhood education; education; elementary education; English/language arts teacher education; family and community services; finance; fine/studio arts; graphic design; health and physical education; history; humanities; information science/studies; interdisciplinary studies; international business/trade/commerce; international marketing; international relations and affairs; journalism; kindergarten/preschool education; kinesiology and exercise science; management information systems; management science; marketing/marketing management; marriage and family therapy/counseling; mass communication/media; mathematics; mathematics teacher education; music; music performance; music teacher education; music theory and composition; natural sciences; nursing (registered nurse training); parks, recreation and leisure; philosophy; physical education teaching and coaching; physics; physiology; political science and government; psychology; religious studies; religious/sacred music; science teacher education; social sciences; social studies teacher education; sociology; Spanish; Spanish language teacher education; special education; speech and rhetoric; sport and fitness administration/management; voice and opera.

Oklahoma City University

Accounting; advertising; American studies; art history, criticism and conservation; art teacher education; arts management; biochemistry; biological and physical sciences; biology/biological sciences; biophysics; broadcast journalism; business administration and management; business/commerce; business/managerial economics; chemistry; cinematography and film/video production; commercial and advertising art; computer science; corrections; criminal justice/law enforcement administration; criminal justice/police science; dance; dramatic/theater arts; education; elementary education; English; finance; fine/studio arts; French; German; history; humanities; international business/trade/commerce; journalism; kindergarten/preschool education; kinesiology and exercise science; liberal arts and sciences/liberal studies; management information systems; marketing/marketing management; mass communication/media; mathematics; Montessori teacher education; music; music management and merchandising; music teacher education; music theory and composition; nursing (registered nurse training); philosophy; physical education teaching and coaching; physics; piano and organ; political science and government; pre-dentistry studies; pre-law studies; pre-pharmacy studies; pre-veterinary studies; premedical studies; prenursing studies; psychology; public relations/image management; radio and television; religious education; religious studies; religious/sacred music; science teacher education; secondary education; sociology; Spanish; speech and rhetoric; speech/theater education; theater design and technology; violin, viola, guitar and other stringed instruments; voice and opera; wind/percussion instruments.

Oklahoma State University

Accounting; aeronautics/aviation/aerospace science and technology; aerospace, aeronautical and astronautical engineering; agricultural business and management; agricultural communication/journalism; agricultural economics; agricultural public services related; agricultural teacher education; agricultural/biological engineering and bioengineering; American studies; animal sciences; architectural engineering; architecture; art; athletic training; biochemistry; biology/biological sciences; botany/plant biology; business administration and management; business/managerial economics; chemical engineering; chemistry; civil engineering; computer and information sciences; computer engineering; construction engineering technology; dramatic/

theater arts; economics; education; electrical, electronic and communications engineering technology; electrical, electronics and communications engineering; elementary education; English; entomology; environmental science; finance; fire protection and safety technology; food science; foods, nutrition, and wellness; forestry; French; general studies; geography; geology/earth science; German; history; horticultural science; hospitality administration; housing and human environments; human development and family studies; industrial engineering; international business/trade/commerce; journalism; landscape architecture; landscaping and groundskeeping; liberal arts and sciences/liberal studies; management information systems; marketing/marketing management; mathematics; mechanical engineering; mechanical engineering/mechanical technology; microbiology; music; music teacher education; parks, recreation and leisure; philosophy; physical education teaching and coaching; physics; physiology; political science and government; psychology; public health education and promotion; Russian; secondary education; sociology; soil science and agronomy; Spanish; speech-language pathology; statistics; technical teacher education; zoology/animal biology.

Pacific Lutheran University

Anthropology; art; biology/biological sciences; business administration and management; chemistry; Chinese; Chinese studies; classics and languages, literatures and linguistics; computer science; economics; education; engineering; English; environmental studies; fine/studio arts; French; geological and earth sciences/geosciences related; geology/earth science; German; history; international/global studies; mathematics; military studies; movement therapy and movement education; music; music teacher education; Norwegian; nursing (registered nurse training); philosophy; physics; political science and government; pre-law; premedical studies; psychology; religious studies; Scandinavian studies; social work; sociology; Spanish; theology; women's studies.

Pacific University

Accounting; art; art teacher education; athletic training; biology/biological sciences; broadcast journalism; business administration and management; chemistry; Chinese; computer science; creative writing; dramatic/theater arts; economics; education; elementary education; English; environmental studies; finance; French; German; health science; history; humanities; international relations and affairs; Japanese; journalism; kindergarten/preschool education; kinesiology and exercise science; liberal arts and sciences/liberal studies; literature; marketing/marketing management; mass communication/media; mathematics; modern languages; music; music performance; music teacher education; philosophy; physics; political science and government; pre-dentistry studies; pre-veterinary studies; premedical studies; psychology; radio and television; secondary education; social work; sociology; Spanish; telecommunications.

Peabody Conservatory of Music of The Johns Hopkins University

Audio engineering; jazz/jazz studies; music; music teacher education; piano and organ; violin, viola, guitar and other stringed instruments; voice and opera; wind/percussion instruments.

Penn State University Park

Accounting; acting; actuarial science; adult and continuing education administration; advertising; aerospace, aeronautical and astronautical engineering; African American/Black studies; agribusiness; agricultural and extension education; agricultural business and management related; agricultural mechanization; agriculture; agronomy and crop science; animal sciences; animal sciences related; anthropology; archeology; architectural engineering; architecture; art; art history, criticism and conservation; art teacher education; Asian studies (East); astronomy; atmospheric sciences and meteorology; biochemistry; biological and biomedical sciences related; biological and physical sciences; biology/biological sciences; biology/biotechnology laboratory technician; biomedical/medical engineering; business/commerce; business/managerial economics; chemical engineering; chemistry; civil engineering; classics and languages, literatures and linguistics; com-

munication and journalism related; communication disorders; communication/speech communication and rhetoric; comparative literature; computer and information sciences; computer engineering; criminal justice/law enforcement administration; dietitian assistant; economics; educational assessment, evaluation, and research related; electrical, electronics and communications engineering; elementary education; engineering related; engineering science; English; environmental/environmental health engineering; film/cinema studies; finance; food science; foreign language teacher education; forensic science and technology; forest sciences and biology; forestry technology; French; geography; geological and earth sciences/geosciences related; geology/earth science; German; graphic design; health/health-care administration; history; horticultural science; hospitality administration related; human development and family studies; human nutrition; industrial engineering; information science/studies; international relations and affairs; Italian; Japanese; Jewish/Judaic studies; journalism; kinesiology and exercise science; labor and industrial relations; landscape architecture; landscaping and groundskeeping; Latin American studies; liberal arts and sciences/liberal studies; management information systems; management sciences and quantitative methods related; marketing/marketing management; materials science; mathematics; mechanical engineering; medical microbiology and bacteriology; medieval and Renaissance studies; mining and mineral engineering; music; music performance; music teacher education; natural resources and conservation related; natural resources/conservation; nuclear engineering; nursing (registered nurse training); organizational behavior; parks, recreation and leisure facilities management; pathology/experimental pathology; petroleum engineering; philosophy; physics; political science and government; premedical studies; psychology; rehabilitation and therapeutic professions related; religious studies; Russian; secondary education; sociology; soil science and agronomy; Spanish; special education; statistics; theater design and technology; toxicology; turf and turfgrass management; visual and performing arts; women's studies.

Pepperdine University

Accounting; advertising; art; art history, criticism and conservation; athletic training; biology/biological sciences; business administration and management; chemistry; communication/speech communication and rhetoric; computer science; dramatic/theater arts; dramatic/theater arts and stagecraft related; economics; education; elementary education; English; foods, nutrition, and wellness; French; German; history; humanities; interdisciplinary studies; international business/trade/commerce; international relations and affairs; journalism; kinesiology and exercise science; liberal arts and sciences/liberal studies; mathematics; mathematics teacher education; music; music teacher education; natural sciences; philosophy; physical education teaching and coaching; political science and government; pre-dentistry studies; pre-law studies; premedical studies; psychology; public relations/image management; religious education; religious studies; secondary education; sociology; Spanish; speech and rhetoric; telecommunications.

Pitzer College

African American/Black studies; American studies; anthropology; art; art history, criticism and conservation; Asian American studies; Asian studies; biochemistry; biology/biological sciences; chemistry; classics; classics and languages, literatures and linguistics; creative writing; dance; dramatic/theater arts; ecology; economics; engineering; English; environmental science; environmental studies; European studies; film/cinema studies; fine/studio arts; foreign languages and literatures; French; German; Hispanic American, Puerto Rican, and Mexican American/Chicano studies; history; interdisciplinary studies; international relations and affairs; international/global studies; Latin American studies; linguistics; literature; mathematics; molecular biology; music; neuroscience; organizational behavior; philosophy; physics; political science and government; premedical studies; psychology; regional studies; religious studies; Romance languages; Russian; science, technology and society; sociology; Spanish; women's studies.

Point Loma Nazarene University

Accounting; art teacher education; athletic training; biblical studies; biochemistry; biology/biological sciences; broadcast journalism; business administration and management; business/corporate communications; chemistry; child development; communication/speech communication and rhetoric; computer science; creative writing; development economics and international development; dietetics; dramatic/theater arts; engineering physics; English; English language and literature related; environmental science; family and consumer sciences/human sciences; fashion/apparel design; fine arts related; fine/studio arts; foods, nutrition, and wellness; graphic communications; graphic design; health and physical education; history; industrial and organizational psychology; interior design; international/global studies; journalism; kinesiology and exercise science; liberal arts and sciences/liberal studies; management information systems; mass communication/media; mathematics; music; music performance; music teacher education; music theory and composition; nursing (registered nurse training); philosophy; philosophy and religious studies related; physics; piano and organ; political science and government; pre-theology/pre-ministerial studies; psychology; religious/sacred music; Romance languages; social sciences; social work; sociology; Spanish; theological and ministerial studies related; voice and opera.

Polytechnic Institute of NYU

Agricultural/biological engineering and bioengineering; bioinformatics; chemistry; civil engineering; computer engineering; computer science; construction management; electrical, electronics and communications engineering; liberal arts and sciences/liberal studies; management information systems; mathematics; mechanical engineering; molecular biochemistry; physics.

Pomona College

African American/Black studies; American studies; anthropology; art; art history, criticism and conservation; Asian American studies; Asian studies; Asian studies (East); astronomy; biochemistry; biology/biological sciences; chemistry; Chinese; classics and languages, literatures and linguistics; cognitive science; computer science; dance; dramatic/theater arts; ecology; economics; English; environmental studies; film/cinema studies; fine/studio arts; French; geology/earth science; German; Hispanic American, Puerto Rican, and Mexican American/Chicano studies; history; humanities; interdisciplinary studies; international relations and affairs; Japanese; Latin American studies; liberal arts and sciences/liberal studies; linguistics; mathematics; medical microbiology and bacteriology; modern languages; molecular biology; music; neuroscience; philosophy; physics; political science and government; premedical studies; psychology; public policy analysis; religious studies; Romance languages; Russian; sociology; Spanish; women's studies.

Presbyterian College

Accounting and business/management; art; art history, criticism and conservation; biology/biological sciences; business administration and management; business/managerial economics; chemistry; computer science; dramatic/theater arts; early childhood education; economics; education; English; fine arts related; fine/studio arts; foreign languages and literatures; French; German; history; mathematics; middle school education; modern languages; music; music performance; music teacher education; philosophy; physics; physics related; political science and government; psychology; religious studies; religious/sacred music; sociology; Spanish; special education.

Princeton University

Anthropology; architecture; art history, criticism and conservation; Asian studies (East); astrophysics; chemical engineering; chemistry; civil engineering; classics and languages, literatures and linguistics; comparative literature; computer engineering; ecology; economics; electrical, electronics and communications engineering; English; French; geological and earth sciences/geosciences related; German; history; mathematics; mechanical engineering; molecular biology; multi-/interdisciplinary studies related; music; Near and Middle Eastern studies;

operations research; philosophy; physics; political science and government; psychology; public policy analysis; religious studies; Slavic languages; sociology; Spanish.

Providence College

Accounting; American studies; art history, criticism and conservation; banking and financial support services; biochemistry; biology/biological sciences; business administration and management; ceramic arts and ceramics; chemistry; community organization and advocacy; computer science; divinity/ministry; drawing; economics; engineering physics; English; finance; fine/studio arts; fire science; French; general studies; health/health-care administration; history; humanities; international/global studies; Italian; liberal arts and sciences/liberal studies; marketing/marketing management; mathematics; multi-/interdisciplinary studies related; music; music teacher education; painting; philosophy; political science and government; psychology; secondary education; social sciences; social work; sociology; Spanish; special education; systems engineering; theology; visual and performing arts; visual and performing arts related.

Purdue University

Accounting; actuarial science; aeronautical/aerospace engineering technology; aeronautics/aviation/aerospace science and technology; aerospace, aeronautical and astronautical engineering; African American/Black studies; agricultural communication/journalism; agricultural economics; agricultural mechanization; agricultural teacher education; agricultural/biological engineering and bioengineering; agriculture; agronomy and crop science; animal sciences; anthropology; apparel and textiles; applied mathematics; architectural engineering technology; art; Asian studies; athletic training; atmospheric sciences and meteorology; audiology and speech-language pathology; biochemistry; biological and physical sciences; biology teacher education; biology/biological sciences; biomedical/medical engineering; botany/plant biology; business administration and management; cell and molecular biology; chemical engineering; chemistry; chemistry teacher education; civil engineering; classics and languages, literatures and linguistics; clinical laboratory science/medical technology; communication/speech communication and rhetoric; computer and information sciences; computer engineering; computer science; construction engineering; construction engineering technology; construction management; creative writing; design and visual communications; dietetic technician; dramatic/theater arts; early childhood education; education; electrical, electronics and communications engineering; elementary education; engineering related; English; entomology; family and consumer sciences/human sciences; farm and ranch management; financial planning and services; fine/studio arts; fishing and fisheries sciences and management; food science; foods, nutrition, and wellness; foreign languages and literatures; forestry; French; French language teacher education; geology/earth science; German language teacher education; German studies; health and physical education; health professions related; health services/allied health/health sciences; health teacher education; history; horticultural science; hospitality administration related; human development and family studies; humanities; industrial engineering; industrial technology; interdisciplinary studies; interior design; Japanese; Japanese studies; journalism; kindergarten/preschool education; kinesiology and exercise science; landscape architecture; liberal arts and sciences and humanities related; liberal arts and sciences/liberal studies; management information systems and services related; manufacturing technology; marketing/marketing management; materials engineering; mathematics; mathematics teacher education; mechanical drafting and CAD/CADD; mechanical engineering; mechanical engineering technologies related; mechanical engineering/mechanical technology; meteorology; microbiology; molecular biology; music; natural resources/conservation; nuclear engineering; nursing (registered nurse training); nutrition sciences; occupational health and industrial hygiene; operations management; pharmacy; philosophy; photography; physical education teaching and coaching; physics; physics teacher education; plant genetics; political science and government; pre-dentistry studies; premedical studies; psychology; public relations/image management; religious studies; robotics technology; Russian; science teacher education; secondary education; social sciences; social studies teacher education; social work; sociology; Spanish; Spanish language teacher education; special education (early childhood); speech-language pathology; statistics; survey technology; surveying engineering; technology/industrial arts teacher education; tourism and travel services management; veterinary/animal health technology; visual and performing arts; wildlife and wildlands science and management; women's studies; zoology/animal biology.

Queen's University at Kingston
American native/native American education; art history, criticism and conservation; biochemistry; biology/biological sciences; business/commerce; Canadian studies; cartography; chemical engineering; chemistry; civil engineering; cognitive science; computer engineering; computer science; dramatic/theater arts; economics; education; education (multiple levels); electrical, electronics and communications engineering; elementary education; engineering; engineering physics; engineering related; English; environmental science; film/cinema studies; French; geography; geological/geophysical engineering; geology/earth science; German; German studies; health and physical education; history; linguistics; mathematics; mechanical engineering; mining and mineral engineering; music; nursing (registered nurse training); occupational therapy; philosophy; physical education teaching and coaching; physical therapy; physics; political science and government; psychology; religious studies; science teacher education; sociology; Spanish; statistics; technical teacher education; theology; women's studies.

Quincy University
Accounting; aviation/airway management; biology/biological sciences; business administration and management; chemistry; clinical laboratory science/medical technology; communication/speech communication and rhetoric; computer and information sciences; computer science; criminal justice/safety; elementary education; English; finance; forensic science and technology; graphic design; history; human services; humanities; management science; marketing/marketing management; mathematics; music; music teacher education; nursing (registered nurse training); philosophy; physical education teaching and coaching; political science and government; psychology; sign language interpretation and translation; special education; sport and fitness administration/management; theology.

Quinnipiac University
Accounting; actuarial science; advertising; applied mathematics; athletic training; biochemistry; biological and physical sciences; biology/biological sciences; broadcast journalism; business administration and management; business/managerial economics; chemistry; child development; cinematography and film/video production; communication and journalism related; computer science; criminal justice/safety; developmental and child psychology; dramatic/theater arts; economics; education; English; entrepreneurship; film/cinema studies; finance; gerontology; history; human resources management; human services; information science/studies; international business/trade/commerce; international relations and affairs; journalism; legal assistant/paralegal; legal studies; liberal arts and sciences/liberal studies; literature; marketing/marketing management; mass communication/media; mathematics; medical microbiology and bacteriology; nursing (registered nurse training); occupational therapy; physical therapy; physician assistant; physiological psychology/psychobiology; political science and government; pre-dentistry studies; pre-law studies; pre-veterinary studies; premedical studies; psychology; public relations/image management; radiologic technology/science; sales, distribution and marketing; social sciences; sociology; Spanish; web page, digital/multimedia and information resources design.

Randolph College
Ancient/classical Greek; art; art history, criticism and conservation; biology/biological sciences; business/commerce; chemistry; classics and languages, literatures and linguistics; communication/speech communication and rhetoric; creative writing; dance; dramatic/theater arts; economics; elementary education; engineering physics; English; environmental studies; fine/studio arts; French; German; health professions related; history; international relations and affairs; Latin; liberal arts and sciences/liberal studies; mathematics; museum studies; music history, literature, and theory; music performance; music theory and composition; philosophy; physics; political science and government; psychology; religious studies; sociology; Spanish.

Reed College
American studies; anthropology; art; biochemistry; biology/biological sciences; chemistry; Chinese; classics and languages, literatures and linguistics; dance; dramatic/theater arts; economics; English; fine/studio arts; French; German; history; international relations and affairs; linguistics; literature; mathematics; music; philosophy; physics; political science and government; psychology; religious studies; Russian; sociology; Spanish.

Regis University
Accounting; biochemistry; biology/biological sciences; business administration and management; chemistry; communication/speech communication and rhetoric; computer science; criminal justice/law enforcement administration; economics; education; elementary education; English; environmental studies; French; health information/medical records administration; history; human ecology; humanities; liberal arts and sciences/liberal studies; mathematics; neuroscience; nursing (registered nurse training); philosophy; political science and government; pre-dentistry studies; pre-law studies; pre-veterinary studies; premedical studies; psychology; religious studies; sociology; Spanish; visual and performing arts.

Rensselaer Polytechnic Institute
Aerospace, aeronautical and astronautical engineering; Air Force R.O.T.C./air science; applied mathematics; architecture; architecture related; Army R.O.T.C./military science; biochemistry; bioinformatics; biological and biomedical sciences related; biological and physical sciences; biology/biological sciences; biomedical/medical engineering; biophysics; building/construction finishing, management, and inspection related; business administration and management; chemical engineering; chemistry; civil engineering; communication/speech communication and rhetoric; computer and information sciences; computer engineering; computer science; economics; electrical, electronics and communications engineering; engineering; engineering physics; engineering science; environmental/environmental health engineering; finance; geology/earth science; hydrology and water resources science; industrial engineering; information technology; interdisciplinary studies; management information systems; management information systems and services related; manufacturing engineering; marketing/marketing management; materials engineering; mathematics; mechanical engineering; Navy/Marine Corps R.O.T.C./naval science; nuclear engineering; philosophy; pre-law studies; premedical studies; psychology; science, technology and society; social sciences; systems engineering; visual and performing arts related.

Rhodes College
Anthropology; art; art history, criticism and conservation; biochemistry; biology/biological sciences; business administration and management; chemistry; classics and languages, literatures and linguistics; computer science; dramatic/theater arts; economics; English; fine/studio arts; French; German; history; interdisciplinary studies; international business/trade/commerce; international economics; international relations and affairs; Latin; mathematics; modern Greek; music; philosophy; physics; political science and government; psychology; religious studies; Russian studies; sociology; Spanish; urban studies/affairs.

Rice University
Ancient/classical Greek; anthropology; applied mathematics; architecture; art; art history, criticism and conservation; Asian studies; astronomy; astrophysics; biochemistry; biology/biological sciences; biomedical/

medical engineering; business administration and management; chemical engineering; chemistry; civil engineering; classics and languages, literatures and linguistics; computer and information sciences; computer engineering; ecology; economics; electrical, electronics and communications engineering; English; environmental/environmental health engineering; evolutionary biology; fine/studio arts; French; geology/earth science; geophysics and seismology; German; history; kinesiology and exercise science; Latin; Latin American studies; linguistics; materials engineering; materials science; mathematics; mechanical engineering; multi-/interdisciplinary studies related; music; music history, literature, and theory; music performance; music theory and composition; neuroscience; philosophy; physical and theoretical chemistry; physics; political science and government; psychology; public policy analysis; religious studies; Russian; Russian studies; sociology; Spanish; statistics; visual and performing arts related; women's studies.

Ripon College

Anthropology; art; biochemistry; biology/biological sciences; business administration and management; chemistry; communication/speech communication and rhetoric; computer science; dramatic/theater arts; early childhood education; economics; education; elementary education; English; environmental studies; French; German; history; interdisciplinary studies; Latin American studies; mathematics; music; music teacher education; philosophy; physical education teaching and coaching; physical sciences; physiological psychology/psychobiology; political science and government; pre-dentistry studies; pre-law studies; pre-veterinary studies; premedical studies; psychology; religious studies; Romance languages; secondary education; sociology; Spanish.

Rochester Institute of Technology

Accounting; advertising; aerospace, aeronautical and astronautical engineering; American Sign Language (ASL); animation, interactive technology, video graphics and special effects; biochemistry; bioinformatics; biological and biomedical sciences related; biology/biological sciences; biomedical sciences; biomedical/medical engineering; biotechnology; business administration and management; business/commerce; ceramic arts and ceramics; chemistry; cinematography and film/video production; civil engineering technology; clinical laboratory science/medical technology; commercial and advertising art; commercial photography; communication and media related; communication/speech communication and rhetoric; computational mathematics; computer and information sciences; computer and information systems security; computer engineering; computer engineering technology; computer graphics; computer science; computer software engineering; computer systems analysis; computer systems networking and telecommunications; crafts, folk art and artisanry; criminal justice/law enforcement administration; criminal justice/safety; data modeling/warehousing and database administration; design and visual communications; desktop publishing and digital imaging design; diagnostic medical sonography and ultrasound technology; digital communication and media/multimedia; economics; electrical and electronic engineering technologies related; electrical, electronics and communications engineering; electromechanical technology; engineering; engineering related; engineering science; engineering-related technologies; environmental science; finance; fine/studio arts; foodservice systems administration; graphic communications; graphic design; hazardous materials management and waste technology; hospitality administration; hospitality and recreation marketing; hotel/motel administration; human nutrition; illustration; industrial design; industrial engineering; industrial safety technology; information technology; interdisciplinary studies; interior design; intermedia/multimedia; international business/trade/commerce; international relations and affairs; journalism; management information systems; manufacturing technology; marketing/marketing management; mathematics; mathematics and computer science; mechanical engineering; medical illustration; metal and jewelry arts; metallurgy; natural resources management and policy; occupational safety and health technology; ophthalmic laboratory technology; painting; philosophy; photographic and film/video technology; photojournalism; physician assistant; pre-dentistry studies; pre-law studies; pre-veterinary studies; premedical studies; printing management; psychology; public policy analysis; public relations, advertising, and applied communication related; public relations/image management; publishing; quality control and safety technologies related; resort management; restaurant/food services management; sculpture; sign language interpretation and translation; special products marketing; statistics; system administration; system, networking, and LAN/WAN management; systems engineering; telecommunications; telecommunications technology; tourism and travel services marketing; web page, digital/multimedia and information resources design; web/multimedia management and webmaster; woodworking.

Rollins College

Anthropology; art history, criticism and conservation; biochemistry; biology/biological sciences; chemistry; classics and languages, literatures and linguistics; communication and media related; computer science; dramatic/theater arts; economics; education; English; environmental studies; fine/studio arts; French; history; international business/trade/commerce; international relations and affairs; Latin American studies; marine biology; mathematics; music; philosophy; physics; political science and government; psychology; religious studies; sociology; Spanish.

Rose-Hulman Institute of Technology

Biology/biological sciences; biomedical/medical engineering; chemical engineering; chemistry; civil engineering; computer engineering; computer science; computer software engineering; economics; electrical, electronics and communications engineering; engineering physics; engineering related; mathematics; mechanical engineering; physics.

Rutgers, The State University of New Jersey, Newark

Accounting; African American/Black studies; allied health diagnostic, intervention, and treatment professions related; American studies; anthropology; applied mathematics; art; biological and biomedical sciences related; biology/biological sciences; botany/plant biology; business administration and management; chemistry; classics and classical languages related; classics and languages, literatures and linguistics; clinical laboratory science/medical technology; computer and information sciences; criminal justice/safety; cultural studies; dramatic/theater arts; economics; engineering; English; environmental studies; finance; fine arts related; French; geological/geophysical engineering; geology/earth science; German; Hispanic American, Puerto Rican, and Mexican American/Chicano studies; history; information science/studies; Italian; journalism; marketing/marketing management; mathematics; multi-/interdisciplinary studies related; music; nursing (registered nurse training); philosophy; physics; physics related; political science and government; psychology; science, technology and society; Slavic, Baltic, and Albanian languages related; social work; sociology; Spanish; women's studies; zoology/animal biology.

Rutgers, The State University of New Jersey, New Brunswick

Accounting; African studies; agricultural/biological engineering and bioengineering; agriculture; American studies; ancient/classical Greek; animal genetics; animal physiology; animal sciences; animal/livestock husbandry and production; anthropology; art; art history, criticism and conservation; Asian studies (East); astrophysics; atmospheric sciences and meteorology; biochemistry; biology/biological sciences; biomedical sciences; biomedical/medical engineering; biometry/biometrics; biotechnology; business administration and management; cell biology and anatomical sciences related; cell biology and histology; ceramic arts and ceramics; ceramic sciences and engineering; chemical engineering; chemistry; Chinese; civil engineering; classics and languages, literatures and linguistics; clinical laboratory science/medical technology; commercial and advertising art; communication/speech communication and rhetoric; comparative literature; computer engineering; computer science; criminal justice/law enforcement administration; cultural studies; dance; dramatic/theater arts; drawing; ecology; economics; electrical, electronics and communications engineering; engineering science; English; environmental design/architecture; environmental studies; equestrian studies;

European studies (Central and Eastern); evolutionary biology; film/cinema studies; finance; food science; foreign languages and literatures; French; geography; geology/earth science; German; Hispanic American, Puerto Rican, and Mexican American/Chicano studies; history; human ecology; industrial engineering; information science/studies; interdisciplinary studies; Italian; jazz/jazz studies; Jewish/Judaic studies; journalism; kinesiology and exercise science; labor and industrial relations; Latin; Latin American studies; liberal arts and sciences/liberal studies; linguistics; management science; management sciences and quantitative methods related; marine biology and biological oceanography; marketing/marketing management; mass communication/media; mathematics; mechanical engineering; medical microbiology and bacteriology; medieval and Renaissance studies; molecular biology; music; music teacher education; natural resources management; natural resources/conservation; Near and Middle Eastern studies; nursing (registered nurse training); nutrition sciences; painting; pharmacy; philosophy; photography; physics; plant science; political science and government; Portuguese; pre-dentistry studies; pre-law studies; premedical studies; printmaking; psychology; public health; religious studies; Russian; Russian studies; sculpture; social sciences related; social work; sociology; Spanish; statistics; turf and turfgrass management; urban studies/affairs; veterinary sciences; visual and performing arts; women's studies.

Saint Francis University

Accounting; accounting and finance; American studies; anthropology; biology teacher education; biology/biological sciences; business administration and management; chemistry; chemistry teacher education; clinical laboratory science/medical technology; computer programming; computer science; criminal justice/law enforcement administration; criminology; economics; education; elementary education; engineering; English; English/language arts teacher education; environmental science; environmental studies; exercise physiology; finance; fine arts related; foreign language teacher education; forensic science and technology; French; French language teacher education; history; history teacher education; human resources management; international business/trade/commerce; international relations and affairs; journalism; labor and industrial relations; literature; management information systems; marine biology and biological oceanography; marketing/marketing management; mass communication/media; mathematics; mathematics and computer science; mathematics teacher education; modern languages; nursing (registered nurse training); occupational therapy; pastoral studies/counseling; philosophy; physical therapy; physician assistant; political science and government; pre-dentistry studies; pre-law studies; pre-veterinary studies; premedical studies; psychology; public administration; public relations/image management; real estate; religious studies; science teacher education; secondary education; social studies teacher education; social work; sociology; Spanish; special education.

St. John's College (MD)

Interdisciplinary studies; liberal arts and sciences/liberal studies; western civilization.

St. John's College (NM)

Ancient/classical Greek; classics and languages, literatures and linguistics; English; ethics; foreign languages and literatures; French; general studies; history; history of philosophy; humanities; liberal arts and sciences and humanities related; liberal arts and sciences/liberal studies; literature; mathematics; philosophy; philosophy and religious studies related; philosophy related; physical sciences; physics; premedical studies; religious studies; western civilization.

Saint John's University (MN)

Accounting; art; biochemistry; biology/biological sciences; business administration and management; chemistry; classics and languages, literatures and linguistics; computer science; dietetics; dramatic/theater arts; economics; education; elementary education; engineering physics; English; environmental studies; fine/studio arts; foods, nutrition, and wellness; forest sciences and biology; French; German; history; humanities; mathematics; mathematics and computer science; music;

natural sciences; nursing (registered nurse training); occupational therapy; peace studies and conflict resolution; philosophy; physical therapy; physics; political science and government; pre-dentistry studies; pre-law studies; pre-pharmacy studies; pre-theology/pre-ministerial studies; pre-veterinary studies; premedical studies; psychology; religious education; secondary education; social sciences; social work; sociology; Spanish; speech and rhetoric; theology.

Saint Joseph's University

Accounting; actuarial science; biochemistry; biology/biological sciences; business administration and management; chemistry; communication/speech communication and rhetoric; computer and information sciences; criminology; economics; elementary education; English; English/language arts teacher education; environmental studies; European studies; finance; foreign language teacher education; French; French studies; German; health services/allied health/health sciences; history; hospital and health-care facilities administration; humanities; information science/studies; international business/trade/commerce; international marketing; international relations and affairs; Italian; Latin; legal studies; liberal arts and sciences/liberal studies; management information systems; marketing/marketing management; mathematics; mathematics teacher education; philosophy; physics; political science and government; psychology; public administration; purchasing, procurement/acquisitions and contracts management; religious studies; science teacher education; secondary education; social sciences; social studies teacher education; sociology; Spanish; special education; special products marketing; visual and performing arts.

St. Lawrence University

African studies; American literature; anthropology; art; art history, criticism and conservation; Asian studies; biochemistry; biology/biological sciences; biophysics; Canadian studies; chemistry; computer science; creative writing; dramatic/theater arts; economics; English; English literature (British and Commonwealth); environmental studies; fine/studio arts; foreign languages and literatures; French; geology/earth science; geophysics and seismology; German; history; international/global studies; mathematics; mathematics and computer science; modern languages; music; neurobiology and neurophysiology; neuroscience; philosophy; physics; political science and government; psychology; religious studies; sociology; Spanish.

St. Louis College of Pharmacy

Pharmacy.

Saint Louis University

Aeronautical/aerospace engineering technology; aerospace, aeronautical and astronautical engineering; airline pilot and flight crew; American studies; art history, criticism and conservation; athletic training; atmospheric sciences and meteorology; audiology and speech-language pathology; aviation/airway management; biochemistry; biology/biological sciences; biomedical/medical engineering; business administration and management; chemistry; classics and classical languages related; clinical laboratory science/medical technology; communication/speech communication and rhetoric; computer and information sciences; computer engineering; corrections; criminal justice/law enforcement administration; cytotechnology; dramatic/theater arts; economics; education (multiple levels); electrical, electronic and communications engineering technology; electrical, electronics and communications engineering; engineering physics; engineering/industrial management; English; environmental science; fine/studio arts; foods, nutrition, and wellness; foreign languages and literatures; French; geology/earth science; geophysics and seismology; German; health information/medical records administration; health/health-care administration; history; human resources management; humanities; international relations and affairs; Italian; kinesiology and exercise science; management information systems; management science; marketing/marketing management; mathematics; mechanical engineering; medical radiologic technology; modern Greek; music; nuclear medical technology; nursing (registered nurse training); organizational behavior; philosophy; physical therapy;

physics; political science and government; psychology; purchasing, procurement/acquisitions and contracts management; Russian; social work; sociology; Spanish; theology; urban studies/affairs; women's studies.

Saint Mary's College

Accounting; applied mathematics related; art; art teacher education; biology/biological sciences; business administration and management; business teacher education; chemistry; clinical laboratory science/medical technology; communication disorders; communication/speech communication and rhetoric; creative writing; dramatic/theater arts; economics; education; elementary education; English literature (British and Commonwealth); French; history; humanities; interdisciplinary studies; Italian; management information systems; marketing/marketing management; mathematics; mathematics and computer science; music; music teacher education; nursing (registered nurse training); philosophy; political science and government; psychology; religious studies; social work; sociology; Spanish.

Saint Mary's College of California

Accounting; accounting related; American studies; anthropology; archeology; area, ethnic, cultural, and gender studies related; art; art history, criticism and conservation; biochemistry; biological and biomedical sciences related; biology/biological sciences; business administration and management; business/commerce; chemistry; chemistry related; communication and journalism related; communication/speech communication and rhetoric; dance; dramatic/theater arts; economics; engineering; English; English language and literature related; European studies; finance and financial management services related; foreign languages related; French; German; health and physical education; health and physical education related; health professions related; historic preservation and conservation; history; industrial and organizational psychology; interdisciplinary studies; international business/trade/commerce; international relations and affairs; Italian; kinesiology and exercise science; Latin; Latin American studies; liberal arts and sciences and humanities related; liberal arts and sciences/liberal studies; literature; mathematics; mathematics and computer science; mathematics and statistics related; modern Greek; modern languages; multi-/interdisciplinary studies related; music; nursing (registered nurse training); philosophy; physics; physiological psychology/psychobiology; political science and government; political science and government related; psychology; psychology related; religious studies; social sciences; social sciences related; sociology; Spanish; sport and fitness administration/management; theater literature, history and criticism; theology; visual and performing arts related; women's studies.

St. Mary's College of Maryland

Anthropology; art; biochemistry; biological and physical sciences; biology/biological sciences; chemistry; computer and information sciences; dramatic/theater arts; economics; English; foreign languages and literatures; history; mathematics; multi-/interdisciplinary studies related; music; philosophy; physics; political science and government; psychology; psychology related; public policy analysis; religious studies; sociology.

St. Norbert College

Accounting; art; biological and physical sciences; biology/biological sciences; business administration and management; chemistry; commercial and advertising art; communication/speech communication and rhetoric; computer and information sciences; dramatic/theater arts; economics; elementary education; English; environmental science; French; geology/earth science; German; history; humanities; international business/trade/commerce; international relations and affairs; mathematics; music; music teacher education; philosophy; physics; political science and government; psychology; religious studies; sociology; Spanish.

St. Olaf College

American studies; ancient studies; ancient/classical Greek; art; art history, criticism and conservation; Asian studies; biology/biological sciences; chemistry; classics and languages, literatures and linguistics; computer science; dance; dramatic/theater arts; economics; English; environmental studies; ethnic, cultural minority, and gender studies related; French; German; history; kinesiology and exercise science; Latin; Latin American studies; liberal arts and sciences/liberal studies; mathematics; multi-/interdisciplinary studies related; music; music performance; music related; music teacher education; music theory and composition; Norwegian; nursing (registered nurse training); philosophy; physics; political science and government; psychology; religious studies; Russian; Russian studies; social studies teacher education; social work; sociology; Spanish; women's studies.

Salem College

Accounting; American studies; art history, criticism and conservation; arts management; biology/biological sciences; business administration and management; chemistry; clinical laboratory science/medical technology; creative writing; economics; education; English; fine/studio arts; French; German; history; interdisciplinary studies; interior design; international business/trade/commerce; international relations and affairs; mass communication/media; mathematics; music; music performance; music teacher education; nonprofit management; philosophy; physician assistant; psychology; religious studies; sociology; Spanish.

Samford University

Accounting; ancient/classical Greek; Asian studies; athletic training; biochemistry; biology/biological sciences; business administration and management; business/managerial economics; cartography; chemistry; classics and languages, literatures and linguistics; communication/speech communication and rhetoric; computer science; counseling psychology; dramatic/theater arts; education (multiple levels); English; English/language arts teacher education; entrepreneurship; environmental science; family and community services; finance; foods and nutrition related; foreign languages and literatures; French; general studies; geography; German; graphic design; history; history teacher education; human development and family studies; human resources development; interior design; international business/trade/commerce; international relations and affairs; journalism; Latin; Latin American studies; marine biology and biological oceanography; marketing/marketing management; mathematics; music performance; music theory and composition; nursing (registered nurse training); philosophy; philosophy and religious studies related; physical education teaching and coaching; physics; piano and organ; political science and government; premedical studies; psychology; public administration; religious studies; religious/sacred music; social sciences; sociology; Spanish; student counseling and personnel services related; visual and performing arts related; voice and opera.

San Diego State University

Accounting; advertising; aerospace, aeronautical and astronautical engineering; African American/Black studies; agricultural business and management; American Indian/Native American studies; American studies; anthropology; applied mathematics; art history, criticism and conservation; Asian studies; astronomy; atomic/molecular physics; bioinformatics; biology/biological sciences; business/commerce; chemistry; child development; civil engineering; classics and classical languages related; classics and languages, literatures and linguistics; communication and journalism related; communication disorders; comparative literature; computer engineering; computer science; construction engineering technology; creative writing; criminal justice/law enforcement administration; criminology; dance; design and visual communications; dietetics; dramatic/theater arts; early childhood education; economics; electrical, electronics and communications engineering; engineering; English; environmental science; environmental studies; environmental/environmental health engineering; European studies; European studies (Central and Eastern); finance; fine/studio arts; French; geography; geology/earth science; German; gerontology; graphic design; health and physical education; health professions related; health services/allied health/health sciences; Hispanic American, Puerto Rican, and Mexican American/Chicano studies; history; hospitality administration; human resources management; humanities; information science/studies; information technology; interior design; international business/trade/commerce; international relations and affairs; Japanese; Jewish/Judaic studies; journalism; Judaic studies; Latin American studies; liberal arts and sciences/liberal studies; linguistics; marketing/marketing management; mass communication/media; mathematics; mechanical engineering; microbiology; multi-/interdisciplinary studies related; music related; music teacher education; nursing (registered nurse training); nursing related; operations management; parks, recreation and leisure; philosophy; physical sciences; physics; political science and government; psychology; public administration; public relations; public relations/image management; radio and television; real estate; religious studies; Russian; Russian studies; social sciences; social work; sociology; Spanish; speech and rhetoric; statistics; trade and industrial teacher education; urban studies/affairs; women's studies.

Santa Clara University

Accounting; accounting and business/management; ancient studies; ancient/classical Greek; anthropology; art history, criticism and conservation; biochemistry; biological and physical sciences; biology/biological sciences; business/managerial economics; chemistry; civil engineering; classics and languages, literatures and linguistics; communication/speech communication and rhetoric; computer engineering; computer science; dramatic/theater arts; economics; electrical, electronics and communications engineering; engineering; engineering physics; English; environmental science; finance; fine/studio arts; French; French studies; German studies; history; interdisciplinary studies; Italian; Italian studies; Latin; liberal arts and sciences/liberal studies; management information systems; marketing/marketing management; mathematics; mechanical engineering; music; organizational behavior; philosophy; physics; political science and government; psychology; religious studies; sociology; Spanish; Spanish and Iberian studies.

Sarah Lawrence College

Acting; African American/Black studies; African studies; American history; American literature; American studies; animal genetics; anthropology; archeology; architectural history and criticism; art; art history, criticism and conservation; Asian history; Asian studies; Asian studies (East); Asian studies (South); astronomy; biological and physical sciences; biology/biological sciences; chemistry; Chinese studies; cinematography and film/video production; classics and languages, literatures and linguistics; comparative literature; computer science; creative writing; dance; dance related; developmental and child psychology; directing and theatrical production; dramatic/theater arts; drawing; early childhood education; ecology; economics; education; elementary education; English; English language and literature related; English literature (British and Commonwealth); environmental studies; European history; European studies; European studies (Central and Eastern); film/cinema studies; fine/studio arts; foreign languages and literatures; French; gay/lesbian studies; geology/earth science; German; history; history and philosophy of science and technology; history related; human development and family studies; human/medical genetics; humanities; interdisciplinary studies; international relations and affairs; Italian; Japanese; jazz/jazz studies; kindergarten/preschool education; Latin; Latin American studies; liberal arts and sciences and humanities related; liberal arts and sciences/liberal studies; literature; marine biology and biological oceanography; mathematics; Middle/Near Eastern and Semitic languages related; modern languages; molecular biology; music; music history, literature, and theory; music performance; music theory and composition; natural sciences; Near and Middle Eastern studies; organic chemistry; painting; philosophy; philosophy and religious studies related; photography; physics; piano and organ; playwriting and screenwriting; political science and government; pre-dentistry studies; pre-law studies; pre-veterinary studies; premedical studies; printmaking; psychology; public policy analysis; religious studies; religious studies related; Romance languages; Russian; sculpture; social sciences; social sciences related; sociology; Spanish; urban studies/affairs; violin, viola, guitar and other stringed instruments; visual and performing arts; visual and performing arts related; voice and opera; western civilization; wind/percussion instruments; women's studies.

Scripps College

African American/Black studies; American studies; anthropology; art; art history, criticism and conservation; Asian American studies; Asian studies; Asian studies (East); biochemistry; biology/biological sciences; chemistry; Chinese; classics and languages, literatures and linguistics; computer science; dance; dramatic/theater arts; economics; English; environmental science; environmental studies; European studies; film/video and photographic arts related; fine/studio arts; foreign languages and literatures; French; geology/earth science; German; Hispanic American, Puerto Rican, and Mexican American/Chicano studies; history; international relations and affairs; Italian; Japanese; Jewish/Judaic studies; Latin; Latin American studies; legal studies; linguistics; mass communication/media; mathematics; modern languages; molecular biology; multi-/interdisciplinary studies related; music; neuroscience; organizational behavior; philosophy; physics; physiological psychology/psychobiology; political science and government; pre-engineering; premedical studies; psychology; public policy analysis; religious studies; Russian; science, technology and society; sociology; Spanish; visual and performing arts related; women's studies.

Seattle Pacific University

Accounting; apparel and textiles; art; art teacher education; biochemistry; biology teacher education; biology/biological sciences; business administration and management; chemistry; classics and languages, literatures and linguistics; communication/speech communication and rhetoric; computer engineering; computer systems analysis; design and visual communications; dramatic/theater arts; economics; electrical, electronics and communications engineering; engineering; English; English/language arts teacher education; European studies; family and consumer sciences/human sciences; foods, nutrition, and wellness; French; general studies; German; history; human development and family studies; interior design; kinesiology and exercise science; Latin; Latin American studies; liberal arts and sciences/liberal studies; linguistics; mathematics; mathematics and statistics related; mathematics teacher education; music; music teacher education; nursing (registered nurse training); philosophy; physical education teaching and coaching; physics; political science and government; pre-dentistry studies; pre-law studies; premedical studies; psychology; religious education; Russian; science teacher education; social science teacher education; sociology; Spanish; special education; theology.

Seattle University

Accounting; applied mathematics; art; art history, criticism and conservation; Asian studies (East); biochemistry; biological and physical sciences; biology/biological sciences; business administration and management; business/managerial economics; chemistry; civil engineering; clinical laboratory science/medical technology; computer science; creative writing; criminal justice/law enforcement administration; diagnostic medical sonography and ultrasound technology; dramatic/theater arts; economics; electrical, electronics and communications engineering; English; environmental studies; environmental/environmental health engineering; European studies (Western); finance; fine/studio arts; forensic science and technology; French; German; history; humanities; industrial engineering; insurance; international business/trade/commerce; international economics; international relations and affairs; journalism; liberal arts and sciences/liberal studies; management information systems; marketing/marketing management; mass communication/media; mathematics; mechanical engineering; nursing (registered nurse training); operations management; philosophy; photography; physics; political science and government; psychology; public administration; public relations/image management; religious studies; social work; sociology; Spanish.

Sewanee: The University of the South

American studies; anthropology; applied art; art; art history, criticism and conservation; Asian studies; biology/biological sciences; chemistry; classics and languages, literatures and linguistics; comparative literature; computer science; dramatic/theater arts; drawing; economics; English; environmental studies; European studies; fine/studio arts; forestry;

French; geology/earth science; German; history; international relations and affairs; Latin; literature; mathematics; medieval and Renaissance studies; modern Greek; music; music history, literature, and theory; natural resources management and policy; philosophy; physics; political science and government; psychology; religious studies; Russian; Russian studies; social sciences; Spanish.

Siena College
Accounting; American studies; biology/biological sciences; chemistry; classics and languages, literatures and linguistics; computer and information sciences; ecology; economics; English; finance; fine/studio arts; French; history; marketing/marketing management; mathematics; philosophy; physics; political science and government; pre-dentistry studies; pre-law studies; premedical studies; psychology; religious studies; secondary education; social work; sociology; Spanish.

Simpson College
Accounting; art; athletic training; biochemistry; biology/biological sciences; business administration and management; chemistry; computer and information sciences; computer science; criminal justice/law enforcement administration; dramatic/theater arts; economics; elementary education; English; environmental science; forensic science and technology; French; German; history; international business/trade/commerce; international relations and affairs; marketing/marketing management; mass communication/media; mathematics; music; music performance; music teacher education; philosophy; physical education teaching and coaching; physics; political science and government; pre-dentistry studies; pre-engineering; pre-law studies; pre-pharmacy studies; pre-theology/pre-ministerial studies; pre-veterinary studies; premedical studies; psychology; religious studies; secondary education; sociology; Spanish; sport and fitness administration/management.

Skidmore College
American studies; anthropology; area, ethnic, cultural, and gender studies related; art; art history, criticism and conservation; Asian studies; biology/biological sciences; business, management, and marketing related; business/commerce; chemistry; classics and languages, literatures and linguistics; computer and information sciences; dance; dramatic/theater arts; economics; elementary education; English; English language and literature related; environmental studies; fine arts related; French; French studies; geology/earth science; German; history; international relations and affairs; kinesiology and exercise science; Latin American studies; law and legal studies related; liberal arts and sciences/liberal studies; mathematics; music history, literature, and theory; neuroscience; philosophy; physics; political science and government; psychology; religious studies; social sciences related; social work; sociology; Spanish; women's studies.

Smith College
African American/Black studies; American studies; ancient/classical Greek; anthropology; architecture; art; art history, criticism and conservation; Asian studies (East); astronomy; biochemistry; biology/biological sciences; chemistry; classics and languages, literatures and linguistics; comparative literature; computer science; dance; dramatic/theater arts; East Asian languages; economics; education; engineering science; English; fine/studio arts; French; French studies; geology/earth science; German; German studies; history; interdisciplinary studies; Italian; Latin; Latin American studies; mathematics; medieval and Renaissance studies; music; Near and Middle Eastern studies; neuroscience; philosophy; physics; political science and government; Portuguese; pre-law studies; premedical studies; psychology; religious studies; Russian; Russian studies; sociology; Spanish; women's studies.

Southern Methodist University
Accounting; advertising; African American/Black studies; anthropology; applied economics; art history, criticism and conservation; biochemistry; biology/biological sciences; business administration and management; business/commerce; chemistry; civil engineering; computer engineering; computer science; creative writing; dance; dramatic/theater arts;

econometrics and quantitative economics; economics; electrical, electronics and communications engineering; English; environmental studies; environmental/environmental health engineering; European studies; film/cinema studies; finance; finance and financial management services related; financial planning and services; fine/studio arts; French; geology/earth science; geophysics and seismology; German; Hispanic American, Puerto Rican, and Mexican American/Chicano studies; history; humanities; information science/studies; international relations and affairs; Italian; journalism; Latin American studies; liberal arts and sciences and humanities related; management science; marketing/marketing management; mathematics; mechanical engineering; medieval and Renaissance studies; multi-/interdisciplinary studies related; music; music performance; music teacher education; music theory and composition; music therapy; philosophy; physics; piano and organ; political science and government; psychology; public policy analysis; public relations; public relations/image management; religious studies; social sciences; sociology; Spanish; statistics; voice and opera.

Southwest Baptist University
Accounting; art; art teacher education; athletic training; biblical studies; biology teacher education; biology/biological sciences; business administration and management; business/commerce; chemistry; chemistry teacher education; clinical laboratory science/medical technology; commercial and advertising art; communication/speech communication and rhetoric; computer and information sciences; computer science; criminal justice/law enforcement administration; customer service management; dramatic/theater arts; early childhood education; elementary education; emergency medical technology (EMT paramedic); English; English/language arts teacher education; finance; general studies; health and physical education; health teacher education; history; human services; marketing/marketing management; mathematics; mathematics teacher education; middle school education; missionary studies and missiology; music; music teacher education; nursing (registered nurse training); occupational safety and health technology; office management; parks, recreation and leisure; pastoral studies/counseling; physical education teaching and coaching; political science and government; psychology; religious education; religious studies; science teacher education; social science teacher education; sociology; Spanish; speech teacher education; sport and fitness administration/management; theology.

Southwestern University
Accounting; American studies; ancient/classical Greek; animal behavior and ethology; anthropology; art; art history, criticism and conservation; biochemistry; biology/biological sciences; business/commerce; chemistry; Chinese; classics and languages, literatures and linguistics; communication/speech communication and rhetoric; computational mathematics; computer and information sciences; dramatic/theater arts; economics; education; elementary education; English; environmental studies; French; German; history; international relations and affairs; kinesiology and exercise science; Latin; Latin American studies; liberal arts and sciences and humanities related; mathematics; music; music teacher education; philosophy; physical sciences; physics; political science and government; psychology; religious studies; sociology; Spanish; special education; women's studies.

Stanford University
Aerospace, aeronautical and astronautical engineering; African American/Black studies; African studies; American Indian/Native American studies; American studies; ancient studies; ancient/classical Greek; anthropology; archeology; art; art history, criticism and conservation; Asian studies; Asian studies (East); biology/biological sciences; biomedical/medical engineering; chemical engineering; chemistry; Chinese; civil engineering; classics and languages, literatures and linguistics; communication/speech communication and rhetoric; comparative literature; computer engineering; computer science; cultural studies; dramatic/theater arts; earth sciences; economics; electrical, electronics and communications engineering; engineering; English; environmental studies; environmental/environmental health engineering; film/cinema studies; fine/studio arts;

French; geological and earth sciences/geosciences related; geology/earth science; geophysics and seismology; German; German studies; Hispanic American, Puerto Rican, and Mexican American/Chicano studies; history; humanities; industrial design; interdisciplinary studies; international relations and affairs; Italian; Japanese; Latin; linguistics; materials science; mathematics; mathematics and computer science; mechanical engineering; medical biomathematics/biometrics; music; philosophy; physics; political science and government; psychology; public policy analysis; religious studies; science, technology and society; Slavic languages; sociology; Spanish; statistics; systems science and theory; urban studies/affairs; women's studies.

State University of New York at Binghamton

Accounting; African American/Black studies; ancient/classical Greek; anthropology; Arabic; archeology; art; art history, criticism and conservation; Asian studies; biochemistry; biology/biological sciences; business administration and management; cartography; cell and molecular biology; chemistry; cinematography and film/video production; classics and classical languages related; classics and languages, literatures and linguistics; community organization and advocacy; comparative literature; computer science; creative writing; dance; directing and theatrical production; ecology; economics; electrical, electronics and communications engineering; engineering; engineering related; English; English language and literature related; entrepreneurship; environmental studies; evolutionary biology; finance; fine/studio arts; French; geography; geology/earth science; German; history; human development and family studies related; industrial engineering; international business/trade/commerce; international relations and affairs; Italian; Jewish/Judaic studies; Latin; Latin American studies; linguistics; management information systems; marketing/marketing management; materials science; mathematics; mechanical engineering; medieval and Renaissance studies; multi-/interdisciplinary studies related; music; music history, literature, and theory; music performance; Near and Middle Eastern studies; nursing (registered nurse training); philosophy; physics; physiological psychology/psychobiology; political science and government; pre-law studies; psychology; sculpture; sociology; Spanish; systems science and theory; theater design and technology; visual and performing arts.

State University of New York College at Geneseo

Accounting; African American/Black studies; American studies; anthropology; art; art history, criticism and conservation; biochemistry; biology/biological sciences; biophysics; business administration and management; chemistry; communication disorders; communication/speech communication and rhetoric; comparative literature; computer science; dramatic/theater arts; early childhood education; economics; education; elementary education; English; fine/studio arts; French; geochemistry; geography; geology/earth science; geophysics and seismology; history; international relations and affairs; mathematics; music; natural sciences; philosophy; physics; political science and government; predentistry studies; pre-law studies; pre-veterinary studies; premedical studies; psychology; sociology; Spanish; special education; special education (early childhood); speech therapy; visual and performing arts related.

State University of New York College of Environmental Science and Forestry

Agricultural/biological engineering and bioengineering; biochemistry; biological and physical sciences; biology teacher education; biology/biological sciences; biotechnology; botany/plant biology; chemical engineering; chemistry; chemistry teacher education; city/urban, community and regional planning; construction engineering; construction management; ecology; entomology; environmental biology; environmental design/architecture; environmental education; environmental studies; environmental/environmental health engineering; fish/game management; fishing and fisheries sciences and management; forest engineering; forest sciences and biology; forest/forest resources management; forestry; hydrology and water resources science; land use planning and management; landscape architecture; natural resources management and policy; natural resources/conservation; parks, recreation

and leisure; physical therapy; plant pathology/phytopathology; plant physiology; plant protection and integrated pest management; plant sciences; polymer chemistry; pre-dentistry studies; pre-law studies; pre-veterinary studies; premedical studies; science teacher education; water resources engineering; wildlife and wildlands science and management; wildlife biology; wood science and wood products/pulp and paper technology; zoology/animal biology.

Stetson University

Accounting; American studies; aquatic biology/limnology; art; biochemistry; biology/biological sciences; business administration and management; business/managerial economics; chemistry; communication/speech communication and rhetoric; computer science; dramatic/theater arts; economics; education; elementary education; English; entrepreneurial and small business related; environmental science; finance; French; geography; German; health services/allied health/health sciences; history; humanities; international business/trade/commerce; international relations and affairs; kinesiology and exercise science; Latin American studies; management information systems; management science; marketing/marketing management; mathematics; molecular biology; music; music performance; music teacher education; music theory and composition; philosophy; physics; piano and organ; political science and government; pre-dentistry studies; pre-law studies; pre-veterinary studies; premedical studies; psychology; religious studies; Russian studies; secondary education; social sciences; sociology; Spanish; sport and fitness administration/management; violin, viola, guitar and other stringed instruments; visual and performing arts related; voice and opera; web page, digital/multimedia and information resources design.

Stevens Institute of Technology

Biochemistry; bioinformatics; biomedical/medical engineering; business administration and management; chemical engineering; chemistry; civil engineering; computational mathematics; computer engineering; computer science; electrical, electronics and communications engineering; engineering physics; engineering/industrial management; English; environmental/environmental health engineering; history; history and philosophy of science and technology; humanities; mathematics; mechanical engineering; naval architecture and marine engineering; Near and Middle Eastern studies; philosophy; physics; pre-dentistry studies; pre-law studies; premedical studies; systems engineering.

Stonehill College

Accounting; American studies; biochemistry; biology/biological sciences; business administration and management; chemistry; communication/speech communication and rhetoric; computer science; criminology; early childhood education; economics; elementary education; English; environmental studies; ethnic, cultural minority, and gender studies related; finance; fine/studio arts; foreign languages and literatures; health/health-care administration; history; international business/trade/commerce; international relations and affairs; marketing/marketing management; mathematics; multi-/interdisciplinary studies related; neuroscience; philosophy; physics; political science and government; psychology; public administration; religious studies; sociology.

Stony Brook University, State University of New York

African American/Black studies; American studies; anthropology; applied mathematics; art history, criticism and conservation; Asian American studies; astronomy; athletic training; atmospheric sciences and meteorology; biochemistry; biology/biological sciences; biomedical/medical engineering; business administration and management; chemistry; chemistry related; clinical laboratory science/medical technology; comparative literature; computer hardware engineering; computer science; cytotechnology; dramatic/theater arts; economics; electrical, electronics and communications engineering; engineering; English; English as a second/foreign language (teaching); environmental studies; European studies; fine/studio arts; French; geology/earth science; German; health professions related; history; humanities; information science/studies; Italian; journalism; linguistics; marine biology; mathematics;

mechanical engineering; multi-/interdisciplinary studies related; music; nursing (registered nurse training); pharmacology; philosophy; physical sciences related; physics; political science and government; psychology; religious studies; respiratory care therapy; Russian; social sciences; social work; sociology; Spanish; women's studies.

Susquehanna University

Accounting; art history, criticism and conservation; biochemistry; biology/biological sciences; business administration and management; business/corporate communications; business/managerial economics; chemistry; communication/speech communication and rhetoric; computer science; creative writing; dramatic/theater arts; ecology; economics; elementary education; English; entrepreneurship; finance; fine/studio arts; French; geology/earth science; German; graphic design; history; human resources management; information science/studies; international business/trade/commerce; international relations and affairs; journalism; kindergarten/preschool education; marketing/marketing management; mass communication/media; mathematics; music; music performance; music teacher education; philosophy; physics; political science and government; pre-dentistry studies; pre-law studies; pre-veterinary studies; premedical studies; psychology; public relations/image management; radio and television; religious studies; secondary education; sociology; Spanish; speech and rhetoric.

Swarthmore College

Ancient studies; ancient/classical Greek; anthropology; art history, criticism and conservation; Asian studies; astronomy; astrophysics; biochemistry; biology/biological sciences; chemical physics; chemistry; Chinese; classics and languages, literatures and linguistics; comparative literature; computer and information sciences; dance; dramatic/theater arts; economics; education related; engineering; English; film/video and photographic arts related; fine/studio arts; French; German; German studies; history; Japanese; Latin; linguistics; mathematics; medieval and Renaissance studies; music; philosophy; physics; physiological psychology/psychobiology; political science and government; psychology; religious studies; Russian; social sciences related; Spanish; women's studies.

Sweet Briar College

Anthropology; archeology; art history, criticism and conservation; biochemistry, biophysics and molecular biology related; biology/biological sciences; business/commerce; chemistry; classics and languages, literatures and linguistics; computer science; creative writing; dance; dramatic/theater arts; economics; engineering science; engineering/industrial management; English; environmental science; environmental studies; fine/studio arts; foreign languages and literatures; French; German; German studies; history; interdisciplinary studies; international relations and affairs; Italian studies; liberal arts and sciences/liberal studies; mathematics; mathematics related; music; philosophy; physics; political science and government; psychology; religious studies; sociology; Spanish; theoretical and mathematical physics.

Syracuse University

Accounting; advertising; aerospace, aeronautical and astronautical engineering; African American/Black studies; American studies; anthropology; apparel and textiles; architecture; area, ethnic, cultural, and gender studies related; art; art history, criticism and conservation; art teacher education; audiology and speech-language pathology; biochemistry; biological and biomedical sciences related; biology/biological sciences; biomedical/medical engineering; business administration and management; business, management, and marketing related; chemical engineering; chemistry; chemistry teacher education; cinematography and film/video production; civil engineering; classics and languages, literatures and linguistics; commercial and advertising art; communication and journalism related; communication/speech communication and rhetoric; computer and information sciences; computer and information sciences and support services related; computer engineering; creative writing; dramatic/theater arts; economics; education (specific subject areas) related; education related; electrical, electronics

and communications engineering; engineering physics; English literature (British and Commonwealth); English/language arts teacher education; entrepreneurship; environmental/environmental health engineering; family and consumer sciences/home economics teacher education; finance; fine arts related; fine/studio arts; foods, nutrition, and wellness; foodservice systems administration; foreign languages and literatures; French; geography; geology/earth science; German; health professions related; history; human development and family studies; information science/studies; interior architecture; international relations and affairs; Italian; journalism; kinesiology and exercise science; Latin American studies; legal professions and studies related; liberal arts and sciences/liberal studies; library science; linguistics; marketing/marketing management; mathematics; mathematics teacher education; mechanical engineering; mechanical engineering/mechanical technology; music; music history, literature, and theory; music performance; music teacher education; music theory and composition; Near and Middle Eastern studies; operations research; philosophy; philosophy and religious studies related; photography; physical education teaching and coaching; physics; physics teacher education; political science and government; psychology; public administration; radio and television; religious studies; Russian; Russian studies; sales, distribution and marketing; social sciences; social studies teacher education; social work; sociology; Spanish; special education; speech and rhetoric; transportation and materials moving related; visual and performing arts related; women's studies.

Tabor College

Accounting; actuarial science; administrative assistant and secretarial science; adult and continuing education; agricultural business and management; art teacher education; athletic training; biblical studies; biological and physical sciences; biology/biological sciences; business administration and management; business teacher education; chemistry; clinical laboratory science/medical technology; communication/speech communication and rhetoric; computer science; divinity/ministry; education; education (K-12); elementary education; English; environmental biology; health teacher education; history; humanities; interdisciplinary studies; international relations and affairs; journalism; kindergarten/preschool education; legal administrative assistant/secretary; marketing/marketing management; mass communication/media; mathematics; medical administrative assistant and medical secretary; music; music management and merchandising; music teacher education; natural sciences; pastoral studies/counseling; philosophy; physical education teaching and coaching; piano and organ; pre-dentistry studies; premedical studies; psychology; public relations/image management; religious studies; science teacher education; secondary education; social sciences; sociology; special education; voice and opera.

Taylor University

Accounting; applied mathematics; art; art teacher education; biblical studies; biology/biological sciences; business administration and management; chemistry; chemistry related; communication/speech communication and rhetoric; computer and information sciences related; computer engineering; computer science; design and applied arts related; development economics and international development; dramatic/theater arts; early childhood education; economics; elementary education; engineering physics; English; English/language arts teacher education; environmental biology; environmental science; environmental/environmental health engineering; finance; French; French language teacher education; geography; geology/earth science; history; international relations and affairs; kinesiology and exercise science; liberal arts and sciences and humanities related; marketing/marketing management; mass communication/media; mathematics; mathematics and statistics related; mathematics teacher education; music; music teacher education; natural sciences; philosophy; physical education teaching and coaching; physics; political science and government; psychology; science teacher education; social studies teacher education; social work; sociology; Spanish; Spanish language teacher education; speech teacher education; sport and fitness administration/management.

Tennessee Technological University

Accounting; agricultural business and management; agricultural teacher education; agricultural/biological engineering and bioengineering; agronomy and crop science; animal sciences; art; art teacher education; biochemistry; biology/biological sciences; business administration and management; chemical engineering; chemistry; child development; civil engineering; clothing/textiles; computer engineering; computer science; dietetics; economics; education; electrical, electronics and communications engineering; elementary education; English; family and consumer sciences/home economics teacher education; family and consumer sciences/human sciences; fashion merchandising; finance; foods, nutrition, and wellness; French; geology/earth science; German; health teacher education; history; horticultural science; industrial engineering; industrial technology; information science/studies; interdisciplinary studies; international business/trade/commerce; journalism; kindergarten/preschool education; labor and industrial relations; landscaping and groundskeeping; marketing/marketing management; mathematics; mechanical engineering; music; music teacher education; nursing (registered nurse training); operations management; physical education teaching and coaching; physics; political science and government; pre-dentistry studies; pre-law studies; pre-veterinary studies; premedical studies; psychology; secondary education; social work; sociology; Spanish; special education; technical and business writing; turf and turfgrass management; web page, digital/multimedia and information resources design; wildlife and wildlands science and management.

Texas A&M University

Accounting; aerospace, aeronautical and astronautical engineering; agribusiness; agricultural and food products processing; agricultural animal breeding; agricultural business and management; agricultural economics; agricultural production; agricultural/biological engineering and bioengineering; agricultural/farm supplies retailing and wholesaling; agriculture; agronomy and crop science; American studies; animal sciences; animal/livestock husbandry and production; anthropology; applied horticulture; applied mathematics; aquaculture; architecture; atmospheric sciences and meteorology; biochemistry; biology/biological sciences; biomedical sciences; biomedical/medical engineering; business administration and management; cartography; cell and molecular biology; chemical engineering; chemistry; civil engineering; community health services counseling; computer engineering; computer science; construction engineering technology; curriculum and instruction; dairy science; digital communication and media/multimedia; dramatic/theater arts; ecology; economics; electrical, electronic and communications engineering technology; electrical, electronics and communications engineering; engineering technology; English; entomology; environmental design/architecture; environmental science; environmental studies; farm and ranch management; finance; fishing and fisheries sciences and management; food science; foods, nutrition, and wellness; forest/forest resources management; forestry; French; geography; geological and earth sciences/geosciences related; geology/earth science; geophysics and seismology; German; health and physical education; history; horticultural science; human resources development; industrial engineering; interdisciplinary studies; international/global studies; landscape architecture; management science; manufacturing technology; marketing/marketing management; mathematics; mechanical engineering; mechanical engineering/mechanical technology; microbiology; molecular genetics; multi-/interdisciplinary studies related; museum studies; music; natural resources/conservation; nuclear engineering; ocean engineering; ornamental horticulture; parks, recreation and leisure; parks, recreation and leisure facilities management; petroleum engineering; philosophy; physics; plant protection and integrated pest management; political science and government; poultry science; pre-veterinary studies; psychology; public relations, advertising, and applied communication related; range science and management; Russian; sales, distribution and marketing; sociology; Spanish; speech and rhetoric; tourism and travel services management; urban forestry; wildlife and wildlands science and management; zoology/animal biology.

Texas Christian University

Accounting; advertising; anthropology; art history, criticism and conservation; art teacher education; astronomy and astrophysics related; athletic training; ballet; bilingual and multilingual education; biochemistry; biology/biological sciences; broadcast journalism; business administration, management and operations related; chemistry; communication/speech communication and rhetoric; computer and information sciences; computer and information sciences related; counselor education/school counseling and guidance; creative writing; criminal justice/safety; dietetics; dietetics and clinical nutrition services related; dramatic/theater arts; e-commerce; early childhood education; economics; educational leadership and administration; elementary education; engineering; English; English/language arts teacher education; environmental science; farm and ranch management; fashion merchandising; finance; fine/studio arts; French; general studies; geography; geology/earth science; health and physical education; health and physical education related; health science; history; interior design; international business/trade/commerce; international economics; international finance; international marketing; international relations and affairs; journalism; Latin American studies; liberal arts and sciences/liberal studies; management science; marketing/marketing management; mass communication/media; mathematics; mathematics teacher education; military studies; movement therapy and movement education; music; music performance; music teacher education; music theory and composition; neuroscience; nursing (registered nurse training); painting; philosophy; photography; physical education teaching and coaching; physics; piano and organ; political science and government; printmaking; psychology; radio and television; real estate; religious studies; science teacher education; sculpture; secondary education; social studies teacher education; social work; sociology; Spanish; special education; special education (gifted and talented); special education (hearing impaired); speech-language pathology; technical teacher education; theater literature, history and criticism.

Texas Tech University

Accounting; acting; advertising; agricultural business and management; agricultural communication/journalism; agricultural economics; agriculture; agronomy and crop science; animal sciences; anthropology; apparel and textiles; applied horticulture; architectural engineering technology; architecture; art; art history, criticism and conservation; biochemistry; biological and physical sciences; biology/biological sciences; business administration and management; business administration, management and operations related; business/commerce; cell and molecular biology; chemical engineering; chemistry; child development; civil engineering; classics and languages, literatures and linguistics; computer and information sciences; computer engineering; dance; dietetics; dramatic/theater arts; economics; electrical, electronic and communications engineering technology; electrical, electronics and communications engineering; engineering; engineering physics; engineering technology; English; environmental/environmental health engineering; family and community services; family and consumer sciences/human sciences; family resource management; family systems; fashion merchandising; fashion/apparel design; finance; fine/studio arts; fishing and fisheries sciences and management; food science; foods, nutrition, and wellness; French; general studies; geography; geology/earth science; geophysics and seismology; German; graphic design; health and physical education; health services/allied health/health sciences; history; hotel/motel administration; human development and family studies; industrial engineering; interdisciplinary studies; interior architecture; international business/trade/commerce; journalism; landscape architecture; Latin American studies; liberal arts and sciences/liberal studies; management information systems; marketing/marketing management; mathematics; mechanical engineering; mechanical engineering/mechanical technology; microbiology; multi-/interdisciplinary studies related; music; music performance; music theory and composition; natural resources/conservation; petroleum engineering; philosophy; photojournalism; physics; political science and government; psychology; public relations/image management; radio and television; range science and management; Russian studies; social work; sociology; Spanish; speech and rhetoric;

technical and business writing; theater design and technology; wildlife and wildlands science and management; zoology/animal biology.

Thomas Aquinas College

Interdisciplinary studies; liberal arts and sciences/liberal studies; multi-/interdisciplinary studies related; western civilization.

Towson University

Accounting; American studies; art; art history, criticism and conservation; art teacher education; athletic training; biochemistry, biophysics and molecular biology related; biology/biological sciences; business administration and management; business administration, management and operations related; chemistry; chemistry related; communication/speech communication and rhetoric; computer and information sciences; dance; dramatic/theater arts; early childhood education; ecology; economics; education related; elementary education; English; family systems; forensic science and technology; geography; geological and earth sciences/geosciences related; geology/earth science; gerontology; health and physical education related; health professions related; health/health-care administration; history; information science/studies; interdisciplinary studies; international relations and affairs; kinesiology and exercise science; mass communication/media; mathematics; music; music teacher education; nursing (registered nurse training) occupational therapy; philosophy; photographic and film/video technology; physical education teaching and coaching; physics; political science and government; psychology; psychology related; religious studies; social sciences; social sciences related; special education; speech-language pathology; sport and fitness administration/management; urban studies/affairs; women's studies.

Transylvania University

Accounting; anthropology; art; art history, criticism and conservation; art teacher education; biology/biological sciences; business administration and management; business/commerce; chemistry; chemistry teacher education; classics and languages, literatures and linguistics; computer and information sciences; computer science; dramatic/theater arts; economics; elementary education; English; French; history; kinesiology and exercise science; mathematics; middle school education; music performance; music related; music teacher education; philosophy; physical education teaching and coaching; physics; political science and government; psychology; religious studies; social sciences related; sociology; Spanish.

Trinity College

American studies; anthropology; art; art history, criticism and conservation; biochemistry; biology/biological sciences; biomedical/medical engineering; chemistry; Chinese; classics and languages, literatures and linguistics; comparative literature; computer engineering; computer science; creative writing; dance; dramatic/theater arts; economics; education; electrical, electronics and communications engineering; engineering; English; environmental science; fine/studio arts; French; gay/lesbian studies; German; history; interdisciplinary studies; international relations and affairs; Italian; Japanese; Jewish/Judaic studies; mathematics; mechanical engineering; modern languages; music; neuroscience; philosophy; physics; political science and government; psychology; public policy analysis; religious studies; Russian; sociology; Spanish; women's studies.

Trinity University

Accounting; acting; anthropology; art; art history, criticism and conservation; Asian studies; biochemistry; biology/biological sciences; business administration and management; chemistry; Chinese; classics and languages, literatures and linguistics; communication/speech communication and rhetoric; computer and information sciences; dramatic/theater arts; economics; engineering science; English; European studies; finance; French; geology/earth science; German; history; humanities; international business/trade/commerce; Latin American studies; management science; marketing/marketing management; mathematics; music; music performance; music theory and composition; neuroscience; philosophy; physics; political science and government; pre-dentistry

studies; pre-law studies; pre-veterinary studies; premedical studies; psychology; religious studies; Russian; sociology; Spanish; speech and rhetoric; theater design and technology; urban studies/affairs; voice and opera.

Truman State University

Accounting; agricultural business and management; agriculture; agronomy and crop science; animal sciences; applied art; art; art history, criticism and conservation; athletic training; biology/biological sciences; business administration and management; chemistry; classics and languages, literatures and linguistics; commercial and advertising art; communication disorders; communication/speech communication and rhetoric; computer and information sciences; criminal justice/police science; criminal justice/safety; design and visual communications; dramatic/theater arts; economics; English; equestrian studies; exercise physiology; finance; fine/studio arts; French; German; health science; health services/allied health/health sciences; history; horticultural science; journalism; kinesiology and exercise science; linguistics; management information systems; marketing/marketing management; mass communication/media; mathematics; multi-/interdisciplinary studies related; music; music performance; nursing (registered nurse training); philosophy; physics; piano and organ; political science and government; pre-dentistry studies; pre-law studies; pre-pharmacy studies; pre-veterinary studies; premedical studies; psychology; public health; religious studies; Romance languages; Russian; sociology; Spanish; speech and rhetoric; visual and performing arts; voice and opera.

Tufts University

African American/Black studies; American studies; anthropology; archeology; architectural engineering; art history, criticism and conservation; Asian studies; Asian studies (Southeast); astronomy; behavioral sciences; biology/biological sciences; chemical engineering; chemistry; child development; Chinese; civil engineering; classics and languages, literatures and linguistics; community health and preventive medicine; computer engineering; computer science; developmental and child psychology; dramatic/theater arts; ecology; economics; electrical, electronics and communications engineering; elementary education; engineering; engineering physics; engineering related; engineering science; English; environmental studies; environmental/environmental health engineering; experimental psychology; French; geological/geophysical engineering; geology/earth science; German; history; industrial engineering; international relations and affairs; Jewish/Judaic studies; kindergarten/preschool education; Latin; mathematics; mechanical engineering; mental health/rehabilitation; modern Greek; music; philosophy; physics; political science and government; psychology; public health; Romance languages; Russian; Russian studies; secondary education; sociobiology; sociology; Spanish; special education; urban studies/affairs; women's studies.

Tulane University

Accounting; African studies; American studies; anatomy; anthropology; architecture; art; art history, criticism and conservation; Asian studies; biochemistry; biology/biological sciences; biomedical/medical engineering; biostatistics; business administration and management; business/commerce; cell biology and anatomical sciences related; cell biology and histology; chemical engineering; chemistry; classics and classical languages related; classics and languages, literatures and linguistics; cognitive psychology and psycholinguistics; communication and journalism related; communication/speech communication and rhetoric; computer and information sciences; computer science; corrections; dance; dramatic/theater arts; ecology; economics; electrical, electronics and communications engineering; engineering science; English; environmental biology; environmental studies; environmental/environmental health engineering; evolutionary biology; finance; fine/studio arts; foreign languages and literatures; French; geology/earth science; German; Hispanic American, Puerto Rican, and Mexican American/Chicano studies; history; information science/studies; international relations and affairs; Italian; Italian studies; Jewish/Judaic studies; Latin; Latin American studies; legal assistant/paralegal; legal professions and studies related; liberal arts and sciences and humanities related; liberal arts and sciences/liberal studies; linguistics; marketing/marketing management; mass communication/media; mathematics; mathematics and statistics related; mechanical engineering; medieval and Renaissance studies; modern Greek; molecular biology; multi-/interdisciplinary studies related; music; music performance; music theory and composition; neuroscience; philosophy; physics; political science and government; Portuguese; psychology; religious studies; Russian; Russian studies; sociology; Spanish; women's studies.

Union College (NE)

Accounting; art; art teacher education; biochemistry; biology teacher education; biology/biological sciences; business administration and management; business teacher education; chemistry; chemistry teacher education; clinical laboratory science/medical technology; commercial and advertising art; computer science; computer teacher education; education; elementary education; engineering; English; English/language arts teacher education; entrepreneurship; fine/studio arts; French; German; graphic design; health science; health/medical preparatory programs related; history; history teacher education; information science/studies; international relations and affairs; journalism; kinesiology and exercise science; mathematics; mathematics teacher education; music; music performance; music teacher education; nursing (registered nurse training); pastoral studies/counseling; physical education teaching and coaching; physician assistant; physics; physics teacher education; psychology; public relations/image management; religious education; religious studies; secondary education; social science teacher education; social sciences; social work; Spanish; sport and fitness administration/management; theology.

Union College (NY)

American studies; anthropology; astronomy; biochemistry; biological and biomedical sciences related; biological and physical sciences; biology/biological sciences; chemistry; classics and languages, literatures and linguistics; computer and information sciences; economics; electrical, electronics and communications engineering; English; fine/studio arts; foreign languages and literatures; geology/earth science; history; humanities; liberal arts and sciences/liberal studies; mathematics; mechanical engineering; neuroscience; philosophy; physics; political science and government; psychology; social sciences; sociology.

Union University

Accounting; advertising; ancient Near Eastern and biblical languages; art; art teacher education; athletic training; biblical studies; biological and physical sciences; biology/biological sciences; broadcast journalism; business administration and management; business teacher education; business/managerial economics; chemistry; clinical laboratory science/medical technology; computer science; dramatic/theater arts; economics; education; elementary education; English; English as a second/foreign language (teaching); family and community services; finance; foreign languages and literatures; French; history; information science/studies; journalism; kindergarten/preschool education; kinesiology and exercise science; marketing/marketing management; mass communication/media; mathematics; music; music management and merchandising; music performance; music teacher education; nursing (registered nurse training); parks, recreation and leisure facilities management; philosophy; philosophy and religious studies related; physical education teaching and coaching; physics; piano and organ; political science and government; pre-dentistry studies; pre-law studies; pre-pharmacy studies; premedical studies; psychology; public relations/image management; radio and television; religious studies; religious/sacred music; science teacher education; secondary education; social work; sociology; Spanish; special education; speech and rhetoric; sport and fitness administration/management; theology; theology and religious vocations related; voice and opera.

United States Air Force Academy

Aerospace, aeronautical and astronautical engineering; area studies; atmospheric sciences and meteorology; behavioral sciences; biochemistry;

biological and physical sciences; biology/biological sciences; business administration and management; chemistry; civil engineering; computer science; economics; electrical, electronics and communications engineering; engineering; engineering mechanics; engineering science; English; environmental/environmental health engineering; geography; history; humanities; interdisciplinary studies; legal studies; materials science; mathematics; mechanical engineering; military studies; operations research; physics; political science and government; social sciences.

United States Coast Guard Academy

Civil engineering; electrical, electronics and communications engineering; management science; mechanical engineering; naval architecture and marine engineering; oceanography (chemical and physical); operations research; political science and government.

United States Merchant Marine Academy

Engineering-related technologies; engineering/industrial management; marine science/merchant marine officer; marine transportation related; maritime science; naval architecture and marine engineering; nuclear engineering technology; transportation and materials moving related.

United States Military Academy

Aerospace, aeronautical and astronautical engineering; American studies; applied mathematics; Arabic; Army R.O.T.C./military science; Asian studies (East); behavioral sciences; biological and physical sciences; biology/biological sciences; business administration and management; chemical engineering; chemistry; Chinese; civil engineering; computer engineering; computer science; economics; electrical, electronics and communications engineering; engineering; engineering physics; engineering/industrial management; environmental studies; environmental/environmental health engineering; European studies; European studies (Central and Eastern); French; geography; German; history; humanities; information science/studies; interdisciplinary studies; Latin American studies; literature; mathematics; mechanical engineering; modern languages; Near and Middle Eastern studies; nuclear engineering; operations research; philosophy; physics; political science and government; Portuguese; pre-law studies; premedical studies; psychology; public policy analysis; Russian; Spanish; systems engineering.

United States Naval Academy

Aerospace, aeronautical and astronautical engineering; Arabic; chemistry; computer and information sciences; computer hardware engineering; computer science; econometrics and quantitative economics; economics; electrical, electronics and communications engineering; engineering; English; French; history; mathematics; mechanical engineering; naval architecture and marine engineering; ocean engineering; oceanography (chemical and physical); physical sciences; physics; political science and government; systems engineering.

University at Buffalo, the State University of New York

Aerospace, aeronautical and astronautical engineering; African American/Black studies; American studies; anthropology; architecture; art; art history, criticism and conservation; Asian studies; audiology and speech-language pathology; biochemistry; bioinformatics; biological and biomedical sciences related; biology/biological sciences; biophysics; biostatistics; biotechnology; business administration and management; chemical engineering; chemistry; chemistry related; civil engineering; classics and languages, literatures and linguistics; clinical laboratory science/medical technology; communication/speech communication and rhetoric; computer engineering; computer science; dance; dramatic/theater arts; dramatic/theater arts and stagecraft related; economics; electrical, electronics and communications engineering; engineering; engineering physics; English; environmental design/architecture; environmental/environmental health engineering; exercise physiology; film/cinema studies; fine/studio arts; French; geography; geology/earth science; German; history; humanities; industrial engineering; information science/studies; Italian; liberal arts and sciences/liberal studies; linguistics; mass communication/media; mathematics; mathematics related;

mechanical engineering; multi-/interdisciplinary studies related; music; music performance; nuclear medical technology; nursing (registered nurse training); occupational therapy; pharmacology and toxicology; pharmacy, pharmaceutical sciences, and administration related; philosophy; physics; political science and government; psychology; sociology; Spanish; structural engineering; theoretical and mathematical physics; women's studies.

The University of Alabama in Huntsville

Accounting; art; biology/biological sciences; business administration and management; chemical engineering; chemistry; civil engineering; computer and information sciences; computer engineering; electrical, electronics and communications engineering; elementary education; engineering related; English; finance; foreign languages and literatures; history; industrial engineering; management information systems; marketing/marketing management; mathematics; mechanical engineering; music; nursing (registered nurse training); philosophy; physical sciences related; physics; political science and government; psychology; sociology; speech and rhetoric.

The University of Arizona

Aerospace, aeronautical and astronautical engineering; agricultural economics; agricultural teacher education; agricultural/biological engineering and bioengineering; anthropology; architecture; art history, criticism and conservation; art teacher education; Asian studies (East); astronomy; atmospheric sciences and meteorology; biochemistry; biology teacher education; biology/biological sciences; business/commerce; cell biology and histology; chemical engineering; chemistry; chemistry teacher education; city/urban, community and regional planning; civil engineering; clinical laboratory science/medical technology; communication disorders; communication/speech communication and rhetoric; computer and information sciences; computer engineering; consumer economics; creative writing; criminal justice/law enforcement administration; dance; drama and dance teacher education; dramatic/theater arts; economics; education (specific subject areas) related; electrical, electronics and communications engineering; elementary education; engineering; engineering physics; engineering related; English; English/language arts teacher education; environmental studies; family and consumer sciences/home economics teacher education; fine/studio arts; foreign language teacher education; French; French language teacher education; geography; geology/earth science; German; German language teacher education; health teacher education; health/health-care administration; Hispanic American, Puerto Rican, and Mexican American/Chicano studies; history teacher education; human development and family studies; Italian; Jewish/Judaic studies; journalism; kindergarten/preschool education; landscape architecture; Latin American studies; liberal arts and sciences/liberal studies; linguistics; marketing/marketing management; materials science; mathematics; mathematics teacher education; mechanical engineering; mining and mineral engineering; multi-/interdisciplinary studies related; music; music performance; music related; music teacher education; Near and Middle Eastern studies; nuclear engineering; nutrition sciences; optical sciences; philosophy; physical education teaching and coaching; physics; physics teacher education; political science and government; pre-veterinary studies; psychology; public administration; radio and television; religious studies; Russian; science teacher education; secondary education; social science teacher education; social studies teacher education; sociology; Spanish; Spanish language teacher education; special education; speech teacher education; systems engineering; theater design and technology; visual and performing arts; water resources engineering; wildlife and wildlands science and management; women's studies.

University of Arkansas

Accounting; agribusiness; agricultural teacher education; agricultural/biological engineering and bioengineering; agronomy and crop science; American studies; animal sciences; anthropology; apparel and textiles; architecture; art; audiology and speech-language pathology; biology/biological sciences; business administration and management; business/commerce; business/managerial economics; chemical engineering;

chemistry; civil engineering; classics and languages, literatures and linguistics; communication/speech communication and rhetoric; computer and information sciences; computer engineering; criminal justice/safety; data processing and data processing technology; dramatic/theater arts; early childhood education; economics; electrical, electronics and communications engineering; English; environmental science; family and consumer sciences/human sciences; finance; food science; foods, nutrition, and wellness; French; geography; geological and earth sciences/geosciences related; geology/earth science; German; health and physical education; health professions related; history; housing and human environments; human development and family studies; human resources development; industrial engineering; international business/trade/commerce; international relations and affairs; journalism; kindergarten/preschool education; landscape architecture; logistics and materials management; marketing/marketing management; mathematics; mechanical engineering; music performance; nursing (registered nurse training); parks, recreation and leisure; philosophy; physics; political science and government; poultry science; premedical studies; psychology; social work; sociology; Spanish; technical teacher education.

University of California, Berkeley

African American/Black studies; American Indian/Native American studies; American studies; ancient/classical Greek; anthropology; applied mathematics; architecture; art; art history, criticism and conservation; Asian American studies; Asian studies; Asian studies (Southeast); astrophysics; atmospheric sciences and meteorology; biology/biological sciences; biomedical/medical engineering; botany/plant biology; business administration and management; cell and molecular biology; Celtic languages; chemical engineering; chemistry; chemistry related; Chinese; civil engineering; classical, ancient Mediterranean and Near Eastern studies and archaeology; classics and languages, literatures and linguistics; cognitive science; comparative literature; computer science; dance; dramatic/theater arts; Dutch/Flemish; economics; electrical, electronics and communications engineering; engineering physics; engineering science; English; environmental science; environmental studies; environmental/environmental health engineering; ethnic, cultural minority, and gender studies related; film/cinema studies; foreign languages related; forest/forest resources management; forestry; French; geography; geological/geophysical engineering; geology/earth science; German; Hispanic American, Puerto Rican, and Mexican American/Chicano studies; history; Italian; Japanese; landscape architecture; Latin; Latin American studies; legal studies; linguistics; manufacturing engineering; mass communication/media; materials science; mathematics; mechanical engineering; microbiology; multi-/interdisciplinary studies related; music; natural resources management and policy; natural resources/conservation; Near and Middle Eastern studies; nuclear engineering; nutrition sciences; operations research; peace studies and conflict resolution; philosophy; physical sciences; physics; political science and government; psychology; public health related; religious studies; Scandinavian languages; Slavic languages; social sciences related; social work; sociology; Spanish; speech and rhetoric; statistics; toxicology; urban studies/affairs; women's studies.

University of California, Davis

Aerospace, aeronautical and astronautical engineering; African American/Black studies; agricultural business and management related; agriculture and agriculture operations related; American Indian/Native American studies; American studies; animal sciences; animal sciences related; anthropology; apparel and textiles; applied mathematics; art history, criticism and conservation; Asian American studies; Asian studies (East); atmospheric sciences and meteorology; biology/biological sciences; biomedical/medical engineering; biotechnology; botany/plant biology; cell biology and histology; chemical engineering; chemistry; Chinese; city/urban, community and regional planning; civil engineering; classical, ancient Mediterranean and Near Eastern studies and archaeology; communication/speech communication and rhetoric; comparative literature; computational mathematics; ecology, evolution, systematics and population biology related; economics; electrical, electronics and communications engineering; engineering related; English; entomology; environmental studies; environmental toxicology; exercise physiology;

film/cinema studies; fine/studio arts; food science; French; genetics; geology/earth science; German; Hispanic American, Puerto Rican, and Mexican American/Chicano studies; history; human development and family studies; hydrology and water resources science; international agriculture; international relations and affairs; Italian; Japanese; landscape architecture; linguistics; materials engineering; mathematics; mechanical engineering; microbiology; molecular biochemistry; multi-/interdisciplinary studies related; music; natural resources and conservation related; natural resources/conservation; neurobiology and neurophysiology; nutrition sciences; philosophy; physical sciences related; physics; physics related; political science and government; political science and government related; psychology; religious studies; Russian; sociology; soil science and agronomy; Spanish; statistics; urban forestry; visual and performing arts related; women's studies; zoology/animal biology.

University of California, Irvine

Aerospace, aeronautical and astronautical engineering; African American/Black studies; anthropology; area, ethnic, cultural, and gender studies related; art history, criticism and conservation; Asian American studies; Asian studies (East); biochemistry/biophysics and molecular biology; biology/biological sciences; biomedical/medical engineering; business/managerial economics; cell biology and histology; chemical engineering; chemistry; Chinese; civil engineering; classical, ancient Mediterranean and Near Eastern studies and archaeology; classics and languages, literatures and linguistics; comparative literature; computer and information sciences; computer and information sciences and support services related; computer and information sciences related; computer engineering; computer science; criminology; dance; dramatic/theater arts; ecology; ecology, evolution, systematics and population biology related; econometrics and quantitative economics; economics; electrical, electronics and communications engineering; English; environmental design/architecture; environmental/environmental health engineering; European studies; film/cinema studies; fine/studio arts; French; geology/earth science; German; German studies; Hispanic American, Puerto Rican, and Mexican American/Chicano studies; history; human ecology; humanities; information science/studies; international/global studies; Japanese; journalism; Korean; linguistics; literature; materials engineering; mathematics; mechanical engineering; microbiological sciences and immunology related; microbiology; multi-/interdisciplinary studies related; music; music performance; neuroscience; nursing related; pharmacy, pharmaceutical sciences, and administration related; philosophy; physics; political science and government; psychology; public health related; religious studies; Russian; social psychology; social sciences; sociology; Spanish; women's studies.

University of California, Los Angeles

Aerospace, aeronautical and astronautical engineering; African American/Black studies; African languages; agricultural/biological engineering and bioengineering; American Indian/Native American studies; American literature; ancient/classical Greek; anthropology; applied mathematics; Arabic; architecture; area studies related; area, ethnic, cultural, and gender studies related; art; art history, criticism and conservation; Asian American studies; Asian studies; Asian studies (East); Asian studies (Southeast); astrophysics; atmospheric sciences and meteorology related; biochemistry; biology/biological sciences; biomathematics and bioinformatics related; biophysics; business/managerial economics; cell and molecular biology; chemical engineering; chemistry; Chinese; civil engineering; classical, ancient Mediterranean and Near Eastern studies and archaeology; classics and classical languages related; cognitive science; comparative literature; computational mathematics; computer and information sciences; computer engineering; design and applied arts related; development economics and international development; dramatic/theater arts; ecology; economics; electrical, electronics and communications engineering; English; environmental science; European studies; film/cinema studies; fine arts related; foreign languages related; French; geography; geography related; geological and earth sciences/geosciences related; geological/geophysical engineering; geology/earth science; geophysics and seismology; German; Hebrew; Hispanic American, Puerto Rican, and Mexican American/Chicano studies; history; international economics; inter-

national/global studies; Italian; Japanese; Jewish/Judaic studies; Korean; Latin American studies; liberal arts and sciences and humanities related; linguistic and comparative language studies related; linguistics; marine biology and biological oceanography; materials engineering; materials science; mathematics; mathematics related; mechanical engineering; medical microbiology and bacteriology; multi-/interdisciplinary studies related; music; music history, literature, and theory; musicology and ethnomusicology; neuroscience; nursing related; philosophy; physics; physiological psychology/psychobiology; physiology; political science and government; Portuguese; psychology; religious studies; Russian; Russian studies; Scandinavian languages; Slavic languages; sociology; Spanish; statistics; women's studies.

University of California, Riverside

African American/Black studies; American Indian/Native American studies; anthropology; anthropology related; art; art history, criticism and conservation; Asian American studies; Asian studies; biochemistry; biology/biological sciences; biomedical sciences; biomedical/medical engineering; botany/plant biology; business administration and management; business/managerial economics; chemical engineering; chemistry; Chinese; classics and languages, literatures and linguistics; comparative literature; computer engineering; computer science; creative writing; cultural studies; dance; dramatic/theater arts; economics; economics related; electrical, electronics and communications engineering; English; entomology; environmental studies; environmental/environmental health engineering; ethnic, cultural minority, and gender studies related; fine/studio arts; foreign languages and literatures; foreign languages related; French; geology/earth science; geophysics and seismology; German; Hispanic American, Puerto Rican, and Mexican American/Chicano studies; history; history related; human development and family studies; humanities; information science/studies; international relations and affairs; international/global studies; Latin American studies; legal studies; liberal arts and sciences/liberal studies; linguistics; materials science; mathematics; mechanical engineering; multi-/interdisciplinary studies related; music; music related; neuroscience; philosophy; philosophy related; physical sciences; physics; physiological psychology/psychobiology; political science and government; political science and government related; pre-law studies; psychology; psychology related; public administration; public policy analysis; religious studies; Russian; Russian studies; social sciences; social sciences related; sociology; Spanish; statistics; women's studies.

University of California, San Diego

Aerospace, aeronautical and astronautical engineering; animal physiology; anthropology; applied mathematics; archeology; art; art history, criticism and conservation; atomic/molecular physics; biochemistry; biology/biological sciences; biomedical/medical engineering; biophysics; biotechnology; cell biology and histology; chemical engineering; chemistry; chemistry teacher education; Chinese; classics and languages, literatures and linguistics; cognitive psychology and psycholinguistics; computer engineering; computer science; creative writing; cultural studies; dance; dramatic/theater arts; ecology; econometrics and quantitative economics; economics; electrical, electronics and communications engineering; engineering; engineering physics; engineering science; English; environmental studies; film/cinema studies; fine/studio arts; foreign languages and literatures; French; geology/earth science; German; history; human ecology; interdisciplinary studies; intermedia/multimedia; Italian; Japanese; Jewish/Judaic studies; Latin American studies; linguistics; literature; management science; mass communication/media; mathematics; mathematics teacher education; mechanical engineering; medical microbiology and bacteriology; medicinal and pharmaceutical chemistry; molecular biology; music; music history, literature, and theory; natural resources management and policy; philosophy; physics; physics teacher education; political science and government; psychology; religious studies; Russian; Russian studies; sociology; Spanish; structural engineering; systems engineering; urban studies/affairs; women's studies.

University of California, Santa Barbara

African American/Black studies; anthropology; applied mathematics related; aquatic biology/limnology; area studies related; art history,

Majors by College

criticism and conservation; Asian American studies; Asian studies; biochemistry; biochemistry, biophysics and molecular biology related; biology/biological sciences; biopsychology; business/managerial economics; cell biology and histology; chemical engineering; chemistry; chemistry related; Chinese; classics and languages, literatures and linguistics; communication/speech communication and rhetoric; comparative literature; computer engineering; computer science; dance; dramatic/theater arts; ecology, evolution, systematics and population biology related; econometrics and quantitative economics; economics; electrical, electronics and communications engineering; English; environmental studies; film/cinema studies; fine/studio arts; French; geography; geology/earth science; geophysics and seismology; German; Hispanic American, Puerto Rican, and Mexican American/Chicano studies; history; hydrology and water resources science; interdisciplinary studies; international/global studies; Italian; Japanese; legal studies; liberal arts and sciences and humanities related; liberal arts and sciences/liberal studies; linguistics; marine biology and biological oceanography; mathematics; mechanical engineering; medical microbiology and bacteriology; medieval and Renaissance studies; microbiology; molecular biology; multi-/interdisciplinary studies related; music; Near and Middle Eastern studies; pharmacology; philosophy; physics; physiology; political science and government; Portuguese; pre-law studies; psychology; public/applied history and archival administration; religious studies; Slavic languages; sociology; Spanish; statistics; women's studies; zoology/animal biology.

University of California, Santa Cruz
Agricultural/biological engineering and bioengineering; American studies; anthropology; art; art history, criticism and conservation; biochemistry; bioinformatics; biology/biological sciences; biomedical/medical engineering; business/managerial economics; cell biology and histology; chemistry; classics and languages, literatures and linguistics; cognitive psychology and psycholinguistics; computer engineering; computer graphics; computer science; creative writing; developmental and child psychology; dramatic/theater arts; ecology; economics; education; electrical, electronics and communications engineering; environmental studies; family and community services; family/community studies; film/cinema studies; foreign languages and literatures; geology/earth science; German; health science; Hispanic American, Puerto Rican, and Mexican American/Chicano studies; history; information science/studies; international economics; Italian studies; Latin American studies; legal studies; linguistics; literature; marine biology and biological oceanography; mathematics; molecular biology; music; neuroscience; philosophy; physics; plant sciences; political science and government; pre-law; premedical studies; psychology; Russian studies; sociology; women's studies.

University of Central Arkansas
Accounting; African American/Black studies; art; athletic training; audiology and speech-language pathology; biological and physical sciences; biology/biological sciences; business administration and management; business teacher education; business/commerce; cardiovascular technology; chemistry; cinematography and film/video production; clinical laboratory science/medical technology; community health services counseling; computer and information sciences; dramatic/theater arts; economics; English composition; English/language arts teacher education; environmental studies; family and consumer sciences/home economics teacher education; family and consumer sciences/human sciences; finance; French; general studies; geography; health professions related; history; insurance; international/global studies; journalism; kindergarten/preschool education; kinesiology and exercise science; management information systems; marketing/marketing management; mathematics; mathematics teacher education; middle school education; multi-/interdisciplinary studies related; music; music performance; nuclear medical technology; nursing (registered nurse training); philosophy; physical education teaching and coaching; physics; political science and government; psychology; public administration; public relations, advertising, and applied communication related; religious

studies; science teacher education; social studies teacher education; sociology; Spanish; speech and rhetoric; substance abuse/addiction counseling.

University of Central Florida
Accounting; actuarial science; advertising; aerospace, aeronautical and astronautical engineering; anthropology; art; art teacher education; audiology and speech-language pathology; biology/biological sciences; biotechnology; business administration and management; business/commerce; business/managerial economics; chemistry; cinematography and film/video production; civil engineering; clinical laboratory science/medical technology; communication/speech communication and rhetoric; computer and information sciences; computer engineering; computer engineering technology; computer technology/computer systems technology; criminal justice/safety; dramatic/theater arts; early childhood education; economics; electrical, electronic and communications engineering; electrical, electronics and communications engineering technology; elementary education; English; English/language arts teacher education; environmental/environmental health engineering; finance; fine/studio arts; foreign language teacher education; foreign languages and literatures; forensic science and technology; French; general studies; health information/medical records administration; health services/allied health/health sciences; health/health-care administration; history; hospitality administration; hospitality administration related; humanities; industrial engineering; information technology; intermedia/multimedia; international/global studies; journalism; legal assistant/paralegal; liberal arts and sciences/liberal studies; management information systems; marketing/marketing management; mathematics; mathematics teacher education; mechanical engineering; mechanical engineering technologies related; medical microbiology and bacteriology; medical radiologic technology; music performance; music teacher education; nursing (registered nurse training); philosophy; photography; physical education teaching and coaching; physics; political science and government; psychology; public administration; radio and television; real estate; religious studies; respiratory care therapy; restaurant/food services management; science teacher education; social science teacher education; social sciences; social work; sociology; Spanish; special education; statistics; structural engineering; tourism and travel services management; trade and industrial teacher education.

University of Chicago
African American/Black studies; African studies; American studies; ancient Near Eastern and biblical languages; ancient/classical Greek; anthropology; applied mathematics; Arabic; area, ethnic, cultural, and gender studies related; art; art history, criticism and conservation; Asian studies (East); Asian studies (South); Asian studies (Southeast); behavioral sciences; Bengali; biochemistry; biology/biological sciences; chemistry; Chinese; classics and languages, literatures and linguistics; comparative literature; computer science; creative writing; economics; English; English language and literature related; environmental studies; European studies (Central and Eastern); film/cinema studies; fine/studio arts; French; geography; geophysics and seismology; German; Hindi; history; human development and family studies; humanities; interdisciplinary studies; international/global studies; Italian; Japanese; Jewish/Judaic studies; Latin; Latin American studies; liberal arts and sciences/liberal studies; linguistics; mathematics; medieval and Renaissance studies; modern languages; music; music history, literature, and theory; Near and Middle Eastern studies; philosophy; physics; political science and government; psychology; public policy analysis; religious studies; Romance languages; Russian; Russian studies; Sanskrit and classical Indian languages; Slavic languages; social sciences; sociology; South Asian languages; Spanish; statistics; Tamil; Tibetan; Turkish; Urdu.

University of Colorado at Boulder
Accounting; advertising; aerospace, aeronautical and astronautical engineering; anthropology; applied mathematics; architectural engineering; art history, criticism and conservation; Asian studies; astronomy; audiology and hearing sciences; biochemistry; broadcast journalism; cell and molecular biology; chemical engineering; chemistry;

Chinese; civil engineering; classics and languages, literatures and linguistics; communication and media related; communication/speech communication and rhetoric; computer engineering; computer science; dance; dramatic/theater arts; ecology, evolution, systematics and population biology related; economics; electrical, electronics and communications engineering; engineering physics; English; environmental design/architecture; environmental studies; environmental/environmental health engineering; ethnic, cultural minority, and gender studies related; film/cinema studies; finance; fine/studio arts; French; geography; geology/earth science; Germanic languages; history; humanities; international/global studies; Italian; Japanese; journalism; linguistics; marketing/marketing management; mathematics; mechanical engineering; music; music performance; music teacher education; philosophy; physics; physiology; political science and government; psychology; religious studies; Russian studies; sociology; Spanish; women's studies.

University of Connecticut

Accounting; acting; actuarial science; agricultural economics; agricultural teacher education; agriculture; agronomy and crop science; allied health diagnostic, intervention, and treatment professions related; American studies; animal physiology; animal sciences; animal/livestock husbandry and production; anthropology; applied horticulture; applied mathematics; art history, criticism and conservation; biology/biological sciences; biomedical/medical engineering; biophysics; business/commerce; cell biology and anatomical sciences related; chemical engineering; chemistry; civil engineering; classics and languages, literatures and linguistics; clinical laboratory science/medical technology; cognitive science; communication/speech communication and rhetoric; computer engineering; computer science; cytotechnology; dietetics; dramatic/theater arts; dramatic/theater arts and stagecraft related; ecology; economics; electrical, electronics and communications engineering; elementary education; engineering physics; engineering related; English; environmental studies; environmental/environmental health engineering; finance; fine/studio arts; French; general studies; geography; geology/earth science; German; health/health-care administration; history; horticultural science; human development and family studies; industrial engineering; insurance; Italian; journalism; landscape architecture; Latin American studies; linguistics; management information systems; management science; manufacturing engineering; marine biology and biological oceanography; marketing/marketing management; materials engineering; mathematics; mechanical engineering; multi-/interdisciplinary studies related; music; music teacher education; natural resources/conservation; nursing (registered nurse training); nutrition sciences; parks, recreation and leisure facilities management; pathology/experimental pathology; pharmacy; pharmacy, pharmaceutical sciences, and administration related; philosophy; physical education teaching and coaching; physical therapy; physics; political science and government; pre-pharmacy studies; psychology; real estate; sociology; Spanish; special education; statistics; structural biology; theater design and technology; theater literature, history and criticism; urban studies/affairs; women's studies.

University of Dallas

Art; art history, criticism and conservation; biochemistry; biology/biological sciences; business administration and management; ceramic arts and ceramics; chemistry; classics and languages, literatures and linguistics; dramatic/theater arts; economics; education; elementary education; English; fine/studio arts; French; German; history; mathematics; painting; philosophy; physics; political science and government; pre-dentistry studies; pre-law studies; pre-theology/pre-ministerial studies; premedical studies; printmaking; psychology; sculpture; secondary education; Spanish; theology.

University of Dayton

Accounting; American studies; applied art; applied mathematics related; art history, criticism and conservation; art teacher education; biochemistry; biology/biological sciences; broadcast journalism; business administration and management; business/managerial economics; chemical engineering; chemistry; civil engineering; commercial and

advertising art; computer engineering; computer engineering technology; computer science; criminal justice/law enforcement administration; dietetics; dramatic/theater arts; economics; education; electrical, electronic and communications engineering technology; electrical, electronics and communications engineering; elementary education; English; environmental biology; environmental studies; finance; fine/studio arts; foods, nutrition, and wellness; French; general studies; geology/earth science; German; health teacher education; history; industrial technology; information science/studies; international business/trade/commerce; international relations and affairs; journalism; kindergarten/preschool education; kinesiology and exercise science; management information systems; marketing/marketing management; mass communication/media; mathematics; mechanical engineering; mechanical engineering/mechanical technology; music; music teacher education; music therapy; philosophy; photography; physical education teaching and coaching; physical sciences; physics; political science and government; pre-dentistry studies; pre-law studies; premedical studies; psychology; public relations/image management; radio and television; religious education; religious studies; science teacher education; secondary education; sociology; Spanish; special education; sport and fitness administration/management.

University of Delaware

Accounting; agribusiness; agricultural business and management; agricultural economics; agricultural teacher education; agricultural/biological engineering and bioengineering; agriculture; agronomy and crop science; animal sciences; anthropology; art; art history, criticism and conservation; Asian studies (East); athletic training; bilingual and multilingual education; biochemistry; biology teacher education; biology/biological sciences; biology/biotechnology laboratory technician; biotechnology; botany/plant biology; business administration and management; business/managerial economics; chemical engineering; chemistry; chemistry teacher education; civil engineering; clinical laboratory science/medical technology; commercial and advertising art; communication/speech communication and rhetoric; community organization and advocacy; comparative literature; computer and information sciences; computer engineering; computer science; consumer economics; criminal justice/law enforcement administration; developmental and child psychology; dietetics; ecology; economics; education; electrical, electronics and communications engineering; elementary education; engineering; English; English as a second/foreign language (teaching); English/language arts teacher education; entomology; environmental engineering technology; environmental studies; environmental/environmental health engineering; family and community services; family and consumer economics related; fashion merchandising; fashion/apparel design; finance; food science; foods, nutrition, and wellness; foreign language teacher education; foreign languages and literatures; French; geography; geology/earth science; geophysics and seismology; German; health and physical education; health teacher education; history; history teacher education; horticultural science; hospitality and recreation marketing; hotel/motel administration; human development and family studies; international relations and affairs; Italian; journalism; kindergarten/preschool education; kinesiology and exercise science; Latin; Latin American studies; liberal arts and sciences/liberal studies; linguistics; management information systems; marketing/marketing management; mass communication/media; mathematics; mathematics teacher education; mechanical engineering; music; music pedagogy; music teacher education; music theory and composition; natural resources management and policy; neuroscience; nursing (registered nurse training); nursing science; nutrition sciences; operations management; ornamental horticulture; philosophy; physical education teaching and coaching; physics; physics teacher education; piano and organ; plant protection and integrated pest management; political science and government; psychology; public relations/image management; sociology; soil conservation; soil science and agronomy; Spanish; sport and fitness administration/management; theater design and technology; wildlife and wildlands science and management; women's studies.

University of Denver

Accounting; animal sciences; anthropology; area, ethnic, cultural, and gender studies related; art; art history, criticism and conservation; art teacher education; Asian American studies; biochemistry; bioinformatics; biological and physical sciences; biology/biological sciences; business administration and management; business statistics; business/commerce; business/managerial economics; chemistry; chemistry related; commercial and advertising art; communication/speech communication and rhetoric; computer engineering; computer science; computer software and media applications related; computer systems analysis; construction management; creative writing; criminology; digital communication and media/multimedia; dramatic/theater arts; ecology; economics; electrical, electronics and communications engineering; engineering; English; environmental science; ethnic, cultural minority, and gender studies related; finance; fine arts related; French; geography; German; graphic design; history; hospitality administration; hotel/motel administration; information technology; international business/trade/commerce; inter-national relations and affairs; Italian; journalism; Latin American studies; management information systems; marketing/marketing management; mathematics; mechanical engineering; molecular biology; multi-/interdisciplinary studies related; music; music performance; music related; musicology and ethnomusicology; philosophy; physics; political science and government; psychology; public policy analysis; real estate; religious studies; Russian; social sciences; social sciences related; sociology; Spanish.

University of Evansville

Accounting; archeology; art; art history, criticism and conservation; art teacher education; athletic training; biblical studies; biochemistry; biology teacher education; biology/biological sciences; business administration and management; business/managerial economics; chemistry; chemistry teacher education; civil engineering; classics and languages, literatures and linguistics; clinical laboratory science/medical technology; cognitive science; communication and journalism related; communication and media related; computer and information sciences; computer and information sciences and support services related; computer engineering; creative writing; design and visual communications; drama and dance teacher education; dramatic/theater arts; economics; education; electrical, electronics and communications engineering; elementary education; English; English composition; English/language arts teacher education; environmental science; environmental studies; finance; French; French language teacher education; German; German language teacher education; graphic design; health/health-care administration; health/medical preparatory programs related; history; international business/trade/commerce; international relations and affairs; kinesiology and exercise science; legal professions and studies related; liberal arts and sciences/liberal studies; management information systems; marketing/marketing management; mathematics; mathematics teacher education; mechanical engineering; multi-/interdisciplinary studies related; music; music management and merchandising; music performance; music teacher education; music therapy; neuroscience; nursing (registered nurse training); philosophy; physical education teaching and coaching; physical therapist assistant; physics; physics teacher education; political science and government; pre-dentistry studies; pre-pharmacy studies; pre-veterinary studies; premedical studies; psychology; science teacher education; social science teacher education; social studies teacher education; sociology; Spanish; Spanish language teacher education; special education; sport and fitness administration/management; theater/theater arts management; theology.

University of Florida

Accounting; advertising; aerospace, aeronautical and astronautical engineering; agricultural and food products processing; agricultural economics; agricultural teacher education; agricultural/biological engineering and bioengineering; agronomy and crop science; American studies; animal sciences; anthropology; architecture; art history, criticism and conservation; art teacher education; Asian studies; astronomy; athletic training; audiology and speech-language pathology; biology/biological

sciences; botany/plant biology; business administration and management; chemical engineering; chemistry; civil engineering; classics and languages, literatures and linguistics; community health and preventive medicine; community health services counseling; computer and information sciences; computer engineering; construction engineering technology; criminology; dairy science; dance; dramatic/theater arts; East Asian languages related; economics; electrical, electronics and communications engineering; elementary education; engineering science; English; entomology; environmental science; environmental/environmental health engineering; family and community services; finance; fine/studio arts; fire science; food science; forestry; French; geography; geology/earth science; German; graphic design; health services/allied health/health sciences; health teacher education; history; horticultural science; industrial engineering; insurance; interior design; intermedia/multimedia; Jewish/Judaic studies; journalism; Judaic studies; kinesiology and exercise science; landscape architecture; linguistics; management science; marketing/marketing management; materials engineering; mathematics; mechanical engineering; medical microbiology and bacteriology; middle school education; multi-/interdisciplinary studies related; music; music teacher education; nuclear engineering; nursing (registered nurse training); ornamental horticulture; parks, recreation and leisure facilities management; philosophy; physical education teaching and coaching; physics; plant pathology/phytopathology; plant sciences; political science and government; Portuguese; poultry science; psychology; public relations/image management; radio and television; real estate; religious studies; Russian; sociology; soil science and agronomy; Spanish; special education; sport and fitness administration/management; statistics; survey technology; systems engineering; women's studies; zoology/animal biology.

University of Georgia

Accounting; advertising; African American/Black studies; agribusiness; agricultural communication/journalism; agricultural economics; agricultural teacher education; agricultural/biological engineering and bioengineering; agriculture; ancient/classical Greek; animal sciences; anthropology; applied horticulture; Arabic; art; art history, criticism and conservation; astronomy; biochemistry; biological and physical sciences; biology/biological sciences; biotechnology; botany/plant biology; broadcast journalism; business administration and management; business operations support and secretarial services related; business/commerce; business/managerial economics; cell biology and histology; chemical engineering; chemistry; chemistry related; child development; Chinese; classics and languages, literatures and linguistics; cognitive science; communication disorders; comparative literature; computer engineering; computer science; consumer economics; criminal justice/safety; dairy science; dance; dietetics; dramatic/theater arts; ecology; economics; educational psychology; engineering; English; English/language arts teacher education; entomology; environmental health; environmental studies; environmental/environmental health engineering; family and consumer sciences/home economics teacher education; family and consumer sciences/human sciences communication; family resource management; fashion merchandising; film/cinema studies; finance; fine/studio arts; fishing and fisheries sciences and management; food science; foods, nutrition, and wellness; foreign language teacher education; forestry; French; genetics; geography; geology/earth science; German; health teacher education; history; housing and human environments; insurance; international business/trade/commerce; international relations and affairs; Italian; Japanese; journalism; kindergarten/preschool education; landscape architecture; Latin; Latin American studies; liberal arts and sciences/liberal studies; linguistics; management information systems; marketing/marketing management; mathematics; mathematics teacher education; microbiology; middle school education; music; music performance; music teacher education; music theory and composition; music therapy; natural resources/conservation; philosophy; physical education teaching and coaching; physics; political science and government; poultry science; psychology; public health education and promotion; public relations/image management; radio and television broadcasting technology; real estate; religious studies; Romance languages; Russian; science teacher education; social studies teacher education; social work; sociology; Spanish; special education; speech and rhetoric; sport and fitness administration/management; statistics; technical teacher education; turf and turfgrass management; water, wetlands, and marine resources management; wildlife and wildlands science and management; women's studies.

University of Illinois at Chicago

Accounting; African American/Black studies; anthropology; architecture related; art history, criticism and conservation; art teacher education; biochemistry; biology teacher education; biology/biological sciences; biomedical/medical engineering; business administration and management; chemical engineering; chemistry; chemistry teacher education; cinematography and film/video production; civil engineering; classical, ancient Mediterranean and Near Eastern studies and archaeology; classics and languages, literatures and linguistics; communication/speech communication and rhetoric; computer engineering; computer science; criminal justice/safety; design and applied arts related; dietetics; dramatic/theater arts; economics; electrical, electronics and communications engineering; elementary education; engineering physics; engineering/industrial management; English; English/language arts teacher education; entrepreneurship; ethnic, cultural minority, and gender studies related; film/video and photographic arts related; finance; fine/studio arts; French; French language teacher education; geology/earth science; German language teacher education; German studies; graphic design; health information/medical records administration; history; history teacher education; industrial design; industrial engineering; information science/studies; Italian; kinesiology and exercise science; Latin American studies; management science; marketing/marketing management; mathematics; mathematics and computer science; mathematics teacher education; mechanical engineering; music; neuroscience; nursing (registered nurse training); philosophy; photography; physics; physics teacher education; Polish; political science and government; pre-dentistry studies; psychology; Romance languages; Russian; Slavic languages; social work; sociology; Spanish; Spanish language teacher education; statistics; urban studies/affairs.

University of Illinois at Urbana–Champaign

Accounting; accounting and business/management; actuarial science; advertising; aerospace, aeronautical and astronautical engineering; agricultural and extension education; agricultural business and management; agricultural communication/journalism; agricultural economics; agricultural mechanization; agricultural public services related; agricultural teacher education; agricultural/biological engineering and bioengineering; agronomy and crop science; airline pilot and flight crew; animal sciences; animal sciences related; animal/livestock husbandry and production; anthropology; applied horticulture; architecture; architecture related; area studies related; art history, criticism and conservation; art teacher education; Asian studies (East); astronomy; athletic training; atmospheric sciences and meteorology; audiology and hearing sciences; audiology and speech-language pathology; auditing; aviation/airway management; banking and financial support services; biochemistry; biological and biomedical sciences related; biology/biological sciences; biomedical/medical engineering; biophysics; biotechnology; botany/plant biology; broadcast journalism; business administration and management; business teacher education; business/commerce; cell and molecular biology; cell biology and histology; ceramic sciences and engineering; chemical engineering; chemistry; chemistry teacher education; child development; city/urban, community and regional planning; civil engineering; classics and languages, literatures and linguistics; communication and journalism related; communication/speech communication and rhetoric; community health and preventive medicine; comparative literature; computational mathematics; computer and information sciences; computer and information systems security; computer engineering; computer programming; computer science; computer software engineering; construction engineering; consumer economics; crafts, folk art and artisanry; dance; dietetics; directing and theatrical production; dramatic/theater arts; early childhood education; East Asian languages; ecology; economics; economics related; education (multiple levels); electrical, electronics and communications engineering;

elementary education; engineering; engineering mechanics; engineering physics; English; English composition; English/language arts teacher education; entomology; entrepreneurship; environmental health; environmental science; environmental/environmental health engineering; family and consumer sciences/human sciences business services related; farm and ranch management; fashion merchandising; film/cinema studies; finance; financial planning and services; food science; food science and technology related; food technology and processing; foreign language teacher education; forest sciences and biology; forestry; French; French language teacher education; general studies; geography; geological and earth sciences/geosciences related; geology/earth science; geotechnical engineering; German; German language teacher education; graphic design; health services administration; Hebrew; history; history teacher education; horticultural science; hospitality administration; human development and family studies; human nutrition; human resources management; humanities; industrial and organizational psychology; industrial design; industrial engineering; insurance; international agriculture; international/global studies; Italian; jazz/jazz studies; journalism; kindergarten/preschool education; kinesiology and exercise science; landscape architecture; Latin American studies; Latin teacher education; liberal arts and sciences and humanities related; liberal arts and sciences/liberal studies; linguistics; logistics and materials management; management information systems; management science; manufacturing engineering; marketing research; marketing/marketing management; mass communication/media; materials engineering; materials science; mathematics; mathematics and computer science; mathematics teacher education; mechanical engineering; metallurgical engineering; microbiology; music; music history, literature, and theory; music performance; music teacher education; music theory and composition; natural resources management; natural resources management and policy; natural resources/conservation; natural resources/conservation related; nuclear engineering; operations management; operations research; organizational behavior; organizational communication; ornamental horticulture; painting; parks, recreation and leisure; philosophy; photography; physical education teaching and coaching; physics; physics teacher education; physiology; plant molecular biology; plant protection and integrated pest management; political science and government; polymer/plastics engineering; Portuguese; pre-law studies; pre-veterinary studies; psychology; public health related; purchasing, procurement/acquisitions and contracts management; real estate; religious studies; restaurant, culinary, and catering management; Russian; Russian studies; sales, distribution and marketing; science teacher education; sculpture; secondary education; Slavic languages; social science teacher education; social studies teacher education; sociology; Spanish; Spanish language teacher education; special education; special education (early childhood); special education (multiply disabled); speech and rhetoric; sport and fitness administration/management; statistics; structural engineering; technical teacher education; theater literature, history and criticism; urban forestry; vocational rehabilitation counseling; voice and opera; water resources engineering; wildlife and wildlands science and management; women's studies.

The University of Iowa

Accounting; actuarial science; African American/Black studies; African studies; Air Force R.O.T.C./air science; American Indian/Native American studies; American studies; anthropology; Army R.O.T.C./military science; art; art history, criticism and conservation; art teacher education; arts management; Asian studies; astronomy; athletic training; biochemistry; biology teacher education; biology/biological sciences; biomedical/medical engineering; business administration and management; business/managerial economics; ceramic arts and ceramics; chemical engineering; chemistry; chemistry teacher education; Chinese; cinematography and film/video production; civil engineering; classics and languages, literatures and linguistics; clinical laboratory science/medical technology; comparative literature; computer science; dance; drama and dance teacher education; dramatic/theater arts; drawing; economics; electrical, electronics and communications engineering; elementary education; engineering; English; environmental studies; film/cinema studies; finance; French; French language teacher education; geography;

geology/earth science; German; German language teacher education; history; history teacher education; human resources management; industrial engineering; information science/studies; interdisciplinary studies; Italian; Japanese; jazz/jazz studies; journalism; kinesiology and exercise science; labor and industrial relations; Latin; Latin American studies; linguistics; literature; management information systems; management science; management sciences and quantitative methods related; marketing related; marketing/marketing management; mass communication/media; mathematics; mathematics teacher education; mechanical engineering; medieval and Renaissance studies; metal and jewelry arts; museum studies; music; music teacher education; music therapy; nuclear medical technology; nursing (registered nurse training); painting; parks, recreation and leisure; pharmacy; philosophy; photography; physics; piano and organ; political science and government; Portuguese; pre-dentistry studies; pre-law studies; pre-pharmacy studies; pre-veterinary studies; premedical studies; printmaking; psychology; religious studies; Russian; science teacher education; sculpture; secondary education; social studies teacher education; social work; sociology; Spanish; Spanish language teacher education; speech and rhetoric; speech teacher education; sport and fitness administration/management; statistics; therapeutic recreation; violin, viola, guitar and other stringed instruments; voice and opera; wind/percussion instruments; women's studies.

The University of Kansas

Accounting; aerospace, aeronautical and astronautical engineering; African American/Black studies; African studies; American studies; ancient studies; anthropology; architectural engineering; architectural history and criticism; architecture; art history, criticism and conservation; art teacher education; astronomy; athletic training; atmospheric sciences and meteorology; behavioral sciences; biochemistry; biological and biomedical sciences related; biology/biological sciences; business administration and management; business/commerce; ceramic arts and ceramics; chemical engineering; chemistry; civil engineering; classics and languages, literatures and linguistics; clinical laboratory science/medical technology; cognitive psychology and psycholinguistics; communication disorders; community health services counseling; computer and information sciences; computer engineering; cytotechnology; dance; design and visual communications; developmental and child psychology; dramatic/theater arts; early childhood education; East Asian languages; economics; electrical, electronics and communications engineering; elementary education; engineering physics; English; environmental studies; European studies; fiber, textile and weaving arts; finance; fine/studio arts; French; geography; geology/earth science; Germanic languages; graphic design; health and physical education; health information/medical records administration; history; humanities; illustration; industrial design; interior design; international relations and affairs; journalism; Latin American studies; liberal arts and sciences/liberal studies; linguistics; logistics and materials management; management information systems; marketing/marketing management; mathematics; mechanical engineering; metal and jewelry arts; microbiology; middle school education; molecular biology; music; music performance; music teacher education; music theory and composition; music therapy; musicology and ethnomusicology; nursing science; painting; petroleum engineering; pharmacy; philosophy; physical education teaching and coaching; physics; piano and organ; political science and government; printmaking; psychology; public administration; religious studies; respiratory care therapy; Russian studies; sculpture; secondary education; Slavic languages; social work; sociology; Spanish; speech and rhetoric; stringed instruments; theater design and technology; violin, viola, guitar and other stringed instruments; voice and opera; wind/percussion instruments; women's studies.

University of Kentucky

Accounting; advertising; agricultural economics; agricultural/biological engineering and bioengineering; agriculture and agriculture operations related; agronomy and crop science; animal sciences; anthropology; apparel and textiles; architecture; art history, criticism and conservation; art teacher education; arts management; audiology and speech-language

pathology; biology/biological sciences; business/commerce; business/managerial economics; cell biology and anatomical sciences related; chemical engineering; chemistry; civil engineering; classics and languages, literatures and linguistics; clinical laboratory science/medical technology; communication/speech communication and rhetoric; computer and information sciences; dramatic/theater arts; economics; education (specific subject areas) related; electrical, electronics and communications engineering; elementary education; English; family and consumer sciences/human sciences; finance; fine/studio arts; food science; foods, nutrition, and wellness; forest sciences and biology; French; geography; geology/earth science; German; health teacher education; health/health-care administration; history; hospitality administration; interdisciplinary studies; interior design; journalism; kindergarten/preschool education; landscape architecture; Latin American studies; linguistics; management science; marketing/marketing management; materials engineering; mathematics; mechanical engineering; middle school education; mining and mineral engineering; multi-/interdisciplinary studies related; music history, literature, and theory; music performance; music teacher education; natural resources/conservation; nursing (registered nurse training); nursing related; philosophy; physical education teaching and coaching; physical therapy; physics; political science and government; psychology; radio and television; Russian; science teacher education; social sciences; social work; sociology; Spanish; special education.

University of Maryland, Baltimore County

Acting; African American/Black studies; American studies; ancient studies; anthropology; biochemistry/biophysics and molecular biology; bioinformatics; biology/biological sciences; business administration, management and operations related; chemical engineering; chemistry; computer engineering; computer science; computer/information technology services administration related; dance; dramatic/theater arts; economics; emergency medical technology (EMT paramedic); engineering; English; environmental science; environmental studies; fine arts related; foreign languages and literatures; geography; health professions related; history; information science/studies; mass communication/media; mathematics; mechanical engineering; multi-/interdisciplinary studies related; music; philosophy; physics; physics teacher education; political science and government; psychology; social work; sociology; statistics; visual and performing arts; women's studies.

University of Maryland, College Park

Accounting; aerospace, aeronautical and astronautical engineering; African American/Black studies; agricultural economics; agricultural/biological engineering and bioengineering; agriculture; American studies; animal sciences; anthropology; Arabic; architecture; art history, criticism and conservation; art teacher education; astronomy; biochemistry; biology/biological sciences; business/commerce; chemical engineering; chemistry; Chinese; civil engineering; classics and languages, literatures and linguistics; communication/speech communication and rhetoric; computer and information sciences; computer engineering; criminology; dance; dietetics; dramatic/theater arts; ecology; economics; electrical, electronics and communications engineering; elementary education; engineering related; English; English/language arts teacher education; family and community services; finance; fine/studio arts; food science; foods, nutrition, and wellness; foreign language teacher education; foreign languages and literatures; French; geography; geology/earth science; German; health teacher education; history; information science/studies; international business/trade/commerce; Italian; Japanese; Jewish/Judaic studies; journalism; kindergarten/preschool education; kinesiology and exercise science; landscape architecture; linguistics; logistics and materials management; management science; marketing/marketing management; materials engineering; mathematics; mathematics teacher education; mechanical engineering; microbiology; multi-/interdisciplinary studies related; music; music performance; music teacher education; natural resources/conservation; philosophy; physical education teaching and coaching; physical sciences; physics; plant sciences; political science and government; pre-dentistry studies; pre-law studies; pre-veterinary studies; psychology; Romance languages; Russian;

Russian studies; science teacher education; secondary education; social studies teacher education; sociology; Spanish; special education; speech-language pathology; women's studies.

University of Mary Washington

American studies; anthropology; art history, criticism and conservation; biology/biological sciences; business administration and management; chemistry; classics and languages, literatures and linguistics; computer and information sciences; economics; education; elementary education; English; fine arts related; foreign languages and literatures; geography; historic preservation and conservation; history; international relations and affairs; liberal arts and sciences and humanities related; liberal arts and sciences/liberal studies; mathematics; multi-/interdisciplinary studies related; music; philosophy; philosophy and religious studies related; physical sciences related; physics; political science and government; psychology; religious studies; sociology; visual and performing arts.

University of Miami

Accounting; acting; advertising; aerospace, aeronautical and astronautical engineering; African American/Black studies; American studies; anthropology; architectural engineering; architecture; art; art history, criticism and conservation; athletic training; biochemistry; biology/biological sciences; biomedical/medical engineering; business administration and management; chemistry; cinematography and film/video production; civil engineering; classics and languages, literatures and linguistics; communication/speech communication and rhetoric; computer engineering; computer science; creative writing; criminology; design and visual communications; dramatic/theater arts; economics; electrical, electronics and communications engineering; elementary education; engineering science; English; entrepreneurship; environmental/environmental health engineering; finance; French; general studies; geography; geology/earth science; German; health services/allied health/health sciences; history; human resources management; industrial engineering; information science/studies; international business/trade/commerce; international relations and affairs; jazz/jazz studies; Jewish/Judaic studies; journalism; kinesiology and exercise science; Latin American studies; legal studies; management science; marketing/marketing management; mass communication/media; mathematics; mechanical engineering; medical microbiology and bacteriology; meteorology; music; music performance; music related; music teacher education; music theory and composition; music therapy; natural resources management and policy; neuroscience; nursing (registered nurse training); philosophy; physics; piano and organ; political science and government; psychology; public relations/image management; real estate; religious studies; secondary education; sociology; Spanish; sport and fitness administration/management; voice and opera; women's studies.

University of Michigan

Aerospace, aeronautical and astronautical engineering; African American/Black studies; American studies; ancient studies; anthropology; anthropology related; applied mathematics; architecture; art history, criticism and conservation; Asian studies; astronomy; athletic training; atmospheric sciences and meteorology; biochemistry; biological and biomedical sciences related; biology/biological sciences; biomedical sciences; biomedical/medical engineering; biophysics; business administration and management; ceramic arts and ceramics; chemical engineering; chemistry; civil engineering; classical, ancient Mediterranean and Near Eastern studies and archaeology; classics and languages, literatures and linguistics; clinical laboratory science/medical technology; communication/speech communication and rhetoric; comparative literature; computer and information sciences and support services related; computer engineering; computer science; creative writing; dance; dental hygiene; dramatic/theater arts; drawing; ecology; economics; electrical, electronics and communications engineering; elementary education; engineering; engineering physics; engineering science; English language and literature related; English literature (British and Commonwealth); environmental studies; environmental/environmental health engineering; fiber, textile and weaving arts; film/cinema studies; French; general studies; geological and earth sciences/geosciences related;

geological/geophysical engineering; geology/earth science; German; graphic design; Hebrew; Hispanic American, Puerto Rican, and Mexican American/Chicano studies; history; humanities; industrial design; industrial engineering; intermedia/multimedia; Italian; jazz/jazz studies; Jewish/Judaic studies; kinesiology and exercise science; Latin; Latin American studies; linguistics; materials engineering; materials science; mathematics; mechanical engineering; medical pharmacology and pharmaceutical sciences; medicinal and pharmaceutical chemistry; medieval and Renaissance studies; metal and jewelry arts; Middle/Near Eastern and Semitic languages related; modern Greek; multi-/interdisciplinary studies related; music; music history, literature, and theory; music related; music teacher education; music theory and composition; naval architecture and marine engineering; Near and Middle Eastern studies; neuroscience; nuclear engineering; nursing (registered nurse training); oceanography (chemical and physical); organizational behavior; pharmacy administration/pharmaceutics; philosophy; photography; physical education teaching and coaching; physics; Polish; political science and government; printmaking; psychology; psychology related; religious studies; Romance languages; Russian; Russian studies; sculpture; secondary education; social sciences; sociology; Spanish; sport and fitness administration/management; statistics; theater design and technology; women's studies.

University of Michigan–Dearborn

Accounting; American studies; anthropology; area studies related; art history, criticism and conservation; biochemistry; biology/biological sciences; business administration and management; business administration, management and operations related; chemistry; chemistry teacher education; communication/speech communication and rhetoric; computer and information sciences; computer programming; criminal justice/safety; early childhood education; economics; education; electrical, electronics and communications engineering; elementary education; engineering related; English; environmental science; environmental studies; finance; French; general studies; geology/earth science; health/health-care administration; history; human resources management; humanities; industrial engineering; liberal arts and sciences/liberal studies; management information systems; manufacturing engineering; marketing/marketing management; mathematics; mathematics teacher education; mechanical engineering; microbiology; multi-/interdisciplinary studies related; philosophy; physics; political science and government; psychology; science teacher education; secondary education; social sciences; social studies teacher education; sociology; Spanish; women's studies.

University of Minnesota, Morris

Anthropology; art history, criticism and conservation; biology/biological sciences; business administration and management; chemistry; computer science; dramatic/theater arts; economics; education; education (K-12); elementary education; English; European studies; fine/studio arts; French; geology/earth science; German; history; human services; Latin American studies; liberal arts and sciences/liberal studies; management science; mathematics; music; philosophy; physical therapy; physics; political science and government; pre-dentistry studies; pre-law studies; pre-pharmacy studies; pre-veterinary studies; premedical studies; psychology; secondary education; social sciences; sociology; Spanish; speech and rhetoric; speech/theater education; statistics; women's studies.

University of Minnesota, Twin Cities Campus

Accounting; actuarial science; aerospace, aeronautical and astronautical engineering; African American/Black studies; African studies; agricultural business and management; agricultural teacher education; agricultural/biological engineering and bioengineering; agriculture; agronomy and crop science; American Indian/Native American studies; American studies; animal genetics; animal physiology; animal sciences; anthropology; architecture; art; art history, criticism and conservation; art teacher education; Asian studies (East); Asian studies (South); astronomy; astrophysics; audiology and speech-language pathology; biochemistry; biology/biological sciences; botany/plant biology; business teacher education; cell biology and histology; chemical engineering; chemistry;

Chinese; civil engineering; clinical laboratory science/medical technology; clothing/textiles; commercial and advertising art; comparative literature; computer science; construction management; dance; dental hygiene; developmental and child psychology; dramatic/theater arts; ecology; economics; education; electrical, electronics and communications engineering; elementary education; emergency medical technology (EMT paramedic); English; English/language arts teacher education; environmental studies; European studies; family and community services; family and consumer sciences/home economics teacher education; film/cinema studies; finance; fish/game management; foods, nutrition, and wellness; foreign language teacher education; forest/forest resources management; forestry; French; funeral service and mortuary science; geography; geological/geophysical engineering; geology/earth science; geophysics and seismology; German; health and physical education related; Hebrew; Hispanic American, Puerto Rican, and Mexican American/Chicano studies; history; industrial engineering; insurance; interior design; international business/trade/commerce; international relations and affairs; Italian; Japanese; Jewish/Judaic studies; journalism; kindergarten/preschool education; landscape architecture; Latin; Latin American studies; linguistics; management information systems; marketing/marketing management; mass communication/media; materials engineering; materials science; mathematics; mathematics teacher education; mechanical engineering; medical microbiology and bacteriology; modern Greek; music; music teacher education; music therapy; natural resources management and policy; Near and Middle Eastern studies; neuroscience; nursing (registered nurse training); occupational therapy; parks, recreation and leisure facilities management; philosophy; physical education teaching and coaching; physical therapy; physics; plant sciences; political science and government; Portuguese; pre-dentistry studies; pre-law studies; pre-veterinary studies; premedical studies; psychology; public health; religious studies; Russian; Russian studies; Scandinavian languages; science teacher education; social science teacher education; sociology; soil science and agronomy; Spanish; urban studies/affairs; women's studies; wood science and wood products/pulp and paper technology.

University of Missouri–Columbia

Accounting; advertising; agricultural business and management; agricultural economics; agricultural mechanization; agricultural teacher education; agriculture; animal sciences; anthropology; apparel and textiles; archeology; art; art history, criticism and conservation; art teacher education; Asian studies (East); Asian studies (South); atmospheric sciences and meteorology; behavioral sciences; biochemistry; biology teacher education; biology/biological sciences; broadcast journalism; business administration and management; business teacher education; business/managerial economics; chemical engineering; chemistry; chemistry teacher education; civil engineering; classics and languages, literatures and linguistics; communication disorders sciences and services related; communication/speech communication and rhetoric; computer and information sciences; computer engineering; computer science; diagnostic medical sonography and ultrasound technology; dietetics; dramatic/theater arts; early childhood education; economics; education; electrical, electronics and communications engineering; elementary education; English; environmental studies; European studies; European studies (Central and Eastern); family and consumer economics related; finance; fish/game management; fishing and fisheries sciences and management; food science; foods, nutrition, and wellness; forestry; French; general studies; geography; geology/earth science; German; health/medical preparatory programs related; history; hotel/motel administration; housing and human environments; human development and family studies; industrial engineering; interdisciplinary studies; interior architecture; international agriculture; international business/trade/commerce; journalism; kindergarten/preschool education; Latin; Latin American studies; linguistics; management information systems; marketing/marketing management; mass communication/media; mathematics; mathematics teacher education; mechanical engineering; medical radiologic technology; middle school education; music; music teacher education; natural resources/conservation; nuclear medical technology; nursing (registered nurse training); occupational therapy; parks,

recreation and leisure; peace studies and conflict resolution; philosophy; photojournalism; physics; physics teacher education; plant sciences; political science and government; psychology; publishing; radio and television; radiologic technology/science; real estate; religious studies; respiratory care therapy; restaurant/food services management; Russian; Russian studies; science teacher education; secondary education; social studies teacher education; social work; sociology; Spanish; special education related; statistics; technical teacher education; wildlife and wildlands science and management.

University of Missouri–Kansas City

Accounting; American studies; art; art history, criticism and conservation; biology/biological sciences; business administration and management; chemistry; civil engineering; clinical/medical laboratory technology; communication/speech communication and rhetoric; computer science; criminal justice/law enforcement administration; criminology; dance; dental hygiene; dramatic/theater arts; early childhood education; economics; electrical, electronics and communications engineering; elementary education; English; fine/studio arts; French; geography; geology/earth science; German; history; information technology; interdisciplinary studies; liberal arts and sciences/liberal studies; mass communication/media; mathematics; mechanical engineering; middle school education; music; music performance; music teacher education; music theory and composition; nursing (registered nurse training); pharmacy; philosophy; physics; political science and government; psychology; secondary education; sociology; Spanish; statistics; urban education and leadership; urban studies/affairs.

University of Nebraska–Lincoln

Accounting; actuarial science; advertising; agricultural and food products processing; agricultural business and management; agricultural communication/journalism; agricultural economics; agricultural mechanization; agricultural teacher education; agricultural/biological engineering and bioengineering; agriculture; agronomy and crop science; ancient studies; ancient/classical Greek; animal sciences; anthropology; apparel and textiles; architectural engineering; architecture; art history, criticism and conservation; art teacher education; athletic training; atmospheric sciences and meteorology; audiology and hearing sciences; biochemistry; biology teacher education; biology/biological sciences; biomedical/medical engineering; botany/plant biology; broadcast journalism; business administration and management; business teacher education; business/managerial economics; chemical engineering; chemistry; chemistry teacher education; civil engineering; classics and languages, literatures and linguistics; communication/speech communication and rhetoric; community health services counseling; computer and information sciences; computer engineering; computer teacher education; construction engineering technology; dance; dramatic/theater arts; economics; education (multiple levels); education (specific subject areas) related; electrical, electronics and communications engineering; elementary education; engineering related; English; English as a second/foreign language (teaching); English/language arts teacher education; entomology; environmental studies; European studies (Western); family and consumer economics related; film/cinema studies; finance; fine/studio arts; fire protection and safety technology; food science; foods, nutrition, and wellness; foreign language teacher education; forensic science and technology; French; French language teacher education; geography; geology/earth science; German; German language teacher education; health teacher education; history; history teacher education; horticultural science; hospitality administration; industrial engineering; industrial production technologies related; interior architecture; international business/trade/commerce; international relations and affairs; journalism related; landscape architecture; landscaping and groundskeeping; Latin; Latin American studies; law and legal studies related; legal professions and studies related; liberal arts and sciences/liberal studies; management science; marketing/marketing management; mathematics; mathematics teacher education; mechanical engineering; medieval and Renaissance studies; middle school education; music; music teacher education; natural resources management and policy; natural resources/conservation; philosophy; physical education teaching and coaching; physics; physics teacher education; plant protection and integrated pest management; political science and government; pre-dentistry studies; pre-pharmacy studies; pre-veterinary studies; premedical studies; psychology; range science and management; reading teacher education; Russian; sales and marketing/marketing and distribution teacher education; science teacher education; social science teacher education; sociology; soil science and agronomy; Spanish; Spanish language teacher education; special education (hearing impaired); special education related; speech-language pathology; technology/industrial arts teacher education; trade and industrial teacher education; turf and turfgrass management; veterinary/animal health technology; women's studies.

The University of North Carolina at Asheville

Accounting; art; atmospheric sciences and meteorology; biology/biological sciences; business administration and management; chemistry; classics and languages, literatures and linguistics; computer science; dramatic/theater arts; economics; engineering; English; environmental studies; fine/studio arts; French; German; history; liberal arts and sciences/liberal studies; mass communication/media; mathematics; music; music related; operations management; philosophy; physics; political science and government; psychology; religious studies; sociology; Spanish; web page, digital/multimedia and information resources design; women's studies.

The University of North Carolina at Chapel Hill

African American/Black studies; American studies; anthropology; applied mathematics; archeology; area, ethnic, cultural, and gender studies related; art history, criticism and conservation; Asian studies; biology/biological sciences; biostatistics; business administration and management; chemistry; classics and languages, literatures and linguistics; clinical laboratory science/medical technology; comparative literature; computer science; dental hygiene; dramatic/theater arts; early childhood education; economics; elementary education; English; environmental health; environmental science; environmental studies; European studies; fine/studio arts; foods, nutrition, and wellness; geography; geology/earth science; German; health and physical education; health/health-care administration; history; human resources management; information science/studies; Latin American studies; liberal arts and sciences/liberal studies; linguistics; mass communication/media; mathematics; medical radiologic technology; middle school education; music; music performance; nursing (registered nurse training); parks, recreation and leisure facilities management; pathology/experimental pathology; peace studies and conflict resolution; pharmacy, pharmaceutical sciences, and administration related; philosophy; physical sciences related; physics; political science and government; psychology; public policy analysis; religious studies; Romance languages related; Russian studies; Slavic, Baltic, and Albanian languages related; sociology; women's studies.

The University of North Carolina Wilmington

Accounting; anthropology; art history, criticism and conservation; athletic training; biology teacher education; biology/biological sciences; business administration and management; business/managerial economics; chemistry; chemistry teacher education; cinematography and film/video production; communication/speech communication and rhetoric; computer science; creative writing; criminal justice/safety; dramatic/theater arts; economics; education (specific subject areas) related; elementary education; English; English/language arts teacher education; environmental science; environmental studies; finance; fine/studio arts; French; French language teacher education; geography; geology/earth science; German; health and physical education; health professions related; history; history teacher education; kindergarten/preschool education; management information systems; marine biology and biological oceanography; marketing/marketing management; mathematics; mathematics teacher education; middle school education; music; music performance; music teacher education; nursing (registered nurse training); parks, recreation and leisure facilities management; philosophy and religious studies related; physical education teaching and coaching; physics; political science and government; psychology; social

work; sociology; Spanish; Spanish language teacher education; special education; special education (emotionally disturbed); special education (mentally retarded); special education (multiply disabled); special education (specific learning disabilities); statistics; therapeutic recreation.

University of North Florida

Accounting; anthropology; art; art teacher education; athletic training; banking and financial support services; biology/biological sciences; business administration and management; business/managerial economics; chemistry; civil engineering; computer and information sciences; construction engineering technology; criminal justice/safety; early childhood education; economics; electrical, electronics and communications engineering; elementary education; English; finance; fine/studio arts; general studies; health services/allied health/health sciences; health/health-care administration; history; international business/trade/commerce; international/global studies; jazz/jazz studies; liberal arts and sciences/liberal studies; marketing/marketing management; mass communication/media; mathematics; mathematics teacher education; mechanical engineering; middle school education; music; music performance; music teacher education; nursing (registered nurse training); philosophy; physical education teaching and coaching; physics; political science and government; psychology; science teacher education; secondary education; sign language interpretation and translation; sociology; Spanish; special education; sport and fitness administration/management; statistics; trade and industrial teacher education; transportation management.

University of Notre Dame

Accounting; aerospace, aeronautical and astronautical engineering; African American/Black studies; American studies; ancient/classical Greek; anthropology; Arabic; architecture; art history, criticism and conservation; biochemistry; biological and physical sciences; biology/biological sciences; business/commerce; chemical engineering; chemistry; chemistry related; Chinese; classics and languages, literatures and linguistics; computer and information sciences; computer and information sciences and support services related; computer engineering; design and visual communications; dramatic/theater arts; economics; electrical, electronics and communications engineering; English; environmental science; environmental/environmental health engineering; finance; fine/studio arts; French; German; history; Italian; Japanese; liberal arts and sciences/liberal studies; management information systems; marketing/marketing management; mathematics; mechanical engineering; medieval and Renaissance studies; music; philosophy; philosophy and religious studies related; physics; physics related; political science and government; premedical studies; psychology; Romance languages; Russian; science teacher education; sociology; Spanish; theology.

University of Oklahoma

Accounting; advertising; aeronautics/aviation/aerospace science and technology; aerospace, aeronautical and astronautical engineering; African American/Black studies; American Indian/Native American studies; anthropology; architectural engineering; architecture; art; art history, criticism and conservation; astronomy; astrophysics; biochemistry; botany/plant biology; broadcast journalism; business administration and management; business/managerial economics; chemical engineering; chemistry; Chinese; cinematography and film/video production; civil engineering; classics and languages, literatures and linguistics; clinical laboratory science/medical technology; communication/speech communication and rhetoric; computer engineering; computer science; construction management; criminal justice/law enforcement administration; dance; dramatic/theater arts; early childhood education; economics; electrical, electronics and communications engineering; elementary education; engineering; engineering physics; English; English language and literature related; English/language arts teacher education; environmental design/architecture; environmental science; environmental/environmental health engineering; finance; fine/studio arts; foreign language teacher education; French; geography; geological and earth sciences/geosciences related; geology/earth science; geophysics and seismology; German; health and physical education; history; human resources management and services related; humanities; industrial engineering; information science/studies; interior design; international/global studies; journalism; liberal arts and sciences/liberal studies; linguistics; management information systems; management science; marketing/marketing management; mathematics; mathematics teacher education; mechanical engineering; meteorology; microbiology; multi-/interdisciplinary studies related; music; music pedagogy; music teacher education; petroleum engineering; philosophy; physics; political science and government; psychology; public administration; religious studies; Russian; science teacher education; social studies teacher education; social work; sociology; Spanish; special education; visual and performing arts; women's studies; zoology/animal biology.

University of Pennsylvania
Accounting; actuarial science; African American/Black studies; African studies; American studies; anthropology; architecture; art history, criticism and conservation; Asian studies (East); Asian studies (South); biochemistry; bioinformatics; biology/biological sciences; biomedical sciences; biomedical/medical engineering; biophysics; business administration and management; business administration, management and operations related; chemical engineering; chemistry; classics and languages, literatures and linguistics; cognitive science; communication/speech communication and rhetoric; community health services counseling; comparative literature; computer engineering; computer graphics; computer systems networking and telecommunications; dramatic/theater arts; e-commerce; East Asian languages; economics; electrical, electronics and communications engineering; elementary education; engineering related; English; English language and literature related; environmental design/architecture; environmental studies; environmental/environmental health engineering; film/cinema studies; finance; fine/studio arts; French; geology/earth science; German; health professions related; health/health-care administration; history; history and philosophy of science and technology; human resources management; humanities; insurance; international business/trade/commerce; international relations and affairs; international/global studies; Italian; Jewish/Judaic studies; Latin American studies; legal professions and studies related; liberal arts and sciences/liberal studies; linguistics; logic; management information systems; management sciences and quantitative methods related; marketing/marketing management; materials engineering; materials science; mathematics; mechanical engineering; music; natural sciences; neuroscience; nursing (registered nurse training); nursing related; operations management; philosophy; philosophy related; physics; political science and government; psychology; public policy analysis; real estate; religious studies; Romance languages related; Russian; sales, distribution and marketing; Semitic languages; social sciences; sociology; Spanish; statistics; systems engineering; transportation management; urban studies/affairs; visual and performing arts; women's studies.

University of Pittsburgh
Accounting; African American/Black studies; anthropology; applied mathematics; art history, criticism and conservation; audiology and speech-language pathology; biological and physical sciences; biology/biological sciences; biomedical/medical engineering; business/commerce; chemical engineering; chemistry; Chinese; civil engineering; classics and languages, literatures and linguistics; computer and information sciences and support services related; computer engineering; computer science; corrections; creative writing; dental hygiene; dietetics; dramatic/theater arts; ecology; economics; educational psychology; electrical, electronics and communications engineering; engineering; engineering physics; English; English literature (British and Commonwealth); ethnic, cultural minority, and gender studies related; film/cinema studies; finance; fine/studio arts; French; geological and earth sciences/geosciences related; geology/earth science; German; health information/medical records administration; health professions related; history; history and philosophy of science and technology; humanities; industrial engineering; information science/studies; interdisciplinary studies; Italian; Japanese; legal studies; liberal arts and sciences/liberal studies; linguistics; marketing/marketing management; materials engineering; mathematics;

mathematics and statistics related; mathematics related; mechanical engineering; metallurgical engineering; microbiology; molecular biology; multi-/interdisciplinary studies related; music; neuroscience; nursing (registered nurse training); occupational therapy; pharmacy; philosophy; physical education teaching and coaching; physical sciences; physics; political science and government; psychology; public administration; rehabilitation and therapeutic professions related; religious studies; Russian; Slavic languages; social sciences; social work; sociology; Spanish; speech and rhetoric; statistics; urban studies/affairs.

University of Portland
Accounting; arts management; biology/biological sciences; business administration and management; chemistry; civil engineering; computer engineering; computer science; criminal justice/safety; dramatic/theater arts; education; electrical, electronics and communications engineering; elementary education; engineering; engineering science; engineering/industrial management; English; environmental studies; finance; history; interdisciplinary studies; international business/trade/commerce; journalism; marketing/marketing management; mass communication/media; mathematics; mechanical engineering; music; music teacher education; nursing (registered nurse training); philosophy; physics; political science and government; pre-dentistry studies; pre-law studies; premedical studies; psychology; secondary education; social work; sociology; Spanish; theology.

University of Puget Sound
Art; Asian studies; biochemistry; biology/biological sciences; business/commerce; chemistry; classics and languages, literatures and linguistics; communication/speech communication and rhetoric; computer programming (specific applications); computer science; creative writing; developmental biology and embryology; dramatic/theater arts; economics; English; French; geology/earth science; German; history; interdisciplinary studies; international business/trade/commerce; international economics; international relations and affairs; kinesiology and exercise science; mathematics; molecular biology; music; music management and merchandising; music performance; music teacher education; natural sciences; philosophy; physics; political science and government; pre-dentistry studies; pre-law studies; pre-veterinary studies; premedical studies; psychology; religious studies; science, technology and society; sociology; Spanish.

University of Redlands
Accounting; anthropology; art history, criticism and conservation; Asian studies; audiology and speech-language pathology; biology/biological sciences; business administration and management; business/commerce; chemistry; computer science; creative writing; economics; education; elementary education; English; environmental studies; fine/studio arts; French; German; history; interdisciplinary studies; international relations and affairs; liberal arts and sciences/liberal studies; literature; management information systems; mathematics; music; music history, literature, and theory; music performance; music teacher education; music theory and composition; philosophy; physics; piano and organ; political science and government; psychology; religious studies; secondary education; sociology; Spanish; speech therapy; voice and opera.

University of Rhode Island
Accounting; African American/Black studies; animal sciences; anthropology; apparel and accessories marketing; apparel and textiles; applied economics; art; art history, criticism and conservation; biology/biological sciences; biomedical/medical engineering; business administration and management; chemical engineering; chemistry; civil engineering; classics and languages, literatures and linguistics; clinical laboratory science/medical technology; communication disorders; communication/speech communication and rhetoric; comparative literature; computer and information sciences; computer engineering; consumer economics; econometrics and quantitative economics; economics; electrical, electronics and communications engineering; elementary education; English; environmental studies; finance; fishing and fisheries sciences and management; foods, nutrition, and wellness; French; geol-

ogy/earth science; German; health/health-care administration; history; human development and family studies; human services; industrial engineering; interdisciplinary studies; international business/trade/commerce; Italian; journalism; landscape architecture; Latin American studies; liberal arts and sciences/liberal studies; management information systems; marine biology and biological oceanography; marketing/marketing management; mathematics; mechanical engineering; medical microbiology and bacteriology; music; music performance; music teacher education; music theory and composition; natural resources management and policy; natural resources/conservation; nursing (registered nurse training); ocean engineering; pharmacy; philosophy; physical education teaching and coaching; physics; political science and government; psychology; public policy analysis; secondary education; sociology; Spanish; turf and turfgrass management; wildlife and wildlands science and management; women's studies; zoology/animal biology.

University of Richmond

Accounting; African studies; American studies; ancient studies; ancient/classical Greek; anthropology; area, ethnic, cultural, and gender studies related; art history, criticism and conservation; Asian studies; biology/biological sciences; business administration and management; chemistry; cognitive science; computer science; criminal justice/safety; dramatic/theater arts; economics; economics related; English; environmental studies; European studies; fine/studio arts; French; geography; German studies; history; humanities; international business/trade/commerce; international economics; international relations and affairs; Italian studies; journalism; Latin; Latin American studies; mathematics; molecular biochemistry; multi-/interdisciplinary studies related; music; organizational behavior; philosophy; physics; political science and government; psychology; religious studies; Russian studies; sociology; Spanish; speech and rhetoric; women's studies.

University of Rochester

African American/Black studies; American Sign Language (ASL); anthropology; applied mathematics; art history, criticism and conservation; biochemistry; biological and physical sciences; biology/biological sciences; biomedical/medical engineering; chemical engineering; chemistry; classics and languages, literatures and linguistics; cognitive science; comparative literature; computer science; ecology; economics; electrical, electronics and communications engineering; engineering science; English; environmental science; environmental studies; film/cinema studies; fine/studio arts; foreign languages and literatures; French; geological/geophysical engineering; geology/earth science; German; history; international relations and affairs; Japanese; jazz/jazz studies; linguistics; mathematics; mathematics and statistics related; mechanical engineering; medical microbiology and bacteriology; molecular genetics; music; music teacher education; music theory and composition; neuroscience; nursing (registered nurse training); optical sciences; philosophy; physics; physics related; political science and government; psychology; religious studies; Russian; Russian studies; social sciences related; Spanish; statistics; women's studies.

University of St. Thomas (MN)

Accounting; actuarial science; ancient/classical Greek; art history, criticism and conservation; Asian studies (East); biochemistry; biology teacher education; biology/biological sciences; broadcast journalism; business administration and management; business administration, management and operations related; business/corporate communications; chemistry; chemistry teacher education; classics and classical languages related; classics and languages, literatures and linguistics; clinical/medical social work; communication/speech communication and rhetoric; computer and information sciences; creative writing; criminology; drama and dance teacher education; dramatic/theater arts; econometrics and quantitative economics; economics; education (K-12); education (specific subject areas) related; electrical, electronics and communications engineering; elementary education; English; English/language arts teacher education; entrepreneurship; finance; foreign language teacher education; foreign languages related; French; geography; geology/earth science; German; health and physical education; health science; health

teacher education; history; human resources management; interdisciplinary studies; international business/trade/commerce; international economics; international relations and affairs; Japanese; journalism; journalism related; Latin; marketing/marketing management; mathematics; mathematics teacher education; mechanical engineering; middle school education; multi-/interdisciplinary studies related; music; music teacher education; operations management; peace studies and conflict resolution; philosophy; physical education teaching and coaching; physics; physics teacher education; political science and government; psychology; psychology related; public administration; public health education and promotion; real estate; religious studies; Russian; Russian studies; science teacher education; social sciences; social studies teacher education; social work; sociology; Spanish; speech/theater education; women's studies.

University of St. Thomas (TX)

Accounting; biology/biological sciences; business administration and management; chemistry; communication/speech communication and rhetoric; dramatic/theater arts; economics; education; elementary education; English; environmental science; environmental studies; finance; fine/studio arts; French; general studies; history; international relations and affairs; liberal arts and sciences/liberal studies; management information systems; marketing/marketing management; mathematics; music; music teacher education; pastoral studies/counseling; philosophy; political science and government; pre-dentistry studies; pre-law studies; pre-pharmacy studies; pre-veterinary studies; premedical studies; psychology; secondary education; Spanish; theology; theology and religious vocations related.

University of San Diego

Accounting; anthropology; art history, criticism and conservation; biochemistry; biology/biological sciences; business administration and management; business/managerial economics; chemistry; communication/speech communication and rhetoric; computer science; dramatic/theater arts; economics; electrical, electronics and communications engineering; English; finance; fine/studio arts; French; history; humanities; industrial engineering; intercultural/multicultural and diversity studies; international relations and affairs; liberal arts and sciences/liberal studies; marine biology and biological oceanography; marketing/marketing management; mathematics; mechanical engineering; music; nursing (registered nurse training); philosophy; physics; political science and government; psychology; religious studies; sociology; Spanish.

The University of Scranton

Accounting; ancient/classical Greek; biology/biological sciences; biomathematics and bioinformatics related; biophysics; business administration and management; business administration, management and operations related; chemistry; chemistry related; clinical laboratory science/medical technology; communication/speech communication and rhetoric; communications technologies and support services related; computer and information sciences and support services related; computer engineering; computer science; criminal justice/safety; dramatic/theater arts; early childhood education; economics; electrical, electronics and communications engineering; elementary education; English; entrepreneurship; finance; foreign languages and literatures; French; German; gerontology; health/health-care administration; history; human resources management; human services; information science/studies; international business/trade/commerce; international relations and affairs; Italian; kindergarten/preschool education; kinesiology and exercise science; Latin; management science; marketing/marketing management; mathematics; mathematics and statistics related; neuroscience; nursing (registered nurse training); operations management; philosophy; physics; political science and government; psychology; religious studies; secondary education; sociology; Spanish; special education.

University of South Carolina

Accounting; advertising; African American/Black studies; anthropology; aquatic biology/limnology; art history, criticism and conservation; art teacher education; biology/biological sciences; biomedical/medical engineering; broadcast journalism; business administration and management; business/managerial economics; chemical engineering; chemistry; civil engineering; classics and languages, literatures and linguistics; computer and information sciences; computer engineering; criminal justice/law enforcement administration; dance; dramatic/theater arts; economics; electrical, electronics and communications engineering; English; European studies; experimental psychology; finance; fine/studio arts; French; general retailing/wholesaling; geography; geology/earth science; geophysics and seismology; German; history; hospitality administration; insurance; international relations and affairs; Italian; journalism; kinesiology and exercise science; Latin American studies; liberal arts and sciences/liberal studies; management science; marine biology; marine biology and biological oceanography; marine science/ merchant marine officer; marketing/marketing management; mathematics; mechanical engineering; music; music teacher education; nursing (registered nurse training); oceanography; office management; philosophy; physical education teaching and coaching; physics; political science and government; public relations/image management; real estate; religious studies; Russian; sociology; Spanish; sport and fitness administration/management; statistics; women's studies.

University of Southern California
Accounting; acting; aerospace, aeronautical and astronautical engineering; African American/Black studies; American studies; anthropology; anthropology related; architecture; arts management; Asian American studies; Asian studies (East); astronomy; biochemistry; biology/biological sciences; biomedical/medical engineering; biophysics; broadcast journalism; business administration and management; chemical engineering; chemistry; cinematography and film/video production; civil engineering; classics and languages, literatures and linguistics; communication/speech communication and rhetoric; comparative literature; computational mathematics; computer and information sciences; computer software and media applications related; creative writing; dental hygiene; dramatic/theater arts; drawing; East Asian languages related; economics; electrical, electronics and communications engineering; English; environmental studies; environmental/ environmental health engineering; ethnic, cultural minority, and gender studies related; film/cinema studies; film/video and photographic arts related; French; geography; geology/earth science; German; gerontology; Hispanic American, Puerto Rican, and Mexican American/Chicano studies; history; industrial engineering; international relations and affairs; Italian; jazz/jazz studies; journalism; kinesiology and exercise science; linguistics; mathematics; mechanical engineering; multi-/interdisciplinary studies related; music; music management and merchandising; music performance; music teacher education; music theory and composition; neuroscience; occupational therapy; philosophy; physical sciences; physics; playwriting and screenwriting; political science and government; psychology; public health education and promotion; public policy analysis; public relations/image management; religious studies; Russian; sociology; Spanish.

The University of Tennessee
Accounting; advertising; aerospace, aeronautical and astronautical engineering; agricultural business and management related; agricultural economics; agricultural teacher education; agricultural/biological engineering and bioengineering; animal sciences; anthropology; architecture; area, ethnic, cultural, and gender studies related; art history, criticism and conservation; art teacher education; audiology and hearing sciences; biochemistry; biology/biological sciences; botany/plant biology; business administration and management; business teacher education; business/commerce; business/managerial economics; chemical engineering; chemistry; civil engineering; classics and languages, literatures and linguistics; clinical laboratory science/medical technology; commercial and advertising art; computer engineering; computer science; consumer economics; cultural studies; dramatic/theater arts; ecology; economics; electrical, electronics and communications engineering; engineering physics; engineering science; English; family and consumer sciences/home economics teacher education; family systems; finance; fine/

studio arts; food science; foods, nutrition, and wellness; forestry; French; geography; geology/earth science; German; health teacher education; history; hotel/motel administration; human development and family studies; industrial engineering; interior design; Italian; journalism; kinesiology and exercise science; logistics and materials management; marketing/marketing management; materials engineering; mathematics; mechanical engineering; medical microbiology and bacteriology; multi-/ interdisciplinary studies related; music; music teacher education; nuclear engineering; nursing (registered nurse training); ornamental horticulture; parks, recreation and leisure facilities management; philosophy; physics; plant protection and integrated pest management; plant sciences; political science and government; psychology; public administration; radio and television; religious studies; Russian; social work; sociology; Spanish; special education; speech and rhetoric; speech-language pathology; sport and fitness administration/management; statistics; technical teacher education; wildlife and wildlands science and management; zoology/ animal biology.

The University of Tennessee at Chattanooga
Applied mathematics; art; art teacher education; biology/biological sciences; business administration and management; chemistry; communication/speech communication and rhetoric; computer science; criminal justice/law enforcement administration; dramatic/theater arts; early childhood education; economics; electrical, electronics and communications engineering; engineering; engineering/industrial management; English; English/language arts teacher education; environmental science; foreign language teacher education; foreign languages and literatures; geology/earth science; history; humanities; interior design; kinesiology and exercise science; legal assistant/paralegal; mass communication/ media; mathematics; mechanical engineering; middle school education; music; music teacher education; nursing (registered nurse training); philosophy and religious studies related; physical therapy; physics; political science and government; psychology; science teacher education; secondary education; social sciences related; social work; special education.

The University of Texas at Austin
Accounting; advertising; aerospace, aeronautical and astronautical engineering; American studies; ancient studies; ancient/classical Greek; anthropology; apparel and textiles; Arabic; archeology; architectural engineering; architecture; art; art history, criticism and conservation; Asian studies; astronomy; athletic training; biochemistry; biological and physical sciences; biology/biological sciences; biomedical/medical engineering; business administration and management; business administration, management and operations related; business/commerce; chemical engineering; chemistry; civil engineering; classics and languages, literatures and linguistics; clinical laboratory science/medical technology; communication disorders; communication/speech communication and rhetoric; computer and information sciences; Czech; dance; design and visual communications; dramatic/theater arts; East Asian languages; economics; electrical, electronics and communications engineering; English; English composition; ethnic, cultural minority, and gender studies related; European studies; family and consumer sciences/human sciences; finance; fine/studio arts; foods, nutrition, and wellness; foreign languages and literatures; French; geography; geological and earth sciences/geosciences related; geology/earth science; geophysics and seismology; German; health and physical education; health services/allied health/health sciences; Hebrew; history; human development and family studies; humanities; hydrology and water resources science; interior design; Iranian/Persian languages; Islamic studies; Italian; jazz/jazz studies; Jewish/Judaic studies; journalism; Latin; Latin American studies; liberal arts and sciences/liberal studies; linguistics; logistics and materials management; management information systems; marketing/marketing management; mathematics; mathematics and computer science; mechanical engineering; multi-/interdisciplinary studies related; music; music management and merchandising; music performance; music theory and composition; Near and Middle Eastern studies; nursing (registered nurse training); petroleum engineering; philosophy; physics; political science and government; Portuguese; psychology; public relations/image

management; radio and television; recording arts technology; religious studies; Russian; Russian studies; Scandinavian languages; Semitic languages; social work; sociology; Spanish; sport and fitness administration/management; Turkish; urban studies/affairs; visual and performing arts; women's studies.

The University of Texas at Dallas
Accounting; American studies; applied mathematics; art; audiology and speech-language pathology; biochemistry; biology/biological sciences; business/commerce; chemistry; cognitive science; comparative literature; computer and information sciences; computer software engineering; criminology; developmental and child psychology; economics; electrical, electronics and communications engineering; ethnic, cultural minority, and gender studies related; finance; geography; geology/earth science; history; humanities; interdisciplinary studies; mathematics; mechanical engineering; molecular biology; neuroscience; physics; political science and government; psychology; public administration; public policy analysis; sociology; statistics; visual and performing arts.

University of the Pacific
Art; art history, criticism and conservation; audiology and speech-language pathology; biochemistry; biology/biological sciences; biomedical/medical engineering; business administration and management; chemistry; chemistry related; civil engineering; classics and languages, literatures and linguistics; commercial and advertising art; communication/speech communication and rhetoric; computer engineering; computer science; dramatic/theater arts; economics; education; electrical, electronics and communications engineering; engineering physics; engineering/industrial management; English; environmental studies; fine/studio arts; French; geology/earth science; German; history; information science/studies; interdisciplinary studies; international relations and affairs; Japanese; kinesiology and exercise science; mathematics; mechanical engineering; music; music history, literature, and theory; music management and merchandising; music teacher education; music theory and composition; music therapy; pharmacy; philosophy; physical sciences; physics; piano and organ; political science and government; psychology; religious studies; social sciences; sociology; Spanish; special education; voice and opera.

University of the Sciences in Philadelphia
Biochemistry; bioinformatics; biology/biological sciences; chemistry; clinical laboratory science/medical technology; computer science; environmental science; health services/allied health/health sciences; health/medical psychology; marketing/marketing management; medical pharmacology and pharmaceutical sciences; medicinal and pharmaceutical chemistry; microbiology; occupational therapy; pharmacology and toxicology; pharmacy; pharmacy, pharmaceutical sciences, and administration related; physical therapy; psychology; sport and fitness administration/management.

University of Tulsa
Accounting; anthropology; applied mathematics; art history, criticism and conservation; arts management; athletic training; audiology and speech-language pathology; biochemistry; biology/biological sciences; business administration and management; business/commerce; chemical engineering; chemistry; communication/speech communication and rhetoric; computer science; dramatic/theater arts; early childhood education; economics; education; electrical, electronics and communications engineering; elementary education; engineering physics; English; environmental studies; film/cinema studies; finance; fine/studio arts; French; geology/earth science; geophysics and seismology; German; history; information science/studies; information technology; international business/trade/commerce; kinesiology and exercise science; legal professions and studies related; liberal arts and sciences/liberal studies; management information systems; marketing/marketing management; mathematics; mathematics teacher education; mechanical engineering; music; music performance; music related; music teacher education; music theory and composition; nursing (registered nurse training); organizational behavior; petroleum engineering; philosophy; physics; piano and organ; political science and government; psychology; religious studies; Russian studies; sociology; Spanish; special education (hearing impaired); sport and fitness administration/management; voice and opera.

University of Utah
Accounting; anthropology; Arabic; architecture; art; art history, criticism and conservation; Asian studies; athletic training; audiology and speech-language pathology; ballet; biology/biological sciences; biomedical/medical engineering; business administration and management; chemical engineering; chemistry; Chinese; civil engineering; classics and languages, literatures and linguistics; clinical laboratory science/medical technology; communication/speech communication and rhetoric; comparative literature; computer engineering; computer science; consumer economics; dance; dramatic/theater arts; economics; electrical, electronics and communications engineering; elementary education; English; entrepreneurship; environmental science; environmental studies; film/cinema studies; finance; French; geography; geological/geophysical engineering; geology/earth science; geophysics and seismology; German; health and physical education; health and physical education related; health services/allied health/health sciences; Hebrew; history; human development and family studies; international/global studies; Iranian/Persian languages; Japanese; kinesiology and exercise science; linguistics; management information systems; marketing/marketing management; mass communication/media; materials engineering; mathematics; mechanical engineering; metallurgical engineering; meteorology; mining and mineral engineering; music; Near and Middle Eastern studies; nursing (registered nurse training); occupational therapy; parks, recreation and leisure; pharmacy; philosophy; physical therapy; physics; political science and government; psychology; public health education and promotion; Russian; social science teacher education; social work; sociology; Spanish; special education; speech and rhetoric; Turkish; urban studies/affairs; women's studies.

University of Virginia
Aerospace, aeronautical and astronautical engineering; African American/Black studies; anthropology; architectural history and criticism; architecture; area studies related; art; astronomy; audiology and speech-language pathology; biology/biological sciences; biomedical/medical engineering; business/commerce; chemical engineering; chemistry; city/urban, community and regional planning; civil engineering; classics and languages, literatures and linguistics; comparative literature; computer and information sciences; computer engineering; cultural studies; dramatic/theater arts; economics; electrical, electronics and communications engineering; engineering; English; environmental science; French; German; history; international relations and affairs; Italian; kinesiology and exercise science; liberal arts and sciences/liberal studies; mathematics; mechanical engineering; multi-/interdisciplinary studies related; music; nursing (registered nurse training); philosophy; physics; political science and government; psychology; religious studies; Slavic languages; sociology; Spanish; systems engineering.

University of Washington
Accounting; aerospace, aeronautical and astronautical engineering; African American/Black studies; Air Force R.O.T.C./air science; American Indian/Native American studies; ancient/classical Greek; anthropology; applied mathematics; architecture; Army R.O.T.C./military science; art; art history, criticism and conservation; Asian studies; Asian studies (East); Asian studies (South); Asian studies (Southeast); astronomy; atmospheric sciences and meteorology; audiology and speech-language pathology; bilingual and multilingual education; biochemistry; biology teacher education; biology/biological sciences; biostatistics; botany/plant biology; business administration and management; business/commerce; Canadian studies; cell biology and histology; ceramic arts and ceramics; ceramic sciences and engineering; chemical engineering; chemistry; Chinese; city/urban, community and regional planning; civil engineering; classics and languages, literatures and linguistics; clinical laboratory science/medical technology; commercial and advertising art; communication/speech communication and rhetoric; comparative literature; computer and information sciences; computer engineering; computer

science; construction management; creative writing; criminal justice/law enforcement administration; cultural studies; dance; data processing and data processing technology; dental hygiene; dramatic/theater arts; economics; education; education (multiple levels); electrical, electronics and communications engineering; elementary education; engineering; English; English as a second/foreign language (teaching); environmental health; environmental studies; European studies; fiber, textile and weaving arts; fishing and fisheries sciences and management; forest engineering; forest sciences and biology; forest/forest resources management; forestry; French; general studies; geography; geology/earth science; geophysics and seismology; German; Hispanic American, Puerto Rican, and Mexican American/Chicano studies; history; history and philosophy of science and technology; humanities; industrial design; industrial engineering; information science/studies; interdisciplinary studies; interior architecture; international business/trade/commerce; international relations and affairs; Italian; Japanese; Jewish/Judaic studies; landscape architecture; Latin; Latin American studies; liberal arts and sciences/liberal studies; linguistics; management information systems; management science; materials engineering; maternal/child health and neonatal nursing; mathematics; mechanical engineering; medical microbiology and bacteriology; metal and jewelry arts; metallurgical engineering; molecular biology; music; music history, literature, and theory; music performance; music teacher education; music theory and composition; musical instrument fabrication and repair; musicology and ethnomusicology; natural resources management and policy; Navy/Marine Corps R.O.T.C./naval science; Near and Middle Eastern studies; nursing (registered nurse training); occupational therapy; oceanography (chemical and physical); orthotics/prosthetics; painting; pharmacy; philosophy; photography; physical therapy; physician assistant; physics; piano and organ; political science and government; printmaking; psychology; public administration; public health; public health/community nursing; religious studies; Romance languages; Russian; Russian studies; Scandinavian languages; Scandinavian studies; science teacher education; sculpture; secondary education; Slavic languages; social sciences; social work; sociology; Spanish; speech and rhetoric; statistics; technical and business writing; violin, viola, guitar and other stringed instruments; voice and opera; wildlife and wildlands science and management; women's studies; wood science and wood products/pulp and paper technology; zoology/animal biology.

University of Wisconsin–La Crosse
Accounting; archeology; art teacher education; athletic training; biology/biological sciences; business administration and management; chemistry; clinical laboratory science/medical technology; communication/speech communication and rhetoric; computer and information sciences; dramatic/theater arts; economics; elementary education; English; finance; French; geography; German; health teacher education; history; history; insurance; international business/trade/commerce; liberal arts and sciences and humanities related; management information systems; marketing/marketing management; mathematics; medical microbiology and bacteriology; medical radiologic technology; microbiology/bacteriology; music; parks, recreation and leisure facilities management; philosophy; physical education teaching and coaching; physical sciences; physics; political science and government; psychology; public administration; public health education and promotion; rehabilitation and therapeutic professions related; social sciences; sociology; Spanish; therapeutic recreation; visual and performing arts.

University of Wisconsin–Madison
Accounting; actuarial science; advertising; African American/Black studies; African languages; agricultural teacher education; agricultural/biological engineering and bioengineering; animal genetics; anthropology; applied art; applied mathematics; art; art history, criticism and conservation; art teacher education; astronomy; biochemistry; biology/biological sciences; biomedical/medical engineering; botany/plant biology; broadcast journalism; business administration and management; cartography; cell biology and histology; chemical engineering; chemistry; child development; Chinese; civil engineering; classics and languages, literatures and linguistics; clinical laboratory science/medical technology;

clothing/textiles; comparative literature; computer engineering; computer science; construction management; consumer services and advocacy; developmental and child psychology; dietetics; dramatic/theater arts; electrical, electronics and communications engineering; elementary education; engineering; engineering mechanics; engineering physics; English; entomology; environmental/environmental health engineering; experimental psychology; family and consumer economics related; family and consumer sciences/home economics teacher education; family and consumer sciences/human sciences; fashion merchandising; finance; food science; foods, nutrition, and wellness; French; geography; geology/earth science; geophysics and seismology; German; Hebrew; Hispanic American, Puerto Rican, and Mexican American/Chicano studies; history; history and philosophy of science and technology; hydrology and water resources science; industrial engineering; insurance; interior design; international relations and affairs; Italian; Japanese; journalism; kindergarten/preschool education; labor and industrial relations; linguistics; mass communication/media; mathematics; mechanical engineering; medical microbiology and bacteriology; metallurgical engineering; mining and mineral engineering; modern Greek; molecular biology; music; music teacher education; nuclear engineering; nursing (registered nurse training); occupational therapy; parks, recreation and leisure; pharmacology; pharmacy; philosophy; physical education teaching and coaching; physician assistant; political science and government; Portuguese; psychology; public relations/image management; radio and television; real estate; Russian; Scandinavian languages; science teacher education; secondary education; Slavic languages; social sciences; social work; sociology; Spanish; special education; speech therapy; statistics; survey technology; toxicology; urban studies/affairs; women's studies; zoology/animal biology.

University of Wisconsin–River Falls
Accounting; agricultural business and management; agricultural teacher education; agricultural/biological engineering and bioengineering; agriculture; agronomy and crop science; animal sciences; art; art teacher education; biochemistry; biology teacher education; biology/biological sciences; biotechnology; broadcast journalism; business administration and management; chemistry; chemistry teacher education; communication disorders; computer and information sciences; computer science; computer teacher education; dairy science; dramatic/theater arts; economics; education; elementary education; engineering technology; English; English as a second/foreign language (teaching); English/language arts teacher education; environmental studies; equestrian studies; finance; food science; French; French language teacher education; geography; geology/earth science; German; German language teacher education; history; history teacher education; horticultural science; information science/studies; journalism; land use planning and management; liberal arts and sciences/liberal studies; management information systems; marketing/marketing management; mathematics; mathematics teacher education; music; music teacher education; natural resources/conservation; natural sciences; physical education teaching and coaching; physical sciences; physics; physics teacher education; political science and government; pre-dentistry studies; pre-law studies; pre-pharmacy studies; pre-veterinary studies; premedical studies; psychology; public relations/image management; radio and television; science teacher education; secondary education; social science teacher education; social sciences; social studies teacher education; social work; sociology; soil science and agronomy; Spanish; Spanish language teacher education; speech and rhetoric; speech therapy.

Ursinus College
American studies; anthropology; art; Asian studies (East); biological and physical sciences; biology/biological sciences; business administration and management; chemistry; civil engineering; classics; classics and languages, literatures and linguistics; computer science; economics; electrical, electronics and communications engineering; English; environmental studies; fine arts related; French; German; health and physical education; history; international relations and affairs; mass communication/media; mathematics; mechanical engineering; metallurgical engineering; multi-/

interdisciplinary studies related; neuroscience; philosophy; physics; political science and government; psychology; social sciences related; sociology; Spanish.

Valparaiso University

Accounting; actuarial science; American studies; art; art teacher education; Asian studies (East); atmospheric sciences and meteorology; biochemistry; biological and physical sciences; biology teacher education; biology/biological sciences; chemistry; chemistry teacher education; civil engineering; classics and languages, literatures and linguistics; communication and journalism related; computer engineering; computer science; creative writing; criminology; drama and dance teacher education; dramatic/theater arts; economics; economics related; electrical, electronics and communications engineering; elementary education; English; English/language arts teacher education; environmental science; finance; foreign language teacher education; French; French language teacher education; geography; geography teacher education; geological and earth sciences/geosciences related; geology/earth science; German; German language teacher education; health and physical education; history; history teacher education; humanities; international business/trade/commerce; international economics; international relations and affairs; journalism; kinesiology and exercise science; management science; management sciences and quantitative methods related; marketing/marketing management; mass communication/media; mathematics; mathematics teacher education; mechanical engineering; middle school education; multi-/interdisciplinary studies related; music; music management and merchandising; music performance; music teacher education; music theory and composition; nursing (registered nurse training); organizational communication; philosophy; physical education teaching and coaching; physics; physics teacher education; piano and organ; political science and government; psychology; psychology teacher education; public relations/image management; radio and television; religious/sacred music; science teacher education; secondary education; social science teacher education; social sciences; social work; sociology; Spanish; Spanish language teacher education; sport and fitness administration/management; teacher assistant/aide; technical and business writing; theology; voice and opera.

Vanderbilt University

African American/Black studies; African studies; American studies; anthropology; art; Asian studies (East); astronomy; biology/biological sciences; biomedical/medical engineering; chemical engineering; chemistry; civil engineering; classics and languages, literatures and linguistics; cognitive psychology and psycholinguistics; computer engineering; computer science; dramatic/theater arts; ecology; economics; education; electrical, electronics and communications engineering; elementary education; engineering; engineering science; English; European studies; French; geology/earth science; German; history; human development and family studies; human resources management; interdisciplinary studies; kindergarten/preschool education; Latin American studies; mass communication/media; mathematics; mechanical engineering; molecular biology; music; philosophy; physics; piano and organ; political science and government; Portuguese; psychology; religious studies; Russian; secondary education; sociology; Spanish; special education; urban studies/affairs; violin, viola, guitar and other stringed instruments; voice and opera; wind/percussion instruments.

Vassar College

African studies; American studies; ancient/classical Greek; anthropology; art history, criticism and conservation; Asian studies; astronomy; biochemistry; biology/biological sciences; chemistry; Chinese; classics and languages, literatures and linguistics; cognitive psychology and psycholinguistics; computer and information sciences; dramatic/theater arts; economics; English; environmental science; environmental studies; film/cinema studies; fine/studio arts; French; geography; geology/earth science; German; history; interdisciplinary studies; international relations and affairs; Italian; Japanese; Jewish/Judaic studies; Latin; Latin American studies; liberal arts and sciences and humanities related; mass communication/media; mathematics; medieval and Renaissance studies; multi-/

interdisciplinary studies related; music; philosophy; physics; physiological psychology/psychobiology; political science and government; psychology; religious studies; Russian; science, technology and society; sociology; Spanish; urban studies/affairs; visual and performing arts; women's studies.

Villanova University

Accounting; art history, criticism and conservation; astronomy; astrophysics; biochemistry; biology/biological sciences; business administration and management; business/managerial economics; chemical engineering; chemistry; civil engineering; classics and languages, literatures and linguistics; computer engineering; computer science; criminal justice/law enforcement administration; economics; education; electrical, electronics and communications engineering; English; environmental science; environmental studies; finance; French; geography; history; human services; humanities; international business/trade/commerce; international/global studies; Italian; liberal arts and sciences/liberal studies; management information systems; marketing/marketing management; mass communication/media; mathematics; mechanical engineering; nursing (registered nurse training); philosophy; physics; political science and government; psychology; religious studies; secondary education; sociology; Spanish.

Virginia Military Institute

Biology/biological sciences; chemistry; civil engineering; computer science; economics; electrical, electronics and communications engineering; English; history; international relations and affairs; mathematics; mechanical engineering; modern languages; physics; psychology.

Virginia Polytechnic Institute and State University

Accounting; aerospace, aeronautical and astronautical engineering; agricultural economics; agronomy and crop science; animal sciences; architecture; art; biochemistry; biology/biological sciences; business administration and management; business family and consumer sciences/human sciences; business/managerial economics; chemical engineering; chemistry; civil engineering; clothing/textiles; communication/speech communication and rhetoric; computer and information sciences; computer engineering; computer science; construction management; consumer/homemaking education; dairy science; dramatic/theater arts; economics; electrical, electronics and communications engineering; engineering mechanics; English; environmental studies; finance; food science; foods, nutrition, and wellness; forestry; French; geography; geology/earth science; German; history; horticultural science; hotel/motel administration; human development and family studies; industrial design; industrial engineering; information science/studies; interdisciplinary studies; interior design; international relations and affairs; landscape architecture; management science; marketing/marketing management; materials engineering; mathematics; mechanical engineering; mining and mineral engineering; music; ocean engineering; philosophy; physics; political science and government; poultry science; psychology; public policy analysis; secondary education; sociology; Spanish; statistics.

Wabash College

Art; biology/biological sciences; chemistry; classics and languages, literatures and linguistics; dramatic/theater arts; economics; English; French; German; history; Latin; mathematics; modern Greek; music; philosophy; physics; political science and government; pre-law studies; pre-veterinary studies; premedical studies; psychology; religious studies; Spanish; speech and rhetoric.

Wagner College

Accounting; anthropology; art; arts management; biology/biological sciences; business administration and management; chemistry; computer and information sciences related; computer science; dramatic/theater arts; economics; education; elementary education; English; finance; history; international relations and affairs; kindergarten/preschool education; mathematics; medical microbiology and bacteriology; music; nursing (registered nurse training); philosophy; physician assistant; physics;

political science and government; pre-dentistry studies; pre-engineering; pre-law studies; pre-theology/pre-ministerial studies; premedical studies; psychology; public administration; secondary education; sociology; Spanish.

Wake Forest University
Accounting; ancient/classical Greek; anthropology; art history, criticism and conservation; biology/biological sciences; business/commerce; chemistry; Chinese; classics and languages, literatures and linguistics; clinical laboratory science/medical technology; communication/speech communication and rhetoric; computer and information sciences; dramatic/theater arts; econometrics and quantitative economics; economics; education (multiple levels); engineering; English; finance; fine/studio arts; French; German; history; Japanese; kinesiology and exercise science; Latin; management information systems; management science; mathematics; music; philosophy; physician assistant; physics; political science and government; psychology; religious studies; Russian; sociology; Spanish.

Wartburg College
Accounting; art; art teacher education; arts management; biochemistry; biology/biological sciences; broadcast journalism; business administration and management; chemistry; clinical laboratory science/medical technology; commercial and advertising art; computer science; economics; elementary education; engineering; English; English composition; finance; French; German; history; history teacher education; information science/studies; international business/trade/commerce; international relations and affairs; journalism; kindergarten/preschool education; marketing/marketing management; mass communication/media; mathematics; mathematics teacher education; music; music performance; music teacher education; music theory and composition; music therapy; occupational therapy; philosophy; physical education teaching and coaching; physics; political science and government; psychology; public relations/image management; religious studies; religious/sacred music; secondary education; social science teacher education; social work; sociology; Spanish; speech/theater education; sport and fitness administration/management.

Washington & Jefferson College
Accounting; art; art teacher education; biochemistry; biology/biological sciences; biophysics; business/commerce; cell biology and anatomical sciences related; chemistry; chemistry related; economics; education; English; environmental studies; French; German; history; information technology; international business/trade/commerce; international/global studies; mathematics; multi-/interdisciplinary studies related; music; philosophy; physics; political science and government; psychology; religious studies; sociology; Spanish; theater literature, history and criticism.

Washington and Lee University
Accounting; anthropology; archeology; art history, criticism and conservation; Asian studies (East); biochemistry; biology/biological sciences; business administration and management; chemical engineering; chemistry; classics; computer and information sciences; computer science; dramatic/theater arts; economics; engineering physics; English; environmental studies; fine/studio arts; foreign languages and literatures; French; geological and earth sciences/geosciences related; geology/earth science; German; history; journalism; mathematics; medieval and Renaissance studies; multi-/interdisciplinary studies related; music; neuroscience; philosophy; physics; political science and government; psychology; religious studies; Russian studies; sociology; Spanish.

Washington College
American studies; anthropology; art; biology/biological sciences; business administration and management; chemistry; computer science; dramatic/theater arts; ecology; economics; English; environmental studies; foreign languages and literatures; French; German; history; humanities; international relations and affairs; Latin American studies; liberal arts and sciences/liberal studies; mathematics; multi-/interdisciplinary studies related;

music; philosophy; physics; physiological psychology/psychobiology; political science and government; pre-dentistry studies; pre-law studies; pre-veterinary studies; premedical studies; psychology; sociology; Spanish.

Washington University in St. Louis
Accounting; advertising; African American/Black studies; African studies; American literature; American studies; ancient studies; ancient/classical Greek; anthropology; applied art; applied mathematics; Arabic; archeology; architectural engineering technology; architectural technology; architecture; architecture related; area studies related; area, ethnic, cultural, and gender studies related; art; art history, criticism and conservation; art teacher education; Asian studies; Asian studies (East); biochemistry; biological and biomedical sciences related; biological and physical sciences; biology teacher education; biology/biological sciences; biomedical/medical engineering; biophysics; biopsychology; business administration and management; business administration, management and operations related; business/commerce; business/managerial economics; ceramic arts and ceramics; chemical engineering; chemistry; chemistry related; chemistry teacher education; Chinese; classics and languages, literatures and linguistics; cognitive psychology and psycho-linguistics; commercial and advertising art; communication and journalism related; communication/speech communication and rhetoric; comparative literature; computer and information sciences; computer and information sciences and support services related; computer engineering; computer science; computer/information technology services administration related; creative writing; cultural studies; dance; design and visual communications; drama and dance teacher education; dramatic/theater arts; drawing; East Asian languages related; economics; education; education (K-12); education (specific levels and methods) related; electrical, electronics and communications engineering; elementary education; engineering; English; English language and literature related; English literature (British and Commonwealth); English/language arts teacher education; entrepreneurship; environmental studies; ethnic, cultural minority, and gender studies related; European studies; fashion/apparel design; film/cinema studies; finance; fine/studio arts; French; French language teacher education; geology/earth science; German; German language teacher education; Germanic languages; graphic design; health professions related; Hebrew; history; history teacher education; human resources management; humanities; illustration; industrial and organizational psychology; information science/studies; international business/trade/commerce; international economics; international finance; international relations and affairs; Islamic studies; Italian; Japanese; Jewish/Judaic studies; Latin; Latin American studies; liberal arts and sciences/liberal studies; literature; marketing related; marketing/marketing management; mathematics; mathematics and computer science; mathematics teacher education; mechanical engineering; medieval and Renaissance studies; merchandising, sales, and marketing operations related (general); middle school education; modern languages; multi-/interdisciplinary studies related; music; music history, literature, and theory; music theory and composition; natural resources/conservation; natural sciences; Near and Middle Eastern studies; neuroscience; operations management; painting; philosophy; philosophy and religious studies related; photography; physics; physics teacher education; political science and government; pre-dentistry studies; pre-pharmacy studies; pre-veterinary studies; premedical studies; printmaking; psychology; regional studies; religious studies; Romance languages; Russian; Russian studies; science teacher education; science, technology and society; sculpture; secondary education; social and philosophical foundations of education; social science teacher education; social sciences; social sciences related; social studies teacher education; Spanish; Spanish language teacher education; statistics; systems engineering; systems science and theory; theater literature, history and criticism; urban studies/affairs; voice and opera; women's studies.

Webb Institute
Naval architecture and marine engineering.

Wellesley College

African American/Black studies; African studies; American studies; ancient/classical Greek; anthropology; archeology; architecture; art history, criticism and conservation; Asian studies (East); astronomy; astrophysics; biochemistry; biology/biological sciences; chemistry; Chinese; classics and languages, literatures and linguistics; cognitive psychology and psycholinguistics; comparative literature; computer science; digital communication and media/multimedia; dramatic/theater arts; economics; English; environmental studies; ethnic, cultural minority, and gender studies related; film/cinema studies; film/video and photographic arts related; fine/studio arts; French; French studies; geology/earth science; German; German studies; history; international relations and affairs; Islamic studies; Italian; Italian studies; Japanese; Jewish/Judaic studies; Latin; Latin American studies; linguistics; mathematics; medieval and Renaissance studies; music; Near and Middle Eastern studies; neuroscience; peace studies and conflict resolution; philosophy; physics; political science and government; psychology; religious studies; Russian; Russian studies; sociology; Spanish; women's studies.

Wells College

African American/Black studies; American studies; anthropology; art; art history, criticism and conservation; biochemistry; biology/biological sciences; business administration and management; chemistry; computer science; creative writing; dance; dramatic/theater arts; economics; education; elementary education; engineering; English; environmental studies; fine/studio arts; French; history; international relations and affairs; mathematics; molecular biology; music; philosophy; physics; political science and government; pre-dentistry studies; pre-law studies; pre-veterinary studies; premedical studies; psychology; public policy analysis; religious studies; secondary education; sociology; Spanish; women's studies.

Wesleyan College

Advertising; American studies; art history, criticism and conservation; biology/biological sciences; business administration and management; chemistry; communication/speech communication and rhetoric; computer and information sciences; early childhood education; economics; education; English; environmental science; fine/studio arts; French; history; humanities; interdisciplinary studies; international business/trade/commerce; international relations and affairs; mathematics; middle school education; music; philosophy; physical sciences; physics; political science and government; psychology; religious studies; social sciences; Spanish.

Wesleyan University

African American/Black studies; American studies; anthropology; archeology; art; art history, criticism and conservation; Asian studies (East); astronomy; biochemistry; biology/biological sciences; chemistry; classics and languages, literatures and linguistics; computer science; dance; dramatic/theater arts; economics; English; European studies (Central and Eastern); film/cinema studies; fine/studio arts; French; geology/earth science; German; health and physical education; history; humanities; interdisciplinary studies; Italian; Latin American studies; mathematics; medieval and Renaissance studies; molecular biology; music; philosophy; physics; political science and government; psychology; religious studies; Romance languages; Russian; Russian studies; science, technology and society; social sciences; sociology; Spanish; women's studies.

Western Washington University

American studies; anthropology; anthropology related; applied mathematics; archeology; art; art history, criticism and conservation; art teacher education; Asian studies (East); audiology and speech-language pathology; automotive engineering technology; biochemistry; biological and physical sciences; biology teacher education; biology/biological sciences; business administration and management; business/commerce; Canadian studies; cell and molecular biology; cell biology and histology; ceramic arts and ceramics; chemistry; chemistry teacher education; communication/speech communication and rhetoric; community health

services counseling; computer and information sciences; computer teacher education; creative writing; dance; design and applied arts related; design and visual communications; developmental and child psychology; drama and dance teacher education; dramatic/theater arts; drawing; early childhood education; economics; economics related; education (specific levels and methods) related; education (specific subject areas) related; electrical, electronic and communications engineering technology; elementary education; English; English/language arts teacher education; environmental science; environmental science; environmental studies; fiber, textile and weaving arts; finance; foreign languages and literatures; foreign languages related; French; French language teacher education; general studies; geography; geological and earth sciences/geosciences related; geology/earth science; geophysics and seismology; German; German language teacher education; health and physical education; health/medical preparatory programs related; history; history teacher education; human resources management; human services; human services; humanities; industrial design; industrial technology; intermedia/multimedia; international business/trade/commerce; Japanese; journalism; journalism related; liberal arts and sciences/liberal studies; linguistics; management information systems; manufacturing technology; marine biology and biological oceanography; marketing/marketing management; mathematics; mathematics and computer science; mathematics teacher education; multi-/interdisciplinary studies related; music; music history, literature, and theory; music performance; music teacher education; music theory and composition; neuroscience; operations management; optical sciences; painting; parks, recreation and leisure; philosophy; photography; physical education teaching and coaching; physics; plastics engineering technology; political science and government; printmaking; psychology; science teacher education; sculpture; social science teacher education; social studies teacher education; sociology; Spanish; Spanish language teacher education; special education; speech teacher education; technology/industrial arts teacher education; visual and performing arts.

Westminster College (UT)

Accounting; airline pilot and flight crew; art; arts management; aviation/airway management; biology/biological sciences; business/commerce; business/managerial economics; chemistry; communication/speech communication and rhetoric; computer science; criminal justice/safety; early childhood education; education; elementary education; English; environmental studies; finance; finance and financial management services related; fine/studio arts; health services/allied health/health sciences; history; international business/trade/commerce; management information systems and services related; marketing/marketing management; mathematics; neuroscience; nursing (registered nurse training); philosophy; physics; political science and government; psychology; social sciences; sociology; special education.

Westmont College

Anthropology; art; art teacher education; biology/biological sciences; business/commerce; business/managerial economics; chemistry; communication/speech communication and rhetoric; computer science; dance; dramatic/theater arts; economics; education; elementary education; engineering physics; English; English/language arts teacher education; French; history; kinesiology and exercise science; liberal arts and sciences/liberal studies; mathematics; mathematics teacher education; modern languages; music; neuroscience; philosophy; physical education teaching and coaching; physics; political science and government; pre-dentistry studies; pre-law studies; pre-pharmacy studies; pre-theology/pre-ministerial studies; pre-veterinary studies; premedical studies; psychology; religious studies; secondary education; social science teacher education; social sciences; sociology; Spanish.

Wheaton College (IL)

Anthropology; archeology; art; biblical studies; biology/biological sciences; business/managerial economics; chemistry; classics and classical languages related; communication/speech communication and rhetoric; computer science; economics; elementary education; engineering related; English; environmental studies; French; geology/earth science; German; health services/allied health/health sciences; history; international relations and affairs; mathematics; multi-/interdisciplinary studies related; music; music history, literature, and theory; music performance; music related; music teacher education; music theory and composition; nursing related; philosophy; physics; political science and government; psychology; religious education; secondary education; social studies teacher education; sociology; Spanish.

Wheaton College (MA)
African American/Black studies; African studies; American studies; ancient studies; ancient/classical Greek; anthropology; art history, criticism and conservation; Asian studies; astronomy; biochemistry; bioinformatics; biology/biological sciences; chemistry; classics; classics and languages, literatures and linguistics; computer science; dance; dramatic/theater arts; economics; English; environmental science; fine/studio arts; French studies; German; German studies; Hispanic American, Puerto Rican, and Mexican American/Chicano studies; history; international relations and affairs; Italian studies; Latin; mathematics; music; philosophy; philosophy and religious studies related; physics; physiological psychology/psychobiology; political science and government; psychology; religious studies; Russian; Russian studies; sociology; women's studies.

Whitman College
Anthropology; art; art history, criticism and conservation; Asian studies; astronomy; astrophysics; biochemistry; biochemistry/biophysics and molecular biology; biology/biological sciences; biophysics; chemistry; chemistry related; classics and languages, literatures and linguistics; communication/speech communication and rhetoric; dramatic/theater arts; economics; English; ethnic, cultural minority, and gender studies related; film/cinema studies; French; geological and earth sciences/geosciences related; geology/earth science; German; history; mathematics; mathematics and computer science; molecular biology; music; music history, literature, and theory; music performance; music theory and composition; philosophy; physics; physics related; political science and government; political science and government related; psychology; religious studies; social sciences related; sociology; Spanish.

Whitworth University
Accounting; American studies; art; art teacher education; arts management; athletic training; biology/biological sciences; business administration and management; chemistry; computer science; dramatic/theater arts; economics; elementary education; English; fine/studio arts; French; history; international business/trade/commerce; international relations and affairs; journalism; mass communication/media; mathematics; music; music teacher education; nursing (registered nurse training); peace studies and conflict resolution; philosophy; physical education teaching and coaching; physics; piano and organ; political science and government; pre-dentistry studies; pre-law studies; pre-veterinary studies; premedical studies; psychology; religious studies; secondary education; sociology; Spanish; special education; speech and rhetoric; voice and opera.

Willamette University
American studies; anthropology; art; art history, criticism and conservation; Asian studies; biology/biological sciences; chemistry; classics and languages, literatures and linguistics; comparative literature; computer science; dramatic/theater arts; economics; English; environmental science; fine/studio arts; French; German; history; humanities; international/global studies; Japanese studies; kinesiology and exercise science; Latin American studies; mathematics; music; music performance; music theory and composition; philosophy; physics; piano and organ; political science and government; psychology; religious studies; science technologies related; sociology; Spanish; speech and rhetoric; violin, viola, guitar and other stringed instruments; voice and opera; women's studies.

William Jewell College
Accounting; art; art teacher education; biochemistry; bioethics/medical ethics; biology/biological sciences; business administration and management; business/managerial economics; cell biology and histology;

chemistry; chemistry teacher education; clinical laboratory science/medical technology; communication/speech communication and rhetoric; computer and information sciences; computer science; drama and dance teacher education; dramatic/theater arts; economics; education (multiple levels); elementary education; English; English/language arts teacher education; foreign language teacher education; French; history; information science/studies; international business/trade/commerce; international relations and affairs; mathematics; middle school education; molecular biology; music; music performance; music teacher education; music theory and composition; nursing (registered nurse training); parks, recreation and leisure; philosophy; physical education teaching and coaching; physics; physics teacher education; political science and government; psychology; religious studies; religious/sacred music; secondary education; Spanish; Spanish language teacher education; speech and rhetoric; speech teacher education.

Williams College
American studies; anthropology; art history, criticism and conservation; Asian studies; astronomy; astrophysics; biology/biological sciences; chemistry; Chinese; classics and languages, literatures and linguistics; computer science; dramatic/theater arts; economics; English; ethnic, cultural minority, and gender studies related; fine/studio arts; French; geology/earth science; German; history; Japanese; literature; mathematics; music; philosophy; physics; political science and government; psychology; religious studies; Russian; sociology; Spanish; women's studies.

Winona State University
Accounting; advertising; applied art; applied mathematics; art; art teacher education; athletic training; aviation/airway management; biological and physical sciences; biology/biological sciences; broadcast journalism; business administration and management; business teacher education; business/managerial economics; chemical engineering; chemistry; clinical laboratory science/medical technology; clinical/medical laboratory technology; commercial and advertising art; computer and information sciences; computer programming; computer science; consumer merchandising/retailing management; corrections; criminal justice/law enforcement administration; criminal justice/police science; cytotechnology; dramatic/theater arts; drawing; ecology; economics; education; elementary education; engineering; English; environmental biology; finance; fine/studio arts; French; geology/earth science; German; health science; health teacher education; health/health-care administration; history; human resources management; information science/studies; international relations and affairs; journalism; kindergarten/preschool education; kinesiology and exercise science; labor and industrial relations; legal assistant/paralegal; legal studies; liberal arts and sciences/liberal studies; management information systems; marketing/marketing management; mass communication/media; materials engineering; mathematics; mechanical engineering; middle school education; music; music management and merchandising; music teacher education; natural resources/conservation; natural sciences; nursing (registered nurse training); parks, recreation and leisure; parks, recreation and leisure facilities management; physical education teaching and coaching; physical sciences; physical therapy; physics; political science and government; polymer chemistry; polymer/plastics engineering; pre-dentistry studies; pre-law studies; pre-veterinary studies; premedical studies; psychology; public administration; public health; public relations/image management; quality control technology; radio and television; reading teacher education; science teacher education; secondary education; social sciences; social work; sociology; Spanish; special education; speech and rhetoric; sport and fitness administration/management; statistics; telecommunications; therapeutic recreation; voice and opera; wildlife and wildlands science and management; wildlife biology; zoology/animal biology.

Wisconsin Lutheran College
Art; biochemistry; biology/biological sciences; business administration and management; chemistry; communication/speech communication and rhetoric; dramatic/theater arts; early childhood education; educational statistics and research methods; elementary education; English; German;

history; interdisciplinary studies; mass communications; mathematics; music; nursing (registered nurse training); philosophy; political science and government; psychology; secondary education; social sciences; Spanish; theology.

Wittenberg University
American studies; art; Asian studies (East); biochemistry/biophysics and molecular biology; biology/biological sciences; business administration and management; chemistry; communication/speech communication and rhetoric; computer science; dramatic/theater arts; economics; education; English; French; geography; geological and earth sciences/geosciences related; geology/earth science; German; history; liberal arts and sciences/ liberal studies; mathematics; music; philosophy; physics; political science and government; psychology; religious studies; Russian studies; sociology; Spanish.

Wofford College
Accounting; art history, criticism and conservation; biology/biological sciences; business/managerial economics; chemistry; Chinese; computer science; creative writing; dramatic/theater arts; economics; English; environmental studies; finance; French; German; history; humanities; international business/trade/commerce; international relations and affairs; mathematics; philosophy; physics; political science and government; pre-dentistry studies; pre-law studies; pre-veterinary studies; premedical studies; psychology; religious studies; sociology; Spanish.

Worcester Polytechnic Institute
Actuarial science; aerospace, aeronautical and astronautical engineering; animal genetics; applied mathematics; biochemistry; biology/biological sciences; biology/biotechnology laboratory technician; biomedical sciences; biomedical/medical engineering; business administration and management; cell biology and histology; chemical engineering; chemistry; civil engineering; computer and information sciences; computer engineering; computer science; economics; electrical, electronics and communications engineering; engineering mechanics; engineering physics; engineering related; engineering/industrial management; environmental studies; environmental/environmental health engineering; fluid/thermal sciences; history; history and philosophy of science and technology; humanities; industrial engineering; information science/ studies; interdisciplinary studies; intermedia/multimedia; management information systems; materials engineering; materials science; mathematics; mechanical engineering; medical microbiology and bacteriology; medicinal and pharmaceutical chemistry; molecular biology; music; nuclear engineering; philosophy; physical sciences related; physics; robotics; science, technology and society; social sciences; technical and business writing.

Xavier University
Accounting; advertising; art; athletic training; biological and physical sciences; biology teacher education; biology/biological sciences; business administration and management; business/managerial economics; chemical engineering; chemistry; chemistry teacher education; classics and languages, literatures and linguistics; clinical laboratory science/ medical technology; computer science; corrections; criminal justice/ safety; economics; education; education (specific levels and methods) related; elementary education; English; entrepreneurship; finance; fine/ studio arts; French; German; history; human resources management; international business/trade/commerce; international relations and affairs; liberal arts and sciences/liberal studies; management information systems; marketing/marketing management; mathematics; middle school education; Montessori teacher education; music; music teacher education; natural sciences; nursing science; occupational therapy; philosophy; physics; physics teacher education; political science and government; psychology; public relations/image management; radio and television; science teacher education; social work; sociology; Spanish; special education; sport and fitness administration/management; theology.

Yale University
African American/Black studies; African studies; American studies; ancient/classical Greek; anthropology; applied mathematics; archeology; architecture; art; art history, criticism and conservation; Asian studies (East); astronomy; astrophysics; biology/biological sciences; biomedical/ medical engineering; cell biology and anatomical sciences related; chemical engineering; chemistry; Chinese; classics and languages, literatures and linguistics; cognitive psychology and psycholinguistics; computer and information sciences; cultural studies; dramatic/theater arts; ecology; economics; electrical, electronics and communications engineering; engineering physics; engineering science; English; environmental studies; environmental/environmental health engineering; ethnic, cultural minority, and gender studies related; evolutionary biology; film/ cinema studies; foreign languages related; French; geological and earth sciences/geosciences related; German; history; humanities; Italian; Japanese; Jewish/Judaic studies; Latin; Latin American studies; linguistics; literature; mathematics; mathematics and computer science; mechanical engineering; molecular biology; multi-/interdisciplinary studies related; music; philosophy; physics; political science and government; Portuguese; psychology; religious studies; Russian; Russian studies; sociology; South Asian languages; Spanish; systems science and theory; women's studies.

GEOGRAPHICAL LISTING OF COLLEGES

NOTES

NOTES

NOTES

NOTES

NOTES

NOTES

NOTES

NOTES

NOTES

NOTES

NOTES

NOTES

Peterson's
Book Satisfaction Survey

Give Us Your Feedback

Thank you for choosing Peterson's as your source for personalized solutions for your education and career achievement. Please take a few minutes to answer the following questions. Your answers will go a long way in helping us to produce the most user-friendly and comprehensive resources to meet your individual needs.

When completed, please tear out this page and mail it to us at:

Publishing Department
Peterson's, a Nelnet company
2000 Lenox Drive
Lawrenceville, NJ 08648

You can also complete this survey online at **www.petersons.com/booksurvey**.

1. **What is the ISBN of the book you have purchased? (The ISBN can be found on the book's back cover in the lower right-hand corner.)** _____

2. **Where did you purchase this book?**
   ❑ Retailer, such as Barnes & Noble
   ❑ Online reseller, such as Amazon.com
   ❑ Petersons.com
   ❑ Other (please specify) _____

3. **If you purchased this book on Petersons.com, please rate the following aspects of your online purchasing experience on a scale of 4 to 1 (4 = Excellent and 1 = Poor).**

	4	3	2	1
Comprehensiveness of Peterson's Online Bookstore page	❑	❑	❑	❑
Overall online customer experience	❑	❑	❑	❑

4. **Which category best describes you?**
   ❑ High school student
   ❑ Parent of high school student
   ❑ College student
   ❑ Graduate/professional student
   ❑ Returning adult student
   ❑ Teacher
   ❑ Counselor
   ❑ Working professional/military
   ❑ Other (please specify) _____

5. **Rate your overall satisfaction with this book.**

Extremely Satisfied	Satisfied	Not Satisfied
❑	❑	❑

6. **Rate each of the following aspects of this book on a scale of 4 to 1 (4 = Excellent and 1 = Poor).**

	4	3	2	1
Comprehensiveness of the information	❏	❏	❏	❏
Accuracy of the information	❏	❏	❏	❏
Usability	❏	❏	❏	❏
Cover design	❏	❏	❏	❏
Book layout	❏	❏	❏	❏
Special features (e.g., CD, flashcards, charts, etc.)	❏	❏	❏	❏
Value for the money	❏	❏	❏	❏

7. **This book was recommended by:**
   ❏ Guidance counselor
   ❏ Parent/guardian
   ❏ Family member/relative
   ❏ Friend
   ❏ Teacher
   ❏ Not recommended by anyone—I found the book on my own
   ❏ Other (please specify) _____

8. **Would you recommend this book to others?**

   Yes   Not Sure   No
     ❏   ❏   ❏

9. **Please provide any additional comments.**

   _____

   _____

   _____

   _____

   _____

Remember, you can tear out this page and mail it to us at:

   Publishing Department
   Peterson's, a Nelnet company
   2000 Lenox Drive
   Lawrenceville, NJ 08648

or you can complete the survey online at **www.petersons.com/booksurvey.**

Your feedback is important to us at Peterson's, and we thank you for your time!

If you would like us to keep in touch with you about new products and services, please include your e-mail address here: _____